The Global Prosecution of Core Crimes under International Law

Christopher Soler

The Global Prosecution of Core Crimes under International Law

ASSER PRESS

Springer

Christopher Soler
Faculty of Laws
University of Malta
Valletta, Malta

ISBN 978-94-6265-334-4 ISBN 978-94-6265-335-1 (eBook)
https://doi.org/10.1007/978-94-6265-335-1

Published by T.M.C. ASSER PRESS, The Hague, The Netherlands www.asserpress.nl
Produced and distributed for T.M.C. ASSER PRESS by Springer-Verlag Berlin Heidelberg

This T.M.C. ASSER PRESS imprint is published by the registered company Springer-Verlag GmbH, DE part of Springer Nature.
The registered company address is: Heidelberger Platz 3, 14197 Berlin, Germany

To the wrongly convicted and imprisoned,
in the hope they would be freed;

to all victims who still await criminal justice,
in the belief it shall prevail; and

to all journalists who, at the risk of losing their own lives, courageously expose such sad stories.

Foreword

There are several ways by means of which one could read the book by Dr. Christopher Soler entitled *The Global Prosecution of Core Crimes under International Law*. The book adopts a multi-layered approach in which every part is both autonomous and functional to the larger design. This outcome may correspond to the author's own intellectual maturation while preparing his doctoral dissertation, but has the distinct advantage that the reader can benefit both from each and every chapter on its own, as well as from the entirety of the book as a whole for a unitary vision. To this extent, the book can serve as a valuable frame of reference for jurists, judges, legal practitioners, academics and public administrators who work in the dynamic fields of international human rights law and international criminal law, more so because the book has a noticeable substantive law dimension and a marked procedural law perspective.

Christopher Soler earned his Ph.D. from the prestigious University of Amsterdam, which degree led to this book, after conducting extensive research under the supervision of Prof. Harmen van der Wilt, whose guidance helped him deepen his reasoning relating to some delicate criminal responsibility issues in addition to various institutional matters revolving around the very "architecture" of international criminal justice as a system *per se*.

First, the book offers a bird's-eye view on international criminal justice and describes, in a competent and appropriate way, the diversified scope of jurisdictional avenues which serve to bring to justice those accused of major international crimes (the so-called "core crimes", and the author expresses an interesting view on this very terminology). The author scrutinizes the *aut dedere aut judicare* rule in the detail it deserves. This certainly constitutes an overarching benefit of this work.

Secondly, the book examines some of the most crucial difficulties in international criminal justice, namely the lack of cooperation, in particular in the execution of arrest warrants and in the surrender of defendants. In this regard, the author offers a number of interesting proposals and thought provoking comments with a view to strengthen the cooperation system between states and the International Criminal Court.

Thirdly, the book presents a renewed perspective on domestic efforts to prosecute and punish persons accused of international crimes by supporting the notion that a broader positive obligation for states to repress/punish core crimes is emerging.

Fourthly, there are constructive reflections upon possible improvements to be made to the coordination between the domestic and international level, so as to transform an often confrontational relationship into a more collaborative one. The vertical and horizontal systems of enforcement are thoroughly examined. This, in and of itself, contributes to a better understanding of such systems and is another enveloping benefit of this book. Moreover, both systems are integrated and dissected systematically to provide the answer to the main research question of the analytical study, this being: Which are the juridical obstacles to the surrender and/or extradition of individuals wanted for core crimes? The examination and critical analysis of both systems of enforcement of international criminal law in one and the same work gives this book a significant edge over other studies which only deal with the systems of enforcement individually and separately, just as though they were completely distinct and detached frameworks. This is another underlying asset of this work.

Finally, this book is a timely contribution to the broader debate on the future of international criminal justice and on the possible ways to offer redress to the victims of international crimes. The author combines his extensive practical experience as an attorney involved in criminal law cases with a trans-national dimension (extradition, judicial cooperation and so on), with diplomatic experience as State representative in ICC-related matters, together with an academic approach which leads him to offer both practical and expedient solutions.

In this vein, the author offers several potential options that could improve the current situation. Moreover, reviewing the framework of existing rules, he identifies a number of solutions which could strengthen the overall objective of rendering justice for core crimes in a more efficient and effective manner.

An area where recent developments will potentially benefit from this work is the establishment of mechanisms designed to collect and preserve evidence for possible use in criminal proceedings either at national or international level, before tribunals which are yet to be determined. In this regard, the International, Impartial and Independent Mechanism to Assist in the Investigation and Prosecution of Persons Responsible for the Most Serious Crimes under International Law Committed in the Syrian Arab Republic since March 2011 (also known as the "IIIM") established by the UN General Assembly in December 2016 or the Investigative team to promote accountability for Daesh/ISIL crimes (UNITAD) created by the Security Council in September 2017, at the request of the Government of Iraq, come to mind. These recent mechanisms as well as other nascent initiatives such as the proposed multilateral treaty for mutual legal assistance and extradition for the domestic prosecution of the most serious international crimes launched by the Netherlands together with several other States, as well as the possible draft convention on the prevention and repression of crimes against humanity emerging from the works of the International Law Commission, seem to point to a "new era" for international criminal justice—the era of return to national jurisdiction, coherently—somehow—with the principle of complementarity of the ICC jurisdiction.

Broadly speaking the author does not challenge the main underlying idea behind the notion of complementarity that domestic courts are and remain the essential avenue for the prosecution and punishment of international crimes. However, he makes a clever attempt to offer a broader perspective that apart from domestic courts includes a strengthened role for the ICC, legislative reforms and appropriate implementation of the ICC Statute and domestication of international norms.

The book, which I strongly commend, offers innovative ideas on how to further structure a functioning "global system" of international criminal justice where the various actors involved would cooperate more effectively towards the objective of rendering justice for victims of international crimes.

New York, USA/Catania, Italy
October–November 2018

Salvatore Zappalà
Professor of International and EU Law
University of Catania (Italy)

Editor-in-Chief, Journal of International Criminal Justice

Member of the Steering Committee of the Antonio Cassese Initiative for Justice, Peace & Humanity

Former Legal Adviser (2010–2018) to the Permanent Mission of Italy to the United Nations in New York

Preface

This book deals with the prosecution of core crimes and is aimed at legal practitioners (prosecutors, defence lawyers, magistrates and judges), jurists, experts of criminal justice, researchers, public administrators, law students, human rights activists and journalists. It provides the first comprehensive study of both systems of enforcement of international criminal law, and of the relationship between these systems, in one book by using with the same lens. It examines an under-studied field of law and serves to increase an understanding of the two systems of enforcement of international criminal law, these being the horizontal system of enforcement and the vertical system of enforcement, also known as the supra-national system and the inter-State system respectively. These are dealt with separately, but the interaction between them is also assessed. This book differentiates between various species (categories) of crimes, establishing a frame of reference for the ultimate consideration of the two systems of enforcement. It offers perspectives which, in turn, can be used to improve the prevailing enforcement regime. Moreover, it undertakes an exhaustive jurisprudential overview in assessing the systems of enforcement of international criminal law. In so doing, it offers insights about how the enforcement of international criminal law can be consolidated and improved, both in so far as substantive international criminal law is concerned and in respect of procedural international criminal law. By virtue of the legal analysis therein, this book espouses a human rights law oriented critique to the general enforcement of domestic, regional and international criminal justice.

It is distressing to contemplate why persons are investigated, prosecuted and punished for various crimes such as theft, to give just one example, whereas they are frequently not investigated, prosecuted and punished for mass atrocities (core crimes) which, besides endangering international peace and security, cause immense suffering and hardship to many human beings and to humankind in general. This *realpolitik*, i.e. the failure to investigate, prosecute and punish core crimes, is becoming more common place in view of an increasing number of States which are either unwilling or unable to do so for reasons which I delve into. Upon such failure, the responsibility to protect has to be assumed either by other States which could exercise other forms of jurisdiction, such as universal jurisdiction, over persons found on their territory, or else by the international community in the form of an investigation and prosecution before an international criminal tribunal, a judicial panel, a special court, a hybrid court and/or the International Criminal Court. I research the ways (means) how this could be implemented, and also consider which judicial institution is best positioned (placed) to do so.

By scrutinizing the cooperation regime within both systems of enforcement, the book investigates the extent to which obstacles to the surrender and/or extradition of individuals are insurmountable or otherwise. Where grounds for refusal of extradition are invoked by States, some ideas to restrict their application and effect, without violating international human rights law, are postulated. These can include ways to circumvent the stumbling block, *id est*, the ground for refusal. I suggest ways, methods and ideas which could incentivise and encourage the cooperation of States which are called to surrender or extradite (i.e. physically transfer) an individual wanted for the purposes of an eventual prosecution of core crimes. My proposals are of a juridical (legal) nature and hinge upon the pretext that international criminal law is poorly executed and implemented because of a major stumbling block, this being that individuals wanted for core crimes are not surrendered to the International Criminal Court and are not extradited to the requesting State which intends to prosecute them for their alleged crimes notwithstanding the subsistence of compelling incriminating evidence which could, in all probability, be sufficient to secure their conviction before a competent criminal court. I challenge such grounds for refusal of surrender and/or extradition, where this is possible. Should this not be possible, I examine ways how the stumbling block (i.e. the ground for refusal) could be circumvented, provided these remedial measures do not violate international human rights law.

The book is divided in five (V) parts and organised in twenty-three (23) chapters. Throughout the work, I examine the extent to which grounds for refusal of surrender act as obstacles to hinder or jeopardise the process of surrender from a State to the International Criminal Court. I investigate the extent to which grounds for refusal of extradition act as obstacles to hinder or jeopardise the extradition process between the requesting State and the requested State. The critical analysis is preceded by an inspection of the concept of 'core crimes' which are distinguished from 'transnational organized crimes', 'international crimes' and 'domestic crimes'. I undertake an autopsy of the general State obligation to cooperate, illustrate the extent to which such obligation is binding (both upon State Parties to the International Criminal Court and upon non-State Parties in certain circumstances), and reveal the consequences in cases of a breach thereof.

To achieve the above objective, I avail myself and make use of principles, such as complementarity and subsidiarity, which are crucial to successfully execute rules of international law such as the obligation to extradite or prosecute (*aut dedere aut judicare*), a rule which is also examined in detail. Understanding both systems of enforcement, comprehensively and collectively, unmasks the synergy and inter-relation between them. The work determines the ability and the potential of each one of the two systems of enforcement to fight impunity and, in a secondary manner, the ability and the potential of the remaining system to fight impunity upon the default of the other system. The prospective roles of domestic, hybrid, special (*sui generis*) and international courts (and tribunals) in the fight against impunity for the purposes of the enforcement of international criminal law are discussed and evaluated. The proliferation of such courts and tribunals is a laudable effort of the international community which is aimed to ensure that victims of core crimes can at least have their day in court.

Valletta, Malta
January 2019

Christopher Soler

Acknowledgements

This book is an updated and revised version of the doctoral thesis which I defended at the beautiful *Agnietenkapel, Universiteit van Amsterdam*, on 22 December 2017, a very special day. This project started at the very end of 2010, with the encouragement of the Rector Emeritus of the University of Malta, Prof. Juanito Camilleri, and of the Chancellor of the University of Malta, Prof. David Attard, my role model, now Judge and Vice-President of the International Tribunal for the Law of the Sea. I thank you both for the encouragement and for your belief in me. This project was largely enabled by the financial contribution of the University of Malta, of which I am currently the Director (Legal Services) and which I thank for sponsoring my doctoral research. I hereby express appreciation to Prof. Alfred J. Vella, Rector of the University of Malta. *Rettur*, thank you for allowing me both to pursue my Ph.D. studies and to permit that I chair two important working groups under the auspices of the Maltese Presidency of the Council of the European Union, namely *COJUR* (Public International Law) and *COJUR*-ICC (International Criminal Court) between January and June 2017. I thank the Government of Malta for appointing me both to chair such workshops and also as its delegate to the Assembly of State Parties to the Rome Statute of the International Criminal Court in its 15th session held in The Hague between 16 and 24 November 2016. These were enriching experiences. Furthermore, my judicial role as Chairperson of one of the three Chambers of the Refugee Appeals Board in terms of the Refugees Act, Chapter 420 of the Laws of Malta, has increased my awareness about the distressing human tragedies that underlie the consummation of serious crimes of concern to the international community.

Throughout my doctoral research there have been some special colleagues, close friends of mine, who have shown interest in my project and, occasionally, provided sound advice. Their constructive critique has enabled me to pose some important questions which proved to be fruitful. These include Prof. Kevin Aquilina, my mentor, Prof. Andrew Muscat, Prof. Giuseppe Cataldi, Prof. Stephen Calleya, Judge Prof. Liesbeth Lijnzaad, Assist. Prof. Rosanne van Alebeek, Adjunct Prof. David Donat Cattin, Assoc. Prof. João Casqueira Cardoso, Judge Juan Carlos

Fernández de Aguirre, Dr. Michele Corleto, Dr. Monica Vlad, Dr. Ivan Mifsud, Dr. Omar Grech, Dr. David Friggieri, Dr. Audrey Fino, Dr. Alex Spiteri Gingell, Dr. Kevan Azzopardi, Ms. Zahra Mousavi, Ms. Morgane Nicot, Ms. Irene ter Stege, Mr. Michiel Egeler, Mr. Isaac de Toro Mezquita, Mr. Giuseppe Colasanto and Mr. Graziano Patriarca. I cherish moments where I am able to engage directly with some wise individuals whose commitment to human rights is truly relentless and inspirational. The President of the Republic of Malta, Marie-Louise Coleiro Preca, comes to mind in this regard. *Grazzi mill-qalb Eċċellenza.* Others whom I also know well, and who have contributed to the protection of human rights and the delivery of criminal justice, include Judge Emeritus of the European Court of Human Rights Giovanni Bonello, Judge Emeritus Joseph Galea Debono, Judge Emeritus Lawrence Quintano, Dr. Emmanuel Mallia, and Dr. Tonio Borg. Here I must also thank my lecturers at the University of Sussex, where I obtained my LL.M. in International Criminal Law in 1999, particularly Prof. Richard Vogler, Prof. Paul Omar and Dr. Emily Haslam. They consolidated and secured my passion for international criminal law and the extent to which I value the protection of fundamental human rights.

I show deep appreciation for the patience and dedication of members of staff at the libraries where I conducted my research, namely the T.M.C. Asser Institute in The Hague (especially Mr. Marco van der Harst), the University of Amsterdam, the Peace Palace Library in The Hague, the University of Malta (especially Director Mr. Kevin Ellul), the University of Sussex (United Kingdom), the Institute of Advanced Legal Studies in Russell Square, London, the *Università La Sapienza* of Rome, the University of Maribor, Slovenia (through Prof. Dušan Lesjak), the *Università degli Studi di Ferrara* (through Dr. Rocco Toffaletti), and the International Maritime Law Institute (IMLI) which is housed at the University of Malta. At the latter university, Ms. Daniela Agius Cachia and Ms. Denise Jones helped me coordinate secretarial, administrative and logistical matters which facilitated my tasks. They hereby deserve a note of thanks. Likewise, as an ultimate beneficiary of its informative 'International Crimes Database' website, I express words of praise to the T.M.C. Asser Institute. Furthermore 'DomCLIC' came in very handy especially when I compiled Part IV of my book. In pursuance thereof, I thank The Hague Justice Portal and the other partners involved in 'DomCLIC' for their priceless project. A word of thanks also goes to Springer-Verlag, distributors of my book. I express my heartfelt gratitude to T.M.C. Asser Press and to all its members of staff, especially to Mr. Frank Bakker, Publisher, and Ms. Kiki van Gurp, Production Coordinator, both of whom helped me to finalise the manuscript. Hence, 'thank you, Asser Press' and 'thank you, Springer'.

The insights of Prof. Harmen van der Wilt, my Ph.D. supervisor, were crucial. I wish to express profound appreciation to such a generous gentleman, a brilliant legal mind indeed. I cherish every moment spent with you and I am honoured to have been a recipient of your wisdom and a beneficiary of your frank guidance. You will always be a friend and colleague I will respect and look up to. Moreover, you were the one who recommended my book for publication by T.M.C. Asser Press. Thank you so much, Harmen. My heartfelt thanks goes to Prof. Salvatore

Zappalà, certainly a leading authority in the field, who immediately accepted my invitation to read my book and write a foreword thereto. Your praiseworthy words fill me with pride. *Grazie mille Salvatore.*

I am very grateful to my sister, Sara Bianchi, who left my nephews and niece with my brother-in-law in order to support me throughout the oral defence of my doctoral thesis. That meant a lot to me. I have been truly blessed to have the parents I have, William (an architect-writer, who was a pillar of advice and support), and Natalie, née Woods. They have been inspirational role models. From my decision to become a lawyer at the tender age of 11 to date, they have served as a bastion of respect and empowerment. There are no words which can capture and describe my gratitude in your regard. Thinking about you automatically conjures one thought to my mind: 'you can't light a candle to the sun'. Last but not least, a very special and unique thanks goes to my wife Christine, née Dyer, and to our children Daniel and Nina. You have been so patient and understanding to endure my love affair with international criminal law throughout this long journey which culminated in this opus. To all my family: *'Inħobbkhom ħafna'.*

Contents

Part I Introduction

1 Methodological Framework and Research Questions 3
1.1 Motivation and Objective 4
1.2 Field of Application 8
1.3 Structure, Methodology and Research Questions 10
References 13

2 Preliminary Observations on the Systems of Enforcement 15
2.1 The Vertical System of Enforcement: A Useful Frame of Reference 16
2.2 The Horizontal System of Enforcement: From a *'Ius Prosequi'* to 'Mandatory Prosecutions'? 23
References 25

Part II The Characterisation and Prosecution of Core Crimes: Some Underlying Assumptions

3 Multi-level Prosecutions of Serious Crimes of Concern to the International Community 31
References 37

4 Why Do We Need to Understand the Concept of 'Core Crimes'? 41
4.1 The Salient Features of Core Crimes 43
4.2 Why Are Core Crimes the Most Serious Crimes of Concern to the International Community? 46
References 56

5 What Is Required to Intrude into the Sovereignty of a Defaulting State in Order to Investigate and Prosecute Core Crimes? 59
5.1 The Principles of Human Security and International Harm 61

5.2 Why Do Group (Collective) Crimes Breach Human Security and Why Are They so Harmful? 66
5.3 Interventions Designed to Prevent and Punish Core Crimes by Prosecuting Core Crimes 72
5.4 The Conceptual Genesis of the Responsibility to Protect 73
5.5 The Transformation of the Concept of the Responsibility to Protect into a Legal Principle 76
References 82

6 The Overarching Contextual (Juridical) Elements 89
6.1 Genocide 91
6.2 Crimes Against Humanity 93
6.3 War Crimes 101
6.4 Aggression 104
References 106

7 The Juridical Consequences of Core Crimes: Individual Criminal Liability and State Aggravated Responsibility 111
References 116

8 Detecting the Determining and Distinguishing Factors 117
8.1 Core Crimes Versus Transnational Organized Crimes 118
8.2 Core Crimes Versus Domestic Crimes 131
8.3 Core Crimes Versus International Crimes 133
8.4 Concluding Remarks 138
References 139

Part III The Vertical System of Enforcement

9 Salient Features of the Vertical System of Enforcement 147
9.1 The Meaning of Verticality 148
9.2 Distinguishable Models of the Vertical System of Enforcement 149
9.3 The Line of Demarcation Between a Preference and a Necessity 156
References 160

10 The State Obligation to Cooperate under International Law 165
10.1 The Nature of the General Obligation of An ICC State Party to Cooperate 166
10.2 The Obligations of Non-State Parties under the United Nations Security Council Resolution Regime 175
10.3 The Consequences of a Breach of the State's Obligation to Cooperate 184
References 201

11 Inherent Limitations of the Vertical System of Enforcement 209
11.1 Grounds for Refusal Emerging Directly from Admissibility Challenges 216
11.1.1 Genuine Willingness or Ability to Prosecute 218
11.1.2 *Ne Bis in Idem* 231
11.1.3 Postponement of the Execution of a Request for Surrender 249
11.2 Competing Requests and Conflicting Obligations 251
11.3 Specific Requirements under National Law 255
11.3.1 Abuse of Process 256
11.4 Diplomatic Privileges and Immunities 265
11.4.1 Immunities *Rationae Personae* 278
11.4.2 Immunities *Rationae Materiae* 289
11.5 The Rule of Speciality 296
References 298

12 The Ensuing 'Jurisdictional Joint Venture', A Division of Labour *Par Excellence* 311
References 314

Part IV The Horizontal System of Enforcement

13 *Aut Dedere Aut Judicare* 319
13.1 The Nature, Scope and Status of the *Aut Dedere Aut Judicare* Rule 321
13.2 The Execution of the *Aut Dedere Aut Judicare* Rule in Domestic Criminal Courts 351
13.3 Limitations of the *Aut Dedere Aut Judicare* Rule 367
13.4 Emerging Alternatives to the *Aut Dedere Aut Judicare Formulae* 370
13.5 The Fractional Re-characterisation of the *Aut Dedere Aut Judicare* Rule 380
References 389

14 The Reliance of the Horizontal System of Enforcement on the *Corpus Juris* Relating to Extradition 403
References 408

15 The Impact of Customary International Law and General Principles of Law on the Horizontal System of Enforcement 411
References 413

16 Pitfalls Within the Horizontal System of Enforcement 415
16.1 The Non-extradition of Nationals 428
16.2 The Military Offence Exemption 436

16.3 The Political Offence Exemption 437
16.4 The Double Criminality Rule. 448
16.5 The Exclusion of the Cause of the Criminal Action by Reason of Amnesty 454
16.6 Plea Bargaining 465
16.7 Human Rights General Exceptions to Extraditions 467
16.7.1 The Right to a Fair Trial 470
16.7.2 The *Ne Bis in Idem* Rule 477
16.7.3 The Prohibition of Torture and Other Cruel, Inhuman and Degrading Treatment or Punishment 493
16.7.4 Death Row and the Death Penalty. 507
16.8 Diplomatic Privileges and Immunities 518
16.8.1 Immunities *Rationae Personae* 519
16.8.2 Immunities *Rationae Materiae* 522
References 533

17 Concurrent State Obligations 551
References 553

18 The Self-assumption of Jurisdiction: An Abuse of Process or a Necessary Evil? 555
References 559

Part V Conclusion

19 The Obligation of States to Prevent, Prosecute and Punish Core Crimes 563
References 577

20 The Development of Functional International Constitutionalism 581
References 584

21 The Exercise of *Kompetenz-Kompetenz* in the Determination of Presumptive Jurisdiction 587
21.1 International Courts. 589
21.2 Domestic Courts 592
References 595

22 The Proliferation of Judicial Panels and Judicial Partnerships 597
References 601

23 Concluding Observations and Final Remarks 603
References 615

Table of Cases 619

Index 657

Abbreviations

ABA	American Bar Association
ACIL	Amsterdam Centre for International Law
ACJHR	African Court of Justice and Human Rights
ACmmHPR	African Commission on Human and Peoples' Rights
ACtHPR	African Court of Human and Peoples' Rights
AG	Advocate General
AHRLJ	African Human Rights Law Journal
AHRLR	African Human Rights Law Reports
AI	Amnesty International
AIDP	*Association Internationale de Droit Pénal*
AIDS	Acquired Immune Deficiency Syndrome
AIP	Amnesty International Publications
AJICL	Arizona Journal of International and Comparative Law
AJIL	American Journal of International Law
AJLS	African Journal of Legal Studies
AJPIL	Austrian Journal of Public and International Law
ALJ	Australian Law Journal
Anx.	Annex
A-P JHR	Asia-Pacific Journal on Human Rights
APSR	American Political Science Review
Ashgate	Ashgate Publishing Limited
ASIL	American Society of International Law
ASP	Assembly of State Parties to the Rome Statute of the International Criminal Court
ASR	African Studies Review
Asser Institute	*T.M.C. Asser Instituut*
Asser Press	T.M.C. Asser Press

AUILR	American University International Law Review
AULR	Auckland University Law Review
Basic Principles & Guidelines	Basic Principles and Guidelines on the Right to a Remedy and Reparation for Victims of Gross Violations of International Human Rights Law and Serious Violations of International Humanitarian Law
BCICLR	Boston College International and Comparative Law Review
BEP	Berkeley Electronic Press
BiH	Bosnia and Herzegovina
BIICL	British Institute of International and Comparative Law
BJIL	Berkeley Journal of International Law
BLSR	Berkeley Law Scholarship Repository
Brill	*Koninklijke Brill N.V.*
BUILJ	Boston University International Law Journal
BWCC	Bosnian War Crimes Chamber
BYIL	British Yearbook of International Law
CaLR	California Law Review
CAP	Carolina Academic Press
CAR	Central African Republic
CAT	Convention Against Torture
CgJIL	Chicago Journal of International Law
ChJIL	Chinese Journal of International Law
CIA	Central Intelligence Agency
CILJ	Cornell International Law Journal
CILRAP	Centre for International Law Research and Policy
CISA	Convention Implementing the Schengen Agreement
CJEL	Columbia Journal of European Law
CJTL	Columbia Journal of Transnational Law
CLF	Criminal Law Forum
CLJ	Cambridge Law Journal
CllUP	Cornell University Press
CLP	Current Legal Problems
CLR	Criminal Law Review
CLSC	Crime, Law and Social Change
CMP	Cameron May Publishing Limited
CoE	Council of Europe
COJUR	*Comité Juridique*
CP	Clarendon Press
CPL	Cavendish Publishing Limited
CREMS	Convention Relating to Extradition between the Member States of the European Union

CUP	Cambridge University Press
D & H	*Dunker & Humblot GmbH*
Daesh	*Ad-Dawlah al-Islamiyah fil 'Iraq wa ash-Sham*
DINA	*Dirección de Intelligencia Nacional*, Chile
DJCIL	Duke Journal of Comparative and International Law
Doc.	Document
DPLR	DePaul Law Review
DRC	The Democratic Republic of The Congo
EAC	Extraordinary African Chambers
EAW	European Arrest Warrant
ECCC	Extraordinary Chambers in the Courts of Cambodia for the Prosecution of Crimes Committed During the Period of Democratic Kampuchea
ECE	European Convention on Extradition
ECFI	Court of First Instance of the European Communities
ECJ	Court of Justice of the European Union
ECMAC	European Convention on Mutual Assistance in Criminal Matters
ECtHR	European Court of Human Rights and Fundamental Freedoms
ECvHR	European Convention for the Protection of Human Rights and Fundamental Freedoms
ed.	Editor
edn.	Edition
eds.	Editors
EE	Edward Elgar Publishing Limited
EILR	Emory International Law Review
EJCCLCJ	European Journal of Crime, Criminal Law and Criminal Justice
EJIL	European Journal of International Law
EJIL: Talk!	The Blog of the European Journal of International Law
EJLS	European Journal of Legal Studies
EPPO	European Public Prosecutor's Office
ESPO	Ethiopian Special Prosecutor's Office
ETSPSC	East Timor Special Panels for Serious Crimes
EU	European Union
EUCLR	European Union Constitutional Law Review
FARC	*Fuerzas Armadas Revolucionarias de Colombia*
FEDEFAM	*Federación Latinoamericana de Asociaciones de Familiares de Detenidos-Desaparecidos*

FIDH	*Fédération Internationale des Ligues des Droits de l'Homme*
FILJ	Fordham International Law Journal
FP	The Foundation Press
FRA	European Union Agency for Fundamental Rights
Framework Decision on the European Arrest Warrant	EU Council Framework Decision 2002/584 of the 13th June 2002 on the European Arrest Warrant and the Surrender Procedures Between Member States 2000/584/JHA
FRG	Federal Republic of Germany
FYIL	Finnish Yearbook of International Law
GAOR	General Assembly Official Records
German LJ	German Law Journal
GIP	Graduate Institute Publications
Giuffrè	*Giuffrè Editore S.p.A.*
GJIL	Goettingen Journal of International Law
GLJ	Georgetown Law Journal
GPO	Government Printing Office
GrJIL	Georgetown Journal of International Law
GULC	Georgetown University Law Center
GUP	Goettingen University Press
GYIL	German Yearbook of International Law
HAIL	The Hague Academy of International Law
HCSS	Hybrid Court for South Sudan
HHRJ	Harvard Human Rights Journal
HILJ	Harvard International Law Journal
HIV	Human Immunodeficiency Virus
HJIL	Houston Journal of International Law
HJJ	Hague Justice Journal
HoL	House of Lords
HP	Hart Publishing
HRB	The Human Rights Brief
HRC	Human Rights Committee
HRQ	Human Rights Quarterly
HRW	Human Rights Watch
IACmmHR	Inter-American Commission on Human Rights
IACtHR	Inter-American Court of Human Rights
IACvHR	Inter-American Convention on Human Rights
IBA	International Bar Association
ICC Statute	Rome Statute of the International Criminal Court
ICC	International Criminal Court
ICCPR	International Covenant on Civil and Political Rights
ICD of the HC of Kenya	International Crimes Division of the High Court of Kenya

ICD of the HC of Uganda	International Crimes Division of the High Court of Uganda
ICD	International Crimes Database, T.M.C. Asser Institute
ICJ	International Court of Justice
ICJ Rep.	Annual Reports of the International Court of Justice
ICJ Statute	Statute of the International Court of Justice
ICJR	International Criminal Justice Review
ICLQ	International and Comparative Law Quarterly
ICLR	International Criminal Law Review
ICRC	International Committee of the Red Cross
ICT of Bangladesh	International Crimes Tribunal (Bangladesh)
ICTR	International Criminal Tribunal for Rwanda
ICTY	International Criminal Tribunal for the Former Yugoslavia
IDEA	International Institute for Democracy and Electoral Assistance
IDI	*Institut de Droit International*
IDJHRL	Interdisciplinary Journal of Human Rights Law
IHT	Iraqi High Tribunal
IIIM	International, Impartial and Independent Mechanism to Assist in the Investigation and Prosecution of Those Responsible for the Most Serious Crimes under International Law Committed in the Syrian Arab Republic Since March 2011
ILA	International Law Association
iLawyer	iLawyer, a blog on international justice
ILC Yearbook	Yearbook of the International Law Commission
ILC	International Law Commission
ILJ	Indiana Law Journal
ILR	Israel Law Review
IMO	International Maritime Organization
Intersentia	Intersentia Publishers
IRRC	International Review of the Red Cross
ISSJ	International Social Science Journal
IYIL	Italian Yearbook of International Law
JCL	Journal of Criminal Law
JCS	Journal of Conflict Studies
JEP	*Jurisdicción Especial para la Paz*
JHR	Journal of Human Rights
JHUP	John Hopkins University Press
JICJ	Journal of International Criminal Justice

JITE	Journal of Institutional and Theoretical Economics
JSJ	Journal of Social Justice
JW & SL	John Wiley & Sons Limited
KLI	Kluwer Law International
KRC	Kampala Review Conference of the Rome Statute of the International Criminal Court
KRP	Kosovo Regulation 64 Panels
KSC	Kosovo Specialist Chambers
LCP	Law and Contemporary Problems
LHPS	Long House Publishing Services
LJIL	Leiden Journal of International Law
LLAICLR	Loyola of Los Angeles International Law and Comparative Law Review
Longman	Longman Publishing Group
Ltd.	Limited
Maklu	Maklu Publishers
McGLJ	McGill Law Journal
MEDAC	Mediterranean Academy of Diplomatic Studies, University of Malta
MJECL	Maastricht Journal of European and Comparative Law
MJIL	Michigan Journal of International Law
MLJ	Mississippi Law Journal
MnnJIL	Minnesota Journal of International Law
MNP	Martinus Nijhoff Publishers
MPYUNL	Max Planck Yearbook of United Nations Law
MS	*Mohr Siebeck GmbH & Co. KG*
MUP	Manchester University Press
n.	Footnote
NATO	North Atlantic Treaty Organisation
NEJICL	New England Journal of International and Comparative Law
NELR	New England Law Review
NGO	Non-Governmental Organisation
NILR	Netherlands International Law Review
NJIHR	Northwestern Journal of International Human Rights
NJIL	Nordic Journal of International Law
NlJIL	Netherlands Journal of International Law
No.	Number
Nos.	Numbers
notes	Footnotes
NQHR	Netherlands Quarterly of Human Rights
NY	New York

NYIL	Netherlands Yearbook of International Law
NYUJILP	New York University Journal of International Law and Politics
NZJPIL	New Zealand Journal of Public International Law
OAS	Organization of American States
OJLS	Oxford Journal of Legal Studies
OLAF	*Office Européen de la Lutte Antifraude*
OPI	Oceana Publications Inc.
OTP	Office of the Prosecutor of the International Criminal Court
OUP	Oxford University Press
p.	Page
para	Paragraph
paras	Paragraphs
PB	Penguin Books
PCIJ	Permanent Court of International Justice
PE	Pearson Education Limited
PGA	Parliamentarians for Global Action
P*i*CT	Project on International Courts and Tribunals
pp.	Pages
PRI	Peace Research Institute
PULP	Pretoria University Law Press
RBDI	*Revue Belge de Droit International*
RDI	*Rivista di Diritto Internazionale*
RIDP	*Revue internationale de droit pénal: bulletin de l'Association Internationale de Droit Pénal*
RLP	Rowman and Littlefield Publishers
Round Hall	Round Hall Limited
RPE	Rules of Procedure and Evidence
RUF	Revolutionary United Front
S & M	Sweet & Maxwell
SAJCJ	South African Journal of Criminal Justice
SCJIL	Santa Clara Journal of International law
SCSL	Special Court for Sierra Leone
S-G	Secretary-General of the United Nations
Sijthoff	A.W. Sijthoff International Publishing Company B.V.
SJIL	Stanford Journal of International Law
SJLTA	Southwestern Journal of Law and Trade in the Americas
Springer	*Springer-Verlag*
STL	Special Tribunal for Lebanon
SUP	Stanford University Press
SWCC	Serbian War Crimes Chamber
T & F	Taylor & Francis Group

TBA	Texas Bar Association
TILJ	Texas International Law Journal
TJLR	Thomas Jefferson Law Review
TLR	Texas Law Review
TOAEP	Torkel Opsahl Academic E-Publisher
TP	Transnational Publishers Incorporation
TRAL	Thomson Reuters (Professional) Australia Limited
TRIAL	Track Impunity Always
UCK	Kosovo Liberation Army
UCLALR	University of California Los Angeles Law Review
UDHR	Universal Declaration of Human Rights
UK	United Kingdom
ULR	Utrecht Law Review
UMHRL	University of Minnesota Human Rights Library
UMJLR	University of Michigan Journal of Law Reform
UN	United Nations
UNAFEI	United Nations Asia and Far East Institute for the Prevention and the Treatment of Offenders
UNC	United Nations Charter
UNCATOC	United Nations Convention Against Transnational Organized Crime
UNCHR	United Nations Commission on Human Rights
UNCLOS	United Nations Convention on the Law of the Sea
UNDP	United Nations Development Programme
UNGA	United Nations General Assembly
UNITA	The National Union for the Total Independence of Angola
UNODC	United Nations Office on Drugs and Crime
UNSC	United Nations Security Council
UNTAET	United Nations Transitional Administration in East Timor
UPLR	University of Pennsylvania Law Review
USA	United States of America
UTFLR	University of Toronto Faculty of Law Review
UTLR	The University of Tulsa Law Review
UvA	*Universiteit van Amsterdam* (University of Amsterdam)
Vathek	Vathek Publishing
VCLT	Vienna Convention on the Law of Treaties
VJIL	Virginia Journal of International Law
Vol.	Volume
VUA	*Vrije Universiteit Amsterdam* (Free University of Amsterdam)

WILJ	Wisconsin International Law Journal
WK	Wolters Kluwer
YIHL	Yearbook of International Humanitarian Law
YJIA	Yale Journal of International Affairs
YJIL	Yale Journal of International Law
YLJ	Yale Law Journal
YUP	Yale University Press

Part I
Introduction

Chapter 1
Methodological Framework and Research Questions

Contents

1.1 Motivation and Objective 4
1.2 Field of Application 8
1.3 Structure, Methodology and Research Questions 10
References 13

Abstract This initial chapter introduces the book which portrays the position at law as at 1 January 2019, slightly more than twenty years after the signature of the ICC Statute. It does so by unmasking its objective. The aim of the book is to seek to provide a better understanding of the prevailing enforcement mechanisms within international criminal law by undertaking a normative account thereof which includes an analysis on the extent to which States enjoy leeway to refuse surrender and/or extradition of an individual wanted for core crimes. The chapter poses a research question, and some research sub-questions the reply to which will help to answer the research question, this being 'which are the juridical obstacles to the surrender and/or extradition of individuals wanted for core crimes?' The research sub-questions posed are the following: (1) to what extent, if at all, may international courts and/or States exact the surrender and/or extradition (for the purposes of subsequent prosecution) of those individuals accused of core crimes? (2) to what extent may grounds for refusal of surrender act as bars (obstacles) to hinder or jeopardise the process of surrender from a State to the ICC? (3) to what extent may grounds for refusal of extradition act as bars (obstacles) to hinder or jeopardise the extradition process between the requesting State and the requested State? I explain the methodology used to consider the obstacles which effectively hinder or block the surrender and/or extradition, and consequently the subsequent prosecution, of alleged perpetrators of core crimes.

Keywords Enforcement · Field of application · Methodology · Objective · Position at law · Research questions · Sources · Structure · Research sub-questions · Subject of international law

C. Soler, *The Global Prosecution of Core Crimes under International Law*,
https://doi.org/10.1007/978-94-6265-335-1_1

This book deals with the prosecution of core crimes. My work shall be introduced by means of this chapter which shall cater for the structure I shall adopt and the methodology I shall use. By virtue of this chapter the research question will be posed and the objective of this work, together with its field of application, will be portrayed.

1.1 Motivation and Objective

This book seeks to provide a better understanding of the prevailing enforcement mechanisms within international criminal law by undertaking a normative account thereof which includes an analysis on the extent to which States enjoy leeway to refuse surrender and/or extradition of an individual wanted for core crimes. It examines both systems of enforcement cumulatively and together, both individually and collectively, within the same study. Whilst proposing some improvements to each enforcement system when these are considered separately and autonomously, some conclusions are deduced after integrating both systems. I perform this task by examining pitfalls within the systems of enforcement of international criminal law. Where possible, this book attempts to propose methods which could be adopted to fill such gaps in compliance with international law. Therefore, the main research question can be coherently enunciated as follows: Which are the juridical obstacles to the surrender and/or extradition of individuals wanted for core crimes? Antonio Cassese had asserted that 'criminal justice is among the most civilized responses to such violence'.[1] But criminal justice can only be meted out if persons are brought to trial (*id est*, surrendered or extradited), unless either a State enjoying custodial jurisdiction over these individuals is willing to prosecute them or unless trials *in absentia* are permissible. Thus, the quest for an international rule of law,[2] as opposed to mob rule,[3] may be said to be the fulcrum of this book since it constitutes a primary catalyst the aftermath of which is the intended maintenance of peace and security. This latter goal depends, at least *in partem*, upon an effective but fair

[1] Cassese 2011, p. 271.

[2] Although the dynamic concept of the rule of law can hardly be defined (De Gaetano 2018), it could be construed to signify that:

i. No man is punishable or can be lawfully made to suffer in body and goods except for a distinct breach of law established in the ordinary legal manner before the ordinary courts of the land; and
ii. No man is above the law and that every man, whatever be his rank or condition, is subject to the ordinary law of the realm and amenable to the jurisdiction of the ordinary tribunals.

(Dicey 1982, pp. 110–115). Observing the rule of law 'imposes on the State the positive duty to protect individuals' fundamental rights by providing for a system that can offer protection to any individual present in its territory against violations of his/her fundamental rights by others' (Hirsch Ballin 2012, p. 12).

[3] Aquilina 2017, pp. 107–110.

international criminal law which, *inter alia*, does not allow powerful politicians to act *legibus solutus*.[4]

At the very start one must refer to the term 'enforcement'.[5] Although it is not a keyword which emerges from the title of my book, it pervades my entire analysis, and its understanding and improvement are the ultimate deliverables of my work. 'Enforcement' is not a term which many lawyers have embarked onto defining, maybe because it is intricately linked with the concept of jurisdiction which, in turn, is conflated with the concept of sovereignty.[6] Some jurists have actually explicitly used the term in the title of their book but failed to define it expressly. Mohamed Cherif Bassiouni dedicates a whole volume to his study about international criminal law on 'enforcement' but limits the concept of enforcement to the direct enforcement model.[7] Beth van Schaack and Ronald Slye limit themselves to defining the term 'jurisdiction to enforce' by stating that it 'concerns a State's power to compel persons to comply with its law, such as with respect to the investigation of, or the imposition of a sanction for, international crimes'.[8] Similarly Roger O'Keefe determines that a State's jurisdiction is its 'authority, by reference to international law, to prescribe, adjudicate and enforce legal rules'.[9] Others uphold that the enforcement of international criminal law covers 'not only the international prosecution of international crimes, but also various international aspects of their domestic investigation and prosecution'.[10] I would think that the term 'enforcement' in the context of criminal justice is meant to convey the application, implementation and execution of judicial norms which are intended to repress and suppress crime. Enforcement thus has a broad reach in so far as it embraces any measure which may be legitimately taken to prevent crimes, and to prosecute and punish persons who commit them. This is its import within this book.

Substantively the core crimes necessitate a close analysis, whilst procedural equity and fairness should be safeguarded in pursuance of the enforcement of international criminal law which is imperative for its subsistence. In other words, unless international criminal law is effectively enforced, it remains a dead letter. To prevent such contingency, a robust procedural regime must be devised. It is not surprising to note that publicists have argued that procedural law is more important than substantive law, although in truth both are equally important. Jeremy Lever states that this is because, in the first place, the outcome of cases is in practice more likely to be affected by procedural rules rather than by substantive ones, and secondly, parties are more likely to regard their treatment at the hands of the law as

---

4 Bin 2017, p. 77.

5 Under general international law, its 'lack of an automatic and compulsory enforcement mechanism remains the most striking feature' thereof (Proukaki 2010, p. 1).

6 O'Keefe 2015, p. 3.

7 Bassiouni 1987, p. xvi.

8 van Schaack and Slye 2010, p. 27.

9 O'Keefe 2015, p. 3.

10 Cryer et al. 2010, p. 5.

unjust because of what they perceive to be defects of the law of procedure rather than because of what they perceive to be anomalies derivative of substantive rules of law.[11] This said, for the sake of precision, procedural law, as understood by myself, shall not be narrowly confined to the regulation of a trial. Its reach is broader since it encompasses the ways and means (the *modus operandi*) which may be adopted, and the measures which may be undertaken, to implement international criminal law. In fact, issues relating to surrender (which precedes a trial) and the execution of a sentence (which follows a trial) are stipulated within the ICC RPE, in their eleventh (entitled 'International Cooperation and Judicial Assistance') and twelfth (entitled 'Enforcement') chapters respectively. To this extent, admissibility requirements, jurisdictional issues, competence of courts and tribunals, mutual assistance in criminal matters and cooperation between executive and judicial authorities assume fundamental importance.

In this context, an analysis of the substantive notion of core crimes would be of value for an understanding of the *leitmotif* behind this book. Its underlying *raison d'être* is reflected within its ultimate objective. In other words, a substantive analysis of core crimes is imperative to understand how such crimes can be prosecuted in a fair and effective manner conducive to the desired global bestowal of international criminal justice. After all, it stands to reason that, since core crimes cause specific problems to criminal justice,[12] the substantive nature of such crimes affects the manner in which they can be countered because the enforcement of international criminal law heavily relies on the regime of cooperation for the punishment of core crimes.

At the outset, suffice to mention that international criminal law has developed as a result of the advent of the phenomenon by means of which the individual has become a subject of international law. This has, in turn and over the years, radically changed the remit and jurisdictional reach of diplomacy, international relations, but particularly of international human rights law, international humanitarian law and most significantly of international criminal law. The impact which this categorisation had on crime prevention must not be under-estimated. Until a few decades ago, the application and enforcement of individual rights was considered to be a matter which belonged exclusively to municipal law, although it involved certain fundamental human rights recognized and proclaimed by the international community, in conjunction with other major developments in international law. The phenomenon as a result of which the individual has become a subject of international law and the acknowledgement of human rights on an international scale was crystallized by some important human rights instruments promulgated in 1948, such as the UDHR and the Genocide Convention. These followed the formulation of the doctrine of individual criminal responsibility, the priceless and tangible effect of the so-called Nuremberg Principles which were passed on 21 November 1947 by

[11] Lever 1999, p. 285.

[12] Letschert 2017, p. 472.

means of UNGA Resolution 177.[13] Hence the Nuremberg Principles, besides symbolising the embryonic stages of international criminal law, acted as a catalyst for the progressive restatement of human rights norms.

Nowadays the doctrine of individual criminal responsibility is put into practice by means of the judgments of international criminal courts and tribunals, those of so-called hybrid courts,[14] *dicta* of the ICC, and decisions of domestic criminal courts. Since contemporary international criminal law arguably outlaws trials *in absentia*,[15] the implementation of the doctrine of individual criminal responsibility rests upon the pre-requisite of arrest and surrender[16] of indictees[17] before international criminal courts/tribunals on the one hand, and upon extradition and mutual assistance in criminal matters[18] on the other hand, both systems reflecting the vertical and horizontal approaches to state cooperation respectively. In actual fact, the vertical system of enforcement constitutes a frame of reference *per se* (a platform) upon which the horizontal system of enforcement may rest. The space given to justify this observation within Sect. 2.1, together with the fact that the vertical system of enforcement will precede the horizontal system of enforcement within this book, are symptomatic of the need to justify this contention. The latter (horizontal) system, as the most important prevailing enforcement system, was traditionally used to ensure prosecutions involving the State which apprehended the alleged criminal (the requested State] and the State which intends prosecuting the alleged criminal (the requesting State]. In pursuance of these preliminary observations, I shall pose the research sub-question: to what extent, if at all, may States exact the surrender and/or extradition (for the purposes of subsequent prosecution) of those individuals accused of core crimes? Whereas States are gradually losing the upper hand within the vertical system of enforcement, they are struggling to safeguard their discretion by means of their consensual legal practice within the horizontal system of enforcement. One will note that the intricacies surrounding the concept of core crimes, to be dealt with in Part II, convolute the entire enforcement paradigm.

---

[13] These are Principles of International Law Recognised in the Charter of the Nuremberg Tribunal and in the Judgment of the Tribunal, which were adopted and codified by the ILC at its 29 July 1950 session, and submitted to the UNGA as part of the ILC's report covering the work of that session. To read this report, see ILC Yearbook 1950, pp. 374–378.

[14] These include, *inter alia*, the SCSL, the ECCC, the KRP, the ETSPSC, the STL, the IHT, the SWCC and the BWCC.

[15] This assertion may be partially qualified since Article 22 of the Statute of the STL (Statute of the STL (2007) Statute of the Special Tribunal for Lebanon) (which in any case is not an international criminal tribunal) allows trials *in absentia* (Jenks 2009, p. 61).

[16] In accordance with Article 102(a) of the ICC Statute (ICC Statute (1998) Rome Statute of the International Criminal Court) surrender is 'the delivering up of a person by a State to the Court'.

[17] These are individuals accused of having committed a core crime, this being any of those acts which breach Articles 5 to 8 *bis* of the ICC Statute, above n. 16. These core crimes will be referred to and examined within Chap. 6 of my book.

[18] This includes rendition, transfers of prisoners and exchange of information.

This book will examine whether and how these enforcement systems can constitute a sufficiently watertight structure conducive to bringing accused individuals to justice, or rather whether international criminal law has matured sufficiently or otherwise to procure such a framework. In other words, by means of this work, an analysis will be undertaken in order to understand whether contemporary international criminal law, by virtue of the prevailing complementarity regime[19] and/or by means of grounds of jurisdiction, can combat impunity by ensuring that those accused of core crimes be prosecuted accordingly, be it before an international court/tribunal, before a hybrid court/tribunal or before domestic criminal courts. The latter (indirect) horizontal system is given the prominence it deserves in so far as it is the main enforcement system whereas the relevance of the former (direct) vertical system will also be addressed. In an ancillary manner, the ensuing pitfalls (some of which constitute *lacunae* which hinder the prosecution of individuals who have allegedly committed core crimes] will be identified and, occasionally (where I determine that this is required and/or desirable) methods and remedies intended to fill the gaps which these hurdles/obstacles have caused will be suggested.

1.2 Field of Application

This work, which portrays the position at law as at 1 January 2019 is devised against the backdrop of contemporary public 'international law'. This term may be broadly defined as 'the standard of conduct, at a given time for States and other entities subject thereto'.[20] Contemporary public international law comprises international criminal law *stricto sensu*, international human rights law and international humanitarian law. These three *instituti legis* are considered as branches of public international law, specific fields of study which shall be referred to throughout this work. In fact, this work shall heavily rely on international criminal law,[21] although it shall refer to international human rights law, particularly in Parts III and IV, and seldom to international humanitarian law.[22]

Throughout this process, I make use of the formal sources of public international law by predominantly relying upon primary sources of international law, namely conventional and customary international law, as per Article 38(1) of the Statute of the ICJ. In doing this, precedence will be given to the ICC Statute, applicable

[19] See Articles 17 to 19 of the ICC Statute, above n. 16.

[20] Grant and Barker 2009, p. 300.

[21] Jurists have noted that 'little has been thoughtfully written about the more fundamental questions of what international criminal procedure is' (Boas et al. 2011, p. 2). Throughout this work, any reference to 'international criminal law' is conveyed to comprise 'the law of international criminal procedure' which, in turn, encompasses the enforcement of international criminal law itself.

[22] International humanitarian law refers to the current understanding of the *ius in bello*, the laws concerning the conduct of warfare (Alexander 2015, p. 110).

treaties, general principles and rules of international law, and general rules of law in terms of the *lex specialis*, Article 21 of the ICC Statute. The analysis of the vertical system necessarily relies upon Article 21 of the ICC Statute which delineates the sources of this *lex specialis*, although it fails to identify the 'internationally recognized human rights' which shall be protected and/or their source.[23] Customary international law has the potential of acting as a protagonist especially in the fourth Part, in liaison with general principles of law recognised by the civilised nations. At a horizontal level, general principles of criminal law occasionally assume fundamental importance, especially when certain grounds of refusal of extradition are scrutinized. However, since State practice does vary considerably, making it impossible to analyse all the divergent State practices, certain State practices will be scrutinized more than others both because they may be more influential and prone to set the ball rolling for the eventual formation of customary international law, and also because they are more susceptible to being grouped owing to common denominators they possess. The same may be said about domestic human rights law (most of which is habitually constitutionalised) and practice, and about applicable regional human rights mechanisms which bind the respective contracting parties thereto.

This book also makes appropriate use of secondary sources such as case-law,[24] the works of publicists,[25] resolutions of the UNSC and of the UNGA, drafts of the ILC, works of independent bodies such as the ILA, the *IDI* and the *AIDP*,[26] together with unilateral acts of States. Case-law, termed by Brownlie as 'authoritative evidence of the state of the law,[27] inevitably plays a central role in the fourth Part wherein the horizontal system will be analysed closely, whereas conventional international law is likely to assume more significance within Part III dealing with the vertical system, which can only boast of some relevant jurisprudential outcomes. Although David Maxwell-Fyfe, as prosecutor in the Nuremberg Trials, had said 'we declare what international law is',[28] international criminal law is established, interpreted and applied both by international courts and tribunals, but particularly by domestic criminal courts and tribunals. I frequently refer to the writings of learned publicists, considered to be a subsidiary source. These assume notable significance as a persuasive source especially where jurisprudence is scant. Such is the situation prevailing before the ICC itself, which is still in its age of puberty. Since the ICC is arbiter of its own jurisdictional competence, the opinions of

---

[23] Abels 2012, p. 163. For an analysis of views relating to the extent to which Article 21(3) of the ICC Statute, above n. 16, has a normative effect, see Zeegers 2016, pp. 73–90.

[24] Resorting to jurisprudence is imperative since courts are the ultimate arbiters of international law.

[25] D'Aspremont and van den Herik 2012, *passim*.

[26] For an analysis of the history, philosophy, structure, membership, publications and influence of the *AIDP* by means of the cooperation it undertakes with other institutions, see Bassiouni 1995, pp. 275–294.

[27] Brownlie 2008, p. 19.

[28] Jackson 1945.

publicists predicate a higher value in the vertical system of enforcement, which abundance is not so marked in the examination of the horizontal system since the latter system is jurisprudentially prosperous. The *kompetenz-kompetenz* of the ICC, which shall be dealt with under Sect. 21.1 of Chap. 21, should also provide fertile ground for screening, monitoring, verification and (if necessary) constructive criticism of the exercise of the ICC's powers, especially where the interplay with the UNSC's powers comes to the fore. In these circumstances, *inter alia*, such analysis is best left in the hands of reliable legal literature.

1.3 Structure, Methodology and Research Questions

Having introduced the goal of this work, this chapter will address structural and methodological matters in the light of the research question posed herein. Part II focuses on the ambiguous concept of 'core crimes'. This is done by charting the pretext to the justification of the intervention of the international community when such crimes are not dealt with by the territorial State, and by displaying the features, characteristics and elements of these crimes. Whilst providing a workable definition of core crimes, I attempt to clarify the concept of core crimes by distinguishing core crimes from other species of crimes. The second Part is also intended to postulate some underlying assumptions, especially those which arise directly from the title (subject-matter) of the work itself. This process is important since it provides a solid platform upon which the main body of this work rests, such main body being constituted by means of Part III dealing with the vertical system of enforcement and Part IV dealing with the horizontal system of enforcement. A warrant of arrest for core crimes need not necessarily be issued by the ICC or by an international criminal tribunal. A charge issued by any State against an individual would fall within the purview of this study. This is why, as is explained in the next chapter, prosecutions referred to herein encompass both systems of enforcement (the vertical and the horizontal one) in order to, holistically, cover all sorts of prosecutions which may be undertaken around the globe. Therefore, to pose the relevant research sub-questions: (i) to what extent may grounds for refusal of surrender act as bars (obstacles) to hinder or jeopardise the process of surrender from a State to the ICC? Similarly, (ii) to what extent may grounds for refusal of extradition act as bars (obstacles) to hinder or jeopardise the extradition process between the requesting State and the requested State? Within this analysis I consider the obstacles which effectively hinder or block the surrender and/or extradition and subsequent prosecution of alleged perpetrators of core crimes.

Since some of such grounds of refusal have an intrinsic human rights law connotation, in analysing such grounds of refusal, I will keep norms of international human rights law in mind. Indeed, even international human rights law predicates that international criminal law elicits and binds States to cooperate in the suppression of gross human rights violations especially when such crimes are committed by or tolerated by the acquiescence of States. The role of States in the ensuing conundrum is pivotal. Individuals, often officials of rogue States commit core crimes whereas other individuals, often officials of failed States, close a blind eye to the commission of such crimes. Such States can largely control the administration of criminal justice since they possess the evidence (if and when it is preserved by means of an investigation) and the required data relating to the *locus delicti commissi*, the witnesses, together with all other requisites for the purposes of a successful prosecution. The cooperation of these same (defaulting) States for the surrender and/or extradition of its nationals who are suspected of having committed such core crimes is hence solicited. Such cooperation is requested from the very same people whose major (political and/or personal) interest might be to cast aside every attempt which may smoothen the path to justice. This is why the ICC 'will regularly have to deal with national authorities who have every interest in frustrating and obstructing ongoing investigations'.[29] Just to give a concrete example, members of the ICC prosecutorial team have held *seduta stante* that the Kenyan State, headed by President *Kenyatta* (the accused), has deliberately taken an extensive set of steps to obstruct the emergence of the truth and the course of justice, as a result of which the prospect of a conviction was weak.[30]

Having portrayed this book's objectives by means of this chapter, and after presenting some underlying assumptions in Part II, the body of this book consists in the third and fourth Parts which deal with the vertical system of enforcement and with the horizontal system of enforcement respectively. The counterpart of the horizontal system, by virtue of the new international criminal regime, is the vertical system which constitutes the subject-matter of Part III. Here I will ask: to what extent, under international criminal law, may States be said to be obliged to surrender alleged criminals to the ICC to stand trial for core crimes? What leeway do they enjoy under international law? Such analysis will be undertaken not only with regard to those States which have adhered to the ICC Statute, but also with regard to those which have not yet done so, thus exploring the jurisdictional intricacies emanating therefrom. To this extent, within the entire work, my approach is dictated by virtue of a cosmopolitan and global perspective, examining *in toto* various situations which may lead to fully-fledged indictments issued by the ICC. Therefore, to pose the research sub-question differently (this time, couched in

---

[29] Swart and Sluiter 1999, p. 126.

[30] ICC Status Conference 2015. The prosecutors argued that the Government of Kenya withheld significant evidence (including bank account details) which would have proved that *Uhuru Muigai Kenyatta* personally supplied the perpetrators of crimes against humanity (consisting in the 2007–2008 post-electoral violence in Kenya) with substantial amounts of funds and monies which were funnelled down by means of messengers and intermediaries and delivered in cash to the perpetrators to be used for such purposes, and all this with the knowledge that they would be used for such purposes. On 5 December 2014 the ICC Prosecutor filed a notice withdrawing the charges against the accused (ICC Trial Chamber V(B), *Prosecutor v Uhuru Muigai Kenyatta, Notice of Withdrawal of the Charges Against Uhuru Muigai Kenyatta*, 5 December 2014, Case No. ICC-01/09-02/11) and, on 13 March 2015, the ICC terminated proceedings against *Kenyatta* (ICC Trial Chamber V(B), *Prosecutor v Uhuru Muigai Kenyatta, Decision on the Withdrawal of Charges Against Mr. Kenyatta*, 13 March 2015, Case No. ICC-01/09-02/11).

negative terms): to what extent, if at all, are States allowed to refuse to surrender alleged criminals to the ICC? Within this analysis I scrutinize the pitfalls which act as a hurdle to the surrender of alleged perpetrators of core crimes, and shall occasionally attempt, in so far as this is possible, to propose methods intended to fill the ensuing *lacunae* without violating international law. This examination necessitates a profound understanding of the general State obligation to cooperate, the extent to which it is binding (upon State Parties to the ICC and upon non-State Parties in certain circumstances), and the consequences in cases of a breach thereof. Since the ensuing consequences do little to deter States from failing to cooperate with the ICC, I embark onto identifying new legal avenues which can serve to trigger the criminal liability of those who decide to withhold cooperation.

Whereas terminological issues are considered within Chap. 3 and a frame of reference shall be devised in Part III, the fourth Part will encompass the fulcrum of this work. Within Part IV I shall examine the most widely used system of enforcement, the horizontal system, which relies heavily upon State consent, reciprocity and extradition practice, with due regard being had to important and dynamic principles and doctrines of international law. The extent, if any, of the leeway enjoyed by States to extradite or otherwise will be examined. Here I will pose the research sub-question (this time, couched in negative terms) as follows: to what extent, if at all, may requested States be allowed to refuse to extradite alleged criminals to other requesting States? The replies to the research sub-questions will help to answer the research question. In the process, human rights general exceptions to extradition are dealt with and some diverse evidentiary thresholds (yardsticks) are exposed for consideration. Within this analysis I inspect the pitfalls which act as a hurdle to the extradition of alleged perpetrators of core crimes, and attempt, in so far as this is possible, to suggest methods intended to fill the ensuing *lacunae* without violating international law. For this purpose, I must first undertake an autopsy of the *aut dedere aut judicare* rule.

Within Part V, a recapitulation of the focal issues raised within this book will be undertaken. This process will include the substantiation of points raised throughout the book in order to justify the need for any proposed changes within the entire prevailing *corpus juris.* Besides summarising arguments posited, my recommendations are intended to solidify the existent juridical infrastructure and, provided traces of it may be identified successfully and reliably, to establish the emerging framework likely to induce the applicability of a *ius puniendi* under international law. This will not compel the irreversible defeat of impunity but it is intended to constitute an eye-opener for international lawyers in their quest to ensure firstly that prosecutions for core crimes allegedly committed be conducted, and secondly that such prosecutions be conducted fairly and expeditiously in conformity with due process standards and norms imposed by international human rights law. Understandably, in the examination of both systems of enforcement, reference to fundamental human rights will however only limitedly be made either when a ground of refusal hinges on the application or otherwise of a human rights norm or else when the human rights norm largely influences the position at international criminal law. These observations wrap up the introductory chapter of my book.

References

Abels D (2012) Prisoners of the International Community: The Legal Position of Persons Detained at International Criminal Tribunals. Asser Press, The Hague

Alexander A (2015) A Short History of International Humanitarian Law. EJIL 26(01):109–138

Aquilina K (2017) The Rule of Law *À La Maltaise*: Selected Writings of Kevin Aquilina. Department of Media, Communications and Technology Law, Faculty of Laws, University of Malta, Malta

Bassiouni MC (1987) International Criminal Law Vol. III, Enforcement. TP, Dobbs Ferry, NY

Bassiouni MC (1995) *AIDP*: International Association of Penal Law: Over a Century of Dedication to Criminal Justice and Human Rights. In: Bassiouni MC (ed) The Contributions of Specialized Institutes and Non-Governmental Organizations to the United Nations Criminal Justice Program. In Honour of Adolfo Beria di Argentine. MNP, The Hague/Boston/London, pp. 275–294

Bin R (2017) *Lo Stato di Diritto: Come Imporre Regole e Potere* [The Rule of Law: How to Impose Rule and Power], *Seconda Edizione Aggiornata* [Second Revised Edition]. Il Mulino, Bologna, Italy

Boas G, Bischoff JL, Reid NL, Taylor III BD (2011) International Criminal Procedure. International Criminal Law Practitioner Library, Volume III. CUP, Cambridge

Brownlie I (2008) Principles of Public International Law, 7th edn. OUP, Oxford

Cassese A (2011) Reflections on International Criminal Justice. JICJ 9:271–275

Cryer R, Friman H, Robinson D, Wilmshurst E (2010) An Introduction to International Criminal Law and Procedure, 2nd edn. CUP, Cambridge

D'Aspremont J, van den Herik L (2012) The Public Good of Academic Publishing in International Law. LJIL 26(01):1–6

De Gaetano VA (2018) Keynote Speech on the Occasion of the 70th Anniversary of the Universal Declaration of Human Rights at a Conference entitled 'Marking the 70 Years of the Universal Declaration of Human Rights: Trends and Perspectives', organised by the Faculty of Laws, University of Malta and the President's Foundation for the Wellbeing of Society, held on 7 December 2018 at Antoine de Paule Hall, San Anton Palace, Attard, Malta

Dicey AV (1982) Introduction to the Study of the Law of the Constitution. Liberty Fund, Indianapolis

Genocide Convention (1948) Convention on the Prevention and Punishment of the Crime of Genocide

Grant JP, Barker JC (2009) Parry & Grant Encyclopaedic Dictionary of International Law, 3rd edn. OUP, Oxford

Hirsch Ballin MFH (2012) Anticipative Criminal Investigation: Theory and Counterterrorism Practice in the Netherlands and the United States. Asser Press, The Hague

ICC (2015) ICC Status Conference: Prosecution Admits Weak Case Against President Kenyatta. https://www.youtube.com/watch?v=Tl5ILac5KvA. Accessed 12 April 2015

ICC RPE (2000) Rules of Procedure and Evidence of the International Criminal Court

ICC Statute (1998) Rome Statute of the International Criminal Court

ILC (1950) Report of the International Law Commission to the General Assembly. Document A/1316, Report of the International Law Commission Covering its Second Session, 5 June–29 July 1950. In: ILC Yearbook II:364–385

Jackson RH (1945) US Representative to the International Conference on Military Trials. Washington DC, GPO

Jenks C (2009) Notice Otherwise Given: Will *In Absentia* Trials at the Special Tribunal for Lebanon Violate Human Rights? FILJ 33(1):57–100

Letschert R (2017) International Criminal Proceedings – An Adequate Tool for Victims' Justice? In: Tibori-Szabó K, Hirst M (eds) Victim Participation in International Criminal Justice: Practitioners' Guide. Asser Press, The Hague, pp. 467–472

Lever J (1999) Why Procedure is More Important than Substantive Law. ICLQ 48(2):285–301

Nuremberg Principles (1947) Principles of International Law Recognised in the Charter of the Nuremberg Tribunal and in the Judgment of the Tribunal

O'Keefe R (2015) International Criminal Law. The Oxford International Law Library, OUP, Oxford

Proukaki EK (2010) The Problem of Enforcement in International Law: Countermeasures, the Non-Injured State and the Idea of International Community. Routledge, T & F, London/NY

Swart B, Sluiter G (1999) The International Criminal Court and International Criminal Co-operation. In: von Hebel HAM, Lammers JG, Schuking J (eds) Reflections on the International Criminal Court. Asser Press, The Hague, pp. 91–127

Statute of the STL (2007) Statute of the Special Tribunal for Lebanon

UDHR (1948) Universal Declaration of Human Rights

UNGA (1947) Resolution 177 (1947), UN Doc A/RES/177(II)

van Schaack B, Slye R (2010) International Criminal Law and its Enforcement, Cases and Materials, 2nd edn. FP, NY

Zeegers K (2016) International Criminal Tribunals and Human Rights Law: Adherence and Contextualization. International Criminal Justice Series, Volume 5, Asser Press, The Hague

Chapter 2
Preliminary Observations on the Systems of Enforcement

Contents

2.1 The Vertical System of Enforcement: A Useful Frame of Reference 16
2.2 The Horizontal System of Enforcement: From a *'Ius Prosequi'* to 'Mandatory Prosecutions'? 23
References 25

Abstract This chapter starts by exposing the vertical system of enforcement (also known as the direct system of enforcement) which constitutes a meaningful frame of reference for the purposes of the horizontal system of enforcement (also known as the indirect system of enforcement). The former model of enforcement is the supra-national model whereas the latter system is the inter-State model. This chapter portrays the need to have persons surrendered and/or extradited for criminal justice to be delivered and introduces the concept of the duty of the State to cooperate. The ICC, based on State consent (unlike the *ad hoc* tribunals) cannot constrain non-State Parties to cooperate with it when such States are unwilling to do so, unless it can elicit such cooperation on the pretext of a UNSC Resolution. The relevance of the complementarity principle as a catalyst for compliance is noted. Yet, the vertical system of enforcement is heavily burdened and hampered by the fact that the ICC lacks a police force. In the light of the prohibition of trials *in absentia,* the lack of enforcement powers is a serious limitation which paralyzes the functions of the ICC. The horizontal system of enforcement is presented as the primary system of enforcement. Domestic criminal courts are the *forum conveniens* because national States possess the necessary judicial infrastructure, including a police force, prosecution services, courts and a penitentiary system. Domestic competent authorities are expected to engage in the investigation and prosecution of individuals who are allegedly responsible for having committed core crimes.

Keywords Arrest · Catalyst for compliance · Domestication of international criminal law · Duty to cooperate · Extradition · *Forum conveniens* · Frame of

C. Soler, *The Global Prosecution of Core Crimes under International Law*,
https://doi.org/10.1007/978-94-6265-335-1_2

reference · ICC · Horizontal system of enforcement · Surrender · Vertical system of enforcement · Withdrawal · Police force

Before defining some keywords and indulging into some terminological distinctions, some relevant preliminary remarks are warranted in anticipation of the main body of this book, namely Parts III and IV thereof.

2.1 The Vertical System of Enforcement: A Useful Frame of Reference

This heading is intended to convey the use that can be made of the vertical systems of enforcement. For this purpose, an understanding of the concept of verticality will be undertaken at the very beginning of the third Part. This will enable me to consider the vertical system of enforcement, particularly in the light of the ICC regime. I shall undertake this approach, focusing on the ICC, because I want my book to be forward-looking and also in order to address matters which are still rather debatable and relatively understudied. Any reference to either the *ad hoc* tribunals[1] or to the semi-internationalised tribunals within the third Part is hence intended either to shed a light on a point which I would like to make or to conduct a comparative analysis for the benefit of postulating a divergent state of affairs in order to better understand the contours of the ICC's system of enforcement.

Some distinctions between systems prevailing within the vertical system of enforcement are hereby warranted. Besides being an international, though not universal, criminal court, the ICC, which is anything but a 'prototypical court',[2] is a permanent institution,[3] whereas other courts and tribunals are neither international (because they are geographically and/or regionally confined) and not indefinite (because they are temporary). Since the ICC's terms of reference are indefinite, this places the ICC in a somewhat different, rather than advantageous, situation. The ICC's position is intrinsically *sui generis*. The ICC Statute is not the product of a UNSC Resolution. Having been established by treaty, ICC orders do not prevail over a State's duty under treaty or customary law towards States which are not a party to the ICC Statute.[4] On the other hand, in the *ad hoc* tribunals, the duty to

[1] From a jurisprudential viewpoint, the ICTY and the ICTR are considered as the 'richest source of the law of individual criminal responsibility' (see Boas et al. 2007, p. 5).

[2] This term is used by Hopmann 1996, cited in Caron 2006, p. 408, n. 23.

[3] See Article 1 of the ICC Statute (ICC Statute (1998) Rome Statute of the International Criminal Court); see also ICC Pre-Trial Chamber I, *Situation in the DRC, Decision on the Prosecutor's Application for Warrants of Arrest under Article 58*, 10 February 2006, Case No. ICC-01/04-01/07, para 60, in Klip and Sluiter 2010, p. 64.

[4] Ciampi 2002, p. 1631.

arrest and transfer[5] does not emanate conventionally (by signature and ratification of a legal instrument) but is considered to be the application of an enforcement measure under Chapter VII of the UNC.[6] This duty leads to a situation wherein such State obligations prevail over any other State obligations which derive from any other international agreement, over domestic laws and national security interests.[7] The difference between, on the one hand, the *ad hoc* tribunals, and on the other hand, the ICC, is such that the cause of the jurisdiction of the *ad hoc* tribunals has been termed as 'an enviable genesis not shared by the ICC'.[8] However, one must keep in mind that 'what matters is not that the Council created the Tribunal but the specific powers conferred by the decisions of the Council,' since 'the fact that the Security Council created the Tribunal does not in and of itself empower it. Rather it is the terms of the Council decision and the Statute, as adopted and amended by it, which define the powers that it has'.[9] The ICC, unlike the *ad hoc* tribunals, 'is not a subsidiary organ of the UN in the sense that the principal organ possesses the competence to determine the membership, structure, *vires*, mandate, powers and duration of existence of its subsidiary organ'.[10] The ICC is an independent and self-standing international judicial institution, created by States, which can command respect (and demand cooperation) from its State Parties but not from all UN Members States.[11] This factor, *inter alia*,[12] distinguishes the *ad hoc* tribunals from the ICC,[13] as a result of which 'it may seem difficult to treat cooperation law as a uniform regime',[14] notwithstanding that without the *ad hoc* tribunals 'there might never have been a permanent International Criminal Court'.[15] UN Member States are also vested with a duty to take all measures necessary to implement the provisions of the Statutes of the *ad hoc* tribunals and are precluded

[5] For a thorough understanding of the ICTY regime dealing with arrest and surrender, see Bassiouni and Manikas 1996, pp. 773–793.

[6] Macdonald examines the special nature of the UNC, both as a constitution and as a contract (Macdonald 1991, pp. 63–86).

[7] Bantekas 2010, p. 369.

[8] Sloan 2003, p. 111.

[9] Prost 2011, p. 436.

[10] Rastan 2008, p. 442.

[11] Mackenzie et al. 2010, p. 159.

[12] Another basis for States to cooperate with *ad hoc* tribunals is the Dayton Peace Agreement {Dayton Peace Agreement (1995) The General Framework Agreement for Peace in Bosnia and Herzegovina and the Annexes thereto, initialled in Dayton, Ohio on 21 November 1995 and signed in Paris on 14 December 1995} which has no counterpart within the ICC cooperation regime (Wenqi 2006, pp. 98–99).

[13] May 1999, p. 155.

[14] Sluiter 2009, p. 188.

[15] Guterres A (2017) UN Tribunal for Former Yugoslavia Leaves Behind Culture of Accountability, Says Guterres. https://news.un.org/en/story/2017/12/640162-un-tribunal-former-yugoslavia-leaves-behind-culture-accountability-says. Accessed 9 February 2018.

from invoking provisions of domestic law or human rights treaties as justification for a failure to comply with a request or order of a tribunal.

UN Member State obligations to arrest and transfer individuals subject to an arrest warrant, by virtue of the inapplicability of national legal provisions as per Rule 58 of the ICTY RPE, are thus *erga omnes partes*.[16] On the other hand, non-UN Member States 'may undertake to comply with the obligations laid down in Article 29 by expressly accepting the obligation in writing'.[17] The seminal *Blaškić dictum*[18] found that an 'unconditional and absolute duty for States to co-operate'[19] with the ICTY subsisted. The same applies for the ICTR,[20] as noted by Judge Rafael Nieto-Navia who held that such an absolute obligation 'cannot be overridden in particular circumstances by considerations of convenience or politics'.[21] Whilst such absolute obligation held ground within the *ad hoc* tribunals, the absence, within subsequent jurisprudence, of any reference to the *Blaškić* Appeal's Chamber qualification of the obligation as one which is *erga omnes* 'may be an indication that such a qualification does not have much success'.[22] In fact, 'it is a little misleading to state that the Statute lays down an unconditional obligation for States to co-operate with the Court, to which there are but very few exceptions' particularly because the ICC cannot make certain requests for cooperation and assistance which do not fit easily into the interstate model of cooperation.[23] In practice, precluding the ICC from making certain types of requests is effectively equivalent to implanting grounds for refusal of surrender.[24] In the *ad hoc* tribunals no margin of appreciation[25] is allowed because 'no State can unilaterally invoke a ground of refusal'.[26] This sharply contrasts with the nature of State obligations

---

16 ICTY Appeals Chamber, *Prosecutor v Tihomir Blaškić, ICTY Appeals Chamber Judgment on the Request of the Republic of Croatia for Review of the Decision of the Trial Chamber II of 18 July 1997*, 29 October 1997, Case No. IT-95-14-AR 108*bis*, paras 26 and 65.

17 *Blaškić*, above n. 16, para 26.

18 The concepts of vertical and horizontal cooperation were first introduced by the ICTY's *Blaškić dictum* (*Blaškić*, above n. 16, para 47).

19 Klip and van der Wilt 2002, p. 1122.

20 For the reasons why the ICTR 'has not achieved the same high profile as the Yugoslav tribunal', see Maimouni 2011, pp. 37–38.

21 ICTR Appeals Chamber, *Jean-Bosco Barayagwiza v The Prosecutor*, Decision on the Prosecutor's Request for Review or Reconsideration, 31 March 2000, Case No. ICTR-97-19AR72, Declaration of Judge Rafael Nieto-Navia, para 6.

22 Demirdjian 2010, p. 186.

23 Swart and Sluiter 1999, p. 125.

24 Ibid.

25 'There is no universal formula for determining where and how the margin of appreciation should be applied. The width of the discretion left to the contracting States will vary, according to such factors as the nature of the Convention right in issue, the importance of that right for the individual, the nature of the activity involved in the case, the extent of the interference and the nature of the State's justification' (Emmerson et al. 2007, p. 116).

26 Finkle 2011, p. 421.

emanating from Part 9 of the ICC Statute, as shall be seen in the third Part of this work.

In practice, since trials[27] *in absentia* are prohibited under the ICC Statute,[28] a fugitive would have to be arrested, detained and surrendered to the ICC for it to enjoy the jurisdiction it is entitled to exercise under international law. Any arrest is made with a view to surrender. Consequently a duty to arrest a person is necessarily linked to a duty to surrender such person.[29] Realistically, therefore, 'the Court's greatest legal limitation is that it lacks any means to ensure the arrest and surrender of suspects. Although State Parties face a legal obligation to arrest and surrender indictees within their jurisdiction, their willingness and ability to do so is often questionable'.[30] Antonio Cassese metaphorically referred to the ICTY as a 'giant without arms and legs – it needs artificial limbs to walk and work',[31] stressing that international courts cannot operate without the help of State authorities.[32] Subsequently, Theodor Meron shared Cassese's concerns.[33] One can only imagine what both would say today with reference to the ICC, which is weaker, in this regard, than the ICTY. Other jurists are more critical and pessimistic. They consider the vertical system of enforcement as 'the weakest link of the Court's procedural framework'.[34] Pascal's words come to mind at this point: 'We must make what is just, strong'.[35] The relevance of the above differentiation cries out loud. The ICC, based on State consent[36] (unlike the *ad hoc* tribunals) cannot constrain non-State Parties to cooperate with it when such States are unwilling to do so, unless it can elicit such cooperation on the pretext of a UNSC Resolution.

The ICC's main problems do not simply stem from the differences (with the *ad hoc* tribunals) noted here above. The uphill struggle the ICC faces is the remnant of

---

[27] A trial does not include the confirmation of charges hearing in terms of Article 61(2) of the ICC Statute, above n. 3. In fact, this legal provision is not placed within Part 6 of the ICC Statute, above n. 3, entitled 'the Trial'.

[28] See its Article 63.

[29] Swart 2002, p. 1252.

[30] Burke-White 2008, p. 65

[31] Cassese 1998, p. 13.

[32] Cassese 1999, p. 164.

[33] Meron 2008.

[34] Cryer et al. 2011, p. 529.

[35] Pascal 1660, para 298, cited in Jorda 2004, p. 584.

[36] Nancy Combs clarifies that the 'compromise reached in Rome steers a middle course between universality and consent, and it provides the ICC with jurisdiction over a case if either the territorial State or the State of nationality of the defendant is a State Party or has accepted the ICC's jurisdiction on an ad hoc basis' (see Combs 2005, pp. 353–354).

the role generally played by the State in the commission of core crimes which will be discussed in depth in the forthcoming Part, that is, Part II of this work, and which discloses a *realpolitik*. This may be rephrased as a manifest frailty which is caused by the fact that the ICC 'may be forced to try to induce cooperation from the very governments whose members it is trying to prosecute'.[37] Inevitably, therefore, political considerations are of the essence in this realm,[38] wherein, just to cite a case in point, President Thomas Yayi of Benin lamented the harassment of African leaders by the ICC.[39] The AU's statement, in April 2011, to the effect that 'it would consider withdrawing from the Statute *en masse* if a proposed request for deferral of the post-election violence cases under Article 16 were to fail', is certainly a more worrisome example.[40] The withdrawals of Burundi,[41] South Africa[42] and The Gambia[43] from the ICC Statute could have prompted further moves to such effect in the near future particularly if Afro-centrist objections continue to spread[44] and if the AU's strategy calling for a collective withdrawal from the ICC materialises.[45] This unwanted development might have been avoided by means of the revocation of the

---

[37] Currie 2007, p. 383.

[38] Roach 2011, p. 546 and p. 550; see also Roper and Barria 2008, p. 467; see also Ginsburg 2013, *passim*.

[39] Jalloh 2009, p. 463. The need to uphold the 'principle of prosecutorial fairness' is given importance not only by jurists, but even by political scientists and experts of international relations (Peskin 2005, pp. 227–228).

[40] Brighton 2012, p. 661.

[41] The preliminary examination of the situation in Burundi was announced by the ICC on 25 April 2016 (see website of the ICC 2016. https://www.icc-cpi.int/burundi. Accessed 29 October 2016). On 18 October 2016 Burundi's President signed legislation further to which Burundi became the first State Party to withdraw from the ICC Statute, above n. 3 (Muhumuza (2016) Burundi's President Signs Bill on Withdrawal from the ICC. The Washington Post. https://www.washingtonpost.com/world/africa/burundis-president-signs-bill-on-withdrawal-from-the-icc/2016/10/18/3c212704-9559-11e6-9cae-2a3574e296a6_story.html Accessed 29 October 2016).

[42] On 19 October 2016, South Africa's Minister of International Relations and Cooperation signed a document which outlines the withdrawal plan (Reuters (2016) South Africa to Quit International Criminal Court. The Guardian, Pretoria. https://www.theguardian.com/world/2016/oct/21/south-africa-to-quit-international-criminal-court-document-shows. Accessed 19 April 2018).

[43] *Agence France-Presse* (2016) Gambia is the Latest African Nation to Quit International Criminal Court: Announcement Follows Decisions by South Africa and Burundi Earlier this Month to Withdraw from ICC. The Guardian, Dakar. https://www.theguardian.com/world/2016/oct/26/gambia-becomes-latest-african-nation-to-quit-international-criminal-court. Accessed 19 April 2018.

[44] Vilmer 2016, pp. 1324–1334.

[45] Associated Press (2017) African Leaders Plan Mass Withdrawal from International Criminal Court, The Guardian, Addis Ababa. https://www.theguardian.com/law/2017/jan/31/african-leaders-plan-mass-withdrawal-from-international-criminal-court. Accessed 19 April 2018.

withdrawal by South Africa[46] and The Gambia.[47] Yet, the former African State still threatens withdrawal[48] and the AU, at its thirtieth summit held in Addis Ababa, Ethiopia, has now resolved to ask the UNGA to seek an advisory opinion from the ICJ on the issue of Head of State immunity.[49] It is hoped that this would not overshadow the valid 'contributions to the creation of the ICC'[50] made by African States, whose delegates, as Judge Monageng acknowledged, 'were at the forefront of pressing for a permanent, impartial and strong International Criminal Court that would address international crimes and help with strengthening national judicial systems'.[51] Most importantly, irrespective of the role of the State in the commission of core crimes, the absence of police powers to enforce a request for surrender is a major handicap. Other considerations may, for example, have a deep impact on extraneous and unrelated matters, namely by the exercise of pressure on defaulting States. Former ICTY President Antonio Cassese had called for the expulsion of then Yugoslavia from the Olympic Games for its failure to arrest *Radovan Karadžić* and *Ratko Mladić*.[52] Appeals in these two cases are currently being heard before the UN International Residual Mechanism for Criminal Tribunals.[53] All this shows that the ICC does not operate within a vacuum but within a rather volatile political atmosphere.

Having, at the outset, pinpointed some important variations between the respective vertical systems of enforcement, the third Part of this work, by scrutinizing the content and consequences of the vertical systems of enforcement within the ambit of international criminal law, also referred to by jurists as the 'direct

---

[46] Reuters (2017) South Africa Formally Revokes International Court Withdrawal, Daily World. http://www.internationalcrimesdatabase.org/. Accessed 19 April 2018. This major development followed the decision of the South African High Court (Guateng Division, Pretoria) which found that the government's decision to give notice of withdrawal from the ICC was unconstitutional and invalid (High Court {Guateng Division, Pretoria}, South Africa, *Matter between Democratic Alliance and Minister of International Relations and Cooperation et al.*, 22 February 2017, Case 83145/2016, para 84. http://www.saflii.org/za/cases/ZAGPPHC/2017/53.pdf. Accessed 19 April 2018).

[47] UN News Centre (2015) UN Chief Guterres Welcomes The Gambia's Rescission of its Withdrawal from the International Criminal Court. http://www.un.org/apps/news/story.asp?NewsID=56190#.WM_agVXysdU. Accessed 20 February 2017.

[48] du Plessis M (2017) South Africa's Latest Threat to Withdraw From the ICC or, How to Squander Leadership. Daily Maverick. https://www.dailymaverick.co.za/article/2017-12-11-south-africas-latest-threat-to-withdraw-from-the-icc-or-how-to-squander-leadership/#.WtMrbi5uapo. Accessed 19 April 2018. However, a withdrawal seems unlikely with Zuma having lost the leadership of the African National Congress and with Cyril Ramaphosa at the helm of South Africa (Reinold 2018).

[49] Kersten 2018.

[50] Gissel 2018, p. 747.

[51] Monageng 2014, p. 15.

[52] McDonald 2004, p. 563.

[53] See list of selected ongoing cases at http://www.irmct.org/en. Accessed 29 December 2018.

enforcement system',[54] shall be identifying and parading the utility of such system. This Part shall hence identify the utility of the vertical system of enforcement for the purposes of the implementation of international criminal justice. This utility will become clearer after a reading of the third, fourth and fifth Parts in so far as they shall reveal the synergy and inter-reliance between the respective enforcement systems of international criminal law, these being the vertical system of enforcement and the horizontal system of enforcement. The vertical system of enforcement is useful because it has the potential to shape new rules of customary international law and to forge new general principles of law which can, and should, in turn, be used within the horizontal system of enforcement. In fact, the domestication of international criminal law provides national criminal justice systems with the opportunity to transpose and incorporate laws into their own criminal justice system. This is, however, not only an opportunity. It can assume the nature of a fully-fledged obligation. Whereas, until a few years ago, the lack of implementing legislation led to impunity, nowadays it could safely lead to the enjoyment of jurisdiction by the ICC and/or international criminal tribunals. The case against an individual subsists, only the judicial *forum* changes. Therefore, although the ICC Statute does not necessitate domestic criminalization *de lege*, if State Parties choose not to incorporate the acts or omissions penalized by the ICC Statute into their domestic law, they would *de facto* practically be relinquishing their own jurisdiction. They would not possess the necessary tools to investigate and prosecute a core crime. Upon such failure to investigate and/or prosecute, they would be waiving the rights they enjoy by virtue of the principle of complementarity. The complementarity principle, which is well-embodied in the ICC Statute,[55] and the way it shall be applied by the ICC, could serve as a catalyst for compliance not only with a State's duty to investigate and prosecute core crimes but with a State's duty to undertake such investigation and prosecution fairly. This is more so when one recalls that complementarity (which denotes the primacy of domestic courts) 'has become the rule and not merely the exception',[56] a rule the pretext of which is a presumption in favour of national jurisdictions and the impact of which constitutes a potent threat to State sovereignty.[57] Complementarity acts as a catalyst for compliance especially when the interests of States and the ICC to retain or assume jurisdiction over a case coincide. When such interests are not shared, the relationship between the State and the ICC has been described as antagonistic.[58] This tension will be unmasked within the third Part of this work. The ongoing relationship, with all its ups and downs, is the ultimate proof both of the impact which the vertical system of enforcement can have on the horizontal system of enforcement and of the fact that the ICC, with all

---

[54] Bassiouni 2008, p. 3; Knoops 2002, p. 9.

[55] Scheffer 2000, p. 204.

[56] Otto Triffterer's Tubingen Keynote Address 2010, paras 45–46, cited in Usacka 2011, p. 489, n. 64.

[57] Megret 2006, p. 23.

[58] Kleffner 2006, p. 84.

its bottlenecks, is a meaningful enforcement mechanism.[59] It is undisputed that cross-fertilization and judicial dialogue allows domestic judges to seek guidance from international judges.[60] To this extent, the vertical system of enforcement is a useful frame of reference because the horizontal system of enforcement is most likely to learn from it. Actually, it can provide more than a mere frame of reference for horizontal cooperation. In the words of Harmen van der Wilt, way back at the start of the new millennium, 'it seems fair to state that domestic courts to a large extent lack the capacity and the tools to conduct war crimes trials independently and impartially. Simultaneously, States are bound by international legal provisions to carry out investigations and to prosecute crimes under international law. Caught in this dilemma, States are often left no other option than to seek the assistance of an international criminal court'.[61] Indeed, this observation still holds true today.

2.2 The Horizontal System of Enforcement: From a *'Ius Prosequi'* to 'Mandatory Prosecutions'?

After having identified the utility of the vertical system of enforcement, some introductory remarks about the horizontal system of enforcement are apposite. Before delving into the dynamics of the way the horizontal system of enforcement functions, its relevance must be reiterated. This is necessary particularly because the horizontal system of enforcement is commonly referred to as the 'indirect enforcement system,[62] the cornerstone of which is *aut dedere aut judicare*.[63] To an extent, this misleads one to perceive such a system as, in some way, ancillary or secondary. In truth, the horizontal system of enforcement is not the subsidiary system of international criminal justice, but its fulcrum, its very essence. In footballing terms, the horizontal system of enforcement caters for the first-team players whereas the ICC's players sit on the bench as reserves, and enter the field by way of a substitution when a horizontal system of enforcement player is either injured (unable) or unwilling to play. The horizontal system of enforcement is the primary *coliseum* of international criminal proceedings within a global village wherein international law is increasingly undergoing a domestication process.[64]

The norms prohibiting core crimes 'penetrate the armour of State sovereignty'.[65] In any case, however, international courts operating within the vertical system of enforcement are not obliged to follow judgments arising from the horizontal system

[59] Jensen 2006, pp. 166–168.
[60] van Sliedregt 2012, p. 851.
[61] van der Wilt 2000, p. 336.
[62] Bassiouni and Wise 1995, Preface, p. x; Knoops 2002, p. 9.
[63] Bassiouni 2003, p. 334.
[64] Nollkaemper 2011, p. 245.
[65] Werle and Bung 2010, p. 1; Werle 2009, p. 32.

of enforcement, that is, domestic *dicta*. To this extent, although a municipal court decision is given due weight and may be considered as truly authoritative, it is not legally binding under international law, notwithstanding that it may be said that domestic criminal courts act on behalf of, or in representation of, or as agents of the international community, especially when they exercise universal jurisdiction. André Nollkaemper specifically identifies the constitutional and criminal fields of law in reaching a conclusion that municipal court judgments may be subject to indirect review by a competent international judicial *forum*.[66] This however does not detract from their relevance in that 'the international legal order itself may accept under certain conditions the authority of decisions of national courts'.[67] The influence of decisions of national courts can be expected to increase because more and more domestic courts consider international legal matters and, in doing so, they seek to determine and interpret international law objectively.[68] The horizontal system of enforcement's relevance may be synthesised in the words of Georges Abi-Saab who, notwithstanding the ICC, refers to a 'still largely interstate system of present-day international law'.[69] Though he seems to amplify the point, Benedetto Conforti suggests that the horizontal system of enforcement is the only way to understand the legal function of general international law and its binding force.[70] In a detailed study,[71] Harmen van der Wilt identifies four distinct approaches which manifest the way in which domestic courts are contributing to the development of international criminal law. These four approaches[72] truly reflect the broad purview of the horizontal system of enforcement, a jurisdictionally unparalleled reach, especially when compared to the ICC's role as an emergency, stand-by judicial mechanism.

The centrality of the horizontal system of enforcement has already been posited here above. To this, one may merely add a practical note. Domestic criminal courts within the horizontal system of enforcement are the *forum conveniens* because national States possess the 'necessary judicial infrastructure, namely a police force, prosecution services, courts and a penitentiary system'.[73] Notwithstanding this, some judicial systems portray and perceive differentiations upon the pretext of other determining factors and criteria, such as nationality.[74] A case in point is the DRC which seems to side-line the importance of the *forum conveniens*. In September

[66] Nollkaemper 2011, p. 255.

[67] Ibid.

[68] Nollkaemper 2003, p. 295.

[69] Abi-Saab 2003, p. 601.

[70] Conforti 1993, p. 8.

[71] van der Wilt 2013, p. 209.

[72] These are strict compliance, antagonism, the discovery of new standards of customary international law, and the application of local norms.

[73] Kleffner 2008, p. 27.

[74] For an understanding of the right to a nationality under international human rights law, see Forlati 2013, pp. 19–20.

2003, Minister of Justice Kisimba-Ngoy had declared that 'for crimes committed by Congolese, we will hold them accountable in national courts. For crimes committed by international actors, we will hold them accountable in international courts'.[75] Domestic trials are not only undertaken since the municipal criminal court is the *forum conveniens*. Other reasons, motives and interests, sometimes prevail.

The prevalence of the horizontal system of enforcement *per se* as the predominant *domaine reserve* of the enforcement of international criminal law requires no ulterior elucidation at this stage. What still needs to be done (what the fourth Part will be doing), however, is to assess whether a *ius prosequi* enjoyed by the international community and/or States can (or should) become (be transformed into) a rule requiring mandatory prosecutions when core crimes are concerned. This may be said to be, amidst an in-depth study of the grounds for refusal of State cooperation at a stage preceding surrender (within the vertical system of enforcement) and preceding extradition (within the horizontal system of enforcement), a major thrust of this book. It will reveal how a burgeoning obligation, at least for certain States, to engage in the prosecution of core crimes, is budding, and how it can have repercussions on other States in the field of mandatory cooperation. For this purpose and with such tasks in mind, I shall now pass onto examining the concept of 'core crimes', an understanding of which is essential as a precursor to analyse the strengths and weaknesses of both systems of enforcement. This analysis will serve to answer the research question which was posed in the first chapter.

References

Abi-Saab G (2003) The Proper Role of Universal Jurisdiction. JICJ 1(3):596–602

Bantekas I (2010) International Criminal Law, 4th edn. HP, Oxford

Bassiouni MC (2003) Introduction to International Criminal Law. International and Comparative Criminal Law Series, TP, Ardsley, NY

Bassiouni MC (2008) The Discipline of International Criminal Law. In: Bassiouni MC (ed) International Criminal Law: Sources, Subjects and Contents, Vol. II, 3rd edn. MNP, Leiden, pp. 3–40

Bassiouni MC, Manikas P (1996) The Law of the International Criminal Tribunal for the Former Yugoslavia. TP, NY

Bassiouni MC, Wise EM (1995) *Aut Dedere Aut Judicare*: The Duty to Extradite or Prosecute in International Law. MNP, Dordrecht/Boston/London

Boas G, Bischoff JL, Reid N (2007) International Criminal Law Practitioner Library, Volume I: Forms of Responsibility in International Criminal Law. CUP, Cambridge

Brighton C (2012) Avoiding Unwillingness: Addressing the Political Pitfalls Inherent in the Complementarity Regime of the International Criminal Court. ICLR 12(4):629–664

Burke-White WW (2008) Proactive Complementarity: The ICC and National Courts in the Rome System of International Justice. HILJ 49(1):53–108

Caron DD (2006) Towards a Political Theory of International Courts and Tribunals. BJIL 24 (2):401–422

[75] Tillier 2013, p. 527.

Cassese A (1998) On the Current Trends Towards Criminal Prosecution and Punishment of Breaches of International Humanitarian Law. EJIL 9:2–17

Cassese A (1999) The Statute of the International Criminal Court: Some Preliminary Reflections. EJIL 10:144–171

Ciampi A (2002) The Obligation to Cooperate. In: Cassese A, Gaeta P, Jones JRWD (eds) The Rome Statute of the International Criminal Court: A Commentary, Vol. II. OUP, Oxford, pp. 1607–1638

Combs N (2005) The International Criminal Court. In: van Krieken PJ, McKay D (eds) The Hague: Legal Capital of the World. Asser Press, The Hague, pp. 345–436

Conforti B (1993) International Law and the Role of Domestic Legal Systems. MNP, Dordrecht/Boston/London

Cryer R, Friman H, Robinson H and Wilmshurst E (2011) An Introduction to International Criminal Law and Procedure, 2nd edn. CUP, Cambridge

Currie RJ (2007) Abducted Fugitives Before the International Criminal Court: Problems and Prospects. CLF 18(3–4):349–393

Dayton Peace Agreement (1995) The General Framework Agreement for Peace in Bosnia and Herzegovina

Demirdjian A (2010) Armless Giants: Cooperation, State Responsibility and Suggestions for the ICC Review Conference. ICLR 10(02): 181–208

Emmerson B, Ashworth A and Macdonald A (2007) Human Rights and Criminal Justice, 2nd edn. S & M, London

Finkle E (2011) Subpoena to Witnesses, Commentary on the ICTY Trial Chamber Decision on Application of General Dragoljub Ojdanić for Binding Orders Pursuant to Rule 54*bis*, Prosecutor v Milutinović *et al.*, Case No. IT-99-37-PT, 23 March 2005. In: Klip A, Sluiter G (eds) Annotated Leading Cases of International Criminal Tribunals, The International Criminal Tribunal for the Former Yugoslavia 2005, Vol. 27. Intersentia, Antwerp/Oxford/Portland

Forlati S (2013) Nationality as a Human Right. In Annoni A, Forlati S (eds) The Changing Role of Nationality in International Law. Routledge Research in International Law, Routledge, London/Oxford/NY, pp. 18–36

General Framework Agreement for Peace in BiH and the Annexes thereto (1995)

Ginsburg T (2013) Political Constraints on International Courts. University of Chicago Public Law & Legal Theory Working Paper No. 453, University of Chicago Law School, Chicago

Gissel LE (2018) A Different Kind of Court: Africa's Support for the International Criminal Court, 1993–2003. EJIL 29(3):725–748

Hopmann PT (1996) The Negotiation Process and the Resolution of International Conflicts. University of South Carolina Press, Columbia, South Carolina

ICC Pre-Trial Chamber I, *Situation in the DRC, Decision on the Prosecutor's Application for Warrants of Arrest under Article 58*, 10 February 2006, Case No. ICC-01/04-01/07. In: Klip A, Sluiter G (eds) (2010) Annotated Leading Cases of International Criminal Tribunals: The International Criminal Court 2005–2007. Vol. 23, Intersentia, Antwerp/Oxford/Portland

ICC (2016) ICC Prosecutor Authorised to Open *Proprio Motu* Investigation. https://www.icc-cpi.int/burundi. Accessed 19 April 2016

ICC Statute (1998) Rome Statute of the International Criminal Court

Jalloh CC (2009) Regionalizing International Criminal Law? ICLR 9(3):445–499

Jensen R (2006) Complementarity, "Genuinely" and Article 17: Assessing the Boundaries of an Effective International Criminal Court. In: Kleffner JK and Kor G (eds) Complementary Views on Complementarity: Proceedings of the International Roundtable on the Complementary Nature of the International Criminal Court, Amsterdam, 25/26 June 2004. Asser Press, The Hague, pp. 147–170

Jorda C (2004) The Major Hurdles and Accomplishments of the International Criminal Tribunal for the Former Yugoslavia: What the International Criminal Court Can Learn from Them. JICJ 2:572–584

Kersten M (2018) Negotiated Engagement – The African Union, the International Criminal Court, and Head of State Immunity, Justice in Conflict. https://justiceinconflict.org/2018/03/05/negotiated-engagement-the-african-union-the-international-criminal-court-and-head-of-state-immunity/. Accessed 19 April 2018

Kleffner JK (2006) Complementarity as a Catalyst for Compliance. In: Kleffner JK and Kor G (eds) Complementary Views on Complementarity: Proceedings of the International Roundtable on the Complementary Nature of the International Criminal Court, Amsterdam, 25/26 June 2004. Asser Press, The Hague, pp. 79–104

Kleffner JK (2008) Complementarity in the Rome Statute and National Criminal Jurisdiction. International Courts and Tribunals Series, OUP, Oxford

Klip A, van der Wilt H (2002) Netherlands' Report for the *AIDP*. *RIDP* 73:1091–1137

Knoops G-JA (2002) Surrendering to International Criminal Courts: Contemporary Practice and Procedures. International and Comparative Criminal Law Series, TP, Ardsley/NY

Macdonald RSJ (1991) The United Nations Charter: Constitution or Contract? In: Macdonald RSJ, Johnston DM (eds) The Structure and Process of International Law. MNP, Dordrecht/Boston/London, pp. 63–86

Mackenzie R, Romano C, Shany Y, Sands P (2010), The Manual on International Courts and Tribunals, 2nd edn. International Courts and Tribunals, OUP, Oxford

Maimouni F (2011) (ed) Rwanda Tribunal: Selected Documents. Wolf Legal Publishers, Nijmegen

May R (1999) The Relationship Between the ICC and the ICTY. In: von Hebel HAM, Lammers JG and Schuking J (eds) Reflections on the International Criminal Court. Asser Press, The Hague, pp. 155–162

McDonald GK (2004) Problems, Obstacles and Achievements of the International Criminal Tribunal for the Former Yugoslavia. JICJ 2(2):558–571

Megret F (2006) Why Would States Want to Join the ICC?: A Theoretical Explanation Based on the Legal Nature of Complementarity. In: Kleffner JK and Kor G (eds) Complementary Views on Complementarity: Proceedings of the International Roundtable on the Complementary Nature of the International Criminal Court, Amsterdam, 25/26 June 2004. Asser Press, The Hague, pp. 1–51

Meron T (2008) Key Note Speech, Making the International Criminal Court a Global Reality Through Cooperation: Perspectives, Challenges and Strategies. The Peace Palace, Academy Hall, IBA, London

Monageng SM (2014) Africa and the International Criminal Court: Then and Now. In: Werle G, Fernandez L, Vormbaum M (eds) Africa and the International Criminal Court. International Criminal Justice Series, Vol. 1, Asser Press, The Hague, pp. 13–20

Nollkaemper A (2003) Decisions of National Courts as a Source of International Law: An Analysis of the Practice of the ICTY. In: Boas G, Schabas WA (eds) International Criminal Law Developments in the Case Law of the ICTY. International Humanitarian law Series, MNP, Leiden/Boston, pp. 277–296

Nollkaemper A (2011) National Courts and the International Rule of Law. OUP, Oxford

Pascal B (1660) Justice and the Reasons for Effects: Section V of Selected *Pensees*. EP Dutton & Co. Inc, NY

Peskin V (2005) Beyond Victor's Justice? The Challenge of Prosecuting the Winners at the International Criminal Tribunals for the Former Yugoslavia and Rwanda. JHR 4(2):213–231

Prost K (2011) The ICTY and its Relationship with National Jurisdictions: Powers, Limits, and Misconceptions. In: Swart B, Zahar A, Sluiter G (eds) The Legacy of the International Criminal Tribunal for the Former Yugoslavia. OUP, Oxford, pp. 434–468

Rastan R (2008) Testing Co-operation: The ICC and National Authorities. LJIL 21(2):431–456

Reinold T (2018) African Union v International Criminal Court: Episode MLXIII(?). EJIL: Talk! https://www.ejiltalk.org/african-union-v-international-criminal-court-episode-mlxiii/. Accessed 29 March 2018

Roach SC (2011) The Turbulent Politics of the International Criminal Court. Peace Review: A Journal of Social Justice, 23:546–551

Roper SD and Barria LA (2008) State Co-operation and International Criminal Court Bargaining Influence in the Arrest and the Surrender of Suspects. LJIL 21(2):457–476

Scheffer D (2000) The United States and the ICC. In: Shelton D (ed) International Crimes, Peace, and Human Rights: The Role of the International Criminal Court. TP, Ardsley, NY, pp. 203–206

Sloan J (2003) Prosecutor v Todorović: Illegal Capture as an Obstacle to the Exercise of International Criminal Jurisdiction. LJIL 16(1):85–113

Sluiter G (2009) Cooperation of States, with International Criminal Tribunals. In: Cassese A (ed) The Oxford Companion to International Criminal Justice, OUP, Oxford, pp. 187–200

Swart B (2002) Arrest Proceedings in the Custodial State. In: Cassese A, Gaeta P and Jones JRWD (eds) The Rome Statute of the International Criminal Court: A Commentary. Vol. II, OUP, Oxford, pp. 1247–1255

Swart B, Sluiter G (1999) The International Criminal Court and International Criminal Co-operation. In: von Hebel HAM, Lammers JG, Schuking J (eds) Reflections on the International Criminal Court. Asser Press, The Hague, pp. 91–127

Tillier J (2013) The International Criminal Court Prosecutor and Positive Complementarity: Strengthening the Rule of Law? ICLR 13(3):507–591

Triffterer O (2010) Tubingen Keynote Address, The Court in Danger? Future Perspectives for International Criminal Law and Its Enforcement Mechanisms. In: The Review Conference and the Future of the International Criminal Court: Proceedings of the First *AIDP* Symposium for Young Penalists in Tubingen, Germany, co-organized by the *AIDP* YP Committee. KLI, Dordrecht

UNC (1945) Charter of the United Nations

Usacka A (2011) Promises Fulfilled? Some Reflections on the International Criminal Court in its First Decade. CLF 22(4):473–492

van der Wilt H (2000) The International Criminal Court and Domestic Jurisdictions: Competition or Concerted Action. In: Coomans F, Grunfeld F, Westendorp I, Willems J (eds) Rendering Justice to the Vulnerable, *Liber Amicorum* in Honour of Theo van Boven. KLI, Dordrecht, pp. 323–338

van der Wilt H (2013) Domestic Courts' Contribution to the Development of International Criminal Law; Some Reflections. ILR Vol. 46(2):207–231

van Sliedregt E (2012) Pluralism in International Criminal Law. LJIL 25(4):847–855

Vilmer J-BJ (2016) The African Union and the International Criminal Court: Counteracting the Crisis. International Affairs, 92(6):1319–1342

Wenqi Z (2006) On Co-operation by States not party to the ICC. IRRC 88(861):87–110

Werle G (2009) Principles of International Criminal Law, 2nd edn. Asser Press, The Hague

Werle G, Bung J (2010) Concepts, Tasks and Legitimacy, Summary (Principles of International Criminal Justice). International Criminal Justice, Sommersemester, *Humboldt-Universität* zu Berlin. http://werle.rewi.hu-berlin.de/02_Principles-Summary.pdf. Accessed 19 April 2018

Part II
The Characterisation and Prosecution of Core Crimes: Some Underlying Assumptions

Chapter 3
Multi-level Prosecutions of Serious Crimes of Concern to the International Community

Contents

References 37

Abstract After highlighting that the book will only consider the crucial stage of the procedural iter which can lead to prosecutions, this being either the surrender or extradition of individuals, this chapter unravels the various distinct institutional levels of prosecution. Distinctions are drawn between the domestic, international and hybrid models, whereas the main features of the latter model are explained. With the exception of the African Criminal Court, there is no system which allows for regional prosecutions. When an alleged core crime is not prosecuted, other systems are established. These include special prosecutions which undertake *sui generis* trials before special courts and/or tribunals. Therefore, multi-layered levels (frameworks) of different types and kinds of prosecutions also comprise extraordinary mechanisms of a *sui generis* nature, such as the *Lockerbie* trial. Special courts can be constituted by means of specialized units within the local criminal justice system, such as the ICD of the HC of Uganda and the ICT of Bangladesh. There is no formal relationship between the ICC and the ICD of the HC of Uganda, although the latter can be regarded as a court of complementarity with the ICC. In the case of the ICT of Bangladesh, unlike the KSC which are staffed with international prosecutors and judges, there is no involvement of the international community. These special courts are also distinguished from hybrid tribunals. The determining factor is the involvement or otherwise of external (not domestic) elements. If there is no international involvement at all, the hybrid dimension is missing.

Keywords African Criminal Court · Domestic prosecutions · Hybrid tribunals · Institutional levels of prosecutions · International prosecutions · Malabo Protocol · Regional criminal court · Regional prosecutions · Special prosecutions · Specialized units · *Sui generis* prosecutions

C. Soler, *The Global Prosecution of Core Crimes under International Law*,
https://doi.org/10.1007/978-94-6265-335-1_3

Having established the *modus operandi* which shall be undertaken to accomplish the tasks set out in this book, a few preliminary remarks relating to the subjection of crimes to prosecution (or rather, the extent to which they are prosecutable), are warranted. This is significant when one notes that the purposes and the functions of international criminal law include both extradition and prosecution.[1] These remarks will be made in conjunction with the quest to better understand the import of certain keywords and terminological distinctions. To this effect Part II primarily delves into the concept of 'core crimes' which is central to this work, as attested by the title of this study, this being 'the global prosecution of core crimes under international law'. Before understanding the concept of 'core crimes' it would be appropriate to map out the different geographic and institutional levels of prosecutions which the international community has so far admitted since this book relates to 'the global prosecution of core crimes'. In other words, it is important to note the various permutations which allow for different levels of prosecutions, these being domestic,[2] hybrid and international prosecutions, although regional and special (*sui generis*) prosecutions are also traceable. This importance also stems from the fact that the surge in such judicial mechanisms has radically changed international affairs.[3] This preliminary exercise, coupled with the analysis which is undertaken in this Part, has a duplicate function. Firstly, it sows the seeds for the prospective two Parts which deal with the vertical and the horizontal systems of enforcement respectively. Secondly, it shows the extent to which crimes can be categorized on the basis of the way they are prosecuted and punished, or inversely, the extent to which their prosecution and punishment depends on their distinctive categorization (status). Before proceeding, an important observation is called for. This book only considers a crucial stage of the procedural iter which can lead to prosecutions, that is, either the surrender or the extradition of individuals. Either one of these is necessary for the purposes of an eventual prosecution unless trials *in absentia* are allowed. The book does not consider prosecutions before trial chambers. *Multo magis,* it does not deal with appeals from convictions and/or sentences. Since the prosecution of individuals is entirely reliant either on their prior surrender or on their prior extradition, the surrender or extradition of individuals, in practice, ensures their prosecution. Additionally, the term 'prosecution' has been preferred because a duty to prosecute can also derive from a failure either to surrender or to extradite.

Whereas the international system of prosecutions operates vertically, national systems of prosecutions function horizontally. On the one hand, the prevailing system of international prosecutions is partially reflected within the currently applicable ICC complementarity regime and the primacy of the *ad hoc* international

---

[1] Malekian 2011, p. 138.

[2] The words 'domestic', 'national', 'local' and/or 'municipal' are also used inter-changeably.

[3] de Serpa Soares 2015, p. 672.

criminal tribunals. The vertical system is premised on selective prosecutions[4] and relies on the obligation of State cooperation which is intended to lead to the surrender of suspects to the ICC.[5] Rod Rastan, Legal Officer of the Prosecutor of the ICC, has acknowledged that 'with the establishment of the Rome Statute, the international community has created a global system of international criminal justice'.[6] He adds, justifying the need to galvanise international cooperation to support the work of the ICC, that 'the treaty signed in Rome is not just about a Court, it is about a system; a global system based upon the interaction of international and national authorities'.[7] It is this global system which leads to global prosecutions, as portrayed within the title of my book. On the other hand, the horizontal system is characterised by *a juris tantum* presumption towards effective and fair national criminal justice systems which assume jurisdiction over an alleged crime provided such systems are genuinely willing and able to investigate and prosecute.[8] It is State to State, termed as 'transordinate' by Neil Boister,[9] and relies heavily, though not exclusively, upon the national prosecution of crimes subject to the jurisdiction of the ICC. The two systems are not detached but feed into each other.

In legal discourse prosecutions have generally been associated with domestic processes intended to bring alleged criminals to justice. The term 'prosecutions' has however been broadened considerably within recent scholarship, although this has not been the result of a gradual and consistent escalation. In fact, nowadays, prosecutions exist both nationally and internationally. They hardly exist regionally or continentally. The EU and the OAS, for example, do not possess a prosecution service or office, although recent developments within the EU manifest an intention to develop such structures (limiting however such jurisdiction to crimes against the EU's financial interests) in the near future.[10] Mention must here be made of the CoE

---

[4] Notwithstanding that the gravity threshold within Article 17(1)(d) of the ICC Statute (ICC Statute (1998) Rome Statute of the International Criminal Court) can be said to justify (and possibly demand) selective prosecutions, Charles Chernor Jalloh states that the concept of 'greatest responsibility' was formally introduced into international criminal law by the Statute of the SCSL [Statute of the SCSL (2002) Statute of the Special Court for Sierra Leone] (Jalloh 2011, p. 412). Selectivity has been considered by some as inconsistent with the principle of equality of all persons before the law (Nielsen 2008, pp. 81 and 85, cited in Eberechi 2011, p. 55, n. 24).

[5] Article 59 of the ICC Statute, above n. 4.

[6] Rastan 2007, p. 1.

[7] Rastan 2007, p. 6.

[8] Article 17, sub-article 1, para (a) of the ICC Statute, above n. 4.

[9] Boister 2003, p. 972.

[10] See Article 86 of the Treaty on the Functioning of the European Union, as amended by the Lisbon Treaty, and the subsequent legislative proposal of a Regulation, dealing with the EPPO's Office, undertaken by the European Commission on 17 July 2013. For a background of the concept of the European Public Prosecutor, see Ligeti 2013, pp. 1–6, and Weyembergh and Briere 2016. This legislative proposal was the subject of discussion at European Council level (D'Alfonso 2015). On 12 October 2017 the Regulation establishing the EPPO was adopted by the EU Member States which are part of the EPPO enhanced cooperation. The EPPO will be based in Luxembourg

which, by means of its ECtHR,[11] has extended its jurisdiction to deal with crimes committed outside of the territory of the member States of the CoE, hence vesting itself with extra-territorial jurisdiction.[12] This said, one must keep in mind that the ECtHR is a human rights court which determines the responsibility of the State and grants redress, not a criminal court which prosecutes and punishes. Only the ACJHR[13] may be vested with jurisdiction which is intended to expand to cover core crimes.[14] The African continent is the only one to have moved in such direction. In so far as the ACJHR[15] is concerned, the distinction between a criminal court and a human rights court has faded because this court will have an international criminal chamber (section) which can try core crimes. The African Criminal Court may be considered as 'the first regional criminal court to be established anywhere in the world',[16] especially in view of a clear functional divide which subsists between the respective chambers of the ACJHR.[17]

In some circumstances the international community is faced with the predicament that no court or tribunal acts at all. This may be, *inter alia*, for political reasons, for lack of evidence or for perceived lack of jurisdiction. When this scenario prevails, the international community, or rather some States, have taken the initiative to devise extraordinary mechanisms intended to deliver international

---

and shall assume its investigative and prosecutorial tasks not before the expiration of three years after the entry into force of the Regulation (Council of the EU (2017) 20 Member States Confirm the Creation of a European Public Prosecutor's Office. http://www.consilium.europa.eu/en/press/press-releases/2017/10/12/eppo-20-ms-confirms/. Accessed 25 April 2018).

[11] ECtHR Grand Chamber, *Mazin Jum'Aa Gatteh Al-Skeini and Others v UK*, 7 July 2011, Application No. 55721/07; ECtHR Grand Chamber, *Hilal Abdul Razzaq Ali Al-Jedda v UK*, 7 July 2011, Application No. 27021/08; *vide* also ECtHR Grand Chamber, *Sabah Jaloud v The Netherlands*, 20 November 2014, Application No. 47708/08.

[12] Miko 2013; see also Lopas 2011, cited in Mutyaba 2015, p. 20.

[13] For a thorough analysis of the jurisdiction of the ACJHR, see Magliveras and Naldi 2013, pp. 117–131 and see also Ssenyonjo and Nakitto 2016, pp. 71–102.

[14] Mutyaba 2015, p. 20.

[15] This court, established by means of a Protocol [Malabo Protocol (2014) Protocol on Amendments to the Protocol on the Statute of the African Court of Justice and Human Rights] which is available at http://www.africancourtcoalition.org/images/docs/legal-texts/acjhr_protocol.pdf (accessed 22 April 2018), merges the ACtHPR {Gherari 2010, pp. 780–788}, and the Court of Justice of the AU. Such Protocol was adopted by the AU on 1 July 2008. Before the Protocol was *in vigore*, the AU started the process to amend the Protocol itself. The legal validity of such amendments is questionable since the Protocol can only be amended after having entered into force (*vide* Articles 58–60 of the Protocol itself, cited in Ssenyonko 2013, pp. 414–415, n. 176). Notwithstanding such concerns, the Protocol has been amended in the 23rd ordinary session of the Assembly of the AU, held in Malabo, Equatorial Guinea, on 26 June 2014, as a result of which the AU has decided to specifically exempt senior government officials from prosecution by the proposed regional criminal court, which will otherwise be authorized to try individuals accused of core crimes (International Justice Resource Centre 2014).

[16] Jalloh 2017, p. 801.

[17] The African Criminal Court shall constitute a special Chamber under the 'roof' of the ACJHR (van der Wilt 2017a, p. 969). I concur with van der Wilt to the effect that the ACJHR should focus on transnational crimes, rather than core crimes (van der Wilt 2017b, p. 202).

criminal justice. In fact, multi-layered levels (frameworks) of different types and kinds of prosecutions also comprise extraordinary mechanisms of an *ad hoc* nature, such as the *Lockerbie* trial. These are truly special prosecutions in so far as they are prosecutions undertaken before special courts which are specifically and uniquely set up to deal with a selected number of prosecutions.[18] To this extent they are very *sui generis* and are not to be confused with hybrid courts and/or tribunals, although some jurists occasionally refer to hybrid tribunals as 'special courts.'[19] Some of these co-called 'special courts' are constituted by means of specialized units or divisions within the local criminal justice system.[20] The ICD of the HC of Uganda and the ICT of Bangladesh come to mind. There is no formal relationship between the ICC and the ICD of the HC of Uganda, although the latter can be regarded as a court of complementarity with the ICC.[21] In the case of the ICT of Bangladesh there is no involvement of the international community.[22] Consequently, unlike the KSC,[23] these special courts should not be considered as hybrid tribunals. What counts is the involvement or otherwise of external (not domestic) elements. If there is no international involvement at all, the hybrid dimension is missing. This is the initial premise which shows that although mechanisms may be undertaken to enable prosecutions to take place regionally and in an extraordinary manner (*id est* before special courts), prosecutions are predominantly undertaken either on a national or on a supra-national level. It is difficult to conceive of the hybrid courts,[24] some *dicta* of which shall be cited throughout this work, as regional prosecutions, given their exceptional nature which follows an era of bloodshed within the territory of the respective State or region. Rather than constituting mechanisms for regional prosecutions, they incorporate locals in the judicial structures and are tailored to the needs of certain situations in so far as they are constituted close to the victims,[25] although the trial of former President of Liberia *Charles Taylor* was moved to The Hague, just like the STL.[26] Sarah Williams traces their salient features by identifying their distinctive characteristics, these being that such tribunals:

[18] See Sects. 13.2 and 13.4.

[19] Dixon and Khan 2013, pp. 75–93.

[20] These are sometimes proposed where State cooperation with an international criminal tribunal has not been forthcoming, as in the case of Kenya with the ICC (Kenyans for Peace with Truth & Justice 2014, pp. 11–12, and Kenyans for Peace with Truth & Justice and Kenya Human Rights Commission 2013, pp. 45–51).

[21] ICD 2018.

[22] Ibid.

[23] These are seated in The Hague and are staffed with international prosecutors and judges (KSC & Specialist Prosecutor's Office 2018).

[24] For a thorough understanding of the institutional and procedural aspects of the SCSL, the ECCC, and the STL, see Mackenzie et al. 2010, pp. 212–247; see also Jalloh and Meisenberg 2012, *passim*.

[25] The importance of having hybrid tribunals housed within *the locus delicti commissi* is explained by Padraig McAuliffe in McAuliffe 2008, pp. 370–380.

[26] Mackenzie et al. 2010, p. 244.

1. exercise criminal judicial functions;
2. are of an *ad hoc* nature;
3. allow for participation both by international and national judges;
4. draw funding from the international community;
5. blend national and international aspects in their applicable laws; and
6. include participation by an entity other than the affected State (for example, the UN or a third State).[27]

Sarah Williams opines that the above mentioned third and the fifth characteristics ultimately distinguish such hybrid tribunals both from national courts and from international courts.[28] Yet, some eminent authors do not focus on the hybridity, but merely consider such tribunals as 'other international tribunals'.[29] Sarah Nouwen considers the third feature, the fact that their panels are composed both of domestic and international judges, as their only defining commonality.[30] There are two categories of such hybrid tribunals. On the one hand there are the 'domesticated international courts' (such as the SCSL, the ECCC, and the STL) and on the other hand, there are the 'internationalized domestic courts' (like the Kosovo, East Timor and BiH tribunals) which, besides prosecuting crimes, buttress the national judiciary and the rule of law in the affected country.[31] The IHT and the ESPO, with the latter having been entrusted with 'the power to investigate and prosecute Derg crimes and to establish a historical record of the gross human rights violations',[32] are habitually excluded from the list of hybrid tribunals.[33] The localized features of hybrid tribunals emerge from the constitutive instruments and statutes of such tribunals. The non-regional characteristics and the national dimension of such hybrid tribunals is evident in both types of tribunals but is more marked in the latter type of tribunals (in internationalized domestic courts). This should not mislead one into thinking that such hybrid tribunals are not international criminal tribunals. Reference must be made to the UNSC Resolution 1315 adopted on 14 August 2000, and to the UN and Sierra Leone bilateral agreement signed in Freetown on 16 January 2002. Together with jurisprudence,[34] they point to the SCSL as being, for all intents and purposes of law, an international criminal tribunal. Be that as it may, such tribunals may be said to possess various distinct national and international elements, but hardly any regional features and characteristics. To assemble the collage and fill the impunity gaps left by other international criminal justice

27 Totten 2013, p. 1065.

28 Totten 2013, pp. 1065–1066.

29 Luban et al. 2010, pp. 122–129.

30 Nouwen 2006, p. 213.

31 Mackenzie et al. 2010, p. 245.

32 Tessema 2018, p. 149.

33 Nouwen 2006, p. 192.

34 SCSL Appeals Chamber, *Prosecutor v Charles Ghankay Taylor*, Decision on Immunity from Jurisdiction, 31 May 2004, Case No. SCSL-2003-01-I, paras 40–42.

mechanisms,[35] the hybrid tribunals fall somewhere between, in terms of international involvement, the category of pure international criminal tribunals (such as the ICTY, ICTR and the ICC) and national courts which receive assistance (including the training of judges and the provision of forensic experts for criminal investigations) from third States or international organizations.[36]

Prosecutions of serious crimes of concern to the international community hence occur nationally (domestically), internationally (on a supra-national level), and also by means of hybrid criminal tribunals, although some regional experimentation can be traced. Where no prosecution is undertaken before one of the main three juridical frameworks, extraordinary (special) prosecutions may be instituted before special courts. Yet, this is insufficient in so far as it obviously does not conclusively establish, or at least reflect, why certain crimes fall under one category rather than under another or why certain crimes enjoy a certain status as opposed to other crimes. To establish this conclusively, one must pose the questions: Is the way and manner a crime is prosecuted reflective of its specific categorization and status? Or must one extrapolate other salient features, traits and components (such as its collective dimension) to determine how and why a crime falls under one category rather than under another category and/or how and why a crime, as opposed to others, enjoys a certain status? A reply to these questions will underpin the following chapters within Part II, the objective of which is to articulate a workable definition of 'core crimes' which, in turn, will be conducive to understanding the vertical and horizontal systems of enforcement. Before proceeding as stipulated here above, rather than taking it for granted that an understanding of core crimes is essential, one must pose, *ab initio*, the preliminary question: why do we need to understand the concept of core crimes in the first place? I will now undertake to reply to this question in the next chapter.

References

Boister N (2003) Transnational Criminal Law? EJIL 14(5):953–976

Council of the EU (2017) 20 Member States Confirm the Creation of a European Public Prosecutor's Office. http://www.consilium.europa.eu/en/press/press-releases/2017/10/12/eppo-20-ms-confirms/. Accessed 25 April 2018

D'Alfonso A (2015) The European Public Prosecutor's Office – EPPO, European Parliamentary Research Service. http://epthinktank.eu/2015/01/08/the-european-public-prosecutors-office-eppo/. Accessed 22 April 2018

de Serpa Soares M (2015) An Age of Accountability, Special Editorial. JICJ 13(4):669–676

Dixon R, Khan KAA (2013) Archbold International Criminal Courts: Practice, Procedure and Evidence. S & M, London

[35] Fidelma Donlon notes that most commentators argue that hybrid tribunals can be a powerful mechanism to combat impunity (Donlon 2011, p. 101).

[36] Totten 2013, p. 1066 and p. 1068.

Donlon F (2011) Hybrid Tribunals. In: Schabas WA, Bernaz N (eds) Routledge Handbook of International Criminal Law. T & F, London/NY, pp. 85–105

Eberechi I (2011) Rounding Up the Usual Suspects: Exclusion, Selectivity, and Impunity in the Enforcement of International Criminal Justice and the African Union's Emerging Resistance. AJLS 4(1):51–84

Gherari H (2010) Responsibility for Violations of Human Rights Obligations: African Mechanisms. In: Crawford J, Pellet A, Olleson S (eds) and Parlett K (assistant ed) The Law of International Responsibility. Oxford Commentaries on International Law, OUP, Oxford, pp. 775–789

ICC Statute (1998) Rome Statute of the International Criminal Court

ICD (2018) http://www.internationalcrimesdatabase.org/Courts/Domestic. Accessed 22 April 2018

International Justice Resource Centre (2014) African Union Approves Immunity for Government Officials in Amendment to African Court of Justice and Human Rights' Statute. http://www.ijrcenter.org/2014/07/02/african-union-approves-immunity-for-heads-of-state-in-amendment-to-african-court-of-justice-and-human-rights-statute/. Accessed 4 July 2014

Jalloh CC (2011) Special Court for Sierra Leone: Achieving Justice? MJIL 32(3):395–460

Jalloh CC (2017) The Nature of the Crimes in the African Criminal Court. JICJ 15(04):799–826

Jalloh CC, Meisenberg SM (eds) (2012) The Law Reports of the Special Court for Sierra Leone. MNP, Dordrecht, Boston, London

KSC & Specialist Prosecutor's Office (2018) https://www.scp-ks.org/en. Accessed 22 April 2018

Kenyans for Peace with Truth & Justice (2014) A Real Option for Justice? The International Crimes Division of the High Court of Kenya. Africa Centre for Open Governance

Kenyans for Peace with Truth & Justice and Kenya Human Rights Commission (2013) Securing Justice: Establishing a Domestic Mechanism for the 2007/8 Post-Election Violence in Kenya. Kenyans for Peace with Truth & Justice

Ligeti K (2013) Introduction. In: Ligeti K (ed) Towards a Prosecutor for the European Union: A Comparative Analysis, Vol. I. Modern Studies in European Law, HP, Bloomsbury, pp. 1–6

Lisbon Treaty (2007) Treaty of Lisbon Amending the Treaty on the European Union and the Treaty Establishing the European Community

Lopas M (2011) Two Decisions Expand Extra-Territorial Jurisdiction of European Court. HRB. http://hrbrief.org/hearings/two-decisions-expand-extraterritorial-jurisdiction-of-european-court/. Accessed 22 April 2018

Luban D, O'Sullivan JR, Stewart DP (2010) International and Transnational Criminal Law. Aspen Casebook Series, WK, Austin/Boston/Chicago/NY/The Netherlands

Mackenzie R, Romano C, Shany Y, Sands P (2010) The Manual on International Courts and Tribunals, 2nd edn. OUP, Oxford

Magliveras KD, Naldi GJ (2013) The African Union (AU). WK, Austin/Boston/Chicago/NY/The Netherlands

Malabo Protocol (2014) Protocol on Amendments to the Protocol on the Statute of the African Court of Justice and Human Rights

Malekian F (2011) Principles of Islamic International Criminal Law: A Comparative Search, 2nd edn. Brill, Leiden/Boston

McAuliffe P (2008) Transitional Justice in Transit: Why Transferring a Special Court for Sierra Leone Trial to The Hague Defeats the Purposes of Hybrid Tribunals. NILR 55(3):365–393

Miko S (2013) *Al Skeini v UK* and Extraterritorial Jurisdiction under the European Convention for Human Rights. BCICLR 35(3):63–79

Mutyaba R (2015) The International Criminal Court – Its Impact and the Challenges it Faces in Fulfilling its Mandate. http://www.academia.edu/4019723/The_International_Criminal_Court_Its_Impact_and_the_Challenges_It_Faces. Accessed 22 April 2018

Nielsen C (2008) From Nuremberg to The Hague: The Civilizing Mission of the International Criminal Law. AULR 14:81–114

Nouwen SMH (2006) Hybrid Courts: The Hybrid Category of a New Type of Courts Holding Great Promise. ULR Research Paper 2(2):190–214

Rastan R (2007) The Power of the Prosecutor in Initiating Investigations, A Paper Prepared for the Symposium on the International Criminal Court, 3–4 February 2007, Beijing, China. International Centre for Criminal Law Reform and Criminal Justice Policy, Vancouver, Canada

Ssenyonjo M, Nakitto S (2016) The African Court of Justice and Human and Peoples Rights "International Criminal Law Section": Promoting Impunity for African Union Heads of State and Senior State Officials? ICLR 16(1):71–102

Ssenyonko M (2013) The Rise of the African Union Opposition to the International Criminal Court's Investigations and Prosecutions of African Leaders. ICLR 13(2):385–428

Statute of the SCSL (2002) Statute of the Special Court for Sierra Leone

Tessema M (2018) Prosecution of Politicide in Ethiopia: The Red Terror Trials. International Criminal Justice Series, Vol. 18. Asser Press, The Hague

Totten C (2013) Reviewing Williams S (2012) Hybrid and Internationalised Criminal Tribunals - Selected Jurisdictional Issues, Oxford, HP. In: ICLR 13(5):1065–1068

UNSC (2000) Resolution 1315 (2000) UN Doc. S/RES/1315

van der Wilt (2017a) Unconstitutional Change of Government: A New Crime Within the Jurisdiction of the African Criminal Court. LJIL 30(4):967–986

van der Wilt (2017b) Complementary Jurisdiction (Article 46H). In: Werle G, Vormbaum M (eds) The African Criminal Court: A Commentary on the Malabo Protocol. International Criminal Justice Series, Vol. 10, Asser Press, The Hague, pp. 187–202

Weyembergh A, Briere C (2016) Towards a European Public Prosecutor's Office (EPPO). Study for the LIBE Committee, Directorate Journal for Internal Policies, Policy Department C: Citizens Rights and Constitutional Affairs, Civil Liberties, Justice and Home Affairs, November 2016. http://www.europarl.europa.eu/RegData/etudes/STUD/2016/571399/IPOL_STU(2016)571399_EN.pdf. Accessed 22 April 2018

Chapter 4
Why Do We Need to Understand the Concept of 'Core Crimes'?

Contents

4.1 The Salient Features of Core Crimes 43
4.2 Why Are Core Crimes the Most Serious Crimes of Concern to the International Community? 46
References 56

Abstract This chapter explores whether it is important to understand the concept of 'core crimes' before attempting to reply to the research question posed in Chap. 1. It determines that such an understanding is crucial and identifies the reasons for this predicament. It devises a workable definition of 'core crimes', this being a term which cannot be subjected to a strict legal definition. A core crime may be construed to be either an act of commission or an omission of an individual which is prohibited by customary international law, is accompanied by contextual elements (circumstances) generally requiring a degree of premeditation, habitually involves groups (both in terms of its perpetrators and in terms of its victims), attacks and harms universal values by breaching the security of humans (both individually and collectively), and engenders both individual criminal responsibility and State aggravated (heightened) responsibility. It reaches this conclusion after sifting through the salient features of core crimes, namely State involvement as a phenomenological aspect, rather than as an essential ingredient or constitutive element, thereof. It assesses the reasons why core crimes are the most serious crimes of concern to the international community, which stems from the fact that the perpetrators thereof are not punished by the State best placed and best qualified to do so. In doing so, the chapter distinguishes between a faltering State, a failed State and a rogue State, juxtaposing the structural and systematic default of States and the increasing phenomenon of core crimes being committed by non-State entities.

Keywords *Aut dedere aut judicare* · Core crimes · Legality · Workable definition · System criminality · State involvement · Failure to investigate · Failure to prosecute · Gravity · Non-State entities · Seriousness · Structural failure

C. Soler, *The Global Prosecution of Core Crimes under International Law*,
https://doi.org/10.1007/978-94-6265-335-1_4

Now that the phrase 'the global prosecution' has been explained, the focus of this chapter shifts onto an understanding of the crucial concept of 'core crimes'. The reasons why we need to understand the concept of core crimes might not be so self-evident. Labelling core crimes distinctively from others and identifying their distinguishing characteristics is not largely a matter of taste as Roger O' Keefe rehashes.[1] The forthcoming analysis assumes importance not only because 'core crimes' is a phrase within the title of this work, but because the two keywords are not defined by any legal instrument. Consequently the international community still quarrels over a concise definition thereof. The purpose of this chapter is not to distinguish between one core crime and another but to extrapolate salient features and common denominators therefrom in order to be able to understand their genesis and the reasons why core crimes require special cooperation devices and mechanisms, after which one can understand how they are repressed, both vertically and horizontally in the forthcoming Parts of this book. This extrapolation necessitates that I cover a vast terrain which ranges from principles of political philosophy to the legal qualification of such crimes. This is largely owing to the fact that the proscription of core crimes has multiple legal foundations in international law.[2] Indeed the identification of the characteristics of core crimes will:

I. ease an understanding of the regime of State cooperation (or the lack of it) with the ICC in view of the surrender of individuals for the purposes of the vertical system of enforcement, as shall be seen throughout Part III;
II. facilitate the scrutiny of certain tenets, such as the exercise of universal jurisdiction, which are focal principles for the functioning of the horizontal system of enforcement, as shall be seen throughout Part IV of this work; and
III. project the *aut dedere aut judicare* rule of international law as a main enforcement paradigm which penetrates into every system.

One must also refer to another two factors which impel the need to define key terms, especially those bearing the title of this work, being 'the global prosecution of core crimes under international law'. First of all, legal certainty, and hence definitional accuracy, is a paramount *desideratum* of criminal law since ambiguities 'may create great unfairness, not just to the defendant, but also to the prosecuting authorities'.[3] The international community wants to avoid Nuremberg-like controversies which concerned alleged violations of the *nullum crimen sine lege* and *nulla poena sine lege* principles.[4] If one acknowledges that core crimes have distinguishing features and particular constitutive elements, as shall be explained in Chap. 6, it is inevitable that the principle of legality becomes paramount. Secondly,

[1] O'Keefe 2015, p. 84.

[2] Einarsen 2012, p. 65.

[3] Mettraux 2011, p. 143.

[4] German jurists had argued, after the fall of the Berlin Wall, that it would be possible to abandon the legal principle of *nulla poena sine lege* because they believed that this would be the only effective way to hold the regime of the German Democratic Republic responsible for crimes committed under its responsibility (Eikel 2018, p. 547).

as Gerhard Werle notes, 'only a rough outline has thus far emerged of a specific doctrine of international crimes'[5] which are tagged as 'core crimes' throughout my book. Thus, besides lacking a formal definition, core crimes cannot boast to be grounded on a specific doctrine which gives them a meaningful identity. The need to understand the nature and specificities of core crimes is hence still impending.

4.1 The Salient Features of Core Crimes

I will commence by forging the concept of core crimes and by coining a workable (rather than a legal) definition thereof. This workable definition is not grounded upon the normative proposition for a legal definition of core crimes which may be said to consist of five cumulative and inter-related conditions which need to subsist before any type of proscribed conduct can be considered as a core crime.[6] The concept of core crimes is hardly amenable to a legal definition. It is much easier to describe core crimes rather than define them. Terje Einarsen can hardly claim to have provided a legal definition since most of the elements thereof (such as fundamental universal value, inherent gravity, recognition as a matter of serious international concern) are subjective and do not constitute rigid (strict) pre-requisites which are a *sine qua non* for the purposes of a legal definition. It is also prone to many fluctuations. This is why a workable definition has to be formulated. It may be said to possess a rationale devised upon some theoretical underpinnings but falls short of being classified as a strictly juridical definition. This chapter will show that a core crime may be construed to be either an act of commission or an omission of an individual which is prohibited by customary international law, is accompanied by contextual elements (circumstances) generally requiring a degree of premeditation, habitually involves groups (both in terms of its perpetrators and in terms of its victims), attacks and harms universal values by breaching the security of humans (both individually and collectively), and engenders both individual criminal responsibility and State aggravated (heightened) responsibility. The above may constitute a workable definition of 'core crimes'. Chapters 6, 7 and 8 will focus on the concept of core crimes by dissecting and examining this workable definition and the legal consequences thereof.

---

[5] Werle 2009, p. 139.

[6] These five conditions are:

1. The type of conduct manifestly violates a fundamental universal value or interest;
2. The type of conduct is universally regarded as punishable due to its inherent gravity;
3. The type of conduct is recognised as a matter of serious international concern;
4. The proscriptive norm is anchored in the law-creating sources of international law; and
5. Criminal liability and prosecution is not dependent upon the consent of a concerned State.

(Einarsen 2012, p. 236 and pp. 248–249).

Admittedly, to do justice to the terminology, either of the following two terms could have been used in order to shed a light on the very nature of such crimes: 'crime of State' or 'State crime'. However, the use of the term 'core crime', as opposed to the terms 'crime of State' and 'State crime' is preferred since core crimes are also perpetrated by non-State actors,[7] and hence the above two terms ('crime of State' or 'State crime') are not the most adequate. Core crimes[8] are crimes subject to the jurisdiction of the ICC, being listed in Articles 5 to 8*bis* of the ICC Statute.[9] In fact, some publicists refer to them simply as 'ICC crimes'.[10] The term 'macro-criminality' has been associated to core crimes,[11] though this does not shed any light on their salient features. These may be said to be embodied in 'forms of system criminality which stand out for their contextual elements'.[12] Chapter 6 will disclose the reasons why and how these contextual elements effectively

---

[7] Throughout Part II, the term 'non-State actors' is used interchangeably with the term 'non-State entities'. These are not officially part of the machinery of the State, and whose conduct is not generally attributable to the State (Cerone 2011, p. 18). Hence, the use of such term in this work obviously departs from its classical understanding which 'recognizes three types of non-State actor: non-governmental organizations (NGOs), intergovernmental organizations (IGOs) and transnational corporations(TNCs)...' (Reinalda 2011, p. 3, and also Struett 2009, pp. 187–219). Thus, for the purposes of this book, non-State actors are not 'decentralised, local advocacy networks driven by members and constituencies' (Mihr 2012, p. 321). For this reason, and to avoid any confusion, I shall refer to the term 'non-State entities' rather than 'non-State actors'. This term (*id est* 'non-State entities') is also used by Judge Hans-Peter Kaul [ICC Pre-Trial Chamber II, Situation in the Republic of Kenya, *Decision Pursuant to Article 15 of the Rome Statute on the Authorization of an Investigation into the Situation in the Republic of Kenya*, Dissenting Opinion of Judge Hans-Peter Kaul, 31 March 2010, Case No. ICC-01/09, para 50]. For an understanding of non-State entities, also referred to as insurrectional movements, see Cahin 2010a, pp. 247–256. Examples of such non-State entities include UNITA in Angola, RUF in Sierra Leone (both of which finance their operations by trafficking blood diamonds), Shining Path in Peru, FARC in Colombia and UCK in Kosovo which rely predominantly on drug trafficking (Cahin 2010b, p. 334; see also Luban et al. 2010, p. 122). There exists no clear definition of armed opposition groups under international law (Zegveld 2002, p. 134).

[8] Kai Ambos has used the term 'core crimes' interchangeably with 'supranational crimes' (Ambos 2011, p. 667). A comprehensive study of such core crimes, with accompanying relevant domestic and international jurisprudence, including the prevailing USA law on such core crimes, is provided by Luban et al. 2010, pp. 955–1135.

[9] Article 6 punishes genocide, Article 7 punishes crimes against humanity, Article 8 punishes war crimes whereas Article 8*bis*, introduced after the 2010 Kampala Review Conference of the Rome Statute of the International Criminal Court and potentially applicable as of year 2017, punishes aggression. The ICC Statute [ICC Statute (1998) Rome Statute of the International Criminal Court] was adopted following the UN Diplomatic Conference of Plenipotentiaries on the Establishment of an ICC held in Rome between 15 June 1998 and 17 July 1998 (to which I attended as a member of *Non c'è Pace Senza Giustizia*), the terms of reference and mandate of which were determined by means of a Resolution on the Establishment of an ICC {UNGA (1997) Resolution 52/160 (1997), Establishment of an International Criminal Court. UN Doc. A/RES/52/160} (Benedetti et al. 2014, p. 87).

[10] Terracino 2007, p. 422.

[11] Militello 2007, pp. 944–945.

[12] van der Wilt 2008, pp. 233–234.

transform ordinary crimes into core crimes,[13] portraying such contextual elements as the defining characteristics of core crimes.[14] Therefore the distinctive categorization of crimes does not depend on the amount of perpetrators required for their commission or on the amount of victims of such crimes. The crimes do not become core crimes with reference to their numerical or mathematical dimension. This is noted at the outset since it postulates *a priori* the perceived nature and type of crimes I shall be dealing with under the tag 'core crimes'. Merely stating that core crimes are those expressly penalised by the ICC Statute, or merely calling them 'ICC crimes', is reductive and insufficient. Therefore, one must necessarily query:

(i) what makes such crimes rise to the level of a core crime? and
(ii) why and how did the core crimes manage to obtain their inclusion and find a place within the ICC Statute, whereas other crimes have not?

Replying to such questions is probably the best way to decipher the very nature of core crimes. To answer such questions I will first analyse the salient features of core crimes and I will then distinguish the characteristics of core crimes from those of other crimes. It will be shown that, generally speaking (or rather, with the exception of some war crimes),[15] core crimes are the most serious crimes of concern to the international community because they:

(1) are group-oriented (collective) crimes under customary international law[16] which possess contextual elements which, in turn, breach *jus cogens* norms; and
(2) involve the State either as perpetrator when such State is unwilling to counter them or else when they are perpetrated by non-State entities, in which case the State is usually unable to counter them.

---

[13] Marchuk 2014, p. 114.

[14] Some eminent jurists sideline the importance of contextual elements and seem not to be fully attuned with and sensitive towards the salient and distinctive features of core crimes, as described and as shall be dealt with throughout this chapter. Roger O' Keefe, for example, undertakes a detailed and comprehensive study of the different labels of crimes but opines that the label 'core crime' is 'both formally meaningless and factually misleading' (O'Keefe 2015, pp. 63–64).

[15] These include the three new war crimes which were adopted by the ASP in its 16th session and were inserted thereafter. They relate to the use of prohibited weapons both in international and in non-international armed conflicts. Some States opined that these newly added crimes have not yet been criminalized under customary international law, and should hence not have been included in the ICC Statute, above n. 9. For an analysis of the implications of criminalising conduct under the ICC Statute, above n. 9, which does not constitute a crime under customary international law, see Akande 2018.

[16] Although there is nothing in the ICC Statute, above n. 9, which expressly requires that the core crimes be crimes under existing customary international law, 'the drafters of the Rome Statute were careful to try to restrict the jurisdiction granted to the Court at that time to crimes that were already deemed to be criminalised under customary international law' (Akande 2018).

4.2 Why Are Core Crimes the Most Serious Crimes of Concern to the International Community?

I suggest that the above mentioned salient features are, ultimately, what (conceptually) makes a core crime what it is, that is, a core crime. They intrinsically differentiate the concept of core crimes from other types of crimes. This does not mean that all of these characteristics are tantamount to indispensable ingredients (constitutive elements) of the core crime. With the exception of the contextual elements, they are merely features (but not a requirement or prerequisite) of such core crimes. Therefore, although State involvement is a phenomenological aspect of core crimes which justifies potential intervention by the international community, it is not a hard and fast 'jurisdictional requirement' or an ICC admissibility threshold. It is not a legal pre-requisite thereof. In other words, the involvement of the State is not a necessary ingredient (pre-requisite) of these crimes, but it is an implicit aspect within the contours of these crimes. This is why it may be said that the involvement of the State is not a self-evident proposition emanating directly from the contextual elements of the core crimes, but it hovers in the background of these core crimes. Both of the above two features[17] are largely inter-dependent. Indeed core crimes breach *jus cogens* norms precisely because of their gravity which largely derives both from the involvement of the State and from the contextual elements of these crimes. More so, the contextual elements themselves point to some form of involvement of the State. These observations require some elucidation. Core crimes breach a fundamental norm of international law, violating a *jus cogens* norm. A breach of these hierarchically superior norms is a consequence, not a cause, of core crimes. Here I will pose and address the following question: Why and how do core crimes infringe *jus cogens* norms? Larry May upholds that a *jus cogens* norm must satisfy two principles, the security principle and the international harm principle[18] both of which will be taken into account within Sect. 5.1. Mohammed Cherif Bassiouni, in his pioneering works, upheld that core crimes constitute a threat to the international community and/or shock the conscience of humanity.[19] They henceforth threaten community interests such as international peace and threaten security by means of their collective public nature.[20] Miguel de Serpa Soares does not beat around the bush in asserting that core crimes 'are an inherent threat to international peace and security'.[21] Indeed, core crimes generally possess characteristics which entangle two main (inter-related) reasons, being:

---

[17] These are marked as (1) and (2) here above, at the very end of Sect. 4.1.

[18] May 2005, p. 63.

[19] Bassiouni 1999, p. 42.

[20] Kremnitzer 1992, p. 339.

[21] de Serpa Soares 2015, p. 670.

1. the involvement of the State, be it direct, indirect or otherwise caused by its powerlessness to counter these crimes when they are perpetrated. The phenomenon of State involvement is increasingly receiving more attention although David Luban has remarked that, until some years ago, it had received scant attention probably because, in his opinion, 'international law idolizes States, so that recognizing a category of State criminality would be as heretical as a religion labelling its own gods criminals'.[22] Though this seems exaggerated, if plausible, it would be an unfair proposition because 'just as individuals are unable to hide their guilt behind the State, the State should not be permitted to hide its guilt behind the punishment of individuals'.[23] More eloquently, 'it would not make sense for States to be protected by the notion of individual criminal responsibility. Acts of State may be imputed to individuals, and individual acts may be imputed to States';[24] and/or
2. the lack of involvement of the State after their commission, consisting in the failure to investigate and prosecute such crimes, which failure can either derive from the unwillingness of the State to investigate and prosecute or from its inability to do so. Habitually (though not necessarily) the State is unwilling when its conduct (its omission to investigate and prosecute or its failure to investigate and prosecute properly/diligently) is deliberate. This scenario mirrors the rogue State. It is unable to investigate and prosecute when its omission to investigate and prosecute is dictated by external factors over which the State has lost control (such as due to the power exercised by competing non-State entities).[25] This scenario mirrors the faltering State[26] and is consonant with the contemporary dynamics of armed conflict which commonly display the following characteristics: 'a weak State apparatus, widespread poverty, competition over dwindling natural resources, multiple violent non-State actors, and the involvement of powerful regional States'.[27] The term 'faltering State' can be more appropriate than the term 'failed State' because circumstances in a State may change further to which non-State entities would not necessarily continue to pose a threat to the State. This should hopefully be the case with *FARC* after the agreement signed with the Government of Colombia[28] which followed the rejection of a peace deal by means of a referendum held on 2 October 2016. In

---

[22] Luban 2011, p. 63.

[23] Jørgensen 2000, p. 152.

[24] Jørgensen 2000, p. 158.

[25] Non-State entities which resemble States in terms of their structure and organization (and are in fact called 'quasi-States') benefit from an advantageous position in international law which excludes them from the law applicable to States, creating 'potential imbalances between a quasi-State's capacity and its accountability for abuse of its power' (French 2013, p. 43).

[26] The use of the word 'faltering' was kindly suggested to myself on 22 August 2016 by Stephen Calleya, Professor of International Relations and Director of MEDAC.

[27] Taulbee 2017, p. 72.

[28] Associated Press (2016) Colombia Government Formally Ratifies Revised FARC Peace Deal: New Accord with Rebels has 50 Changes to Initial Deal that was Rejected by Voters in October

Colombia the *JEP* will be prosecuting and adjudicating war crimes committed during the Colombian armed conflict[29] spanning several decades and involving numerous armed actors.[30] This shows that in some circumstances States can find ways and means to prosecute individual members of non-State entities in order to punish such core crimes. Moreover, a State may want to prosecute individuals for core crimes committed on its territory especially when a change in the political administration of the country follows the consummation of such crimes or in furtherance and in pursuance of a peace deal which may cater for some prosecutions. This does not necessarily mean that a State has adhered to its obligations at law. As shall be seen in Part III, a State may prosecute in *mala fides*, devising a *mise en scène* intended to portray its sense of accountability by prosecuting individuals but subsequently pardons them unjustifiably or grants parole prematurely. In such a scenario the genuineness of the trial may be seriously questioned, and the intrusion of the international community occurs legitimately when other (third) States and/or the ICC come to the rescue of the oppressed group (population) by executing international criminal justice. Unwillingness or inability are alternative requirements, as per Article 17(1) of the ICC Statute, whereas investigation and prosecution are cumulative unless a State has diligently investigated (which requirement is a *sine qua non*) and has decided, genuinely, not to prosecute.

Core crimes are crimes which are 'the most serious crimes of concern to the international community as a whole'.[31] They are not merely serious, but they are the most serious, or 'the most troubling crimes',[32] these being the crimes which are *ejusdem generis* within the four enumerated categories.[33] This begs the question: why are such crimes the most serious crimes of concern to the international community? Some commentators have missed the wood for the trees when they rigidly equated the seriousness of the crime in terms of the ensuing concern to the international community simply and exclusively with the grave nature of the acts perpetrated. Margaret de Guzman, for example, in searching for the ICC's objective, asks 'but what is the Court supposed to try to prevent? Certainly it is intended to prevent crimes as serious as the atrocities that motivated its creation - the Holocaust, the Rwandan genocide and ethnic cleansing in the former Yugoslavia in particular. But why stop there? If international prosecution can prevent even a small number of

Referendum, The Guardian. https://www.theguardian.com/world/2016/dec/01/colombias-government-formally-ratifies-revised-farc-peace-deal. Accessed 24 November 2017.

[29] ABA 2018.

[30] Olásolo and Ramirez Mendoza 2017, p. 1012.

[31] See preambular paras 4 and 9 of the ICC Statute, above n. 9. For an understanding of the concept of 'international community in international law', see Sreenivasa Rao 2008, pp. 85–105. For an understanding of the notion of 'international community as a whole', see de Fiumel 1989, pp. 251–252, Ago 1989, pp. 252–253 and Graefrath 1989, pp. 253–255.

[32] Luban et al. 2010, p. 172.

[33] Marchuk 2014, p. 71.

killings, why not include such killings in its jurisdiction? Without a clear conceptual or doctrinal limitation, whether in the form of gravity or otherwise, the goal of preventing crimes pushes in favour of expansion'.[34]

The answer to the question posed here above is scattered all over the ICC Statute, and may be said to constitute a doctrinal understanding of international criminal law. One must look deeper into the ICC Statute and one must read between the lines thereof in order to answer the question. Whereas the object and purpose (hence the spirit) of the ICC Statute is largely reflected within its Preamble, in the light of general rules of treaty interpretation,[35] the multilateral convention should be considered cumulatively. The fact that such 'grave crimes threaten the peace security and well-being of the world'[36] and 'deeply shock the conscience of humanity'[37] does not answer the question posed, nor does it say much about the reason why such crimes made it to the ICC Statute whereas others have not. Most of all and more than anything else, the fact that ICC 'shall be complementary to national criminal jurisdictions'[38] goes to show that the ICC shall not intervene when domestic criminal justice systems are willing and able to mete out justice *in situ*.[39] As shown in Sect. 4.1, crimes become particularly serious (or better, become 'the most serious') when the State where they are committed does not fulfil its duty (a word which the Preamble expressly uses in this context) to 'exercise its criminal jurisdiction over those responsible…'[40] The fact that such crimes are the most serious crimes of concern to the international community hence derives from the fact that the perpetrators thereof are not punished by the State best placed, best qualified and best suited to do so. To confront this distressing reality, the Preamble of the ICC Statute is riddled with phrases such as 'must not go unpunished',[41] 'their effective prosecution must be ensured',[42] 'put an end to impunity for the perpetrators of these crimes and thus to contribute to the prevention of such crimes'[43] and 'guarantee lasting respect for and the enforcement of international justice'.[44]A clear emphasis on the need to punish such crimes is evident and is encapsulated within the words 'their effective prosecution must be ensured'.[45] Punishment can only

[34] de Guzman 2012, p. 49.

[35] See Article 31 of the VCLT [VCLT (1969) Vienna Convention on the Law of Treaties], an explanation thereof in Fatima 2005, pp. 79–128, and a thorough commentary thereof in Sorel and Borè Eveno 2011, pp. 804–837.

[36] See preambular para 3 of the ICC Statute, above n. 9.

[37] See preambular para 2 of the ICC Statute, above n. 9.

[38] See preambular para 10 of the ICC Statute, above n. 9.

[39] See references to Article 17(1)(b) of the ICC Statute, above n. 9, in Sect. 11.1.1.

[40] See preambular para 6 of the ICC Statute, above n. 9.

[41] See preambular para 4 of the ICC Statute, above n. 9.

[42] See preambular para 4 of the ICC Statute, above n. 9.

[43] See preambular para 5 of the ICC Statute, above n. 9.

[44] See preambular para 11 of the ICC Statute, above n. 9.

[45] See preambular para 4 of the ICC Statute, above n. 9.

occur in furtherance of an investigation and a prosecution in terms of the applicable law. In the absence of such investigation and prosecution, a crime will remain of serious concern to the international community. This is the ethos upon which the ICC Statute is ultimately grounded. In the wise words of George Fletcher 'its basic imperative appears to be avoiding the injustice of impunity – i.e. the injustice of systematically failing to respond to the evil of criminal wrongdoing. To avoid impunity, either a national court or – when the national courts are "unwilling or unable" to prosecute - the ICC should intervene to punish the guilty, regardless of national interests'.[46] Fletcher draws inspiration from Kantian philosophy to conclude that 'tolerating the impunity of mass offenders leaves a stain like blood guilt on the conscience of the world'.[47] He convincingly argues that 'the international community has committed itself to avoiding impunity for the most serious crimes of concern. In doing so, it is motivated not by self-interest but by a desire to demonstrate that no offender is above the law and no group of victims should be abandoned simply because its local system of justice is unwilling or unable to secure a conviction of mass offenders'.[48] The above words tendered by George Fletcher capture the *leitmotif* upon which my book rests. It will also explain why I favour a restrictive interpretation of grounds for refusal of surrender and extradition in Parts III and IV of this work respectively. The above doctrinal enunciation gives legitimacy to the entire international criminal justice systems. This is so because it does not rely upon subjective perception relating to the gravity (or otherwise) of crimes. By relying on such subjective tests, there is no way in a million years that one can draw the line between a crime which is serious and one which is not, or between a crime which is very serious and one which is less serious. A more objective, or rather empirical, test can be employed. Kevin Jon Heller categorises what he calls 'international crimes'[49] by measuring the extent to which they are universally criminal under international law. Although he substantiates his theories by relevant State practice,[50] I find such reasoning a bit circular since the 'universality of the act'[51] adds little to the conundrum. He posits, on the one hand, the direct criminalization thesis, which has natural law origins, and criminalizes acts under international law irrespective of whether they are domestically criminalized.[52] On the other hand, the national criminalization thesis, which has positive law origins, obliges domestic States to criminalize and prosecute such crimes.[53] Rather than focusing on its subsidiary nature, which, in all fairness, he appropriately

[46] Fletcher 2005, p. 26.

[47] Kant 1797, reprinted by CUP, Mary Gregor translating, 1991, 14.2, cited in Fletcher 2005, p. 26, n. 23.

[48] Fletcher 2005, p. 26.

[49] Heller 2017, pp. 1–2.

[50] Heller 2017, p. 5.

[51] Heller 2017, p. 4.

[52] Heller 2017, pp. 10–41.

[53] Heller 2017, pp. 41–59.

acknowledges,[54] he emphasises that 'there is a necessary connection between universal jurisdiction and the idea of universal criminality. Universal jurisdiction is the primary international-law vehicle for affirming the idea that certain acts are universally criminal'.[55]

I opine that seriousness resides in the fact that the crimes are not investigated and prosecuted, not that they are universally condemned or universally abhorred. The fact that there is a need to prohibit and penalize core crimes, as shall be seen in Parts III and IV of this book, is because these crimes, habitually, go unpunished. This state of affairs emerges not because such crimes are universally considered as very reprehensible but derives from the extra-ordinary dynamics of system criminality. Their universal condemnation is a side effect of the core crime itself. When core crimes are punished domestically, the core crimes which were committed remain distasteful to the whole world but no need to punish them elsewhere subsists. Their universal dimension, in the broad sense of the word, dwindles. This carries away universal jurisdiction, the need for which instinctively subsides. It is bizarre to punish car theft, misappropriation, fraud and forgery, just to cite some examples, and leave genocide unpunished. This absurd state of affairs runs counter to every sense of justice and righteousness. Other objective factors consisting in the evaluation of the unwilling and/or inability (or otherwise) of the States whose claim of jurisdiction may be deemed to be primary and overriding should be embraced. The litmus test of unwillingness and/or inability ultimately justifies the entire edifice upon which contemporary international criminal justice is grounded and legitimises the prevailing juridical framework, this being the *corpus juris* we may safely nowadays call 'international criminal law'. Whereas the Holocaust might have been its catalyst, this *corpus juris* has evolved to a point whereby it has equipped States with a right (or rather a duty) to intervene when the territorial State fails to deliver criminal justice. This evolution is no more than a crystallization of the customary international law rule of *aut dedere aut judicare*[56] both within the complementarity regime of the ICC Statute, a regime which has become the cornerstone of international criminal justice, and by virtue of the exercise of a ground of jurisdiction (potentially even universal jurisdiction) by third (bystander) States which enjoy custodial jurisdiction over an individual who is suspected of having committed core crimes.

The word 'core' radiates the seriousness [or rather, gravity] of the act or omission.[57] Admittedly, the seriousness or gravity of the act or omission might be

---

[54] Heller 2017, pp. 58–59.

[55] Heller 2017, p. 51.

[56] See Sect. 13.1 and Chap. 15 for an analysis on the customary international law status of the *aut dedere aut judicare* rule and the various *formulae* which shape the diversified forms which the rule has taken over the years.

[57] This is expressly acknowledged by the Preamble to the ICC Statute, above n. 9, which directly refers to 'grave crimes' which 'threaten the peace, security and well-being of the world' and to the 'most serious crimes of concern to the international community as a whole'.

considered as tenuous[58] and nonetheless subjective, but the culprit of the act or omission, being the State (on the one hand) or non-State entities (on the other hand), is neither tenuous nor subjective. These characteristics can be intertwined, as the *Tadić dictum* inferred, in so far as one may be said to cause the other. Here the ICTY Trial Chamber held that 'the reason that crimes against humanity so shock the conscience of mankind and warrant intervention by the international community is because they are not isolated, random acts of individuals but rather result from a deliberate attempt to target a civilian population'.[59] In other words, these are 'core' crimes because they are so heinous as to 'shock the conscience of humanity'[60] and also because they are generally committed either by the players [stakeholders] which compose the very core for which the *corpus juris* of international law was constituted in the first place, or by non-State entities which should be contained within the State and by the State. This is where their utter gravity speaks out loud. The State commits the core crimes, sponsors them, condones them or fails to punish such crimes when they are committed on its own territory, and, *dulcis in fundo,* against the same State's own citizens. Their gravity is hence qualitative, not quantitative. It is the system which is criminal, not the State. However, it is the State which creates or condones the system. Yet, the State is an artificial person which cannot commit tangible crimes because only people can murder people.[61] Its equivalent in the context of State criminality is the government or regime, but not the State *per se* in so far as the State, as a legal person, is constituted both by the government within a territory and by its population.[62] In fact the State survives changes in the government as long as its main elements emanating from the Montevideo Convention continue to subsist. Consequently, a clear distinction must be made between the State, the government or regime (viewed collectively), and the personnel holding power within that government or regime.[63] Against this distressing backdrop, I pose the fundamental question: who would expect a State to prosecute its own leaders and high public officials when those same leaders [and/or high public officials], even in most modern democracies where a separation of powers[64] reigns, appointed and nominated the public prosecutors and judges who are expected to uphold the law of the land? It is self-evident that such prosecutions are a very unlikely prospect, particularly if and when leaders and/or high public officials retain State power, or a substantial portion of it, be it *de lege* or *de facto.* Rwanda is the perfect example of this naked truth. Its vote against the ICTR at UN

[58] This is also because 'any isolated or sporadic misbehaviour, however heinous and revolting, cannot be regarded as a crime against humanity' (Cassese 2002, p. 357).

[59] ICTY Trial Chamber, *Prosecutor v Duško Tadić*, 7 May 1997, Case No. IT-94-1-ICTY, para 653.

[60] See Preamble to the ICC Statute, above n. 9.

[61] Luban 2011, p. 78.

[62] Luban 2011, p. 84.

[63] Ibid.

[64] Montesquieu 1758; see also Maddex 1996, p. 267, and Borg 2016, pp. 6–7.

level[65] fits like a glove in the scenario postulated here above. Similarly competent authorities are habitually either reluctant or impotent when they are faced with mounting pressure to prosecute members of non-State entities either because of the prospect of an escalation of violence or simply owing to an impossibility to arrest, detain and confine such members. Nobody would expect a State to act vigorously to punish crimes which its senior officials have perpetrated or to be willing to cooperate with others who intend doing so.

Now an important qualification must be made, although scant reference to it was previously made. States are not necessarily unwilling to investigate and prosecute. They may be unable to do so. With the exception of some war crimes which can be committed by a single soldier whereupon 'the emphasis on the criminality of certain violations of international humanitarian law makes the war paradigm shift from the collective to the individual plane',[66] core crimes are generally perpetrated either by officers of the State or by organized armed groups (non-State entities). This qualification is important, for the purposes of my book, because it puts one on track for an understanding of the vertical system of enforcement in Part III and for the horizontal system of enforcement in Part IV. Whereas faltering States are considered a cause for concern when they come closer to the brink of collapse (such as Somalia), *id est* when they move closer to becoming failed States, rogue States are viewed as directly threatening international order and stability (as with North Korea),[67]generally owing to their military capabilities.

William Zartman gives a social contract-based definition of State failure which, in his view, subsists when 'the basic functions of the State are no longer performed in so far as the structure, authority (legitimate power), law, and political order have fallen apart'.[68] When the structural and systematic violence perpetrated by the members of groups opposing the State becomes endemic, at that point in time, a State may be said to be divested of any form of control it has over its own territory. Since the administration of criminal justice is a core component of a State's sovereignty,[69] when a State loses control over its own territory, *de facto*, it loses its territorial sovereignty because the 'State authorities are either effectively non-existent or unable to protect their citizens'.[70] It may hence be safely categorized as a failed State, and (for all intents and purposes of the law on universal jurisdiction) it should be placed within the same juridical position of the rogue State which, as shall be seen shortly, loses its legitimacy which is the prelude to its own sovereignty. The inability to counter core crimes generally subsists 'either because of the superior force and authority of the criminal group in a given territory or

---

[65] UNSC (1994) The Situation Concerning Rwanda. UN Doc. S/PV.3453.

[66] Spadaro 2018, p. 137.

[67] Bilgin and Morton 2004, p. 170; see also Hoyt 2000, p. 3.

[68] Zartman 1995, cited in Nguyen 2005, p. 4, notes 10 and 11.

[69] Ferdinandusse 2006, p. 99.

[70] Rodenhauser 2014, p. 928.

because the State apparatus (the executive and/or judiciary) has been corroded…'[71] A State which defaults in its principal duty to exercise territorial sovereignty within a rule of law paradigm may be safely termed as a 'faltering State'. When such default becomes structural and systematic, the term 'failed State' can be used to explain the prevailing state of play. The failure of the State is the gain of those who oppose and confront its legitimacy to exercise power and control over territory. These opponents are non-State entities. Whilst embracing Larry May's security principle, which shall be dealt with in Sect. 5.1, by way of an underlying assumption, Harmen van der Wilt interestingly upholds that a proper exercise of the primary function of the State to protect its citizens necessarily 'requires a monopoly on the use of force. This primary function is the gist of the concept of sovereignty. However, if the State defaults on this primordial task, it thereby forfeits its privileges as a sovereign entity and the international community is authorized, if not obliged, to intervene on behalf of the forsaken and betrayed population'.[72] This default occurs when the State is either too strong or too weak. The former (strong State) is the rogue State which systematically oppresses its citizens in an outright manner, whereas the latter (weak State) is the faltering and/or failed State which is unable to offer sufficient protection to its citizens as a result of which such citizens live in constant peril. Although distinguishable in terms of some refined differences, both predicaments are disturbing in their own ways. Syria, 'where chemical attacks have become a regular occurrence',[73] is a very distressing example where both predicaments are fused. Having allegedly used chemical weapons,[74] sarin gas,[75]

[71] Giorgou 2013, p. 1014.

[72] van der Wilt 2012, pp. 1114–1115.

[73] Solvang O (2017) Dozens Feared Dead From Chemical Exposure in Syria: Exposure After Aircraft Attacked Town of Khan Sheikhoun. HRW. https://www.hrw.org/news/2017/04/04/dozens-feared-dead-chemical-exposure-syria. Accessed 2 May 2018.

[74] Gunter J (2018) Douma 'attack': How do you test for Chemical Weapons? BBC News. http://www.bbc.com/news/world-middle-east-43801091. Accessed 30 April 2018. Chemical weapons are defined in the Article II of the Chemical Weapons Convention [Chemical Weapons Convention (1992) Convention on the Prohibition of the Development, Production, Stockpiling and Use of Chemical Weapons and on Their Destruction], a critical analysis of which may be found in Krutzsch and Trapp 2014, pp. 76–104.

[75] Sanchez R (2017) Syria Chemical Attack: 11 Children Among At Least 58 Reported Killed in Alleged Regime Strike on Idlib. The Telegraph. http://www.telegraph.co.uk/news/2017/04/04/syria-gas-attack-nine-children-among-least-35-people-reported/. Accessed 2 May 2018; MacQueen K (2013) Syria: A Rogue State's New Low. Macleans. http://www.macleans.ca/news/world/syria-a-rogue-states-new-low/. Accessed 17 October 2015; HRW (2013) Syria: Government Likely Culprit in Chemical Attack: New Evidence Based on Rocket Analysis and Witness Accounts. https://www.hrw.org/news/2013/09/10/syria-government-likely-culprit-chemical-attack. Accessed 17 October 2015.

chlorine gas[76] and nerve agents[77] against innocent individuals, it possesses a marked rogue State dimension. Syria can also be used as a *casus classicus* to portray the structural incapacity (inability) to act, as opposed to the incidental failure to act. Syria is therefore also a failed State, not merely a faltering State. Chapter 5 will show how the structural and systematic inability to act triggers the right (or rather, the obligation) of other States and of the international community to intervene. Therefore, core crimes are not necessarily committed by persons who possess control and authority within the organs of the State, nor are they necessarily committed by or with the connivance of State power. They can be committed by non-State entities (generally poised in the form of armed opposition forces, rebel miltia or guerrilla groups) especially when the State lacks the executive and judicial power to counter such groups. Non-State entities develop group dynamics and have the capacity to orchestrate gross, systematic human rights violations especially when they possess State-like resources and infrastructure[78] or elements of governmental power.[79] As shall be noted later on throughout Sect. 6.2, such gross human rights violations can include all core crimes, even crimes against humanity which necessitate a State or organizational policy as a constitutive element of the crime itself. Whereas some jurists, such as Harmen van der Wilt, had argued that core crimes were committed by strong States, nowadays they posit that core crimes are no longer only the prerogative of the repressive and strong State but that they habitually concern the withering away of fragile and weak States upon the menace of ruthless opponents.[80] The cliché' that States are the sole perpetrators of core crimes is hence outdated[81] and the failed (weak) State scenario is increasingly becoming a more worrying prospect than the rogue (strong) State scenario. The gloomy picture ultimately paints core crimes as crimes which are committed by or with the connivance of State power and are also committed when the State is too weak to exercise its power, authority and control in the face of coordinated and violent opposition. All the above shows why we need to understand the concept of core crimes. Indeed the extraordinary dynamics of system criminality expose the need to devise special cooperation devices in order to enforce international criminal law. Having explained the concept of core crimes, the next chapter will explore the intrusion into the sovereignty of a defaulting State in order to investigate and prosecute core crimes.

---

[76] Ross A and Malik S (2015) Syrian Doctors to Show US Evidence of Assad's Use of Chemical Weapons, The Guardian. https://www.theguardian.com/world/2015/jun/16/syria-assad-regime-is-weaponising-chlorine-us-congress-to-hear. Accessed 17 October 2015.

[77] HRW (2017) Syria: New Evidence Shows Pattern of Nerve Agent Use; Government Enters Realm of Crimes Against Humanity. https://www.hrw.org/news/2017/05/01/syria-new-evidence-shows-pattern-nerve-agent-use. Accessed 17 November 2017.

[78] Rodenhauser 2014, pp. 916–917.

[79] Giorgou 2013, p. 1017.

[80] van der Wilt 2015, pp. 225–226.

[81] van der Wilt 2015, p. 227.

References

ABA (2018) Colombia: Special Jurisdiction for Peace. https://www.americanbar.org/groups/human_rights/justice_defenders/articles/colombia-jep/. Accessed 27 November 2018

Ago R (1989) The Concept of "International Community as a Whole": A Guarantee to the Notion of State Crimes. In: Weiler JHH, Cassese A, Spinedi M (eds) International Crimes of State: A Critical Analysis of the ILC's Draft Article 19 on State Responsibility. Walter de Gruyter, Berlin/NY, pp. 252–253

Akande D (2018) Customary International Law and the Addition of New War Crimes to the Statute of the ICC. EJIL: Talk! https://www.ejiltalk.org/customary-international-law-and-the-addition-of-new-war-crimes-to-the-statute-of-the-icc/. Accessed 17 October 2018

Ambos K (2011) Judicial Creativity at the Special Tribunal for Lebanon: Is There a Crime of Terrorism under International Law? LJIL 24(3):655–675

Bassiouni MC (1999) The Sources and Content of International Criminal Law: A Theoretical Framework. In: Bassiouni MC (ed) International Criminal Law: Crime, Vol. 1, 2nd edn. TP, Ardsley, NY, pp. 3–125

Benedetti F, Bonneau K, Washburn JL (2014) Negotiating the ICC: New York to Rome 1994–1998. MNP, Dordrecht/Boston/London

Bilgin P, Morton AD (2004) From Rogue to Failed States? The Fallacy of Short-termism. Politics 24(3):169–180

Borg T (2016) A Commentary on the Constitution of Malta. Kite Group, Malta

Cahin G (2010a) Attribution of Conduct to the State: Insurrectional Movements. In: Crawford J, Pellet A, Olleson S (eds) and Parlett K (assistant ed) The Law of International Responsibility. Oxford Commentaries on International Law, OUP, Oxford, pp. 247–256

Cahin G (2010b) The Responsibility of Other Entities: Armed Bands and Criminal Groups. In: Crawford J, Pellet A, Olleson S (eds) and Parlett K (assistant ed) The Law of International Responsibility. Oxford Commentaries on International Law, OUP, Oxford, pp. 331–341

Cassese A (2002) Crimes Against Humanity. In: Cassese A, Gaeta P, Jones JRWD (eds) The Rome Statute of the International Criminal Court: A Commentary, Vol. I. OUP, Oxford, pp. 353–378

Cerone J (2011) The Vanishing Relevance of State Affiliation in International Criminal Law: Private Security Contractors and Other Non-State Actors. In: Brown BS (ed) Research Handbook on International Criminal Law, Research Handbooks in International Law. EE, Cheltenham, UK/Northampton, MA, USA, pp. 17–33

Chemical Weapons Convention (1992) Convention on the Prohibition of the Development, Production, Stockpiling and Use of Chemical Weapons and on Their Destruction

de Fiumel H (1989) Critical Observations on Crimes of State and the Notion of "International Community as a Whole". In: Weiler JHH, Cassese A, Spinedi M (eds) International Crimes of State: A Critical Analysis of the ILC's Draft Article 19 on State Responsibility. Walter de Gruyter, Berlin/NY, pp. 251–252

de Guzman MM (2012) How Serious are International Crimes? The Gravity Problem in International Criminal Law. CJTL 51(18):18–68

de Serpa Soares M (2015) An Age of Accountability, Special Editorial. JICJ 13(4):669–676

Eikel M (2018) Germany's Global Responsibility and the Creation of the International Criminal Court, 1993–1998. JICJ 16(3):543–570

Einarsen T (2012) The Concept of Universal Crimes in International Law. TOAEP, Oslo

Fatima S (2005) Using International Law in Domestic Courts. HP, Oxford/Portland, Oregon, USA

Ferdinandusse WN (2006) Direct Application of International Criminal Law in National Courts. Asser Press, The Hague

Fletcher GP (2005) Parochial *versus* Universal Criminal Law. JICJ 3(1):20–34

French D (2013) Statehood and Self-Determination: Reconciling Tradition and Modernity in International Law. CUP, Cambridge

Giorgou I (2013) State Involvement in the Perpetration of Enforced Disappearance and the Rome Statute. JICJ 11(5):1001–1021
Graefrath B (1989) On the Reaction of the "International Community as a Whole": A Perspective of Survival. In: Weiler JHH, Cassese A, Spinedi M (eds) International Crimes of State: A Critical Analysis of the ILC's Draft Article 19 on State Responsibility. Walter de Gruyter, Berlin/NY, pp. 253–255
Heller KJ (2017) What is an International Crime? (A Revisionist History). HILJ 58(2):1–71
Hoyt PD (2000) Rogue States and International Relations Theory. JCS 20(2):1–12
ICC Statute (1998) Rome Statute of the International Criminal Court
Jørgensen NHB (2000) The Responsibility of States for International Crimes. Oxford Monographs in International Law, OUP, Oxford
Kant I (1797) The Metaphysics of Morals. In: Gregor M (transl.) (1991) Reprinted by CUP, Cambridge
Kremnitzer M (1992) The World Community as an International Legislator in Competition with National Legislators. In: Eser A and Lagondy O (eds) Principles and Procedures for a New Transnational Criminal Law, Documentation of an International Workshop in 1991: Society for the Reform of Criminal Law and the Max Planck Institute for Foreign and International Criminal Law, *Freiburg im Breisgau*, pp. 337–349
Krutzsch W, Trapp R (2014) Article II: Definitions and Criteria. In: Krutzsch W, Trapp R (2014) Krutzsch W, Myjer E, Trapp R (eds) Herbach J (assistant ed) The Chemical Weapons Convention: A Commentary. OUP, Oxford, pp. 73–104
Luban D (2011) State Criminality and the Ambition of International Criminal Law. In: Isaacs T and Vernon R (eds) Accountability for Collective Wrongdoing. CUP, Cambridge, pp. 61–91
Luban D, O'Sullivan JR and Stewart DP (2010) International and Transnational Criminal Law. WK, Austin/Boston/Chicago/NY/The Netherlands
Maddex RL (1996) The Illustrated Dictionary of Constitutional Concepts. Routledge, London
Marchuk I (2014) The Fundamental Concept of Crime in International Law: A Comparative Law Analysis. Springer, Berlin/Heidelberg
May L (2005), Crimes Against Humanity: A Normative Account. CUP, Cambridge
Mettraux G (2011) The Definition of Crimes Against Humanity and the Question of a "Policy" Element. In: Sadat LN (eds) Forging a Convention for Crimes Against Humanity. CUP, Cambridge, pp. 142–176
Mihr A (2012) Non-State Actors in Conflict. In: Boeretijn I, Henderson L, Janse R and Weaner R (eds) Human Rights and Conflict: Essays in Honour of Bas de Gaay Fortman. Intersentia, Cambridge, pp. 305–323
Militello V (2007) The Personal Nature of Individual Criminal Responsibility and the ICC Statute. JICJ 5(4):941–952
Montesquieu C-L (1758) *De l'Esprit des Lois* Chareles de Secondat, Baron de Montesquieu (originally published anonymously)
Montevideo Convention (1933) Montevideo Convention on the Rights and Duties of States
Nguyen M (2005) The Question of Failed States: Australia and the Notion of State Failure. View on Asia: Briefing Series, Uniya, Jesuit Social Justice Centre. http://www.grocjusz.edu.pl/Materials/_archiwum/archiwum2009/pd_sem_2603_B.pdf. Accessed 2 May 2018
O'Keefe R (2015) International Criminal Law. OUP, Oxford
Olásolo H, Ramirez Mendoza JMF (2017) The Colombia Integrated System of Truth, Justice, Reparation and Non-Repetition. JICJ 15(5):1011–1047
Reinalda B (2011) Non-State Actors in the International System of States. In: Reinalda B (ed) The Ashgate Research Companion to Non-State Actors. Ashgate, Farnham, Surrey, UK, pp. 3–17
Rodenhauser T (2014) Beyond State Crimes: Non-State Entities and Crimes Against Humanity. LJIL 27(4):913–928
Sorel J-M, Borè Eveno V (2011) Article 31: Convention of 1969. In: Corten O, Klein P (eds) The Vienna Convention on the Law of Treaties: A Commentary, Vol. I. OUP, Oxford, pp. 804–837

Spadaro A (2018) International Criminal Law in the Jurisprudence of International Criminal Tribunals and Courts. In: Djukic D, Pons N (eds) The Companion to International Humanitarian Law. International Humanitarian Law Series MNP, Leiden/Boston, pp. 135–153

Sreenivasa Rao P (2008) The Concept of International Community in International Law: Theory and Reality. In: Buffard I, Crawford J, Pellet A, Wittich S (eds) International Law Between Universalism and Fragmentation: Festschrift in Honour of Gerhard Hafner. MNP, Leiden/Boston, pp. 85–105

Struett MJ (2009) NGOs, the International Criminal Court, and the Politics of Writing International Law. In: Bianchi A (ed) Non-State Actors and International Law. The Library of Essays in International Law, Ashgate, Farnham, Surrey, UK, pp. 187–219

Taulbee JL (2017) Genocide, Mass Atrocity, and War Crimes in Modern History: Blood and Conscience, Vol. 2, War Crimes. Praeger Security International, Santa Barbara, California/Denver, Colorado

Terracino JB (2007) National Implementation of ICC Crimes: Impact on National Jurisdictions and the ICC. JICJ 5(2):421–440

UNGA (1997) Resolution 52/160 (1997), UN Doc. A/RES/52/160

UNSC (1994) The Situation Concerning Rwanda. UN Doc. S/PV.3453

van der Wilt H (2008) Equal Standards? On the Dialectics Between National Jurisdictions and the International Criminal Court. ICLR 8(1):229–272

van der Wilt H (2012) War Crimes and the Requirement of a Nexus with an Armed Conflict. JICJ 10(5):1113–1128

van der Wilt H (2015) Self-Referrals as an Indication of the Inability of States to Cope with Non-State Actors. In: Stahn C (ed) The Law and Practice of the International Criminal Court. OUP, Oxford, pp. 210–227

VCLT (1969) Vienna Convention on the Law of Treaties

Werle G (2009) Principles of International Criminal Law, 2nd edn. Asser Press, The Hague

Zartman IW (1995) Introduction: Posing the Problem of State Collapse. In: Zartman IW (ed) Collapsed States: The Disintegration and Restoration of Legitimate Authority. Lynne Riener Publishers, Boulder, Colorado/London, pp. 1–15

Zegveld L (2002) The Accountability of Armed Opposition Groups in International Law. Cambridge Studies in International and Comparative Law, CUP, Cambridge

Chapter 5
What Is Required to Intrude into the Sovereignty of a Defaulting State in Order to Investigate and Prosecute Core Crimes?

Contents

5.1 The Principles of Human Security and International Harm 61
5.2 Why Do Group (Collective) Crimes Breach Human Security and Why Are They so Harmful? 66
5.3 Interventions Designed to Prevent and Punish Core Crimes by Prosecuting Core Crimes 72
5.4 The Conceptual Genesis of the Responsibility to Protect 73
5.5 The Transformation of the Concept of the Responsibility to Protect into a Legal Principle 76
References 82

Abstract When the ultimate protector of the citizen defaults to such extent as to jeopardize the human security of individuals, the (international) harm caused to the groups becomes systematic, at which point the risk of ulterior infringements and of a spill-over effect increases. The legal injury sustained by the group becomes universal, a juridical interest is presumed and the *locus standi* requirement is dispensed with as a result of the breach of *erga omnes* obligations. The fine line between a right to intervene and a duty to intervene is evaluated by tracing the journey of the 'responsibility to protect' principle from an idea to a norm. The ICC Statute, designed to defeat structural impunity, has contributed towards this journey. When core crimes are committed on their territory, States forfeit their legitimacy *ipso facto* because of a blatant conflict of interest. A State cannot be perpetrator, prosecutor, judge and jury of its own cause, whereupon the State's officials themselves are also accused. Owing to this conflict of interest, States auto-delegitimize themselves, opening the floodgates for external prosecutions. The seeds are sown for the consideration of the unwillingness or inability of States to prosecute core crimes committed within their territory, which will be assessed in the context of the complementarity principle and will be mentioned in the light of the

C. Soler, *The Global Prosecution of Core Crimes under International Law*,
https://doi.org/10.1007/978-94-6265-335-1_5

positive obligations of States. The complementarity test operates at a vertical level, *id est* international institution versus State. The subsidiarity test operates at a horizontal (inter-State) level. Complementarity and subsidiarity mirror each other.

Keywords Sovereignty · Self-delegitimization process · Human security · International harm · External intervention · Collective crimes · Group-based crimes · Group-oriented crimes · Systematic harm · Structural impunity · Responsibility to protect · Universal legal injury · *Locus standi* · *Erga omnes* obligations · Complementarity · Subsidiarity

This chapter will show that when the ultimate protector of the citizen defaults to such extent as to seriously jeopardize the security of individuals, the oppressed population needs another protector to come to the rescue. At such point in time[1] the intrusion of the international community is solicited to guarantee the security of helpless citizens and to prevent the ensuing harm. In Win-Chiat Lee's gripping words, the State, by committing, condoning or not prosecuting such crimes, loses its political authority (sovereignty) over such crimes, an authority which is *ipso facto* transferrable to other States.[2] In this way States lose their own legitimacy which is the pretext to their sovereignty. This legitimacy is forfeited *ipso facto* because of a blatant conflict of interest. A State, the essence of political authority,[3] has a vested interest in ensuring that its organs of government remain intact. It cannot be perpetrator, prosecutor, judge and jury of its own cause, whereupon the State's officials themselves are also accused. In a nutshell, owing to this palpable conflict of interest, States auto-delegitimize themselves, opening the floodgates for external prosecutions. Such point in time assumes the characteristics of what Danilo Turk calls the 'internationalization of sovereignty'.[4] It is this self-delegitimization process which, in my opinion, triggers either international criminal prosecutions (as shall be seen in Part III of this work) or proceedings before another State on the basis of universal jurisdiction (as shall be seen in Part IV of this work). By virtue of 'the self-delegitimization process' States lose a portion of their sovereign bundle to the international community as a whole and forfeit their right to protest against the exercise of universal jurisdiction,[5] the rationale of which has remained elusive,[6] and/or against the establishment of an international criminal tribunal, a special court or the ICC. This is the point at which 'the mobilization of the international

[1] Monica Lugato suggests that external interference should occur only when there has been a 'manifest failure' of the territorial State to protect its populations from atrocities (Lugato 2017, p. 256).

[2] Lee 2010, p. 18.

[3] For an examination of alternatives to the present States system for the purposes of universal political organisation, see Bull 2012.

[4] Turk 2003, p. 758.

[5] Ryngaert 2008, pp. 114–115.

[6] Reeves 2018, p. 1049.

community as a whole'[7] becomes warranted. At such stage *jus cogens* norms 'dethrone States as the ultimate masters of the world's legal order'[8] and a *droit d'ingérence* kicks in.[9]

On these lines, the inability of States to prosecute core crimes committed within their territory will hence surface in the context of the complementarity principle within the next (the third) Part, will be mentioned in the light of the positive obligations of States within the fourth Part, and will come to the fore in the concluding observations of this book. The complementarity test, which will be analysed in Part III of this book, operates at a vertical level, *id est* international institution versus State. The subsidiarity test, which will be analysed in Part IV of this work, operates at a horizontal (inter-State) level.[10] The complementarity and the subsidiarity principle mirror each other.[11] The extent of such mirroring is so conspicuous that 'the ICC's defining complementarity test has been, for all intents and purposes, directly incorporated into South African law by the Constitutional Court' which endorsed the principle of subsidiarity in the *Zimbabwe Torture Docket* case.[12] It is thus only by way of exception, and when the State fails to provide physical security and subsistence to its subjects,[13] that State sovereignty may be legitimately perforated. Yet this is not automatic. It requires some steps which shall be explained shortly.

5.1 The Principles of Human Security and International Harm

Physical, or better, human security comprises two sets of twin concepts, these being 'a traditional (narrow) and a "renewed" (broad) version of security, on the one hand, and the interlinked freedoms – from fear and from want, on the other hand'.[14] Sandra Fredman gives the principle of human security both a negative and a positive dimension consisting of the imposition of a duty restraining the State and the requirement of action by the State respectively.[15] The failure to intervene by

[7] Jørgensen 2000, pp. 180–181.

[8] Tomuschat 2015, cited in Kleinlein 2017, p. 310.

[9] This was promoted by Bernard Kouchner, representative of NGO *Médecins Sans Frontières*, various decades ago (Ciciriello and Borgia 2017, p. 243).

[10] Burke-White 2002–2003, pp. 86–94, cited in Ryngaert 2007, p. 154, n. 2.

[11] Ryngaert 2007, p. 178.

[12] Constitutional Court, South Africa, *National Commission of the South African Police Service and Another v Southern African Human Rights Litigation Centre and Another* (*Zimbabwe Torture Docket Case*), 30 October 2014, [CCT 02/14] ZACC 30, para 61, cited in Ventura 2015, p. 882.

[13] May 2005, p. 68.

[14] Gal-Or 2015, p. 673. For a thorough understanding of the concept of human security in an international law context, see von Tigerstrom 2007, pp. 59–90.

[15] Fredman 2007, p. 308.

investigating and prosecuting is tantamount to the ultimate abdication of international responsibility and rekindles the gesture by means of which Pontius Pilate washed his hands in front of the crowd. It is an omission which, in turn, entitles the *civitas maxima* to disown the defaulting custodial State and to dismember such State from what political philosophers call 'humanity'. Similarly, whilst analysing the concept of 'humankind', Geoffrey Robertson considers freedom from the wanton State infliction of death and torture as a right of humankind which is universally accepted.[16] He upholds that these freedoms 'are designed to keep the State at a distance, to ring-fence every adult from interference with his body or his mind, until a defined point at which social dangerousness justifies intervention'.[17] Most importantly Robertson predicates that 'normally it will be the State itself that is the violator, through police or army or security services, but the State may also be obliged to exercise its power to stop violations by third parties – whether they be vigilante groups, death squads or potent private organizations like media groups or multinationals or trade unions. It follows that the pivotal technical right, which must be implemented as a precondition of the enjoyment of basic liberties, is the right to an effective remedy'.[18] It is, as noted here above, the total lack of such internal (domestic) remedy which triggers external intervention in the form of a prosecution by the ICC or of the exercise of universal jurisdiction, the latter being a 'stop-gap measure to address impunity'.[19] The inexistence of such remedy renders victims completely helpless and just as vulnerable as when an earthquake demolishes every standing object or living person. Larry May argues that 'when a Hobbesian State sovereign is not protecting, or is actively oppressing, his subjects, this opens the door for the possibility that another State or international institution could intervene to protect these people who are not having their security protected'.[20] Such door, in May's words, is left open 'in those cases where a sovereign is unwilling or unable to provide the protection to his subjects'.[21] Larry May concludes that Immanuel Kant's work 'Perpetual Peace' resembles those of Hobbes to the effect that 'sovereignty can be legitimately abrogated when security is jeopardized by the sovereign', and that this, in turn, partially supports and justifies the existence of international criminal law in the first place.[22] He places emphasis on the security principle to the extent that he argues that institutions of international criminal justice, the ICC being a prime example thereof, 'are aimed at providing collective security for all the State members'.[23] As a matter of fact the principle of security encircles 'the centrality of the safety of the person and security of communities and

[16] Robertson 2012, p. 125.
[17] Ibid.
[18] Robertson 2012, pp. 125–126.
[19] Peter 2016, p. 3.
[20] May 2014, p. 768.
[21] May 2014, p. 784.
[22] May 2014, p. 768.
[23] May 2014, p. 778.

their protection against physical violence'.[24] To this effect, the fiasco of the State consisting in the non-fulfilment of its primary duty to provide a minimum level of security has been termed as an 'excellent conceptual tool to sustain the international community's right of interference'.[25] These developments stem from the process by means of which sovereignty has evolved from being an absolute right to becoming a responsibility towards a State's own citizens.[26] Sovereignty is intricately linked to responsibility.[27] Like anything else, sovereignty connotes both duties and rights to States and is premised on the willingness and ability of a State to protect its subjects.[28] It should not be misused or abused by the territorial State to shield the perpetration of gross human rights violations from external intervention, but, as a general rule, besides authorizing the State to exercise its criminal jurisdiction over those within its territory, it also implies that a State is not responsible for acts of another State (or more generally another legal person). Larry May adds that 'sovereignty can be legitimately abrogated when security is jeopardized by the sovereign, thereby also providing a partial support for international criminal law'[29] because the protection of one's subjects 'is the hallmark of sovereignty'.[30] He reiterates that the intrusion by other States or the undertaking of international criminal prosecutions requires the involvement of two normative principles which possess a moral dimension,[31] these being a breach of the security principle and the harm to the international community. The breach of the security principle is the essence of crimes against humanity and may be captured as follows: 'the death and deprivation, suffered by the population as a result of the State's defaulting on its primary obligations, is the gist of "crimes against humanity", violates *eo ipso facto* the interests of the international community and authorizes both other States and international tribunals to intervene'.[32] In full view of the link between the two principles, 'only the most egregious harms warrant international prosecution'.[33] These are the harms that violate the security principle.[34] The collective violence which characterises core crimes is systematic, organized and goal-directed, as a result of which unplanned, reactionary, impulsive acts are ruled out[35] of the equation.

---

[24] Gal-Or 2015, p. 690.
[25] van der Wilt 2012a, p. 1127.
[26] Birdsall 2015, p. 51.
[27] Turk 2003, p. 757.
[28] May 2005, p. 68.
[29] May 2014, p. 768.
[30] May 2014, p. 784.
[31] May 2005, p. 79.
[32] van der Wilt 2012b, p. 2.
[33] May 2005, p. 75.
[34] May 2005, p. 77.
[35] Olusanya 2014, p. 231.

Larry May's two-pronged approach was partially criticized by Harmen van der Wilt, Andrew Altman and Christopher Wellman who opined that the international harm principle is not required as an additional and separate condition to warrant international prosecutions.[36] In van der Wilt's view the international harm principle is embedded within the security principle. Now since the security principle encapsulates the international harm principle, the latter principle should not be used as an analytical tool in the identification of core crimes. This is because the collective dimension of core crimes is already implicit in the security principle in view of the collective nature of the ways and methods which either States or non-State entities undertake to commit such core crimes.[37] Other reasons should determine the point at which external intervention would be required and the reasons why it would be required in the first place.

Fletcher distinguishes between two types of crimes. Some crimes are so categorized by force of the international treaty which defines them. Others are so categorized since they are wrongs in themselves in so far as they are inherently wrong. The former are parochial crimes which endanger and habitually jeopardize 'the purely parochial interests of particular nations or of their political leadership'.[38] The latter are universal crimes[39] which 'are not, or should not be, dependent on parochial interests'.[40] They are crimes regardless of their domestic criminalization. Harry Hobbs examines legal literature to identify five theoretical bases which trigger the international interest in repressing such crimes, these being their nature and gravity, their scale, the fact that they capture the particular evil consisting in the abuse of State power to harm, rather than to protect, their being directed against groups and their constituting an assault on human dignity.[41] These are the same crimes which are prohibited by the ICC Statute (which I refer to as 'core crimes'). To explain the nature of these 'universal crimes' an extract from the interlocutory decision of the Appeals Chamber of the STL should be cited.[42] It held that 'the fact that all States of the world punish murder through their legislation does not entail that murder has become an international crime. To turn into an international crime, a domestic offence needs to be regarded by the world community as an attack on universal values (such as peace or human rights) or on values held to be of

---

[36] Altman and Wellman 2004, pp. 40 and 45, cited in van der Wilt 2012b, p. 2, n. 9.

[37] van der Wilt 2012a, pp. 1114–1117.

[38] Fletcher 2005, p. 23.

[39] He clarifies that the nature of the crime as universal should not be confused with the ground of universal jurisdiction. Just because a crime is a universal crime, it does not necessarily mean that it is subject to universal jurisdiction or that States are entitled to exercise universal jurisdiction to suppress such crimes (Fletcher 2005, pp. 23 and 24).

[40] Fletcher 2005, p. 23.

[41] Hobbs 2017, p. 189.

[42] Chiara Ragni pinpoints that the Appeals Chamber of the STL 'made a very important and valuable contribution to the progressive development of the customary international law on terrorism (and more generally of international criminal law)…' (Ragni 2013, pp. 682–683).

paramount importance in that community;...'[43] These are hence the same crimes which, in the words of Larry May, fulfil the principle of harm to humanity or international harm in so far as they possess two crucial and identifiable criteria:

1. that the person who is harmed by the crime is so harmed owing to his membership in a particular group or to his ownership of a characteristic not particular to the person's individual self, these being the crimes which require the *dolus specialis*[44] (namely genocide and persecution as a crime against humanity); or
2. that the crime is committed by a group (such as the State itself).[45]

These alternative criteria[46] disclose a very important feature of core crimes, this being their group-based and/or group-oriented nature. Core crimes are inherently and ineliminably group crimes. Group membership is pivotal to understand both why the victims are selected and why the perpetrators acted as they did.[47] Core crimes are 'marked by their collectivity; orders are given, plans made, weapons provided, detainees rounded up, and only then does someone pull the trigger'.[48] The group element is less conspicuous in the case of war crimes. On the contrary, genocide is a paradigmatic group crime which is directed against an entire group and perpetrated by a State or other organized group.[49] This is so to the extent that the term 'victim groups' is used to designate the aggrieved parties in core crimes.[50] Safeguarding the protected groups (national, ethnic, racial or religious)[51] is the objective of the proscription of genocide which refers to the word 'group' in each and every prohibited act (in all the five prohibited modes of conduct), these being the *actus reus* of the crime. In the groups safeguarded by the legal proscription, and most of all, in their protection by means of the prohibition of core crimes such as genocide, one also finds features which are absent in the other categories of crimes (such as transnational organized crimes). In fact, legal regimes which prohibit transnational organized crimes (such as suppression conventions) do not always contain provisions [similar to Article 25(3)(d) of the ICC Statute] which specifically

---

43 STL Appeals Chamber, *Interlocutory Decision on the Applicable Law*, 16 February 2011, Case No. STL-11-01/1, para 91.

44 This is the specific intent to destroy either a protected group or a part of that group.

45 May 2005, pp. 80–86.

46 There is no strict requirement that these criteria be satisfied, but if they subsist cumulatively, the case for the categorization of the harm as an international harm is far more compelling.

47 May 2005, p. 91.

48 ICTY Appeals Chamber, *Prosecutor v Duško Tadić*, 15 July 1999, Case No. IT-94-1-A, para 191, cited in Jackson 2015, p. 17, n. 54.

49 May 2005, p. 157.

50 Barth 2013, pp. 258–260.

51 Negative definitions of groups (for example 'non-Serbs') do not suffice. There must be a positive group identification [ICC Pre-Trial Chamber I, *Prosecutor v Omar Hassan Ahmad Al Bashir, Decision on the Prosecution's Application for a Warrant of Arrest Against Omar Hassan Ahmad Al Bashir*, 4 March 2009, Case No. ICC-02/05-01/09, para 135, cited in Cryer 2009, p. 292, n. 58].

establish individual criminal responsibility for someone who contributes to the commission or attempted commission of a crime by a group of persons acting with a common purpose. One would have to now ask why group crimes breach human security and why are they so harmful.

5.2 Why Do Group (Collective) Crimes Breach Human Security and Why Are They so Harmful?

Group crimes breach human security and are so harmful to humanity because of the intrinsic value of groups. As Raphael Lemkin upheld, 'national or ethnic groups as such are essential to humanity, because they have value over and above individuals who make them up. Lemkin was the first scholar who mapped the jurisprudential journey of genocide after drafting and lobbying for the Genocide Convention.[52] He emphasised the contributions that members of different national groups have made to world culture'.[53] There is therefore a cosmopolitan dimension to such groups, in the sense that generally such groups cannot be solely and exclusively confined to the borders of one State. Consequently, such groups deserve special protection in so far as such groups enrich humanness and humanity. The worthiness of such protection stems from the diversities of such groups,[54] all of which should harmoniously encircle what Giuseppe Mazzini referred to as the 'symphony of nations'.[55] The other categories of crimes, these being transnational organized crimes, domestic crimes and international crimes, do not seek to safeguard such groups. Therefore, since groups have an important value consisting in their ability to produce distinctiveness and to enhance pluralism, in turn colouring the globe, they are, arguably, prone and susceptible to be recipients of arbitrary violence. The international community must protect members of groups not only because groups contribute to civilization but predominantly also because groups, whilst being depersonalized phenomena, epitomize the *civitas maxima* itself, the subsistence of life within a collective undertaking in so far as (since they are groups, as opposed to States) they permeate State boundaries and survive within political communities which are not necessarily confined to one State. Groups are the collective embodiment of individual units of action and the aggregate reproduction of the uniqueness of each and every individual. Irrespective of the contribution they may offer to humankind, groups deserve special protection particularly because they

---

[52] Luban et al. 2010, p. 987.

[53] Lemkin 1944, p. 91, cited in Luban 2011a, p. 631, n. 49. However, David Luban disagrees when he opines that groups have value only through the political life they create (Luban 2006, pp. 303–320, cited in Luban 2011a, p. 635, n. 67).

[54] Lemkin 1944, p. 91, cited in Tams et al. 2014, p. 85, n. 32.

[55] Kreß 2013, min 22, cited in Tams et al. 2014, p. 85, n. 33.

have a right to exist.[56] The cross-border capacity which is inherent in the existence of groups may be said to be the very reason why groups deserve special protection. The Indo-Aryan ethnic group commonly known as Rom (or Romani) people, for example, live in various States, particularly the USA, the Balkan States, Spain, France, Russia and Ukraine.[57] Similarly the Kurdish religious community known as Yezidis predominantly live in Iraq but large Yezidi communities may be found in Syria, Armenia, Georgia, Russia and Germany.[58] Groups may be deemed to be a miniature version of the international community itself, or more precisely a minority thereof. In other words, the physical persons targeted are not so targeted because of their individual traits but because they are members of such group, meaning that it is the group which is the ultimate target whereas the individuals composing such group are merely a means to an end, the latter being the destruction of the group. The individual victims are simply the 'representative of the entire set'.[59] To this extent some core crimes, such as genocide,[60] violate human dignity[61] by giving value to individuals solely in their capacity as group-members, reducing them to instruments for the protection of the group they belong to and depersonalizing the violence in the process.[62] The crimes are also committed by groups, either by the State or by non-State entities. Quintessentially, the group, be it the victims who are targeted for their characteristics as members of the group, or the perpetrators who are systematically organized into and within a group structure, is all-pervading in core crimes. The forthcoming analysis of the contextual elements within Chap. 6 will show the extent to which the fact that core crimes are really and truly group-based crimes is anchored not only in their conceptual foundation but is also transplanted within their juridical (legal) elements.

Moreover the collective dimension of core crimes poses multi-faceted risks. If one were to conduct a thorough impact assessment of core crimes, one would realise that the harm which ensues there from is tremendous, at times catastrophic. Jann Kleffner aptly notes that 'system crimes habitually have a paralyzing effect on the national judicial system of the State or States, which are primarily envisaged to conduct proceedings: first and foremost, not only the State on whose territory core crimes occurred, but also the State whose nationality the alleged perpetrator and victim possess'.[63] In his words, 'most of the system crimes under consideration constitute serious breaches, if not per definition, then at least whenever they are

56 Tams et al. 2014, pp. 81–83.

57 See http://en.wikipedia.org/wiki/Romani_people. Accessed 13 March 2012.

58 See http://en.wikipedia.org/wiki/Yazidis. Accessed 13 March 2012.

59 Arens 2013, p. 9.

60 Here the crime of genocide is not being selected to suggest that its contextual elements are more or less determinative for the genus of core crimes as a whole but merely to emphasize the inevitable connection with its collective dimension which is more so apparent in the light of the groups protected by the definition of genocide.

61 Werle 2009, p. 257.

62 Murray 2011, p. 589 and p. 611, cited in Tams et al. 2014, p. 83, n. 20.

63 Kleffner 2008, p. 2.

committed on a gross or systematic scale'.[64] At that stage, one would pose the question: Is an individual acting alone, or in concert with a few others within a group, capable of producing such devastation? Answering affirmatively would be incongruous and ludicrous, although the *Kenya* decision[65] contemplates relatively small groups consisting in political alliances, militias and criminal gangs (such as Mungiki and the Luo Taliban),[66] creating havoc and causing devastation.[67] The group element is partially implicit in the 'involvement of the State' element and/or in the organizational requirement which goes to show that the perpetrators thereof are generally organised armed groups. If the State is an active perpetrator it is an organized group. Usually only strong organized groups would be able to challenge the power of the State.

Crimes against humanity may be said to be subject to universal jurisdiction since they affect and harm the interests of the international community as a whole because they 'strike at the core of the human condition, by shattering the political realm'[68] and in so far as they 'are crimes against humanness as well as crimes against humankind'.[69] They violate the security principle because 'group-based harm violates a strong interest of the international community, and can even be said to harm humanity'[70] since 'they focus on a non-individualized feature of the victim, and thereby risking widespread harm'.[71] In such circumstances, 'there is a much greater likelihood that the harms will spread throughout a population', this having already occurred amidst ethnic cleansing in various parts of the world.[72] The risk of a spill over effect drastically increases. Consequently, the more coordinated and orchestrated the attacks are, the more they are likely to affect groups rather than just individuals, and the more they possess characteristics of core crimes. Their goal-oriented nature[73] renders group-based harms more serious and dangerous than individualized harms caused by random acts of violence, no matter how heinous they may be. With these types of harms the 'risk of harm to the members of humanity concerning their peace and security'[74] lingers. In fact the international harm principle has a marked preventive dimension which consists in the knowledge that systematic harm which is structurally committed is likely to involve more victims. A direct relationship between the concept of 'harm' and the qualification as

[64] Kleffner 2009, p. 267.

[65] See Chap. 4, n. 7.

[66] Materu 2015, pp. 34–35.

[67] For a detailed examination of the *Kenya* situation before the ICC, see Materu 2015, pp. 177–256.

[68] van der Wilt 2012b, p. 5.

[69] Luban 2004, pp. 159–160.

[70] May 2005, p. 80.

[71] May 2005, p. 81.

[72] May 2005, p. 86.

[73] Tams et al. 2014, pp. 94–95.

[74] May 2005, p. 84.

'victim' subsists even in terms of Rule 85 of the ICC RPE.[75] The above construct provides 'a legitimate basis for intervention so as to protect the larger community also likely to be harmed by the plan'.[76] In Larry May's opinion, for a crime to be group-based, there must subsist coordinated systematic harm which is perpetrated either by a State or by a State-alike body, such as the governmental use of rape as a weapon of war, *id est* to ethnically cleanse an area.[77] One notes that widespread and systematic harm mirrors the widespread and systematic attack against a civilian population which characterises the penal proscription of crimes against humanity. To harm humanity such harm must either be inflicted against an individual because of the individual's group membership or else it must occur due to the involvement of a group such as the State or other collective entity.[78] Therefore, what renders the harms group-based is either the nature of the crime or the status of the perpetrator.[79] These crimes hence infringe a focal interest of humanity, being 'that its members, as members, not be harmed'.[80] In other words, when groups are involved the harm becomes systematic. At such point humanity is directly involved, and in a sense victimized, when the person enduring the violence merely stands in for larger segments of the population.[81] He does not suffer owing to his individual attributes, conduct (actions) or choices, but because of his membership in a targeted civilian population,[82] a membership over which he has no control and which he was not able to dictate. Consequently, such harms 'are more likely to assault the common humanity of the victims and to risk crossing borders and damaging the broader international community'.[83] In view of the broad potential of international harm, universal jurisdiction basically entails that 'other States are equally qualified and entitled to intervene if the territorial State defaults on its primary obligations'.[84] Now, since crimes against humanity (such as torture and enslavement)[85] dehumanize human beings by divesting them of all and any dignity they have, they are prime examples of what van der Wilt considers to be a direct 'strike at the core of the human condition'. Carla Ferstman is categoric when she writes that 'part of the trauma and dislocation relates to the fact that the crimes are generally perpetrated by, or at the behest of, the State. The calculated abuse of the integrity of individuals,

[75] Calvo-Goller foresees that certain questions will arise, namely queries relating to the degree of harm necessary in order to qualify as a victim and how direct the harm must be (Calvo-Goller 2006, p. 245).

[76] May 2005, p. 88.

[77] May 2005, pp. 88–89.

[78] May 2005, p. 83.

[79] Ibid.

[80] May 2005, p. 82.

[81] May 2005, pp. 85–86.

[82] The phrase 'civilian population' is ably analysed in Garbett 2015, pp. 118–147.

[83] May 2005, p. 83.

[84] van der Wilt 2012b, p. 9.

[85] For a thorough understanding of the crime of enslavement as a form of system criminality, see van der Wilt 2016, pp. 269–283.

in a way that is designed specifically to undermine their dignity, is particularly horrible when it is perpetrated by or on behalf of those with the very responsibility to protect individuals' rights'.[86]

Whilst undertaking a phenomenological analysis by using the sub-title 'politics gone cancerous', David Luban, whose analysis is also largely inspired by Hobbesian thought but is focused on other salient features, explains that crimes against humanity transform political communities into death traps because they violate 'the fact that to be human is to live in groups with other humans'.[87] Luban shows how crimes against humanity involve a perversion of politics and a perversion of the political animal. In his view the international community's right of criminal law enforcement is directly linked to the way the perversion of politics, which is inherent to crimes against humanity, backfires on the entire international community and affects all human beings.[88] Crimes against humanity are generally committed at home, when 'the State has turned against its own citizens',[89] transforming the territory of a State 'from a place of refuge into a trap'.[90] Indeed, most crimes against humanity are 'committed by professional soldiers, blessed by religious leaders and tacitly approved by governments'.[91] This explains why it is State leaders who 'are the most likely to end up in the international dock'.[92] The gist of Luban's analysis parallels that of Richard Vernon who considers crimes against humanity as an inversion of politics.[93] Indeed politics is designed to bring people (and their ideas) together in search of the common good and the public interest.[94] Core crimes shatter such mosaic, in most cases, irremediably. They necessarily imply the negation of human security and freedom, the latter being, in the words of Jean-Jacques Rousseau and Immanuel Kant, the supreme moral value.[95] 'Human security' has a 'freedom from fear' dimension which encompasses personal security and collective security within the general ambit of freedom from physical violence.[96] At the level of core crimes, Diana Amneus, with reference to the 1994 Human Development Report,[97] upholds that 'human security' is elevated to a 'community security' and 'political security' dimension.[98] They are the most severe

86 Ferstman 2007, p. 149.

87 Luban 2004, p. 117 and p. 160.

88 van der Wilt 2012b, p. 8.

89 Sadat 2011, p. 464.

90 Sadat 2011, p. 467.

91 Robertson 2012, p. 798.

92 May and Hoskins 2010, pp. 2–3.

93 Vernon 2002, pp. 241–246, cited in Luban et al. 2010, p. 983.

94 Rousseau, in his *Lettres Ecrites de la Montagne*, upheld that 'the first and foremost public interest is always justice' (Rapaczynski 1987, p. 245).

95 Rapaczynski 1987, p. 243.

96 Amneus 2013, p. 6.

97 UN Development Programme 1994, p. 23, cited in Amneus 2013, p. 5, n. 10.

98 Amneus 2013, p. 6.

and abominable acts of violence in that they have an 'added dimension of cruelty and barbarism'.[99] Commenting on the phrase 'politics gone cancerous', Darryl Robinson explains that crimes against humanity hence occur when human beings use organisations to harm other human beings.[100] He stresses on two dimensions of such crimes, these being scale (denoting the commission of multiple acts) and collectivity (denoting the State or organizational policy).[101] Really and truly these mirror the 'widespread and systematic' chapeau elements. This is probably why David Luban goes further than stating that States have an interest in repressing crimes against humanity. He adds that crimes against humanity are treated as universal jurisdiction offences because all individual persons have an interest in repressing them.[102] Case-law has acknowledged, for example, that Argentina has a particular role in the international community, purportedly deriving from its ratification of the VCLT which crystallizes *jus cogens* norms, to recognise crimes against humanity and prosecute them, irrespective of Article 118 of the Argentine Constitution.[103] In David Luban's view, the jurisdiction is universal among people, not necessarily universal among States.[104] This is also inferred by Jo Stigen who, in examining the functionalist theory in an ICC context, upholds that 'one should perhaps not so readily assume *a priori* that the effective prosecution of perpetrators of international crimes is a "public interest" among States'.[105] The *partie civile*[106] (the *querellantes*)[107] is humankind itself, not the international community of States. Such perpetrators become anyone's fair target since 'they threaten humanity as a whole'.[108] These *hostis humani generis* become 'anyone's and everyone's legitimate enemy'.[109] Such *vigilante* jurisdiction, as David Luban calls it, should be delegated 'to any officially constituted tribunal, national or international, that satisfies the requirements of natural justice', which include the right to a fair trial.[110] David Luban acknowledges, though he does not fully agree, that 'exterminations, enslavements, and other murder-type crimes are so intrinsically atrocious that they will count as crimes against humanity whenever they are inflicted on a population,

[99] Supreme Court, Canada, *Regina v Imre Finta*, 24 March 1994, Case No. 23023, 23097, paras 701, 818, cited in Luban 2004, p. 98, n. 47.

[100] Robinson 2014.

[101] Ibid.

[102] Luban 2004, p. 91.

[103] Buenos Aires Federal Court, *Simón, Julio, Del Cerro, Juan Antonio, sustracción de menores de 10 años*, Decision of Judge Gabriel Cavallo, 6 March 2001, Case No. 8686/2002000/B, para 598, cited in Ferdinandusse 2006, p. 210, n. 1242 and also p. 75.

[104] Luban 2004, p. 141.

[105] Stigen 2010, p. 189.

[106] Sulzer 2007, pp. 135–137.

[107] These are those injured by the crime, the complainants/stakeholders who have a juridical interest in the punishment of the crime (Kemp 2014, p. 153).

[108] de Serpa Soares 2015, p. 670.

[109] Luban 2004, p. 140.

[110] Luban 2004, p. 91.

regardless of the nature of the population, whereas persecutions that are not so atrocious will be crimes against humanity only when they are inflicted on "suspect classes", that is, groups whose commonalities have historically formed the basis for targeting by outsiders'.[111]

5.3 Interventions Designed to Prevent and Punish Core Crimes by Prosecuting Core Crimes

In the light of the above, a recurring problem is the identification of the point in time at which the continued and primary obligation of the territorial State should give way to external intervention. Though this is not the subject of this book, suffice to say that the continued obligations of the territorial State to investigate and prosecute crimes on the one hand, and the obligation to protect (by investigating and prosecuting) of the third State enjoying custodial jurisdiction over an individual suspected of having committed core crimes within the territorial State on the other hand, are parallel obligations which co-exist. Obviously the right or duty to intervene may also include the adoption of military means, especially when this is expressly authorized by a UNSC Resolution, but for the purposes of this work, intervention (or intrusion) is to be equated to investigation and prosecution. Kai Ambos acknowledges that effective criminal prosecution constitutes one (non-military) level which, as in the case of *Daesh*,[112] needs to be complemented with military action.[113] Therefore, the obligation of the State to take all reasonable measures to prevent genocide is not limited to military intervention.[114] Common Article 1 of the four Geneva Conventions, *inter alia,* establishes 'a clear duty of States to use non-military means to prevent and halt the commission of war crimes and to bring the perpetrators to justice'.[115] In a nutshell, 'humanitarian intervention is only one part of the toolbox of the responsibility to react…The international community should also pursue other measures…and the use of international criminal prosecutions (e.g. referral to the International Criminal Court)'.[116] Criminal prosecutions can constitute both positive anticipatory measures designed

---

[111] Luban 2004, pp. 105–106.

[112] These are also known as Islamic State and rely on a 'robust, multi-level organisational structure designed to exercise central control over the terrorist groups' external messaging' (Milton 2014, cited in Badar 2016, p. 365, n. 13). Müllerson warns that 'even if *Daesh* (ISIS) and other currently existing Islamic terrorist groups would be destroyed in the Middle East, their metastases have already reached societies far beyond this region' (Müllerson 2018, p. 939). For an analysis of the way armed conflicts in Iraq and Syria involving *Daesh* should be classified, see Koutroulis 2016, pp. 829–843.

[113] Ambos 2015.

[114] Bellamy and Reike 2011, p. 95.

[115] Ibid.

[116] Pattison 2010, p. 13.

to prevent genocide especially when such prosecutions (for incitement and/or conspiracy) precede the genocide and remedial measures designed to punish the perpetrators thereof. Whereas the former anticipatory measures are undertaken domestically, the latter remedial measures are not necessarily undertaken on a national basis since the 'State's duty to prevent genocide is not limited only to populations within its own jurisdiction, but extends beyond its borders'.[117] The parallel obligations are triggered upon the consummation of the first core crime, *id est* of the first act (mode of conduct) which constitutes a core crime (by and of itself) or which is perpetrated in furtherance of the consummation of other core crimes. The right to intervene cannot be questioned. What might be questionable is whether there subsists a duty to intervene. Stating that 'the duty to intervene… seems to be a logical corollary of the right to intervene' is reductive.[118] The security principle and the international harm principle can engender a duty to intervene in order to protect a civilian population. Sections 5.4 and 5.5 will reveal how this right to intervene becomes a duty to act of the international community which may be considered as an actor of a unique character.[119] For the forthcoming reasons, *inter alia*, being postulated herein, an entitlement, a mere *faculté*, is transformed into an obligation, an assigned duty to act.

5.4 The Conceptual Genesis of the Responsibility to Protect

The duty to act finds partial refuge in the responsibility to protect principle[120] consisting in the idea that 'no State must be allowed to use the argument of sovereignty to shield the perpetration of massive human rights violations on its territory from external intervention'.[121] The principle itself encompasses the responsibility to react, the responsibility to rebuild and the responsibility to prevent[122] and has sometimes been used inter-changeably with the responsibility to prosecute.[123] Although praiseworthy, the principle has been criticised for many

---

[117] Zyberi 2013, p. 515.

[118] Pattison 2010, p. 16.

[119] Thurer 2011, p. 289.

[120] The phrase 'responsibility to protect' encapsulates the idea that if a State cannot or will not protect its people from such harm, then coercive intervention for human protection purposes, including ultimate military intervention, by others in the international community may be warranted in extreme cases (International Commission on Intervention and State Sovereignty 2001, p. 69, cited in Thurer 2011, pp. 289–290). For an understanding of the principle from an international relations perspective which encourages an obligation to negotiate directly with incumbent leaders of States marred by armed conflict, see De Groof 2016, pp. 30–48.

[121] Thurer 2011, p. 289.

[122] Thurer 2011, p. 291.

[123] Ralph 2015, p. 11.

reasons.[124] The principle was forged when it was unanimously reaffirmed by the UNSC by means of its Resolution 1674 in 2006 and reiterated by an overwhelming majority of States that contributed to the UNGA's debate in July 2009.[125] Some of its features are already well embedded in international law, whereas others are still developing and it hence would be premature to speak of a crystallizing practice[126] particularly because the doctrine is not devoid of what Carlo Focarelli calls 'legal bugs'.[127] This is especially so because the principle 'has gained little traction by way of legal incorporation.'[128] It stands for a wide variety of conduct ranging from preventive acts to swift action when mass atrocities are perpetrated and is the mirror image of the term 'failure to protect'.[129] To this effect, 'the principle of non-intervention yields to the international Responsibility to Protect when the State in question is "unwilling or unable" to halt or avert a population suffering serious harm, as a result of internal war, insurgency, repression or State failure'.[130] In fact nowadays mass atrocities, such as those occurring in Syria, may be deemed to 'result from a combination of acts by perpetrators and omissions by bystanders'.[131]

The responsibility to protect principle did not emerge *in abstracto* and out of the blue. The roots of this transformation may be traced to Hannah Arendt's epic work 'Organized Guilt and Universal Responsibility'.[132] Here Arendt expresses that 'for many years now we have met Germans who declare that they are ashamed of being Germans. I have often felt tempted to answer that I am ashamed of being human. This elemental shame, which many people of the most various nationalities share with one another today, is what finally is left of our sense of international solidarity; and it has not yet found an adequate political expression'.[133] She continues to uphold that the concept of humanity intrinsically 'implies the obligation of a general responsibility… For the idea of humanity, when purged of all sentimentality, has the very serious consequence that in one form or another men must assume responsibility for all crimes committed by men and that all nations share the onus of evil committed by all others. Shame at being a human being is the purely

---

124 Besides the controversy on its implementation, some scholars and politicians have expressed that, in the absence of a 'duty of care', it can allow powerful States to determine the conditions under which the responsibility may be discharged (Tharuk 2016, pp. 432–433). Kofi Annan had held that it can create perverse incentives for rebels and dissidents to provoke State retaliation to armed challenges in order to internationalise local conflicts (Annan 2000, para 216, cited in Tharuk 2016, p. 433, n. 118).

125 Bellamy and Reike 2011, p. 81.

126 Amneus 2013, pp. 13–14, n. 59. See also Stahn 2007, p. 101.

127 Focarelli 2015, pp. 418–423.

128 Pandiaraj 2016, p. 813.

129 Nollkaemper 2013, p. 1, n. 4.

130 International Commission on Intervention and State Sovereignty 2001, p. xi, cited in Amneus 2013, p. 8, n. 24.

131 Nollkaemper 2013, p. 2.

132 Arendt 1945.

133 Ibid.

individual and still non-political expression of this insight'.[134] Commenting thereupon, David Luban detects two sides of the same responsibility. The first is that to realise the concept of humanity 'requires taking responsibility for crime committed in corners of the world to which we have no interest-based ties; but it also requires us to refrain from dehumanizing even the most monstrous evil-doers'.[135] The explanation which David Luban gives to the theories of Hannah Arendt is pivotal both to the justification of international intervention and the duty to intrude when core crimes remain unpunished. Luban, a staunch supporter of norm projection as being the aim of international criminal justice,[136] analyses the ideas of Arendt as follows:

> 'When Arendt says that "men must assume responsibility for all crimes committed by men and that all nations share the onus of evil committed by others", she does not mean the fatuous and false sentiment that we are all collectively guilty for the evil of others – a view that Arendt actively scorned (286). We take responsibility for the crimes of others by holding them accountable, and so the practical way we constitute humanity will conspicuously include the construction of new institutions to hold wrongdoers accountable… The normative commitment to humanity carries the need for international criminal justice as a consequence'.[137] In simple terms, it is only by prosecuting that 'we become members of humanity'.[138]

In a nutshell, though detached and distant from the *locus delicti commissi*, responsibility is triggered by being indifferent and looking away. The above extract can be translated into specific duties for various States. The territorial State has a primary obligation to investigate and prosecute. The bystander (third) State would have such an ancillary obligation if the territorial State has failed to adhere to its obligation and if it enjoys custodial jurisdiction over the suspect.[139] Holding perpetrators accountable therefore is an act which fulfils the primary obligations of States. The obvious consequence of this is manifold: (1) the failure to prosecute by the State best suited (positioned) to do so constitutes a violation of the international responsibilities of such State; (2) the failure of the State which is best suited (qualified) to prosecute engenders the duty of third States to prosecute; and (3) the failure of such third State to prosecute can divest humanity of its intrinsic nature,[140] dehumanizing humanity in the process, at which point the international community (the global village) becomes like a journal with no subscriptions, an association

---

[134] Ibid.

[135] Luban 2015, p. 23.

[136] Norm projection can occur when States revise their criminal codes to reflect the ICC Statute by incorporating new norms within their domestic law. It radiates a task which brings people closer to the law where, for example, an under-enforced domestic law against war crimes can be effective if it becomes part of military training (Luban 2013, p. 511 and p. 515).

[137] Luban 2015, pp. 24–25.

[138] Luban 2015, pp. 25–26.

[139] See the reasons in support of this assertion under Sect. 5.5.

[140] The reasons for this are postulated particularly within Luban's analysis of Arendt's works (see Luban 2015, pp. 24–26).

without associates, a club without members or a company without shareholders. In fact Luban goes a step further in sharing his insight and understanding of the striking theories of Hannah Arendt. He argues, in my view, rather convincingly, that Arendt did not contemplate a pre-existing collective entity called 'humanity' since humanity only exists when 'we shoulder the demanding forms of cross-border responsibility'.[141] If and when States do not shoulder responsibility by judging and repressing such atrocious crimes, the very concept of humanity (which is at the epicentre of the nature of such crimes in the first place) crumbles like a house of cards. In this way, the international intervention of States enjoying custodial jurisdiction by virtue of the undertaking of a prosecution becomes a duty, not merely an entitlement (a right). Third States are hence curators and custodians of humanity. This duty consists in the fact that the failure to intervene by prosecuting is not merely an assault at the direct victims of the crime but an attack against humanity.

5.5 The Transformation of the Concept of the Responsibility to Protect into a Legal Principle

It has been submitted that the responsibility to protect is a political doctrine.[142] This heading will analyse the extent to which one may now consider it as a legal doctrine. This metamorphosis saw the concept travel to become a normative principle of a legal nature. A journey from idea to norm[143] has been undertaken by the responsibility to protect principle since its formal inception in the World Summit Outcome Document in NY in 2005.[144] This journey is reflected in the security shift from State security to human security, a paradigm shift which owes its existence to the responsibility to protect principle.[145] The successful completion of this journey may be said to forge a 'correlative collective duty or responsibility of States'[146] to ensure the protection of the security of human beings, this being the responsibility to protect which 'has a strong basis in treaty and customary international law'.[147] In other words and most importantly, the mere presence of the individual (suspected of having committed core crimes elsewhere) within the territorial jurisdiction of another (third/bystander) State can trigger the responsibility to protect of that other third/bystander State, especially if and when the international

[141] Luban 2015, p. 24.

[142] Donat Cattin 2017, p. 377.

[143] Amneus 2012, pp. 157–171 and Amneus 2013, p. 4, n. 3.

[144] Amneus 2013, pp. 4 and 5.

[145] International Commission on Intervention and State Sovereignty 2001, p. 15, cited in Amneus 2013, p. 7, n. 18.

[146] Amneus 2013, p. 8.

[147] Zyberi 2013, p. 528.

community has failed to act by means of its institutional framework, namely the prevailing UN protective mechanisms. If such third/bystander State decides not to investigate and prosecute the individual suspected of having committed core crimes, its duties flowing from its responsibility to protect require that it either extradites the individual to a State which enjoys jurisdiction over such individual or that it surrenders the individual to the ICC (if the admissibility test is satisfied). Therefore the intrusion can take the form of an extradition of an individual to an international criminal tribunal.[148] In this way, the responsibility to protect principle can assume the shape and form of *aut dedere aut judicare*. This is not necessarily so since although the prohibition of core crimes partake of *jus cogens* status, the obligation to prosecute such core crimes on the basis of *aut dedere aut judicare* does not enjoy the same status.[149] In any case, the responsibility to protect principle includes 'an obligation to facilitate prevention and suppression of certain crimes if necessary through international criminal prosecution'.[150] This conclusion can be drawn from the *Genocide Case*, where the ICJ upheld that while States are not obliged to succeed in their efforts to prevent genocide, they must employ the means which are reasonably available to them to do so.[151] Since 'it is unlikely that each individual State now has a responsibility to intervene militarily to end genocide, and it should be remembered that measures to end genocide must be consistent with international law, which prohibits the use of force except in self-defence or with the express authorization of the UN Security Council',[152] one can safely deduce that such measures, at the very least, should include prosecution, and upon the non-fulfilment of the obligation to prosecute, the expected measure entails the obligation to either surrender or extradite for the purposes of submitting an individual for prosecution elsewhere.

The journey from political concept to legal norm received a massive boost by virtue of the constitutive instrument which established core crimes in the first place, the ICC Statute, this being the document which crystallised the concept of 'core crimes' and which hence should be the yardstick thereof. The *raison d'être* behind their penalization lies within the Preamble itself which also refers to its complementary jurisdiction. Therefore, the serious concern is the direct result of States which, though enjoying jurisdiction over the crime, are either unwilling or

---

[148] May 2005, p. 63.

[149] This conclusion can be safely reached by noting that although the prohibition of torture is *jus cogens*, 'the obligation to prosecute the alleged perpetrators of acts of torture under the Convention applies only to facts having occurred after its entry into force for the State concerned' [ICJ, *Questions Relating to the Obligation to Extradite or Prosecute* (*Belgium v Senegal*), 20 July 2012, ICJ Rep. 2012, p. 422, para 100].

[150] Einarsen 2012, p. 62.

[151] ICJ, *Application of the Convention on the Prevention and Punishment of the Crime of Genocide* (*BiH v Serbia and Montenegro*), 26 February 2007, ICJ Reports 2007 p. 43, para 166.

[152] Gibney 2007, p. 767, cited in Bellamy and Reike, p. 98, n. 56.

unable[153] to investigate and prosecute. The concern stems from the impunity of such crimes at national level, which impunity smells of utter and uninterrupted lawlessness.[154] Since this state of affairs protrudes throughout the consummation (and subsequent consummation) of patterns of similar conduct, such impunity can be considered to be structural. This is so because core crimes 'are always integrated by multiple commissions of acts by several offenders'.[155] Structural impunity may be said to subsist when a State manifestly and persistently fails to protect its population from core crimes in a timely and decisive manner. Such structural impunity is particularly anguishing because most jurists concur that punishment acts as a deterrent which, in turn, can spare the commission of other crimes in the future.[156] The focus on deterrence is not inconsistent with David Luban's expressivist theories connoting that punishment conveys the message that 'political violence, mystified by States, is nothing but crime',[157] notwithstanding that David Luban (like myself) opines that the most plausible among the standard rationales for punishment is retribution.[158] In fact, the Preamble explicitly acknowledges that the determination of the State Parties to put an end to impunity for the perpetrators of these crimes contributes to the prevention of such crimes.[159] Impunity has a marked anti-preventive effect. The non-prosecution of such crimes, in and of itself, is distressing and troublesome since the harm caused lingers and a remedy at law is inexistent. This argument is substantiated by means of the complementarity regime which also allows self-referrals[160] whereby States outsource their conflicts with political contenders to the ICC, suggesting that they consider themselves insufficiently equipped to rigorously enforce the criminal law within their sovereign

---

[153] The concept of 'unwilling or unable' is not employed in the same way, manner and context as it appears as a test within Article 1(2) of the Refugee Convention [Refugee Convention (1951) Convention Relating to the Status of Refugees]. Likewise, it is not employed in terms of the USA formula advocated in a letter sent by the USA to the UNSC on 23 September 2011 justifying the launch of an air campaign against *Daesh* on Syrian territory. In relation to the latter letter, see Corten 2016, pp. 777–780.

[154] This idea is not shared by some eminent jurists. Roger O' Keefe opines that 'the qualifiers of "international concern" and "of concern to the international community as a whole" are once more without formal legal significance, being merely descriptive. Nor do they necessarily imply that no other crimes are of international concern or of concern to the international community as a whole' (O'Keefe 2015, p. 65).

[155] Meloni 2010, p. 19.

[156] Grono and de Courcy Wheeler 2015, p. 1225. Others, to which I do not subscribe, posit that core crimes are resistant to deterrence and that the record of international prosecutions suggest that they offer little hope of preventing future atrocities besides risking to prolong conflicts (Branch 2007, p. 2, cited in Grono and de Courcy Wheeler 2015, pp. 1225–1226, n. 5).

[157] Luban 2011b, p. 70.

[158] Luban 2011b, pp. 72–73.

[159] See preambular para 5 of the ICC Statute.

[160] ICC Appeals Chamber, *Situation in the DRC, Prosecutor v Germain Katanga and Mathieu Ngudjolo Chui, Judgment on the Appeal of Mr. Germain Katanga against the Oral Decision of Trial Chamber II of 12 June 2009 on the Admissibility of the Case,* 25 September 2009, Case No. ICC-01/04-01/07 OA8, para 78; see Akhavan 2010, p. 103 and p. 110, and see also Sect. 11.4.

realm,[161] evidencing a rapidly changing world order characterised by dwindling State authority.[162] When a State resorts to refer its own situation to the ICC, its government contends that it is unable to conduct fair and effective criminal proceedings against non-State actors over whom they do not wield control.[163] Indeed 'the complementarity principle at the ICC is directly analogous to the main pillar of the R2P, namely that States have the primary responsibility for protecting their citizens, and that other bodies can step in only if the State in question is manifestly failing to offer such protection. The responsibility to prevent, subsumed within the R2P, is analogous to the positive complementarity agenda'.[164] There seems to be general consensus that if a State is unable or unwilling to exercise its responsibility to protect, this responsibility is shifted to 'international organisations, including the United Nations, or any other authority controlling the territory and its population'.[165] James Pattison distinguishes between two instances, both of which trigger the responsibility to protect. In the first the responsibility to protect is transferred to the international community when the State involved is unable or unwilling to look after its citizens' human rights, whereas in the second it is transferred to the international community when national authorities are manifestly failing to protect their populations.[166] The latter scenario has the hallmarks of what I call 'the structural inability of the failed State'. This shifting process may have a counterpart in the broad realm of sovereignty which embraces the authority (power) to prosecute individuals and punish convicted criminals. The counterpart can be the responsibility to protect of the third (non-territorial/bystander) State which gets to enjoy custodial jurisdiction over an individual. Hence the custodial State which enjoys jurisdiction over an individual can be placed in the same basket just as the UN or a State controlling the territory and the population of the State wherein the core crimes were perpetrated.

In any case, the intrusion into the sovereignty of a State to investigate and prosecute core crimes is justified by an application of the principle of international harm,[167] dealt with earlier on, which encompasses a breach of the principle of human security. This same 'international harm'[168] can be equated to a 'universal legal injury'. Third States become injured States which can demonstrate a universal

---

[161] van der Wilt and Braber 2015, p. 17. For a detailed examination of the lacking juridical infrastructure in States and consequent inability of such States which auto-refer these cases, see van der Wilt 2015, pp. 210–212.

[162] van der Wilt 2015, p. 211.

[163] van der Wilt 2015, pp. 211–212.

[164] Ainley 2015, p. 50.

[165] Gierycz 2011, p. 101.

[166] The first was advocated by the International Commission on Intervention and State Sovereignty, whereas the second was the agreement reached within the 2005 World Summit (Pattison 2010, p. 14).

[167] May 2005, p. 63.

[168] The principle of harm lies at the very core of penal proscription. Criminal laws, including international criminal law, are legitimate only if they address the prevention of harm, (May 2005,

legal injury.[169] This may subsist, *inter alia,* when third State remedies become necessary to meet the world's needs, so to say, such as 'when no directly injured State would have traditional standing to seek a remedy'.[170] The logical question which follows is how and why can a third (bystander) State be considered as an injured State when a core crime is committed very far away from such third State? This heading will address this question, the reply to which portrays the journey from concept to legal principle. André Nollkaemper and Dov Jacobs do not refer to the phrase 'universal legal injury' but convey its thrust when they analyse the ambiguous concept of *erga omnes* obligations, these being obligations owed to the international community as a whole. They perceptively remark that there exist two types of *erga omnes* obligations, depending on the interest protected by the obligation and the legal regime of responsibility applied. Their analysis seems to differentiate between *erga omnes* obligations *in abstracto* and *erga omnes* obligations *in concreto*, although they do not use the latter term. The former (*erga omnes* obligations *in abstracto*) are obligations which only entitle the injured State to claim the responsibility of the defaulting State. Therefore, the obligation to respect diplomatic immunity is owed to all States, but upon its breach, it is only the injured State that can bring a claim or vaunt a pretension. On the other hand, the obligation to refrain from committing genocide is an obligation *in concreto* because its breach will grant *locus standi* not only to the injured State, but also to any other State acting on behalf of the international community'.[171] Now one must reconsider these submissions by thinking outside the box in so far as they may seem to contain a contradiction or imprecision. A *locus standi in judicio* is an entitlement which emanates from a juridical (legally protected) interest, not an obligation. Yet, *erga omnes* obligations are duties owed by States to all the international community, not merely entitlements. How can one reconcile one with the other? In other words, how can one speak of an *erga omnes* obligation *in concreto* when all that this conveys is a mere *locus standi*? Would the breach of an *erga omnes* obligation by a State merely grant an entitlement to other States to avail themselves of their *locus standi* and/or intervene, or would it impose an obligation upon such other third States to exercise their *locus standi* and/or intervene? In the context of the questions posed here above and of my book, a *locus standi* can be effectively[172] exercised in three ways. A third State may enjoy custodial jurisdiction over an individual, at which point it may decide to exercise the *aut dedere aut judicare* rule either by

p. 66 and p. 67) which can be considered to be a denial of rights (Feinburg 1984, pp. 105–106, cited in May 2005, p. 67, n. 15).

169 Jean D'Aspremont uses the phrase 'universal legal injury' in reviewing James Crawford's book 'State Responsibility: The General Part' (D'Aspremont 2015, p. 983).

170 Quigley 2006, p. 259.

171 Kolb and Krahenmann 2009, p. 429, cited in Nollkaemper and Jacobs 2012–2013, p. 420, n. 319.

172 The word 'effectively' is being used to signify that the *locus standi* must lead to tangible results consisting in the investigation and prosecution of the individual, not merely to orders by the ICJ as to which State should prosecute and as to which is the *forum conveniens*.

extraditing the individual to a State enjoying jurisdiction over the individual, or by prosecuting the individual on its own soil. In the absence of any ground of jurisdiction, the custodial State may resort to universal jurisdiction, as shall be seen within the fourth Part of this work. Should there have been a request for surrender, the third State may have surrendered the individual to the ICC in terms of the prevailing rules which shall be dealt with in the next (third) Part of this work. Now the power and effect of *erga omnes* obligations is that when they are at stake the juridical (legally protected) interest is presumed to be present. These obligations therefore have a marked procedural impact which dispenses with the traditional requirement of *locus standi*.[173] Notwithstanding that only in exceptional situations a bystander (third) State can become responsible for failing to act on the basis of a breach of an obligation to protect,[174] since the *erga omnes* character of an obligation presupposes a common interest rooted in the prohibition of the violation of *jus cogens* norms, as shall be analysed further in Part IV of this work, the entitlement may be said to have been transformed into a duty, for all the reasons which are being disclosed within this heading, when the third State enjoys custodial jurisdiction over the individual. André Nollkaemper, an ardent promoter of the concept of shared (diffused) responsibility,[175] qualifies the obligation to intervene of States which occupy the territory of another State by confining it to instances wherein such States exercise some form of personal, territorial or extra-territorial jurisdiction. He provides the example of the Netherlands when it failed to protect individuals who were actively deported from its compound in *Srebrenica*,[176] and compares it to the obligation of the Netherlands to, *ab initio*, prevent the genocide in *Srebrenica*.[177] The Netherlands may be held responsible for the former but not for the latter.[178] Yet he does not limit the performance of the obligation to protect solely to States exercising territorial control, but expands it to States which have the capacity to exert influence over perpetrators or the capacity to avert the genocide, drawing such a proposition from the *Genocide* case.[179] Using Libya as an example, Nollkaemper argues that further to UNSC Resolution 1973, 'both the territorial State and outside actors then may be obliged to act – and in principle these responsibilities do not exclude or undermine each other'.[180] The corollary of these

[173] Kolb and Krahenmann 2009, p. 429.

[174] Nollkaemper 2013, pp. 4–5.

[175] This connotes that all actors who/which refrain from acting are a cause in the sense that they had to do something, 'and their omissions are empirically connected to the outcome – along with the acts of perpetrators' (Nollkaemper 2013, p. 20).

[176] The Hague Court of Appeal, *Hasan Nuhanović v The Netherlands*, 5 July 2011, Case No. 200.020.174/01, cited in Nollkaemper 2013, p. 6, n. 19.

[177] *Hoge Raad* [Supreme Court], The Netherlands, *Stichting Mothers of Srebrenica v The Netherlands and United Nations*, 13 April 2012, Case No. 10/04437, cited in Nollkaemper 2013, p. 6, n. 20.

[178] Nollkaemper 2013, p. 6.

[179] Nollkaemper 2013, p. 7.

[180] Nollkaemper 2013, p. 21.

propositions is that if a person is suspected of having somehow participated in a core crime committed in State X, and if such person somehow ends up within the custodial jurisdiction of another State (State Y), State Y would possess the capacity to exert influence over perpetrators or the capacity to avert the genocide, especially if one embraces the theory that the prevention of genocide is partially accomplished by the prosecution and punishment thereof, in so far as the prosecution thereof is likely to deter others from committing genocide. The same can be said about the UN itself, although the contribution to mass atrocities by its omission may not necessarily lead to the establishment of international responsibility for the breach of its obligation to protect.[181] The ICJ has found that the capacity of States to prevent genocide outside their territory 'depends, among other things, on the geographical distance of the State concerned from the scene of the events, and on the strength of the political links, as well as links of all other kinds, between the authorities of that State and the main actors in the events'.[182]

This chapter has shown that it is legitimate for a bystander State to intrude into the sovereignty of a defaulting State when systematic harm is structurally inflicted against a group. More so, circumstances may dictate that a bystander State which has custodial jurisdiction over a person who has allegedly committed core crimes could come under an obligation to either prosecute or extradite such individual. To determine the extent to which such duty may thrive, one would have to monitor the progressive development of international law and the willingness, or otherwise, of the ILC to codify the 'responsibility to protect' principle, at least in so far as core crimes are concerned. The need for such codification becomes more pertinent when one realises the extent to which the juridical elements of core crimes reflect their main features and characteristics, this being a task I will undertake in the next chapter.

References

Ainley K (2015) The Responsibility to Protect and the International Criminal Court: Counteracting the Crisis. International Affairs 91(1):37–54

Akhavan P (2010) Self-Referrals before the International Criminal Court: Are States the Villains or the Victims of Atrocities? CLF 21:103–120

Altman A, Wellman C (2004) A Defence of International Criminal Law. Ethics 115(1):35–67

Ambos K (2015) The New Enemy of Mankind: The Jurisdiction of the ICC over Members of "Islamic State"'. EJILTalk! http://www.ejiltalk.org/the-new-enemy-of-mankind-the-jurisdiction-of-the-icc-over-members-of-islamic-state/. Accessed 1 February 2017

Amneus D (2012) Has Humanitarian Intervention Become Part of International Law under the Responsibility to Protect Doctrine? In: Hoffmann J, Nollkaemper A (eds) Responsibility to

[181] Nollkaemper 2013, p. 15.

[182] *BiH v Serbia and Montenegro* 2007, above n. 151, para 430, cited in Ruvebana 2014, p. 171, n. 759.

Protect: From Principle to Practice. Pallas Publications, Amsterdam University Press, pp. 157–171
Amneus D (2013) The Coining and Evolution of Responsibility to Protect: The Protection Responsibilities of the State. In: Zyberi G (ed) An Institutional Approach to the Responsibility to Protect. CUP, Cambridge, pp. 3–32
Annan KA (2000) We the Peoples: The Role of the United Nations in the Twenty-First Century, Report of the S-G, NY. UN Doc. A/54/2000
Arendt H (1945) Organised Guilt and Universal Responsibility. In: Essays in Understanding 1930–1954: Formation, Exile and Totalitarianism. Shocken Books, NY, published in 1994, originally published in Jewish Frontier, no. 12, as 'German Guilt'. http://home.earthlink.net/~lstenmark/Hum2B/ArendtOrgGuilt.pdf. Accessed 2 February 2012
Arens L (2013) International Jurisdiction: An Analysis of Larry May's Theory on Crimes Against Humanity. 2013 Tananbaum Prize Winner of Philosophy, Politics and Law, Binghamton University, The State University of NY. http://www.binghamton.edu/philosophy-politics-and-law/pdfs/Larisa%20Arens%20Tanenbaum%20Prize%20Paper.pdf. Accessed 3 August 2016
Badar ME (2016) The Road to Genocide: The Propaganda Machine of the Self-Declared Islamic State (IS). ICLR 16:361–511
Barth B (2013) Victims of Genocide and Crimes Against Humanity. In: Bonacker T, Safferling C (eds) Victims of International Crimes: An Interdisciplinary Discourse. Springer/Asser Press, Berlin/Heidelberg, The Hague, pp. 253–262
Bellamy AJ, Reike R (2011) The Responsibility to Protect and International Law. In: Bellamy AJ, Davies SE, Glanville L (eds) The Responsibility to Protect and International Law. MNP, Leiden/Boston pp. 81–100
Birdsall A (2015) The Responsibility to Prosecute and the ICC: A Problematic Relationship? CLF 26(1):51–72
Branch A (2007) Uganda's Civil War and the Politics of ICC Intervention. Ethics and International Affairs 21(2):179–198
Bull H (2012) The Anarchical Society: A Study of World Order in Politics, 4th edn. Palgrave Macmillan, Basingstoke, UK
Burke-White WW (2002–2003) A Community of Courts: Toward a System of International Criminal Law Enforcement. MJIL 24(1):86–94
Calvo-Goller KN (2006) The Trial Proceedings of the International Criminal Court: ICTY and ICTR Precedents. MNP, Leiden/Boston
Ciciriello MC, Borgia F (2017) Deconstructing the Responsibility to Protect Doctrine: Looking for a New Legal Basis. In: Acconci P, Donat Cattin D, Marchesi A, Palmisano G, Santoni V (eds) International Law and the Protection of Humanity: Essays in Honour of Flavia Lattanzi. MNP, Leiden, pp. 225–244
Corten O (2016) The "Unwilling or Unable" Test: Has it Been and Could it Be, Accepted? LJIL 29 (3):777–799
Cryer R (2009) The Definitions of International Crimes in the Al Bashir Arrest Warrant Decision. JICJ 7(2):283–296
D'Aspremont J (2015) Reviewing Crawford J (2014) State Responsibility: The General Part. CUP, Cambridge. In: ICLQ 64(4):982–984
De Groof E (2016) First Things First: R2P Starts with Direct Negotiations. The International Spectator, Special Issue on the Responsibility to Protect, The Quarterly Journal of *Istituto Affari Internazionali* 51(2):30–48
de Serpa Soares M (2015) An Age of Accountability, Special Editorial. JICJ 13(4):669–676
Donat Cattin D (2017) Intervention of Humanity or the Use of Force to Halt Mass-Atrocity Crimes, the Peremptory Prohibition of Aggression and the Interplay Between *Jus Ad Bellum, Jus in Bello* and Individual Criminal Responsibility on the Crime of Aggression. In: Acconci P, Donat Cattin D, Marchesi A, Palmisano G, Santoni V (eds) International Law and the Protection of Humanity: Essays in Honour of Flavia Lattanzi. MNP, Leiden, pp. 353–396
Einarsen T (2012) The Concept of Universal Crimes in International Law. TOAEP, Oslo
Feinburg J (1984) The Moral Limits of the Criminal Law, Vol. I, Harm to Others. OUP, Oxford

Ferdinandusse WN (2006) Direct Application of International Criminal Law in National Courts. Asser Press, The Hague

Ferstman C (2007) The Approach of the United Kingdom to Crimes under International Law: The Application of Extraterritorial Jurisdiction. In: Kaleck W, Ratner M, Singelnstein T, Weiss P (eds) International Prosecution of Human Rights Crimes. Springer, 2007, pp. 149–158

Fletcher GP (2005) Parochial *versus* Universal Criminal Law. JICJ 3(1):20–34

Focarelli C (2015) The Responsibility to Protect in the Global System. In: Hilpold P (ed) The Responsibility to Protect (R2P): A New Paradigm of International Law? Brill/Nijhoff, Leiden/Boston, pp. 417–438

Fredman S (2007) The Positive Right to Security. In: Goold BJ, Lazarus L (eds) Security and Human Rights. HP, London, pp. 307–324

Gal-Or N (2015) The Formation of a Customary International Crime: Global Terrorism Human (In) Security. ICLR 15(4):665–699

Garbett C (2015) The Concept of the Civilian: Legal Recognition, Adjudication and the Trials of International Criminal Justice. Routledge, T & F, Milton Park, Didcot, UK

Geneva Convention (1949a) Geneva Convention (I) for the Amelioration of the Condition of the Wounded and Sick in Armed Forces in the Field

Geneva Convention (1949b) Geneva Convention (II) for the Amelioration of the Condition of the Wounded, Sick and Shipwrecked Members of Armed Forces at Sea

Geneva Convention (1949c) Geneva Convention (III) relative to the Treatment of Prisoners of War

Geneva Convention (1949d) Geneva Convention (IV) relative to the Protection of Civilian Persons in Time of War

Genocide Convention (1948) Convention on the Prevention and Punishment of the Crime of Genocide

Gibney M (2007) Genocide and State Responsibility. Human Rights Law Review 7(4):760–773

Gierycz D (2011) The Responsibility to Protect: A Legal and Rights-Based Perspective. In: Bellamy J, SE Davies, Glanville L (eds) The Responsibility to Protect and International Law. MNP, Leiden/Boston, pp. 101–117

Grono N, de Courcy Wheeler A (2015) The Deterrent Effect of the ICC on the Commission of International Crimes by Government Leaders. In: Stahn C (ed) The Law and Practice of the International Criminal Court. OUP, Oxford, pp. 1225–1244

Hobbs H (2017) Towards a Principled Justification for the Mixed Composition of Hybrid International Criminal Tribunals. LJIL 30(1):177–197

ICC Statute (1998) Rome Statute of the International Criminal Court

International Commission on Intervention and State Sovereignty (2001) The Responsibility to Protect. Report Published by International Development Research Centre, Ottawa, Canada. http://responsibilitytoprotect.org/ICISS%20Report.pdf. Accessed 7 December 2012

Jackson M (2015) Complicity in International Law. Oxford Monographs in International Law, OUP, Oxford

Jørgensen NHB (2000) The Responsibility of States for International Crimes, Oxford Monographs in International Law. OUP, Oxford

Kemp S (2014) Guatemala Prosecutes Former President Rios Montt: New Perspectives on Genocide and Domestic Criminal Justice. JICJ 12(1):133–156

Kleffner JK (2008) Complementarity in the Rome Statute and National Criminal Jurisdictions. International Courts and Tribunals Series. OUP, Oxford

Kleffner JK (2009) The Collective Accountability of Organised Armed Groups for System Crimes. In: Nollkaemper A, van der Wilt H (eds) System Criminality in International Law. CUP, Cambridge, pp. 238–269

Kleinlein T (2017) *Jus Cogens* Re-examined: Value Formalism in International Law. EJIL 28(1): 295–315

Kolb R, Krahenmann S (2009) The Scope *Rationae Personae* of the Compulsory Jurisdiction of the International Court of Justice. In: Gaeta P (ed) The UN Genocide Convention: A Commentary. OUP, Oxford, pp. 425–441

Koutroulis V (2016) The Fight Against the Islamic State and *Jus in Bello.* LJIL 29(3):827–852

Kreß C (2013) Commentary on S.6 German Code of International Criminal Law *(Volkerstrafgesetzbuch)*. In: Wolfgang J, Miebach K (eds) *Munchener Kommentar zum Strafgesetzbuch*, Band 6/2: *Nebenstrafrecht* III, *Volkerstrafgesetzbuch*, 2nd edn. C.H. Beck, Munchen

Lee W-C (2010) International Crimes and Universal Jurisdiction. In: May L, Hoskins Z (eds) International Criminal Law and Philosophy. ASIL Studies in International Legal Theory, CUP, Cambridge, pp. 15–38

Lemkin R (1944) Axis Rule in Occupied Europe: Laws of Occupation, Analysis of Government, Proposals for Redress. Carnegie Endowment for International Peace, Divisions of International Law, Washington DC

Luban D (2004) A Theory of Crimes Against Humanity. YJIL 29(1):85–167

Luban D (2006) Calling Genocide by its Rightful Name: Lemkin's Word, Darfur, and the U.N. Report. *CgJIL* 7(1):303–320

Luban D (2011a) Hannah Arendt as a Theorist of International Criminal Law. ICLR 11(3):621–641

Luban D (2011b) State Criminality and the Ambition of International Criminal Law. In: Isaacs T and Vernon R (eds) Accountability for Collective Wrongdoing. CUP, Cambridge, pp. 61–91

Luban D (2013) After the Honeymoon: Reflections on the Current State of International Criminal Justice. JICJ 11(3):505–515

Luban D (2015) Arendt on the Crime of Crimes, Georgetown Law Faculty Publications and Other Works, Paper 1473, GULC. http://scholarship.law.georgetown.edu/facpub/1473/. Accessed 8 September 2016

Luban D, O'Sullivan JR, Stewart DP (2010) International and Transnational Criminal Law. WK, Alphen aan den Rijn

Lugato M (2017) Conceptualizing the Responsibility to Protect: A Short Contribution. In: Acconci P, Donat Cattin D, Marchesi A, Palmisano G, Santoni V (eds) International Law and the Protection of Humanity: Essays in Honour of Flavia Lattanzi. MNP, Leiden, pp. 245–261

Materu SF (2015) The Post-Election Violence in Kenya: Domestic and International Legal Responses, International Criminal Justice Series, Vol. 2. Asser Press, The Hague

May L (2005) Crimes Against Humanity: A Normative Account. CUP, Cambridge

May L (2014) A Hobbesian Defence of International Criminal Law. ICLR 14(4–5):768–788

May L, Hoskins Z (2010) Introduction. In: May L, Hoskins Z (eds) International Criminal Law and Philosophy. ASIL Studies in International Legal Theory, CUP, Cambridge, pp. 1–12

Meloni C (2010) Command Responsibility in International Criminal Law. Asser Press, The Hague

Milton D (2014) The Islamic State: An Adaptive Organization Facing Increasing Challenges, The Group that Calls Itself a State: Understanding the Evolution and Challenges of the Islamic State. The Combatting Terrorism Centre at West Point, US Military Academy, Department of Defence, US Government. https://ctc.usma.edu/app/uploads/2014/12/CTC-The-Group-That-Calls-Itself-A-State-December20141.pdf. Accessed on 29 July 2018

Müllerson R (2018) Human Rights are Neither Universal nor Natural. ChJIL 17(4):925–942

Murray A (2011) Does International Criminal Law Still Require a Crime of Crimes? A Comparative Review of Genocide and Crimes Against Humanity. GJIL 3(2):589–615

Nollkaemper A (2013) Failures to Protect in International Law, Amsterdam Law School Legal Studies Research Paper No. 2013-46, ACIL, UvA, Amsterdam. https://papers.ssrn.com/sol3/papers.cfm?abstract_id=2319317. Accessed 3 January 2014

Nollkaemper A, Jacobs D (2013) Shared Responsibility in International Law: A Conceptual Framework. MJIL 34(2):359–438

O'Keefe R (2015) International Criminal Law. OUP, Oxford

Olusanya O (2014) Using the Macro-Micro Integrated Theoretical Model to Understand the Dynamics of Collective Violence. In: Bantekas I, Mylonaki E (eds) Criminological Approaches to International Criminal Law. CUP, Cambridge, pp. 222–239

Pandiaraj S (2016) Sovereignty as Responsibility: Reflections on the Legal Status of the Doctrine of Responsibility to Protect. ChJIL 15(4):795–815

Pattison J (2010) Humanitarian Intervention and the Responsibility to Protect: Who Should Intervene? OUP, Oxford

Peter CM (2016) Fighting Impunity: African States and the International Criminal Court. In: Ankumah EA (ed) The International Criminal Court and Africa: One Decade On. Africa Legal Aid Series, Vol. 4. Intersentia, Cambridge, pp. 1–62

Quigley J (2006) The Genocide Convention: An International Law Analysis. International and Comparative Criminal Justice, Ashgate, Aldershot, Hampshire, UK/Burlington, VT, USA

Ragni C (2013) The Contribution of the Special Tribunal for Lebanon to the Notion of Terrorism: Judicial Creativity or Progressive Development of International Law? In: Boschiero N, Scovazzi T, Pitea C, Ragni C (eds) International Courts and the Development of International Law: Essays in Honour of Tullio Treves. Asser Press, The Hague, pp. 671–684

Ralph J (2015) Symposium: International Criminal Justice and the Responsibility to Protect. CLF 26(1):1–12

Rapaczynski A (1987) Nature and Politics: Liberalism in the Philosophies of Hobbes, Locke and Rousseau. CIlUP, Ithaca, NY

Reeves AR (2018) Liability to International Prosecution: The Nature of Universal Jurisdiction. EJIL 28(4):1047–1067

Refugee Convention (1951) Convention Relating to the Status of Refugees

Robertson G (2012) Crimes Against Humanity: The Struggle for Global Justice, 4th edn. PB, London

Robinson D (2014) Supranational Criminal Law Lecture held at the Asser Institute on 17 September 2014. https://www.youtube.com/watch?v=ddjlVo7G0Sw. Accessed 9 July 2017

Ruvebana E (2014) Prevention of Genocide under International Law: An Analysis of the Obligations of States and the united Nations to Prevent Genocide at the Primary, Secondary and Tertiary Levels. School of Human Rights Research, Intersentia, Antwerp

Ryngaert C (2007) Applying the Rome Statute's Complementarity Principle: Drawing Lessons from the Prosecution of Core Crimes by States Acting under the Universality Principle. CLF 19:153–180

Ryngaert C (2008) Jurisdiction in International Law. OUP, Oxford

Sadat LN (2011) A Comprehensive History of the Proposed International Convention on the Prevention and Punishment of Crimes Against Humanity. In: Sadat LN (eds) Forging a Convention for Crimes Against Humanity. CUP, Cambridge, pp. 455–501

Stahn C (2007) Responsibility to Protect: Political Rhetoric or Emerging Legal Norm. AJIL 101 (1):99–120

Stigen J (2010) What's in the ICC for States? In: Eriksen CC, Emberland M (eds) The New International Law – An Anthology. The Raoul Wallenberg Institute, Human Rights Library, Vol. 36. MNP, Leiden/Boston, pp. 183–199

Sulzer J (2007) Implementing the Principle of Universal Jurisdiction in France. In: Kaleck W, Ratner M, Singelnstein T, Weiss P (eds) International Prosecution of Human Rights Crimes. Springer, Berlin/Heidelberg, pp. 125–137

Tams CJ, Berster L, Schiffbauer B (2014) Convention on the Prevention and Punishment of the Crime of Genocide: A Commentary. Verlag C.H. Beck/Hart/Nomos, Munchen/Oxford/Baden-Baden/Portland, Oregon

Tharuk R (2016) The Responsibility to Protect at 15, Review Article. International Affairs 92 (2):415–434

Thurer D (2011) International Humanitarian Law: Theory, Practice, Context. Ail-Pocket, Pocketbooks of the HAIL, The Hague

Tomuschat C (2015) The Security Council and *Jus Cogens*. In: Cannizzaro E (ed) The Present and Future of *Jus Cogens. Sapienza Università Editrice*, Rome, pp. 7–97

Turk D (2003) Reflections on Human Rights, Sovereignty of States and the Principle of Non-Intervention. In: Bergsmo M (ed) Human Rights and Criminal Justice for the Downtrodden: Essays in Honour of Asbjorn Eide. MNP, Leiden, pp. 753–766

UN Development Programme (1994) Human Development Report. OUP, NY. http://hdr.undp.org/sites/default/files/reports/255/hdr_1994_en_complete_nostats.pdf Accessed 2 February 2012

UNSC (2006) Resolution 1674 (2006), UN Doc. S/RES/1674
UNSC (2011) Resolution 1973 (2011), UN Doc. S/RES/1973
van der Wilt (2015) Self-Referrals as an Indication of the Inability of States to Cope with Non-State Actors. In: Stahn C (ed) The Law and Practice of the International Criminal Court. OUP, Oxford, pp. 210–227
van der Wilt H (2012a) War Crimes and the Requirement of a Nexus with an Armed Conflict. JICJ 10(5):1113–1128
van der Wilt H (2012b) Crimes Against Humanity: A Category *Hors Concours* in International Criminal Law? Faculty of Law, UvA, Amsterdam Law School, Amsterdam, Research Paper 2012-24, ACIL 2012-06, General Subserie Research Paper 2012-03 http://papers.ssrn.com/sol3/papers.cfm?abstract_id=2005728. Accessed 27 July 2015
van der Wilt H (2016) Slavery Prosecutions in International Criminal Jurisdictions. JICJ 14 (2):269–283.
van der Wilt H, Braber I (2015) The Case for Inclusion of Terrorism in the Jurisdiction of the International Criminal Court. In: Mariniello T (ed) The International Criminal Court in Search of its Purpose and Identity. Routledge Research in International law, Routledge, London/NY, pp. 17–38
Ventura MJ (2015) The Duty to Investigate Zimbabwe Crimes Against Humanity (Torture) Allegations: The Constitutional Court of South Africa Speaks on Universal Jurisdiction and the ICC Act. JICJ 13(4):861–889
Vernon R (2002) What is a Crime Against Humanity? Journal of Political Philosophy 10(3):231–249
von Tigerstrom B (2007) Human Security and International Law: Prospects and Problems. Studies in International Law, Vol. 14, HP, Bloomsbury
Werle G (2009) Principles of International Criminal Law, 2nd edn. Asser Press, The Hague
Zyberi G (2013) Sharing the Responsibility to Protect: Taking Stock and Moving Forward. In: Zyberi G (ed) An Institutional Approach to the Responsibility to Protect. CUP, Cambridge, pp. 511–530

Chapter 6
The Overarching Contextual (Juridical) Elements

Contents

6.1 Genocide 91
6.2 Crimes Against Humanity 93
6.3 War Crimes 101
6.4 Aggression 104
References 106

Abstract Core crimes possess some overarching juridical elements which are also called 'contextual circumstances'. These mirror the unwillingness and/or inability of States to investigate and prosecute. In the crimes of genocide the contextual elements are implicit in the *dolus specialis*, this being the intent to destroy, in whole or in part, a protected group. The existence of a genocidal plan or policy is not a necessary ingredient of the crime, but it is still important evidentiary material wherefrom the *dolus specialis* may be inferred. Crimes against humanity require that the perpetrator knew that the conduct was part of or intended the conduct to be part of a widespread or systematic attack which must be pursuant to or in furtherance of a State or organizational policy to commit such attack. *Dicta* show how the group-oriented nature of such crimes is implicit in the role of the State. War crimes require an armed conflict which, in turn, presupposes either that the State is a contending party to the conflict itself or else that it is incapable to extinguish such conflict. Although distinct, crimes against humanity and war crimes possess some common features when the perpetrators thereof, namely organizational requirements, are analysed. Being a leadership crime, aggression conjures that the perpetrator must be in a position by means of which he can exercise control over or direct the political or military action of a State. These overarching juridical elements reveal the intrinsic difficulties which are connected with the investigation and/or prosecution of core crimes.

Keywords Contextual elements · Group · Genocide · *Dolus specialis* · Crimes against humanity · Widespread or systematic attack · *Jean-Pierre Bemba Gombo* · Organization · State or organizational policy · Private entity · *Kenya* ·

C. Soler, *The Global Prosecution of Core Crimes under International Law*,
https://doi.org/10.1007/978-94-6265-335-1_6

State-likeness · War crimes · Armed conflict · Threshold · Aggression · Leadership crime

The observations in the preceding three chapters pave the way to consider the contextual elements which can reflect a degree of State involvement within core crimes, and can also, in turn, reveal other important features and characteristics of core crimes. Since 'contextual elements can be independent of the alleged criminal act or omission on which the criminal charges are based,' their 'constituent boundaries remain difficult to define with any degree of certainty required in criminal law'.[1] The contextual elements form part of the so-called ICC Elements of Crimes which assist the ICC in the interpretation and application of the substantive crimes.[2] The ICC Elements of Crimes are particularly important also since the ICC has indicated that it will not easily deviate from the stipulations contained therein.[3] The ICC Elements of Crimes are imbued with so-called 'contextual circumstances' (or, as they are commonly referred to, 'contextual elements').[4] I shall make use of the term 'contextual elements' because it is more appropriate from a criminal law perspective. These contextual elements profoundly mirror the nature, features and characteristics of such core crimes. In fact, the macro-criminal nature of these crimes implies that their occurrence 'is by definition linked to the existence of a particular political and social context.'[5] Only these contextual elements elevate crimes to the level of core crimes.[6] Thus, whereas domestic crimes and transnational organised crimes require an organic combination of *actus reus* and *mens rea*, core crimes, over and above this organic combination, require the subsistence of the contextual elements.[7] The ensuing combination of constitutive elements is two-layered.[8] An analysis of the core crimes, one by one, will show the extent to which the contextual elements may be deemed to be overarching in so far as they mirror the unwillingness and/or inability of States to investigate and prosecute.

---

[1] Koursami 2018, p. 26.

[2] For a thorough understanding of the ICC Elements of Crimes (ICC Elements of Crimes (1998) International Criminal Court, Elements of Crimes), see Kelt and von Hebel 2001, pp. 19–40.

[3] ICC Pre-Trial Chamber I, Prosecutor v *Omar Hassan Ahmad Al Bashir*, *Decision on the Prosecution's Application for a Warrant of Arrest Against Omar Hassan Ahmad Al Bashir*, 4 March 2009, Case No. ICC-02/05-01/09, cited in Akhavan 2012, p. 34, n. 28.

[4] Kreß 2009, p. 297.

[5] Meloni 2010, p. 14.

[6] van der Wilt 2008, p. 234.

[7] Marchuk 2014, p. 70.

[8] Marchuk 2014, p. 92.

6.1 Genocide

Genocide,[9] the conduct of which is clearly defined under general international law[10] by virtue of a treaty which is universally ratified, is considered to be the 'crime of crimes',[11] or, in the words of the UN, 'the ultimate crime'.[12] Genocide 'is most likely to be contained within a State's borders',[13] because 'generally system crimes are committed by a State against its own nationals'.[14] It does not expressly require the policy of a State or State-like organization, but it requires and is generally committed 'in the context of a manifest pattern of similar conduct directed against that group or was conduct that could itself effect such destruction'.[15] It also requires that the intended victim be the group 'as such', not just its individual members.[16] Although genocide can be committed by a lone *génocidaire* where such individual is capable of 'effecting the destruction' of one of the protected groups,[17] this is 'little more than a sophomoric *hypothèse d'école* and a distraction for judicial institutions'.[18] The above mentioned contextual circumstance [the context of a manifest pattern of similar conduct directed against that group or was conduct that could itself effect such destruction] seems to exclude the possibility of a lone *génocidaire*.[19] Negating the contextual element and presupposing that the *actus reus* and the *dolus specialis*[20] of a lone *génocidaire* are detached from a particular setting (background/surrounding scenario) is unrealistic. Therefore, in the case of

---

[9] ICJ, *Case Concerning Armed Activities on the Territory of Congo (DRC v Rwanda)*, 3 February 2006, ICJ Rep. 2006, General List No. 126, para 64, wherein the ICJ held that, because of its ethical necessity, the prohibition of genocide had evolved into a norm of customary international law, is a superior norm of *jus cogens*, and that the rights and obligations enshrined in the Genocide Convention (Genocide Convention (1948) Convention on the Prevention and Punishment of the Crime of Genocide) are rights and obligations *erga omnes*.

[10] Article 2 of the Genocide Convention, above n. 9, and Article 6 of the ICC Statute (ICC Statute (1998) Rome Statute of the International Criminal Court). See also Schabas 2012, pp. 3–14, and see also van den Herik 2012, pp. 51–58.

[11] ICTY Trial Chamber, *Prosecutor v Radislav Krstić*, 2 August 2001, Case No. IT-98-33-T, para 541.

[12] UN Economic and Social Council 1985, p. 5, para 14.

[13] Simbeye 2004, p. 36.

[14] Scobbie 2009, p. 272.

[15] Element 4 of Article 6(a), Element 4 of Article 6(b), Element 5 of Article 6(c), Element 5 of Article 6(d) and Element 7 of Article 6(e), ICC Elements of Crimes, above n. 2.

[16] Akhavan 2012, p. 43.

[17] See Article 6 of the ICC Statute, above n. 10; see ICTY Appeals Chamber, *Prosecutor v Goran Jelisić*, 5 July 2001, Case No. IT-95-10-A, paras 16, 42, 45, 46 and 51, and see also Kreß 2010, p. 871.

[18] Schabas 2005, p. 877.

[19] Akhavan 2012, p. 46.

[20] This intent to destroy is being increasingly identified by means of circumstantial evidence and inferred upon the existence of overall patterns of persecution towards specific protected groups (Sterio 2017, p. 298).

genocide the contextual elements are implicit in the *dolus specialis*, the aggravated *mens rea* constituting the formal/mental/subjective element of the crime. The contextual element, the existence of a genocidal plan or policy, is not a necessary ingredient of the crime of genocide, but it is still important evidentiary material wherefrom the *dolus specialis* may be inferred.[21] In the words of Claus Kreß, it is 'an objective point of reference for the determination of a realistic genocidal intent'.[22] It is the *dolus specialis*, rather than the genocidal plan or policy, which is the ingredient of the crime. Thus, the *dolus specialis* is the unique and conspicuous feature of the goal-oriented crime of genocide.[23] The *Karadžić and Mladić* case confirmed the subsistence of the requirement of a plan as an evidentiary matter notwithstanding that the Genocide Convention does not explicitly necessitate its fulfilment as an ingredient of the crime[24] whereas the ICTR, citing Morris and Scharf, upheld that 'it is virtually impossible for the crime of genocide to be committed without some or indirect involvement on the part of the State given the magnitude of this crime'.[25] Consequently 'it is not easy to carry out genocide without a plan or organisation'.[26] However, in terms of juridical pre-requisites, genocide just requires a single act in execution of the crime accompanied by the *dolus specialis*. Therefore, killing a single victim could qualify as genocide.[27] The *dolus specialis*, together with some principles emerging therefrom, may be said to infer the involvement of an organization behind the consummation of genocide. In fact Larry May goes as far as saying that 'genocide – the intent to destroy a group or a people – is ultimately a collective crime rather than an individual crime'.[28] The ICC has declared that 'the crime of genocide is only completed when the relevant conduct presents a concrete threat to the existence of the targeted group, or a part thereof. In other words, the protection afforded by the penal norm defining the crime of genocide – as an *ultima ratio* mechanism to preserve the highest values of the international community – is only triggered when the threat against the existence of the targeted group, or part thereof, becomes concrete and real, as opposed to just being latent or hypothetical'.[29] This line of thought partially substantiates the controversial *Jelisić dictum* which established that 'it will be very difficult in practice to provide proof of the genocidal intent of an individual if the crimes committed are not widespread and if the crime charged is not backed by an

---

[21] Marchuk 2014, p. 110.

[22] Kreß 2009, p. 297.

[23] Ambos 2009, p. 835, cited in Akhavan 2012, p. 45, n. 78.

[24] ICTY, *Prosecutor v Radovan Karadžić and Ratko Mladić, Consideration of the Indictment Within the Framework of Rule 61 of the Rules of Procedure and Evidence*, 11 July 1996, Case No. IT-95-5-R61 & IT-95-18-R61, para 94.

[25] ICTR Trial Chamber, *Prosecutor v Kayishema and Ruzindana*, 21 May1999, Case No. ICTR-95-1-T, para 94.

[26] Ibid.

[27] Akhavan 2012, p. 45.

[28] May 2005, p. 175.

[29] *Prosecutor v Al Bashir*, above n. 3, para 124, cited in Akhavan 2012, p. 43, n. 93.

organization or a system'.[30] Even the ILC conceded that crimes such as genocide 'are of such magnitude that they often require some type of involvement on the part of high level government officials or military commanders as well as their subordinates'.[31] It can hence be implicitly inferred that the consummation of genocide would need a structured organizational set-up in order to pose such a concrete threat. A loose structure comprising a few people who possess the *dolus specialis* might not be enough to concretely threaten the targeted group. Even if one were to discard the criterion of the 'concrete threat', one must anyway acknowledge that the *dolus specialis*, of its own nature, infers the functional involvement of a pre-ordained, organized and fully-fledged set-up, the effectiveness of which lies within its own infrastructural framework.

6.2 Crimes Against Humanity

Crimes against humanity are committed when the 'perpetrator knew that the conduct was part of or intended the conduct to be part of a widespread or systematic attack directed against a civilian population'.[32] A *nexus* must hence subsist between the act (conduct) of the accused and the attack consisting in the fact that the act of the accused must have been committed 'pursuant to or in furtherance of a State or organizational policy to commit such attack'.[33] Most importantly, within the context of this work, Article 7, para 1 of the ICC Statute refers to 'the plan or policy of the State or organization'. The 'policy to commit such attack requires that the State or organisation actively promote or encourage such an attack against a civilian population'.[34] The mental element of the crime requires that the accused must have had knowledge of the widespread or systematic attack. Therefore, it is the knowledge of the accused that his act/s occurred in the broader context of a widespread or systematic attack against a civilian population which transforms an ordinary crime into a crime against humanity.[35] The selection of the civilian population accompanied by the requisite knowledge, in and of itself, endangers the human security of individual members of the targeted civilian population.[36] More

[30] ICTY Trial Chamber, *Prosecutor v Goran Jelisić*, 14 December 1999, Case No. IT-95-10-T, para 101, cited in Akhavan 2012, p. 163, n. 111.

[31] ILC 1996, p. 45, para 10, cited in Akhavan 2012, p. 154, n. 60.

[32] See Article 7, para 2 of the ICC Elements of Crimes, above n. 2.

[33] See Article 7(2)(a) of the ICC Statute, above n. 10.

[34] See Article 7, para 3.

[35] Akhavan 2012, p. 40.

[36] I have made ample reference to the principle of human security from a conceptual viewpoint and from the perspective of political philosophy. The right to security of person, deriving from Article 9 of the ICCPR and Article 5 of the ECvHR, has also been recognised jurisprudentially [ICTY Trial Chamber I, Section A, *Prosecutor v Vidoje Blagojević and Dragan Jokić*, 17 January 2005, Case No. IT-02-60-T, para 592].

than in any other core crime, the involvement of the State is paramount in crimes against humanity. Besides the clear reference to the 'plan or policy of the State or organization', the role of the State may be implicitly inferred from the important phrase 'widespread or systematic attack'. The attack is widespread if it is massive, frequent, carried out collectively with considerable seriousness and directed against a multiplicity of victims.[37] The attack can be carried out either over a large geographical area or in a small geographical area when it is directed against a large number of civilians.[38] It is systematic when the violent acts are undertaken in a coordinated and in a structured manner. An ILC report construes the concept of a 'systematic act' to denote an act 'committed pursuant to a preconceived plan or policy'.[39] There must be 'an organised plan in furtherance of a common policy, which follows a regular pattern and results in a continuous commission of acts or a "pattern of crimes" such that the crimes constitute a non-accidental repetition of similar criminal conduct on a regular basis'.[40] The 'widespread and systematic' requirement clearly infer that in order to commit such crimes, an underlying robust structure conducive to the preparation, planning and premeditation of such crimes must be in place. This structure can either be the infrastructural framework of the State or that of an organized group (a non-State entity). Darryl Robinson refers to the systematic nature of such crimes as the requisite associative aspect of crimes against humanity, in the absence of which the crimes will not be crimes against humanity notwithstanding a high degree of scale (their widespread nature).[41] The 'widespread and systematic' requirement adds a lot to the nature of the crimes by connoting the strength of the organization, its capacity to wreak havoc and the powerlessness of official State authorities to counter such conduct.

I must now make reference to an ICC judgment which explicitly evidences the contextual elements of crimes against humanity and war crimes. The contextual elements of crimes against humanity are vividly captured within paras 148–169 of the ICC Trial Chamber's judgment in the *Jean-Pierre Bemba Gombo* case.[42] Although Bemba Gombo was acquitted on appeal,[43] the findings of the Trial

---

[37] ICC Trial Chamber III, Situation in the CAR, *Prosecutor v Jean-Pierre Bemba Gombo, Judgment Pursuant to Article 74 of the Statute*, 21 March 2016, Case No. ICC-01/05-01/08, para 163.

[38] ICC, Pre-Trial Chamber II, *Prosecutor v Jean-Pierre Bemba Gombo, Decision Pursuant to Article 61(7)(a) and (b) of the Rome Statute on the Charges of the Prosecutor Against Jean-Pierre Bemba Gombo*, 15 June 2009, Case No. ICC-01/05-01/08, para 83.

[39] ILC 1996, p. 47, para 3, cited in Hwang 1998, p. 467, n. 65.

[40] ICC Pre-Trial Chamber I, *Prosecutor v Germain Katanga and Mathieu Ngudjolo Chui, Decision on the Confirmation of Charges*, 30 September 2008, Case No. ICC-01/04-01/07, para 397.

[41] Robinson 2015, p. 711, n. 19.

[42] *Prosecutor v Bemba Gombo*, above n. 37.

[43] ICC Appeals Chamber, Situation in the CAR, *Prosecutor v Jean-Pierre Bemba Gombo, Judgment on the Appeal of Mr. Jean-Pierre Bemba Gombo against Trial Chamber III's 'Judgment Pursuant to Article 74 of the Statute'*, 8 June 2018, ICC-01/05-01/08 A.

Chamber, at least in so far as the contextual elements of such crimes are involved, were not impugned. In fact direct reference to the doctrinal foundations and the normative requirements of the contextual elements of crimes against humanity were only made in the separate opinion of Judges Christine van den Wyngaert and Howard Morrison.[44] The Trial Chamber enlisted the following contextual elements:

1. Existence of an attack directed against any civilian population;
   (a) Course of conduct involving the multiple commission of acts referred to in Article 7(1) of the ICC Statute;
   (b) Directed against any civilian population;
   (c) Pursuant to or in furtherance of a State or organizational policy to commit such attack;
2. Widespread nature of the attack;
3. Acts committed as part of the attack (*nexus*);
4. Knowledge of the attack.

Although each and every contextual element deserves attention, I shall only make reference to the contextual elements which support my theories, as portrayed within Part II. In pursuance of this, I shall focus on the contextual element which qualifies the attack as being directed pursuant to or in furtherance of a State or organizational policy to commit such attack. Most of the other contextual elements within the ICC Statute are hardly subject to interpretation and, in any case, have been settled jurisprudentially. Moreover the prevailing 'organizational' threshold seems to be the lingering bone of contention especially because the Trial Chamber III has now loosened this threshold when one compares the *Bemba Gombo* judgment with the compelling dissenting opinion of Hans-Peter Kaul.[45] The contextual element presupposes the existence of either a 'State' or an 'organization'. Although the latter term must be considered in conjunction with the term 'policy',[46] it is the latter term, *id est* 'organization', which causes controversy and which merits scrutiny. The intention to loosen the remit of the term is immediately evidenced by the Trial Chamber's citation of the broad definition of 'organization' in the concise Oxford English dictionary.[47] I strongly doubt whether the drafters of the ICC Statute had this definition in mind when the important phrase 'organizational policy' was promulgated. The Trial Chamber motivates its decision to widen the parameters of the organizational requirement largely by quoting the *Katanga* decision of Trial Chamber II to such effect:

---

[44] *Prosecutor v Bemba Gombo*, above n. 43, Separate Opinion of Judge Christine van den Wyngaert and Judge Howard Morrison, paras 57–72.

[45] This dissenting opinion will be analysed later on in this same heading.

[46] I fully subscribe to the meaning of the concept of policy, as articulated in *Prosecutor v Bemba Gombo*, above n. 37, paras 159–161.

[47] Here organization is tautologically defined as 'an organized body of people with a particular purpose' (Concise Oxford English Dictionary 2006, cited in *Prosecutor v Bemba Gombo*, above n. 37, para 158, n. 354).

> It therefore suffices that the organization have (*sic*) a set of structures or mechanisms, whatever those may be, that are sufficiently efficient to ensure the coordination necessary to carry out an attack directed against a civilian population. Accordingly, as aforementioned, the organisation concerned must have sufficient means to promote or encourage the attack, with no further requirement necessary. Indeed, by no means can it be ruled out, particularly in view of modern asymmetric warfare, that an attack against a civilian population may also be the doing of a private entity consisting of a group of persons pursuing the objective of attacking a civilian population; in other words, of a group not necessarily endowed with a well-developed structure that could be described as a quasi-State.[48]

The ICC has not conclusively determined what qualifies as an 'organization' for the purposes of satisfying the organizational policy requirement which prevails in Article 7 of the ICC Statute.[49] This leads to uncertainty and to diverse interpretations, particularly in so far as required thresholds are concerned.[50] It seems to me that the Trial Chamber disconnects the organizational requirement both from the policy element and from the *chapeau* elements of crimes against humanity, the widespread or systematic attack against a civilian population. These are the major flaws of this judgment. A policy requires, in terms of the ICC Elements of Crimes, the active promotion or encouragement of an attack against a civilian population by a State or an organization.[51] Although it is correct to uphold that there is no requirement that the perpetrators necessarily be motivated by the policy or that they themselves be members of the State or organization,[52] one can hardly imagine that a private entity with a mediocre structural framework could possibly vex the State to such extent as to imperil the security of its citizens. Here one must keep in mind that if the vexing challenge posed against the State is not significant, the complementarity regime, the cornerstone of the ICC Statute,[53] would become redundant. It is because of this complementarity regime, and owing to the 'unable' and 'unwilling' criteria,[54] that one may reasonably conclude that the policy must be furthered by an organization with some mettle, not merely by 'a private entity consisting of a group of persons pursuing the objective of attacking a civilian population'.[55] If this were not so, any group consisting of a few people could become perpetrators of core crimes if such people pursue the aim of attacking a civilian population. Needless to

48 *Prosecutor v Katanga and Chui*, above n. 40, para 119, cited in *Prosecutor v Bemba Gombo*, above n. 37, para 158, n. 355.

49 Corrie 2016, pp. 292–293.

50 See, for example, an analysis as to whether *Los Zetas* cartel in Mexico meets the required threshold in Open Society Justice Initiative 2016, pp. 87–95.

51 Article 7, para 3, ICC Elements of Crimes, above n. 2, cited in *Prosecutor v Bemba Gombo*, above n. 37, para 159, n. 357.

52 *Prosecutor v Katanga and Chui*, above n. 40, para 1115, cited in *Prosecutor v Bemba Gombo*, above n. 37, para 161, n. 366.

53 Swart and Sluiter 1999, p. 105; see also Williams 1999, pp. 383, 390 and 392.

54 These have been dealt with in Chaps. 4 and 5. A juridical consideration thereof will be undertaken in Part III.

55 *Prosecutor v Katanga and Chui*, above n. 40, para 119, cited in *Prosecutor v Bemba Gombo*, above n. 37, para 158, n. 355.

say, this understanding will flood the ICC with a backlog of cases which are most unlikely to meet the gravity threshold[56] anyway. It seems that this could not have been the intention of the ICC drafters since it cannot be reconciled with the very *leitmotif* of the ICC when its whole *raison d'être* is that its functions shall be auxiliary to the administration of criminal justice by domestic courts.[57] Moreover a private entity is most unlikely to undertake a widespread or systematic attack against a civilian population. If it is not so well-structured, by the time a member of the organization perpetrates the first inhumane act, the State would react thereto by suppressing the commencement of execution of other associated/related crimes in furtherance of the attack against the civilian population. Hence such attacks are not likely to be large-scale. They are most unlikely to be systematic since the violent (inhumane) acts would not have been undertaken in a coordinated and in a structured manner. As the ICTY expressed in *Limaj and Others:*

> due to structural factors and organisational and military capabilities, an attack directed against a civilian population will most often be found to have occurred at the behest of the State. Being the locus of organized authority within a given territory, able to mobilize and direct military and civilian power, a sovereign State by its very nature possesses the attributes that permit it to organise and deliver an attack against a civilian population; it is States which can most easily and efficiently marshal the resources to launch an attack against a civilian population on a 'widespread' scale or upon a "systematic" basis.[58]

Hence although Trial Chamber III's effort to enlist, as exhaustively as possible, the contextual elements of core crimes, this being an exercise which has not been frequently undertaken by the ICC, is laudable, I am at odds with its understanding of the organizational requirement.

After having tested the concept of organization against the essentials of core crimes, one must remark that in the consummation of core crimes, whether it likes it or not, the State remains implicated anyway, albeit in a distinctive and differentiated form of responsibility. Thus, the same group element is partially implicit in the 'involvement of the State' element. In other words, if the State is an active perpetrator it is an organized group. If not, *id est* if the core crime is perpetrated by non-State entities, these would have to be strong and powerful organized groups in order to challenge the power of the State. These conclusions may be reached following an examination of the *Kenya dictum*.[59] Tilman Rodenhauser upholds that 'specific criteria that qualify a non-State entity as an organization can be deduced from the very definition of crimes against humanity under the Rome Statute'.[60] He enlists the following requisites which ought to be fulfilled in order to establish that a

---

56 For a succinct explanation thereof, see ICC, War Crimes Research Office 2008, pp. 1–57.

57 Greve 2003, p. 85.

58 ICTY Trial Chamber II, *Prosecutor v Fatmir Limaj et al.*, 30 November 2005, Case No. IT-03-66-T, para 191, cited in Cassese et al. 2013, p. 93, n. 27.

59 ICC, Pre-Trial Chamber II, Situation in the Republic of Kenya, *Decision Pursuant to Article 15 of the Rome Statute on the Authorization of an Investigation into the Situation in the Republic of Kenya*, 31 March 2010, Case No. ICC-01/09.

60 Rodenhauser 2014, p. 923.

non-State entity qualifies as an 'organization' in terms of Article 7 of the ICC Statute (which requirement also subsists under customary international law). The non-State entity should:

(i) consist of a number of people;
(ii) pursue a common purpose;
(iii) have the ability to develop and promulgate a policy suitable to direct an attack against a particular population and which is sufficient to orchestrate the attack against the civilian populations;
(iv) have sufficient capacity to commit crimes on a significant scale or have the capacity to plan and organize an attack; and
(v) possess an internal structure to implement the policy and ensure its concise execution.[61]

Most of these criteria were carefully and distinctively articulated by the ICC Pre-Trial Chamber II in its ground-breaking *Kenya* decision.[62] The ICC Pre-Trial Chamber II determined that the fact that collective entities (such as local leaders, businessmen, members of the police force and politicians associated with the two leading political parties)[63] behind the post-election violence were not of a State-like nature does not pose a hurdle to considering them as organizations in terms of Article 7(2)(a) of the ICC Statute. The ICC Pre-Trial Chamber II adopted a capacity-oriented approach by first acknowledging that the ICC Statute is unclear as to the criteria pursuant to which a group may qualify as an organization. Whereas William Schabas and Mohamed Cherif Bassiouni argued that only State-like organizations may qualify, the ICC Pre-Trial Chamber II upheld that the formal nature of a group and the level of its organization should not be the defining criterion. Instead, supporting the reasoning and arguments presented by Marcello DiFilippo, Darryl Robinson, Steven Ratner, Benedetto Conforti and Peter Burns, a distinction should be drawn on whether a group has the capability to perform acts which violate basic human values.[64] Such assessment must be made on a case-by-case basis, and should be made by taking into account a number of factors, including:

(a) whether the group is under a responsible command, or has an established hierarchy;
(b) whether the group possesses, in fact, the means to carry out a widespread or systematic attack against a civilian population;
(c) whether the group exercises control over part of the territory of a State;
(d) whether the group has criminal activities against the civilian population as a primary purpose;

---

[61] Rodenhauser 2014, p. 928.

[62] *Kenya*, above n. 59.

[63] *Kenya*, above n. 59, para 117.

[64] *Kenya*, above n. 59, para 90, notes 83 and 84.

(e) whether the group articulates, explicitly or implicitly, an intention to attack a civilian population; and
(f) whether the group is part of a larger group, which fulfils some or all of the above mentioned criteria.

The ICC Pre-Trial Chamber II made it a point to clarify that such criteria are not exhaustive and that they are intended to assist the ICC in its determinations but do not constitute a rigid legal definition.[65] In other words, such criteria are indicative, not conclusive. They are neither mandatory nor cumulative. Their simultaneous fulfilment is not a *sine qua non*. Judge Hans-Peter Kaul dissented by means of a detailed opinion which, just like the judgment, exceeds eighty pages. This dissenting opinion is backed by some prominent jurists, including Claus Kreß, who considers it to be more carefully reasoned, supported by references and more methodologically transparent than the judgment itself.[66] Larissa van den Herik and Nico Schrijver acknowledge that most jurists consider Kaul's opinion as the most compelling view.[67] Judge Kaul's dissent is predominantly based upon the demarcation line between crimes against humanity pursuant to Article 7 of the ICC Statute, and crimes under national (Kenyan) law, this being the pivotal juridical issue. In Judge Kaul's view, the demarcation line between these crimes (the distinction between which should not be blurred) should not be marginalized or downgraded, even in an incremental way.[68] Kaul rightly advanced that it is exactly a threat emanating from a State policy that renders crimes against humanity fundamentally different in nature and scale when compared to domestic crimes.[69] This assertion may provide basic guidelines as a result of which one can develop tools conducive to distinguishing between a core crime (termed as an 'international crime' within the dissenting opinion), namely a crime against humanity on the one hand. and a transnational organized crime (termed as 'human rights violations' within the dissenting opinion) on the other hand, this distinction being a major thrust of this second Part. The distinction is more blurred when the core crime at stake is a crime against humanity, precisely because of the organizational policy requirement which bears a resemblance (both literally, and in so far as their accompanying infrastructure is concerned) with transnational organized crimes committed by criminal organizations. This is the main reason why more words are devoted to crimes against humanity when compared to war crimes in this part of the chapter. Judge Kaul's dissent might not remove the fog which causes the blurred vision,[70] but can provide the necessary acumen to reduce the resultant haze. His

---

65 *Kenya*, above n. 59, para 93.

66 Kreß 2010, p. 862.

67 van den Herik and Schrijver 2013, p. 19.

68 *Kenya*, above n. 59, Dissenting Opinion of Judge Hans-Peter Kaul, para 9.

69 *Kenya*, above n. 59, Dissenting Opinion of Judge Hans-Peter Kaul, para 60, cited in Marchuk 2014, pp. 102–103.

70 This is especially so since Judge Kaul does not make reference to the factor/indicator of territorial control within his dissent.

interpretation of the term 'organization' might be considered as far too narrow and restrictive by some jurists[71] (especially when compared to the majority decision).[72] The gist of the most important (operative) extracts of Judge Kaul's dissenting opinion[73] can be paraphrased to convey that core crimes can be committed by State-like entities (non-State entities) but that the degree and extent of the State-likeness of the organization itself must be cogent and compelling, not merely considerable and convincing. Basically, the organization must be a 'para-State' or a state within a State[74] which is based on furthering its criminal enterprise in a spirited and determined fashion and which employs stratagems to seriously challenge the sovereignty of the State. The entity must have so many State-alike features that, in normal circumstances and beyond criminal law considerations, it would be categorised as a quasi-State entity, rather than a mere non-State entity or a simple private organization. The organization should effectively, or at least nearly, be deemed to be a state within the State. It can be, for example, a *de facto* regime. In other words, for such an organization to qualify as an organization for the purposes of the law on crimes against humanity, a scale of criteria must be climbed. Therefore, an amorphous alliance of co-ordinating members of a tribe with a predisposition towards violence with fluctuating membership acting more as a network is not transformed into an organisation merely by having planned and co-ordinated violence during a series of meetings.[75] Similarly, Irena Giorgou upholds that 'a restrictive interpretation of the concept of "political organization" in the Rome Statute definition – limiting it to "State-like" organizations – is warranted, both *de lege lata* and *de lege ferenda*. Based on this premise, attaining consistency between the *chapeau* and the definition leads to the conclusion that the *Kenya* interpretation of "organizational policy" is flawed, insofar as it does not restrict this element to "State-like" organizations'.[76] The approach of Judge Kaul is hence qualitative, not quantitative.

[71] On 18 November 2016, during a side event of the 15th Session of the ICC ASP in The World Forum, Hague, to which I attended on behalf of Malta's delegation, Darryl Robinson expressed this view. The side event, entitled 'Crimes Against Humanity, Sex Crimes and Command Responsibility: Developments and Boundaries in Core International Crimes Practice', was co-hosted by CILRAP, Norway, the DRC, and the UK.

[72] This established that the *chapeau* requirement for crimes against humanity of a 'widespread or systematic attack' carried out 'pursuant to or in furtherance of a State or organizational policy' refers to any organization, including private or criminal, with the capacity to carry out such a widespread or systematic attack (*Kenya*, above n. 59, para 90).

[73] *Kenya*, above n. 59, dissenting opinion of Judge Hans-Peter Kaul, paras 52–53.

[74] Jain 2014, p. 145.

[75] ICC Pre-Trial Chamber II, *Decision on the Prosecutor's Application for Summons to Appear for William Samoei Ruto, Henry Kiprono Kosgey and Joshua Arap Sang in Prosecutor v Ruto, Kosgey and Sang*, Dissenting Opinion of Judge Hans-Peter Kaul, 15 March 2011, Case No. ICC-01/09-01/11-2, paras 18–49, cited in Jain 2014, p. 92, n. 76.

[76] Giorgou 2013, p. 1004.

6.3 War Crimes

War crimes are the only core crimes which must necessarily be committed in armed conflict. They cannot be committed in peacetime. Whereas an armed conflict does not necessarily require the involvement of a State, when non-State entities undertake such armed conflicts, these are generally undertaken against the armed forces of a State or else against other non-State entities with the State trying to disarm such rebel militias, guerrillas and organized armed groups.[77] Hence the subsistence of the armed conflict presupposes either that the State is a contending party to the conflict or that it is incapable to extinguish it, these being two predicaments which justify external intervention. In relation to war crimes, the *actus reus* symbolises the contextual element, this being a *nexus* with an armed conflict, precisely entailing that the war crime must have been committed 'in the context of and associated with' an armed conflict.[78] The '*nexus* with armed conflict' constitutes a requirement of war crimes in terms of the ICC Elements of Crimes. These Elements of Crimes further require that the 'perpetrator was aware of the factual circumstances that established that protected status'[79] and was 'aware of factual circumstances that established the existence of an armed conflict'.[80]

The existence of the armed conflict 'makes humanitarian law applicable to a particular State or territory, transforming otherwise ordinary crimes into war crimes.'[81] This illustrates that the determination of whether an armed conflict subsists or otherwise is crucial for the application of international humanitarian law and international criminal law. The main difficulty is distinguishing between mere internal disturbances and protracted armed violence which could fulfil such

---

[77] Such organized armed groups differ widely and range from *de facto* regimes (quasi-States), to groups which possess highly organized armed forces and have the ability to establish and maintain a stable control over territory and persons within it, and finally to those organized armed groups which lack the ability to control territory (Kleffner 2009, pp. 241–242). Sometimes these groups may be unidentified armed groups (*FIDH* 2016, pp. 61–62).

[78] van der Wilt 2012, p. 4.

[79] *Vide* Articles 8(2)(a)(i)–(viii), ICC Elements of Crimes, above n. 2. Common Article 3 to the 1949 Geneva Conventions (Geneva Convention (1949a) Geneva Convention (I) for the Amelioration of the Condition of the Wounded and Sick in Armed Forces in the Field;

Geneva Convention (1949b) Geneva Convention (II) for the Amelioration of the Condition of the Wounded, Sick and Shipwrecked Members of Armed Forces at Sea; Geneva Convention (1949c) Geneva Convention (III) relative to the Treatment of Prisoners of War; Geneva Convention (1949d) Geneva Convention (IV) relative to the Protection of Civilian Persons in Time of War), which applies to non-international armed conflicts, confers protected person status on civilians who are 'taking no active part in the hostilities, including members of armed forces who have laid down their arms and those placed *hors de combat* by sickness, wounds, detention or any other cause'.

[80] See this requirement which prevails in Articles 8(2)(a)(ii)-1, 8(2)(a)(ii)-2, 8(2)(a)(ii)-3, 8(2)(a)(iii), and 8(2)(a)(iv) of the ICC Elements of Crimes, above n. 2.

[81] Akhavan 2012, p. 31; see also Akande 2016.

threshold.[82] War crimes and crimes against humanity are separate and distinct crimes, but they possess some common features when the perpetrator thereof is analysed. As stated by van der Wilt and Braber:

> the organizational requirements for the assessment of crimes against humanity… are strongly reminiscent of the corresponding conditions for belligerent groups in armed conflicts. It follows that a non-State group which lacks the organizational proficiency to trigger an "armed conflict" - and is therefore technically unable to commit war crimes - would equally fail to qualify as a perpetrator of crimes against humanity in "peace time".[83]

In simpler terms, the organizational requirement serves to differentiate between sporadic outbursts of violence (such as riots) on the one hand and armed conflict on the other hand. If there exists a conflict between the official power within the State and a State-alike organisation, and if protracted violence subsists, the threshold of an armed conflict may be said to have been reached. Armed conflicts are no longer always a contest between two contending parties where it takes two to tango, but can be characterised by many stakeholders as a result of which it is the multiplier effect which intensifies the conflict and guarantees a certain equality of arms rather than the organizational and/or military capacity of the main stakeholders. By way of example, in Syria, for various months, besides the Syrian government, Russia, a US-led coalition (which includes Saudi Arabia, Jordan, Australia, Canada, Turkey and France), moderate rebels and armed factions, the *Daesh* and the Kurds are the major stakeholders.[84]

This dividing line is, sometimes, very hazy indeed, at which point placing the crime under one basket (category/species of crime) instead of another becomes an arduous task. The same haziness subsists between an act of war and a terrorist attack[85] in so far as 'terrorism and terrorists come in all shapes and sizes'.[86] In truth this distinction is also mirrored in another distinction between the various facets of terrorism, the legal definition of which 'has acquired a special reputation for

[82] Another difficulty is the identification of the dividing line between combatants and non-combatants. This has been termed as the weak spot of international humanitarian law (van der Wilt 2009, pp. 534–537).

[83] van der Wilt and Braber 2015, p. 26.

[84] Associated Press (2015) In Increasingly Complex Syria Conflict, a Look at Who is in the Air, Who is on the Ground. http://www.foxnews.com/world/2015/10/01/in-increasingly-complex-syria-conflict-look-at-who-is-in-air-who-is-on-ground.html. Accessed 13 March 2016; see also BBC News (2017) Syria: a Brief Guide to Who's Fighting Whom. http://www.bbc.com/news/world-middle-east-39528673. Accessed 14 June 2017.

[85] Marco Sassòli argues in favour of the disconnection between terrorism and war in so far as this is *de lege lata* not correct and *de lege ferenda* not useful. He admits of two exceptions to his general argument. *De lege lata*, when terrorist acts are committed in an armed conflict as defined under international humanitarian law, they are covered by international humanitarian law and all acts that could reasonably be labelled as terrorist are prohibited by that law. *De lege ferenda* it might be useful to define terrorist acts in peace time by analogy to what is prohibited in war time (Sassòli 2006, p. 980).

[86] Garraway 2013, p. 447.

controversy and elusiveness.'[87] The fact that this distinction is mirrored in yet another distinction, as stated here above, is so because terrorism in peacetime consisting in 'acts taking place beyond the framework of an armed conflict',[88] would retain its designation as 'terrorism', whereas terrorist acts in wartime are subject to the laws of armed conflict. The latter is worth fleshing out since the international community stands to gain therefrom. Prosecutions on the basis of *jus in bello*[89] have multi-faceted advantages. The Geneva Conventions and their two Additional Protocols of 1977 are universally binding. In so far as grave breaches committed in international armed conflicts are concerned,[90] they apply indistinctively and regardless of their political motivation to all the parties to a conflict and they entail individual criminal responsibility subject to the ground of universal jurisdiction.[91] Certainly to benefit from their field of application, an armed conflict must subsist. Yet, there are other situations which need to be assessed in an *ad hoc* manner to determine instances wherein terrorist attacks could still fall under the rubric of 'armed conflict' when they are not committed in theater. Roberta Arnold perceptively upholds that these attacks refer to acts related to an armed conflict but which occur beyond the territorial boundaries of the parties to the conflict, giving the 1985 hijacking of the Italian cruise ship Achille Lauro as an example.[92] Thus, this species of war crimes can potentially be made used of, by way of example, to ground prosecutions of the Paris attacks[93] on the basis of violations of *jus in bello* particularly because the requirement of an armed conflict 'is the ordinary trigger of international humanitarian law'.[94] In fact, some of the acts constituting the Paris attacks (particularly those involving bombings rather than shootings and/or hostage-taking)[95] are tantamount to systematic terrorism (or systematic terror) in terms of Article 33 of the Fourth Geneva Convention. Hence, although terrorism is

---

[87] Becker 2006, p. 84.

[88] Arnold 2014, p. 261.

[89] Literally translated, this conveys 'laws within warfare' (Fife 2003, p. 57).

[90] ICTY Appeals Chamber, *Prosecutor v Duško Tadić, Decision on the Defence Motion for Interlocutory Appeal on Jurisdiction*, 2 October 1995, Case No. IT-94-1, para 79.

[91] Arnold 2014, p. 262.

[92] Ibid.

[93] These include the wilful killing and serious injuries to persons throughout various parts of Paris, and its northern suburd *Saint-Denis* (these being attacks which took place next to the *Stade de France*, *Le Petit Cambodge*, *Le Carillon*, *Café Bonne Bière*, *La Casa Nostra*, *La Belle Équipe*, and *Le Comptoir Voltaire* on *Boulevard Voltaire)* (BBC News (2015) Paris Attacks: What Happened on the Night. http://www.bbc.com/news/world-europe-34818994. Accessed 23 March 2016), together with the hostage-taking at the *Bataclan* theatre (Nossiter (2016) Hostage at *Bataclan* Recalls Terrorists During Paris Attacks.http://www.nytimes.com/2016/01/01/world/europe/bataclan-hostage-paris-terror-attack.html?_r=0. Accessed 19 August 2016).

[94] Kolb 2014, p. 96.

[95] Since the bombings undertaken were suicide bombings, given that the death of the suspect extingushes any potential criminal action against such suspect, only accomplices of the deceased suicide bombers could be prosecuted.

not encompassed by the grave breaches provisions in international humanitarian law, it can fall within the parameters of other serious violations of international humanitarian law which form part of the larger category of war crimes.[96] Any ulterior considerations go beyond the scope of this book.

6.4 Aggression

The general prohibition of resort to military force in contravention of the purposes of the UNC 'was recognized as one of customary international law…'[97] Aggression, deemed as 'the supreme international crime, differing only from other war crimes in that it contains within itself the accumulated evil of the whole',[98] has become a prosecutable core crime, as of 17 July 2018, now that a two-thirds majority of the ASP resolved and voted to such effect in the 16th ASP which was held in NY between 4–14 December 2017. During the 2010 KRC it was defined in terms of amended Article 8*bis* of the ICC Statute[99] which limits the scope of application of the crime of aggression to the most serious conduct violating the prohibition to use armed force.[100] At the 16th ASP, which secured its activation, it was narrowly defined in so far as, *inter alia*, it only applies to 'manifest' violations of the UNC measured by character, gravity and scale. The contextual element, in so far as the crime of aggression is concerned, is very conspicuous since aggression can only be committed by State leaders. In the words of the Preparatory Commission aggression can be committed by those 'being in a position effectively to exercise control over or to direct the political and military action of a State'.[101] A leadership crime conjures that the perpetrator has to be 'in a position effectively to exercise control over or to direct the political or military action of a State',[102] this being the requirement eventually established by the resolution itself. In fact the conduct of the individuals committing aggression must produce a clear result consisting in the execution of an act of aggression against another sovereign State, as stipulated by the second paragraph of Article 8*bis* which contains an exhaustive

[96] Arnold 2004, p. 86.

[97] Sayapin 2014, p. 46.

[98] International Military Tribunal, *The Trial of the German Major War Criminals, Proceedings of the International Military Tribunal Sitting at Nuremberg, Germany*, Part 22 (22 August 1946 to 1 October 1946), para 426.

[99] Its first paragraph stipulates that a 'crime of aggression means the planning, preparation, initiation or execution, by a person in a position effectively to exercise control over or to direct the political or military action of a State, of an act of aggression which, by its character, gravity and scale, constitutes a manifest violation of the Charter of the United Nations'.

[100] Donat Cattin 2017, pp. 380 and 383.

[101] ASP 2003, p. 234, cited in Bonafè 2009, p. 211, n. 90.

[102] Clark 2015, p. 782.

list of incriminated acts which mirrors the list of the UNGA Resolution 3314.[103] Aggression 'is characterized by a complete overlap between aggravated State responsibility and individual criminal liability as far as the material element is concerned. The same is true with respect to the subjective element'.[104] The overlap is so substantial that both forms of responsibility almost coincide to the point of equivalence.[105] This is more so if the determination of a State act of aggression by means of a UNSC Resolution could corroborate a charge alleging the commission of the crime of aggression before the ICC, this being an interpretation which is supported by the ICC's preparatory works.[106] Yet, practice shows 'that the record of the Security Council in stating that a situation is one of aggression is, at best, sporadic.'[107] This can have wide-ranging consequences when one reverberates that it may be safely argued that the UNSC has the exclusive, pre-emptive, right to identify acts of aggression,[108] a prerogative which, however, does not extend to international criminal law.[109] Owing to the relevance of the 'leadership requirement', there is no need to elaborate further on aggression. Its connection with the State is self-evident to the extent that it is the only crime of the four core crimes which cannot be committed by members of non-State entities unless these are leaders of a *de facto* regime. Unlike the other three core crimes which do not require State action as a *sine qua non* element of the crimes, aggression is explicitly tied to State acts.[110] Although a prosecution of the crime of aggression is most unlikely since, *inter alia*,[111] both the crime and the ICC's jurisdiction have been narrowly defined,[112] it is now up to the ICC, when and if it will be given the opportunity, 'to determine the extent of its jurisdiction over acts of aggression committed by nationals or on the territory of non-ratifying State Parties',[113] this being still a moot and controversial point[114] which is beyond the scope of my book.

The distinguishing features of core crimes have been paraded in Chaps. 4 and 5. The involvement of the State is all-pervading. This chapter has shown how the characteristics of core crimes are reflected in their contextual (juridical) elements. The ingredients of core crimes reveal the intrinsic difficulties which are connected

---

103 Donat Cattin 2017, p. 383.

104 Bonafè 2009, p. 138.

105 Bonafè 2009, p. 143.

106 Bonafè 2009, pp. 142, 212 and 215.

107 Escarameia, 2004, p. 140.

108 McDougall 2013, pp. 208–214.

109 McDougall 2013, pp. 214–234.

110 Getgen Kestenbaum 2016, p. 62.

111 Zimmermann aptly notes that 'it does not seem realistic to expect that a relevant number of additional State Parties to the Rome Statute, in particular States involved in the use of military force, will ratify the Kampala amendment any time soon' (Zimmermann 2018, p. 28).

112 Whiting 2018.

113 Sturchler 2018.

114 For an analysis of the competing arguments, see Akande 2017.

with their investigation and/or prosecution. Indeed, the consummation of core crimes does not only engender individual criminal responsibility. Before distinguishing core crimes from other species of crimes, I shall now show how and why they elicit State aggravated responsibility since this enables us to understand better both the role of the State and the legal pedigree of such crimes.

References

Additional Protocol I to the Geneva Conventions (1977) Protocol Additional to the Geneva Conventions of 12 August 1949, and relating to the Protection of Victims of International Armed Conflicts

Additional Protocol II to the Geneva Conventions (1977) Protocol Additional to the Geneva Conventions of 12 August 1949, and relating to the Protection of Victims of Non-International Armed Conflicts

Akande D (2016) When Does the Use of Force Against a Non-State Armed Group Trigger an International Armed Conflict and Why Does This Matter? EJIL Talk! http://www.ejiltalk.org/when-does-the-use-of-force-against-a-non-state-armed-group-trigger-an-international-armed-conflict-and-why-does-this-matter/. Accessed 28 January 2017

Akande D (2017) The International Criminal Court Gets Jurisdiction Over the Crime of Aggression. EJIL: Talk! https://www.ejiltalk.org/the-international-criminal-court-gets-jurisdiction-over-the-crime-of-aggression/. Accessed 17 October 2018

Akhavan P (2012) Reducing Genocide to Law: Definition, Meaning, and the Ultimate Crime. Cambridge Studies in International and Comparative Law, CUP, Cambridge

Ambos K (2009) What Does 'Intent to Destroy' in Genocide Mean? IRRC 91(876):833–858

Arnold R (2004) The ICC as a New Instrument for Repressing Terrorism. International and Comparative Criminal Law Series, TP, Ardsley, NY

Arnold R (2014) The Judicial Contribution of the Special Court for Sierra Leone to the Prosecution of Terrorism. In: Jalloh CC (ed) The Sierra Leone Special Court and Its Legacy: The Impact For Africa and International Criminal Law. CUP, Cambridge, pp. 260–288

ASP (2003) Report of the Second Session. Official Records of the ASP. Doc. No. ICC-ASP/2/10

Becker T (2006) Terrorism and the State: Rethinking the Rules of State Responsibility. Hart Monographs in Transnational & International Law, HP, Oxford/Portland, Oregon

Bonafè BI (2009) The Relationship Between State and Individual Responsibility for International Crimes. MNP, Leiden/Boston

Cassese A, Gaeta P, Baig L, Fan M, Gosnell C, Whiting A (2013) Cassese's International Criminal Law. OUP, Oxford

Clark RS (2015) The Crime of Aggression. In: Stahn C (ed) The Law and Practice of the International Criminal Court. OUP, Oxford, pp. 778–800

Concise Oxford English Dictionary (2006) 11th edn. Oxford Dictionaries, OUP, Oxford

Corrie KL (2016) Could the International Criminal Court Strategically Prosecute Modern Day Slavery? JICJ 14(2):285–303

Donat Cattin D (2017) Intervention of Humanity or the Use of Force to Halt Mass-Atrocity Crimes, the Peremptory Prohibition of Aggression and the Interplay Between *Jus Ad Bellum, Jus in Bello* and Individual Criminal Responsibility on the Crime of Aggression. In: Acconci P, Donat Cattin D, Marchesi A, Palmisano G, Santoni V (eds) International Law and the Protection of Humanity: Essays in Honour of Flavia Lattanzi. MNP, Leiden/Boston, pp. 353–396

ECvHR (1950) European Convention for the Protection of Human Rights and Fundamental Freedoms

Fife RE (2003) Criminalizing Individuals for Acts of Aggression Committed by States, Part One: International Criminal Law. In: Bergsmo M (ed) Human Rights and Criminal Justice for the Downtrodden: Essays in Honour of Asbjorn Eide. MNP, Leiden/Boston, pp. 53–73
Escarameia P (2004) The ICC and the Security Council on Aggression: Overlapping Competencies? In: Politi M, Nesi G (ed) The International Criminal Court and the Crime of Aggression. Ashgate, Aldershot, England/Burlington, Vermont, USA, pp. 133–143
FIDH (2016) Repression and Genocidal Dynamics in Burundi. Ligue Iteka
Garraway C (2013) Armed Conflict and Terrorist Organizations. In: van den Herik L, Schrijver N (eds) Counter-Terrorism Strategies in a Fragmented International Legal Order: Meeting the Challenges. CUP, Cambridge, pp. 425–453
Geneva Convention (1949a) Geneva Convention (I) for the Amelioration of the Condition of the Wounded and Sick in Armed Forces in the Field
Geneva Convention (1949b) Geneva Convention (II) for the Amelioration of the Condition of the Wounded, Sick and Shipwrecked Members of Armed Forces at Sea
Geneva Convention (1949c) Geneva Convention (III) relative to the Treatment of Prisoners of War
Geneva Convention (1949d) Geneva Convention (IV) relative to the Protection of Civilian Persons in Time of War
Genocide Convention (1948) Convention on the Prevention and Punishment of the Crime of Genocide
Getgen Kestenbaum J (2016) Closing Impunity Gaps for the Crime of Aggression. CgJIL 17 (1):51–79
Giorgou I (2013) State Involvement in the Perpetration of Enforced Disappearance and the Rome Statute. JICJ 11(5):1001–1021
Greve HS (2003) Acts of Terrorism and Crimes Within the Jurisdiction of the International Criminal Court. In: Bergsmo M (ed) Human Rights and Criminal Justice for the Downtrodden: Essays in Honour of Asbjorn Eide. MNP, Leiden/Boston, pp. 75–110
Hwang P (1998) Defining Crimes Against Humanity in the Rome Statute of the International Criminal Court. FILJ 22(02):456–504
ICC Elements of Crimes (1998) International Criminal Court, Elements of Crimes
ICC Statute (1998) Rome Statute of the International Criminal Court
ICCPR (1966) International Covenant on Civil and Political Rights
ILC (1996) Report of the ILC on the Work of its Forty-Eight Session. GAOR 51st Session, Supp. No. 10, UN Doc.A/51/10
Jain N (2014) Perpetrators and Accessories in International Criminal Law: Individual Modes of Responsibility for Collective Crimes. HP, Bloomsbury
Kelt M, von Hebel H (2001) General Principles of Criminal Law and the Elements of Crimes. In: Lee RS (ed) Friman H, Fernandez de Gurmendi S, von Hebel H, Robinson D (assistant eds) The International Criminal Court: Elements of Crimes and Rules of Procedure and Evidence. TP, Ardsley, NY, pp. 19–40
Kleffner JK (2009) The Collective Accountability of Organized Armed Groups for System Crimes. In: Nollkaemper A, van der Wilt H (eds) System Criminality in International Law. CUP, Cambridge, pp. 238–269
Kolb R (2014) Advanced Introduction to International Humanitarian Law. Elgar Advanced Introductions, EE, Cheltenham/Camberley/Northampton, Massachusetts
Koursami N (2018) The 'Contextual Elements' of the Crime of Genocide. International Criminal Justice Series, Vol. 17. Asser Press, The Hague
Kreß C (2009) The Crime of Genocide and Contextual Elements: A Comment on the ICC Pre-Trial Chamber's Decision in the *Al Bashir* Case. JICJ 7(2):297–306
Kreß C (2010) On the Outer Limits of Crimes Against Humanity: The Concept of Organization Within the Policy Requirement: Some Reflections on the March 2010 ICC Kenya Decision. LJIL 23(4): 855–873
Marchuk I (2014) The Fundamental Concept of Crime in International Law: A Comparative Law Analysis. Springer, Berlin/Heidelberg
May L (2005) Crimes Against Humanity: A Normative Account. CUP, Cambridge

McDougall C (2013) The Crime of Aggression under the Rome Statute of the International Criminal Court. Cambridge Studies in International and Comparative Law, CUP, Cambridge

Meloni C (2010) Command Responsibility in International Criminal Law. Asser Press, The Hague

Open Society Justice Initiative (2016) Undeniable Atrocities: Confronting Crimes Against Humanity in Mexico. Open Society Foundations, NY

Robinson D (2015) Crimes Against Humanity: A Better Policy on Policy. In: Stahn C (ed) The Law and Practice of the International Criminal Court. OUP, Oxford, pp. 705–731

Rodenhauser T (2014) Beyond State Crimes: Non-State Entities and Crimes Against Humanity. LJIL 27(4):913–928

Sassòli M (2006) Terrorism and War. JICJ 4(5):959–981

Sayapin S (2014) The Crime of Aggression in International Criminal Law: Historical Development, Comparative Analysis and Present State. Asser Press, The Hague

Schabas W (2005) Darfur and the Odious Scourge: The Commission of Inquiry's Findings on Genocide. LJIL 18(4):871–885

Schabas W (2012) Genocide and Crimes Against Humanity: Clarifying the Relationship. In: van der Wilt H, Vervliet J, Sluiter GK, Houwink ten Cate JThM (eds) The Genocide Convention: The Legacy of 60 Years. MNP, Leiden/Boston, pp. 3–14

Scobbie I (2009) Assumptions and Presuppositions: State Responsibility for System Crimes. In: Nollkaemper A, van der Wilt H (eds) System Criminality in International Law. CUP, Cambridge, pp. 270–297

Simbeye Y (2004) Immunity and International Criminal Law. Ashgate, Farnham, Surrey, UK

Sterio M (2017) The Karadzic Genocide Conviction: Inferences, Intent, and the Necessity to Redefine Genocide. EILR 31(2):271–298

Sturchler N (2018) The Activation of the Crime of Aggression in Perspective. EJIL:Talk! https://www.ejiltalk.org/the-activation-of-the-crime-of-aggression-in-perspective/. Accessed 17 October 2018

Swart B, Sluiter G (1999) The International Criminal Court and International Criminal Co-operation. In: von Hebel HAM, Lammers JG, Schuking J (eds) Reflections on the International Criminal Court. Asser Press, The Hague, pp. 91–127

UN Economic and Social Council (1985) Revised and Updated Report on the Question of the Prevention and Punishment of the Crime of Genocide. UN Doc. E/CN.4Sub.2/1985/6

UNC (1945) Charter of the United Nations

UNGA Resolution (1974) Resolution 3314 (XXIX) (1974), UN Doc. A/RES/29/3314

van den Herik L (2012) The Meaning of the Word "Destroy" and its Implications for the Wider Understanding of the Concept of Genocide. In: van der Wilt H, Vervliet J, Sluiter GK, Houwink ten Cate JThM (eds) The Genocide Convention: The Legacy of 60 Years. MNP, Leiden/Boston, pp. 51–58

van den Herik L, Schrijver N (2013) The Fragmented International Legal Response to Terrorism. In: van den Herik L, Schrijver N (eds) Counter-Terrorism Strategies in a Fragmented International Legal Order: Meeting the Challenges. CUP, Cambridge, pp. 1–25

van der Wilt H (2008) Equal Standards? On the Dialectics Between National Jurisdictions and the International Criminal Courts. ICLR 8(1):229–272

van der Wilt H (2012) War Crimes and the Requirement of a *Nexus* with an Armed Conflict. JICJ 10(5):1113–1128

van der Wilt H, Braber I (2015) The Case for Inclusion of Terrorism in the Jurisdiction of the International Criminal Court. In: Mariniello T (ed) The International Criminal Court in Search of its Purpose and Identity. Routledge Research in International law, Routledge, London/New York, pp. 17–38

van der Wilt HG (2009) Can Romantics and Liberals be Reconciled?: Some Further Reflections on Defending Humanity. JICJ 7(3):529–539

War Crimes Research Office (2008) The Gravity Threshold of the International Criminal Court. Legal Analysis and Education Project. American University Washington College of Law, Washington DC, USA

Whiting A (2018) Crime of Aggression Activated at the ICC: Does it Matter? https://www.justsecurity.org/49859/crime-aggression-activated-icc-matter/. Accessed 17 October 2018

Williams SA (1999) Article 17: Issues of Admissibility. In: Triffterer O (ed) Commentary on the Rome Statute of the International Criminal Court. Nomos, Baden-Baden, pp. 383–394

Zimmermann A (2018) A Victory for International Rule of Law? Or: All's Well that Ends Well? The 2017 ASP Decision to Amend the Kampala Amendment on the Crime of Aggression. JICJ 16(1):19–29

Chapter 7
The Juridical Consequences of Core Crimes: Individual Criminal Liability and State Aggravated Responsibility

Contents

References 116

Abstract Core crimes, unlike other species of crimes, elicit State aggravated responsibility, which explains both why the State is failing to live up to its duties and justifies the external intervention of the international community. State aggravated responsibility is a consequential characteristic of the commission of core crimes especially when the State is involved as an active perpetrator. These consequences are so unique and conspicuous that they may safely be said to constitute characteristics in their own right, particularly since they (cumulatively) do not belong to other categories/species of crime (such as domestic crimes, transnational organized crimes and international crimes). When cumulatively considered, these consequential characteristics belong solely and exclusively to core crimes. To this extent, although they cannot be directly equated to State aggravated responsibility, these consequential characteristics constitute evidence of aggravated State responsibility. Inversely, the subsistence of State aggravated responsibility serves to corroborate the contention that the State is somehow involved, directly or indirectly, in the perpetration of core crimes. Individual criminal liability on one hand and aggravated State responsibility on the other hand, although distinct, can concur. The idea that the State is somehow involved, directly or indirectly, in the perpetration of core crimes has a parallel in State responsibility. Not only will the State be held responsible for not preventing the core crime and, once perpetrated, for not prosecuting and punishing it, but it will be faced with a continuing obligation to ensure that an individual suspected of having committed a core crime be submitted to prosecution.

Keywords Juridical consequences · Consequential characteristics · *BiH v Serbia* · Ordinary responsibility · Aggravated responsibility · Dual responsibility · *Milošević* · State involvement · Continuing obligations · Concurrent jurisdiction · Law of international responsibility

C. Soler, *The Global Prosecution of Core Crimes under International Law*,
https://doi.org/10.1007/978-94-6265-335-1_7

Chapters 4, 5 and 6 have illustrated the gravity of core crimes which largely results from their contextual elements, their group-oriented nature and their group-based features and characteristics. Having examined the nature of core crimes and having unmasked the inevitable State connection, it is now easier to understand some very important consequences of the commission of such core crimes. It might seem strange that crimes which don't easily partake of a legal definition anyway engender significant legal consequences. This portrays the specificity of core crimes and their extra-ordinary nature. This chapter will show that core crimes, unlike other species of crimes, elicit State aggravated responsibility, which both explains why the State is failing to live up to its duties and justifies the external intervention of the international community. State aggravated responsibility is a consequential characteristic of the commission of core crimes especially when the State is involved as an active perpetrator. These consequences are so unique and conspicuous that they may safely be said to constitute characteristics in their own right, particularly since they (cumulatively) do not belong to other categories/species of crime (such as domestic crimes, transnational organized crimes and international crimes). They (when cumulatively considered) belong solely and exclusively to core crimes. To this extent, although they cannot be directly equated (or considered equivalent) to State aggravated responsibility, they constitute evidence of aggravated State responsibility. Inversely, the subsistence of State aggravated responsibility serves to corroborate the contention that the State is somehow involved, directly or indirectly, in the perpetration of core crimes.

The determination of responsibility, and/or the extent of such responsibility in international law, can be a very complex matter, the intricacies of which are epitomised when multiple States and/or international organizations, including the UN, are engaged in a peace-keeping operation wherein wrongful acts which harm civilians were committed.[1] Ultimately, from a rather generalized viewpoint, one may contend that responsibility flows from attribution.[2] Yet, an analysis of the respective responsibilities of the stakeholders exceeds the scope of this chapter. Limitedly, its aim is to show how core crimes usually engender both individual criminal liability and aggravated State responsibility. The former pervades this entire work and is most manifest in the third and fourth Parts which shall deal with the ways alleged perpetrators may be brought to justice under the vertical and horizontal systems of enforcement respectively. These two forms of responsibility are not mutually exclusive. Instead, they can concur, they can coincide and they can feed into one another. In the words of Chantal Meloni, they 'cohabit in the current

[1] Nollkaemper 2016.

[2] Oto Spijkers, lecturer of public international law at *Universiteit Utrecht* and senior researcher associate at the Netherlands Institute for the Law of the Sea, analysing *Hoge Raad* [Supreme Court], The Netherlands, *Nuhanović v the Netherlands*, 6 September 2013, Case No. 12/03324, during a series of guest lectures held at the University of Malta on 5–9 February 2018, which were entitled 'Responsibility of the UN and troop-contributing State for acts of peacekeeping operations: The case of Srebrenica'.

international system.'[3] The idea that the State is somehow involved, directly or indirectly, in the perpetration of core crimes has a parallel in State responsibility. Not only they will be held responsible for not preventing the core crime and, once perpetrated, for not prosecuting and punishing it, but they will be faced with a continuing obligation to ensure that an individual suspected of having committed a core crime be submitted to prosecution. This continuing obligation vests unto the territorial State. In other words, the State *locus delicti commissi* should preserve and produce any evidence which could be relevant for the purposes of either an eventual prosecution before an international criminal court/tribunal or an eventual prosecution before another State which enjoys custodial jurisdiction over the individual.

The concept of dual responsibility, looked upon favourably by Andrea Bianchi,[4] was also deemed to be a 'constant feature of international law' by the ICJ in the *BiH v Serbia*[5] case. The ICJ observed, *inter alia*, that the Genocide Convention goes beyond the criminal responsibility of individuals in order to contemplate and comprise State responsibility for genocide, hence affirming that individual criminal responsibility and State responsibility are not mutually exclusive but complementary in nature and scope. Evidently, the dual responsibility is not limited to aggression but can indeed subsist in relation to other core crimes. Both forms of responsibility (that of the State and that of the individual), can function independently of one another since one does not extinguish the other, and can generate parallel judicial proceedings. Concurrent jurisdiction may therefore be exercised, by the international criminal tribunal or ICC and by the ICJ, over the same set of facts,[6] when the parallel responsibilities of the individual (the representative of the State) and of the State[7] are respectively subjected to judicial scrutiny. Incidentally, it is therefore not surprising that, on 27 February 2006, two cases were being heard contemporaneously in The Hague, these being the *BiH v Serbia* case before the ICJ and the *Prosecutor v Milošević* case before the ICTY wherein *Slobodan Milošević* was accused of genocide, crimes against humanity, grave breaches of the Geneva Conventions and violations of the laws or customs of war. Iryna Marchuk is hence correct to state that it would be unreasonable to consider the regime of individual criminal responsibility and that of State responsibility as two separate regimes, 'given that the law on individual criminal responsibility is logically complemented

[3] Meloni 2010, p. 8.

[4] Bianchi 2009, p. 24.

[5] ICJ, *Application of the Convention on the Prevention and Punishment of the Crime of Genocide (BiH v Serbia and Montenegro)*, 26 February 2007, ICJ Rep. 2007, p. 43, para 173.

[6] ICTY Trial Chamber I, *Prosecutor v Miroslav Kvočka et al., Decision on the Defence Motion Regarding Concurrent Procedures Before International Criminal Tribunal for the Former Yugoslavia and International Court of Justice on the Same Questions,* 5 December 2000, Case No. IT-98-30/1, subsequently confirmed by the ICTY Appeals Chamber, *Prosecutor v Miroslav Kvočka et al., Decision on Interlocutory Appeal by the Accused Zoran Žigić Against the Decision of the Trial Chamber I dated 5 December 2000*, 25 May 2001, Case No. IT-98-30/1, para 17.

[7] Pellet 1999, p. 432.

by international State responsibility'.[8] Certainly, although they are two distinct regimes, ultimately 'State responsibility is engaged by the acts or omissions of individuals.'[9] In this context, State responsibility and individual liability have been referred to as 'symbiotic'.[10] Likewise, the *Furundžija dictum* taught us that 'under current international humanitarian law, in addition to individual criminal liability, State responsibility may ensue as a result of State officials engaging in torture or failing to prevent torture or to punish torturers'.[11] Analysing the opinion of the three Lords in the UK *Pinochet* case, Rosanne van Alebeek submits that 'a number of scholars argued that the violation of human rights by State officials should be considered an official act since it would otherwise be impossible to assert the international responsibility of the home State for that act'.[12]

Though they may subsist *pari passu*, both modes of liability are different in various ways and should not be confused with one another. From a *rationae temporis* perspective, the acceptance of the *institutum legis* of State responsibility predated the establishment of individual criminal responsibility under international law. However, 'the individual responsibility system has expanded faster than the law of State responsibility'.[13] The standard of proof involved also varies in both. Keeping apart the high threshold[14] provided for by the *BiH v Serbia* and by the *Croatia v Serbia dicta*, State ordinary responsibility is generally proved on the basis of a balance of probabilities,[15] whereas individual criminal responsibility requires proof beyond reasonable doubt. Their ultimate objectives also differ. Whereas State responsibility elicits reparation by attempting to attain the *status quo ante*, individual criminal responsibility usually generates a criminal sanction of a personal nature, incarceration. The former is reparatory, whereas the latter is punitive. André Nollkaemper perceptively observes that 'in cases of partial transparency, that distinction loses some of its ground. Punishment of individuals can then be part of the remedy for State responsibility', which obligation to prosecute results in a continued duty of performance.[16] In this way individual criminal responsibility and State responsibility are integrated into one and the same thing where 'the

[8] Marchuk 2014, p. 90.

[9] Kaczorowska-Ireland 2015, p. 460.

[10] Simpson 2009, p. 71.

[11] ICTY Trial Chamber, *Prosecutor v Anto Furundžija*, 10 December 1998, Case No. IT-95-17/1-T, para 142.

[12] van Alebeek 2008, p. 146.

[13] Wyler and Castellanos-Jankiewicz 2011, p. 400.

[14] Having been considered as excessive by some, it 'contributes directly to limiting attribution of responsibility for genocide' (Aquilina and Mulaj 2017).

[15] One must recall that States are often responsible for many kinds of wrongs (delictual acts) which certainly do not constitute core crimes.

[16] Nollkaemper 2003, p. 636.

implementation of an obligation to punish is at the same time a remedy against both the State and the individual'.[17] The ICJ has already established that it has the *vires* to order the prosecution of perpetrators or, alternatively, to order the State to cooperate with international criminal tribunals for the purposes of such prosecution.[18] A law of international responsibility, of which individual criminal responsibility and State responsibility are component parts and which, occasionally, are interrelated, may be said to have materialized.[19] This is particularly so when one keeps in mind that the State's omission to punish individuals engenders its international responsibility, this being neither public nor private and neither penal nor civil. Since this type of responsibility is 'simply international'[20] it entitles (or more precisely, obliges,) the international community to step in. The duty of the international community is more compelling after a subsequent failure of the territorial State to investigate and prosecute further to an order of reparation by the relevant judicial authority consisting in the demand to investigate and prosecute. State and individual responsibility coincide and interact with each other. More precisely, State responsibility intersects with international criminal law by virtue of the State obligations to prevent core crimes and to prosecute and punish perpetrators of core crimes.[21] The State, however, for all intents and purposes of law, remains a separate juridical person and a subject, *sua sponte* and *qua* State, of international law in its own right. They are therefore autonomous, complementary and, although they don't directly compete with one another, they may at times overlap,[22] as is evident within the notion of 'complicity in genocide' under Article III(e) of the Genocide Convention and the parallel concept of 'aid and assistance of a State' in the commission of an internationally wrongful act by another State in terms of Article 16 of the ILC's Articles on State Responsibility.

Having embarked onto an analysis as to why some crimes rise to the level of core crimes, having justified the circumstances when international (external) intervention is warranted and expected, having analysed the contextual elements of core crimes, and having disclosed the multiple consequences of the commission of core crimes, the above observations lead me to distinguish specifically between, on the one hand a core crime, and on the other hand, a 'transnational organized crime', a 'national crime' and an 'international crime' respectively within the next chapter.

---

[17] Nollkaemper 2003, p. 638.

[18] ICJ, *United States Diplomatic and Consular Staff in Tehran (USA v Iran) (Iranian Hostage Case)*, 24 May 1980, ICJ Reports [1980]. ICJ Reps. 3, cited by Nollkaemper 2003, p. 638, fn. 111.

[19] Nollkaemper 2003, p. 639.

[20] Pellet 1999, pp. 433–434.

[21] Boas 2010, p. 506.

[22] Crawford and Olleson 2005, p. 909; see also Spinedi 2002, p. 895.

References

Aquilina K, Mulaj K (2017) Limitations in Attributing State Responsibility under the Genocide Convention. JHR, Taylor & Francis. http://www.tandfonline.com/doi/abs/10.1080/14754835.2017.1300521?journalCode=cjhr20. Accessed 12 January 2017
Bianchi A (2009) State Responsibility and Criminal Liability of Individuals. In: Cassese A (ed) The Oxford Companion to International Criminal Justice, OUP, Oxford, pp. 16–24
Boas G (2010) The Difficulty with Individual Criminal Responsibility in International Criminal Law In: Stahn C, van den Herik L (eds) Future Perspectives on International Criminal Justice. Asser Press, The Hague, pp. 501–519
Crawford J, Olleson S (2005) State Responsibility. In: Shelton DL (ed) Encyclopedia of Genocide and Crimes Against Humanity, Thomson Gale, Detroit/Munich, pp. 904–910
Geneva Convention (1949a) Geneva Convention (I) for the Amelioration of the Condition of the Wounded and Sick in Armed Forces in the Field
Geneva Convention (1949b) Geneva Convention (II) for the Amelioration of the Condition of the Wounded, Sick and Shipwrecked Members of Armed Forces at Sea
Geneva Convention (1949c) Geneva Convention (III) relative to the Treatment of Prisoners of War
Geneva Convention (1949d) Geneva Convention (IV) relative to the Protection of Civilian Persons in Time of War
Genocide Convention (1948) Convention on the Prevention and Punishment of the Crime of Genocide
ILC's Articles on State Responsibility (2001) Draft Articles on the Responsibility of States for Internationally Wrongful Acts, UN Doc. A/56/10
Kaczorowska-Ireland A (2015) Public International Law, 5th edn. Routledge, T & F, London & NY
Marchuk I (2014) The Fundamental Concept of Crime in International Law: A Comparative Law Analysis. Springer, Berlin/Heidelberg
Meloni C (2010) Command Responsibility in International Criminal Law. Asser Press, The Hague
Nollkaemper A (2003) Concurrence Between Individual Responsibility and State Responsibility in International Law. ICLQ 52(3):615–640
Nollkaemper A (2016) UN Audiovisual Library of International Law Lecture Series, André Nollkaemper on Shared Responsibility in International Law. https://www.youtube.com/watch?v=1Vj64HnBIz0. Accessed 11 April 2018
Pellet A (1999) Can a State Commit a Crime? Definitely, Yes! EJIL 10(2):425–434
Simpson G (2009) Men and Abstract Entities: Individual Responsibility and Collective Guilt in International Criminal Law. In: Nollkaemper A, van der Wilt H (eds) System Criminality in International Law. CUP, Cambridge, pp. 69–100
Spijkers O (2018) Responsibility of the UN and troop-contributing State for acts of peacekeeping operations: The case of Srebrenica. Guest lectures held at the Faculty of Laws, University of Malta between 5–9 February 2018
Spinedi M (2002) State Responsibility v Individual Responsibility for International Crimes: *Tertium non Datur?* EJIL 13(4):895–899
van Alebeek R (2008) The Immunity of States and Their Officials in International Criminal Law and International Human Rights Law. Oxford Monographs in International Law, OUP, Oxford
Wyler E, Castellanos-Jankiewicz A (2011) State Responsibility and International Crimes. In: Schabas WA, Bernaz N (eds) Routledge Handbook of International Criminal Law, T & F, London & NY, pp. 385–405

Chapter 8
Detecting the Determining and Distinguishing Factors

Contents

8.1 Core Crimes Versus Transnational Organized Crimes 118
8.2 Core Crimes Versus Domestic Crimes 131
8.3 Core Crimes Versus International Crimes 133
8.4 Concluding Remarks 138
References 139

Abstract Some common denominators are juxtaposed to distinguish between one species of crime and another. Core crimes are first put against the backdrop of 'transnational organised crimes'. Besides other differences which are brought to the fore, the latter possess no contextual elements. Yet, in so far as the crimes of terrorism and trafficking in human beings are concerned, the demarcation line is very tenuous with both crimes changing colour like chameleons by moving to and fro between one species and another. Terrorism can be encompassed in and constituted by the crime against humanity of inhumane acts of a similar character which cause great suffering, or serious injury to body, or to mental or physical health. Trafficking in human beings can overlap with the crime against humanity of enslavement. Some determining factors, including the concept of an 'organization' and the dexterity thereof, or otherwise, are considered. The mode of repression of the crime can shed a light on its nature which, in turn, influences the choice of the prosecuting forum. Core crimes are also 'domestic crimes' since they have been incorporated into national law. Yet many domestic crimes are localised and do not injure the rights of the international community. 'International crimes', a misleading term, are punishable under suppression conventions. They resemble core crimes but do not possess contextual elements and do not generally elicit State-aggravated responsibility. Piracy can be selected as an example thereof. The chapter develops some underlying assumptions in preparation for Parts III and IV of the book.

Keywords Common denominators · Cause of criminalization · Suppression conventions · Prosecuting forum · Legal consequences · Special cooperation devices · Treaty crimes · State cooperation · Organizational policy · Terrorism ·

C. Soler, *The Global Prosecution of Core Crimes under International Law*,
https://doi.org/10.1007/978-94-6265-335-1_8

Trafficking in human beings · Transnational organized crimes · International crimes · Equality of arms · Armed conflict · Domestic crimes

To fully understand the concept of 'core crime' and the reasons why they are subject to a specific system of law enforcement, it is not sufficient to merely delve into the concept itself and into the juridical elements thereof. The concept must also be differentiated from other concepts such as the concepts of 'transnational organized crime', 'domestic crime' and 'international crime'. The genus of 'crimes' is divided into various species which may be considered as labels of crimes. Moreover, some prevalent characteristics do not serve as definitional criteria for core crimes.[1] Avoiding such confusion and differentiating accordingly is meaningful since it may have a bearing on the level and manner of enforcement of the respective criminal sanction. This exercise will be undertaken within Sects. 8.1–8.3. To understand better such distinctions, I juxtapose (and make use of) some common denominators of crimes in general, such as, *inter alia*, the cause of their criminalization, the mode of repression, the perpetrators thereof, the victims thereof, the *locus delicti commissi*, the harm caused, and the effects of the crime. The following excursus will consider these common denominators in so far as the different categories of crimes is concerned, these being 'core crimes', 'transnational organized crimes', 'international crimes' and 'domestic crimes'. It will enable me to detect differences by using a comparative lens, *id est*, by comparing like with like.[2] Within this exercise, I shall attempt to extrapolate differences between the way and the extent to which such common denominators apply to each and every respective category. The cause (reason) for the criminalization of modes of conduct can largely subsume the other common denominators, although express reference to such other common denominators can, occasionally, be important in and of itself.

8.1 Core Crimes Versus Transnational Organized Crimes

Whereas national crimes are habitually committed by an individual acting alone, transnational organized crime is generally committed by individuals functioning within the remit and under the auspices of their criminal organizations.[3] Domestic crimes and transnational organised crimes require an organic combination of *actus*

---

[1] Gravity, for example, does not distinguish a core crime from a domestic crime (O'Keefe 2015, pp. 57–59).

[2] Such an analysis can have many benefits. 'For the legislator, it can be a source of possible approaches to a specific issue or even to the enterprise of criminal law reform and criminal law-making in general. For the judge, it can suggest different solutions to tricky problems of interpretation or common-law adjudication' (Heller and Dubber 2011, p. 1).

[3] Andreas Schloenhardt opines that although there is no prototypical crime cartel, criminal organizations depend on shared ideology, loyalty and terror (Schloenhardt 2008, p. 946).

reus and *mens rea*, whereas core crimes, over and above this organic combination, require the subsistence of contextual elements. Chapters 5, 6 and 7 have evidenced that core crimes require meticulous planning, preparation, organization and the involvement both of material and human resources which can be mobilized either by the State or by mighty contenders which challenge the powers of the State, these being non-State entities. To this extent, these core crimes require a certain degree of malice aforethought (premeditation) which, in turn, marginalises some forms of criminal intent such as *dolus eventualis*. The same cannot be said about most domestic crimes. Whereas, because of the contextual elements, core crimes are the most serious crimes of concern to the international community as a whole, transnational organized crimes are 'common crimes against internationally protected interests'.[4]

Citing Bassiouni, Neil Boister explains that (i) trans-boundary criminality is criminal activity which crosses borders and has a factual or phenomenological element consisting in the planning or commission beyond national borders and that (ii) transnational crimes may be penalized when there is a sufficiently influential cosmopolitan belief that the conduct in question should be outlawed in all States owing to its moral repugnance.[5] To this extent, transnational organized crime are *mala in se* (evil in themselves),[6] rather than *mala prohibita* (regulatory offences). Cyrille Fijnaut contends that the term 'transnational crime' is a container-type concept which includes different types of crimes ranging from corporate crimes (tax evasion and social security fraud), to professional crimes (serious theft and kidnapping) and onto political crimes (terrorist related offences).[7] Neil Boister cites Mueller who states that the term 'transnational crime' is a criminological rather than a juridical term which was coined by UN Crime Prevention and Criminal Justice Branch and may be defined as 'criminal phenomena transcending international borders, transgressing the laws of several States or having an impact on another country'.[8] Boister, amalgamating 'transnational crime' and 'transnational law', has shown preference to the term 'transnational criminal law'.[9] Such categorisation is laudable, but for the purposes of this work, the author shall make use of the term 'transnational organized crime' since this is being deliberately differentiated from national crime, international crime and core crime accordingly. Additionally, the regulatory legal framework makes reference to 'transnational organized crime', which term infers the role of the underlying criminal organization. Though the role of the underlying criminal organization is not explicitly deemed to be a prerequisite for the consummation of such crimes within various domestic criminal justice

[4] Bassiouni 1999, cited in Boister 2003, p. 955, n. 11.

[5] Bassiouni 1999, p. 4 and pp. 39–46, cited in Boister 2003, pp. 966–968.

[6] The expression *malum in se* denotes that the crime is made criminal by reason rather than only by statute (Ristroph 2012, p. 100).

[7] Fijnaut 2000, pp. 120–122.

[8] Mueller 2001, p. 13, cited in Boister 2003, p. 954.

[9] Boister 2012a.

systems[10] and in terms of the relevant suppression conventions,[11] such criminal organizations are generally the culprits thereof. Sometimes they are powerful enough to challenge the State. This goes to show the underlying and growing fusion between core crimes and transnational organized crimes, a fusion which is also conspicuous in the jurisdictional framework of the African Criminal Court.[12] It will be shown that the crimes of trafficking in human beings and terrorism can exemplify this fascinating fusion. Mueller, who coined the term 'transnational crime',[13] contends that transnational crimes are invariably organised.[14] Here the term 'organization' should not be confused with the systematic nature of crimes against humanity and the State and/or organizational policy requirement which characterises crimes against humanity. Although the transnational dimension derives from the nature and impact of the crimes, some jurists describe them by directly associating their nature with the need to combat such crimes on a common basis.[15] They have a corrosive effect on civil society, invading and tainting legitimate enterprises (including businesses and governments) as a front for or an instrument through which such criminal organizations conduct illicit activities, generally accompanied by violence, for profit.[16] Such crimes are prohibited by States which have ratified a suppression convention, most of which contain a common but crucial legal provision, the *aut dedere aut judicare* rule introduced therein to restrict and limit safe havens.

Unlike both core crimes and international crimes, transnational organised crimes are not prohibited and punished by customary international law, but are many a time treaty based and only impose individual criminal responsibility in terms and by virtue of domestic law.[17] Therefore, although the origin of the norm is international,

[10] See UNCATOC (UNCATOC (2000) UN Convention Against Transnational Organised Crime) adopted by means of a UNGA Resolution 55/25 of 15 November 2000 (UNGA (2000) Resolution 55/25 (2000), UN Doc. A/RES/55/25), and the Protocols thereto (Trafficking Protocol (2000) Protocol to Prevent, Suppress and Punish Trafficking in Persons, Especially Women and Children, supplementing the United Nations Convention against Transnational Organized Crime; Smuggling Protocol (2000) Protocol against the Smuggling of Migrants by Land, Sea and Air, supplementing the United Nations Convention against Transnational Organized Crime; Manufacturing Protocol (2001) Protocol against the Illicit Manufacturing of and Trafficking in Firearms, Their Parts and Components and Ammunition, supplementing the United Nations Convention against Transnational Organized Crime). By virtue of its Article 38, the UNCATOC entered into force on 29 September 2003. One hundred and eighty-nine States are parties to it [https://treaties.un.org/Pages/ViewDetails.aspx?src=IND&mtdsg_no=XVIII-12&chapter=18&lang=en. Accessed 31 December 2018].

[11] These are enlisted in n. 28 here below.

[12] van der Wilt 2017, p. 202.

[13] Bassiouni and Vetere 1998, p. xxxi.

[14] Mueller 2001, p. 13, cited in Obokata 2010, p. 29, n. 130.

[15] Militello 2015, p. 207.

[16] Luban et al. 2010, p. 506.

[17] Boister 2012b, p. 298.

penal proscription is national[18] and individual criminal responsibility depends on explicit domestic criminalization. The *corpus* of multilateral treaties suppressing transnational organized crimes may serve as a juridical framework for the analysis of the horizontal system of enforcement in so far as core crimes are concerned, especially in so far as the *aut dedere aut judicare* rule is made use of therein. The final deliverable of these suppression conventions is localized since their focal purpose is to build a juridical infrastructure within national law in order to facilitate international cooperation intended to suppress the modes of conduct constituting the prohibited acts which amount to transnational organized crimes. Since treaties are multilateral legal instruments, they presuppose an intended broad jurisdictional reach. Suppression conventions are targeted to have domestic impetus by imposing obligations on States which, in turn, and by adhering to such obligations, are likely to curb the transnational organized crime. In fact, such suppression conventions aim to suppress 'inter- and intra-State criminal activity that threatens shared national interests or cosmopolitan values'.[19] Technically they create a State obligation to penalise acts domestically but fail to bind individuals directly,[20] and, unlike both international crimes[21] and core crimes, they are only punishable if they are criminalized domestically. In fact, in most circumstances, such States invariably penalize the acts which they are asked and obliged to criminalize in terms of these suppression conventions and by virtue of the ratification thereof. Yet, reference to the term 'treaty crime' could be misleading since transnational organized crimes may have other sources, not necessarily international conventions.[22] Such crimes are habitually referred to as 'treaty crimes' since they are penalised under conventional international law by means of the so-called suppression conventions.[23] Moreover, the term 'treaty crimes' could cause confusion with the term 'international crime'. In my view, the term 'treaty crime' confines the crime to a particular and specific treaty. Transnational organized crimes are generally inter-connected, inter-related and inter-dependent. Narcoterrorism, for example, is the means by which terrorist organizations engage in lucrative drug trafficking activity to fund their criminal operations, gain recruits, networks and expertise, and fulfil their politically motivated objectives.[24] Hence the term 'transnational organized crimes' is more appropriate than the term 'treaty crime', especially for the purposes of this work. It also stands to reason that such crimes be punished by the State because these crimes are habitually committed by organized groups which oppose the State. Whereas core crimes are committed, as noted here above, with some form of State

---

[18] Boister 2003, p. 954.

[19] Boister 2003, p. 968.

[20] Milanović 2011, p. 28.

[21] See Sect. 8.3.

[22] Boister cites Stessens 2000, who refers to the influence of soft law in the creation of anti-money-laundering norms (Boister 2003, p. 963).

[23] These comprise the legal instruments referred to in n. 28, here below.

[24] For a better understanding of diverse forms of terrorism, see van Krieken 2002, pp. 200–219.

involvement, by means of the commission of transnational organized crime the State may be said to be involved in its capacity of collective victim and/or stakeholder. Unlike in the case of core crimes, transnational organised crimes do not take place in the context of fierce political struggle wherein perpetrators and their allies interpret punishment as political victimization.[25]

Examples of transnational organized crimes include trafficking [be it of firearms, drugs[26] or human beings], terrorism, migrant smuggling,[27] and money-laundering. These phenomena are criminalized by means of *ad hoc* multilateral legal instruments[28] (sectoral conventions) which contain various common provisions generally intended to penalize the acts under domestic law, provide for extra-territorial jurisdiction and the *aut dedere aut judicare* rule. A transnational organized crime is defined as a crime which:

(a) is committed in more than one State;
(b) is committed in one State but a substantial part of its preparation, planning, direction, or control takes place in another State;
(c) is committed in one State but involves an organized criminal group that engages in criminal activities in more than one State; or
(d) is committed in one State but has substantial effects in another State.[29]

There also exists the regional counterpart of some of these instruments.[30] States hence have incentives to cooperate with the aim of suppressing transnational

---

[25] Golash 2010, p. 221.

[26] Drug use which habitually results from drug trafficking is the main route of HIV transmission (Kroll 2007).

[27] For a better understanding of this phenomenon, see Mallia 2010, *passim.*

[28] These legal instruments include the following: Convention for the Suppression of Counterfeiting (1929); Single Convention on Narcotic Drugs (1961); Convention on Offences and Certain Other Acts Committed on Board Aircraft (1963); Convention for the Suppression of Unlawful Seizure of Aircraft (1970); Convention for the Suppression of Unlawful Acts against the Safety of Civil Aviation (1971); Convention on Psychotropic Substances (1971); Convention on the Physical Protection of Nuclear Material (1980); Protocol for the Suppression of Unlawful Acts of Violence at Airports Serving International Civil Aviation (1988); Convention on the Prevention and Punishment of Crimes against Internationally Protected Persons, including Diplomatic Agents (1973); Convention Against the Taking of Hostages (1979); Convention Against Illicit Traffic in Narcotic Drugs and Psychotropic Substances (1988); Convention for the Suppression of Unlawful Acts against the Safety of Maritime Navigation and the Protocol for the Suppression of Unlawful Acts against the Safety of Fixed Platforms located on the Continental Shelf (1988); Convention on the Marking of Plastic Explosives for the Purpose of Detection (1991); Convention on the Safety of United Nations and Associated Personnel (1994); Convention for the Suppression of Terrorist Bombings (1997); Convention Against the Recruitment, Use, Financing and Training of Mercenaries (1989); Convention for the Suppression of the Financing of Terrorism (1999); Convention Against Corruption (2003); Trafficking Protocol, above n. 10; Smuggling Protocol, above n. 10; Manufacturing Protocol, above n. 10.

[29] Article 3 of the UNCATOC, above n. 10.

[30] See, for example, *inter alia*, the European Convention on the Suppression of Terrorism (1977), the Protocol Supplementing the European Convention on the Suppression of Terrorism (2003),

organized crimes. The *aut dedere aut judicare* rule (the obligation to extradite or prosecute, which will be dealt with in depth in the fourth Part of this work) is important for the suppression of transnational organized crimes. In these types of crimes, more than in others (and unlike in the case of core crimes), cooperation by States is more forthcoming. The entire repressive regime, in fact, heavily relies on cooperation obligations[31] which occasionally may only apply to transnational crimes involving an organized criminal group[32] and on other duties emanating from legal instruments intended to curb such crimes.[33] This is probably because States perceive that these crimes cannot be localised, but have trans-boundary aspects and effects which can haunt them in the near future. States also tend to protect reciprocity by complying with the requests of other States because they know that they can and probably will be in the same situation of such other States one day or another.

Some commentators consider human trafficking as a form of modern day slavery to the extent that they argue that human trafficking should be reclassified as a form of slavery, submitting that it is not so classified because of racial and gender assumptions within the term 'slavery' itself.[34] To justify their assertions, such authors tend to argue that each and every type of human trafficking necessarily offends the conscience of humankind and strikes at the heart of the international order.[35] Yet, the position at law is somewhat different because while the crime of trafficking in human beings and the crime against humanity of enslavement are increasingly overlapping,[36] they do not coincide.[37] The Trafficking Protocol treats trafficking as a transnational crime of international concern. Article 4 of the Trafficking Protocol provides that the offence must be transnational in nature

and Inter-American Convention Against Terrorism (2002). In certain fields, regional mechanisms have been pre-emptive in their quest to curb certain transnational organized crime (see, for example, CoE Convention on Laundering, Search, Seizure and Confiscation of the Proceeds from Crime (1990), CoE Convention on the Protection of the Environment Through Criminal Law (1998), and the CoE Convention on Cybercrime (2001)).

31 These include forms of assistance such as mutual legal assistance, judicial assistance, seizure and confiscation of the proceeds of crime, and extradition (Boister 2016, pp. 52–69).

32 Article 16 of the UNCATOC, above n. 10, for example, requires State Parties to consider trafficking as an extraditable offence (van der Wilt 2014, p. 324).

33 By way of example, some transnational organized crimes (including trafficking in human beings) feature in the list of offences in respect of which the Framework Decision on the EAW has partially abolished the double criminality requirement (van der Wilt 2014, p. 325).

34 Tavakoli 2009, p. 77.

35 Tavakoli 2009, abstract, p. 77.

36 Furthermore, to complicate matters, the expanded notion of slavery in the *Kunarac* decision [ICTY Trial Chamber, *Prosecutor v Dragoljub Kunarac et al.*, 22 February 2001, Case No. IT-96-23-T & IT-96-23/1-T] has blurred the dividing line between trafficking in human beings and slavery (van der Wilt 2014, p. 314).

37 van der Wilt 2014, abstract, p. 297.

outlining four criteria for this purpose.[38] These four criteria provide a solid baseline to elicit definitional clarity, and tally with the differentiations I postulated. In fact, crimes committed by non-State entities which do not operate beyond national borders do not fall within the rubric and parameters of this definition and are consequently not punishable under the UNCATOC[39] which was signed in the 'symbolically significant Sicilian capital of Palermo'.[40] They could, instead, be punishable as core crimes.

The above has shown that whereas core crimes may be committed by persons in high public office (especially in rogue States), transnational organized crimes are generally committed by non-State entities and/or criminal organizations. Since non-State entities, as seen here above, can also commit core crimes, the first distinction is not necessarily watertight and decisive. Moreover the crime of trafficking in human beings shows that core crimes on the one hand and transnational organized crimes on the other hand are committed, so to say, in different playing fields. Their *locus delicti commissi* is not one and the same. Human trafficking is not always carried out transnationally.[41] In fact the act of human trafficking[42] can constitute both a domestic crime and a core crime when committed within the State's borders. Human trafficking is an ordinary 'national crime' since it is punishable domestically and it can also be territorially limited, that is, perpetrated internally, within States, thus exacting territorial jurisdiction of the State wherein it is committed. More importantly, it can be committed by just one person. Human trafficking is a 'transnational organized crime' when it involves migrants who were smuggled from one State to another with the ulterior purposes of, for example, sexual exploitation or prostitution. This shows that human trafficking and migrant smuggling are not one and the same crime, although the former can follow the consummation of the latter crime. In as much as it can constitute slave trade by virtue of the subsequent exploitation of the victim, human trafficking[43] is a fully-fledged 'international crime' for all intents and purposes of law. If, however, the elements of the crime against humanity of enslavement are present, the escalation of human trafficking would project it onto the status of a core crime.[44] It can also constitute the war crime of sexual slavery under 8(2)(e)(vi) of the ICC Statute if committed in armed conflict. Human trafficking is therefore like a chameleon

[38] The transnational nature and dimension of the act can be deduced and extracted from the definition of 'transnational organized crime' which is found in Article 3 of the UNCATOC, above n. 10, and is cited at the top of this page.

[39] Obokata 2010, p. 29.

[40] Findlay and Hanif 2013, p. 699.

[41] Tavakoli 2009, p. 82.

[42] Generally these acts involve the luring of people from other jurisdictions with false promises of legitimate work (USA Department of State 2015, p. 8, also cited in Tolbert and Smith 2016, p. 446, n. 93).

[43] For an analysis of how jurisprudence distinguishes enslavement and slavery from trafficking, see Siller 2016, pp. 418–426.

[44] *Prosecutor v Dragoljub Kunarac et al.*, above n. 36, cited in Obokata 2005, p. 445.

which changes colour depending upon its environment and surrounding circumstances, or rather, the general context of the crime, *id est* its contextual circumstances. For the sake of clarity, trafficking in human beings constitutes slavery only when the perpetrator arrogates control (over movement) and establishes complete financial subservience of the victim as if he owns the victim as a thing or commodity.[45] This is important not only to understand the constitutive elements of the crimes (which goes beyond the scope of this book)[46] but to learn that the mode of repression of the crime (as a common denominator) can shed a light on its nature. Inversely, the nature of the crime influences the choice of the appropriate forum which shall punish perpetrators who commit the crime in question.[47] Moreover, and most importantly for the purposes of this work, trafficking in human beings connotes private enterprise whereas the crime against humanity of enslavement implies institutionalized repression with governmental approval or even involvement.[48] It is true that human trafficking can (and habitually does) involve the corruption of State officials,[49] but it is not a crime that is usually committed or condoned on a massive scale by the State.[50] In fact enslavement, like other crimes against humanity is only a crime against humanity when it is combined with the contextual elements.[51] A common denominator of crimes, that is, its perpetrator, varies considerably when trafficking and enslavement are compared. Indeed the divergences in the perpetrator are more than meets the eye. Even if one were to apply the more flexible standards of the majority in the Kenya *dictum* and the Trial Chamber III in the *Bemba Gombo* case (as opposed to Hans Peter Kaul's dissent), the vast majority of criminal organizations that engage in human trafficking would by no means meet the threshold required by the ICC Statute in so far as they lack the power, resources and institutional features (which the State enjoys as a result of its dominant position)[52] required to carry our large scale attacks on civilian populations.[53] Harmen van der Wilt reaches such conclusion by comparing the requirements of 'organization' within the *Kenya* decision (which requirements have already been explained here above) with the definition of 'organization' in Article 2 of the UNCATOC.[54] The latter legal instrument defines 'organized criminal group' as 'a structured group of three or more persons, existing for a period of time and acting in concert with the

45 van der Wilt 2014, p. 314.

46 A detailed analysis on the law and practice (which includes jurisprudence of the ICC, the *ad hoc* tribunals and the ECtHR) of trafficking in human beings on the one hand and the crime against humanity of enslavement on the other hand has been recently undertaken by Harmen van der Wilt (van der Wilt 2014, pp. 297–334).

47 van der Wilt 2014, p. 299.

48 van der Wilt 2014, p. 298.

49 Gallagher 2010, pp. 442–443.

50 van der Wilt 2014, p. 331.

51 van der Wilt 2014, p. 314.

52 van der Wilt 2014, p. 331.

53 van der Wilt 2014, p. 307.

54 Ibid.

aim of committing one or more serious crimes or offences, established in accordance with this Convention, in order to obtain, directly or indirectly, a financial or other material benefit'. Hence the divergence between the two is evident.

The crime of terrorism does not only lie in between core crimes and transnational organized crimes, but also lies in between the dichotomy of State crimes and individual crimes. As noted by Nina Jørgensen, the recruitment, use, financing, training of mercenaries and international terrorism fall in between and come under the revised 1996 Draft Code of Crimes Against the Peace and Security of Mankind whenever therein agents or representatives of a State were involved.[55] Rather than stopping when wars commence, 'the risk of terrorist tactics is exacerbated as perpetrators exploit the fog of war and accompanying lawlessness to menace opposing populations'.[56] This predicament may also have been a reason why certain crimes are not adequately redressed. It therefore merits some close scrutiny, also because most jurists tend to analyse terrorist acts in isolation and to focus on their quest to achieve a legally acceptable and/or universal definition[57] rather than comparatively (*id est* by undertaking a comparative study of the elements of the crime of terrorism with the elements of other crimes which cause massive levels of pain and human suffering). Kai Ambos, whilst conceding that terrorism is on the brink of becoming a core crime, forges the elements of an emerging core crime by inferring them from the various definitions of international and national sources by way of their systematic comparison.[58] Harmen van der Wilt and Inez Braber construct a solid case to motivate the inclusion of a stand-alone crime of terrorism[59] within the ICC's jurisdiction, hence elevating it to the status of a core crime *stricto sensu* which need not necessarily be committed only in times of peace. Their edifice relies on the identification of significant parallels between core crimes (namely war crimes and crimes against humanity) and the crime of terrorism.[60] The edifice built by van der Wilt and Braber rests on two important pillars. Firstly 'intermittent terrorist attacks

---

55 Jørgensen 2000, p. 152.

56 Gillett and Schuster 2011, p. 1011.

57 Vojin Dimitrijevic compiles a list of instruments generally designated as anti-terrorist but notes that none of them defines 'terrorism' (Dimitrijevic 2003, p. 607). Seeking a definition is particularly difficult since terrorists are perceived as freedom fighters by some but as criminals by others (Alì 2013, pp. 299–303), just like, in David Luban's words (Luban 2011a, b, p. 64) the biblical sacrifice of Isaac can be perceived either as a nation-founding act (proof) of faith or as an attempted murder (see, *inter alia*, Ventura 2011, pp. 1025–1027; Fletcher 2006, pp. 894–911; DiFilippo 2008, pp. 540–548; Cassese 2006, pp. 936–937; van der Vyver 2010, pp. 528–530; Hmoud 2006, pp. 1032–1034).

58 Ambos 2011, pp. 667–675.

59 It must be recalled that terrorism was considered as a crime under international law by the ILC until the 1996 Draft Code of Crimes Against the Peace and Security of Mankind {Draft Code of Crimes Against the Peace and Security of Mankind (1996)} (Heller 2015) and that acts of terrorism were subsequently considered as the most serious threats to peace and security by means of UNSC Resolution 1566 [UNSC (2004) Resolution 1566 (2004), UN Doc. S/RES/1566], para 1, cited in Martin 2013, p. 641 and p. 646.

60 van der Wilt and Braber 2015, p. 33.

on civilians in a context of virtual anarchy breeds similar human suffering and social disruption as analogous attacks in an armed conflict', and secondly 'the impotence of the State to protect its own citizens has always been advanced as one of the strongest justifications of legal intervention by the international community – next to the State's oppression of its citizens - and the former is precisely the situation which we are facing in large parts of Africa'.[61] The second pillar can, *inter alia*, be made use of to decipher features and characteristics (outlined here above) which shed a light on the concept of core crimes. The adoption of their line of argumentation would effectively plug a jurisdictional loophole consisting in the ability of the ICC to try terrorist acts. This it could do irrespective of the definition of the crime of terrorism under customary international law in view of its tenth legal provision which allows it to depart from international law.[62] Their arguments fascinatingly encapsulate the awareness of the substantial broadening of the scope of the concept and jurisdictional reach of 'armed conflict' adopted particularly by the *ad hoc* tribunals.[63] Drawing upon the practice of the *ad hoc* tribunals, on the Statute of the SCSL and developments in customary international law,[64] van der Wilt and Braber note that although terrorism *per se* is not a war crime, both State officials and non-State entities could be subjected to prosecution by the ICC if they have been involved in 'intentionally directing attacks against the civilian population as such or against individual civilians not taking direct part in hostilities'.[65] In actual fact they pinpoint that although terrorism is not a core crime, there are equivalent (counterpart) war crimes, one of which is hostage-taking (this being a war crime which closely resembles an act of terrorism in peace time), that cover materially the same unlawful conduct.[66] They pose the question: 'can non-state armed groups commit war crimes?', to which they reply affirmatively. They contend that this is so when non-State entities have sufficient prowess to do so. This depends partially on their capacity to engage against State armies in protracted

---

[61] van der Wilt and Braber 2015, p. 18 and p. 30.

[62] van der Wilt and Braber 2015, pp. 35–36.

[63] van der Wilt and Braber 2015, p. 21. Helen Duffy similarly refers to 'an unduly broad approach to armed conflict and to notions of "association" with the conflict' (Duffy 2013, p. 524).

[64] It seems that the test of 'overall control' as a basis for the internationalization of armed conflict is far from settled [ICC Trial Chamber II, *Situation in The DRC, Prosecutor v Germain Katanga, Judgment Pursuant to Article 74 of the Statute,* Minority Opinion of Judge Christine van den Wyngaert, Anx. I, 7 March 2014, Case No. ICC-01/04-01/07, para 276 and n. 382, cited in Cullen 2015, p. 774, n. 54.] Robert Kolb, whilst noting that it is not necessarily limited to the qualification of a conflict as international, is curious as to whether it will make real or putative contributions to the law of armed conflict (Kolb 2009, p. 1027). The same scepticism has been voiced about the qualification of armed conflict under the ICC Statute {ICC Statute (1998) Rome Statute of the International Criminal Court} and the distinction between international and non-international armed conflict (Cullen 2015, p. 774).

[65] This prohibition applies both to international armed conflicts {Article 8(2)(b)(i) of the ICC Statute, above n. 64} and to non-international (*id est* internal) armed conflicts {Article 8(2)(e)(i) of the ICC Statute, above n. 64} (see van der Wilt and Braber 2015, p. 20).

[66] van der Wilt and Braber 2015, p. 20; see also van der Wilt 2015, pp. 221–222.

clashes. If they do reach that threshold (when they only apply needlepin attacks) the mess and human misery can be as bad. Weak states may be equally impotent to do something against it. To paraphrase their thrust, why shouldn't the ICC come to their rescue? Their argument heavily relies on a study of thresholds of armed conflicts, because it is the extent of such armed conflict which, in turn, determines whether an act can qualify to constitute a core crime or otherwise. Whereas they acknowledge the *Tadić dictum*[67] as an authoritative *point de depart*, the *Limaj dictum*[68] as an analysis of standards introduced in *Tadić*, and the *Boškoski & Tarčulovski dictum*[69] as a comprehensive synthesis of the leading practice, van der Wilt and Braber make another step which is crucial for the purposes of understanding the subsistence or otherwise of an armed conflict. They submit that unless there is a certain equality of arms (in the literal, not juridical, sense) between adversaries vying for power and resources, there would be no armed conflict but merely protracted violence by splinter groups. In other words, for there to be an armed conflict, the rebel groups must have a fighting chance, a prospect of success. They must stand a reasonable chance to succeed in defeating governmental forces. If, however, the military strength such groups possess is not sufficient to defy governmental forces or other similar groups vying for territorial power and control, an armed conflict would not subsist because the prevailing military imbalance would necessarily entail that the State can still vaunt its control over its territory and that it has the ability to investigate and prosecute those who attempt to jeopardize such control and power. I note that the above contentions are further substantiated by the views of the ICRC,[70] which are, in turn, supported by many States and non-governmental organizations. These views predicate that loosely organized groups/networks[71] or individuals which share a common ideology would not fulfil the threshold of parties to a conflict within the meaning of international humanitarian law, as a consequence of which their actions do not amount to core crimes but to terrorist offences which should be dealt with by domestic means rather than by the application of the laws of war.[72] Robert Kolb, citing Meyrowitz,[73] refers to the term 'equality of belligerents' when he examines how international humanitarian law relating to non-international armed conflicts (armed conflicts between governmental forces and insurgents or between armed groups) is in an unbalanced and

[67] ICTY Appeals Chamber, *Prosecutor v Duško Tadić, Decision on the Defence Motion for Interlocutory Appeal on Jurisdiction*, 2 October 1995, Case No. IT-94-1, particularly para 72.

[68] ICTY Trial Chamber II, *Prosecutor v Fatmir Limaj et al.*, 30 November 2005, Case No. IT-03-66-T, particularly paras 146, 150, 166.

[69] ICTY Trial Chamber II, *Prosecutor v Ljube Boškoski & Johan Tarčulovski,* 10 July 2008, Case No. IT-04-82-T, para 177.

[70] The status, role and functions of the ICRC are explained in Voneky 2013, pp. 690–691.

[71] Some examples include the Mai Mai in the DRC, the anti-Balaka in CAR and various vigilante groups in the Lake Chad region (Bellal 2017).

[72] ICRC 2011, cited in Garraway 2013, p. 439, n. 44.

[73] Meyrowitz 1970, cited in Kolb 2014, p. 30, n. 17.

chaotic state.[74] No further argument on the lines of the 'equality of arms' criterion used by Braber and van der Wilt is made. In contrast, Emily Crawford and Alison Pert, in making reference to Article 1(1) of Additional Protocol II to the Geneva Conventions, infer that the establishment of the 'equality of arms', in the sense and as juxtaposed here above, could be dependent on the intensity of the fighting (conflict),[75] implying that an intense conflict may reveal that there subsisted a certain equality of arms.[76] Trafficking in human beings and terrorism exemplify two separate crimes which lie on the fence and possess many shades of grey.

There exists a striking difference between the cause of criminalization of core crimes and the cause of criminalization of transnational organized crimes. The cause for criminalization of core crimes, which is dealt with extensively in Chap. 4, can be largely attributed to their gravity which resides in the fact that these crimes are not investigated and prosecuted owing to the unwillingness or inability of the State which is most qualified and expected to ensure their punishment. On the other hand, the same may not be said about transnational organized crimes, about international crimes and about domestic crimes. The former crimes will be considered first. Unwillingness to investigate and prosecute hardly and remotely applies to transnational organized crimes. Inability could apply to such crimes, this being why the suppression of transnational organized crimes heavily relies on close judicial and extra-judicial cooperation between States. With the exception of a very few grey areas which have been dealt with here above, as a general rule, transnational organized crimes are punished at national level by States enjoying a ground of jurisdiction, sometimes even extra-territorially. It is true that these crimes are very difficult to curb and hence require concerted action, but this is not owing to the State's unwillingness or inability to investigate and prosecute such crimes. These crimes are somewhere in between ordinary (domestic) crimes and core crimes.[77] In so far as it becomes a victim, yet another common denominator distinguishes a crime within one category/species from the other. The State thus wears a different hat because its role is considerably different. This role (the hat which the State wears) largely dictates the mode of repression of the crime which is, in turn, largely dependent upon the heads of responsibility prevailing under the applicable law. Being the victim (rather than the perpetrator), the State is generally not unwilling to investigate and prosecute the transnational organized crime. On the contrary, it is in its ultimate interest to investigate and prosecute such transnational organized crime.

---

[74] Kolb 2014, pp. 28–33.

[75] Crawford and Pert 2015, p. 258.

[76] In a different context, *id est* that of an international armed conflict, Robert Kolb an eminent international humanitarian law expert, places less emphasis on the intensity of the conflict, submitting that 'any time there is hostile action between armed forces of States, international humanitarian law shall apply. A border incident is an "armed conflict" in the sense of the Geneva Conventions. There is no reason to say that the first injured soldier shall not be cared for under Geneva Convention I, simply because he or she is for the moment only one, and thus the armed conflict is not yet sufficiently intense' (Kolb 2014, pp. 96–100, particularly p. 98).

[77] van der Wilt 2014, p. 315.

In fact these crimes are prosecuted by national courts.[78] This is so unless the transnational organized crime partakes of heavy State involvement such as when State-sponsored terrorism[79] subsists, in which case it would move closer to the category of 'core crimes' rather than remain under the parameters of 'transnational organized crimes'.[80]

Transnational organized crimes are fought by suppression conventions which do not directly establish individual criminal responsibility but create inter-State obligations which generate penal laws.[81] The enforcement jurisdiction of suppression conventions which penalize transnational organised crimes 'is often exercised by a State other than (or perhaps more accurately, in addition to) the State desirous of exercising its prescriptive/adjudicative jurisdiction'.[82] The same does not apply with regards to core crimes in so far as the ICC exercises jurisdiction to prescribe, jurisdiction to adjudicate and jurisdiction to enforce all by virtue of one and the same instrument,[83] this being the ICC Statute. Now the difference in the manner of law enforcement is a symptom of the difference in the nature of these diverse species of crimes. In fact, the distinction between a core crime on the one hand and a transnational organized crime on the other hand is predominantly prevalent in terms of the manner such crimes are fought, a difference which unmasks the diverse natures thereof. The manner by means of which international criminal law curbs transnational organised crimes is completely different to the way it combats core crimes. Domestic crimes are punished within the national territory, transnational organised crimes are punishable both territorially and extra-territorially whereas core crimes may also be punished in the absence of a jurisdictional link, *id est* on the basis of universal jurisdiction.[84] Even case-law has established that unlike core crimes, transnational organized crimes are not subject to universal jurisdiction in terms of customary international law.[85] Therefore jurisdiction over transnational organised crimes is more limited 'because it is ordinarily only established when a direct injury is threatened or caused to the State taking responsibility', and is 'dependent on the terms of a particular suppression convention'.[86] In the case of

---

78 Ibid.

79 Antonio Cassese contended that State-sponsored terrorism amounted to a core crime not because it constituted a crime which was directly and actively perpetrated by persons possessing an official capacity in high public offices (*id est* by the State) but because of its implications for international peace and security (Cassese 2001, pp. 993–994).

80 See references to trafficking in human beings and terrorism under this heading (*id est* 8.1).

81 Boister 2003, p. 962.

82 Clark 2015, p. 93.

83 Nyamuya Maogoto 2016, p. 50.

84 Marchuk 2014, p. 70.

85 USA District Court for the Southern District of Florida, *USA v Cesar James-Robinson*, 11 June 1981, 515 F Supp 1340 (SD Fla. 1981), 1344 n. 6, and USA Court of Appeals, 11th Circuit, *USA v Esteban Marino-Garcia*, 9 July 1982, 679 F.2d 1373, 1382 n. 16, both cited in Boister 2012a, p. 151, n. 102.

86 Boister 2003, p. 964.

core crimes, the right to criminalize becomes a right of the international community once the State *de facto* decriminalizes core crimes by either being unable or unwilling to investigate and prosecute the perpetrators thereof. As noted in Chap. 5 and as shall be postulated in Chap. 19 the right verges on a duty in certain circumstances. On the contrary, in transnational organized crimes the right to criminalize remains a prerogative of the State which would have ratified the relative suppression convention. The breach of such State obligations results in an international tort or delict and entails State (ordinary, not aggravated) responsibility.[87] They are hence fought indirectly by imposing obligations on States to enact legislation intended to penalize conduct[88] which 'threatens shared national interests or cosmopolitan values'.[89] Thus, the jurisdictional reach of core crimes on one hand and of transnational organized crimes on the other hand is also different.

In the emphasis on groups, and most of all, in their protection by means of the prohibition of core crimes, one also finds features which are absent in the other categories of crimes (such as transnational organized crimes). Furthermore, whereas individuals are the objects of suppression conventions which punish transnational organized crimes, individuals are the subjects of domestic laws and the ICC Statute which punish core crimes. More specifically, the ICC Statute crystallizes a direct customary international law based obligation on individuals irrespective of the position in domestic law.[90] The prohibition of core crimes hence protects the *civitas maxima* against *hostis humani generis*.[91] This sharply contrasts with transnational organized crimes which possess an indirect public nature, more commonly involve private individual conduct with accompanying private motives (even when committed by small groups), and harm persons or private interests,[92] not the international community as a whole.

8.2 Core Crimes Versus Domestic Crimes

The large majority of domestic crimes, serious as they may be,[93] do not injure the rights and interest of the international community, do not threaten the peace and security of mankind and do not shock the conscience of humanity. A major

---

87 Boister 2003, p. 962.

88 Obokata 2010, p. 31.

89 Boister 2003, p. 968.

90 Boister 2012a, p. 18.

91 Bassiouni 1974, p. 405.

92 Bassiouni 1974, p. 421.

93 Some domestic crimes, such as ordinary wilful homicide (murder), can be considered as the most serious in terms of the punishment they carry. Wilful homicide is punished either by life imprisonment and/or the death penalty in the majority of States around the globe but this factor does not render it a crime of concern to the international community, let alone a crime of serious concern to the international community. The international community does not lose any sleep by

difference between this body of laws and the conventions which penalize transnational organised crimes is that domestic crimes are criminalized solely at the election of the State and do not emerge from an international treaty. This is not to mention yet another obvious distinction connoting that domestic crimes need not necessarily be transnational in nature or possess any transnational element. Astrid Kjeldgaard-Pedersen upholds that the distinction between domestic and international criminal courts should resolve solely around the nature of the founding document rather than around the involvement of the international community, as a result of which a court set up under international law is international, whereas a court set up under domestic law is domestic.[94] Yet, concluding that a domestic crime is simply a crime which is dealt with by a domestic court whereas an international crime is a crime which is dealt with by an international court is a tautological conclusion which can be misleading, and also incorrect, in so far as domestic courts habitually prosecute persons for having committed core crimes, international crimes and transnational organized crimes. Since these species of crimes, in one way or another, have become domestic crimes, differentiation on the basis of the prosecuting forum is superfluous. In any case, the fact that a crime is tried before an international criminal tribunal, though descriptive of a core crime, is not determinative of it.[95]

The term 'domestic crime' can be used inter-changeably with the terms 'local crime', 'national crime' and 'municipal crime'. A domestic crime may be construed to mean an act or omission which constitutes a crime and which is prosecuted domestically by virtue of the prevailing provisions within the relevant national criminal law which penalise such modes of conduct [either crimes by commission or crimes by omission]. For the purposes of clarity, since my above mentioned definition presupposes the existence of a crime, a definition of 'crime' is warranted. A law dictionary defines a crime as 'an act that the law makes punishable; the breach of a legal duty treated as the subject matter of a criminal proceeding'.[96] The corollary of this definition entails that a domestic crime is an act that is made punishable by national law. In other words, a domestic crime is the breach of a legal duty imposed by national law and treated as a subject matter of domestic criminal proceedings. Municipal law habitually defines crimes as given conduct constituting an offence and punishable by a given penalty.[97]

---

such murders, no matter how cruel (heinous) they may be, because the territorial State investigates them and prosecutes them.

[94] Kjeldgaard-Pedersen 2015, p. 131.

[95] The SCSL has been conferred with jurisdiction over some crimes under Sierra Leone's Prevention of Cruelty to Children Act {Prevention of Cruelty to Children Act (1926) Chapter 31, Law of Sierra Leone} and its Malicious Damage Act {Malicious Damage Act (1861) Chapter 97, Law of Sierra Leone}, whereas the STL is vested with jurisdiction solely over crimes under Lebanese law (O'Keefe 2015, p. 60).

[96] Garner 2004, p. 399.

[97] O'Keefe 2015, p. 49.

Although national criminal codes contain a multitude of offences which are purely local, in their cause, content, nature and effects, the national implementation of crimes falling within the jurisdiction of the ICC has, to an extent, internationalized domestic crimes. This occurred owing to the fact that the crimes subject to the jurisdiction of the ICC have become, in various states, fully-fledged domestic crimes. Although they partake of an international nature and dimension, they retain their domestic features since they are prosecutable locally. Hence, their breach constitutes a violation of the local criminal code and subjects the law-breaker to national prosecution. This is an important development in the enforcement of international criminal law *per se* which is aided by the fact that 'criminal codes are usually thought to have a number of benefits – accessibility, comprehensiveness, certainty and consistency'.[98] Harmen van der Wilt also largely attributes the success of international criminal law to domestic jurisdictions, stating that they 'contribute to the further evolution of international criminal law'.[99] In the context of the legality principle,[100] he adds that 'domestic jurisdictions are simply better equipped to abide by the principle – and therefore have a better record – than international tribunals'.[101] Moreover, the perpetrator of ordinary domestic crimes is generally an individual, acting alone or in concert with other perpetrators who are disentangled from armed factions, and hence posing a less serious threat to the international community than an individual carrying out orders of a head of State and/or military superior or an individual who forms part of an organized armed group.

8.3 Core Crimes Versus International Crimes

The above mentioned characteristic, this being the conduct of a single individual, is also reminiscent of 'international crimes' which resemble (but are not identical to) core crimes. 'International crimes' is a very misleading term. This is because, as correctly upheld by Roger O'Keefe, the 'epithet "international" denotes, as before, merely the body of law by reference to which the act is considered punishable'.[102] William Schabas refers to the research conducted by Mohammed Cherif Bassiouni who gives examples such as piracy, unlawful use of the mail, counterfeiting, destruction of submarine cables and bribery of foreign officials in order to conclude that 'many crimes are international because they are declared to be criminal in an international treaty'.[103] I shall identify the fine line of demarcation between the two

[98] de Burca and Gardner 1990, p. 559.

[99] van der Wilt 2008, p. 252.

[100] The legality principle is considered as the guiding interpretative principle for core crimes (Grover 2014, p. 102).

[101] van der Wilt 2008, p. 258.

[102] O'Keefe 2015, p. 59.

[103] Schabas 2008, pp. 268–269.

categories (species). International crimes are acts which are criminalized by multilateral conventions but which do not constitute core crimes owing to the non-subsistence of features and characteristics with which core crimes are deeply associated, namely the contextual elements (circumstances) and their group-based nature. International crimes can engender State responsibility under domestic, regional and/or international human rights law. Yet, unlike core crimes, they do not generally engender State aggravated responsibility, but at most State ordinary responsibility. 'International crimes' are habitually used to refer to 'transnational crimes'.[104] The need to distinguish between 'international crime' and 'core crime,' at least for the purposes of this work, is hence underscored, although some jurists speak of either 'core international crime'[105] or 'international core crime'.[106] Although she may have done so for different reasons, Paola Gaeta also distinguishes between 'international crimes' on the one hand and 'core crimes' on the other. In fact she uses the term 'international crimes proper' to designate core crimes, implying that when she refers to 'treaty-based crimes' she is not referring to 'international crimes proper'.[107] Likewise, this position is reiterated in the third edition of 'Cassese's International Criminal Law', of which Paola Gaeta is one of the revisers.[108] Larry May and Zachary Hoskins resort to the same terminology, contending that 'international crimes proper', unlike crimes against States, are subject to universal jurisdiction.[109] The above differentiation is also subtly and, by implication, accepted by André Nollkaemper who refers to a 'narrow category of crimes that international law recognises as international crimes under customary law. This category also has been referred to as core crimes'.[110]

The lack of a definition of the concept of 'international crime' within legal instruments has also occasionally led to the use, or misuse, of the term itself.[111] The term 'international crime' may be used inter-changeably with the following terms:

(a) crime under international law; and
(b) crime against international law.

Terje Einarsen has distinguished between three kinds of crimes:

i. core international crimes;
ii. other international crimes against the peace and security of mankind; and

[104] Lee 2010, p. 20, n. 9.

[105] See, for example, Bergsmo 2010, p. 23, see Wyler and Castellanos-Jankiewicz 2011, pp. 395–400, see Damgaard 2008, *passim*, and see also Bantekas and Oette 2016, pp. 705–711.

[106] Ambos 2007, pp. 55–68.

[107] Gaeta 2009, pp. 70–71.

[108] Cassese et al. 2013, p. 21.

[109] May and Hoskins 2010, p. 3.

[110] Nollkaemper 2009, p. 19.

[111] Mark Allan Gray speaks of an international crime of ecocide, James Odek so categorizes bio-piracy, whereas Ndiva Kofele-Kale defines patrimonicide as the 'international economic crime of indigenous spoliation' (Pakos 2003, pp. 215, 141 and 45 respectively).

iii. international crimes not dependent on the existence of threats to international peace and security.[112]

The former are the core crimes, which have just been dealt with in Chap. 6. The second class of crimes are, largely speaking, those which I call 'international crimes', whereas the third (latter) category constitutes a similar (though not identical) classification of transnational organized crimes. Terje Einarsen postulates that the above mentioned three classes are not mutually exclusive sets. In his view, they are best represented as the areas delimited by the three concentric circles, juxtaposed here below. The core crimes are indicated within the black innermost circle. The middle circle encompasses all crimes against the peace and security of mankind. This includes both the core crimes (the black circle) and other crimes against the peace and security of mankind (the grey circle). The outer circle encompasses all international crimes, including the first two, as well as international crimes not dependent on the existence of threats to international peace and security (the white circle).[113] In so far as he attempts to identify core crimes on the basis of legal consequences attached to them, Einarsen's study could represent a laudable effort to articulate definitional clarity. Yet, in my opinion, his views are highly indicative, rather than conclusive, in so far as they do not provide determining factors and/or criteria which may be made use of in order to categorize the different classes (sets/species) of crimes in a definitive manner. Just to provide an example, Einarsen enlists the following consequences of core crimes:

1. direct (individual) liability under international law applies;
2. no statute of limitations applies;
3. no *ex post facto* limitation on implementing statutes applies;
4. limited amnesty protection from prosecution applies;
5. the territorial State of the crime scene has a right and a duty to investigate and prosecute;
6. the nationality State of perpetrators/victims has a right to investigate and prosecute;
7. the nationality State of perpetrators may have a duty to investigate and prosecute;
8. third States may have universal jurisdiction to investigate and prosecute;
9. States may have a duty to extradite or prosecute a suspected resident perpetrator;
10. prosecutions must adhere to the international legality principle;
11. prosecutions must adhere to international procedural standards of fair trial;
12. the UN may facilitate prosecution in cooperation with the territorial State;
13. the UN may establish criminal courts without consent of the territorial/national State;
14. the UN may refer the situation to the prosecutor of the ICC;
15. the UN may authorize armed intervention for the protection of civilians.

---

112 Einarsen 2012, p. 224; Currie 2014, p. 163.

113 Einarsen 2012, p. 225.

He then acknowledges that some of the listed consequences may apply to non-international crimes as well as to core crimes, which he calls 'international crimes'.[114] The above consequences, therefore, cannot serve to conclusively distinguish one type (species/category) of crime from another.

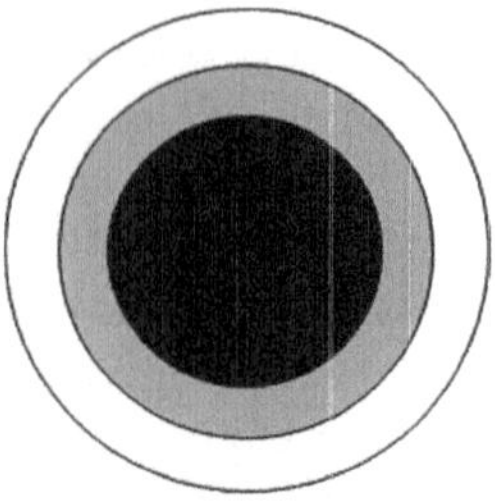

Probably the most vivid example which may be made use of to justify the need to distinguish between 'international crimes' and 'core crimes' is the crime of piracy *jure gentium.*[115] This does not necessarily constitute a transnational organized crime[116] and is not tantamount to a core crime.[117] Unlike core crimes, piracy does not even give rise to criminal responsibility under customary international law,[118] although it was 'the first crime over which there was "universal" jurisdiction.'[119] In fact it is not punished by the ICC Statute in so far as it punishable only under an international convention, by territorial States and by the prospect of a specialised anti-piracy Court[120] in Somalia and other States in the region with

[114] Einarsen 2012, p. 233.

[115] This crime is defined by virtue of Article 15 of the Convention on the High Seas (Convention on the High Seas (1958) Geneva Convention on the High Seas) signed on 29 April 1958 and reaffirmed in Article 101 of the UNCLOS (UNCLOS (1982) UN Convention on the Law of the Sea) which was signed on 10 December 1982.

[116] Piracy, the international crime *par excellence*, is exceptional in that it is habitually committed within the high seas, not within territorially defined geographical or identifiable areas. The UNODC Counter-Piracy Programme began in 2009 with a mandate to help just one country, namely Kenya, in order to assist it in dealing with an increase of attacks by Somali pirates.

[117] The ICC Statute, above n. 64, makes no reference at all to piracy. Likewise it does not even refer to Article 101 of UNCLOS, above n. 115.

[118] O'Keefe 2015, p. 51.

[119] Slomanson 2011, p. 253

[120] This was about to be established following a Report of the UN S-G on Possible Options to Further the Aim of Prosecuting and Imprisoning Persons Responsible for Acts of Piracy and Armed Robbery of the Coast of Somalia, Including, in particular, options for Creating Special Domestic Chambers possibly with International Components, a Regional Tribunal or an International Tribunal and Corresponding Imprisonment Arrangements, taking into Account the Work of the Contact Group on Piracy off the Coast of Somalia, the Existing Practice in Establishing International and Mixed Tribunals and the Time and Resources Necessary to Achieve and Sustain Substantive Results, which was triggered by the UNSC Resolution 1918 of 2010, para 110, cited in van der Wilt 2014, pp. 331–332, n. 112; see also Boister 2012a, p. 269.

substantial international participation and/or support in terms of UNSC Resolution 2015 (2011).[121] UNSC Resolution 2316 (2016) reiterated the commitment to establish the specialised anti-piracy court.[122] It stands at a considerable distance from the species of core crimes. Piracy, the definition of which 'is somehow obscured, ostensibly due to the difference in interpretation between national laws and those set down by various international treaties,'[123] is indeed a crime which puts in jeopardy safety at high sea,[124] affecting and disrupting, in turn, international trade. This geographical feature (the fact that it is committed beyond State borders) renders it so difficult to suppress. The harm it causes to the international community, coupled with the inapplicability of territorial jurisdiction (given that piracy is committed on the high seas), has traditionally permitted the exercise of universal jurisdiction over it. Res Jorge Schuerch notes that piracy is the only crime over which universal jurisdiction is explicitly established in conventional law.[125] Yet, evidence shows that 'prosecuting pirates seems to be more difficult than catching them'[126] and that 'States have in fact never accepted a general obligation to prosecute pirates'.[127] Pirates are a nuisance in so far as they jeopardize commerce which, in turn, generates socio-economic growth and reduces unemployment. Pirates 'by definition are private actors',[128] being professional anarchists, the actions of whom cause a spilling-over effect. For the above mentioned reasons, and although piracy is committed for private ends,[129] a common and mutual interest in prosecuting and punishing pirates hence subsists on a global scale.[130] Suffice to

[121] This was adopted on 24 October 2011 by the UNSC in its 6635th meeting [para 16].

[122] UNSC Resolution 2316 was adopted in its 7805th meeting held on 9 November 2016 [para 19].

[123] de Than and Shorts 2003, p. 257.

[124] Cassese et al. 2013, p. 19.

[125] In the view of Res Jorge Schuerch, the Geneva Conventions {Geneva Convention (1949a) Geneva Convention (I) for the Amelioration of the Condition of the Wounded and Sick in Armed Forces in the Field; Geneva Convention (1949b) Geneva Convention (II) for the Amelioration of the Condition of the Wounded, Sick and Shipwrecked Members of Armed Forces at Sea; Geneva Convention (1949c) Geneva Convention (III) relative to the Treatment of Prisoners of War; Geneva Convention (1949d) Geneva Convention (IV) relative to the Protection of Civilian Persons in Time of War}, their Additional Protocol I {Additional Protocol I (1977) Protocol Additional to the Geneva Conventions of 12 August 1949, and relating to the Protection of Victims of International Armed Conflicts, 8 June 1977], the Genocide Convention {Genocide Convention (1948) Convention on the Prevention and Punishment of the Crime of Genocide} and the CAT {CAT (1984) Convention Against Torture and Other Cruel, Inhuman or Degrading Treatment or Punishment} implicitly allow for the exercise of universal jurisdiction (Schuerch 2016, p. 75).

[126] Karim 2011, p. 393.

[127] Karim 2011, pp. 396–397.

[128] Luban 2011ab, p. 629.

[129] Kulyk 2016, pp. 392–393.

[130] For this purpose, as of 1998, the IMO has undertaken the implementation of an anti-piracy project [IMO, Piracy and Armed Robbery Against Ships. http://www.imo.org/OurWork/Security/PiracyArmedRobbery/Pages/Default.aspx (accessed 24 October 2018)], which includes a reference to 'Save our Seafarers' and to various statistics relating to the perpetration of piracy around the

mention the 1825 *Antelope* case wherein the USA Supreme Court defined a crime against all nations as an offence which engenders 'the duty of all States to seek out and punish offenders, as in the case of piracy'.[131] Indeed piracy affects the interests of States, but not necessarily of the entire international community. It is 'solely a crime against the victims'.[132] It does not breach the principle of human security and its effects fall short of being classified as 'international harm' in terms of the principles explained earlier on.[133] Consequently, it does not reach the threshold required to be categorised as one of the most serious crimes of concern to the international community. The same may be said about terrorism which does not reach the organizational requirement for the purposes of crimes against humanity and which does not fall within the parameters of international humanitarian law since it does not qualify as an armed conflict. In the absence of subject-matter jurisdiction by the ICC, there has been a recommendation to punish such terrorist acts by virtue of the establishment of an International Court Against Terrorism or a Special Court Against Terrorism.[134]

8.4 Concluding Remarks

Having understood the terms of reference of the concept of 'core crime' within this work, a final note is required. These four different types of crimes {core crimes, transnational organized crimes, domestic crimes and international crimes} are not written herein in ascending or descending order in terms of gravity (although core crimes are the most serious), nor are they written herein chronologically, depending on the time of their recognition, *id est* with the first crime which subsisted (existed) juxtaposed before the second, third and so on and so forth. The purpose of this chapter was not to consider which, of the four of them, is the gravest (although reasons why core crimes are the most serious crimes of concern to the international community were provided) or the eldest but to elicit definitional precision in view of the forthcoming two Parts which shall constitute the main thrust of this work. Notwithstanding the fact that a general understanding may be traced to the effect that, hierarchically, core crimes are the gravest of such crimes, there are yet another two reasons in support of my choice to avoid any classification in terms of gravity of these above mentioned four types of crimes. The above has shown that a crime can simultaneously be a core crime and a domestic crime, as a result of which

globe. Such statistics may be viewed at http://www.imo.org/KnowledgeCentre/ShipsAndShippingFactsAndFigures/Statisticalresources/Piracy/Pages/default.aspx. Accessed 24 October 2018].

131 Micallef 1991, pp. 65–66.

132 Luban 2011ab, p. 629.

133 See Sect. 5.1.

134 See the joint Romanian-Spanish initiative which was discussed by Asser Institute throughout an event which was reported in Pantaleo and Ribbelink 2016.

distinguishing between the two is less relevant than distinguishing between a core crime and a transnational organized crime, although (with regard to some crimes such as trafficking in human beings and terrorism) a fine and thin line divides these two species of crime. International crimes may be considered as the species most akin to core crimes but they do not possess contextual elements.

What is imperative is to understand the features and characteristics of core crimes in order to ground and develop underlying assumptions further to which the two main systems of enforcement (the vertical and the horizontal systems) can be now analysed by undergoing a stress test which will determine the extent to which they can be resilient amidst fragile cooperation frameworks which increasingly require more robust cooperation devices. Without understanding the dynamics of core crimes the legal limbo will persist since the focus on the establishment of special devices, methods and mechanisms would vanish into thin air. It is the understanding of these special devices, methods and mechanisms which I shall now embark upon.

References

Additional Protocol I (1977) Protocol Additional to the Geneva Conventions of 12 August 1949, and relating to the Protection of Victims of International Armed Conflicts, 8 June 1977

Alì A (2013) The Relevance of International Humanitarian Law in National Case Law on Terrorism. In: Pocar F, Pedrazzi M, Frulli M (eds) War Crimes and the Conduct of Hostilities: Challenges to Adjudication and Investigation. EE, Cheltenham, UK/Northampton, MA, USA, pp. 293–310

Ambos K (2007) Prosecuting International Crimes at the National and International Level: Between Justice and Realpolitik. In: Kaleck W, Ratner M, Singelnstein T, Weiss P (eds) International Prosecution of Human Rights Crimes. Springer, Berlin/Heidelberg, pp. 55–68

Ambos K (2011) Judicial Creativity at the Special Tribunal for Lebanon: Is There a Crime of Terrorism under International Law? LJIL 24(3):655–675

Bantekas I, Oette L (2016) International Human Rights Law and Practice, 2nd edn. CUP, Cambridge

Bassiouni MC (1974) An Appraisal of the Growth and Developing Trends of International Criminal Law. *RIDP* 45:405–433

Bassiouni MC (1999) The Sources and Content of International Criminal Law: A Theoretical Framework. In: Bassiouni MC (ed) International Criminal Law: Crime, Vol. 1, 2nd edn. TP, Ardsley, NY, pp. 3–125

Bassiouni MC, Vetere E (1998) Towards Understanding Organized Crime and its Transnational Manifestations. In: Bassiouni MC, Vetere E (eds) Organized Crime: A Compilation of UN Documents, 1975–1998. MNP, Leiden/Boston, pp. xxvii–xlix

Bellal A (2017) ICRC Commentary of Common Article 3: Some Questions Relating to Organized Armed Groups and the Applicability of IHL. EJIL: Talk! https://www.ejiltalk.org/icrc-commentary-of-common-article-3-some-questions-relating-to-organized-armed-groups-and-the-applicability-of-ihl/. Accessed 16 October 2018

Bergsmo M (2010) Criteria for Prioritizing and Selecting Core International Crimes Cases. Forum for International Criminal and Humanitarian Law, Publication Series, 2nd edn. TOAEP, Oslo

Boister N (2003) Transnational Criminal Law? EJIL 14(5):953–976

Boister N (2012a) An Introduction to Transnational Criminal Law. OUP, Oxford

Boister N (2012b) International Tribunals for Transnational Crimes: Towards a Transnational Criminal Court? CLF 23(4):295–318
Boister N (2016) The Cooperation Provisions of the UN Convention Against Transnational Organised Crime: A 'Toolbox' Rarely Used? ICLR 16(1):39–70
Cassese A (2001) Terrorism is Also Disrupting Some Crucial Legal Categories of International Law. EJIL 12(5):993–1001
Cassese A (2006) The Multifaceted Criminal Notion of Terrorism in International Law. JICJ 4 (5):933–958
Cassese A, Gaeta P, Baig L, Fan M, Gosnell C, Whiting A (2013) Cassese's International Criminal Law. OUP, Oxford
CAT (1984) Convention Against Torture and Other Cruel, Inhuman or Degrading Treatment or Punishment
Clark RS (2015) Jurisdiction Over Transnational Crime. In: Boister N, Currie RJ (eds) Routledge Handbook of Transnational Criminal Law, Routledge, T & F, pp. 91–106
CoE Convention on Cybercrime (2001)
CoE Convention on Laundering, Search, Seizure and Confiscation of the Proceeds from Crime (1990)
CoE Convention on the Protection of the Environment Through Criminal Law (1998)
Convention Against Corruption (2003)
Convention Against Illicit Traffic in Narcotic Drugs and Psychotropic Substances (1988)
Convention Against the Recruitment, Use, Financing and Training of Mercenaries (1989)
Convention Against the Taking of Hostages (1979)
Convention Against Torture (1984) Convention Against Torture and Other Cruel, Inhuman or Degrading Treatment or Punishment
Convention for the Suppression of Counterfeiting (1929)
Convention for the Suppression of Terrorist Bombings (1997)
Convention for the Suppression of the Financing of Terrorism (1999)
Convention for the Suppression of Unlawful Acts against the Safety of Civil Aviation (1971)
Convention for the Suppression of Unlawful Acts against the Safety of Maritime Navigation and the Protocol for the Suppression of Unlawful Acts against the Safety of Fixed Platforms located on the Continental Shelf (1988)
Convention for the Suppression of Unlawful Seizure of Aircraft (1970)
Convention on Offences and Certain Other Acts Committed on Board Aircraft (1963)
Convention on Psychotropic Substances, the 1980 Convention on the Physical Protection of Nuclear Material (1971)
Convention on the High Seas (1958) Geneva Convention on the High Seas
Convention on the Marking of Plastic Explosives for the Purpose of Detection (1991)
Convention on the Physical Protection of Nuclear Material (1980)
Convention on the Prevention and Punishment of Crimes against Internationally Protected Persons, including Diplomatic Agents (1973)
Convention on the Safety of United Nations and Associated Personnel (1994)
Council Framework Decision on the EAW (2002) Council Framework Decision on the European Arrest Warrant and the Surrender Procedures Between the Member States, Doc. 2002/584/JHA
Crawford E, Pert A (2015) International Humanitarian Law. CUP, Cambridge
Cullen A (2015) The Characterization of Armed Conflict under the Rome Statute. In: Stahn C (ed) The Law and Practice of the International Criminal Court. OUP, Oxford, pp. 762–777
Currie RJ (2014) Reviewing Einarsen T (2012) The Concept of Universal Crimes in International Law. TOAEP, Oslo. In: JICJ 12(1):162–163.
Damgaard C (2008) Individual Criminal Responsibility for Core International Crimes. Springer, Berlin/Heidelberg
de Burca G, Gardner S (1990) The Codification of the Criminal Law. OJLS 10(4):559–571
de Than C, Shorts E (2003) International Criminal Law and Human Rights, 1st edn. S & M, London

DiFilippo M (2008) Terrorist Crimes and International Co-operation: Critical Remarks on the Definition and Inclusion of Terrorism in the Category of International Crimes. EJIL 19(3):533–570

Dimitrijevic V (2003) Terrorism and Human Rights After 2001. In: Bergsmo M (ed) Human Rights and Criminal Justice for the Downtrodden: Essays in Honour of Asbjorn Eide. MNP, Dordrecht/Boston/London, pp. 603–620

Draft Code of Crimes Against the Peace and Security of Mankind (1996)

Duffy H (2013) Harmony or Conflict? The Interplay Between Human Rights and Humanitarian Law in the Fight Against Terrorism. In: van den Herik L, Schrijver N (eds) Counter-Terrorism Strategies in a Fragmented International Legal Order: Meeting the Challenges. CUP, Cambridge, pp. 482–526

Einarsen T (2012) The Concept of Universal Crimes in International Law. TOAEP, Oslo

European Convention on the Suppression of Terrorism (1977)

Fijnaut C (2000) Transnational Crime and the Role of the United Nations, in its Containment Through International Cooperation: A Challenge for the 21st Century. EJCCLCJ 8(2):119–127

Findlay M, Hanif N (2013) International Conventions and the Failure to a Transnational Approach to Controlling Crime Business. ICLR 13(3):697–724

Fletcher GP (2006) Responding to Terrorism: The Quest for a Legal Definition: The Indefinable Concept of Terrorism. JICJ 4(5):894–911

Gaeta P (2009) International Criminalization of Prohibited Conduct. In: Cassese A (ed) The Oxford Companion to International Criminal Justice. OUP, Oxford, pp. 63–74

Garner BA (2004) Black's Law Dictionary, 8th edn. Thomson West, Saint Paul, Minnesota, USA

Garraway C (2013) Armed Conflict and Terrorist Organizations. In: van den Herik L, Schrijver N (eds) Counter-Terrorism Strategies in a Fragmented International Legal Order: Meeting the Challenges. CUP, Cambridge, pp. 425–453

Geneva Convention (1949a) Geneva Convention (I) for the Amelioration of the Condition of the Wounded and Sick in Armed Forces in the Field

Geneva Convention (1949b) Geneva Convention (II) for the Amelioration of the Condition of the Wounded, Sick and Shipwrecked Members of Armed Forces at Sea

Geneva Convention (1949c) Geneva Convention (III) relative to the Treatment of Prisoners of War

Geneva Convention (1949d) Geneva Convention (IV) relative to the Protection of Civilian Persons in Time of War

Genocide Convention (1948) Convention on the Prevention and Punishment of the Crime of Genocide

Gillett M, Schuster M (2011) Fast-Track Justice: The Special Tribunal for Lebanon Defines Terrorism. JICJ 9(5):989–1020

Golash D (2010) The Justification of Punishment in the International Context. In: May L, Hoskins Z (eds) International Criminal Law and Philosophy. ASIL Studies in International Legal Theory, CUP, Cambridge, pp. 201–223

Grover L (2014) Interpreting Crimes in the Rome Statute of the International Criminal Court. CUP, Cambridge

Heller KJ (2015) Supranational Criminal Law Lecture held at Asser Institute. https://www.youtube.com/watch?v=GZ3t_tlPsWg. Accessed 19 March 2018

Heller KJ, Dubber MD (2011) Introduction: Comparative Criminal Law In: Heller KJ, Dubber MD (eds) The Handbook of Comparative Criminal Law. SUP, Stanford, California, USA, pp. 1-11

Hmoud M (2006) Countering Terrorism on a Global Scale: Negotiating the Draft Comprehensive Convention on International Terrorism: Major Bones of Contention. JICJ 4(5):1031–1043

ICC Statute (1998) Rome Statute of the International Criminal Court

ICRC (2011) International Humanitarian Law and Terrorism: Questions and Answers. www.icrc.org/web/eng/siteeng0.nsf/htmlall/terrorism-faq-050504?opendocument≠a3. Accessed 1 November 2018

Inter-American Convention Against Terrorism (2002)

Jørgensen NHB (2000) The Responsibility of States for International Crimes. Oxford Monographs in International Law. OUP, Oxford

Karim S (2011) Is There an International Obligation to Prosecute Pirates? NILR 58(3):387–407
Kjeldgaard-Pedersen A (2015) What Defines an International Criminal Court? A Critical Assessment of "the Involvement of the International Community" as a Deciding Factor. LJIL 28(1):113–131
Kolb R (2009) International Humanitarian Law and Its Implementation by the Court. In Doria J, Gasser H-P, Bassiouni MC (eds) International Humanitarian Law Series: The Legal Regime of the International Criminal Court: Essays in Honour of Professor Igor Blishchenko, MNP, Leiden/Boston, pp. 1015–1038
Kolb R (2014) Advanced Introduction to International Humanitarian Law. Elgar Advanced Introductions, EE, Cheltenham, UK/Northampton, MA, USA
Kroll C (2007) Speech at UNODC by the Global Coordinator for HIV/AIDS http://www.unodc.org/unodc/en/hiv-aids/what-is-being-done.html. Accessed 9 January 2011
Kulyk MZ (2016) Piracy, Hijacking and Armed Robbery Against Ships. In: Attard D (general ed), Fitzmaurice M, Martinez Gutierrez NA, Hamza R (eds) The IMLI Manual of International Maritime Law, Vol. III, Marine Environmental Law and Maritime Security Law. IMO International Maritime Law Institute, Malta. OUP, Oxford, pp. 387–413
Lee W-C (2010) International Crimes and Universal Jurisdiction. In: May L, Hoskins Z (eds) International Criminal Law and Philosophy. ASIL Studies in International Legal Theory, CUP, Cambridge, pp. 15–38
Luban D (2011a) Hannah Ardent as a Theorist of International Criminal Law. ICLR 11(3):621–641
Luban D (2011b) State Criminality and the Ambition of International Criminal Law. In: Isaacs T and Vernon R (eds) Accountability for Collective Wrongdoing. CUP, Cambridge, pp. 61–91
Luban D, O'Sullivan JR, Stewart DP (2010) International and Transnational Criminal Law. WK, Alphen aan den Rijn, The Netherlands
Malicious Damage Act (1861) Chapter 97, Law of Sierra Leone
Mallia P (2010) Migrant Smuggling By Sea: Combating a Current Threat to Maritime Security Through the Creation of a Cooperative Framework. MNP, Boston/Leiden
Manufacturing Protocol (2001) Protocol against the Illicit Manufacturing of and Trafficking in Firearms, Their Parts and Components and Ammunition, supplementing the United Nations Convention against Transnational Organized Crime
Marchuk I (2014) The Fundamental Concept of Crime in International Law: A Comparative Law Analysis. Springer, Berlin/Heidelberg
Martin C (2013) Terrorism as a Crime in International and Domestic Law: Open Issues. In: van den Herik L, Schrijver N (eds) Counter-Terrorism Strategies in a Fragmented International Legal Order: Meeting the Challenges. CUP, Cambridge, pp. 639–666
May L, Hoskins Z (2010) Introduction. In: May L, Hoskins Z (eds) International Criminal Law and Philosophy. ASIL Studies in International Legal Theory, CUP, Cambridge, pp. 1–12
Meyrowitz H (1970) *Le Principe de l'Égalité des Belligérants Devant le Droit de la Guerre*. Pedone, Paris
Micallef AE (1991) The Criminal Offence in International Law. Thesis defended before the London School of Economics and Political Science for the Conferment of the Degree of Doctor of Philosophy (Ph.D.) in International Law. http://etheses.lse.ac.uk/1179/1/U048646.pdf. Accessed 25 July 2011
Milanović M (2011) Is the Rome Statute Binding on Individuals? (And Why Should We Care). JICJ 9(1):25–52
Militello V (2015) Transnational Organized Crime and European Union: Aspects and Problems. In: Ruggeri S (ed) Human Rights in European Criminal Law: New Developments in European Legislation and Case Law After the Lisbon Treaty. Springer, Berlin/Heidelberg, pp. 201–214
Mueller GOW (2001) Transnational Crime: Definitions and Concepts in "Combating Transnational Crime". In: Williams P, Vlassis D (eds) Combating Transnational Crime: Concepts, Activities and Responses. Frank Cass, London/Portland, Oregon, pp. 13–21
Nollkaemper A (2009) Introduction. In: Nollkaemper A, van der Wilt H (eds) System Criminality in International Law. CUP, Cambridge, pp. 1–25

Nyamuya Maogoto J (2016) Taming Westphalian Sovereignty: International Penal Process and the Expansion of Universal Jurisdiction. In: Petrovic J (ed) Accountability for Violations of International Humanitarian Law: Essays in Honour of Jim McCormack. Routledge, T & F, Milton Park, Abingdon, pp. 26–52

O'Keefe R (2015) International Criminal Law. OUP, Oxford

Obokata T (2005) Trafficking of Human Beings as a Crime Against Humanity: Some Implications for the International Legal System. ICLQ 54(2):445–457

Obokata T (2010) Transnational Organised Crime in International Law, Studies in International and Comparative Criminal Law: Volume 5. HP, Bloomsbury

Pakos N (2003) International Crimes. Ashgate, Farnham, Surrey, UK

Pantaleo L, Ribbelink O (2016) The Establishment of a Special Court Against Terrorism. EJIL: Talk! http://www.ejiltalk.org/the-establishment-of-a-special-court-against-terrorism/. Accessed 21 November 2017

Prevention of Cruelty to Children Act (1926) Chapter 31, Law of Sierra Leone

Protocol for the Suppression of Unlawful Acts of Violence at Airports Serving International Civil Aviation (1988)

Protocol Supplementing the European Convention on the Suppression of Terrorism (2003)

Ristroph A (2012) Criminal Law for Humans. In: Dyzenhaus D, Poole T (eds) Hobbes and the Law. CUP, Cambridge

Schabas WA (2008) International Crimes. In: Armstrong D (ed) Routledge Handbook of International Law. Routledge International Handbooks, Routledge, T & F, Milton Park, Abingdon, pp. 268–280

Schloenhardt A (2008) Transnational Organized Crime and International Criminal Law. In Bassiouni MC (ed) International Criminal Law: Sources, Subjects, and Contents, Vol. 1, 3rd edn. MNP, Leiden/Boston, pp. 939–962

Schuerch RJ (2016) The International Criminal Court at the Mercy of Powerful States: How the Rome Statute Promotes Legal Neo-Colonialism. Thesis defended before the Faculty of Law, *UvA*, Amsterdam, for the Conferment of the Degree of Doctor of Philosophy (Ph.D.)

Siller N (2016) Modern Slavery: Does International Law Distinguish Between Slavery, Enslavement and Trafficking?' JICJ 14(2):405–427

Single Convention on Narcotic Drugs (1961)

Slomanson WR (2011) Fundamental Perspectives on International Law, 6th edn. Wadsworth Cengage Learning, Boston

Smuggling Protocol (2000) Protocol against the Smuggling of Migrants by Land, Sea and Air, supplementing the United Nations Convention against Transnational Organized Crime

Stessens G (2000) Money Laundering: A New International Law Enforcement. CUP, Cambridge

Tavakoli N (2009) A Crime that Offends the Conscience of Humanity: A Proposal to Reclassify Trafficking in Women as an International Crime. ICLR 9(1):77–98

Tolbert D, Smith LA (2016) Complementarity and the Investigation and Prosecution of Slavery Crimes. JICJ 14(2):429–451

Trafficking Protocol (2000) Protocol to Prevent, Suppress and Punish Trafficking in Persons, Especially Women and Children, supplementing the United Nations Convention against Transnational Organized Crime

UN S-G (2010) Report of the S-G on Possible Options to Further the Aim of Prosecuting and Imprisoning Persons Responsible for Acts of Piracy and Armed Robbery of the Coast of Somalia, Including, in particular, options for Creating Special Domestic Chambers possibly with International Components, a Regional Tribunal or an International Tribunal and Corresponding Imprisonment Arrangements, taking into Account the Work of the Contact Group on Piracy off the Coast of Somalia, the Existing Practice in Establishing International and Mixed Tribunals and the Time and Resources Necessary to Achieve and Sustain Substantive Results. UN Doc. S/2010/394

UNCATOC (2000) UN Convention Against Transnational Organised Crime

UNCLOS (1982) UN Convention on the Law of the Sea

UNGA (2000) Resolution 55/25 (2000), UN Doc. A/RES/55/25

UNSC (2004) Resolution 1566 (2004), UN Doc. S/RES/1566
UNSC (2010) Resolution 1918 (2010), UN Doc. S/RES/1918
UNSC (2011) Resolution 2015 (2011), UN Doc. S/RES/2015
UNSC (2016) Resolution 2316 (2016), UN Doc. SC/12582
USA Department of State (2015) Trafficking in Persons Report. https://www.state.gov/documents/organization/245365.pdf. Accessed 18 March 2016
van der Vyver JD (2010) Prosecuting Terrorism in International Tribunals. EILR 24(2):527–547
van der Wilt (2017) Complementary Jurisdiction (Article 46H). In: Werle G, Vormbaum M (eds) The African Criminal Court: A Commentary on the Malabo Protocol. International Criminal Justice Series, Vol. 10, Asser Press, The Hague, pp. 187–202
van der Wilt H (2008) Equal Standards? On the Dialectics Between National Jurisdictions and the International Criminal Courts. ICLR 8(1):229–272
van der Wilt H (2014) Trafficking in Human Being, Enslavement, Crimes Against Humanity: Unravelling the Concepts. ChJIL 13(2):297–334
van der Wilt H (2015) Self-Referrals as an Indication of the Inability of States to Cope with Non-State Actors. In: Stahn C (ed) The Law and Practice of the International Criminal Court. OUP, Oxford, pp. 210–227
van der Wilt H, Braber I (2015) The Case for Inclusion of Terrorism in the Jurisdiction of the International Criminal Court. In: Mariniello T (ed) The International Criminal Court in Search of its Purpose and Identity. Routledge Research in International law, Routledge, pp. 17–38
van Krieken PJ (2002) Terrorism and the International Legal Order: With Special Reference to the UN, the EU and Cross-Border Aspects. Asser Press, The Hague
Ventura MJ (2011) Terrorism According to the Special Tribunal for Lebanon's Interlocutory Decision on the Applicable Law: A Defining Moment or a Moment of Defining. JICJ 9 (5):1021–1042
Voneky S (2013) Implementation and Enforcement of International Humanitarian Law. In: Fleck D (ed) The Handbook of International Humanitarian Law, 3rd edn. OUP, Oxford, pp. 647–700
Wyler E, Castellanos-Jankiewicz A (2011) State Responsibility and International Crimes. In: Schabas WA, Bernaz N (eds) Routledge Handbook of International Criminal Law. T & F, Milton Park, Abingdon, UK, pp. 385–405

Part III
The Vertical System of Enforcement

Chapter 9
Salient Features of the Vertical System of Enforcement

Contents

9.1 The Meaning of Verticality 148
9.2 Distinguishable Models of the Vertical System of Enforcement 149
9.3 The Line of Demarcation Between a Preference and a Necessity 156
References 160

Abstract Verticality is characterised by the lack of reciprocity. The vertical system of enforcement is the solid platform for the horizontal system of enforcement to rest upon, especially when and if the latter system is ineffective. Surrender and extradition are distinct in character but their effects are similar. Yet, whereas the *corpus juris* of extradition generally allows an array of grounds for refusal, the vertical system of enforcement limits these. The latter system portrays the internationalized model of criminal justice and encompasses distinguishable fora, namely the ICC, the *ad hoc* tribunals and the hybrid courts and/or tribunals. Part III of this work will focus on the ICC which is the only permanent court in the supra-national system. There subsist three circumstances, being the *Milošević* exception, the UNSC referral and the unfair trial syndrome, which illustrate that the vertical system of enforcement can play a crucial role in the administration of criminal justice. It completes the patchwork even if just one of these above mentioned three circumstances would subsist. The case for its existence is obviously much stronger when the need for two out of the three circumstances subsists. The horizontal system of enforcement, in various circumstances ranging from a lack of political will to investigate and prosecute crimes, to a lack of financial and technical resources necessary to conduct prosecutions, may be divested of the necessary acumen to fight impunity. International prosecutions should have a (qualitatively) precedential and (quantitatively) subsidiary function. International courts/tribunals fulfil a threefold task: prosecution, stimulation and oversight.

C. Soler, *The Global Prosecution of Core Crimes under International Law*,
https://doi.org/10.1007/978-94-6265-335-1_9

Keywords Verticality · Frame of reference · Surrender · Extradition · Hybrid courts · Community of courts · Complementarity · Subsidiarity · Cooperation · Unwillingness · Inability · *Aut dedere aut judicare* · UNSC resolution · Referral · *Milošević* exception · Unfair trial · ICC

To begin with I shall examine the distinguishing characteristics of the vertical system of enforcement. This exercise will be undertaken by analysing the true meaning of verticality, by delimiting the field of application of the vertical system of enforcement and by identifying instances when such system becomes necessary, rather than merely desirable. By undertaking such process, the utility of the vertical system of enforcement, already referred to within the Sect. 2.1, will be reiterated.

9.1 The Meaning of Verticality

To deal with the vertical system of enforcement, one must first understand the concept of verticality *per se*. A definition of verticality can be traced in the communitarian regime of EU Law, which defines the 'co-operation between national authorities and the Commission' as vertical[1] co-operation.[2] The clearest demonstration of verticality is the power of the 'international court to compel the rendering of co-operation under pain of sanction'.[3] In fact, Göran Sluiter regards the role of the requesting tribunal/court as final arbiter over cooperation disputes as 'the unique and most prominent feature of the vertical cooperation regime'.[4] The German Federal Constitutional Court described vertical interdependence as a cooperative relationship in which both courts are engaged in a similar enterprise, but in which the ECJ has responsibility for the entire area of the Community.[5] The ICTY Trial Chamber, examining its vertical relationship with UN member States, held that its status 'as an enforcement measure under Chapter VII' meant that 'sovereignty by definition cannot play the same role'.[6] The primacy over national courts and the ability to issue binding orders to States also reflected that the ICTY State cooperation regime was a vertical one.[7] The effect of this primacy firstly entails a State obligation to cooperate. It further connotes that the *ad hoc* tribunals, by virtue of

---

1 The term 'supranational' is also, at times, used inter-changeably (Sluiter 2003, p. 611).

2 Klip 2009, p. 354.

3 Rastan 2008, p. 435.

4 Sluiter 2008, p. 875, n. 12.

5 German Federal Constitutional Court, *Solange II*, Order, 22 October 1986, 2 BvR 197/83, *BVerfGE* 73, 339 (387), cited in Burke-White 2002, p. 91.

6 ICTY Trial Chamber II, *Prosecutor v Dragan Nikolić, Decision on Defence Motion Challenging the Exercise of Jurisdiction by the Tribunal*, 9 October 2002, IT-94-2-PT, para 100.

7 ICTY Appeals Chamber, *Prosecutor v Tihomir Blaškić, ICTY Appeals Chamber Judgment on the Request of the Republic of Croatia for Review of the Decision of the Trial Chamber II of 18*

their own statutory provisions, may formally request States to defer to the competence of such *ad hoc* tribunals.[8] In principle, 'by ratifying the Statute, in particular by accepting Article 119 of the ICC Statute State parties have granted the authority to decide on the interpretation of the extent of the duty to cooperate to the requesting side, namely the ICC'.[9] This compulsory dispute settlement mechanism is yet another salient feature of the vertical system of enforcement.[10] It is imperative to ask 'what distinguishes the vertical system of enforcement from the horizontal system of enforcement of international criminal law?' A basic distinction is self-evident. Whereas the former constitutes a supra-national system wherein the ICC and the requested State are stakeholders, the latter is premised upon State sovereignty, as a result of which *par in parem non habet imperium*,[11] and upon reciprocity. The lack of such reciprocity, *per se*, is a major and salient feature of the vertical system of enforcement,[12] the surrender law of which is still at an evolutionary stage.[13] Other salient features of the vertical system of enforcement are the scope of the State duty to cooperate and the unilateral model of dispute settlement.[14]

9.2 Distinguishable Models of the Vertical System of Enforcement

In primis, it must be stated that an analysis of the relevant legal provisions of the ICC Statute does not constitute the ultimate purpose neither of this Part nor of this book, in its entirety. This analysis will only be undertaken in so far as, and in as much as, it may shed a light or have a consequence on the horizontal system of enforcement as a model of cooperation.[15] This is because, as stated within the first Part of this book, the global prosecution of core crimes under international law, is predominantly ensured horizontally. Therefore, Chaps. 10 and 11 are intended to

July 1997, 29 October 1997, Case No. IT-95-14-AR 108*bis*, para 47, cited in Den-Racsmany 2007, p. 176.

8 Ryngaert 2013, p. 128.

9 Sluiter 2009, p. 191.

10 Ibid.

11 An equal has no power over an equal.

12 Sluiter 2009, p. 190; Sluiter 2003, p. 613.

13 Knoops 2002, p. 90.

14 Stahn 2010, p. 663.

15 Whereas the horizontal system of enforcement is often referred to as an interstate model of cooperation, the vertical system of cooperation is also referred to as the supranational model of cooperation (Swart and Sluiter 1999, p. 98).

provide a frame of reference[16] for the forthcoming Part which focuses on the horizontal system of enforcement. This is also consonant with the general perception that 'verticality is typically associated with effectiveness, whilst horizontalism is perceived as weakness'.[17] It is also true physically, or rather, visually. It thus stands to reason that the vertical system of enforcement can provide a frame of reference for the horizontal system of enforcement, rather than vice-versa. The vertical system of enforcement is the solid platform for the horizontal system of enforcement to rest upon, especially when and if the horizontal system of enforcement is ineffective. Carsten Stahn goes as far as arguing that, although perceived as weaker than the pure vertical model of cooperation (exemplified by the *ad hoc* tribunals), 'the ICC regime is, to some extent, more nuanced and receptive to long-term systemic change', and consequently stronger than meets the eye.[18] The nature and functions of the ICC system of cooperation shall be examined shortly in Chap. 10.

Whereas the *corpus juris* of extradition generally allows an array of grounds for refusal, the vertical system of enforcement restricts these. In fact, differences exist in relation to the actual consequences of the entire process leading to the subjection of an individual before a court or tribunal. Whereas, for example, Articles 29 and 28 of the ICTY and the ICTR Statutes respectively preclude States from advancing human rights challenges to surrender within the vertical system of enforcement, the same preclusion does not subsist within the horizontal system of enforcement. Therefore, the terminological divergences between surrender and extradition also subsist when one adopts such a consequentialist approach. Similarly, whereas various conditions may be imposed by the requested State within the extradition process, surrender under the vertical system of enforcement may only be made subject to some conditions. In other words, whereas extradition can largely depend upon the fulfilment of a unilateral demand by the requested State, such as for example, the non-execution of the death penalty if the extraditable offence is one subject to the capital punishment, more than a mere demand for an assurance would have to be brought to justify the refusal of surrender. Jurists, such as Bert Swart,

---

[16] In truth, in and of itself, the vertical system of enforcement constitutes a frame of reference also *inter se*. Kimberly Prost, for example, assessing the benefits that the ICC may draw from the ICTY, states that the 'strongest contribution from the ICTY experience may ultimately come from the mistakes made and lessons learned in the development of the relationship between the States and the Tribunal and the co-operation regime' (Prost 2011, p. 468). In a more positive tone, Alexander Zahar and Goran Sluiter argue that the ICTY jurisprudence 'served as an important precedent for shaping the cooperation regime of the ICC' (Zahar and Sluiter 2008, p. 459) whereas Bert Swart and Goran Sluiter felt that 'the main weakness of Part 9 of the Statute lies in the fact that not enough lessons have been drawn from the ICTY's experience' (Swart and Sluiter 1999, p. 126). This should not be construed to convey the exclusion of the contrary. As Ken Roberts noted, 'there would appear to be an emerging symbiotic relationship between the two institutions in which the permanent court is also likely to exert influence upon the ICTY' (Roberts 2001, p. 560).

[17] Kreß et al. 2008, p. 1509.

[18] Stahn 2010, p. 666.

have admitted that there exist several weighty arguments as to why the handing over of a person to an international judicial body, including the ICC, 'should not be subjected to the same restrictions and conditions and should not be decided upon in conformity with the same procedural rules as are standard in ordinary extradition cases',[19] referring to this achievement as a major merit of the ICC Statute and motivating its distinct categorisation as 'surrender', as opposed to 'extradition'. Some, including Bert Swart,[20] have opined that the codification of the obligation to surrender upon States is the 'major achievement of the Statute'[21] since such obligation cannot result from customary international law.

Surrender and extradition are distinct in character[22] though their effects are similar.[23] Claus Kreß and Kimberly Prost uphold that the terminological distinction should, 'as was the underlying thinking, at the same time contribute to a growing awareness on the national level for the substantial differences between horizontal and vertical cooperation'.[24] The distinction has been sanctioned conventionally[25] and has also been domesticated (nationalized/localized).[26] In fact, it has been held that 'cooperation is an obligatory consequence of extradition in view of its end result, namely surrender of the accused'.[27] This is why the surrender of suspects is considered to be 'the most important form of assistance',[28] revealing that jurisdiction and cooperation cannot be simply detached from one another.[29] The conceptual difference between these terms stems from the very nature of the normative frameworks within which they function. Surrender, commonly also referred to as 'transfer' especially in the context of ICTY and ICTR, entails the physical and actual delivery of a person to the ICC and, in a more general context, may be said to

---

[19] See such arguments in Swart 2002, pp. 1679–1686.

[20] Swart and Sluiter 1999, p. 98.

[21] Swart 2002, p. 1701.

[22] ECtHR Fourth Section, *Mladen Naletilić v Croatia, Decision as to the Admissibility of the Application*, 4 May 2000, Application No. 51891/99. Important distinctive traits can also be traced in the communitarian regime of the EAW (Klimek 2015, pp. 311–321).

[23] To assess the prevailing terminological distinctions, see Swart 2002, pp. 1678–1680.

[24] Kreß and Prost 2008, pp. 1645–1646.

[25] Article 102 of the ICC Statute (1998) Rome Statute of the International Criminal Court.

[26] See, for example, the replacement of the term 'extradition' (*Ueberstellung*) by 'surrender' (*Auslieferung*) in the German Law to Implement the Rome Statute of the ICC of 17 July 1998 [*Entwurfeines Gesetzeszur Ausfuehrung des Roemischen Statuts des Internationalen Strafgerichtshofes vom 17 Juli 1998*] {Draft Act Implementing the Rome Statute for the International Criminal Court of 17 July 1998}, Act Amending the Basic Law (Federal Law Gazette 2000, I 1633) 29 November 2000, and also Canada's Amendment to the Extradition Act 1999 (2005) Amendments to the 1999 Extradition Act (Statutes of Canada 1999, c.18), 19 July 2005, particularly its Chap. 18, in order to incorporate surrender to the ICC (see Bekou and Shah 2006, p. 526).

[27] Knoops 2002, p. 16.

[28] Godinho 2003, p. 502.

[29] It is not surprising that some major works in the field refer to both terms within their title, their subject-matter (see, *inter alia*, Kaul and Kreß 1999, *passim*).

presuppose that the vertical system of enforcement is exercising its functions by virtue of either of the following *sui generis* regimes:

(a) the ICC;
(b) the ICTY and the ICTR, both of which are hereinafter being jointly referred to as 'the *ad hoc* tribunals'; and
(c) the hybrid[30] courts and/or tribunals,[31]

all of which cumulatively elucidate the proliferation of international criminal tribunals.[32] This juxtaposition is shared by Carsten Stahn and Larissa van den Herik who refer to three models of international criminal justice: *ad hoc* justice, hybrid courts, and the ICC Statute.[33] In relation to the hybrid courts and/or tribunals, however, one must note that the SCSL, the STL, the ECCC and the ETSPSC should not be regarded as international justice systems since the duty to cooperate is generally confined to the *locus delicti commissi* (the State where the crimes were committed).[34] This is predominantly because the pretext to such tribunals, unlike the pretext to the *ad hoc* tribunals, is not a resolution of the UNSC. For the purposes of this work, such hybrid courts [sometimes referred to as internationalized criminal tribunals] are being considered within the parameters of the vertical system of enforcement, although (just like the ICC) they contain features and characteristics of the horizontal system of enforcement. They hence exemplify the overlap between the vertical and the horizontal systems of enforcement. Such tribunals fall within the rubric of the vertical system of enforcement particularly because such courts/tribunals make use of international judges, international jurisprudence, international resources, and were financed by the UN itself. To this extent, they form part of the internationalized model of criminal justice. My decision to categorise hybrid courts within the parameters of the vertical system of enforcement is also supported jurisprudentially and in legal literature. The Appeals Chamber of the SCSL held, in no unclear terms, that 'there is no reason to conclude that the Special Court should be treated as anything other than an international tribunal or court'.[35] Their belonging to the remit of the vertical system of enforcement is also reminiscent of the fact that they are habitually categorized either as semi-internationalized

---

[30] These have also been called, *inter alia*, mixed courts and/or tribunals (Nouwen 2006, p. 192).

[31] See Chap. 3.

[32] A similar, though not quite marked, proliferation may be traced within the horizontal system of enforcement. Alternative mechanisms such as *gacaca* trials in Rwanda (Werle 2009, pp. 111–113), and the very extra-ordinary *Pan Am 103* tribunal, being the *Camp Zeist* court, which tried the *Lockerbie* suspects under Scottish Law (Scharf 2008, pp. 521–527) will be referred to within Part IV.

[33] Stahn and van den Herik 2012, cited in van Sliedregt 2012, p. 848.

[34] Sluiter 2009, p. 189.

[35] SCSL Appeals Chamber, *Prosecutor v Charles Ghankay Taylor, Decision on Immunity from Jurisdiction*, 31 May 2004, Case No. SCSL-2003-01-I, para 41(d). For a concise analysis of the *Charles Taylor* case, see Jalloh 2016, pp. 312–332.

tribunals[36] or as sibling tribunals.[37] Recourse to and use of *dicta* of these courts/tribunals to determine the theoretical and doctrinal contours of cooperation within the system of enforcement in international criminal law will therefore occasionally be made within this Part dealing with the vertical system of enforcement, rather than in the next Part dealing with the horizontal system of enforcement. The hybrid nature of such courts is not a coincidence. It goes to reflect the inter-dependence and inter-connection between the vertical system of enforcement and the horizontal system of enforcement, exemplifying the overlap between both systems of enforcement. These elements are sufficiently notable and have led jurists to describe the courts comprising the emerging system of international criminal law enforcement as 'interactive'.[38] It has also been stated that the current system, comprising the vertical system of enforcement and the horizontal system of enforcement, constitutes a network which is referred to as a 'community of courts'.[39] This network engenders overlapping jurisdictions which are mutually supportive and dependent, intersecting each other. In fact, 'international courts are also interpreting, applying, and developing the same legal principles'.[40] These jurisdictions are hence linked both vertically and horizontally, and apply a common set of laws. This inevitable link, crystallized in practice by means of the exchange of information, ideas and personnel, solidifies the international system of enforcement, rendering it significantly global and far-reaching. Such power emanates from the core principle of subsidiarity and the fluid, dynamic concept of complementarity[41] which 'hinges on the presence of actual investigations or prosecutions, not prospective ones'.[42]

Although, as has been shown in Sect. 2.1, significant differences can be traced within (and between) the above vertical systems of enforcement,[43] their common denominator is the inapplicability of the horizontal system of enforcement,[44] that is, of inter-state cooperation.[45] Unlike the vertical system of enforcement, the horizontal system of enforcement depends exclusively upon cooperation between one State and another, which cooperation, in the context of core crimes, is mirrored by the *aut dedere aut judicare* rule of customary international law.[46] This rule has been

---

[36] Burke-White 2002, p. 5.

[37] O'Callaghan 2008, p. 536.

[38] Burke-White 2002, p. 75.

[39] Burke-White 2002, p. 3.

[40] Webb 2013, p. 8.

[41] Stahn 2015, p. 230.

[42] Sriram and Brown 2012, p. 229.

[43] These comprise the ICC, the *ad hoc* tribunals and the hybrid courts/tribunals.

[44] The major consequence of this is the inapplicability (be it complete or partial) of the traditional grounds for refusal (Sluiter 2009, p. 190).

[45] On the other hand, within the supranational co-operation model, the vertical system of enforcement, 'the unconditional and absolute character of the duty to co-operate' subsists (Swart and Sluiter 1999, p. 98).

[46] In the realm of State cooperation, besides mandatory rules, discretionary networks created by means of an inter-governmental initiative, such as Justice Rapid Response, are intended to

deemed to constitute 'the basis of international criminal law enforcement'.[47] Therefore, whereas extradition[48] follows a process of cooperation[49] between States, surrender follows a process of cooperation not between States but between a State and either of the above mentioned international judicial institutions.

It stands to reason that the attainment of such cooperation is the ICC's major challenge. The previous Part has shown how core crimes are generally committed with the connivance of State power. It is therefore not surprising at all that 'the very nature of international crimes, which are crimes of State as much as crimes of individuals, makes it likely that the Court will regularly have to deal with national authorities who have every interest in frustrating and obstructing ongoing investigations'.[50] To complicate matters, cooperation requests may become a sensitive matter especially when they 'involve evidence controlled by the said States that originates in the area of the secret service or intelligence authorities'.[51] Such cooperation is of the essence since the ICC, a nascent court, has no sovereign powers on any territory, nor does it have any autonomous enforcement capacity. It is constrained to rely exclusively upon State cooperation. Similarly, 'without state cooperation, the work of the Tribunal would be rendered impossible'.[52] The extent to which the inverse could be true is a matter which is being given some attention within legal literature. The Belgian Government has, before the ICTR, submitted that the duty of cooperation is not one-sided, but necessarily reciprocal, and hence *ad hoc* Tribunals must cooperate with States too.[53] This is termed 'reverse cooperation'[54] and actually happens with an eye to boosting positive complementarity.[55]

---

facilitate the expeditious exchange of information and the proper conduct of full-scale investigations [http://www.justicerapidresponse.org/. Accessed 25 October 2018].

47 Gamarra and Vicente 2008, p. 630.

48 In the USA, the term 'interstate rendition' is used to refer to extradition.

49 Cooperation may also be obtained by means of the information and support directly provided by non-State actors, such as international or inter-governmental organizations and civil society. Such information and support may include the relocation of witnesses, provision for support services for the purposes of witness protection, monitoring of the conditions of detention of prisoners, general supervision of sentence enforcement, and the release from the custody of the ICC.

50 Swart and Sluiter 1999, p. 126.

51 Wenqi 2006, p. 100.

52 ICTR Appeals Chamber, *Jean Bosco Barayagwiza v Prosecutor, Decision on the Prosecutor's Request for Review or Reconsideration*, Declaration by Judge Rafael Nieto-Navia, 31 March 2000, Case No. ICTR-97-19AR72, para 4.

53 ICTR Trial Chamber I, *Prosecutor v Bernard Ntuyahaga, Decision on the Prosecutor's Motion to Withdraw the Indictment*, 18 March 1999, Case No. ICTR-98-40-T, sub-title 1. The judgment has no paragraphs.

54 Gioia 2011, p. 807.

55 Positive complementarity is referred to by Burke-White as 'pro-active complementarity' (Owuor 2014, p. 31) and is a tool to promote national proceedings (see Sriram and Brown 2012, p. 229). If abused by States which delay matters by establishing tribunals (which turn out to be sham tribunals) with great fanfare, and which enact seriously flawed legislation, it can lead to what Christopher Keith Hall calls 'perverse complementarity' (Hall 2010, p. 1034).

Positive complementarity relates to the ways how international assistance can be directed towards the strengthening of national jurisdictions in the investigation and prosecution of core crimes[56] and in the restoration of justice systems capable of protecting human rights.[57] It assists domestic criminal justice systems to bring criminal justice home, close to comfort. Various measures can be adopted at national level to combat unwillingness and/or inability. These include legislative assistance, strengthening specialized police investigation and prosecutorial services skills, training and capacity development, victim support and witness protection, public outreach and communications, legal aid services, strengthening forensic capacities, documentation and archives, reparation programmes, establishing channels of communication and cooperation with courts, together with erecting physical infrastructures.[58] In the absence of such domestic measures, the ICC will continue to play a role in the overall enforcement of international criminal law. The ICC furnishes cooperation to States in the following three ways:

(a) in terms of Article 93(1) of the ICC Statute, the Prosecutor can share documents gathered in the course of her investigation;
(b) The OTP policy papers support the sharing of best practices; and
(c) ICC Legal Tools,[59] consisting of a database of basic information, are made available to judicial institutions willing to prosecute core crimes. The latter method assists States in ensuring fair trials at a domestic level,[60] which assistance is also offered to non-State Parties.[61]

In the above scenario the vertical system of enforcement assists and provides a service to the horizontal system of enforcement. In the words of James Cockayne, 'international cooperation must cut both ways'.[62] In fact, 'lack of State cooperation on a prosecutor's side can have an impact on the outcome of a case as well'.[63] The ICC Statute seems to recognize this only limitedly and *in partem* since its Article 93(10) confers discretion (not a duty) upon the ICC to cooperate with and provide assistance to State Parties. Owing to the lack of such an explicit obligation, it is correct to conclude that the self-contained ICC cooperation regime,[64] the details

[56] ASP 2012, and ASP 2013, cited in Evenson and Smith 2015, pp. 1273–1274, n. 57.

[57] Seils 2015, p. 327.

[58] UNDP 2012, p. 11.

[59] For a detailed analysis of such ICC Legal Tools, see Bergsmo et al. 2010, pp. 804–808; see also Cohen 2012, p. 1018.

[60] Tillier 2013, pp. 554–555.

[61] Tillier 2013, p. 515.

[62] Cockayne 2004, p. 636.

[63] Wartanian 2005, p. 1301.

[64] Sluiter 2003, p. 631.

of which 'are set out in sixteen complex and delicately worded articles',[65] is modelled in such a way as to deny reciprocity.[66] This contrasts sharply with the horizontal system of enforcement, as stated here above.

9.3 The Line of Demarcation Between a Preference and a Necessity

The mere relevance of the vertical system of enforcement turns into a necessity upon the subsistence of certain external factors, as a result of which the vertical system of enforcement becomes truly indispensable. This is the point at which the vertical system of enforcement becomes a system that really matters. Therefore, in the light of the relative primacy of the horizontal system of enforcement, which may be considered a residuum of the complementarity principle, I pose, *ab initio*, the following questions: (i) why is the vertical system of enforcement required in the first place and why can the international community not do away with it? Additionally, (ii) if we cannot stay without the vertical system of enforcement, when is it that we really need it? The first question has, to a large extent, already been answered in Sect. 2.1. The second question will be addressed now. I identify three distinct and separate circumstances, which are not hierarchically juxtaposed, necessitating the existence of the vertical system of enforcement in its purest form [wherein the competent *forum* is the ICC], the corollary of which is the *a priori* stifling of the horizontal system of enforcement.

(A) Firstly, where a brutal dictator is prosecuted for core crimes, the entire international community will have an interest in making use of the vertical system of enforcement, also because the process of democratization and the reinstatement of regional stability within a post-conflict situation would be seriously jeopardized by *in situ* prosecutions.[67] This first circumstance may be termed as 'the *Milošević* exception'.[68] Here again the term 'exception' portrays the negation of a general rule, being the primary application of the horizontal system of enforcement. A domestic trial, in such case, would entail the risk of reprisals during the period of post-conflict transitional justice. On the other hand, subjecting one's national to an international trial portrays a willingness to waive one's sovereignty, a sense of trust in the international system and an acknowledgment of the gravity of the crimes allegedly committed. It also dispels concerns of domestic unfair trials.

[65] Schabas 2016, p. 1265.
[66] Zahar and Sluiter 2008, p. 460.
[67] Murray 2011, p. 612.
[68] Burke-White 2002, p. 93.

(B) Secondly, one of the three triggering procedures within the vertical system of enforcement involves the referral of a situation by the UNSC.[69] This trigger mechanism, the UNSC Resolution, enables the UNSC to 'occupy a privileged position'[70] in the ICC statutory regime. It has already been availed of twice so far, in accordance with Article 13(b) of the ICC Statute, in relation to the alleged core crimes committed in Darfur and in Libya, on 31 March 2005 by virtue of UNSC Resolution 1593[71] and on 26 February 2011 by virtue of UNSC Resolution 1970[72] respectively. The legal weight of such UNSC Resolutions is considerable particularly because it may be safely argued that non-State Parties to the ICC Statute which are UN Member States are obliged to cooperate with the ICC since the international arrest warrant stems directly from a UNSC Resolution which was made under Chapter VII powers emanating from the UNC itself. Non-State Parties cannot any longer, if they ever could, ignore the ICC Statute.[73] Article 19(2) of the ICC Statute also infers this because it seems to suggest that both jurisdiction and admissibility can be challenged by non-States Parties.[74] I shall come back to this matter later on, within Sect. 10.

(C) Thirdly, there exist circumstances (also duly accepted by Britta Lisa Krings)[75] where, in my view, due process of law[76] is, for all intents and purposes of domestic criminal proceedings, a near-impossibility. This undermines the whole system of enforcement because 'the guarantee of a fair trial and protection of the rights of the accused have paramount importance before the ICC'.[77] Suffice to note, in the context of the vertical system of enforcement, that 'there is inherent jurisdiction to reopen an appeal if a party had been subjected to an unfair procedure'.[78] In a few post-conflict situations wherein a change in

---

[69] For a thorough understanding of such triggering procedures, see Olásolo 2005, pp. 123–126 and 129–137 respectively.

[70] Ralph 2016, p. 645.

[71] UNSC (2005b) Resolution 1593 (2005), UN Doc. S/RES/1593. The USA and China abstained from voting, but did not exercise their veto power. This Resolution, in its second paragraph upholds that Sudan 'shall cooperate fully with and provide any necessary assistance to the Court and the Prosecutor' (UNSC (2005a) Press Release SC/8351, Security Council, 5158th Meeting (Night). http://www.un.org/News/Press/docs/2005/sc8351.doc.htm. Accessed 21 June 2011).

[72] UNSC (2011) Resolution 1970 (2011), UN Doc. S/RES/1970. This resolution was unanimous.

[73] Cryer 2015, p. 280.

[74] Schabas 2010, p. 368.

[75] Krings 2012, p. 763.

[76] For a detailed understanding of the concept of due process and accompanying cases and materials, see Martin et al. 1997, pp. 527–634.

[77] Kirsch 2007, p. 544.

[78] ICTR Appeals Chamber, *Jean Bosco Barayagwiza v Prosecutor, Decision on the Prosecutor's Request for Review or Reconsideration*, Separate Opinion of Judge Shahabuddeen, 31 March 2000, Case No. ICTR-97-19AR72, para 5.

regime has been experienced,[79] where a new or diverse criminal justice system is either emerging or is in its embryonic stages, there subsists what I call 'the unfair trial syndrome', meaning that a fair trial is excludable *ab initio*. By way of example, the conviction *in absentia* of *Saif Al-Islam Gaddafi*, who was condemned to death by firing squad by a Libyan court, was (in the opinion of many human rights groups) anything but fair.[80] The International Commission of Jurists has had no qualms in claiming that the imposition of the death penalty after such an unfair trial also violates the right to life of *Saif Al-Islam Gaddafi*.[81] Yet, it has always been unlikely that the capital punishment would be administered since the Zintanis had anyway shown no intention of handing over *Saif Al-Islam Gaddafi* to the competent authorities, given that Libya had no single government but two waring factions, an internationally-recognized parliament based in Tobruk and the capital (Tripoli) held by rivals Libya Dawn. Instead, for some years, the Zintanis considered *Saif Al-Islam Gaddafi* as a precious political commodity and could have and/or may have used him as a bargaining chip with Libya's newly formed government.[82] This hardly changed when reliable evidence showed that *Saif Al-Islam Gaddafi* was no longer within the custody of Al-Ajami Al-Atiri, Commander of the Abu-Bakr al-Siddiq Battalion in Zintan, but was within the custody of the Zintan Revolutionaries' Military Council.[83] At the time of writing of this book, a mystery still surrounds *Saif Al-Islam Gaddafi* in that his current whereabouts are still unknown to the OTP of the ICC.[84] One can also refer to the trial of Saddam Hussein where 'there are good reasons to criticize the conduct of the trial, in particular the lack of support for defence counsel and the security breaches experienced by them, and the apparent interference with the judicial process by various parts of the Iraqi government'.[85] Notwithstanding the fact that there is no correlation between an unfair trial and either the death penalty *per se* or the death-row phenomenon, the *Dujail* trial[86] was marred, *inter alia*, by various aspects which evidently

[79] The best contemporary example is Libya, where *Saif Al-Islam Gaddafi*'s fate is still unclear.

[80] Stephen C (2015) *Gaddafi*'s son *Saif Al-Islam* Sentenced to Death by Court in Libya, The Guardian. http://www.theguardian.com/world/2015/jul/28/saif-al-islam-sentenced-death-by-court-in-libya-gaddafi-son. Accessed 16 July 2018. See also AI (2015) Flawed Trial of *Al-Gaddafi* Officials Leads to Appalling Death Sentences. https://www.amnesty.org/en/latest/news/2015/07/libya-flawed-trial-of-al-gaddafi-officials/. Accessed 11 January 2016.

[81] Ansbro 2015.

[82] BBC News (2015) Gaddafi Son Sentenced to Death Over War Crimes. http://www.bbc.com/news/world-africa-33688391. Accessed 12 July 2016.

[83] ICC 2017, paras 16 and 17, brought to my attention by the Embassy of the Republic of Malta, Carnegielaan, 4-14, The Hague, The Netherlands.

[84] OTP 2018, para 11. See also Sect. 11.1.1.

[85] Alford 2008, p. 475; see also Ghoshray 2011, p. 11.

[86] This trial, wherein eight persons were accused of crimes against humanity committed as from 1982 onwards, commenced on 19 October 2005.

negated due process of law.[87] The extent, if any, to which the ICC should serve as a supra-national human rights court or otherwise will be examined within Sects. 11.1.1–11.1.3.

At this stage, suffice to mention that these three above mentioned circumstances, being the Milošević exception, the UNSC referral and the unfair trial syndrome, can illustrate, both alternatively and cumulatively, that the vertical system of enforcement cannot be overlooked and that it has been vested with a crucial role to play in the completion of the 'jigsaw puzzle of international criminal law', as I put it. This jigsaw puzzle, which displays various novel and hybrid criminal courts and tribunals, symbolically portrays a see-saw which is pivoted in the middle and which contains the vertical system of enforcement on one side and the horizontal system of enforcement on the other. To put it differently, the vertical system of enforcement would complete the patchwork even if just one of these above mentioned three circumstances would subsist. The case for the vertical system of enforcement is obviously much stronger when the need for two out of the three circumstances subsists. Thus, the horizontal system of enforcement, in various circumstances ranging from a lack of political will to investigate and prosecute crimes, to a lack of financial and technical resources necessary to conduct prosecutions, may be divested of the intuition required to fight impunity. Others have drawn similar conclusions, arguing that 'international prosecutions should have a (qualitatively) precedential and (quantitatively) subsidiary function. Ideally international courts should fulfil a threefold task: prosecution, stimulation, oversight'.[88]

Succinctly, and this will become clearer *en passant*, the complementarity principle, whilst encircling the prevailing juridical labyrinth[89] which can be an inevitable source of delay,[90] sets the demarcation line between a domestic and an international trial. States which are unable or unwilling to engage in the prosecution of core crimes set the stage for the ICC. Hence, categorising the complementarity

---

[87] These aspects include the following:

(a) after the commencement of the trial in October 2005 two defence lawyers were killed and another was seriously wounded;
(b) another defence counsel was assassinated in June 2006;
(c) access to witnesses who may have been produced by the defence was severely hampered;
(d) although a hybrid, internationalized court, the Statute of the Iraqi High Tribunal did not expressly deal with judicial independence;
(e) in January 2006, Judge Rizgar resigned, complaining of government interference;
(f) he was not replaced by the most senior judge from within the five-man Trial Chamber because the Supreme National Baathification Commission, an external and political body, opposed his appointment by over-ruling his regular and legitimate nomination as President of the IHT.

[88] Jeßberger 2009, pp. 214–215.

[89] Complementarity is deemed to have been waived upon a State's inactivity when, for example, the State does not even investigate. Such inactivity has also been termed as co-operative complementarity and uncontested admissibility (Cross and Williams 2010, p. 339; see also Schabas 2010, p. 343).

[90] Swart and Sluiter 1999, p. 107.

principle as the cornerstone of the ICC Statute[91] is sensible. After all, the vertical system of enforcement (particularly the ICC itself) exists because of complementarity which boils down to the unwillingness or inability of States to genuinely engage in criminal prosecutions of core crimes. The willingness or ability of States to conduct prosecutions as a ground for refusal will be dealt with in Sect. 11.1.1. What should be said at this stage is that the OTP has enlisted various indicia of unwillingness and some on inability to genuinely carry out proceedings.[92] It has also provided indicators of shielding, of unjustified delays and of lack of independence and impartiality in criminal proceedings.[93] Some of such indicators could, in their own right, constitute a *presumptio iuris tantum*. Departures from normal legal procedures of a State (such as by circumventing the applicable criminal procedures by appointing a special investigator who is politically aligned with persons close to the accused, or transferring the case to a tribunal which conducts secret trials) are most likely to create a presumption of shielding[94] which the State would have to rebut by means of evidence to the contrary or by objectively justifying such departures. In *Côte d'Ivoire*'s admissibility challenge the Office of Public Counsel for Victims argued that the release of several members of the former government of *Laurent Gbagbo* indicated lack of real and genuine willingness to bring *Simone Gbagbo* to justice.[95] In circumstances where shielding subsists it is not only desirable to expect the vertical system of enforcement to do the job. It becomes imperative and necessary that this occurs. The contours and boundaries of the task with which the ICC is entrusted will shortly be examined.

References

AI (2015) Flawed Trial of *Al-Gaddafi* Officials Leads to Appalling Death Sentences. https://www.amnesty.org/en/latest/news/2015/07/libya-flawed-trial-of-al-gaddafi-officials/. Accessed 11 January 2016

Alford S (2008) Some Thoughts on the Trial of Saddam Hussein: The Realities of the Complementarity Principle. ICLR 8(3):463–475

Ansbro D (2015) International Commission of Jurists, Libya: Unfair Trial of *Saif Al-Islam Gadhafi* and Others; A Missed Opportunity to Establish Truth, Violates Right to Life. http://www.icj.org/libya-unfair-trial-of-saif-al-islam-gadhafi-and-others-a-missed-opportunity-to-establish-truth-violates-right-to-life/. Accessed 12 July 2016

ASP (2012) Report of the Bureau on Complementarity, Eleventh Session of the ASP, 7 November 2012, ICC-ASP/11/24

---

[91] Swart and Sluiter 1999, p. 105; see also Williams 1999, pp. 383, 390 and 392.

[92] OTP 2003, pp. 28–31.

[93] OTP 2013, pp. 13–14.

[94] Holmes 2002, pp. 667–668.

[95] ICC Pre-Trial Chamber I, *Situation in the Republic of Côte d'Ivoire, Prosecutor v Simone Gbagbo, Decision on Côte d'Ivoire's challenge to the admissibility of the case against Simone Gbagbo*, 11 December 2014, Case No. ICC-02/11-01/12, para 25.

ASP (2013) Report of the Bureau on Complementarity, Twelfth Session of the ASP, 15 October 2013, ICC-ASP/12/31

Bekou O, Shah S (2006) Realising the Potential of the International Criminal Court: The African Experience. HRLR 6(3):499–544

Bergsmo M, Bekou O, Jones A (2010) Complementarity After Kampala: Capacity Building and the ICC's Legal Tools. GJIL 2(2):791–811

Burke-White WW (2002) A Community of Courts: Toward a System of International Criminal Law Enforcement. MJIL 24(1):1–101

Canada's Amendment to the Extradition Act 1999 (2005) Amendments to the 1999 Extradition Act [Statutes of Canada 1999, c.18], 19 July 2005

Cockayne J (2004) The Fraying Shoestring: Rethinking Hybrid War Crimes Tribunals. FILJ 28 (3):616–680

Cohen D (2012) Reviewing Bergsmo M (ed) Complementarity: Legal Information Transfer. TOAEP, Oslo. In: JICJ 10(4):1017–1019

Cross ME, Williams S (2010) Recent Developments at the International Criminal Court: *Prosecutor v Germain Katanga and Mathieu Ngudjolo Chui* - A Boost for Co-Operative Complementarity? HRLR 10(2):336–345

Cryer R (2015) The ICC and its Relationship to Non-State Parties. In: Stahn C (ed) The Law and Practice of the International Criminal Court. OUP, Oxford, pp. 260–280

Den-Racsmany Z (2007) Lessons of the European Arrest Warrant for Domestic Implementation of the Obligation to Surrender Nationals to the International Criminal Court. LJIL 20(1):167–191

Evenson E, Smith A (2015) Completion, Legacy, and Complementarity at the ICC. In: Stahn C (ed) The Law and Practice of the International Criminal Court. OUP, Oxford, pp. 1259–1276

Gamarra Y, Vicente A (2008) United Nations Member States' Obligations Towards the International Criminal Tribunal for the Former Yugoslavia: Arresting and Transferring Lukić, Gotovina and Zelenović. ICLR 8(4):627–653

German Law to Implement the Rome Statute of the ICC of 17 July 1998 [*Entwurfeines Gesetzeszur Ausfuehrung des Roemischen Statuts des Internationalen Strafgerichtshofes vom 17 Juli 1998*] {Draft Act Implementing the Rome Statute for the International Criminal Court of 17 July 1998}, Act Amending the Basic Law (Federal Law Gazette 2000, I 1633) 29 November 2000

Ghoshray S (2011) Enforcing International Criminal Law in the Iraqi Special Tribunal: An Analysis of the Scope, Jurisdiction and Legitimacy of the Proposed Legal Framework. International Society for the Reform of Criminal Law. http://www.isrcl.org/Papers/2004/Ghoshray.pdf, p. 11. Accessed 3 February 2011

Gioia F (2011) Complementarity and 'Reverse Cooperation'. In: Stahn C, El Zeidy MM (eds) The International Criminal Court and Complementarity: From Theory to Practice, Volume II. CUP, Cambridge, pp. 807–829

Godinho JAF (2003) The Surrender Agreements Between the United States and the International Criminal Tribunal for the Former Yugoslavia and the International Criminal Tribunal for Rwanda: A Critical View. JICJ 1(2):502–516

Hall CK (2010) Positive Complementarity in Action. In: Stahn C, El Zeidy M (eds) The International Criminal Court and Complementarity: From Theory to Practice, Vol. II. CUP, Cambridge, pp. 1014–1051

Holmes JT (2002) Complementarity: National Courts *versus* the International Criminal Court. In: Cassese A, Gaeta P, Jones JRWD (eds) The Rome Statute of the International Criminal Court: A Commentary, Vol. I. OUP, Oxford, pp. 667–686

ICC (2017) Statement of Chief Prosecutor Fatou Bensouda to the UNSC on the Situation in Libya Pursuant to UNSC Resolution 1970 (2011), 8 May 2017

ICC Statute (1998) Rome Statute of the International Criminal Court

ICTR Statute (1994) Statute of the International Criminal Tribunal for Rwanda

ICTY Statute (1993) Statute of the International Criminal Tribunal for the Former Yugoslavia

Jalloh CC (2016) Charles Taylor. In: Schabas WA (ed) The Cambridge Companion to International Criminal Law. CUP, Cambridge, pp. 312–332

Jeßberger F (2009) International v. National Prosecution of International Crimes. In: Cassese A (ed) The Oxford Companion of International Criminal Justice, OUP, Oxford, pp. 208–215

Kaul H-P, Kreß C (1999) Jurisdiction and Cooperation in the Statute of the International Criminal Court: Principles and Compromises. YIHL 2:143–175

Kirsch P (2007) The Role of the ICC in Enforcing International Criminal Law. AUILR 22(4):539–547

Klimek L (2015) European Arrest Warrant. Springer, Springer International Publishing, Switzerland

Klip A (2009) European Criminal Law: An Integrative Approach, Intersentia, *Ius Communitatis* Series, Vol. 2. Intersentia, Cambridge

Knoops G-JA (2002) Surrendering to International Criminal Courts: Contemporary Practice and Procedures. International and Comparative Criminal Law Series, TP, Ardsley, NY

Kreß C, Prost K (2008) Article 102: Use of Terms. In: Triffterer O (ed) Commentary on the Rome Statute of the International Criminal Court, Observers' Notes, Article by Article, Preliminary Remarks, 2nd edn. CH Beck/Hart/Nomos, Munchen/Oxford/Baden-Baden, pp. 1645–1646

Kreß C, Prost K, Wilkitzki P (2008) On Part 9: International Cooperation and Judicial Assistance: Preliminary Remarks. In: Triffterer O (ed) Commentary on the Rome Statute of the International Criminal Court, 2nd edn. CH Beck/Hart/Nomos, Munchen/Oxford/Baden-Baden, pp. 1503–1512

Krings BL (2012) The Principles of Complementarity and Universal Jurisdiction in International Criminal Law: Antagonists or Perfect Match? GJIL 4(3):737–763

Martin FF, Schnably SJ, Slye RC, Wilson R, Falk R, Simon JS, Koren E (1997) International Human Rights Law and Practice: Cases, Treaties and Materials. KLI, Alphen aan den Rijn, The Netherlands, published under the auspices of Rights International, the Centre for International Human Rights Law Inc.

Murray ARJ (2011) Does International Criminal Law Still Require a 'Crime of Crimes?': A Comparative Review of Genocide and Crimes Against Humanity. GJIL 3(2):589–615

Nouwen SMH (2006) Hybrid Courts: The Hybrid Category of a New Type of International Crimes Courts. ULR 2(2):190–214

O'Callaghan D (2008) Is the International Criminal Court the Way Ahead? ICLR 8(3):533–556

Olásolo H (2005) The Triggering Procedure of the International Criminal Court. MNP, Dordrecht/Boston/London

OTP (2003) Informal Expert Paper: The Principle of Complementarity in Practice. ICC-01/04-01/07-1015-Anx. https://www.icc-cpi.int/RelatedRecords/CR2009_02250.PDF. Accessed 17 July 2017

OTP (2013) Policy Paper on Preliminary Examinations. ICC-OTP, November 2013. https://www.icc-cpi.int/iccdocs/otp/otp-policy_paper_preliminary_examinations_2013-eng.pdf. Accessed 10 March 2016

OTP (2018) Sixteenth Report of the OTP of the ICC to the UNSC Pursuant to UNSCR 1970 (2011). https://www.icc-cpi.int/itemsDocuments/181102-rep-otp-UNSC-libya_ENG.pdf. Accessed 29 December 2018

Owuor MO (2014) The International Criminal Court and Positive Complementarity: Institutional and Legal Framework, Thesis submitted in fulfilment of the degree of Doctor of Laws in International Criminal Law at the University of South Africa. http://www.academia.edu/7483015/THE_INTERNATIONAL_CRIMINAL_COURT_AND_POSITIVE_COMPLEMENTARITY_INSTITUTIONAL_AND_LEGAL_FRAMEWORK._-_RESEARCH_PROPOSAL_IN_LAW_-_DOCTOR_OF_LAWS_LL.D_DEGREE_By_OWUOR_MILTON_O. (link no longer active) Accessed 20 September 2016

Prost K (2011) The International Criminal Tribunal for the Former Yugoslavia and its Relationship with National Jurisdictions: Powers, Limits, and Misconceptions. In: Swart B, Zahar A, Sluiter G (eds) The Legacy of the International Criminal Tribunal for the Former Yugoslavia. OUP, Oxford, pp. 434–468

Ralph J (2016) The International Criminal Court. In: Bellamy AJ, Dunne T (eds) The Oxford Handbook of the Responsibility to Protect. OUP, Oxford, pp. 638–654

Rastan R (2008) Testing Co-operation: The International Criminal Court and National Authorities. LJIL 21(2):431–456

Roberts K (2001) Aspects of the ICTY Contribution to the Criminal Procedure of the ICC. In: May R, Tolbert D, Hocking J, Roberts K, Jia BB, Mundis D, Oosthuizen G (eds) Essays on ICTY Procedure and Evidence In Honour of Gabrielle Kirk McDonald. International Humanitarian Law Series, KLI, The Hague/London/Boston, pp. 559–572

Ryngaert C (2013) State Cooperation with the International Criminal Tribunal for Rwanda. ICLR 13(1):125–146

Schabas WA (2010) The International Criminal Court: A Commentary on the Rome Statute. Oxford Commentaries on International Law, OUP, Oxford

Schabas WA (2016) The International Criminal Court: A Commentary on the Rome Statute, 2nd edn. Oxford Commentaries on International Law, OUP, Oxford

Scharf MP (2008) The Lockerbie Model of Transfer of Proceedings. In: Bassiouni MC (ed) International Criminal Law: Multilateral and Bilateral Enforcement Mechanisms, Vol. II, 3rd edn. MNP, Leiden, pp. 521–527

Seils P (2015) Putting Complementarity in its Place. In: Stahn C (ed) The Law and Practice of the International Criminal Court. OUP, Oxford, pp. 305–327

Sluiter G (2003) The Surrender of War Criminals to the International Criminal Court. LLAICLR 25:605–651

Sluiter G (2008) Obtaining Cooperation From Sudan–Where is the Law? JICJ 6(5):871–884

Sluiter G (2009) Cooperation of States with International Criminal Tribunals. In: Cassese A (ed) The Oxford Companion to International Criminal Justice. OUP, Oxford, pp. 187–200

Sriram CL, Brown S (2012) Kenya in the Shadow of the ICC: Complementarity, Gravity and Impact. ICLR 12(2):219–244

Stahn C (2010) Arrest and Surrender under the ICC Statute: A Contextual Reading. In: Stahn C, van den Herik L (eds) Future Perspectives on International Criminal Justice. Asser Press, The Hague, pp. 659–685

Stahn C (2015) Admissibility Challenges before the ICC: From Quasi-Primacy to Qualified Deference? In: Stahn C (ed) The Law and Practice of the International Criminal Court. OUP, Oxford, pp. 228–259

Stahn C, van den Herik L (2012) Fragmentation, Diversification and 3D Legal Pluralism: International Criminal Law as the Jack-in-the-box? In: van den Herik L, Stahn C (eds) The Diversification and Fragmentation of International Criminal Law. MNP, Leiden/Boston, pp. 21–89

Statute of the IHT (2003) Statute of the Iraqi High Tribunal

Swart B (2002) Arrest and Surrender. In: Cassese A, Gaeta P, Jones JRWD (eds) The Rome Statute of the International Criminal Court: A Commentary, Vol. II. OUP, Oxford, pp. 1639–1703

Swart B, Sluiter G (1999) The International Criminal Court and International Criminal Co-operation. In: von Hebel HAM, Lammers JG, Schuking J (eds) Reflections on the International Criminal Court. Asser Press, The Hague, pp. 91–127

Tillier J (2013) The International Criminal Court Prosecutor and Positive Complementarity: Strengthening the Rule of Law? ICLR 13(3):507–591

UNC (1945) Charter of the United Nations

UNDP (2012) Discussion Paper: Complementarity and Transitional Justice: Synthesis of Key Emerging Issues for Development: New Opportunities Arising from the Principle of Complementarity and Support for National Capacities to Investigate and Prosecute Serious Crimes of International Concern. http://www.undp.org/content/dam/undp/library/Democratic%20Governance/Access%20to%20Justice%20and%20Rule%20of%20Law/Discussion%20Paper%20%E2%80%93%20Complementarity%20and%20Transitional%20Justice%20%E2%80%93%202012%20_%20EN.pdf. Accessed 19 April 2013

UNSC (2005a) Press Release SC/8351, Security Council, 5158th Meeting (Night). http://www.un.org/News/Press/docs/2005/sc8351.doc.htm. Accessed 21 June 2011

UNSC (2005b) Resolution 1593 (2005b), UN Doc. S/RES/1593

UNSC (2011) Resolution 1970 (2011), UN Doc. S/RES/1970
van Sliedregt E (2012) Pluralism in International Criminal Law. LJIL 25(4):847–855
Wartanian A (2005) The International Criminal Court Prosecutor's Battlefield: Combating Atrocities While Fighting for States' Cooperation: Lesson from the United Nations Tribunals Applied to the Case of Uganda. GrJIL 36(4):1289–1316
Webb P (2013) International Judicial Integration and Fragmentation. OUP, Oxford
Wenqi Z (2006) On Co-operation by States not party to the ICC. IRRC 88(861):87–110
Werle G (2009) Principles of International Criminal Law, 2nd edn. Asser Press, The Hague
Williams SA (1999) Article 17: Issues of Admissibility. In: Triffterer O (ed) Commentary on the Rome Statute of the International Criminal Court. HP/Nomos, Oxford/Baden-Baden, pp. 383–394
Zahar A, Sluiter G (2008) International Criminal Law: A Critical Introduction. OUP, Oxford

Chapter 10
The State Obligation to Cooperate under International Law

Contents

10.1 The Nature of the General Obligation of An ICC State Party to Cooperate 166
10.2 The Obligations of Non-State Parties under the United Nations Security Council Resolution Regime 175
10.3 The Consequences of a Breach of the State's Obligation to Cooperate........................ 184
References 201

Abstract This chapter seeks to establish the extent to which States are entitled to assess if the ICC enjoys jurisdiction in order to determine whether they are obliged to surrender a suspect thereto. The ICC Statute only imposes direct obligations on States which have ratified such treaty. The ICC cooperation model is best described as slanted, neither vertical nor horizontal. There is no harmonised international procedure relating to the national execution of an ICC cooperation request. Although States cannot rely on the absence of domestic law to justify non-compliance, the effect of ICC requests largely hinges on the degree to which States have domestically promulgated procedures intended to facilitate cooperation. The complementarity regime prevailing therein endows States with some discretion. Non-State Parties may only be invited by the ICC to cooperate. Yet, even non-State Parties to the ICC would need to implement legislation to execute a UNSC Resolution which directly invokes the cooperation of States. The potential repercussions of the failure to cooperate by the State may lead to the finding of a violation either by the ICC and a referral of the matter to the ASP in terms of Article 87(7) of the ICC Statute and Regulation 109 of the ICC, or else to a referral to the UNSC when the case had been triggered by a UNSC Resolution. Notwithstanding recent jurisprudence, it is still unclear whether the ASP can take any action beyond making the finding of non-compliance. Some ideas to strengthen the fragile ICC cooperation regime are suggested.

Keywords State Parties · Non-State Parties · *Kompetenz-kompetenz* · Inherent powers · Implied powers · Judicial activism · *Modus operandi* · State discretion · Manner of execution · Complementarity · Orders ·

C. Soler, *The Global Prosecution of Core Crimes under International Law*,
https://doi.org/10.1007/978-94-6265-335-1_10

Jurisdiction · Grounds for refusal · Admissibility · Trigger mechanism · *Aut dedere aut judicare* · Inactivity · State obligation · UNSC resolution · Referral · Deferral · Review · Agreements · Arrangements · Finding of non-compliance · ASP · Collective countermeasures · Non-enforcement · Impunity · Threat to the peace · Responsibility to protect · Part 9 · Sanctions · International peace and security · Remedy · Unwilling · Unable · Chapter VII enforcement mechanisms

At the risk of sounding presumptuous, having understood the relevance of and the need for the vertical system of enforcement within the general enforcement of international criminal law, at this stage, the juridical framework which embodies the vertical system of enforcement will be assessed. Subsequently its major shortcomings will be detected particularly with reference to the ICC Statute, also by virtue of case-law.

10.1 The Nature of the General Obligation of An ICC State Party to Cooperate

Owing to its nature as an international convention, the ICC Statute only imposes obligations on States which have ratified such treaty in accordance with the legal maxims *pacta sunt servanda* and *res inter alios acta*, both derivative of the VCLT. The former maxim denotes that every treaty in force binds the parties to the treaty to perform their obligations in good faith, whereas the latter maxim conveys the existence of a matter or rule which does not create third party rights or duties. To this extent, State 'commitment tends to lead towards compliance'.[1] This is why this heading refers to State Parties rather than States. This does not mean that *dicta* of the ICC are binding on its State Parties.[2] In any case, the ICC cannot impose obligations of surrender on States which have not ratified the ICC Statute. Non-State Parties have no such cooperation obligations, and may only be invited by the ICC to cooperate.[3] This remains so as long as one continues to disregard any obligations which may flow from customary international law.[4] I however opine that it is doubtful whether such obligations may be said to emanate from customary international law, although Kenneth Gallant seems to open a window for this possibility, by not excluding such contingency, when he states that 'any obligation of a State not party to the ICC Statute (and which has not accepted the jurisdiction of the Court) to co-operate with the Court or obey its orders must therefore come

[1] Meernik and Aloisi 2009, pp. 267–268.

[2] Harmen van der Wilt states that Article 21 of the ICC Statute (ICC Statute (1998) Rome Statute of the International Criminal Court), fails to give ICC *dicta* such effect (van der Wilt 2008, p. 256).

[3] Article 87(5) of the ICC Statute, above n. 2.

[4] Wenqi 2006, p. 108.

from another source'.[5] Were this so (that is, should a customary international law rule to this effect be said to subsist), the UNSC (which is also bound by customary international law),[6] when referring a situation to the ICC, would not have resolved by recognizing that 'States not party to the Rome Statute have no obligation under the Statute'.[7] Kimberly Prost, following the observations of Bert Swart and Göran Sluiter,[8] is fully correct when she states that the ICC cooperation model is 'best described as slanted – neither vertical nor horizontal'.[9] When the ICC's cooperation regime is discussed, given that it 'should be positioned between the traditional inter-state cooperation regime and that of the *ad hoc* tribunals',[10] the leaning Tower of Pisa immediately comes to my mind. The Tower of Pisa alikeness is intriguing because such building truly mirrors the ICC cooperation regime which constitutes 'a unique mixture of the horizontal and vertical regimes',[11] whilst being 'predominantly vertical'.[12] Whereas the architectural marvel of the Tower of Pisa was partially straightened by experts to solidify its structure and ensure its integrity,[13] the juridical marvel of the ICC Statute's cooperation regime will have to become more robust by means of the ICC's jurisprudence. This will obviously have a significant effect on the general obligation of a State Party to cooperate. Although such an obligation has to be fulfilled by States, it emanates directly from the ICC Statute. Hence, its contours can, to an extent, be determined by the ICC. Here, one must not underestimate the privileged position that the ICC holds within the playing field of the global enforcement of international criminal justice. This stems from an inherent, competitive advantage, the fact that the ICC is arbiter of its own jurisdiction.[14] As a result of this it is entitled to scrutinise domestic proceedings in order to 'satisfy itself' that it enjoys such jurisdiction in terms of Article 19 of the ICC Statute itself, leaving States without the final say. To a large extent the ICC is a master of its own destiny. It holds the ultimate authority to interpret and apply the

[5] Gallant 2003, p. 583.

[6] As a matter of fact, '*jus cogens* norms recognized by customary international law and the Vienna Convention on the Law of Treaties, and the purposes and principles of the UN itself, impose limits on the powers of the Security Council that should be monitored' {ECFI, Second Chamber (Extended Composition) *Ahmed Ali Yusuf and Al Barkakaat International Foundation v Council of the European Union and Commission of the European Communities* [2005], 21 September 2005, T-306/01, paras 277–282; ECFI, Second Chamber (Extended Composition) *Yasin Abdullah Kadi v Council of the European Union and Commission of the European Communities* [2005], 21 September 2005, T-315/01, paras 226–231, both judgments being cited in Gordillo 2012, p. 292, n. 12}.

[7] UNSC (2005) Resolution 1593 (2005), S/RES/1593, para 2.

[8] Swart and Sluiter 1999, pp. 105–110.

[9] Prost 2011, p. 464.

[10] Zahar and Sluiter 2008, p. 459.

[11] Rastan 2008, p. 432.

[12] Zahar and Sluiter 2008, p. 461; Sluiter 2003a, p. 651.

[13] BBC (2011) Leaning Tower of Pisa: A Work in Progress. http://news.bbc.co.uk/2/hi/programmes/fast_track/9568633.stm. Accessed 11 April 2012.

[14] Holmes 2002, p. 672.

provisions governing the complementarity regime once its jurisdiction has been triggered.[15] It is only bound by the legal provisions of its own Statute in accordance with the *kompetenz-kompetenz*[16] principle,[17] whose specific conditions of implementation are stipulated in Articles 18 and 19 of the ICC Statute and thoroughly explained by the ICC itself.[18] The *kompetenz-kompetenz* principle is also closely linked to the vertical system of enforcement since it is a powerful feature of verticality.[19] In the context of the above power-oriented discourse, Yitiha Simbeye opines that 'notwithstanding the ICC's lack of express coercive powers to bind States that the *ad hoc* Tribunals have, it can, perhaps, attempt to extend its powers by implication'.[20] He adds that 'perhaps the ICC will determine that its powers to issue certain binding orders are not inherent. However, if it is to operate effectively, a time will come when it will have to rely on implication to extend its capacity to act. A particular area where this may occur is with the surrender of suspects'.[21] This assumes legal validity when one keeps in mind that the assumption of inherent[22] powers[23] is also partially derivative of the very concepts of judicial discretion and judicial activism.[24] The latter 'consists in using and developing law to achieve certain results or objectives', hence using law as 'a means to achieve a certain end'.[25]

In this way and by exercising such powers, judges could make judge-made law, just as ICTY judges modelled the ICTY cooperation regime which turned out to be of 'important precedential value for the drafters of the ICC Statute.'[26] This might be

[15] ICC Pre-Trial Chamber II, *Situation in Uganda, Prosecutor v Joseph Kony, Vincent Otti, Okot Odhiambo, Dominic Ongwen, Decision on the Admissibility of the Case under Article 19(1) of the Statute*, 10 March 2009, Case No. ICC-02/04-01/05, para 45, cited in Stahn 2011, p. 240, n. 34.

[16] This is known as '*la compétence de la compétence*' in French (see Chap. 21).

[17] ICTY Appeals Chamber, *Prosecutor v Duško Tadić, Decision on the Defence Motion for Interlocutory Appeal on Jurisdiction*, 2 October 1995, Case No. IT-94-1, para 17.

[18] *Prosecutor v Joseph Kony et al.*, above n. 15, para 45.

[19] Sluiter 2002a, p. 131.

[20] Simbeye 2004, p. 29.

[21] Simbeye 2004, p. 33.

[22] In the context of judicial powers and as described here above, the words 'implied', 'implicit' and 'inherent' are used inter-changeably.

[23] The *telos* of such powers is that 'if an organ has been endowed with specific powers, it may solicit State cooperation if this is necessary for an effective exercise of these powers' (Sluiter 2003b, p. 121). In other words, inherent powers are 'those powers which are derived from the very existence of the organization' (ICJ, *Nuclear Tests Case (Australia v France)*, 20 December 1974, ICJ Rep 1974, p. 253, para 23).

[24] Even where the vertical relationship is strong and effective, such as in the case of the *ad hoc* tribunals, 'the system of State cooperation within these criminal tribunals is mainly 'judge-made', meaning that as the Statutes of these tribunals are not conclusive with respect to these criteria, the judges before these tribunals ultimately created more clarity through their judgments' (Cassese 2003, p. 356).

[25] Merrills 1993, para 231, cited in Forowicz 2010, pp. 13–14, notes 59 and 60.

[26] Sluiter 2009, p. 188.

inevitable due to the bottlenecks prevailing within the ICC Statute,[27] most of which shall be addressed within Sect. 11.1–11.5. The ICC therefore seems to need some form of expeditious surgical intervention. Salvatore Zappalà, in support of judicial activism by the ICC, whilst recognizing that the ICC has already shown some signs of activism by virtue of its case-law,[28] gives three reasons to justify the need for judges to approach their task teleologically:

i. international criminal law supplements national criminal law in such a way that it steps in under exceptional circumstances, where nothing has been done at the domestic level to bring perpetrators to justice;
ii. international criminal law must take into account a variety of national legal systems and legal doctrines, both in terms of substantive and procedural criminal law, necessitating further flexibility; and
iii. since often high level State officials are involved in the perpetration of core crimes, legal issues arising throughout the criminal proceedings are complex and 'therefore require judges to display a great deal of activism to disentangle the intricacies of proceedings'.[29]

He appropriately concludes by noting that should ICC judges be perceived as being excessively activists, this would provide an incentive for States to 'exercise jurisdiction at a national level thereby obliging the Court to refrain from hearing a case'.[30] The extent to which ICC judges may adopt a teleological approach to substantive international criminal law seems rather restricted in view of the detail prevailing within the ICC Elements of Crimes.[31] However, 'the ICC regime allows considerable room for flexibility and judicial creativity in relation to procedural matters designated for that purpose by the negotiators'.[32] Certainly, although matters dealing with State cooperation, such as arrest and surrender, can partake of

[27] Kreß 2003, pp. 603–617.

[28] ICC, Pre-Trial Chamber I, *Situation in the DRC, Decision to Convene a Status Conference*, 17 February 2005, Case No. ICC-01/04; ICC Pre-Trial Chamber I, *Situation in the DRC, Decision on the Applications for Participation in the Proceedings of VPRS 1, VPRS 2, VPRS 3, VPRS 4, VPRS 5 and VPRS 6*, 17 January 2006, Case No. ICC-01/04, cited by Zappalà 2009, p. 221, n. 24.

[29] Zappalà 2009, pp. 220–221.

[30] Zappalà 2009, p. 223.

[31] These are an internal source of law and are constituted by means of a legal text the status of which is regulated by Article 9 of the ICC Statute, above n. 2. This legal provision stipulates that the ICC Elements of Crimes (1998) International Criminal Court, Elements of Crimes, must be applied by the ICC but are not binding upon it. Instead, they are meant to be of assistance to the ICC in the interpretation and application of Articles 6, 7 and 8 of the ICC Statute, above n. 2. The ICC Pre-Trial Chamber has concluded that they must be applied unless the competent Chamber finds an irreconcilable contradiction between the ICC Elements of Crimes (see above) on the one hand and the ICC Statute (above n. 2) on the other hand, in which case the ICC Statute, above n. 2, shall prevail (ICC Pre-Trial Chamber I, *Situation in Darfur, Sudan, Decision on the Prosecution's Application for a Warrant of Arrest Against Omar Hassan Al Bashir*, 4 March 2009, Case No. ICC-02/05-01/09, paras 128 and 131, cited in Bitti 2015, p. 421, notes 46 and 47).

[32] Vasiliev 2014, p. 46.

substantive law issues, they fall more squarely within the procedural realm of law. In the context of the interplay between the vertical system of enforcement and the horizontal system of enforcement, an example of such synergy is called for. William Schabas already pointed to 'one good example of judicial activism' within the *Lubanga* seminal decision[33] wherein inactivity (commonly referred to as State inaction, which omission unambiguously leads to admissibility of the case)[34] was inserted together with the two prongs of complementarity, these being unwilling or unable genuinely to investigate or prosecute. The consequence of examining complementarity from the viewpoint of 'inactivity' amounts to rendering the 'unable' criterion relatively insignificant, because, as Schabas notes, 'if a State is unable, it will also, presumably, be inactive'.[35] Although the latter finding is correct, Schabas over-estimates the teleological dimension since a close reading of the ICC Statute leads one to conclude that admissibility issues, namely the question of unwillingness or inability, do not arise *ab initio* when a State remains inactive. This was also duly confirmed by the *Katanga* appellate chamber.[36] In any case, the extent to which ICC judges will, to use a term applied by Nina Jørgensen, 'descend into the arena'[37] to minimise the impact caused by the shortcomings of the ICC Statute, is a matter which will capture everyone's attention in the coming years and decades. It seems that this privileged position, being the faculty to provide a useful guideline for the assessment of a State's willingness and ability to carry out effective investigations into gross human rights violations, does not however belong to States, separately, that is one by one. It is highly questionable whether a State itself can shed a light on its own willingness and/or ability to investigate and/or prosecute crimes. If this were possible, one would have to assess to what extent this would be fair and to what degree a State's juridical infrastructure would be impartial and independent of the current political forces. Therefore, this privileged position can be enjoyed by a court, like the ECtHR, which scrutinizes State action and/or inaction, not by the State whose action and/or inaction is questioned.

The above should not be understood as leaving absolutely no leeway to States. Some legal literature[38] reveals that the point whether States are entitled to assess whether the ICC enjoys jurisdiction in order to determine whether it is obliged to surrender a suspect or otherwise, will largely depend upon the prevailing legal

---

[33] ICC Pre-Trial Chamber I, *Situation in the DRC, Prosecutor v Thomas Lubanga Dyilo, Decision on the Prosecutor's Application for a Warrant of Arrest under Article 58*, 10 February 2006, Case No. ICC-01/04-01/06, cited in Schabas 2008, p. 757, n. 119.

[34] Robinson 2010, p. 102.

[35] Schabas 2010, p. 344.

[36] ICC Appeals Chamber, *Situation in the DRC, Prosecutor v Germain Katanaga and Mathieu Ngudjolo Chui, Judgment on the Appeal of Mr. Germain Katanga against the Oral Decision of Trial Chamber II of 12 June 2009 on the Admissibility of the Case*, 25 September 2009, Case No. ICC-01/04-01/07 OA8, paras 75–78 confirming the Prosecutor's submissions outlined in para 66.

[37] Jørgensen 2009, p. 123.

[38] See, *inter alia*, Duffy 2001, pp. 6–8.

(particularly constitutional)[39] provisions within the State which is called upon to decide such a matter.[40] However, this may not be perfectly correct in view of the *kompetenz-kompetenz* enjoyed by the ICC. It is true that the *modus operandi*, the manner in which the obligation to surrender should be implemented, is a matter pertaining to domestic law.[41] Specific guidelines to aid public sector employees in the understanding and implementation of such domestic legislation have also been introduced within some jurisdictions.[42] Hence the importance of national law is highlighted.[43] This is accentuated by those State Parties to the ICC Statute which have adopted implementing laws which solicit national courts to fill in the *lacunae* emanating from the functioning of the ICC.[44] Olympia Bekou argues in favour of extending the spirit of Article 88 of the ICC Statute to include provisions of substantive law.[45] Article 88 postulates an important positive obligation upon State Parties, by means of which States undertake to ensure that there are procedures available in their national laws enabling them to comply with the prevailing ICC framework of cooperation. In other words, States must promulgate legislation in order to equip themselves with the required legal infrastructure which would allow them to fulfil their cooperation obligations emanating directly from the ICC Statute. The lack of such legislation cannot constitute a ground for refusal of cooperation. States, in turn, have the discretion as to the *modus operandi* of the manner of execution. One must hence distinguish between, on the one hand, the assessment of whether a State is free to comply with the request (which it is not unless the ICC Statute so permits) and, on the other hand, the manner/way as to how to execute such request. There is no harmonised or common international procedure relating to the national execution of an ICC cooperation request.

Be that as it may, however, the correct assessment denotes that, irrespective of the above and as shall result from this Part, the buck stops at the ICC. In the context

[39] For an analysis of the related doctrine of constitutional autonomy and case-law connected thereto, see d'Aspremont and Brolmann 2010, pp. 130–133; see also Tzanakopoulos 2010, pp. 70–72.

[40] By way of example, 'the rejection of a request for surrender by the ICC is virtually impossible' due to the legal provisions of German Law to Implement the Rome Statute of the ICC of 17 July 1998 [*Entwurfeines Gesetzeszur Ausfuehrung des Roemischen Statuts des Internationalen Strafgerichtshofes vom 17 Juli 1998*] {Draft Act Implementing the Rome Statute for the International Criminal Court of 17 July 1998}, Act Amending the Basic Law (Federal Law Gazette 2000, I 1633) 29 November 2000 (Wilkitzki 2001, p. 201; see also Ambos and Stegmiller 2008, pp. 181–198).

[41] d'Aspremont and Brolmann 2010, p. 118.

[42] Jensen 2003, pp. 4–55.

[43] Mark Ellis, Executive Director of the IBA, held that 'implementing legislation is currently the missing link between the obligations within the Rome Statute and their implementation by State Parties' (Ellis (2008) IBA, News Release, 14 November 2008, London. http://www.iccnow.org/documents/IBA_NEWS_RELEASE.pdf. Accessed 3 July 2011).

[44] This process is called 'reverse complementarity' and has been adopted by Spain, Belgium and Germany (Pinto Soares 2012, p. 190, n. 68).

[45] Bekou 2009a, p. 468.

of this Part, the question: 'are States entitled to assess whether the ICC enjoys jurisdiction in order to determine whether they are obliged to surrender a suspect or otherwise?' is pervasive. Attempting to address the question posed necessitates an understanding of the ICC's peculiar cooperation regime, this being the subject-matter of this sub-heading. Admittedly the question posed is a tricky issue, from a vertical system of enforcement perspective, because the ICC Statute, the ninth part of which deals with 'international cooperation and judicial assistance',[46] is silent on the matter and because the line of demarcation between the dividing point where exclusive domestic jurisdiction makes way for ICC jurisdiction is a bit hazy. It seems that this entitlement of States to assess jurisdiction is not possible in so far as the *ad hoc* tribunals are concerned. In fact, a District Court in The Hague has held that ICTY orders[47] cannot be reviewed by Dutch national courts,[48] although a State can (only) implicitly undertake a review of ICTR orders, having applied a presumption of conformity to human rights.[49] Would this however necessarily equally apply to the ICC? ICC orders are, comparatively with orders of the two *ad hoc* tribunals (these being Chapter VII enforcement mechanisms), not as mandatory, even upon State Parties to the ICC itself. States are still allowed some discretion.[50] This leeway is, to an extent applicable to States, also within their own constitutional (human rights law)[51] regime. In fact, the ECtHR is not authorized to determine the local authorities' assessment of their own national law unless it is flagrantly and manifestly arbitrary.[52] States thus enjoy a noteworthy discretion both regionally and internationally. This leeway has led Antonio Cassese to conclude that, in drafting the ICC Statute, a 'mostly State-oriented approach,' which contrasts with the way the UNSC has moulded the *ad hoc* tribunals,[53] was adopted. There are others reasons why the reply to the question posed within this paragraph would

---

[46] The term 'cooperation' used within the Statute 'carries insufficient weight and leads States to misinterpret the meaning of the obligation' since it 'implies willingness to assist and work towards the same end' (Demirdjian 2010, pp. 182–183).

[47] A distinction should be drawn between, on the one hand, the challenge of orders, *id est* the objection to requests for cooperation on the basis of a ground for refusal and, on the other hand, the challenge of jurisdiction. The *Opacić* and *Rukundo* cases are merely intended to illustrate, by analogy, the difference between the regimes of the *ad hoc* tribunals and that of the ICC.

[48] District Court of The Hague, *Dragan Opacić v the Netherlands*, 30 May 1997, KG 97/742.

[49] Federal Supreme Court of Switzerland, Appeal Judgment, *Rukundo v Federal Office of Justice*, 3 September 2001, Case Numbers 1A.129/2001 and 1A.130/2001.

[50] The fact that the admissibility of a case is not a pre-requisite for the issuance of an international arrest warrant (see also Chap. 11, n. 12) manifests such discretion. As Dov Jacobs points out in his criticism of the fact that 'the review of admissibility is not compulsory,' timing is of the essence (Jacobs 2010, p. 116). Likewise, the ICC Statute, above n. 2, 'acknowledges that the timing of arrest and surrender requires strategy and policy-oriented decision-making' (Stahn 2010, p. 671).

[51] Christian Tomuschat defines this *corpus juris* as one which aims to 'reconcile the effectiveness of State power with the protection against the same State power' (Tomuschat 2008, p. 8).

[52] ECtHR Former Third Division, *Vasiliy Kononov v Latvia*, 24 July 2008, Application No. 36376/04, para 108.

[53] Cassese 1999, p. 165.

probably be in the negative, denoting an inequality between orders of the *ad hoc* tribunals on the one hand and orders of the ICC on the other. First of all, these are grounded upon different juridical foundations. The ICC cannot be placed in the same basket as the *ad hoc* tribunals not only because, unlike the *ad hoc* tribunals, it portrays both vertical and horizontal features,[54] denoting a mixed legal regime[55] by means of which its major strength 'is its capacity to combine dialogue among overlapping jurisdictions with incentives for compliance',[56] but also because its conventional jurisdictional framework is substantially distinctive thereto (since, as shown previously, it does not emanate from a UNSC Resolution). Besides enjoying both vertical and horizontal features, with the former being predominant,[57] the ICC may also vaunt a lateral viewpoint which mirrors the complementarity regime and is a derivative of the same.[58] Roberto Bellelli eloquently explains the relationship between the ICC Statute and State Parties by using a contradiction in terms, categorising it as a 'mandatory option'.[59] In theory, an option exists, but in practice, 'the absence in domestic criminal legal systems of any of the crimes under the Statute would raise an Article 17 ICC Statute issue of admissibility: the State might be found unable to carry out its proceedings',[60] shifting *ipso jure* jurisdiction from a domestic criminal court unto the ICC. In all fairness, however, the term 'mandatory option' can fit perfectly within the *sui generis* ICC cooperation regime because the system relies on 'mandatory State co-operation by way of consent', entailing that 'States agree in advance, either through treaty accession or *ad hoc* consent, to assume a duty of co-operation'.[61] Frédéric Mégret, emphasizing the element of mandatory compliance, asserts that vertical cooperation is a misnomer since cooperation presupposes voluntarism and equality, both of which are inconsistent with verticality which suggests the giving of orders.[62]

All this leads to the following scenario. State Parties are strongly encouraged and incentivised to prosecute core crimes. If the ratification of the ICC Statute conveyed something, this is a major consequence thereof. If, however, they fail to do so or fail to ensure the prosecution of such core crimes by extraditing the person concerned to a requesting State which enjoys jurisdiction, they are duty bound to fulfil the obligation to cooperate in terms of the cooperation regime within the ICC Statute. Effectively, this is a *tertium non datur*. It is a form of *aut dedere aut iudicare* in so far as 'surrender of an accused to an international court constitutes compliance with

---

54 Knoops and Amsterdam 2006, p. 264; Young 2001, p. 340; see also Mutyaba 2012, p. 944.
55 Stahn 2010, pp. 666–670.
56 Stahn 2010, p. 661.
57 Sluiter 2003a, p. 651.
58 Currie 2007, pp. 378–379.
59 Bellelli 2010, p. 212.
60 Ibid.
61 Stahn 2010, p. 666.
62 Mégret 2010, p. 187.

the treaty obligation to extradite or prosecute'.[63] Indeed, 'the duty to "exercise criminal jurisdiction" should be read in a manner consistent with the customary obligation *aut dedere aut judicare*, and is therefore satisfied by extradition and surrender, since those are criminal proceedings that result in prosecution'.[64] *Aut dedere aut judicare* hence becomes the bridge between the vertical and horizontal systems of enforcement. Both systems are engrafted upon *aut dedere aut judicare*. In a nutshell, all this reveals that *aut dedere aut judicare* is not merely confined to the horizontal system of enforcement. It is the pivot upon which the general enforcement of international criminal justice hinges.[65] An OTP policy paper in fact found that 'the duty to exercise criminal jurisdiction should be read in a manner consistent with the customary obligation *aut dedere aut judicare*, and is therefore satisfied by extradition and surrender, since those are criminal proceedings that result in prosecution'.[66] It is hence not surprising that the historical roots of complementarity derive directly from the *aut dedere aut judicare* rule.[67] The net effect of this is that a State which declines to exercise jurisdiction favours an ICC prosecution to the extent that William Schabas paradoxically deems such State conduct as reflective of a theory whereby 'a State respected its obligation to prosecute by failing to prosecute'.[68]

The triggering mechanisms can have a measure of significance. Daniel Nsereko argues that by surrendering suspects to the ICC, States legitimately exercise their own sovereignty because the process of surrender, by and of itself, is not a breach of the duty to prosecute.[69] Because of this form of *aut dedere aut judicare*, the State in question loses its primacy and the ICC gains control over the situation once the case has been rendered admissible. In fact, complementarity is often viewed both as an actual right of primacy of States but also as an obligation of States to become active.[70] A State's complete inactivity, habitually referred to as 'the inaction scenario' by the OTP[71] and manifested by a State's refusal to undertake, at least, preliminary and initial investigative steps, in practice circumvents the admissibility test, rendering it futile. Domestic inactivity (the lack of national proceedings) is sufficient to make the case admissible,[72] which determination is case specific since it requires an examination of whether the national proceedings encompass the same person for the same conduct as that which forms the basis of the proceedings before

63 Swart 2002, p. 1688.

64 OTP 2003, p. 19, n. 24, and also cited in Schabas 2010, pp. 342–343.

65 Soler 2014, p. 292.

66 OTP 2003, p. 19, n. 24.

67 Buchan and Johnsson 2012, p. 105.

68 Schabas 2007, p. 2.

69 Nsereko 2013, p. 446.

70 Krings 2012, pp. 748 and 749.

71 OTP 2003, p. 7.

72 *Prosecutor v Germain Katanga and Mathieu Ngudjolo Chui*, above n. 36, para 78.

the ICC.[73] Concisely put, Harmen van der Wilt notes that inactivity or 'complete inertia will leave the International Criminal Court a free hand to start investigations itself'.[74] I will come back to this inaction scenario later on within Sect. 11.1.1.

Indeed the complementarity regime prevailing therein endows States with some discretion amidst their general legal obligation to cooperate with the ICC itself,[75] an obligation which has rendered the relationship with State Parties a vertical one of a *sui generis* nature, as is evident from a reading of this chapter. By virtue of this relationship, the ICC is entitled to call upon States to exercise its cooperation requests as if they were a mere extension of the ICC's direct authority. State Parties should ensure that adequate implementing legislation and supplementary agreements are in place to enable cooperation and ensure that appropriate structures and procedures are established to make such cooperation run smoothly. States can delay compliance if the accused was being prosecuted for a serious crime or was serving a sentence elsewhere.[76] Should hurdles and obstacles subsist for the grant of cooperation, State Parties are duty bound to consult with the ICC promptly with a view to eliminating such obstacles. Göran Sluiter advances, by way of a general rule, that 'if an organ has been endowed with specific powers, it may solicit State cooperation if this is necessary for an effective exercise of these powers'.[77] Should the requested cooperation not be forthcoming, the ICC can register a finding of non-compliance,[78] this being the subject-matter of Sect. 10.3. Göran Sluiter's studies stress the importance of State cooperation to the extent that he speaks of 'an effective regime of State cooperation'.[79] This leads me to analyse such regime in so far as it can also have an effect upon non-State Parties to the ICC Statute.

10.2 The Obligations of Non-State Parties under the United Nations Security Council Resolution Regime

The above has shown that a general 'duty of states to arrest and surrender persons whose presence before the Court is needed is one of the cornerstones on which the Rome Statute rests'.[80] By imposing obligations on States the ICC was aware (at the time the ICC Statute was promulgated) that, as Madam Justice Louise Arbour had already stated in a 1998 interview, the 'arrest problem was endemic, it was crucial,

[73] OTP 2013, p. 12.

[74] van der Wilt 2011, p. 688.

[75] Article 86 of the ICC Statute, above n. 2.

[76] This is connected to the *ne bis in idem* rule which will be considered under Sect. 11.1.2.

[77] Sluiter 2003b, p. 121.

[78] Regulation 109(2) of the ICC.

[79] Sluiter 1999, p. 285.

[80] Swart 2002, p. 1640.

and it was paralysing to the Yugloslav Tribunal'.[81] The ICC was also aware that (unlike the *ad hoc* tribunals) it would not easily benefit from other factors, such as domestic legislation, financial and political incentives to States and individuals, socio-economic and geo-strategic incentives, for the purposes of facilitating arrests.[82] The ICC held that there exists a 'duty of every State to exercise its criminal jurisdiction over those responsible for international crimes'.[83] State Parties must cooperate with the ICC's investigations,[84] they are to devise appropriate procedures under their domestic laws to facilitate such cooperation,[85] and besides undertaking various forms of judicial cooperation,[86] they are bound to surrender persons to the ICC if legal requirements are satisfied.[87] This is true, however, only in so far as State Parties are concerned. The ICC Statute itself only contemplates jurisdiction over nationals of non-State Parties in three circumstances, an analysis of which enables one to appreciate the pivotal preponderance of State consent in matters of cooperation.[88] Here, consent is either unilateral in so far as the State undertakes to cooperate, or bi-lateral since an agreement is reached with the ICC. It is not equivalent to consensus of States which, being a replacement for custom,[89] is another matter. Nor is it a manifestation of the dual functions of consent in the law on State responsibility.[90] The only instance where the ICC may assert jurisdiction irrespective of State consent is upon a UNSC referral.[91] An analysis of the UNSC Resolution regime is hence called for.

Crude as it may seem from their viewpoint, even non-State Parties to the ICC would need to implement legislation to execute a UNSC Resolution which directly invokes the cooperation of States.[92] Although States cannot rely on the absence of domestic law to justify non-compliance, the effect of ICC requests largely hinges on the degree to which States have domestically promulgated procedures intended to

---

[81] Llewllyn and Raponi 1999, pp. 83–84.

[82] Ruiz Verduzco 2015, p. 43.

[83] *Prosecutor v Germain Katanga and Mathieu Ngudjolo Chui*, above n. 36, para 59.

[84] Article 86 of the ICC Statute, above n. 2, should not be considered as tantamount to a residual obligation to cooperate in situations other than those addressed by specific obligations.

[85] Article 88 of the ICC Statute, above n. 2.

[86] Article 93 of the ICC Statute, above n. 2.

[87] Articles 59 and 89 of the ICC Statute, above n. 2.

[88] *Vide* Article 12(2)(a) dealing with territorial jurisdiction, Article 12(3) concerning the acceptance of ICC jurisdiction by a non-State Party {with the situations in *Côte d'Ivoire* and Ukraine constituting classical examples of this}, and Article 13 which deals with the trigger mechanisms; see also van der Wilt 2005, p. 100.

[89] D'Amato 2004, p. 185.

[90] '...when operative as a circumstance precluding wrongfulness, consent suspends the international obligations which are incumbent on States, whereas when functional pursuant to the law of treaties, consent creates, modifies, or extinguishes the rules whence such obligations stem forth' (Farhang 2014, p. 55).

[91] Heyder 2006, pp. 652–653.

[92] d'Aspremont and Brolmann 2010, p. 117.

facilitate cooperation.[93] Indeed, UNSC Resolutions can directly affect the horizontal system of enforcement too. France is a case in point. Universal jurisdiction over core crimes is generally not allowed in France.[94] UNSC Resolutions 827 and 955, establishing ICTY and ICTR respectively, have triggered the promulgation of French Law Number 95-1 of 2 January 1995 and Law Number 96-432 of 22 May 1996 'which allow for the exercise of absolute universal jurisdiction in relation to international crimes committed in Yugoslavia and Rwanda respectively'.[95] The national discretion of States is hence underscored, but this not to the detriment of the ICC's powers. To all this, Göran Sluiter underlines the way the applicable cooperation regime fluctuates as a result of the variables and permutations. He sums up matters, in a concise way, by correctly noting that 'which regime applies depends on the State whose assistance is sought, as well as on the manner in which the investigation has been triggered'.[96]

The dilemma, within the context of the need for cooperation, caused by the non-ratification of the ICC Statute by certain States, these being non-State Parties, is not however, always unsurmountable. The recognition of unlimited jurisdiction of the ICC (irrespective of State consent) has a direct bearing on the duty of non-State Parties to cooperate. In any case, notwithstanding non-ratification of the ICC Statute, there are other means (deriving, *inter alia*, from UNSC Resolutions and from customary international law) of ensuring surrender of those subjected to an international arrest warrant. Such means can permit the legitimate circumvention of the jurisdictional hurdle in the ultimate quest to ensure surrender. Whilst Bert Swart, when referring to the Genocide and Apartheid Conventions, opines that these 'two conventions may well strengthen the position of the Court',[97] Göran Sluiter makes a solid and credible case for the use of Article VI of the Genocide Convention[98] in order to elicit State cooperation for the arrest and surrender of an

[93] Stahn 2010, p. 667.

[94] Sulzer 2007, p. 125.

[95] Ibid.

[96] Sluiter 2003a, p. 611.

[97] Swart 2002, p. 1687.

[98] This portrays that 'persons charged with genocide or any of the other acts enumerated in Article III shall be tried by a competent tribunal of the State in the territory of which the act was committed, or by such international penal tribunal as may have jurisdiction with respect to those Contracting Parties which shall have accepted its jurisdiction'. Göran Sluiter, whilst disagreeing with the ICJ's interpretation {ICJ, Application of the Convention on the Prevention and Punishment of the Crime of Genocide, 26 February 2007, ICJ Rep. 2007, p. 43} of Article VI which presupposes that the duty to cooperate under international law is a pre-requisite for the acceptance of jurisdiction of an international penal tribunal, argues that the ICC, a beneficiary of Article VI, constitutes an international penal tribunal and that the requirements of 'acceptance of jurisdiction' on the one hand, and 'the existence of a duty to cooperate on the other' should be separated (Sluiter 2010, pp. 370–371).

alleged *génocidaire*.[99] A striking feature of the edifice he constructs is the fact that as a result of UNSC Resolution 1593 the need of further acceptance of jurisdiction is nullified. His argumentation, supported by Matthew Gillet's conclusion to the effect that Resolution 1593 estopped Sudan from asserting Head of state immunity by activating latent obligations under the Genocide Convention,[100] finds refuge in the combination of two crucial legal provisions. Firstly, Article 12 of the ICC Statute stipulates that if the trigger mechanism used is a UNSC Resolution [hence representing the entire international community], no further requisites to the exercise of jurisdiction can be imposed. Therefore, in this case, there is no need to rely upon Article VI of the Genocide Convention. It was still rather unclear whether the complementarity principle, which as shown regulates the relationship between the ICC and national jurisdictions, should be considered as applicable to UNSC referrals. This moot point is caused by the fact that Article 17 'does not distinguish between the provenance of referrals'.[101] No ICC Statute provision excludes the application of the admissibility test to UNSC referrals. On the other hand, one may argue that the UNSC could set the ICC aside as a result of its primacy in so far both as the ICC Statute recognises that the ICC itself affirms the purposes and principles of the UNC, and also by virtue of Article 103 of the UNC which, besides establishing a hierarchy among sources of international law, has elevated the UN Charter 'to the status of a superior international treaty'.[102] In practice, the UNSC has already passed resolutions which are at odds both with the ICC Statute and with the obligations of State Parties when it called on the ICC not to institute any investigation or prosecution for conduct by UN peacekeeping troops from nationals of non-State Parties.[103] These measures, called deferrals, are contemplated by Article 16 of the ICC Statute, a legal provision which has been contested since its inception.[104] The Pre-Trial Chamber of the ICC has determined that the complementarity principle should also be applied in cases triggered by UNSC Resolutions, this being a matter which shall be dealt with under Sects. 11.1 and 11.1.1. This conclusion was reached with reference to Article 13 of the ICC Statute which provides that the ICC may exercise its jurisdiction over core crimes 'in accordance with the Statute'. Now, since the ICC Statute includes the complementarity

---

99 Others, including Paola Gaeta, concur, though Paola Gaeta argues that *Omar Al Bashir* is shielded by diplomatic privileges and immunities as a sitting Head of State. However, William Schabas disagrees (Schabas 2011). This matter has sparked a lot of debate at all levels in international criminal law circles, including before the *COJUR*-ICC Working Group of the EU Council which was chaired by myself between January and June 2017.

100 Gillet 2012, pp. 63–96, but particularly pp. 93 and 95.

101 Dascalopoulou-Livada 2008, p. 59.

102 Vidmar 2012, pp. 18–19.

103 Coalition for the ICC 2008.

104 For a thorough legal analysis of deferrals, particularly the conditions and criteria which are required to invoke Article 16 of the ICC Statute, above n. 2, see Ruiz Verduzco 2015, pp. 52–60.

provisions, the complementarity principle applies thereto.[105] Similarly, Justine Tillier seems to conclude that 'the mere fact that complementarity is considered as a central principle of the existence of the Court means it should apply implicitly to Security Council referrals'.[106] Secondly, Article 25 of the UNC imposes upon UN member States the obligation to accept and carry out UNSC Resolutions, irrespective of whether a State agrees or disagrees with such resolutions. A decision by the UNSC, taken *intra vires*, is binding on States.[107] This legal provision manifests the subtle interaction between the UNC and the ICC Statute.[108] When these two crucial legal provisions coincide or overlap, they lead to significant legal consequences, including:

(a) States are precluded from challenging the ICC's jurisdiction;[109] and
(b) States are bound to cooperate. Whether they have ratified the ICC Statute, whether they are State Parties or non-State Parties, becomes immaterial.

In principle, I agree with Göran Sluiter's observations, but I qualify the second pretext (*id est* Article 25 of the UNC) to the effect that a State would potentially be entitled to refuse to carry out a UNSC Resolution either if and when the implementation of the UNSC Resolution violates a *jus cogens* norm[110] or is likely to violate a *jus cogens* norm, or else if and when the implementation of the UNSC Resolution constrains it to violate a conventional provision to which it is already bound, or when such implementation leads it to violate customary international law, unless that same State which is called to carry out such UNSC is a persistent objector. To this extent (and only to this extent), States may be entitled to assess and determine the human rights record of the ICC itself throughout their evaluation as to whether to surrender an individual to the ICC or not. My assertion is, though unsupported by evidence, substantiated by the fact that the drafting history of the ICC Statute also concedes that 'the Statute should permit the involvement of national courts in the application of national law where those requirements were considered fundamental, especially to protect the rights of individuals, as well as to

[105] ICC Pre-Trial Chamber I, *Prosecutor v Saif Al-Islam Gaddafi and Abdullah Al-Senussi, Decision on the Postponement of the Execution of the Request to Surrender of Saif Al-Islam Gaddafi Pursuant to Article 95 of the Rome Statute*, 1 June 2012, Case No. ICC-01/11-01/11, para 28.

[106] Tillier 2013, p. 515.

[107] Oberg 2005, pp. 879 and 891, cited in Akande 2009, p. 347, n. 44.

[108] Gallant 2003, p. 583.

[109] There is, however, some evidence that domestic and regional courts have found themselves competent to review Chapter VII resolutions in order to determine whether the Security Council has acted *ultra vires* or otherwise (de Wet and Nollkaemper 2002, p. 166, cited by Tzanakopoulos 2012, p. 50, n. 47). Such review, however, is most unlikely in such case since the UNSC has been rather cautious in using its powers of referral to the ICC on the pretext of the alleged commission of core crimes. In fact, since the ICC has been established, the UNSC has only resolved so twice.

[110] These norms, their nature and characteristics, are dealt with in Parts II and IV of this book.

verify procedural legality'.[111] The non-recognition of such qualifications would render the UNSC the ultimate, hierarchical supreme international organ. Additionally, as Jochen Frowein and Nico Krisch suggest, 'quasi-judicial determinations should remain exceptional and should be confined to cases where they are indispensable for the exercise of the police function of the Security Council.'[112] It must be recalled that the UNSC might be the supreme political organ, but it has no judicial standing and/or authority, and hence, arguably, the validity of its resolutions can be reviewed by the ICJ,[113] although such review would be valid only if incidental and if effected in a non-binding manner.[114] Additionally a UNSC Resolution *per se* is a subsidiary/secondary source of international law, as articulated by Article 38(1) of the Statute of the ICJ itself. All this seems to allow the facultative, though slight, leeway for State discretion. In all fairness, Göran Sluiter suggests some qualifications to his conclusion. Firstly, he contemplates the situation wherein the language of the relevant UNSC Resolution restricts the acceptance of jurisdiction. Besides being very unlikely, such UNSC Resolution would probably be defective *ad validitatem.* One cannot but here query: how could a UNSC Resolution trigger the ICC's jurisdiction, hence *de facto* necessitating State cooperation for such jurisdiction to bear fruits, whilst simultaneously limiting the acceptance of the same jurisdiction which the same UNSC Resolution has triggered? Secondly, Göran Sluiter acknowledges that the ICJ 'restricted the duty to cooperate to what States can reasonably do'.[115] This mirrors Articles 57(3)(d),[116] 86, 89(1), 93(1), 97, 99(4) of the ICC Statute, all of which promote an optimal degree of cooperation between State Parties and the ICC. Notwithstanding such qualifications, I go a step further in so far as Sluiter's observations can contribute to shape a reliable obligation to cooperate which is extraneous to and detached from the ratification of the ICC Statute. It seems in fact that, at least in so far as war crimes and the crime against humanity of torture are concerned, the Geneva Conventions and the CAT can serve the same purpose identified by Göran Sluiter in connection specifically and limitedly to the Genocide Convention. Moreover, being

[111] UNGA 1996, para 323, cited in Young 2001, p. 344.

[112] Frowein and Krisch 2002, p. 708.

[113] For an examination as to whether this is at all possible, see references to the *Lockerbie* case [ICJ, *Questions of Interpretation and Application of the 1971 Montreal Convention Arising from the Aerial Incident at Lockerbie (Libyan Arab Jamahiriya v UK), Provisional Measures,* Order of 14 April 1992, ICJ Rep. 1992, p. 114] in Sect. 13.4.

[114] Tzanakopoulos 2011, p. 110.

[115] Sluiter 2010, p. 377.

[116] This legal provision is important since it arguably constitutes the only exception to the fact that the ICC Prosecutor does not have the power to rely on coercive measures without ensuring State cooperation. In fact, this legal provision allows the ICC Pre-Trial Chamber to authorise the ICC Prosecutor to take coercive measures without ensuring State cooperation in failed State situations (de Meester 2009, p. 280). Göran Sluiter upheld that the discharge of the ICC's mandate and the need to ensure effective prosecutions might justify the exercise of such powers (Sluiter 2002b, p. 309). For an understanding of failed State situations, see Chaps. 5 and 6.

multi-lateral treaties, the Genocide Convention,[117] the Geneva Convention, the CAT, and the UNC itself, just like the ICC Statute, could be relied upon if and when their prevailing cooperation regime is more reliable and/or effective than the one belonging to the ICC Statute. No rule of international law precludes the application of these legal instruments, which can be said to embody international criminal law to a large extent, to the benefit of the ICC Statute itself. I present the need to scrutinize whether the non-applicability of statutory limitations,[118] together with the fact that, as shall be seen within the fourth Part of this work, the *aut dedere aut iudicare* rule can be said to apply in relation to the commission of core crimes, might lead to a conclusion that an obligation of cooperation is anyway indirectly inferred. Göran Sluiter does not state the above, but his categorization of Article VI of the Genocide Convention as a 'unique form of *aut dedere aut iudicare*'[119] can be said to adduce such observation.

From a purely jurisdictional viewpoint, though a fully-fledged convention, thus regulated by the VCLT, the ICC Statute does not only affect its own signatories. As noted, agreements of cooperation may be concluded with the ICC itself by virtue of Article 87(5) of the ICC Statute, together with *ad hoc* arrangements, and agreements or any other appropriate basis.[120] The existence of a *locus standi* of any State goes to show that 'complementarity is of a universal nature comprising also third States'.[121] There is no doubt that the assistance of third states[122] can also be crucial in the apprehension of suspects. Other States, not necessarily the State referring the matter to the ICC in terms of Article 14 of the ICC Statute, can exercise an important influence upon the surrender process. By way of example, 'French authorities assisted the Court in transporting Mr. *Lubanga* to The Hague'.[123] Additionally, 'Article 72 applies also to third States insofar as the relevant information is a matter of national security. Hence, any third State is entitled to intervene in the proceedings according to paragraph 4'.[124] Most importantly, 'the duty of cooperation, however, reaches beyond the States Parties since it includes States not parties which otherwise have accepted the exercise of jurisdiction by the Court with respect to the crime in question; they are consequently not third States in relation to the duty of cooperation, limited, however, to these crimes'.[125]

---

[117] For a comprehensive analysis of this important Convention, see van der Wilt et al. 2012, *passim*.

[118] Article 29 of the ICC Statute, above n. 2.

[119] Sluiter 2010, p. 366.

[120] Regulation 107 of the ICC.

[121] Hafner 2001, p. 245.

[122] In terms of Article 2 of the VCLT (1969) Vienna Convention on the Law of Treaties, these are States not party to a treaty, hence non-State Parties.

[123] UN (2004) Press Release: Prosecutor Receives Referral of the Situation in the DRC. 19 April 2004, Doc. AFR/903-L/3067, cited in Mutyaba 2012, p. 956.

[124] Hafner 2001, p. 252.

[125] Hafner 2001, p. 244.

UNSC Resolutions[126] adopted under Chapter VII of the UNC are binding on all UN member States (including ICC non-State Parties), these being 'the formal medium of the Council to express its collective will'.[127] Such obligations can be equated to the general obligation to cooperate of State Parties,[128] particularly that obligation which flows from Article 86 of the ICC Statute. The words 'cooperate fully' in UNSC Resolutions 1593 and 1970 are identical to the relevant phrase in Article 86 of the ICC Statute. This infers that, although the non-State Party's obligations subsist, such non-State Party enjoys the same rights as those of State Parties in so far as the invocation of grounds of refusal is concerned. In Göran Sluiter's words, 'when the Security Council, by a binding decision taken under Chapter VII, submits a situation to the ICC, thereby creating jurisdiction for that Court, United Nations members must be regarded as having accepted the jurisdiction of the ICC in respect of that situation'.[129] This does tally with the fact that under Chapter VII of the UNC, the UNSC can impose legal obligations on all UN member States, thereby significantly affecting the rights and obligations of States,[130] with Chapter VII constituting an important *caveat* which nullifies the principle of non-intervention protected by Article 2(7) of the UNC.[131] Finally, notwithstanding the fact that the UNSC's powers are regulated exclusively by the UNC, since the UNSC resolution is modelled upon the ICC Statute and made in terms of such legal instrument, the UNSC cannot, in making a referral, modify the obligation of the State to cooperate in a way which is substantially different to the prevailing obligations of State Parties under the ICC Statute. This is largely because of two reasons.

(I) Firstly, the UNSC referrals, wherein usually the referred situation deals with one prevailing within a non-State Party, were always intended to extend the ICC's jurisdiction to situations occurring outside the territory of a State Party and with respect to acts committed by non-nationals of a State Party. If this were not so, and hence if the UNSC can modify the contours of State cooperation, the prevailing rules should be more rigorous and less rudimentary, but not vice-versa. In connection with State obligations to cooperate, 'pursuant to Article 25 of the Charter, they acquire the character of obligations *erga omnes* while, as a consequence of Article 103 of the Charter, they prevail over obligations member States may have assumed under any other international

[126] For an understanding of the impact of UNSC Resolutions on the ICJ, see Greenwood 1999, pp. 81–86.

[127] Duijzentkunst 2008, p. 190.

[128] Akande 2012, p. 299.

[129] Sluiter 2010, p. 372.

[130] Orakhelashvili 2005, p. 61.

[131] Duijzentkunst 2008, p. 196.

agreement'.[132] In any case, 'a denial of fundamental human rights is a flagrant violation of the purposes and principles of the Charter',[133] being the maintenance of international peace and security. Moreover, the fact that the UNSC is vested with authority to deal with the protection of human rights is a settled matter in international law.[134] Therefore, such conclusions may be reached since, by virtue of Article 103 of the UNC, by means of Article 25 of the UNC as a result of which obligations of cooperation acquire an *erga omnes* character,[135] and last but not least, further to important jurisprudence,[136] UNC obligations prevail over treaty obligations. They would, however, have to be expressly stipulated to be more rigid than those prevailing under the ICC Statute. In such case one would need to determine whether the ICC would be able to enforce an additional obligation which does not derive from its own Statute. This is a moot point, a hypothetical and (so far) unprecedented scenario which is not the object of this work. If however such additional obligations are not so expressly stipulated, the UNSC Resolution, although it does not go beyond the ICC Statute, should not be presumed to impose less onerous obligations on the States which are called upon to comply with such obligations.

(II) Secondly, the UNSC does not have any *ad hoc* procedure to address investigations following a referral to the ICC by itself. In the absence of such express rules, the UNSC implicitly acknowledged that the ICC Statute shall govern investigations and prosecutions which follow its referral. This, in turn, strengthens and substantiates the above assertion, being that the obligation of States emanating from a UNSC Resolution can be equated to the general obligation to cooperate of State Parties to the ICC Statute. What's good for the goose is good for the gander. *Ergo*, States which have been subjected to the obligation to cooperate further to a UNSC referral must also be entitled to challenge the admissibility of a case by invoking grounds for refusal to cooperate accordingly. The concept of the 'admissibility of a case' shows that admissibility is about the exercise of jurisdiction, which exercise is undertaken by means of the act of prosecution, rather than about the existence of jurisdiction. In other words, the ICC may have jurisdiction over a case, but for the

---

[132] Swart 2002, p. 1677. For a contrary view, as a result of which human rights instruments possess a normative superiority vis-à-vis binding UNSC Resolutions, see *Rukundo v Federal Office of Justice*, above n. 49.

[133] ICJ, Advisory Opinion, *Legal Consequences for States of the Continued Presence of South Africa in Namibia Notwithstanding Security Council Resolution 276 (1970)* (*Namibia* case), 21 June 1971, 1971 ICJ 16, para 131, cited in Paust 2010, p. 3.

[134] ICTR, Trial Chamber II, *Prosecutor v Joseph Kanyabashi, Decision on the Defence Motion on Jurisdiction*, 18 June 1997, Case No. ICTR-96-15-T, paras 28–29

[135] Swart 2002, p. 1677.

[136] ICJ, *Questions of Interpretation and Application of the 1971 Montreal Convention Arising from the Aerial Incident at Lockerbie (Libyan Arab Jamahiriya v UK), Provisional Measures*, Order of 14 April 1992, ICJ Rep. 1992, p. 114, para 39.

reasons postulated in Article 17 of the ICC Statute, it may decide not to exercise such jurisdiction.[137] Admissibility may be challenged, in terms of Article 18 of the ICC Statute, when what can eventually become a 'case' is still a 'situation'.[138] For admissibility to be challenged a case need not be identified. On the other hand, the ICC's jurisdiction can be challenged only when a case subsists. This means that a State which contends that the ICC does not enjoy jurisdiction to entertain a referral by the UNSC, 'would need to wait until an arrest warrant had been issued before launching its contestation'.[139] One cannot, however, disentangle admissibility from jurisdiction completely since, occasionally, they overlap. By way of example, a State can submit that the ICC does not enjoy jurisdiction *rationae materiae* in so far as the conduct in question constitutes a mere ordinary crime (rather than a core crime), and on this basis, contest the admissibility of the case by claiming its primacy, *id est* that the ICC should not interfere with the exercise of its jurisdiction by the domestic State, be it territorial or otherwise. As stated above, just as the UNSC cannot, in making a referral, modify the obligation of the State to cooperate in a way which is substantially different to the prevailing obligations of State Parties under the ICC Statute, similarly the ICC may not question the validity or otherwise of the UNSC referral. In other words the ICC is not entitled to check whether the UNSC acted legitimately, when it used its Chapter VII powers, or otherwise. Arguably, only the ICJ may decide upon the constitutionality, being the formal and substantive legality, of such UNSC Resolutions.[140]

10.3 The Consequences of a Breach of the State's Obligation to Cooperate

It is settled that State Parties are obliged to cooperate with the ICC. Non-State Parties may, in certain circumstances,[141] be so obliged too. The crucial questions, which must be posed at this stage, are therefore: What happens if and when States (which are obliged to cooperate, be they State Parties or non-State Parties) do not cooperate with the ICC? What sanctions can be imposed on defaulting States?

---

137 Schabas 2010, p. 340.

138 A situation refers to a larger set of circumstances, whereas a case refers to circumstances in which an individual suspect has been identified. For an explanation as to the relevance of the distinction for the purposes of the admissibility test, see Olásolo 2003, pp. 99–100; see also Rastan 2011, pp. 421–459.

139 Schabas 2010, p. 365.

140 Graefrath 1993, p. 201.

141 See Sect. 10.2.

These questions, the importance of which stems from the ICC's relative silence on the repercussions of non-cooperation,[142] will be replied to within this heading.

The potential repercussions of the failure to cooperate by the State, which is either obliged to cooperate or obliged to provide a sufficient degree of cooperation, by means of which the ICC is prevented from exercising its functions and powers, may lead to the finding of a violation either by the ICC and a referral of the matter to the ASP[143] in terms of Article 87(7)[144] of the ICC Statute and Regulation 109 of the ICC, or else to a referral to the UNSC when the case had been triggered by a UNSC Resolution. The ICC can merely record the default by detecting the breach and, at best, draw an adverse inference therefrom.[145] In so far as State Parties are concerned, the report (or rather notification) to the ASP and/or to the UNSC,[146] depending on whether the request for cooperation was tendered on the basis of a State referral, an auto-referral (a self-referral) or else *proprio motu* investigations on the one hand and, on the other hand, the UNSC respectively, does not constitute direct punitive measures but is tantamount to an insufficient political censure[147] very much akin to a mere 'naming and shaming' exercise,[148] practically just a verbal admonition. This exercise is premised on the fact that 'cooperating with the ICC is a signal of States' commitments to human rights and the rule of law'.[149] The corollary of this is that non-cooperation is the antithesis of such commitment. It is indeed disappointing that the UNSC does not even have an established procedure to deal with a finding of non-cooperation.[150] It seems that, at some institutional levels, cooperation is lacking. In fact, the ICC reported that 'closer cooperation between the Security Council Sanctions Committee and the Court would have a positive impact on the pursuit of the common goals of the Council and the Court.'[151] To add insult to injury, as of 2015, two non-permanent members of the UNSC are

---

[142] Barnes 2011, p. 1595.

[143] The ASP, established by Article 112(1) of the ICC Statute, above n. 2, is not an organ of the ICC and is separate and distinct therefrom [*vide* Article 34 of the ICC Statute, above n. 2]. Its role and function in the cooperation saga is best explained in terms of its political clout. The more States ratify the ICC Statute, above n. 2, the more influential the ASP would be, and consequently the more likely it would affect co-operative relations between third States [non-State Parties] and the ICC (Wenqi 2006, p. 108).

[144] This is commonly referred to as a judicial finding of non-compliance (Sluiter 2011) and may not be appealed (Sluiter 2018a, p. 387). Article 87(7) proceedings are administrative in nature (Sluiter 2018a, p. 387).

[145] OTP 2003, p. 18.

[146] Such measures follow the negotiation mechanism contemplated by Article 119(2) of the ICC Statute, above n. 2.

[147] Mutyaba 2012, p. 953.

[148] Schabas 2004, p. 130.

[149] Kelley 2007, p. 573, cited in Hillebrecht and Straus 2017, p. 171, n. 14.

[150] Ruiz Verduzco 2015, p. 49.

[151] UNGA 2018, pp. 6–113, also cited in ICC Report 2017, pp. 6–99 – 6–118.

defaulting States Chad and Nigeria,[152] with the latter State enjoying the Presidency thereof in August 2015.[153] Visits by *Omar Al Bashir*, such as that in South Africa, sparked political outrage and ignited legal literature.[154] These incidents reflect the resolution of the AU Assembly which determined that *Al Bashir*, as a serving head of State, is entitled to immunity for as long as he remains in office.[155] The frustration of the ICC, which seems to be losing its patience,[156] has been eloquently portrayed when it reiterated that, unlike domestic courts, it has no direct enforcement mechanism, meaning that it lacks a police force.[157] Consequently, 'if there is no follow up action on the part of the Security Council, any referral by the Council to the ICC under Chapter VII of the UN Charter would never achieve its ultimate goal, namely, to put an end to impunity. Accordingly, any such referral would become futile'.[158]

There is not much more the ICC can do apart from formally and judicially denouncing lack of compliance.[159] This is hardly viewed as influential for the reasons which shall be explained shortly. In fact, even when the ICC had the opportunity to do so, it decided not to pursue such path. Drawing widespread criticism, the ICC initially had not referred the matter to the ASP after the ICC Prosecutor was constrained to decide, upon pressure coming from the ICC itself, to withdraw the charges against *Uhuru Muigai Kenyatta*, the first acting Head of State who appeared before the ICC.[160] Subsequently the ICC Appeals Chamber remanded the impugned decision to the Trial Chamber for it to determine whether there has been a failure to comply with a cooperation request and, if so, 'whether a referral of *Kenya* to the ASP would be an appropriate measure to seek assistance to obtain the requested cooperation or otherwise address the lack of compliance by

---

152 UNSC (2017) http://www.un.org/en/sc/members/. Accessed 11 November 2017.

153 Permanent Mission of the Federal Republic of Nigeria to the UN (2015) http://redesign.nigeriaunmission.org/. Accessed 12 January 2016.

154 Tladi 2015, pp. 1027–1047; see also de Wet 2015, pp. 1049–1071; see also Ventura 2015, pp. 995–1025, all of which were articles published for the purposes of the symposium entitled 'On President Al-Bashir's Presence at the AU Summit in South Africa and the Non-Execution of the ICC Arrest Warrant'.

155 The resolution stipulates that '…African Union member States shall not cooperate pursuant to the provisions of Article 98 of the Rome Statute of the ICC relating to immunities, for the arrest and surrender of President Omar El Bashir of the Sudan' (AU 2009, cited in Okowa 2014, p. 236, n. 35).

156 Boschiero 2015, pp. 625–653.

157 ICC Pre-Trial Chamber II, *Situation in Darfur, Sudan, Prosecutor v Omar Hassan Ahmad Al Bashir, Decision on the Cooperation of the DRC Regarding Omar Al Bashir's Arrest and Surrender to the Court*, 9 April 2014, Case No. ICC-02/05-01/09, para 33.

158 Ibid.

159 Ruiz Verduzco 2015, p. 45.

160 ICC 2014, also cited in Zakerhossein and DeBrouwer 2015, pp. 218–219, n. 138.

Kenya...'[161] It has been noted that *Kenya*'s efforts illustrate 'that the risk of Member States using the ASP's powers to improperly influence judicial decision-making is most acute when Member States' own interests are affected by ICC proceedings'.[162] The ICC was not convinced that a referral to the ASP and/or the UNSC would be warranted in order to achieve cooperation from South Africa because the South African Government, which was the first State Party to approach the ICC with a request for consultations, accepted its obligation to cooperate with the ICC. In the words of the ICC Pre-Trial Chamber II, since 'any possible ambiguity as to the law concerning South Africa's obligations has been removed, a referral of South Africa's non-compliance with the Court's request for the arrest and surrender of *Omar Al Bashir* would be of no consequence as a mechanism for the Court to obtain cooperation'.[163] There would have been a distinct outcome if, as Göran Sluiter recommends, 'all findings of non-compliance under Article 87 of the Statute are automatically referred to the ASP'.[164] The ICC was of a different view when it referred Jordan's non-compliance to the ASP and the UNSC in so far as there was no uncertainty with respect to the obligations of Jordan,[165] 'the first Arab State to ratify the Rome Statute',[166] which, in any case, had not requested consultations with the ICC in terms of Article 97 of the ICC Statute.[167] The differential treatment accorded by the ICC to South Africa, on one hand, and Jordan, on the other hand, has been considered as puzzling and harshly criticised.[168] In Sluiter's view, the South Africa and Jordan rulings constitute 'an encroachment by the Court on the role and prerogatives of the ASP'.[169]

In the absence of coercive powers enjoyed by the ICC or support by the UNSC,[170] cooperation becomes reliant solely on goodwill which, in a world in

---

[161] ICC Appeals Chamber, *Situation in the Republic of Kenya, Prosecutor v Uhuru Muigai Kenyatta, Judgment on the Prosecutor's Appeal Against Trial Chamber's V(B)'s 'Decision on Prosecution's Application for a Finding of Non-Compliance under Article 87(7) of the Statute'*, 19 August 2015, Case No. ICC-01/09-02/11 OA 5, paras 94–96.

[162] Woolaver and Palmer 2017, p. 656.

[163] ICC, Pre-Trial Chamber II, *Situation in Darfur, Sudan, Prosecutor v Omar Hassan Ahmad Al Bashir, Decision under Article 87(7) of the Rome Statute on the Non-compliance by South Africa with the Request by the Court for the Arrest and Surrender of Omar Al Bashir*, 6 July 2017, Case No. ICC-02/05-01/09, para 137.

[164] Sluiter 2018b.

[165] ICC, Pre-Trial Chamber II, *Situation in Darfur, Sudan, Prosecutor v Omar Hassan Ahmad Al Bashir, Decision under Article 87(7) of the Rome Statute on the non-compliance by Jordan with the Request by the Court for the Arrest and Surrender of Omar Al-Bashir*, 11 December 2017, Case No. ICC-02/05-01/09, para 53.

[166] du Plessis 2017.

[167] *Decision on Jordan's non-compliance*, above n. 165, para 47.

[168] Sluiter 2018a, pp. 390–393.

[169] Sluiter 2018a, p. 399.

[170] The ICC, using a critical tone, has noted that 'the past 24 meetings of the Security Council of the United Nations following the adoption of Resolution 1593 (2005), including meetings held on the occasion of the biannual reports made by the Prosecutor to the Security Council of the United

which power politics is rife, is often in short supply.[171] Sometimes such report does not emanate from the State, but from defence counsel.[172] Whereas the ASP can, in turn, escalate the matter to a dispute settlement method, including a referral to the ICJ,[173] the UNSC can, at best, have a political impact which would isolate the defaulting State.[174] One must here recall that the UNSC has enforcement powers vis-à-vis States which do not implement its binding orders, which orders could include ICC requests for surrender.[175] The same powers may not be exercised on international institutions, such as the ICC itself. In practice, all the ASP can do is to revoke the right to vote of a State Party within the ASP itself and within the Bureau,[176] although such measures are specifically intended to sanction defaults relating to financial and budgetary matters. It could also ask for the immediate cessation of the default, whilst considering collective countermeasures on the strength of the general rules on State responsibility.[177] Indeed, there is no doubt that it would be appropriate to conclude that the enforcement mechanisms under the ICC Statute are weak,[178] especially because 'it is unclear whether the Assembly of State Parties can take any action beyond making the finding of non-compliance'.[179] Owing to this undesirable reality, other initiatives, new efforts to develop arrest strategies[180] and the setting up of an innovative complementarity

Nations, have not resulted in measures against State Parties that have failed to comply with their obligations to cooperate with the Court, despite proposals from different States to develop a follow-up mechanism concerning the referral of States to the Security Council by the Court' [*Decision on South Africa's non-compliance*, above n. 163, para 138].

171 Cryer 2015, p. 280.

172 ICC 2013.

173 For this purpose, some basis of jurisdiction must be laid pursuant to Article 36 of the ICJ Statute [ICJ Statute (1946) Statute of the International Court of Justice]. Moreover, a referral of the matter to the ICJ would most likely decelerate the entire procedure (Demirdjian 2010, p. 189).

174 Sluiter 2009, p. 198.

175 Articles 25, 41 and 103 of the UNC.

176 Article 112(8) of the ICC Statute, above n. 2.

177 Ciampi 2002, p. 1635.

178 Jurists have attempted to counteract the ICC's vulnerability by proposing the following alternative enforcement mechanisms:

(a) the use of economic aid inducements;
(b) the use of diplomatic and economic sanctions on uncooperative governments;
(c) freezing the assets of indicted individuals;
(d) offering individual cash rewards for information or assistance leading to the arrest or the conviction of indicted individuals;
(e) the use of luring by deception for locating and apprehending suspects; and
(f) the use of military force to execute apprehension and confinement of suspects.

(Scharf 2000, pp. 925–927). Others have suggested that the ICC should possess its own police force (see, *inter alia*, Scheffer 1995, pp. 649–660; see also Perritt 1999, pp. 281–324).

179 Danner 2003, p. 529. Three laudable recommendations for the improvement of the cooper ation regime have been proposed by Göran Sluiter (Sluiter 2008, p. 884).

180 ASP 2013a, paras 26–27, cited in O'Donohue 2015, p. 133, n. 209.

website,[181] have been developed to incentivise cooperate and promote complementarity. The ASP would have to ensure that an amendment to the UN-ICC Negotiated Relationship Agreement should be undertaken in order to allow the possibility of a referral to the ICJ to obtain an advisory opinion.[182] Comparatively, when analysed in the light of the *ad hoc* tribunals, the ICC punitive infrastructure, when it is not backed by a UNSC Resolution, is disappointing.[183] There exists no ICC counterpart of Rule 59(A) which provides a means of enforcing Article 29(2)(e) of the ICTY Statute by requiring States to report their failures to execute an arrest warrant. Rule 59(B) thereof deems a failure to report as a failure to execute the warrant itself.[184] Neither ICC State Parties nor the ASP enjoys this luxury. The ICC's enforcement regime is also long-winded and can lead to ambiguities. By way of example, 'it is not clear whether the Assembly of State Parties can take up the issue of non-compliance on its own initiative, without referral by the Court or by the Security Council'.[185] The fact that no State referrals have subsisted so far shows the reluctance of States to denounce other States. This same reluctance is likely to surface at ASP level. After all the ASP, although the management oversight of the ICC, is nothing more than a legislative body composed of the same States that have ratified and acceded to the ICC Statute, the State Parties themselves. It will not and 'cannot replace the Court as the judicial body charged with applying the law in complete independence'.[186]

Other potential measures must not be discarded and will be proposed at this stage. A glance thereto is pertinent. Firstly, the ICC, may, in so far as this is worth the time, effort and energy, confirm the charges in the absence of the non-surrendered person even prior to such person's initial appearance before the ICC.[187] Secondly, nothing stops State Parties from adopting countermeasures vis-à-vis the defaulting State. Philipp Ambach asserts that ICC State Parties can collectively hold each other accountable for compliance with the ICC's cooperation regime.[188] Their juridical interest is unquestioned. In any case, the breach of a treaty[189] is an internationally wrongful act entailing State responsibility under

---

[181] ASP 2011, para 10, cited in O'Donohue 2015, p. 137, n. 240.

[182] Demirdjian 2010, p. 189.

[183] Sluiter 2003a, pp. 650–651.

[184] Bassiouni and Manikas 1996, p. 792.

[185] Schabas 2010, p. 1124.

[186] Kreß 2018, p. 12.

[187] See Article 61(2) of the ICC Statute, above n. 2, which, in Carsen Stahn's rather optimistic view, is a more powerful tool than Rule 61 proceedings in the context of the *ad hoc* tribunals (Stahn 2010, p. 669).

[188] Ambach 2015, p. 1280.

[189] Just as the ICC Statute, above n. 2, triggers the obligation to cooperate, such obligation equally stems from *ad hoc* agreements and/or arrangements. Their breach would hence equally entail the State responsibility of the defaulting State just as though the defaulting State were a signatory of (and would have ratified) the ICC Statute, above n. 2, in the first place. In substantiation of this, Zhu Wenqi upholds that 'if a non-Party State has expressed a willingness to co-operate and has

general international law.[190] Hence, in so far as ICC State Parties are concerned, other State Parties which might have a juridical interest in ensuring that the defaulting State Party actually surrenders the individual to the ICC (such 'specially affected State' or 'injured State' could include a State whose nationals are victims of the core crime in question), might invoke the general rules of State responsibility for the consummation of an internationally wrongful act consisting in the refusal to surrender the individual to the ICC further to the international arrest warrant. Such rules comport that the breach of a treaty constitutes an internationally wrongful act which entails the responsibility of the defaulting State under international law. The consequence of this is the right of State Parties to adopt countermeasures when the following pre-requisites subsist cumulatively:

a. a finding by the ICC to the effect that a State Party has committed a characterized infringement of the obligation to cooperate;
b. the ASP has taken no action to remedy the default; and
c. the UNSC has taken no action to remedy the default.[191]

Thirdly, it might be legitimate for international institutions to exercise economic pressure on defaulting States in order to entice their cooperation with the ICC. Kai Ambos, giving the example of the EU which could exercise such pressure on unwilling African States in times of debt reduction and the fight against global poverty, infers that this would however violate development aid policies and goals.[192] Such economic pressure could include the imposition of sanctions and asset freezing.[193]

Moreover, Article 112(4) of the ICC Statute could be used to establish a 'Compliance Committee' as a subsidiary body of the ASP.[194] Nothing seems to preclude or impede the Compliance Committee to consider non-compliance of a State *proprio motu*, even in the absence of a report by the ICC or the UNSC. Such moves would allow the ICC cooperation regime to rest upon a more robust structure. It would not be so unprecedented within the realm of the vertical system of enforcement that a particular organ/unit be set up with specific terms of reference. By way of analogy, the ICTY President had established a special Referral Bench to hear all motions for transfer of cases.[195] Finally, though various States might be reluctant, one should not exclude the possibility of an amendment to the ninth part of the ICC Statute. This could, as a start and at the very least, send a

reached agreement with the ICC on a specific case, it has consequently incurred an obligation to co-operate in that particular case just like the State parties. The ICC or State parties to the Court are entitled to ask it to perform its co-operation obligations' (Wenqi 2006, pp. 107–108).

[190] See Chap. 7.

[191] Ciampi 2002, p. 1636.

[192] Ambos 2007, p. 61.

[193] ASP 2013b, paras 49–50, and Stagno Ugarte 2012, cited in Ruiz Verduzco 2015, p. 61, n. 185.

[194] The ASP has already established the Committee on Budget and Finance, the Staff Pension Committee, the Trust Fund for Victims, and the Oversight Committee on Permanent Premises.

[195] Tolbert and Kontić 2011, p. 905.

message to the effect that priority should be given to mandatory compliance and adherence to obligations rather than to mere cooperation and assistance by prior consent. Besides undertaking amendments to some legal provisions, the title of Part 9 could be changed to read, unequivocally, 'State Obligations'.

Unfortunately, precedents at the UNSC are not comforting at all. By way of example, various ICTY Presidents have repeatedly reported State non-compliance in very clear terms to the UNSC to no avail.[196] The UNSC Resolution has also failed to provide follow up support to the ICC once it has referred to it a situation.[197] The UNSC has not responded to any of the eight communications which the ICC has sent to the UNSC alleging the non-cooperation of Argentina, Australia and Luxembourg.[198] It was questioned why, for example, the UNSC 'did not issue any kind of statement in relation to the arrest of *Saif Al-Islam Gaddafi*, against whom the ICC has issued an arrest warrant in relation to the situation in Libya, referred by the Security Council'.[199] Similarly, after the Darfur UNSC referral, no measures were taken following the notification of non-cooperation which had been brought to its formal cognisance.[200] These omissions are indeed disappointing particularly because had certain measures been taken at UN level, these would have been binding.[201] Effectively, the UN, faced with a persistent default of a State to cooperate further to a referral by the UNSC itself, can, by means of a two-thirds majority of the UNGA following a recommendation of the UNSC,[202] expel a UN member State 'for persistent violations of the principles of the Charter'.[203] Such sanctions are particularly plausible since impunity can be considered as a 'threat to the peace' in terms of Article 39 of the UNC and as a menace to the maintenance of international peace and security.[204] To this effect, a deterrence rationale which has

---

196 Former ICTY President McDonald, in her final letter as ICTY President to the UNSC, expressed the serious problem of non-enforcement of its orders as follows:

> During the past four years, my predecessor, Judge Antonio Cassese and I have reported, on numerous occasions, State non-compliance and many of these matters remain unresolved. In fact, notwithstanding action by the Security Council, including resolutions 940 and 1207 and several Presidential Statements, the States concerned have continued to flaunt the will of the international community, refusing to co-operate with the Tribunal and failing to carry out their legal obligations. This is simply unacceptable, and I respectfully request that the Security Council take steps to address the troubling situation (Harmon and Gaynor 2004, p. 420).

197 See above n. 170.

198 Knottnerus 2014, p. 221.

199 Mistry and Ruiz Verduzco 2012, p. 9.

200 Ibid.

201 By virtue of Article 103 of the UNC, the legality of UN sanctions cannot be reviewed {*Yusuf and Al Barakaat International Foundation*, above n. 6; *Kadi*, above n. 6, paras 281, 299 and 316}.

202 Article 18 of the UNC.

203 Article 6 of the UNC.

204 Murray 2011, p. 612.

been strategically deployed as a logic that links justice to peace through its ability to prevent atrocities[205] substantiates calls that the ICC serves as an entity to strengthen international peace and security.[206] This rationale ultimately rests upon the ICC's ability to pursue successful prosecutions.[207] Prosecutions set a precedent establishing international norms and deterring those who would commit core crimes by demonstrating an end to impunity.[208] Such conclusion cannot be drawn by the ICC but only by the UNSC since an Article 39 determination is not subject to judicial review by the ICC. This does not mean that the UNSC acts *legibus solutus.* It is anyway bound to respect the limits of the powers conferred upon it by means of the UNC.[209] In the context of a deferral, the most the ICC could do is to assess whether the UNSC's decision adheres to the four conditions stipulated in Article 16 of the ICC Statute.[210] The importance of a categorization of a situation as a 'threat to the peace' is significant. An obligation to cooperate with the ICC can stem directly from such a categorization by the UNSC even in instances where a case is triggered by a State referral or by the Prosecutor *proprio motu.*[211] However, even in such case, in the face of such default, 'there is not necessarily an express responsibility in the Charter for the Security Council to act'.[212] Only a sprouting[213] (and preferably depoliticized)[214] responsibility to protect can be legitimate ground to exact the

205 Vinjamuri 2015, p. 15.

206 Ruiz Verduzco 2015, p. 31.

207 Grono and de Courcy Wheeler 2015, p. 1243.

208 Grono and de Courcy Wheeler 2015, p. 1225. One must here acknowledge that these views have been criticized by some who contend that the very nature of core crimes renders them resistant to deterrence through prosecutions which risk prolonging conflicts (Branch 2007, p. 2, cited in Grono and de Courcy Wheeler 2015, pp. 1225–1226, n. 5).

209 Knottnerus 2014, p. 204; see also Condorelli and Villalpando 2002, p. 579.

210 A valid deferral (i) should be limited to a period of twelve months; (ii) should include an express request by the UNSC to the ICC so that such ICC does not commence or proceed with an investigation or prosecution; (iii) must be issued by means of a resolution adopted under Chapter VII of the UNC; and (iv) such UNSC's powers must be so exercised on a case-by-case basis (Knottnerus 2014, pp. 198–200).

211 Ciampi 2002, p. 1611.

212 Trahan 2013, p. 425.

213 The word 'sprouting' is hereby used by myself to reflect the (arguably) shaky foundation of the responsibility to protect which, in the views of some jurists, consistitutes a mere aspiration rather than a fully-fledged duty. In fact it has been stated that many critics, one of whom is Philip Cunliffe (see Cunliffe 2010) '...argue either that the responsibility to protect is a dangerous and imperialist doctrine that threatens to undermine the national sovereignty and political autonomy of the weak or that it is little other than rhetorical posturing that promises little tangible improvement in the protection of vulnerable people. To complicate matters, profound disagreements have emerged about the function, meaning and proper use of responsibility to protect' (Bellamy et al. 2011, pp. 2–3).

214 Schiff argues that the responsibility to protect hinges on international political mobilization whereas the ICC depends on legal judgment (Schiff 2015, p. 8, cited in Birdsall 2015, p. 55, n. 7).

taking of measures. In such case a link of causation would have to subsist.[215] In other words, it would have to be proved that impunity infringes the responsibility to protect by jeopardizing, or by potentially jeopardizing, international peace and security itself. This is plausible since evidence shows that where amnesties were granted political killings and death squads increased.[216] Moreover, many parallels have been traced between the ICC's goal to end impunity and the responsibility to protect.[217] Over and above all this, the responsibility to protect principle and the ICC share some key assumptions and provisions, including the projection of a normative framework of responsibility of the international community (a facet of which is constituted by the complementarity regime) to hold perpetrators of core crimes to account.[218] If, therefore, justice is not properly meted out, it seems reasonable to argue that the responsibility to protect would be violated. This is more so when one keeps in mind that the responsibility to protect connotes nothing more than: 'sovereignty is not an absolute right of national governments, but is rather an earned right, based upon fulfilment of government's responsibility to protect its people from violence'.[219] Consequently, 'the belief that preventing atrocity crimes is a responsibility of both national governments and the international community also underlay the establishment of the International Criminal Court'.[220] The ICC Statute, by means of its Preamble and especially the complementarity regime prevailing within Article 17 of the ICC Statute, also affirms 'that when governments fail to protect people, the responsibility to do so befalls the international community'.[221] This international community is embodied within the UNSC which 'should be the international body responsible for identifying, preventing and stopping violations of the R2P norm – in other words, for determining when a government has failed to protect its citizens, and for mobilising international action to protect suffering populations'.[222] Such action should encompass measures intended to fulfil the following responsibilities:

---

[215] This connotes 'a naturalistic relationship between the result of a crime and wilful action' (Murmann 2014, p. 283), and may be defined as 'the process of connecting an act (or omission) with an outcome as cause and effect' (Plakokefalos 2015, p. 471).

[216] HRW 1991, p. 87.

[217] The 2009 UN Secretary-General's report stipulates that 'by seeking to end impunity, the ICC and the UN-assisted tribunals have added an essential tool for implementing the responsibility to protect' and considers the ICC as 'one of the key instruments relating to the responsibility to protect' (UNGA 2009, para 10, cited in Birdsall 2015, p. 54, n. 4).

[218] Birdsall 2015, pp. 54–55.

[219] Contarino and Lucent 2011, p. 196.

[220] Ibid.

[221] Contarino and Lucent 2011, p. 197.

[222] International Commission on Intervention and State Sovereignty 2001, also cited in Contarino and Lucent 2011, p. 197.

1. The responsibility to prevent atrocities from occurring;
2. The responsibility to react once atrocities occur; and
3. The responsibility to rebuild after the atrocities have ceased to occur.[223]

The second responsibility mentioned here above clearly necessitates a robust sanctioning mechanism in order to punish defaults imputable to States which inhibit the adherence to UNSC Resolutions and/or orders of the ICC which follow such a resolution. Now if the UN fails to so act notwithstanding such domestic default, nothing precludes concerned States from acting in its stead.[224] The word 'concerned' is broader than the terms 'interested States' or than 'injured States'. A State can hence intervene without having a juridical interest and/or without feeling directly aggrieved by another State's conduct and actions, which conduct and actions can include a State's omission to investigate and prosecute. This widens the parameters of such potential measures significantly because it is hardly conceivable that a State would not be concerned with ongoing impunity in the face of the continued commission of core crimes especially when such core crime either leads to an influx of migrants to the detriment of such other State and/or its political allies, or to the death of such other State's citizens. Antonios Tzanakopoulos rightly contends that 'if it is accepted that violations of the obligations of the United Nations under the Charter result in all Member States of the Organization being injured, then the countermeasure of disobedience is virtually always available in response'.[225] Countermeasures by States which are not directly injured but are 'concerned States' also seem permissible since the request to arrest and surrender, though triggered by a UNSC Resolution, ultimately derives from the ICC itself. In the light of this, I refer to Akehurst who 'has argued that third-State countermeasures are admissible when they aim at enforcing a judicial decision'.[226] The Preamble to the ICC Statute itself refers to such core crimes as being of serious concern to the international community as a whole, which community comprises all States. *Ergo*, any State can claim that it is concerned by a default of the system, entailing and presupposing a default of the domestic State enjoying jurisdiction over the core crime and a subsequent default of the UNSC. Whether any such 'concerned State' would have the political will to adopt measures intended to incentivise and spark the process leading to the execution of national or international criminal justice is another matter which ought to be scrutinized by political scientists and experts of international relations, not by myself. This said, in the lack of such political will, no rule of law stops such 'concerned States' from teaming up to solicit effective measures which may be undertaken by international

[223] International Commission on Intervention and State Sovereignty 2001, also cited in Contarino and Lucent 2011, p. 195, n. 9.

[224] International Commission on Intervention and State Sovereignty 2001, also cited in Contarino and Lucent 2011, pp. 197–198, n. 15.

[225] Tzanakopoulos 2011, p. 198.

[226] Tzanakopoulos 2011, p. 200.

organisations[227] or multilateral coalitions, even in matters involving arrest and surrender of those suspected of having committed core crimes.

There might exist yet another way to compel cooperation. It is pertinent to detect it at this stage. The UNSC could have availed itself of Article 87(5)(a) of the ICC Statute which stipulates that the ICC may invite non-State Parties to cooperate with it on the basis of an *ad hoc* arrangement with such State or on any other appropriate basis. Whereas the former *ad hoc* arrangement necessitates State consent, the latter appropriate basis could be constituted by means of the *vires* of the UNSC emanating from Article 41 of the UNC. This important legal provision is intended to ensure compliance with UNSC decisions. In fact it stipulates that the UNSC may decide what measures to employ to give effect to its decisions and may call upon UN members to apply such measures. In my view, the measures contemplated by the UNC are tantamount to an appropriate basis in terms of Article 87(5)(a) of the ICC Statute. The only problem with this submission is the import of the word 'invite' within Article 87(5)(a) of the ICC Statute, in so far as this connotes the discretionary approval of the invitee, the State whose cooperation is solicited.

Considered cumulatively, since the non-ratification of the ICC Statute by various States and the fact that the regulation of the power to issue cooperation requests is flawed,[228] the ICC cooperation regime cannot be deemed to be compact. Comparatively speaking, 'the supranational model of the *ad hoc* Tribunals may well be superior, in a number of respects, to the mixture of models in Part 9' of the ICC Statute[229] which is a compromise between traditional extradition law and the 'new law' of the *ad hoc* Tribunals.[230] Vertical cooperation under Part 9 has been described 'as a triangular legal relationship between the requesting Court, the requested State and the individual or individuals concerned.'[231] Amidst this peculiar 'triangular relationship the ICC and the requested State have a joint responsibility for the rights of the individual or individuals concerned'.[232] What is important, at least for the purpose of this heading, is that the ICC 'has the final authority to adjudicate disputes over failures of compliance'.[233] This is substantiated by Article 59(4) of the ICC Statute which divests custodial States of their jurisdiction and/or authority and/or *vires* to consider whether a warrant of arrest was issued in accordance with Article 58 of the ICC Statute. On the same vein, Rule 117 (3) allows the arrested person to impugn the warrant of arrest only directly before the Pre-Trial Chamber, that is, after surrender to the ICC which enjoys exclusive

[227] See an analysis of the status of international organisations in Voetelink 2015, pp. 169–187.

[228] Sluiter 2009, p. 200.

[229] Swart and Sluiter 1999, p. 101.

[230] Swart 2002, p. 1640.

[231] Kreß and Prost 2016, p. 2011

[232] Ibid.

[233] Stahn 2010, p. 667.

jurisdiction over the matter. The handcuffs used on the arrested individual are not only the custodial State's property, but are also the same handcuffs which tie the hands of the same custodial State, severely restraining its flexibility. Article 59(4) of the ICC Statute obliges national authorities to ensure that the custodial State can fulfil its duty to surrender the person to the ICC, which legal provision implies that a breach of the suspect's human rights cannot constitute a ground for refusal (an impediment to surrender) but must be raised as a bar to proceedings before the ICC where abuse of process[234] can be complained of.[235]

In so far as Article 87(7) of the ICC Statute, mentioned here above, is concerned Göran Sluiter appropriately notes that the finding of non-compliance can be issued by the same Chamber which requested the cooperation in the first place. This, in his view, would entail a violation of the rules of natural justice, namely the *nemo iudex in causa propria*[236] rule, 'especially since there appears to be no right of review for the affected state'.[237] Göran Sluiter, making use of Article 11*bis* of the ICTY Statute,[238] recommends the creation of a mechanism of review by a Chamber that is not directly involved. Although it is by means of his works that a better understanding on the law of cooperation today exists, in this matter, I beg to differ. First of all, granting a specific *vires* to a 'sister' Chamber would not guarantee the independence and impartiality of the adjudicating Chamber. Such decision would have to be taken by a judicial body which is completely extraneous and unrelated to the ICC, such as, for example, the ICJ, which, after all, is entitled to apply international law and scrutinizes State conduct. So, if an adjudicator were to hear the contending parties to the dispute and decide there upon, this should not be another ICC Chamber. It seems to me, however, that a State whose default is alleged might not necessarily be afflicted by prejudice as a result of the existent framework. First of all, a State can produce and tender repeated representations before the organ which initially requested its cooperation, be it the Prosecutor[239] and/or the Registrar,[240] whose re-consideration can henceforth be solicited. William Schabas opines that since Article 87 of the ICC Statute does not specify which organ of the ICC has the authority to make requests for measures of cooperation, 'the answer

---

[234] See Sect. 11.3.1.

[235] Hall 2008, p. 1152.

[236] No person can judge a case in which he or she is a party.

[237] Sluiter 2008, p. 875.

[238] For a detailed analysis of Article 11*bis* of the ICTY Statute see Bekou 2009b, pp. 726–769.

[239] ICC Pre-Trial Chamber II, *Situation in Uganda, Decision on Prosecutor's Application for Leave to Appeal in Part Pre-Trial Chamber II's Decision on the Prosecutor's Applications for Warrants under Article 58, Unsealed Pursuant to Decision ICC-02/04-01/05-52 dated 13 October 2005, Situation in Uganda*, 19 August 2005, Case No. ICC-02/04-01/05-20-US-Exp, paras 7–8.

[240] ICC Pre-Trial Chamber I, *Situation in Darfur, Sudan, Prosecutor v Ahmad Muhammad Harun (Ahmad Harun) and Ali Muhammad Ali Abd-Al Rahman (Ali Kushayb), Decision on the Prosecution Application under Article 58(7) of the Statute*, 27 April 2007, Case No. ICC-02/05-01/07, paras 56–57.

will vary depending upon the nature of the request'.[241] This power of re-consideration, besides reflecting abundant judicial discretion, is also apparent in other circumstances, within the ICC Statute itself.[242] Only the ICC, by way of example, can 'determine the precise content of the duty to cooperate'.[243] To this extent, in my view, it may be said to constitute an inherent power of the ICC, with the ultimate power being the fact that it is arbiter of its own jurisdiction. In other words, the ICC (and only the ICC), has *kompetenz-kompetenz*, which, in the context of the ICC's functions, may be said to be the power of the ICC to decide whether it enjoys the power (legal authority) to deal with a case *ab initio*. This power of the ICC, in turn and of itself, divests States of any power. Indeed, the ICC's Appeals Chamber has found that the ICC may also vaunt implied powers by reason of the purport and function of Article 21(3) of the ICC Statute.[244] Sergey Vasiliev, referring to Article 21, notes that it could have 'an overt generative (gap-filling) function, a power-conferring function' but that it could also serve to 'enable the Court to deduce - rather than generate – remedies that are already implicit in its applicable law and follow from it as a matter of course'.[245] Nothing precludes a State from bringing to the Registrar's consideration the reasons and grounds for refusing to comply with the Prosecutor's request, and vice-versa. In fact, one can also identify a 'rigid but highly artificial distinction between the law concerning the power to request and the duty to provide assistance'.[246] A system of review, in my opinion, is therefore in-built, though inadvertently, as a result of the fact that the organ responsible for the transmission of requests for co-operation is not unequivocally and not unambiguously established particularly because Rule 176(2) is very much subject to interpretation.[247] Such review may also be said to result from the consultation process which the ICC Statute expressly implants.[248]

Secondly, the grounds for constituting such a default (this being non-compliance itself) as one carrying strict liability[249] seem to subsist. Although this might not

---

[241] Schabas 2010, p. 981.

[242] Article 119(1) allows the ICC to determine and conclusively settle any dispute relating to its own judicial functions.

[243] Sluiter 2003a, p. 651.

[244] ICC Appeals Chamber, *Situation in the DRC, Prosecutor v Thomas Lubanga Dyilo, Judgment on the Appeal of the Prosecutor Against the Decision of Trial Chamber I Entitled 'Decision on the Consequences of Non-Disclosure of Exculpatory Materials Covered by Article 54(3)(e) Agreements and the Application to Stay the Prosecution of the Accused, Together with Certain Other Issues Raised at the Status Conference on 10 June 2008'*, 21 October 2008, Case No. ICC-01/04-01/06 OA 13, para 77, cited in Vasiliev 2014, p. 135.

[245] Vasiliev 2014, p. 135.

[246] Sluiter 2008, p. 878.

[247] Rastan 2008, pp. 447–449.

[248] Swart and Sluiter 1999, pp. 103–105.

[249] Sometimes, the term 'absolute liability' is inter-changeably used (Simester et al. 2010, p. 173).

directly obviate the need for impartial review all together, it is noteworthy especially because the Preamble to the ICC Statute, and more specifically the words 'fully cooperate'[250] within Article 86[251] point to a situation entailing strict liability. Transposed within an international ambit, anything which falls short of one's duty to 'fully cooperate' would *ipso facto* trigger such strict liability. Hence, for a State to be free from liability it must provide unconditional and unencumbered cooperation to the ICC, which includes its constituent organs, amongst which and most importantly, the Prosecutor. Limitless and prompt cooperation, due diligence and good faith, are the rule, whereas the grounds for refusal enlisted within the ICC Statute would be the only exceptions. This does not, however, necessarily exclude other avenues for refusal. Circumstances might subsist, for example, wherein upon a request to cooperate with the ICC, a State questions the actual parameters of the situation and/or the remit of the investigation, the contours of which might be equivocal and/or ambiguous. The wording of the ICC Statute, however, does not seem to permit such challenges. No provision allows a State to question the parameters of a situation and/or the remit of the investigation. Such permission cannot be presumed or deduced merely from the sovereign powers of States under international law, especially when the referral is triggered by a UNSC Resolution, in which case all UN member States are presumed to have consented to such referral. This can be said to result from Article 25 of the UNC according to which UN member States undertake to carry out the decisions of the UNSC in accordance with the UNC. Some have opined that such phrase regulates the *modus operandi* as to how UNSC decisions are to be implemented, whereas others have expressed the view that such phrase conveys the binding nature of UNSC decisions. Citing the *Namibia* case, Antonios Tzanakopoulos upholds that 'the preponderant view seems to be that the members are obliged to carry out all resolutions which the Security Council is authorized by the Charter to issue with the intention to bind the members at whom they are directed'.[252] The reservations which States may potentially (and maybe legitimately) make in this context relate to the fact that a valid (*intra vires*) UNSC Resolution constitutes a referral to the ICC which is not predominantly intended to bind all UN member States but is intended to trigger the ICC's jurisdiction in terms of Article 13(b) of the ICC Statute.

To go back to the main issue within this heading, there are instances where States have less leeway (or no leeway at all) in determining whether they shall cooperate or otherwise. In these circumstances the obligations of State Parties on one hand and those of non-State Parties on the other hand, more or less converge. Whereas non-State Parties[253] are under no general duty to cooperate with the

[250] This is a 'complex legal notion, and may be subject to various interpretations' (Sluiter 2008, p. 877).

[251] This phrase has not been given a precise meaning within the meeting preceding the adoption of UNSC Resolution 1593 (Sluiter 2008, p. 876).

[252] Tzanakopoulos 2011, p. 58.

[253] Non-State Parties and/or third parties should be construed to mean those States which have not ratified the ICC Statute, above n. 2.

ICC,[254] such duty to cooperate becomes mandatory and unconditional (even upon non-State Parties) when the ICC's jurisdiction is triggered by a UNSC Resolution, provided such States are UN Member States. Such resolution would be 'binding on all United Nations Member States'.[255] At this stage and by virtue of such resolution 'the equivalent primacy over other international obligations should apply'.[256] Upon such resolution, the cooperation regime, for all intents and purposes of law, becomes coercive to the extent that Luis Moreno Ocampo, fully aware of Sudan's non-compliance, upheld that 'as soon as Mr. *Al Bashir* travels in international airspace[257] his plane could be intercepted and he could be arrested. That is what I expect',[258] he categorically demanded. In other words, keeping aside, for the moment, issues relating to al-Bashir's personal immunity which shall be dealt with under Sect. 11.4.1, the obligation to cooperate becomes as absolute[259] as the obligation to cooperate of State Parties in general circumstances. However, further to a State Party referral, the ASP, in terms of its competence arising from Regulation 109,[260] cannot inflict any sanctions upon the defaulting State other than the declaratory finding of a violation and a concomitant reprimand warning of consequences for ulterior non-compliance.

To sum up, nothing precludes the UNSC from stepping in and adopting sanctions, including military action, in terms of Chapter VII of the UNC, namely Articles 41 and 42: 'if a State refuses to cooperate and such refusal amounts to a threat to the peace, even in cases previously referred to the Court by a State or initiated by the Prosecutor *proprio motu*'.[261] This would not be far-fetched at all because, as shown here above, there subsists an inevitable and 'intrinsic relation between the commission of core crimes and threats to international peace and security'.[262] After all, as already stated, such State behaviour could also potentially expose the defaulting State to actions for damages arising from an international delict before the ICJ. Further to a referral by the UNSC, the UNSC may impose sanctions and other measures on the basis of the relevant provisions of Chapter VII of the UNC. Naturally, the State Party referral cannot affect non-State Parties, whereas the UNSC referral can lead to sanctions even upon those States which have not ratified the ICC Statute but which are UN member States. This is not to mention

[254] These include both populous and powerful States such as Egypt, India, Indonesia, Iran, Israel, Pakistan, China, Russia, Sudan and the USA.

[255] Wenqi 2006, p. 108.

[256] Cryer et al. 2011, p. 512.

[257] The former ICC Chief Prosecutor clarified that 'international airspace' meant 'outside of Sudan'.

[258] See http://www.huffingtonpost.com/2009/03/04/albashir-arrest-warrant-i_n_171703.html. Accessed 13 January 2011.

[259] Mutyaba 2012, p. 937.

[260] See Regulations of the International Criminal Court (2004) Regulations of the Court, ICC-BD/01-01-04.

[261] Cassese 1999, p. 166.

[262] Mistry and Ruiz Verduzco 2012, p. 10.

the pressure that is generally exercised politically and diplomatically by other States and institutions upon the defaulting State, which pressure, coupled with the influence habitually exercised by mass media, can potentially lead to remedial action by the defaulting State. In other words, the remedy at international law for non-cooperation therefore largely depends on the trigger mechanism, unless such non-cooperation could be such as to constitute a threat to the peace, an unlikely scenario requiring international political consensus at UNSC level.

In any case, it seems that, given the absence of sanctions which can be imposed on defaulting States, the ICC would have to, by means of a teleological approach, devise strategies to ensure that it sufficiently equips itself with the required intuition to start biting rather than continue barking to no avail. Moreover, if the USA punished 'small States for working with the Court',[263] one would expect the ICC to have the means required to punish States which are obliged to work with it but breach such obligation and choose instead not to work with it. The ICC cooperation regime is quite extra-ordinary in that it allows some leeway to States, depending on the prevailing circumstances. This is so with regard to State Parties. No one-size-fits-all formula subsists since negotiations are generally marred by *realpolitik.* The final outcome of negotiations would depend on the strength or weakness of the negotiating State, keeping in mind that the State would commonly enjoy a significant amount of bargaining power especially if and when the ICC cannot effectively prosecute without its cooperation. The ICC, in such a state of affairs, would be a beggar, not a chooser, especially where the State enjoys hefty political clout at international level. In the case of non-State Parties, unfortunately, should a State default by failing to cooperate notwithstanding *ad hoc* arrangements, no sanctions can directly be imposed upon the breaching party, especially if and when the *ad hoc* arrangement, consisting in an agreement, stipulates that a breach thereof would not lead to any remedial actions or measures. In any case, 'there is no vote in the Assembly to take away, and no financial contribution to increase',[264] but only political pressure, if it could be worth something. This is not to say that the ICC's efforts are fruitless. The ICC would rather have an *ad hoc* arrangement with a non-State Party, albeit without any sanctioning powers, than have nothing at all. One must here echo the words of the ICC itself when it found that non-compliance by States 'prevents the Court from exercising its functions and powers under the Statute'.[265] This is why corollaries of the absence of State cooperation are the negation of criminal justice and the violation of the rights of victims. The fragile ICC cooperation regime requires an overhaul. Time will tell whether this will be brought to fruition either directly by amendments to the ICC Statute or indirectly by virtue of the ICC's jurisprudence, if at all.

---

263 Hawkins 2008, p. 107.

264 Zahar and Sluiter 2008, p. 475; see also Sluiter 2009, p. 199.

265 *Decision on Jordan's non-compliance*, above n. 165, para 24.

References

Akande D (2009) The Legal Nature of Security Council Referrals to the ICC and its Impact on Al Bashir's Immunities. JICJ 7(2):333–352

Akande D (2012) The Effect of Security Council Resolutions and Domestic Proceedings on State Obligations to Cooperate with the International Criminal Court. JICJ 10(2):299–324

Ambach P (2015) A Look Towards the Future – The ICC and "Lessons Learnt" In: Stahn C (ed) The Law and Practice of the International Criminal Court. OUP, Oxford, pp. 1277–1295

Ambos K (2007) Prosecuting International Crimes at the National and International Level: Between Justice and Realpolitik. In: Kaleck W, Ratner M, Singelnstein T, Weiss P (eds) International Prosecution of Human Rights Crimes. Springer, Berlin/Heidelberg, pp. 55–68

Ambos K, Stegmiller I (2008) German Research on International Criminal Law: Book Reviews. CLF 19(1):181–198

Apartheid Convention (1973) Convention on the Suppression and Punishment of the Crime of Apartheid

ASP (2011) Report of the Secretariat on Complementarity, Official Records, Vol. I, Tenth Session of the ASP, 12–21 December 2011, Doc. ICC-ASP/10/2

ASP (2013a) Report of the Bureau on Non-Cooperation. Twelfth Session, 20–28 November 2013, Doc. ICC-ASP/12/34

ASP (2013b) Report of the Court on the Status of Ongoing Cooperation between the International Criminal Court and the United Nations, including in the Field. Twelfth Session, 20–28 November 2013, Doc. ICC-ASP/12/42

AU (2009) Decision of the 13th Ordinary Session of the Assembly of Heads of State and Government. Assembly/AU/Dec. 245 (XIII)

Barnes GP (2011) The International Criminal Court's Ineffective Enforcement Mechanisms: The Indictment of President Omar Al Bashir. FILJ 34(6):1585–1619

Bassiouni MC, Manikas P (1996) The Law of the International Criminal Tribunal for the Former Yugoslavia. TP, Irvington-on-Hudson, NY

Bekou O (2009a) A Case for Review of Article 88, ICC Statute: Strengthening A Forgotten Provision. NCLR 12(3):468–483

Bekou O (2009b) Rule 11*Bis*: An Examination of the Process of Referrals to National Courts in ICTY Jurisprudence. FILJ 33(3):723–791

Bellamy AJ, Davies SE, Glanville L, Introduction. In: Bellamy AJ, Davies SE, Glanville L (eds) The Responsibility to Protect and International Law. MNP, Leiden/Boston, pp. 1–12

Bellelli R (2010) Obligation to Cooperate and Duty to Implement. In: Bellelli R (ed) International Criminal Justice: Law and Practice from the Rome Statute to Its Review. MPG Books Group, Ashgate, Farnham, Surrey, pp. 211–240

Birdsall A (2015) The Responsibility to Prosecute and the ICC: A Problematic Relationship? CLF 26(1):51–72

Bitti G (2015) Article 21 and the Hierarchy of Sources of Law Before the International Criminal Court. In: Stahn C (ed) The Law and Practice of the International Criminal Court. OUP, Oxford, pp. 421–443

Boschiero N (2015) The ICC Judicial Finding on Non-Cooperation Against the DRC and No Immunity for Al Bashir Based on UNSC Resolution 1593. JICJ 13(3):625–653

Branch A (2007) Uganda's Civil War and the Politics of ICC Intervention. Ethics and International Affairs 21(2):179–198

Buchan R, Johnsson C-EJ (2012) Reviewing Jurdi NN (2011) The International Criminal Court and National Courts: A Contentious Relationship. Ashgate, Farnham. ICLR 12(1):104–109

Cassese A (1999) The Statute of the International Criminal Court: Some Preliminary Reflections. EJIL 10(1):144–171

Cassese A (2003) International Criminal Law. OUP, Oxford

Ciampi A (2002) The Obligation to Cooperate. In: Cassese A, Gaeta P, Jones JRWD (eds) The Rome Statute of the International Criminal Court: A Commentary, Vol. II. OUP, Oxford, pp. 1607–1638

Coalition for the ICC (2008) Factsheet: Chronology of the Adoption of Security Council Resolutions 1422/1487 and Withdrawal of the Proposed Renewal in 2004. http://www.iccnow.org/documents/FS-1422and1487Chronology_26March2008.pdf. Accessed 30 November 2011

Condorelli L, Villalpando S (2002) Can the Security Council Extend the ICC'S Jurisdiction? In: Cassese A, Gaeta P, Jones JRWD (eds) The Rome Statute of the International Criminal Court: A Commentary, Vol. I. OUP, Oxford, pp. 571–582

Contarino M, Lucent S (2011) Stopping the Killing: The International Criminal Court and Judicial Determination of the Responsibility to Protect. In: Bellamy AJ, Davies SE, Glanville L (eds) The Responsibility to Protect and International Law. MNP, Leiden/Boston, pp. 196–198

CAT (1984) Convention Against Torture and Other Cruel, Inhuman or Degrading Treatment or Punishment

Cryer R (2015) The ICC and its Relationship to Non-State Parties. In: Stahn C (ed) The Law and Practice of the International Criminal Court. OUP, Oxford, pp. 260–280

Cryer R, Friman H, Robinson D, Wilmshurst E (2011) An Introduction to International Criminal Law and Procedure, 2nd edn. CUP, Cambridge

Cunliffe P (2010) Critical Perspectives on the Responsibility to Protect. Routledge, London

Currie RJ (2007) Abducted Fugitives Before the International Criminal Court: Problems and Prospects. CLF 18(3–4):349–393

D'Amato A (2004) International Law: Sources; Collected Papers, Vol. III. MNP, Leiden/Boston

d'Aspremont J, Brolmann C (2010) Challenging International Criminal Tribunals Before Domestic Courts. In: Reinisch A (ed) Challenging Acts of International Organizations Before National Courts. OUP, Oxford, pp. 111–136

Danner AM (2003) Enhancing the Legitimacy and Accountability of Prosecutorial Discretion at the International Criminal Court. AJIL 97(3):510–552

Dascalopoulou-Livada P (2008) The Principle of Complementarity and Security Council Referrals. In: Politi M, Gioia F (eds) The International Criminal Court and National Jurisdictions. Ashgate, Farnham, Surrey, UK, pp. 57–62

de Meester K (2009) Coercive Measures, Privacy Rights and Judicial Supervision in International Criminal Investigations: In Need of Further Regulation. In: Sluiter G, Vasilev S (eds) International Criminal Procedure: Towards a Coherent Body of Law. CMP, London, pp. 273–309

de Wet E (2015) The Implications of President Al Bashir's Visit to South Africa for International and Domestic Law. JICJ 13(5):1049–1071

de Wet E, Nollkaemper A (2002) Review of Security Council Decisions by National Courts. GYIL 45:166–202

Demirdjian A (2010) Armless Giants: Cooperation, State Responsibility and Suggestions for the ICC Review Conference. ICLR 10(2):181–208

du Plessis M (2017) Time to Resolve the Debate Over Immunity and the International Criminal Court. Chatham House, The Royal Institute of International Affairs. https://www.chathamhouse.org/expert/comment/time-resolve-debate-over-immunity-and-international-criminal-court. Accessed 3 December 2018

Duffy H (2001) National Constitutional Compatibility and the International Criminal Court. DJCIL 11(5):5–38

Duijzentkunst BS (2008) Interpretation of Legislative Security Council Resolutions: Student Paper. ULR 4(3):188–209

Farhang C (2014) The Notion of Consent in Part One of the Draft Articles on State Responsibility. LJIL 27(1):55–73

Forowicz M (2010) The Reception of International Law in the European Court of Human Rights. International Court and Tribunals Series, OUP, Oxford

French Law No. 95-1 on adapting French Law to the Provisions of United Nations Security Council Resolution 827 Establishing an International Tribunal for the Prosecution of Persons

Responsible for Serious Violations of International Humanitarian Law Committed in the Territory of Former Yugoslavia Since 1991, 2 January 1995
French Law No. 96-432 on adapting French Law to the Provisions of United Nations Security Council Resolution 955 Establishing the International Tribunal for Rwanda, 22 May 1996
Frowein JA, Krisch N (2002) Chapter VII. Action with Respect to Threats to the Peace, Breaches of the Peace, and Acts of Aggression. In: Simma B, Mosler H, Randelzhofer A, Tomuschat C, Wolfrum R (eds) Paulus A, Chaitidou E (assistant eds) The Charter of the United Nations: A Commentary, Volume I, 2nd edn. OUP, Oxford, pp. 701–763
Gallant KS (2003) The International Criminal Court in the System of States and International Organizations. LJIL 16(3):553–591
Geneva Convention (1949a) Geneva Convention (I) for the Amelioration of the Condition of the Wounded and Sick in Armed Forces in the Field
Geneva Convention (1949b) Geneva Convention (II) for the Amelioration of the Condition of the Wounded, Sick and Shipwrecked Members of Armed Forces at Sea
Geneva Convention (1949c) Geneva Convention (III) relative to the Treatment of Prisoners of War
Geneva Convention (1949d) Geneva Convention (IV) relative to the Protection of Civilian Persons in Time of War
Genocide Convention (1948) Convention on the Prevention and Punishment of the Crime of Genocide
German Law to Implement the Rome Statute of the ICC of 17 July 1998 [*Entwurfeines Gesetzeszur Ausfuehrung des Roemischen Statuts des Internationalen Strafgerichtshofes vom 17 Juli 1998*] {Draft Act Implementing the Rome Statute for the International Criminal Court of 17 July 1998}, Act Amending the Basic Law (Federal Law Gazette 2000, I 1633) 29 November 2000
Gillet M (2012) The Call of Justice: Obligations under the Genocide Convention to Cooperate with the International Criminal Court. CLF 23(1–3):63–96
Gordillo LI (2012) Interlocking Constitutions: Towards an Interordinal Theory of National, European and United Nations Law. HP, Oxford
Graefrath B (1993) Leave to the Court What Belongs to the Court: The Libyan Case. EJIL 4 (2):184–205
Greenwood CJ (1999) The Impact of Decisions and Resolutions of the Security Council on the ICJ. In: Heere WP (ed) International Law and The Hague's 750th Anniversary. Asser Press, The Hague, pp. 81–86.
Grono N, de Courcy Wheeler A (2015) The Deterrent Effect of the ICC on the Commission of International Crimes by Government Leaders. In: Stahn C (ed) The Law and Practice of the International Criminal Court. OUP, Oxford, pp. 1225–1244
Hafner G (2001) The Status of Third States Before the International Criminal Court. In: Politi M, Nesi G (eds) The Rome Statute of the International Criminal Court: A Challenge to Impunity. Ashgate, Farnham, Surrey, UK, pp. 239–253
Hall C (2008) On Article 59. In: Triffterer O (ed) Commentary on the Rome Statute of the International Criminal Court. 2nd edn. CH Beck/Hart/Nomos, Munchen/Oxford/Baden-Baden, pp. 1147–1158
Harmon MB, Gaynor F (2004) Prosecuting Massive Crimes with Primitive Tools: Three Difficulties Encountered by Prosecutors in International Criminal Proceedings. JICJ 2(2):403–426
Hawkins D (2008) Power and Interests at the International Criminal Court. The SAIS Review of International Affairs 28(2):107–119
Heyder C (2006) The U.N. Security Council's Referral of the Crimes in Darfur to the International Criminal Court in Light of U.S. Opposition to the Court: Implications for the International Criminal Court's Functions and Status. BJIL 24(2):650–671
Hillebrecht C, Straus S (2017) Who Pursues the Perpetrators? State Cooperation with the ICC. HRQ 39(1):162–188

Holmes JT (2002) Complementarity: National Courts versus the International Criminal Court. In: Cassese A, Gaeta P, Jones JRWD (eds) The Rome Statute of the International Criminal Court: A Commentary, Vol. I. OUP, Oxford, pp. 667–686

HRW (1991) El Salvador's Decade of Terror: Human Rights Watch Since the Assassination of Archbishop Romero, HRW Report. http://www.hrw.org/reports/1991/10/01/el-salvador-s-decade-terror-human-rights-assassination-archbishop-romero. Accessed 13 August 2011

ICC (2013) Press Statement of the Defence for *Saif Al-Islam Gaddafi*, ICC, The Hague, 25 November 2013. http://www.iccnow.org/documents/Libya_Defense_PR.pdf. Accessed 2 September 2015

ICC (2014) Statement of the Prosecutor of the ICC, Fatou Bensouda, on the Withdrawal of Charges Against Mr. *Uhuru Muigai Kenyatta*, 5 December 2014. https://www.icc-cpi.int/Pages/item.aspx?name=otp-statement-05-12-2014-2. Accessed 13 May 2015

ICC Elements of Crimes (1998) International Criminal Court, Elements of Crimes

ICC Report (2017) 1 August 2016 – 31 July 2017, A/72/349, 17 August 2017. In: Muller J, Sauvant KP (2018) Annual Review of United Nations Affairs 2016/2017, Volume VI. OUP, Oxford, pp. 6-99–6-118

ICC Statute (1998) Rome Statute of the International Criminal Court

ICJ Statute (1946) Statute of the International Court of Justice

ICTY Statute (1993) Statute of the International Criminal Tribunal for the Former Yugoslavia

International Commission on Intervention and State Sovereignty (2001) The Responsibility to Protect. Report adopted by the UNGA in the 2005 World Summit Outcome Document. International Development Research Centre. Ottawa, Canada. http://responsibilitytoprotect.org/ICISS%20Report.pdf. Accessed 30 December 2011

Jacobs D (2010) Commentary on Arrest Warrants and Admissibility. In: Klip A, Sluiter G (eds) Annotated Leading Cases of International Criminal Tribunals: The International Criminal Court 2005–2007, Vol. 23. Intersentia, Antwerp/Oxford/Portland, pp. 113–122

Jensen R (2003) Cooperating with the International Criminal Court: Potential Implications for National Criminal Justice Personnel. http://www.icclr.law.ubc.ca/Publications/Reports/ICC%20Reports/NCJP_Guide_English.PDF. Accessed 22 June 2011

Jørgensen NHB (2009) The *Proprio Motu* and Interventionist Powers of Judges at International Criminal Tribunals. In: Sluiter G, Vasiliev S (eds) International Criminal Procedure: Towards a Coherent Body of Law. CMP, London, pp. 121–147

Kelley J (2007) Who Keeps International Commitments and Why? The International Criminal Court and Bilateral Non-Surrender Agreements. American Political Science Review 101 (3):573–589

Knoops G-JA, Amsterdam RR (2006) The Duality of State Cooperation within International and National Criminal Cases. FILJ 30(2):260–295

Knottnerus AS (2014) The Security Council and the International Criminal Court: The Unsolved Puzzle of Article 16. NILR 61(2):195–224

Kreß C (2003) The Procedural Law of the International Criminal Court in Outline: Anatomy of a Unique Compromise. JICJ 1(3):603–617.

Kreß C (2018) On the Activation of ICC Jurisdiction Over the Crime of Aggression. JICJ 16(1):1–17

Kreß C, Prost K (2016) Part 9: International Cooperation and Judicial Assistance. In: Triffterer O, Ambos K (eds) The Rome Statute of the International Criminal Court: A Commentary, 3rd edn. CH Beck/Hart/Nomos, Munchen/Oxford/Baden-Baden, pp. 2003–2157

Krings BL (2012) The Principles of Complementarity and Universal Jurisdiction in International Criminal Law: Antagonists or Perfect Match? GJIL 4(3):737–763

Llewllyn J, Raponi S (1999) The Protection of Human Rights Through International Criminal Law: A Conversation with Madam Justice Louise Arbour, Chief Prosecutor for the International Criminal Tribunals for the Former Yugoslavia and Rwanda. UTFLR 57(1):83–99

Meernik J, Aloisi R (2009) I Do Declare: Politics, Declarations and the International Criminal Court. ICLR 9(2):253–273

Mégret F (2010) In Search of the 'Vertical': Towards an Institutional Theory of International Criminal Justice's Core. In: Stahn C, van den Herik L (eds) Future Perspectives on International Criminal Justice. Asser Press, The Hague, pp. 178–224

Merrills JG (1993) The Development of International Law by the European Court of Human Rights, 2nd edn. MUP, Manchester

Mistry H, Ruiz Verduzco D (Rapporteurs) (2012) The United Nations Security Council and the International Criminal Court. International Law Meeting Summary, with Parliamentarians for Global Action, Chatham House, London. http://www.pgaction.org/pdf/activity/Chatham-ICC-SC.pdf. Accessed 1 September 2016

Murmann U (2014) Problems of Causation with regards to (Potential) Actions of Multiple Protagonists. JICJ 12(2):283–294

Murray ARJ (2011) Does International Criminal Law Still Require a 'Crime of Crimes'? A Comparative Review of Genocide and Crimes Against Humanity. GJIL 3(2):589–615

Mutyaba R (2012) An Analysis of the Cooperation Regime of the ICC and its Effectiveness in the Court's Objective in Securing Suspects in its Ongoing Investigations and Prosecutions. ICLR 12(5):937–962

Nsereko D (2013) The International Criminal Court and Complementarity in Practice. LJIL 26 (2):427–447

O'Donohue J (2015) The ICC and the ASP. In: Stahn C (ed) The Law and Practice of the International Criminal Court. OUP, Oxford, pp. 105–138

Oberg E (2005) The Legal Effects of Resolutions of the UN Security Council and General Assembly in the Jurisprudence of the ICJ. EJIL 16(5):879–906

Okowa P (2014) The Security Council, the African Union and the International Criminal Court: Anatomy of a Problematic Relationship. In: Ebbesson J, Jacobsson M, Klamberg M, Langlet D, Wrange P (eds) International Law and Changing Perceptions of Security, Liber Amicorum Said Mahmoudi. MNP, Leiden/Boston

Olásolo H (2003) The Prosecutor of the International Criminal Court Before the Initiation of Investigations: A Quasi-Judicial or a Political Body? ICLR 3(2):87–150

Orakhelashvili A (2005) The Impact of Peremptory Norms on the Interpretation and Application of United Nations Security Council Resolutions. EJIL 16(1):59–88

OTP (2003) Informal Expert Paper: The Principle of Complementarity in Practice. ICC-01/04-01/07-1015-Anx. https://www.icc-cpi.int/RelatedRecords/CR2009_02250.PDF. Accessed 17 July 2017

OTP (2013) Policy Paper on Preliminary Examinations. ICC-OTP, November 2013. https://www.icc-cpi.int/iccdocs/otp/otp-policy_paper_preliminary_examinations_2013-eng.pdf. Accessed 10 March 2016

Paust JJ (2010) The United Nations is Bound by Human Rights: Understanding the Full Reach of Human Rights, Remedies, and Non-immunity. HILJ 51:1–13

Permanent Mission of the Federal Republic of Nigeria to the UN (2015) http://redesign.nigeriaunmission.org/. Accessed 12 January 2016

Perritt HH (1999) Policing International Peace and Security: International Police Forces. WILJ 17:281–324

Pinto Soares P (2012) Tangling Human Rights and International Criminal Law: The Practice of International Tribunals and the Call for Rationalized Legal Pluralism. CLF 23(1–3):161–191

Plakokefalos I (2015) Causation in the Law of State Responsibility and the Problem of Overdetermination: In Search of Clarity. EJIL 26(2):471–492

Prost K (2011) The International Criminal Tribunal for the Former Yugoslavia and its Relationship with National Jurisdictions: Powers, Limits, and Misconceptions. In: Swart B, Zahar A, Sluiter G (eds) The Legacy of the International Criminal Tribunal for the Former Yugoslavia. OUP, Oxford, pp. 434–468

Rastan R (2008) Testing Co-operation: The International Criminal Court and National Authorities. LJIL 21(2):431–456

Rastan R (2011) Situation and Case: Defining the Parameters. In: Stahn C, El Zeidy MM (eds) The International Criminal Court and Complementarity: From Theory to Practice, Volume I. CUP, Cambridge, pp. 421–459

Regulations of the International Criminal Court (2004) Regulations of the Court, ICC-BD/01-01-04

Robinson D (2010) The Mysterious Mysteriousness of Complementarity. CLF 21(1):67–102.

Ruiz Verduzco D (2015) The Relationship Between the ICC and the Security Council. In: Stahn C (ed) The Law and Practice of the International Criminal Court. OUP, Oxford, pp. 30–64

Schabas W (2004) An Introduction to the International Criminal Court, 2nd edn. CUP, Cambridge

Schabas W (2008) Prosecutorial Discretion v Judicial Activism. JICJ 6(4):731–761

Schabas WA (2007) Complementarity in Practice: Some Uncomplimentary Thoughts. Paper for Presentation at the 20th Anniversary Conference for the International Society for the Reform of Criminal Law, Vancouver. http://www.isrcl.org/Papers/2007/Schabas.pdf. Accessed 19 June 2011

Schabas WA (2010) The International Criminal Court: A Commentary on the Rome Statute. Oxford Commentaries on International Law. OUP, Oxford

Schabas WA (2011) What Should the ICC do About the ICC Situation? Human Rights and International Criminal Law ICC Forum, University of California, Los Angeles, School of Law with the support of the OTP of the ICC. http://iccforum.com/darfur. Accessed 31 March 2013

Scharf MP (2000) The Tools for Enforcing International Criminal Justice in the New Millennium: Lesson from the Yugoslavia Tribunal. DPLR 49(4):925–979

Scheffer DJ (1995) UN Peace Operations and Prospects for a Standby Force. CILJ 28(3):649–660

Schiff B (2015) The ICC and the R2P: Problems of Individual Culpability and State Responsibility. International Studies Association Annual Meeting, Montreal 2011 Conference

Simbeye Y (2004) Immunity and International Criminal Law. Ashgate, Farnham, Surrey, UK

Simester AP, Spencer JR, Sullivan GR, Virgo GJ (2010) Simester and Sullivan's Criminal Law: Theory and Doctrine, 4th edn. HP, Oxford/Portland, Oregon

Sluiter G (1999) *Prosecutor v Blaškić*, State Cooperation and Subpoena, Commentary following ICTY Appeals Chamber Judgment on the Request of the Republic of Croatia for Review of the Decision of the Trial Chamber II of 18 July 1997, IT-95-14-AR 108*bis*, 29 October 1997. In: Klip A, Sluiter G (eds) Annotated Leading Cases of International Criminal Tribunals: The International Criminal Tribunal for the Former Yugoslavia 1993–1998, Vol. 1. Intersentia, Antwerp/Groningen/Oxford/Vienna, pp. 247–285

Sluiter G (2002a) State Cooperation with the International Criminal Court. In: Yepes-Enriquez R (ed) Treaty Enforcement and International Cooperation in Criminal Matters. Asser Press, The Hague, pp. 127–137

Sluiter G (2002b) International Criminal Adjudication and the Collection of Evidence: Obligations of States. Intersentia, Cambridge

Sluiter G (2003a) The Surrender of War Criminals to the International Criminal Court. LLAICLR 25:605–651

Sluiter G (2003b) Commentary on Release of Ntuyahaga. In: Klip A, Sluiter G (eds) Annotated Leading Cases of International Criminal Tribunals: The International Criminal Tribunal for Rwanda 1994–1999, Vol. 2. Intersentia, Antwerp/Groningen/Oxford/Vienna, pp. 118–122

Sluiter G (2008) Obtaining Cooperation From Sudan – Where is the Law? JICJ 6(5):871–884

Sluiter G (2009) Cooperation with International Criminal Tribunals. In: Cassese A (ed) The Oxford Companion to International Criminal Justice. OUP, Oxford, pp. 187–200

Sluiter G (2010) Using the Genocide Convention to Strengthen Cooperation with the International Criminal Court in the Al Bashir Case. JICJ 8(2):365–382

Sluiter G (2011) There is a Duty to Cooperate for States in the Arrest and Surrender of Al Bashir, under the Genocide Convention and/or the ICC Statute and/or UN Security Council Resolution 1593. Human Rights and International Criminal Law International Criminal Court Forum, University of California, Los Angeles School of Law with the support of the OTP of the ICC. https://iccforum.com/darfur#Sluiter. Accessed 23 December 2016

Sluiter G (2018a) Enforcing Cooperation: Did the Drafters Approach It the Wrong Way? JICJ 16 (2):383–402

Sluiter G (2018b) Key Reforms for the Next Decade of the ICC (International Criminal Court) – Towards a Stronger Judicial Role in the Investigations and a More Robust System of Enforcing State Cooperation. Anniversary Debate, Human Rights and International Criminal Law ICC Forum, University of California, Los Angeles, School of Law with the support of the OTP of the ICC. https://iccforum.com/anniversary. Accessed 17 December 2018

Soler C (2014) A Conceptual Re-characterisation of Universal Criminal Jurisdiction. *Id-Dritt* 24:285–315

Stagno Ugarte B (2012) Strengthening the Rule of Law through the United Nations Security Council, Workshop held at the Australian National University on 17–18 December 2012 by the Australian Government's Australian Civil-Military Centre and the ANU Centre for International Governance and Justice, Working Paper No. 6.2. http://regnet.anu.edu.au/sites/default/files/publications/attachments/2015-05/Ugarte_6.2_0_0.pdf. Accessed 3 October 2013

Stahn C (2010) Arrest and Surrender under the ICC Statute: A Contextual Reading. In: Stahn C, van den Herik L (eds) Future Perspectives on International Criminal Justice. Asser Press, The Hague, pp. 659–685

Stahn C (2011) Taking Complementarity Seriously: On the Sense and Sensibility of "Classical", "Positive" and "Negative" Complementarity. In: Stahn C, El Zeidy MM (eds) The International Criminal Court and Complementarity: From Theory to Practice, Volume I, CUP, Cambridge, pp. 233–282

Sulzer J (2007) Implementing the Principle of Universal Jurisdiction in France. In: Kaleck W, Ratner M, Singelnstein T, Weiss P (eds) International Prosecution of Human Rights Crimes. Springer, Berlin/Heidelberg, pp. 125–137

Swart B (2002) Arrest and Surrender. In: Cassese A, Gaeta P, Jones JRWD (eds) The Rome Statute of the International Criminal Court: A Commentary, Vol. II. OUP, Oxford, pp. 1639–1703

Swart B, Sluiter G (1999) The International Criminal Court and International Criminal Co-operation. In: von Hebel HAM, Lammers JG, Schuking J (eds) Reflections on the International Criminal Court. Asser Press, The Hague, pp. 91–127

Tillier J (2013) The ICC Prosecutor and Positive Complementarity: Strengthening the Rule of Law? ICLR 13(3):507–591

Tladi D (2015) The Duty on South Africa to Arrest and Surrender President *Al Bashir* under South African and International Law: A Perspective from International Law. JICJ 13(5):1027–1047

Tolbert D, Kontić A (2011) The International Criminal Tribunal for the Former Yugoslavia ('ICTY') and the Transfer of Cases and Materials to National Judicial Authorities: Lessons in Complementarity. In: Stahn C, El Zeidy MM (eds) The International Criminal Court and Complementarity: From Theory to Practice, Volume II. CUP, Cambridge, pp. 888–919

Tomuschat C (2008) Human Rights: Between Idealism and Realism, 2nd edn. OUP, Oxford

Trahan J (2013) The Relationship Between the International Criminal Court and the United Nations Security Council: Parameters and Best Practices. CLF 24(4):417–473

Tzanakopoulos A (2010) Domestic Court Reactions to United Nations Security Council Sanctions. In: Reinisch A (ed) Challenging Acts of International Organizations Before National Courts. OUP, Oxford, pp. 54–76

Tzanakopoulos A (2011) Disobeying the Security Council: Countermeasures Against Wrongful Sanctions. Oxford Monographs in International Law, OUP, Oxford

Tzanakopoulos A (2012) Collective Security and Human Rights. In: de Wet E, Vidmar J (eds) Hierarchy in International Law: The Place of Human Rights. OUP, Oxford, pp. 42–70

UN (2004) Press Release: Prosecutor Receives Referral of the Situation in the DRC. 19 April 2004, Doc. AFR/903-L/3067

UNC (1945) Charter of the United Nations

UNGA (1996) Report of the Preparatory Committee on the Establishment of an International Criminal Court Committee Report, Vol. I, Proceedings of the Preparatory Committee During March-April and August 1996. GAOR Fifty-First Session, Supplement No. 22, UN Doc. A/51/22

UNGA (2009) Report of the Secretary-General, Implementing the Responsibility to Protect. Sixty-Third Session. Follow-up to the Outcome of the Millennium Summit, UN Doc. A/63/677
UNGA (2018) Report of the ICC on its Activities 2016/17, 1 August 2016 – 31 July 2017, 17 August 2017, UN Doc. A/72/349. https://www.icc-cpi.int/itemsDocuments/A72349/170817-rep-UNSC_ENG.pdf. Accessed 30 November 2018
UN-ICC Negotiated Relationship Agreement (2004) Negotiated Relationship Agreement Between the International Criminal Court and the United Nations
UNSC (1993) Resolution 827 (1993), UN Doc. S/RES/827
UNSC (1994) Resolution 955 (1994), UN Doc. S/RES/955
UNSC (2005) Resolution 1593 (2005), UN Doc. S/RES/1593
UNSC (2011) Resolution 1970 (2011), UN Doc. S/RES/1970
van der Wilt H (2005) Bilateral Agreements Between the United States and State Parties to the Rome Statute: Are They Compatible with the Object and Purpose of the Statute? LJIL 18 (1):93–111
van der Wilt H (2008) Equal Standards? On the Dialectics Between National Jurisdictions and the International Criminal Court. ICLR 8(1):229–272
van der Wilt H (2011) States' Obligations to Investigate and Prosecute Perpetrators of International Crimes: The Perspective of the European Court of Human Rights. In: Stahn C, El Zeidy MM (eds) The International Criminal Court and Complementarity: From Theory to Practice, Volume II. CUP, Cambridge, pp. 685–706
van der Wilt HG, Vervliet J, Sluiter GK, Houwink ten Cate JThM (eds) The Genocide Convention: The Legacy of 60 Years. MNP, Leiden/Boston
Vasiliev S (2014) International Criminal Trials: A Normative Theory, Vol. 1: Nature, Thesis Submitted in Fulfilment of the Degree of Doctor of Philosophy at the UvA, Amsterdam
VCLT (1969) Vienna Convention on the Law of Treaties
Ventura MJ (2015) Escape from Johannesburg?: Sudanese President Al Bashir Visits South Africa, and the Implicit Removal of Head of State Immunity by the UN Security Council in Light of Al-Jedda. JICJ 13(5):995–1025
Vidmar J (2012) Norm Conflicts and Hierarchy in International Law: Towards a Vertical International System? In: de Wet E, Vidmar J (eds) Hierarchy in International Law: The Place of Human Rights. OUP, Oxford, pp. 13–41
Vinjamuri L (2015) The ICC and the Politics of Peace and Justice. In: Stahn C (ed) The Law and Practice of the International Criminal Court. OUP, Oxford, pp. 13–29
Voetelink J (2015) Status of Forces: Criminal Jurisdiction Over Military Personnel Abroad. Asser Press, The Hague
Wenqi Z (2006) On Co-operation by States not Party to the International Criminal Court. IRRC 88 (861):87–110
Wilkitzki P (2001) The German Law on Co-operation with the International Criminal Court. ICLR 2(2):195–212
Woolaver H, Palmer E (2017) Challenges to the Independence of the International Criminal Court from the Assembly of State Parties. JICJ 15(4):641–665
Young SNM (2001) Surrendering the Accused to the International Criminal Court. BYIL 71 (1):317–356
Zahar A, Sluiter G (2008) International Criminal Law: A Critical Introduction. OUP, Oxford
Zakerhossein MH, DeBrouwer A-M (2015) Diverse Approaches to Total and Partial *In Absentia* Trials by International Criminal Tribunals. CLF 26(2):181–224
Zappalà S (2009) Judicial Activism v Judicial Restraint in International Criminal Justice. In: Cassese A (ed) The Oxford Companion to International Criminal Justice. OUP, Oxford, pp. 216–223

Chapter 11
Inherent Limitations of the Vertical System of Enforcement

Contents

11.1 Grounds for Refusal Emerging Directly from Admissibility Challenges 216
11.1.1 Genuine Willingness or Ability to Prosecute 218
11.1.2 *Ne Bis in Idem* 231
11.1.3 Postponement of the Execution of a Request for Surrender 249
11.2 Competing Requests and Conflicting Obligations 251
11.3 Specific Requirements under National Law 255
11.3.1 Abuse of Process 256
11.4 Diplomatic Privileges and Immunities 265
11.4.1 Immunities *Rationae Personae* 278
11.4.2 Immunities *Rationae Materiae* 289
11.4.2.1 Bilateral Immunity Agreements 292
11.5 The Rule of Speciality 296
References 298

Abstract This chapter studies the grounds which States may invoke to refuse to surrender individuals under the ICC Statute. States can challenge the admissibility of a case before the ICC which undertakes a two-pronged appraisal of complementarity, namely the State action assessment and the genuineness assessment. The latter test need not be undertaken if there subsists State inaction. Inactivity and gravity generate admissibility. The genuineness assessment necessitates an assessment of the State's conduct with a human rights lens. Various permutations are examined especially in the light of the *Saif Al-Islam* conundrum and in the context of the 'same conduct' requirement with a special focus on the proceedings against *Simone Gbagbo*. The three facets of *ne bis in idem*, namely the *res judicata* facet, the concurrence facet and the complementarity facet, are analysed. Other grounds for refusal include the postponement of the execution of a request for surrender, competing requests and conflicting obligations, and specific requirements under national law. In terms of the latter, emphasis is placed on the doctrine of abuse of process in a plural-State hypothetical scenario. Likewise, such scenario sheds a light on the application of diplomatic privileges and immunities, both personal and functional. Three main arguments are deployed to make a case against

C. Soler, *The Global Prosecution of Core Crimes under International Law*,
https://doi.org/10.1007/978-94-6265-335-1_11

the latter type of immunities where proceedings before the ICC are concerned. The tension between Articles 27 and 98 is exposed. The extent to which the rule of speciality, the only traditional extradition-based ground for refusal in the ICC Statute, can be invoked, is examined.

Keywords Grounds for refusal · Vertical system of enforcement · Competing requests · Same case · State obligations · Execution of a request · Independence · Impartiality · Flagrant human rights violation · Postponement · Cooperation · Challenge of admissibility · Genuine willingness or ability · Investigate and prosecute · *Ne bis in idem* · Abuse of process · Diplomatic privileges and immunities · Speciality · Effective investigation · *Forum conveniens* · National procedural law · Arrest · Surrender · Complementarity · Gravity threshold · Indirect waiver argument · Customary law argument · Immunities *rationae materiae* · Immunities *rationae personae* · Due process · Same conduct · Investigative steps · Inadmissibility · *Bona fide* trial · Substantially collapsed · Triggering mechanism · Official acts · Bilateral immunity agreements · *Ultra vires* acts · Flagrant denial of justice · Non-cooperation · Egregious violation · *Mala fide* prosecution · Genuineness assessment · State action assessment · Inaction · Fair trial assessment · *Res judicata* facet · Complementarity facet · Concurrence facet · Constitutive elements · *Mise en scène* · Shielding · Amnesty · Pardon · Same person · Jurisdictional pointsman · Parole · Interests of justice · Sham trials · *Simone Gbagbo* · *Saif Al-Islam Gaddafi*

The failure to surrender, at a stage when the State is entitled to legitimately challenge the ICC's jurisdiction, should not engender criminal liability. Instances in fact subsist where a State is legitimately entitled to reject a request for surrender by the ICC. After having introduced novel ways as to how the failure to surrender *per se* could engender criminal liability, I shall now proceed to determine the ways and means, at the State's disposal, justifying a failure to surrender. At this stage, a close analysis of the grounds for the refusal of the request to surrender in terms of the ICC Statute will follow. Since these are expressly stipulated within the ICC Statute, as opposed to the Statutes of the *ad hoc* tribunals which contain no grounds for refusal, States can hardly raise any other grounds (not contained in the ICC Statute) to justify their failure to cooperate with the ICC although legitimate obstacles to implementation of a request by the ICC to a State may arise.[1] This chapter will analyse how and why the vertical system of enforcement could be impaired to the extent that it might not be able to fill in the missing parts of the jigsaw puzzle which was mentioned previously. Hence, are the juridical restrictions and limitations surrounding the vertical system of enforcement such that it might be, occasionally, precluded from performing its main functions? If so, can such *lacunae* be filled in such a way as to safeguard the effective application of international criminal law?

[1] Sluiter 2002, pp. 175–176.

What grounds for refusal may States invoke to justify non-cooperation? These issues, all of which are important for an understanding of the vertical system of enforcement, will be scrutinized shortly. Earlier on, I explained the role and relevance of the vertical system of enforcement in the global enforcement of international criminal law. This presupposes that the vertical system of enforcement will step in when the horizontal system of enforcement does not perform its functions. In all truth, however, there exist circumstances wherein the vertical system of enforcement, called upon to act upon the default of the horizontal system of enforcement, might be impotent or constrained to inaction by means of the very mechanism that created the vertical system of enforcement in the first place. It is at this stage that impunity is likely to continue to reign.

This contingency leads me to examine the counterparts of the grounds for refusal of extradition within the vertical system of enforcement. In other words, the reasons for which surrender of an individual may not be effected will now be examined. Put differently, I will now pose the crucial question: what leeway, if any, do States have to refuse or postpone cooperation[2] with the ICC or any other court enjoying international criminal jurisdiction? Keeping in mind that ICTY, ICTR and the hybrid courts are not of a permanent nature, unlike the ICC, for the purposes of this work (as stated in Sect. 2.1), such surrender is viewed in the light of the prevailing provisions of the ICC Statute which reflect the very essence of the vertical system of enforcement. The Mechanism for International Criminal Tribunals[3] pursuant to their Completion Strategy[4] also dictates that the main focus, at this stage, should be the ICC as a permanent criminal court. This led me to undertake an exercise conducive to the understanding of the ICC cooperation model within Chap. 10. In the context of such ICC model, which, as has already been shown, is the one that interests us most, one must start off by acknowledging that the main achievement of the ICC Statute 'is that the duty of State Parties to comply with requests of the Court is not made subject to a number of exceptions which are normal in extradition law and practice'.[5] In fact, unlike within the horizontal system of enforcement which shall be considered in Part IV, seven main hurdles to the execution of the vertical system of enforcement may be detected, these being:

---

[2] Occasionally, some jurists use the term 'compliance' inter-changeably (Cumes 2006, p. 347).

[3] This is also known as the 'Residual Mechanism for Criminal Tribunals' and was set to begin functioning on 1 July 2013 [see Briefing by Presidents (2011) SC/10476, 6678th Meeting entitled 'Funding Shortfalls, Lack of State Cooperation, Personnel Retention Threaten Timely Completion of International Tribunals' Tasks'. http://www.un.org/News/Press/docs/2011/sc10476.doc.htm. Accessed 13 May 2014]. The date set for completion of cases was 31 December 2014. For a time it was felt that this target had become a realistic possibility since, as held by ICTY Prosecutor Serge Brammertz, ICTY has managed to secure the surrender of all requested indictees [see Briefing by Presidents (2011) SC/10476, 6678th Meeting entitled 'Funding Shortfalls, lack of State Cooperation, Personnel Retention Threaten Timely Completion of International Tribunals' Tasks'. http://www.un.org/News/Press/docs/2011/sc10476.doc.htm. Accessed 13 May 2014].

[4] See http://www.icty.org/sid/10874. Accessed 13 May 2014; see also Tolbert and Kontić 2009, pp. 135–138.

[5] Mochochoko 1999, pp. 310–314, cited in Swart 2002a, p. 1596, n. 24.

(1) the challenge of admissibility due to the genuine willingness or ability to investigate or prosecute;
(2) *ne bis in idem*;
(3) postponement of the execution of a request for surrender;
(4) competing requests and conflicting obligations;
(5) abuse of process by a custodial State;
(6) diplomatic privileges and immunities; and
(7) the rule of speciality.

The above mentioned seven hurdles (grounds for refusal) are inevitably inter-linked, occasionally inter-dependent and are not deemed to be impediments *strictu sensu* in so far as they are not always insurmountable hurdles. With the exception of the above mentioned third ground which is dealt with in Part 9 of the ICC Statute, the grounds of refusal follow their placing/juxtaposition within the ICC Statute. They are not hierarchically juxtaposed herein. The order of their significance will largely depend upon the contextual circumstances of each case. Most of these grounds for refusal might not have a lasting effect. Some of such grounds may subsist until a challenge of admissibility is decided upon by the ICC. Others may await a successful completion of the consultative process of negotiations. Some others can be put in abeyance until specific conditions are satisfied, specific assurances are given or until a contractual arrangement is conclusively reached. A commentator identifies 'three kinds of objections to surrender requests',[6] initially postulating them somewhat differently from the above,[7] but

[6] Young 2001, p. 338.

[7] Simon Young states that the following are the three grounds for refusal of cooperation:

i. States might argue that their domestic procedural requirements for arrest and surrender have not been met in the particular case, giving Senator Pinochet's unfitness to stand trial as a typical example;
ii. States might resort to substantive grounds for refusal which are constitutionally entrenched, such as the non-extradition of its own nationals;
iii. States may object to the Court's failure to provide the same human rights and fair trial standards as the custodial state. He gives the constitutional prohibition of life imprisonment (applicable in Colombia) or the mandatory provision of a trial by jury as examples, concluding that 'surrender should only be possible if the International Criminal Court provided the same degree of rights protection as in the custodial state' (Young 2001, pp. 338–339).

I will show, throughout this chapter, that these should not be tantamount to substantive impediments *per se*, as Simon Young contends whilst seemingly conflating extradition and surrender. Although this chapter will manifest that State discretion is significant, that the measuring tape is in the hands of States, and that ultimately the process of surrender heavily relies on local norms and domestic laws, the power and discretion of the State seem to be exaggerated by Young, whose study is probably one of the most comprehensive in the field of surrender law. Admittedly however, Simon Young's observations find refuge in the fact that the ICC Statute does not have a counterpart to ICTY's Rule 58 which expressly obliges States to surrender notwithstanding any legal impediment under national law and/or any extradition treaty. His approach by means of which 'the precise scope of legitimate national law objections to surrender will have to be determined in the context of the Statute, its drafting history and underlying purpose', is certainly subsequently partially mirroring the above,[8] whereas Rita Mutyaba contended that 'States may raise several grounds for non-compliance with the Court's cooperation request'.[9] These seven above mentioned hurdles constitute the main barriers[10] to surrendering individuals who are subject to an international arrest warrant[11] issued by the ICC.[12] The emphasis on the process of surrender *per se* is relevant because although some other grounds are very significant, they do not generally precede surrender. They are hence not being considered for the purposes of this work. National security[13] is a case in point. It is a particularly thorny concept because 'individual States may claim secrecy for relevant information and documents with the argument, the disclosure would prejudice their national security, while the Court may claim to need just this evidence to establish or to deny individual responsibility for crimes falling within its jurisdiction…'[14] It has been said that 'of the grounds for refusal still included in the Statute, national security is by far the most important',[15]

---

praiseworthy and goes to show that any domestic hurdles to surrender cannot be considered in isolation. (Young 2001, p. 340).

8 Towards the end of his thought-provoking study, Simon Young postulates four categories of objections, these being:

I. procedural;
II. substantive;
III. human rights; and
IV. conflicting international obligations.

(Young 2001, pp. 349–355).

9 'These include competing requests for extradition of a suspect, problems with the request which may impede or prevent the execution of the request, execution of the request may affect an ongoing investigation or prosecution, the cooperation request would make the State Party act inconsistently with its obligations under international law or diplomatic immunity of a person or international agreements, concerns about the accused's human rights being violated and sovereignty claims' (Mutyaba 2012, p. 946).

10 These are stumbling blocks, hurdles, obstacles which hinder surrender.

11 It is important to note that 'the issuance of a warrant of arrest or a summons to appear marks the demarcation line between proceedings concerning the situation and proceedings concerning the case' [ICC Pre-Trial Chamber I, *Situation in the DRC, Decision on the Applications for the Participation in the Proceedings of VPRS 1, VPRS 2, VPRS 3, VPRS 4, VPRS 5 and VPRS 6,* 17 January 2006, Case No. ICC-01/04, para 65, cited in Olásolo 2007, p. 194].

12 The admissibility of a case is not a pre-requisite for the issuance of an international arrest warrant [*Judgement on the Prosecutor's Appeal Against the Decision of Pre-Trial Chamber I Entitled "Decision on the Prosecutor's Application for Warrants of Arrest under Article 58", Situation in the DRC*, Case No. ICC-01/04, Appeals Chamber, 13 July 2006, Ground of Appeal B (a), paras 42–45. In: Klip A, Sluiter G (2010) (eds) Annotated Leading Cases of International Criminal Tribunals: The International Criminal Court: 2005–2007, Vol. 23, Intersentia, Cambridge, pp. 85–100].

13 For an analysis of the history of negotiations relating to Article 72 of the ICC Statute, see Behrens 2002, pp. 116–119. For a comprehensive analysis of this ground for refusal, see Roggemann 2002, pp. 1–24.

14 Triffterer 2002, p. 74.

15 Swart and Sluiter 1999, p. 124.

but this is particularly so only in the context of the production of evidence when the suspect is already within the ICC's control. One can also deduce *ictu oculi* that, having been located in Part 6 of the ICC Statute entitled 'the trial', this ground is mostly invoked after the commencement of the trial, when documentary evidence is subjected to disclosure, not pre-surrender.[16] In the context of this work national security can only assume relevance in the determination of the whereabouts of the suspect who is the subject of a request for surrender by the ICC. In fact an obvious barrier to surrender is the absconding or concealment of fugitives. Rather than being a legal impediment, this barrier is a logistical and practical one which should not fall within the purview of the juridical analysis being accomplished herein, although it demonstrates that it is not unlikely that the ICC's jurisdiction 'be exercised over other persons falling within the sanctions lists of the Security Council',[17] thus reflecting the broad jurisdictional reach of the ICC itself. Similarly, other fair trial pleas which supervene and/or follow the surrender process will be decided upon by the ICC and do not fall within the remit of this work. In fact the State has no sphere of competence over such matters, unless the arrest and surrender are impugned on the basis of a domestic procedural guarantee, the validity of which should be reviewed by a domestic court in so far as the arrest was consummated at the hands of domestic authorities. In practice, other grounds for refusal subsist, but these are more of an operational and/or logistical nature, rather than juridical hurdles. Article 97 of the ICC Statute, for example, allows the refusal of State cooperation if the person sought cannot be located or where the investigation conducted has determined that the person in the requested State is clearly not the person named in the warrant. In any case, in such circumstances, the State is duty bound to consult with the ICC without delay with an eye to resolving the matter. Göran Sluiter also lifts a veil by drawing everyone's attention to, and hence disclosing, '"hidden obstacles" that may be (ab) used by States to withhold or delay surrender', amongst which he includes the reference to national procedural law in Article 89(1) of the ICC Statute, the grounds to postpone assistance stipulated within Articles 94 and 95, and the requirements imposed on the ICC by Articles 87 (dealing with the language and transmission of the request) and 91 (concerning the contents of the request for arrest and surrender).[18] Some of these will be considered within this chapter at a later stage. Needless to say, but death extinguishes the criminal action. Hence the demise of an individual against whom an international arrest warrant has been issued necessarily entails the non-fulfilment of such request for cooperation. In sum, the

[16] See, for example, Klip 2010, p. 286.

[17] Ciampi 2010, p. 543.

[18] Sluiter 2009, p. 252.

entire *iter* prevailing within the ICC is a far cry from the 'form of privileged extradition, like special fast lanes in the extradition highway'.[19]

Before making express reference to jurisprudence which sheds a light on the intriguing peculiarities of the vertical system of enforcement, whilst applying and interpreting the legal provisions which embody it, one must note that no fully-fledged system of binding precedent subsists between the vertical system of enforcement and the horizontal system of enforcement under international law. Thus, States are not duty bound to follow *dicta* of international criminal tribunals and/or the ICC. They will not follow such *dicta* since they are faced with a different juridical, contextual and political situation. To this extent, the vertical system of enforcement only permeates into the horizontal system of enforcement in a limited manner, without necessarily encroaching upon it. The complementarity regime entails that, since State Parties to the ICC generally incorporate international criminal law into their own domestic legislation, such States are, first and foremost, bound by the provisions of their own legislation. Consequently, from the standpoint of States, international criminal law consists of their own national legal provisions, which, at times, may vary from the legal provisions of the ICC Statute itself. Whilst reflecting a deeply-embedded primacy of national jurisdictions, this state of affairs manifests that *dicta* of international criminal tribunals and/or the ICC may be said to constitute a persuasive and authoritative[20] source of international criminal law. This should not be equated to the assertion that such judgments have never been seriously questioned.[21] This said, it is unlikely that State Parties will be permitted to deviate from the explicit standards deriving from the ICC Statute in so far as international cooperation is concerned. This sets the stage for the consideration of the main hurdles to the vertical system of enforcement. Such analysis shall be undertaken with reference to the positioning of such hurdles within the ICC Statute, which does not contain a specific part or sub-title dealing with 'grounds for refusal' *per se,* in so far as such grounds are not always explicitly stipulated as grounds for refusal.

---

[19] Knoops 2002, p. 15.

[20] André Nollkaemper explains that the authority of *dicta* cannot be presumed but must be earned. He postulates four conditions for this purpose, these being:

i. institutional effectiveness;
ii. substantive effectiveness;
iii. remedial effectiveness; and
iv. the quality of individual decisions.

(Nollkaemper 2011, pp. 256–264).

[21] ICC Pre-Trial Chamber II, Situation in the Republic of Kenya, *Decision Pursuant to Article 15 of the Rome Statute on the Authorization of an Investigation into the Situation in the Republic of Kenya,* Dissenting Opinion of Judge Hans-Peter Kaul, 31 March 2010, Case No. ICC-01/09, paras 28–32.

11.1 Grounds for Refusal Emerging Directly from Admissibility Challenges

This heading is not intended to detect *lacunae* and/or suggest improvements to the admissibility test[22] but is intended to highlight the way grounds for refusal of surrender can sprout directly therefrom. The admissibility test is crucial to the very existence of the ICC. Admissibility challenges task the ICC with striking the right balance between its role as a watchdog and its function as gentle incentivizer of domestic criminal proceedings.[23] Under the ICC Statute, both the ICC Registrar and the Prosecutor may issue a request for State cooperation which may be transmitted either by diplomatic channels or through Interpol.[24] Arrest and surrender of the accused after the indictment generally require the following *iter*, by means of which the Prosecutor requests an order which the Registrar transmits to the State where the accused is found. As shall be noted shortly, State Parties may postpone compliance with ICC requests when an admissibility challenge is pending.[25] If proceedings fail the dynamic admissibility test,[26] which test encompasses two pillars of admissibility,[27] these being both the complementarity principle[28] and the gravity threshold, State Parties are relieved from their obligation to provide assistance to the ICC. This is because, for a time, it was being held by the ICC Pre-Trial Chamber that 'the determination of admissibility is a prerequisite for the assumption of jurisdiction and to deal with an arrest warrant'.[29] In practice, Pre-Trial Chambers consider the question of jurisdiction prior to the issuance of an

[22] Carsten Stahn's development of the concept of 'qualified deference' merits close scrutiny. Stahn opines that, rather than abolishing the 'same conduct' test altogether, three techniques can be employed to give sufficient space to domestic investigations and prosecutions, whilst retaining checks and balances inherent in the complementarity regime. These are (1) flexibility towards domestic jurisdictions to investigate and build the case after the filing of an admissibility challenge; (2) greater monitoring after deference; and (3) consideration of conditions to admissibility (Stahn 2015, p. 258).

[23] Stahn 2015, p. 231.

[24] Article 176(2) of the ICC RPR (2002) Rules of Procedure and Evidence of the International Criminal Court.

[25] Article 89(2) of the ICC Statute [ICC Statute (1998) Rome Statute of the International Criminal Court].

[26] Nouwen 2011, p. 227.

[27] For a user-friendly, simplistic but comprehensive, analysis of the admissibility test, including a step-by-step set of guidelines, see El Zeidy 2011, pp. 217–222; see also Stegmiller 2010, pp. 160–173; see also Stegmiller 2013, pp. 484–488. For a thorough textual analysis of the same, see Robinson 2010, pp. 81–88; see also Robinson 2011, pp. 463–475.

[28] This principle is not defined within the ICC Statute. Its historical roots derive from the *aut dedere aut judicare* rule (Buchan and Johnsson 2012, pp. 102).

[29] ICC Pre-Trial Chamber I, *Situation in the DRC, Prosecutor v Thomas Lubanga Dyilo, Decision on the Prosecutor's Application for a Warrant of Arrest under Article 58,* 10 February 2006, Case No. ICC-01/04-01/06, para 4.

arrest warrant.[30] The Appeals Chamber held that a Pre-Trial Chamber should only consider admissibility on an exceptional basis when issuing an arrest warrant, such exceptional basis being when it is appropriate in the circumstances, bearing in mind the interests of the suspect.[31]

Upon a State referral, the third State the national of which is investigated (and/or the State enjoying territorial jurisdiction) may challenge admissibility on the basis of its genuine willingness and ability to investigate or prosecute the person being investigated. The Prosecutor's trigger will not occur *a priori* if and when a State which enjoys jurisdiction shows a genuine willingness and ability to investigate and prosecute. To date the Prosecutor exercised such *proprio motu* powers rarely, namely in the situation relating to post-electoral violence in *Kenya* wherein, on 8 March 2011, the ICC Pre-Trial Chamber II issued summons to appear for six Kenyans,[32] then known as the 'Ocampo six', and subsequently known as the 'Bensouda three',[33] in the situation in *Côte d'Ivoire* and in the Georgia investigation. It remains to be seen, this time in more detail than simply by means of a scant reference (as undertaken in Sect. 10.2), whether the UNSC Resolution trigger allows for an admissibility challenge by the involved non-State Party or whether it presupposes *ab initio* the admissibility of the case before the ICC. Whereas the right to challenge the admissibility of a case was always abundantly clear in so far as State Parties are concerned, it is now also the case when non-State Parties are concerned. This emanates further from Libya's admissibility challenge[34] in the *Saif Al-Islam Gaddafi* case,[35] the outcome of which was confirmed on appeal.[36] In fact, Article 95 of the ICC Statute equally applies to non-State Parties. Consequently, a

---

[30] ICC Pre-Trial Chamber I, *Prosecutor v Ahmad Muhammad Harun et al.*, Decision on the Prosecution Application under Article 58(7) of the Statute, 27 April 2007, Case No. ICC-02/05-01/07, paras 12–17, cited in Schabas 2010, p. 366, n. 28.

[31] *Situation in the DRC*, above n. 12, para 52; ICC Pre-Trial Chamber I, *Situation in the DRC, Prosecutor v Katanga, Decision on the Evidence and Information Provided by the Prosecution for the Issuance of a Warrant of Arrest for Germain Katanga*, 5 November 2007, Case No. ICC-01/04-01/07, para 17; *Prosecutor v Harun et al.*, above n. 30, para 18, all cited in Schabas 2010, pp. 366–367, n. 35.

[32] Muthoni Wanyeki 2012, pp. 1 and 13.

[33] Capital News (2013) From the 'Ocampo Six' to the 'Bensouda Three'. http://www.capitalfm.co.ke/news/2013/09/from-the-ocampo-six-to-bensouda-three/. Accessed 3 June 2014.

[34] Such challenge does not invalidate substantive decisions to issue an international arrest warrant delivered prior to the making of the challenge [see Article 19(9) of the ICC Statute, above n. 25, and ICC Pre-Trial Chamber I, *Situation in the DRC, Prosecutor v Callixte Mbarushimana, Decision on the Defence Challenge to the Validity of the Arrest Warrant,* 9 January 2011, Case No. ICC-01/04-01/10, para 10].

[35] ICC Pre-Trial Chamber I, *Situation in Libya, Prosecutor v Saif Al-Islam Gaddafi and Abdullah Al-Senussi, Decision on the Postponement of the Execution of the Request for Surrender of Saif Al-Islam Pursuant to Article 95 of the Rome Statute*, 1 June 2012, Case No. ICC-01/11-01/11, para 28.

[36] ICC Appeals Chamber, *Situation in Libya, Prosecutor v Saif Al-Islam Gaddafi and Abdullah Al-Senussi, Decision on the Request for Suspensive Effect and Related Issues,* 18 July 2013, Case No. ICC-01/11-01/11.

UNSC Resolution, for example UNSC Resolution 1970, does not *ipso facto* entail and engender immediate mandatory compliance since complementarity also applies to non-State Parties. It would anyway need to be filtered by the ICC admissibility test. In other words, the complementarity regime also applies in the event of a UNSC referral.[37] Daniel Nsereko, emphasizing the priority of trial of States, asserts that the *Saif Al-Islam Gaddafi* case has shown that States which are the subject of a UNSC referral are entitled to invoke the complementarity principle and may resist the ICC's jurisdiction when they enjoy territorial jurisdiction over a core crime.[38] This gives the States a certain control over inter-jurisdictional issues. It gives the State, which, in a private law context would enjoy the 'right of first refusal',[39] the upper hand in jurisdictional matters. This also stems further to a literal interpretation of the ICC Statute because the *chapeau* is couched negatively, entrenching a presumption of inadmissibility. Hence inadmissibility seems to be the rule, whereas admissibility, paras (a) to (d) of Article 17(1) of the ICC Statute, would be the exception to the rule. Obviously, the room for manoeuvre of States is dependent upon a successful admissibility challenge. It assumes significance only if and when the ICC, the ultimate arbiter, determines that a case over which it (the ICC itself) could have jurisdiction is inadmissible.

The grounds of refusal here below will show that the admissibility test, largely encapsulated within Articles 17, 18 and 19 of the ICC Statute, provides the main breeding ground for the latitude of States. In truth, whilst reading through the ICC Statute, (in) admissibility pops up like an advert whilst someone browses on a website. In fact reference to the admissibility test is not confined and limited to grounds which are considered in Sect. 11.1.1, 11.1.2 and 11.1.3. I shall now consider these grounds one by one.

11.1.1 Genuine Willingness or Ability to Prosecute

This sub-heading is not intended to analyse in detail the concept of willingness and/ or ability as an end in itself but only to understand the extent to which these can constitute a ground for refusal to surrender an individual wanted by the ICC. Good guidance is already provided by the ICC Statute itself,[40] and this is supplemented with the ICC's case-law,[41] by the ICC's Prosecutor's policy papers[42] and by legal

---

[37] OTP 2003, p. 21.

[38] Nsereko 2013, p. 432.

[39] This is a 'potential buyer's contractual right to meet the terms of a third party's higher offer' (Garner 2004, p. 1350).

[40] See Article 17(2) of the ICC Statute, above n. 25, which deals specifically with the determination of unwillingness.

[41] *Prosecutor v Thomas Lubanga Dyilo,* above n. 29.

[42] OTP 2003.

literature, with Mohamed El Zeidy's comprehensive study probably constituting the best study thereof.[43] In colloquial terms, if and when States act diligently by prosecuting properly (in good faith), the ICC's jurisdiction is virtually negated. States, therefore, can to a large extent nullify the ICC's jurisdictional competence. The genuine willingness and ability of States to investigate or prosecute practically disallows the application and execution of all the three trigger mechanisms. Having established that all cases, irrespective of their respective trigger mechanism, should be filtered by the admissibility test, I shall now turn onto analysing the elements and effects of the ground for refusal which allows States not to surrender an individual when such States are genuinely able and willing to prosecute. Many commentators and, as shall be shortly noted, now the ICC too, opine that when deciding upon admissibility, the ICC first determines whether inability subsists. To undertake such task the ICC must determine whether the national judicial system has totally or substantially collapsed. Article 17(3) of the ICC Statute guides the ICC by stipulating three factors (the first two being objective)[44] which the ICC is to consider for the purposes of such determination, these being:

1. the State is unable to obtain the accused;
2. the State is unable to obtain the necessary evidence and testimony;
3. the State is unable to otherwise carry out its proceedings.

This, in their view, is the first exercise the ICC should undertake. If it does not find inability in terms of the above requirements, it must pass onto considering unwillingness.

Mohamed El Zeidy, citing *Lubanga*,[45] summary records of meetings of the *Ad Hoc* Committee[46] and OTP reports,[47] refers to an admissibility test which encompasses a twofold approach, this being (1) complementarity and (2) gravity.[48] The first assessment dealing with complementarity is also, in turn, sub-divided into two parts. It firstly involves an assessment as to whether the State has dealt with a situation or case in a manner which satisfies Articles 17(1)(a)–(c) of the ICC Statute. If the requirements emanating from such legal provisions are fulfilled, the ICC must declare the case inadmissible. If not, *id est* if the criteria set out in sub-paragraphs (a)–(c) of Article 17 of the ICC Statute are not met, the situation or case is admissible, in which case there is no need to determine a State's unwillingness or inability in terms of Article 17(2) and 17(3) of the ICC Statute. The

[43] El Zeidy 2008, pp. 157–207 on unwillingness and pp. 222–237 on inability.

[44] Greppi 2008, p. 65.

[45] *Prosecutor v Thomas Lubanga Dyilo*, above n. 29, para 29, unsealed pursuant to ICC Pre-Trial Chamber I, *Situation in the DRC, Prosecutor v Thomas Lubanga Dyilo, Decision to Unseal the Warrant of Arrest Against Mr. Thomas Lubanga Dyilo and Related Documents,* 17 March 2006, Case No. ICC-01/04-01/06.

[46] UN Diplomatic Conference of Plenipotentiaries on the Establishment of an International Criminal Court 1998, para 19.

[47] Ocampo 2005, pp. 3–4.

[48] El Zeidy 2008, p. 160.

second assessment must be undertaken only if domestic proceedings subsist, in which case they must be qualitatively screened.[49] Here their genuineness (or otherwise) is put to the test. I favour the steps identified by Mohamed El Zeidy in so far as these steps best reflect the language of the ICC Statute and the intention of its drafters, hence incorporating both a literal and a logical/purposive approach of the ICC Statute. The view that admissibility rests upon a two-prong test based on the distinction between inaction and domestic action is, by now (after the *Katanga* judgment),[50] largely uncontested. A more user-friendly way of explaining the above mentioned two-pronged appraisal of complementarity identified by Mohamed El Zeidy is by dividing it into two general stages which may be designated as follows: (1) 'the State action assessment' and (2) 'the genuineness assessment.' In other words, if the State did not act at all, *id est* if the State has remained inactive (passive) either by not investigating or by not prosecuting, and provided that the gravity threshold[51] has been satisfied, the situation and/or case is admissible, and hence there is no need to undertake the genuineness assessment. The issue of genuineness does not need to be considered if there is inaction, because the unwillingness or inability of a State having jurisdiction over the case becomes relevant only where the first limb of the test has been satisfied.[52] Simply put, State inaction plus gravity generates admissibility. If the State action assessment is in the negative, the genuineness assessment becomes superfluous. It therefore becomes 'unnecessary to set out the Chamber's understanding of the criteria of unwillingness and inability within the meaning of Article 17(1)(a) and as detailed in Article 17(2) and (3) of the Statute'.[53] The case is admissible because 'inaction on the part of a State having jurisdiction (that is, the fact that a State is not investigating or prosecuting, or has not done so), renders a case admissible before the Court'.[54] The burden of proving State action rests on the State challenging admissibility. To do so successfully, the State must provide evidence with a sufficient degree of specificity and probative value that demonstrates that it is investigating or prosecuting the case, not merely that the State is asserting that investigations are ongoing.[55] These

---

[49] El Zeidy 2008, p. 161.

[50] ICC Appeals Chamber, *Situation in the DRC, Prosecutor v Germain Katanga and Mathieu Ngudjolo Chui, Judgment on the Appeal of Mr. Germain Katanga Against the Oral Decision of Trial Chamber II of 12 June 2009 on the Admissibility of the Case*, 25 September 2009, Case No. ICC-01/04-01/07 OA8, para 78, cited in Stahn 2015, p. 229, n. 6.

[51] The term 'gravity threshold' is sometimes used inter-changeably with the term 'threshold of criminality' (Russo 2012, p. 447), probably to denote the level of moral opprobrium in the act or omission.

[52] ICC Pre-Trial Chamber I, *Prosecutor v Simone Gbagbo, Decision on Côte d'Ivoire Challenge to the Admissibility of the Case Against Simone Gbagbo*, 11 December 2014, Case No. ICC-02/11-01/12, para 19.

[53] *Prosecutor v Simone Gbagbo*, above n. 52, para 36.

[54] *Prosecutor v Simone Gbagbo*, above n. 52, para 27.

[55] ICC Appeals Chamber, *Situation in the Republic of Kenya, Prosecutor v Francis Kirimi Muthaura, Uhuru Muigai Kenyatta and Mohammed Hussein Ali, Judgment on the Appeal of the Republic of Kenya Against the Decision of Pre-Trial Chamber II of 30 May 2011 entitled*

assessments are burdensome and onerous exercises, not only politically but also in terms of resources. As aptly noted by Morten Bergsmo the OTP will spend more time, effort and energy in preparing submissions on admissibility than in proving the guilt of an alleged perpetrator.[56] If, on the other hand, the State action assessment is in the affirmative, the genuineness assessment must be meticulously undertaken to decipher whether the State action was undertaken in *mala fide* or in *bona fide*. If the latter subsists, the case is inadmissible. Here one must emphasize that 'although the ICC is not a human rights court, human rights standards may still be of relevance and utility in assessing whether the proceedings are carried out "genuinely"',[57] the latter word (which bears a resemblance with the concept of *bona fides*) being the least subjective concept considered throughout the negotiations which led to the adoption of the ICC Statute since it excluded effectiveness and efficiency.[58] The genuineness assessment is intrinsically a fair trial assessment wherein due process is interpreted rather broadly. It has been held that 'the success of a challenge to the ICC's jurisdiction depends on a consideration of whether a fair trial can be held'.[59] In fact, for this purpose, Mohamed El Zeidy scrutinizes *dicta* of human rights regional courts dealing with a violation of the positive obligations of a State consisting either in the failure to investigate or prosecute or else in an investigation or prosecution conducted improperly and/or insufficiently.[60] Mohamed El Zeidy adopts the same method of analysis[61] in considering shielding in terms of Article 17(2)(a) of the ICC Statute. This is appropriate because to examine genuine unwillingness in terms of Article 17(1)(a), one of the criteria to be used is a determination as to whether a national decision was made for the purpose of shielding in terms of Article 17(2)(a) of the ICC Statute. To motivate his methods of analysis, Mohamed El Zeidy also specifically dedicates part 2 of the third chapter of

---

'Decision on the Application by the Government of *Kenya Challenging the Admissibility of the Case Pursuant to Article 19(2)(b) of the Statute'*, 30 August 2011, Case No. ICC-01/09-02/11 OA, paras 2 and 61, cited in *Prosecutor v Simone Gbagbo*, above n. 52, para 28, notes 46–47.

56 Bergsmo 1998, pp. 29 and 43.

57 OTP 2003, pp. 8–9.

58 Holmes 2002, p. 674.

59 Čengić 2010, p. 187.

60 In IACtHR, *Paniagua Morales et al. v Guatemala (Panel Blanca* {The case of the *White Van}),* 8 March 1998, Series C, No. 37, paras 94, 139, 160, 169, 171, 178, and in IACtHR, *Maritza Urrutia v Guatemala*, 27 November 2003, Series C, No. 103, paras 104, 119, 124–126, the IACtHR found that a genuine investigation requires the State to use all the legal means at its disposal in the conduct of a serious criminal process that identifies the suspects involved and leads to actual trial and appropriate punishment if necessary (El Zeidy 2008, p. 167, n. 56).

61 Mohamed El Zeidy analyses ECtHR Grand Chamber, *McCann and Others v UK*, 27 September 1995, Application No. 18984/91, para 161; ECtHR Grand Chamber, *Anelia Kunchova Nachova et al. v Bulgaria*, 6 July 2005, Application Numbers 43577/98 and 43579/98, para 113; ECtHR Fourth Section, *Borislav Yevgenyevich Poltoratskiy v Ukraine*, 29 April 2003, Application No. 38812/97, para 126; ECtHR, *Sergey Kuznetsov v Ukraine* 29 April 2003, Application No. 39042/97, para 106; ECtHR Former Second Section, *İsak Tepe v Turkey,* 9 May 2003, Application No. 27244/95, paras 181–182; and IACtHR, *Velásquez-Rodríguez v Honduras*, 29 July 1988, Series C, No. 4, para 177.

his book to an examination of the impact of human rights bodies' decisions on complementarity determinations.[62] Hence, when proceedings are 'so inadequate they cannot be considered genuine proceedings'[63] in terms of Article 17(1)(a) of the ICC Statute. This begs the question: but where does one draw the line in relation to the extent/degree of such inadequacy? Ultimately, how can a case become admissible before the ICC when blatant bias subsists *ab initio* (before the actual commencement of a trial)? Whose word is final, in such cases: the ICC's word or the word of the State which has clearly resolved to prosecute? I opine that there is no one-size-fits-all formula which may be adopted to reply to such questions. A case-by-case analysis is required. A lot will largely depend upon the prevailing human rights monitoring mechanisms. If a State's Constitution envisions a remedy at law for an individual should a human rights violation subsist, if the State is a signatory to a regional human rights convention (such as the ECvHR), if the State is a signatory to the ICCPR (hence subject to the judicial scrutinty of the HRC), a blatant human rights violation is most likely to lead to the dismissal of the case altogether. To this extent, a gross human rights violation will benefit, rather than prejudice the accused since a conviction would be overturned on appeal and/or at a subsequent court instance (at some stage of the entire procedural *iter*). In such cases the State can, inadvertently and not deliberately, tacitly and informally absolve the individual of a crime for reasons beyond the individual's control and for reasons imputable to the State itself which, paradoxically, accuses such individual of the same crime. At this point, the State could be deemed to be unwilling to prosecute although, ironically, its actions constitute the very embodiment of willingness.[64] This is because, in terms of Article 17(2)(c) of the ICC Statute, the proceedings could be said to have been conducted in a manner which, in the circumstances, is inconsistent with an intent to bring the person concerned to justice.

The case of *Saif Al-Islam* has already been referred to in Sects. 9.3, 10.3 and 11.1. It assumes fundamental importance within the context of this sub-heading and of Sect. 11.1.2, both of which are intricately linked. The *nexus* between the ground of 'genuine willingness or ability to prosecute' and '*ne bis in idem*' is even stronger in the *Saif Al-Islam* case because the grounds and circumstances of his release remain a mystery. It is hence unclear whether an amnesty was issued, and if so, 'the effect of this purported amnesty on his domestic proceedings',[65] whether he was pardoned, or whether he was released without any legal basis. I will, later on in this chapter, show how and why amnesties most probably will not escape Article 17 of the ICC Statute and that the permissibility of amnesties is doubtful in the light of the admissibility test. In practice, amnesties 'deserve the same treatment as sham trials' and do not qualify as judgments for the purposes of Article 20 of the ICC Statute.[66]

---

62 El Zeidy 2008, pp. 207–211.

63 OTP 2003, p. 8.

64 This theory is also put forward by Kevin Jon Heller (Heller 2012).

65 OTP 2018, para 10.

66 van den Wyngaert and Ongena 2002, p. 726.

I will, at this stage, deal with the *Saif Al-Islam* conundrum because it significantly enlightens one's understanding of the ground for refusal entitled 'genuine willingness or ability to prosecute'. In considering this ground for refusal, one must constantly keep in mind that 'the principle of complementarity only addressed situations where breaches of human rights standards, more precisely the right to an independent and impartial judiciary, work in favour of the accused'.[67] For the sake of non-repetition, matters which I shall be dealing with under this sub-heading will not be dealt with again under Sect. 11.1.2. Before indulging in purely legal considerations, the current state of affairs must be referred to. After arresting him, the Zintan militia seemed very eager to prosecute *Saif Al-Islam Gaddafi*. *Saif Al-Islam*, by virtue of an admissibility challenge filed on 5 June 2018, claims to have been released from custody in Zintan on 12 April 2016. Yet, Libya does not confirm that he was released and still seeks to arrest him. Libya claims that 'efforts were continuing in order to transfer him into the custody of the competent authorities of Libya'.[68] An OTP Report issued in November 2018 confirms that *Saif Al-Islam*'s whereabouts are still unknown.[69] The OTP contests *Saif Al-Islam*'s admissibility challenge. It claims that Pre-Trial Chamber I should find *Saif Al-Islam*'s case admissible since he has not been tried in Libya for the purposes of Articles 17(1)(c) and 20(3) of the ICC Statute.[70] The OTP goes as far as claiming that, 'as a fugitive from justice both in Libya and before the ICC, Mr. *Gaddafi* does not have procedural standing to challenge admissibility'[71] in the first place. At the time of writing of this book, the admissibility challenge of *Saif Al-Islam* is still *sub iudice*.

Assuming just for a moment that circumstances shall change, and that *Saif Al-Islam* would be re-captured by the Zintanis and/or any other group willing to prosecute him, a few observations must be made. A few comments will be made with the assumption that the Zintanis and/or any other group willing to prosecute him re-capture *Saif Al-Islam*. In this context, the overt determination of the Zintanis might be their own demise. It is unlikely that a conviction of Saif Al-Islam will withstand an appeal. Naturally, to draw such a conclusion one must presume that the Libyan Supreme Court has the power to and would dismiss a case on the grounds of a flagrant violation of due process rights. This would necessitate an in-depth analysis of Libyan legislation. A cursory look, however, is enough to conclude that Article 304 of Libya's Code of Criminal Procedure stipulates that the 'breach of any disposition of law concerning essential procedures gives rise to the nullity of the procedure'. Such nullity, in terms of Article 309 of Libya's Code of Criminal Procedure entails that the procedure would have no effect or

[67] Pichon 2008, p. 194.
[68] OTP 2018, para 12.
[69] OTP 2018, para 11.
[70] OTP 2018, para 8.
[71] Ibid.

consequence.[72] Moreover, in any case, Libya has not defined war crimes or crimes against humanity under its domestic law.[73] The *nullum crimen sine lege* rule anyway conjures Libya's inability to prosecute. It seems clear that whichever way one looks at the matter, the *Saif Al-Islam* case is admissible. The complementarity test therefore connotes that the effect of the primacy of the State is that the State becomes the first port of call, but will not necessarily be the safest port where to anchor the ship. If the flagrant human rights violations can lead to the nullity of the procedure and the non-execution of any punishment inflicted as a consequence of such procedure, this would constitute unwillingness by virtue of Article 17(1)(b). This seems to have been the defensive strategy when Saif Al-Islam's lawyers, in support of ICC admissibility, contended that justice will not be served by domestic proceedings since these are 'so ineliminably tainted by violations of domestic law that either the defendant would have to be released, or, the proceedings will go down in history as a manipulated spectacle of victor's revenge'.[74] If the Libyan Courts fail to nullify procedures which are blatantly in conflict with Libyan domestic human rights law, such Court's lack of independence and/or impartiality might also lead to unwillingess since it would anyway probably fall within the remit of Article 17(2)(c) of the ICC Statute. In the latter case, however, for unwillingness in terms of the ICC Statute to subsist, it would have to be proved that the same proceedings were conducted in a manner which, in the circumstances, is inconsistent with an intent to bring the person concerned to justice, this being an important qualification. Whether this ulterior requisite would be satisfied on the pretext of the prior knowledge of the Libyan State that the outcome of the proceedings will not lead to justice is a matter which goes beyond this study. This view is also consonant with a logical and purposive interpretation of the ICC Statute in so far as, firstly, any prosecution has to be one which protects human rights, and secondly, genuineness[75] applies to the 'willingness' or the 'ability' and should not be misconstrued to constitute an open invitation to investigate what is tantamount to a genuine trial.[76] In the *Saif Al-Islam* case, the ICC, whilst avoiding to undertake an analysis of due process in Libya, decided that Libya had not provided sufficient evidence to prove that its investigation covers the same conduct as the ICC indictment or that it is able genuinely to carry out its investigations or proceed to

---

[72] ICC Pre-Trial Chamber I, *Situation in Libya, Prosecutor v Saif Al-Islam Gaddafi and Abdullah Al-Senussi, Public Redacted Version of the Corrigendum to the 'Defence Response to the Application on Behalf of the Government of Libya Pursuant to Article 19 of the ICC Statute'*, 31 July 2012, Case No. ICC-01/11-01/11, para 217.

[73] Powles 2012, p. 8.

[74] ICC Pre-Trial Chamber I, *Situation in Libya, Prosecutor v Saif Al-Islam Gaddafi and Abdullah Al-Senussi, Public Redacted Version of the Response to the Libyan Government's Further Submissions on Issues Related to Admissibility of the Case Against Saif Al-Islam Gaddafi*, 18 February 2013, Case No. ICC-01/11-01/11, para 11, cited in Stahn 2015, p. 235, n. 49.

[75] For an analysis of the concept of genuineness in terms of Article 17(1)(b), see Nouwen 2011, pp. 216–220.

[76] O'Donohue and Rigney 2012.

trial.[77] In the light of the above, amidst the *Saif Al-Islam* conundrum, Frédéric Mégret and Marika Giles Samson conclude by stating that 'the selection of the former golden playboy of the Libyan establishment for an upgrade to a business class trial in The Hague may well be seen as indicating that those responsible for the worst crimes benefit from preferential treatment. Conversely, a domestic *Gaddafi* trial would reflect well on a fundamental tenet of justice, equality (be it equality in misfortune)'.[78]

In the absence of mechanisms designed to safeguard basic human rights, it might be permissible to contend that no trial at all may be said to subsist because a flawed and unfair trial could be null *ab initio*. It assumes and possesses no legal validity. It thus not only portrays unwillingess but may be deemed to be, arguably, also an inability[79] to try the accused since trying the accused presupposes that such trial would, at the very least, respect rudimentary due process guarantees. This so-called 'due process theory'[80] is the view adopted by the majority of international criminal law scholars.[81] Marina Aksenova contends that the ICC admissibility provisions 'are at the very last unclear with respect to the level of human rights protection they grant to suspects or any other parties to the domestic proceedings. The other provisions of the Rome Statute and the Rules of Procedure and Evidence expressly upholding human rights and due process guarantees do not dispel this ambiguity'.[82] Steven Powles goes as far as saying that 'it is inherent in the concepts of "unwilling" and "unable" that a State should be required to provide not only a trial, but a fair trial. It is crucial, I would say, that a State not only be able to put someone on trial but give them a fair trial'.[83] Frédéric Mégret and Marika Giles Samson have similarly concluded that 'there may be a point where violations of due process (based on domestic or international law) do nullify an ability or intent to prosecute'.[84] Admittedly, however, all this might lead to a State's unwillingness to investigate and prosecute, not to its inability *strictu sensu*, in terms of the ICC Statute. This is because the ICC Statute expressly stipulates that for inability to

[77] ICC Pre-Trial Chamber I, *Situation in Libya, Prosecutor v Saif Al-Islam Gaddafi and Abdullah Al-Senussi, Decision on the Admissibility of the Case Against Saif Al-Islam Gaddafi*, 31 May 2013, Case No. ICC-01/11-01/11, paras 216–219.

[78] Mégret and Samson 2013, Abstract, p. 581.

[79] For a thorough analysis of this criterion, see El Zeidy 2008, pp. 222–237.

[80] This theory postulates that the concepts of independence and impartiality in Article 17(2)(c) of the ICC Statute, above n. 25, create a due process requirement, whereby proceedings in which an individual is easier to convict because of violations of his due process guarantees are not conducted independently or impartially. Anne Bishop however rightly advocates that for a State to be deemed to be unwilling in terms of Article 17(1)(b) of the ICC Statute, above n. 25, the proceedings must not merely not be conducted impartially and independently, but they must also be conducted in a manner which, in the circumstances, is inconsistent with an intent to bring the person concerned to justice (Bishop 2013, pp. 411–412).

[81] A list of such scholars, together with their works, may be found in Bishop 2013, p. 398, n. 65.

[82] Aksenova 2017, pp. 80–81.

[83] Powles 2012, p. 7.

[84] Mégret and Samson 2013, p. 583.

subsist there must be a total or substantial collapse of the national justice system.[85] A criminal justice system which:

(a) does not incorporate due process guarantees; or
(b) protects them on paper, but never applies and exercises them; or
(c) protects them on paper, applies and exercise them nearly always, but chooses to discard or ignore them in a particular case,

is not one which, in terms of the ICC Statute, has collapsed, or at least, has substantially collapsed. Jurists take opposing views on the matter. Whereas Nidal Nabil Jurid seems to equate such collapse with a system which is on the brink of physical obliteration, Russel Buchan and Clae-Erik Joakim Johnsson opine that 'unless a judicial system strictly complies with settled international standards relating to due process (such as impartiality of the judiciary, fairness of procedure etc.) it should be determined to be in substantial collapse for the purposes of Article 17(3)' of the ICC Statute.[86] I favour the former view as the correct interpretation, although this effectively limits the ICC's jurisdiction and its quest to defeat impunity. However, should the latter interpretation be correct, an important facet of the complementarity regime (substantial collapse) could become entirely dependent on due process. Nevertheless, even though it may sound weird, by means of the second limb of Article 17(2)(c),[87]at least for admissibility purposes, it would seem that matters relating to due process should be considered when it is designed to make the accused more difficult to convict, not, as Jennifer Trahan suggests, 'when there are both due process violations and potential imposition of the death penalty'.[88] Trahan's argument that the problem is compounded when fair trial concerns are accompanied by the potential imposition of a death penalty[89] certainly cannot apply to Libya anyway since the death penalty imposed by the Tripoli Court of Assize on 28 July 2015 shall be annulled because it was delivered *in absentia*.[90] This is not the norm because usually fair trial violations facilitate the conviction of the accused, in which case the second limb of Article 17(2)(c) would not apply since, irrespective of the extent of their unfairness, such proceedings would not be inconsistent with the intent to bring the defendant to justice. In principle, unfairness of the proceedings which renders the accused easier to convict (and which is hence detrimental to the accused) does not satisfy Article 17(2)(b) and (c) of the ICC Statute. There exists 'clear evidence that there was no agreement for the idea of granting the ICC jurisdiction to look into stand-alone due process violations during

---

[85] Article 17(3) of the ICC Statute, above n. 25.

[86] Buchan and Johnsson 2012, pp. 105.

[87] This states that the proceedings in the domestic State must be conducted in a manner which, in the circumstances, is inconsistent with an intent to bring the person concerned to justice, for unwillingness to subsist.

[88] Trahan 2017, p. 843.

[89] Ibid.

[90] Court of Assize, Tripoli, Libya, *Prosecutor v Saif Al-Islam Gaddafi and Abdullah Al-Senussi et al., Death Sentence*, 28 July 2015, 630/2012; see also OTP 2018, para 12.

the drafting of the Rome Statute'.[91] The ICC Appeals Chamber has asserted that challenges relating to the fairness of proceedings and violation of due process rights of defendants in domestic proceedings do not *per se* constitute grounds for a finding of unwillingness.[92] However, whilst not excluding the validity of the 'due process thesis', Article 17 could be read in such way as to leave enough leeway for a 'ruling on admissibility in instances when national law makes it easier or harder to convict an individual'.[93] In my opinion such flexibility to rule on the admissibility of a case in instances when the domestic State makes it easier to convict the individual can only subsist when the ease to convict is such as to literally leave no option to an appellate or constitutional court but to nullify the entire proceedings and quash the conviction. In other words, the ease used to convict under a particular criminal justice system ultimately makes it harder to enforce the conviction of the individual under that same criminal justice system. As stated throughout this Part, this would require an assessment of the domestic *corpus juris*, particularly the domestic remedies which are available to an individual upon a finding of a fair trial violation in terms of the relevant constitutional provisions. Therefore, of particular interest is the observation of the prospect of what two jurists call a 'clumsy State' which undertakes a trial with such ineptness that it 'shoots itself in the foot and thus needs to be rescued from its own incompetence'.[94] Effectively, therefore, just as the ECvHR has to delve into the applicable domestic law to fulfil its functions, the ICC would probably have to do so too in such cases. In fact, to assess admissibility, the ICC must necessarily determine whether the case which the State is investigating sufficiently mirrors the one which is before the ICC.[95] This, in and of itself, presupposes that the contours of the case being investigated domestically must be clear[96] in such way that the ICC can unequivocally identify what the national

[91] Jurdi 2017, p. 205.

[92] ICC Appeals Chamber, *Situation in Libya, Judgment on the Appeal of Abdullah Al-Senussi against the decision of Pre-Trial Chamber I of 11 October 2013 entitled 'Decision on the Admissibility of the Case against Abdullah Al-Senussi, Gaddafi and Al-Senussi'*, 24 July 2014, Case No. ICC-01/11-01 OA6, paras 230–231, cited in Stahn 2015, p. 232, n. 22.

[93] Aksenova 2017, p. 80.

[94] Mégret and Samson 2013, pp. 583–584.

[95] Although this is a settled matter, it is not devoid of being subjected to diverse views. Kevin Jon Heller, in defence of radical complementarity, opines that 'as long as a State is making a genuine effort to bring a suspect to justice, the ICC should find his or her case inadmissible regardless of the conduct the State investigates or the prosecutorial strategy the State pursues' (Heller 2016, p. 664). In supporting Heller's idea, Miles Jackson advances the concept of regional complementarity, this being tantamount to an institutional or geographical extension of radical complementarity, conveying that a genuine prosecution by a lawfully constituted regional tribunal should be considered as a prosecution by a State such that the case is inadmissible before the ICC (Jackson 2016, pp. 1069–1071).

[96] ICC Appeals Chamber, Situation in Libya, *Prosecutor v Saif Al-Islam Gaddafi and Abdullah Al-Senussi, Judgment on the Appeal of Libya Against the Decision of Pre-Trial Chamber I of 31 May 2013 entitled 'Decision on the Admissibility of the Case Against Saif Al-Islam Gaddafi'*, 21 May 2014, Case No. ICC-01/11-01/11 OA4, paras 83–84.

authorities were investigating.[97] Thus, for the purposes of this assessment the ICC must know about the parameters of the investigation being carried out both by the Prosecutor and by the State, and only when the terms of reference for the relevant comparison are satisfactorily identified can the ICC proceed to the determination of whether there is sufficient overlap such that the domestic case can be said to be the same as the case before the ICC.[98] If a State is unable to present such parameters to the ICC, no assessment of whether the same case is being investigated can be meaningfully made by the ICC.[99] In such circumstances, the State would not have discharged its burden of proof and consequently, the ICC is divested of any tools to do the job. If the State challenging admissibility fails to spell out the contours of the case, such failure constitutes a basis for rejecting the admissibility challenge, 'even if investigative steps are being taken'.[100] The State is hence left with no choice but to furnish the relevant information faithfully if it wants to succeed in its admissibility challenge. The Pre-Trial Chamber has dedicated more than two pages of its judgment in examining significant features of Ivorian criminal law of procedure.[101] It concluded that Cote d'Ivoire had not demonstrated that concrete, tangible and progressive investigative steps are being undertaken in order to ascertain *Simone Gbagbo*'s criminal responsibility for the same conduct as that alleged in the proceedings before the ICC, nor did the documentation indicate that *Simone Gbagbo* is currently being prosecuted by *Côte d'Ivoire* for the same conduct attributed to her in the case before the ICC.[102] After being amnestied and freed by President Alassane Ouattara in August 2018 as part of a large Ivorian amnesty process,[103] the ICC is currently evaluating the request of the OTP to access 'information and material to be transmitted by Côte d'Ivoire and to provide observations on the admissibility of Ms *Gbagbo*'s case'.[104] This goes to show the dynamic nature of the admissibility test.

Rather than considering international human rights law *per se*, this being a job that may potentially be left in the hands of a prospective international court of human rights, the ICC would have to consider whether the conduct and actions of State authorities are such as to run afoul of the domestic law of the State which intends (and asserts its willingness) to prosecute. In the case of Libya, for example, the ICC had to consider the Libyan Code of Criminal Procedure and the recently

---

97 *Prosecutor v Saif Al-Islam Gaddafi and Abdullah Al-Senussi*, above n. 77, para 135.

98 *Prosecutor v Simone Gbagbo*, above n. 52, para 32.

99 *Prosecutor v Simone Gbagbo*, above n. 52, para 34.

100 Rastan 2017, p. 26.

101 *Prosecutor v Simone Gbagbo*, above n. 52, paras 39–42.

102 *Prosecutor v Simone Gbagbo*, above n. 52, para 78.

103 *Le Monde Afrique* (2018) Côte d'Ivoire: Simone Gbagbo *Recouvre la Liberté*. https://www.lemonde.fr/afrique/article/2018/08/08/cote-d-ivoire-simone-gbagbo-recouvre-la-liberte_5340499_3212.html. Accessed 30 August 2018.

104 ICC Pre-Trial Chamber II, *Situation in the Republic of Côte d'Ivoire, Prosecutor v Simone Gbagbo, Prosecution's Request to Access Material and Provide Observations in the Article 19(1) Admissibility Proceedings*, 25 September 2018, Case No. ICC-02/11-01/12, paras 2 and 3.

enacted Libyan Constitutional Declaration which, cumulatively, protect the right to a fair trial in Libya.[105] All this renders the admissibility test very dynamic. It moves to and fro according to the underlying juridical framework. In fact a decision on admissibility must be based on the circumstances prevailing at the time the national proceedings are issued,[106] which national proceedings are ambulatory.[107] This is why both the ICC Pre-Trial Chamber and the Appeals Chamber stressed that Libya could initiate a second admissibility challenge.[108] The flagrant violation test can be used for such purpose in as much as such violation 'makes the accused more difficult to convict'.[109] The ICC cannot find a State unwilling or unable simply because it violates fair trial rights.[110] The violation would have to be such as to possibly constitute the war crime of depriving a prisoner of war from a fair trial (had an armed conflict been ongoing). It must be irremediable, one that cannot be regularised, salvaged or cured since it will not be possible to revert to the *staus quo ante*. This threshold, which bears the characteristics of 'gross inadequacy' and possesses a degree of objectivity, might seem higher than the (more subjective) 'so inadequate' threshold established by the OTP.[111] Frédéric Mégret and Marika Giles Samson opine, and I concur, that 'the litmus test is not whether the right to a fair trial has been violated in itself, but whether the degree to which it has been violated is such that one cannot realistically say that there has been a trial at all, thus revealing an unwillingness or inability'.[112] In other words the domestic trial must be so flawed as to not be a trial at all. This is not saying the same as Payam Akhavan who opines that when there is a high probability of a wrongful conviction because the trial is so flawed, it is manifestly inconsistent with the object and purpose of complementarity, which is to bring perpetrators to justice rather than to punish the innocent.[113] In my view, if it is marred by a *fait accompli* before it commences, if it bears signs of a flagrant violation *in limine litis,* it is no trial at all *ab initio*. These signs can include the arrest, detention and mistreatment of legal counsel of the accused, pre-trial detention *incommunicado*, the prohibition of access to a lawyer, the solitary confinement which is not judicially permissible and/or which does not follow a judgment by a Court established by law, the preparation of the room and facilities for the execution of the death penalty, the constant intimidation of witnesses, the evident bias of judges (possibly further to statements/

[105] Bishop 2013, pp. 407–408.

[106] ICC Pre-Trial Chamber I, *Prosecutor v Saif Al-Islam Gaddafi and Abdullah Al-Senussi, Decision on the OPCD Requests in relation to the Hearing on the Admissibility of the Case,* 2 October 2012, Case No. ICC-01/11-01/11, para 9, cited in Akhavan 2016, p. 1047, n. 16.

[107] *Prosecutor v Katanga*, above n. 50, para 56, cited in Akhavan 2016, p. 1045, n. 15.

[108] *Prosecutor v Saif Al-Islam Gaddafi and Abdullah Al-Senussi*, above n. 96, para 44, cited in Akhavan 2016, p. 1054, n. 39.

[109] Bishop 2013, p. 389.

[110] Heller 2006, pp. 255–280.

[111] OTP 2003, p. 8.

[112] Mégret and Samson 2013, p. 585.

[113] Akhavan 2016, p. 1058.

declarations made), the production of inadmissible evidence which is vitiated by torture, and the confidential information which is disclosed to the press and becomes available on mass-media. Such signs can be apparent from the very start of an investigation. In the *Saif Al-Islam* case, Melinda Taylor, the Office of Public Counsel for the Defence had filed two rather damning and confidential reports following her meeting with *Saif Al-Islam* held in the detention facility in Zintan between 29 February 2012 and 4 March 2012.[114] Such signs call into question the willingness and ability to prosecute the accused because they unmask a masquerade, a blatant perversion of the law. As recalled by Frédéric Mégret and Marika Giles Samson, the *Caucescu* trial in Rumania is a fair example thereof.[115] To this extent, the ICC, though not a human rights court, must use a human rights lens, especially when it undertakes the admissibility test. It has already provided such a vivid example in the admissibility challenges by Libya where it dealt with 'inability' by *de facto* entering into the realm of human rights which is ordinarily explored in the context of the 'unwillingness' assessment.[116] The ICC Pre-Trial Chamber I found that Libya's failure to secure adequate witness protection, that torture and death resulting from torture in detention facilities were reported, and that these cumulatively manifested Libya's inability to obtain the necessary testimony. Such factors, coupled with *Saif Al-Islam Gaddafi*'s denial of his right to a defence, cemented Libya's inability.[117] This begs the questions whether such a flagrant violation can ever be remedied by means of a trial at the ICC, and whether this would fall within the remit of Article 20(3)(b) of the ICC Statute. It seems not to be the case, owing to the qualification in this legal provision to the effect that the domestic criminal proceedings must have been conducted in a manner which is inconsistent with an intent to bring *Saif Al-Islam* to justice. A negative reply to such questions reveals that the ICC has no remedial functions and is not tasked with repairing miscarriages of justice and/or directly redressing human rights violations which occurred at the hands of domestic criminal courts.

Due process issues hence may seem to permeate both the 'inability' and the 'unwillingness' assessments, although the ICC Statute does not expressly allow the ICC to undertake such assessment from a purely human rights law viewpoint. This is because, as Marta Bo perceptively notes, it is arduous to imagine that a domestic breach of due process could somehow 'justify a qualification as 'unavailability' from which an objective impossibility to carry out proceedings might derive'.[118] Nevertheless, the ICC's admissibility test procedurally resembles the admissibility regime in human rights (regional and international) mechanisms wherein an applicant must first exhaust ordinary and domestic remedies at law.[119] Whereas,

114 Bishop 2013, pp. 403–404 and 409–410.

115 Mégret and Samson 2013, Abstract, p. 581.

116 Bo 2014, p. 531.

117 Bo 2014, p. 532.

118 Bo 2014, p. 533.

119 El Zeidy 2008, pp. 158–159.

notwithstanding the Pre-Trial Chamber's judgment,[120] a breach of due process rights could be said not to fall directly within the rubric of the 'inability' assesssment,[121] the same is less evident in relation to the 'unwillingness' assessment, as shown here above. Due process considerations may undoubtedly surface for the purposes of subparagraphs (a)–(c) of Article 17(2) of the ICC Statute. More specifically, an infringement of due process rights under subparagraphs (b) and (c) of Article 17(2) of the ICC Statute would influence the admissibility test if such infringment is intended to shelter[122] the accused from criminal liability.

In dealing with admissibility, due process rights resemble a rotational symbiotogram. In fact, for the purposes of this ground for refusal, due process must be considered from a completely different angle. It assumes the characteristics of a number 116 which, when written on a piece of paper and remaining untouched, becomes a number 911 once the piece of paper is inverted (turned upside down). Similarly, it assumes the features of a 'W' on a tennis racket which becomes an 'M' when dropped on the floor and inverted at the beginning of a tennis match to determine who serves first. The above shows that although the breach of the right to a fair trial cannot be considered *per se* as a distinct ground for inadmissibility, due process considerations can, albeit limitedly and from a different perspective, sigificantly affect the outcome of the admissibility test.

11.1.2 Ne Bis in Idem

This ground for refusal is uniquely multi-dimensional. It constitutes an international human right within a domestic context, but not within an international context. It is undisputed that '*ne bis in idem* brings to the foreground issues of fairness and human rights'.[123] The principle itself has been loosely categorized as an international human right[124] *per se*, although this should have been qualified and limited to the national context. A detailed analysis of the international human rights law on *ne bis in idem* is not however the main thrust of this sub-heading. Besides the unfairness stemming from the fact that a person would be prosecuted twice for the

---

120 *Prosecutor v Saif Al-Islam Gaddafi and Abdullah Al-Senussi*, above n. 77.

121 Such assessment is more objective and fact-driven than the unwillingness assessment (Holmes 2002, p. 677).

122 In practice, to shelter is to shield. However 'shelter' is here being used to distinguish between shielding (the first criterion) and the other two separate criteria in Article 17(2) of the ICC Statute, above n. 25, especially since the latter two criteria (unjustified delay, and independence and impartiality) are 'simply corollaries of the concept' of shielding (Holmes 2002, p. 675). In fact, proceedings which shield a person are also proceedings which are not independent and impartial. There is thus an overlap between such criteria (Holmes 2002, p. 676).

123 Young 2001, p. 337.

124 Vervaele 2005, pp. 101–106.

same crime,[125] the rationale of the rule also pragmatically ensures the avoidance of inefficiency and conflicting judgments.[126] Nevertheless, this sub-heading will show that, in the light of this work and in its entirety, *ne bis in idem* is less important when it is taken into account in its traditional and classical conception, as a human right. The fact that *ne bis in idem* does not only have a human rights connotation and dimension obviously renders the ground for refusal more relevant for the purposes of this work. This is because, before international criminal tribunals, *ne bis in idem*, as a human right, has occasionally been considered as applicable only 'at the time of the trial, and not before. Accordingly, the earliest stage at which *ne bis in idem* can be raised is after the issuance of the warrant of arrest'.[127] Given that it may precede surrender, the need to consider it for the purposes of this work is hereby identified, and hence subsists. Succinclty, the *ne bis in idem* issue may arise before a person is surrendered, at which point in time the State may have discretion whether to cooperate (surrender the individual) or otherwise because *ne bis in idem* looms on the horizon. Although *ne bis in idem* may be regarded as quite compelling at the domestic level, it is nowhere close to being an absolute right internationally, in horizontal relations. By way of example the IACtHR, considering cases where individuals were deliberately shielded (or, at least, not diligently prosecuted) in Latin American States, upheld that 'a judgment issued in the circumstances described above only provides fictitious or fraudulent grounds for double jeopardy'.[128] It seems, in fact, that some judgments of the IACtHR which was asked to consider a dispute emanating from the horizontal system of enforcement, were influenced by the ICC Statute in so far as they relate to the commission of core crimes and other considerations connected thereto.[129]

Ne *bis in idem* has three important facets which bring it close to other important principles, including complementarity, which, in turn, encapsulates matters such as amnesties, all of which are central to modern discourse within international criminal law. As a matter of fact, the *ne bis in idem* provision in the ICC Statute 'must be read together with the principle of complementarity, contained in Article 17'[130] of the ICC Statute. The first facet, which I refer to as the '*res judicata* facet', prevails

---

[125] *Nemo debet bis vexari pro eadem causa.*

[126] van den Wyngaert and Ongena 2002, p. 707.

[127] The Special Panel for Serious Crimes, *República Democrática de Timor-Leste,* Dili District Court, *The Deputy General Prosecutor for Serious Crimes v Wiranto et al., Legal Ruling Concerning the Applicability of Ne Bis in Idem at the Arrest Warrant Stage of the Proceedings*, 5 May 2005, Case No. 05/2003, para 19, cited in Warrant of Arrest for Wiranto, *Deputy General Prosecutor v Wiranto*, Case No 05/2003, The Special Panels for Serious Crime. In: Klip A, Sluiter G (2009) (eds) Annotated Leading Cases of International Criminal Tribunals: Timor Leste: The Special Panels for Serious Crimes 2003–2005, Vol. 16. Intersentia, Antwerp/Oxford/Portland, pp. 64 and 82.

[128] IACtHR, *La Cantuta v Perú* (Merits, Reparations and Costs), 29 November 2006, Series C No. 162, para 153.

[129] See references to the impotant *La Cantuta* case in Sects. 13.5 and 16.7.2.

[130] van den Wyngaert and Ongena 2002, p. 721.

within the same jurisdiction, irrespective of whether this jurisdiction is domestic or international.[131] Liu Daqun, citing *Krstić,* notes that cumulative convictions and appeals on acquittal are exceptions to this general rule.[132] The second facet, which I refer to as the 'concurrence facet', surfaces between two different jurisdictions where concurrent jurisdiction subsists, that is, where the following permutations may arise:

i. when more than one State enjoys jurisdiction over the same person; and/or
ii. when more than one international criminal tribunal and/or ICC enjoys jurisdiction over the same person, and/or
iii. when one State and one international criminal tribunal enjoy jurisdiction over the same person.

The second permutation, this being the one pointed in (ii) here above, is unlikely owing to the distinction in criminal jurisdictions between the various international tribunals and/or courts.[133] The third facet, which I refer to as the 'complementarity facet' largely depends on the regulating statutory regime and emerges between a requested State and an international criminal tribunal and/or ICC. The fact that a due process guarantee was placed within the second part of the ICC Statute entitled 'jurisdiction, admissibility and applicable law', rather than in Part III and/or Part VI thereof, is significant. It goes to show that whereas the *ne bis in idem* rule protects the requirement of a fair trial, it has the potential of, *de facto*, suppressing prosecutions. This was not a coincidence but a a deliberate relocation effected at Zutphen, the Netherlands, in 1998, when the structure of the then draft ICC Statute was considered by the Preparatory Committee.

The *ne bis in idem* rule, whilst being tantamount to a fair trial requisite, can therefore hamper the jurisdiction of the ICC by virtue of the *chapeau* of Article 17 of the ICC Statute wherein it can constitute a ground for rendering a case inadmissible.[134] This also reflects the dynamic nature of the admissibility test,[135] an

[131] Article 20(1) of the ICC Statute, above n. 25.

[132] ICTY Appeals Chamber, *Prosecutor v Radislav Krstić*, 19 April 2004, IT-98-33-A, para 218, cited by Daqun 2009, p. 305.

[133] Daqun 2009, p. 305.

[134] The ICC has devised a testing mechanism to determine (in) admissibility under Article 17(1) (a) and(b) of the ICC Statute. The ICC held that the following questions must be posed and replied to:

i. whether there are ongoing investigations or prosecutions; and
ii. whether there have been investigations in the past, and the State having jurisdiction has decided not to prosecute the person concerned.

[*Prosecutor v Germain Katanga and Mathieu Ngudjolo Chui*, above n. 50, para 78].

[135] Nsereko 2013, p. 443.

assessment persistently absorbed by fluctuations beyond the control of the prosecutor of the ICC. This test, described by Kai Ambos as an 'on-going process',[136] is reflected in the intention of the Libyan Government to challenge admissibility once again if and when Saif Al-Islam Gaddafi shall be transferred from Zintan to Tripoli.[137] However, now that the death penalty has been imposed *in absentia*[138] further to a trial which has been considered as unfair by the UN,[139] and especially because he has been released by the Zintanis, as stated here above, this prospect has become very unlikely.[140] Were this to happen, there is no doubt that a change in circumstances allows the ICC to determine admissibility *de novo*.[141] This is also why the admissibility test is appropriately considered to be of a dynamic and ongoing nature. Diane Bernard cites Heller who states that the respect of guarantees of due process does not constitute an explicit, positive obligation, but a ground for reinforcing the case for admissibility before the ICC.[142] This discloses the attributes of the *ne bis in idem* prohibition within the ICC Statute in that the rule performs some estimable multi-tasking. It resembles a multi-purpose building which can be transformed accordingly, depending on the needs and exigencies of a particular moment in time. In doing so, it can constitute the best showcase for the internationalization of criminal law. Its dual *telos*, its protective and the jurisdictional features, has also been acknowledged by the ICC.[143]

[136] Ambos 2010, p. 35.

[137] Jehani A (2013) Declaration of Libya's representative to the ICC. http://www.presstv.com/detail/2013/07/18/314481/libya-must-hand-over-gaddafis-son-icc/. Accessed 11 October 2015.

[138] This was 'due to the failure of his transfer from the custody of the Zintan rebels to the central authorities in Tripoli' (Jurdi 2017 p. 211).

[139] Nebehay S (2017) Gaddafi Son's Trial Unfair, Should be Sent to ICC: UN, Reuters, World News. http://www.reuters.com/article/us-libya-gaddafi-un-idUSKBN1600W8. Accessed 10 April 2018, cited in ICD (2017) http://www.internationalcrimesdatabase.org/. Accessed 10 April 2018.

[140] See Sect. 9.3.

[141] ICC Pre-Trial Chamber II, *Situation in Uganda, Prosecutor v Joseph Kony, Vincent Otti, Okot Odhiambo, Dominic Ongwen, Decision on the Admissibility of the Case under Article 19(1) of the Statute*, 10 March 2009, Case No. ICC-02/04-01/05, para 28.

[142] Heller 2005, p. 257, cited in Bernard 2011a, b, p. 879.

[143] ICC Trial Chamber II, *Situation in the DRC, Prosecutor v Germain Katanga and Mathieu Ngudjolo Chui, Reasons for the Oral Decision on the Motion Challenging the Admissibility of the Case (Article 19 of the Statute)*, 16 June 2009, Case No. ICC-01/04-01/07, para 48.

Since the intricate *ne bis in idem*[144] rule is applicable both vertically and horizontally,[145] a rather rigid application of such rule could effectively hinder surrender under the vertical system of enforcement. The vertical effect can be felt both upward[146] (externally, from the ICC perspective) and downward[147] (internally, always from the ICC perspective). The latter governs instances when a State cannot prosecute a person after the ICC has already tried such person on the basis of the imputed acts. The former, which falls within the parameters of this chapter and may be considered to be upward (not downward) *ne bis in idem*,[148] limits the ICC from prosecuting after a prosecution was already conducted domestically by a State, provided that such State did not either shield the accused or else did not conduct proceedings independently or impartially in terms of Article 20(3) of the ICC Statute.[149]

All this also shows how the vertical system of enforcement [namely certain ICC statutory provisions] can provide a frame of reference for the horizontal system of enforcement. The ICC's statutory provisions can constitute a litmus test which scrutinizes whether a State has diligently investigated and/or prosecuted or otherwise. The ICC's findings can largely influence the defences pleaded by States before a regional human rights mechanism such as the ECtHR, the IACtHR and the ACtHPR which delivered its first major substantive judgment in the names *Tanganyika Law Society et al v United Republic of Tanzania* on 14 June 2013.[150] This is owing to the intrinsic overlap of both *instituti legis*. In fact, it is most likely

---

[144] There are terminological differences between '*non bis in idem*' and '*ne bis in idem*'. The *ad hoc* tribunals adopt the former phrase, whereas the ICC Statute adopts the latter phrase (Naqvi 2010, n. 27, p. 291). The *ne bis in idem* rule, commonly referred to by jurists as the prohibition of double jeopardy or *autrefois acquit* (Harris et al. 2009, p. 270) is considered to be a fundamental human right which partakes of the due process [fair trial] guarantees. Although some jurists use the terms inter-changeably (Bohlander 2008, p. 541; Conway 2003, p. 217), double jeopardy and *ne bis in idem* are not identical concepts. 'Double jeopardy operates only within a single legal system while the identity of the prosecuting power is not relevant to the application of *non bis in idem*. *Non bis in idem* relates to numerous issues including the recharging of an accused with the same or another offence, the framing of an indictment, the sentencing of an accused on multiple convictions (double punishment), new trials, appeals, revision, the relationship between courts and between States' (Daniels 2006, pp. 2–3). The difference is exposed simplistically but concretely by Sean Murphy who states that *'[n]on bis in idem* addresses the possibility of repeated prosecutions for the same conduct in different legal systems, whereas double jeopardy generally refers to repeated prosecutions for the same conduct in the same legal system' (Murphy 1999, pp. 81–82).

[145] Spinellis 2002, pp. 1151–1161.

[146] This portrays the right not to be tried again by the ICC after the acquittal or conviction by another court.

[147] This denotes the right not to be tried again by another court after acquittal or conviction by the ICC [Article 20(2) of the ICC Statute, above n. 25].

[148] Kleffner 2008, p. 119.

[149] This legal provision encompasses any proceedings before any court (with the exception of the ICC), not necessarily a domestic court.

[150] Neuman 2014, p. 323. The pretext to the expansion in jurisdiction of such court is explained in Paulussen and Dorsey 2012, p. 235.

that the same State which challenges the ICC's admissibility (possibly on the basis of what it claims to be its willingness and ability to prosecute) is the very same State which is faced with a human rights action by an individual who claims to be a victim of the State's (then) inactivity. The alleged victim, who has no *locus standi* before the ICC and cannot directly trigger its jurisdiction, exercises his right to individual petition on the pretext of the fact that the State has, for example, failed to investigate and prosecute the enforced disappearance of his son when such enforced disappearance can, on the one hand, constitute a crime against humanity, and on the other hand, it can simultaneously violate the right to life and the prohibition of torture of the applicant. The failure to investigate and prosecute such crime would not only potentially demonstrate unwillingness and/or inability, but it could also, *inter alia,* breach the positive obligations of the State which enjoys jurisdiction over such crime, manifesting the intrinsic overlap referred to here above. As aforesaid, the exceptions to the *ne bis in idem* rule emerge directly from the complementarity principle and fall within the ambit of the admissibility test,[151] so much so that Mohamed El Zeidy identifies a relationship between the two and observes that '*ne bis in idem* is a corollary of the principle of complementarity'.[152] Consequently, the exceptions to *ne bis in idem* merit close and separate attention. Merely for the sake of non-repetition, they have not been directly included also within Sect. 11.1.1 dealing with genuine willingness or ability to investigate and prosecute. Jann Kleffner aptly notes that the two instances mentioned here above (upward and downward *ne bis in idem*) resemble the two forms of unwillingness in terms of Article 17(2)(a) of the ICC Statute.[153] What the ICC Statute does in a non-derogable manner is to impede a trial before the ICC following prior or subsequent proceedings before the ICC which relate to the same conduct[154] proscribed under the substantive legal provisions of the ICC Statute, namely

---

[151] Article 17(1)(c) of the ICC Statute, above n. 25.

[152] El Zeidy 2008, p. 285.

[153] Kleffner 2008, p. 119.

[154] The reference to conduct as opposed to crimes entails that the ICC *ne bis in idem* rule prohibits the re-trial for the same fact, not for the same offence. This is further made clear owing to the use of the term 'crime' in Article 20(2) of the ICC Statute. Andre de Hoogh unequivocally equates 'conduct' to 'fact' (De Hoogh 2009, p. 92). This conclusion is also confirmed by Jann Kleffner who equates conduct to behaviour, meaning that conduct 'thus involves a *de facto* as opposed to a *de jure* appraisal' (Kleffner 2008, p. 119). It also echoes the decision ECtHR Third Section, *Franz Fischer v Austria*, 29 May 2001, Application No. 37950/97, para 25, to the effect that 'the wording of Article 4 of Protocol No. 7 does not refer to the same offence but rather to the trial and punishment again for an offence for which the applicant has already been finally acquitted or convicted. Jurists have detected a danger to this approach, consisting in the fact that a person may be tried on the same facts but for a lesser charge' (van den Wyngaert and Stessens 1999, p. 791). In other words, the facts remain the same but the other lesser offence would be comprised and involved within the greater offence, just like a *Matryroshka* doll which fits perfectly within the others. Distinctively, however, Article 14(7) of the ICCPR [ICCPR (1966) International Covenant on Civil and Political Rights] refers to the same offence. This complicates matters since the latter treaty may be said to constitute 'the only universal definition one may identify' (Naqvi 2010, p. 293, n. 27). On the other hand, it is doubted whether the ICCPR (see above) should constitute

Articles 6, 7, 8, and 8*bis*. Therefore, put within a jurisdictional context, 'if a person has been tried by another court, the case is inadmissible before the ICC regardless of the legal qualification of the conduct in the other court'.[155] The importance of all this is epitomised by the 'same person/same conduct' test. This test, described as incident-specific,[156] is at the heart of the ICC system, as will be noted when other grounds for refusal will be dealt with. In a few words, in terms of Article 20(1) of the ICC Statute which reflects the '*res judicata* facet', 'the "*idem*" relates to the same conduct being re-tried by the ICC itself under a different categorisation, that is, murder as a war crime being subsequently re-tried as a crime against humanity or genocide. The provision would be without prejudice to cumulative charging which, according to ICTY practice, has been permitted where the crimes charged protect different values or contain different elements'.[157] In terms of Article 20(3) of the ICC Statute, which reflects the 'complementarity facet,' symbolising upward *ne bis in idem*,[158] the *idem* that is protected relates to 'conduct also prescribed under articles 6,7 or 8' for which the person has already been tried by another Court, based upon the above mentioned assessment of genuineness, this entailing the permissibility of a new trial before the ICC if and when the domestic proceedings were not genuine.[159] The only *idem* which relates to the crime, rather than the conduct, emanates from Article 20(2) of the ICC Statute which, by prohibiting downward *ne bis in idem*,[160] prevents the trial, this time by another Court, for a crime that one has been already tried for by the ICC. By way of example, if the ICC has tried someone for rape as a war crime, it could later try him for rape as a crime against humanity, depending on whether such crime would require the subsistence of other constitutive elements. That same accused might also be subjected to prosecution by a domestic court for the ordinary crime of rape if such ordinary crime necessitates the subsistence of ingredients which are not directly incorporated within the more complex core crime

---

the litmus test which ensures that *ne bis in idem* rights are safeguarded. The ICCPR (see above), in fact, does not guarantee *ne bis in idem* with respect to national jurisdictions of two or more States, but only outlaws double jeopardy in relation to an offence already adjudicated within a given State [HRC, *A.R.J. v Australia*, 28 July 1997, Communication No. 692/1996, para 6.4]. The effect of all this uncertainty is that '*ne bis in idem* is subject to too many variants as to qualify as a general principle of law or a clear customary rule', (Naqvi 2010, p. 306) although low common denominators may be identified in the pursuit of a future rule of general international law. (Conway 2003, pp. 237–238). In terms of the *ius prosequi*, this equates to a less burdensome journey towards the desired tangible crystallization of the defeat of impunity for core crimes. This is further accentuated by the fact that the ICC Statute considers *ne bis in idem* as a procedural bar to jurisdiction, and not a fair trial guarantee in its own right.

155 Nouwen 2011, p. 213.

156 *Prosecutor v Saif Al-Islam Gaddafi* and Abdullah Al-Senussi, above n. 96, paras 71–73; *Prosecutor v Saif Al-Islam Gaddafi* and Abdullah Al-Senussi, above n. 92, para 119, both cited in Stahn 2015, p. 229.

157 Rastan 2010, p. 91, n. 30.

158 van den Wyngaert and Ongena 2002, pp. 724–726.

159 Rastan 2010, pp. 92–93.

160 van den Wyngaert and Ongena 2002, pp. 723–724.

[be it a war crime or a crime against humanity].[161] For example, whereas slight penetration suffices to prove the core crime of rape in terms of Articles 7(I)(g)-I and 8 (2)(b)(xxii)-I (the crime against humanity and the war crime respectively),[162] on the other hand, penetration is not required for the crime of statutory rape to subsist in the State of California, USA. Mere sexual activity with a person under the legal age of consent suffices.[163]

It is pertinent, in the light of the following excursus, to highlight that the contents of this paragraph could have figured in the former sub-heading, *id est* Sect. 11.1.1. This is because Articles 17(1)(a) and 19(2)(b) of the ICC Statute intersect one another especially where the concept of a case being prosecuted in Article 17(1)(a) of the ICC Statute overlaps with the concept of a State having prosecuted under Article 19(2)(b) of the ICC Statute. In fact, Articles 19(1) and 19(2) of the ICC Statute refer explicitly to Article 17 of the ICC Statute. For the sake of non-repetition, this paragraph is only present within this sub-heading. If the case which is being investigated or prosecuted by a State possessing jurisdiction over it is substantially the same as the case before the ICC, such case would be inadmissible and the ICC would enjoy no jurisdiction over it. The case is deemed to be substantially the same if the national investigation covers the same individual and the same conduct as alleged in the proceedings before the ICC.[164] The 'same person' test is very easy in so far as such person is easily identifiable since he or she is necessarily a (one and unique) natural person. Legal persons such as corporate entities and/or companies are not subject to individual criminal responsibility under the ICC Statute. The 'same person' test simply involves the same individual. It would be correct to conclude that the term 'substantially' only applies with reference to the 'same conduct' test, and not to the 'same person' test.[165] The ICC Appeals Chamber has found that a case is only inadmissible before the ICC if the same suspects are being investigated by *Kenya* for substantially the same conduct, adding that for the purposes of a challenge under Article 19(2)(b) of the ICC Statute concrete investigative steps are required.[166]

---

161 Rastan 2010, p. 92.

162 ICC Elements of Crimes (1998) International Criminal Court, Elements of Crimes.

163 Aizman 2016. This sharply contrasts with Pakistan, which requires full penetration to prove rape, where courts have gone as far as holding that the presence of semen in the victim's vagina is an insufficient indication of rape (HRW 1999, p. 36, n. 79).

164 *Prosecutor v Francis Kirimi Muthaura and Others*, above n. 55, paras 39–40.

165 *Prosecutor v Francis Kirimi Muthaura and Others*, above n. 55, paras 39 and 40.

166 Such steps include measures directed at ascertaining whether suspects are responsible for that conduct, interviews of witnesses or suspects, the collection of documentary evidence and the carrying out of forensic analyses [*Prosecutor v Francis Kirimi Muthaura and Others*, above n. 55, paras 40–42, cited in Stahn 2015, p. 236, notes 53 and 54].

Ergo, the mere readiness to take steps or the investigation of other suspects were insufficient.[167] The ICC Pre-Trial Chamber qualified this in a seemingly restrictive manner. It found that the expression 'the case is being investigated' within the meaning of Article 17(1)(a) of the ICC Statute connotes that 'concrete, tangible and progressive investigative steps are being undertaken by the domestic authorities in *Côte d'Ivoire* in order to ascertain *Simone Gbagbo*'s criminal responsibility for the same conduct as that alleged in the proceedings before the Court'.[168] The investigative steps must hence be concrete, tangible and progressive, as opposed to 'sparse and disparate'.[169] They are sparse when they lack in progression.[170] They are disparate when the overall factual contours of the alleged domestic investigations remain indiscernible in so far as they contain generic descriptions of the alleged crimes and provide extremely vague information on the factual parameters of the purported investigations which remain unclear and undefined.[171] They remain indiscernible if the factual criminal conduct attributed to *Simone Gbagbo* or the facts underlying the accusations that are purportedly being investigated, do not assist the ICC's understanding on the subject-matter of proceedings undertaken against *Simone Gbagbo* consisting in the limited and discrete investigative steps undertaken by the Ivorian domestic authorities.[172] Yet, one notes that the word 'tangible', as opposed to 'concrete and progressive', is not used by the Pre-Trial Chamber earlier on within the same judgment.[173] Whereas 'concrete' and 'tangible' could possibly be used inter-changeably, the term 'progressive' seems to indicate that, to a large extent, the investigative steps undertaken [or being undertaken] should be such as to lead to a successful prosecution [or at least to the likelihood of a successful prosecution]. This does not mean that the ICC Pre-Trial Chamber is called to determine whether the evidence on the merits of the national case collected by the domestic authorities is strong enough to establish the criminal responsibility of the individual.[174] Yet, in my view, to demonstrate the progressive undertaking of investigative steps the domestic State must maximise the use it could make of any available evidence which it is expected to preserve because the word 'progressive' presupposes that the investigation will progress to yet another stage. In other words, if, for example, scene of crime officers [either inadvertently or deliberately] fail to preserve available evidence which could prove the subsistence of a core crime, even

---

[167] *Prosecutor v Francis Kirimi Muthaura and Others*, above n. 55, paras 40–42, cited in Stahn 2015, p. 236, n. 55.

[168] *Prosecutor v Simone Gbagbo*, above n. 52, para 78.

[169] *Prosecutor v Simone Gbagbo*, above n. 52, para 65.

[170] *Prosecutor v Simone Gbagbo*, above n. 52, para 70.

[171] *Prosecutor v Simone Gbagbo*, above n. 52, paras 70–71.

[172] *Prosecutor v Simone Gbagbo*, above n. 52, paras 73 and 76.

[173] *Prosecutor v Simone Gbagbo*, above n. 52, para 30.

[174] ICC Pre-Trial Chamber I, *Situation in Libya*, *Prosecutor v Saif Al-Islam Gaddafi* and Abdullah Al-Senussi, *Decision Requesting Further Submissions on Issues Related to the Admissibility of the Case Against Saif Al-Islam Gaddafi*, 7 December 2012, Case No. ICC-01/11-01/11, para 122, cited in *Prosecutor v Simone Gbagbo*, above n. 52, para 31, n. 53.

if the State subsequently tries to reconstruct the crime scene with an intent to secure a conviction, in the absence of the best evidence, no progressive investigative steps can be recorded and proved by the domestic State. This is especially so when a State's domestic system rigorously upholds the 'best evidence rule'.[175] The ICC Pre-Trial Chamber also explicitly qualified the requirements to demonstrate that 'the case is being investigated' *rationae temporis*. It upheld that for the purposes of a successful admissibility challenge the State must 'substantiate that an investigation or prosecution is in progress at this moment'.[176] The 'same conduct' test is not so straight-forward at all. It seems that the conduct in question must be defined with reference to the constitutive elements (the essential ingredients)[177] of the crime as proscribed and penalized by the ICC Statute and the ICC Elements of Crimes. To this extent, 'conduct' in the light of an investigation and/prosecution in terms of Article 17(1)(a) of the ICC Statute, is more akin to 'fact' rather than 'offence'. It hence seems that the domestic case must largely concern the same conduct, not necessarily the same crime,[178] a position which departs significantly from 'the specificity test' adopted by Pre-Trial Chamber I in *Lubanga*.[179] In fact, more recently, the ICC Appeals Chamber has determined that 'conduct' is constituted by incidents under investigation, which incidents are a central aspect of such conduct.[180] The level of sameness may be assessed by examining the degree and extent of overlap between the incidents investigated domestically and at ICC level.[181] The Appeals Chamber found that domestic investigations need to sufficiently mirror the ICC investigations,[182] using such phrase which, in the words of Marta Bo, constitutes a rather vague threshold which hardly illuminates or simplifies matters.[183] A speculative or potential investigation is insufficient.[184] A lot can be learnt when one reads the *Saif Al-Islam* appellate judgment on the one hand and the recent *Simone Gbagbo* Pre-Trial Chamber *dictum* on the other hand. A comparative analysis of the thresholds adopted by both Chambers shows that, although the Pre-Trial Chamber

---

175 Divisional Court, UK, *Smakowski and Zestfair Ltd v Westminster City Council*, (1990), 154 J. P. 345 DC, Crim. L.R. 1990 Jun 419–421, cited in Richardson 2007, pp. 1307–1308.

176 ICC Pre-Trial Chamber I, *Situation in Libya, Prosecutor v Saif Al-Islam Gaddafi* and Abdullah Al-Senussi, *Decision Requesting Further Submissions on Issues Related to the Admissibility of the Case Against Saif Al-Islam Gaddafi*, 7 December 2012, Case No. ICC-01/11-01/11, para 14, cited in *Prosecutor v Simone Gbagbo*, above n. 52, para 35, n. 65.

177 Nsereko 2013, p. 444.

178 Nouwen 2011, pp. 212–214.

179 *Prosecutor v Thomas Lubanga* Dyilo, above n. 29, paras 38–40.

180 *Prosecutor v Saif Al-Islam Gaddafi* and Abdullah Al-Senussi, above n. 96, para 62.

181 *Prosecutor v Saif Al-Islam Gaddafi* and Abdullah Al-Senussi, above n. 96, para 72.

182 Payam Akhavan contends that 'even an ongoing investigation in its early stages (i.e. that relates to "aspects" of the ICC case but does not yet reveal its full contours) will not satisfy the "same conduct test"' (Akhavan 2016, p. 1054).

183 Bo 2014, p. 521.

184 *Prosecutor v Francis Kirimi Muthaura, Uhuru Muigai Kenyatta and Mohammed Hussein Ali*, para 40, cited in Akhavan 2016, p. 1045, n. 9.

largely adopted the views of the Appellate Chamber and in fact cites this appellate judgment repeatedly, on some counts, it seems to impose a higher *onus probandi* on the State challenging admissibility.

Similarly, 'domestic jurisdictions may thus pursue prosecution under the label of ordinary crimes without fear of re-trial, if the offences charged domestically are based on essential elements of crimes listed under article 6,7 or 8, or at least not substantially different from them'.[185] Thus a convict is protected by the *ne bis in idem* rule if he has been sentenced for an ordinary crime. This reverberates the *Ponsetti and Chesnel v France*[186] *dictum* by the ECtHR which added that the offences had to differ in their constitutive elements, a decision which supplemented the laudable *Oliveira v Switzerland*[187] judgment by the same Court, wherein a single act [a mode of conduct] could be prosecuted under different offences that had been committed contemporaneously. In sum, the prevailing *ne bis in idem* prohibition is of a vertical (not of a horizontal) nature, and can have a deep impact on the admissibility test which effectively determines the ICC's jurisdiction or otherwise. Within the international context (both horizontal and vertical), it is therefore essential to start from the conduct, particularly because legal systems differ. In the light of this prevailing state of affairs, the importance of *ne bis in idem*[188] for the purposes of this work should be stressed. Suffice to recall that the 'Trial Chamber noted that, with the exception of grounds based on the *ne bis in idem* principle, the violation of an accused person's human rights is not a ground for the inadmissibility of a case'.[189] This is consonant with Articles 17(1)(c), 19(4) and 20 of the ICC Statute as a result of which the *ne bis in idem* rule is the only ground of inadmissibility for which the ICC may grant leave to bring a challenge post-trial or on multiple occasions. Its characteristics as a peremptory plea which is capable of extinguishing the criminal action are thus underlined.

Since the ICC must determine *autrefois convict* and/or *autrefois acquit,* that is whether a person has been tried already or otherwise, the ICC (not the State, the national courts of which must defer the issue until the ICC has decided on the admissibility of the case) shall be the ultimate arbiter on the applicability of a *ne bis in idem* plea, in the same way as it has the final say on its own jurisdiction, post-admissibility. This is crucially important for the purposes of the

---

[185] Tallgren and Reisinger Coracini 2008, p. 692, n. 129.

[186] ECtHR Third Section, *Ponsetti and Chesnel v France,* 14 September 1999, Application Numbers 36855/97 and 41731/98, para 5 of 'The Law'.

[187] ECtHR, *Maria Celeste Vieira Veloso de Oliveira v Switzerland,* 30 July 1998, Application No. 84/1997/868/1080, para 26.

[188] The rule of *ne bis in idem* in criminal matters is also applied within EU Law, as a consequence of the incorporation of the Schengen *acquis* in the European Community [*Schengen Acquis* (1999) The Schengen Convention to Implement the Schengen Agreement of 14 June 1985] and EU legal order by the Amsterdam Treaty (1997) Treaty of Amsterdam amending the Treaty of the European Union, the Treaties establishing the European Communities and certain related acts (Mitsilegas 2009, p. 143).

[189] *Prosecutor v Germain Katanga and Mathieu Ngudjolo Chui,* above n. 50, para 99.

complementarity principle. By virtue of a *mise en scène*, a State may deliberately prosecute an individual to enable him to benefit from the *ne bis in idem* rule. In actual fact, by prosecuting him the State would be attempting to shield such person. The State may alternatively prosecute but punish by inflicting very mild and lenient terms of imprisonment. A State could do this to afford protection to an individual (or to attempt to afford such protection) both on an intra-jurisdictional level, *id est* should another domestic political regime decide to prosecute the same individual, and on an inter-jurisdictional scale, *id est* within the EU and/or before the ICC. These manoeuvres unmask 'a devious intent on the part of the State, contrary to its apparent actions'.[190] This would render the case admissible before the ICC since it would trigger the exception to the principle in Article 20(3)(b) of the ICC Statute because the case previously judged domestically adopted a procedure which lacked impartiality and independence, it did not respect due process norms and/or did not radiate an intent to judge the accused. For the purposes of determining whether Colombia was willing to exercise domestic jurisdiction over core crimes, the ICC noted that the OTP 'has informed the Colombian authorities that a sentence that is grossly or manifestly inadequate, in light of the gravity of the crimes and the form of participation of the accused, would vitiate the genuineness of national proceedings'.[191]

Distinctively from 'the unjustified delay in proceedings' {Article 17(2)(b) of the ICC Statute} and the 'lack of independence or impartiality' {Article 17(2)(c) of the ICC Statute}, both of which draw objective boundaries, the determination of 'shielding[192] or otherwise'{Article 17(2)(a) of the ICC Statute} embodies an element of subjectivity.[193] Yet, different approaches and tests, be they objective or subjective, do not preclude overlap. Sub-paragraphs (b) and (c) of Article 17(2) of the ICC Statute 'are contributing factors to the determination that domestic proceedings are sham, aiming to shield the accused from criminal responsibility, in accordance with sub-paragraph (a)'[194] of Article 17(2) of the ICC Statute. The ICC Statute devised a protective cover to prevent multiple prosecutions by the ICC itself. It may be said to act effectively in an intra-jurisdictional setting. The same may not be said when an inter-jurisdictional setting is considered, in that, within such context, rather than protecting the rights of the accused, the *ne bis in idem* rule is focused on organizing the inter-jurisdictional concurrence by regulating the relationship between national and international jurisdictions.[195] This is so to the extent that the rule has been equated to the role of a pointsman between concurrently competent jurisdictions.[196] The goalposts are hence shifted from the State to

190 Arbour and Bergsmo 1999, p. 131.

191 OTP 2014, para 114, cited in Weiner 2016, p. 233, n. 94.

192 For guidelines reflecting the notion of shielding, see El Zeidy 2008, pp. 175–180.

193 El Zeidy 2008, p. 168.

194 El Zeidy 2008, p. 170.

195 Shany 2007, pp. 159–163.

196 Bernard 2011a, b, p. 871.

the ICC which is to determine the same prior to surrender itself and *ab initio*. In practice, therefore, 'ratification of the Statute grants the ICC an independent right of assessment over the situation and the choices made in the domestic context'.[197] The shifting process resembles the preliminary reference procedure within EU Law,[198] because the arrested person can raise the *ne bis in idem* plea before the domestic court which postpones the surrender proceedings until the ICC decides there upon. As Héctor Olásolo explains, 'it is likely that the violation from a national perspective of the *ne bis in idem* principle will prevent the States Parties concerned, and particularly those in which the *ne bis in idem* principle has constitutional rank, from complying with their obligations to cooperate with the ICC'.[199] Furthermore, and just to highlight the importance of this ground for refusal, whereas challenges on admissibility must be filed before the Pre-Trial Chamber, those based upon the *ne bis in idem* rule could be allowed with the leave of the Trial Chamber in exceptional circumstances.[200] Such pleas are, in common law jargon, of a strictly peremptory nature in that they *ab initio* preclude the commencement of a trial.

In relation specifically to the *ne bis in idem* rule (applied in a broad and general context),[201] which minimum guarantee could effectively hinder surrender and thus jeopardize the vertical system of enforcement of international criminal law, the ICC Statute is not silent. As shown, it is, to an extent, both pro-active and pre-emptive. It caters, by virtue of its Articles 20(3)(a) and 20(3)(b), for the assumption of 'international jurisdiction' where a person has been previously tried but where either such sham trial was conducted to shield such person from prosecution or was not conducted in an independent and impartial manner which is inconsistent with an intent to bring such person to justice. The ability of this rule to suppress surrender is hence restricted,[202] especially when one considers such rule in the light of the complementarity provisions of the ICC Statute, summarily analysed here above. Additionally, the ICC is not precluded from exercising jurisdiction over the conduct of persons who have been granted an amnesty.[203] This is because 'amnesties most probably will not escape Article 17, and they will be, in most cases, admissible before the ICC'.[204] This is also confirmed by Jann Kleffner who, whilst studying complementarity, upholds that the permissibility of amnesties is doubtful in the

---

[197] Stahn 2010, p. 669.

[198] Chalmers et al. 2006, pp. 273–301.

[199] Olásolo 2005, p. 154.

[200] ICC Appeals Chamber, Situation in the DRC in the case of the *Prosecutor v Germain Katanga and Mathieu Ngudjolo Chui*, Judgment on the Appeal of Mr. Katanga Against the Decision of the Trial Chamber II of 20 November 2009 entitled 'Decision on the Motion of the Defence for Germain Katanga for a Declaration on Unlawful Detention and Stay of Proceedings', Dissenting Opinion of Judge Erkki Kourula and Judge Ekaterina Trendafilova, 12 July 2010, Case No. ICC-01/04-01/07 OA 10, n. 147.

[201] Article 14(7) of the ICCPR, above n. 154.

[202] Daniels 2006, p. 11.

[203] Amnesties will also be considered under Sect. 16.5.

[204] Jurdi 2011, p. 84.

light of the admissibility test.[205] In practice, amnesties 'deserve the same treatment as sham trials' and do not qualify as judgments for the purposes of Article 20 of the ICC Statute.[206] Likewise, the same may be said about decisions rendered by truth and reconciliation commissions in so far as their trials are not trials in the sense of Article 20 of the ICC Statute. Yet, Iain Scobbie, citing Schabas, suggests that 'a sincere attempt at non-judicial accountability would be respected by the Prosecutor, exercising discretion under Article 53.1.c, by concluding that an investigation of the alleged offences "would not serve the interests of justice"'.[207] I doubt whether an inquiry conducted by such commission, no matter how 'sincere' it may be, could fall within the legal rubric of an investigation in terms of the ICC Statute especially because an investigation necessarily presupposes the possibility of criminal proceedings rather than a mere fact-finding inquiry into the conduct and responsibilities.[208] In any case, it will be up to the Prosecutor to determine whether, in terms of Article 53(1)(c) of the ICC Statute, such prosecution would serve the interests of justice or otherwise.[209] Therefore, the interests of justice tests need only be considered where positive determinations have been made on both jurisdiction and admissibility.[210] These tests are negatively couched. The Prosecutor is not required to establish that an investigation or a prosecution is in the interests of justice, but 'shall proceed with an investigation unless there are specific circumstances which provide substantial reasons to believe it is not in the interests of justice to do so at that time'.[211] OTP papers rightly seem to favour a restrictive interpretation of Article 53 which would not encompass factors such as fostering peace and national reconciliation in post-conflict societies.[212] The pretext for such restrictive interpretation emanates from treaty law itself, namely from Article 31 of the VCLT which stipulates that the terms of the treaty ought to be interpreted in the light of the objects and purposes of the treaty, these being the prevention of serious crimes by ending impunity in so far as 'justice is an essential component of a stable peace'.[213] In fact, the ICC Statute may be said to have two overarching goals: the ending of impunity, by encouraging genuine national proceedings, and the prevention of crimes.[214] Since 'a treaty interpreter must read all applicable provisions of a treaty

---

205 Kleffner 2006, pp. 94–95.

206 van den Wyngaert and Ongena 2002, p. 726.

207 Schabas 2001, p. 69, cited in Scobbie 2003, p. 34, n. 77.

208 Vladimir Tochilovsky has also proposed the merging of investigative and prosecutorial functions within international criminal justice systems (Tochilovsky 2011, pp. 599–601); see also Robinson 2006, p. 144.

209 For a thorough analysis of Article 53 of the ICC Statute, above n. 25, see Robinson 2003, pp. 486–498.

210 OTP 2007, p. 2.

211 OTP 2007, p. 3.

212 Buchan and Johnsson 2012, p. 106.

213 OTP 2007, p. 8.

214 OTP 2013, p. 4.

in a way which gives meaning to all of them harmoniously',[215] it would be erroneous to reach any other conclusion. Consequently, a prosecution can only be dismissed 'where the specific characteristics of the victim or perpetrator indicate that justice would not be served by continuing the prosecution'.[216] A strong *iuris tantum* presumption to the effect that investigations and prosecutions will be in the interest of justice may be deemed to subsist.[217] If and when such presumption is rebutted by the Prosecutor, the Pre-Trial Chamber will, in terms of Article 53(3) of the ICC Statute, review the Prosecutor's decision not to investigate or prosecute.

Christine van den Wyngaert and Tom Ongena perceptively detect a serious *lacuna*, a loophole also noted by John T. Holmes within the same publication.[218] The ICC Statute is silent on what will happen in the case where persons have been pardoned (or paroled) in a State after their conviction has been pronounced. Article 20(2) thereof addresses a state of affairs wherein criminal proceedings have been conducted in an unacceptable way, but fails to address a state of affairs wherein unacceptable measures are taken after procedures have come to an end. I concur with one of the ways, proposed by Christine van den Wyngaert and Tom Ongena, as to how this *lacuna* can be filled. Essentially, as will be shown in the forthcoming Part, customary international law prohibits blanket amnesties for core crimes. Hence, (arguably) such amnesties are null and void *ab initio* and can have no material effect on ICC proceedings.[219]Admittedly, this line of argumentation might have a flaw in that it conflates amnesties on the one hand with pardons (and/or paroles) on the other hand, when both are different in terms of their timing and in terms of their contextual circumstances. However, in any case, there might be no need to fill such *lacuna* in the first place since, as John Holmes upholds, the pardon or parole can be 'conclusive evidence of a lack of genuineness from the outset' especially if the State actions vary significantly from the usual national practice for similar conduct.[220] Such solution is not necessarily watertight. Mohamed El Zeidy notes the arguments postulated by William Schabas to the effect that a State may genuinely investigate, prosecute, convict and sentence an individual, but a change in the political administration of that State can lead to a subsequent pardon. Mohamed El Zeidy concedes that, in such circumstances, notwithstanding the suspicious or foul intentions of the new political administration, the *bona fide* trial may bar the ICC from asserting jurisdiction in terms of Article 20(3) of the ICC Statute. Examining John Holmes' divergent opinion, Mohamed El Zeidy pinpoints that the conjunction 'and', used in Article 20(3)(b) of the ICC Statute, 'seems to suggest that the Court must look not only to the manner in which the proceedings were conducted, but also to a factor such as the administration's intentions at the

215 Akande 2009, p. 338.

216 Buchan and Johnsson 2012, p. 106.

217 OTP 2013, p. 17; see also OTP 2007, p. 3.

218 Holmes 2002, p. 678.

219 van den Wyngaert and Ongena 2002, pp. 726–727.

220 Holmes 2002, pp. 678–679.

time the proceedings took place'.[221] He concludes that John Holmes' interpretation 'may be valid in a situation where the administration that oversaw the trial proceeding is the same one granting the pardon'.[222] The above explains why amnesties can hardly figure as a ground for refusal *per se* within the vertical system of enforcement, as opposed to the horizontal system of enforcement. In all fairness, as noted above, Article 53(1)(c) confers discretion upon the ICC Prosecutor to dismiss prosecutions previously covered by a national amnesty when such prosecution would not be in the interest of justice. But this is not tantamount to a ground for refusal which can be invoked by States. It is just a measure entailing specific and unfettered prosecutorial discretion. Besides valid reservations as to whether the phrase 'interest of justice' could be made use of to enable the execution of amnesties,[223] as noted above, (on the same lines of the OTP's restrictive interpretation of Article 53) I doubt whether, in the light of the ICC's Preamble and the emerging duty to prosecute (which pervades this work), one could ever successfully submit (and sufficiently motivate a claim to the effect) that not prosecuting can serve the interests of justice more than prosecuting, even amidst a post-conflict, democratization process. A similar, though less convincing, argument can be postulated in connection with the UNSC's powers to prevent a prosecution from coming before the ICC where this would be in the ultimate interest of fostering peace and national reconciliation.[224] The explicit regulation of the ICC Statute, which after all, being a convention, is the primary source of international law, was particularly important because 'most commentators agree that the international application of *non bis in idem* cannot be considered customary international law nor can it be considered a general principle of international law',[225] although it has been incorporated within a multitude of treaties, of which only the CISA attaches an *erga omnes* status thereto.[226]

Delving onto case-law relating directly to cooperation, in *Prosecutor versus Duško Tadić*,[227] the ICTY was called upon to examine the *ne bis in idem* plea of the defendant based upon the defence's submission that national criminal proceedings[228] (in this case in Germany) had already been instituted against the defendant. The ICTY Trial Chamber dismissed the claim on the grounds that the accused has

221 El Zeidy 2008, p. 298.

222 Ibid.

223 Buchan and Johnsson 2012, p. 103.

224 See the deferral mechanism contemplated by Article 16 of the ICC Statute which is eloquently analysed in Knottnerus 2014.

225 Daniels 2006, p. 11; see also Conway 2003, pp. 217–218.

226 Conway 2003, pp. 219–221.

227 ICTY Trial Chamber, *Prosecutor v Duško Tadić, Decision on the Defence Motion on the Principle of Non Bis in Idem*, 14 November 1995, Case No IT-94-1-T.

228 National proceedings must encompass both the person and the conduct which is the subject of the case before the Court. This means that the person must be investigated and prosecuted for the specific crimes under consideration by the ICC [*Prosecutor v Thomas Lubanga* Dyilo, above n. 29, paras 38 and 40 cited in Klip and Sluiter 2010, p. 61].

not yet been the subject of a judgment on the merits of any of the charges[229] for which he had been indicted, but held that Germany, which had deferred the case to the ICTY, could not again prosecute *Tadić* for the same facts[230] after a *res judicata* emanated from the ICTY. Surprisingly, another State was precluded from trying *Tadić* again, but the same impediment would not have had the same effect had *Tadić* been re-tried by the ICTY itself. In fact, the ICTY Statute does not provide for any internal *ne bis in idem* because 'nothing in the Statute or Rules explicitly prohibits the Prosecutor from retrying the accused, after acquittal, on the same facts'.[231]

The ICC has already dealt with the *ne bis in idem* rule in the case of *Thomas Lubanga* Dyilo. These criminal proceedings were preceded by an arrest warrant issued by the Courts of the DRC against *Lubanga* Dyilo. Criminal proceedings in the DRC were not pursued. Thus, technically, *ne bis in idem* did not apply since *Dyilo* was not tried in the DRC. Carter opines that, had criminal proceedings been instituted, most probably the rule would not have barred a prosecution since it is unlikely that the conduct would have been viewed as the same, given that the recruitment of child soldiers varies from the charges instituted in the DRC. In fact no reference is made to the recruitment of child soldiers in the DRC arrest warrants.[232] In support of this, the ICC has held that 'since the warrants of arrest issued in the DRC contained no reference to the charges brought by the Prosecutor and no other State with jurisdiction was investigating, prosecuting or had investigated and prosecuted the same crimes, the case was considered admissible'.[233] Therefore the ICC adopted a two-pronged approach, the 'same offence test' in conjunction with the 'same fact test'. This seems to tally with a rigid interpretation of Article 20(3) of the ICC Statute which refers to a person being 'tried by another Court for conduct also proscribed under articles 6,7 or 8'. The term 'conduct' might lead one to conclude that it can be inter-changeably used with the word 'fact'. However the word 'conduct' is deliberately qualified with the phrase 'also proscribed under articles 6,7 or 8', these being the core crimes, the punishable criminal offences.

The *ne bis in idem* principle was also raised by the defence in the *Bemba* case, wherein inadmissibility was claimed on such ground since, in the defence's view,

---

[229] For an understanding of the meaning of a 'criminal charge', see Gomien et al. 1996, p. 163.

[230] The preclusion of prosecution on the same facts is also referred to as *ne bis in idem* in concreto, this being adopted generally within civil law countries, whereas such prohibition on the basis of the same offence, generally adopted within common law jurisdictions, is referred to as *ne bis in idem* in abstracto (Conway 2003, p. 227).

[231] Bassiouni and Manikas 1996, p. 334.

[232] Carter 2010, pp. 15–16.

[233] ICC Pre-Trial Chamber I, *Prosecutor v Bosco Ntanganda, Decision on the Prosecutor's Application for Warrants of Arrest under Article 58,* 10 February 2006, Case No. ICC-01/04-02/06-20-Anx2, paras 29–41.

investigations of the national authorities were conducted in relation to allegations which are identical to the charges brought by the ICC itself. It must be stated, in this context, that Sarah Nouwen emphasizes that the domestic case must concern the same conduct, not necessarily the same crime.[234] In the *Bemba* case, the defence submitted that ICC proceedings violated the *res judicata* principle and that the *ne bis in idem* principle did not require an acquittal or a conviction. An agreement between the accused and the prosecution sufficed. The prosecution astutely transformed diplomatic immunities in its favour, by arguing that such immunity, security concerns and the difficulty in collecting the necessary evidence resulted in the overall 'unavailability' of the CAR national judicial system rendering such CAR authorities genuinely unable to prosecute the case domestically. It further argued that for *ne bis in idem* to bar proceedings a previous acquittal or conviction must necessarily subsist. Principal counsel for victims, referring to case-law in international humanitarian law, international human rights law and international criminal law, followed suit. CAR legal representatives also backed the Prosecutor's view on the need for a previous acquittal or conviction. The ICC, *inter alia*, concluding that a case was not being investigated or prosecuted by the CAR and that no trial had taken place, decided that the dismissal of the charges by the Senior Investigating Judge did not constitute a final decision on the merits of the case,[235] but was still *sub iudice* because on the following day the Deputy Prosecutor of the *Tribunal de Grand Instance* lodged a *prima facie* valid appeal against all the accused persons. The case before the ICC was thus admissible. The *Chui* case[236] before the ICC might have led to a clearer understanding of the *ne bis in idem* rule. *Chui* was acquitted in 2004 of a charge of murder of an individual in Bunia in the DRC. At his initial appearance before the ICC in 2008, he claimed that he had previously been tried and acquitted for the same conduct on the basis of which he was facing charges before the ICC. The Pre-Trial Chamber had given the defence an opportunity to file a written motion challenging admissibility based on *ne bis in idem*. The defence, however, failed to follow this motion. Consequently, the ICC did not take further cognisance of the principle in the light of the facts of the case, and the possibility of a formal and judicial acknowledgment that the doctrine now constitutes a general principle of criminal law faded into the background. One can only hope for an imminent and possibly conclusive elucidation of the *ne bis in idem* hurdle within the forthcoming jurisprudence of the ICC.

---

[234] Nouwen 2011, p. 212.

[235] ICC Pre-Trial Chamber III, *Situation in the CAR, Prosecutor v Jean-Pierre Bemba* Gombo, *Decision on the Admissibility and Abuse of Process Challenges,* 24 June 2010, Case No. ICC-01/05-01/08, para 261.

[236] ICC Pre-Trial Chamber I, *Situation in the DRC*, Prosecutor v Germain Katanga and Mathieu Ngudjolo Chui, Initial Appearance of Mathieu Ngudjolo Chui, 11 February 2008, Case No. ICC-01/04-01/07.

11.1.3 Postponement of the Execution of a Request for Surrender

Though this relates to Article 94, a legal provision within Part 9 of the ICC Statute, it is being considered now and within the heading entitled 'grounds for refusal emerging directly from admissibility challenges', for the reasons which shall be shortly explained. At the outset, one must clarify that a right to postpone is not tantamount to a right to deny/refuse. Postponement of the execution of requests for arrest is not permissible under the ICC Statute.[237] On the other hand, postponement of the execution of requests for surrender has a dual dimension. It can occur in respect of ongoing investigations or prosecutions, but can also occur pending a challenge to the admissibility of a case before the ICC. These dimensions are not completely detached. Dapo Akande eloquently posits that 'Article 94 deals with a domestic case that deals with different conduct while Article 95 deals with a domestic case that deals with the same conduct'.[238] With regard to the former type of postponement, this takes place irrespective of any admissibility challenge. Article 94 of the ICC Statute, which enables the ICC investigation to carry on and the Prosecutor to seek measures to preserve evidence,[239] necessitates that for an execution of a request to be postponed, domestic proceedings that are somehow related to the forthcoming (potential) ICC proceedings would have to be pending. More precisely, there must be an ongoing investigation or prosecution of a case, different from that to which the request relates, within the domestic State. Hence no interference with an ongoing national investigation is allowed. This adheres to the complementarity principle. However, the domestic case must not involve the same person/same conduct[240] as that being investigated by the ICC. Otherwise it would be eligible to constituting an admissibility challenge or lead to the suspension of a State's obligations which would circumvent the need to make an admissibility challenge. Were this possible, it would pervert the ICC jurisdictional regime and bypass the ICC itself. The drafting history of Article 94 of the ICC Statute also reveals that it was not intended to apply to requests for surrender.[241]

All the above goes to show how such grounds for refusal could be inter-linked and inter-dependent. In so far as the latter form of postponement is concerned, the suspension of an investigation, this being the postponement of a request, can lead to a fully-fledged refusal if a case is subsequently deemed inadmissible by the ICC. In other words, faced with an ICC request, if a State vaunts jurisdiction and proves it has the willingness and ability to exercise such jurisdiction, the ICC's jurisdiction is nullified. Consequently the requested person is not surrendered to the ICC. Hence,

[237] Swart 2002b, p. 1694.

[238] Akande 2012a, p. 322.

[239] Article 93(1)(j) of the ICC Statute, above n. 25.

[240] See Sects. 11.1.1 and 11.1.2.

[241] Akande 2012a, p. 322.

on the basis of Article 19(7) of the ICC Statute, the execution of a request for surrender is suspended by the Prosecutor until a decision on the admissibility of a case is reached by the ICC. Such challenge would have to be made by the State, not the accused. Such an admissibility challenge *ipso facto* leads to the suspension of the Prosecutor's investigation.[242] It stands to reason that an admissibility challenge is accompanied by a postponement of the obligations of the State to cooperate. This is because at that moment in time (upon the admissibility challenge) a State is privy to whether it is legally entitled to retain jurisdiction or whether it should comply with the ICC's request to cooperate and surrender the individual. At that stage the State's obligation is frozen, and is only to be resumed if the case is declared admissible by the ICC. The above mentioned justifies the need to consider this ground for refusal at this stage, *id est* as a ground emerging directly from the admissibility test, rather than in terms of its positioning within the ICC Statute. Here one must not forget the content of Sect. 11.1 wherein it was concluded that whereas the right to challenge the admissibility of a case was always abundantly clear in so far as State Parties are concerned, it is now also the case when non-State Parties are concerned. This emanates further from Libya's admissibility challenge[243] in the *Saif Al-Islam Gaddafi* case,[244] the outcome of which was confirmed on appeal.[245]

The importance which Article 95 could have for the purposes of this work can be nullified if Article 95 is not deemed to extend to obligations for arrest and surrender. It seems, however, that Dapo Akande is correct when he concludes that the postponement of the execution of requests is not limited to 'other forms of cooperation'[246] in terms of Article 93, that it applies to the entire Part of the ICC Statute, Part 9, which includes requests for arrest and surrender, and also in the light of Article 89(2) of the ICC Statute which permits the suspension of the surrender obligation upon a *ne bis in idem* challenge.[247] Here again, the link with *ne bis in idem*, yet another distinct ground for refusal, sticks out. Geert-Jan Alexander Knoops opines that the fate of the *ne bis in idem* defence raised pursuant to Article 89(2) largely depends on the way Rule 181 of the RPE shall be applied by the ICC.[248] The above considerations emphasize the pivotal role of the admissibility test.

To wrap up the analysis of grounds for refusal emerging from admissibility challenges,[249] it would be appropriate to refer to the existing matrix which was recently drawn up by the ICC Appeals Chamber, further to which domestic action

---

242 Article 19(7) of the ICC Statute.

243 See n. 260 here below.

244 *Prosecutor v Saif Al-Islam Gaddafi* and Abdullah Al-Senussi, above n. 35, para 28.

245 *Prosecutor v Saif Al-Islam Gaddafi* and Abdullah Al-Senussi, above n. 36.

246 For a detailed and comprehensive examination of this phrase in the context of the ICC Statute, see Ciampi 2002a, pp. 1705–1747.

247 Akande 2012a, pp. 317–321.

248 Knoops 2002, p. 327.

249 See Sects. 11.1, 11.1.1, 11.1.2 and 11.1.3.

must mirror ICC practice.[250] The prevailing law on admissibility which somehow impinges upon the grounds for refusal of surrender, as shown here above, may be concisely summarised as follows:

1. admissibility determinations are case-specific, with the constitutive elements of a case before the ICC being the person and the alleged conduct. For a domestic case to be considered as the 'same case' before the ICC it must involve the same person (individual) and substantially the same conduct. The latter requirement is dependent on the factual parameters of each individual case and hence necessitates a case-by-case analysis which must focus on the alleged conduct, rather than on its legal characterisation. The contours or parameters of the case must be clear even during an investigation and irrespective of its stage;
2. the expression 'the case is being investigated' must be construed to require the undertaking of tangible, concrete and progressive investigative steps to ascertain whether the person is responsible for the conduct alleged against him before the ICC; and
3. a decision on the admissibility of the case must be based on the circumstances prevailing at the time of its issuance. For a State to discharge its burden of proof to the effect that currently there does not subsist a situation of 'inaction' [inactivity] at domestic level, it needs to substantiate its claim that an investigation is currently ongoing by providing evidence of a sufficient degree of specificity and probative value demonstrating that it is indeed investigating the case.[251]

11.2 Competing Requests and Conflicting Obligations

The ICC Statute's Article 90 caters for situations wherein a State Party may be faced with various obligations, one of which is the obligation to surrender a person to the ICC. Hence, where the duty to surrender, which includes the duty to authorize transit,[252] conflicts with another international obligation of the State, the State may refuse to surrender a person to the ICC, but must respect the *aut dedere aut judicare* rule, which shall be analysed in depth in Part IV, by extraditing the suspect, whose custodial jurisdiction it enjoys, to the requesting non-State Party. To this extent, one must recall that 'a variant of the *aut dedere aut judicare* model allows contracting States to deliver an alleged offender to a competent international

[250] *Prosecutor v Saif Al-Islam Gaddafi* and Abdullah Al-Senussi, above n. 96, para 73, cited in Stahn 2015, p. 239, n. 68.

[251] *Prosecutor v Simone Gbagbo*, above n. 52, paras 33–34 and 75–78; see also ICC Pre-Trial Chamber I, *Situation in Libya, Prosecutor v Saif Al-Islam Gaddafi* and Abdullah Al-Senussi, Decision on the Admissibility of the Case Against Abdullah Al-Senussi, 11 October 2013, Case No. ICC-01/11-01/11, para 66, cited in Stahn 2015, p. 238, n. 67.

[252] See Article 89(3) of the ICC Statute, above n. 25.

criminal tribunal, rather than prosecute him or extradite him'.[253] This heading shall determine which of the perpendicular obligations the requested State must adhere to. Although it has not yet developed a firm strategy in relation to parallel proceedings at the national level,[254] the ICC Statute has anticipated the possibility of conflicting obligations,[255] and has tried to offer a solution to the conundrum by means of its various legal provisions, including Articles 90 and 96.[256] Where this ensues anyway, State Parties are obliged to 'consult with the Court without delay in order to resolve the matter'.[257] Bert Swart states that where the conflict endures, the solution would have to be found by applying the general principles of international law relating to conflicting treaty obligations, where, similarly, a determining factor might be whether the third State, whose rights would be breached by the surrender of a person to the ICC, is itself a State Party or otherwise.[258]

Indeed, the situation might become complicated when the competing requests are multiple. *Al-Senussi*, for example, was subject to an extradition request to Mauritania, filed by France to serve his life sentence in France. Simultaneously, Libya tendered an extradition request to Mauritania for *Al-Senussi*'s alleged crimes in connection with the 2011 uprising. *Al-Senussi* was extradited to Libya by Mauritania on the 5 September 2012.[259] The ICC, for a time, also requested the surrender of *Al-Senussi* on the same basis as it requested *Saif Al-Islam*'s surrender, this being UNSC Resolution 1970, more so when its Pre-Trial Chamber and the Appeals Chamber had confirmed that the case against Al-Senussi was admissible.[260] Olympia Bekou aptly notes that national laws are most unlikely to include provisions relating to competing requests with priority awarded to the ICC in certain circumstances in terms of Article 90 of the ICC Statute. This, in her view, limits the use that can be made of Article 88 of the ICC Statute which ought to be amended in pursuance of incrementing 'positive complementarity',[261] with the

[253] Caligiuri 2018, p. 254.

[254] Ambos and Stegmiller 2012, p. 403.

[255] Ciampi 2002b, p. 1632.

[256] Swart 2002b, p. 1681.

[257] Article 97 of the ICC Statute, above n. 25.

[258] Swart 2002b, p. 1681.

[259] Bishop 2013, p. 405.

[260] It must be noted, however, that Libya's admissibility challenge was only directed at the *Saif Al-Islam* case. Libya argued that both cases should be considered separately. On 11 October 2013 the ICC [*Prosecutor v Saif Al-Islam Gaddafi* and Abdullah Al-Senussi, above n. 251], in the first successful admissibility challenge (see Stahn 2015, p. 232) held that the *Al-Senussi* case was inadmissible and was hence to proceed in Libya. The different outcomes of the *Saif Al-Islam* and *Al-Senussi* cases (wherein the former, unlike the latter, was considered admissible) has quelled fears that the ICC would interpret the admissibility threshold overly restrictively in order to keep any case once received in its docket in an effort of self-preservation (Bernard 2011a, b, p. 203, cited in Ambach 2015, p. 1281, n. 27).

[261] Bekou 2009, pp. 468 and 470.

latter term conveying that 'it always promotes national proceedings first'.[262] I further remark that the absence of a domestic legislative counterpart might lead to some incompatibility with national law.

The in-built ICC mechanism, concisely explained by Bert Swart and Göran Sluiter,[263] leaves the solution for competing requests up to a number of relevant and casuistic factors, the main criteria of which distinguish both between State Parties and non-State Parties to the ICC Statute, and also between requests for the same conduct and requests for different conduct.[264] It stipulates that a requested State Party is obliged to effect surrender to the ICC in the case of a competing request for extradition filed by another State Party if the ICC has determined such case is admissible.[265] Therefore, the general rule is that when there exists more than one request for surrender and extradition emanating from other State Parties, the requested State is to give priority to the ICC's request if the ICC has determined that the case in respect of which surrender is sought is admissible. Thus, by ratifying the ICC Statute, State Parties agreed that any extradition obligations they are owed become subordinate to a superior obligation of surrender to the ICC.[266] This ground of refusal, thus, unambiguously ropes in admissibility too, presenting yet another instance where admissibility pops up like an advert whilst browsing on a website. If, for example, the extradition request is tendered when the determination of admissibility is pending, the requested State must postpone its decision on the extradition request until the ICC has determined that the case is inadmissible. From a logical perspective, in competing requests, a lawyer would be inclined to favour the *forum conveniens*, this generally being either the State enjoying territorial jurisdiction or the State whose national is the accused. This is not always the case. The ICC may have accumulated strong evidence against a leadership group. Where one of the suspects flees to a third State, the third State is not compelled to compete with the ICC for jurisdiction. All stakeholders may agree that the ICC has developed and preserved superior evidence consisting in witnesses and expertise relating to that situation, 'making the ICC the more effective forum'.[267] It seems safe to conclude that the *forum conveniens* should be the one possessing 'the most promising prospect for an effective investigation and prosecution'.[268] Some criteria to determine such promising prospect include:

1. the availability of and access to witnesses;
2. the presence of the alleged perpetrator on the State's territory; and
3. the independence and impartiality of the judiciary.[269]

---

[262] Stegmiller 2013, p. 483.

[263] Swart and Sluiter 1999, p. 109.

[264] Knoops 2002, pp. 291–292.

[265] Article 90(2) of the ICC Statute, above n. 25.

[266] Schabas 2010, p. 1005.

[267] OTP 2003, p. 19.

[268] OTP 2003, p. 24.

[269] Ibid.

Hence, due process standards can be evaluated even for the purposes of establishing the *forum conveniens*. However, the admissibility test, with all its intricacies, may ultimately occasionally negate the inclination to opt for the *forum conveniens*. The determining factors become, to a large extent, the criteria to determine (in) admissibility.

The obligation of the State Party to extradite subsists when there exists an international obligation. A State Party may, subject to a number of procedural conditions, give priority to a competing extradition obligation. This reflects the primacy of the horizontal system of enforcement and corresponds with the preliminary points raised in Sect. 2.2. The State, here, is burdened with a choice to make: either surrender to the ICC or extradite to the requesting State. What it definitely cannot do is fail to choose either one of these. In making this choice, in accordance with Article 90(6) of the ICC Statute, it would have to take relevant factors into account, including:

(1) the respective dates of the requests;
(2) the interest of the requesting State (including the *locus delicti commissi* and the nationality of the accused); and
(3) the possibility of subsequent surrender between the ICC and the requesting State,[270] which is likely to depend upon whether the requesting State itself is a State Party to the ICC Statute or otherwise.

The rules are different when non-State Parties are concerned, with the fundamental factor being whether or not the requested State Party is under an international obligation to extradite the person to the requesting non-State Party. Bert Swart opines that the prevailing formula seems to cover the situation in which an international agreement on the extradition of persons is in force between the two States but does not create an obligation to extradite the person requested. He adds that this may be due to the fact that the person requested possesses the nationality of the requested State or because the offence for which the extradition has been requested is subject to the capital punishment under the law of the requesting State.[271] In the absence of such international obligation for the requested State Party to extradite the person, the requested State must give priority to the ICC's request if the ICC has determined that the case is admissible. In the absence of such determination on admissibility, the requested State is entitled to extradite the person sought to the requesting State. Bert Swart aptly notes that a *lacuna* prevails since Articles 90(4) and 90(5) of the ICC Statute are silent on the position at law when the determination of admissibility is still pending.[272]

What has been stated here above relates to competing requests where the same conduct is concerned. In the case where other conduct is the subject of the request, the determining criterion is whether there subsists an international obligation for the

270 Swart 2002b, p. 1696.

271 Ibid.

272 Ibid.

requested State Party to extradite the person sought or otherwise. If no such international obligation exists, the person sought should be surrendered to the ICC. If the international obligation exists, the requested State has to make the choice referred to here above.

11.3 Specific Requirements under National Law

Whereas the grounds for refusal dealt with so far focused on the international law of the ICC, national law can impose requirements which, if not satisfied, can impede the domestic competent authorities from adhering to the ICC's request for surrender. Such imposition could be constitutionally entrenched within national law. In terms of Article 91(4) of the ICC Statute, however, the most a State could do is consult the ICC with a view to solving the matter. For this purpose, the State itself would have to draw the ICC's attention to (and flag) the matter since any ensuing consultation would have to occur upon the ICC's request. Although Article 91(4) of the ICC Statute does not explicitly refer to human rights *per se*, such requirements could also specifically deal with human rights issues especially since the duty to safeguard some human rights may override the duty to surrender because the protection of such human rights prevails over other State obligations. This is more so when the human right at stake enjoys a *jus cogens* status. Article 91(4) in fact makes a cross-reference to para 2(c) of Article 91 which refers to 'documents, statements or information as may be necessary to meet the requirements for the surrendered person in the requested State'. The 'documents, statements or information' may include a confession (be it extra-judicial or otherwise) by the suspect since such confession is habitually made use of by requesting States in order to justify (to the standard of proof required by the respective national law) the extradition of the suspect to the requested State. Really and truly, issues dealing with the protection of human rights can also be (indirectly) availed of as a ground of refusal by the requested State on the basis of the phrase 'in accordance with its national procedural law' stipulated within Article 89(3) of the ICC Statute. Most importantly, such pleas can be tendered by a requested State in terms of the main provision within the Statute which deals specifically with the surrender of persons to the ICC. In fact Article 89(1) of the ICC Statute, whilst referring to the provisions of Part 9 of the ICC Statute relating to 'international cooperation and judicial assistance', stipulates that compliance with the request for arrest and surrender must be undertaken in accordance with the procedure under the national law of the requested State.

Indeed, the synergy between the law on cooperation and human rights is multi-functional and operates on various layers with each one capable of intersecting the others. State cooperation can be limited by human rights law. This is, indeed, the thrust of this heading. On the other hand, cooperation with the ICC can both enhance respect for human rights by domestic States and ensure that the UNSC targeted sanctions comply with human rights law and practice.[273] Nevertheless the leeway of States which derives from Articles 89(3) and 91(4) of the ICC Statute is very limited indeed, not to say inexistent. This is because the mandatory wording of such legal provisions connotes that States must comply with requests for surrender anyhow and anyway. They are simply authorised to undertake surrender in a way which does not breach their own legislative requirements. It is hence the manner (*modus operandi*) of surrender which may be negotiated amidst a consultation process, but not the surrender *per se*. This position may be less straight-forward when human rights violations which simultaneously breach a *jus cogens* norm are involved. However, for a ground of refusal of cooperation to subsist the pretext to the human rights violation must not have been provoked by the same State which is about to consider whether the individual should be surrendered or otherwise. If a State violates human rights of an individual flagrantly at the pre-trial stage it should not be permitted to use the same violation to justify non-surrender. If this were not so, States would be incentivised to breach human rights of individuals over whom they enjoy custodial jurisdiction, a juridical absurdity indeed. Whereas this position relating to a State (unilaterally) may be said to be a settled matter, complexities arise in a plural-State scenario, as shall be seen shortly in the following sub-heading.

11.3.1 Abuse of Process

The doctrine of abuse of process[274] safeguards the procedural rights of the accused throughout the entire procedural *iter*, commencing from the issuance of the international arrest warrant unto sentencing.[275] Irrespective of the remedy granted for a violation,[276] what is crucial for the purposes of this work is that due process rights do not commence to apply when a trial starts, but when the situation of a person is substantially affected by acts intended to bring him or her on trial, hence also covering the initial stages of arrest and surrender. In other words a trial or hearing does not only take place inside the courtroom. Its precursor precedes the trial itself. Therefore, the blatant violations of pre-trial human rights can constitute grounds for refusal of cooperation. Abuse of process thus has the potential to affect cooperation practice. This can also be deduced from the ICC Statute itself because it establishes

---

[273] Ciampi 2008, pp. 103–111.

[274] Another jurist considers the 'misuse of the criminal process' on the basis of *mala fides* (bad faith) as sufficient for proceedings to be stayed (Naqvi 2010, p. 361).

[275] Wherever there is a right, there is a remedy (Fellmeth and Horwitz 2009, p. 281).

[276] Such remedy, which should be proportionate to the violation and the harm endured, can range from the reduction of a sentence, in case of a conviction, to pecuniary compensation in the case of an acquittal.

a hierarchy of applicable law, with Article 21(3)[277] thereof being at the very top of the pyramid.[278] The fact that it pervades throughout all stages of the procedural *iter*, that is, from the moment the international arrest warrant is issued, renders it a matter which should be scrutinized for the purposes of this book. Such state of affairs leads me to consider this ground of refusal. Its consideration entails, as will become evident in Part IV, looking at *Soering* upside down, or rather, analysing the *Soering* seminal *dictum* within a vertical context.

Having established its (not so apparent) relevance for the purposes of this work, a basic understanding thereof is solicited. The use of the abuse of process doctrine[279] arguably comprises any act or decision which, of its own nature, is capable of violating the rights of the suspect or accused and consequently having a bearing on the fair administration of criminal justice. The doctrine, which originates from Common Law,[280] confers powers of a broad nature (such as the staying of a prosecution) upon courts[281] and also certainly includes and encapsulates issues dealing with unfair trials. In fact, a landmark case wherein the HoL stayed the prosecution and ordered the release of the accused affirmed that 'a Court has a discretion to stay any criminal proceedings on the ground that to try those proceedings will amount to an abuse of its own process either (i) because it will be impossible (usually by reason of delay) to give the accused a fair trial or (ii) because it offends the court's sense of justice and propriety to be asked to try the accused in the circumstances of a particular case'.[282]

In the light of the sufficient protection afforded to individuals by means of the ICC Statute (this being the first and only multi-lateral legal instrument which regulates the rights of suspects at a pre-trial stage), rather than being invoked vertically, fundamental human rights constituting barriers to surrender, with the exceptions of the *ne bis in idem* rule and the doctrine of 'abuse of process', are likely to be invoked horizontally. In fact, the *travaux preparatoires* show that the drafters of the ICC Statute intended the ICC to 'adhere scrupulously to international human rights standards in exercising its functions'.[283] Although the term 'internationally recognized human rights'[284] is not defined by the ICC Statute, 'a teleological approach indicates that the ICC is always bound by the highest human rights standards'.[285] After all 'internationally recognized human rights take

[277] This legal provision unequivocally stipulates that 'the application and interpretation of law pursuant to this article must be consistent with internationally recognized human rights…'.

[278] Deprez 2012, p. 729.

[279] Currie 2007, p. 362.

[280] Knoops 2002, pp. 236–238.

[281] Spencer 2014, p. 14.

[282] HoL, *Regina v Horseferry Road Magistrates' Court ex parte Bennett*, 24 June 1993 [1993] 3 WLR 90.

[283] McAuliffe de Guzman 1999, p. 445, cited in Usacka 2016, p. 287, n. 26.

[284] Article 21(3) of the ICC Statute, above n. 25.

[285] Viebig 2016, pp. 141–142.

precedence over any other conflicting rule of the ICC legal system, including those laid out in the Statute'.[286] The above is simply being stated not to strengthen the research theme which has already been identified in Sect. 1.3, but to acknowledge that State cooperation could have a bearing on the doctrine of equality of arms, an important characteristic of due process. State cooperation, therefore, has a constitutional (not only a penal and/or procedural) dimension, because 'it conditions the conduct of a fair trial'.[287] This *nexus* is emulated by Enrique Carnero Rojo's study which echoes the deep connection between the fair trial requirement and the admissibility criteria under the ICC Statute.[288] Having dealt with *ne bis in idem* within the context of the admissibility test in Sect. 11.1.2, this heading will only take into account the doctrine of 'abuse of process'.

Allegations of unfair trials by defendants before the ICC are not so uncommon,[289] but these relate predominantly to the actual proceedings, after [not preceding] surrender, *id est ex post facto*. Hence they shall not be considered for the purposes of this work. Furthermore, it is being made clear, at this stage, that this sub-heading will deal with circumstances which could vitiate the obligation to cooperate, but not directly with the situation whereby the illegality of a prior detention affects the legality of a subsequent detention order by another court, these being issues relating to the doctrine *male captus bene detentus*. This is why landmark cases such as *Duch*'s,[290] *Eichmann*'s,[291] *Alvarez-Machain*'s[292] and *Ebrahim*'s[293] cannot substantiate an understanding of the role of the vertical system of enforcement. The task of examining such *dicta* is an endeavour beyond the scope of this chapter.

It is not a common occurrence that the ICC would be called to decide upon an allegation that the ICC itself cannot furnish a fair trial or a similar allegation that a

[286] Gradoni et al. 2013, p. 83.

[287] Jorda 2004, p. 574.

[288] Carnero Rojo 2005, pp. 829–869.

[289] See, for example, ICC Pre-Trial Chamber II, *Situation in Uganda, Decision on Prosecutor's Application for Leave to Appeal in Part Pre-Trial Chamber II's Decision on the Prosecutor's Applications for Warrants of Arrest under Article 58*, 19 August 2005, Case No. ICC-02/04-01/05, para 24–51.

[290] *Kaing Guek Eav, alias Duch* was one of the main suspects for the atrocities committed by the regime of Democratic Kampuchea in the 1970s (Ryngaert 2008, p. 719). The case [ECCC, *Prosecutor v. Kaing Guek Eav alias Duch*, 3 February 2012, 001/18-07-2007-ECCC/SC] is eloquently explained by Eckelmans 2016, pp. 159–179.

[291] Adolf Eichmann complained of the illegality of his capture in Argentina by Israeli agents, arguing it affected the legality of his detention and trial (Ryngaert 2008, p. 728).

[292] Alvarez-Machain [USA Supreme Court, *USA v Humberto Alvarez-Machain*, 15 June 1992, 504 U.S. 655 (112 S.Ct. 2188, 119 L.Ed.2d 441) 91/712] argued that the illegality of his capture in Mexico by USA drug enforcement agents affected the legality of his detention and trial (Ryngaert 2008, p. 728; see also Reisman et al. 2004, pp. 1504–1512).

[293] Ebrahim was abducted from Swaziland to South Africa [Supreme Court of Appeal, South Africa, *State v Ebrahim Ismail Ebrahim*, 26 February 1991, 279/89, cited in Nsereko 2009, p. 991, n. 65].

trial before it should be considered null and void on the basis of an unfair hearing resulting from blatant *a priori* political bias. This is not to say that such allegations have never been made under the vertical system of enforcement. In fact, by way of example, in the case *'Prosecutor v Joseph Kanyabashi',* the defence unsuccessfully argued that the 'Tribunal is not, and cannot be impartial and independent'.[294] The extent to which such allegations, claims and pretensions can lead to a ground for refusal of surrender is not crystal clear. It sets the scene to pose a crucial question: can 'abuse of process' serve as a ground for refusal of surrender? The reply to this should probably be in the affirmative particularly if the continued pre-trial detention of the individual violates the domestic law of the custodial State which is being asked to surrender the individual. Such specific requirements of national law can include the prohibition of arbitrary detention especially when this follows the consummation of acts of torture in another State.

As a general rule, 'where the breaches of the rights of the accused are such as to make it impossible for him or her to make his or her defence within the framework of his rights, no fair trial can take place and the proceedings can be stayed'.[295] There need not have been *mala fides* by the prosecution.[296] What is required is that this led to a violation of the rights of the accused in bringing him to justice.[297] Yet, at the ICC, this does not necessarily presuppose the halting or discontinuance of the proceedings since 'the ICC draws a distinction between permanent and non-permanent – "conditional" – stays of proceedings, depending on whether the damage caused to the fairness of the proceedings is reparable'[298] or otherwise. Mention must, at this stage, be made of Article 59 of the ICC Statute which involves the direct role of the competent judicial authority of the custodial State, a role vividly portrayed by the ICC's Pre-Trial Chamber in the *Lubanga Dyilo* case. The ICC Appeals Chamber, also seemingly agreed that 'it would look into irregularities when these are committed in the context of 'concerted action' between the ICC and third parties, even before the sending of the ICC request for arrest and surrender (hence before the constructive custody)'. This term, 'concerted action', is very general and could encompass any involvement of the ICC in irregularities. It was also this term which arguably confirmed the assumption made in the context of the *Lubanga Dyilo* Pre-Trial Chamber's views on Article 59 of the ICC Statute to the effect that the judges of the Pre-Trial Chamber were probably of the opinion that they would have to examine irregularities in the context of a national arrest/

[294] ICTR Trial Chamber II, *Prosecutor v Joseph Kanyabashi, Decision on the Defence Motion on Jurisdiction*, 18 June 1997, Case No. ICTR-96-15-T, para B7 (v).

[295] Tochilovsky 2014, p. 1326.

[296] Ibid.

[297] ICC Trial Chamber I, *Situation in the DRC*, Prosecutor v Thomas Lubanga Dyilo, Decision on the Consequences of Non-Disclosure of Exculpatory Materials Covered by Article 54(3)(E) Agreements and the Application to Stay the Prosecution of the Accused, Together with Certain Other Issues Raised at the Status Conference on 10 June 2008, 13 June 2008, Case No. ICC-01/04-01/06, para 90, cited in Tochilovsky 2014, p. 1326, n. 30.

[298] Pitcher 2018, p. 305.

detention prior to the official ICC arrest in so far as these irregularities were somehow related to the ICC proceedings. However even though the Appeals Chamber thus accepted the concerted action term, a term which could encompass a national arrest/detention if that arrest/detention were somehow related to the ICC proceedings, the Appeals Chamber also presented an additional requirement, namely that only violations of the suspect's rights which are related to the 'process of bringing the appellant to justice for the crimes that form the subject-matter of the proceedings before the Court (…) may provide ground for halting the process'.[299] The above scenario (the concerted action paradigm) partially resonates the following plural-States hypothetical setting which is hereby juxtaposed by myself. State X requests Mr. A from neighbouring State Y which, enjoying custodial jurisdiction of Mr. A [and before the request for extradition from State Y, and with the intent to prosecute him on the basis of a ground of jurisdiction], tortures Mr. A in order to extract a confession. State Y subsequently extradites Mr. A to State X. When in the custody of State X, an ICC State Party, the ICC issues an international arrest warrant against Mr. A, State X would be entitled to assess whether to surrender or not to the ICC on the basis of the 'abuse of process' doctrine. Hence the ground of refusal of 'abuse of process' would fall within the parameters of this work because its consideration precedes the decision to surrender or otherwise. To put this into practice, the custodial State might determine that the initial arrest and detention of the suspect in the first State (this being either the State which has transferred the suspect to the custodial State for investigation and prosecution, or the State where the fugitive was found after absconding from the State which arrested and detained the suspect first) seriously infringed the human rights of the suspect. A similar scenario might arise whereby the custodial State is the same State which arrested and detained the suspect in the first place. However, if a change in the political administration occurred after the arrest and during the continued detention of the suspect, such custodial State, at some stage, may deem that arrest questionable, shedding a bad light on the arrest committed by the previous political administration.[300] These scenarios beg the questions: will the prior unlawful detention and/or torture be taken into account during the ICC proceedings? Would that be a possible and legitimate reason for the custodial State to refuse surrender?

It seems that non-cooperation may hardly be justified even when another State [this being the State extraneous to and not responsible for the infringement of human rights] is concerned, unless the requested State deems the violation the suspect was made to endure as so grave as to breach a *jus cogens* norm and constitute a sufficient punishment in itself. If, however, another State (not the defaulting State) is not involved within this legal scenario, the ICC would always be

[299] ICC Appeals Chamber, *Situation in the DRC*, Prosecutor v Thomas Lubanga Dyilo, Judgment on the Appeal of Mr. Thomas Lubanga Dyilo Against the Decision on the Defence Challenge to the Jurisdiction *of the Court Pursuant to Article 19(2) of the Statute of 3 October 2006*, 14 December 2006, Case No. ICC-01/04-01/06(OA4), para 44, cited in Paulussen 2010, p. 970.

[300] In Latin America the contrary has occurred when changes of government brought a change of policy and prosecutions for past official conduct (Akande and Shah 2011, p. 816).

the final arbiter as to whether, post-surrender, the individual, now in ICC custody, should be granted an effective remedy for the violation s/he was constrained to endure. In this context, it should not be forgotten that the criminal process, after all, is the ICC's, and it is hence the ICC which is entrusted to 'decide whether it would be "repugnant" or "odious" to the administration of justice to allow the case to continue',[301] or otherwise. Ultimately, besides the obvious risk posed unto the individual, the ICC's credibility and fairness (not that of the State which arrested and surrendered the individual) is at stake. Such conclusions may also be inferred when one considers Article 85(1) of the ICC Statute itself[302] which stipulates that victims of unlawful arrest or detention have an enforceable right to compensation. It does not specify where and at what stage such unlawful arrest or detention occurred. Whereas a request for surrender presupposes an arrest elsewhere (not in Scheveningen), detention is a continuous state of affairs which commences upon the deprivation of liberty/confinement (which follows the arrest itself) and protracts throughout the entire process until either bail or discharge/acquittal. Hence, although detention may be undertaken at the hands of the ICC itself, the same may not be said in so far as arrest is concerned. It is therefore sound to conclude that Article 85(1), which is the legal provision preceding the commencement of Part 9 of the ICC Statute, covers abuses which occurred in the requested State and beyond the ICC's control. Admittedly, the main problem with such an interpretation is the placing of Article 85 within Part VIII which deals with 'appeal and revision'. The object and purpose of the entire legal provision (which comprises three paragraphs) also seem to infer that the provision was intended to remedy injustices committed by the ICC itself. This being so, Article 85 seems to further restrict the ICC's remedial powers because the right to compensation does not include the right to acquit. Thus, even if Article 85(1) is deemed to cover acts/measures of requested States, there is a limit as to how the ICC can remedy such abuses.

Complications would arise when, directly as a result of the human rights violations endured by the individual, such individual was acquitted by a domestic court. Where it is not so evident, from the judgment of the domestic court, that the acquittal occurred on the basis of a finding of lack of guilt after having dealt with the merits of the case, an issue relating to *ne bis in idem* is likely to surface, in which case the admissibility test would come into play. Where, however, the individual was released in a *Barayagwiza*-like scenario, commonly described as a controversial episode,[303] *id est* exclusively owing to the human rights violation and not after having dealt with the merits of the case, or better not after having assessed guilt or innocence, the requested State would generally not be entitled to refuse surrender. In my view, where a breach of the fair trial rights of the individual was

[301] Tochilovsky 2014, p. 1327.

[302] See also Zappalà 2002, p. 1577.

[303] Schabas 2006, p. 379.

involved (such as in the *Barayagwiza* case),[304] refusal of surrender is not a State option. The State, however, may enjoy some rights to refuse where the violation at stake breaches a *jus cogens* norm, such as where the individual was tortured in a third State to extract a confession and where such confession (generally in the form of a written and signed statement) has already been sent to the ICC's Prosecutor and will be submitted/produced as documentary evidence throughout the proceedings before the ICC. The ground for refusal would not be the prospect of an unfair trial before the ICC, where the OTP would rely on an involuntary confession (since fair trial rights are not protected by a *jus cogens* norm), but would be the egregious breach of the individual's right to freedom from torture which, in and of itself, indemnifies the victim of torture to an extent that he should no longer be subjected to any action or measure which can be deemed to be committed in furtherance of such torture, the torture being an unlawful and disproportionate punishment in and of itself. In this context, the so-called doctrine of the forbidden fruit comes to mind. ICTY determined that, 'where an accused is very seriously mistreated, maybe even subject to inhuman, cruel or degrading treatment, or torture, before being handed over to the Tribunal',[305] the case may warrant a dismissal, although the remedy would usually be disproportionate. If therefore egregious violations of the accused's rights are detrimental to the Court's integrity, such Court may decline to exercise jurisdiction[306] because 'it would be inappropriate for a court of law to try the victims of these abuses. This is particularly so when the violation is attributable (imputable) to a court of law or to any of its organs.[307] An egregious violation under the ICC system may be said to be equivalent to a flagrant denial of justice[308] under the ECvHR system.[309] Apart from such exceptional cases, however, the

[304] *Barayagwiza* was released before trial when the Appeals Chamber dismissed the charges against him by means of its decision [ICTR Appeals Chamber, *Jean Bosco Barayagwiza v Prosecutor, Prosecutor's Request for Review or Reconsideration*, 31 March 2000, Case No. ICTR-97-19-AR72]. The Appeals Chamber declared that the length of time (over three years) which *Barayagwiza* spent in detention in Cameroon at the behest of the ICTR without being indicted violated the 90-day rule as set forth by Rule 40*bis* and established human rights jurisprudence. The Appeals Chamber reached the conclusion that 'to proceed with the trial of the Appellant would amount to an act of injustice [...] forcing him to undergo a lengthy and costly trial, only to have him raise, once again the very issues currently pending before this Chamber. Moreover, in the event the Appellant was to be acquitted after trial we can foresee no effective remedy for the violation of his rights. Therefore, on the basis of these findings, the Appeals Chamber will decline to exercise jurisdiction over the Appellant, on the basis of the abuse of process doctrine...' [para 72 of the above mentioned judgment, cited in http://www.icty.org/x/file/Legal%20Library/jud_supplement/supp9-e/barayagwiza.htm. Accessed 22 March 2011].

[305] ICTY Trial Chamber II, *Prosecutor v Dragan Nikolić, Decision on the Defence Motion Challenging the Exercise of Jurisdiction by the Tribunal*, 9 October 2002, Case No. IT-94-2, para 114].

[306] ICTR Appeals Chamber, *Jean Bosco Barayagwiza v Prosecutor, Decision*, 3 November 1999, Case No. ICTR-97-19-AR72, para 74.

[307] Smeulers 2007, p. 110.

[308] See Sect. 16.7.1.

[309] This is suggested by Göran Sluiter (Sluiter 2016).

remedy of setting aside jurisdiction will, in the Appeals Chamber's view, usually be disproportionate'.[310] The conclusion which must be drawn is that violations throughout the pre-trial stage can hardly serve as a pretext for non-cooperation by the requested State. This remains a tricky area of the law. Blatant breaches of freedom from torture consummated in a third State may have been deliberately perpetrated to extract confessions with an eye to prosecuting at that time. They may also have been consummated since the suspect allegedly committed crimes against nationals of such other third State. However, such torture may have been perpetrated to shield the accused from prosecution if and when the State enjoying custodial jurisdiction is made aware (via diplomatic channels) that an extradition request is imminent. In such case the State enjoying custodial jurisdiction may deliberately torture the accused to allow him to benefit from 'abuse of process' in the State which is about to request his extradition especially if such requesting State has rigid laws catering for drastic remedies upon the finding of human rights breaches.

This said, even where breaches of *jus cogens* norms are concerned, the ground for refusal of the State would only be partial. This is because the requested State enjoying custodial jurisdiction over the individual may decide to surrender only upon the fulfilment of a resolutive condition, this being the undertaking of an obligation by the OTP not to make use of and not to submit/produce the individual's written statement (as documentary evidence), since the consent thereto was vitiated, having been precipitated by threats/torture, intimidation, promises or suggestions.[311] The confession is hence involuntary. This reveals the importance of a consultation process which can be undertaken between the ICC and the requested State in terms of the ICC Statute. Article 97 of the ICC Statute is an illustrative (rather than exhaustive) legal provision, and stipulates that where the requested State identifies problems which may impede or prevent the execution of the ICC's request for surrender, such State is to consult with the ICC to resolve the matter. It is the State which identifies the hurdles/obstacles. No time limit (which commences to run from the date of the ICC request for surrender) is fixed for the identification of such hurdles/obstacles. The term 'without delay', which requires less expeditious action than the term 'promptly',[312] refers to the undertaking of the consultation process, not to the identification of the hurdle/obstacle. The legal provision

---

[310] ICTY Appeals Chamber, *Prosecutor v Dragan Nikolić, Decision on Interlocutory Appeal Concerning Legality of Arrest*, 5 June 2003, Case No. IT-94-2-AR73, para 30.

[311] In the *Duch* case before the ECCC, it was held that the ICC Appeals Chamber in *Lubanga Dyilo* would also refuse jurisdiction, under the abuse of process doctrine, in the case of grave violations of the suspect's rights (thereby focusing on the more 'physical' serious mistreatment and torture) as such, hence irrespective of the entity responsible (Paulussen 2010, p. 968).

[312] This term is used in Articles 36(2)(a), 59(2), 67(1)(a) and 93(3), 93(6), 103(1)(c), 121(1), 122 (1) of the ICC Statute, above n. 25. Article 93(3) is particularly important since this legal provision uses such a term in a very similar context to the one prevailing within Article 97, *id est* where consultations to resolve a matter are involved. The substitution of the word 'promptly' with the words 'without delay' within Article 97, as opposed to Article 93(3) [both of which are stipulated within Part 9 of the ICC Statute], connotes that the drafters of the ICC Statute, above n. 25, did not

demands that the State consults with the ICC rather than imposing a fixed requirement for the State to adhere to the ICC's orders in so far as surmounting the hurdles/obstacles and solving the problems is concerned. Whereas abuse of process would require the breach of a *jus cogens* norm where the rights of the accused are egregiously violated, it would not need to reach such threshold where cogent and incontrovertible evidence exists pointing towards a sham trial and hence a miscarriage of justice, the outcome of which could anyway jeopardize the rights and interests of the accused and of the victims whose pleas for justice would remain unanswered. In the former case the State which enjoys custodial jurisdiction of the accused could legitimately expect to be the ultimate arbiter,[313] whereas in the latter case, the ICC would, besides determining (in)admissibility, decide whether circumstances to warrant a transfer of proceedings subsist or otherwise. Nevertheless, the State's discretion in the former situation is not cast in stone, but can be seriously questioned. The Appeals Chamber in *Lubanga Dyilo* had ample opportunity to crystallize such discretionary powers, but failed to address the extent to which the judicial authority of the custodial State, in terms of Article 59 of the ICC Statute, can look into irregularities prior to the official arrest/detention.[314]Although he does not say so in so many words, Cedric Ryngaert, on the same lines, opines that 'abuse of process can, and should, only be successfully applied in case of torture or serious mistreatment of the suspect'.[315] The ICC's recourse to various interlocutory decrees certainly delays proceedings but also shows that problems must be solved, not placed under the carpet until they resurface. Rather than letting the damage be or letting the damage proliferate and spread, the ICC should deal with allegations of abuse of process immediately when it is faced with such allegations, not after a formal decision of its Pre-Trial Chamber or of its Appeals Chamber.

To conclude, abuse of process, broadly interpreted, should be construed to include the pre-emption of circumstances which stultify the proper administration of justice. Such circumstances should be grave enough possibly to warrant the transfer of proceedings from a domestic court [within the horizontal system of enforcement] to an international court [within the vertical system of enforcement]. In truth, within the process by means of which proceedings are duly transferred, abuse of process acts as a catalyst to the jurisdiction of an international court and/or tribunal rather than as a hurdle/obstacle thereto. By way of example, 'when in 1998 a military court in Belgrade started proceedings against those indicted in the *Vukovar* case, the Prosecutor argued that a request for the transfer of proceedings

want to impose strict time requirements on the requested State in the catch-all provision, *id est* in Article 97.

[313] Partial exception to this may arise from ordinary law, such as for example, Section 5(8) of the UK International Criminal Court Act of 2001 [UK ICC Act (2001) International Criminal Court Act, United Kingdom], whereby the ICC is ultimately the court to stipulate whether and what remedy should be provided in the case of abuse of process [HoL, *Stockdale v Hansard*, 15 June 1839, vol. 48 cc301/6, cited in Cryer and Bekou 2007, pp. 454–455, n. 83].

[314] Paulussen 2010, p. 974.

[315] Ryngaert 2008, p. 719.

should be made because such proceedings 'would merely be a sham in order to put off the international community, in order to reduce the pressure that is being placed upon them because of their failure to comply with their international obligations', and because 'five minutes after the pressure from the international community eases on the Federal Republic of Yugoslavia, these three accused persons w[ould] be released and...any other order made would not be genuine'.[316] Such requests for transfer of proceedings generally relate to human rights matters, namely due process guarantees.[317] Although, as a general rule and as shown here above, issues relating to abuse of process are the ICC's prerogative (which fact significantly limits the discretion of the requested State), the juridical intricacies unmasked within this sub-heading manifest that this is a sensitive/delicate field of law where a *lex ferenda* (a law to be proposed), which would hopefully whiten or blacken the many shades of grey, cries out loud. In all fairness, since the ICC's decision, ultimately, boils down to a matter of extent and degree, it may (befittingly) prefer to deal with the matter on a case-by-case basis. One hence awaits the ICC's guidance, after the confirmation of charges hearing to be held on 20 April 2019, now that an individual in its custody, *Alfred Yekatom*, is alleging torture, amongst other human rights violations, by the CAR authorities before he was transferred to the ICC.[318]

11.4 Diplomatic Privileges and Immunities

The sixth hurdle to the execution of the vertical system of enforcement is the exercise and applicability of diplomatic privileges and immunities. Such privileges and immunities may be waived by the State[319] and/or regional organizations[320]

---

[316] ICTY, *Prosecutor v Mrkšić et al.*, Transcript, 9 December 1998, Case No. IT-95-13/1, paras 22–23, cited in Carnero Rojo 2005, p. 857.

[317] ICTY, *Decision on the Prosecutor's Request for Deferral and Motion for Order to the Former Yugoslav Republic of Macedonia*, 4 October 2002, Case No. IT-02-55-MISC.6, paras 13 and 18; see also ICTR Trial Chamber designated under Rule 11bis, *Prosecutor v Fulgence Kayishema, Decision on the Request by Human Rights Watch for Leave to Appear as Amicus Curiae in the Proceedings for Referral of the Indictment Against Fulgence Kayishema to Rwanda: Rule 11bis and 74 of the Rules of Procedure and Evidence*, 8 November 2007, Case No. ICTR-2001-67-I, cited in Klip A, Sluiter G (2010) (eds) Annotated Leading Cases of International Criminal Tribunals: The International Criminal Tribunal for Rwanda 2006–2007, Vol. 25. Intersentia, Cambridge, pp. 281–285.

[318] Al Jazeera (2018) News: CAR. https://www.aljazeera.com/news/2018/11/car-war-crimes-suspect-yekatom-appears-icc-alleges-torture-181123111318110.html. Accessed 23 December 2018.

[319] Mutyaba 2012, p. 949.

[320] Article 18 of the Protocol on the Privileges and Immunities of the European Communities [Protocol on the Privileges and Immunities of the European Communities (1967) Official Journal, No. 167, 13 July 1967] caters for such waivers when these are compatible with the ultimate interests of the EU.

when these are the ultimate beneficiary thereof. The susceptibility of immunities to waivers is important not only since it would allow the undertaking of prosecutions, but also because it can infer that immunities do not have the character of *jus cogens* and that therefore they do not override the UN Charter's provisions.[321] They are not exceptionless norms. On the contrary, other *jus cogens* rights, such as freedom from torture, cannot be waived. One might be inclined to think that since the main rule connected thereto is stipulated at the beginning of the ICC Statute, in Article 27, this ground for refusal should have been considered first. In actual fact, this is being considered at this stage because Article 98 of the ICC Statute, which may be tantamount to a ground for refusal *per se*, might be deemed to neutralize Article 27 of the ICC Statute. Article 98(1) of the ICC Statute[322] becomes important when the exercise of jurisdiction by the ICC entails the prosecution of a Head of State of a non-State Party, at which point the question of personal immunity might validly arise.[323]

The immunity barrier makes its presence felt also horizontally, or rather, more so horizontally. This is because 'immunity from jurisdiction protects the equality of states in accordance with the maxim *par in parem non habet imperium*'.[324] In other words, 'immunity appears as a classical institution of relations between States'[325] within a horizontal, rather than a vertical/supranational, context. However, to the extent that it paves the way to understanding better the horizontal system of enforcement, since it has horizontal ramifications and since it was pleaded before the ICC, this obstacle merits consideration. This is also important because it is undisputed that, only once a person is brought before the ICC for the purpose of trial,[326] no immunities can be invoked.[327] Hence the question of immunity precedes

---

[321] Gillet 2012, p. 93.

[322] This deals with conflicting international obligations, outside of competing requests (Prost 2005, p. 76).

[323] ICC Pre-Trial Chamber II, *Situation in Darfur, Sudan, Prosecutor v Omar Hassan Ahmad Al Bashir, Decision on the Cooperation of the DRC Regarding Omar Al Bashir's Arrest and Surrender to the Court*, 9 April 2014, Case No. ICC-02/05-01/09, para 27.

[324] Voetelink 2013, p. 241.

[325] Prouveze 2011, p. 361.

[326] This requirement differentiates indictees from ICC staff and officials. The latter are protected by means of their status [see Article 48 of the ICC Statute, the Agreement on Privileges and Immunities of the ICC [Agreement on Privileges and Immunities of the ICC (2002) Agreement on the Privileges and Immunities of the International Criminal Court, ICC/ASP/1/3], and the Resolution of the ASP on Cooperation, adopted at the 8th Plenary Meeting, held on 21 November 2012, by consensus [ASP (2012) Resolution ICC-ASP/11/Res.5, Doc. ICC/ASP/11/20], paras 7–9. http://www.icc-cpi.int/iccdocs/asp_docs/Resolutions/ASP11/ICC-ASP-11-Res5-ENG.pdf. Accessed 22 July 2014. An important point must be raised in relation to the Agreement on Privileges and Immunities of the ICC. This offers a possibility to States not parties to the ICC Statute to become parties to such agreement irrespective of their ratification of the ICC Statute or otherwise. By virtue of this States are allowed to foster cooperation with the ICC without being subject to its jurisdiction (Nilsson 2004, p. 577).

[327] See Article 27 of the ICC Statute, above n. 25.

surrender to the ICC and can constitute a hurdle thereto. The same may not be said in relation to the horizontal system of enforcement, wherein immunities can generally be invoked *in limine litis,* that is, once a trial commences and way after the completion of the extradition process. The fact that the law on immunities is largely of a customary nature, coupled with the juridical uncertainties thereto (including the conflicting nature of Articles 27 and 98 of the ICC Statute), not to mention contrasting and inconsistent decisions of national and international courts, renders the role of legal literature more important in order to understand such ground for refusal.

Although the purpose of this heading is not to delve into the law on diplomatic privileges and immunities but merely to assess the extent to which such immunities can constitute a ground for refusal of the request for surrender, I need to make three crucial preliminary distinctions. (I) Firstly a distinction should be drawn between the two main types of immunities, something which both the ICC Statute and the *Yerodia dictum* have failed to do explicitly. Personal immunities, or immunities *rationae personae*, relate to the person holding a specific function and apply to certain high-level State officials (particularly Heads of State) only during their term in office.[328] Functional immunities, or immunities *rationae materiae*, attach to the official underlying act rather than the person possessing it, and can therefore avail former State officials too.[329] Consequently, 'given that the purpose of immunities is to facilitate the conduct of international relations, the community of States may decide to remove them in particular instances where they no longer serve this purpose and moreover endanger international peace and security'.[330] This means that the ICC might be faced with a situation whereby the ICC's Prosecutor may elect to exercise her discretion under Article 53 of the ICC Statute not to proceed in a case where immunity has been granted at the national level for the purposes of a transition to democratization, in which case such decision would have no direct ramifications on international cooperation *per se*.[331]

(II) Secondly, a distinction should be drawn between national and international criminal courts/tribunals, such distinction having been vividly undertaken within the *Taylor dictum*,[332] and endorsed by prominent jurists, such as Gerhard Werle.[333] Yitiha Simbeye confirms that 'it is anticipated that internationally constituted criminal courts have an advantage over their domestic counterparts, in not being hampered by the issue of immunities of State officials'.[334] In fact, the ICTY Trial

328 Cassese 2008, p. 304.

329 Akande 2004, p. 412.

330 Bantekas 2010, p. 133.

331 Drumbl 2008, pp. 236–237.

332 SCSL Appeals Chamber, *Prosecutor v Charles Ghankay Taylor, Decision on Immunity from Jurisdiction*, 31 May 2004, Case No. SCSL-2003-01-I, paras 52–53. The SCSL held that the principle of sovereign equality of States, which underlies Head of State immunity before national courts, is irrelevant in respect of international tribunals (Kreß 2009, p. 951).

333 Werle 2009, p. 61.

334 Simbeye 2004, p. 90.

Chamber upheld that no person, in whatever official capacity, enjoys immunity before an international tribunal when he or she is accused of core crimes.[335] This conclusion can be reached both on the basis of legal interpretation but also as a result of State practice[336] which 'clearly demonstrates that the drafters of the statutes of contemporary international criminal tribunals removed both functional and personal immunities therein'.[337] It is also supported by the ICC which recently held that 'it is not disputed that under international law a sitting Head of State enjoys personal immunities from criminal jurisdiction and inviolability before national courts of foreign States even when suspected of having committed one or more of the crimes that fall within the jurisdiction of the Court'.[338] Micaela Frulli, considering personal immunities, held that 'international criminal tribunals may indict and charge high state officials, such as Heads of state, suspected of crimes under their jurisdiction even if they are still in office'.[339]

I postulate that all this may be said to be caused by the following two factors:

i. the *nexus* between the commission of core crimes and the connivance of State power;[340] and
ii. the principle of *pacta sunt servanda* which, in these circumstances, obliges State Parties to perform their obligations which stem from the treaty they have signed and ratified.[341]

Consequently, if States are the architects of core crimes, be it directly or indirectly, it would be fallacious and absurd for States to create an ICC in order to defeat impunity whilst simultaneously conferring immunity to the very same persons who stand accused with the very same crimes which the ICC is meant to prevent, suppress and/or punish. The SCSL's categorisation of itself as an international criminal court has enabled it to conclude that, as a result of such categorisation, 'the paragraph in its Statute that denies immunity to officials is not in conflict with any peremptory norm of general international law and its provisions must be given effect by this Court.'[342] The final decision reached by the Special Court for Sierra Leone embossed that 'the official position of the applicant as an

---

335 ICTY Trial Chamber III, *Prosecutor v Slobodan Milošević, Decision on Preliminary Motions*, 8 November 2001, Case No. IT-02-54, paras 26–34.

336 'A number of States, including the United Kingdom, have interpreted such immunities as having been waived by States party to the Rome Statute' (Cryer 2002, p. 738).

337 Bantekas 2010, p. 133.

338 *Prosecutor v Omar Hassan Ahmad Al Bashir*, above n. 323, para 25.

339 Frulli 2009a, p. 368.

340 These characteristics have been dealt with in Chap. 5.

341 Similarly, since it derived from an agreement between all UN Member States and Sierra Leone, the Statute of the SCSL was binding also on Liberia, which 'could then be said to have indirectly waived any non-peremptory customary immunity right'. Admittedly, however, Claus Kreß sheds doubts on the *Taylor dictum* in so far as it unsuccessfully tried to combine the customary law argument and the indirect waiver argument (Kreß 2005, p. 204).

342 Nouwen 2005, p. 648.

incumbent Head of State at the time when the criminal proceedings were initiated against him is not a bar to his prosecution by the Court'.[343] The SCSL was not established by the UNSC under Chapter VII powers, but by means of an Agreement between Sierra Leone and an international organization, the UN.[344] This further internationalizes its nature, as a result of which the defendants' position was distinct from *Yerodia*'s who was prosecuted by a domestic court instead. Since the ICJ in *Yerodia*, as shall be seen in Part IV dealing with the horizontal system of enforcement, acknowledged that 'an incumbent or former Minister for Foreign Affairs may be subject to criminal proceedings before certain international criminal courts, where they have jurisdiction',[345] the SCSL could fall within the parameters of the classification of 'certain international criminal courts'. The impact of the distinction between a national and international court must be assessed in the light of the nature, *leitmotif* and *raison d'être* behind diplomatic privileges and immunities, particularly of functional immunity.[346] This is because international courts and tribunals have declared that 'immunities from foreign domestic jurisdiction are not the same as immunities from international jurisdiction.'[347] In fact this stems particularly from the SCSL's Taylor *dictum*.[348] This corollary is explained by Sarah Nouwen who correctly opines that, 'international criminal tribunals would derive their mandate from the international community and hence do not, unlike national courts would, violate the principle that sovereign states do not adjudicate on the conduct of another State.'[349] On the strength of this, Antonio Cassese remarked that a customary rule removing personal immunities of Heads of State for core crimes when jurisdiction over such crimes vests onto international courts had budded.[350]

---

[343] *Prosecutor v Charles Ghankay Taylor*, above n. 332, para 53, duly analysed in Heller 2013, pp. 835–855.

[344] As per Article 24(1) of the UNC itself, the UNSC acts on behalf of the members of the UN. Consequently, the Agreement between Sierra Leone and the UN is an agreement between Sierra Leone and all the members of the UN [*Prosecutor v Charles Ghankay Taylor*, above n. 332, para 38, n. 31].

[345] ICJ, *Arrest Warrant of 11 April 2000 (DRC v Belgium)*, 14 February 2002, ICJ Rep. 2002, p. 3, para 61. The mark it would have left on contemporary international law could have largely depended upon its confirmation or revocation when the judgment in the case Concerning Certain Criminal Proceedings in France (DRC v France), further to an application before the ICJ dated 9 December 2002, would be delivered [see the ICJ order {Order No. 129} of 16 November 2009, authorising the submission of written pleadings by not later than 17 May 2010]. Succinctly, in this case, the DRC claimed that the exercise of jurisdiction by French courts over some Congolese nationals, including the Head of State, for alleged torture, infringed international law. However, the case was dropped by the plaintiff by means of a note filed before the ICJ on the 5 November 2010 [see ICJ, *Case Concerning Certain Criminal Proceedings in France (DRC v France)*, Order of Removal of the Case from the List, 16 November 2010].

[346] van Alebeek 2008, pp. 103–157.

[347] Skander Galand 2014, p. 626.

[348] *Prosecutor v Charles Ghankay Taylor*, above n. 332.

[349] Nouwen 2005, p. 656.

[350] Cassese 2008, p. 311.

More than merely budding, Mettraux, Dugard and du Plessis now refer to a systematic exclusion of the possibility to raise immunities as a defence or as a jurisdictional bar to charges involving allegations of core crimes.[351] On the same lines, the ICC Pre-Trial Chamber had controversially[352] decided that 'customary international law creates an exception to Head of State immunity when international courts seek a Head of State's arrest for the commission of international crimes. There is no conflict between *Malawi*'s obligations towards the Court and its obligations under customary international law; therefore article 98(1) of the Statute does not apply.'[353] The ICC Pre-Trial Chamber, in fact, cited Antonio Cassese to the effect that the rationale for foreign State officials being entitled to raise personal immunity before national courts is that otherwise national authorities might use prosecutions to unduly impede or limit a foreign state's ability to engage in international action. Cassese emphasised that this danger does not arise with international courts and tribunals, which are 'totally independent of states and subject to strict rules of impartiality'[354] since they do not act and function at the behest of States. Paola Gaeta strongly suggests that persons are only entitled to immunities *rationae personae* before domestic courts of foreign (this being the State of which the person is not an official) States, where they are authorized to discharge official functions.[355] The above reveals that the exercise and application of diplomatic privileges and immunities within the horizontal system of enforcement (where national courts have a final say as to whether to extradite or otherwise) is rather different to that prevailing within the vertical system of enforcement (where international courts enjoy such prerogative). Dapo Akande, however, minimises the need to distinguish between national and international courts. He highlights that 'international courts', a term which is not defined by international law, are, after all, the making of States and hence not so independent therefrom. He emphasizes that the *Malawi* decision ignores Article 98 of the ICC Statute, rendering it redundant, this being 'contrary to a basic principle of treaty interpretation'.[356] Similarly Michael Ramsden and Isaac Yeung complained about a faulty interpretation of Article 98(1) of the ICC Statute.[357]

(III) A third distinction pervades this heading and various bits of Part III. In so far as the legal consequences vary, one must also distinguish between State Parties to the ICC Statute and non-State Parties (commonly referred to as 'third States'), a

[351] Mettraux et al. 2018, p. 591.

[352] Dapo Akande has vociferously criticised this decision (Akande 2011).

[353] ICC Pre-Trial Chamber I, *Prosecutor v Omar Hassan Ahmad Al Bashir, Decision Pursuant to Article 87(7) of the Rome Statute on the Failure by the Republic of Malawi to Comply with the Cooperation Requests Issued by the Court with Respect to the Arrest and Surrender of Omar Hassan Ahmad Al Bashir (Malawi* case), 12 December 2011, Case No. ICC-02/05-01/09, para 43.

[354] Cassese 2008, p. 312, cited in the *Malawi* case, above n. 353, para 34.

[355] Gaeta 2002, p. 991.

[356] Akande 2011.

[357] Ramsden and Yeung 2016, p. 709.

distinction also habitually made in the national legislation of ICC State Parties[358] which domestically incorporates the ICC Statute itself.[359]

I shall now submit some preliminary remarks by analysing the tension resulting from two seemingly conflicting legal provisions, Articles 27 and 98 of the ICC Statute. Article 27(2) of the ICC Statute, which seemingly applies to State Parties, establishes that immunities shall not bar the ICC from exercising its jurisdiction over a person. Article 98 of the ICC Statute, a controversial legal provision, may be said to preserve the immunities of non-State Parties[360] by allowing State Parties to give effect to immunity obligations they owe to non-State Parties.[361] It has led to a myriad of legal literature. Undoubtedly a certain amount of tension (and an uneasy relationship) prevails between, on the one hand Article 27, and on the other hand, Article 98 of the ICC Statute. This could be alleviated depending on whether Article 27 of the ICC Statute is deemed to reflect customary international law[362] or otherwise. The extent to which Article 27(2) of the ICC Statute is far-reaching (*id est* whether such an exception for lifting immunities applies to Heads of all States, including non-State Parties to the ICC Statute [third States], or whether it is only confined to those States which have adhered to the ICC Statute), was examined by the ICC Pre-Trial Chamber,[363] and shall be referred to later on. Suffice to say, at this stage, that Article 27(2) of the ICC Statute has horizontal effects[364] although some have argued otherwise in view of the placement of Article 27(2) which does not fall within the purview of Part 9 within the ICC Statute.[365] The tension mentioned here above derives from opposing and contested values.[366] Article 27 combats impunity and promotes equality within the realm of international criminal justice, hence, in the process upholding an international rule of law. Article 98 of the ICC Statute promotes State sovereignty and stable relations between States. Kimberly Prost acknowledges that 'with the benefit of hindsight, the language of Article 98 could have been more clearly articulated to reflect the narrow purposes envisaged at the time of its drafting'.[367] This might have reduced the difficulty involved in balancing 'the obligations owed to the ICC to arrest Heads of State,

---

358 The UK, Ireland, Malta and Samoa are cases in point (Akande 2009, p. 339, n. 23).

359 Akande 2011.

360 Akande 2012b, p. 10.

361 Akande 2009, p. 339.

362 'Customary international law abrogates immunity in the case of core crimes' (Day 2004, p. 510).

363 *Prosecutor v Omar Hassan Ahmad Al Bashir*, above n. 323, paras 26–34.

364 ICC Pre-Trial Chamber II, *Situation in Darfur, Sudan, in the Case of the Prosecutor v Omar Hassan Ahmad Al Bashir, Decision under Article 87(7) of the Rome Statute on the Non-Compliance by South Africa with the Request by the Court for the Arrest and Surrender of Omar Al Bashir (Decision on South Africa's non-compliance)*, 6 July 2017, Case No. ICC-02/05-01/09, para 94.

365 Akande and de Souza Dias 2018.

366 Tladi 2013, p. 203.

367 Prost 2018, p. 366.

with the customary international law immunities that are ordinarily accorded to such officials'.[368]

Yet, the ICC Pre-Trial Chamber has demonstrated that Article 98(1) of the ICC Statute actually serves to resolve conflicts between international obligations, rather than to augment tensions prevailing by seemingly inconsistent and/or conflicting legal provisions. This is so since Article 98(1) of the ICC Statute directs the ICC to secure the cooperation of the third State for the waiver or lifting the immunity of its Head of State, which course of action is aimed 'at preventing the requested State from acting inconsistently with its international obligations towards the non-State Party with respect to the immunities attached to the latter's Head of State'.[369] There is yet another interpretation by means of which the prevailing tension could subside. It can be circumvented if one chooses to interpret Article 27(2) of the ICC Statute in an exclusive manner and by highlighting that Article 27 does not distinguish between State Parties and non-State Parties. This line of thinking can find refuge in the fact that Article 27 is not technically addressed to States[370] and is supported by the ICC's current practice,[371] which conveys that Article 27 is clear and binding and that it substantiates the object and purpose of the ICC Statute to fight impunity.[372] As Dov Jacobs explains, undertaking this approach [*id est* just applying Article 27(2) of the ICC Statute] would mean that the ICC could exercise jurisdiction against nationals of non-State Parties irrespective of the way in which the case has been brought before the ICC.[373] With such interpretation, the triggering mechanism becomes immaterial.

Some influential views are worth a mention here. Obviously, which, if any, of these views will be conclusively adopted by the ICC is a shot in the dark. Dapo Akande suggests that only non-State Parties can benefit from Article 98 of the ICC Statute. For State Parties, Article 98 was rendered inapplicable by Article 27 of the ICC Statute. The pretext to his observations emanates from treaty law and treaty interpretation. He contends that due to *res inter alios acta*,[374] a treaty establishing an international criminal tribunal cannot remove immunities that international law grants to officials of States that are not party to that treaty. Consequently, although the ICC may exercise jurisdiction over nationals of non-State Parties, these would still be entitled to enjoy immunities.[375] Specifically in relation to the ICC,

---

[368] du Plessis and Tladi 2017.

[369] *Prosecutor v Omar Hassan Ahmad Al Bashir*, above n. 323, para 27.

[370] Jacobs 2015, p. 292.

[371] ICC, Pre-Trial Chamber I, *Situation in Darfur, Sudan, Prosecutor v Omar Al Bashir, Decision on the Prosecution's Application for a Warrant of Arrest Against Omar Hassan Ahmad Al Bashir*, 4 March 2009, Case No. ICC-02/05-01/09, cited in Jacobs 2015, p. 292.

[372] *Prosecutor v Omar Al Bashir,* above n. 371, paras 43–44, cited in Jacobs 2015, pp. 292–293.

[373] Jacobs 2015, p. 292.

[374] Article 34 of the VCLT (1969) Vienna Convention on the Law of Treaties.

[375] Akande 2004, pp. 420–433.

commentators[376] have posited that State Parties, by their own ratification of the ICC Statute, have already relinquished any immunities against ICC proceedings. Thus, no obligations under international law hinder the surrender of those subject to an international arrest warrant. Hence, the ICC State Parties can be deemed to have waived the immunity of their own officials in case they are prosecuted before the ICC,[377] 'by virtue of their having accepted Article 27, which waives immunity based on official capacity'.[378] In other words, the official capacity does not exempt a person from criminal liability, this being a 'core principle'.[379] This 'reflects the current view of international and internationalized criminal courts'.[380] Non-State Parties may waive such immunities by virtue of *ad hoc* agreements with the ICC itself, as per Article 87(5) of the ICC Statute. This is particularly relevant since States which would have just experienced a change in regime and either undertake auto-referrals (self-referrals) or subject themselves to the ICC's jurisdiction, are also very likely to waive such immunities. Now that self-referrals[381] have been considered legitimate, it would seem that, of its own nature, such auto-referral, anyway strips the Head of the State (with such State making the referral to investigate its nationals) of any immunity which such Head of State would be entitled to in the absence of such auto-referral. In any case one must not underestimate the legal weight of the *Pinochet dictum* which 'ruled that international crimes are exempt from traditional international immunities'.[382] Despite this and notwithstanding its praiseworthy outcome, one cannot fail to acknowledge that it was poorly reasoned.[383] Although this judgment was delivered in a horizontal context, it may be said to apply *a fortiori* when the ICC is involved. In a supplementary fashion, if immunities *rationae personae* no longer apply owing to a waiver, the same holds *a fortriori* true for immunities *rationae materiae*. Keeping *Pinochet* in mind, one must remember however that whereas *jus cogens* belongs to the substantive part of international criminal law, immunities, as shall be seen in Sect. 16.8, have more of a procedural character.[384] Micaela Frulli is categoric when stating that 'it is universally acknowledged, whatever theoretical perspective one may choose, that functional immunity cannot be invoked by a State official suspected of international

---

376 Cryer et al. 2011, p. 555.

377 Nouwen 2005, p. 656.

378 Dembowski 2003, p. 150.

379 *Prosecutor v Omar Al Bashir,* above n. 371, para 43.

380 Knoops 2008, p. 128.

381 For a comprehensive examination of the practice of self-referrals, see van der Wilt 2015, pp. 210–227, and El Zeidy 2008, pp. 228–235 and 274–283. For a critique of self-referrals and an opinion about the extent to which they signal a departure from the purposive rationale of the principle of complementarity which, in turn, could be detrimental to the credibility and impartiality of the ICC, see Hassanein 2017, pp. 107–134.

382 Swart and Sluiter 1999, p. 121.

383 See Sect. 11.4.2.

384 Jia 2012, p. 1315.

crimes, whether before a domestic or an international court'.[385] Her study is well researched, but her statement seems too sweeping and simplistic, although, in all fairness, it may be deduced from the Pinochet *dictum* of the House of Lords. Ademola Abass contends that, by referring to obligations under international law with respect to State or diplomatic immunity, the ICC Statute cannot be applied to State Parties and non-State Parties equally, and that the legal provision does not necessarily coincide with international law. 'Thus, a third State, that is, the State that has not ratified the Rome Statute and likely to be most affected, is encouraged to waive its rights under international law as a precondition for the application of Article 27 to its nationals'.[386] This might be so but does not apply to cases triggered by virtue of a UNSC Resolution which, in any case, prevails over such consensual arrangements. This is where the matter of diplomatic privileges and immunities becomes particularly relevant for the purposes of this work. It is where the matter has horizontal ramifications, that is, where it can have an influence on the horizontal system of enforcement. The proper inter-relationship between Articles 27 and 98(1) becomes critical when an ICC State Party has custodial jurisdiction over a national of a non-State Party (who would normally enjoy immunity) and the ICC requests the surrender thereof. This requires a combined consideration of Articles 27 and 98 (1) of the ICC Statute,[387] with the former having a deep impact on domestic law,[388] whereas the latter is a legal provision which 'principally concerns individuals or objects of a third State that are entitled to immunity under customary international law, as well as any immunities established by treaty'.[389] The impact on domestic law is perceptible in many States, including Italy, where fundamental principles emanating from Articles 2, 10 and 11 of the Constitution appear to permit an interpretation that would render immunities from prosecution no longer enforceable in a national court when they relate to core crimes.[390] Although these legal provisions of Italy's Constitution deal with immunity from prosecution, such immunity can affect the cooperation regime because the preclusion of the prospect of a prosecution is most likely to impede cooperation itself.

It is settled that 'Article 98(1) cannot however, be a possible ground for refusal of the arrest and surrender of a Head of State who has committed crimes within the Court's jurisdiction. When *Malawi* and *Chad* refused to cooperate with the Pre-Trial Chamber I in the arrest and surrender of *Al Bashir* based on Article 98(1),

385 Frulli 2009b.

386 Abass 2005, p. 281.

387 Frulli 2009a, p. 369.

388 Article 27 takes into account national rules on immunities of certain State officials. Considered in the light of other ICC Statute provisions, particularly the crucial Articles 17 and 88, it could make it incumbent upon the State Parties to change their national legislation on immunities belonging to some State officials in order to enable national courts to institute proceedings against those State officials and to enable domestic competent authorities to execute an order to arrest and surrender by the ICC (Gaeta 2002, p. 997).

389 Schabas 2010, p. 1041.

390 Lee 2005, p. 18.

the Chamber found that 'immunity of either former or sitting Heads of State cannot be invoked to oppose prosecution by an international court'. This principle is equally applicable to former or sitting heads of State that are not party to the Rome Statute whenever the Court may exercise jurisdiction'.[391] Carsten Stahn argues that the inapplicability of immunities might be justified in the light of the wording of the ICC Statute and the fact that the situation was referred to the ICC by the UNSC. He questioned, however, the reasoning and findings on customary international law.[392] Whereas the customary international law status of the inapplicability of immunities will be considered under Sect. 16.8, it seems to be settled (as stated earlier on) that the exception envisaged by Article 98 of the ICC Statute cannot be invoked when the case was triggered by a UNSC Resolution. In such circumstances, 'any immunity afforded to the accused by reason of a pre-existing treaty is inapplicable'.[393] Others have postulated that Article 98, rather than being a ground for refusal, constitutes a *sui generis* ICC obligation.[394]

The theory of implied waivers,[395] to be examined particularly under Sect. 11.4.2, has also been proposed to circumvent the negative effects that Article 98 of the ICC Statute may have on Article 27 of the ICC Statute which does not recognize any exception from prosecution or confer any immunity on public officials. Incidentally, and not surprisingly at all, Articles 27 and 98 of the ICC Statute (with the latter being classified as a miscellaneous provision) were drafted by different committees during the negotiation process.[396] Kimberly Prost upholds that 'neither the placement nor content of Article 98 suggests that it was intended as a substantive article or that it was designed to conflict with, amend or countermand the clear obligations on States parties flowing from the adoption of Article 27 on official capacity'.[397] Hugh King opines that when the suspect is from another State Party, immunities are inapplicable and the suspect must be surrendered to the ICC. The same may not be said if the suspect is a national of a non-State Party since, in this case, the applicability of Article 98(1) would be set in motion.[398] In fact, Article 98(1) of the ICC Statute may be said to have been designed to apply only to non-State Parties.[399] Hugh King does not believe that the way the ICC acquires jurisdiction should have a bearing on the applicability of Article 27 to non-State Parties since even a UNSC referral is still subject to the limits on its powers as per the ICC Statute. In line with the well-established principle of conferred powers, the UNSC cannot confer

---

[391] *Malawi* case, above n. 353, para 36, cited in Mutyaba 2012, n. 85 at p. 949.

[392] Stahn 2012, n. 47 at p. 331.

[393] Bantekas 2010, p. 134.

[394] Sluiter 2011.

[395] 'At the heart of this notion lies the issue of a hierarchy of norms' (Simbeye 2004, p. 136) which has been dealt with in Part II, and shall also referred to under Part IV.

[396] van Schaack and Slye 2010, p. 978.

[397] Prost 2011, p. 314.

[398] King 2006, p. 270.

[399] Cryer 2009a, p. 202.

additional powers on the ICC. Hence, if the ICC cannot apply Article 27 to non-State Parties since such parties have not consented to be bound thereby, the limit on the ICC's ability to exercise its jurisdiction over such non-State Party officials enjoying immunity remains constant, irrespective of a referral by means of a UNSC Resolution. This certainly does not hold ground in all the vertical systems of enforcement since the same may not be said about the *ad hoc* tribunals. In fact, international criminal tribunals can try certain State officials and disregard immunities. It is hence the constitutive basis/instrument of such international criminal tribunals (rather than whether they are called/designated as 'international tribunals' or 'international courts'), which makes the whole difference, this being the fact that the *ad hoc* tribunals were adopted by the UNSC under its Chapter VII powers and consequently:

i. bind all UN member States; and
ii. override States' other obligations by virtue of Article 103 of the UNC.

It could be plausible to argue that UN Member States have indirectly consented to the waiving of their immunities. On the other hand, the treaty-based ICC means that only State Parties have consented to the lifting of immunities. Non-State Parties have not waived their immunities before the ICC.[400] This state of affairs cannot be overruled unless a UNSC referral subsists. *Ergo*, the ICC would have to convince State Party Z to obtain the waiver of the immunity of the official who is a national of non-State Party Y in order to permit surrender. Without such waiver, requesting surrender would not be possible since it would be tantamount to imposing duties on State Party Y which are conflicting with international obligations, this running counter to Article 98(1) of the ICC Statute.[401] Since the ICC Statute does not and cannot oblige non-State Parties to waive the immunities of their officials, and since the ICC Statute does not oblige non-State Parties to consent to the surrender of their officials, (with the exception of a UNSC referral) the only way this could be effected is if and when the State in question, the non-State Party, had, on the basis of Article 87(5) and at an earlier date, entered into some form of agreement with the ICC to such effect.[402]

Charles Chernor Jalloh notes that the *Slobodan Milošević* and *Jean Kambanda* examples cannot be compared to the *Al Bashir* state of affairs, because in the former cases the 'relevant countries did not seem to object to the nullification of the immunity'.[403] In any case, any immunity *Omar Al Bashir* may claim or enjoy can only be exercised when he is on foreign soil. Hence, Sudan can be said to be obliged to arrest him and surrender him to the ICC. Pre-Trial Chamber judges also endorsed this by finding that 'the Security Council, by referring Sudan, "accepted" that investigations and prosecutions arising therefrom will be conducted under the

400 King 2006, pp. 277–280.
401 King 2006, p. 284.
402 Swart and Sluiter 1999, p. 121.
403 Jalloh 2009, p. 485.

statutory framework provided for in the Court's primary and secondary legal instruments'.[404] Having analysed the above jurisprudence, one must keep in mind that former heads of State have drastically different immunities than incumbents such as *Al-Bashir*. Sudan's refusal to waive *Al Bashir*'s immunity means that his legal position cannot be compared to those of others, such as *decuius Slobodan Milošević*. To this extent, Asad Kiyani rightly highlights that 'relying on past cases as precedents is therefore unhelpful to the ICC position'.[405] Mark Drumbl submits that the inapplicability of immunities before international court and/or tribunals has become customary international law. The deliberate insertion of legal provisions eliminating immunities within the vertical system of enforcement (Article 27 of the ICC Statute being a prime example thereof) together with the increasing number of ICC Statute's ratifications seem to have crystallized the inapplicability of immunities into a rule of customary international law,[406] with such customary international law being obviously applicable, in the absence of a persistent objector, both to State Parties and to non-State Parties equally. This assertion is more convincing in view of the diffused State practice which, implicitly or explicitly, renders immunities inapplicable when a request for arrest has been made by the ICC.[407]

To date, the ICC has very scarcely dealt with immunities.[408]Although one of its judgments related to the fact that the Trial Chamber had not erred when it determined that there was no decision not to prosecute within the meaning of Article 17 (1)(b) of the ICC Statute, the ICC took into account the Order of the 16th September 2004 of the Senior Investigating Judge concluding that prosecution of the vice-President *Jean-Pierre Bemba Gombo* was barred by diplomatic immunity and that *Bemba* was thus protected from prosecution for complicity in the crimes of premeditated murder, rape, theft *et al.*, committed by his fighters in the CAR.[409] In this case, the defence argued that the ICC Statute did not envisage that diplomatic immunity of an accused residing outside the territorial jurisdiction of the CAR were factors that could be taken into account when assessing the 'inability to prosecute criterion' for admissibility purposes.

[404] *Prosecutor v Omar Al Bashir*, above n. 371, para 45.

[405] Kiyani 2013, pp. 471–472.

[406] Drumbl 2008, p. 238.

[407] Domestic implementing legislation has been promulgated in Canada, New Zealand, UK, Switzerland, Malta, South Africa, Croatia, Trinidad and Tobago, Ireland, Samoa and Estonia. (Akande 2009, pp. 338–339, n. 19).

[408] See, *inter alia, Prosecutor v Omar Hassan Ahmad Al Bashir*, above n. 323; see also *Malawi* case, above n. 353; see also *Prosecutor v Omar Al Bashir*, above n. 371. For a thorough analysis of the ICC's approach to immunities, see Jacobs 2015, pp. 281–302.

[409] ICC Appeals Chamber, *Situation in the CAR, Prosecutor v Jean-Pierre Bemba Gombo, Corrigendum to Judgment on the appeal of Mr. Jean Pierre Bemba Gombo Against the Decision of Trial Chamber III of 24 June 2010 entitled 'Decision on the Admissibility and Abuse of Process Challenges'*, 19 October 2010, Case No. ICC-01/05-01/08 OA 3, paras 34 *et seq.*

11.4.1 Immunities Rationae Personae

Having made such important preliminary distinctions, duly substantiated by relevant jurisprudence, and having unveiled the tension between Articles 27 and 98 of the ICC Statute, for the purposes of the law on immunities, the moot juridical issue is also likely to involve a plural-State hypothetical scenario in a similar way to the one juxtaposed within the former ground for refusal (abuse of process) which was dealt with in Sect. 11.3.1. This is where horizontal ramifications are felt, and hence this is where the vertical system of enforcement can serve as a frame of reference to the horizontal system of enforcement. To this effect, I postulate a hypothetical setting wherein State X, an ICC State Party, is the requested State enjoying custodial jurisdiction over person Z who happens to be the Head of State Y (which is a non-State Party). State X is faced with an impending dilemma: either fulfil its obligations deriving from the ICC Statute by surrendering person Z, which decision could expose it to State liability in so far as it would have committed an internationally wrongful act to the detriment of State Y (besides breaching the inviolability of person Z), or else infringe its statutory obligations to surrender and respect the diplomatic immunities and privileges of person Z who, as incumbent Head of State, enjoys immunities *rationae personae*. In other words, should the requesting State (enjoying custodial jurisdiction over the person subject to an international arrest warrant), faced with such dilemma, surrender the individual to the ICC or should such State respect the inviolability of the Head of State? Now, if both States X and Y were to be ICC State Parties no issue arises since ICC State Parties have waived their right to invoke immunity by becoming an ICC State Party in the first place. States which have signed the ICC Statute [and hence accepted its Article 27(2)] have waived their immunities for the purposes of Article 98(1) of the ICC Statute with respect to proceedings conducted by the ICC.[410]

The matter is convoluted, as per the hypothetical setting postulated here above, when a non-State Party is involved because non-State Parties did not accept Article 27(2) of the ICC Statute. In truth, there can be no hard and fast rule which answers the question posed above. The reply thereto can largely depend upon a shifting of goalposts. In such circumstances, the trigger mechanism can change matters significantly, even in so far as personal immunities are concerned. The UNSC Resolution 1593 can be deemed to have implicitly stripped *Al-Bashir* of any and all immunities he might have been entitled to in the absence of such a Resolution. This position was endorsed by the ICC when it determined that South Africa could not 'invoke any other decision, including that of the AU, providing for any obligation to the contrary'.[411] Sudan's UN membership may infer that it has already waived

---

[410] *Malawi* case, above n. 353, para 18.

[411] ICC Pre-Trial Chamber II, *Situation in Darfur, Sudan, Prosecutor v Omar Hassan Ahmad Al Bashir, Decision following the Prosecutor's request for an order further clarifying that the Republic of South Africa is under the obligation to immediately arrest and surrender Omar Al Bashir*, 13 June 2015, Case No. ICC-02/05-01/09, para 9.

personal immunities for circumstances involving the UNSC acting under UNC Chapter VII powers due to the UNSC's broad powers in such circumstances, just as ICC State Parties have waived their right to invoke immunity by becoming an ICC State Party in the first place. The UNSC referral is a resolution taken in terms and in pursuance of Article 13(b) of the ICC Statute, the twenty-seventh article of which applies in cases of a UNSC referral which was undertaken in the light/context of the ICC Statute. Hence, 'based on a United Nations members' waiver, it should be interpreted as removing personal immunities towards other States, otherwise its effect would be nullified by Article 98(1) of the ICC Statute'.[412] The current position of the ICC 'appears to accept that President *Al Bashir* would enjoy head of State immunity, were it not, so it believes, for the fact that it had been waived by the Security Council'.[413] William Schabas was therefore correct to assume that the ICC Pre-Trial Chamber determined,[414] at least implicitly, that by referring the situation of Darfur to the ICC, the UNSC 'intended to lift any immunity to which Sudan might be entitled'.[415] In other words, when a case is referred to the ICC by means of a UNSC Resolution, the custodial State enjoying the jurisdiction of the suspect may be said to be duty bound to surrender a Head of State of a non-State party for the following reasons. This is so even when such State claims to have international obligations emanating from an AU resolution which conflict with its international obligations arising from the UNSC referral. The ICC Pre-Trial Chamber has unequivocally found that the UNSC has implicitly lifted the immunities of *Omar Al Bashir* by virtue of resolution 1593(2005), as a consequence of which the DRC 'cannot invoke any other decision, including that of the African Union, providing for any obligation to the contrary'.[416] This is because immunities attached to *Omar Al Bashir* are a procedural bar from prosecution before the ICC and because the cooperation envisaged within the UNSC Resolution 'was meant to eliminate any impediment to the proceedings before the Court, including the lifting of immunities. Any other interpretation would render the Security Council decision requiring that Sudan "cooperate fully" and "provide any necessary assistance to the Court" senseless'.[417] The ICC Pre-Trial Chamber clarified that, besides a conflict between the AU and the ICC, the conflict subsisted between the AU's decision to retain the immunity of *Omar Al Bashir* and the UNSC Resolution which removed such immunity for the purpose of the proceedings before the ICC.[418] The ICC Pre-Trial

412 Papillon 2010, p. 288.

413 Supreme Court of Appeal, South Africa, *The Minister of Justice and Constitutional Development v The Southern African Litigation Centre*, 15 March 2016, 867/15 [2016] ZASCA 17, para 82.

414 *Prosecutor v Omar Hassan Ahmad Al Bashir*, above n. 371.

415 Schabas 2010, p. 1042.

416 *Prosecutor v Omar Hassan Ahmad Al Bashir*, above n. 323, para 31.

417 *Prosecutor v Omar Hassan Ahmad Al Bashir*, above n. 323, para 29.

418 *Prosecutor v Omar Hassan Ahmad Al Bashir*, above n. 323, para 30.

Chamber correctly resolved such conflict by resorting to Articles 25 and 103 of the UNC.[419]

In the first place, in the absence of any immunity enjoyed by Sudan, other (third) States are under no obligation to respect inexistent immunities. Furthermore, besides its obligation to uphold UNSC Resolutions in terms of Article 103 of the UNC, the resolution in itself may be worded in such a manner as to negate, *ab initio*, the immunity *rationae personae* of the incumbent Head of State. One must here remark that in the field of international law and international relations, the recognition of a particular status by other States and other international organizations is of the essence. Just as considerations relating to 'State recognition' count in so far as States may be considered as fully-fledged States in terms of the Montevideo Convention, these considerations count for the privileges and immunities of Heads of States. By way of example, the actions undertaken by the UN in its Resolution 1970, which actions include an arms embargo, a travel ban and the freezing of assets belonging to various members of the then Libyan regime, including the then *de facto* Head of State *Muammar Gheddafi*, are clearly intended to divest such Head of State of any immunity *rationae personae*. The custodial State enjoying jurisdiction may be said not to be breaching the inviolability of the Head of State Y since State Y, a UN member State, is anyway bound by Article 103 of the UNC. In this way, though ICC law, alone and unaided, might not trump diplomatic privileges and immunities, UN law does override such immunities which may be said to evaporate once the UNSC resolution is passed. This is more unquestionably so when the wording of such resolution is mandatory and intended to trump such privileges and immunities. This was not the case with UNSC Resolution 1593 which did not explicitly impose a legal obligation on non-State Parties (besides Sudan itself) to cooperate with the ICC, but merely urged them to do so.[420] The term 'urge' connotes a mere recommendation or exhortation to take certain action.[421] Its nature is discretionary, not mandatory. The detrimental effects of the use of the term 'urge' do not lie in the use of the term itself. They lie in the lack of an obligation, and hence a consequential absence of any conflict of obligations, as envisaged by Article 103 of the UNC.[422] Matthew Gillet notes that in UNSC Resolution 1593 no exception was made for Head of State immunity or the application of Article 98(1) of the ICC Statute, upholding that the omission was deliberate because Resolution 1593 explicitly referred to the separate obligations emanating from Article 98(2) of the ICC Statute.[423] Such a Resolution (when it

419 *Prosecutor v Omar Hassan Ahmad Al Bashir*, above n. 323, paras 30–31.

420 See para 2 of UNSC Resolution 1593 {UNSC (2005) Resolution 1593 (2005) UN Doc. S/RES/1593}. For an analysis relating to the extent to which UNSC Resolutions must be explicit, see de Souza Dias 2018.

421 Akande 2009, p. 344.

422 Ibid.

423 Gillet 2012, p. 92.

makes use of mandatory wording)[424] hence eradicates the distinction between a State Party and a non-State Party because the net effect of such resolution is that non-State Parties are to be regarded as in the analogous position to a State Party. For all intents and purposes, they are to be treated equally as State Parties since, upon the subsistence of a UNSC referral, the ICC Statute no longer operates as a treaty.[425] Hence, Article 34 of the VCLT ceases to stand in the way. The resolution which is passed in the light and context of Article 13(b) of the ICC Statute,[426] this legal provision being its governing framework,[427] binds the non-State Party with Article 27 of the ICC Statute just as though the non-State Party had decided to sign and ratify the ICC Statute. Since 'the jurisdiction and functioning of the Court must take place in accordance with the Statute, a decision to confer jurisdiction is a decision to confer it in accordance with the Statute. Thus, all States (including non-Parties) are bound to accept that the Court can act in accordance with its Statute. In this sense, at least, a non-Party to the Statute is bound by the Statute in the case of a referral – in the sense that it is bound to accept the jurisdiction of the Court and legality of the Court's operation in accordance with its Statute'.[428] It is only at this point that the third distinction postulated within Sect. 11.4 becomes immaterial. This line of thought can still hold ground, though it might be less compelling, when the wording of the UNSC Resolution is discretionary. Whether a binding decision is made under Article 25 of the UNC is to be determined by looking not just at the wording of the resolution but at the totality of the circumstances surrounding it,[429] and in a cumulative manner.

In the case of such trigger mechanism, for the reasons elucidated here above, the same conclusion may be reached irrespective of whether the custodial State has signed a bilateral immunity agreement because such agreement cannot eliminate or limit the supreme nature of the UNC. Article 103 of the UNC stipulates, in no uncertain terms that, 'in the event of a conflict between the obligations of members of the United Nations under the present Charter and their obligations under any other international agreement, their obligations under the present Charter shall prevail'. If State X signed a bilateral immunity agreement, it would anyway have to surrender the head of State Y when the ICC's request for surrender is triggered by a UNSC resolution. In this field of law, the effect on such other States constitutes the horizontal ramifications thereof. The same conclusion cannot be reached when the trigger mechanism is the exercise of the Prosecutor's *proprio motu* powers or else

---

[424] A contrary view, equating recommendations to authorizations to take specific action under Chapter VII of the UNC, has been adopted by the English HoL in HoL, *Regina (on the application of Al-Jedda) (FC) (Appellant) v Secretary of State for Defence (Respondent)*, 12 December 2007, 2007 UKHL 58, paras 30–34, cited in Akande 2009, pp. 344–345, n. 38.

[425] Akande 2009, abstract, p. 333.

[426] See, for example, paras 4–8, entitled 'ICC Referral', of UNSC Resolution 1970 {UNSC (2011) Resolution 1970 (2011), UN Doc. S/RES/1970}.

[427] Akande 2009, p. 340.

[428] Akande 2009, p. 341.

[429] Akande 2009, p. 347.

when it is a State referral, irrespective of the State (this could be any third State, not State X and/or State Y) which referred the case to the ICC. In such case, the obligations of State X vis-à-vis State Y do not evaporate but remain intact. This is more so when a bilateral immunity agreement subsists, in which case the request for surrender is nullified *ab initio* in terms of Article 98(2) of the ICC Statute and the ICC, in the words of this legal provision, 'may not proceed with a request for surrender'. There are two arguments by means of which one may rebut the above contention.

The first argument largely depends on an underlying assumption which has been introduced within the second Part of this work when the features and characteristics of core crimes were analysed. In Chap. 5, I submitted that by committing core crimes States lose their own legitimacy which is the pretext to their sovereignty. This legitimacy is forfeited *ipso facto* because of a blatant conflict of interest. A State, the essence of political authority, has a vested interest in ensuring that its organs of government remain intact. It cannot be perpetrator, prosecutor, judge and jury of its own cause, whereupon the State's officials themselves are also accused. In a nutshell, owing to this palpable conflict of interest States auto-delegitimize themselves, opening the floodgates for external prosecutions. It is, what the author calls, this self-delegitimization process that triggers universal jurisdiction, and it is this same process which can erode immunities, both *rationae personae* but especially *rationae materiae*. In other words, since the commission of core crimes creates a process of self-delegitimization of the State, its Head of State no longer remains such Head of State (the State now having been delegitimized) and hence may no longer benefit from immunities *rationae personae*. This argument, admittedly a bit stretched, is fraught with difficulties since it might be deemed to infringe the presumption of innocence and it is also dependent on a pretext, the link between the core crime itself and the State, a pretext which is not always so evident especially when non-State actors are involved as perpetrators of such core crimes. The difficulties which stand in the way of such argument can however be eclipsed if the ICC's Pre-Trial Chamber paves the way for the issuance of an international arrest warrant in terms of Article 15(4) of the ICC Statute, in which case it would have already established a reasonable basis to proceed against an identifiable person (the incumbent Head of State). Such problematic features can also be overshadowed if one accepts the view, posited, *inter alia*, by Alexander Orakhelashvili, that *jus cogens* anyway overrides and abrogates immunities.[430] In this context, I have already shown, in Part II, that core crimes are prohibited by a *jus cogens* norm. Orakhelashvili's theory can hence fit like a glove in the context of my book.

The second argument relies upon an explicit stipulation within a treaty and is dependent upon the express prohibition and penalization of a particular crime by that same treaty (the respective suppression convention). The Genocide Convention can provide a classical example thereof.[431] Its Article IV provides that even Heads

[430] Orakhelashvili 2011, pp. 849–855.

[431] Akande 2009, p. 351.

of State and public officials are to be punished. The Genocide Convention hence imposes a clear obligation on its Member States (which are not necessarily ICC State Parties) to arrest those charged with genocide although they may be serving heads of State who enjoy personal immunities. The imposition can, arguably, have a duplicate juridical effect. Besides being conventionally proscribed, it may be said to have crystallized into a rule of customary international law, as a result of which a State enjoying custodial jurisdiction is constrained to arrest and surrender an individual who has been indicted with genocide. For some African States, tension also subsists between the requirement to adhere to the ICC Statute and simultaneously to adhere to AU resolutions.[432] In fact, the AU itself concluded that 'although the Rome Statute specifies that heads of State do not have immunity, it does not specify whether the provision only applies to member States. It is confusing because the Rome Statute includes that there is both no immunity for Heads of State and that there can be diplomatic immunity under Article 98(1). Additionally, Article 98(2) provides that States do not have to comply with the ICC when they have prior agreements. Because Chad and Kenya are members of the AU, they have an agreement with the AU. Chad and Kenya could attempt to continue to argue that because the AU's position conflicts with the ICC, they do not have to follow the ICC's requests. The Rome Statute is vague in regard to immunity and leaves its member States with little certainty and a lot of flexibility'.[433] Yet, the legal weight of such resolutions, as shown here above, is questionable.

In support of *Al Bashir*'s assertion for immunities, Asad Kiyani examines the extent to which Article 27(2) of the ICC Statute could be rendered inoperative. He states, opposing Dapo Akande's views, that there are only two circumstances which could render this important legal provision as inapplicable, these being the following two circumstances, both of which *Al-Bashir* could be said to benefit from:

I. a non-State party has not voluntarily accepted the ICC's jurisdiction; and
II. when persons clothed with personal immunity are indicted.[434]

Claus Kreß, a member of the German delegation at the Rome Conference, analysing *Taylor* and stressing the significance of the UN-ICC Relationship Agreement, reaches the following conclusions:

> All in all, there are weighty factors supporting the view that the ICC is not a joint organ of the States Party to the Rome Statute, but rather is a court which, irrespective of its formal creation by treaty, substantially derives its "mandate from the international community" as para 51 of the Taylor decision puts it. It is submitted that, if this legal proposition is correct, the ICC must, as a consequence, be empowered to request a State party to arrest and surrender a non-State party national serving in a capacity to which immunity *rationae personae* is normally attached, provided that there are reasonable grounds to believe that such person has committed a crime within the ICC's jurisdiction (in the full meaning of the

432 For a detailed analysis thereof, see Maunganidze and du Plessis 2015, pp. 65–83.

433 Barnes 2010–2011, pp. 1615–1616; see also Odero 2011, pp. 150–154.

434 Kiyani 2013, p. 484.

term): The requested State would not be required "to act inconsistently with its obligations under international law" (Article 98, para 1, of the ICC Statute), because the absence of customary immunity rights *rationae personae* before the ICC would have to be extended to the relationship with a State party where the latter does not act unilaterally but rather is requested to cooperate within the ICC's framework of vertical cooperation.[435]

Mark Drumbl refers to the language of the constitutive instruments of courts functioning within the vertical system of enforcement as a ground for the inapplicability of immunity *rationae personae* by way of a defence before such international fora.[436] Citing the ICTY Statute,[437] the ICTR Statute,[438] the SCSL,[439] the Law on the ECCC,[440] and the ICC Statute's twenty-seventh legal provision,[441] he notes that within the vertical system of enforcement immunities have been largely eliminated.[442] In pursuit of the same inapplicability of immunities *rationae personae* to core crimes, Ademola Abass cites case-law, including *Eichmann, Furundžija, Tadić, Cavallo and Filártiga v Peña-Irala.*[443] Literature conveys that international criminal tribunals have, *de facto,* empowered States to supersede personal immunities,[444] thwarting the personal immunity of Heads of other (third) States. In other words, personal immunities are irrelevant, and hence always inapplicable (as a defence, post-surrender), before the vertical system of enforcement. Contemporary literature, detecting a 'trend to limiting immunity and strengthening accountability',[445] has acknowledged that 'the shift in the law towards the narrowing of immunities is readily seen',[446] but has cast a penumbra of doubt on the *raison d'etre* of the *Taylor dictum.*[447]Although verticality is correctly presupposed and hierarchically juxtaposed, this is only so because States have granted international courts the ability to issue orders to States, either by treaty or under UNC Chapter VII powers. Such critics are however right to note that 'the Special Court for Sierra Leone would have been on much sounder ground if it had simply observed that Taylor was no longer a Head of State at the time of the

435 Kreß 2005, p. 208.

436 Drumbl 2008, p. 235.

437 Article 7(2).

438 See its Article 6(2).

439 See its Article 6(2).

440 See its Article 29.

441 In its second paragraph, this legal provision explicitly eliminates immunity *rationae personae* by means of an express waiver of State Parties.

442 Drumbl 2008, pp. 235–236.

443 Abass 2005, p. 279.

444 Cryer et al. 2011, p. 459.

445 Cryer et al. 2011, p. 559.

446 Cryer et al. 2011, p. 558.

447 Cryer et al. 2011, p. 551.

decision, having stepped down in August 2003, and hence that he no longer enjoyed personal immunity and was liable to arrest and prosecution for international crimes'.[448] Irrespective of this, the *Taylor* precedent is a laudable piece of legal literature.[449]

Asad Kiyani rebuts arguments that the UNSC Chapter VII powers have rendered *Al Bashir*'s immunity inoperative for the purposes of the ICC Statute. He identified three ways how this could have occurred:

(1) through the delegation of the UNSC Chapter VII powers to the ICC, which it would then exercise;
(2) by binding Sudan to the ICC Statute, hence including Article 2(2), by means of a UN Chapter VII resolution; and
(3) by deleting the immunity through the direct action by the UNSC itself.

He then rebuts all these arguments on the basis of the fact that neither Chapter VII nor Article 103 of the UNC allows the UNSC to extend the ICC's jurisdiction. The ICC, he opines, cannot exercise Chapter VII powers and the UNSC has no authority to revise the rules of international law in order to negate *Al Bashir*'s immunity.[450] Moreover, no customary international law exception for the application of immunities (before international criminal courts or tribunals)[451] which can trump yet another customary international law rule protecting the immunities of heads of States subsists. He notes that the practice of international criminal tribunals cannot support such customary international law exception since *Gbagbo, Gaddafi, Taylor* and *Milošević* were all former Heads of State when warrants for their arrest were issued. Consequently they lacked personal immunities at the time of their arrest and trial.[452] It seems that the immunity of Heads of State from the ICC is not yet customary international law.[453]Anyhow, solutions must be found to negate such immunity (in order to prevent the crystallization thereof into customary international law) and the consequential impunity which would flow therefrom. Legal literature seems to point to some potential solutions which may be used to circumvent Head of State immunity, such as *Al Bashir*'s. Claus Kreß concluded that 'under the modern positivist approach to customary international law… a weighty case can be made for the crystallization of a customary international criminal law exception from the international law immunity *rationae*

---

448 Cryer et al. 2011, p. 552.

449 Claus Kreß, whose commentary postulates the so-called 'indirect waiver argument' and the 'customary law argument' [see n. 341], considers it to be tantamount to a 'noteworthy piece of international case law on the question of immunity *rationae personae* before an international criminal court' (Kreß 2005, p. 204).

450 Kiyani 2013, p. 474.

451 One must here reiterate that Article 27 of the ICC Statute departs from customary international law with detrimental effects since it does not even distinguish between immunities *rationae materiae* and immunities *rationae personae* (Abass 2005, p. 281).

452 Kiyani 2013, pp. 487–489.

453 Skander Galand 2014, p. 627.

personae in proceedings before a judicial organ of the international community'.[454] Rather than a customary international law rule proclaiming such immunities, a customary international law exception to immunities (in criminal proceedings before an international court/tribunal) subsists. Dapo Akande argues that UNSC Resolution 1593 implies that Sudan must, in the interests of effective investigation and prosecution of Darfur, be equated with an ICC State Party. By ratifying the ICC Statute, hence also its twenty-seventh article, Dapo Akande contends that State Parties waived the immunities of their own officials, 'such that, not only is the official barred from pleading immunity, but State parties themselves are barred from claiming the immunity of their officials in the context of Article 98'.[455] In so far as Article 98 is concerned, it must be highlighted that the AU decision referred to here above[456] does not fall within the remit of Article 98 because it does not represent one of the types of (immunity) obligations which fall within the parameters of that provision.[457] Concisely put, Dapo Akande submits that since the *Omar Al Bashir* case emanates from a UNSC referral, the ICC Statute (including its Article 27) must be regarded as binding on Sudan just as though Sudan were a State Party. Dapo Akande's views are not unsupported. Examining the legislative history of Article 98, Dire Tladi postulates that many States stressed a restrictive approach to exceptions to the general duty to cooperate, requesting that such exceptions be enumerated within an exhaustive list. This calls for a broad system of State co-operation wherein the insistence to limit and specify grounds for refusal of cooperation 'lends support to a restrictive interpretation of Article 98(1), including the phrase "'State or diplomatic immunity'".[458] Both reach the same conclusion, but whereas Akande focuses on the position of Sudan, Tladi emphasizes the position of State Parties. The ICC has not allowed the dust to settle by means of its inconsistent string of judgments. First, in the *Chad* and *Malawi* decisions, it found that *Al Bashir* does not enjoy immunity because of an exception under customary international law for the prosecution of core crimes by an international court.[459] Then, in the *DRC* decision, it revised its position by finding that the UNSC, by virtue of Resolution 1593, implicitly waived *Al Bashir*'s immunity.[460] Subsequently, in the *South Africa* decision the ICC determined that *Al Bashir* does not enjoy immunity because the UNSC's referral placed Sudan in a similar position as a State Party,[461] as a result of which 'no immunity needs to be waived'.[462] The ICC essentially retained this reasoning in its decision on *Jordan's* non-compliance, which case, as

[454] Kreß 2012, p. 254.
[455] Dapo Akande being cited by Tladi 2013, p. 210.
[456] See Sect. 10.2.
[457] Sluiter 2011.
[458] Tladi 2013, pp. 217–218.
[459] Knottnerus 2017.
[460] Ibid.
[461] Ibid.
[462] *Decision on South Africa's non-compliance*, above n. 364, para 93.

stated in Chap. 10, is still *sub iudice*. In other words, the ICC's position to date seems to be that 'Article 27(2) of the Statute applies equally with respect to Sudan, rendering inapplicable any immunity on the ground of official capacity belonging to Sudan that would otherwise exist under international law'.[463]

In any case, irrespective of whether non-State Parties actually ratify the ICC Statute, by virtue of the above assertions, their citizens are not immune *in toto* from being prosecuted by the ICC. To begin with, as explained previously, when the ICC's jurisdiction is triggered by a UNSC Resolution, the ICC Statute could be deemed to bind the non-State Party. In the case of *Omar Al Bashir*, 'by requiring Sudan to cooperate with the Court, the resolution explicitly subjects Sudan to the requests and decisions of the Court. Since the Court must, under its own Statute, act in accordance with the Statute, making the decisions of the Court binding on Sudan is to subject Sudan to the provisions of the Statute indirectly'.[464] Hence, the UNSC, by means of its resolution, stripped all Sudanese nationals, including *Omar Al Bashir*, of any immunity they may have previously enjoyed.[465] UNSC referrals could thus lead to a concomitant obligation of the territorial State, this being the *locus delicti commissi*.[466] Whether such State is a State Party or otherwise to the ICC Statute would become immaterial.

However, in as much as Sudan might be so bound, although the Pre-Trial Chamber of the ICC directed the Registry to transmit a request for the arrest and surrender of *Omar Al Bashir* to all UNSC members that are not State Parties to the ICC Statute,[467] one cannot conclude that had *Omar Al Bashir* been on their territory, such non-State Parties would have had an obligation to arrest and surrender him. This is true only to a certain point. If the UNSC referral contains an accompanying obligation, also imposed by the UNSC Resolution, for the non-State Party to cooperate with the ICC in the discharge of the ICC's mandate, such obligation would bind the non-State Party. This has occurred by virtue of the operative para 2 of the UNSC Resolution 1593 of 2005[468] wherein the UNSC referred the situation of Darfur to the ICC, requesting the Government of Sudan to cooperate fully with

---

463 ICC, Pre-Trial Chamber II, Situation in Darfur, Sudan, *Prosecutor v Omar Hassan Ahmad Al Bashir, Decision under Article 87(7) of the Rome Statute on the non-compliance by Jordan with the request by the Court for the arrest and surrender of Omar Al-Bashir (Decision on Jordan's non-compliance)*, 11 December 2017, ICC-02/05-01/09, para 38.

464 Akande 2009.

465 du Plessis 2010, pp. 78–79.

466 The territorially-based paradigm is still the prevalent theory of jurisdiction in general international law (Paliouras 2014, p. 37).

467 Such decision conflicts with the Decision on the Prosecutor's Application for Warrants of Arrest under Article 58 in relation to the situation in Uganda [ICC Pre-Trial Chamber II, *Situation in Uganda, Decision on the Prosecutor's Application for Warrants of Arrest under Article 58 in Relation to the Situation in Uganda*, 8 July 2005, Case No. ICC-02/04].

468 Critics of this resolution argue that 'it discriminates on the basis of nationality' since it ensures that nationals of other States are excluded from the ICC's jurisdiction (Ssenyonjo 2009, p. 399 and p. 403). William Schabas speaks of a 'defective Security Council resolution' (Schabas 2007, p. 51).

the ICC. Additionally, the mere referral of the situation by the UNSC, besides automatically binding Sudan to cooperate as if it were a party to the ICC Statute, abrogated immunities,[469] the latter being creatures of custom rather than treaty.[470] Dapo Akande, on this basis, contends that UNSC practice, which paved the way for the ICTY to prosecute *Slobodan Milošević* and for the ICTR to convict Prime Minister *Jean Kambanda*, as a result of Chapter VII powers, abrogated immunities.[471] Although *Omar Al Bashir* is still not within the ICC's custody,[472] the attempts to have him surrender to the ICC and prosecuted before the ICC, coupled with the prosecutions of *Taylor*, *Milošević* and *Gbabgo* may dissuade future leaders (Heads of States) from committing core crimes.[473]

To recapitulate, before international courts/tribunals, immunities *rationae personae* are still applicable unless the case was triggered by a UNSC referral, at which point they evaporate into thin air. Inherent characteristics of international jurisdictions (which include a UN member's waiver of immunities when an international tribunal is set up by virtue of a UNSC Resolution) render immunities *rationae personae* inapplicable.[474] This is why Thomas Weatherall contends that 'according to either understanding, the international arrest warrants and subsequent criminal proceedings against *Taylor, Al-Bashir,* and *Gaddafi* suggest that immunity *rationae personae* does not apply in proceedings for violations of *jus cogens* instituted by international judicial organs such as the ICC'.[475] If and where the case was triggered diversely, immunities *rationae personae*, though still applicable to date, are suffering some blows by the perceived existence of the customary international law exception to personal immunities which Claus Kreß has masterfully detected. Although the ICC is the only international court which explicitly denies immunity *rationae personae*,[476] such immunities are still solidly rooted within the international legal system, especially because the ICJ and domestic courts take the consistent position that there is absolute immunity *rationae personae* for persons accused of core crimes,[477] but also due to Article 98(1) of the ICC Statute which prevents the prosecution of Heads of State who benefit from such personal immunities.[478] Owing to such a blurred picture, it would be premature (and probably incorrect) to conclude that personal immunities cannot be invoked within the vertical system of enforcement. They are still solidly grounded. States are not precluded from invoking such immunities as a ground for refusal unless such ICC

---

469 Akande 2008, p. 2.

470 van Schaack and Slye 2010, p. 978.

471 Akande 2008, p. 3.

472 For a detailed examination of the case against *Omar Al Bashir*, see Kreß 2015, pp. 669–704.

473 Grono and de Courcy Wheeler 2015, pp. 1243–1244.

474 Papillon 2010, p. 276.

475 Weatherall 2015, p. 293.

476 Webb 2013, p. 79.

477 Webb 2013, p. 76.

478 Papillon 2010, p. 283.

request for surrender follows a UNSC referral, in which case the hands of the requested State are certainly tied. Yet, the position at law might shift depending on the stance which shall be taken by the ICC Appeals Chamber when it shall deliver a decision on the legal questions raised further to *Jordan*'s appeal.[479]

11.4.2 Immunities Rationae Materiae

Immunities *rationae materiae* are more vulnerable than personal immunities. Judicial inconsistency and conflicting legal provisions (which have hardly been tested and applied), enabled me (within Sect. 11.4, more than within others) to make ample reference to the works of jurists. It is true that individual criminal responsibility has increasingly pursued the deconstruction of strong bonds between States and their officials.[480] It is equally true that 'courts have set aside immunity *rationae materiae* when officials are accused of international crimes'.[481] However, although some practice is comforting and the trend is to restrict the applicability of immunities, it does not seem that, at least in the near future, as Rémy Prouveze predicts, 'immunity from criminal jurisdiction in international law may become still more questioned or even disappear completely'.[482]

Three related and inter-twined arguments are normally deployed to make a case against the applicability of immunities *rationae materiae* from the criminal process. Firstly, since immunities *rationae materiae* are accorded only to sovereign (official) acts, the atrocious nature of the core crimes violates *jus cogens* norms and cannot be deemed to constitute sovereign (official) acts. This argument would subsist only if Krystyna Marek's statement, to the effect that *jus cogens* is an obscure notion,[483] is rejected. The excursus postulated by myself here above and in Part II fits like a glove in this context. I have already expressed that since the commission of core crimes creates a process of self-delegitimization of the State, such State 'waives any right to immunity as the State has stepped out of the sphere of sovereignty'.[484] For such reasons, Lords Browne-Wilkinson and Hutton concluded that *Pinochet*, a former Head of State, is not immune in respect of torture committed whilst in office,[485] with the former Law Lord categorically eliciting the *aut dedere aut*

---

[479] ICC Appeals Chamber, *Situation in Darfur, Sudan, The Hashemite Kingdom of Jordan's Appeal Against the 'Decision under Article 87(7) of the Rome Statute on the Non-Compliance by Jordan with the Request by the Court for the Arrest and Surrender [of] Omar Al-Bashir'*, 12 March 2018, Case No. ICC-02/05-01/09.

[480] van der Wilt 2005, p. 110.

[481] Webb 2012, p. 121; see also HoL, *Regina v Bow Street Stipendiary Magistrate and Others, Ex Parte Pinochet* (*Spanish request for extradition* case), 24 March 1999, (No.3) [1999], 2 WLR 827.

[482] Prouveze 2011, p. 362.

[483] Marek 2002, p. 351.

[484] Belsky et al. 1989, p. 394, cited in Akande and Shah 2011, pp. 828–829, n. 59.

[485] *Spanish request for extradition* case, above n. 481, paras 113 and 166.

judicare rule.[486] Moreover, besides the above mentioned two Law Lords, Lords Hope and Millett placed emphasis on the idea that since torture is a core crime *per se*, immunity was removed,[487] whereas Lord Phillips upheld that 'customary international law had progressed to the point that a former Head of State could not claim immunity for crimes against international law such as torture'.[488] All these Law Lords referred to *jus cogens* in their opinions, although such references were 'not always apposite or clear'.[489] Secondly, core crimes, though acts of States or crimes committed with the connivance of State power, cannot be considered as sovereign (official) acts since 'international crimes are always *ultra vires* acts'.[490] Hence they cannot be cloaked by immunities *rationae materiae* since such immunities, whilst diverting responsibility to the State, attach only to official acts. Thirdly, the theory of implied waivers, such waivers being undertaken by States, relies upon the issue of hierarchy of norms, which is also central to this work. In other words, should the norms prohibiting core crimes be considered hierarchically supreme they will override and take precedence over and above the inconsistent rules regulating immunities, thus negating the need for waivers.[491] This rests upon the premise that *jus cogens* norms 'prevail over and invalidate ... other rules of international law in conflict with them... since sovereign immunity itself is a principle of international law, it is trumped by *jus cogens*. In short...when a State violates *jus cogens*, the cloak of immunity provided by international law falls away, leaving the State amenable to suit'.[492] As Christine van den Wyngaert correctly stated in her dissenting opinion in *Yerodia*, the *erga omnes* obligations to prosecute and punish crimes prohibited by a *jus cogens* norm necessarily trump the lower order obligation to respect immunity.[493] I believe that this argument has a very solid basis. In domestic law, Constitutions prevail over ordinary legislation. Similarly, in the absence of an international constitutional law or a centralized legal mechanism, it stands to reason that the law by means of which the doctrine of individual criminal responsibility has been cast in stone should prevail over any other international convention because this law, the ICC Statute, has penalized core crimes and, to an extent, expropriated domestic criminal jurisdiction, besides constitutionalizing both the denationalization of the administration of criminal justice and

486 Brody 2000, p. 15.

487 Cryer 2009b, p. 875.

488 Brody 2000, p. 15.

489 Cryer 2009b, p. 875.

490 Frulli 2009a, p. 369.

491 A waiver has been defined as 'the permission given by the State of the individual concerned, authorizing the State with custodial enforcement jurisdiction to proceed with investigation, arrest and trial of the individual concerned' (Simbeye 2004, p. 136).

492 USA Court of Appeals, 9th Circuit, *Susan Siderman de Blake et al. v Argentina*, 22 May 1992, 85 5773, 1992, 965 F. 2d 699.

493 ICJ, *Arrest Warrant of 11 April 2000 (DRC v Belgium)*, Dissenting Opinion of Judge Christine van den Wyngaert, 14 February 2002, ICJ Rep. 2002, p. 3, para 28, cited in Tladi 2013, p. 220.

the internationalization of a global rule of law.[494] Besides the ICCPR, the ICC Statute, arguably, is the international instrument which contains most elements, features and characteristics akin to those of a domestic Constitution. To this extent, together with the UNC, it is the counterpart of various Constitutions on an international scale and with a global dimension. Considering hierarchies, various publicists have acknowledged that international *jus cogens* norms supersede domestic legislation,[495] and that they do not admit of any persistent objection since the principle of persistent objector is incompatible with the concept of *jus cogens*.[496] All this substantiates and supports the theory of implied waivers which has been juxtaposed here above.

Dapo Akande and Sangeeta Shah also identify the inapplicability of immunities *rationae materiae* when core crimes are being prosecuted, but do so upon a different pretext. They largely disagree with the three arguments postulated here above. They submit that rules conferring extra-territorial jurisdiction displace immunities.[497] Thus, when a rule permitting the exercise of extra-territorial jurisdiction over a crime (and the consequential prosecution of its perpetrators) develops, immunities *rationae materiae* subside. Likewise, since the CAT established universal jurisdiction for torture, *Pinochet* was divested of any immunity *rationae materiae*[498] since such extra-territorial (universal) jurisdiction cannot be reconciled with immunities which blatantly run counter to the object and purpose of the CAT which so categorically prohibits and unequivocally penalizes torture. Extra-territorial jurisdiction (*multo magis*, universal jurisdiction) and immunities *rationae materiae* are therefore mutually exclusive. They simply cannot co-exist. Consequently, immunities *rationae materiae* cannot subsist where universal jurisdiction applies to core crimes.[499] This means that since core crimes are subject to universal jurisdiction, as shown in Part II, immunities *rationae materiae* can be nullified. For the sake of non-repetition within this heading, Part IV will thoroughly examine the concept of universal jurisdiction, and may be relied upon for a better understanding thereof.

Quintessentially, irrespective of which, if any (of the above four arguments) one opts to adhere to, immunities *rationae materiae* from the criminal process wherein individuals are charged with core crimes are skating on thin ice. They can no longer be relied upon to evade criminal liability since contemporary 'developments in international law now mean that the reasons for which immunity *rationae materiae* are conferred simply do not apply to prosecutions'[500] for core crimes.

---

494 See Chap. 1, n. 2.

495 Haffke 1994, cited in Simbeye 2004, p. 140.

496 Brownlie, van Hoof, Rozakis, Ruiz, Robledo, Ronzitti and Barberis, cited in Ragazzi 1997, p. 67, n. 96.

497 Akande and Shah 2011, p. 817.

498 Opinions of Lords Browne-Wilkinson, Saville, Millet and Phillips, in *Spanish request for extradition* case, above n. 481, paras 114, 169–170, 178–179 and 190.

499 Akande and Shah 2011, p. 849.

500 Akande and Shah 2011, p. 840.

11.4.2.1 Bilateral Immunity Agreements

I shall now pass onto considering the second sub-article/paragraph of Article 98 which deals with bilateral immunity agreements, the analysis of which is intricately linked to prior discourse on the consequential differences between, State Parties on the one hand, and non-State Parties on the other hand. This legal provision does impose duties on State Parties, but binds the ICC to refrain from requesting the surrender of an individual when the State has entered into a bilateral immunity agreement.[501] Were such State to comply with the request for surrender, it would be acting 'inconsistently with its obligations under international agreements pursuant to which the consent of a sending State is required to surrender a person of that State to the Court, unless the Court can first obtain the cooperation of the sending State for the giving of consent for the surrender'. Article 98(2) of the ICC Statute, according to Kimberley Prost and Angelika Schlunck, is only applicable to State Parties to the ICC Statute.[502] To be precise, Article 98(2) of the ICC Statute can have the effect of a ground for refusal, but it would also be slightly misleading to consider it as one such ground for refusal. This is because the prevailing obligation is not couched on the State party but vests directly on the ICC which should refrain from requesting the surrender of an individual when a State Party has entered into a bilateral immunity agreement within the scope of Article 98(2) of the ICC Statute. Article 98 of the ICC Statute speaks about 'what the Court may not do, not what State Parties may do'.[503] Rather than refusing State cooperation, such cooperation is not requested and is not requestable by the ICC in the first place. It cannot be demanded by the ICC *ab initio*. To this extent, Article 98 of the ICC Statute is the clearest demonstration of the obligations of the ICC, notwithstanding its *kompetenz-kompetenz*. Besides Article 17, Article 98 is, most probably, from the perspective of the ICC, the most onerous statutory provision which the Kampala Conference was not capable of addressing effectively. From the viewpoint of scholars and jurists, Article 98 of the ICC Statute is probably the most controversial, grey area of the ICC Statute. Looked upon by States, it is a legal provision which provides fertile grounds for enduring juridical and political wrestling. The absence of terms such as 'arrest' therein means that the ICC will have yet a tougher task to undertake when it shall be faced with its obligation, arising from Article 119 (1) of the ICC Statute, to settle disputes concerning its judicial functions. Yet, Article 98 of the ICC Statute clearly restricts and hinders cooperation. In influencing the State's obligation to cooperate, its net effect is equivalent to any other ground for refusal. Bilateral immunity agreements have not been rescinded. On the contrary, the USA-ICC relationship has deteriorated severely after Donald Trump's election as President and, more so, since the OTP has requested the ICC Pre-Trial Chamber authorisation to commence an investigation into the situation in

---

[501] King 2006, p. 302.

[502] Prost and Schlunck 1999, p. 1132, cited in Sluiter 2003, n. 95 at p. 633.

[503] Iverson 2012, p. 137.

the Islamic Republic of Afghanistan,[504] an ICC State Party, for core crimes allegedly committed by the Taliban, the Kabul government, and the American forces and CIA officers, despite the threat of US sanctions.[505] The rotting of the relationship culminated when the USA boycotted an informal UNSC meeting to mark the 20th anniversary of the ICC Statute, a meeting attended to by many opponents of the ICC, including Russia and China.[506] Bilateral immunity agreements, also known as 'Article 98 agreements', are intended to exempt USA citizens from potential surrender to the ICC.[507] Effectively, they 'bar the Court from exercising its jurisdiction',[508] to the extent that they should have been referred to as impunity (rather than immunity) agreements, particularly in the light of Article 98 (2) of the ICC Statute.[509] Such bilateral immunity agreements therefore have the potential to significantly hinder State cooperation and act as a ground for the refusal of the surrender of an individual.

Article 98(2) of the ICC Statute was inserted primarily to cover the situation of troops abroad under Status of Forces Agreements.[510] However, Dieter Fleck concludes that no conflicts between Status of Forces Agreements[511] and the ICC should arise in view of the fact that 'Article 98(2) is not applicable to standard Status of Forces Agreements'.[512] He reaches such conclusions on the basis of the fact that Status of Forces Agreements and Article 98(2) of the ICC Statute deal with different matters. Whereas Status of Forces Agreements stipulate the conditions under which the sending and the receiving State respectively may exercise both civil and criminal jurisdiction over offences allegedly perpetrated by members of the armed forces of the sending State, Article 98(2) deals with international agreements

---

[504] ICC Pre-Trial Chamber III, *Situation in the Islamic Republic of Afghanistan, Public Redacted Version of 'Request for Authorisation of an Investigation Pursuant to Article 15'*, 20 November 2017, Case No. ICC-02/17, para 376.

[505] Cobain 2018.

[506] Lederer EM (2018) US Boycotts Informal UN Meeting on ICC's 20th Anniversary. Associated Press. https://www.apnews.com/f1ca6338ccc34a00982036d41d46aaaa. Accessed 7 October 2018.

[507] For a better understanding of the impact of such agreements, see Scheffer 2005; see also Deen-Racsmany 2004; see also Fleck 2003.

[508] Triffterer 1999, p. 513.

[509] This important legal provision stipulates that:

'The Court may not proceed with a request for surrender which would require the requested State to act inconsistently with its obligations under international agreements pursuant to which the consent of a sending State is required to surrender a person of that State to the Court unless the Court can first obtain the cooperation of the sending State for the giving of consent for the surrender'.

[510] Cryer 2005, p. 154.

[511] The purpose and effect of Status of Forces Agreements is to limit, and not extend, the functional immunity of foreign armed forces as the result of a balance between the law of the sending State and the law of the receiving State (Fleck 2003, p. 656).

[512] Fleck 2003, p. 651.

pursuant to which the consent[513] of the sending State is required to surrender a person of that State to the ICC.[514] Harmen van der Wilt, whilst critical of Dieter Fleck's arguments, adopts an objective analysis built upon assumptions to decipher the intention of the drafters. He concludes, basing himself predominantly on the reference to 'sending State' in Article 98(2) of the ICC Statute, that the most plausible assumption is that when Article 98 was framed the drafters 'had situations in mind which were governed by Status of Forces Agreements – peacekeeping operations and the stationing of troops in foreign countries – and would allow the adjustment of these agreements to take into account of the coming into being of the ICC, respecting claims of primary jurisdiction of the sending State'.[515] To the extent that they attack the very heart of the complementarity system, this being the essence of the ICC regime, he opines that 'the current exemption agreements are in contravention of the Rome Statute in general and are not compatible with Article 98 (2) in particular'.[516]

Whereas Status of Forces Agreements are agreements concluded when one State (the host State) is hosting military forces of another State (the sending State), bilateral immunity agreements are broader because they do not merely cover military personnel but also all nationals, including private individuals. When ICC State Parties sign bilateral immunity agreements they bind themselves to undertake obligations which conflict with their ICC obligations, placing the ICC in a situation whereby it will 'have to refrain from requesting the surrender of United States nationals unless the consent of the United States can be obtained'.[517] William Schabas refers to negotiated immunity agreements between States and State-like entities or *sui generis* organizations, such as, for example, the ICRC, and contends that these agreements are not contemplated by Article 98.[518] Opponents of the USA position have sustained that Article 98(2) applies only to Status of Forces Agreements, or at best, only to USA nationals who have been sent to the relevant State, whereas others uphold that such legal provision applies only to existing agreements[519]and not to agreements concluded after a State has become a State Party.[520] Undoubtedly Article 98(2) can provide States with a reason to deny surrender or other forms of cooperation where such agreements exist and nationals of a non-State Party are concerned.[521]Although the validity of such bilateral

513 It is undisputed that 'consent plays a pivotal role in determining the authority and legitimacy of the International Criminal Court' (Brighton 2012, p. 632).

514 Fleck 2003, p. 656.

515 van der Wilt 2005, p. 102.

516 van der Wilt 2005, p. 105.

517 King 2006, pp. 298–299.

518 Schabas, 2010, p. 1040.

519 The negotiating history, however, does not reveal such intention at all (van der Wilt 2005, p. 101).

520 King 2006, p. 300.

521 Schabas 2010, p. 1045.

immunity agreements under international law is highly questionable,[522] such bilateral immunity agreements, together with the American Servicemembers' Protection Act,[523] cumulatively create a scenario which precludes material assistance to the ICC, including investigations, arrests, detentions and surrender. However, Markus Benzig upholds that 'the non-surrender agreements concluded by the United States generally are too broad in scope and too lax with respect to duties of investigation and prosecution of the parties to be in conformity with Article 98'.[524] In any case, considered conjointly, they constitute 'a dangerous precedent as to the good faith interpretation of cooperation duties'.[525] Additional legislation, such as the American Servicemembers' Protection Act, mentioned here above, 'basically prohibits the United States from cooperating with the ICC'.[526] The adoption of such measures is intended to ensure that the ICC will not assert jurisdiction over nationals of the State adopting such countermeasures without its consent.[527] To this extent, it constitutes 'the most principled and most decisive rejection of the International Criminal Court's jurisdiction by a non-State Party thus far'.[528] This indicates that although 'the role of State consent in the new international law has become less important because of the combination of *jus cogens* obligations and international human rights law',[529] it still leaves an indelible mark.

It has been shown how both paragraphs of Article 98 of the ICC Statute are inter-related and can offset the State's obligation to surrender. Bing Bing Jia stresses the difference in wording between Articles 98(1) and 98(2) of the ICC Statute, and concludes that such 'change of wording in Article 98(2) gives rise to the question as to whether a State party, which may be a 'sending State' at the same time, may avoid executing a request for assistance from the Court, thus in breach of the terms of Articles 86 and 87'.[530] He argues that Article 98(1) may provide yet another basis {and independently from Article 98(2)} for any third State, which could well be a sending State, to claim that State immunity applies to its officials, including members of its armed forces in foreign territory.[531] All this shows that Article 98 of

522 Council of the EU 2002; see also Mutyaba 2012, p. 950.

523 For an analysis of some of the political consequences of this piece of legislation, see Magliveras and Bourantonis 2003, pp. 32–42; see also Everett 2000, pp. 137–151.

524 Benzig 2009, p. 253.

525 Zahar and Sluiter 2008, p. 471.

526 Chet 2003, p. 1122.

527 Besides the American Servicemembers' Protection Act (2002) Title II of Public Law 107-206, the USA concluded agreements with other States prohibiting the transfer of USA nationals to the ICC, and adopted UNSC Resolutions preventing the ICC from exercising jurisdiction over those nationals of non-State Parties that are involved in UN-authorized operations {UNSC (2002) Resolution 1422 (2002), UN Doc. S/RES/1422, and UNSC (2003) Resolution 1487 (2003), UN Doc. S/RES/1487}.

528 Kochler 2003, p. 241.

529 Ku and Yoo 2013, p. 225.

530 Jia 2009, p. 166.

531 Ibid.

the ICC Statute (together with its *nexus* with and impact upon, other ancillary matters) is still a grey area within international criminal law. This is still so in view of the fact that unfortunately recent ICC jurisprudence has 'not entirely cleared up the ambiguity regarding the correct interpretation of Article 98(1)'[532] and Article 98 (2) of the ICC Statute. A guiding *dictum* beckons.

11.5 The Rule of Speciality

The last ground for refusal is the rule of speciality which deserves to be considered as a ground for refusal in as much as it can be invoked at a stage preceding surrender and also because, in any case, it has attained the status of customary international law.[533] Just like other grounds for refusal may overlap, as seen here above, the rule of speciality could fall within the purview of the abuse of process doctrine since the ICC would be committing prosecutorial abuse were it to benefit from the formal processes of the requested State to secure the surrender of a person for any other offence than the one for which surrender was granted.[534] It also ensures and safeguards all other grounds for refusal, including the extradition principles of reciprocity and dual criminality.[535] The rule of speciality, anchored in Article 101 of the ICC Statute, conveys that persons surrendered to the ICC may be tried only for the conduct which was the basis for their surrender to the ICC.[536] Its rationale lies in the fact that 'the investigation of a person who has been surrendered to the Court for a specific crime might lead to the discovery of evidence that the surrendered person has also committed another crime or that the evidence for the crime for which the person was surrendered, while insufficient for conviction, is sufficient for a lesser crime'.[537] The ramifications thereof (the consequences of an examination of the extent to which the rule of speciality applies in a given situation), could have relevance, for the purposes of this work, also in so far as they shed a light on the criteria necessary for 'national proceedings' to subsist in terms of the *ne bis in idem* plea.

The rule of speciality[538] is the only traditional extradition-based ground for refusal which the ICC Statute expressly admits. Whereas William Schabas reveals that it was inserted to alleviate concerns by States to the effect that the ICC co-operation regime (surrender law) would not be so different from the horizontal

[532] *Malawi* case, above n. 353, cited in Mistry and Ruiz Verduzco 2012, p. 11.

[533] Wilkitzki 1999.

[534] Knoops 2002, p. 173.

[535] Ibid.

[536] Arsanjani 1999, p. 73.

[537] Ibid.

[538] This derives its 'right of existence' from the principle of legality (Sluiter 2003, p. 639).

system of enforcement (extradition law operating between sovereign States),[539] Bert Swart thinks that the drafters of the ICC Statute overlooked the fact that the rule had a distinct and legitimate purpose in the ILC's draft which it no longer had in the ICC Statute.[540] Whatever the reason, it seems that the rule of speciality should not have been included in the ICC Statute.[541] In terms of the legal maxim *ubi lex voluit lex dixit*, I opine that the ICC Statute wanted to preclude the other traditional extradition-based grounds for refusal from the vertical system of enforcement. This line of thought is supported by jurists,[542] and by the fact that, 'in the light of the negotiating history, these should be considered as exhaustive'.[543] It has been said that speciality 'cannot serve as a ground to refuse surrender. Rather, it imposes conditions on the legal consequences of surrender'.[544] This should be qualified and explained because, in actual fact, if the requested State does not obtain the necessary guarantees it could be entitled to refuse surrender. The ICC, however, rather than providing assurances, may request a waiver of the speciality requirement. In terms of Article 101(2) of the ICC Statute, States may, at their discretion, waive such requirement, and are also encouraged to do so. This is notwithstanding its customary international law status, noted here above. In the case of the speciality ground for refusal, the 'same conduct' test is also relevant. This is because 'the rule of speciality does not forbid the conviction for a lesser offence if that conviction is based on the same set of facts'.[545] Bert Swart aptly notes that there is no need for the speciality rule in the relations between State Parties and the ICC. If a State Party objects to the person being tried for a new offence, the State Party can challenge the jurisdiction of the ICC or the admissibility of the case in terms of Article 19 of the ICC Statute.[546]

Matters are different in so far as non-State Parties are concerned since such States may object to the person surrendered being tried for offences which were not covered by the agreement on the basis of which it was willing to surrender the person sought. Such matters can be agreed to contractually.[547] The agreement between the non-State Party and the ICC would hence regulate the position at law on a case-by-case basis. Such agreement would be enforceable unless it violates the human rights of the person sought, especially if and when it impinges, albeit indirectly, on the legality principle. Rule 196 of the ICC Rules of Procedure and Evidence entitles the surrendered person to provide his views on a perceived violation of the above mentioned Article 101 of the ICC Statute.

---

[539] Schabas 2010, p. 1055.
[540] Swart 2002b, p. 1700.
[541] Swart 2002b, p. 1702.
[542] Cryer 2005, p. 150.
[543] Cryer et al. 2011, p. 511.
[544] Sluiter 2003, p. 643.
[545] Swart 2002b, p. 1700.
[546] Ibid.
[547] Swart 2002b, p. 1701.

The ICC is well placed, in terms of resources, to conduct investigations and prosecutions. Yet, although arbiter of its own jurisdiction, its powers to prosecute and judge individuals are limited by the grounds for refusal which the ICC Statute allows. The extent to which these grounds are robust, or otherwise, will depend on the ICC's tendency, either to trust or to distrust the criminal justice systems of domestic States, and on the ICC's interpretation and application of the relevant provisions of the ICC Statute. This concludes the examination of the grounds of refusal within the vertical system of enforcement.

References

Abass A (2005) The Competence of the Security Council to Terminate the Jurisdiction of the International Criminal Court. TILJ 40(2):263–297

Agreement between all UN Member States and Sierra Leone (2002) Agreement between the United Nations and the Government of Sierra Leone on the Establishment of a Special Court for Sierra Leone

Agreement on Privileges and Immunities of the ICC (2002) Agreement on the Privileges and Immunities of the International Criminal Court, ICC/ASP/1/3

Aizman DW (2016) Aizman Law Firm, Criminal Defence Practice. http://www.lacriminaldefensepartners.com/sex-crimes/rape-defense/#.Vc80RS4eOuo. Accessed 12 January 2016

Akande D (2004) International Law Immunities and the International Criminal Court. AJIL 98 (3):407–433

Akande D (2008) The Bashir Indictment: Are Serving Heads of State Immune from International Criminal Court Prosecution. Oxford Transitional Justice Research Working Paper Series. https://www.law.ox.ac.uk/sites/files/oxlaw/akande1.pdf. Accessed 1 June 2012

Akande D (2009) The Legal Nature of Security Council Referrals to the ICC and its Impact on *Al Bashir*'s Immunities. JICJ 7(2):333–352

Akande D (2011) ICC Issues Detailed Decision on Bashir's Immunity (…At Long Last…) But Gets the Law Wrong, EJIL Talk! http://www.ejiltalk.org/icc-issues-detailed-decision-on-bashir%E2%80%99s-immunity-at-long-last-but-gets-the-law-wrong/. Accessed 11 August 2013

Akande D (2012a) The Effect of Security Council Resolutions and Domestic Proceedings on State Obligations to Cooperate with the International Criminal Court. JICJ 10(2):299–324

Akande D (2012b) Problems with Immunities and the ICC. In: Wilmshurst E, Akande D, Bekou O, Powles S (eds) International Law Meeting Summary, Milestones in International Criminal Justice: Recent Judgments and New Developments, Chatham House, London

Akande D, de Souza Dias T (2018) Does the ICC Statute Remove Immunities of State Officials in National Proceedings? Some Observations From the Drafting History of Article 27(2) of the Rome Statute. EJIL:Talk! https://www.ejiltalk.org/does-the-icc-statute-remove-immunities-of-state-officials-in-national-proceedings-some-observations-from-the-drafting-history-of-article-272-of-the-rome-statute/. Accessed 24 December 2018

Akande D, Shah S (2011) Immunities of State Officials, International Crimes, and Foreign Domestic Courts. EJIL 21(4):815–852

Akhavan P (2016) Complementarity Conundrums: The ICC Clock in Transitional Times. JICJ 14 (5):1043–1059

Aksenova M (2017) Human Rights at the International Criminal Court: Testing the Limits of Judicial Discretion. NJIL 86(1):68–90

Ambach P (2015) A Look Towards the Future – The ICC and "Lessons Learnt". In: Stahn C (ed) The Law and Practice of the International Criminal Court. OUP, Oxford, pp. 1277–1295

Ambos K (2010) The Colombian Peace Process and the Principle of Complementarity of the International Criminal Court: An Inductive Situation-Based Approach. Springer, Berlin/Heidelberg

Ambos K, Stegmiller I (2012) Prosecuting International Crimes at the International Criminal Court: Is There a Coherent and Comprehensive Prosecution Strategy? CLSC 58(4):391–413

American Servicemembers' Protection Act (2002) Title II of Public Law 107-206

Amsterdam Treaty (1997) Treaty of Amsterdam amending the Treaty of the European Union, the Treaties establishing the European Communities and certain related acts

Arbour L, Bergsmo M (1999) Conspicuous Absence of Jurisdictional Overreach. In: von Hebel HAM, Lammers JG, Schuking J (eds) Reflections on the International Criminal Court. Asser Press, The Hague, pp. 129–140

Arsanjani MH (1999) Reflections on the Jurisdiction and Trigger Mechanism of the International Criminal Court. In: von Hebel HAM, Lammers JG, Schuking J (eds) Reflections on the International Criminal Court. Asser Press, The Hague

ASP (2012) Resolution ICC-ASP/11/Res.5, Doc. ICC/ASP/11/20

Bantekas I (2010) International Criminal Law. HP, Oxford

Barnes GP (2011) The International Criminal Court's Ineffective Enforcement Mechanisms: The Indictment of President *Omar Al Bashir*. FILJ 34(6):1584–1619

Bassiouni MC, Manikas P (1996) The Law of the International Criminal Tribunal for the Former Yugoslavia. TP, Irvington-on-Hudson, NY

Behren H-J (2002) Protection of National Security Information in the ICC: A Guide to Article 72 of the Rome Statute. In: Roggemann H, Šarcevic P (eds) National Security and International Criminal Justice. KLI, The Hague/London/NY, pp. 115–126

Bekou O (2009) A Case for Review of Article 88, ICC Statute: Strengthening A Forgotten Provision. NCLR 12(3):468–483

Belsky AC, Merva M, Roht-Arriaza N (1989) Implied Waiver under the FSIA: A Proposed Exception to Immunity for Violations of Peremptory Norms of International Law. CaLR 77 (2):365–415

Benzig M (2009) Article 98 (ICC St.) Agreements. In: Cassese A (ed) The Oxford Companion to International Criminal Justice. OUP, Oxford, pp. 252–253

Bergsmo M (1998) The Jurisdictional Regime of the International Criminal Court (Part II, Articles 11–19). EJCCLCJ 6(4)29–47

Bernard D (2011a) *Ne Bis In Idem* - Protector of Defendant's Rights or Jurisdictional Pointsman*?* JICJ 9(4):863–880

Bernard P (2011b) The Paradox of Institutional Conversion: The Evolution of Complementarity in the International Criminal Court. International Journal of Humanities and Social Science 1 (19):203–216

Bishop A (2013) Failure of Complementarity: The Future of the International Criminal Court Following the Libyan Admissibility Challenge. MnnJIL 22:388–421

Bo M (2014) The Situation in Libya and the ICC's Understanding of Complementarity in the Context of UNSC-Referred Cases. CLF, 25(3–4):505–540

Bohlander M (2008) *Ne Bis in Idem*. In: Bassiouni MC (ed) International Criminal Law: International Enforcement, Vol. III, 3rd edn. MNP, Leiden/Boston

Brighton C (2012) Avoiding Unwillingness: Addressing the Political Pitfalls Inherent in the Complementarity Regime of the International Criminal Court. ICLR 12(4):629–664

Brody R (2000) The Case of Augusto Pinochet. In: Brody R, Ratner M (eds) The Pinochet Papers: The Case of Augusto Pinochet in Spain and Britain. KLI, Alphen aan den Rijn, The Netherlands, pp. 7–22

Buchan R, Johnsson C-EJ (2012) Reviewing Jurdi NN (2011) The International Criminal Court and National Courts: A Contentious Relationship. Ashgate, Farnham. In: ICLR 12(1):104–109

Caligiuri A (2018) Governing International Cooperation in Criminal Matters: The Role of the *Aut Dedere Aut Judicare* Principle. ICLR 18(2):244–274

Capital News (2013) From the 'Ocampo Six' to the 'Bensouda Three. http://www.capitalfm.co.ke/news/2013/09/from-the-ocampo-six-to-bensouda-three/. Accessed 3 November 2015

Carnero Rojo E (2005) The Role of Fair Trial Considerations in the Complementarity Regime of the International Criminal Court: From "No Peace Without Justice" to "No Peace with Victor's Justice?" LJIL18(4):829–869
Carter LE (2010) The Principle of Complementarity and the International Criminal Court: The Role of *Ne Bis in Idem.* SCJIL 8(1):165–198
Cassese A (2008) International Criminal Law, 2nd edn. OUP, Oxford
Čengić A (2010) Commentary: *Habeas Corpus* at the ICC: The Ways in Which a Person Detained by the ICC may Challenge his or her Detention – a Study of the Dyilo case. In: Klip A, Sluiter G (eds) Annotated Leading Cases of International Criminal Tribunals: The International Criminal Court: 2005–2007, Vol. 23. Intersentia, Cambridge, pp. 182–192
Chalmers D, Hadjiemmanuil C, Monti G, Tomkins A (2006) European Union Law. CUP, Cambridge
Chet JT (2003) The Proliferation of Bilateral non-Surrender Agreements Among non-Ratifiers of the Rome Statute of the International Criminal Court. AUILR 19(5):1115–1180
Ciampi A (2002a) Other Forms of Cooperation. In: Cassese A, Gaeta P, Jones JRWD (eds) The Rome Statute of the International Criminal Court: A Commentary, Vol. II. OUP, Oxford, pp. 1705–1747
Ciampi A (2002b) The Obligation to Cooperate. In: Cassese A, Gaeta P, Jones JRWD (eds) The Rome Statute of the International Criminal Court: A Commentary, Vol. II. OUP, Oxford, pp. 1607–1638
Ciampi A (2008) State Cooperation with the International Criminal Court and Human Rights. In: Politi M, Gioia F (eds) The International Criminal Court and National Jurisdictions. Ashgate, Farnham, Surrey, UK pp. 103–111
Ciampi A (2010) Commentary on State Cooperation. In: Klip A, Sluiter G (eds) Annotated Leading Cases of International Criminal Tribunals: The International Criminal Court: 2005–2007, Vol. 23. Intersentia, Cambridge, pp. 538–543
CISA (1990) Convention Implementing the Schengen Agreement, 19 June 1990, [2000] OJ L239/19
Cobain I (2018) ICC on Collision Course with US over Looming Afghan War Crimes Probe. Middle East Eye. https://www.middleeasteye.net/news/icc-collision-course-us-over-looming-afghanistan-war-crimes-probe-366131245. Accessed 11 November 2018
Conway G (2003) *Ne Bis In Idem* in International Law. ICLR 3(3):217–244
Council of the EU (2002) Conclusions on the ICC, 30 September 2002, CEU 12134/02. http://www.consilium.europa.eu/uedocs/cmsUpload/ICC34EN.pdf. Accessed 22 May 2016
Cryer R (2002) Implementation of the International Criminal Court Statute in England and Wales. ICLQ 51(3):733–743
Cryer R (2005) Prosecuting International Crimes: Selectivity and the International Criminal Law Regime. Cambridge Studies in International and Comparative Law, CUP, Cambridge
Cryer R (2009a) Means of Gathering Evidence and Arresting Suspects in Situations of States' Failure to Cooperate. In: Cassese A (ed) The Oxford Companion to International Criminal Justice. OUP, Oxford, pp. 201–207
Cryer R (2009b) Pinochet. In: Cassese A (ed) The Oxford Companion to International Criminal Justice. OUP, Oxford, pp. 872–875
Cryer R, Bekou O (2007) International Crimes and International Criminal Court Cooperation in England and Wales. JICJ 5(2):441–459
Cryer R, Friman H, Robinson D, Wilmshurst E (2011) An Introduction to International Criminal Law and Procedure, 2nd edn. CUP, Cambridge
Cumes G (2006) *Ad Hoc* Tribunals, Reviewing Otham MC (2005) Accountability for International Humanitarian Law Violations: The Case of Rwanda and East Timor. In: CLF 17(3):345–353
Currie RJ (2007) Abducted Fugitives Before the International Criminal Court: Problems and Prospects. CLF 18(3–4):349–393
Daniels RN (2006) *Non Bis in Idem* and the International Criminal Court, *BEP,* Working Paper 1365. http://law.bepress.com/cgi/viewcontent.cgi?article=6282&context=expresso. Accessed 28 October 2012

Daqun L (2009) Double Jeopardy. In: Cassese A (ed) The Oxford Companion to International Criminal Justice. OUP, Oxford, pp. 304–305

Day A (2004) Crimes Against Humanity as a *Nexus* of Individual and State Responsibility: Why the ICJ Got Belgium v. Congo Wrong. BJIL 22(3):489–512

De Hoogh A (2009) The (lack of) Accountability of Indonesian Commanders and Political Authorities. In: Klip A, Sluiter G (eds) Annotated Leading Cases of International Criminal Tribunals: Timor Leste: The Special Panels for Serious Crimes 2003–2005, Vol. 16. Intersentia, Antwerp/Oxford/Portland, pp. 85–95

de Souza Dias T (2018) The 'Security Council Route' to the Derogation from Personal Head of State Immunity in the *Al Bashir* Case: How Explicit Must Security Council Resolutions be? EJIL: Talk! https://www.ejiltalk.org/the-discussion-of-the-security-council-roots-to-the-derogation-from-personal-immunities-in-the-al-bashir-case-how-explicit-must-security-council-resolutions-be/. Accessed 19 November 2018

Decision on the Prosecutor's Application for Warrants of Arrest, Article 58, Situation in the Democratic Republic of the Congo, Case No. ICC-01/04-01/07, Pre-Trial Chamber I, 10 February 2006. In: Klip A, Sluiter G (2010) (eds) Annotated Leading Cases of International Criminal Tribunals: The International Criminal Court 2005–2007, Vol. 23. Intersentia, Cambridge, pp. 53–84

Decision on the Request by Human Rights Watch for Leave to Appear as Amicus Curiae in the Proceedings for Referral of the Indictment Against Fulgence Kayishema to Rwanda (Rules 11bis and 74 of the Rules of Procedure and Evidence), *Prosecutor v. Fulgence Kayishema*, Case no. ICTR-2001-67-I, Trial Chamber III, 8 November 2007. In: Klip A, Sluiter G (2010) (eds) Annotated Leading Cases of International Criminal Tribunals: The International Criminal Tribunal for Rwanda 2006–2007, Vol. 25. Intersentia, Cambridge, pp. 281–285

Deen-Racsmany Z (2004) A New Passport to Impunity?: Non-Extradition of Naturalised Citizens versus Criminal Justice. JICJ 2(3):761–784

Dembowski LC (2003) The International Criminal Court: Complementarity and its Consequences. In: Stromseth JE (eds) Accountability for Atrocities: National and International Responses. International and Comparative Law Series, TP, Irvington-on-Hudson, NY, pp. 135–169

Deprez C (2012) Extent of Applicability of Human Rights Standards to Proceedings Before the International Criminal Court: On Possible Reductive Factors. ICLR 12(4):721–741

Donohue JO, Rigney S (2012) The International Criminal Court Must Consider Fair Trial Concerns in Determining Libya's Application to Prosecute *Saif al-Islam Gaddafi* Nationally. EJIL: Talk! http://www.ejiltalk.org/the-icc-must-consider-fair-trial-concerns-in-determining-libyas-application-to-prosecute-saif-al-islam-gaddafi-nationally/. Accessed 31 October 2014

Drumbl MA (2008) Immunities and Exceptions. In: Bassiouni MC (ed) International Criminal Law: Multilateral and Bilateral Enforcement Mechanisms, Vol. II, 3rd edn. MNP, Leiden/Boston, pp. 231–242

du Plessis M (2010) The International Criminal Court that Africa Wants. Institute for Security Studies, Pretoria, South Africa. http://www.issafrica.org/uploads/Mono172.pdf. Accessed 30 June 2012

du Plessis M, Tladi D (2017) The ICC's Immunity Debate – the Need for Finality. EJIL:Talk! https://www.ejiltalk.org/the-iccs-immunity-debate-the-need-for-finality/. Accessed 2 September 2017

Eckelmans FC (2016) The *Duch* Case: The ECCC Supreme Court's Chamber Review of Case 001. In: Meisenberg SM, Stegmiller I (eds) The Extraordinary Chambers in the Courts of Cambodia: Assessing their Contribution to International Criminal Law. International Criminal Justice Series, Vol. 6, Asser Press, The Hague

ECvHR (1950) European Convention for the Protection of Human Rights and Fundamental Freedoms

El Zeidy M (2008) The Principle of Complementarity in International Criminal Law: Origin, Development and Practice. MNP, Leiden/Boston

El Zeidy MM (2011) Admissibility in International Criminal Law. In: Schabas WA, Bernaz N (eds) Routledge Handbook of International Criminal Law. Routledge, T & F, Milton Park, Abingdon, UK, pp. 211–229

Everett RO (2000) American Servicemembers and the International Criminal Court. In: Sewall SB, Kaysen C (eds) The United States and the International Criminal Court: National Security and International Law. American Academy of Arts and Sciences, RLP, Lanham, Maryland, pp. 137–151

Fellmeth AX, Horwitz M (2009) Guide to Latin in International Law. OUP, Oxford

Fleck D (2003) Are Foreign Military Personnel Exempt from International Criminal Jurisdiction under Status of Forces Agreements? JICJ 1(3):651–670

Frulli M (2009a) Personal Immunities and International Crimes. In: Cassese A (ed) The Oxford Companion to International Criminal Justice. OUP, Oxford, pp. 368–369

Frulli M (2009b) Some Reflections on the Functional Immunity of State Officials. Symposium: International Law in Italian Courts. IYIL 19(1):91–99

Gaeta P (2002) Official Capacity and Immunities. In: Cassese A, Gaeta P, Jones JRWD (eds) The Rome Statute of the International Criminal Court: A Commentary, Vol. II. OUP, Oxford, pp. 975–1002

Garner BA (2004) Black's Law Dictionary, 8th edn. Thomson West, Saint Paul, Minnesota, USA

Genocide Convention (1948) Convention on the Prevention and Punishment of the Crime of Genocide

Gillet M (2012) The Call of Justice: Obligations under the Genocide Convention to Cooperate with the International Criminal Court. CLF 23(1–3):63–96

Gomien D, Harris DJ, Zwaak L (1996) Law and Practice of the European Convention on Human Rights and the European Social Charter. CoE Publishing, Strasbourg, France

Gradoni L, Lewis DA, Megret F, Nouwen SMH, Ohlin JD, Reisinger-Coracani A, Zappalà S (2013) In: Sluiter G, Friman H, Linton S, Vasiliev S, Zappalà S (eds) International Criminal Procedure: Principles and Rules. OUP, Oxford, pp. 39–129

Greppi E (2008) Inability to Investigate and Prosecute under Article 17. In: Politi M, Gioia F (eds) The International Criminal Court and National Jurisdictions. Ashgate, Farnham, Surrey, UK, pp. 63–70

Grono N, de Courcy Wheeler A (2015) The Deterrent Effect of the ICC on the Commission of International Crimes by Government Leaders. In: Stahn C (ed) The Law and Practice of the International Criminal Court. OUP, Oxford, pp. 1225–1244

Haffke CW (1994) The Torture Victim Protection Act: More Symbol than Substance. Emory Law Journal 43:1467–1517

Harris DJ, O'Boyle M, Bates EP, Buckley CM (2009) Law of the European Convention on Human Rights, 2nd Edn. OUP, Oxford

Hassanein AS (2017) Self-Referral of Situations to the International Criminal Court: Complementarity in Practice – Complementarity in Crisis. ICLR 17(1):107–134

Heller KJ (2006) The Shadow Side of Complementarity: The Effect of Article 17 of the Rome Statute on National Due Process. CLF 17(3–4):255–280

Heller KJ (2012) Why the Failure to Provide *Saif* with Due Process Is Relevant to Libya's Admissibility Challenge. *Opinio Juris*. http://opiniojuris.org/2012/08/02/why-the-failure-to-provide-saif-with-due-process-is-relevant-to-libyas-admissibility-challenge/. Accessed 30 September 2014

Heller KJ (2013) The Taylor Sentencing Judgment: A Critical Analysis. JICJ 11(4):835–855

Heller KJ (2016) Radical Complementarity. JICJ 14(3):637–665

Holmes JT (2002) Complementarity: National Courts versus the ICC. In: Cassese A, Gaeta P, Jones JRWD (ed) The Rome Statute of the International Criminal Court: A Commentary, Vol. I. OUP, Oxford, pp. 667–686

HRW (1999) *Crime or Custom?: Violence Against Women in Pakistan*. https://books.google.com.mt/books?id=DbA8oe0NmtUC&pg=PA36&lpg=PA36&dq=rape+requires+full+penetration&source=bl&ots=P6QCN_wYSO&sig=56_7dLMEzw1tu4hpwX6RaD3WtI8&hl=en&sa=X&ei=7L9HVLXHI43ZatbGgtgE#v=onepage&q=rape%20requires%20full%20penetration&f=false. Accessed 2 February 2011

ICC Elements of Crimes (1998) International Criminal Court, Elements of Crimes

ICC RPR (2002) Rules of Procedure and Evidence of the International Criminal Court

ICC Statute (1998) Rome Statute of the International Criminal Court
ICCPR (1966) International Covenant on Civil and Political Rights
ICTR Statute (1994) Statute of the International Criminal Tribunal for Rwanda
ICTY Statute (1993) Statute of the International Criminal Tribunal for the Former Yugoslavia
Italy's Constitution (1947) *Costituzione della Repubblica Italiana*
Iverson JM (2012) The Continuing Functions of Article 98. GJIL 4(1):131–151
Jackson M (2016) Regional Complementarity: The Rome Statute and Public International Law. JICJ 14(5):1061–1072
Jacobs D (2015) The Frog that Wanted to be an Ox: The ICC's Approach to Immunities and Cooperation. In: Stahn C (ed) The Law and Practice of the International Criminal Court. OUP, Oxford, pp. 281–302
Jalloh CC (2009) Regionalizing International Criminal Law? ICLR 9(3):445–499
Jia BB (2009) The International Criminal Court and Third States. In: Cassese A (ed) The Oxford Companion to International Criminal Justice. OUP, Oxford, pp. 160–167
Jia BB (2012) The Immunity of State Officials for International Crimes Revisited. JICJ 10 (5):1303–1321
Jorda C (2004) The Major Hurdles and Accomplishments of the International Criminal Tribunal for the Former Yugoslavia: What the International Criminal Court Can Learn from Them. JICJ 2(2):572–584
Judgement on the Prosecutor's Appeal Against the Decision of Pre-Trial Chamber 1 Entitled "Decision on the Prosecutor's Application for Warrants of Arrest, Article 58", Situation in the DRC, Case No. ICC-01/04, Appeals Chamber, 13 July 2006. In: Klip A, Sluiter G (2010) (eds) Annotated Leading Cases of International Criminal Tribunals: The International Criminal Court: 2005–2007, Vol. 23, Intersentia, Cambridge, pp. 85–100
Jurdi NN (2011) The International Criminal Court and National Courts: A Contentious Relationship. Ashgate, Farnham, Surrey, UK
Jurdi NN (2017) The Complementarity Regime of the International Criminal Court in Practice: Is it Truly Serving the Purpose? Some Lessons From Libya. LJIL 30(1):199–220
King H (2006) Immunities and Bilateral Immunity Agreements: Issues Arising from Articles 27 and 98 of the Rome Statute. NZJPIL 4(2):269–310
Kiyani AG (2013) Al-Bashir and the International Criminal Court: The Problem of Head of State Immunity. ChJIL 12(3):467–508
Kleffner JK (2006) Complementarity as a Catalyst for Compliance. In: Kleffner JK and Kor G (eds) Complementary Views on Complementarity: Proceedings of the International Roundtable on the Complementary Nature of the International Criminal Court, Amsterdam, 25/26 June 2004. Asser Press, The Hague, pp. 79–104
Kleffner JK (2008) Complementarity in the Rome Statute and National Criminal Jurisdictions. OUP, Oxford
Klip A (2010) Cooperation of States, with reference to *Prosecutor v Bagosora, Kabiligi, Ntabakuze and Nsengiyumva*, Modalities for Presentation of a Witness,' Case No. ICTR-98-41-T, Trial Chamber I, 20th September 2006. In: Klip A, Sluiter G (eds) Annotated Leading Cases of International Criminal Tribunals: The International Criminal Tribunal for Rwanda 2006–2007, Vol. 25. Intersentia, Antwerp/Oxford/Portland, pp. 286–289
Knoops G-JA (2002) Surrendering to International Criminal Courts: Contemporary Practice and Procedures. International and Comparative Criminal Law Series, TP, Irvington-on-Hudson, NY
Knoops G-JA (2008) Defences in Contemporary International Criminal Law. International and Comparative Criminal Law Series, MNP, Leiden/Boston
Knottnerus A (2017) The Immunity of Al Bashir: The Latest Turn in the Jurisprudence of the ICC. EJIL:Talk! https://www.ejiltalk.org/the-immunity-of-al-bashir-the-latest-turn-in-the-jurisprudence-of-the-icc/. Accessed 9 March 2018
Knottnerus AS (2014) The Security Council and the International Criminal Court: The Unsolved Puzzle of Article 16. NILR 61(2):195–224

Kochler H (2003) Global Justice or Global Revenge?: International Criminal Justice at the Crossroads. Springer, Vienna/NY

Kreß C (2005) Commentary on Immunity from Jurisdiction. In: Klip A, Sluiter G (eds) Annotated Leading Cases of International Criminal Tribunals: The Special Court for Sierra Leone 2003–2004, Vol. 9. Intersentia, Antwerp/Oxford, pp. 202–208

Kreß C (2009) Taylor. In: Cassese A (ed) The Oxford Companion to International Criminal Justice. OUP, Oxford, pp. 951–952

Kreß C (2012) The International Criminal Court and Immunities under International law for States Not Party to the Court's Statute. In: Bergsmo M, Yan L (eds) State Sovereignty and International Criminal Law, Beijing, TOAEP, Biejing, pp. 223–265

Kreß C (2015) The ICC's First Encounter with the Crime of Genocide, The Case Against *Al Bashir*. In: Stahn C (ed) The Law and Practice of the International Criminal Court. OUP, Oxford, pp. 669–704

Ku J, Yoo J (2013) Globalization and Sovereignty. BJIL 31(1):210–234

Lee RS (2005) States' Responses: Issues and Solutions. In Lee RS (ed.) States' Responses to Issues Arising From the ICC Statute: Constitutional, Sovereignty, Judicial Cooperation and Criminal Law, International and Comparative Criminal Law Series. TP, Irvington-on-Hudson, NY, pp. 1–46

Libyan Code of Criminal Procedure (1955)

Libyan Constitutional Declaration (2011) الإعلان الدستوري, 3 August 2011

Magliveras K, Bourantonis D (2003) Rescinding the Signature of an International Treaty: The United States and the Rome Statute Establishing the International Criminal Court. Diplomacy & Statecraft 14(4):21–49

Marek K (2002) Criminalizing State Responsibility. In: Provost R (ed) State Responsibility in International Law. Ashgate, Aldershot, UK/Burlington, VT, USA, pp. 343–368

Maunganidze OA, du Plessis A (2015) The International Criminal Court and the African Union. In: Stahn C (ed) The Law and Practice of the International Criminal Court. OUP, Oxford, pp. 65–83

McAuliffe de Guzman M (1999) Article 21: Applicable Law. In: Triffterer O (ed) Commentary on the Rome Statute of the International Criminal Court: Observers' Notes, Article by Article. Nomos, Baden-Baden, pp. 435–446

Megret F, Samson MG (2013) Holding the Line on Complementarity in Libya: The Case for Tolerating Flawed Domestic Trials. JICJ 11(3):571–589

Mettraux G, Dugard J, du Plessis M (2018) Head of State Immunities, International Crimes and President *Bashir*'s Visit to South Africa. ICLR 18(4):577–622

Mistry H, Ruiz Verduzco D (Rapporteurs) (2012) The United Nations Security Council and the International Criminal Court. International Law Meeting Summary, with Parliamentarians for Global Action, Chatham House, London. http://www.pgaction.org/pdf/activity/Chatham-ICC-SC.pdf. Accessed 11 September 2014

Mitsilegas V (2009) European Union Criminal Law, Vol. 17, in the series Modern Studies in European Law. HP, Oxford

Mochochoko P (1999) International Cooperation and Judicial Assistance. In: Lee RS (ed) The International Criminal Court: The Making of the Rome Statute: Issues, Negotiations, Results. KLI, The Hague/London/Boston, pp. 305–317

Montevideo Convention (1933) Montevideo Convention on the Rights and Duties of States

Murphy SD (1999) Progress and Jurisprudence of the International Tribunal for the Former Yugoslavia. AJIL 93(1):57–97

Muthoni Wanyeki L (2012) Institute for Security Studies, The International Criminal Court's Cases in Kenya: Origin and Impact. Paper No. 237. file:///C:/Users/csol1/Downloads/Paper237.pdf. Accessed 14 May 2018

Mutyaba R (2012) An Analysis of the Cooperation Regime of the International Criminal Court and its Effectiveness in the Court's Objective in Securing Suspects in its Ongoing Investigations and Prosecutions. ICLR 12(5):937–962

Naqvi YQ (2010) Impediments to Exercising Jurisdiction Over International Crimes. Asser Press, The Hague

Neuman GL (2014) Bi-level Remedies for Human Rights Violations. HILJ 55(2):323–360

Nilsson C (2004) Contextualizing the Agreement on the Privileges and Immunities of the International Criminal Court. LJIL17(3):559–578

Nollkaemper A (2011) National Courts and the International Rule of Law. OUP, Oxford

Nouwen SMH (2005) The Special Court for Sierra Leone and the Immunity of Taylor: The Arrest Warrant Case Continued. LJIL 18(3):645–669

Nouwen SMH (2011) Fine-Tuning Complementarity. In: Brown BS (ed) Research Handbook on International Criminal Law. EE, Cheltenham, UK/Northampton, MA, USA, pp. 206–231

Nsereko D (2009) Cooperation with the Court on Matters of Arrest and Surrender of Indicted Fugitives: Lessons from the *Ad Hoc* Tribunals and National Jurisdictions. In: Doria J, Gasser H-P, Bassiouni MC (eds) The Legal Regime of the International Criminal Court: Essays in Honour of Professor Igor Blishchenko. MNP, Leiden/Boston, pp. 975–999

Nsereko D (2013) The International Criminal Court and Complementarity in Practice. LJIL 26 (2):427–447

Ocampo LM (2005) First Report of the Prosecutor of the International Criminal Court, Mr. Luis Moreno Ocampo, To the Security Council Pursuant to UNSCR 1593 (2005). https://www.legal-tools.org/uploads/tx_ltpdb/ICC_Darfur_UNSC_Report_290605_EN.pdf. Accessed 2 January 2016

Odero S (2011) Politics of International Criminal Justice: The ICC's Arrest Warrant for *Al Bashir* and the African Union's Neo-Colonial Conspirator Thesis. In: Murungu C, Biegon J (eds) Prosecuting International Crimes in Africa. PULP, Pretoria, pp. 145–160

Olásolo H (2005) The Triggering Procedure of the International Criminal Court. MNP, Leiden/Boston

Olásolo H (2007) The Lack of Attention to the Distinction Between Situations and Cases in National Laws on Co-operation with the ICC with Particular Reference to the Spanish Case. LJIL 20(1):193–205

Orakhelashvili A (2011) Immunities of State Officials, International Crimes, and Foreign Domestic Courts: A Reply to Dapo Akande and Sangeeta Shah. EJIL 22(3):849–855

OTP (2003) Informal Expert Paper: The Principle of Complementarity in Practice. ICC-01/04-01/07-1015-Anx. https://www.icc-cpi.int/RelatedRecords/CR2009_02250.PDF. Accessed 17 July 2017

OTP (2007) Policy Paper on the Interests of Justice. ICC-OTP-2007. https://www.icc-cpi.int/nr/rdonlyres/772c95c9-f54d-4321-bf09-73422bb23528/143640/iccotpinterestsofjustice.pdf. Accessed 17 July 2017

OTP (2013) Policy Paper on Preliminary Examinations. ICC-OTP-2013. https://www.icc-cpi.int/iccdocs/otp/otp-policy_paper_preliminary_examinations_2013-eng.pdf. Accessed 10 March 2016

OTP (2014) Report on Preliminary Examination Activities, 2014. https://www.icc-cpi.int/iccdocs/otp/otp-pre-exam-2014.pdf. Accessed 11 November 2016

OTP (2018) Sixteenth Report of the OTP of the ICC to the UNSC Pursuant to UNSCR 1970 (2011). https://www.icc-cpi.int/itemsDocuments/181102-rep-otp-UNSC-libya_ENG.pdf. Accessed 19 December 2018

Paliouras ZA (2014) The Non-Appropriation Principle: The *Grundnorm* of International Space Law. LJIL 27(1):37–54

Papillon S (2010) Has the United Nations Security Council Implicitly Removed Al Bashir's Immunity? ICLR 10(5):275–288

Paulussen C (2010) *Male Captus Bene Detentus?* Surrendering Suspects to the International Criminal Court. Thesis Submitted In Fulfilment of the Conferment of the degree of Doctor of Philosophy (Ph.D.) at Tilburg University

Paulussen C, Dorsey J (2012) Year in Review 2012. YIHL 15:187–236

Pichon J (2008) The Principle of Complementarity in the Cases of the Sudanese Nationals Ahmad Harun and Ali Kushayb Before the International Criminal Court. ICLR 8(1)185–228

Pitcher K (2018) Judicial Responses to Pre-Trial Procedural Violations in International Criminal Proceedings. International Criminal Justice Series, Vol. 16. Asser Press, The Hague

Powles S (2012) Complementarity in the ICC: Libya. In: Wilmshurst E, Akande D, Bekou O, Powles S (eds) International Law Meeting Summary, Milestones in International Criminal Justice: Recent Judgments and New Developments. Chatham House, London

Prost K (2005) Co-operation with the International Criminal Court: Arrests and Surrender, the Gathering of Evidence and Asset Forfeiture. In: Brandon B, du Plessis M (eds) The Prosecution of International Crimes: A Practical Guide to Prosecuting International Criminal Court Crimes in Commonwealth States. Commonwealth Secretariat, London, pp. 73–93

Prost K (2011) State Cooperation and Transfers. In: Schabas WA, Bernaz N (eds) Routledge Handbook of International Criminal Law, Routledge, T & F, Milton Park, Abingdon, UK, pp. 305–322

Prost K (2018) The Surprises of Part 9 of the Rome Statute on International Cooperation and Judicial Assistance. JICJ 16(2):363–382

Prost K, Schlunck A (1999) Article 98: Cooperation with Respect to Waiver of Immunity and Consent to Surrender. In: Triffterer O (ed) Commentary on the Rome Statute of the International Criminal Court: Observers' Notes, Article by Article. Nomos, Baden-Baden, pp. 1131–1133

Protocol No. 7 to the European Convention for the Protection of Human Rights and Fundamental Freedoms (1984)

Protocol on the Privileges and Immunities of the European Communities (1967) [Official Journal, No. 167, 13th July 1967]

Prouveze R (2011) Immunities. In: Schabas WA, Bernaz N (eds) Routledge Handbook of International Criminal Law. Routledge, T & F, Milton Park, Abingdon, UK, pp. 355–367

Ragazzi M (1997) The Concept of International Obligations *Erga Omnes*. CP, Oxford

Ramsden M, Yeung I (2016) Head of State Immunity and the Rome Statute: A Critique of the Pre-Trial Chamber's *Malawi* and *DRC* Decisions. ICLR 16(4):703–729

Rastan R (2010) Complementarity: Contest or Collaboration? In: Bergsmo M (ed) Complementarity and the Exercise of Universal Jurisdiction for Core International Crimes. Forum for International Criminal and Humanitarian Law, Publication Series No. 7, TOAEP, Oslo, pp. 83–132

Rastan R (2017) What is "Substantially the Same Conduct"?: Unpacking the ICC's "First Limb" Complementarity Jurisprudence. JICJ 15(1):1–29

Reisman WM, Arsanjani MH, Wiessner S, Westerman GD (2004) International Law in Contemporary Perspective. FP, NY

Richardson PJ (ed) (2007) Archbold: Criminal Pleading, Evidence and Practice. S & M, London

Robinson D (2003) Serving the Interests of Justice: Amnesties, Truth Commissions and the International Criminal Court. EJIL14(3):481–505

Robinson D (2006) Comments on Chapter 4 of Claudia Cardenas Aravena. In: Kleffner JK, Kor G (eds) Complementary Views on Complementarity: Proceedings of the International Roundtable on the Complementary Nature of the International Criminal Court, Amsterdam, 25/26 June 2004. Asser Press, The Hague, pp. 141–146

Robinson D (2010) The Mysterious Mysteriousness of Complementarity. CLF 21(1):67–102

Robinson D (2011) The Inaction Controversy: Neglected Words and New Opportunities. In: Stahn C, El Zeidy MM (eds) The International Criminal Court and Complementarity: From Theory to Practice, Volume I. CUP, Cambridge, pp. 460–502

Roggemann H (2002) National Security and Protection of the State in National and International Criminal Procedure: Systematic and Comparative Aspects. In: Roggemann H, Šarcevic P (eds) National Security and International Criminal Justice. KLI, Alphen aan den Rijn, The Netherlands, pp. 1–24

Russo F (2012) Disaster Through the Lens of International Criminal Law. In: de Guttry A, Gestri M, Venturini G (eds) International Disaster Response Law. Asser Press, The Hague, pp. 441–462

Ryngaert C (2008) The Doctrine of Abuse of Process: A Comment on The Cambodia Tribunal's Decisions in the Case Against Duch (2007). LJIL 21(3):719–737

Schabas W (2001) An Introduction to the International Criminal Court. CUP, Cambridge

Schabas W (2007) An Introduction to the International Criminal Court, 3rd edn. CUP, Cambridge

Schabas WA (2006) The UN International Criminal Tribunals: The Former Yugoslavia, Rwanda and Sierra Leone. CUP, Cambridge

Schabas WA (2010) The International Criminal Court: A Commentary on the Rome Statute. Oxford Commentaries on International Law, OUP, Oxford

Scheffer D (2005) Article 98(2) of the Rome Statute: America's Original Intent. JICJ 3(2):333–353

Schengen Acquis (1999) The Schengen Convention to Implement the Schengen Agreement of 14 June 1985

Scobbie I (2003) New Wine in Old Bottles or Old Wine in New Bottles? Reflections on the Assertion of Jurisdiction in Public International Law. In: Capps P, Evans M, Konstadinidis S (eds) Asserting Jurisdiction: International and European Legal Perspectives. HP, Oxford/ Portland, Oregon, pp. 17–37

Shany Y (2007) Regulating Jurisdictional Relations Between National and International Courts. OUP, Oxford

Simbeye Y (2004) Immunity and International Criminal Law. Ashgate, Farnham, Surrey, UK

Skander Galand A (2014) Reviewing Bergsmo M, Yan L (eds) (2012) State Sovereignty and International Criminal Law. Beijing, TOAEP. In: EJIL 25(2):625–629

Sluiter G (2002) International Criminal Adjudication and the Collection of Evidence: Obligations of States. Intersentia, Cambridge

Sluiter G (2003) The Surrender of War Criminals to the International Criminal Court. LLAICLR 25:605–651

Sluiter G (2009) Arrest and Surrender. In: Cassese A (ed) The Oxford Companion to International Criminal Justice. OUP, Oxford, pp. 250–252

Sluiter G (2011) There is a Duty to Cooperate for States in the Arrest and Surrender of Al Bashir, under the Genocide Convention and/or the ICC Statute and/or UN Security Council Resolution 1593. Human Rights and International Criminal Law International Criminal Court Forum, University of California, Los Angeles School of Law with the support of the OTP of the ICC. https://iccforum.com/darfur#Sluiter. Accessed 23 December 2016

Sluiter G (2016) The Practice of Shared Responsibility in Relation to International Criminal Tribunals and their Relation to States. Amsterdam Law School Legal Studies Research Paper No. 2016-24, ACIL No. 2016-10, SHARES Research Paper 98 (2016). http://www.sharesproject.nl/wp-content/uploads/2016/05/98-Sluiter-Practice-vol.-2016.pdf. Accessed 15 May 2017

Smeulers A (2007) Jurisdiction –Legality of Arrest. In: Klip A, Sluiter G (eds) Annotated Leading Cases, The International Criminal Tribunal for the Former Yugoslavia 2002–2003, Vol. 11. Intersentia, Cambridge, pp. 106–112

Spencer JR (2014) International Law, People Trafficking and the Power to Stay Criminal Proceedings for Abuse of Process. CLJ 73(1):11–14

Spinellis D (2002) Global Report: The *Ne Bis in Idem* Principle in "Global" Instruments. *RIDP* 73:1149–1162

Ssenyonjo M (2009) The International Criminal Court and the Warrant of Arrest for Sudan's President *Al-Bashir*: A Crucial Step Towards Challenging Impunity or a Political Decision?' NJIL 78(3):397–431

Stahn C (2010) Arrest and Surrender under the ICC Statute: A Contextual Reading. In: Stahn C, van den Herik L (eds) Future Perspectives on International Criminal Justice. Asser Press, The Hague, pp. 659–685

Stahn C (2012) Libya, The International Criminal Court and Complementarity: A Test for 'Shared Responsibility'. JICJ 10(2):325–349

Stahn C (2015) Admissibility Challenges before the ICC: From Quasi-Primacy to Qualified Deference? In: Stahn C (ed) The Law and Practice of the International Criminal Court. OUP, Oxford, pp. 228–259

Statute of the SCSL (2002) Statute of the Special Court for Sierra Leone
Stegmiller I (2010) Complementarity Thoughts. CLF 21(1):159–174
Stegmiller I (2013) The International Criminal Court and Mali: Towards More Transparency in International Criminal Law Investigations? CLF 24(4):475–499
Swart B (2002a) General Problems In: Cassese A, Gaeta P, Jones JRWD (eds) The Rome Statute of the International Criminal Court: A Commentary, Vol. II. OUP, Oxford, pp. 1589–1605
Swart B (2002b) Arrest and Surrender In: Cassese A, Gaeta P, Jones JRWD (eds) The Rome Statute of the International Criminal Court: A Commentary, Vol. II. OUP, Oxford, pp. 1639–1703
Swart B, Sluiter G (1999) The International Criminal Court and International Criminal Co-operation. In: von Hebel HAM, Lammers JG, Schuking J (eds) Reflections on the International Criminal Court. Asser Press, The Hague, pp. 91–127
Tallgren I, Reisinger Coracini A (2008) On Article 20. In: Triffterer O (ed) Commentary on the Rome Statute of the International Criminal Court, 2nd edn. Nomos, Baden-Baden, pp. 669–699
Tladi D (2013) The International Criminal Court Decisions on Chad and Malawi: On Cooperation, Immunities, and Article 98. JICJ 11(1):199–221
Tochilovsky V (2011) Special Commentary: International Criminal Justice – Some Flaws and Misperceptions. CLF 22(4):593–607
Tochilovsky V (2014) The Law and Jurisprudence of the International Criminal Tribunals and Courts: Procedure and Human Rights Aspects, 2nd edn. Intersentia, Cambridge, Antwerp, Portland
Tolbert D, Kontić A (2009) The ICTY: Transitional Justice, the Transfer of Cases to National Courts, and Lessons for the International Criminal Court. In: Stahn C, Sluiter G (eds) The Emerging Practice of the International Criminal Court. MNP, Leiden/Boston, pp. 135–162.
Trahan J (2017) The International Criminal Court's Libya Cases(s) – The Need for Consistency with International Human Rights as to Due Process and the Death Penalty. ICLR 17(5):803–843
Triffterer O (1999) Irrelevance of official capacity. In: Triffterer O (ed) Commentary on the Rome Statute of the International Criminal Court: Observers' Notes, Article by Article. Nomos, Baden-Baden, pp. 501–514
Triffterer O (2002) Security Interests of the Community of States, Basis and Justification of an International Criminal Jurisdiction versus 'Protection of National Security Information', Article 72 Rome Statute. In: Roggemann H, Šarcevic P (eds) National Security and International Criminal Justice. KLI, The Hague/London/NY, pp. 53–82
UK ICC Act (2001) International Criminal Court Act, United Kingdom
UN Diplomatic Conference of Plenipotentiaries on the Establishment of an International Criminal Court, *Ad Hoc* Committee, Summary Record of the 11th Meeting, 22 June 1998, UN Doc. A/CONF.183/C.1/SR.11
UNC (1945) Charter of the United Nations
UN-ICC Relationship Agreement (2004) Negotiated Relationship Agreement Between the International Criminal Court and the United Nations
UN Diplomatic Conference of Plenipotentiaries on the Establishment of an International Criminal Court (1998) *Ad Hoc* Committee, Summary Record of the 11th Meeting, 22 June 1998, UN Doc. A/CONF.183/C.1/SR.11
UNSC (2002) Resolution 1422 (2002), UN Doc. S/RES/1422
UNSC (2003) Resolution 1487 (2003), UN Doc. S/RES/1487
UNSC (2005) Resolution 1593 (2005), UN Doc. S/RES/1593
UNSC (2011) Resolution 1970 (2011), UN Doc. S/RES/1970
Usacka A (2016) Constitutionalism and Human Rights at the International Criminal Court. In: Scheinin M, Krunke H, Aksenova M (eds) Judges as Guardians of Constitutionalism and Human Rights. EE, Cheltenham, UK/Northampton, MA, USA, pp. 281–305
van Alebeek R (2008) The Immunity of States and Their Officials in International Criminal Law and International Human Rights Law. Oxford Monographs in International Law, OUP, Oxford

van den Wyngaert C, Ongena T (2002) *Ne Bis in Idem* Principle, Including the Issue of Amnesty. In: Cassese A, Gaeta P, Jones JRWD (eds) The Rome Statute of the International Criminal Court: A Commentary, Vol. I. OUP, Oxford, pp. 705–729

van den Wyngaert C, Stessens G (1999) The International *Non Bis In Idem* Principle: Resolving Some of the Unanswered Questions. ICLQ 48(4):779–804

van der Wilt H (2005) Bilateral Agreements Between the United States and State Parties to the Rome Statute: Are They Compatible with the Object and Purpose of the Statute? LJIL 18 (1):93–111

van der Wilt H (2015) Self-Referrals as an Indication of the Inability of States. In: Stahn C (ed) The Law and Practice of the International Criminal Court. OUP, Oxford, pp. 210–227

van Schaack B, Slye RC (2010) International Criminal Law and its Enforcement: Cases and Materials, 2nd edn. FP, St. Paul, Minnesota

VCLT (1969) Vienna Convention on the Law of Treaties

Vervaele JAE (2005) The Transnational *Ne Bis In Idem* Principle in the European Union: Mutual Recognition and Equivalent Protection of Human Rights. ULR 1(2):100–118

Viebig P (2016) Illicitly Obtained Evidence at the International Criminal Court. International Criminal Justice Series, Vol. 4. Asser Press, The Hague

Voetelink J (2013) Status of Forces and Criminal Jurisdiction. NILR 60(2):231–250

Warrant of Arrest for Wiranto, *Deputy General Prosecutor v Wiranto*, Case No 05/2003, The Special Panels for Serious Crime. In: Klip A, Sluiter G (2009) (eds) Annotated Leading Cases of International Criminal Tribunals: Timor Leste: The Special Panels for Serious Crimes 2003–2005, Vol. 16. Intersentia, Antwerp/Oxford/Portland, pp. 63–74

Weatherall T (2015) *Jus Cogens*: International Law and Social Contract. CUP, Cambridge

Webb P (2012) Human Rights and the Immunities of State Officials. In: de Wet E, Vidmar J (eds) Hierarchy in International Law: The Place of Human Rights. OUP, Oxford, pp. 114–147

Webb P (2013) International Judicial Integration and Fragmentation. OUP, Oxford

Weiner AS (2016) Ending Wars, Doing Justice: Colombia, Transitional Justice, and the International Criminal Court. SJIL 52(2):211–241

Werle G (2009) General Principles of International Criminal Law. In: Cassese A (ed) The Oxford Companion to International Criminal Justice. OUP, Oxford, pp. 54–62

Wilkitzki P (1999) Commentary on Article 101: Rule of Speciality. In: Triffterer O (ed) Commentary on the Rome Statute of the International Criminal Court. Nomos, Baden-Baden, pp. 1147–1156

Young SNM (2001) Surrendering the Accused to the International Criminal Court. BYIL 71 (1):317–356

Zahar A, Sluiter G (2008) International Criminal Law: A Critical Introduction. OUP, Oxford

Zappalà S (2002) Compensation to an Arrested or Convicted Person. In: Cassese A, Gaeta P, Jones JRWD (eds) The Rome Statute of the International Criminal Court: A Commentary, Vol. II. OUP, Oxford, pp. 1577–1585

Chapter 12
The Ensuing 'Jurisdictional Joint Venture', A Division of Labour *Par Excellence*

Contents

References 314

Abstract There subsists a 'jurisdictional joint venture', this being a division of labour, or rather a burden shifting exercise between the vertical system of enforcement and the horizontal system of enforcement. Part III has shown that the ICC has a noteworthy role to play in the completion of the jigsaw-puzzle of international criminal justice. The vertical system of enforcement provides a solid platform for an understanding of the horizontal system of enforcement. The ICC Statute's regime on the surrender of persons has eliminated virtually all grounds for refusal which can be found at the inter-State level. By way of example, throughout the drafting process of the ICC Statute, the non-extradition of nationals was deliberately removed from the grounds for refusal. State Parties to the ICC Statute are called upon to remove domestic barriers to surrender to the ICC which, in turn, must have good knowledge of the law of the requested State and must frame its request in such a way as to try to obtain the most favourable outcome therefrom. The constitution of a ground of refusal which is based upon the respect for human rights is increasingly being rendered superfluous with the advent of a solid infrastructure of human rights protection within the vertical system of enforcement. Besides the damaging lack of a police force which could execute arrests and surrenders, there exists a noticeable *lacuna* consisting in the absence of a procedural framework to cater for the effective steps which should follow a finding of a State's non-compliance.

Keywords Vertical system of enforcement · Horizontal system of enforcement · Domestic barriers to surrender · Grounds for refusal · Non-extradition of nationals · Solid platform · Burden shifting exercise · Jurisdictional joint venture · Division of labour · Fundamental human rights · Legislation · Responsibility to enforce · Impunity · Police force

C. Soler, *The Global Prosecution of Core Crimes under International Law*,
https://doi.org/10.1007/978-94-6265-335-1_12

The absence of traditional grounds for refusal has been identified as the major feature of the vertical relationship between the ICC and States.[1] On the basis of the *Blaškić* Appeals Chamber ruling (subpoena), such grounds have been regarded as 'rooted in State sovereignty and therefore inappropriate in a vertical cooperation relationship'.[2] In fact, one can now safely say that 'the ICC Statute's regime on the surrender of persons has successfully eliminated virtually all grounds for refusal that can be found at the inter-State level'.[3] Though this is an intrinsic feature of the vertical system of enforcement, State Parties to the ICC Statute are also called upon, not for the purposes of the horizontal system of enforcement, but, in the first place, to equip the vertical system of enforcement. In other words, States Parties to the ICC Statute are solicited to remove domestic barriers to surrender to the ICC. In substantiation of this, throughout the drafting process of the ICC Statute,[4] the non-extradition of nationals was actually deliberately removed from the grounds for refusal.[5] It would be absurd to allow the non-extradition of nationals when the ICC's jurisdiction is premised either upon territoriality or the nationality of the accused. In relation to the latter, whether the ICC's jurisdiction is based upon the nationality at the time of the crime or at the time of the prosecution, or both, is still unsettled.[6] Additionally, there is less cause of concern when one is tried before the ICC rather than before an unfair foreign forum whereby the accused is more susceptible to being discriminated against. In any case, a trend has been detected, at least in Europe, by means of which a more flexible interpretation of the non-extradition of nationals rule has been advocated. Göran Sluiter, in fact, illustrates that certain States may extradite their nationals on the condition that the nationals serve their sentences in the requested State.[7]

Part III has shown that the vertical system of enforcement can provide a solid platform for an understanding of the horizontal system of enforcement. The final outcome is constituted by a 'jurisdictional joint venture',[8] this being a division of labour or rather a burden shifting exercise between the vertical system of enforcement and the horizontal system of enforcement, which division of labour is

---

[1] Den-Racsmany 2007, p. 177.

[2] Sluiter 2009, p. 252.

[3] Kreß and Prost 1999, cited in Kreß 2003, p. 615, n. 29.

[4] The Rome Negotiating Text initially contained eleven grounds for refusal (Swart and Sluiter 1999, p. 124).

[5] UN Diplomatic Conference of Plenipotentiaries on the Establishment of an ICC 1998, cited in Young 2001, p. 345.

[6] Skander Galand 2018.

[7] Sluiter 2003a, p. 641.

[8] A joint venture is 'a business undertaking by two or more persons engaged in a single defined project' (Garner 2004, p. 856). This metaphor is used to reflect the various types of criminal courts and tribunals within the vertical system of enforcement which join forces with those prevailing within the horizontal system of enforcement (as shall be seen within the Part IV) to undertake a common goal, *id est* to attempt to defeat impunity. Conjointly they epitomize and illustrate, as the title of this work exemplifies, 'the global prosecution of core crimes under international law'.

ultimately designed to defeat impunity. These are the instructions (referred to by Darryl Robinson as 'marching orders')[9] which the international community has given to the ICC. *Dicta* of courts and tribunals which function within the parameters of the vertical system of enforcement have forged some principles which the horizontal system of enforcement can benefit from and which have contributed to the crystallization of customary international law, even in so far as immunities are concerned. Moreover, the application of international and fundamental human rights, though still a Pandora's box in terms of their implementation, is likely to solidify the importance of the safeguard and retention of human rights standards within international criminal proceedings. This is also, to an extent, because the constitution of a ground of refusal which is based upon the respect of human rights is increasingly being rendered superfluous with the advent of a solid infrastructure of human rights protection within the vertical system of enforcement whereby criminal procedure is dispersed over various jurisdictions.[10]

Besides the damaging lack of a police force[11] which could execute arrests and surrenders,[12] there exists a noticeable *lacuna* consisting in the absence of a procedural framework to cater for the necessary and effective steps which should follow a finding of a State's non-compliance,[13] the latter being a matter which goes far beyond the terms of reference and functions of the Law Enforcement Network established by the ICC's OTP.[14] Hence, special ICC cooperation legislation is desireable especially because jurisprudence on jurisdictional issues, immunity and the relationship to non-State parties remains contested.[15] This legislation should allow for a flexible approach to the applicable procedures when State authorities are acting upon an ICC request for cooperation. The ICC, in turn, must have good knowledge of the law of the requested State and it must frame its request in such a way as to try to obtain the most favourable outcome.[16]

At the risk of sounding presumptuous, Part III has attempted to minimise the consequences of the assertion of Geert-Jan Alexander Knoops who stated that 'it is

---

[9] Robinson 2003, p. 485.

[10] Sluiter 2003b, p. 941.

[11] Yitiha Simbeye drafted an additional protocol to the ICC Statute of the International Constabulary, proposing such an international constabulary as an organ of the ICC itself, (Simbeye 2004, pp. 150–155; see also Kaul 2009, pp. 34–38), whereas Alexis Demirjian favoured an International Marshals Service (Demirdjian 2010, p. 186).

[12] This may be countered by the ICC itself should it decide, by means of cooperation agreements, to allow the use of alternative enforcement measures such as multinational organizations (multinational forces) which are capable of executing arrest warrants and apprehending suspects. ICTY's successful engagement of military or peace-keeping forces which apprehended suspects as a result of the execution of ICTY orders by NATO troops could serve as a guiding model for the ICC to counterbalance this major shortcoming (Mutyaba 2012, pp. 942, 953, 954).

[13] Sluiter 2011.

[14] Tolbert and Kontić 2011, p. 918.

[15] Stahn 2015, p. xciii.

[16] Friman 2008, p. 95.

difficult to see any enumeration of surrender defences as a complete and rigid catalogue since many of the substantive surrender rights and potential defences elaborated hereinafter are still at an experimental stage'.[17] It has also shown that the ICC, though plagued by inescapable dyads,[18] has a noteworthy role to play in the completion of the jigsaw-puzzle of international criminal justice. Whereas Part IV will also deal, *inter alia*, with a responsibility to protect, a notional responsibility to enforce[19] may be said to be budding, at least in so far as the vertical system of enforcement is concerned. This sets the scene for a detailed examination of the indirect, but, as a result of the complementarity regime, the most widely resorted to method of enforcement (the horizontal system of enforcement), to be considered under Part IV.

References

Demirdjian A (2010) Armless Giants: Cooperation, State Responsibility and Suggestions for the ICC Review Conference. ICLR 10(2):181–208

Den-Racsmany Z (2007) Lessons of the European Arrest Warrant for Domestic Implementation of the Obligation to Surrender Nationals to the International Criminal Court. LJIL 20(1):167–191

Friman H (2008) Cooperation with the International Criminal Court: Some Thoughts on Improvements under the Current Regime. In: Politi M, Gioia F (eds) The International Criminal Court and National Jurisdictions. Ashgate, Farnham, Surrey, UK, pp. 93–102

Garner BA (2004) Black's Law Dictionary, 8th edn. Thomson West, St. Paul, Minnesota

Kaul H-P (2009) The International Criminal Court – Its Relationship to Domestic Jurisdictions. In: Stahn C, Sluiter G (eds) The Emerging Practice of the International Criminal Court. MNP, Leiden/Boston, pp. 31–38

Knoops G-JA (2002) Surrendering to International Criminal Courts: Contemporary Practice and Procedures. International and Comparative Criminal Law Series, TP, Irvington-on-Hudson, NY

Kreß C (2003) The Procedural Law of the International Criminal Court in Outline: Anatomy of a Unique Compromise. JICJ 1(3):603–617

Kreß C, Prost K (1999) Article 89: Surrender of Persons to the Court. In: Triffterer O (ed) Commentary on the Rome Statute of the International Criminal Court, Observer's Notes, Article by Article. Nomos, Baden-Baden, pp. 1071–1079

Mutyaba R (2012) An Analysis of the Cooperation Regime of the ICC and its Effectiveness in the Court's Objective in Securing Suspects in its Ongoing Investigations and Prosecutions. ICLR 12(5):937–962

Rastan R (2009) The Responsibility to Enforce – Connecting Justice with Unity. In: Stahn C, Sluiter G (eds) The Emerging Practice of the International Criminal Court. MNP, Leiden/Boston, pp. 163–182

Robinson D (2003) Serving the Interests of Justice: Amnesties, Truth Commissions and the International Criminal Court. EJIL 14(3):481–505

Robinson D (2015) Inescapable Dyads: Why the International Criminal Court Cannot Win. LJIL 28(2):323–347

[17] Knoops 2002, p. 167.

[18] Robinson 2015, pp. 333–343.

[19] Rastan 2009, pp. 163–182. See also Stahn and Nerlich 2008, p. 429

Simbeye Y (2004) Immunity and International Criminal Law. Ashgate, Farnham, Surrey, UK
Skander Galand A (2018) Prosecuting 'The Beatles' Before the ICC: A Gateway for the Opening of an Investigation in Syria? EJIL:Talk! https://www.ejiltalk.org/prosecuting-the-beatles-before-the-icc-a-gateway-for-the-opening-of-an-investigation-in-syria/. Accessed 9 September 2018
Sluiter G (2003a) The Surrender of War Criminals to the International Criminal Court. LLAICLR 25:605–651
Sluiter G (2003b) International Criminal Proceedings and the Protection of Human Rights. NELR 37(4):935–948
Sluiter G (2009) Arrest and Surrender. In: Cassese A (ed) The Oxford Companion to International Criminal Justice. OUP, Oxford, pp. 250–252
Sluiter G (2011) There is a Duty to Cooperate for States in the Arrest and Surrender of Al Bashir, under the Genocide Convention and/or the ICC Statute and/or UN Security Council Resolution 1593. Human Rights and International Criminal Law International Criminal Court Forum, University of California, Los Angeles School of Law with the support of the OTP of the ICC. https://iccforum.com/darfur#Sluiter. Accessed 23 December 2016
Stahn C (2015) Introduction. In: Stahn C (ed) The Law and Practice of the International Criminal Court. OUP, Oxford, pp. lxxxiii–c
Stahn C, Nerlich V (2008) The International Criminal Court and Co-operation: Introductory Note. LJIL 21(2):429–430
Swart B, Sluiter G (1999) The International Criminal Court and International Criminal Co-operation. In: von Hebel HAM, Lammers JG, Schuking J (eds) Reflections on the International Criminal Court. Asser Press, The Hague, pp. 91–127
Tolbert D, Kontić A (2011) The International Criminal Tribunal for the Former Yugoslavia ("ICTY") and the Transfer of Cases and Materials to National Judicial Authorities: Lessons in Complementarity. In: Stahn C, El Zeidy MM (eds) The International Criminal Court and Complementarity: From Theory to Practice, Volume II. CUP, Cambridge, pp. 888–919
UN Diplomatic Conference of Plenipotentiaries on the Establishment of an ICC (1998) Rome 15 June – 17 July 1998, Official Records, Vol. I. Report of the Working Group on General Principles of Criminal Law, U.N. Doc. A/CONF.183/C.I/WGIC/L.11/Add.4/Corr.I
Young SNM (2001) Surrendering the Accused to the International Criminal Court. BYIL 71 (1):317–356

Part IV
The Horizontal System of Enforcement

Chapter 13
Aut Dedere Aut Judicare

Contents

13.1 The Nature, Scope and Status of the *Aut Dedere Aut Judicare* Rule 321
13.2 The Execution of the *Aut Dedere Aut Judicare* Rule in Domestic Criminal Courts 351
13.3 Limitations of the *Aut Dedere Aut Judicare* Rule 367
13.4 Emerging Alternatives to the *Aut Dedere Aut Judicare Formulae* 370
13.5 The Fractional Re-characterisation of the *Aut Dedere Aut Judicare* Rule 380
References 389

Abstract Core crimes constitute violations of customary international law which allows for universal jurisdiction thereupon. Yet, we cannot extrapolate the applicability of the *aut dedere aut judicare rule* therefrom, nor can we extract it from their *jus cogens* status. This can be done by virtue of some determining factors. One of these relates to the qualitative gravity of core crimes, another emanates from an insufficient reach of international human rights law and a third can be triggered by acknowledging that non-prosecution could be tantamount to a threat to the peace. If a core crime is protected by a *jus cogens* norm and is subject to universal jurisdiction it is *ipso facto*, exercisable *erga omnes*. The execution of the *aut dedere aut judicare* rule in domestic courts may be equated to the assertion of universal jurisdiction by such domestic courts. The Hague *formula* favours a choice of the *forum deprehensionis* to either extradite or prosecute. It admits of two important variables, with the first variant being 'the terrorism *formula*' and the second off-shoot being 'the drugs *formula*'. The fourth Geneva formula postulates the prioritization of prosecution over extradition. Limitations to the *aut dedere aut judicare* rule deriving from the principle of non-*refoulement* are also considered. The obligation to surrender which arises once the admissibility issue has been decided by the ICC, the *Lockerbie* incident (*aut dedere aut transferre*), gacaca tribunals, and the proposed EU *corpus juris criminalis*, may fall within the special category of alternatives to the *aut dedere aut judicare formulae*.

C. Soler, *The Global Prosecution of Core Crimes under International Law*,
https://doi.org/10.1007/978-94-6265-335-1_13

Keywords *Aut dedere aut judicare* · Submit to prosecution · Treaty law · Customary international law · International community · General principles of law · *Jus cogens* norms · Obligation to prosecute · Custodial State · Qualified *erga omnes* obligation · Gravity · State power · Subsidiary universal jurisdiction · Failure to investigate · Failure to prosecute · International human rights law · International peace and security · Non-prosecution · UNSC referral · Deterrence · Default mechanism · Bystander States · Failure to punish · Third States · Hierarchy · *Formulae* · Injured State · Prioritization · Complementarity regime · State practice · Multiple States · *Forum deprehensionis* · ICC · Extradite · Surrender · Horizontal complementarity · Vertical complementarity · Frame of reference · *Eichmann* · *Pinochet* · CAT · Geneva Conventions · *Barcelona Traction* case · State acquiescence · Impunity · *Bouterse* · *Hostis humani generis* · Mandatory prosecutions · *Nicaragua* case · *Actio criminalis popularis* · Universal jurisdiction *in absentia* · *Yerodia* case · Conditional universal jurisdiction · Quasi-universal jurisdiction · Domestic criminal courts · The Hague *formula* · Sub-*formulae* · Terrorism formula · Drugs formula · Geneva formula · *Forum conveniens* · Princeton Project · *Hissène Habré* · *Belgium v Senegal* · EAC · *Guatemala Genocide* case · *Scilingo* case · Domestic *dicta* · Limitations · Non-*refoulement* · Emerging alternatives · *Lockerbie* case · *Aut dedere aut transferre* · *Gacaca* courts · Fair trial rights · *Corpus juris criminalis* · European criminal law · Fractional re-characterisation · IACtHR · *Zimbabwe Torture Docket* case · Positive obligations · Right to a national effective remedy · *Velásquez-Rodríguez v Honduras* · Private prosecution · *Cyprus v Turkey* · *Street Children* case · Fundamental human rights · Extra-territorial jurisdiction · ECtHR · Dynamic interaction · Duty to investigate

In primis, suffice to say that it might be hard to conceive of the enforcement of international criminal justice as predominantly dependent upon the execution of 'something' embodied merely in four Latin words. In practice, however, this is not a figment of one's imagination. Scholars identified seventy-two instances wherein the *aut dedere aut judicare* rule appears, after having examined three hundred and twelve international legal instruments.[1] At the outset, therefore, the first task that should be undertaken is to determine the nature, scope and status of this rule.

---

[1] Paust et al. 2007, p. 12.

13.1 The Nature, Scope and Status of the *Aut Dedere Aut Judicare* Rule

The complex nature of *aut dedere aut judicare*[2] is not cast in stone but is still clouded by controversy. *Aut dedere aut judicare* may be referred to in many ways ranging from:

i. a customary obligation[3] of international law;[4]
ii. a customary[5] right, an entitlement, under international law;[6]
iii. a general principle of law which bestows rights and obligations bilaterally, between the State where an offender is present and the State directly linked to the offence;[7]
iv. a principle[8] of customary international law;[9]
v. an obligation, habitually by States and prosecutors;[10]
vi. an obligation specifically deriving from the UNC;[11]
vii. an *erga omnes* obligation;[12]

---

[2] Sometimes jurists use *aut dedere aut judicare* on the one hand, and *aut dedere aut prosequi* on the other hand, inter-changeably (Kolb 2004, p. 232). Kolb justifies his preference to the latter term, that is, *aut dedere aut prosequi*, since 'the obligation of the State is not to try, but to submit the case to the competent authorities in view of prosecution' (Kolb 2004, p. 263). Though Kolb's choice of words is valid, the former, that is, *aut dedere aut judicare*, shall be used for the purposes of my book.

[3] Obokata 2010, p. 46.

[4] ICTY Appeals Chamber, *Prosecutor v Tihomir Blaškić, Judgment on the Request of the Republic of Croatia for Review of the Decision of the Trial Chamber II of 18 July 1997*, 29 October 1997, Case No. IT-95-14-AR 108*bis*, para 29.

[5] Such rule acquires customary status, *inter alia*, when States sign and ratify a significant number of treaties containing the *aut dedere aut judicare* rule, hence articulating the belief that *aut dedere aut judicare* is a recognized and accepted rule which is conducive to the suppression of core crimes. The customary status of such rule has been originally propounded by Bassiouni (Bassiouni and Wise 1995, Preface, pp. 22–25; see pp. 43–48 thereof for a contrary view).

[6] ICTY Trial Chamber, *Prosecutor v Anto Furundžija*, 10 December 1998, Case No. IT-95-17/1-T.

[7] Reydams 2003, p. 115; Plachta 2001a, pp. 68–69.

[8] Bassiouni and Wise 1995, Preface, p. 24.

[9] ICJ, *Case Concerning Questions of Interpretation and Application of the 1971 Montreal Convention Arising from the Aerial Incident at Lockerbie, Request for the Indication of Provisional Measures (Libyan Arab Jamahiriya v USA)*, Provisional Measures, Order of 14 April 1992, Dissenting Opinion of Judge Weeramantry, ICJ Rep. 1992, p. 114.

[10] ILC 2011, p. 318.

[11] Enache-Brown and Fried 1998, p. 632.

[12] African Commission, *Various Communications vs Mauritania*, 11 May 2000, Communications 54/91, 61/91, 96/93, 98/93, 164/97, 210/98, para 83, reproduced in p. 27 of the *amicus* brief on the Legality of Amnesties in International Law which is referred to in the appeal judgment in SCSL Appeals Chamber, *Prosecutor v Morris Kallon, Decision on Challenge to Jurisdiction Lomé*

viii. a corollary of the principle of complementarity;[13]
ix. a defence, by counsel before the ICC;[14]
x. a *jus cogens* norm, by a few publicists;[15]
xi. a 'dead letter';[16]
xii. a general norm of international law;[17]
xiii. a ground of jurisdiction;[18]
xiv. a form of universality;[19]
xv. a jurisdiction-bestowing device;[20]
xvi. a system;[21]
xvii. a communitarian principle;[22] to
xviii. an open-ended concept,[23]

the intricacies of which I shall shortly consider. An examination of its nature is crucial to understand its weight for the purposes of the enforcement of international criminal justice, because only by understanding its nature, one can decipher its consequences. Though reference will be made to the sources of international law which were referred to in Sect. 1.2, the scope of Part IV is not to complete a definitive study on all bi-lateral and multi-lateral extradition treaties which include the *aut dedere aut judicare* obligation, or else to enlist all UNSC Resolutions which refer to it. These will be mentioned only when they can shed a light on the nature, status and scope of *aut dedere aut judicare*.

In so far as it is explicitly provided for within treaties, *aut dedere aut judicare*, the origins of which are attributable to the Dutch jurist Hugo Grotius,[24] is a fully-fledged conventional international law, *id est,* it possesses the feaures of a treaty and therefore it only binds those States which have ratified the treaty. It is thus only valid *inter partes*. It has no force of law in relation to non-State parties to the treaty, which consequently do not have an obligation to implement it.[25] To the

Accord Amnesty, 13 March 2004, SCSL-2004-15-AR72(E), and is also cited in Abass 2006, p. 355, n. 31.

13 El Zeidy 2008, pp. 220–221.

14 Knoops 2002, p. 313.

15 See Bassiouni's main arguments in Bassiouni and Wise 1995, preface, p. 25.

16 Cassese 1986, p. 275.

17 Enache-Brown and Fried 1998, pp. 631–632.

18 Benavides 2001, p. 19; Henzelin 2000; Bassiouni 2001, p. 81.

19 Kolb 2004, p. 281. Jann Kleffner refers to treaty-based war crimes which attract universal jurisdiction in the form of *aut dedere aut judicare* (Kleffner 2008, p. 275).

20 Boed 2000, pp. 311–312.

21 van Steenberghe 2011, pp. 1091 and 1103.

22 Article 7(3) of the Treaty of Amsterdam enshrines *aut dedere aut judicare* when EU Member States fail to extradite their nationals.

23 Plachta 2001a, p. 85.

24 '*...la cui paternitá è attribuita a Ugo Grozio...*' (Dean et al. 2003, p. 518).

25 Migliorino 1995, p. 970.

extent that it may be deemed to constitute customary international law, *aut dedere aut judicare* may be said to be an important unwritten rule.[26] It is a settled matter that customary law is the most suitable source for grounding the non-treaty based nature of the obligation to extradite or prosecute.[27] This theory finds support in the works of jurists who argue, *inter alia*, that suppression conventions which have secured a substantial degree of ratifications have led to a general pattern of treaty practice, and hence a rule of customary international law.[28] Another jurist opines that the duty to extradite or prosecute is inherent in the concept of an international criminal act, a *delictum iuris gentium*, and that, in the absence of centralized legislative, executive and judicial international institutions, it is incumbent on each State, through compulsory *dédoublement fonctionnel*,[29] to act on behalf of the international community and to repress such acts.[30] Such rules have a broader jurisdictional reach and more weight than the fully-fledged law created by treaties, because although treaties admit of unilateral reservations, customary international law[31] is only inapplicable if the persistent objector subsists. Such rules 'by their very nature…must have equal force for all members of the international community, and cannot therefore be the subject of any right of unilateral exclusion exercisable at will by any one of them in its own favour'.[32] It therefore seems apparent that the *aut dedere aut judicare* rule acquires further force when it constitutes a rule of customary international law. Now one must here add that the persistent objector is rather unlikely in circumstances dealing with the obligation to extradite or prosecute because although States may be reluctant to extradite or prosecute in some circumstances, they are constantly aware of the likelihood that, some day or another, they will want to exact prosecution by virtue of an extradition request. Since 'what goes around comes around', the persistent objector is not likely to figure when such issues are at stake. Consequently, it is safe to conclude, as Raphael van Steenberghe does after a detailed study, that 'a customary obligation to extradite or prosecute may be derived from the State practice but only with respect to a limited number of crimes, namely core international crimes such as genocide,

---

[26] A rule has been described as something which 'typically lays down a fairly specific binding obligation, although it can also define a reasonably specific persuasive obligation' (Lepard 2010, p. 162).

[27] van Steenberghe 2011, p. 1091.

[28] Freestone 1997, p. 60.

[29] This means 'role splitting' (Cassese 1990, p. 213).

[30] Scelle 1932, pp. 55–57.

[31] 'Traditional public international law posits that two elements are required to manifest the existence of a rule in customary international law: an established, consistent, and widespread State practice in the international realm, and *opinio juris* - that is, a conviction on the part of these States that they are bound to behave in such a way by an already existing rule' {ICJ, *Federal Republic of Germany v Denmark*; *Federal Republic of Germany v The Netherlands* [*North Sea Continental Shelf* cases], 20 February 1969, ICJ Rep. 1969 p. 3, para 77}, cited in Boas et al. 2007, p. 21.

[32] *North Sea Continental Shelf Cases*, above n. 31, para 63.

crimes against humanity or war crimes, and only to the extent that such a customary nature is ascribed to the obligation as it is correctly understood'.[33]

From a judicial perspective, be it within domestic, regional or international courts or tribunals, *aut dedere aut judicare* certainly constitutes a general principle of law,[34] otherwise barely described as general international law.[35] For those, such as Mohammed Cherif Bassiouni,[36] who advocate that it has reached *jus cogens* status,[37] it is a norm.[38] This assertion is counter-productive and self-defeating. As Edward Wise points out, 'if every State under any circumstances had this alternative obligation (either to surrender or to prosecute) treaty stipulations notwithstanding, that would invalidate both international instruments providing exclusively for '*dedere*' and treaties providing for the extradition of nationals'.[39] One must keep in mind that although the prohibition of torture is *jus cogens*, 'the obligation to prosecute the alleged perpetrators of acts of torture under the Convention applies only to facts having occurred after its entry into force for the State concerned'.[40] Moreover, States cannot be said to be under an obligation to prosecute when, for reasons beyond their control, they have no access at all to evidence inculpating the accused. Similarly, States cannot be said to be under an obligation to extradite since this 'will often depend on matters beyond the custodial State's control – including whether there is any extradition request to accede to or whether requesting States are States that will not engage in torture'.[41] Citing the CAT Committee's decision in *Marcos Roitman Rosenmann v Spain* in connection with the extradition of *Pinochet*, Nowak and McArthur assert that 'while prosecution constitutes an

---

[33] van Steenberghe 2011, p. 1095.

[34] Lepard states that 'a principle is less specific and normally establishes a persuasive obligation to give some value or action great weight in decision-making. A general principle is a principle that is broad in scope and applies across a wide range of subject areas' (Lepard 2010).

[35] The ICJ has occasionally drawn no difference between general principles of law and customary law, hence amalgamating both sources by coining the term 'general international law' {ICJ, *Case Concerning the Barcelona Traction, Light and Power Company Limited (Belgium v Spain)*, 5 February 1970, ICJ Rep. 1970, p. 3, para 34, which articulated the concept of *erga omnes* obligations, and ICJ, *United States Diplomatic and Consular Staff in Tehran (USA v Iran)* [*Iranian Hostages* Case], 24 May 1980, ICJ Rep. 1980, p. 3, para 62}. This is not to say that these are one and the same thing. General principles of law include general principles both of international law and of national law, whereas customary international law must be looked for primarily at the actual practice and *opinio juris* of States.

[36] Bassiouni 1987, p. 22.

[37] I am not one of these.

[38] A norm is 'a model or standard accepted (voluntarily or involuntarily) by society or other large group, against which society judges someone or something' (Garner 2009, p. 1159).

[39] Wise 1993, p. 280.

[40] ICJ, *Questions Relating to the Obligation to Extradite or Prosecute* (*Belgium v Senegal*), 20 July 2012, ICJ Rep. 2012, p. 422, para 100.

[41] Trapp 2011, p. 88.

obligation for the forum State, no other State, i.e. not even the territorial State, is under an obligation to request extradition'.[42]

From the viewpoint of contemporary international criminal law, *aut dedere aut judicare* is a means to an end, a tool in the enforcement paradigm which is the object of this book. It is tantamount to an obligation in the minds of various jurists, that is, squarely reproduced, a duty States must fulfil. However, in so far as core crimes are concerned,[43] the obligation to extradite or prosecute,[44] is not a simple one, but indeed a qualified *erga omnes* obligation. This is particularly so for three main reasons which shall now be presented.

(1) Firstly, core crimes are indeed crimes under customary international law,[45] as affirmed, *inter alia*, in *Prosecutor v Duško Tadić*,[46] by the *Čelebići* Trial Chamber,[47] and by the *Jelisić* Trial Chamber.[48] Jann Kleffner upholds that 'one of the sources used to establish such customary rules are national laws relating to, and prosecutions of, the conduct in question',[49] whereas Yitiha Simbeye, in no unclear terms, reiterates that 'the ICC's four crimes are international customary crimes based on international customary rules'.[50] This is partially so because 'custom plays an even greater role in the field of international criminal

[42] Nowak and McArthur 2008, p. 346

[43] Some jurists reach my conclusion in relation to a broader range of serious crimes (Steven 1999, pp. 425 and 440).

[44] Prosecution under contemporary international criminal law does not merely entail the possibility of the imposition of a sanction, such as, for example, a pecuniary sanction. It denotes the undertaking of criminal proceedings, a conclusion reached by analogical interpretation of the linguistic terminology used within the ICC Statute (1998) Rome Statute of the International Criminal Court which refers to the French word '*poursuites*', a term which is used in the context of criminal proceedings, to which it is inherently connected. This is substantiated by the Preamble of the ICC Statute itself which, whilst postulating, as a main objective of the ICC Statute, the effective prosecution of the most serious crimes of concern to the international community as a whole, refers to the duty of every State to exercise criminal jurisdiction in its sixth paragraph.

[45] Orna Ben-Naftali states that the wide and diverse membership of most Conventions, relevant resolutions of the UNSC, the UNGA and other international bodies, international and domestic jurisprudence and strong scholarly support 'further suggest that an obligation to exercise complementary universal jurisdiction over international crimes in general and over genocide in particular, enjoys customary status' (Ben-Naftali 2009, pp. 50–51). Amongst others, 'the offence of enforced disappearance carries individual criminal liability under customary international law' (Finucane 2010, p. 176).

[46] ICTY Appeals Chamber, *Prosecutor v Duško Tadić*, Decision on the Defence Motion for Interlocutory Appeal on Jurisdiction, 2 October 1995, Case No. IT-94-1-AR72, para 138. This judicial pronouncement dealt with crimes against humanity.

[47] See ICTY Trial Chamber, *Prosecutor v Zejnil Delalić et al*., (*Čelebići* case), 16 November 1998, Case No. IT-96-21-T, which concerned the crime of torture.

[48] ICTY Trial Chamber, *Prosecutor v Goran Jelisić*, 14 December 1999, Case No. IT-95-10-T, para 60, which categorically affirmed the customary international law and *jus cogens* nature of genocide.

[49] Kleffner 2008, p.15.

[50] Simbeye 2004, p. 37.

law'[51] and is the reason why 'customary international law is the most important source of international criminal law'.[52] The preponderance of customary international law is being scrutinized by scholars, particularly in the field of the protection of fundamental human rights.[53] This notwithstanding the fact that genocide, slavery, torture, enforced disappearance of persons and some war crimes which fall within the remit of the four Geneva Conventions are also conventionally proscribed.[54] Moreover, in the context of the peculiarities of genocide, one must add that the customary regime applicable to the domestic suppression of genocide is not identical to that of the Genocide Convention since the former municipal enforcement system, unlike the Genocide Convention,[55] allows for universal jurisdiction,[56] a principle of jurisdiction which does not require any *nexus* between the *forum* State and the crime,[57] and which is not defined neither by treaty law nor by customary international law.[58] This is not the same as 'indirect jurisdiction'.[59] Universal jurisdiction is a very powerful mechanism in the hands of States in that it permits the trial of core crimes 'committed anywhere in the world by and against anybody'.[60] To this extent, it augments, as the title of this book portrays, the 'global prosecution of core crimes under international law.' This, however, does not solve the

[51] Schlutter 2010, p. 2.

[52] See the back-cover of Schlutter 2010.

[53] Roberts 2001, p. 757.

[54] Although it recognised that 'the prohibition of genocide is a peremptory norm of customary international law, giving rise to a non-derogable obligation by each nation State to the entire international community', which obligation is 'independent of the Convention on the Prevention and Punishment of the Crime of Genocide' [para 18 of the judgment], the Federal Court of Australia sitting in Canberra, in *Nulyarimma v Thompson*, dismissed the appeal on the basis of the lack of Australian legislation penalizing genocide. The Federal Court held that 'it is not enough to say that, under international law, an international crime is punishable in a domestic tribunal even in the absence of a domestic law declaring that conduct to be punishable. If genocide is to be regarded as punishable in Australia, on the basis that it is an international crime, it must be shown that Australian law permits that result' [Federal Court of Australia, Canberra, *Nulyarimma v Thompson*, 1 September 1999, [1999] FCA 1192, 165 ALR 621, para 22].

[55] In ICJ, *Application of the Convention on the Prevention and Punishment of the Crime of Genocide (BiH v Serbia and Montenegro)*, 26 February 2007, ICJ Rep. 2007, p. 43, para 442, the ICJ held that 'an obligation to try the perpetrators of the Srebrenica massacre in Serbia's domestic courts cannot be deduced from Article VI'.

[56] This is implicit in the ICTRs recognition of the applicability of universal jurisdiction over the crime of genocide in ICTR Trial Chamber I, *Prosecutor v Bernard Ntuyahaga, Decision on the Prosecutor's Motion to Withdraw the Indictment*, 18 March 1999, Case No. ICTR-98-40-T.

[57] O'Keefe 2004, pp. 745–746; see also Adanan 2013, pp. 3–7.

[58] Hoover 2011, p. 6.

[59] In terms of Article 4a of the Dutch Criminal Code, this subsists where a foreign State requests The Netherlands to take over prosecution of a criminal case and a treaty exists between the foreign State and The Netherlands foreseeing prosecution in the case, *Hoge Raad* [Supreme Court], The Netherlands, *Public Prosecutor v Joseph Mpambara*, 21 October 2008, Case No. 09-750007-07.

[60] Pocar and Maystre 2010, p. 263.

dilemma. That core crimes are abhorrent and condemnable is neither new nor controversial. This does not automatically render them subject to universal jurisdiction. We cannot simply extrapolate the applicability of the *aut dedere aut judicare rule* therefrom. Nor can we extract it merely because such crimes violate a *jus cogens* norm, although Bing Bing Jia found that 'there is in reality an obvious link between the doctrine of universal jurisdiction and *jus cogens*'.[61] It seems to me that there are some determining factors which could be used to undertake such extraction. These are rather latent and relatively unexplored. I shall delve into them now.

(A) One of such determining factors relates to the qualitative (rather then the quantitative) gravity of core crimes. This has been explained in Chap. 5 by means of the theory of self-delegitimization (auto-deligitimization) which I have already postulated. The link with the State, the fact that such core crimes are generally committed with the connivance of State power, is however just a part of the picture. Merely referring to this link, on its own, is not enough to trigger universal jurisdiction *per se*. What is required is what Andre de Hoogh considers to be a correlative right of the entire international community to compensate for the failure of States which do not investigate and prosecute core crimes.[62] This right becomes less controversial when States which have a primary obligation to investigate and prosecute were directly involved in the commission of the same very crimes which they were obliged to prevent and punish in the first place. It is this correlative right which opens the door for universal jurisdiction. Harmen van der Wilt captures the gist of such conclusions by stating that 'if the State most responsible for suppressing international crimes flouts its obligations, other States, as trustees of the international community, are at least allowed to redress the situation'.[63] In this way the claim of universal jurisdiction gains legitimacy, because it is directly tagged to, and emanates from, original sovereign rights that have been turned into obligations and contributes to a watertight system of international criminal law enforcement. *Pascal Simbikangwa*'s trial is a classical example of the juridical value of the principle of universal jurisdiction. It might not be the best example of the subsidiary nature of universal jurisdiction since Rwanda was willing to prosecute, but it still illustrates subsidiarity since Rwanda's willingness to prosecute was curtailed by serious deficiencies within its juridical framework. The Rwandan, whose case is still *sub iudice*,[64] was not tried by the ICTR because when he was arrested in Mayotte in 2008, the ICTR had already commenced its

---

[61] Jia 2012, p. 1315.

[62] de Hoogh 1996, p. 146.

[63] van der Wilt 2011, p. 1051.

[64] *Cour d'Assises de Paris, 2ème Section* [*Second Chamber of the Criminal Court of Paris], Public Prosecutor v Pascal Senyamuhara Safari (alias Pascal Simbikangwa)*, 14 March 2014, Case No. 13/0033. *Simbikangwa* was convicted of genocide and condemned to twenty-five years of imprisonment (see also Trouille 2016, p. 213, n. 89). His appeal was set to commence before the

completion strategy.[65] Trying *Simbikangwa* before the UN Mechanism for International Criminal Tribunals, though theoretically possible, was not recommended since it would have incremented the obstacles the ICTR was facing in completing its work and satisfying deadlines/timeframes until such time it closes its doors.[66] The ICC has no jurisdiction *rationae temporis* since the Rwandan genocide preceded the entry into force of the ICC Statute, and extradition to Rwanda was rejected by France both for fear of an unfair trial, notwithstanding the abolition of the death penalty in Rwanda and since Rwanda had not criminalized genocide and crimes againsy humanity in 1994 (when the genocide took place).[67] Hence a potential violation of the principle of legality in the requesting State can also act to bar an extradition request. The *Cour de Cassation* decided likewise in the *Muhayimana* case.[68]

(B) The second determining factor emanates from an insufficient reach of international human rights law itself. Where this *corpus juris* is ill-equipped to curb such core crimes and grant a remedy to victims thereof, the applicability of *aut dedere aut judicare*, a form of universal jurisdiction, becomes more cogent and compelling. This is also because it facilitates and allows access to justice in the first place, the protection of which would be stultified when *aut dedere aut judicare* is not undertaken further to an insufficient consideration by international human rights law. There is indeed an intrinsic connection between the suppression of core crimes by international criminal law and the protection of fundamental human rights by international human rights law. Stef Vandeginste appreciates that this link has been best exposed by Anja Seibert-Fohr in her work 'Prosecuting Serious Human Rights Violations', as a result of which she identifies a clear 'role of criminal justice in international human rights protection'.[69] It is consequential to think that if this link is weakened, a bottleneck subsists. As aptly put by Mayeul Hieramente, there is a 'certainly well-founded fear that human rights protection in the hands of the Nation State is far from being guaranteed'.[70] Hieramente, however, whilst scrapping the 'nature of the crime' requirement, advocates a general consensus theory by means of which 'third State prosecutions based on universal jurisdiction can only be deemed legal if it can be established that there is international consensus that every State should have the right to prosecute the crime in question'.[71] He goes as far as

Assize Court of Bobigny on 24 October 2014 (Ntwari 2015) but instead commenced on 24 October 2016 (Ntwari 2015).

[65] Trouille 2016, p. 201.

[66] Trouille 2016, p. 202.

[67] Trouille 2016, pp. 202–209.

[68] *Cour de Cassation, Chambre Criminelle* [Court of Cassation, Criminal Division], France, *Muhayimana*, Judgment No. 810, 26 February 2014, 13-87888, also cited in Trouille 2016, p. 208, n. 69.

[69] Vandeginste 2012, p. 239.

[70] Hieramente 2011, p. 577.

[71] Ibid.

saying that 'once consensus is established even minor crimes could theoretically be prosecuted universally'.[72] I doubt the practicality and validity of this approach. Firstly, one asks, how would States manifest their approval or disapproval, if at all, they intend manifesting it? Secondly, where is the line drawn if most, but not all, UN Member States approve, whereas the only State which disapproves would, for example, be an important UNSC Member State? Thirdly, what if States approve unilaterally but disapprove multi-laterally by means of a resolution of an international organization they form part of. For example, Turkey and Rumania would both approve by means of unilateral declarations of their respective Ministers of Foreign Affairs, but NATO publicly and formally disapproves since a prosecution in Bulgaria (another NATO member, and neighbouring State of both Turkey and Rumania) could have trans-border, detrimental effects whilst seriously endangering regional stability. Finally, what if widespread consensus is not forthcoming? Do we simply say goodbye to universal jurisdiction? These questions may show that Mayeul Hieramente's theory is fraught with difficulties.

(C) The third determining factor identified by the author can be triggered by an understanding, possibly at UN level, that non-prosecution could be tantamount to a threat to the peace. It seems that Mayeul Hieramente accepts this as possible in view of the set-up of the STL.[73] He quotes Bassiouni who acknowledges that if the international community and its core values are put at risk by the way a State addresses the crimes committed, one can legitimately call for international action.[74] Naturally, such international action can take the shape either of a UNSC referral (within the vertical axis) or of a prosecution based upon universal jurisdiction (within the horizontal axis). Such threat to the peace can partake of a more durable and permanent nature if one considers non-prosecution as a breeding ground for future gross human rights violations elsewhere.[75] This third determining factor, therefore, presupposes that deterrence can be made use of in order to maintain international peace and security.

Having explained the doctrinal foundations and pretext of universal jurisdiction in Part II, I advocate that the right of third States (not those enjoying territorial jurisdiction over the core crime, and not those whose national has allegedly committed the core crime) to exercise universal jurisdiction is triggered when the territorial State and/or the State of nationality fails to investigate and/or prosecute core crimes or does not do so properly/diligently. This infers that territorial jurisdiction

[72] Ibid.

[73] Ibid.

[74] Bassiouni 2001, p. 97, cited in Hieramente 2011, p. 577.

[75] For an argument on these lines, see Guénaël Mettraux who, with reference to the *Hadžihasanović* trial judgment [ICTY Trial Chamber, *Prosecutor v Enver Hadžihasanović and Amir Kubura*, 15 March 2006, IT-01-47-T], appropriately held that 'a proven failure to punish crimes may be relevant to establishing a failure to prevent subsequent criminal occurrences by the same group of subordinates' (Mettraux 2009, p. 234).

and the active nationality principle of jurisdiction are predominant in international criminal law.[76] To put this in the context of this book, one must note that this may be said to be the horizontal counterpart of the vertical system. In fact, it is the point at which universal jurisdiction becomes 'analogous to the complementary jurisdiction of the ICC' in so far as it truly serves as a (subsidiary) default mechanism.[77] I will return to subsidiarity at a later stage throughout this chapter. The proposition by means of which third States act as trustees of the international community projects universal jurisdiction as an expression of international solidarity.[78] After all the ICC and bystander States operate as agents of the international community when they intervene to prosecute core crimes.[79]

It is uncontested that customary international law does impose a duty on States to prosecute all core crimes committed within their territorial jurisdiction.[80] It is undisputed that customary international law allows for universal jurisdiction over core crimes[81] although the Supreme Court of Senegal had found that the presence of *Hissène Habré* on Senegalese territory does not by itself suffice as a legal basis to institute criminal proceedings against him for torture committed in the Republic of Chad since Senegalese law does not provide for universal jurisdiction over torture.[82] This partially contrasts with the State obligation, prevailing under CAT, to start investigating irrespective of whether it has custodial jurisdiction over the suspected torturer.[83] Now, this right of third States (not being the territorial State and not being the State of the alleged perpetrator) can move closer to becoming a duty only if and when the territorial State and/or the State of nationality owe the customary international law obligation to investigate and prosecute the core crime in question towards all other third States, *id est* towards the international community. Such *erga omnes* obligations stemming from the general prohibition to engage in core crimes has already been explicitly endorsed in so far as genocide[84] and torture[85] are concerned. Ward Ferdinandusse goes a step further by concluding that both international criminal law and human rights law base the need for punishment on the State customary obligation to prosecute all core crimes, and questions whether such obligation, in and of itself, is a *jus cogens* norm, opining that

---

76 van der Wilt 2011, p. 1048.

77 van der Wilt 2011, p. 1046.

78 Vajda 2010, p. 330.

79 Burens 2016, p. 79.

80 Ambos 1999, pp. 353–354, cited in Ferdinandusse 2006, p. 202, n. 1195.

81 van der Wilt 2011, p. 1049.

82 *Cour Suprême du Sénégal* [Supreme Court, Senegal], *Association des Victimes des Crimes et Répressions Politiques au Tchad (AVCRP) et al. v Hissène Habré*, 20 March 2001, Case No. 14, p. 5.

83 Nowak and McArthur 2008, p. 345.

84 *Barcelona Traction* case, above n. 35, and ICJ, *Reservations to the Convention on the Prevention and Punishment of the Crime of Genocide*, Advisory Opinion, 28 May 1951, 1951-ICJ Reports, p. 15, the latter case being cited in van der Wilt 2000, p. 328.

85 *Prosecutor v Furundžija*, above n. 6, para 151.

'the better view seems to be that the duty does not have *jus cogens* status'.[86] Although it is acknowledged that the duty to abide by *jus cogens* norms applies *erga omnes*,[87] and notwithstanding that 'both concepts are somehow related',[88] it is undisputed (though occasionally rendered unclear in legal literature) that *jus cogens* norms and *erga omnes* obligations are not one and the same thing, but two sides of the same coin.[89] They have different meanings, different scopes and different consequences.[90] The former presupposes a hierarchy and priority of standards, whereas the latter 'refers to the (extended) circle of States having a legal interest in the observance of such obligations'.[91] To this extent, *erga omnes* obligations gel both *jus cogens* norms (which after all prohibit core crimes) and core crimes themselves, because *erga omnes* obligations (like a gravity anchored suspension bridge which connects two steel towers) are the common denominating factor between the two (*id est* between *jus cogens* norms and core crimes). This said, the *aut dedere aut judicare* rule is not, *per se* (in and of itself), *jus cogens*. By being a binding obligation upon States under customary international law, it does not automatically attain *jus cogens* status.[92] This is even more so as a result of its innate lack of a common and uniform obligation that is generalizable to core crimes, a fact which is evident by the different *formulae* which proscribe it, and which shall be considered shortly. This further proves that an *erga omnes* obligation need not necessarily always protect and safeguard a *jus cogens* norm, although some jurists do not endorse such conclusion.[93] It can exist on its own, irrespective of whether the obligation it imposes is linked or otherwise to a *jus cogens* norm. By way of example, the ICJ has declared that the rights of peoples to self-determination is an *erga omnes* right,[94] but does not go on to declare that a corollary of such right is the direct acquisition of *jus cogens* status. Instead, it acknowledges that the right of peoples to self-determination is irreproachable whereas the principle of

[86] Ferdinandusse 2006, p. 183, n. 1084.

[87] van der Wilt 2000, p. 329.

[88] Tams 2005, p. 139.

[89] van der Wilt 2000, p. 329.

[90] Ibid.

[91] Ibid.

[92] However, the converse seems to be true, although Ragazzi is in disagreement (Ragazzi 1997, p. 194). A *jus cogens* norm would inevitably lead to an obligation *erga omnes* [IACmmHR, *Michael Domingues v USA*, 22 October 2002, Report No. 62/02, Case 12.285, para 49; see also Judge Bravo's dissenting opinion in ECtHR, *Sulaiman Al-Adsani v UK*, 21 November 2001, Application No. 35763/97, Reports 2000-XI]. Some jurists have gone much further not only by subscribing to my view but by stating that 'many contend that all customary human rights norms are *erga omnes*' (Lepard 2010, p. 342).

[93] De Hoogh, analysing the *Barcelona Traction* Case, states that 'the Court had the concept of *jus cogens* in mind when speaking of obligations *erga omnes*', whereas Sinclair held, again with reference to the *Barcelona Traction* Case, that 'obligations *erga omnes* are examples of what the Court would consider to be norms of *jus cogens*' (De Hoogh 1996, pp. 55–56; see also Sinclair 1984, p. 213, respectively).

[94] ICJ, *Portugal v Australia* [*East Timor* case], 30 June 1995, ICJ Rep. 1995, p. 90, para 29.

self-determination 'is one of the essential principles of contemporary international law'.[95] Likewise, Guido de Marco, the former President of the forty-fifth session of the UNGA, with reference to the Yugoslav wars, wrote that '*non erano minoranze che volevano fare uno Stato, ma nazioni che volevano fare uno Stato. Questo è il frutto dell'autodeterminazione. E si può realizzare la pace in un popolo e tra i popoli solo se vi è il diritto alla autodeterminazione*'.[96] The discernment between the two has also been accepted by the ILC which has repeatedly drawn a distinction between *jus cogens* norms and *erga omnes* obligations.[97] In other words, whereas *jus cogens* categorically prohibits and outlaws the consummation of the core crime, *erga omnes* relates to the method of enforcing the sanction for the consummation of the core crime. This contrasts with the expansive list of human rights which have been repeatedly associated to *jus cogens* norms within legal literature,[98] which list justifies the categorisation of *jus cogens* norms as 'constitutional norms of the international order'.[99] Such list may be traced jurisprudentially,[100] and has also been endorsed by an influential communitarian regime.[101] It is inconsistent with the contention that even general principles of law[102] can qualify as *jus cogens*.[103]

Therefore, the *erga omnes* nature of the obligation to investigate and prosecute can seem to transform itself into a fully-fledged obligation to extradite or prosecute, into an *aut dedere aut judicare*. It gives rights to multiple States because 'all States are, in a legal sense, injured by the violation'.[104] Although one may perceive that many States should not be effected by a genocide occurring very far away from them (within another continent), Sect. 5.2 has shown how and why all the international community is somehow affected. Therefore, the default of the territorial State or the State of nationality entitles third States to step in without having to give prior notice and without having to seek authorization from the defaulting State. This is the whole thrust of *erga omnes* rules, these being 'those that give third-party States, rather than just the victim, legal claims against States that violate them'.[105]

---

[95] Ibid.

[96] de Marco 2007, p. 17 [There were no minorities which wanted to create a State, but nations. This is the consequence of self-determination. Peace within and amongst peoples is possible only if the right to self-determination is safeguarded: my translation].

[97] Kadelbach 2006, p. 28.

[98] McDougal and others contend that all rights stipulated within the UDHR are norms of *jus cogens* and that they constitute the heart of a global bill of rights (McDougal et al. 1980, p. 274).

[99] Schwobel 2011, p. 39.

[100] Judge Tanaka's dissenting opinion in ICJ, *Ethiopia v South Africa; Liberia v South Africa* [*South West Africa* cases], 18 July 1966, ICJ Rep. 6.

[101] ECFI, Second Chamber (Extended Composition) *Yasin Abdullah Kadi v Council of the European Union and Commission of the European Communities* [2005], 21 September 2005, T-315/01, paras 226–231.

[102] Examples of such principles are the principle of good faith and the requirement of reparation.

[103] For a contrary view, see Byers 1997, pp. 211–223.

[104] Posner 2009, p. 14.

[105] Posner 2009, p. 5.

These third States could be said to be obliged to step in provided they enjoy custodial jurisdiction over an individual suspected of having committed a crime prohibited by a *jus cogens* norm. To this extent, a State 'obligation to retaliate against States that violate *jus cogens* norms' has been identified.[106] It would comport that States could be said to have an obligation to prosecute even if the only possible basis is universal jurisdiction. This might however be too sweeping a statement. Even the complementarity regime which binds ICC State Parties does not oblige State Parties to prescribe universal jurisdiction. This means that 'a State, such as Germany, in the example, is not obliged but rather allowed to prosecute an alleged perpetrator under universal jurisdiction, since there is no internationally recognized obligation to implement universal jurisdiction into their legislative system, even if there may be a trend towards such implementation in some States'.[107] Now if universal jurisdiction is a mere entitlement, rather than a duty, the ensuing conundrum, perceptively noted by Britta Lisa Krings, would entail a prioritization between on the one hand the State wanting to exercise universal jurisdiction (being any State with no connection to the crime) within the horizontal system of enforcement and, on the other hand, another State's right of complementarity. Krings reaches a practical conclusion with which I fully concur. She states that it seems reasonable to consider the State of presence of the alleged perpetrators (the *forum deprehensionis*, the custodial State) as the privileged State to prosecute the perpetrators.[108] Therefore when one State avails itself of its right to undertake a prosecution on the pretext of universal jurisdiction, it does not violate the right of another State to complementarity.[109] In hindsight, it must be noted that the *forum deprehensionis* might not necessarily be the *forum conveniens*, but as Britta Lisa Krings acknowledges, 'in such situations some rule of subsidiary jurisdiction needs to be applied'.[110]

In this context, the stepping in referred to here above assumes the characteristics of a process which might not have been triggered by the third State itself. This is because the third State might be faced with the reality of having a person suspected of core crimes on its own soil. At this point, since it enjoys custodial jurisdiction over such person, it can choose to extradite him to the *forum conveniens*,[111] or to surrender him to the ICC if the case is admissible before the ICC, or else to subject him to prosecution. What it cannot do is leave matters as is, *id est* do absolutely nothing. Leaving such suspected person reside in such third State without, at the

[106] Posner 2009, p. 14.

[107] Rau 2003, p. 214, cited in Krings 2012, p. 761, n. 67.

[108] Krings 2012, p. 762.

[109] Krings 2012, pp. 762–763.

[110] Ibid.

[111] The twelfth legal provision of the ICC Statute, above n. 44, seems to imply, without prejudice to the exercise of universal jurisdiction, that the forum which ought to be given priority should be either the territorial State or the State whose nationals are allegedly involved in the core crime in question. This is also the prevailing position under customary international law (van der Wilt 2011, pp. 1047–1049).

very least, attempting to obtain evidence and information in relation to the crimes he may have committed and/or without consulting with the ICC (if the case is admissible), is not permissible. In fact such third State should first evaluate whether an extradition request is pending. If not, it should determine whether a request for surrender has been made by the ICC. If no extradition and no surrender requests have been made, the third State should seek investigative material with an eye to subject the suspect to prosecution, and at the very least preserve any existing evidence.

It is to be noted that, at the beginning of the preceding paragraph, the above argument is predicated upon a crucial premise. This premise entails that the obligation to investigate and prosecute is a customary international law obligation. Naturally, where the *aut dedere aut judicare rule* is conventionally proscribed, the State obligation clearly subsists as a result of ratification of the particular treaty. It is only in the absence of such stipulation that one must gauge whether a customary international law obligation to investigate and prosecute such core crimes subsists or otherwise. The analysis as to whether such State obligation anyway derives from customary international law or otherwise is of such a focal nature to my book that it may be said to pervade it. It is however more marked in this chapter and in Chap. 15, although the prevailing State practice which deals with the grounds for refusal of extradition (to be dealt with in Chap. 16) points, quite incontrovertibly, to such a customary international law obligation. This does not mean that State obligations derive exclusively from customary international law. Extra-territorial jurisdiction and the Genocide Convention can co-exist. In *Public Prosecutor v Duško Cvjetković*,[112] the first trial by a domestic court exercising universal jurisdiction over the ethnic violence in the Balkans in the beginning of the 1990s, the Austrian Supreme Court upheld that universal jurisdiction is compatible with the purposes [rather than the text] of the Genocide Convention. Similarly, in *Public Prosecutor v Jorgić*, the German Federal Supreme Court[113] analysed the text of the Genocide Convention to conclude that, having failed to mention certain forms of jurisdiction, no mandatory universal jurisdiction to prosecute is thereby imposed. However universal jurisdiction, a ground of jurisdiction established in the landmark *Eichmann case* (which moved the law forward on the question of universal jurisdiction, effectively setting aside the narrow jurisdictional frame set by the Genocide Convention),[114] was permissible since the underlying object and purpose of the Genocide Convention presupposes a principle of jurisdiction the function of which 'is precisely to close all loopholes in the prosecution of crimes against the

[112] *Oberste Gerichtshof* [Supreme Court], Vienna, Austria, *Public Prosecutor v Cvjetković*, Judgment on Interlocutory Appeal Upholding Jurisdiction, 13 July 1994, 150s99/94. The trial judgment was delivered by Salzburg Court [*Landesgericht* {Trial Court}, Salzburg, Austria *Public Prosecutor v Cvjetković*, Acquittal, 31 May 1995, 150s99/94].

[113] *Bundesgerichtshof* [German Federal Supreme Court], *Public Prosecutor v Nikola Jorgić*, 30 April 1999, 2 BvR 1290/99.

[114] ווילעה טפשמה תיב [Supreme Court], Israel, *Attorney-General of Israel v Adolf Eichmann*, 29 May 1962, Criminal Appeal 336/61, and Schabas 2013a, p. 667.

fundamental legal interests of the community of States'.[115] The Constitutional Court confirmed the *Jorgić* judgment on appeal.[116] More prominently and on the same stratagem, *Unión Progresista de Fiscales de España et al. v Pinochet*[117] has led to various legal actions to this effect and on this pretext in Chile itself. However, it was qualified by a subsequent decision[118] which, in terms of Article VI of the Genocide Convention which imposes *subsidiaridad*,[119] limited the exercise of universal jurisdiction over genocide on the ground that Spanish jurisdiction is subsidiary to the jurisdiction of the territorial State. Harmen van der Wilt juxtaposes that subsidiary universal jurisdiction emanates from the primary obligations of the territorial State or the State of the perpetrator, to initiate criminal investigations and the prosecution of core crimes. Such States owe their obligation towards the entire international community. To this extent such obligations are *erga omnes*. What triggers the exercise of universal jurisdiction is the 'inadequate performance by the States bearing prior responsibility' to investigate and prosecute.[120] In fact subsidiary universal jurisdiction, which denotes that 'priority of prosecution should be given to the States having a direct link to the crimes due to the territoriality or nationality of the perpetrator, is in the process of developing into a rule of customary international law'.[121] Cedric Ryngaert also notes that important treaties, such as the CAT, do not prioritise between grounds of jurisdiction which States ought to exercise.[122] He favours (and I concur), on the premise of State practice,[123] a customary law principle of subsidiarity before States effectively exercise universal jurisdiction.[124] In practice, by virtue of subsidiarity, universal jurisdiction becomes exercisable only when the State enjoying territorial jurisdiction (or another ground of jurisdiction, excluding universal jurisdiction itself) is unable or unwilling to

---

115 *Public Prosecutor v Nikola Jorgić*, above n. 113, para 39.

116 *Bundesverfassungsgericht* [Federal Constitutional Court, 4th Chamber of the Second Senate, Germany], *Public Prosecutor v Nikola Jorgić*, 12 December 2000, 2 BvR 1290/99.

117 *Audiencia Nacional* [Criminal Chamber, Plenary Session] Spain, *Unión Progresista de Fiscales de España et al. v. Pinochet, 5* November 1998 (see also Brody and Ratner 2000, pp. 95–107).

118 *Audiencia Nacional*, Spain, *Rigoberta Menchu Tum et al. v Ríos Montt et al. (Guatemala Genocide* case), 13 December 2000, 331/99.

119 This term, used by the *Audiencia Nacional*, means 'subsidiarity'.

120 van der Wilt 2011, abstract at p. 1043.

121 Burens 2016, p. 77.

122 Ryngaert 2005, pp. 600–601.

123 He cites Belgian [Belgium's Law Concerning the Repression of Grave Breaches of the Geneva Conventions (1878) as amended on 18 July 2001 (*Loi Portant Modification de l'Article 12bis de la Loi du 17 avril 1878 Contenant le Titre Préliminaire du Code de Procedure Pénale*) and on 7 August 2003 (*Loi relative aux violations graves du droit international humanitaire*)] and German legislation {para 153(f) of the *Strafprozeßordnung* [Code of Criminal Procedure], Germany (1987)}, although in so far as the latter is concerned, such subsidiarity principle only applies to crimes under international humanitarian law (Ryngaert 2005, pp. 602–605).

124 Ryngaert 2005, p. 601.

prosecute core crimes.[125] This determines the jurisdictional priority of the territorial State in case of competing jurisdictional claims and reminds us of the complementarity principle which prevails within the ICC regime (dealt with in Part III).[126] It comes as no surprise that 'subsidiary universal jurisdiction is also called "horizontal complementarity" if similar requirements to Article 17 of the ICC Statute are applied'.[127] Although it may be premature to uphold that the subsidiarity principle is required by international law, 'it clearly serves as a restraining device, allowing for the exercise of jurisdiction only where the most interested State unduly fails to live up to its responsibilities'.[128] Vertical complementarity, juxtaposed in Part III of this book, can thus be used to define subsidiarity[129] which is being dealt with under Part IV. This further shows how the vertical system of enforcement can provide a frame of reference for the horizontal system of enforcement and justifies why it precedes the horizontal system of enforcement in my book. The latter may feel deprived of the counterpart of the admissibility test, since there is no universally agreed mechanism to determine whether a State is unable or unwilling to prosecute, but a hotchpotch of ill-equipped provisions sporadically placed within extradition laws, extradition treaties, domestic legislation and State practice. The fact that extradition laws protect human rights of the extraditee but largely fail to consider the exigencies for the effective prosecution of core crimes[130] convolutes the scenario. Nor is there a mechanism to determine whether, when a State is willing to prosecute, it will conduct such proceedings diligently. Furthermore, no judicial framework on a global level is in place to decipher whether a State has prosecuted genuinely or otherwise. All this is left in the hands of States involved within an extradition request. This state of affairs may call for a special (*ad hoc*) mechanism (possibly an International Chamber of Horizontal Complementarity) which delves into the above mentioned matters. Such judicial institution could:

1. function as a counterpart of the ICC Pre-Trial Chamber within the horizontal system of enforcement;
2. develop its objective criteria to prioritize jurisdictional claims without jeopardizing the *corpus juris* which encompasses what may be termed as 'International Extradition Law';
3. define the scope of the phrase 'unwilling and unable', in turn assisting the ICC in its lengthy admissibility procedure; and
4. relocate the decision-making power to determine the admissibility of a case from the *nexus*-State (which, as seen in Part II, usually has blood on its hands) to an independent and impartial judicial institution.

---

[125] Roht-Arriaza 2007, p. 117.

[126] Ryngaert 2005, p. 601.

[127] Kleffner 2003, p. 109, cited in Burens 2016, p. 79, n. 12.

[128] Ryngaert 2015, p. 69.

[129] Geneuss 2013, p. 179, cited by Burens 2016, p. 79, n. 14.

[130] Burens 2016, pp. 89–90.

This suggested framework would not burden the ICC with more tasks (as suggested in so far as ICC State Parties are concerned),[131] nor would it project the ICJ as a final arbiter to apply horizontal complementarity once it is duly codified conventionally between ICC State Parties or once it is open to non-State Parties, as suggested by Laura Burens.[132] It would also circumvent the need for the forum State to cater for mechanisms intended to incentivise compliance by the *nexus*-State.

One must further note, however, that only the CAT and the four Geneva Conventions directly provide for a repressive system which envisages an *aut dedere aut judicare*-based universal jurisdiction.[133] The latter Conventions regularly contain various State undertakings, including the penalization of crimes, the promulgation of legislation for such purpose, the establishment of certain forms of jurisdiction and the exercise of that same jurisdiction. The penalization of such crimes on a domestic level has wide ramifications which are relevant to this study. If a core crime is a domestic crime, when the State in question has jurisdiction over such crimes penalized by treaties it has ratified, that State acquires jurisdiction not only over crimes in *aut dedere aut judicare* treaties but also over treaties which do not contain an express obligation to exercise universal jurisdiction.[134] In sum, *aut dedere aut judicare* is a qualified *erga omnes* obligation owing to the nature of core crimes as crimes under customary international law. This first reason must be supplemented by another two reasons which shall be considered now.

(2) Secondly, *jus cogens* norms,[135] though still controversial,[136] encapsulate binding, not merely persuasive, obligations. The ICJ taught that 'obligations *erga omnes* may derive, in general, from the principles and rules concerning the basic rights of the human person'.[137] In other words, rules and principles cause obligations. Such duties originate from fundamental human rights, because these basic rights, in turn, derive from high moral and ethical values which are inalienable. Therefore, such obligation stems directly from the rights and dignity inherently enjoyed by the very fact that human beings are humans. *Qua* humans they are the *aventi diritto*, the holders of such vested and acquired

[131] Kreß 2006, p. 584f, n. 111, cited in Burens 2016, p. 92, n. 68.

[132] Burens 2016, pp. 92–93.

[133] The State obligation to bring persons, regardless of their nationality, before its own courts constitutes a form of universal jurisdiction (Henzelin 2000, pp. 351–356). Vanessa Thalmann reaches the same conclusion although she does so predominantly with reference to the *travaux préparatoires* of the four Geneva Conventions (Thalmann 2009, p. 252).

[134] AI 2011, p. 9.

[135] For an objective analysis of the meaning of *jus cogens*, of the source of such norms and of their content, see Stephens 2004, pp. 247–255.

[136] Linderfalk 2009, p. 963.

[137] *Barcelona Traction* case, above n. 35, paras 33–34.

rights, the recipients of the fulfilment of State obligations.[138] To an extent, in so far as the prosecution of core crimes is concerned, this compelling overtone is the mettle which the *aut dedere aut judicare* rule is made of, the same moral underpinning which is the antecedent of its power and the guarantor of its legitimacy. These hierarchically superior and self-evident values override other principles, norms and rules to attain the status of *jus cogens*, nowadays recognised by an overwhelming number of States which are signatories to the VCLT, the fifty-third article of which relates specifically to *jus cogens*. Birgit Schlutter acknowledges that 'customary international criminal law is often cited as containing so-called norms of "universal" international law, that is, norms which are of a high normative value, which contain rules of a high moral character'.[139] Tom Obokata synthesises my above mentioned first two reasons [grounds] by stating that the prohibition of core crimes is 'firmly established in customary international law, and constitutes *jus cogens*'.[140] Establishing a connection between the hierarchy-driven *jus cogens* norms and the relations-driven obligations *erga omnes*, Maurizio Ragazzi appropriately notes that 'like obligations *erga omnes*, norms of *jus cogens* are meant to protect the common interests of States and basic moral values', that the 'classical examples of norms of *jus cogens* which emerged during the codification of the law of treaties largely coincide with the examples of obligations *erga omnes* given in the *Barcelona Traction* case' and finally that 'characteristic expressions attaching to the concept of *jus cogens* (such as the international community "as a whole") occur also in the International Court's *dictum* on obligations *erga omnes*'.[141] In fact 'the *Barcelona Traction* case which expressly refers to *erga omnes* obligations is often also cited as a reference for *jus cogens*'.[142] The prominent *nexus* between *jus cogens* and *erga omnes* was expounded by Randall's logical *formula*,[143] by means of which what is compelling law must necessarily engender an obligation flowing to all. Such *formula* was however deemed to be simplistic and circular.[144] It seems that, with the exception of the points raised by myself here above, Payam Akhavan's conclusions are fitting

[138] Sergio Cotta firmly holds '*dove c'è l'uomo c'è il diritto*'. {where there is man, there is law: my translation}. He adds that *'parallelamente, ma secondo un ordine roversciato, si riscontra che dove c'è il diritto, c'è l'uomo. Non soltanto per la banale constatazione estrinseca che l'uomo è l'oggetto, e il destinatario, delle prescrizioni giuridiche "poste"; bensì per una ragione più profonda: per la oggettiva logica interna alla giuridicità'* {In parallel, but by reverse order, where there is law, there is man. This is not only due to the intrinsic conclusion that man is the object and beneficiary of the legal provisions, but for a more significant reason: this being the objective and internal logic of legality itself: my translation} (Cotta 1997, p. 111).

[139] Schlutter 2010, p. 3.

[140] Obokata 2010, p. 30.

[141] Ragazzi 1997, p. 72.

[142] Kadelbach 2006, p. 26.

[143] Randall 1988, p. 785.

[144] Bassiouni 1996, p. 72.

when he concedes that 'the jurisprudence thus far only suggests that *jus cogens* status gives rise to a right to prosecute based on universal jurisdiction, but not a duty'.[145]

(3) Thirdly if a core crime is protected by a *jus cogens* norm and is subject to universal jurisdiction[146] also further to it being a crime under customary international law, it is *ipso facto*, exercisable *erga omnes*[147] unless the prosecution of such crime somehow domestically conflicts with the constitutionally-entrenched principle of *nullum crimen sine lege*. Such conflict is highly improbable given the nature of ordinary crimes punishable as core crimes, for example, murder and bodily harm. Whereas the act or mode of conduct might be domestically designated with a different nomenclature, the act or mode of conduct still constitutes a domestic crime and is punishable as such. Core crimes are, after all, 'municipal crimes subject to municipal criminal law'.[148] The conflict may potentially subsist only rarely in crimes, such as enforced disappearance, where the rules of customary international law might seem inconsistent with the strict requirements necessary as a basis for the conviction of individuals municipally. The customary law[149] element is therefore crucial. This is particularly so for two underlying reasons, the first of which is a corollary of the above stated:

   (i) *aut dedere aut judicare*-based jurisdiction may become a form of universal jurisdiction if the underlying crime constitutes a violation of *jus cogens*.[150] In fact, 'the duty to prosecute or extradite (*aut dedere aut judicare)* applies to international crimes and more particularly to *jus cogens* crimes';[151] and
   (ii) by means of sufficient time and State practice, it may be argued that universal jurisdiction over certain crimes, including hostage-taking and hijacking,[152] has passed onto customary international law as a result of

---

145 Akhavan 2010, p. 1259.

146 Universal jurisdiction is presumptively lawful provided that no prohibitive rule to the contrary has crystallized [PCIJ Twelfth Ordinary Session, *Case of S.S. Lotus (France v Turkey)*, 7 September 1927, PCIJ Series A, no. 10].

147 'The difference between a customary universal jurisdiction and a conventional one is merely one of range of application: one is valid *erga omnes*, the other possibly only *inter partes*' (Kolb 2004, p. 253).

148 Lee 2010, p. 15.

149 Claus Kreß suggests that the desire of the international community to defeat impunity may be 'seen as a strong indication in favour of a customary State competence to exercise universal jurisdiction' (Kreß 2006, p. 573).

150 Randall 1988, p. 821.

151 Bassiouni 2008a, p. 483.

152 See, *inter alia,* USA District Court, District of Columbia, *USA v Fawaz Yunis*, 12 February 1988, 681 F.Supp. 896 (D.D.C. 1988) Crim. A No. 87-0377; USA District Court for the Southern District of New York, *USA v Ramzi Ahmed Yousef et al*, 29 May 1996, 927 F.Supp. 673 (S.D.N.Y.

> State acquiescence[153] by virtue of the absence of international protest[154] against the exercise of such jurisdiction over nationals of States which are not necessarily parties to the treaties penalizing such conduct.[155] It may thus be stated that 'in view of the widespread State practice as to the exercise of universal jurisdiction over core crimes, such jurisdiction is lawful under customary international law'.[156] Lord Slynn of Hadley, in the *Pinochet* case, went as far as noting that 'universality of jurisdiction is subject to customary international law rules'.[157] Paradoxically universal jurisdiction depends, to a large extent, as shown here above, upon State practice, but State practice renders universal jurisdiction not homogeneous. This is because 'States are entitled to grant their own courts universal jurisdiction over certain crimes as a result of a national decision.... Consequently, the universal jurisdiction principle is not uniformly applied everywhere'.[158] This, *in partem*, explains why no international convention dealing with universal jurisdiction,[159] though desirable for the sake of legal certainty, is in place.

The above sequential frame of thought finds support in the (widely criticised) judgment of the Tribunal of First Instance of Brussels[160] which upheld that 'as a matter of customary international law, or even more strongly as a matter of *jus cogens*, universal jurisdiction over crimes against humanity exists, authorizing national judicial authorities to prosecute and punish the perpetrators in all circumstances'.[161] Most significantly, by linking the above mentioned concepts, the Brussels Tribunal of First Instance upheld that:

1996), S12 93 Cr.180 (KTD); USA Court of Appeals, District of Columbia Circuit, *USA v Omar Mohammed Ali Rezaq*, 6 February 1998, 134 F.3d 1121 (D.C. Cir. 1998), 96-3127.

153 Watson notes that it is indeed difficult to determine whether a government has, in fact, acquiesced to another government's actions or practices (Watson 1993, p. 39).

154 Zimmerman upholds that 'no State has with regard to the exercise of universal jurisdiction concerning genocide, crimes against humanity or war crimes, so far acted as a persistent objector' (Zimmermann 2006, p. 353). One must also remember that the tacit acquiescence of a State is relevant for the purposes of such State practice.

155 Morris 2001, p. 64.

156 Ryngaert 2008a, p. 117.

157 Poels 2005, p. 69.

158 Philippe 2006, p. 379.

159 The complexity surrounding universal jurisdiction is accentuated by its very nature. Alexander Poels, a supporter of universal jurisdiction *in absentia*, distinguishes between 'unilateral universal jurisdiction', 'delegated universal jurisdiction' and absolute universal jurisdiction' (Poels 2005, pp. 67–69). The latter term is defined as 'universal jurisdiction which does not require the prosecuting State to have the alleged perpetrator in custody...' (Kluwen 2017, p. 37)

160 Tribunal of First Instance of Brussels, *Aguilar Diaz et al. v Pinochet*, Order, 6 November 1998.

161 *Aguilar Diaz et al. v Pinochet*, above n. 160, para 288.

> We find that, before being codified in treaty or statute, the prohibition of crimes against humanity was part of customary international law and of international *jus cogens*, and this norm imposes imperatively an *erga omnes* on our domestic legal order....The general principle of international law *aut dedere aut judicare* imports the necessity of combating impunity of crimes under international law and the responsibility of State authorities to ensure punishment of such crimes irrespective of the place of commission.[162]

UNSC resolutions point in the same direction when they require States to deny safe havens.[163] It must be clarified that this does not mean that *jus cogens* and customary international law are one and the same thing. This is not the case, although Kennedy terms *jus cogens* as a 'super-customary norm',[164] Klein refers to it as 'super-customary law',[165] whereas D'Amato inappropriately equates customary international law to *jus cogens*.[166] The net effect of the above mentioned is that once it is protected by a *jus cogens* norm and once it is subject to universal jurisdiction, States are vested with an obligation *erga omnes* to extradite or prosecute those who have allegedly committed such crime, that is, to implement the *aut dedere aut judicare* rule.[167] These may be said to constitute sequential steps in the argument postulating the obligation to fulfil the *aut dedere aut judicare* rule. Indeed, the fact that it can be prosecuted on the basis of universal jurisdiction need not necessarily emerge from its *jus cogens* status. South African legal expert John Dugard, appointed by the Amsterdam Court of Appeals in the case of Surinam commander *Desi Bouterse*, found, in the year 2000, that torture was a crime under customary international law and that customary international law authorised universal jurisdiction over torture.[168] Though the *Hoge Raad* (the Dutch Supreme Court) circumvented the issue whether torture, way back in 1982, was a crime under customary international law by finding that customary international law could not prevail over contrary domestic law pursuant to Article 94 of the Dutch Constitution,[169] Dugard's conclusions must be kept in mind in so far as they constitute a detailed exposition of the status and position of torture under international criminal law.

---

162 *Aguilar Diaz et al. v Pinochet*, above n. 160, cited in Paust et al. 2007, p. 139.

163 Article 2(c) of UNSC (2001) Resolution 1373 (2001), UN Doc. S/RES/1373.

164 Kennedy 1987, cited in Hossain 2005, p. 79.

165 Klein 1988, p. 351.

166 D'Amato 1971, cited in Bassiouni 1996, p. 275, n. 17 and in Bassiouni 2008b, p. 14.

167 Some jurists have gone a step further positing that in the future, international criminal law is most likely to be enforced neither by the ICC nor by States enjoying territorial jurisdiction but by third States willing to prosecute (Jeßberger and Powell 2001, pp. 347 et. seq.; Sands 2003, pp. 40 et seq.).

168 Court of Appeal, Amsterdam, *R. Wijngaarde and R.A.L. Hoost v Desiré Delano Bouterse*, Order of 20 November 2000, LJN: AA8395, cited in *Nederlands Juristenblad*, 2001, p. 51, reprinted in NYIL (2001) Vol. 32, pp. 278–279.

169 *Hoge Raad* [Supreme Court], the Netherlands, *Prosecutor-General of the Supreme Court v Desiré Delano Bouterse*, 18 September 2001, LJN: AB1471, cited in *NYIL* (2001) Vol. 32, pp. 287–292.

A partial differentiation to the above submission could also lead to a correct conclusion. Rather than the fact that the core crime is prosecutable under universal jurisdiction renders the core crime subject to *erga omnes* State obligations, the inverse could also be true. In other words, it is the *erga omnes* nature of the State obligations, derivative from its *jus cogens* status, which triggers universal jurisdiction. To this extent, 'the *Barcelona Traction dictum* has nevertheless entered legal folk-culture as an authorization for wide-ranging protection of human rights, including universal jurisdiction'.[170] Therefore, the following steps can be identified. If a crime violates a *jus cogens* norm, it presupposes a concomitant *obligatio erga omnes* of States to extradite or prosecute the perpetrator, with the latter (the prosecution) occuring on the most favourable jurisdictional pretext such as territorial, active nationality or passive nationality, *id est* by the State best qualified[171] to engage in criminal proceedings by undertaking such prosecution, and failing either such jurisdictional pretext or such engagement, on the basis of universal jurisdiction. On a similar vein, the *IDI* found that there exists 'a universal criminal jurisdiction for genocide, crimes against humanity, and war crimes' and 'the forum State should carefully consider any extradition request from a State having a significant link with the crime, offender, or victim'.[172]

At this stage, two divergent views should be noted since they enrich one's understanding of the matter under scrutiny. George Fletcher, a prominent opponent of universal jurisdiction, in a thought-provoking and concise article which just exceeds only four pages, opines that such disconnected jurisdiction violates the *ne bis in idem* rights of accused persons. In his words, 'there is no guarantee whatsoever against hounding an accused in one court after another until the victims are satisfied that justice has been done'.[173] Albin Eser tackles each and every point raised by Fletcher, rebutting such points in a comprehensive twenty-four page article which, in my view, raises various valid reasons. He concedes that the 'parallel assumption of universal jurisdiction by national courts on the same crime can lead to an overlapping of concurrent national jurisdictions with the risk of international conflicts'.[174] However, he shows that the concerns raised by Fletcher would apply anyway even when universal jurisdiction is not invoked. These concerns subsist when concurrent national jurisdictions strive to exercise legal authority and control over an individual.[175] He forcefully argues that international criminal law, including the ICC Statute, or better, especially the ICC Statute, prohibit double jeopardy and sufficiently protect accused individuals from such contingency.[176] He identifies ways how the *ne bis in idem*

[170] Luban 2004, p. 135.

[171] The term 'best qualified' is habitually used by Harmen van der Wilt in his writings (van der Wilt 2000, p. 334).

[172] *IDI* 2006, pp. 297–301, cited in Webb 2012, pp. 116–117, n. 16.

[173] Fletcher 2003, p. 582.

[174] Eser 2004, p. 976.

[175] Eser 2004, pp. 957–958 and 965.

[176] Eser 2004, pp. 961–963.

protection would not be misused or abused. The nullification of an acquittal if it was procured by fraud and/or collusion is just one of them.[177] He disagrees with Fletcher's views that the American double jeopardy standards are more comprehensive than those of their European counterparts,[178] and, with reference to the *Rodney King* case,[179] he explains that 'a prior State prosecution is no bar to a federal prosecution, and vice-versa'.[180] I appreciate the concerns expressed by a Cardozo Professor of Jurisprudence, whose epic work entitled 'Rethinking Criminal Law' merits praise. However, rather on a conceptual level, I question the basis upon which Fletcher's presumptive order of priorities places the accused before the victim, the State and the international community. I glean Fletcher's intrinsic distrust of the ICC and of various national criminal justice systems, a distrust one may objectively tag as disproportionate and maybe even rather unfair, especially when one recalls that a representative of the ABA acknowledged that 'the Treaty of Rome contains the most comprehensive list of due process protections which has so far been promulgated'.[181] Part III demonstrated the veracity of such statement. Yet again on a conceptual level, Fletcher seems to value the *ne bis in idem* rule as an absolute right, as the very apex and culmination of the pyramid which he considers to be a 'presumptive order of priorities'.[182] However, it does not seem to cross his mind whether he should ask a question before indulging into such prioritisation. Fletcher seems to fail to ask himself whether, in the face of core crimes, the *ne bis in idem* rule should apply in the first place, instead of whether it is sufficiently safeguarded when universal jurisdiction is invoked. The fact that, in the context of 'abuse of process', 'the interest in effectively prosecuting the core international crimes outweights any messiness left behind',[183] should have led Fletcher (at least) to contemplate (though not necessarily to concur with or share) such contingency. Taking for granted the application of, and/or the need to apply, *ne bis in idem* at all costs defeats the fight against impunity (of and for which universal jurisdiction is probably the main tool) which permeates contemporary international criminal law and which the ICC Statute, as seen in the previous Part of this book, makes great strides in addressing.

Rod Rastan's work mirrors the above mentioned sequential steps. He states that 'the offender is treated as an outlaw, an enemy of all mankind – *hostis humanis generis*- whom any nation may in the interest of all capture and punish. This echoes the well-known dictum in the *Barcelona Traction* case regarding the observance of

---

177 Eser 2004, pp. 968–969.

178 Eser 2004, p. 970.

179 District Court for the Central District of California, Los Angeles, California, USA, *The State v Sergeant Stacey Koon, Officer Theodore J. Briseno, Officer Timothy E. Wind, Officer Laurence Powell, (Rodney King* case), 29 April 1992. In this case police officers, after having been acquitted by a Californian jury of beating *Rodney King* nearly to death, were subsequently retried and convicted by a federal court (Herman 1994, cited in Eser 2004, pp. 968–969, n. 74).

180 Eser 2004, p. 968.

181 Eser 2004, p. 963.

182 Fletcher 2003, p. 581.

183 Currie 2007, p. 370.

obligations *erga omnes*. A limited number of crimes attract universal jurisdiction'.[184] Such steps are not however, automatic. Nor are they mandatory and uncontested. Bassiouni, an ardent advocate of *jus cogens* and *obligatio erga omnes*, admitted that:

> The practice of States evidences that, more often than not, impunity has been allowed for *jus cogens* crimes, the theory of universality has been far from being universally recognized and applied, and the duty to prosecute or extradite is more inchoate than established, other than when it arises out of specific treaty obligations.[185]

However, Kenneth Randall sustains a progressive argument to the effect that, when committed by individuals, violations of *erga omnes* obligatons and peremptory norms 'may be punishable by any State under the universality principle'.[186] In the light of the case-law which shall be considered in Chap. 16, it seems that what Randall stated before the new millennium stands on relatively solid ground today because State practice has started to reveal that *jus cogens* violations do not only allow for the assertion of universal jurisdiction, but instead seem to require it. In Cedric Ryngaert's words, this escalation requires a 'moral leap'.[187] Cedric Ryngaert cites works of Paust, Bassiouni, Wise, Myers and Bottini to draw the attention of his readers to the fact that 'it has been argued that States have the authority to exercise universal jurisdiction over core crimes on the basis of the *jus cogens* character of the prohibition of "core crimes". It has even been submitted that the prosecution of violations of *jus cogens* is itself endowed with the status of *jus cogens*'.[188] He also objectively presents the counter-argument to this which is based upon a strict reading of the VCLT and upon State practice, as a result of which 'not many States have acted upon the purported obligation to exercise universal jurisdiction over violations of *jus cogens*, nor actually acted upon conventional obligations to exercise universal jurisdiction over such violations'.[189] Favouring the latter view rather than the former, he suggests that 'even if they have exercised universal jurisdiction, they have ordinarily done so by attaching a string of restraining conditions (most notably the presence requirement), and by excluding the principle of mandatory prosecution'.[190] However, he legitimises universal jurisdiction over core crimes by acknowledging that because any State is expected to prevent and punish core crimes, 'their being amenable to universal jurisdiction may not spark international protest'.[191] Weeramantry, precluding a persistent objector from undermining universal customary norms, goes as far as stating that 'one does not need to go all the way up to the level of *jus cogens* to achieve the

---

184 Rastan 2010, p. 123.

185 Bassiouni 1996, p. 66.

186 Randall 1988, p. 821.

187 Ryngaert 2008a, p. 113.

188 Ryngaert 2008a, p. 112.

189 Ibid.

190 Ryngaert 2008a, p. 113.

191 Ryngaert 2008a, p. 115.

result of a universally binding rule'.[192] By way of parenthesis, universality may be said to find reinforcement in various religions.[193] In this context, Shelton confers that the *leitmotif* and *raison d'être* of categorizing a norm as *jus cogens* is 'to override the will of persistent objectors to a norm of customary international law'.[194] However, in practice, in as much as customary international law is important to identify *jus cogens* norms, such norms, in turn, are more likely to affect conventional international law by invalidating treaties rather than affecting customary international law itself. Lepard argues that the recognition of *jus cogens*, to an extent, is reflective of those who support customary international law.[195] This may be said to emerge from the *Nicaragua dictum*[196] which implied that to determine the status of a customary norm as *jus cogens*, State views and State practice must be considered. Similarly, in order to identify *erga omnes* obligations, the usual method is to analyse State practice with respect to cases in which States not directly affected by an international wrong took counter-measures without being held liable for a wrongful act themselves.[197]

In truth, however, in as much as they are constantly shrouded by controversy, *jus cogens* norms, besides being mysterious, might not be so compelling in nature. Suffice to recall that the ILC, in its commentary on the rules of the VCLT, acknowledged that 'there is no simple criterion by which to identify a general rule of international law as having the character of *jus cogens*'.[198] Additionally, Asia, the most densely populated continent with just under five thousand million

[192] Weeramantry 2004, p. 226.

[193] Lepard notes that the *Bhgavad-Gita*, the most revered book in Hinduism, refers to a united world, the Hebrew Scriptures speak of one Father and one God, Buddhists demand that human beings should care for others as a mother protects her child, Christianity requests the love of neighbours as oneself, whereas the *Qur'an* preaches that all of humanity was one community wherein the whole universe is the family of *Allah* (Lepard 2010, pp. 80–81). This rather spiritual, ethical note should not be construed so as to minimise the sharp differences prevailing between criminal justice systems. Professors of Stanford University, for example, held that 'the People's Republic of China provides an example of a society with a set of values very different from ours, where self-criticism is the norm and a privilege against self-incrimination would be unthinkable' (Cohen and Danelski 1997, p. 815). Moreover, the revised version of the Arab Charter on Human Rights (2004), signed in Tunis on 22 May 2004, in Article 3(3), refers to Islamic *Sharī'ah* {شريعة} and other divine laws (Akram 2006, translated by Al-Midani and Cabanettes, p. 151).

[194] Shelton 2014, p. 172.

[195] Lepard 2010, p. 244.

[196] ICJ, *Case Concerning Military and Paramilitary Activities in and Against Nicaragua (Nicaragua v United States of America)* [*Nicaragua* Case], 27 June 1986, ICJ Rep. 1986, p. 14, para 190.

[197] ILC 2000, paras 386 et seq.

[198] ILC 1996, pp. 247–248. This has not stopped commentators from developing their own criteria for the establishment of peremptory norms (see the seven criteria postulated in Criddle and Fox-Decent 2009, pp. 361–362).

people,[199] does not have a counterpart to the three regional human rights mechanisms. An objective glance at this dichotomy, encompassing on the one hand the naturalist school of thought, and on the other hand, the positivistic school of thought should attract interest. However, since this work is not intended to scrutinize such dichotomy from a philosophy of law viewpoint, I shall not be considering such publications.[200] In this context, Theodor Meron objectively admits that the process of choosing which rights are more important than others, which rights override others, which rights prevail over others, which rights are superior to others, 'is fraught with personal, cultural and political bias'.[201] It is, occasionally, also evident that certain State declarations, actions and inactions have political underpinnings. For example, in 'the constructive dialogue with the Committee the United Kingdom also took the opportunity to express the position that it regarded the detention conditions at Guantanamo as unacceptable, but stopped short of recognizing the applicability of the Convention Against Torture to them'.[202] The Bavarian *Oberlandesgericht*, making a clear statement, referred to the need to show the international community that Germany does not shelter those who commit core crimes.[203] The same may be said in relation to the politically-oriented March 2009 'Bush six'[204] criminal complaints. In this case the Sixth Central Court for Preliminary Criminal Proceedings[205] was called upon to evaluate the jurisdiction of Spain over the 'Bush six' for alleged violations of the Geneva Conventions and the CAT by virtue of participation or facilitation of torture and other cruel, inhuman and/or degrading treatment of detainees at the USA detention facility at Guantanamo Bay.[206] The 'Bush Six' case followed the landmark judgment of the Supreme Court of the USA which determined that Guantanamo detainees enjoy the

---

[199] See http://www.nationsonline.org/oneworld/world_population.htm. Accessed 12 January 2015

[200] Maritain 2012; Finnis 2011; Kramer 2003; Campbell 2004.

[201] Meron 1986, p. 4.

[202] UN Committee Against Torture 2004, paras 41–42, cited in Gondek 2009, p. 251.

[203] Bavarian High Court (*Oberlandesgericht*), Munich, *Novislav Djajic case,* 23 May 1997, 2 St 20/96, 51 *Neue Jusistische Wochenschrisft* (1998), p. 392.

[204] David Addington (former Counsel to, and Chief of Staff for, former Vice President Cheney); Jay S. Bybee (former Assistant Attorney General, Office of Legal Counsel (OLC), U.S. Department of Justice {DOJ}); Douglas Feith (former under Secretary of Defence for Policy, Department of Defence {DOD}); Alberto R. Gonzales (former Counsel to former President George W. Bush, and former Attorney General of the USA); William J. Haynes (former General Counsel, DOD); and John Yoo (former Deputy Assistant Attorney General, OLC, DOJ).

[205] *Juzgado Central de Instrucción* No. 006 [Sixth Central Court for Preliminary Criminal Proceedings], Madrid, Spain, *Bush Six* case, 13 April 2011.

[206] DomCLIC (2016) http://www.asser.nl/default.aspx?site_id=36&level1=15248&level2=&level3=&textid=40126. Accessed 13 July 2016. A report revealed findings of torture in Guantanamo Bay detention facilities. http://www.independent.co.uk/news/world/americas/cia-torture-report-timeline-from-911-to-dianne-feinsteins-findings-9913178.html. Accessed 13 July 2016.

right to *habeas corpus*.[207] In connection with the prosecution of the genocide in Tibet, 'political considerations might lead the relevant Spanish authorities not to request the extradition of the accused'.[208]

Indeed core crimes are on the *jus cogens* radar because they are the most serious crimes of concern to the international community, as postulated earlier on in Chap. 4. Core crimes[209] may be said to attract universal jurisdiction,[210] a principle of jurisdiction which may be said to demand the concept of *iudex (loci) deprehensionis*, the custodial State necessitating the presence of the alleged offender. In this context universal jurisdiction becomes a reflection of an indispensable ingredient of obligations *erga omnes*. This conspicuous feature connotes that 'for a norm to qualify as *erga omnes* States must also generally believe that it creates a legal interest in every other State and that every other State should have the right to bring a legal action against the putative offender in a forum with jurisdiction'.[211] This conclusion is substantiated by the ICJ's judgment wherein the term *erga omnes* was coined, the *Barcelona Traction* case[212] itself. In fact, in this case, the ICJ, by means of its reference to the 'basic rights of the human person' seems to infer that not all human rights partake of an *erga omnes* character. These rudimentary rights certainly include the right to be free from core crimes.

Universal jurisdiction and *erga omnes* obligations hence bestow a *locus standi* because they presuppose an underlying juridical interest. Were they to be transposed domestically, on a local scale, their counterpart would be an *actio criminalis popularis*. They mirror a collectivity of action intended to safeguard the *ordre public*.[213] This conclusion is substantiated by the fact that the exercise of universal jurisdiction

---

[207] USA Supreme Court, *Lakhdar Boumediene et al. v Bush et al.*, 12 June 2008, 06-1195. This case is also cited in para 20 of the report on admissibility following the petition of Algerian national *Djamel Ameziane* before the IACmmHR, which decision was the first time the IACmmHR accepted jurisdiction in a case relating to a Guantanamo detainee [IACmmHR, *Djamel Ameziane v USA, Report No. 17/12 (Admissibility)*, 20 March 2012, P-900-8].

[208] Bakker 2006, p. 599.

[209] States are entitled to assert jurisdiction over all core crimes which are currently prosecutable before the ICC because these are defined in customary international law (Cryer et al. 2010, p. 51). This finds support in a decision of the Peruvian Constitutional Court [*Tribunal Constitucional*, Perú, *Huaura, José Enrique Crousillat López Torres*, 8 August 2008, Decision 01271-2008-PHC/TC, para 6].

[210] A regulation adopted by the UN Transitory Authority for Eastern Timor on the Establishment of Panels with Exclusive Jurisdiction Over Serious Criminal Offences in East Timor establishes that universal jurisdiction means 'jurisdiction irrespective of whether (a) the offence at issue was committed within the territory of East Timor; (b) the offence was committed by an East Timorese citizen; (c) the victim of the offence was an East Timorese citizen' [UNTAET Regulation (2000) Doc. No. UNTAET/REG/2000/15].

[211] Lepard 2010, p. 24.

[212] *Barcelona Traction* case, above n. 35.

[213] Ganshof van der Meersch upholds that when the concept of *ordre public* is elevated to a level of mandatory requirement, it comes near to the concept of *jus cogens* in international law (van der Meersch 1977, p. 59).

is discretionary, not mandatory, upon the custodial State.[214] The extent to which universal jurisdiction may be invoked also depends upon the contours of this ground of jurisdiction. Universal jurisdiction *in absentia*,[215] foreseen as the 'next great

[214] The custodial State is the State wherein a person who is alleged to have committed a core crime or who is the subject of an international arrest warrant is found.

[215] Owing to the lack of consensus as to whether the principles set out in the *Lotus case* continue to apply or not, it seems 'impossible at this time to say whether or not universal jurisdiction *in absentia* is permissible or not as a matter of international law' (Rabinovitch 2004, p. 529). Trials *in absentia* are still allowed in various States, including the Netherlands [Article 280 of the *Wetboek van Strafvordering* (1969) Code of Penal Procedure, the Netherlands]. One must however clarify that for the Netherlands to exercise universal jurisdiction, it seems that the presence of the accused is necessary. This conclusion may be reached from the decision of the Public Prosecutor, subsequently confirmed by the Court of Appeal, not to investigate and prosecute *Pinochet* whose transitory presence in Amsterdam triggered a complaint by *Chili Komitee Nederland* [Public Prosecutor of Amsterdam, *Chili Komitee Nederland v Pinochet*, 6 June 1994; Court of Appeal, Amsterdam, *Chili Komitee Nederland v Pinochet*, 4 January 1995, published in the *NYIL*, Vol. 28, Asser Press, pp. 363–365]. Contrarily, however, *Wijngaarde et al. v Bouterse* [above n. 168], considering core crimes committed in Paramaribo, Surinam, throughout the night of the 8 and 9 December 1982, allowed universal jurisdiction *in absentia* {commonly referred to either as absolute or pure universal jurisdiction} only to be revoked by the Supreme Court which established that under the CAT the Netherlands enjoyed jurisdiction to prosecute either when the offender or victim is a Dutch citizen or else when the suspect is present in the Netherlands at the time of his arrest [*Prosecutor-General of the Supreme Court v Desiré Delano Bouterse*, above n. 169, para 8.5]. The matter seems to have been settled by the *Hoge Raad der Nederlanden*, the Supreme Court of the Netherlands, which, in *Public Prosecutor v Habibullah Jalalzoy* {*Hoge Raad* [Supreme Court], The Netherlands, Criminal Division, *Public Prosecutor v Habibullah Jalalzoy*, 8 July 2008, 07/10064 (LJN: BC7418)}, has outlined that 'in view of the *aut dedere aut judicare* principle (either extradite or punish), the present case involves the exercise of secondary jurisdiction based on the universality principle. Moreover, the importance of the presence of the defendant in the territory of the prosecuting State is also emphasized in the Explanatory Memorandum to the International Crimes Act' [proviso to para 6.4 in DomCLIC (2017) http://www.asser.nl/upload/documents/DomCLIC/Docs/NLP/Netherlands/Jalalzoy_Supreme_Court_08-07-2008_EN.pdf. Accessed 14 April 2017]. The presence requirement was ingrained by the ECtHR in *Nikola Jorgić v Germany* [ECtHR Fifth Section, *Nikola Jorgić v Germany*, 12 July 2007, Application No. 74613/01]. Another State, namely Italy, has convicted the so-called 'Beast of Bolzano', Ukranian-born Michael Seifert, *in absentia*, and has subsequently obtained his extradition from Canada [DomCLIC (2016) http://www.asser.nl/default.aspx?site_id=36&level1=15246&level2=15248&level3=&textid=40085. Accessed 23 October 2016, and The Telegraph (2008) Nazi Beast of Bolzano Faces Justice at 83. https://www.telegraph.co.uk/news/worldnews/1578962/Nazi-Beast-of-Bolzano-faces-justice-at-83.html. Accessed 3 June 2016]. Reydams, referring to *Pinochet* in Denmark [*Opinion of the Director of Public Prosecution of Denmark, Lee Urzúa et al. v Pinochet*, 3 December 1998, 555/98], *Javor* in France {*Cour de Cassation, Chambre Criminelle* [Court of Cassation (Criminal Chamber)], France, *Elvir Javor et al. contre X, Arrêt (Rejet du pourvoi)*, 26 March 1996, 95-81527}, *Sharon* [*Chambre de mises en accusation* [Pre-Trial Chamber of the Belgian Court of Appeal], Brussels, *Samiha Abbas Hijazi et al. v Ariel Sharon*, 26 June 2002] and *Ndombasi* [Court of Appeal, Brussels, *Public Prosecutor v Abdulaye Yerodia Ndombasi et al.*, 16 April 2002] in Belgium, notes that *dicta* in other States follow the same legal principles necessitating the presence of the accused (Reydams 2003, p. 178). Universal jurisdiction with presence is commonly referred to as 'conditional universal jurisdiction' (Cryer et al. 2010, p. 52). The presence requirement is not of a global nature. By way of example, Article 8 of the International Crimes and International Criminal Court Act (2000), New Zealand, Public Act 2000 No. 26, does not require presence.

revolution in international criminal law',[216] can be made permissible by a State under its own legislation. However, this seems to be a far cry from current State practice.[217] The main differential characteristic is that under universal jurisdiction,

---

[216] Poels 2005, p. 84.

[217] In their joint separate opinion, Judges Higgins, Kooijmans and Buergenthal argued that universal jurisdiction *in absentia* is permitted under international law provided that the following criteria are fulfilled:

1. the national State of the accused must be given an opportunity to act on the allegations;
2. the prosecution must be initiated by a prosecutor or *juge d'instruction* who is independent from control by the rest of the government;
3. special circumstances must exist to justify the assertion of jurisdiction, such as a request by the victims for the initiation of such a case; and
4. such jurisdiction must only be asserted over the most heinous crimes.

[ICJ, *Arrest Warrant of 11 April 2000* (*DRC v Belgium*), Dissenting Opinion of Judge Christine van den Wyngaert, 14 February 2002, ICJ Rep. 2002, p. 3]. This contrasts with Cassese's conclusions which find comfort in the absence of a treaty which provides for a legal basis for universal jurisdiction *in absentia* (Cassese 2003, p. 589). The HRC has not outlawed trials which are not based upon universal jurisdiction *in absentia*, even when the death penalty is inflicted. It qualified this by stating that, at least, serious efforts to notify the accused must be undertaken by the State which prosecutes him *in absentia* [HRC, *Daniel Monguya Mbenge v Zaire*, 8 September 1977, Communication No. 16/1977, pp. 76–78]. All this infers that no customary international law rule exists necessitating the presence of the accused in trials. I am not a supporter of universal jurisdiction *in absentia*. This is not because of the principle of non-intervention in the internal affairs of a State, but because it could prejudice the right to a fair trial, it purportedly creates judicial chaos and would probably encourage arbitrary decisions by powerful States leading to a global community wherein 'might is right' instead of an international community which upholds the internationalization of the rule of law. It can also elicit forum-shopping. Cedric Ryngaert acknowledges that 'the bystander State may stand accused of infringing upon the sovereignty of the territorial State, given the absence of any legitimizing link with the case' (Ryngaert 2006, p. 54). Such legitimizing link *(ein legitimierender Anknupfungspunkt)* is eloquently explained in Vajda 2010, pp. 336–338, and also in Jeßberger 2007, p. 215. Even States most supportive of universal jurisdiction such as Belgium, which had promulgated its War Crimes Act, (1999) Act Concerning the Punishment of Grave Breaches of International Humanitarian law, necessitated the voluntary presence of the foreign suspect in Belgium for the purposes of prosecution [*Public Prosecutor v Ndombasi et al.*, above n. 215]. A few months later, on 26 June 2002, in *Samiha Abbas Hijazi et al. v Ariel Sharon*, above n. 215, the *Chambre de mises en accusation* determined that the exercise of universal jurisdiction *in absentia* violates the Genocide Convention (1948) Convention for the Prevention and Punishment of the Crime of Genocide, Geneva Convention (1949a) Geneva Convention (I) for the Amelioration of the Condition of the Wounded and Sick in Armed Forces in the Field, Geneva Convention (1949b) Geneva Convention (II) for the Amelioration of the Condition of the Wounded, Sick and Shipwrecked Members of Armed Forces at Sea, Geneva Convention (1949c) Geneva Convention (III) relative to the Treatment of Prisoners of War, Geneva Convention (1949d) Geneva Convention (IV) relative to the Protection of Civilian Persons in Time of War, the ECvHR (1950) European Convention for the Protection of Human Rights and Fundamental Freedoms, and the principle of sovereign equality of States [*vide* Section A, para 9]. For a thorough examination of Belgium's law on universal jurisdiction, see Langer 2011, pp. 26–32; see also above n. 123. Canada's universal jurisdiction over genocide by means of the Act Respecting Genocide, Crimes Against Humanity and War Crimes and to Implement the Rome Statute of the International Criminal Court and to make Consequential Amendments to Other Acts, Canada (2000) Annual Statutes of Canada, Chap. 24, 29 June 2000, also necessitates the same pre-requisite, *id est* presence. Similarly, the Director of Public Prosecution of Denmark opined that

individual criminal responsibility is at stake, whereas in *erga omnes* obligations, States are the major stakeholders. In other words, universal jurisdiction for the above mentioned core crimes, being all *delicta iuris gentium*, is, first and foremost, a right, because under conventional international law, it is permissive, not mandatory. However, it is simultaneously accompanied by an obligation [possessing *erga omnes* character] of a custodial State under customary international law. This is why it has occasionally been referred to as an 'obligatory territorial jurisdiction over persons, albeit in relation to acts committed elsewhere'.[218] The exercise of the right and fulfilment of this obligation is ultimately one and the same thing, namely the extradition or prosecution of the suspect, the individual alleged to have committed core crimes.

One might rebut this by arguing that a claim alleging a violation of an *erga omnes* obligation may only be brought in a forum enjoying jurisdiction, because otherwise the injured State requirement would be lacking. This criticism would be unsuccessful. The reason for such state of affairs has already been considered in Sect. 5.5 and in an excursus here above. Core crimes are so reprehensible and heinous that whosoever commits them is *hostis humani generis*, an enemy of humankind.[219] Hence, by way of conclusion, *aut dedere aut judicare* may be defined in many ways because it does not encompass a 'one size fits all' prototype. Its nature and status largely depend on underlying and surrounding circumstances. Its clout in general international law, especially in as much as it constitutes a rule of customary international law, is significant, as will be shown in Sects. 13.2–13.5.

Danish jurisdiction under Article 8(1)(5) of *Straffeloven* [Criminal Code], Denmark (1930) Law number 126, only subsists if the suspect is physically present in Denmark [*Lee Urzúa et al. v Pinochet*, above n. 215]. Other jurists, however, have taken a diametrically opposed standpoint (Roht-Arriaza 2006, pp. 207–213). This said, the EU transnational network of information-sharing is a laudable effort intended to facilitate the investigation and prosecution of core crimes [Decisions of the EU Council of Ministers {2002} OJ L 167/1-2 and {2003} OJ L 118/12-14]. Such networks are also conducive to the investigation and prosecution of transnational organised crimes, such as those committed by extensive criminal networks. These include the Italian *mafias*, *La Cosa Nostra* in the USA, this being an off-shoot of the Sicilian mafia (see Bassiouni and Vetere 1998, p. xxxi, n. 17), the Colombian and Mexican drug cartels, the Russian *mafias* and the Japanese *Yakuza* (Obokata 2010, p. 4 and 17). To the criminal networks based in Italy, besides the mafia mentioned here above, some of the actions of which were investigated and noted in a red diary/notebook which belonged to Paolo Borsellino and went missing after his assassination on 19 July 1992 (see Lo Bianco and Rizza 2007, pp. 197–202), one must add the *Camorra*, aptly analysed by Roberto Saviano (see Saviano 2006), the *'Ndrangheta* (see Ciconte 2015) and the *Anonima Sarda* (see Casalunga 2007).

[218] *DRC v Belgium*, above n. 217, para 42 cited in Mitchell 2009, para 20, n. 274.

[219] Ronald Sly and Beth van Schaack acknowledge that 'those responsible of the most serious provisions of international criminal law today join pirates as "enemies of all humankind"' (Slye and van Schaack 2009, p. 73).

13.2 The Execution of the *Aut Dedere Aut Judicare* Rule in Domestic Criminal Courts

At the start of this heading, I highlight that reference to the execution of the *aut dedere aut judicare* rule in domestic courts may be equated to the assertion of universal jurisdiction by such domestic courts.[220] Robert Cryer refers to jurisprudence to portray the existence of 'authority for the idea that national courts are acting as organs of global justice in prosecuting international crimes in case-law'.[221] In practice, this entails that certain domestic courts prosecute, hence avail themselves of the second limb of the *aut dedere aut judicare formula,* on the basis of universal jurisdiction. An examination of such *formulae* renders it easier to understand the connection between *aut dedere aut judicare* and universal jurisdiction.

Before considering such *formulae*, it must be pointed out that the scope of this heading is not to examine each and every prosecution of core crimes undertaken domestically,[222] but to analyse the effect that domestic prosecutions have on the horizontal system of enforcement and to understand how, and to what extent, they could shed a light on the general enforcement of international criminal law. In any case, 'very few national courts have tried individuals for genocide; fewer still have convicted anyone for the offence. Rwanda stands out as an exception…Information about these cases is patchy and insufficiently detailed…. In the Rwandan system there are the added complications of the victors trying the vanquished in the context of a political system that is not exactly a democracy; of evidence that the victors themselves committed serious crimes whose investigation they have resisted or derailed; of pressure having been exerted by the Rwandan government on the ICTR to influence judicial decision-making, and of a less than satisfactory government record for respecting human rights in general'.[223] William Schabas reaches the same conclusion by stating that the prosecution of genocide in domestic courts, with the exception of Rwanda, has been 'symbolic, lightweight and superficial'.[224] This relates to the prosecution of genocide under the traditional/classical grounds of jurisdiction. The same may not be said about the prosecution of other core crimes

---

220 Court of Appeal, The Hague, *Public Prosecutor v Habibullah Jalalzoy*, 29 January 2007, 09-751005-04 (LJN: AZ9366); and Court of Appeal, The Hague, *Public Prosecutor v Hesamuddin Hesam*, 29 January 2007, LJN AZ9365, cited in Ryngaert 2007, p. 15. Antonio Cassese infers that the *aut dedere aut judicare* rule is a principle of quasi-universal jurisdiction (Cassese 1989, p. 593). Michael Scharf endorsed this position (Scharf 2001, paras 99–103, cited in Abass 2006, p. 353, n. 18). Such designation is probably correct particularly because whereas treaties are only binding *inter partes*, they could anyway bind non-parties when their provisions are of a customary character.

221 Cryer 2005, p. 85.

222 For a comprehensive analysis of such prosecutions, until 10 March 2010, see Rikhof 2010, pp. 7–81.

223 Zahar 2009, p. 148.

224 Schabas 2003, pp. 40, 62–63.

on the basis of universal jurisdiction. Joseph Rikhof refers to 13 countries in Europe which have 'initiated criminal investigations and criminal prosecutions for international crimes committed elsewhere between 1994 and 10 March 2010'.[225] Since this work does not solely and exclusively deal with universal jurisdiction, I have adopted a selective approach in choosing cases which, in his opinion, pave the way for an understanding of the manner in which the horizontal system of enforcement functions and of its major shortcomings. A selective approach to such jurisprudence is thus inevitable. In performing such selection, I give priority to recent case-law, not necessarily because such case-law is more authoritative or important, but particularly because a lot has been scrutinized and written in relation to the domestic prosecutions which immediately followed World War II.[226] Additionally, general contemporary international law, including prospective international law, is more likely to be affected by recent jurisprudence than by case-law which precedes the ICC Statute by nearly half a century. Such selection also partially justifies this work in that it motivates my choice to resort to quoting certain decisions rather than others. To this effect, one must not forget that 'the authority of a decision of a national court cannot be presumed, but has to be earned'.[227] In citing such case-law, particularly in relation to the underlying *lacunae* within the horizontal system of enforcement's extradition regime, I have attempted to use, adequately and equitably, the thresholds and criteria adopted by Andre Nollkaemper, these being:

1. institutional effectiveness;
2. substantive effectiveness;

[225] Rikhof 2010, pp. 45–46.

[226] For a succinct but thorough and chronological analysis of such case-law, ranging from the American prosecutions {International (Nuremberg) Military Tribunal, *USA v Karl Brandt et al. (the Medical case)*, 19 August 1947; International (Nuremberg) Military Tribunal, *USA v Erhard Milch et al. (the Milch case)*, 16 April 1947; International (Nuremberg) Military Tribunal, *USA v Josef Altstötter et al. (the Justice case)*, 3 December 1947; International (Nuremberg) Military Tribunal, *USA v Oswald Pohl et al. (the Pohl case)*, 3 November 1947; International (Nuremberg) Military Tribunal, *USA v Friedrich Flick et al. (the Flick case)*, 22 December 1947; International (Nuremberg) Military Tribunal, *USA v Carl Krauch et al. (the I.G. Fabren case)*, 29 July 1948; International (Nuremberg) Military Tribunal, *USA v Wilhelm List et al. (the Hostages case)*, 19 February 1948; International (Nuremberg) Military Tribunal, *USA v Ulrich Greifelt et al. (the Rusha case)*, 10 March 1948; International (Nuremberg) Military Tribunal, *USA v Otto Ohlendorf et al. (the Einsatzgruppen case)*, 8 April 1948; International (Nuremberg) Military Tribunal, *USA v Alfried Krupp et al. (the Krupp case)*, 31 July 1948; International (Nuremberg) Military Tribunal, *USA v Ernst von Weizsäcker et al. (the Ministries case)*, 11–13 April 1949; International (Nuremberg) Military Tribunal, *USA v Wilhelm von Leeb et al. (the High Command case)*, 27 & 28 October 1948}, to the important French prosecutions of *Klaus Barbie, Paul Touvier* and *Maurice Papon* {*Cour de Cassation, Chambre Criminelle* [Court of Cassation (Criminal Law Chamber)], France, *Prosecutor v Klaus Barbie*, 6 October 1983, 83-93194; *Cour de Cassation, Chambre Criminelle* [Court of Cassation (Criminal Law Chamber)], France, *France v Paul Touvier*, 27 November 1992, 92-82409; *Cour de Cassation, Chambre Criminelle*, France, *Prosecutor v Maurice Papon*, 11 June 2004, 98-82.323} (see Bernaz and Prouvèze 2010, pp. 344–365).

[227] Nollkaemper 2011, p. 256.

3. remedial effectiveness; and
4. the quality of individual decisions.[228]

Naturally, throughout the performance of this exercise, a degree of subjectivity is inevitable. In this context, my legal background[229] should have acted to provide a sufficient degree of objectivity. However, in any case, municipal jurisprudence *per se* constitutes a subsidiary means for the determination of rules of law in its function as a fully-fledged source, albeit secondary, of international law.[230] The degree and extent of its accessory nature is also questionable. Antonio Cassese went as far as saying that the role of domestic courts 'has become crucial for the gradual evolution of legal standards better suited to the emerging concerns and values of the world community. It is plausible to believe that courts can gradually contribute to the evolution of an international obligation for States to take action at the national judicial level when acts of genocide are perpetrated in other States'.[231]

The Hague *formula*[232] favours a choice of the *forum deprehensionis*, the custodial state, to either extradite or prosecute. Opting for the former generally guarantees that the trial occurs in the *forum conveniens*, the place where the crime was consummated, although this is not always the case since occasionally the *forum deprehensionis* and the *forum conveniens* vary, as when an individual commits a crime in State A and escapes to State Z. Should it opt for the latter, *id est* to submit the case to its competent authorities for the purposes of prosecution, trials within the custodial State should not be unfair or ineffective. This is problematic since it seems to necessitate a self-appraisal of one's own judicial structure and systems. The *forum deprehensionis* thus becomes arbiter of its own judicial system. Obviously, no formal monitoring mechanism whereby a State may obtain authorization to prosecute by means of an advisory opinion of the ICJ or an explicit authorization of the Pre-Trial Chamber of the ICC is in place. This *formula* finds support in the Draft Code of Crimes Against the Peace and Security of Mankind.[233] It enhances State discretion and was followed in various international conventions, including the

[228] Nollkaemper 2011, pp. 257–264.

[229] Having studied law predominantly at the University of Malta and having practiced as a criminal defence lawyer and human rights lawyer in Malta, I was constantly exposed to a hybrid system of law which fascinatingly fuses Common Law and Continental Law, both substantively and procedurally. Malta is a CoE, EU and Commonwealth member State. However, until 1934, Italian was the official language which was used in judicial proceedings in Malta, and to date, Maltese laws, whilst being based upon the *Code Napoléon* (1804) Napoleonic Code and *Corpus Juris Civilis Romani* (534), posit a largely adversarial system particularly in trials by jury and before the Courts of Criminal Appeal as a result of the legal culture instilled by the English before Malta's independence gained on 21 September 1964.

[230] See Article 38(1)(d) of the ICJ Statute (1946) Statute of the International Court of Justice.

[231] Cassese 2009, p. 543.

[232] This *formula* was postulated in the Convention for the Suppression of Unlawful Seizure of Aircraft (1970) which was signed in The Hague on 16 December 1970.

[233] This was adopted in 1996 by the ILC at its forty-eight session [UNGA Official Records 51st Session, Doc. A/51/10].

Montreal Convention and the Hostages Convention, rendering it the most consistent *formula.*[234] Within the context of the Montreal Convention, Judge Patricia Wald eloquently delved into the intricacies of this *formula* in the *Omar Mohammed Ali Rezaq* case. In her well-drafted opinion,[235] she held that:

> The first step in *Rezaq*'s argument is flawed: the Hague Convention's requirement that a State either prosecutes offenders or extradites them does not imply a bar on (at different times) doing both. In general, a requirement to "do A or B" does not necessarily imply a bar on doing both A and B; one must look at the context and the purpose of the requirement to decide whether such a bar is meant. Here, the context makes clear that the statute's injunction to extradite or prosecute is not meant to state mutually exclusive alternatives. The extradite-or-prosecute requirement is intended to ensure that States make some effort to bring hijackers to justice, either through prosecution or extradition.
>
> A reading of Article 4 that focuses on bringing hijackers to justice is also consistent with the Convention's (short) preamble, one clause of which states that 'for the purpose of deterring [acts of air piracy], there is an urgent need to provide appropriate measures for punishment of offenders.
>
> A reading under which the options of prosecution and extradition are mutually exclusive could also undermine the Convention's goal of ensuring 'punishment of offenders'. For instance, if a person is extradited from State A to State B, and B then discovers that a technical obstacle prevents it from prosecuting her, B should be able to return her to A for prosecution; any other reading of the treaty might allow a suspect to escape prosecution altogether. Or, to choose an example closer to the facts of this case, if State A tries and convicts a defendant for certain crimes associated with a hijacking (as Malta tried Rezaq for murder, attempted murder, and hostage-taking), there is no indication that A is barred from then extraditing her to B once she has served her sentence, so that B may try the defendant for different crimes associated with the same hijacking (as the United States tried Rezaq for air piracy).

The widely used[236] Hague *formula* admits of two important variables, which can be said to constitute another two different *formulae* rather than two sub-*formulae*. The first variant can be referred to as 'the terrorism *formula*'. The CoE treaties, namely the European Convention on the Suppression of Terrorism, and the European Convention on the Protection of the Environment, provide for a *formula* which infers a preference to extradition rather than to prosecution, and is called 'the disjunctive conception'.[237] In other words this *formula* entails *primo dedere secundo prosequi* and hence conveys that States should first extradite a suspect, and only if they cannot do so, they should prosecute him. Such treaties 'make the application of the alternative obligation to prosecute dependent upon the denial of a prior request for extradition'.[238] Therefore, the either/or obligation is of a conditional nature.[239] Additionally, by way of differentiation to other multi-lateral treaties

---

234 Mitchell 2009, para 15.

235 *USA v Omar Mohammed Ali Rezaq*, above n. 152.

236 It has been applied in at least 15 multi-lateral conventions (Mitchell 2009, para 7).

237 Roth 2009, p. 307.

238 van Steenberghe 2011, p. 1111.

239 Trapp 2011, p. 84.

(international conventions),[240] the alternative duty to prosecute within the European Convention on the Suppression of Terrorism is dependent upon a previous extradition request which has been denied.[241] Hence, in this case, the *aut judicare* limb is of a subsidiary nature. It stands to reason that in such case the aggrieved State's interest are prioritised because terrorism is generally committed against, and to the detriment of, the State. In terrorism, the State is generally the victim of an attack by an international criminal organization, whereas in core crimes, as shown already, the State is generally involved as either the perpetrator or owing to its inability to counteract non-State entities. The *aut dedere aut judicare* rule is hence juxtaposed according to the prevailing exigencies. It is deliberately tailored and made to measure the specific crime which ought to be curbed.

Technically, this terrorism *formula* admits of a particular variant which is triggered by means of a constitutional impediment to extradition, and which may hence be designated as 'the constitutional formula'. Such permutation postulates that the duty to extradite should generally be regarded as primary, with the duty to prosecute[242] arising if the domestic legislation contains a bar to extradition. This would entail that the State *locus delicti commissi*, wherein most evidence is preserved, has the primary responsibility to prosecute and punish the offender, whereas the prosecuting authorities and courts of the custodial State have only a secondary duty.[243]

The second off-shoot of the Hague *formula* may be referred to as 'the drugs *formula*'. This entails that an alternative obligation to submit a case for prosecution is subject, where a foreigner is involved, to whether a State has elected to authorise the exercise of extra-territorial jurisdiction. It is mirrored in the UN Convention Against Illicit Traffic in Narcotic Drugs and Psychotropic Substances.[244]

The fourth and last *formula* postulates the prioritization of prosecution over extradition. This presupposes 'a primary or even unconditional obligation of searching presumed perpetrators and bringing them to trial'.[245] Only should this not occur, the State may elect to hand over such persons for trial, provided that the requesting State has made out a *prima facie* case. Since the Geneva Conventions were modelled upon this *primo prosequi* approach, one can refer to it as 'the Geneva *formula*'. Within the system provided under the four Geneva Conventions and the Additional Protocol I, the obligation to extradite or prosecute which is enshrined in

---

240 In these UN treaties, such as Article 7 of the The Hague Hijacking Convention (1970) The Hague Convention for Suppression of Unlawful Seizure of Aircraft, Article 7 of the Montreal Convention (1971) Convention for the Suppression of Unlawful Acts Against the Safety of Civil Aviation and Article 8 of the Hostages Convention (1979) Convention Against the Taking of Hostages, the duty to prosecute exists regardless of a previous extradition request, rendering the *aut judicare* limb absolute.

241 See Article 7 of the European Convention on the Suppression of Terrorism (1977).

242 van der Voort and Zwanenburg 2003, pp. 308–309.

243 Plachta 2001a, p. 75.

244 See Article 6, para 9.

245 Roth 2009, p. 307.

those conventions with respect to the grave breaches of their provisions does not make prosecution subsidiary. It provides that States must prosecute suspects of those breaches or, if they prefer, extradite them to another State. Spain made use of this formula when it rejected the extradition to Argentina of twenty (Francisco Franco era) former Spanish officials on the basis of the 'principle of preferential jurisdiction, according to which a State may refuse to extradite if it is able to prosecute itself'.[246] What therefore matters is to prosecute the prohibited conduct, extradition being presented as an alternative offered to the custodial State to enable it to comply with its prosecution obligations.[247] Effectively, instead of *aut dedere aut judicare*, as traditionally understood, the Geneva *formula* postulates *prosequi vel dedere* because 'States bound by this obligation have a free choice between prosecution and extradition, while emphasis is put on prosecution since extradition appears only as a means at the disposal of the custodial State for complying with its obligation to prosecute'.[248] *De facto*, as rightly highlighted by Robert Roth, the Geneva formula implies 'a duty to establish universal jurisdiction based on the reversal of *aut dedere*'.[249] Indeed this *formula* seems to have been preferred over its the Hague counterpart by the ICJ[250] and is also reflected in UNGA resolutions.[251]

In assessing such *formulae* a Canadian court ably established some important factors which ought to be taken into account to identify the *forum conveniens*, these being:

i. the place where the effects of the crime were most felt;
ii. the jurisdiction which has the greatest juridical interest in prosecuting the crime;
iii. the police force which played a major role in the development of the case;
iv. the jurisdiction that has laid charges;
v. the jurisdiction that has the most comprehensive case;
vi. the jurisdiction which is ready to proceed to trial;
vii. the place where the evidence is located;
viii. the places where the evidence could be transferred to, if any;[252]
ix. the accused persons involved and whether they can be tried jointly;
x. the nationality and residence of the accused;

246 ICD (2017) News Archive. http://www.internationalcrimesdatabase.org/home/newsarchive#p19. Accessed 3 February 2017.

247 van Steenberghe 2011, pp. 1113–1114.

248 van Steenberghe 2011, p. 1114.

249 Roth 2009, p. 308.

250 *BiH v Serbia and Montenegro*, above n. 55, para 443.

251 See UNGA Resolutions 2840 (XXVI) and 3074 (XXVIII), both cited in van Steenberghe 2011, p. 1115.

252 This might be problematic for three main reasons, these being:
1. logistical movement of witnesses is expensive and burdensome;
2. unavailability of some evidence, especially accesses on-site; and
3. procedural restrictions on the tendering of evidence in another jurisdiction.

xi. the severity of the sentence the accused is likely to receive in each jurisdiction; and
xii. the legal infrastructure in the requested State.[253]

To these one may add a consideration of each and every ground for refusal of extradition, particularly the likelihood or otherwise of an unfair trial which should not be discarded when the *forum conveniens* is being identified. In truth, there is not a 'one size fits all' general and rigid rule. Each and every case will depend upon its particular prevailing circumstances and peculiarities, to be considered cumulatively depending on the above mentioned factors. Robert Kolb best explains the connection between *aut dedere aut judicare* and universal jurisdiction by concluding that *aut dedere aut judicare* is a universal jurisdiction which is relative (both *rationae personae* and *rationae materiae*), compulsory and subsidiary, hence equating the *aut dedere aut judicare* rule to conventional universal jurisdiction.[254] Steven Becker, analysing the Princeton Project Steering Committee's work on universal jurisdiction, commented that universal jurisdiction reflects the *aut dedere aut judicare* rule,[255] this conclusion being shared by Tom Obokata.[256] Cedric Ryngaert also refers to 'universal jurisdiction on the basis of an *aut dedere aut judicare* obligation'.[257] This is not to say that, conceptually, there are no differences between the two. On the contrary:

1. *aut dedere aut judicare* is not universal but limited to State parties to the treaty;[258]
2. universal jurisdiction is a right, an entitlement, whereas *aut dedere aut judicare* is a duty, a mandatory obligation, the non-fulfilment of which results in an internationally wrongful act entailing State liability;[259]
3. universal jurisdiction constitutes an entitlement to prosecute, whereas *aut dedere aut judicare* is an alternative of either extraditing or prosecuting;[260] and
4. universal jurisdiction applies only to a limited number of core crimes, whereas *aut dedere aut judicare* is contemplated in a number of treaties which proscribe a larger category of crimes.[261]

---

[253] Court of Queen's Bench of Manitoba, Canada, *Harvey Swystun v USA*, 30 October 1987, 50 Man.R.(2d) 129 (QB).

[254] Kolb 2004, pp. 249–254.

[255] Becker 2001, p. 55.

[256] Obokata 2010, p. 51.

[257] Ryngaert 2008a, p. 101.

[258] This is qualified by the fact that, given the diffuse State practice, the *aut dedere aut judicare* rule 'has the effect of potentially legitimising a claim of universality by a non-State party to suppress a terrorist offence defined in an anti-terrorist convention' (Kolb 2004, p. 275).

[259] Mitchell 2009, para 13.

[260] Examining Article 11 of the Convention for the Protection of All Persons from Enforced Disappearance (2006) signed in NY on 20 December 2006, Lisa Ott states that 'if a State is not willing to extradite a suspected perpetrator, it is under the obligation to prosecute the individual' (Ott 2011, p. 240).

[261] Kolb 2004, p. 252.

The difference between the two is best explained with reference to States, such as South Korea and Nicaragua, which permit universal jurisdiction but do not undertake to follow the *aut dedere aut judicare* rule.[262] The recourse to universal jurisdiction has been quite inconsistent over the past decades. It is rather interrupted and sporadic. It also seems to be, to a small extent, geographically confined since most attempts in support of universal jurisdiction[263] have been undertaken in Europe,[264] where universal jurisdiction has been exercised particularly as a result of enabling Spanish and Belgian laws to this effect.[265] Some important cases outside Europe are also noteworthy.[266]

[262] Hesenov 2013

[263] For a historical, descriptive and critical analysis of such national prosecutions, see Ratner et al. 2009, pp. 185–202. For a regional and/or geographical approach to such study, see Rikhof 2010, pp. 7–81.

[264] During deliberations of the Commission on Human Rights' Working Groups in 1980 [Documents E/CN.4/1408 and E/1980/13], Sweden and Austria favoured the insertion of the *aut dedere aut judicare* rule within the CAT whereas the Netherlands supported the inclusion of universal jurisdiction without the dependence of a rejection of a prior request for extradition within the CAT, throughout deliberations of the Commission on Human Rights' Working Group in 1981 {Documents E.CN.4/1475 and E/1981/25} (Burgers and Danelius 1988, pp. 62–64 and 72).

[265] Article 23.4 (genocide) of the Spanish Organic Law of the Judicial Power (1985) Organic Law No. 6/1985; Belgian Act Concerning the Punishment of Grave Breaches of the Geneva Conventions of 12 August 1949 and their Additional Protocols I and II of 18 June 1977 (1993), Official Journal of 5 August 1993, at 17751–17755, as amended by the Act Concerning the Punishment of Grave Breaches of International Humanitarian Law (1999) Official Journal of 23 March 1999, at 9286–9287, (adopted in 1993, expanded in 1999 and repealed on 5 August 2003). Other important similar laws include Article 1 of the German Act to Introduce the Code of Crimes Against International Law {*Völkerstrafgesetzbuch, VStGB*} (2002), 26 June 2002 (violations of international humanitarian laws); French Law No. 96-432 on adapting French Law to the Provisions of United Nations Security Council Resolution 955 Establishing the International Tribunal for Rwanda, 22 May 1996 and French Law No. 95-1 on adapting French Law to the Provisions of United Nations Security Council Resolution 827 Establishing an International Tribunal for the Prosecution of Persons Responsible for Serious Violations of International Humanitarian Law Committed in the Territory of Former Yugoslavia Since 1991, 2 January 1995 (crimes against international humanitarian law committed in Rwanda and the former Yugoslavia) and Article 689-2 of the French Law (1999) No. 99-115, 23 June 1999 amending Article 689 of the French Code of Criminal Procedure (torture), Official Journal of 24 June 1999; Article 2,1(a) of the Netherlands International Crimes Act (2003) Act of 19 June 2003 Containing Rules Concerning Serious Violations of International Humanitarian Law (International Crimes Act) (crimes against international humanitarian law and torture); Article 134 of the United Kingdom Criminal Justice Act (Torture) (Overseas Territories) Order (1988), 21 December 1988; and Article 6(1) of the Act Respecting Genocide, Crimes Against Humanity and War Crimes and to Implement the Rome Statute of the International Criminal Court and to make Consequential Amendments to Other Acts, Canada (2000) (crimes against international humanitarian law).

[266] See, *inter alia*, Ethiopia Federal High Court, *The Special Prosecutor v Col Mengistu Hailemariam and 173 Others*, 9 October 1995, Criminal File No. 1/87, 1988 EC [GC], ILDC 555 (ET 1995), cited in Tronvoll et al. 2009, pp. 136–152; see also Langer 2015, pp. 251–252.

The *Adolf Eichmann* case paved the way for universal jurisdiction of a penal nature.[267] Here some caution must be employed. The doctrine *male captus bene detentus*, signifying that an irregular capture can nonetheless result in valid detention, was also endorsed by the ICTY both in *Prosecutor v Dragan Nikolić*[268] and in *Prosecutor v Slavko Dokmanović*.[269] The consequence of this is dire. It transforms universal jurisdiction into a very powerful tool by means of which all that is needed for an alleged perpetrator of core crimes to be prosecuted is just one country which permits absolute universal jurisdiction. It is also acknowledged that 'individual nations are increasingly acting in the name of the international community by invoking universal jurisdiction for *jus cogens* violations of international law, bringing charges against foreign individuals in domestic courts for atrocities committed abroad'.[270] There exists a trend 'towards bases of jurisdiction other than territoriality'.[271] The past decades have witnessed, for example, the attempted prosecution[272] in Spain of former Chilean dictator Senator *Augusto Pinochet Ugarte*[273] and the prosecution of former Chadian dictator *Hissène Habré*.[274] The latter case juxtaposed concurrent universal jurisdiction since both Belgium and Senegal instituted criminal proceedings against *Hissène Habré*, nicknamed 'the African Pinochet', responsible, according to a Chadian Truth Commission, for the

---

[267] *Attorney-General of Israel v Adolf Eichmann*, above n. 114. *Eichmann*, a German national, was kidnapped in Argentina and brought to face justice in Israel. The Israeli Supreme Court held that the notion of universal jurisdiction is firmly based on customary international law, and that consequently it existed independently of the Genocide Convention, as a result of which neither Argentina nor Germany questioned the exercise of universal jurisdiction by Israel. The *Demjanjuk* case followed suit [USA Court of Appeals, 6th Circuit, John *Demjanjuk v Joseph Petrowsky et al.*, 31 October 1985, 776 F.2d 571, 85-3435, in International Law Reports, Vol. 79]. Similarly, USA courts have asserted that they enjoy jurisdiction over individuals even if such individuals were abducted and forcibly brought on USA territory [USA Supreme Court, *USA v Humberto Alvarez-Machain*, 15 June 1992, 504 U.S. 655 (112 S.Ct. 2188, 119 L.Ed.2d 441) 91/712]. Luring and trickery, leading to abductions, are practices commonly used by the USA Government as an alternative to extradition (Paust et al. 2007, p. 413; Norberg 2006, pp. 387–400). Such measures have been used for a number of decades. *Adolf Eichmann*, for example, way back on 11 May 1960, was snatched by Mossad agents as he returned home from work as a foreman at the Mercedes Benz plant outside Buenos Aires in Argentina (Schabas 2013b, pp. 683–684; see also Seret 2014, p. 3).

[268] ICTY Trial Chamber II, *Prosecutor v Dragan Nikolić, Decision on the Defence Motion Challenging the Exercise of Jurisdiction by the Tribunal*, 9 October 2002, Case No. IT-94-2.

[269] ICTY Trial Chamber, *Prosecutor v Slavko Dokmanović, Decision on the Motion for Release by the Accused*, 27 October 1997, Case No. ICTY-95-13a.

[270] Tallman 2003, p. 375.

[271] van Schaack and Slye 2010, p. 123.

[272] Reydams refers to such cases as virtual ones, since they 'produced little more than headlines and diplomatic headaches', whereas he refers to cases which led to extraditions and convictions for crimes committed abroad as 'hard cases' (Reydams 2011, pp. 347–349).

[273] Roht-Arriaza 2009a, pp. 77–94.

[274] For a succinct historical and chronological account of domestic prosecutions of core crimes pre-dating the Second World War until year 2008, see Kleffner 2008, pp. 33–38.

systematic torture and murder of over 40,000 people.[275] Senegalese courts initially dismissed the case on the grounds of lack of jurisdiction resulting from the fact that Senegal had not yet incorporated international criminal law into its domestic legislation. Subsequently Belgium[276] requested his extradition under Belgium's universal jurisdiction law,[277] as a result of which *Hissène Habré* was re-arrested in

[275] UN Committee Against Torture, *Suleymane Guengueng and Others v Senegal*, 19 May 2006, CAT/C/36/D/181/2001, cited in AHRLR 56, *AHRLR*, JUTA Law on behalf of the Centre for Human Rights at the University of Pretoria, 2006, para 2.1.

[276] Article 6(1)(1*bis*) of the Law of 17 April 1878, Code of Criminal Procedure, as amended on 7 August 2003 (see above n. 123), necessitates, for the exercise of universal jurisdiction over core crimes, that:

i. the alleged accused is Belgian or has his primary residence in Belgium;

ii. the victim is Belgian or has lived in Belgium for at last three years at the time the crimes were committed; or

iii. Belgium is required by treaty to exercise jurisdiction over the case.

[277] States which have initiated or enacted comparable legislation include Australia [Australian ICC (Consequential Amendments) Act (2002) International Criminal Court (Consequential Amendments Act, 28 June 2002, No. 42, 2002], Canada [Act Respecting Genocide, Crimes Against Humanity and War Crimes and to Implement the Rome Statute of the International Criminal Court and to make Consequential Amendments to Other Acts, Canada (2000) Annual Statutes of Canada, Chap. 24, 29 June 2000], Costa Rica [Costa Rican Penal Code, as amended by Law 8272, 2 May 2003], Croatia [Article 10(2) of the Croatian Law on the Application of the Statute of the International Criminal Court and the Prosecution of Crimes Against International Laws of War and Humanitarian Law (2003) Official Gazette No. 175/2003, Article 14], the DRC [the DRC's Military Justice Code (2002) The Democratic Republic of the Congo Military Justice Code, Act No. 023-2002, 18 November 2002], Finland [Finnish Criminal Code (2008) 13/1889, *Laki rikoslain muuttamisesta* (Law Amending the Criminal Code), as amended under Chap. 11, 212/2008, Sections 1–7, 11 April 2008], France [French Law (1999) No. 99-115, 23 June 1999 amending Article 689 of the French Code of Criminal Procedure, Official Journal of 24 June 1999], Germany [Section 1 of the German Act to Introduce the Code of Crimes Against International Law *{Völkerstrafgesetzbuch, VStGB}* (2002), 26 June 2002], Italy [Italy's *Codice Penale* [Criminal Code] (1889), amendment to Article 7, *decreto legge* 208, 30 July 2004], Malta [Article 54G of the Maltese *Kodiċi Kriminali, Kapitolu 9 tal-Liġijiet ta' Malta* (Criminal Code, Chap. 9 of the Laws of Malta), as amended in 2002], the Netherlands [Section 2(1)(a) of the Netherlands International Crimes Act (2003) Act of 19 June 2003 Containing Rules Concerning Serious Violations of International Humanitarian Law (International Crimes Act), New Zealand [Section 8(1)(c) of the New Zealand International Crimes and ICC Act (2000) International Crimes and International Criminal Court Act, 1 October 2000], Norway [Norway's Criminal Code (1982) Norwegian General Civil Penal Code, Article 12.4], Portugal [Article 5 of Portugal's Criminal Law Relating to Violations of International Humanitarian Law, 22 July 2004, No. 31/ 2004, amending Article 5 of the Penal Code], Scotland [Section 1(2)(b) of the Scotland ICC Act (2001) International Criminal Court (Scotland) Act, 13 September 2001, 2001 asp 13], Slovenia (Slovenia's Criminal Code (1994), amended on 15 June 2005), South Africa [Section 4(2)(b) and (c) of the South African law (2002) Implementation of the Rome Statute of the International Criminal Court, Act No. 27 of 2002], Spain [Article 23.4 of the Spanish Organic Law of the Judicial Power (1985) Organic Law No. 6/1985], Switzerland [Swiss Penal Code (*Strafgesetzbuch*) (1937), as amended, SR 311.0], Trinidad and Tobago [Section 8 of the Trinidad and Tobago International Criminal Court Act (2006) Laws No. 4, § 10, 24 February 2006], the UK [Sections 51(2)(b) and 58(2)(b) of the UK ICC Act (2001) International Criminal Court Act, United Kingdom, 1 September 2001] and Uruguay [Uruguay's Law (2006) No. 18025, 25

Senegal in 2005, only to be released by court order on the basis of the *DRC v Belgium*[278] case, hereinafter referred to as the *Yerodia* case or simply *Yerodia*, described as 'awful' by Alain Pellet.[279] Further to mounting international pressure, the AU recommended that Senegal amends its legislation to be able to assert jurisdiction over *Hissène Habré*. The ICJ has delivered a decision as to whether Senegal is obliged to extradite *Hissène Habré* to Belgium unless it prosecutes him, or otherwise.[280] The ICJ has ordered Senegal to prosecute the former Chadian President by means of a ruling which 'could affect exiled political leaders in other countries'.[281] The ICJ's judgment is likely to have a tremendous impact on the power of the *aut dedere aut judicare* rule. The world Court unanimously decided that Senegal must comply with the *aut dedere aut judicare* rule by either prosecuting *Hissène Habré* on its own soil without further delay or else by extraditing him to a State which can assert jurisdiction over *Hissène Habré*. In the ICJ's words, Senegal should 'without further delay refer the case of Mr *Hissène Habré* to its competent authorities for the purpose of prosecution if it does not extradite him'.[282] Senegal incurred State responsibility by ignoring the charges against *Hissène Habré* which led to a breach of the CAT, a treaty which requires its State Parties to promulgate municipal laws based upon universal jurisdiction by means of its Article 5, para 2. The judgment cannot however shed a light on the customary international law status of the *aut dedere aut judicare* rule since 'at the time of the filing of the application, the dispute between the Parties did not relate to breaches of obligations under customary international law'.[283] Consequently, the ICJ 'has no jurisdiction to decide on Belgium's claims related thereto'.[284] In line with this, the ICJ considers the *aut dedere aut judicare* rule only conventionally, *id est* in the

September 2006] {see references to some of the above mentioned legal instruments in Kochler 2003, p. 85 and in Kleffner 2008, p. 276 n. 201]. In relation to Spain, Rikhof appropriately stresses that the scope of universal jurisdiction has been limited by 2009 amendments to the Organic Law of the Judiciary which require a more substantial connection of the perpetrator to Spain (Rikhof 2010, p. 56). The decision of many other States not to expressly provide for universal jurisdiction within their municipal law does 'not imply that these States consider universal jurisdiction to be unlawful under international law' (Ryngaert 2008a, p. 119). In fact, some of these States have undertaken certain prosecutions, supposedly on the basis of universal jurisdiction [Stockholm District Court, *Prosecutor v Jackie Arklöf*, 18 December 2006, B 4084-04]. Should States abuse of the principle of universal jurisdiction, the aggrieved State would most likely seek the redress of the ICJ on the basis of a violation of its sovereignty.

278 *DRC v Belgium*, above n. 217.

279 Pellet 2006, p. 88.

280 ICJ (2012) Press release on *Questions Relating to the Obligation to Prosecute or Extradite (Belgium v Senegal)*. http://www.icj-cij.org/docket/files/144/16953.pdf. Accessed 3 May 2013

281 The Global Edition of the New York Times (2014) World News, Saturday–Sunday, July 21–22, 2012, p. 3. http://www.nytimes.com/marketing/globaledition/. Accessed 12 May 2014

282 *Belgium v Senegal*, above n. 40, sub-para 6 of final para 122.

283 *Belgium v Senegal*, above n. 40.

284 Ibid.

context of Article 7, para 1 of the CAT, in paras 89–122 of its judgment.[285] Such a unanimous decision contrasts with the ICJ's divergent opinions in the *Yerodia dictum*, which in Göran Sluiter's words did little for a better understanding of certain concepts such as the scope of universal jurisdiction.[286] Had the trial been undertaken by Senegal, it would have been the first time a head of State would be tried before a criminal court of another State. In practice, the exact same did not happen. Instead, *Hissène Habré*, on 2 July 2013, was charged with crimes against humanity and war crimes before the EAC, a special Court created by agreement between Senegal and the AU on 22 August 2012. He was found guilty of having committed crimes against humanity and was sentenced to life imprisonment by the EAC on 30 May 2016 in the first time a State has prosecuted a former leader of another State for gross human rights violations.[287] Although he was acquitted of rape, the convictions and the infliction of life imprisonment were upheld on appeal.[288] Yet another Court housed in Abuja, Nigeria,[289] dismissed, on 5 November 2013, the request of *Hissène Habré*'s lawyers for provisional measures consisting in the immediate suspension of the prosecution on the grounds of the illegitimacy of the EAC and a likely unfair trial.[290] Since such EAC, the jurisdiction of which is limited *rationae temporis* (with crimes committed between 7 June 1982 and 1 December 1990) and *rationae loci* (with crimes committed on Chadian territory), were created contractually between a State and a regional Union, since they have been set-up within the Senegalese judicial system (both operationally and logistically),[291] and also since such EAC apply their own Statute and Senegalese law, they seem to partake of the horizontal system of enforcement more than of the vertical system of enforcement.[292] Unlike the Special Criminal Court for Events in

[285] Ibid.

[286] Sluiter 2004, pp. 176–177.

[287] Maclean R (2016) Chad's *Hissène Habré* Found Guilty of Crimes Against Humanity: Verdict in Senegal Makes Habre First Former Head of State to be Convicted of the Charge by the Courts of Another Country, Dakar. The Guardian. https://www.theguardian.com/world/2016/may/30/chad-hissene-habre-guilty-crimes-against-humanity-senegal. Accessed 9 February 2018.

[288] AI (2017) *Hissène Habré* Appeal Ruling Closes Dark Chapter for Victims. https://www.amnesty.org/en/pressreleases/2017/04/chad-hissene-habre-appeal-ruling-closes-dark-chapter-for-victims/. Accessed 9 July 2018

[289] This is the Court of Justice of the Economic Community of West African States. See its decision [The Court of Justice of the Economic Community of the States of West Africa (ECOWAS), *Hissène Habré v Republic of Senegal*, 18 November 2010, Case No. ECJ/CCJ/JUD/06/10] rejecting *Hissène Habré's* claims dealing with human rights violations.

[290] See http://www.hrw.org/news/2013/11/05/senegal-case-against-habre-set-continue-0. Accessed 24 November 2016.

[291] They comprise an Extraordinary African Investigation Chamber within the Dakar Regional Court (*Tribunal Régional Hors Classe*), an Extraordinary African Indictments Chamber at the Dakar Court of Appeal, an Extraordinary African Assize Chamber at the Dakar Court of Appeal and an Extraordinary African Assize Appeal Chamber at the Dakar Court of Appeal.

[292] However, they have been categorized as a hybrid tribunal by TRIAL [see ICD (2017) News Archive. http://www.internationalcrimesdatabase.org/Courts/Hybrid. Accessed 9 March 2017].

Darfur, created by Sudan on 7 June 2005[293] and pertaining exclusively to the horizontal realm, the EAC would still be somewhere in between the vertical and horizontal grid, though in the proximity of the horizontal baseline. The fact that investigative judges (the tasks of whom are currently pending and ongoing) and prosecutors were nominated by the Senegalese Minister of Justice and appointed by the Chairperson of the AU Commission, coupled with the Judicial Cooperation Agreement between the Republic of Chad and the Republic of Senegal for the Prosecution of International Crimes Committed in Chad between 7 June 1982 to 1 December 1990, which was signed on 3 May 2013,[294] reinforces the contention that these EAC possess more municipal/domestic features rather than international ones. The same may be said about the IHT which was presided by Iraqi judges and applied Iraqi criminal procedural law. However, this was considered within the former Part dealing with the vertical system of enforcement since it was established further to the invasion of Iraq by coalition forces in 2003 and also because 'behind the scenes a large amount of international advice and support was provided to the process'.[295] It thus possessed a heightened international element.

There seems to be a growing inclination to resort to universal jurisdiction where, due to a variety of factors (particularly immunities, especially personal immunities, of high-level individuals), States cannot exercise jurisdiction over certain core crimes. It is interesting to note, in this context, that paradoxically universal jurisdiction conveys the consummation of serious crimes habitually containing an international or trans-national dimension but simultaneously presupposes that the common law rule entailing that 'all crime is local'[296] subsists. In as much as it entitles a State to prosecute by vesting such State with such jurisdictional authority, universal jurisdiction, to a certain extent, localizes crime. The same may not be said about the ICC or international criminal tribunals falling within the remit of the vertical systems of enforcement. On the contrary, these internationalize the dimension of the criminal act or omission and the reproach thereof.

Spain has unsuccessfully attempted to exercise universal jurisdiction over *José Efraín Ríos Montt*, former *de facto* President of Guatemala. The *Audiencia Nacional* determined that for Spain to exercise universal jurisdiction, domestic remedies must first be exhausted both since Guatemalan law permitted the prosecution of genocide and also because the Genocide Convention asserts territorial jurisdiction.[297] It concluded that Guatemalan Courts were not necessarily unwilling

293 Tillier 2013, p. 518.

294 HRW (2014) Q&A: The Case of *Hissène Habré* Before the Extraordinary African Chambers in Senegal. http://www.hrw.org/news/2012/09/11/qa-case-hiss-ne-habr-extraordinary-african-chambers-senegal. Accessed 10 July 2014.

295 IBA (2018) Iraqi High Tribunal. http://www.ibanet.org/Committees/WCC_IHT.aspx. Accessed 3 September 2018.

296 Reydams 2003, p. 86.

297 Ascencio 2003, p. 692.

or unable to prosecute genocide.[298] *Ríos Montt* died at the age of 91[299] whilst standing accused of genocide in two separate trials before Guatemalan criminal courts, one for the genocide of the Mayan Ixil population, the other for the December 1982 Dos Erres massacre.[300] Thus, universal jurisdiction is subsidiary to territorial jurisdiction in so far as the crime of genocide is concerned, in the view of Spain's *Audiencia Nacional.* Ultimately, brushing off the rule necessitating the exhaustion of domestic remedies, a decision of its Constitutional Court established that Spain may try those accused of genocide, crimes against humanity and torture regardless of:

i. the nationality of the victims;
ii. the nationality of the alleged perpetrators;
iii. the presence of the alleged perpetrators; and
iv. of Spanish national interest or otherwise.[301]

As a side note, the subsidiary nature of Spanish universal jurisdiction was corroborated by the *Audiencia Nacional* in the *Scilingo* case[302] wherein the Spanish Supreme Court referred to *'la no persecución penal de los hechos en Argentina como elemento justificante de segundo grado de la actuación de la jurisdicción española'*.[303] This was the first case in which a non-citizen, an Argentine, 'has been found guilty in a fully litigated trial of crimes against humanity committed in Argentina, *id est,* outside the country exercising jurisdiction, and sentenced to serve a prison term of 640 years in the country exercising jurisdiction'.[304] However, upon a *volte-face*, such relatively broad universal jurisdiction was curtailed by virtue of a legislative reform of Article 23(4) of the Law of 1985[305] limiting the exercise of universal jurisdiction to cases where:

(i) the alleged perpetrator is present in Spain;
(ii) the victims are of Spanish nationality; and
(iii) there is a demonstrated relevant *nexus* with Spain.

---

[298] *Rigoberta Menchu et. al. v Ríos Montt et al.*, above n. 118, para 208, cited in Robinson 2016, p. 117, n. 80.

[299] The Economist (2018) https://www.economist.com/the-americas/2018/04/05/the-death-and-cruel-life-of-efrain-rios-montt. Accessed 2 June 2018.

[300] Barreto B, Freed D, Fabi R (2017) Former Guatemalan Dictator *Ríos Montt* to Face Second Genocide Trial. Reuters. http://www.reuters.com/article/us-guatemala-rights-montt-idUSKBN17402W. Accessed 2 August 2017.

[301] *Rigoberta Menchu et. al. v Rios Montt et. al,* above n. 118; see also Roht-Arriaza 2006, pp. 207–213.

[302] *Audiencia Nacional*, Spain, *Graciela P de L and Others v Scilingo*, 19 April 2005, ILDC 136 (ES 2005), para 6, cited in van der Wilt 2011, pp. 1055–1056, n. 51.

[303] This is translated by Harmen van der Wilt to the effect that it conveys 'the failure to criminally prosecute the crimes in Argentina as a justificatory element of the second degree for the activation of Spanish jurisdiction' (van der Wilt 2011, p. 1055, n. 51).

[304] Weiss 2007, p. 31.

[305] de la Rasilla del Moral 2009.

This amendment to the *Ley Orgánica del Poder Judicial* embodies the subsidiary principle, incorporating it directly into Spanish statutory law.[306] In the meantime, Spanish Courts have tended to assert that the territorial State (the State *locus delicti commissi*) enjoys priority of jurisdiction. Spain used the complementarity principle as a guiding framework for its own domestic criminal justice system.[307] Germany also catered for the subsidiarity principle statutorily, modelling it upon the ICC's complementarity principle in such manner as to provide for subsidiary jurisdiction to prevent impunity, 'but not otherwise inappropriately interfere with the primary responsible jurisdiction'.[308] This is probably the best example of the utility of the vertical system of enforcement for the purposes and benefit of the horizontal system of enforcement, although it suggests that national courts should yield to the ICC,[309] which is the antithesis of complementarity. Spain asserted that if the territorial State (the State *locus delicti commissi*) is unwilling or unable to investigate and prosecute,[310] it should intervene, especially because the ICC had no jurisdiction *rationae temporis* over the case. Subsequently, in January 2012, a court in Guatemala City had ordered that *Montt* may be prosecuted in Guatemala on charges of genocide and crimes against humanity.[311] On 10 May 2013, *Montt* was found guilty of crimes committed against the indigenous Mayan population between 1960 and 1966.[312] He was sentenced to a total 80 years imprisonment, 50 years imprisonment for the crime of genocide and 30 years for the *delitos contra los deberes de humanidad* (crimes against the duties of humanity), these being a hybrid form of crimes against humanity and war crimes contained in Guatemala's Criminal Code.[313] He hence became the first former Head of State to be convicted of genocide in his own country, which decision was however overturned by means of the partial annulment of the trial by the divided Constitutional Court on 27 May 2013.[314] This controversial 3-2 decision ordered that the final stages of the trial (from final submissions onwards) be

---

306 van der Wilt 2011, p. 1056.

307 For a comprehensive understanding of Spain's rapport with universal jurisdiction, both legislatively and jurisprudentially, see Ryngaert 2008b, pp. 160–166.

308 Explanations on the Draft of an Act to Introduce the Code of Crimes Against International Law, p. 82, cited in Ryngaert 2008b, p.170, n. 49.

309 van der Wilt 2011, p. 1056.

310 Bassiouni has consistently referred to circumstances 'when that State cannot fairly and effectively prosecute' (Bassiouni 1999, p. 220, cited in Olson 2011, p. 328).

311 See http://ipsnews.net/news.asp?idnews=106575. Accessed 27 January 2017

312 *Tribunal Primero de Sentencia Penal*, Guatemala City, Guatemala, *Ríos Montt* Judgment, 10 May 2013, No C01076-2011-00015, containing 718 pages, referred to in Kemp 2014, p. 134, n. 2.

313 Kemp 2014, p. 134 and 135.

314 Constitutional Court, Guatemala, *Tribunal Primero A*, Guatemala, *Rigoberta Menchu et al. v Ríos Montt et al. (Genocide in Guatemala),* 20 May 2013, Case No. Exp 1904-2013, a summary of which is available in Spanish. http://www.prensalibre.com/noticias/justicia/Resolucion-CC-Exp1904_PREFIL20130522_0004.pdf. Accessed 9 May 2016.

repeated.[315] The re-trial was supposed to take place in January 2016, but has been definitively suspended.[316] The prevailing uncertainty, however, did not decrease the impetus of the prosecution and of the judgment since 'it makes a rich contribution to the historical narrative, with extensive references to victim, expert and documentary evidence, showing the context and multi-faceted nature of State criminality during the *Rios Montt* regime. It has energized civil society with thousands of copies distributed and *querellantes* presenting the findings through community radio in local languages…This prosecution follows other notable Guatemalan cases in recent years and forms part of the wave of domestic prosecutions of international crimes in Latin America, dating from the Argentine *junta* trials'.[317] Civil society has hailed the judgment which convicted Montt for core crimes against the *Ixil* people as a tremendous victory.[318]

The above mentioned legislation *per se*, not to mention Spanish jurisprudence, is a written expression of the will of the people, and it is hence tantamount to State practice.[319] Together with the domestic jurisprudence cited herein, it has the potential to form customary international law because 'for the purposes of the sources of international law, domestic judicial decisions are formally valued ultimately no differently, all other things being equal, than legislation or conduct by the executive. They are State practice capable of reflecting an *opinio juris* relevant to the existence and precise content of a customary international rule or to the interpretation of a treaty provision'.[320] Effectively they further interpret open-ended norms and 'provide building blocks for customary international law or "general principles"'.[321] When such *dicta* are more general and less specific, the more they will have global validity, and hence they possess a broader reach.[322] In this context, it is important to note that three out of every four UN member States 'have authorized their courts to exercise universal jurisdiction over one or more crimes under international law'.[323] Disagreement however exists as to whether the

---

[315] Kemp 2014, p. 133 and pp. 154–155.

[316] Burt 2016.

[317] Kemp 2014, pp. 155–156.

[318] Robinson 2016, p. 132.

[319] Roger O'Keefe identifies three ways how, as manifestations of practice and *opinio juris* on the part of the forum State, domestic *dicta* may contribute to the development of international jurisdictional rules, these being:

(a) domestic *dicta* are, in and of themselves, practice of the forum State;

(b) domestic *dicta* trigger practice by other States because the reaction of one State to the practice by another State itself constitutes State practice; and

(c) domestic *dicta* trigger international *dicta* which develop international rules on jurisdiction and pronouncements by international courts which, in turn, clarify rules of international law.

O'Keefe 2013, pp. 542–556.

[320] O'Keefe 2013, p. 557.

[321] van der Wilt 2013, p. 228 and 210.

[322] van der Wilt 2013, p. 228.

[323] AI 2011, p. 2.

technique of universal jurisdiction is mandatory or otherwise,[324] if and when the exercise of territorial jurisdiction is unfulfilled. Matters have become more obscure as a result of legislation, promulgated on 11 February 2014, by virtue of which the power of Spanish judges to exercise universal jurisdiction has been significantly watered down. This followed the issue of arrest warrants for former Chinese President Jiàng Zemin and four senior Chinese officials over alleged core crimes committed decades ago in Tibet.[325] One must here keep in mind that both China and Tibet are non-State Parties to the ICC Statute.[326] This State practice is a severe setback for supporters of universal jurisdiction, and can divest Spain of symbolic titles (and the ensuing status) which commonly belonged to it, these being 'a champion of human rights' and a 'temple of international justice'.[327] Although I favour a universal jurisdiction exercised cautiously by the *forum deprehensionis*, which would challenge impunity without upsetting international relations drastically,[328] I acknowledge that the practice of universal jurisdiction is not problem-free. Besides issues dealing with political sensitivities, universal jurisdiction proliferates jurisdictional claims and increases conflicts of jurisdiction, augmenting, in turn, the risk of double jeopardy,[329] this being a ground for refusal of extradition *per se.*

13.3 Limitations of the *Aut Dedere Aut Judicare* Rule

At the outset it must be stated that such limitations could also technically constitute grounds for refusal of extradition. They are, however, being considered autonomously under this heading both because they don't necessarily relate exclusively to extradition *per se*, and because they contemporaneously demand multiple levels of protection,[330] ranging from asylum to refugee protection unto *non-refoulement.*

---

[324] Orentlicher 1991, p. 2565.

[325] Stewart 2014.

[326] *Audiencia Nacional*, Spain, *Fundación Casa del Tibet and Others v Jiang Zemin and Others*, Appeal Judgment on Admissibility, 10 January 2006, ILDC 1002 (ES 2006), cited in van der Wilt 2011, p. 1056, n. 53.

[327] Kassam A (2014) Spain Moves to Curb Legal Convention Allowing Trials of Foreign Rights Abuses. The Guardian http://www.theguardian.com/world/2014/feb/11/spain-end-judges-trials-foreign-human-rights-abuses. Accessed 9 August 2016.

[328] Soler 2014, pp. 285–315.

[329] van der Wilt 2011, p. 1062.

[330] See, for example, demands made by Madelaine Mangabu Bukumba and Garcia Mukumba in Federal Court of Canada, Trial Division, Ottawa, Ontario, Canada, *Madeleine Mangabu Bukumba and Gracia Mukumba v Canada (Minister of Citizenship and Immigration)*, 22 January 2004, [2004] FC 93, and requests for refugee status by *Agathe Habyarimana* leading to the decision of the Appeals Commission for Refugees, 2nd Division, France, *Agathe Habyarimana neé Kanziga*, 15 February 2007, 564776.

Whereas States can potentially detour the *aut dedere aut judicare* rule, paradoxically non-adherence to the rule has generally been consummated at the hands of judicial institutions. When an asylum seeker is charged with a criminal offence in the non-custodial State and simultaneously subjected both to an order for deportation and a request for extradition, the principle of non-*refoulement* might act to override both the repatriation to his place of origin and the extradition to the requesting State.[331] It has been held that 'the inclusion of the principle *aut dedere aut judicare* in instruments aimed at suppressing certain crimes with an international dimension is further acknowledgment that even the serious criminal may deserve protection against persecution or prejudice, while not escaping trial or punishment. Where non-extradition in such cases is prescribed as an obligation, the discretion of the State is significantly confined. *Non-refoulement* becomes obligatory in respect of a class of alleged serious offenders, and no less should be required for the non-serious criminal who would otherwise fall within the exception'.[332] The likelihood of this happening once more has been increased by virtue of the recent judgment in the case of *Hirsi Jamaa and Others v Italy*,[333] wherein a concurring opinion[334] elevated the principle of non-*refoulement* to *jus cogens*. Most relevant for the purposes of my book is the fact that the absoluteness or otherwise of this principle depends upon the underlying protected human rights. It was thus held that:

> since refugee status determination is instrumental in protecting primary human rights, the nature of the prohibition of *refoulement* depends on the nature of the human right being protected by it. When there is a risk of serious harm as a result of foreign aggression, internal armed conflict, extrajudicial death, forced disappearance, death penalty, torture, inhuman or degrading treatment, forced labour, trafficking in human beings, persecution, or trial based on a retroactive penal law or on evidence gathered by torture or inhuman and degrading treatment in the receiving State, the obligation of *non-refoulement* is an absolute obligation of all States. When there is a risk of a violation of any European Convention right (other than the right to life and physical integrity, and the principle of legality in criminal law) in the receiving State, the State may derogate from its duty to provide for international protection, depending on the assessment of the proportionality of the competing values involved. There is an exception to this proportionality test: when the risk of a violation of any European Convention right (other than the right to life and physical integrity and the principle of legality in criminal law) in the receiving State is "flagrant" and the very essence of that right is at stake, the State is unavoidably bound by the obligation of *non-refoulement*.
>
> With this extension and content, the prohibition of *refoulement* is a principle of customary international law, binding on all States, even those not parties to the UN Refugee Convention or any other treaty for the protection of refugees. In addition, it has been argued that it is a rule of *jus cogens*, on account of the fact that no derogation is permitted and of its peremptory nature, since no reservations to it are admitted (Article 53 of the Vienna

---

[331] 'An important limitation to extradition is the prohibition of *refoulement*' (Ott 2011, p. 230).

[332] Goodwin-Gill and McAdam 2007, p. 259.

[333] ECtHR Grand Chamber, *Hirsi Jamaa and Others v Italy*, 23 February 2012, Application No. 27765/09.

[334] *Hirsi Jamaa and Others v Italy*, above n. 333, Concurring Opinion of Judge Pinto de Albuquerque.

Convention on the Law of Treaties and Article 42, § 1 of the Refugee Convention and Article VII, § 1 of the 1967 Protocol). This is now the prevailing position in international refugee law as well.[335]

Jus cogens status can attach to the principle of *non-refoulement* only when the violation of yet another *jus cogens* norm (such as the prohibition of torture) is at stake. In this context, asylum seekers have frequently managed to link the application of two separate human rights to avoid deportation and extradition, these being, on the one hand, the right to personal liberty and security, and on the other, the prohibition of torture.[336] This has been done with reference to conditions of detention, wherein the prohibition of torture was invoked further to claims of overcrowding, inadequate heating, inadequate ventilation, inadequate sleeping and toilet facilities, insufficient food, insufficient recreation and insufficient medical treatment.[337] A classical example of such a phenomenon is illustrated in *Saadi v Italy*[338] concerning a Tunisian national, married to an Italian woman, who was to be deported to Tunisia where he had been sentenced to 20 years' imprisonment for membership of a terrorist organisation. Moreover, the Committee Against Torture ruled that Canada could not deport an individual to Pakistan because he would be threatened with torture or other ill-treatment, and because Pakistan had not ratified the CAT.[339] The provisions of the CAT, however, might give rise to uncertainty. Senegal, for example, has argued[340] that the underlying obligation stipulated therein is not a mandatory one, but a duty to 'try to extradite'.[341] It further submitted that it was taking appropriate measures and steps to prepare for the trial of *Hissène Habré*.[342] The limitations explained here above lead me to consider sprouting alternatives to the *aut dedere aut judicare* rule, some of which can, *in partem*, diminish the restrictive effect of such limitations.

[335] *Hirsi Jamaa and Others v Italy*, above n. 334, Concurring Opinion of Judge Pinto de Albuquerque, pp. 64–64.

[336] For a comprehensive analysis of the intriguing interaction between international criminal law and international refugee law, especially in the context of the law on State cooperation, see Yabasun and Holvoet 2013, pp. 742–744.

[337] See, for example, ECtHR First Section, *Iovchev v Bulgaria*, 2 February 2006, Application No. 41211/98, paras 83–93; ECtHR Second Section, *Peers v Greece*, 19 April 2001, Application No. 28524/95, para 275; ECtHR Third Section, *Dougoz v Greece*, 6 March 2001, Application No. 40907/98, para 255.

[338] ECtHR Grand Chamber, *Nassim Saadi v Italy*, 28 February 2008, Application No. 37201/06.

[339] UN Committee Against Torture, *Tahir Hussain Khan v Canada*, 4 July 1994, Communication No. 15/1994, para 12.1.

[340] ICJ (2012) Press Release No. 2012/13 issued on 21 March 2012 in relation to *Belgium v Senegal*, above n. 40.

[341] Article 6, para 2 and Article 7, para 1 of the CAT.

[342] ICJ (2012) Press Release No. 2012/13 issued on 21 March 2012 in relation to *Belgium v Senegal*, above n. 40.

13.4 Emerging Alternatives to the *Aut Dedere Aut Judicare Formulae*

The absence of an internationally recognised definition of core crimes,[343] together with the complexity of the matter under scrutiny, symbolized by the varying permutations arising from the use of distinct *formulae* considered here above, enable me to conclude that criminal conduct of a very serious nature may not be subsumed into a *chapeau* offence which carries the *aut dedere aut judicare* obligation. In other words, because of its intricate nature amidst contemporary international criminal law, an *aut dedere aut judicare*-offence-like theory or school of thought cannot subsist. At first glance, at least in practice, one cannot refer to an offence as an *aut dedere aut judicare*-offence in order to delineate or determine its main elements, features and characteristics. Stating that an offence is an *aut dedere aut judicare*-offence does not explain or clarify the content of Pandora's box, nor does it lead one to conclude that the offence in question is necessarily a serious crime of concern to the international community, a core crime. The *aut dedere aut judicare* component is therefore inconclusive. By way of example, cybercrimes entail *aut dedere aut judicare*[344] though they manifestly fall very short of attaining core crime status, whereas the Former Yugoslav Republic of Macedonia includes *aut dedere aut judicare* for all crimes provided that the conduct committed abroad by a foreigner found in Macedonia is punishable with at least a five-year term of imprisonment.[345]

Some other alternatives to the traditional *aut dedere aut judicare formulae*, considered here above, are traceable. (I) Firstly, mention must be here made of the obligation to surrender which arises once the admissibility issue has been decided by the ICC, a duty which was examined in the light of the vertical system of enforcement within Sect. 11.1. Section 11.2 deals with competing requests analysing whether the State offering to exercise universal jurisdiction is exempt or otherwise from such admissibility issues. The ICC statutory rules on competing requests[346] provide a tenacious frame of reference in this context. Notwithstanding such coherence, one must question their relevance in the light of the fact that the ICC is only binding on State Parties and is hence inapplicable in relation to non-signatories. The potential effect of such statutory rules is hence restrictive.

(II) Secondly, the *Lockerbie* incident[347] may have given rise to another permutation, *aut dedere aut transferre*. Guido Acquaviva defines it as the surrender of alleged perpetrators to a third State,[348] and considers this variant as an alternative to

[343] See Chap. 4.

[344] Cottim 2010.

[345] AI 2009, p. 14.

[346] See Article 90 of the ICC Statute, above n. 44.

[347] This case involved the terrorist bombing of Pan American trans-atlantic flight 103 from Heathrow Airport, London to JFK Airport in NY on 21 December 1988.

[348] Plachta defines it as the 'delivery of the accused to a third state' (Plachta 2001b, p. 136).

the *aut dedere aut judicare* principle.[349] The *Lockerbie* case was tagged as one possessing a new dimension deemed to constitute 'political international criminal law'.[350] In effect, in an unprecedented manner, it dealt with the prosecution of two Libyan nationals before a criminal tribunal composed of Scottish judges, in Camp Zeist, the Netherlands, which applied Scottish Criminal Law. Michael Plachta, examining the *Lockerbie* case, queried whether this permutation could constitute a 'newly emerging rule of international law of extradition'.[351] I think that *aut dedere aut transferre*, a novel course of action, was truly extra-ordinary but failed to acquire the needed impetus. Its life expectancy is very minimal, if not negligible. Besides being the most expensive domestic trial in history, the *Lockerbie* trial can be considered as no more than a mere 'change of location'.[352] Its detailed examination, for the purposes of my book, is therefore superfluous, unless the international community decides to use a similar juridical framework (as done in the *Lockerbie* case) when and if the prosecution of pro-Russian rebels in eastern Ukraine (for the 17 July 2014 destruction of Malaysia Airlines flight MH17)[353] will be undertaken. This is an unlikely predicament,[354] although both the Netherlands and Australia, on the strength of the conclusions of the international joint investigative team, have attributed the downing thereof to Russia's deployment of the Buk installation.[355] Where such *sui generis* (special) courts are not created, other courts, including hybrid tribunals, are generally introduced. Just to give an example thereof, the Kosovo Relocated Specialist Judicial Institution, which is funded by the EU and housed in The Hague, will try war crimes committed by members of the UCK against ethnic minorities and political opponents during the 1999–2000 war in Kosovo.[356] Likewise, on 29 September 2015, the AU announced the establishment of the HCSS to investigate and prosecute individuals bearing responsibility for violations of international law and/or South Sudanese law, committed from 15 December 2013 through the end of the Transitional Period in South Sudan,[357] the formation of which has been delayed by South Sudan's insistence that it will undermine peace efforts.[358] However, *aut dedere aut transferre* is the living proof

[349] Acquaviva 2009, p. 254.

[350] Aoude 2014, para 5.2.

[351] Plachta 2001b, p. 135.

[352] Scharf 2008, pp. 521–527.

[353] See http://online.wsj.com/articles/west-raises-pressure-on-russia-in-downing-of-malaysia-airlines-flight-17-1405909097. Accessed 31 January 2018

[354] ICD (2014) News Archive, 30 July 2014. http://www.internationalcrimesdatabase.org/home/newsarchive#p27. Accessed 30 March 2016.

[355] Milanovic 2018.

[356] ICD (2016) News Archive, 30 July 2014. http://www.internationalcrimesdatabase.org/home/newsarchive#p27. Accessed 30 March 2016.

[357] Holvoet 2016, p. 36, n. 6.

[358] Sudan Tribune (2017) Plural News and Views on Sudan, South Sudan Says Establishing Hybrid Courts Undermines Peace, Juba. http://sudantribune.com/spip.php?article61533. Accessed 23 March 2017

of the fact that the *aut dedere aut judicare* rule is not exempt from metamorphosis. Indeed, it is, albeit rarely, susceptible to change, no matter how *de minimis* this may be.

(III) Thirdly, it is true that a comparative study must be engendered by considering two or more situations which exist in an analogous context, whereby 'like is compared with like'. However, *gacaca*[359] tribunals,[360] described as traditional forms of communal justice which are nearing their definitive completion,[361] might possess the potential which could enable them to fall within the special category of alternatives to the *aut dedere aut judicare formula*. *Gacaca* courts are State-sanctioned criminal tribunals created by statute, the legitimacy of which derived from their status as government institutions,[362] and which closed officially on 18 June 2012 after the prosecution of a little over than a million *génocidaires*.[363] The second limb of the *formula*, the *judicare* limb, presupposes a prosecution whereby an individual is tried (*aut judicare*). It does not however presuppose any kind of prosecution but a prosecution which adheres to international standards of justice, fairness and equity. In other words, for the second limb to be satisfied, the prosecution must be fair, manifest and effective rather than unfair, latent or by means of a sham prosecution conducted amidst procedural defects which occurred in *mala fides*. A prosecution which does not satisfy such standards might be considered as a non-prosecution by any other State that opts to exercise universal jurisdiction by the requesting State which might request the extradition of the prosecuted individual, or by the ICC's Prosecutor who might argue that a prosecution which does not meet such international standards does not fulfil the willingness criterion which is so crucially important for admissibility, and hence for jurisdictional purposes. As shown in Sect. 11.1.1, the latter will however be particularly difficult since even though it may sound weird, by means of the second limb of Article 17(2)(c) of the ICC Statute,[364] due process, at least for admissibility purposes, is only applicable when it is designed to make the accused more difficult to convict. This is not the norm because usually fair trial violations facilitate the conviction of the accused, in which case the second limb of Article 17(2)(c) would not apply since, irrespective of the extent of their unfairness, such proceedings would not be inconsistent with the intent to bring the defendant to justice. All this shows that the ICC is no supra-national human rights court. *Gacaca* criminal

[359] This connotes a meeting on the grass (Carter 2008, p. 41).

[360] These were established in Rwanda in March 2001, heard cases of genocide, and had the power to sentence criminals up to life imprisonment.

[361] Powers 2011.

[362] Le Mon 2007, p. 16

[363] de Brouwer and Ruvebana 2013, pp. 937–938.

[364] This stipulates that the proceedings in the domestic State must be conducted in a manner which, in the circumstances, is inconsistent with an intent to bring the person concerned to justice, for unwillingness to subsist.

proceedings,[365] described as 'an ingenious solution to an overwhelming problem',[366] would not fulfil such international standards whereby fully-fledged fair trial rights are safeguarded, administered and executed within a scenario which enforces the equality of arms. But does this necessarily mean that such proceedings are unfair? Does this necessarily mean that such proceedings cannot constitute a prosecution in terms of the *aut dedere aut judicare* rule? The answer to such questions would probably not be in the affirmative. Hence, other forms of prosecuting alleged perpetrators of core crimes 'which have the potential to spawn new legal responses to gross violations of human rights'[367] might be budding, especially in as much as low-profile criminals are concerned. These juridical infrastructures are more akin to the inquisitorial criminal justice system rather than the adversarial one. To what extent such proceedings and decisions would be considered persuasive and/or authoritative by the 'westernized juridical world' is another matter, but irrespective of this, *gacaca* tribunals, besides being faster and cheaper socio-legal experiments, may be considered as a third sprouting alternative to the second limb of the *aut dedere aut judicare* global enigma. This is more so because there exists a perception that 'the *gacaca* procedure could produce more truth than the formal justice system has so far managed to do'.[368] Moreover, such proceedings have incentivised confessions which have, in turn, skyrocketed, and have been locally preferred.[369] *Gacaca* tribunals 'apply both customary and statutory law'[370] and may be said to provide certain fundamental safeguards anyway. For example, 'the play of argument and counter-argument and of witness and counter-witness by the community basically amounts to a fair defence, possibly producing better results than the formal justice system has until now been able to achieve'.[371] *Gacaca* proceedings, the jurisdiction of which does not overlap with that of domestic Rwandan courts and/or with ICTR's,[372] may be deemed to be 'locally appropriate and popularly legitimate forms of justice' which 'should not be dismissed outright as inappropriate or unjust'.[373] To this effect, it has been juxtaposed that 'the innovations represented by the system could establish a precedent for local retributive justice if care is taken to ensure minimum standards of fairness'.[374]

365 These don't admit of a separation between prosecutors and judges (referred to as person of integrity, *inyangamugayo*), there is no legal counsel, no procedural rules forbidding the admission of hearsay evidence, and no motivated verdict, whereas self-incrimination is greatly encouraged. Such lay people of integrity were appointed from the local community in view of the fact that most Rwandan lawyers were killed during the genocide itself [de Brouwer and Ruvebana 2013, p. 941].

366 Carter 2008, p. 49.

367 Mibenge 2005, p. 195

368 Uvin 2003, p. 118

369 Uvin 2003, p. 119.

370 Kindiki 2001, p. 69.

371 Uvin 2003, p. 119.

372 So-called 'category one *génocidaires*' are not tried by *gacaca* courts (Gaparayi 2001, p. 83).

373 Uvin 2003, p. 119.

374 Wahid Hanna 2008, p. 320.

Comparatively, 'they can be considered more successful in Rwanda than the ICTR has been'.[375]

This said, *gacaca* courts have been criticised for various reasons, including the undermining of the presumption of innocence. The ECtHR remarked that:

'After a pilot phase when approximately 700,000 individuals were identified for prosecution for having participated in the genocide, the *gacaca* courts began trials nationwide in July 2006. The trials have been public but there have been concerns about their fairness, among other things because of a perceived lack of impartiality and reports that defendants have not been given the opportunity to defend themselves. In addition, some courts have spent only a few hours hearing each case and poorly qualified, ill-trained and corrupt *gacaca* judges in certain districts have fuelled widespread distrust of the system. There have been reports of local *gacaca* officials and citizens abusing the process to pursue personal matters and settle grudges unrelated to the genocide, including making false accusations in order to acquire land. However, in some reported cases where judges had acted inappropriately, *gacaca* officials have intervened and held that the procedure had been illegal'.[376]

Detailed NGO reports[377] reveal that there is material upon which the independence and impartiality of such courts can be seriously questioned.[378] Some go as far as contending that the system is 'fundamentally flawed'.[379] More specifically, international fair trial rights have been violated in some cases, particularly as a result of the following breaches:

i. defence lawyers are excluded from *gacaca* courts, negating the right to counsel (legal representation);
ii. the presumption of innocence has been habitually violated by senior Rwandan government officials;
iii. the accuracy and completeness of confessions have almost always been challenged;[380]
iv. accused persons have not been informed on the case and have not been given adequate time to prepare a defence. In many cases the 'accused only learned of the real nature of the allegations against them on the day of their trial. The

[375] Powers 2011.

[376] ECtHR Fifth Section, *Sylvère Ahorugeze v Sweden*, 27 October 2011, Application No. 37075/09, para 37.

[377] HRW (2011) Justice Compromised: The Legacy of Rwanda's Community-Based Gacaca Courts, pp. 27–64. http://www.hrw.org/sites/default/files/reports/rwanda0511webwcover.pdf. Accessed 2 July 2012.

[378] HRW (2011) Justice Compromised: The Legacy of Rwanda's Community-Based Gacaca Courts, pp. 104–111. http://www.hrw.org/sites/default/files/reports/rwanda0511webwcover.pdf. Accessed 2 July 2012.

[379] Chakravarty 2006, p. 135.

[380] Rettig 2008, p. 39.

inability of the accused to involve a lawyer only aggravated these problems';[381]

v. the 2004 *Gacaca* Law does not guarantee the privilege against self-incrimination but imposes a legal duty to testify. *Avocats Sans Frontières*, operating a gacaca-monitoring program nationwide from 2005 until 2010, repeatedly expressed concern on this matter;[382]
vi. the 2004 *Gacaca* Law allowed *gacaca* courts to prosecute persons for crimes for which they had already been tried in first and second instance conventional courts, regardless of whether they had been convicted or acquitted;
vii. *gacaca* courts prosecuted hundreds, perhaps thousands, of individuals *in absentia*, a number of which were politically-motivated cases;
viii. Sovu residents have used *gacaca* courts as a forum to settle old disputes;[383]
ix. more than 60% of Sovu residents admitted that 'people are afraid of defending the accused';[384]
x. transferring category 1 rape cases to *gacaca* courts backfired since most rape victims were reluctant to testify because they perceived that confidentiality would not be respected, they feared corruption, they believed that their cases would not be judged fairly and impartially, given the judges' ties with the community, and they also felt that such transfer of cases minimized the gravity of the rape they had endured.[385]

Finally, in any case, one cannot exclude *ab initio* that substantive justice can be meted out even when procedural unfairness subsists. Frankly, it is arduous to contest the fact that *gacaca* is probably the best example of territorial jurisdiction (a showcase for the *forum conveniens*) at the pinnacle of criminal justice since it is the most home-made solution which caters for the prevailing exigencies in Rwanda and the needs of the Rwandan society at large. This conclusion can fairly be reached also because 'through its participatory nature and having the hearings at the locations where the crimes had taken place and where eyewitnesses were largely available, *gacaca* made it possible to have trials of people whose participation in the genocide would not have been easily known if the (lengthy and costly) rules of procedure and evidence of (for most people far away) ordinary courts would have

---

[381] HRW (2011) Justice Compromised: The Legacy of Rwanda's Community-Based Gacaca Courts, p. 34. http://www.hrw.org/sites/default/files/reports/rwanda0511webwcover.pdf. Accessed 2 July 2012.

[382] *Avocats Sans Frontières* (2010) *Monitoring des Jurisdiction Gacaca, Phase de Jugement, Rapport Analytique no 5: Janvier 2008-Mars 2010* [Monitoring of the Gacaca Courts, Judgment Phase: Analytical Report No. 5, January 2008–March 2010] http://www.asf.be/wp-content/publications/Rwanda_MonitoringGacaca_RapportAnalytique5_Light.pdf. Accessed 30 December 2014; see also Chakravarty 2006, pp. 136–137.

[383] Rettig 2008, p. 39.

[384] Rettig 2008, pp. 40–41.

[385] HRW (2011) Justice Compromised: The Legacy of Rwanda's Community-Based Gacaca Courts, pp. 112–116. http://www.hrw.org/sites/default/files/reports/rwanda0511webwcover.pdf. Accessed 2 July 2012.

been applied'.[386] Moreover, if justice is seen from a wider lens and with a broader perspective, it may have been meted out simply by ensuring that 'for many of the survivors interviewed, knowing the truth, even sometimes only partly, in regard to what happened to their loved ones (how they were killed, where, when and by whom) and where they were buried was a very important result from *gacaca*, whereby locating the bones gave them the opportunity to rebury their relatives in dignity',[387] this being a state of affairs which many relatives of Central and South American *desaparecidos* understandably envy.[388] Interviews and reliable studies have revealed that *gacaca* courts also had a therapeutic effect on victims and their relatives. Anne-Marie de Brouwer and Etienne Ruvebana upheld that 'in spite of how difficult it was to participate and testify in *gacaca*, many also felt that doing so had unburdened their hearts, healed and empowered them'.[389] The conceptual reorientation of Rwandan criminal justice, to which gacaca gave a partial contribution, is a mark containing a value-driven connotation. Confession, apology and forgiveness, values which are nearly-universally recognised, are commonplace in *gacaca* proceedings.[390] In Phil Clark's study, truth, peace, justice, healing, forgiveness and reconciliation are the 'profound objectives' of *gacaca* (a dynamic and kinetic social institution) which, to this extent, is a prime example of restorative justice intended to initiate the process of the reconstruction of the social fabric.[391] *Gacaca* courts also eradicated the culture of impunity to such extent that Rwanda 'became the first post-conflict country ever to seriously follow up on the maxim that there should not be impunity for perpetrators' of core crimes.[392] It is hence not surprising that 'most survivors interviewed have viewed *gacaca* as positive overall', these being findings also confirmed in recent literature and reports.[393]

This said, although the concept of *gacaca* courts might have been laudable (at least conceptually), it is argued that *gacaca*, 'fraught with corruption and violence', might have achieved neither justice nor reconciliation.[394] Worse than this, some,

---

[386] de Brouwer and Ruvebana 2013, p. 950.

[387] de Brouwer and Ruvebana 2013, p. 946.

[388] See the objectives of FEDEFAM (The Latin American Federation of Associations for Relatives of the Detained-Disappeared), a NGO founded in January 1981 in San Jose, Costa Rica and formalized in Caracas, Venezuela, in November 1981, and comprising various countries with member associations, including Argentina, Bolivia, Brasil, Colombia, Chile, Ecuador, El Salvador, Guatemala, Honduras, Mexico, Nicaragua, Paraguay, Peru and Uruguay, in *FEDEFAM* (1981) *Desaparecidos:* Fighting Against Forced Disappearances in Latin America. http://www.desaparecidos.org/fedefam/eng.html. Accessed 3 January 2013.

[389] de Brouwer and Ruvebana 2013, p. 971.

[390] de Brouwer and Ruvebana 2013, pp. 938–943; see also Rettig 2008, p. 44.

[391] Panepinto 2012, pp. 101–102.

[392] de Brouwer and Ruvebana 2013, p. 950.

[393] de Brouwer and Ruvebana 2013, p. 974.

[394] Le Mon 2007, p. 19.

not myself, opine that gacaca courts may have blocked possibilities for other transitional justice institutions which could have been more successful in achieving either justice or reconciliation, or both.[395] Although the question which will always be posed is, whether *gacaca* can be measured against the legal principles and characteristics that can be found in classical penal court systems, [396] and although 'the *gacaca*'s contribution to national reconciliation is actually difficult to define or anticipate,'[397] I consider *gacaca* as a valid alternative to the rather rigid *aut dedere aut judicare formulae*.

(IV) Fourthly, new phenomena imply that new ideas must be introduced just as modern crimes necessitate innovative ways of combating such crimes. In as much as it is an international institution and hence a subject of international law, the EU, which has already established *OLAF*,[398] is consistently constructing a *corpus juris criminalis* designed to combat transnational organised crimes, some of which, as described in Sect 8.1, overlap with or verge onto being considered as core crimes. This proposed novel *corpus juris criminalis*,[399] European Criminal Law, that is, criminal law within the parameters of the EU or EU-devised criminal law, falls short of the European Criminal Code and the European Code of Criminal Procedure contemplated, albeit unfavourably, by André Klip.[400] It is predominantly merely intended to suppress crimes which jeopardize the financial interests of the EU[401] rather than to harmonise or Europeanize criminal law, yet it received vehement objections especially by British journalists and political scientists.[402] To this extent it is a very *sui generis*, non-exhaustive, juridical *ensemble*[403] consisting of a supranational body within the Area of Freedom, Security and Justice.[404] As a result of such objectives which have been crystallized in the Stockholm

---

[395] Ibid.

[396] de Brouwer and Ruvebana 2013, p. 972.

[397] Magsam 2007, p. 162.

[398] This is the European Anti-Fraud Office established on 28 April 1999 by virtue of Decision 1999/352 EC, ECSC, Euratom.

[399] In July 2013 the European Commission proposed a Regulation on the establishment of a EPPO in terms of Article 86 of the Treaty on the Functioning of the EU (2007) Treaty on the Functioning of the European Union. http://eur-lex.europa.eu/legal-content/EN/TXT/?uri=celex:52013PC0534. Accessed 2 March 2014.

[400] Klip 2002, p. 111.

[401] See http://ec.europa.eu/anti_fraud/. Accessed 31 March 2015.

[402] Rowlands D (2012) Centurean 2/'s Weblog, EU-Style Justice *Corpus Juris*. http://centurean2.wordpress.com/2012/02/16/eu-style-justice-corpus-juris-by-david-rowlands-ret-magistrate/. Accessed 30 July 2013.

[403] Such developments, but particularly the EAW, have led Michael Plachta to compare the EU to a laboratory where 'several new and interesting ideas have developed and some experiments have been carried out' (Plachta 2003, p. 179).

[404] Ligeti 2013, p. 3.

Programme,[405] it also curbs the financing of terrorism[406] which can be tantamount to a core crime,[407] together with other crimes, such as human trafficking,[408] which could also constitute core crimes,[409] by:

i. strengthening the roles, functions and powers of EUROJUST;[410]
ii. creating a EPPO;[411]
iii. facilitating mutual cooperation and ensuring mutual recognition in criminal matters;[412]
iv. executing a more coherent approach to criminal sanctions, even across borders;[413] and
v. granting more efficient forms of relief to victims, including effective remedies, compensation and satisfaction to victims.

These inter-State measures introduce internalized mechanisms which rely upon a network of information-sharing and cooperation on a regional sphere in a rather novel manner. This fascinating body of laws has, occasionally, permeated *terra incognita*. Framework Decision 2002/475 on Combating Terrorism stipulates that:

---

[405] European Council (2010) The Stockholm Programme: An Open and Secure Europe Serving and Protecting Citizens, 2010/C 115/01. http://eur-lex.europa.eu/LexUriServ/LexUriServ.do?uri=OJ:C:2010:115:0001:0038:en:PDF. Accessed 12 January 2012.

[406] Terrorism is punishable directly under the Statute of the STL (2007) Statute of the Special Tribunal for Lebanon by virtue of its Article 2(a) (Serra 2008, pp. 350–351). For an in-depth analysis of the circumstances wherein terrorism may constitute a core crime, see Kaikobad 2007, pp. 187–276.

[407] Saul 2006, p. 183. Fiona de Londras states that ‘the absence of a crime of terrorism within the Rome Statute does not mean, however, that no argument can be made that terrorism *per se* is in fact an international crime as a matter of customary international law’ (De Londras 2011, p. 175).

[408] See Sect. 8.1.

[409] Obokata 2005, p. 445; see also Bassiouni 2008c, pp. 593.

[410] EUROJUST, housed in The Hague, is a EU body established by a Council Decision 2002/187/JHA to improve judicial cooperation in the fight against serious crime (amended by Council Decision 2003/659/JHA and Council Decision 2009/426/JHA).

[411] To this effect, four options were assessed. These are (1) the creation of a EPPO within Eurojust, (2) a college-type EPPO, (3) a decentralised EPPO and (4) a centralised EPPO (van Ballegooij 2018, p. 30). Article 86 of the Treaty on the Functioning of the EU establishes that such an office would function within the auspices of EUROJUST [Consolidated Versions of the Treaty on EU and the Treaty on the Functioning of the EU {2008/C 115/01}]. http://eur-lex.europa.eu/LexUriServ/LexUriServ.do?uri=OJ:C:2008:115:0001:01:en:HTML. Accessed 12 January 2012.

[412] For an analysis of the legal instruments which are aimed at implementing the mutual recognition principle, see Weyembergh 2013, pp. 957–975.

[413] Article 86(4) of the Treaty on the Functioning of the EU, above n. 399, which is a provision of the Lisbon Treaty (2007) Treaty of Lisbon Amending the Treaty on European Union and the Treaty Establishing the European Community, allows the extension of the competence of the EPPO, by unanimous decision of the European Council, to include serious crimes having a cross-border dimension. (Ligeti 2013, p. 2).

> Each Member State shall take the necessary measures also to establish its jurisdiction over the offences referred to in Articles 1–4 in cases where it refuses to hand over or extradite a person suspected or convicted of such an offence to another Member State or to a third country.[414]

Hence rather than requiring a prosecution in terms of the second limb which imposes the *judicare* requirement, the above legal provision merely refers to the establishment of jurisdiction. However, the word 'also' seems to infer that the establishment of jurisdiction is the end of a process, the destination point, rather than the *point de départ*. This could suggest that the 'necessary measures' contemplated therein might include other measures which exceed prosecutorial discretion, such as arbitrary detentions, *incommunicado* detentions or detentions without trial for the purposes of justice, liberty and security,[415] a common reality in the USA-controlled Guantanamo Bay detention facility.[416] Whilst, on the one hand, ECJ case-law impliedly precludes such extra-ordinary measures by safeguarding the rights of the defence,[417] it stresses the non-absoluteness of the right to a fair trial, necessitating the striking of a balance between the rights of the accused and those of victims.[418]

(V) Last but not least, the contemporary complex structure of judicial institutions, ranging from the domestic (national), to the special, to the regional (continental) and to the international (supra-national), coupled with the political nature of the matter under scrutiny, enables States to consider their *aut dedere aut judicare* obligations holistically and cumulatively. By way of example, the Supreme Court of the Netherlands[419] considered the fact that former Zairian army officer *Sebastien Nzapali* obtained a valid residence permit in Belgium in January 2008, and awaited the decision of the ECtHR in the case *Nzapali v The Netherlands*[420] until 17 November 2005 when the Strasbourg Court considered *Nzapali*'s claims as inadmissible and manifestly ill-founded.[421] *Ricardo Cavallo*, a former Argentine Intelligence Officer who served in the notorious *Escuela de Suboficiales de*

---

414 Article 9, para 3.

415 This falls within the EU's third pillar of Police and Judicial Cooperation in Criminal Matters.

416 HRW (2018) Detention Without Trial. https://www.hrw.org/topic/terrorism-counterterrorism/detention-without-trial. Accessed 17 November 2018.

417 ECJ, Fourth Chamber, *SGL Carbon AG v Commission of the European Communities*, 10 May 2007, Case C-328/05 P, para 59.

418 ECJ, *Criminal Proceedings Against Maria Pupino*, Opinion of Advocate General Kokott, 11 November 2004, Case C-105/03, para 67; ECJ, Third Chamber, *Varec SA v Belgian State*, 14 February 2008, Case C-450/06.

419 *Hoge Raad* [Supreme Court], the Netherlands, *Public Prosecutor v Sebastien Nzapali*, 1 December 2009, S/07-12112.

420 DomCLIC (2016) http://www.asser.nl/default.aspx?site_id=36&level1=15248&level2=&level3=&textid=39989. Accessed 4 September 2016 and ICD (2016), http://www.internationalcrimesdatabase.org/Case/1128. Accessed 4 September 2016.

421 ECtHR (2015) Information Notes on the Court's Case-Law, No. 191, pp. 9–10. http://www.echr.coe.int/Documents/CLIN_2015_12_191_ENG.pdf. Accessed 30 December 2015.

Mecánica de la Armada,[422] and was known as 'the angel of death',[423] was subjected to an indictment for genocide and terrorism by Spanish Judge Baltasar Garzón in 1999, arrested in Mexico on 24 August 2000, extradited to Spain on 28 June 2003, but finally extradited to Argentina, with the agreement of Mexico, notwithstanding a decision of the Spanish Supreme Court of 18 July 2007 authorising the continuation of proceedings in Spain.[424] *Cavallo* was sentenced to life imprisonment on 26 October 2011 by the Criminal Tribunal of *Buenos Aires* for various crimes against humanity, including murder and torture.[425] This case marked the 'first instance of universal jurisdiction extradition under the age-old principle of *aut dedere aut judicare*'.[426] Although what is suggested hereinafter did not materialise, these situations could have led either to a procrastination of the execution of the *aut dedere aut judicare* rule or to diplomatic and consular negotiations as a result of which a State might potentially circumvent its *aut dedere aut judicare* obligations, albeit limitedly.

13.5 The Fractional Re-characterisation of the *Aut Dedere Aut Judicare* Rule

Only time will tell whether the *aut dedere aut judicare* rule is here to stay, and if so, to what extent and in what way. In any case, some other novelties might be welcomed too. These do not clarify or elaborate the rule. They are ancillary to it, but somehow connected, albeit indirectly. Their underlying thrust might seem, at first glance, segmented, but their long-term influence could leverage the fight against impunity. Whilst not directly boosting the rule, they tweak it in such a way as to upgrade its potential stimulus, hence fractionally re-characterising it. Scant reference is here made to the potential rekindling of the *aut dedere aut transferre* rule, considered in Sect. 13.4. Though its potential is extremely limited, technically it possesses some acumen required to re-characterise the *aut dedere aut judicare* rule.

Contemporary human rights discourse and the enforcement of accessorial human rights can affect the *aut dedere aut judicare* rule. By way of example, the IACtHR

---

422 This was the most important secret detention centre in Buenos Aires at the time of the military *juntas*, being years 1976–1983 (Roht-Arriaza 2009a, p. 50).

423 Weiss 2007, p. 32.

424 *Suprema Corte de Justicia de la Nación* [Supreme Court], Mexico, *Ricardo Miguel Cavallo, Amparo en Revision*, 10 June 2003, Case No. 14/2002.

425 See Tribunal Oral Federal Nº 5, *Prosecutor v Ricardo Miguel Cavallo*, 26 October 2011, Case No. 1298; *Poder Judicial de la Nación*, Buenos Aires, *Prosecutor v Ricardo Miguel Cavallo*, Full Verdict, 28 December 2011, Case No. 1298. The 2005-page full verdict is available in Spanish at http://www.asser.nl/upload/documents/20121101T041309-Cavallo%20Tribunal%20Buenos%20Aires%20Fallo%2028-12-2011.pdf. Accessed 22 July 2016.

426 Weiss 2007, p. 32.

has upheld that the prohibition of forced disappearance……and the corresponding obligation to investigate and punish those responsible has attained the status of *jus cogens*, and that therefore the State *locus delicti commissi* has the obligation not to leave these crimes unpunished by ensuring effective prosecution and punishment of perpetrators.[427] Such regional court has determined that the duty to investigate is particularly intense and significant in cases of crimes against humanity,[428] whereas the HRC, establishing a mandatory duty to investigate and prosecute criminally, has prioritized the forced disappearances of persons and the right to life.[429] The type of crime, however, is not the determining factor which would establish the degree of the duty to investigate, or rather, the extent to which the investigation must be carried out and the time within which it should be completed. The duty, especially for the ICC State Parties, becomes more compelling when it concerns citizens and territory of States which are not ICC State Parties 'because to do otherwise would permit impunity'.[430]

Jurists, arguing against a theory which conclusively establishes that the positive duties under human rights treaties 'create an absolute duty to prosecute all international crimes in all circumstances',[431] have warned that the jurisprudence of the IACtHR 'should not be borrowed directly, in its uncompromising formula and legal reasoning, by other human rights bodies for situations which are structurally different'.[432] I hence take into account the counterpart of the IACtHR in Europe, with due caution. Nowadays, in so far as regional human rights systems are concerned, a general duty to investigate serious violations of fundamental human rights[433] is emerging steadily. It can safely be posited that competent authorities of States are required 'to investigate allegations of ill-treatment when they are "arguable" and

---

427 IACtHR, *Goiburú et al. v Paraguay*, 22 September 2006, Series C No. 153, para 84; IACtHR, *Miguel Castro-Castro Prison v Perú*, 25 November 2006, Series C No. 160.

428 IACtHR, *La Cantuta v Perú* (Merits, Reparations and Costs), 29 November 2006, Series C No. 162.

429 HRC, *Bautista de Arellana v Colombia*, 27 October 1995, Communication No. 563/1993, para 8.6.

430 Constitutional Court, South Africa, *National Commission of the South African Police Service and Another v Southern African Human Rights Litigation Centre and Another (Zimbabwe Torture Docket* case*)*, 30 October 2014 [2014] ZACC 30, para 32, cited in Ventura 2015, p. 869, n. 41 and p. 871, n. 54.

431 Scharf 1996, p. 1.

432 Cryer et al. 2010, p. 71.

433 For the purposes of my book, I shall use the term 'fundamental human rights', rather than 'human rights' or 'fundamental rights', the latter being the EU counterpart of the internationally used term 'human rights'. The term 'fundamental human rights' encompasses the international understanding of 'human rights' and the communitarian regime of 'fundamental rights', typified by the designation of one of its advisory bodies, the FRA, housed in Vienna and set up by means of a legal act in 2007. The nomenclature used herein, 'fundamental human rights', clearly presupposes a level of gravity which is commensurate to the designation of core crimes, being the 'most serious crimes of concern to the international community as a whole' [see the Preamble to the ICC Statute, above n. 44].

"raise a reasonable suspicion"', the corollary of which is the obligation to take all the necessary steps to secure evidence such as detailed statements from victims, eyewitness testimony, forensic evidence and medical reports.[434] Some qualifications must, however, be made.

Firstly, a duty to investigate is discernible, but no fully-fledged duty to prosecute unequivocally subsists. The duty to investigate can owe its origin to the cumulative interpretation of constitutional provisions and of the ICC Statute (if and when this is ratified by a State Party) in the light of and in relation to international law. This firm stand was taken by the South African Constitutional Court in the *Zimbabwe Torture Docket* case.[435] Irrespective of its grounding in the law and/or its jurisprudential (teleological) genesis, the duty to investigate serious crimes (which should encompass core crimes) is recognized in Germany, Lebanon, Azerbaijan, BiH, Japan, England and Wales, Estonia, Armenia, Malta, Canada, South Korea, Perú, India, Mongolia, Italy, Ghana, Argentina and Israel.[436] Fifteen EU Member States confer a right to institute a private prosecution to victims if the public prosecutor has declined to prosecute.[437] Here the 'unable or unwilling' paradigm assumes significance. Yet allowing victims to engage in private prosecutions is not equivalent to a duty of the competent authorities to prosecute, especially when the right to institute a private prosecution arises only upon a waiver or renunciation thereof by a public prosecutor. This is even more so where the waiver is tacit and simply consists in absolute inaction by the public prosecutor. In such cases the rights of victims are endangered in many ways. It is unclear at which point in time may the victim determine conclusively that the public prosecutor has waived or renounced to his right to prosecute. This can lead to risks of time-barring of the criminal action where domestic jurisdictions allow for statutory limitations,[438] not to mention the hazard which the failure to preserve evidence adequately may bring about. Here one must recall that statutory limitations can serve an ultimate purpose, that of guaranteeing a fair trial.[439] Even if a right to institute a private prosecution might be discernible in some States, in the case of some States this right is severely

---

[434] ECtHR, Third Section, *Carol Ciorcan and Others v Romania*, 27 January 2015, Application Numbers 29414/09 and 44841/09, para 147.

[435] *Zimbabwe Torture Docket* case, above n. 430, paras 55 and 47, cited in Ventura 2015, p. 877, n. 76.

[436] Ventura 2015, pp. 880–881, notes 82–99.

[437] FRA (2014) Challenging the Decision Not to Prosecute, cited in Mujuzi 2016, p. 108, n. 2. See also Chap. 21, Sect. 21.2.

[438] France dropped criminal charges of torture and additional charges in terms of Articles 222-1 and 222-6 of the *Code Pénal* against *Pascal Simbikangwa*, a Rwandan living in France, owing to its failure to satisfy the domestic statute of limitations {namely Article 7 of the *Code de Procédure Pénale*, France (1957)} which bars criminal action after the lapse of ten years from the consummation of the crime if, during such ten year period, no investigation or legal proceedings were commenced (Trouille 2016, p. 200, n. 28).

[439] The High Court of Justice, Queen's Bench Division, UK, Ndiki Mutua, Paulo Nzili, *Wambugu Wa Nyigi, Jane Muthoni Mara and Susan Ngondi v The Foreign and Commonwealth Office*, 5 October 2012, HQ09X02666, para 9.

compromised where certain core crimes are concerned since the exercise of the right is dependent upon the approval of the State's chief prosecuting officer. In the case of the UK, for example, the Director of Public Prosecutions must consent to such private prosecution in terms of Section 153(1)(4A) of the Police Reform and Social Responsibility Act.[440] If private prosecutions depend on the whims of public prosecutors they can be aborted quite easily by States which have controlling power and authority either over the offices of the public prosecutor or over the public prosecutor himself, and particularly when his appointment and removal from office is a prerogative either of the Head of State or of the head of Government. Sometimes the right to institute a private prosecution may also be curtailed by the fact that only the victim can mount a private prosecution.[441] It seems more plausible to avail oneself of this right within jurisdictions, like Spain, which allow for professional associations/bodies to institute a private prosecution on behalf of one of its members.[442]Admittedly, the recognition of a duty to prosecute (in terms of international human rights law) both by the IACtHR[443] and by domestic courts in Argentina,[444] Bolivia,[445] Chile,[446] Colombia[447] and México,[448] would not be enough to consider such duty under international law as unequivocal. Undoubtedly an investigation must always be carried out before a prosecution is undertaken.[449] Thus, the role of an investigation is pivotal, but, from a penological perspective, an

[440] Mujuzi 2016, p. 123, n. 110.

[441] ECtHR Chamber, *Alecos Modinos v Cyprus*, Dissenting Opinion of Judge Pikis, 22 April 1993, Application Number 15070/89, pp. 19–20, cited in Mujuzi 2016, p. 122, n. 95.

[442] ECtHR Grand Chamber, *Tejedor García v Spain*, 16 December 1997, Application No. 142/1996/761/962, paras 8 and 25, cited in Mujuzi 2016, p. 122, n. 99.

[443] IACtHR, *Velásquez-Rodríguez v Honduras*, 29 July 1988, Series C, No. 4, para 166. A particularly significant development signalled by this judgment is that 'States may even incur responsibility for abuses committed by individuals acting in a private capacity' as a result of 'the lack of due diligence to prevent the violation or to respond to it as required by the American Convention on Human Rights' [van der Wilt 2000, p. 327]. The ground-breaking judgment was also invoked by the Colombian State Council in Colombian State Council, *Hector Jaime Beltran Parra, Clara Patricia, Nidia Amanda, Jose Antonio and Mario Beltran Fuentes*, 19 July 2007 (Ayala 2016, p. 312, n. 27).

[444] *Corte Suprema de Argentina* [Supreme Court], Argentina, *Arancibia Clavel, Enrique Lautaro Homicidio Calificado y Asociación Ilicita y Otros*, 24 August 2004, Case No. 259, paras 4 and 13, cited in Ferdinandusse 2006, p. 198, n. 1172, and p. 75.

[445] *Tribunal Constitucional, Estado de Bolivia, José Carlos Trujillo Oroza José contra Luis Dabdoub López y Jacinto Morón Sánchez, Sentencia,* 12 November 2001, *Resolucion* 1190/01-R, cited in Ferdinandusse 2006, p. 198, n. 1173.

[446] Court of Appeals, Santiago, Chile, *Fernando Laureani Maturana and Miguel Krassnoff Marchenko v. Miguel Ángel Sandoval Rodríguez*, 5 January 2004, 517-2004, paras 49 and 84, cited in Ferdinandusse 2006, p. 198, n. 1174.

[447] *Corte Constitucional* [Constitutional Court], *Sala Plena*, Bogotá, Colombia, *Sentencia (In re Corte Penal Internacional)*, 30 July 2002, C-578/02, paras 2265, 2268–2269 and 2275–2277, cited in Ferdinandusse 2006, p. 198, n. 1175.

[448] *Cavallo*, above n. 424, para 909, cited in Ferdinandusse 2006, p. 198, n. 1176.

[449] Ventura 2015, p. 869, n. 41 and pp. 875–876.

investigation *per se* is grossly insufficient since it falls short of prosecution. Secondly, no individual right to demand a prosecution, or to see another person criminally prosecuted, subsists internationally.[450] In fact, such right is not provided for either 'in any human rights instrument of the European Union nor in any regional or international human rights instrument in the world'.[451] Although various States allow for the right to institute a private prosecution, the violation of such right does not translate into a violation of the right to a fair trial, but, at most, into a violation of the right to a national effective remedy.[452] Consequently, the reparation involved to remedy the breach is not likely to consist in the order to undertake adversarial proceedings with adequate due process guarantees, including *audi alterm partem*. Thirdly, within a constitutional [rather than a penal] context, such obligations are commonly referred to as 'positive obligations'[453] probably because they necessitate a direct act of the will of the State which has committed some form of omission by virtue of its failure to investigate in the first place. Indeed there exists a direct relationship between the concept of the rule of law and the State's role in punishing culpable wrongdoing.[454] Last but not least, generally,[455] the scope of such obligations is territorially limited in that States are only duty bound to investigate and prosecute those serious human rights violations that have occurred either on their territory or against individuals subject to their jurisdiction.[456] The duty is confined to acts perpetrated within the State's jurisdiction,[457] as a result of which a State is not obliged to exercise extra-territorial and/or universal jurisdiction.

I presuppose, solely for the purposes of my book, that a serious violation of a fundamental human right constitutes a core crime, though this might not necessarily always be the case. In fact, in substantiation of this underlying assumption, most cases dealing with positive obligations relate to the right to life and to the general prohibition of torture, both of which could constitute the core crime of murder/killing[458] [this being either genocide, a crime against humanity or a war crime, depending on the fulfilment of the constitutive elements of the crime], the core

---

[450] HRC, *Hugo Rodríguez v Uruguay*, 9 August 1994, Communication No. 322/1988 (1994), para 6.4.

[451] Mujuzi 2016, p. 108 and p. 117.

[452] ECtHR, *Remetin v Croatia*, 11 December 2012, Application Number 29525/10, para 104, cited in Mujuzi 2016, pp. 119–120, n. 72.

[453] Xenos 2012.

[454] Stark 2014, p. 222.

[455] The ACHPR (1981) African Charter on Human and Peoples' Rights does not fall within this category [see Article 1].

[456] Article 2 of the ICCPR (1966) International Covenant on Civil and Political Rights, Article 1 of the ECvHR, above n. 217, and Article 1, para (1) of the IACvHR (1969) Inter-American Convention on Human Rights.

[457] Schabas 2013b, p. 219.

[458] Under the ICC Statute, above n. 44, murder can constitute a crime against humanity, killing could be tantamount to genocide, whereas wilful killing can be punishable as a war crime, should all the constitutive ingredients of these core crimes be met.

crime of torture [be it a crime against humanity or a war crime, as stated here above][459] or else the *sui generis* core crime of enforced disappearance which is tantamount to a crime against humanity. In the context of the latter, Lisa Ott concludes that 'while the right to the truth was initially referred to explicitly with respect to missing persons, its existence is today generally confirmed in the context of crimes against humanity, genocide, war crimes and gross human rights violations'.[460] This 'right to the truth', a developing concept and a legally enforceable right in international law,[461] is not to be confused with the broader societal (public) interest in knowing the truth.[462] A classical example of such peculiarity is the inter-State case of *Cyprus v Turkey* decided by the ECtHR to the effect that, by sixteen votes to one, Article 2 of the ECvHR had been violated continuously 'on account of the failure of the authorities of the respondent State to conduct an effective investigation into the whereabouts and fate of Greek-Cypriot missing persons who disappeared in life-threatening circumstances'.[463] Such conduct is reminiscent of the crime against humanity of enforced disappearance of persons punishable by Article 7(1)(i) of the ICC Statute, referred to here above. It reminds us of the role of the State within the consummation of core crimes, which role has been examined thoroughly within the second Part of my book. This role, either as perpetrator of core crimes in the midst of a rogue State or as a defaulter of the

[459] Mowbray contends that the State obligation to effectively investigate claims of torture is less well developed than the corresponding obligation to investigate claims by relatives or friends on behalf of a *decuius* or a disappeared person (Mowbray 2004, p. 64).

[460] Ott 2011, p. 112.

[461] This right has been recognized by the ECtHR [ECtHR Grand Chamber, *Cyprus v Turkey*, 10 May 2001, Application No. 25781/94], by the IACtHR [IACtHR, *Nicholas Chapman Blake v Guatemala*, 24 January 1998, Series C No. 36; see also IACtHR, *Anstraum Aman Villagrán-Morales et al. v Guatemala* (Case of the *'Street Children'*), 19 November 1999, Series C No. 63], and by the Human Rights Chamber of BiH [Human Rights Chamber for BiH, *Ferida Selimović et al. v Republika Srpska* (*Srebrenica* cases), 7 March 2003, Case numbers CH/01/8365 etc]. It is premised on two underlying categories of protection:

i. a State's failure to disclose the fate of a person in the custody of the State constitutes inhuman treatment with respect to family members and is a continuing violation of applicable protections against such treatment;

ii. a State's failure to adequately investigate and prosecute crimes committed against a person in its custody constitutes a violation of the family's right of access to justice.

Groome 2011, p. 177.

A continuing violation subsists when 'a violation that began before the State's ratification of the treaty or acceptance of jurisdiction continues or has effects thereafter' (Pasqualucci 2013, p. 138).

[462] Groome 2011, p. 175.

[463] *Cyprus v Turkey*, above n. 461, para 136. In this case although the evidence that 1,485 missing persons were unlawfully killed was highly insufficient, the ECtHR held, in para 132, that the procedural obligation to conduct an effective official investigation 'also arises upon proof of an arguable claim that an individual, who was last seen in the custody of agents of the State, subsequently disappeared in a context which may be considered life-threatening'.

responsibility to protect principle[464] in the midst of a failed State, is pivotal to an understanding of this text.

Naturally, fundamental human rights actions are constitutionally exercisable against the State but their impact is multi-faceted, and can lead to the implementation of individual criminal responsibility. In order to enforce such *dicta,* States may need to implement penal legislation, arrest individuals, investigate situations and either prosecute or extradite. In other words, the net effect of a fundamental human rights action can be the prosecution or extradition of individuals, hence ultimate compliance with the *aut dedere aut judicare* rule. The *actio* is different and its procedural *iter* varies too, but the end domestic product can be one and the same. In any case, should this not be the case, *arguendo*, the case-law of the ECtHR,[465] being relatively authoritative,[466] carries enough weight to be able to ignite an international law rule, at least regionally,[467] which necessitates the undertaking of effective investigations where murder, torture and enforced disappearances of persons subsist. This is more so now that the EU has acceded to the ECvHR,[468] rendering the EU itself directly liable for the violation of a fundamental human right of an individual. The *Kelly and Others v UK dictum*[469] fits like a glove within this intriguing scenario because it conclusively clarifies the purpose of the positive State obligation to carry out effective investigations. It states, in no uncertain terms, that this is 'to ensure accountability for deaths occurring under their responsibility,'[470] adding that for an investigation to be effective it must be capable of leading 'to the identification and punishment of those responsible'.[471] Furthermore, where a *nolle prosequi* subsists, this must be sufficiently motivated since such situation, 'to borrow the words of the domestic courts, cries out for an explanation'.[472] The ECtHR failed to specify the 'procedures the authorities should adopt in providing

---

464 For an understanding of this principle, see Serrano 2011, pp. 92–101; see also Evans 2011, pp. 1–7; see also Scheffer 2011, pp. 305–322.

465 Andrew Drzemczewski, speaking of its unique and *sui generis* characteristics, refers to the ECtHR as an autonomous source within domestic legal *fora* (Drzemczewski 1983, p. 11).

466 For a thorough understanding of the weight that ought to be given to certain judicial pronouncements, which matter is comparable to the recognition of foreign judgments, see Nollkaemper 2011, pp. 244–279.

467 A customary rule may have been established on a regional scale. Lepard refers to such rules as local or special customary norms (Lepard 2010, p. 108).

468 See Article 6, para 2 of the Lisbon Treaty. The reasons for such accession and the modalities thereof are eloquently explained in a speech delivered by former Judge and vice-President of the ECtHR, Francoise Tulkens, to the National School of Judiciary and Public Prosecution (in Krakow, Poland) in a European Judicial Training Network – Human Rights and Access to Justice Seminar, held on 1 March 2013. http://www.ejtn.eu/Documents/About%20EJTN/Independent%20Seminars/Human%20Rights%20and%20Access%20to%20Justice%20Seminar/Krakow_Tulkens_final.pdf. Accessed 19 October 2013.

469 ECtHR, Third Section, *Kelly and Others v UK*, 4 May 2001, Application No. 30054/96.

470 *Kelly and Others v UK*, above n. 469, para 94.

471 *Kelly and Others v UK*, above n. 469, para 96.

472 *Kelly and Others v UK*, above n. 469, para 118, and see also Chap. 21, Sect. 21.2.

for the proper examination of the circumstances of a killing by State agents'.[473] Likewise, it did not favour a harmonised approach encompassing a unified procedure providing all requirements.[474] However its judgments entail that States would not be fulfilling their obligations upon failing to conduct effective investigations which are capable of leading to the prosecution of alleged law-breakers when individuals perish as a result of use of force. Section 13.1 has shown that the instances where a right of third States to investigate and prosecute becomes an obligation are the exception, rather than the rule. No such obligation, as yet, subsists under international law.

Positive obligations may result directly from ratification of a treaty. By way of example, the CAT, by virtue of Articles 12 and 13, obliges States to ensure that any individuals who allege that they have been tortured within the territory of the jurisdiction of the State, have the right to complain and to have their cases 'promptly and impartially examined' by the competent authorities of the State enjoying territorial jurisdiction. The positive obligation of the State to investigate was unanimously endorsed by the ECtHR in the case of *Assenov and Others v Bulgaria*.[475] This emanated predominantly from Article 3 of the ECvHR and implicitly from its first Article, prompting the Strasbourg Court to decide that the effective official investigation should be capable of leading to the identification and punishment of those responsible for any ill-treatment. The *Assenov* positive obligation, though followed in *Sevtap Veznedaroğlu v Turkey*,[476] was debilitated *in partem* in *İlhan v Turkey*,[477] only to find unfading refuge in *Satik and Others v Turkey*,[478] and, scantily, more recently in *Anguelova v Bulgaria*.[479] Such obligation, however, does not seem to bind the State whose soldier is killed in a battlefield, especially because the 1998 UK Human Rights Act does not protect UK soldiers on foreign soil.[480] Yet, owing to its peremptory nature, Article 3 of the ECvHR 'may also apply where the danger emanates from persons or groups of persons who are not public officials. However it must be shown that the risk is real

473 *Kelly and Others v UK*, above n. 469, para 137.

474 This also emerged from ECtHR, Fourth Section, *Anya Velikova v Bulgaria*, 18 May 2000, Application No. 41488/98, para 80. Such requirements generally relate to the institutional independence of investigators, the means and processes of inquiries, together with promptness and reasonable expedition.

475 ECtHR, *Anton Assenov and Others v Bulgaria*, 28 October 1998, Application No. 90/1997/874/1086.

476 ECtHR Second Section, *Sevtap Veznedaroğlu v Turkey*, 11 April 2000, Application No. 32357/96.

477 ECtHR Second Section, *Hasan İlhan v Turkey*, 9 November 2004, Application No. 22494/93.

478 ECtHR First Section, *Kadir Satik and Others v Turkey*, 10 October 2000, Application No. 31866/96.

479 ECtHR, *Assya Anguelova v Bulgaria*, 13 June 2002, Application No. 38361/97.

480 UK Supreme Court, *R (on the application of Smith (FC) (Respondent)) v Secretary of State for Defence (Appellant) and another*, 30 June 2010, [2009] EWCA Civ 441.

and that the authorities of the receiving State are not able to obviate the risk by providing appropriate protection'.[481]

The above discourse on State positive obligations goes to show that international human rights law can and should be used as a tool not only for truth-finding purposes but to effectively combat impunity. Indeed, although they constitute bars to extradition [as shall be seen in Sects. 16.7.1–16.7.4], fundamental human rights can forge the extradition process itself, facilitating its execution. Whereas human rights law and criminal law are two sides of the same coin,[482] and cannot really be separated from each other, international human rights law and international criminal law are two branches of international law which function reciprocally alongside each other, assisting each other mutually in their quest for a durable sophistication. Summarily, as noted here above, international human rights law equips the edifice of international criminal law with a potential tool for extradition and prosecution, whereas international criminal law assists international human rights law by deterring gross, systematic human rights violations. Within the auspices of international law, the dynamic interaction between international criminal law and international human rights law culminates into their inevitable symbiosis, an example of which is the categorisation of core crimes as 'human rights offences'.[483] This is why they can be viewed as complementary *instituti legis.*[484] In fact, although prosecutions belong directly to the realm of criminal law, Anja Seibert-Fohr acknowledges that 'whether there is, in fact, a duty to prosecute should be answered on the basis of international human rights law'.[485] *Ergo*, the State's duty to investigate under international human rights law has a counterpart in international criminal law, the 'right to know', or, put differently, 'a right to truth', which emanates directly from the Geneva Conventions and Additional Protocol I.[486] This concludes my detailed consideration of *aut dedere aut judicare*, a fundamental rule the understanding of which is pivotal for the analysis I undertake throughout this book.

---

[481] ECtHR, Second Section, *M.E. v Denmark*, Application No. 58363/10, 8 July 2014, para 50.

[482] Under the first paragraph within the title 'criminal law provisions', the Resolution on Criminal Procedures in the EU (*Corpus Juris*) 'recalls that the European Convention for the Protection of Human Rights and Fundamental Freedoms constitutes the foundation stone of European integration in the field of criminal law from which it has been possible to derive fundamental principles to serve henceforth as the common legal and cultural denominator of the Member States of the European Union' [European Parliament Resolution (1999) Resolution on Criminal Procedures in the European Union (*Corpus Juris*), 30 July 1999, A4-0091/99, OJ C/219/106]. Moreover, by way of example, Judge John Hedigan held that the codification of criminal law in Ireland can make use of various benefits deriving directly from the ECvHR (Hedigan 2008). Rehman acknowledged that 'international human rights law has advanced in various forms to have a substantial interaction with an influence on domestic criminal justice processes' (Rehman 2002, p. 517).

[483] Kamminga 2001, pp. 944–949.

[484] For a contrary view, see Margueritte 2011, pp. 436–438.

[485] Seibert-Fohr 2005, p. 555.

[486] Wiebelhaus-Brahm 2011, pp. 370–372.

References

ACHPR (1981) African Charter on Human and Peoples' Rights

AI (2017) *Hissène Habré* Appeal Ruling Closes Dark Chapter for Victims. https://www.amnesty.org/en/press-releases/2017/04/chad-hissene-habre-appeal-ruling-closes-dark-chapter-for-victims/. Accessed 9 July 2018

AI (2009) The International Law Commission: The Obligation to Extradite or Prosecute *(Aut Dedere Aut Judicare)*, IOR 40/001/2009, AIP. https://www.amnesty.org/download/Documents/48000/ior400012009en.pdf. Accessed 3 February 2012

AI (2011) Universal Jurisdiction: A Preliminary Survey of Legislation Around the World. IOR 53/004/2011, AIP. https://www.amnesty.org/en/documents/IOR53/004/2011/en/. Accessed 14 January 2016

Abass A (2006) The International Criminal Court and Universal Jurisdiction. ICLR 6(3):349–385

Acquaviva G (2009) *Aut Dedere Aut Judicare*. In Cassese A (eds) The Oxford Companion to International Criminal Justice. OUP, Oxford, pp. 253–254

Act Respecting Genocide, Crimes Against Humanity and War Crimes and to Implement the Rome Statute of the International Criminal Court and to make Consequential Amendments to Other Acts, Canada (2000) Annual Statutes of Canada, Chapter 24, 29 June 2000

Adanan A (2013) Universal Jurisdiction as a Tool for Seeking Accountability for Serious Human Rights Violations. Irish Centre for Human Rights

Akhavan P (2010) Whither National Courts? The Rome Statute's Missing Half: Towards an Express and Enforceable Obligation for the National Repression of International Crimes. JICJ 8(5):1245–1266

Akram SM (2006) The Arab Charter on Human Rights 2004. Translated by Al-Midani MA, Cabanettes M In: *BUILJ* 24:147–164

Ambos K (1999) *Volkerrechtliche Bestrafungspflichten bein schweren Menschenrechtsverletzungen. Archiv des Völkerrechts.* 37(3):318–356

Aoude S (2014) The *Lockerbie* Legality: What Went Wrong in International Criminal Law? http://mathaba.net/info/locker-leg.htm. Accessed 3 October 2015

Arab Charter on Human Rights (2004)

Ascencio H (2003) Are Spanish Courts Backing Down on Universality? The Supreme Tribunals' Decision in Guatemalan Generals. JICJ 1(3):690–702

ASF (2010) *Monitoring des Jurisdiction Gacaca, Phase de Jugement, Rapport Analytique no 5: Janvier 2008–Mars 2010.* http://www.asf.be/wp-content/publications/Rwanda_Monitoring Gacaca_RapportAnalytique5_Light.pdf. Accessed 30 December 2014

Australian ICC (Consequential Amendments) Act (2002) International Criminal Court (Consequential Amendments Act, 28 June 2002, No. 42, 2002

Ayala C (2016) The Judicial Dialogue Between International and National Courts in the Inter-American Human Rights System. In: Scheinin M, Krunke H, Aksenova M (eds) Judges as Guardians of Constitutionalism and Human Rights. EE, Cheltenham, UK/Northampton, MA, USA, pp. 306–328

Bakker CAE (2006) Universal Jurisdiction of Spanish Courts over Genocide in Tibet: Can it Work? JICJ 4(3):595–601

Bassiouni MC (1987) International Extradition, United States Law and Practice, 2nd revised edn. OPI, Dobbs Ferry, NY

Bassiouni MC (1996) International Crimes *Jus Cogens* and *Obligatio Erga Omnes.* LCP 59(4):63–74

Bassiouni MC (1999) Crimes Against Humanity in International Criminal Law, 2nd revised edn. In: Bassiouni MC (ed) International Criminal Law: Procedural and Enforcement Mechanisms, Vol. II, 2nd edn. TP, NY, pp. 521–588

Bassiouni MC (2001) Universal Jurisdiction for International Crimes: Historical Perspectives and Contemporary Practice. VJIL 42(1):81–161

Bassiouni MC (2008a) Crimes Against Humanity, In: Bassiouni MC (ed) International Criminal Law: Sources, Subjects and Contents, Vol. I, 3rd edn. MNP, Ledien, pp. 437–492

Bassiouni MC (2008b) The Need for International Accountability. In: Bassiouni MC (ed) International Criminal Law: International Enforcement, Vol. III, 3rd edn. MNP, Leiden, pp. 3–28

Bassiouni MC (2008c) Enslavement: Slavery, Slave-Related Practices, and Trafficking in Persons for Sexual Exploitation. In: Bassiouni MC (ed) International Criminal Law, Sources, Subjects and Contents, Vol. I, 3rd edn. MNP, Leiden, pp. 535–598

Bassiouni MC, Vetere E (1998) Towards Understanding Organized Crime and its Transnational Manifestations. In: Bassiouni MC, Vetere E (eds) Organized Crime: A Compilation of UN Documents, 1975–1998. TP, Ardsley, NY

Bassiouni MC, Wise EM (1995) *Aut Dedere Aut Judicare*: The Duty to Extradite or Prosecute in International Law. MNP, Leiden/Boston

Becker SW (2001) Commentary on the Princeton Principles. Princeton Project on Universal Jurisdiction, Princeton University, Princeton, New Jersey, USA. https://lapa.princeton.edu/hosteddocs/unive_jur.pdf. Accessed 1 May 2011

Belgian Act Concerning the Punishment of Grave Breaches of the Geneva Conventions of 12 August 1949 and their Additional Protocols I and II of 18 June 1977 (1993), Official Journal of 5 August 1993, at 17751–17755, as amended by the Act Concerning the Punishment of Grave Breaches of International Humanitarian Law (1999) Official Journal of 23 March 1999, at 9286–9287

Belgium's Law Concerning the Repression of Grave Breaches of the Geneva Conventions (1878) as amended on 18 July 2001 (*Loi Portant Modification de l'Article 12bis de la Loi du 17 avril 1878 Contenant le Titre Préliminaire du Code de Procedure Pénale*) and on 7 August 2003 (*Loi relative aux violations graves du droit international humanitaire*)

Ben-Naftali O (2009) The Obligations to Prevent and Punish Genocide. In: Gaeta P (ed) The United Nations Genocide Convention: A Commentary. Oxford Commentaries on International Law, OUP, pp. 27–57

Benavides L (2001) The Universal Jurisdiction Principle: Nature and Scope. *Annuario Mexicano de derecho internacional* 1:19–96

Bernaz N, Prouvèze R (2010) International and Domestic Prosecutions. In: Bassiouni MC (ed) The Pursuit of International Criminal Justice: A World Study on Conflicts, Victimization, and Post-Conflict Justice, Volume 1. Intersentia, Antwerp, Oxford, Portland, pp. 269–398

Boas G, Bischoff JJ, Reid NL (2007) Forms of Responsibility in International Criminal Law, Vol. 1. International Criminal Law Practitioner Library Series, CUP, Cambridge

Boed R (2000) The Effect of a Domestic Amnesty on the Ability of Foreign States to Prosecute Alleged Perpetrators of Serious Human Rights Violations. CILJ 33(2):297–329

Brody R, Ratner M (2000) (eds) The Pinochet Papers: The Case of Augusto Pinochet in Spain and Britain. KLI, Alphen aan den Rijn, The Netherlands

Burens L (2016) Universal Jurisdiction Meets Complementarity: An Approach Towards a Desirable Future Codification of Horizontal Complementarity Between the Member States of the International Criminal Court. CLF 27(1):75–97

Burgers JH, Danelius H (1988) The United Nations Convention Against Torture: A Handbook on the Convention Against Torture and Other Cruel, Inhuman or Degrading Treatment or Punishment. International Studies in Human Rights, MNP, Leiden/Boston

Burt J-M (2016) Appeals Court Upholds Suspension of Ríos Montt Genocide Trial, International Justice Monitor: A Project of the Open Society Justice Initiative, Summary from Guatemala Trials at the National Courts of Guatemala. http://www.ijmonitor.org/2016/06/appeals-court-upholds-suspension-of-rios-montt-genocide-trial/. Accessed 13 May 2017

Byers M (1997) Conceptualising the Relationship Between *Jus Cogens* and *Erga Omnes* Rules. NJIL 66(2-3):211-239

CAT (1984) Convention Against Torture and Other Cruel, Inhuman or Degrading Treatment or Punishment

Campbell T (2004) Prescriptive Legal Positivism: Law, Rights and Democracy. Routledge, T & F, London/NY

Carter LE (2008) Justice and Reconciliation on Trial: *Gacaca* Proceedings in Rwanda. NEJICL 14 (1):41–55

Casalunga L (2007) *Anonima Sequestri Sarda: L'Archivio dei Crimini* (1960–1997) [Kidnaps by Anonima Sarda: Archives of the Crimes (1960–1997)]. *Fratelli Frilli Editori*, Genova, Italy

Cassese A (1986) International Law in a Divided World. Thomson/West, CP, Wotton-under-Edge, UK

Cassese A (1989) The International Community's Legal Response to Terrorism. ICLQ 38(3):589–608

Cassese A (1990) Remarks on Scelle's Theory of "Role Splitting". EJIL 1:210–231

Cassese A (2003) Is the Bell Tolling for Universality? A Plea for a Sensible Notion of Universal Jurisdiction. JICJ 1(3):589–595

Cassese A (2009) Taking Stock of the Genocide Convention and Looking Ahead. In: Gaeta P (ed) The UN Genocide Convention: A Commentary, Oxford Commentaries on International Law, OUP, pp. 531–544

Chakravarty A (2006) Gacaca Courts in Rwanda: Explaining Divisions Within the Human Rights Community. YJIA 1(2):132–148

Ciconte E (2015) *Riti Criminali: I Codici di Affiliazione alla 'Ndrangheta* [Criminal Rituals: The Code of Membership with the 'Ndrangheta]. Rubbettino, Catanzaro, Italy

Code de Procédure Pénale, France (1957)

Code Napoléon (1804) Napoleonic Code

Code Pénal, France (1810)

Cohen W, Danelski DJ (1997) Constitutional Law: Civil Liberties and Individual Rights, 4th edn. FP, Westbury, NY

Consolidated Version of the Treaty on the Functioning of the EU (2012) Consolidated Version of the Treaty on the Functioning of the European Union, C 326/47

Convention for the Protection of All Persons from Enforced Disappearance (2006)

Convention for the Suppression of Unlawful Seizure of Aircraft (1970)

Corpus Juris Civilis Romani (534)

Costa Rican Penal Code, as amended by Law 8272, 2 May 2003

Cotta S (1997) *Soggetto Umano: Soggetto Giuridico* [Human Being: Subject of the Law]. *Giuffre` Editore spa*, Milano, Italia

Cottim AA (2010) Cybercrime, Cyberterrorism and Jurisdiction: An Analysis of Article 22 of the Council of Europe Convention on Cybercrime. EJLS, European University Institute, MNP, Leiden. http://www.ejls.eu/6/78UK.pdf. Accessed 6 July 2016

Council Framework Decision (2002) on Combating Terrorism, Doc. 2002/475/JHA

Council Framework Decision on the EAW (2002) Council Framework Decision on the European Arrest Warrant and the Surrender Procedures Between the Member States, Doc. 2002/584/JHA

Criddle EJ, Fox-Decent E (2009) A Fiduciary Theory of *Jus Cogens.* YJIL 34(2):331–387

Croatian Law on the Application of the Statute of the International Criminal Court and the Prosecution of Crimes Against International Laws of War and Humanitarian Law (2003) Official Gazette No. 175/2003, Article 14

Cryer R (2005) Prosecuting International Crimes: Selectivity and the International Criminal Law Regime. Cambridge Studies in International and Comparative Law, CUP, Cambridge

Cryer R, Friman H, Robinson D, Wilmshurst E (2010) An Introduction to International Criminal Law and Procedure, 2nd edn. CUP, Cambridge

Currie RJ (2007) Abducted Fugitives Before the International Criminal Court: Problems and Prospects. *CLF* 18(3-4):349–393

de Brouwer A-M, Ruvebana E (2013) The Legacy of the Gacaca Courts in Rwanda: Survivors' Views. ICLR 13(5):937–976

de Hoogh A (1996) Obligations *Erga Omnes* and International Crimes: A Theoretical Inquiry into the Implementation and Enforcement of the International Responsibility of States. KLI, Alphen aan den Rijn, The Netherlands de la Rasilla del Moral I (2009) The Swan Song of Universal Jurisdiction in Spain. ICLR 9 (5):777–808

de Londras F (2011) Terrorism as an International Crime. In: Schabas WA, Bernaz N (eds) Routledge Handbook of International Criminal Law. Routledge, T & F, London/NY, pp. 169–180

de Marco G (2007) Foreword. In: Fachinetti G, Franci F, Mastroleo G, Pagliaro V, Ricci G, *Illogica di un Conflitto: La Logica* Fuzzy *Applicata Alla Crisi Tra Israele e Libano* [An Illogical Conflict: Fuzzy Logic Applied to the Arab-Israeli Conflict]. Eurlink Editori, Rome

Dean F, D'Innocenzio M, Pugliese P, Ricci A (2003) *Diritto Penale Internazionale: Lezioni agli Studenti* [International Criminal Law: Lectures for Students], *Terza Edizione. Marghiacci, Galeno Editrice*, Roma

Draft Code of Crimes Against the Peace and Security of Mankind (1996)

Drzemczewski AZ (1983) European Human Rights Convention in Domestic Law: A Comparative Study. CP, Oxford

Dutch Constitution (2008) Constitution of the Kingdom of the Netherlands

Dutch Criminal Code (1881) Criminal Code of the Kingdom of the Netherlands

D'Amato A (1971) The Concept of Custom in International Law. CllUP, Ithaca, NY

ECvHR (1950) European Convention for the Protection of Human Rights and Fundamental Freedoms

El Zeidy M (2008) The Principle of Complementarity in International Criminal Law: Origin, Development and Practice. MNP, Leiden/Boston

Enache-Brown C, Fried A (1998) Universal Crime, Jurisdiction and Duty: The Obligation of *Aut Dedere Aut Judicare* in International Law. McGLJ 43:613–633

Eser A (2004) For Universal Jurisdiction: Against Fletcher's Antagonism. UTLR 39(4):955–978

European Convention on the Suppression of Terrorism (1977)

European Parliament Resolution (1999) Resolution on Criminal Procedures in the European Union (*Corpus Juris*), 30 July 1999, A4-0091/99, OJ C/219/106

Evans G (2011) Crimes Against Humanity and the Responsibility to Protect. In: Sadat LN (ed) Forging a Convention for Crimes Against Humanity. CUP, Cambridge, pp. 1–7

FEDEFAM (1981) *Desaparecidos:* Fighting Against Forced Disappearances in Latin America. http://www.desaparecidos.org/fedefam/eng.html. Accessed 3 January 2013

Ferdinandusse WN (2006) Direct Application of International Criminal Law in National Courts. Asser Press, The Hague

Finnis J (2011) Natural Law and Natural Rights, 2nd edn. OUP, Oxford

Finnish Criminal Code (2008) 13/1889, *Laki rikoslain muuttamisesta* [Law Amending the Criminal Code], as amended under Chapter 11, 212/2008, Sections 1 to 7, 11 April 2008

Finucane B (2010) Enforced Disappearance as a Crime under International Law: A Neglected Origin in the Laws of War. YJIL 35(1):171–197

Fletcher GP (2003) Against Universal Jurisdiction, Editorial Comments. JICJ 1(3):580–584

Freestone D (1997) International Cooperation Against Terrorism and the Development of International Law Principles of Jurisdiction. In: Higgins R, Flory M (eds) Terrorism and International Law. T & F, Routledge, London, pp. 43–67

French Law No. 96-432 on adapting French Law to the Provisions of United Nations Security Council Resolution 955 Establishing the International Tribunal for Rwanda, 22 May 1996

French *Code Pénal* (1810)

French Law (1999) No. 99-115, 23 June 1999 amending Article 689 of the French Code of Criminal Procedure, Official Journal of 24 June 1999

French Law No. 95-1 on adapting French Law to the Provisions of United Nations Security Council Resolution 827 Establishing an International Tribunal for the Prosecution of Persons Responsible for Serious Violations of International Humanitarian Law Committed in the Territory of Former Yugoslavia Since 1991, 2 January 1995

Gaparayi IT (2001) Justice and Social Reconstruction in the Aftermath of Genocide in Rwanda: An Evolution of the Possible Role of the Gacaca Tribunals. AHRLJ 1(1):78–106

Garner BA (2009) Black's Law Dictionary, 9th edn. Thomson West, Saint Paul, Minnesota, USA

Geneuss J (2013) *Volkerrechtsverbrechen und Verfolgungsermessen: § 153f StPO im System volkerrechtlicher Strafrechtspflege*. Nomos, Baden-Baden

Geneva Convention (1949a) Geneva Convention (I) for the Amelioration of the Condition of the Wounded and Sick in Armed Forces in the Field

Geneva Convention (1949b) Geneva Convention (II) for the Amelioration of the Condition of the Wounded, Sick and Shipwrecked Members of Armed Forces at Sea

Geneva Convention (1949c) Geneva Convention (III) relative to the Treatment of Prisoners of War

Geneva Convention (1949d) Geneva Convention (IV) relative to the Protection of Civilian Persons in Time of War

Genocide Convention (1948) Convention on the Prevention and Punishment of the Crime of Genocide

German Act to Introduce the Code of Crimes Against International Law *{Völkerstrafgesetzbuch, VStGB}* (2002), 26 June 2002

Gondek M (2009) The Reach of Human Rights in a Globalizing World: Extraterritorial Application of Human Rights Treaties, Intersentia, Antwerp/Oxford/Portland

Goodwin-Gill GS, McAdam J (2007) The Refugee in International Law. 3rd edn. OUP, Oxford

Groome D (2011) The Right to Truth in the Fight Against Impunity. BJIL 29(1):175–199

HRW (2011) Justice Compromised: The Legacy of Rwanda's Community-Based Gacaca Courts. http://www.hrw.org/sites/default/files/reports/rwanda0511webwcover.pdf. Accessed 2 July 2012

HRW (2014) Q&A: The Case of *Hissène Habré* Before the Extraordinary African Chambers in Senegal. http://www.hrw.org/news/2012/09/11/qa-case-hiss-ne-habr-extraordinary-african-chambers-senegal. Accessed 12 July 2015

HRW (2018) Detention Without Trial. https://www.hrw.org/topic/terrorism-counterterrorism/detention-without-trial. Accessed 17 November 2018

Hedigan J (2008) Codification of the Criminal Law and the European Convention on Human Rights. Paper submitted at the 22nd International Conference of the International Society for the Reform of Criminal Law held in Dublin, 11–15 July 2008. http://www.isrcl.org/Papers/2008/Hedigan.pdf. Accessed 9 March 2012

Henzelin M (2000) *Le Principe de l'Universalité en Droit Pénal International: Droit et Obligation pour les États de Poursuivre et Juger Selon le Principe de l'Universalité* [The Principle of Universality under International Criminal Law: Law and Obligations for States to Prosecute and Judge in Terms of the Principle of Universality], Helbin and Lichtenhahn, Munich, Geneva, Brussels

Herman S (1994) Double Jeopardy All Over Again: Dual Sovereignty, Rodney King, and the ACLU. University of California Los Angeles Law Review 41:609–647

Hesenov R (2013) *Aut Dedere Aut Judicare* as a Principle in International Criminal Law. Azerbaijan National Academy of Sciences. http://jg.kiev.ua/pages/data/18/5.pdf. Accessed 11 December 2013

Hieramente M (2011) The Myth of "International Crimes": Dialectics and International Criminal Law. GJIL 3(2):551–588

Holvoet M (2016) The Continuing Relevance of the Hybrid or Internationalized Justice Model: The Example of the Kosovo Specialist Chambers. CLF 28(1):35–73

Hoover DV (2011) Universal Jurisdiction Not So Universal: A Time to Delegate to the International Criminal Court. Cornell Law School Inter-University Graduate, Student Conference Papers, Paper 52, Cornell Law Library

Hossain K (2005) The Concept of *Jus Cogens* and the Obligation under the United Nations Charter. SCJIL 3(1):72–98

Hostages Convention (1979) Convention Against the Taking of Hostages

IACvHR (1969) Inter-American Convention on Human Rights

IBA (2018) Iraqi High Tribunal. http://www.ibanet.org/Committees/WCC_IHT.aspx. Accessed 3 September 2018

ICC Statute (1998) Rome Statute of the International Criminal Court

ICCPR (1966) International Covenant on Civil and Political Rights

ICJ Statute (1946) Statute of the International Court of Justice

IDI (2006) Krakow Session Resolution III: Universal Criminal Jurisdiction with Respect to the Crime of Genocide, Crimes Against Humanity and War Crimes. *Annuaire de l'Institut de Droit International*, 7I-II: 297-301

ILC (1996) Report of the International Law Commission on the work of its forty-eighth session, 6 May–26 July 1996, Official Records of the General Assembly, Fifty-first session, Supplement No.10, UN Doc. A/51/10

ILC (2000) Third Report on State Responsibility by James Crawford, Special Rapporteur, UN Doc. A/CN.4/507/Add. 1–4

ILC (2011) Concluding Remarks (Report) of the Special Rapporteur Zdzisław Galicki, Sixty-Third Session. The Obligation to Extradite or Prosecute *(aut dedere aut judicare*). ILC Report A/66/10. http://untreaty.un.org/ilc/reports/2011/All%20languages/A_66_10_E.pdf. Accessed 9 December 2013

ILC Yearbook (1966) Vol. II. Documents of the Second Part of the Seventeenth Session and of the Eighteenth Session Including the Reports of the Commission to the General Assembly, UN Doc. A/CN.4/SER.A/1966/Add.1

International Crimes and International Criminal Court Act, New Zealand (2000), Public Act 2000 No. 26

Islamic *Sharīʿah* Law {شري عة}

Italy's *Codice Penale* [Criminal Code] (1889), amendment to Article 7, *decreto legge* 208, 30 July 2004

Jeßberger F (2007) Universality, Complementarity, and the Duty to Prosecute Crimes under International Law in Germany. In: Kaleck W, Ratner M, Singelnstein T, Weiss P (eds) International Prosecution of Human Rights Crimes. Springer, Berlin/Heidelberg, pp. 213–222

Jeßberger F, Powell C (2001) Prosecuting Pinochet in South Africa - Implementing the Rome Statute of the International Criminal Court. SAJCJ 14:344–362

Jia BB (2012) The Immunity of State Officials for International Crimes Revisited. JICJ 10 (5):1303–1321

Kadelbach S (2006) *Jus Cogens*, 'Obligations *Erga Omnes* and Other Rules - The Identification of Fundamental Norms. In: Tomuschat C, Thouvenin J-M (eds) The Fundamental Rules of the International Legal Order: *Jus Cogens* and Obligations *Erga Omnes*. MNP, Leiden/Boston, pp. 21–40

Kaikobad KH (2007) Crimes Against International Peace and Security, Acts of Terrorism and Other Serious Crimes: A Theory on Distinction and Overlap. ICLR 7(2-3):187–276

Kamminga MT (2001) Lessons Learned from the Exercise of Universal Jurisdiction in Respect of Gross Human Rights Offences. HRQ 23(4):940–974

Kemp S (2014) Guatemala Prosecutes Former President Rios Montt: New Perspectives on Genocide and Domestic Criminal Justice. JICJ 12(1):133–156

Kennedy D (1987) International Legal Structures. Nomos, Baden Baden

Kindiki K (2001) Prosecuting the Perpetrators of the 1994 Genocide in Rwanda: Its Basis in International Law and the Implications for the Protection of Human Rights in Africa. AHRLJ 1 (1):64–77

Kleffner JK (2003) The Impact of Complementarity on National Implementation of Substantive Criminal Law. JICJ 1(1):86–113

Kleffner JK (2008) Complementarity in the Rome Statute and National Criminal Jurisdiction, International Courts and Tribunals Series. OUP, Oxford

Klein D (1988) A Theory for the Application of the Customary International Law of Human Rights by Domestic Courts. YJIL 13(2):332–365

Klip A (2002) Conditions for a European *Corpus Juris Criminalis*. In: Faure M, Smits J, Schneider H (eds) Towards a European *Ius Commune* in Legal Education and Research. Maastricht Faculty of Law, Interesentia, Antwerpen/Groningen, pp. 109–123

Kluwen T (2017) Universal Jurisdiction *in Absentia* Before Domestic Courts Prosecuting International Crimes: A Suitable Weapon to Fight Impunity? GTIL 8(1):7–38

Knoops G-J A (2002) Surrendering to International Criminal Courts: Contemporary Practice and Procedures. International and Comparative Criminal Law Series, TP, Ardsley, NY
Kochler H (2003) Global Justice or Global Revenge? International Criminal Justice at the Crossroads. Springer, Vienna/NY
Kolb R (2004) The Exercise of Criminal Jurisdiction over International Terrorists. In: Bianchi A (ed) Enforcing International Law Norms Against Terrorism. HP, Oxford and Portland, Oregon, USA, 2004, pp. 227–281
Kramer MH (2003) In Defense of Legal Positivism: Law Without Trimmings. OUP, Oxford
Kreß C (2006) Universal Jurisdiction Over International Crimes and the *Institut de Droit International*. JICJ 4(3):561–585
Krings BL (2012) The Principles of Complementarity and Universal Jurisdiction in International Criminal Law: Antagonists or Perfect Match? GJIL 4(3):737–763
Langer M (2011) The Diplomacy of Universal Jurisdiction: The Political Branches and the Transnational Prosecution of International Crimes. AJIL 105(1):1–49
Langer M (2015) Universal Jurisdiction is Not Disappearing: The Shift From "Global Enforcer" to "No Safe Haven" Universal Jurisdiction. JICJ 13(2):245–256
Le Mon CL (2007) Rwanda's Troubled Gacaca Courts. The Human Rights Brief, Centre for Human Rights and Humanitarian Law. 14(2):16–20
Lee W-C (2010) International Crimes and Universal Jurisdiction. In: May L, Hoskins Z (eds) International Criminal Law and Philosophy. ASIL Studies in International Legal Theory, CUP, Cambridge, pp. 15–38
Lepard BD (2010) Customary International Law: A New Theory with Practical Applications. ASIL Studies in International Legal Theory, CUP, Cambridge
Ligeti K (2013) Introduction. In Ligeti K (ed) Towards a Prosecutor for the European Union: A Comparative Analysis, Vol. I. Modern Studies in European Law, HP, Bloomsbury, pp. 1–6
Linderfalk U (2009) Normative Conflict and the Fuzziness of the International *Ius Cogens* Regime. *Max-Planck Institut fur auslandisches offentliches Recht und Volkerrecht* 69(4):961–979
Lisbon Treaty (2007) Treaty of Lisbon Amending the Treaty on European Union and the Treaty Establishing the European Community
Lo Bianco G, Rizza S (2007) *L'Agenda Rossa di Paolo Borsellino* [Paolo Borsellino's Red Diary]. *Chiarelettere Editore*, Milano, Italy
Luban D (2004) A Theory of Crimes Against Humanity. YJIL 29(1):85–167
Magsam D (2007) Coming to Terms with Genocide in Rwanda: The Role of International and National Justice. In: Kaleck W, Ratner M, Singelnstein T, Weiss P (eds) International Prosecution of Human Rights Crimes, Springer, Berlin/Heidelberg, pp. 159–165
Maltese *Kodiċi Kriminali, Kapitolu 9 tal-Liġijiet ta' Malta* [Criminal Code, Chapter 9 of the Laws of Malta], as amended in 2002, Article 54G
Margueritte T (2011) International Criminal Law and Human Rights. In: Schabas WA, Bernaz N (eds) Routledge Handbook of International Criminal Law. Routledge, T & F, London and NY, 2011, pp. 435–452
Maritain J (2012) Christianity and Democracy: The Rights of Man and Natural Law. Ignatius Press, San Francisco, California, USA
McDougal MS, Myers S, Harold D, Lasswell HD, Chen L-C (1980) Human Rights and World Public Order: The Basic Policies of an International Law of Human Dignity. YUP, New Haven, Connecticut, USA
Meron T (1986) On a Hierarchy of International Human Rights. *AJIL* 80(1):1–23
Mettraux G (2009) The Law of Command Responsibility. OUP, Oxford
Mibenge C (2005) Alternative Forms of Justice: Lessons Learned From Rwanda. In: Ankumah EA, Kwakwa EK (eds) African Perspective on International Criminal Justice. Africa Legal Aid, Accra/Maastricht/Pretoria, pp. 187–195
Migliorino L (1995) *La Dichiarazione delle Nazioni Unite sulle Misure per Eliminare il Terrorismo Internazionale* [The United Nations Declaration on Measures Aimed to Suppress International Terrorism]. *RDI* 78:962–972

Milanovic M (2018) The Netherlands and Australia Attribute the Downing of MH17 to Russia. EJIL: Talk! https://www.ejiltalk.org/the-netherlands-and-australia-attribute-the-downing-of-mh17-to-russia/. Accessed 1 October 2018

Mitchell C (2009) *Aut Dedere Aut Judicare*: The Extradite or Prosecute Clause in International Law: The Scope and the Operation of the Obligation. *Collections Électroniques de l'Institut de Hautes Études Internationales et du Développement*, GIP. http://iheid.revues.org/302. Accessed 30 March 2018

Montreal Convention (1971) Convention for the Suppression of Unlawful Acts Against the Safety of Civil Aviation

Morris M (2001) High Crimes and Misconceptions: the International Criminal Court and non-Party States. LCP 64(1):13–66

Mowbray A (2004) The Development of Positive Obligations under the European Convention on Human Rights by the European Court of Human Rights. HP, Oxford/Portland, Oregon

Mujuzi JD (2016) Victim Participation in the Criminal Justice System in the European Union Through Private Prosecutions: Issues Emerging from the Jurisprudence of the European Court of Human Rights. EJCCLCJ 24(2-3):107–134

New Zealand International Crimes and ICC Act (2000) International Crimes and International Criminal Court Act, 1 October 2000

Nollkaemper A (2011) National Courts and the International Rule of Law. OUP, Oxford

Norberg N (2006) The United States Supreme Court Affirms the Filartiga Paradigm. JICJ 4 (2):387–400

Norway's Criminal Code (1982) Norwegian General Civil Penal Code, Article 12.4

Nowak M, McArthur E with the contribution of Buchinger K, Kozma J, Schmidt R, Tschan I, Ludwig Boltzmann Institute of Human Rights Vienna (2008) The United Nations Convention Against Torture: A Commentary. OUP, Oxford/NY

Ntwari DS (2015) Rwandan Genocide: Pascal Simbikangwa Appeal Set: as DRC Arrests Key Suspect. Afrika Reporter. http://www.afrikareporter.com/rwandan-genocide-pascal-simbikangwa-appeal-set-as-drc-arrests-key-suspect/. Accessed 4 May 2017

Obokata T (2005) Trafficking of Human Beings as a Crime Against Humanity: Some Implications for the International Legal System. ICLQ 54(2):445–457

Obokata T (2010) Transnational Organised Crime in International Law, Studies in International and Comparative Criminal Law, Vol. 5. HP, Oxford/Portland, Oregon

Olson LM (2011) Re-enforcing Enforcement in a Specialized Convention on Crimes Against Humanity: Inter-State Cooperation, Mutual Legal Assistance, and the *Aut Dedere Aut Judicare* Obligation. In: Sadat LN (ed) Forging a Convention for Crimes Against Humanity. CUP, Cambridge, pp. 323–344

Orentlicher DF (1991) Settling Accounts: The Duty to Prosecute Human Rights Violations of a Prior Regime. YLJ 100(8):2537–2615

Ott L (2011) Enforced Disappearance in International Law. Intersentia, Cambridge/Antwerp/ Portland

O'Keefe R (2004) Universal Jurisdiction: Clarifying the Basic Concept. JICJ 2(3):735–760

O'Keefe R (2013) Domestic Courts as Agents of Development of the International Law of Jurisdiction. LJIL 26(3):541–558

Panepinto A (2012) Reviewing Clark P (2010) The Gacaca Courts, Post-Genocide Justice and Reconciliation in Rwanda: Justice Without Lawyers. CUP, Cambridge. In: ICLR 12(1):101–103

Pasqualucci JM (2013) The Practice and Procedure of the Inter-American Court of Human Rights, 2nd edn. CUP, Cambridge

Paust JJ, Bassiouni MC, Scharf M, Gurulè J, Sadat L, Zagaris B (2007) International Criminal Law: Cases and Materials, 3rd edn. CAP, Durham, North Carolina, USA

Pellet A (2006) Comments in Response to Christine Chinkin and in Defence of *Jus Cogens* as the Best Bastion Against the Excesses of Fragmentation. FYIL XVII:83–90

Philippe X (2006) The Principles of Universal Jurisdiction and Complementarity: How Do the Two Principles Intermesh? IRRC 88(862):375–398

Plachta M (2001a) The Lockerbie Case: The Role of the Security Council in Enforcing the Principle *Aut Dedere Aut Judicare.* EJIL 12(1):125–140

Plachta M (2001b) Contemporary Problems of Extradition: Human Rights, Grounds for Refusal and the Principle *Aut Dedere Aut Judicare*, UNAFEI Annual Report for 1999 and Resource Material Series No. 57. http://www.unafei.or.jp/english/pdf/PDF_rms/no57/57-07.pdf. Accessed 21 August 2011

Plachta M (2003) European Arrest Warrant: Revolution in Extradition? EJCCLCJ 11(2):178–194

Pocar F, Maystre M (2010) The Principle of Complementarity: A Means Towards a More Pragmatic Enforcement of the Goal Pursued by Universal Jurisdiction? In: Bergsmo M (ed) Complementarity and the Exercise of Jurisdiction for Core International Crimes. Forum for International Criminal and Humanitarian Law Publication Series No. 7, TOAEP, Oslo, pp. 247–303

Poels A (2005) Universal Jurisdiction *In Absentia.* NQHR 23(1):65–84

Police Reform and Social Responsibility Act, United Kingdom (2011)

Portugal 's Criminal Law Relating to Violations of International Humanitarian Law, 22 July 2004, No. 31/2004, amending Article 5 of the Penal Code

Posner EA (2009) *Erga Omnes* Norms, Institutionalization, and Constitutionalism in International Law. Journal of Institutional and Theoretical Economics 165(1):5–23

Powers SE (2011) Rwanda's Gacaca Courts: Implications for International Criminal Law. ASIL Insights 15(17). http://www.asil.org/insights110623.cfm. Accessed 23 June 2014

Rabinovitch R (2004) Universal Jurisdiction *In Absentia.* FILJ 28(2):500–530

Ragazzi M (1997) The Concept of International Obligations *Erga Omnes.* Oxford Monographs in International Law, CP, Oxford

Randall K (1988) Universal Jurisdiction under International Law. TLR 66:785–837

Rastan R (2010) Complementarity: Contest or Collaboration? In: Bergsmo M (ed) Complementarity and the Exercise of Universal Jurisdiction for Core International Crimes. Forum for International Criminal and Humanitarian Law Publication Series No. 7, TOAEP, Oslo, pp. 83–132

Ratner SR, Abrams JS, Bischoff JL (2009) Accountability for Human Rights Atrocities in International Law: Beyond the Nuremberg Legacy. 3rd edn. OUP, Oxford

Rau M (2003) *Das Ende der Weltrechtspflege? : zur Abschaffung des belgischen Gesetzes über die universelle Verfolgung völkerrechtlicher Verbrechen. Humanitäres Völkerrecht : Informationsschriften* 16(4): 212–216

Rehman J (2002) The Influence of International Human Rights Law upon Criminal Justice Systems. JCL 66:510–527

Rettig M (2008) Gacaca: Truth, Justice and Reconciliation in Post-Conflict Rwanda? ASR 51 (3):25–50

Reydams L (2003) Universal Jurisdiction: International and Municipal Legal Perspectives. OUP, Oxford

Reydams L (2011) The Rise and Fall of Universal Jurisdiction. In: Schabas WA, Bernaz N (ed) Routledge Handbook of International Criminal Law. Routledge, T & F, London and NY, pp. 337–354

Rikhof J (2010) Fewer Places to Hide?: The Impact of Domestic War Crimes Prosecutions on International Impunity. In: Bergsmo M (ed) Complementarity and the Exercise of Jurisdiction for Core International Crimes. Forum for International Criminal and Humanitarian Law Publication Series No. 7, TOAEP, Oslo, pp. 7–81.

Roberts AE (2001) Traditional and Modern Approaches to Customary International Law: A Reconciliation. AJIL 95(4):757–791

Robinson A (2016) Challenges to Justice at Home: The Domestic Prosecution of Efrain Rios Montt. ICLR 16(1):103–133

Roht-Arriaza N (2006) Comment on the Spanish Constitutional Court, Guatemala Genocide Case. AJIL 100(1):207–213

Roht-Arriaza N (2007) The Pinochet Effect and the Spanish Contribution to Universal Jurisdiction. In: Kaleck W, Ratner M, Singelnstein T, Weiss P (eds) International Prosecution of Human Rights Crimes, Springer, Berlin/Heidelberg, pp. 113–123

Roht-Arriaza N (2009a) The Multiple Prosecutions of Augusto Pinochet. In: Lutz EL, Reiger C (eds) Prosecuting Heads of State. CUP, Cambridge, pp. 77–94

Roht-Arriaza N (2009b) Prosecution of Heads of State in Latin America. In: Lutz EL, Reiger C (eds) Prosecuting Heads of State. CUP, Cambridge, pp. 48–76

Roth R (2009) The Extradition of *Genocidaires*. In: Gaeta P (ed) The United Nations Genocide Convention: A Commentary. Oxford Commentaries on International Law, OUP, Oxford, pp. 278–309

Rowlands D (2012) Centurean 2/'s Weblog, EU-Style Justice *Corpus Juris*. http://centurean2.wordpress.com/2012/02/16/eu-style-justice-corpus-juris-by-david-rowlands-ret-magistrate/. Accessed 30 July 2013

Ryngaert C (2005) Universal Criminal Jurisdiction Over Torture: A State of Affairs After 20 Years United Nations Torture Convention. NQHR 23(4):571–611

Ryngaert C (2006) Universal Jurisdiction in an International Criminal Court Era: A Role to Play for EU member States with the Support of the European Union. EJCCLCJ 14(1):46–80

Ryngaert C (2007) Universal Jurisdiction Over Genocide and Wartime Torture in Dutch Courts: An Appraisal of the Afghan and Rwandan Cases. HJJ 2(2):14–36

Ryngaert C (2008a) Jurisdiction in International Law. Oxford Monographs in International Law, OUP, Oxford

Ryngaert C (2008b) Applying the Rome Statute's Complementarity Principle: Drawing Lessons from the Prosecution of Core Crimes by States Acting under the Universality Principle. CLF 19 (1):153–180

Ryngaert C (2015) The Concept of Jurisdiction in International Law. In: Orakhelashvili A (ed) Research Handbook on Jurisdiction and Immunities in International Law. Research Handbook in International Law, EE, pp. 50–75

Sands P (2003) International Law Transformed? From Pinochet to Congo? LJIL 16(1):37–53

Saul B (2006) Defining Terrorism in International Law. OUP, Oxford

Saviano R (2006) *Gomorra: Viaggio nell'Impero Economico e nel Sogno di Dominio della Camorra* [Gomorra: Journey Through the Economic Empire and the Dream of Dominion of the Camorra]. *Arnoldo Mondadori Editore*, Milano, Italy

Scelle G (1932) *Précis de Droit des Gens* [Human Rights Brief], *Librairie du Recueil Sirey (Société anonyme),* Paris

Schabas WA (2003) National Courts Finally Begin to Prosecute Genocide. JICJ 1(1):39–63

Schabas W (2013a) International Criminal Law and Tribunals and Human Rights. In: Sheeran S, Rodley N (eds) Routledge Handbook of International Human Rights Law. Routledge Handbooks, Routledge, T & F, pp. 215–229

Schabas W (2013b) The Contribution of the Eichmann Trial to International Law. LJIL 26(3):667–699

Scharf M (1996) The Letter of the Law: The Scope of the International Legal Obligation to Prosecute Human Rights Crimes. LCP 59(4):41–62

Scharf MP (2001) The ICC's Jurisdiction Over the National of Non-Party States: A Critique of the US Position. LCP 64(1):67–117

Scharf M (2008) The Lockerbie Model of Transfer of Proceedings. In: Bassiouni MC (ed) International Criminal Law: Multilateral and Bilateral Enforcement Mechanisms, Vol. II, 3rd edn. MNP, Leiden, pp. 521–527.

Scheffer D (2011) Crimes Against Humanity and the Responsibility to Protect. In: Sadat LN (ed) Forging a Convention for Crimes Against Humanity. CUP, Cambridge, pp. 305–322

Schlutter B (2010) Developments in Customary International Law: Theory and Practice of the International Court of Justice and the International *Ad Hoc* Criminal Tribunals for Rwanda and Yugoslavia. MNP, Leiden/Boston

Schwobel CEJ (2011) Global Constitutionalism in International Legal Perspective. MNP, Leiden/Boston

Scotland ICC Act (2001) International Criminal Court (Scotland) Act, 13 September 2001, 2001 asp 13
Seibert-Fohr A (2005) Reconstruction Through Accountability. MPYUNL 9:555–578
Seret R (2014) Hannah Ardent and Crimes Against Humanity Editorial. JICJ 12(1):3–5
Serra G (2008) Special Tribunal for Lebanon: A Commentary on its Major Legal Aspects. ICJR 18 (3):344–355
Serrano M (2011) The Responsibility to Protect: Libya and *Côte d'Ivoire*. Amsterdam Law Forum, VUA 3:3:92–101
Shelton D (2014) International Law and Relative Normativity. In: Evans MD (ed) International Law, 2nd edn. OUP, Oxford, 159–185
Simbeye Y (2004) Immunity and International Criminal Law. Ashgate, Farnham, UK
Sinclair I (1984) The Vienna Convention on the Law of Treaties, 2nd edn. MUP, Manchester
Slovenia's Criminal Code (1994), amended on 15 June 2005
Sluiter G (2004) Implementation of the ICC Statute in the Dutch Legal Order. JICJ 2(1):158–178
Slye RC, van Schaack B (2009) Essentials: International Criminal Law. WK, Alphen aan den Rijn, The Netherlands
Soler C (2014) A Conceptual Re-Characterization of Universal Criminal Jurisdiction. *Id-Dritt* XXIV:285–315. http://www.ghsl.org/en/products/webshop/28/id-dritt-xxiv.htm. Accessed 13 January 2018
South African law (2002) Implementation of the Rome Statute of the International Criminal Court, Act No. 27 of 2002
Spanish Organic Law of the Judicial Power (1985) Organic Law No. 6/1985, Article 23.4
Stark F (2014) Reviewing Ashworth A (2013) Positive Obligations in Criminal Law. Hart, Oxford. In: CLJ 73(1):220–224
Statute of the STL (2007) Statute of the Special Tribunal for Lebanon
Stephens PJ (2004) A Categorical Approach to Human Rights Claims: *Jus Cogens* as a Limitation on Enforcement? WILJ 22(2):245–272
Steven LA (1999) Genocide and the Duty to Extradite or Prosecute: Why the United States is in Breach of Its International Obligations. VJIL 39(2):425–466
Stewart MP (2014) The Internationalist, Council on Foreign Relations, Spain Welcomes Retreat on Universal Jurisdiction. http://blogs.cfr.org/patrick/2014/02/14/spains-welcome-retreat-on-universal-jurisdiction/. Accessed 9 August 2016
Straffeloven [Criminal Code], Denmark (1930) Law number 126
Strafprozeßordnung [Code of Criminal Procedure], Germany (1987)
Swiss Penal Code (*Strafgesetzbuch*) (1937), as amended, SR 311.0
Tallman DA (2003) Universal Jurisdiction: Lessons from Belgium's Experience. In: Stromseth JE (ed) Accountability for Atrocities: National and International Responses. International and Comparative Criminal Law Series, TP, Ardsley, NY, pp. 375–409
Tams CJ (2005) Enforcing Obligations *Erga Omnes* in International Law. Cambridge Studies in International and Comparative Law, CUP, Cambridge
Thalmann V (2009) National Criminal Jurisdiction Over Genocide. In: Gaeta P (ed) The United Nations Genocide Convention: A Commentary. Oxford Commentaries on International Law, OUP, pp. 231–258
The DRC's Military Justice Code (2002) The Democratic Republic of the Congo Military Justice Code, Act No. 023-2002, 18 November 2002
The Economist (2018) From Dictator to Defendant: The Death and the Cruel Life of Efraín Ríos Montt. https://www.economist.com/the-americas/2018/04/05/the-death-and-cruel-life-of-efrain-rios-montt. Accessed 2 June 2018
The Hague Hijacking Convention (1970) The Hague Convention for Suppression of Unlawful Seizure of Aircraft
The Netherlands International Crimes Act (2003) Act of 19 June 2003 Containing Rules Concerning Serious Violations of International Humanitarian Law (International Crimes Act)
Tillier J (2013) The International Criminal Court Prosecutor and Positive Complementarity: Strengthening the Rule of Law? ICLR 13(3):507–591

Trapp KN (2011) State Responsibility for International Terrorism: Problems and Prospects. OUP, Oxford

Treaty of Amsterdam Amending the Treaty on European Union, the Treaties Establishing the European Communities and Certain Related Acts (1997)

Treaty on the Functioning of the EU (2007) Treaty on the Functioning of the European Union

Trinidad and Tobago International Criminal Court Act (2006) Laws No. 4, § 10, 24 February 2006

Tronvoll K, Schaefer C, Aneme GA (2009) Concluding the Main Red Terror Trial. In: Tronvoll K, Schaefer C, Aneme G (eds) The Ethiopian Red Terror Trials: Transitional Justice Challenged. LHPS, Currey, Woodbridge, pp. 136–152

Trouille HL (2016) Universal Jurisdiction and Rwandan *Genocidaires*: The Simbikangwa Trial. JICJ 14(1):195–217

Tulkens F (2013) Speech delivered to the National School of Judiciary and Public Prosecution (in Krakow, Poland) in a European Judicial Training Network – Human Rights and Access to Justice Seminar. http://www.ejtn.eu/Documents/About%20EJTN/Independent%20Seminars/Human%20Rights%20and%20Access%20to%20Justice%20Seminar/Krakow_Tulkens_final.pdf. Accessed 29 November 2016

UDHR (1948) Universal Declaration of Human Rights

UK ICC Act (2001) International Criminal Court Act, United Kingdom, 1 September 2001

UN Committee Against Torture (2004) Thirty-Third Session, Doc. CAT/C/SR.624

UNGA (1971) Resolution 2840 (XXVI) (1971), UN Doc. A/8429

UNGA (1973) Resolution 3074 (XXVIII) (1973), UN Doc. A/RES/3074

UNSC (2001) Resolution 1373 (2001), UN Doc. S/RES/1373

UNTAET Regulation (2000) Doc. No. UNTAET/REG/2000/15

United Kingdom Criminal Justice Act (Torture) (Overseas Territories) Order (1988), 21 December 1988

Uruguay's Law (2006) No. 18025, 25 September 2006

Usacka A (2016) Constitutionalism and Human Rights at the International Criminal Court. In: Scheinin M, Krunke H, Aksenova M (eds) Judges as Guardians of Constitutionalism and Human Rights. EE, Cheltenham, UK/Northampton, MA, USA, pp. 281–305

Uvin P (2003) The Gacaca Tribunals in Rwanda: Case Study. In: Bloomfield D, Barnes T, Huyse L (eds) Reconciliation After Conflict, International Institute for Democracy and Electoral Assistance, Stockholm, Sweden, International IDEA. https://www.idea.int/sites/default/files/publications/reconciliation-after-violent-conflict-handbook.pdf. Accessed on 2 April 2017

Vajda MM (2010) The 2009 *AIDP*'s Resolution on Universal Jurisdiction – An Epitaph or a Revival Call?! ICLR 10(3):325–344

van Ballegooij W (2018) European Public Prosecutor's Office - A View on the State of Play and Perspectives from the European Parliament. In: Geelhoed W, Erkelens LH, Meij AWH (eds) Shifting Perspectives on the European Public Prosecutor's Office. Asser Press, The Hague, pp. 27–38

van der Meersch G (1977) Memorandum/Paper entitled 'Questions of Common Interest which may Form the Subject of Exchanges of Views and Information'. Information on the Court of Justice of the European Communities 1977 – III. Information Office, Court of Justice of the European Communities, Luxembourg. http://aei.pitt.edu/36612/1/A2709.pdf. Accessed 13 July 2011

van der Voort K, Zwanenburg MC (2003) Amnesty and the Implementation of the ICC: Some Country Studies. In: Haveman R, Kavran O, Nicholls J (eds) Supranational Criminal Law: A System *Sui Generis*, Intersentia, Antwerp/Oxford/NY, pp. 305–345

van der Wilt H (2000) The International Criminal Court and Domestic Jurisdictions: Competition or Concerted Action? In: Coomans F, Grunfeld F, Westendorp I, Willems J (eds) Rendering Justice to the Vulnerable: *Liber Amicorum* in Honour of Theo van Boven. KLI, Dordrecht, pp. 328–338 van der Wilt H (2011) Universal Jurisdiction under Attack: An Assessment of African Misgivings Towards International Criminal Justice as Administered by Western States. JICJ 9(5):1043–1066

van der Wilt H (2013) Domestic Courts' Contribution to the Development of International Criminal law: Some Reflections. ILR 46(2):207–231

van Schaack B, Slye RC (2010) International Criminal Law and its Enforcement: Cases and Materials, 2nd edn. Thomas Reuters, FP, NY

van Steenberghe R (2011) The Obligation to Extradite or Prosecute: Clarifying its Nature. JICJ 9 (5):1089–1116

Vandeginste S (2012) Reviewing Siebert-Fohr A (2009) Prosecuting Serious Human Rights Violations. OUP, Oxford. In: LJIL 25(1):239–243

Ventura MJ (2015) The Duty to Investigate Zimbabwe Crimes Against Humanity (Torture) Allegations: The Constitutional Court of South Africa Speaks on Universal Jurisdiction and the ICC Act. JICJ 13(4):861–889

Wahid Hanna M (2008) A Historical Overview of National Prosecutions for International Crimes. In: Bassiouni MC (ed) International Criminal Law: International Enforcement, Vol. III, 3rd edn. MNP, Leiden, p. 297–328

War Crimes Act (1999) Act Concerning the Punishment of Grave Breaches of International Humanitarian law, Belgium

Watson GR (1993) The Passive Personality Principle. TILJ 28(1):1–46

Webb P (2012) Human Rights and the Immunities of State Officials. In: de Wet E, Vidmar J (eds) Hierarchy in International Law: The Place of Human Rights. OUP, Oxford, pp. 114–147

Weeramantry CG (2004) Universalising International Law. MNP, Leiden

Weiss P (2007) The Future of Universal Jurisdiction. In: Kaleck W, Ratner M, Singelnstein T, Weiss P (eds) International Prosecution of Human Rights Crimes. Springer, Berlin/Heidelberg, pp. 29–36

Wetboek van Strafvordering (1969) Code of Penal Procedure, the Netherlands

Weyembergh A (2013) Transverse Report on Judicial Control in Cooperation in Criminal Matters: The Evolution from Traditional Judicial Cooperation to Mutual Recognition. In: Ligeti K (ed) Towards a Prosecutor for the European Union, Volume I, A Comparative Analysis. Modern Studies in European law, HP, Bloomsbury, pp. 945–985

Wiebelhaus-Brahm E (2011) Truth Commissions. In: Schabas WA, Bernaz N (eds) Routledge Handbook of International Criminal Law. Routledge, T & F, London and NY, pp. 369–383

Wise EM (1993) The Obligation to Extradite or Prosecute. ILR 27(1–2):268–287

Xenos D (2012) The Positive Obligations of the State under the European Convention on Human Rights. Routledge Research in Human Rights Law, Routledge, T & F, London/NY

Yabasun D, Holvoet M (2013) Seeking Asylum Before the International Criminal Court. Another Challenge for a Court in Need of Credibility. ICLR 13(3):725–745

Zahar A (2009) Perpetrators and Co-Perpetrators of Genocide. In: Gaeta P (ed) The United Nations Genocide Convention: A Commentary. Oxford Commentaries on International Law, OUP, pp. 139–161

Zimmermann A (2006) Violations of Fundamental Norms of International Law and the Exercise of Universal Jurisdiction in Criminal Matters. In: Tomuschat C, Thouvenin J-M (eds) The Fundamental Rules of the International Legal Order: *Jus Cogens* and Obligations *Erga Omnes*. MNP, Leiden/Boston, pp. 335–353

Chapter 14
The Reliance of the Horizontal System of Enforcement on the *Corpus Juris* Relating to Extradition

Contents

References 408

Abstract The horizontal system of enforcement is largely dependent upon bilateral and multilateral extradition treaties. Whereas multilateral treaties generally target specific crimes, States are increasingly extraditing on the basis of regional treaties. Some rules are phrased in a mandatory way throughout certain treaties, but other similar rules are more leniently (flexibly) drafted within other treaties, leaving therein a considerable amount of discretion upon States. A mandatory provision contrasts sharply with the discretionary nature of another provision, even when like is compared to like, that is, when the *aut dedere aut judicare* rule is under scrutiny. Indeed the obligation to extradite or prosecute may either be alternative or subsidiary. There may be many reasons to favour the prioritization of the *judicare* limb over the *dedere* limb. Yet, practice shows that a prosecution being conducted in the *forum conveniens,* besides being a very common occurrence, is more likely to be both effective and fair. The *dedere limb* should be favoured especially when extradition to the *forum conveniens* is to be undertaken. However, it is equivocal since treaties which either render universal jurisdiction mandatory, facultative, or which seem to permit universal jurisdiction, whilst stipulating the *aut dedere aut judicare* rule, do not shed a light as to whether such extradition should be effected to the requesting State, to another State party to the treaty, to another State which enjoys non-universal jurisdiction over the extraditee, or to any other State which is willing to exercise universal jurisdiction notwithstanding no connection at all with the crime.

Keywords Horizontal system of enforcement · Multilateral treaties · Bilateral treaties · Customary international law · *Aut dedere aut judicare* · Extradition · Alternative obligation · Subsidiary obligation · *Judicare* limb · *Dedere* limb · Duty to prosecute · Prioritization · Suppression conventions · *Forum conveniens*

C. Soler, *The Global Prosecution of Core Crimes under International Law*,
https://doi.org/10.1007/978-94-6265-335-1_14

The horizontal system of enforcement is largely dependent upon bilateral and multilateral extradition treaties, most of which generally epitomize the principle of reciprocity,[1] which principle either serves as a device to sanctify international relations or as a precept in the absence of any extradition treaty.[2] Whereas multilateral treaties generally target specific crimes, States are increasingly extraditing on the basis of regional treaties.[3] Bilateral treaties comport two main consequences. States subject their potential extradition partners to due diligence scrutiny during the process of treaty negotiation, embedding conditional requirements for extradition, and can justify maintaining a duty of non-inquiry into the quality of the criminal justice likely to be administered in the requesting State upon extradition of the fugitive.[4] Fabio Dean, for example, analysing Italy's laws on extradition, admits that although extradition is regulated by Constitutional Law, ordinary law and the signature of treaties, the latter is by far the *fonte normativa principale in materia*.[5] This has a dual effect. Such treaties bind the signatories thereto, but when they are ratified by an overwhelming majority of States they either provide evidence of customary international law[6] or actually entrench customary international law. Customary international norms of extradition can thus be forged by treaty ratification, especially when an accumulation of treaties bind States with a particular rule, although such rule may not be identically proscribed in each and every treaty.[7] Since treaties have caused customary international law, one may argue that the *corpus juris* of extradition, to an extent, relies upon the ratification of international conventions. Likewise, in the field of international humanitarian law, humanitarian principles have crystallized into customary international law.[8] Additionally, in cases of overlap between a treaty rule and a customary rule, the treaty rule overrides the customary one.[9] Thus, this work merits a glance at the main treaties which have paved the way for the extradition and prosecution of those who have allegedly violated conventional international law which proscribes genocide, various war crimes and transnational organized crimes which could be tantamount to crimes against humanity. Such treaties, as shown already, postulate some significant permutations.[10]

---

[1] van der Wilt 2005, p. 71.

[2] van der Wilt 2005, p. 80.

[3] Boister 2016, p. 5.

[4] Boister 2016, p. 5.

[5] This means that treaties are the most important source of extradition law in Italy (Dean et al. 2003, p. 499).

[6] ICJ, *Continental Shelf Case (Libya Arab Jamahiriya v Malta)*, 3 June 1985, [1985] ICJ Rep. 13, para 27.

[7] ILC 2011.

[8] ICJ, *Legality of the Threat or Use of Nuclear Weapons (Nuclear Weapons Advisory Opinion)*, 8 July 1996, ICJ Rep. 1996, p. 226, para 82.

[9] Wolfke 1993, pp. 112–113.

[10] Most jurists have categorized such variables in a distinctively mathematical way, tagging them as '*formulae*', a term also used by myself [see Sect. 13.2].

The prevailing legal wording within treaties is riddled with different degrees of force or weakness.[11] Whereas some rules are phrased in a mandatory way throughout certain treaties, other similar rules are more leniently or flexibly drafted within other treaties, leaving therein a considerable amount of discretion upon States. A mandatory provision contrasts sharply with the discretionary nature of another provision, even when like is compared to like, that is, when the *aut dedere aut judicare* rule is under scrutiny.

In the light of the above, it is worthwhile considering the various combinations which partake of the *aut dedere aut judicare* rule not only for the sake of understanding such combinations but, at this stage, in order to understand how and to what extent the obligations that flow therefrom may be fulfilled by States. Indeed the obligation to extradite or prosecute may either be alternative[12] or subsidiary wherein '*lo Stato richiesto instaura un procedimento per quel fatto qualora abbia rifiutato l'estradizione: primo dedere, secundo iudicare*'.[13]

At this point one should take another snapshot which postulates the dilemma relating to the *formulae* to be used, as examined earlier on, but this time not simply to postulate them but indeed to identify the most favourable one in the light of the crime which is subject to prosecution. Analysing conventions which curb terrorism, which suppression treaties have been the main foundation of the *aut dedere aut judicare* rule, Robert Kolb presents two different viewpoints. The first leans towards the *judicare* limb since there exists in any case a subsidiary obligation to prosecute, conveying that prosecution must take place, subject only to the possibility of setting it aside if extradition happens to take place. In this first interpretation, 'extradition is only a device for trial, it has no value in itself except to guarantee the most convenient forum'.[14] The other interpretation, which (although largely favourable) carries some negative implications,[15] is imbalanced in favour of the *dedere* limb in order to facilitate the prosecution in the *forum conveniens*, which is generally the *locus delicti commissi*, which besides possessing a strong *nexus* to the crime, also happens to be the place where most evidence proving the crime is available.[16] By means of this school of thought, since extradition extinguishes the

---

[11] For example, Elagab states that 'the most comprehensive and far reaching obligations imposed on States came with the adoption of the Hostages Convention of 1979' (Elagab 1995, p. 517).

[12] To extradite or prosecute.

[13] (the requested State undertakes criminal proceedings for the act if it refused to extradite: first extradite, second prosecute: my translation), see Dean et al. 2003, p. 518.

[14] Kolb 2004, p. 257.

[15] These include the fact that, as shall be postulated shortly, whereas prosecution is a direct system of enforcement since it necessitates no further steps, *id est* a one-stop shop, extradition is the preliminary step leading to eventual prosecution. Prosecution is thus a faster way of consummating justice. Additionally, it could also be more favourable to the charged individual since by being prosecuted in the requested State, he is more likely to be tried without undue delay, *id est* within a reasonable time, rather than after the execution of an extradition process to the requesting State.

[16] Analysing the verdict of the trial by jury delivered by the Central Criminal Court in the case of *Faryadi Sarwar Zardad* [Central Criminal Court (Old Bailey), London, *Regina v Faryadi Sarwar Zardad*, 18 July 2005, 200505339/D3], Cedric Ryngaert states that such a case 'highlighted the

duty to prosecute, extradition overrides the duty to prosecute. Prosecution is therefore obligatory in the absence of extradition, and only by default. Marc Henzelin seems to favour the former interpretation. He concludes that 'the conventions establish an original obligation to prosecute, unless extradition takes place. In particular, this means that prosecution is not dependent on the existence of a request to extradite that was not acted upon (*primo dedere secundo prosequi*). Nevertheless, a State may on its own initiative take up contacts with other interested States in order to see if an extradition is possible, desired or otherwise recommended. Its primary obligation to prosecute does not mean that it is precluded to actively seek extradition'.[17] However, Robert Kolb notes that, in as much as this may be true on an international level, the same may not be said in relation to regional treaties which aim to suppress terrorism. Indeed, at European level,[18] the priorities are reversed,[19] privileging extradition over prosecution within the tight extradite-or-prosecute regime.

There may be many reasons to favour the prioritization of the *judicare* limb over the *dedere* limb, including:

I. the inherent nature of such treaties shows that their ultimate aim is the prosecution for conduct constituting the acts or omissions penalized therein. This is why they are habitually referred to as 'suppression conventions'. Suppression can generally be achieved by prosecution because prosecution can lead to effective punishment. Mere extradition does not suffice since it does not directly trigger the infliction of sanctions, except where extradition is undertaken specifically for the purpose of the execution of a sentence, often by virtue and in compliance with a bilateral treaty;
II. extradition, by its own inherent nature, is a means to an end, the end being ultimate prosecution amidst an emerging rule of international law favouring a *ius prosequi*.[20] In fact extradition is generally effected for the purposes of prosecution in the requesting State or, for the execution of a custodial sentence;
III. principles of jurisdiction under international law, including universal jurisdiction itself, have been devised in order to ensure that judicial institutions can legitimately enjoy legal authority over individuals, and not merely to guarantee the transfer of an individual from a State to another further to an executive and political decision-making process; and

---

practical problems encountered in trials on the basis of universal jurisdiction, where much of the evidence and many witnesses are located abroad, in the State where the crimes occurred' (Ryngaert 2005, p. 608).

[17] Henzelin 2000, p. 298.

[18] European Convention on the Suppression of Terrorism (1977).

[19] *Primo dedere secundo prosequi.*

[20] Kai Ambos makes the step from 'right' to 'duty' when he upholds that 'international treaty and customary law provides for a general duty of States to investigate, prosecute and punish international core crimes' (Ambos 2010, p. 55).

IV. the *dedere* limb is ambiguous and equivocal in that treaties which either render universal jurisdiction mandatory,[21] facultative[22] or which seem to permit universal jurisdiction,[23] whilst stipulating the *aut dedere aut judicare* rule, do not shed a light as to whether such extradition should be effected to the requesting State, to another State party to the treaty, to another State which enjoys non-universal jurisdiction over the extraditee, or to any other State which is willing to exercise universal jurisdiction notwithstanding no connection at all with the crime. Such choices emanate from the actual wording of such treaties which do not expressly restrict the scope of extradition *inter partes*. Owing to the rules on treaty interpretation emanating from the VCLT and a relevant legal maxim,[24] there exists a *presumptio juris tantum* that in the absence of a qualified extradition mechanism, any such mechanism is allowed, and therefore extradition *tout court* is envisaged. Therefore, in the spirit of the suppression conventions, applying a purposive interpretation thereto, it could be argued that the *dedere* limb should be considered to be subservient to the *judicare* limb.

Nevertheless, practice shows that a prosecution being conducted in the *forum conveniens*, besides being a very common occurrence, is more likely to be both effective and fair. The *dedere limb* should therefore be favoured especially when extradition to the *forum conveniens* is to be undertaken. Other permutations, possibly reflecting a differential linguistic and structural style of drafting, subsist. For example, the 2005 CoE Convention on Action Against Trafficking in Human Beings stipulates that State parties 'shall adopt such measures as may be necessary to establish jurisdiction over the offences referred to in this Convention, in cases where an alleged offender is present in its territory and it does not extradite him/her to another Party, solely on the basis of his/her nationality, after a request for extradition'.[25] It is noticeable that in this *aut dedere aut judicare* legal provision, no mention is made of prosecution *per se*, but of the establishment of jurisdiction over offences.

The regulatory framework which governs extradition largely affects the success or otherwise of the horizontal system of enforcement. More than being a measure of

[21] Article 49 of the First Geneva Convention, Article 50 of the Second Geneva Convention, Article 129 of the Third Convention and Article 146 of the Fourth Geneva Convention.

[22] Articles 4(b) and 5 of the International Convention on the Suppression and Punishment of the Crime of Apartheid signed in NY on 30 November 1973.

[23] Article 4 sub-article 2 (h) and Article 8 sub-article 4 of the Organization of African Unity Convention on the Prevention and Combating of Terrorism (1999); Article 7 of the Convention for the Suppression of Unlawful Acts Against the Safety of Civil Aviation (1971); Article 8 of the Convention Against the Taking of Hostages (1979); Article 10 sub-article 1 of the Convention for the Suppression of Unlawful Acts Against the Safety of Maritime Navigation (1988); Article 8 sub-article 1 of the Convention for the Suppression of Terrorist Bombings (1997), and Article 10 sub-article 1 of the Convention for the Suppression of the Financing of Terrorism (1999).

[24] *Ubi lex voluit lex dixit.*

[25] Article 31 sub-article 3 in Paust et al. 2007, p. 511.

the success of the horizontal system of enforcement, the ultimate objective of the *corpus juris* relating to extradition is to ensure that those individuals who should be extradited are actually extradited whereas those who should not be extradited, for compelling reasons which must be objectively justified, are not constrained to endure such process. To this extent, conventional international law, which comprises relevant multilateral treaties and applicable bilateral treaties, secures its status as the main source of extradition law, and of the validity, interpretation, execution, implementation and enforcement thereof.

References

Ambos K (2010) The Colombian Peace Process and the Principle of Complementarity of the International Criminal Court: An Inductive, Situation-Based Approach. Springer, Heidelberg

Boister N (2016) The Simplification of the Law of Extradition at a Global Level: Some Reflections on the Implications of the Move Towards a No Dress Rehearsal Rule. Paper submitted for the purposes of an ACIL lecture, UvA, Amsterdam

CoE Convention on Action Against Trafficking in Human Beings (2005)

Convention Against the Taking of Hostages (1979)

Convention for the Suppression of Terrorist Bombings (1997)

Convention for the Suppression of the Financing of Terrorism (1999)

Convention for the Suppression of Unlawful Acts Against the Safety of Maritime Navigation (1988)

Convention for the Suppression of Unlawful Acts Against the Safety of Civil Aviation (1971)

Convention on the Suppression and Punishment of the Crime of Apartheid (1973)

Dean F, D'Innocenzio M, Pugliese P, Ricci A (2003) *Diritto Penale Internazionale: Lezioni agli Studenti* [International Criminal Law: Lectures for Students], *Terza Edizione* [3rd edn.]. *Marghiacci, Galeno Editrice, Roma*

Elagab OY (1995) International Law Documents Relating to Terrorism. CPL, London

European Convention on the Suppression of Terrorism (1977)

Geneva Convention (1949a) Geneva Convention (I) for the Amelioration of the Condition of the Wounded and Sick in Armed Forces in the Field

Geneva Convention (1949b) Geneva Convention (II) for the Amelioration of the Condition of the Wounded, Sick and Shipwrecked Members of Armed Forces at Sea

Geneva Convention (1949c) Geneva Convention (III) relative to the Treatment of Prisoners of War

Geneva Convention (1949d) Geneva Convention (IV) relative to the Protection of Civilian Persons in Time of War

Henzelin M (2000) *Le Principe de l'Universalité en Droit Pénal International: Droit et Obligation pour les États de Poursuivre et Juger Selon le Principe de l'Universalité* [The Principle of Universality under International Criminal Law: Law and Obligations for States to Prosecute and Judge in Terms of the Principle of Universality]. Helbin and Lichtenhahn, Munich, Geneva, Brussels

ILC (2011) Concluding Remarks (Report) of the Special Rapporteur Zdzisław Galicki, Sixty-Third Session. The Obligation to Extradite or Prosecute *(aut dedere aut judicare)*. ILC Report A/66/10. http://untreaty.un.org/ilc/reports/2011/All%20languages/A_66_10_E.pdf. Accessed 9 December 2013

Kolb R (2004) The Exercise of Criminal Jurisdiction over International Terrorists. In: Bianchi A (ed) Enforcing International Law Norms Against Terrorism. HP, Oxford/Portland, Oregon, USA, pp. 227–281

Organization of African Unity Convention on the Prevention and Combating of Terrorism (1999)

Paust JJ, Bassiouni MC, Scharf M, Gurule` J, Sadat L, Zagaris B (2007) International Criminal Law: Cases and Materials, 3rd edn. CAP, Durham, North Carolina, USA
Ryngaert C (2005) Universal Criminal Jurisdiction Over Torture: A State of Affairs After 20 Years United Nations Torture Convention. NQHR 23(4):571–611
van der Wilt H (2005) The Principle of Reciprocity. In: Blekxtoon R, van Ballegooij W (eds) Handbook on the European Arrest Warrant. Asser Press, The Hague, pp. 71–81
VCLT (1969) Vienne Convention on the Law of Treaties
Wolfke K (1993) Custom in Present International Law, 2nd edn. MNP, Dordrecht

Chapter 15
The Impact of Customary International Law and General Principles of Law on the Horizontal System of Enforcement

Contents

References 413

Abstract This chapter considers the influence which sources of international law, with the exception of treaty law, have on the horizontal system of enforcement. There exists relatively widespread consensus to the effect that important treaty provisions, such as the *aut dedere aut judicare* rule, have passed into customary international law. Such consensus, although broad, cannot be considered as overwhelming particularly because, in the first place, even conventionally, the *aut dedere aut judicare* rule presents itself in many forms. Such different *formulae* and their subsequent differentiated adherence could have a prejudicial impact on the customary status of the *aut dedere aut judicare* rule. This is because, since the 1985 *Continental Shelf* case, the ICJ asserted that the substance of customary international law must be looked for primarily at the actual practice and *opinio juris* of States. A traceable and influential *nexus* also exists between customary international law, on the one hand, and general principles of law, on the other hand. Domestic courts can play a role in forming customary international law, in that their decisions constitute State practice. Such *dicta* can constitute both State practice and *opinio juris*. Municipal judgments also have the potential to form and identify general principles of law. This is particularly so in relation to substantive international criminal law (especially the constitutive elements of core crimes), but it is not so self-evident when State practice on extradition is examined with the sources of international law (for such purpose, customary international law and general principles of law) in mind.

Keywords Horizontal system of enforcement · Customary international law · *Aut dedere aut judicare* · *Formulae* · *Continental Shelf* case · *Libyan Arab Jamahiriya v Malta* · Extradition · General principles of law · *Opinio juris* · Sources · State practice

C. Soler, *The Global Prosecution of Core Crimes under International Law*,
https://doi.org/10.1007/978-94-6265-335-1_15

Having examined the way conventional international law deeply affects the horizontal system of enforcement, I shall now pass onto consider the influence that other sources of international law have on such system. Before delving into the intricacies of customary international law, suffice to say that there exists relatively widespread consensus to the effect that important treaty provisions, such as the *aut dedere aut judicare* rule, have passed into customary international law. Such consensus, although broad, cannot be considered as overwhelming particularly because, in the first place, even conventionally, as has been stated in Sect. 13.2, the *aut dedere aut judicare* rule presents itself in a multitude of forms. The link between treaty law and customary international law, in as much as it promotes the *aut dedere aut judicare* rule, is thus enhanced.

To begin with, as Theodor Meron highlights, 'there is a point at which contrary practice reaches such a critical mass that the norm in question cannot be said to be customary'.[1] Such different *formulae* (outlined in Sect. 13.2) and their subsequent differentiated adherence could have a prejudicial impact on the customary status of the *aut dedere aut judicare* rule. This is because, since the *Continental Shelf dictum*, the ICJ asserted that the substance of customary international law must be 'looked for primarily at the actual practice and *opinio juris* of States'.[2]

A traceable and influential *nexus* also exists between customary international law, on the one hand, and general principles of law, on the other.[3] Hugh Thirlway acknowledges that 'there is a somewhat blurred distinction between a rule deriving from the "customary practice" of international tribunals, and a rule constituting a "general principle of law"'.[4] Referring to commentators, Brian Lepard considers this *nexus* as a fully-fledged relationship and suggests that 'customary norms are uniquely based on State practice, whereas general principles do not have to be supported by practice'.[5] One must keep in mind the fact that domestic courts can play a role in forming customary international law, in that their decisions constitute State practice.[6] This is firmly acknowledged[7] by André Nollkaemper who, besides stating that such *dicta* can constitute both State practice and *opinio juris*,[8] goes as far as saying that 'it is a plausible presumption that in certain respects the legal relevance of decisions of domestic courts in regard to international claims may extend, beyond the legal order of the forum State, to the international legal order'.[9] On similar lines, municipal judgments have the potential to form and identify

---

1 Meron 2005, p. 820.

2 ICJ, *Continental Shelf* case *(Libyan Arab Jamahiriya v Malta)*, 3 June 1985, [1985] ICJ Rep. 13, para 27.

3 Schlutter 2010, pp. 71–86.

4 Thirlway 1984, p. 624.

5 Lepard 2010, p. 162.

6 ILC 1950, para 54.

7 Nollkaemper 2011, p. 267.

8 Nollkaemper 2011, p. 268.

9 Nollkaemper 2011, p. 245.

general principles of law.[10] This is particularly so in relation to substantive international criminal law (especially the constitutive elements of core crimes), but it is not so self-evident when State practice on extradition is examined with the sources of international law (for such purpose, customary international law and general principles of law) in mind. In other words, in certain identifiable circumstances, such *dicta* resemble water percolating through a cracked wall. The importance of the horizontal system of enforcement for the general enforcement of international criminal law is hence, once again, underlined.

The above mentioned shows how the multi-faceted *aut dedere aut judicare* rule possesses the potential of rendering the traditional sources of international law[11] different from what they actually constitute and bestow. Its elements and features can truly re-shape the use and application of the sources of international law. The following chapter shall constitute the counterpart to Chap. 11. I shall now hence determine the extent to which States may refuse to extradite an individual over whom they have custodial jurisdiction to another (requesting) State. In other words, I shall now proceed to examine the pitfalls in the horizontal system of enforcement.

References

ICJ Statute (1946) Statute of the International Court of Justice

ILC (1950) Ways and Means for Making the Evidence of Customary International Law More Readily Available. Report of the ILC to the UNGA. http://legal.un.org/ilc/texts/instruments/english/reports/1_4_1950.pdf. Accessed 19 January 2011

Lepard BD (2010) Customary International Law: A New Theory with Practical Applications. ASIL Studies in International Legal Theory, CUP, Cambridge

Meron T (2005) Revival of Customary Humanitarian Law. AJIL 99(4):817–834

Nollkaemper A (2011) National Courts and the International Rule of Law. OUP, Oxford

Schlutter B (2010) Developments in Customary International Law: Theory and Practice of the International Court of Justice and the International *Ad Hoc* Criminal Tribunals for Rwanda and Yugoslavia. MNP, Leiden/Boston

Thirlway H (1984) Dilemma or Chimera? Admissibility of Illegally Obtained Evidence in International Adjudication. AJIL 78(3):622–641

---

[10] Nollkaemper 2011, p. 272.

[11] Article 38(1) of the ICJ Statute (1946) Statute of the International Court of Justice.

Chapter 16
Pitfalls Within the Horizontal System of Enforcement

Contents

16.1 The Non-extradition of Nationals ... 428
16.2 The Military Offence Exemption ... 436
16.3 The Political Offence Exemption ... 437
16.4 The Double Criminality Rule ... 448
16.5 The Exclusion of the Cause of the Criminal Action by Reason of Amnesty ... 454
16.6 Plea Bargaining ... 465
16.7 Human Rights General Exceptions to Extraditions ... 467
16.7.1 The Right to a Fair Trial ... 470
16.7.2 The *Ne Bis in Idem* Rule ... 477
16.7.3 The Prohibition of Torture and Other Cruel, Inhuman and Degrading Treatment or Punishment ... 493
16.7.4 Death Row and the Death Penalty ... 507
16.7.4.1 International Refugee Law: A New and Reliable Measuring Tape? ... 515
16.8 Diplomatic Privileges and Immunities ... 518
16.8.1 Immunities *Rationae Personae* ... 519
16.8.2 Immunities *Rationae Materiae* ... 522
References ... 533

Abstract The non-extradition of nationals has been discarded by the EAW procedure. The military offence exemption is hardly applicable nowadays. The political offence exemption is being eroded by a depoliticizing formula. The double criminality rule has been softened by the EAW which no longer requires it for some offences, including core crimes. Blanket amnesties are being nullified by domestic Constitutional Courts in so far as they breach the duty to prosecute which was municipally sanctioned. Plea-bargains can hardly figure when core crimes are concerned. The most resilient grounds for refusal of extradition are the human rights general exceptions. The likelihood of a flagrant violation of a fair trial can block an extradition. The *ne bis in idem* rule can hinder an extradition on a domestic level, more than on an international level. There could be the need to consider *ne bis in idem* in the light of other grounds for refusal, such as amnesties and double criminality, to which it is connected. Due to its *jus cogens* status, the likelihood of a

C. Soler, *The Global Prosecution of Core Crimes under International Law*,
https://doi.org/10.1007/978-94-6265-335-1_16

breach of the prohibition of torture constitutes the major impediment to an extradition request. This ground has been tested in the context of the prospect of a judicial sentence imposing life imprisonment. The infliction of the death penalty in the requesting State blocks an extradition request, more so when execution can occur after an unfair trial. A trend points to a developing exception to diplomatic privileges and immunities as grounds for refusal of extradition when core crimes are involved.

Keywords Pitfalls · Horizontal system of enforcement · Assurances · *Aut dedere aut judicare* · Speciality · *Pinochet* · *Jus cogens* norms · Obligations *erga omnes* · Fair trial · Shielding · Admissibility test · Death penalty · Non-extradition of nationals · *Fujimori* · EAW · *Zentai* · Torture · Military offence exemption · Political offence exemption · Depoliticizing formula · *Doctrine de gravité* · British political incidence theory · Swiss proportionality theory · ECMAC · Anglo-American incidence test · Multi-lateral legal instruments · ECE · CREMS · State practice · Double criminality rule · *Nullum crimen sine lege* · *Nulla poena sine lege* · Forseeability requirement · Verification · Assessment *in concreto* · Assessment *in abstracto* · Amnesty · *Nolle Prosequi* · *Ne bis in idem* · *Azapo* · Right to a national effective remedy · Impunity · *Barrios Altos* · *Gomes Lund* · Lomé Peace Accords · *Kallon and Kamara* · *Sandoval Rodríguez* · *Simón* · *Obediencia debida* · *Punto final* · Plea bargaining · Due process · *Soering* · *Ng* · *Kindler* · *Ahorugeze* · Flagrant denial of justice test · *Mamatkulov* · *Abu Qatada* · *Al-Moayad* · *Connelly* principles · *Videla* · *Ali Rezaq* · Committee Against Torture · Inhuman and degrading treatment · Non-*refoulement* · *Kafkaris* · Life imprisonment · *Babar Ahmad* · Periodic review · Sentence review · *Öcalan* · Comorbidity · *Plan Sistemático* · *Campo de Mayo* · *Zakaev* · *Ireland v UK* · *Kindler* · Capital punishment · Death row · Method of execution · *Kigula* · Likelihood of a violation · Flagrant violation test · *La Cantuta* massacre · International refugee law · Diplomatic privileges and immunities · Immunities *rationae materiae* · Immunities *rationae personae* · Functional immunities · Personal immunities · Head of State · *Taylor* · *Yerodia* · *Ghaddafi* · *Bouterse* · Implied waiver theory · Developing exception · International Convention for the Prevention, Prosecution and Punishment of Core Crimes · Multilateral Treaty for Mutual Legal Assistance and Extradition for Domestic Prosecution of Crimes of Genocide, Crimes Against Humanity and War Crimes

Being 'an uneasy marriage between law and politics',[1] extradition has its pitfalls.[2] Although some pitfalls can effectively impede an extradition request especially

---

[1] Plachta 2001a, p. 128.

[2] A pitfall is defined as 'trap for the capture of birds in which a trap-door or the like falls over a cavity or hollow; a concealed pit into which animals or men may fall and be captured; an ambush or a natural trap in which a force may be surrounded and overpowered' (Simpson and Weiner 1989, pp. 925–926).

when they are of an absolute nature, such as in the case of the prohibition of torture,[3] it might not necessarily be so because such pitfalls may be circumvented, in certain circumstances, as shall be seen shortly. The word 'pitfall' is more appropriate than the word 'impediment', as used by Yasmin Naqvi,[4] in the context of the horizontal system of enforcement when the grounds for refusal are cumulatively considered, because:

I. when an extradition request is tendered the executive police and prosecutors are not necessarily aware of the defence [grounds to combat extradition] strategy, whereas an impediment is more appropriate in the harmonised vertical system of enforcement with the ICC Statute's provisions;
II. an impediment presupposes something that is fixed, definite and previously established, whereas a pitfall is an unsuspected difficulty, a concealed trap, a reason or ground which a State may postulate at a late stage of an extradition saga, not necessarily *in limine litis*;
III. impediments block extradition, whereas pitfalls merely disturb it without necessarily impeding it, such as when assurances are given by the requesting State to the effect that a death sentence will not be executed against the extraditee. An impediment, in fact, is defined as 'a hindrance or obstruction, especially some fact, such as legal minority that bars a marriage if known beforehand and, if discovered after the ceremony, renders the marriage void or voidable'.[5] In other words, extradition, represented by the king in a chess game, is constantly under check, but the king may avoid a checkmate if he is astute and agile, just as a requesting State can avoid falling into the pitfall;
IV. impediments are of a mandatory nature, whereas pitfalls can allow a limited amount of State discretion;
V. impediments precede the contentious fact, whereas pitfalls are considered *ex post facto*. By way of example, for the prohibition of torture to effectively block an extradition, an examination of the prevailing judicial and penitentiary systems of the requesting State is effected after the request for extradition is tendered by the requesting State. To borrow a financial term, a due diligence exercise is undertaken when the company is insolvent, *id est* undergoing liquidation proceedings, not when it is set-up. Although *jus cogens*, the prohibition of torture, or rather the risk of torture in the requesting State, might not necessarily always be an *a priori* bar to extradition. This contrasts with other grounds for refusal, such as double criminality, which is more apparent at early stages of the entire procedural *iter*;

---

[3] Soler 2004, pp. 379–380.

[4] Naqvi 2010, *passim*. This should not be misconstrued so as to level a criticism of such an impressive work, especially because Yasmin Naqvi, in the ninth page of her book, posits that the 'book is concerned with barriers of a legal nature which operate to stay the exercise of adjudicatory jurisdiction', hence justifying her focus on what she considers as 'six principal impediments'.

[5] Garner 2009, p. 821.

VI. in the absence of an international convention on extradition and an international extradition court, the idea of a pitfall is more commensurate with the greyness of such a complex and multi-faceted matter.

The main hurdles to extraditing individuals who are subject to a request for extradition from the requested State to the requesting State are the following:

1. the non-extradition of nationals;
2. the military offence exemption;
3. the political offence exemption;
4. the double criminality rule;
5. the exclusion of the cause of criminal action by reason of amnesty;
6. plea-bargaining;
7. the right to a fair trial;[6]
8. the *ne bis in idem* rule;
9. the prohibition of torture and other cruel, inhuman and degrading treatment or punishment;
10. death row and the death penalty; and
11. diplomatic privileges and immunities.

These grounds are not so enlisted to reflect a hierarchical or chronological order, or to entail ascending or descending importance. Nor are they so enlisted to portray that the first ground is domestically availed of and resorted to by States more than the second, and so on and so forth. It is further to be noted that some of these grounds are interlinked, as shall be shown hereunder. My analysis should lead to a better understanding of the extent to which such grounds:

i. overlap;
ii. are either mandatory or discretionary;
iii. are likely to be confined, restricted or limited; and
iv. are applicable or otherwise.

These grounds are not cast in stone. Michael Plachta examines them in a peculiar way by enlisting criteria for their classification, containing sources, subject-matter, State's interests involved, together with their rationale, and upholds that they have a potential to grow.[7] In his view, *aut dedere aut judicare* 'may become an effective countermeasure that will, to a certain degree, compensate for the expansionist approach towards the grounds for refusal'.[8] Examining Polish legislation with a 'crime control' perspective which slightly overlooks the human rights *leitmotif* behind such hurdles (obstacles) to extradition, he concludes that 'since there are so many various grounds for refusal of the surrender of the relator it would be unrealistic to expect that all the problems associated with bringing criminals to justice

---

[6] Slye and van Schaack postulate 'concerns about the lack of due process in the requesting State' as one of four grounds of refusal of extradition (Slye and van Schaack 2009, p. 80).

[7] Plachta 2001b.

[8] Plachta 2001b.

will disappear as if by magic. The solution to the problems caused by the denial of extradition requests should be based on the differentiation among the grounds for refusal using the *ratio legis* of each of them as a criterion'.[9] Yasmin Naqvi limits such grounds to:

(a) amnesties;
(b) pardons;
(c) statutes of limitations;
(d) immunities;
(e) *ne bis in idem*; and
(f) abuse of process.[10]

Besides the above mentioned eleven grounds identified by myself, Mohammed Cherif Bassiouni also includes the following, within the list of what he deems to be 'grounds for denial of extradition':[11]

i. exclusion for prosecution based on certain discriminatory grounds;[12]
ii. immunity from prosecution;[13]
iii. double jeopardy;[14]
iv. statutes of limitations;
v. exclusions concerning certain penalties and treatment of offenders.[15]

Moreover, the rule of speciality,[16] 'accepted by most States as a customary rule of extradition law',[17] is often referred to, albeit imprecisely, as a potential obstacle to extradition. It is generally inapplicable where the requested person voluntarily chooses to consent to his own surrender. In fact, speciality can be waived by the requested/surrendered person in terms of Articles 27–28 of the Framework Decision on the EAW. As noted in Part III, this rule entails that a fugitive may only be prosecuted in the requesting State for those offences for which extradition was

---

9 Plachta 1998, p. 105.

10 Naqvi 2010, pp. 75–364.

11 Bassiouni 1986, pp. 413–417. However, in the Model Treaty on Extradition [UN Model Treaty on Extradition (1990) Model Treaty on Extradition 45/116, UNGA, 68th Plenary Meeting, 14 December 1990, UN Doc. A/RES/45/116] brought forth at the eight UN Congress on the Prevention of Crime and the Treatment of Offenders held in Havana, Cuba, he postulated a distinction between 'mandatory grounds for refusal' in Article 3 and 'optional grounds for refusal' in Article 4 (Bassiouni 1994, pp. 460–462).

12 Bassiouni links this ground, commonly referred to as the non-discrimination clause, with the political offence exemption, and in fact states that one is the pure political offence and the other one is the relative political offence.

13 This relates to plea-bargaining, the ground for refusal considered in Sect. 16.6.

14 Its prohibition is considered within the ground for refusal which is dealt with in Sect. 16.7.2.

15 Such constitutional guarantees indirectly feature within the consideration of the ground of refusal which is analysed in Sect. 16.7.3.

16 Article 14 of the ECE (1957) European Convention on Extradition, signed in Paris on 13 December 1957. This rule is occasionally and inter-changeably referred to as 'speciality'.

17 Borelli 2004, cited in Kolb 2004, p. 335.

sought. In other words, it protects the extradited person against prosecution for offences for which the extradition has not been sought. This traditional rule has undergone a substantial re-shaping, in that regional extradition agreements provide for the possibility that the requesting State may charge the individual with further extraditable offences after extradition, provided that the requested State consents.[18] In any case, this rule does not have a significant impact on my book in as much as it does not act to effectively bar extradition but merely to qualify it. It does not constitute a fully-fledged pitfall within the horizontal system of enforcement. Its further examination is hence superfluous, for the following reasons. The fine line which distinguishes a core crime from another, aided by the ICC's Elements of Crimes and by customary international law, nowadays equips States with the necessary utensils required to charge an extraditee with a core crime rather than another crime. The rule applies to the vertical system of enforcement too,[19] as is evident from Part III where it was shown that the ICC Statute incorporates this rule[20] which may be waived by States.[21] However it is clear that speciality bars an indictment on the basis of a charge alleging the commission of a crime which did not form the basis of the surrender or extradition in the first place. Hence it does not bar the extradition to a requesting State *per se* but bars eventual prosecution resulting from an extradition. It merely carries weight *ex post facto*, after the extradition, and is therefore not a pitfall within the horizontal system of enforcement. It does not hinder the formal transfer of the individual who is about to be extradited, but protects such individual from multiple, undisclosed and/or arbitrary charges after the extradition is consummated and once such individual is already in the custody of the requesting State. Similarly, many jurists do not enlist it within 'grounds for denial of extradition', but as a separate 'speciality doctrine'.[22] This is why I shall not take further cognisance of it for the purposes of Part IV.

Before delving into each and every ground, one must add that, being a relatively discretionary and executive matter,[23] reasons motivating the rejection of an extradition request need not necessarily be strictly of a juridical nature. In some States executive discretion is more pronounced than others. For example, 'the long-standing rule of non-inquiry prohibits United States Courts from examining the motivation behind an extradition request and from considering the likely treatment of the accused following surrender to the requesting country, these being

---

[18] Article 14 of the ECE, above n. 16, and Article 2 of the ECMAC (1959) European Convention on Mutual Assistance in Criminal Matters.

[19] ICTY, *Prosecutor v Milan Martić*, ICTY Trial Chamber, Decision on the Prosecutor's Motion to Request Leave to File a Corrected Amended Indictment, 18 December 2002, Case No. IT-95-11.

[20] Article 101(1) of the ICC Statute (1998) Rome Statute of the International Criminal Court.

[21] Article 101(2) of the ICC Statute, above n. 20.

[22] Paust et al. 2007, pp. 348 and 341 respectively.

[23] It has been stated that 'the executive branch has the ultimate authority to decide whether to extradite the accused after a judicial determination that the individual is, in fact, extraditable' (Paust 2007, p. 372).

issues which may be considered by the Secretary of State'.[24] Once again, by way of example, the UK, in March 2000, cited humanitarian concerns arising from *Pinochet's* age, health and lack of mental fitness to stand trial in allowing *Pinochet* to return to Chile rather than being extradited to Spain. Jann Kleffner, citing the former Israeli Prime Minister (*Ariel Sharon*) case in Belgium,[25] notes that the 'political implications of a core crime prosecution may very well be a cause for third States to refrain from conducting or abandoning proceedings'.[26]

Other grounds of refusal could be spotted, but these are not relevant for the subject matter under scrutiny. For example, fiscal offences[27] are immaterial to this work since corruption, money laundering, fraud, counterfeiting, cybercrime, insider trading, and such white-collar crimes are not considered to be core crimes, but transnational organised crimes[28] to which a different cooperation regime, heavily reliant upon mutual legal assistance, applies.[29] Thus, the legal instruments[30] which bar extradition on the basis of the fiscal offence exemption or on banking secrecy

---

[24] USA Courts of Appeals for the Second Circuit, *Muhamed Sacirbey, Petitioner-Appellant, v. Joseph R. Guccione, United States Marshal for the SDNY; Officer Dennis Spitzer, Chief Pretrial Services for the Southern District of New York, Respondents-Appellees*, 9 December 2009, Docket Nos. 06-5137-pr (L), 07-0018-pr (con), 589 F.3d 52, cited in Bederman and Semmelman 2010, p. 647, n. 29.

[25] Besides being considered as the heart of the EU, the Benelux State has endured a deep connection with Rwanda probably as a result of the fact that it was Rwanda's former colonial ruler. Moreover, Belgian nationals were killed in Rwanda during the early days of the massacres, the Belgian government unilaterally withdrew from the UN peace-keeping force, and suspected Rwandan *génocidaires* still reside in Belgium further to the repeal of the War Crimes Act (1999) Act Concerning the Punishment of Grave Breaches of International Humanitarian law, Belgium, which followed the *Yerodia dictum*, leading to what Luc Reydams refers to as a 'juridical soap opera' (Reydams 2003a, p. 109). Such connections are reflected in the case before the Assize Court of Brussels, *Public Prosecutor v Alphonse Higaniro, Vincent Ntezimana, Consolata Mukangango (Sister Gertrude) and Julienne Mukabutera (Sister Maria Kisito), Verdict*, 8 June 2001, critically analysed in Reydams 2003b, pp. 428–436. This case {*Acte d'accusation du Procureur général près la Cour d'appel de Bruxelles du 12 février 2001* [Bill of Indictment of the Prosecutor filed before the Court of Appeal on 12 February 2001], *Prosecutor v. Vincent Ntezimana, Alphonse Higaniro, Consolata Mukangango & Julienne Mukabutera*, Case No. 23764} is particularly noteworthy not only because it led to the first conviction under Belgium's then universal jurisdiction law, but because, on 22 May 2011, the Attorney-General, in his opening trial statement, clarified that he was representing the international community which has the right and duty not to tolerate the commission of barbarous acts, wherever they may be committed (Ongena and van Daele 2002, p. 687).

[26] Kleffner 2008, pp. 44–45.

[27] Article 6 of the CREMS (1996) Convention Relating to Extradition between the Member States of the EU, drawn up on the basis of Article K.3 of the Treaty on European Union, relating to extradition between the Member States of the European Union, signed in Brussels on 27 September 1996.

[28] See the distinction between transnational organised crimes and core crimes in Sect. 8.1.

[29] Plachta 2005, pp. 287–294.

[30] These include Article 5 of the ECE, above n. 16.

legislation will not be considered herein. Moreover, time-barring[31] constitutes such a ground in terms of Article 10 of the ECE, but it is hard to conceive of a core crime which is time-barred,[32] particularly as a result of both the International and the European Convention on the non-Applicability of Statutory Limitations[33] to War Crimes and Crimes Against Humanity.[34] The ECtHR has cited the *Furundžija dictum* to support its contention that statutory limitations of criminal liability do not apply to core crimes.[35] It must be pointed out that, for the purposes of these legal instruments, genocide constitutes a crime against humanity.[36] The Strasbourg Court has also substantiated its view that 'criminal punishability of crimes against humanity without any time-limit can be considered as a principle of customary international law, binding on all States' by providing solid evidence to such effect.[37] The fact that core crimes have risen to the status of *jus cogens*, in Bassiouni's words, entails the following *obligatio erga omnes*:

i. the obligation to prosecute or extradite;
ii. the obligation to provide legal assistance;
iii. the obligation to eliminate statutes of limitations; and
iv. the obligation to eliminate immunities of superiors up to and including Heads of State.[38]

Yasmin Naqvi acknowledges that 'courts have rejected statutes of limitations as a bar to the prosecution of international crimes' for four main reasons:

---

[31] This is also known as the extinctive prescription of the criminal action.

[32] 'Prescription does not seem to be a principle of international criminal law and appears to be irreconcilable with the character of the offences…Their imprescriptibility is inherent in their nature' [Articles 21 and 22 of the preliminary title of the Belgian Code of Criminal Procedure (1808) Book III, Title I, Articles 137–216, amended 30 November 2011].

[33] For a solid understanding of 'statutory limitations', see Kok 2007.

[34] The former was signed in NY on 26 November 1968, whereas the latter was signed in Strasbourg on 25 January 1974.

[35] ICTY Trial Chamber, *Prosecutor v Anto Furundžija*, 10 December 1998, Case No. IT-95-17/1-T, cited in ECtHR Grand Chamber, *Mocanu and Others v Romania*, 17 September 2014, Application Numbers 10865/09, 45886/07 and 32431/08, para 313.

[36] This does not mean that courts which enjoy jurisdiction over crimes against humanity or war crimes necessarily enjoy jurisdiction over genocide. On the contrary, recent practice occasionally precludes the applicability of the Matryoshka [*Babushka*] dolls scenario whereby the jurisdiction of the latter (genocide) is comprised and included within the aegis and parameters of the jurisdiction of the former (crimes against humanity or war crimes) [The Hague District Court, *Public Prosecutor v Joseph Mpambara*, Interlocutory Decision, 24 July 2007, 09/750009-06 and 09/750007-07], confirmed both by the Appeals Court [Appeals Court, The Hague, *Public Prosecutor v Joseph Mpambara*, 17 December 2007, 09-750007-07] and by the Supreme Court of the Netherlands {*Hoge Raad* [Supreme Court], The Netherlands, *Public Prosecutor v Joseph Mpambara*, 21 October 2008, 09-750007-07}.

[37] *Mocanu and Others v Romania*, above n. 35, Concurring Opinion of Judge Pinto de Albuquerque, Joined by Judge Vučinić, paras 5 and 6.

[38] Bassiouni 2008, pp. 10–14; Bassiouni 1996, p. 63; Bassiouni 2001, pp. 85 and 159.

1. firstly, customary international law precludes such time bars because of the nature of the crimes at issue;
2. obligations to prosecute core crimes or to ensure fundamental human rights are incompatible with statutes of limitations;
3. the purposes and principles underlying the use of statutes of limitation do not account for the specificities of cases dealing with core crimes; and
4. time may be tolled in many cases where core crimes have been commited.[39]

Alexander Zahar and Goran Sluiter refer to the *Barbie* case to demonstrate the customary international law status of the rule on the non-applicability of statutory limitations, whereas they refer to two judgments of Italian courts, namely *Hass* and *Priebke*, as a result of which the rule is said to have attained *jus cogens* status.[40] Other important State practice discloses the non-applicability of statutory limitations to core crimes. The case *Chief Prosecutor v Moulana Abul Kalam Azad* before the ICT of Bangladesh relates to genocide and crimes against humanity committed during the 1971 Bangladesh Liberation War. The accused was notified with the charges against him on 25 September 2012, more than forty years after the alleged crimes.[41] Rather than being barred by time in line with and on the basis of the *institutum legis* of extinctive prescription, a significant passage of time can raise fair trial concerns. In fact, the UK High Court of Justice, with reference to events occurring in Kenya during the Mau Mau uprising against British colonial rule between 1952 and 1960, has expressed that 'a fair trial of this part of the case does remain possible and that the evidence on both sides remains significantly cogent for the Court to complete its task satisfactorily'.[42] In the *Pascal Simbikangwa* case, French lawyers expressed concern at the apparent difficulty of prosecuting a case involving events that had taken place twenty years before and nearly 4,000 miles away from France.[43] Cumulatively, when one considers State practice and *opinio juris*, it seems that one can argue that the currently punishable core crimes[44] are not subject to such statutory limitations.[45] In fact it has been argued that 'the duty to prosecute or extradite could not be effective if statutes of limitations applied…

---

[39] Naqvi 2010, p. 192.

[40] *Corte Supreme di Cassazione, Sezione Prima Penale* [Supreme Court, Criminal Chamber I], Italy, *Public Prosecutor v Karl Hass & Erich Priebke, Sentenza sul ricorso* [Judgment following the application], 16 November 1998, referred to in Zahar and Sluiter 2008, p. 518.

[41] ICT of Bangladesh, Second Chamber, *Chief Prosecutor v. Moulana Abul Kalam Azad*, 21 January 2013, 05 (2012).

[42] The High Court of Justice, Queen's Bench Division, UK, *Ndiki Mutua, Paulo Nzili, Wambugu Wa Nyigi, Jane Muthoni Mara and Susan Ngondi v The Foreign and Commonwealth Office*, 5 October 2012, HQ09X02666, para 95.

[43] The New York Times (2014) France Convicts Rwandan Ex-Officer of Genocide. http://www.nytimes.com/2014/03/15/world/africa/france-convicts-rwandan-ex-officer-of-genocide.html?_r=0. Accessed 1 September 2017.

[44] See Chap. 6.

[45] *Audiencia Nacional*, Spain, *Graciela P de L and Others v Adolfo Francisco Scilingo Manzorro*, 19 April 2005, ILDC 136 (ES 2005); Pinzauti 2005, pp. 1092–1105.

Surely, the existence of statutes of limitations weakens the underpinnings of a normative scheme which already has troublesome gaps'.[46] In her comprehensive study on the matter, Ruth Kok upholds that statutes of limitations for core crimes are prohibited under customary international law.[47] This has not stopped a Mexican court from applying statutory limitations to core crimes.[48] Some uncertainty, in so far as the horizontal system of enforcement is concerned, thus still pervades. In any case, I posit that, especially given the 'little State practice in this area',[49]Article 29 of the ICC Statute, which bars the applicability of the statutes of limitations, should be given weight and significance even by non-State parties to the ICC Statute.

Luc Reydams refers to the prohibition of discrimination to the effect that it effectively thwarts extradition.[50] However, in as much as equality and non-discrimination are already protected under Article 14 of the ICCPR, this ground shall not be considered autonomously and distinctively from the other fundamental human rights such as the prohibition of torture and the right to a fair trial. This is particularly because if, for example, States are unwilling to extradite persons to other States that openly discriminate on grounds of race, religion or political opinion, the extradition would be refused primarily because the extraditee would be divested of his right to be tried before an independent and impartial tribunal established by law, which is a due process right. The apartheid era in South Africa, wherein discrimination was authorized or condoned,[51] provides an example of this stark reality. The *nexus* with other fundamental human rights violations is not only established for the purposes of this work, but is an approach consistently adopted in contemporary case-law.[52] Technically speaking, States may make reservations to treaties, which reservations could be tantamount to grounds for refusal in and of themselves, but in so doing they could either jeopardize their international obligations, such as their duty to execute the *aut dedere aut judicare* rule, or else inadvertently impugn or nullify the very existence of the treaty signed when and if such reservation diametrically opposes the object and purpose of the treaty itself. Any such extra-ordinary reservation would thus have to be justifiably sufficient, validly contracted, would be required not to violate the *raison d'être* and *leitmotif* of the treaty itself, and must be proportionate to the ultimate objective of the State demanding such reservation. In other words, its use must be absolutely

---

[46] Bassiouni 2008, p. 9.

[47] Kok 2007, cited in Erikson 2009, p. 58.

[48] *Juez Sexto de Distrito de Procesos Penales Federales en el Distrito Federal* [Sixth District Judge in Criminal Matters of the First Circuit, Mexican Federal Court], *Miguel Angel Cavallo* case, 11 January 2001, Resolution 5/2000.

[49] Werle 2009, p. 249.

[50] Reydams 2003a, p. 19.

[51] Dugard and van den Wyngaert 1998, p. 202.

[52] Analysing jurisprudence of the ECtHR, jurists determined that 'the reach of Article 14 is restricted to discrimination only with respect to the rights and freedoms set out elsewhere in the Convention. So, as a parasitic provision, Article 14 is not a general proscription against every kind of discrimination' (Harris et al. 2009, p. 580).

necessary for the State to attain a legitimate objective which overrides other aims forming the essence of the treaty itself. It is thus very difficult to conceive of such reservations in relation to core crimes, given the international stigma which surrounds them and the international framework which prohibits and punishes them, being the vertical system of enforcement considered in Part III and the horizontal system of enforcement which is being considered within this Part. In the light of the above, reservations to treaties are not being considered as a hurdle/obstacle to extradition for the purposes of this book.

At this stage a practical consideration is appropriate. States may reluctantly extradite an individual, be it conditionally or not, but subsequently fail to cooperate with the requesting State in matters relating to the handing over of evidence, the whereabouts of witnesses and the disclosure of information. Although extradition would have occurred, *de facto*, any prosecution by the requesting State would be substantially jeopardized by the requested State. In essence, therefore, the requested State would have followed the *aut dedere aut judicare* rule, it would have, by extraditing the suspect, contemporaneously relieved itself of its obligation to prosecute, but would have effectively hampered a successful prosecution which could lead to a conviction. Such default might incur consequences for the requested State as a result of such internationally wrongful omissions, but the extraditee would be effectively, at least to a certain degree, shielded. This hypothetical scenario accentuates the sharp distinction between an extradition with a view to or for the purposes of prosecution on the one hand, and a prosecution on the other hand. Requested States which enjoy the custody of the extraditee could alternatively decide to prosecute such individual before its own criminal courts and inflict a very lenient prison sentence, at times below the legally required minimum,[53] or adopt other measures to shield the convict, such as, *inter alia*, commute such sentence, replace it with house arrest, fail to execute it, grant clemency, parole or pardon. However, in such cases, should surrender to the ICC be eventually effected, the ICC Prosecutor would be able to argue that such measures showed a genuine unwillingness to prosecute and that a case before the ICC is thus admissible, possibly diminishing the potential applicability of *ne bis in idem*. This is the stage where exclusive reliance on the horizontal system of enforcement of international criminal law becomes illusive, as has been shown in Part III.

In anticipation of a study on the grounds for refusal, mention must be made of the fact that these grounds convey horizontal obligations exercisable between a State and another. Hence this state of affairs, which I refer to as the horizontal system of enforcement of international criminal law, subsists. The preliminary question to be posed would be: to what extent, if at all, may individuals make use of a breach of an extradition treaty by way of a defence before a domestic criminal court? Traditionally, extradition laws were devised to protect State sovereignty,

[53] Kleffner provides the example of sentences of several defendants in Indonesia (Kleffner 2008, p. 55, n. 262).

rather than individual rights.[54] However, with the advent of the individual *qua* subject of international law,[55] the individual was vested, be it directly or indirectly, with acquired rights as a result of which he has become a beneficiary of State obligations. The process as a result of which the individual has become a fully-fledged subject of international law is eloquently explained by Antônio Augusto Cançado Trindade in his comprehensive works.[56] However, this entire gradual evolution of the status of the individual has not precluded municipal courts from nullifying consequential rights emanating from an infringement of an extradition treaty.[57]

Another final premise is hereby warranted. Whereas more than a decade ago John Dugard and Christine van den Wyngaert stated that 'there is no certainty about the content and scope of the rights that are most likely to block extradition',[58] whether this is still true today, and if so, to what extent, will be seen shortly. These pitfalls may be either of a normative or factual type, the former being established *de*

---

[54] Schwarzenberger 1950, p. 272.

[55] Direct conferment of international legal personality and *locus standi* upon an individual was pursued by a gradual escalation by means of various important legal instruments over a significant span of time, including the General Treaty of Peace and Amity (1907); the Versailles Treaty (1919) *Traité de Versailles*; the German-Polish Upper Silesian Convention (1922) German-Polish Convention concerning Upper Silesia; London Agreement (1945), the Agreement by the Government of the United States of America, the Provisional Government of the French Republic, the Government of the United Kingdom of Great Britain and Northern Ireland and the Government of the Union of Soviet Socialist Republics for the Prosecution and Punishment of the Major War Criminals of the European Axis {which led to the Nuremberg Trials}; the Hague Convention XII (1907) Convention (XII) Relative to the Creation of an International Prize Court; the Constitution of the International Labour Organization (1946) Instrument for the Amendment of the Constitution of the International Labour Organization, adopted by the International Labour Conference at its 29th Session, International Labour Office Official Bulletin, Vol. XXIX, No. 4; the UNC (1945), Charter of the United Nations; the ECvHR (1950) European Convention for the Protection of Human Rights and Fundamental Freedoms; the IACvHR (1969) Inter-American Convention on Human Rights; the Draft Code of Offences Against the Peace and Security of Mankind (1954) International Law Commission Draft Code of Offences Against the Peace and Security of Mankind, adopted in the ILC's sixth session; the ICCPR (1966) International Covenant on Civil and Political Rights; the European Communities Convention (1952) Treaty Establishing the European Coal and Steel Community; the European Communities Convention (1957) Treaty Establishing the European Economic Community; the Inter-American Convention to Prevent and Punish Torture (1985); the ACHPR (1981) African Charter on Human and Peoples' Rights; and the Charter of Paris for a New Europe (1990).

[56] Cançado Trindade 2001a, pp. 17–96; Cançado Trindade 2001b, pp. 207–239; Cançado Trindade 2001c, pp. 45–71.

[57] USA District Court for the Southern District of Florida, *United States of America v Manuel Antonio Noriega*, 8 June 1990, 88-79-CR, 746 F Supp 1506 (1990). In this case the court held that 'as a general principle of international law, individuals have no standing to challenge violations of international treaties in the absence of protest by the sovereign involved' [DomCLIC (2016) http://www.asser.nl/default.aspx?site_id=36&level1=15246&level2=15248&level3=&textid=39982. Accessed 22 November 2016].

[58] Dugard and van den Wyngaert 1998, p. 205.

lege, the latter by *consuetudo*. They may constitute absolute obstacles or partial obstacles to extradition. They are absolute when they are based either upon a norm of *jus cogens*, such as in the prohibition of torture, or when they emanate from a mandatory ground for refusal, as is the case with double criminality. They are only partial when they may be circumvented by means of the satisfaction of suspensive or resolutive conditions and guarantees or assurances,[59] such as the declaration by the requesting State that the death penalty would not be imposed on the extraditee should he be found guilty.[60] An analysis of State practice reveals that the use of conditional extradition is on the rise.[61] In some instances, possibly when the assurances are not deemed sufficient or else when a requesting State needs to be properly tested, requested States may introduce monitoring mechanisms. The Court of Appeal of The Hague allowed the extradition of *Jean Claude Iyamuremye* to Rwanda provided that his trial be closely observed and monitored on behalf of The Netherlands by the International Commission of Jurists (Kenya), 'which means that

[59] Such assurances constitute the second of four 'avoidance techniques' identified by Harmen van der Wilt in the context of a request for the extradition of an individual and the risk of a prospective violation. Their bearing is partially dependent on the nature of the potential violations involved. The ECtHR has attached importance to previous performances (the track record) of the requesting State in its assessment of the value and reliability of such assurances (van der Wilt 2012a, pp. 150, 164 and 165).

[60] *Conseil d'Etat, Assemblée, Affaire Aylor (Joy Aylor-Davis)*, 15 October 1993, 144950, found that France cannot extradite a suspect *génocidaire* for a capital offence unless the requesting State gives an assurance that the death penalty will not be imposed, or if imposed, would not be executed. The main reasons motivating such judgment include, *inter alia*, the fact that the Special Genocide Law of the requesting State, Rwanda {Special Genocide Law of Rwanda (1996) *Loi organique no. 8196 du 30/08/1996 sur l'organisation des poursuites des infractions constitutives du crimes de génocide ou de crimes contre l'humanité, commises à partir du 1er octobre 1990* [Organic Law no. 8196 of 30/08/1996 on the Prosecution of Offences Constituting the Crimes of Genocide or Crimes against humanity, Committed as of 1 October 1990], Official Gazette of the Republic of Rwanda, 1 September 1996}, prescribes the death penalty for certain types of genocide, and France's ratification of the Sixth Protocol to the ECvHR Concerning the Abolition of the Death Penalty [Sixth Protocol to the ECvHR Concerning the Abolition of the Death Penalty (1983) Protocol No. 6 to the Convention for the Protection of Human Rights and Fundamental Freedoms Concerning the Abolition of the Death Penalty as Amended by Protocol No. 11]. In *Corte Costituzionale Italiana* [Italian Constitutional Court], *Pietro Venezia v Ministero di Grazia e Giustizia*, 27 June 1996, 223-1996, the Italian Constitutional Court held that the USA-Italy Extradition Treaty did not provide a sufficient guarantee that the accused would not suffer the death penalty, which is banned in Italy, because an agreement by federal prosecutors to seek the capital punishment was supposedly not binding on States within the USA (Ronco and Ardizzone 2007, p. 158). The USA federal system, its structure, role and functions, hence may complicate matters further in the quest of the USA for the extradition of individuals especially from abolitionist States.

[61] Dugard and van den Wyngaert 1998, p. 188.

the Rwandan authorities will be aware that any violations of a fair trial will be disclosed'.[62] This is certainly a veritable way of how to keep the requesting State on its toes. I shall now turn onto separately examining such pitfalls (hurdles/obstacles).

16.1 The Non-extradition of Nationals

Such ground was contemplated by Article 6(1)(a) of the ECE and by the Benelux Treaty on Extradition and Mutual Assistance in Criminal Matters.[63] Its rationale can be explained as follows:

1. 'the fugitive ought not to be withdrawn from his natural judges;
2. the State owes its subjects the protection of its laws;
3. it is impossible to have complete confidence in the justice meted out by a foreign State, especially with regard to a foreigner;
4. it is disadvantageous to be tried in a foreign language, separated from friends, resources and character witnesses'.[64]

At the outset, jurists have acknowledged that this ground is not constitutive of customary international law,[65] although many States still refuse the extradition of their nationals on the basis of this ground.[66] Japan, for example, persistently denied *Alberto Fujimori's*[67] extradition by claiming that he was its nationalized citizen and

---

62 Court of Appeal, The Hague, *The State of The Netherlands (Ministry of Security and Justice) v Jean Claude I.*, 5 July 2016, Case No. 200.182.281/01, para 3.3, brought to my attention throughout a meeting of the *COJUR*-ICC Working Group held on 15 September 2016 in *Justus Lipsius* Building, Brussels, by Nienke de Lange, Senior Policy Advisor at Ministry of Security and Justice, The Hague, and translated by Wietske Dijkstra, Senior Legal Advisor at the Department of International Affairs and Mutual Legal Assistance in Criminal Matters, Ministry of Security and Justice, The Hague.

63 Benelux Treaty on Extradition and Mutual Assistance in Criminal Matters (1962) T2064 41.8, 27 June 1962.

64 Williams 1991, p. 259 and pp. 260–261, quoting the findings of the 1878 British Royal Commission into Extradition, cited in Boister 2016, p. 22, n. 127.

65 Deen-Racsmany and Blekxtoon 2005, pp. 320–321.

66 Dean et al. 2003, p. 517.

67 Fujimori unexpectedly became President of Perú on 28 July 1990. He declared a state of emergency in 1992, disbanding Congress, suspending constitutional provisions, censoring the press, and allowing the police and military to detain individuals arbitrarily. He ensured that so-called 'faceless trials' would preclude accused persons from any judicial safeguards, subsequently enacted a Law of General Amnesties for Military, Police and Civil Personnel for Diverse Cases in 1995 and was re-elected for a third term in 2000 amidst claims of bribery, fraud and vote rigging when the Peruvian Constitution precluded the retention of such public office for a third time, after which he fled to Japan. The new Peruvian government filed various charges against him including the carrying out of extra-judicial executions of 15 persons in the *Barrios Altos* district of Lima in 1991 and students at *La Cantuta* University in 1992. An international arrest warrant was issued by the Supreme Court of Perú in September 2001 (Bernaz and Prouvèze 2010, pp. 376–380;

that no extradition treaty existed between Japan and Perú,[68] the latter probably being the decisive reason for such denial. Some States, such as the USA, reserve the option not to extradite their own nationals to States which consistently refuse to reciprocate, a discretionary power habitually vested onto the executive organs of government.[69] Other States seem to allow some discretion to themselves in evaluating the gravity of the offence. As a general rule, for example, Denmark does not permit the extradition of its nationals, a restriction which is not prescribed by the Danish Constitution. However, the Nordic Extradition Act allows the extradition of Danish citizens in more serious cases. In 2002, the general Extradition Act was amended to enable the extradition of a Danish national outside the territories of the Nordic countries. Further to the Framework decision on the EAW, 'extradition from Denmark to another member State can no longer be refused for the reason that the person is a Danish national'.[70] For the purposes of this work, it is important to highlight that, besides another thirty-one offences,[71] 'crimes within the jurisdiction of the International Criminal Court' expressly fall within the parameters of the EAW, which has been considered by the Polish Constitutional Court as a 'form of extradition'.[72] Other crimes covered by the EAW include:

i. participation in a criminal organisation;
ii. terrorism;
iii. trafficking in human beings;
iv. murder;

see also Anderson 2002). Fujimori was arrested in Chile in November 2005 and extradited to face trial in Perú by virtue of a judgment of the Chilean Supreme Court of 21 September 2007. On 7 April 2009, a three-judge panel of Perú's Supreme Court convicted Fujimori on charges of abuses of fundamental human rights. The panel found him guilty of ordering the *Grupo Colina* death squad to execute the November 1991 *Barrios Altos* massacre and the July 1992 *La Cantuta* massacre, and for taking part in the kidnappings of Peruvian journalist Gustavo Gorriti and businessman Samuel Dyer. Fujimori's conviction marked the first time in history that a democratically elected president had been tried and found guilty of human rights abuses in his own country (Gamarra 2009, pp. 95–110) {*Corte Suprema de Justicia de la República, Sala Penal Especial* [Supreme Court, Special Criminal Chamber], Perú, *Ministerio Público v Alberto Fujimori Fujimori*, 7 April 2009, A.V. 19-2001}. He was pardoned on 24 December 2017 by President Pedro Pablo Kuczynski, after serving 12 years of his 25-year sentence for crimes against humanity (Ambos and Urquizo 2018). However, Court B of the National Criminal Court of Perú has decided not to apply the pardon and has cleared the way for *Fujimori* to be tried for the murders of six people in Pativilca constituting crimes against humanity (AI 2018).

[68] Bernaz and Prouvèze 2010, p. 379.

[69] Paust et al. 2007, p. 350.

[70] Vestergaard 2003, pp. 91–92.

[71] See such list in Article 2 para 2 of the Framework Decision on the EAW (2002) Council Framework Decision on the European Arrest Warrant and the Surrender Procedures Between the Member States, Doc. 2002/584/JHA, which is intended, *inter alia*, to create a system of free movement of judicial decisions in criminal matters.

[72] *Trybunał Konstytucyjny* [Polish Constitutional Court], *Constitutionality of Laws Implementing the Secondary Law of the European Union*, 27 April 2005, Case Number P1/05, OTK-A 2005, No. 4, Item 42.

v. grievous bodily harm;
vi. illicit trade in human organs and tissue;
vii. kidnapping;
viii. illegal restraint and hostage-taking, and
ix. rape,

all of which could, should the constitutive elements of the crime subsist, constitute core crimes. By way of example, *Hussain Osman*, one of the major suspects in the July 2004 London terrorist bombings, was sent back from Italy to the UK in execution of a EAW. As correctly stated by Antonio Cassese, 'terrorist acts are prohibited as war crimes when directed against civilians or civilian objects; when they fall under the category of crimes against humanity, they are normally banned if they target civilians'.[73] However, the framework and implementation of the EAW, 'a milestone in the history of the extradition of nationals',[74] has been criticised since it 'may in fact increase rather than reduce controversies related to requests for the surrender of nationals in Europe'.[75] In fact some EU member States, such as Denmark and Lithuania, have promulgated additional mandatory grounds for the non-execution of the EAW,[76] whereas the Netherlands undertook to refuse surrender, by way of an exceptional measure, if the Dutch executing authority finds that there can be no doubt that the requested person is innocent.[77]

Nationality is not a straight-forward concept. Some individuals can be stateless *de jure* which equates to 'not having a nationality'.[78] Others can become nationals by means of the recognition of a particular status. For the purposes of the non-extradition of nationals, the Dutch, for example, recognise that refugees are entitled to the same rights as their own nationals,[79] whereas the Nordic States, namely Denmark, Sweden, Iceland, Norway and Finland, upon ratification of the ECE, made declarations protecting domiciled aliens.[80] Moreover, a dispute may arise as to the nationality or otherwise of an individual or as to the subsistence of his dual nationality. *Karoly Zentai* argued that he had lost his Hungarian citizenship as a result of his failure to return to Hungary, of his residing outside Hungary for more than 10 years and also owing to his acquired Australian citizenship. Hungarian competent authorities, however, still considered him as a Hungarian citizen, for all intents and purposes of law. *Karoly Zentai* submitted that, even if he were a dual citizen, the ground of non-extradition of a national is triggered by the *Nottebohm*

73 Cassese 2004a, p. 220.
74 Deen-Racsmany and Blekxtoon 2005, p. 340.
75 Deen-Racsmany and Blekxtoon 2005, p. 317.
76 Klimek 2015, p. 215.
77 Ibid.
78 Zimmermann and Mahler 2011, p. 462.
79 Gilbert 2017, p. 67.
80 Gilbert 2017, pp. 67–68, n. 29.

principle[81] which renders his claim to Australian nationality superior to his supposed Hungarian one. The Federal Court of Australia clarified that this ground for refusal is not a mandatory one but a discretionary one which 'highlights the responsibility of Australia to have regard to the fact that a person requested for extradition is an Australian citizen. It is not contended that this fact can block an extradition. Clearly, Australian citizens are extradited from time to time'.[82] The Federal Court of Australia, applying *aut dedere aut judicare* to the letter, made an important qualification. It held that if Australia refuses the extradition of its national upon this ground of refusal, 'it must, if requested by Hungary, submit the case to the competent authorities in order that proceedings for the prosecution of the person in respect of the offence for which extradition was sought may be taken'.[83] This shows that nationality can be an important element/criterion in the process of extradition and/or in the extent to which a person can be subjected to prosecution. It is not only important, as seen in Sect. 11.2 and Chap. 12, in the context of the ICC's jurisdiction. The Dutch nationality acquired by *Yvonne Basebya* (a high-ranking member of the Hutu extremist party, *Coalition pour la Défense de la République*) on 7 December 2004, for example, was pivotal in her conviction for incitement to genocide by the District Court of The Hague.[84]

Nowadays, as a result of the *jus cogens* prohibition of torture and random spot-checks in prisons by the UN Sub-Committee on the Prevention of Torture,[85] the main *leitmotif* of the non-extradition of nationals is dwindling. Consequently, the non-extradition of nationals is gradually losing its potential to obstruct extradition. One may therefore, at this stage, start doubting whether there is still room left for what has been considered to be a 'form of legal xenophobia'.[86] The only continuing relevance of this pitfall may stem from another principal *raison d'être*, this being the existence of strong bonds between States and their own nationals. To the extent that such innate bonds may be captured within the *jus de non evocando* principle,[87] they can be resilient and may attain a certain degree of permanence.

[81] ICJ, *Liechtenstein v Guatemala* (*Nottebohm* case), 6 April 1855, I.C.J. Reports 1955, p. 4, General List No. 18. This case established that nationality under international law is dependent upon a genuine link (the connecting factor) between the individual and the State (O'Brien 1999, p. 94, n. 12).

[82] Federal Court of Australia, *Zentai v Honourable Brendan O'Connor* (No. 3), 2 July 2010, [2010] FCA 691, para 224.

[83] *Zentai v Honourable Brendan O'Connor*, above n. 82, para 225.

[84] District Court of The Hague, *Prosecutor v Yvonne Basebya*, 1 March 2013, LJN BZ4292.

[85] http://www.apt.ch/index.php?option=com_k2&view=item&id=692:the-un-subcommittee-on-prevention-of-torture-spt&Itemid=251&lang=en. Accessed 30 June 2016

[86] Williams 1991, p. 261.

[87] This entails that the accused has the right to be tried in a domestic court. It was pleaded, unsuccessfully, as a defence before the ICTR in ICTR Trial Chamber II, *Prosecutor v. Joseph Kanyabashi*, Decision on the Defence Motion on Jurisdiction, 18 June 1997, Case No. ICTR-96-15.

Domestic rules prohibiting the extradition of nationals[88] have already suffered a severe blow as a result of Article 7 sub-article 1 of the CREMS which prohibits the refusal of extradition on the ground that a 'person is a national of the requested Member State'. The initial rationale behind this rule stems from a distrust of other States' criminal justice systems. With an ever-closer European Criminal Law which could harmonise such systems, this distrust is increasingly becoming less evident. Such examples were followed by other States. The USA signed an extradition treaty with Italy on 13 October 1983 which expressly prohibits the refusal of extradition on the grounds of nationality. Like most Common Law States, the USA has consistently favoured the exercise of jurisdiction on the basis of territoriality and has always been rather skeptical about the non-extradition of nationals. Furthermore, it seems that since prisoners are being repatriated to serve their sentence in their own country, this traditional ground for refusal is drastically losing its initial impetus. It must be noted that the practice of repatriation of prisoners does not belong exclusively to Europe. It was also implemented in the Arab League Agreement of 1952. Jurists have written that civil law countries 'persist in retaining the rule of non-extradition of nationals' because 'they wish to protect their nationals from sub-standard prison conditions abroad'.[89] States like Mexico, for example, have continuously refused to extradite their own nationals.[90] An interesting case-study of constitutional challenges[91] within the context of the EAW has been undertaken by Zsuzsanna Deen-Racsmany, who notes, with surprise, that although 'one might have expected a wave of constitutional amendments to accommodate the obligation under the European Arrest Warrant to surrender even nationals...only three member States' have done so, these being Germany, Portugal and Slovenia.[92] Zsuzsanna Deen-Racsmany concludes that 'the attempt under the European Arrest Warrant to circumvent the application of the (constitutional) ban known to many European Union member States appears successful, within limits'.[93] This is correct since the Polish Constitutional Court found that the EAW breached the constitutional ban on extraditing Polish nationals to the competent authorities of another member State.[94] Similarly, the German Federal Constitutional Court annulled Germany's law transposing the Framework Decision on the grounds that it did not protect the non-extradition of nationals rule whereas the Cypriot Supreme Court decided that the EAW scheme breached a Cypriot constitutional provision prohibiting citizens

[88] These are more pronounced in civil law countries, rather than in common law countries.

[89] Dugard and van den Wyngaert 1998, p. 201.

[90] Spector 1998, p. 1007, cited in McDermott 2015, p. 291, n. 184.

[91] The challenges examined were filed in Poland, Germany, Greece and Cyprus.

[92] Deen-Racsmany 2006, pp. 293–294.

[93] Deen-Racsmany 2006, p. 305.

[94] *Constitutionality of Laws Implementing the Secondary Law of the European Union*, above n. 72, cited in van Sliedregt 2009, p. 60.

from being transferred abroad for prosecution.[95] Though correct, the above conclusion can be questioned since some States expressly allow for grounds of refusal under their own ordinary law. Under UK law, for example, Article 21 of the 2003 Extradition Act allows the Judge to decide whether the person's surrender would be compatible with the rights emanating from the ECvHR, within the meaning (and under the auspices of) the 1998 Human Rights Act. In *Krolik v Regional Court in Czestochowa*, a *presumptio juris tantum* favouring surrender existed. This was deemed to be a presumption, only rebuttable to the extent that clear, cogent and compelling evidence be tendered in support of the contention that the Polish persons would be put at risk of inhuman and degrading treatment as a result of the awful Polish prison conditions.[96] The obvious question one should pose is therefore: Is it permissible for a State to invoke other grounds of refusal, besides those emanating from the EU Framework Decision of June 2002 (2002/584/JHA)? It seems that the correct answer would be in the affirmative, particularly because the EU is now also bound by the provisions of the ECvHR of the CoE. Advocate-General Sharpston's opinion in the *Ciprian Vasile Radu* case (decided by the Grand Chamber of the ECJ)[97] reveals that the Framework Decision must, as a matter of EU law, be read as subject to the provisions of both the ECvHR and the EU Charter of Fundamental Rights. Therefore, it seems that EU law does permit a member State to refuse to execute a EAW if, to do so, would infringe the wanted person's human rights,[98] although this is still a moot point. It would also seem that national legislation implementing the EAW can be deemed to be unconstitutional, and consequently null and void, in so far as it allegedly conflicts with 'the respective constitutional prohibitions against extraditing nationals'.[99] Even where this is not the case, the legality and legitimacy of local legislation does not mean it shall be problem-free. Inter-State tensions and frictions might arise as a result of the promulgation of domestic legislation and differentiated structures of competences prevailing within the respective member States.[100] To this extent, practice suggests that States seem to be allowed significant latitude. Italy is a case in point since it

[95] *Bundesverfassungsgericht* [German Federal Constitutional Court], *Decision on the German European Arrest Warrant Law*, 18 July 2005, 2 BvR 2236/04, and *Ανώτατο Δικαστήριο Κύπρου* [Cyprus Supreme Court], *Cypriot European Arrest Warrant Law Ruling*, 7 November 2005, Civil Action No. 294/2005. Both decisions are cited in van Sliedregt 2009, p. 60.

[96] High Court of Justice, Queen's Bench Division, Administrative Court, UK, *Artur Krolik v Regional Court in Czestochowa*, Poland, 17 August 2012, CO/2864/2012, CO/2915/2012, CO/2868/2012, CO/2918/2012, CO/2861/2012, CO/2747/2012, [2012] EWHC 2357, [2013] 1 W.L.R. 2390, cited in Spencer 2013, p. 252.

[97] ECJ, *Ciprian Vasile Radu, Request for a preliminary ruling from the Curtea de Apel Constanța*, 29 January 2013, Case No. C-396/11.

[98] Spencer 2013, p. 252.

[99] *Constitutionality of Laws Implementing the Secondary Law of the European Union*, above n. 72, *Decision on the German European Arrest Warrant Law*, above n. 95, and *Cypriot European Arrest Warrant Law Ruling*, above n. 95, all cited in Pollicino 2008, pp. 1314–1315, notes 6, 7 and 8.

[100] van der Wilt 2005a, p. 79.

disregards the list contained in the Framework Decision altogether and has replaced it with its own list of corresponding offences under Italian Law, effectively reintroducing the double criminality verification[101] through the backdoor.

With specific reference to the EAW, it is apt to note that the Framework Decision has shifted responsibilities and decision-making powers from the executive to the judicial branch of governments. In other words, the procedure has been judicialised.[102] Harmen van der Wilt is sceptical as to whether the judicial branches of the member States would be 'fully equipped to do the job'.[103] He favours the application of the principle of reciprocity (which is predicated on State policy) by the executive branch of government since it involves issues dealing with international relations, rather than demands for justice.[104] The Framework Decision itself evidences some disparities pertaining to the ambit of optional grounds for refusal. Harmen van der Wilt pinpointed that some member States were willing to converse such optional grounds into mandatory grounds under their domestic law, whereas others left it to the discretion of their judiciary. Such disparities might lead to varied interpretations and different legal situations,[105] all of which defeat the purposes and scope of the EAW. Moreover, internal friction may subsist (for example between the prosecutors and judges) because responsibilities as to the emission and execution of arrest warrants are divided between such authorities.[106]

This ground of refusal, and various others, was expressly discarded by the EAW[107] procedure which only retained three mandatory grounds for non-execution of the EAW,[108] two of which (amnesties in the executing Member State and *ne bis in idem*[109] respectively) are explained in Sects. 16.5 and 16.7.2.[110] It stands to

[101] van Sliedregt 2009, p. 64.

[102] Klimek 2015, p. 320.

[103] van der Wilt 2005a, p. 77.

[104] van der Wilt 2005a, p. 80 and 81.

[105] van der Wilt 2005a, p. 78.

[106] van der Wilt 2005a, pp. 78–79.

[107] Article 1 of the Framework Decision on the EAW, above n. 71, defines such warrant as 'any judicial decision issued by a Member State ("issuing State") with a view to the arrest or surrender by another Member State ('executing State') of a requested person, for the purposes of conducting a criminal prosecution or executing a custodial sentence or detention order'.

[108] See Article 3, paras 1–3 thereof. The Framework Decision on the EAW uses the term 'surrender', and notwithstanding the distinction pointed out in Sect. 9.2 between 'surrender' under the vertical system of enforcement and 'extradition' under the horizontal system of enforcement, the term 'surrender' in the EAW may be equated to and can be used inter-changeably with the term 'extradition'. André Klip, analysing the EAW, states that 'the material act of surrender is no different from that of extradition' (Klip 2009, p. 368).

[109] This protection is triggered when a *res judicata* has been delivered in any other EU Member State with respect of the same acts provided that, where there has been such sentence, the sentence has been served or is currently being served or may no longer be executed under the law of the sentencing member State.

[110] The other ground prohibits the execution of a EAW where the suspect is a minor and cannot be held criminally liable in the executing State.

reason that this ground be set aside in the light of the higher standards of human rights protection prevailing within the EU member States. The Czech Constitutional Court held that 'if the Czech citizens can enjoy advantages connected with the status of the European Union citizenship, it is natural in such a context that it is necessary to accept also the certain level of responsibility. Current standard of protection of fundamental rights in the European Union does not give the occasion to presume that a protection of fundamental rights of our nationals in another member State will be lower than in the Czech Republic'.[111] Adam Gorski upholds that 'hiding behind the prohibition on extradition of a citizen is a mediaeval right of a feudal lord *(ius de non evocando)*, therefore it constitutes a total lack of trust to other legal systems and the presumption of its enmity or at least the *desinteeressement* in cooperation'.[112] Most of the other grounds mentioned here above,[113] including the ground under scrutiny within this heading, are voluntary grounds, that is, of an optional and discretionary nature. It must be noted, however, that such grounds are either mandatory or discretionary for all intents and purposes of EU law. Thus, one must have a look at each and every supreme law prevailing within the member States, generally Constitutions, to determine whether whatever is discretionary for EU purposes may be rendered compulsory at national level. Glancing at practice, it seems that so far, supreme Courts have been reluctant to nullify the provisions of the EAW on the basis of their inconsistency with domestic extradition, or ordinary law, and with their Constitutional law.[114] In any case, even if they were willing to do so, they might be precluded from doing so by EU law.[115] The end result, in so far as the non-extradition of nationals is concerned, is that nationals of EU member States are not protected against surrender to another EU member State.[116]

The partial removal of the double criminality requirement has augmented the non-extradition of nationals.[117] Indeed, double criminality may come to the fore anyway if the requested State demands that the national is allowed to return in order to serve his sentence in his home country, this practice being common especially when it results directly from a legal provision of the same extradition bi-lateral agreement between the requested and the requesting State. Apparently 'the ambitions of the drafters were too high and/or the drafting process too speedy.

---

[111] Klouckova 2006, p. 4.

[112] Gorski 2008, p. 386.

[113] See such grounds, duly numbered as 1–11, at the very start of this chapter.

[114] HoL, *Office of the King's Prosecutor (Brussels) v Cando Armas et al.*, 17 November 2005, [2005] UKHL 67, 2005 3 WLR 1079, and HoL, *Dabas v High Court of Justice in Madrid*, Spain, 28 February 2007, [2007] 2 WLR 254, cited in Padfield 2007, pp. 253–268.

[115] See issues dealing with direct effect of EU Law in ECJ, *van Gend en Loos (NV Algemene Transporten Expeditie Onderneming v Nederlandse Administratie der Belastingen)*, 5 February 1963, Case 26/62, and in ECJ, *Andrea Francovich and Danila Bonifaci et al. v Italy*, 19 November 1991 Cases C-6 and 9/90, [1991] ECR I-5357.

[116] Klimek 2015, p. 320.

[117] Deen-Racsmany and Blekxtoon 2005, p. 322.

Consequently, the end result contains some loopholes which are created due to the wish to abolish two of the traditional exceptions in extradition (nationality and dual criminality) at the same time'.[118] The *lacunae* must now be filled by the domestic legislatures and municipal criminal courts of the Member States which are obliged to implement the EAW. Thus, although scholars are acknowledging that this ground for refusal is 'becoming less frequent',[119] it does not follow that this necessarily entails a general elimination of such a hurdle in the extradition process.

16.2 The Military Offence Exemption

This exemption surfaces in important treaties such as the ECE[120] and the ECMAC.[121] A rigid application of 'military offences' is increasingly placing this ground for refusal on the wane. In fact, extradition treaties, such as the one between France and Algeria and also the 1990 Commonwealth Scheme for the Rendition of Fugitive Offenders, expressly provide that an offence will only fall within the military offence exemption if it consists merely and solely of a breach of military law, and not also a crime under ordinary criminal law. This *per se* precludes the categorisation of any core crime as an exclusively military offence because all core crimes necessarily also constitute a violation of domestic ordinary criminal law either because they have been incorporated therein or because such conduct would anyway constitute murder, grievous bodily harm, torture or any other crime under ordinary domestic law. Additionally, more often than not (since core crimes can also be committed by officers in the performance of their functions), core crimes are also tantamount to a violation of constitutionally-entrenched human rights, including, *inter alia*, the ECvHR, the IACvHR and the ACHPR. This observation reflects the position under most domestic criminal justice systems, wherein 'military offences' are defined as '*quelli previsti soltanto dalla normativa penale militare e che non costituiscono, pertanto, anche reati comuni*'.[122] Their essential feature is the '*connotazione giuridica del fatto*',[123] not their military status.

In the *Karoly Zentai* case, the Federal Court of Australia held that the range of military offences (exclusive to military law) include offences such as desertion, being absent without leave and disobedience of a direct order. Zentai was wanted in Hungary for prosecution for a war crimes offence under the Hungarian Criminal

118 Deen-Racsmany and Blekxtoon 2005, p. 339.

119 Ciampi 2009, p. 322.

120 Article 4 of the ECE, above n. 16.

121 Article 1 para 2 of the ECMAC, above n. 18.

122 These are those offences which are solely and exclusively prescribed by the military laws and which, hence, do not constitute ordinary offences at law: (my translation) (Dean et al. 2003, p. 513).

123 Their essential features are the juridical characteristics of the fact itself: (my translation) (Dean et al. 2003, p. 513).

Code, alleging his involvement in the death of a man while providing patrol service in Budapest as a member of the Hungarian Royal Army. Hungary confirmed that under Hungary's Code of Criminal Procedure *Zentai* was to be prosecuted for the offence before the Military Division of the Budapest Metropolitan Court (a county court) by reason of his membership of the armed forces at the time the alleged conduct took place, not because the offence of a war crime was a military offence. The Court's conclusion echoes the relevance of this ground for refusal and its potential impact on extradition law. The Court held that 'you can therefore be satisfied that Zentai's surrender is not sought for a military offence within the meaning of subsection 7(d) and this objection is not made out in this case'.[124] It may thus be safely held that the relevance of the military offence exception as a ground for refusal of an extradition request has considerably decreased.

16.3 The Political Offence Exemption

This is commonly referred to as an 'exception' by many jurists. However, I shall refer to it as an 'exemption', a term also used by Silvia Borelli, since this is more appropriate.[125] The use of the term 'exemption' also eliminates the confusion that can be created by the examination of the depoliticizing formula[126] which entails the subsistence of an 'exception to the exception'.[127] Moreover, the *Furundžija dictum* established that other consequences of the *jus cogens* nature of the prohibition against torture include the fact that torture 'must not be excluded from extradition under any political offence exemption'.[128] Indeed, it is not only linked to torture but to other grounds for refusal of extradition. Justice Francis Murphy of the Irish Supreme Court analyses its triple rationale:

1. firstly, the political argument that States should remain neutral vis-à-vis the internal political affairs of other States;
2. secondly, the moral argument provides that resistance to oppression is legitimate and that, therefore, political crimes can be justified; and
3. thirdly, the humanitarian argument provides that a political offender should not be extradited to a State in which he risks an unfair trial.[129]

---

124 *Zentai v Honourable Brendan O'Connor*, above n. 82, para 297.

125 Borelli 2004 cited in Kolb 2004, p. 334.

126 van den Wyngaert 1980, p. 141.

127 Bassiouni 1999, p. 243.

128 *Prosecutor v Anto Furundžija*, above n. 35, para 157.

129 Kelly 2003, p. 494, n. 17.

Harmen van der Wilt, in analysing its rationale,[130] has considered the domestic application thereof, giving pertinent examples from municipal case-law, including the British political incidence theory[131] and the Swiss proportionality theory (which found expression in the French *doctrine de gravité*), discerning that both the Brits and the Swiss have deduced the political character of an offence from the general circumstances in which it was committed, these being circumstances which necessitate a general political conflict with which the offence is directly related.[132] His study also umasks the link between the political offence exemption and fears of biased and unfair trials, and considers the *aut dedere aut judicare* option and the discrimination clause within the European Convention on Terrorism as safety valves which manifest an inclination (deemed unfavourable and problematic by Harmen van der Wilt) to abolish the political offence exemption and substitute it with a general human rights clause.[133] To this extent, it brings together two grounds for refusal of extradition being dealt with within Part IV. Indeed the exemption has been habitually applied with specific limitations, or upon the fulfilment of certain pre-requisites. The Nordic Extradition Act limited the exemption solely to Danish nationals.[134] This shows that a ground for refusal may be intricately linked with another ground for refusal, in this case, the non-extradition of nationals. Actually, a ground of refusal may complement another ground for refusal.

The ground for refusal under scrutiny must be distinguished from the 'political opinion' ground or objection[135] whereby a person is not extradited to the requesting State if the requested State has substantial grounds for believing that the extradition request had been made for purposes of prosecuting or punishing the extraditee on account of his political opinion.[136] The political motivations of prosecutors may also constitute grounds to refuse an extradition and discharge the individual sought by the requesting State.[137] Demonstrated differential treatment may support an

[130] This comprises, besides its humanitarian motivation, the principle of the liberal democratic State and that of the nation State (van der Wilt 1997, p. 58).

[131] This theory, which is also known as the Anglo-American incidence test, provides that in order for the exemption to apply there must be (1) a political disturbance, and (2) the political offence must be incidental to or form part of that disturbance {Divisional Court, UK, *In re Castioni*, 11 November 1890, [1891] 1Q.B. 149} cited in McDermott 2015, p. 284, n. 144. It therefore weighs the circumstances in which the offence occurs (Petersen 1992, p. 775).

[132] van der Wilt 1997, p. 38, pp. 29–35 and p. 37 respectively.

[133] van der Wilt 1997, pp. 47–48.

[134] Vestergaard 2003, p. 92.

[135] See Article 3.2 of the ECE, above n. 120.

[136] Bow Street Magistrates' Court, UK, *The Government of the Russian Federation v Akhmed Zakaev*, Judgment, 23 November 2003, pp. 3–6, particularly p. 5.

[137] Kay A (2016) Former Georgian Minister of Defence and Aide to President Misha Saakashvili Discharged in UK Extradition Proceedings. Bedford Row International. http://9bri.com/former-georgian-minister-of-defence-and-aide-to-president-misha-saakashvili-discharged-in-uk-extradition-proceedings/. Accessed 11 January 2018, citing Senior District Judge Howard Riddle, Chief Magistrate, United Kingdom, *Davit Kezerashvili Extradition Proceedings, Discharge*, 21 March 2016.

inference and a finding to the effect that the requisite *nexus* (causal connection) exists between the initial prosecution or eventual punishment and the political opinion itself.[138] However, some jurists have deeply associated it with the non-discrimination clause, preferring the latter rather than the political offence exemption.[139] It is thus of no surprise that it has been referred to as a vague principle which varies between States.[140]

Furthermore, a distinction is generally drawn between a 'pure political crime' (commonly referred to as an 'absolute political offence')[141] and a 'related political crime'. Whereas the former crimes are directly aimed at the government,[142] the latter are 'connected with political crimes in such a manner that it was meant thereby to prepare for, secure, conceal or prevent the latter'.[143] Complications arise when such 'connected crimes'[144] are considered. These 'constitute the most problematic group of political crimes'.[145] Pure political offences traditionally fell within the parameters of the French objective test which considered an offence not extraditable only if it directly injured the rights of the State whereupon the motives of the accused are here irrelevant.[146] The attempted *coup d'état* of 15 July 2016 in Turkey[147] would be a classical example thereof. Until some decades ago, it seemed that various States adopted a rigid definition of a political offence, such that 'it would be available to the accused if he could show that the offence charged took place during a political uprising and that he was a member of the political group participating in that uprising'.[148] It seems that the related offence would nowadays find it difficult to retain its categorisation as a political offence. Prominent jurists assert that the same may be said in relation to the former in the context of core crimes. They state that 'there is also an exception to this exception, namely core crimes which are excluded from the 'political offense exception'.[149] Whereas the lack of a universally agreed definition might seem to hamper the execution of the exemption, it can boost the application of the exemption if the concept of political

[138] High Court, Australia, *Republic of Croatia (Appellant) v Daniel Snedden aka Dragan Vasiljkovic (Respondent)*, 19 May 2010, [2010] HCA 14, para 21.

[139] Poncet and Hart 1999, p. 294.

[140] Gilbert 1991, p. 114.

[141] Some jurists, such as van den Wyngaert, use the term 'absolute' (van den Wyngaert 1980, p. 105).

[142] Paust et al. 2007, p. 373.

[143] van den Wyngaert 1980, p. 104.

[144] These are crimes 'directed against public order, such as murder, larceny, fraud and arson, but which are committed with a political motive' (Haas 2002, p. 201).

[145] Ibid.

[146] Kielsgard 2013.

[147] BBC News (2016) Turkey's *Coup* Attempt: What You Need to Know. http://www.bbc.com/news/world-europe-36816045. Accessed on 2 January 2017.

[148] USA District Court, *In the Matter of the Extradition of McMullen*, 11 May 1979, 3-78-1099 MG, cited in Evans 1980, p. 434.

[149] Paust et al. 2007, p. 348.

offence is interpreted broadly by the Courts of the requested State. If such requested States are not bound by multi-lateral treaties which clarify the concept of political offence, such as for example the London Scheme for Extradition Within the Commonwealth[150] these States could garner significant leeway. Other treaties, such as the Economic Community of West African States Convention on Extradition, just cater for a prohibition which is shrouded in very broad wording in the general form of 'a political offence' or 'an offence connected with a political offence'.[151]

In her detailed study,[152] Christine van den Wyngaert writes that 'several States have agreed not to consider as political crimes the attempt on the life of a Head of State, war crimes or genocide'.[153] At the time, such State practice, in her view, constituted theoretical 'negative definitions',[154] emanated from conventional obligations[155] and was not being consistently applied in practice.[156] Such wording reflects the extra-ordinary nature of such core crimes and justifies my use of the word 'exemption', which use enables the reader to distinguish between the exemption itself and exceptions to it, the latter being exceptions to the exemption itself. Eventually, some State practice gradually started to reveal the inapplicability of the political offence exemption to crimes against humanity and genocide.[157] Furthermore, although armed conflict is undertaken for ultimately political reasons, 'crimes against the laws and customs of war cannot be considered political offences, as they do not harm a political interest of a particular State, nor a political right of a

150 See Article 4 sub-article 1 of the London Scheme for Extradition Within the Commonwealth (2002).

151 Although Article 12 of the Economic Community of West African States Convention on Extradition (1994) Convention on Extradition of the Governments of the Member States of the Economic Community of West African States, A/P.1/8/94, does not provide a definition of a 'political offence', Article 12(2)(a) thereof allows States to legislate to exclude the political offence exemption for certain particular crimes, hence creating an exception to the exemption.

152 This study encompasses the following distinctions:

i. inherent and non-inherent;
ii. connex and complex; and
iii. subjective and objective.

The ulterior following two distinctions are partially reflected within this book:

i. purely and mixed; and
ii. absolute and relative.

153 van den Wyngaert 1980, pp. 103–104.

154 van den Wyngaert 1980, p. 104.

155 Articles 1(a), (b) and (c) of the Additional Protocol to the ECE (1975) Additional Protocol 1975 to the European Convention on Extradition, ETS No. 086, and the Genocide Convention (1948) Convention on the Prevention and Punishment of the Crime of Genocide.

156 van den Wyngaert 1980, p. 104.

157 Court of Appeals, Ninth Circuit, USA, *William Joseph Quinn v Glen Robinson*, 18 February 1986, 83/2455, 783 F.2d 776 (9th Cir. 1986), ILDC 1584 (US 1986).

particular citizen'.[158] Such State practice triggered the negotiations of the USA Supplementary Extradition Treaties with Canada, UK, Belgium, Germany and Spain, intended to eliminate the application of the political offence exemption to serious crimes, including core crimes.[159]

Nowadays, this exemption, though still not expressly defined,[160] is not uncommon in multi-lateral legal instruments[161] but is explicitly rendered inapplicable by some important international criminal law treaties[162] which cater for, what Christine van den Wyngaert calls, 'a depoliticizing formula'.[163] An exception to the exemption generally subsists where the crime is one 'which the Contracting Parties or the Requesting State have the obligation to prosecute by reason of a multi-lateral international agreement'.[164] With the exception of crimes against humanity which are not yet conventionally proscribed, this applies to all core crimes. Where core crimes are concerned, the political offence exemption does not hold 'even if T's motive for committing the charged acts might be considered of a political nature…'.[165] Adam Gorski opines that such depoliticising of cooperation in criminal matters is tantamount to a process of judiciarisation.[166] All this happened notwithstanding the designation of a core crime, namely genocide, as 'the political crime *par excellence*'.[167] Following the *Furundžija* case, the political offence exemption experienced a gradual but consistent erosion. Robert Roth goes as far as saying that 'the political offence objection should be regarded as a non-issue with respect to international crimes'.[168] Effectively, States have learnt to circumvent the political offence, at least in so far as they deem this imperative. This may be done either by means of a teleological approach which is dependent upon a judicial law-making spree, or else by legislating. The latter method was successfully

---

[158] *Prosecutor v Tadić*, Decision on the Defence Motion for Interlocutory Appeal on Jurisdiction, in Klip and Sluiter 2001, cited in Sluiter 2003, pp. 637–638, n. 112.

[159] Paust et al. 2007, p. 390.

[160] Non-definition was not an oversight. It was deliberate. Such omission occurred since by defining it the concept would not be delimited, this being desired by States to allow them sufficient latitude. Because the exception was dealt with on a case-by-case basis, defining it would restrict the requested State's potential to assess its opinion from case to case (van der Wilt 1997, p. 40).

[161] See Article 3 of the ECE, above n. 16, and Article 2 of the ECMAC, above n. 18.

[162] See Article VII(1) of the Genocide Convention, above n. 155, Article XI(1) of the Apartheid Convention (1973) Convention on the Suppression and Punishment of the Crime of Apartheid, Article 11 of the Convention for the Suppression of Terrorist Bombings (1997), adopted by the UNGA on 15 December 1997, and Article 14 of the Convention for the Suppression of the Financing of Terrorism (1999) adopted by the UNGA on 9 December 1999.

[163] van den Wyngaert 1980, p. 141.

[164] Treaty Between the United States and the Federal Republic of Germany Concerning Extradition (1978), at 300.10, cited in Petersen 1992, p. 775.

[165] *Højesteret* [Supreme Court of Denmark], *Prosecution Service v T* (Attorney Bjørn Elmquist, appointed), Order, 6 November 2013, Case 105/2013, para 6.

[166] Gorski 2008, p. 387.

[167] Schabas 2000, p. 407.

[168] Roth 2009, p. 286.

accomplished in the requested extradition of *Smyth*. After the USA refusal to extradite Irish Republican Army members to the UK on the basis of the political offence exemption, both States negotiated a new Supplementary Treaty 'which technically kept the political offence exception but effectively eviscerated it by listing offences to which the exception would not apply'.[169]

Christine van den Wyngaert has opined that this exemption has been extended too far and has been stretched to include too many categories of fugitives.[170] Being too wide, likewise Geoff Gilbert believes it 'needs to be circumscribed, or, possibly, even abolished',[171] and notes that 'academics have attempted to delimit its boundaries'.[172] Similarly, Harmen van der Wilt identified efforts (which, at the time, were not deemed to be particularly successful) to restrict the scope of the political offence exception by excluding therefrom certain categories of offenders, such as *hostis humani generis*.[173] He does, in fact, opine that the political offence exemption should not cover core crimes.[174] The elimination of the scope of the political offence exemption would be possible because this barrier to extradition is a matter of State Practice, not a general principle of international law.[175] In fact, this was consummated because legal practice and theory disclosed a decline in the political offence exemption, predominantly caused by the *civitas maxima* and by the process of economic, political and legal integration in Europe.[176] Various extradition treaties concluded in the late sixties, seventies and eighties did not contain any protection for political offenders. Jurisprudence also conveyed that it was not possible to review whether the extradition court in the requested State had erred in granting surrender if it turned out at the full trial that the offence was indeed of a political character.[177] It was not appropriate for the Court in the requesting State to query the validity of the fugitive's surrender from the requested State.[178] Similarly,

---

[169] USA Court of Appeals, Ninth Circuit, *Matter of the Extradition of Smyth*, 27 July 1995, 61 F.3d 711, cited in Epps 1996, p. 297.

[170] van den Wyngaert 1980, p. 204.

[171] Gilbert 1998, p. 207.

[172] Gilbert 1998, p. 214.

[173] van der Wilt 1997, p. 41.

[174] van der Wilt 1997, p. 55.

[175] Supreme Court, Ireland, *The State {Duggan} vs Tapley*, 1952, Irish Reports 62, cited in Gilbert 1998, p. 212, n. 38.

[176] van der Wilt 1997, pp. 45–47.

[177] First Senate in Criminal Matters of the German *Reichsgericht*, *Spanish-German Extradition Treaty* case, 1925–1926, Annual Digest of Public International Law Cases 308, cited in Gilbert 1998, p. 213, n. 42.

[178] Court Martial, Khartoum, Sudan, *Trial of Rolf Steiner*, August-September 1971, 74 International Law Reports 478 (1971), cited in Gilbert 1998, pp. 213–214, n. 44 and 39.

extradition treaties create rights for States alone, unless there is an express provision which can benefit the fugitive.[179]

Mere political motive alone is insufficient to categorize a common crime as political.[180] In the *Sindona* case,[181] the Courts of the USA rejected the political offence defence, settling the matter conclusively after adhering to the judgment in *Koskotas v Roche*[182] and that in the *Matter of the Extradition of Locatelli.*[183] Hence, Geoff Gilbert rightly concludes that 'it is difficult to sustain the argument that it is a rule of customary international law',[184] and that 'the balance of authority is against the exemption being a rule of international law and against it conferring effective rights directly on the fugitive'.[185] He had aptly noted, in relation to certain core crimes, that 'such abominable crimes should not otherwise be left unpunished; indeed, if the alleged war criminal is not extradited, then it will be argued in Chap. 8 that he ought to be tried in the requested State or before an international criminal tribunal, such as the *ad hoc* tribunals for the former Yugoslavia and Rwanda or the proposed permanent International Criminal Court'.[186]

Whilst keeping in mind that most core crimes partake of a violent nature, Abraham Sofaer, in support of the Anglo-USA Supplementary Extradition Treaty asserted that 'the rationale for this new Supplementary Treaty is simple: with respect to violent crimes, the political offence has no place in extradition treaties between stable democracies, in which the political system is available to redress legitimate grievances and the judicial process provides fair treatment'.[187] In fact, the CREMS abolishes the political offence exemption by means of its Article 5, because the governments of the Member States comply with obligations stipulated in the ECvHR, and necessitates the rapid and effective operation of extradition between Member States. Harmen van der Wilt, whilst proposing the draft of a new treaty which would expressly define terrorist acts and exclude them from the

---

179 German Federal Constitutional Court, *Baader-Meinhof Gang {Rote Armee Fraktion}(Red Army Faction)* case, 1 August 1978, 1977, BVerfGE 54, 208 1 BvR 797/78 Böll-decision, cited in Gilbert 1998, p. 214, notes 45 and 46.

180 Gilbert 1998, pp. 216–217.

181 USA Court of Appeals, Second Circuit, *Michele Sindona v George V. Grant*, 21 March 1980, Nos. 618, 764, Dockets 78-2155, 79-2175, 619 F.2d 167 (178).

182 USA Court of Appeals, First Circuit, *George Koskotas, Petitioner, v James B. Roche, United States Marshal for the District of Massachusetts, Respondent*, 30 April 1991, 931 F.2d 169, and is cited in Gilbert 1998, p. 266, n. 286.

183 USA District Court for the Southern District of New York, *In the Matter of the Extradition of Sergio Locatelli, a/k/a "Sergio Luigi Locatelli", a/k/a "Guido Zaccaria"*, 6 March 1979, No. 78 Cr. Misc. No. 1 (KTD), 468 F. Supp. 568 (1979), cited in Gilbert 1998, p. 266, n. 287 and 120. The USA Court, by means of this judgment, established that USA Courts will not generally inquire into the motives of the requesting State, this being commonly referred to as 'the rule of non-inquiry' (Paust et al. 2007, pp. 391–404).

184 Gilbert 1998, p. 213.

185 Gilbert 1998, p. 214.

186 Gilbert 1998, p. 251.

187 Gilbert 1998, p. 269.

category of political offences, criticised the CREMS in so far as firstly it leaves Member States no choice other than to grant extradition for numerous elusive offences under the guise of terrorist activity, and secondly it abolishes the *aut dedere aut judicare* option which is fundamental to balance the need for the international repression of terrorism with the protection of the extraditee.[188]

It has been submitted that 'given that abolition would be predicated on the fugitive political offender receiving a fair trial in the requesting State instead, then it should be possible on the basis of the *Bovensmilde* incident for the Netherlands to abolish the political offence exemption'.[189] Although the Framework Decision on the EAW abolished the political offence exemption, which elimination is generally stipulated within the domestic legislation of the EU Member States, this does not necessarily mean that it can never be invoked. In Denmark, 'execution of an arrest warrant shall continue to be refused if there is a 'serious risk that the person will be persecuted for political reasons'.[190] It will ultimately be the requested State's prerogative and discretion whether to extradite or not, *id est* whether to apply the political offence exemption or not. In the light of such broad discretionary powers of States, the exemption's ability to bar extraditions is not neligible at all. It is not of a *de minimis* nature. Thus, what in this work is considered to be constitutive of a pitfall, being the right to a fair trial, paradoxically acts as an obstacle to the largest barrier to extradition, the political offence exemption, which, in Evans's words, for many decades (though, I add, not to date) constituted the 'hot issue of extradition law'.[191]

No doubt that, in contemporary international law, further to the ICC's Preamble, the executive discretion of States should be exercised in order to facilitate prosecution and defeat impunity. This is consonant with a developing world wherein human rights standards are being gradually raised to provide adequate protection for the suspect, indictee, accused and convict. Since today most States have signed, ratified and/or incorporated into their domestic legislation regional human rights instruments [such as the ACHPR, the IACvHR, the ECvHR and/or the ICCPR], suspects, accused persons, indictees and convicts can exercise their rights of individual petition should they be the victims of an unfair trial, possibly a political farce, within the requested State further to an extradition. Hence, in a world where due process safeguards are more pronounced and a judicial remedy to their

188 van der Wilt 1997, pp. 55–58.

189 The trial of the *South Moluccans* in the Netherlands is cited by Gilbert 1998, p. 280. For a relevant judgment connected to the Republic of South Moluccas, which had filed a complaint in the Netherlands requesting that the Indonesian President be arrested upon arrival in the Netherlands, and furthermore, that he would be prosecuted for human rights violations committed against Moluccan detainees, see Court of Appeal, The Hague, The Netherlands, *Government in exile of the Republic of South Moluccas (RMS) v The Netherlands*, 22 November 2011, LJN: BU5105, 200.077.445/01.

190 Vestergaard 2003, pp. 92–93.

191 Evans 1980, cited in Gilbert 1998, p. 203.

violation subsists, the *raison d'être, leitmotif* and intrinsic value of the political offence exemption is indeed becoming questionable.

Moreover, one can safely argue that the political offence exemption, at least in so far as the core crimes are concerned, has already been abolished because the fact that the ICC Statute has categorized such core crimes as crimes under international law has rendered them, for all intents and purpose of law, 'international crimes' rather than political crimes. After all core crimes are crimes *jure gentium*, crimes that have been universally proscribed, even at UN level, this portraying their international element, features, characteristics, dimension and effects. In pursuance of this line of thinking, the French *Conseil d'Etat*'s decision in the case of *Lujambio, Galdeano, Garcia Ramirez and Martinez Beiztegui*[192] and the Irish Supreme Court in the case *McGlinchey v Wren* held that the gravity of certain criminal offences deprived them of any political character because the violence undertaken is the antithesis of what could be regarded as political.[193] It may thus be reasonably concluded that, at least in so far as core crimes are concerned, the gravity of the act outweighs the underlying political motives and that consequently the political offence exemption has become redundant and/or obsolete.[194] This is widely accepted.[195] Yet, in my view, if an individual has been convicted of a core crime *in absentia*, the exemption may still be applied when the requesting State is the State which tried the individual *in absentia* although the laws of the requesting State allow for trials *in absentia*. In other words, if the subject of the extradition request can directly vaunt a claim which has a human rights dimension, the requested State may infer ulterior motives of the requesting State which lead the requested State to believe that the crime over which the extradition is sought has a marked political character. This conclusion may be inferred from a case which dealt with the alleged killing of a British officer in Belfast by an Irish citizen.[196] In politically volatile circumstances requested States may show distrust of the requesting State. The former States habitually fear that political offenders will be subjected to torture and/or harsh punishments in the requested States.[197]

Even if one were to discard the theory of abolition or the affirmation that the political offence exemption is now redundant, one cannot dispute that an unequivocal trend to limit the application of the political offence exception or to increase the exceptions to the exemption is rapidly gaining ground in international

---

192 *Conseil d'Etat*, France, *Lujambio, Galdeano, Garcia Ramirez and Martinez Beiztegui*, 26 September 1984, 62847. This case involved three Basque separatists.

193 Supreme Court, Ireland, *McGlinchey v Wren*, 7 December 1982, Irish Reports 154. German jurist, Carl Schmitt, however disagrees (Frazer 2010).

194 Gilbert 1998, p. 302.

195 Duffy 2007, p. 109.

196 USA Court of Appeals, Second Circuit, *Joseph Patrick Thomas Doherty v Department of Justice, Immigration and Naturalization Service*, 29 June 1990, Nos. 662, 880, Dockets 88-4084, 89-4092, also cited in McDermott 2015, p. 285, n. 147.

197 Petersen 1992, p. 776 and p. 792.

law discourse.[198] In this context, once again, the differentiation between a crime and another has had a large effect on the depoliticization of certain crimes. In fact, '*si è passati alla redazione di apposite convenzioni che hanno come scopo la depoliticizzazione a fini estradizionali di alcune tipologie di reati. Particolarmente rilevante la portata della Convenzione europea per la repressione del terrorismo (Strasburgo, 1977) che fornisce un ampio elenco di reati che gli Stati aderenti alla convenzione stessa si obbligano a considerare 'non politici' ai fini dell'estradizione. Un ulteriore ampliamento rationae materiae della clausola in questione ha progressivamente investito anche i crimini di guerra, i crimini contro l'umanità (genocidio) e gli atti di tortura*'.[199] Robert Kolb refers to USA, English and Dutch jurisprudence to show that State practice is moving towards restricting the political offence exemption.[200] This is so notwithstanding the fact that some important treaties ratified by such States still retain the political offence exemption.[201] The European Convention on the Suppression of Terrorism,[202] lists, in its initial provision, a range of offences which are not to be recognised as political.[203] However, by virtue of its fifth article, it simultaneously permits the refusal of extradition where the requested State has substantial grounds for believing that the request for extradition for an offence has been made for certain purposes, including political

---

[198] Article 2 of the Irish Extradition (Amendment) Act (1994), No. 6 of 1994; Article 1 of the European Convention on the Suppression of Terrorism (1977); Article 1 of the South Asian Association for Regional Cooperation Regional Convention on Suppression of Terrorism (1987); Article 5 of the Anglo-Indian Extradition Treaty (1992) Extradition Treaty Between the United Kingdom and India, Extradition Treaty Between the Government of the United States of America and the Government of Jamaica (1983); Extradition Treaty Between the Government of the United States of America and the Government of the Republic of Costa Rica (1982) and; *in partem*, Article 3 of the Model American Convention (1980) Model American Convention on the Prevention and Punishment of Serious Forms of Violence Jeopardizing Fundamental Rights and Freedoms, Division of Public Service Activities, ABA.

[199] There has been an increasing trend to draw up treaties which depoliticize certain offences for extradition purposes. The European Convention for the Suppression of Terrorism (signed in Strasbourg in 1977) is particularly relevant since it stipulates a broad list of offences which the State Parties undertake not to consider as political for extradition purposes. A further widening *rationae materiae* of such provision has progressively included war crimes, crimes against humanity (genocide) and acts of torture (my translation) (Dean et al. 2003, p. 512).

[200] Kolb 2004, p. 265.

[201] Article 4(1)(iii) of the Extradition Treaty between the Government of Canada and the Government of the USA (1971), signed in Washington DC, on 3 December 1971.

[202] Above n. 198.

[203] These include an offence within the scope of the Convention for the Suppression of Unlawful Seizure of Aircraft (1970), signed at The Hague on 16 December 1970; an offence within the scope of the Convention for the Suppression of Unlawful Acts against the Safety of Civil Aviation (1971), signed at Montreal on 23 September 1971; a serious offence involving an attack against the life, physical integrity or liberty of internationally protected persons, including diplomatic agents; an offence involving kidnapping, the taking of a hostage or serious unlawful detention; an offence involving the use of a bomb, grenade, rocket, automatic firearm or letter or parcel bomb if this use endangers persons; and an attempt to commit any of the foregoing offences or participation as an accomplice of a person who commits or attempts to commit such an offence.

opinion. Though these resemble the equality and non-discrimination clauses expressed in many treaties and human rights instruments, they can undermine the impact of the above list whereby the exceptions to the political offence exemption are stipulated.

The Inter-American Convention Against Terrorism, by virtue of its Article 11, renders the crimes which are expressly penalised by various treaties[204] not subject to the political offence exemption. The treaties encompass various modes of conduct which could, in identifiable circumstances, amount to core crimes. Most importantly a large majority of these treaties adopts, in one way or another, the *aut dedere aut judicare* rule. Consequently, at least in so far as these crimes are concerned, the political offence exemption does not directly stand in the way of the extradition or prosecution of alleged terrorists, bombers, hijackers, kidnappers and hostage-takers. This is obviously subject to the signature and ratification of such conventions by the respective Member States. The Convention for the Suppression of Terrorist Bombings was the catalyst of the process of depoliticization of certain crimes. Besides expressly catering for the exception to the political offence exemption,[205] it stresses such an exception by ensuring that the non-applicability of the political offence exemption prevails over any other extradition treaty which allows for the political offence exemption.[206] Similar legal provisions feature in the Convention for the Suppression of the Financing of Terrorism.[207] One must acknowledge that, to date, the political offence exemption could still be resorted to indirectly. By way of example, Article 8 of the International Convention for the Suppression of Unlawful Acts Against the Safety of Civil Aviation provides that any extradition is subject to the extradition treaties amongst the States concerned, which treaties normally include the political offence exemption, or, if extradition takes place outside such a treaty, that it is subject to the 'conditions provided by the law of the requested State', which would probably also include such limitation.

---

[204] Convention for the Suppression of Unlawful Seizure of Aircraft, above n. 203, Convention for the Suppression of Unlawful Acts against the Safety of Civil Aviation, above n. 203; Convention on the Prevention and Punishment of Crimes against Internationally Protected Persons, including Diplomatic Agents (1973), adopted by the UNGA on 14 December 1973; Convention Against the Taking of Hostages (1979), adopted by the UNGA on 17 December 1979; Convention on the Physical Protection of Nuclear Material (1980), signed in Vienna on 3 March 1980; Protocol on the Suppression of Unlawful Acts of Violence at Airports Serving International Civil Aviation (1988) supplementary to the Convention for the Suppression of Unlawful Acts against the Safety of Civil Aviation, signed in Montreal on 24 February 1988; Convention for the Suppression of Unlawful Acts against the Safety of Maritime Navigation (1988), done at Rome on 10 March 1988; Protocol for the Suppression of Unlawful Acts against the Safety of Fixed Platforms Located on the Continental Shelf (1988) supplementary to the Convention for the Suppression of Unlawful Acts against the Safety of Maritime Navigation, done at Rome on 10 March 1988; Convention for the Suppression of Terrorist Bombings, above n. 162, and the Convention for the Suppression of the Financing of Terrorism, above n. 162.

[205] Article 11, above n. 162.

[206] Article 9 sub-article 5, above n. 162.

[207] Articles 11 sub-article 5 and 14, above n. 162.

Other States have somehow re-introduced the exemption through the backdoor, allegedly justifying its application in line with the general prohibition of discrimination.[208] Just to cite one, Portugal is bound by domestic law to refuse surrender if the EAW is issued on account of political reasons.[209]

Finally, whereas it has been shown that the relevance of the political offence exemption is gradually subsiding, as stated at the commencement of this heading, mention must be made of the principle of non-*refoulement* which can be invoked on the basis of a well-founded fear of being persecuted for one's political opinion, a ground (protected category) for refugee status in terms of Article 1A(2) of the Convention Relating to the Status of Refugees and its 1967 Protocol. States which are precluded from invoking the exemption, possibly by means of an express provision within a bi-lateral or multi-lateral extradition treaty which regulates the requested extradition, may not invoke the exemption at all but may be able to rely on this principle. An individual, a potential extraditee, may become an asylum seeker and eventually (upon the conferement of refugee status) a refugee if such person proves that he will be constrained to undergo criminal proceedings for his diverse political opinions, this being a broader concept than that of a political offence. Indeed, political persecution may subsist even when one will not be constrained to undergo criminal proceedings. In this way, a State may exit a building from the window rather than from its main door. Obviously this escape route can only be utilised when the requesting State is the country of origin of the individual (not another third State).

16.4 The Double Criminality Rule

This rule, which is often referred to as 'dual criminality',[210] is a classical feature of extradition law[211] which found expression in the ECE.[212] Under this treaty, the absence of double criminality is a mandatory ground for refusing the requested extradition.[213] Where core crimes are concerned, civil law countries have the power to waive the double criminality requirement.[214] This requirement entails that the conduct which constitutes the subject of the extradition request must constitute a crime both in the requesting and in the requested State. Silvia Borelli upholds that, barring an

208 Klimek 2015, p. 215.

209 Ibid.

210 Paust et al. 2007, p. 351; see also Deen-Racsmany and Blekxtoon 2005, p. 322. Distinctively, Sam Rugege and Aime M. Karimunda refer to it as 'dual incrimination' (Rugege and Karimunda 2014, pp. 86–88).

211 Plachta 1989, p. 84.

212 Klimek 2015, p. 317.

213 Klimek 2015, p. 81.

214 REDRESS and African Rights 2008, p. 21, n. 64.

express and specific conventional derogation, the double criminality rule should be considered as a 'tacit precondition for extradition'.[215] Some States have used the double criminality rule, within their own extradition legislation, to restrict extra-territorial jurisdiction.[216] It has been argued that the *raison d'être* of this rule is rooted in the principles of State sovereignty and reciprocity.[217] Another dimension of this rule is constituted by means of the principle of legality,[218] namely the *nullum crimen sine lege* and *nulla poena sine lege* rules.[219] This is probably why 'double criminality' is also occasionally referred to as 'double punishability' in case-law.[220] In this way the double criminality rules have a subordinate function which elevates it to the status of a human rights safeguard.[221] The link between double criminality and the principle of legality (particularly *nulla poena sine lege*) is not self-evident because extradition cannot be equated to punishment.[222] It is, in the opinion of Swart, mere assistance to criminal proceedings elsewhere,[223] this being a conclusion which is however not shared by Elies van Sliedregt who postulates that recent developments in extradition law show that 'extradition is part of the criminal process and should be treated as such'.[224] Bassiouni links double criminality with the principle of legality by upholding that a person who is the subject of a request for extradition may claim that, at the time of the alleged offence, it was not a crime under the laws either of the requesting or requested State.[225] Adam Gorski upholds that the fact that double criminality 'should be based on the rights of an individual and therefore represent a sort of international-law consequence of the *nullum crimen sine lege* principle seems to prevail at least in the discussion on the European Arrest Warrant'.[226] He adds that when double criminality is identified with *nullum crimen sine lege*, the *locus delicti* is more important than the place where a legal cooperation is rendered.[227] The link between the two (double criminality and legality) was claimed in the *Advocaten voor*

---

[215] Borelli 2004, cited in Kolb 2004, p. 336.

[216] Article 7(Part II)(a), Section 2(b) of the Brazilian Criminal Code {Brazilian Criminal Code (1940) *Código Penal, Decreto-Lei n.° 2.848 de 7 de Dezembro de 1940* [Decree-Law No. 2.848 of 7 December 1940]}, cited in Kleffner 2008, p. 42, n. 188.

[217] Shearer 1971, p. 137.

[218] This principle, together with the principle of culpability (moral blameworthiness) are the most fundamental principles of criminal law (Ambos 2009a, p. 333).

[219] Dean et al. 2003, p. 502; see also Obokata 2010, p. 58.

[220] District Court, Criminal Law Section, Extradition Division, The Hague, *Public Prosecutor v Ahmatasevic*, Judgment, 5 May 2009, 08-3524, para 6.2.

[221] Dugard and van den Wyngaert 1998, p. 188, cited in Boister 2016, p. 10.

[222] van Sliedregt 2009, p. 53.

[223] Swart 1992, pp. 505–534, cited in van Sliedregt 2009, p. 53, n. 11.

[224] van Sliedregt 2009, p. 53.

[225] Bassiouni 2007, p. 747.

[226] Gorski 2008, p. 387.

[227] Ibid.

de Wereld case.[228] Such lawyers argued that the Framework Decision on the EAW violated the principle of legality by abolishing, as shall be seen shortly, the double criminality requirement with regard to the offences listed in its Article 2(2) and also by listing vague categories of crimes therein. Rejecting the complaint, the ECJ found that the principle of legality can only be violated at State level.[229] Elies van Sliedregt perceptively notes that the abolition of the double criminality verification 'affects the foreseeability requirement that stems from the legality principle'.[230] Double criminality plays a special role consisting in ensuring that 'conduct violating foreign norms is foreseeable as "criminal" and protects against arrest and surrender for conduct not "criminal"'.[231] In other words, such abolition infringes the legality principle especially in the case of offences subject to the EAW which have been committed outside the territory of the issuing Member State.[232] Matters can be more convoluted if the requested State has no legislation which determines the stage at which the act would have to be criminal. Under the law of Sierra Leone, just to mention one of such States, the domestic criminality requirements do not indicate whether the act would have to be criminal at the time of the commission of the crime, or at the time of the extradition request, or when the extradition is to be effected.[233]

Italian jurists have suggested that for the double criminality rule to be satisfied 'è *quindi sufficiente una generica ed astratta previsione del fatto come illecito penale; non si ritiene, peraltro, necessaria neanche la coincidenza in astratto delle fattispecie incriminanti*'.[234] This seems to be the current prevailing position which militates under customary international law. The double criminality rule itself is said to have become customary international law due to its widespread nature.[235] It does not necessitate that the conduct, which is a subject of a request for extradition, constitutes a crime with the same name or designation in both the requesting and the requested State.[236] Citing Deane J in *Riley v The Commonwealth*, the High Court of Australia upheld that 'the principle of double criminality is satisfied where, and only where, any alleged offence against the law of the requesting State in respect of which extradition is sought would necessarily involve a criminal offence against the law of the requested State if the acts constituting it had been done in that

---

228 ECJ, *Advocaten voor de Wereld VZW v Leden van de Ministeraad, Reference for a preliminary ruling from the Arbitragehof*, 3 May 2007, Case C/303-05.

229 *Advocaten voor de Wereld VZW v Leden van de Ministeraad*, above n. 228; see also van Sliedregt 2009, p. 60.

230 van Sliedregt 2009, p. 60.

231 Ibid.

232 Ibid.

233 AI 2012, p. 74, cited in Thompson 2015, p. 113, n. 133.

234 It is enough if a generic fact which is illegal subsists; it is not even necessary to have the same constitutive elements which trigger criminal liability: (my translation) (Dean et al. 2003, p. 502).

235 High Court, Australia, *Minister for Home Affairs of the Commonwealth v Charles Zentai*, 15 August 2012, P56/2011, [2012] HCA 28, para 22.

236 *Minister for Home Affairs of the Commonwealth v Charles Zentai*, above n. 235, para 21.

State'.[237] In other words, as stated by Bassiouni, the conduct must be criminal under the laws and jurisprudence of both States, although it might not be defined identically within both States.[238]

Hence, since the conduct proscribed by core crimes necessarily constitutes a violation of domestic criminal law both because core crimes are habitually penalized under local/national criminal laws and because, should this not be the case, such conduct would anyway constitute murder, grievous bodily harm, torture or any other crime under ordinary domestic law, the double criminality rule is not likely to act any further as a barrier to extradition.[239] This assertion may be threatened, in rare occasions, since:

1. domestic laws punishing core crimes may not correspond to international criminal law;[240]
2. throughout the incorporation process, States may depart from the prevailing international rule;[241] and
3. domestic *obiter dicta* may give precedence to the differential domestic rule in cases of an inconsistency with international criminal law,[242] probably owing to impending constitutional constraints.

The three observations here above may shed doubts on the argument that 'by virtue of the *jus cogens* and the *obligatio erga omnes* doctrines, there should normatively be no requirement of double criminality for the prosecution or extradition of crimes under international law'.[243] The trend to do away with, as far as practicable, the double criminality rule, is even more apparent within EU circles because of Article 2 para 2 of the EAW. The Framework Decision on the EAW has softened the double criminality requirement by not requiring it for a list of thirty-two offences, which comprise core crimes. Whilst enlisting the thirty-two criminal offences[244] that may be subject to the EAW, it states that such procedure is to be undertaken 'without verification of the double criminality of the act',[245] the

---

237 *Minister for Home Affairs of the Commonwealth v Charles Zentai*, above n. 235, para 23.

238 Bassiouni 2007, p. 504.

239 André Klip, analysing the EAW, acknowledges that 'most of the crimes on the list refer to offences criminalised by Union act or other international obligations' (Klip 2009, p. 333), adds that 'the vast majority of offences on the list are offences which are criminal in all member States, anyway' (Klip 2009, p. 335), and concludes that 'for the offences on the list, for which there is no common legal instrument, there is an assumption of double criminality' (Klip 2009, p. 336).

240 By way of example, Article 320 of the Paraguayan Penal Code [Paraguayan Penal Code (1997) *Ley N° 1.160/97, Código Penal*, Law No. 1.160/97, Criminal Code] expressly incorporates a number of war crimes but does not cover several war crimes (Kleffner 2008, p. 39, n. 173).

241 The way the crime of genocide has been incorporated in Germany constitutes a fair example of this dichotomy (Kleffner 2008, p. 40, n. 174).

242 Kleffner 2008, p. 40.

243 AI 2012, p. 63, cited in Thompson 2015, p. 99, n. 70.

244 These include core crimes subject to the jurisdiction of the ICC. Such a list of offences partakes of what has been traditionally called the 'enumerative method' (Shearer 1971, p. 133).

245 *Advocaten voor de Wereld VZW v Leden van de Ministeraad*, above n. 228, para 51.

absence of which does not violate the principle of legality[246] in as much as criminal liability is dependent upon the applicable law of the member State issuing the EAW. The above statement is subject to a qualification which may emerge from Lagondy's valid assertion that since the thirty-two offences provided in the EAW list are punishable throughout the EU, double criminality may be presumed. In his view, double criminality becomes an issue within 'no list' treaties, the Framework Decision on the EAW not being one of such treaties.[247]

Article C of the repealed Joint Action 97/154 on Trafficking in Human Beings solicited the re-consideration of the need of the double criminality requirement. It has been held that 'the abolition of this double criminality check for certain serious offences is a logical application of the principle of mutual recognition within a single area of criminal justice. On the basis that member States share a sufficiently common approach towards the basic elements of criminality such that there is a 'high level of confidence between member States', any differences in approach that do exist vis-à-vis this list of more serious crimes should not be an obstacle to judicial cooperation'.[248] Hence, within EU law, 'although the principle of double criminality is preserved in its general scope, it is excluded, that is, it cannot be opposed as a justified ground for refusing extradition'.[249] In practice, however, various important States such as Belgium, Germany, Italy, Poland, Slovenia and the UK still rely on this principle throughout their decision-making process in certain identifiable circumstances,[250] hence *de facto* aborting the successful achievement of a harmonized European approach. EAW practice shows that 'there is still some form of dual criminality assessment with regard to list offences'.[251] Here the act must constitute an offence under the law of the executing member State, whatever the constitutive elements or however it is described.[252] Consequently, it is fair to conclude that whereas 'at the European level the European Arrest Warrant scheme may seem a radical departure from extradition, in national reality it is not'[253] because it has not entirely abandoned the double criminality rule.[254] Whether this occurred owing to 'language barriers and translation difficulties'[255] is beyond the scope of my book. Such States may give precedence to their obligations deriving from Article 2 of the ECE which prescribes the double criminality requirement. The execution of this legal provision is still somewhat convoluted in view of the fact that it is still unclear how one should assess the extent to which concrete acts fit the

---

[246] *Advocaten voor de Wereld VZW v Leden van de Ministeraad*, above n. 228, para 54.
[247] Lagondy 2009, p. 4, cited in van Sliedregt 2009, p. 68.
[248] Fletcher et al. 2008, p. 114.
[249] Bellelli 2010, p. 233.
[250] Long 2009, p. 21.
[251] van Sliedregt 2009, p. 64.
[252] de Bondt and Vermeulen 2010, p. 23.
[253] van Sliedregt 2009, p. 67.
[254] Boister 2016, p. 15.
[255] Filletti 2017, p. 83.

prevalent legal qualification, that is, whether by virtue of the law of the requesting State or the law of the requested State. Moreover, as shown here above, although the majority of member States have faithfully implemented the Framework Decision on the EAW,[256] some national legislation which transposed and implemented the EAW did, in fact, reintroduce a double criminality criterion by virtue of a mandatory requirement necessitating that the national legislation of the requested State criminalizes conduct falling within the ICC's jurisdiction, which conduct is identical to that which is the subject of the demand contained in the request of execution of a EAW by another member State.[257]

It has been stated that 'some States require that the exact counterpart crime exists, or that the same elements of the offence charged exist in the counterpart crime in the requested State, or that the crime charged be prosecutable under the laws of the requested State'.[258] Silvia Borelli suggests that the double criminality rule requires that, if the same case were to be presented before the courts of the requested State, it should be prosecutable on the same facts. Although the double criminality rule, *per se*, is a customary rule of international extradition law,[259] the consequence of which is that it can be expressly derogated from by extradition treaties[260] culminating into a persistent objector, I do not subscribe to Borelli's view. A fact, namely a particular act, omission or conduct, may constitute an offence in one State and a completely different offence in another. This does not entail that Borelli's conclusions are erroneous. On the contrary, Borelli interprets the double criminality rule *in concreto*, that is objectively, whereas I favour a subjective interpretation to this rule[261] mainly because it considers the criteria satisfied once the conduct is deemed criminal in both jurisdictions which means that there would no longer be the need to compare the constitutive elements of the crime in the requested State with the constitutive elements of the crime in the requesting State.[262] In all fairness Borelli, who performs an assessment *in concreto* (rather than

---

[256] van Sliedregt 2009, p. 68.

[257] Article 8(1)(ii), 8(2) and 8(3) of the Italian Law on the EAW (2005) *Mandato d'arresto europeo e procedure di consegna tra Stati membri* [EAW and Transfer Procedures Between Member States], Law No. 69, 22 April 2005, dealing with '*consegna obbligatoria*' (mandatory surrender).

[258] Bassiouni 1986, p. 412.

[259] Jennings and Watts 1992, p. 107.

[260] High Court, Australia, *Riley v The Commonwealth of Australia*, 18 December 1985, [1985] HCA 82, 159 CLR 1, 62 ALR 497.

[261] The objective interpretation relies on the label of the offences and a strict interpretation of its constitutive elements. The subjective (*in abstracto*) approach relies on the nature of the act, the criminal character of the activity, regardless of its specified label and irrespective of the fulfilment of all the constitutive elements of the crime in the respective laws of the two States (Bassiouni 1974, p. 322). In simpler terms the objective approach necessitates the strict matching of the definition of crimes in both States, whereas the subjective approach (adopted in the UN Model Treaty on Extradition, above n. 11) requires that the underlying conduct is regarded as criminal in both States (Boister 2016, p. 12).

[262] McDermott 2015, p. 289.

in abstracto), admits that 'recent trends in international practice show that the domestic courts are more inclined towards the application of the subjective approach'.[263] Neil Boister refers to a potential danger that specific emergency measures against particular offences such as terrorism will also abandon double criminality.[264] If such emergency measures would cover the most serious crimes of concern to the international community, hence core crimes, double criminality will no longer bar extradition. Until this happens, a clear direction of an international dimension is warranted because the matter seems to be rather unsettled.

16.5 The Exclusion of the Cause of the Criminal Action by Reason of Amnesty

Amnesties are intended to restore peace and facilitate reconciliation[265] throughout the democratization process. Their principal justification is captured by Ben Chigara who refers to 'the perceived opportunity for peace and tranquillity' as an alibi for 'privileging the amnesia effect over the juridical process'.[266] Far from being a novelty in contemporary international law,[267] they are generally accorded post-conflict,[268] and entail a *nolle prosequi* with a consequent waiver of punishment. In most cases, they effectively also deny the right to seek an official investigation into fundamental human rights abuses.[269] With the aim of ensuring a political compromise in order to supposedly mete out national unity and reconciliation, otherwise referred to as 'post-conflict transitional justice',[270] occasionally, they are made subject to the fulfilment of a resolutive or suspensive condition.[271] By way of example, the Constitutional Court of South Africa, considering an amnesty in respect of acts performed by the South African Defence Force members in Namibia, upheld that the amnesty was specifically limited to prosecutions in respect of offences committed within the territory of Namibia.[272] They have been granted in various States, including Algeria, Angola, Argentina, Chile, Croatia, El Salvador, Haiti, Lebanon, Perú, Sierra Leone, South Africa, Uruguay and Yemen,

[263] Borelli 2004, cited in Kolb 2004, p. 336.

[264] Boister 2016, p. 18.

[265] Dugard 1999a, pp. 1001 et seq.

[266] Chigara 2000, p. 125.

[267] They may be traced back to the Westphalian Peace Treaties (1648) Peace Treaties of Westphalia, 14–24 October 1648 (Bernhardt 1981, pp. 148–150).

[268] O'Shea 2002; see also Dugard 1999b.

[269] Seibert-Fohr 2002, p. 335.

[270] Teitel 2002.

[271] Ambos 2009b, pp. 19 and pp. 71 et seq.

[272] Constitutional Court, South Africa, *The State vs Wouter Basson*, 9 September 2005, Case CCT 30/03, para 243.

sometimes with the UN's tacit acquiescence or explicit consent. They were, unsuccessfully, challenged constitutionally in *Azapo et al. v President of the Republic of South Africa et al.*[273] The judgment comprises a comprehensive examination, at times historical and psychological, of the content and consequences of amnesties, acknowledging that amnesties obliterate fundamental human rights,[274] that 'there is no single or uniform international practice in relation to amnesty',[275] and further establishing some important principles:

(a) the offender can no longer be held 'criminally liable' for such offence and no prosecution in respect thereof can be maintained against him or her;
(b) such an offender can also no longer be held civilly liable personally for any damages sustained by the victim and no such civil proceedings can successfully be pursued against him or her;
(c) if the wrongdoer is an employee of the State, the State is equally discharged from any civil liability in respect of any act or omission of such an employee, even if the relevant act or omission was effected during the course and within the scope of his or her employment; and
(d) other bodies, organisations or persons are also exempt from any liability for any of the acts or omissions of a wrongdoer which would ordinarily have arisen in consequence of their vicarious liability for such acts or omissions.[276]

Initially, it must be premised that amnesties do not constitute a determination of a criminal charge,[277] leading to an acquittal or a conviction. For such a determination to subsist the individual's position must have initially been 'substantially affected' by such official notification[278] or by his arrest.[279] Amnesties 'do not qualify as judgments'[280] and they don't encompass an arrest or the notification of criminal proceedings. They actually decriminalize conduct. Since they do not determine guilt or innocence,[281] they cannot be used to trigger the application of the

---

[273] Constitutional Court, South Africa, *Azanian Peoples Organization (AZAPO) and Others v President of the Republic of South Africa and Others*, 25 July 1996, CCT 17/96 [1996] ZACC 16, 1996 (8) BCLR 1015, 1996 (4) SA 672.

[274] See para 9, above n. 273.

[275] See para 24, above n. 273.

[276] See para 7, above n. 273.

[277] ECtHR, *Hans Eckle and Marianne Eckle v FRG*, 15 July 1982, Application No. 8130/78, Serie A No. 51, para 77.

[278] ECtHR Grand Chamber, *Jørgen Pedersen and Sten Kristian Baadsgaard v Denmark*, 17 December 2004, Application No. 49017/99, cited in Harris et al. 2009, p. 209.

[279] ECtHR, *Karl-Heinz Wemhoff v FRG*, 25 April 1968, Application No. 2122/64.

[280] van den Wyngaert and Ongena 2002, p. 726.

[281] *Auto de la Sala de lo Penal de la Audiencia Nacional Confirmando la Jurisdicción de España para Conocer de los Crímenes de Genocidio y Terrorismo Cometido Durante la Dictadura Chilena* [*Decision of the Penal Chamber Confirming Spanish Jurisdiction to Investigate Genocide in Chile*], First Section, 5 November 1998, Appeal 173/98, File 1/98 from Judicial Chamber 6, cited in Wilson 1999, p. 950, n. 83.

ne bis in idem rule.[282] They are the very antithesis of a determination of guilt or otherwise. Moreover, they do not emerge from judicial institutions but from legislative, executive or quasi-judicial *ad hoc* entities, such as parliaments or truth commissions.[283] The latter 'tend to replace the adversarial character of criminal proceedings with a "victim-centred" approach emphasizing emphatic listening to private and public testimonies that catalogue atrocities inflicted on innocent victims'.[284] The same may not be said for pardons which connote that an individual is exempted from serving the sentence or from completing it *in toto*, wherein a sanction emanates directly from a trial.[285] Since pardons are granted *ex post facto*, upon an acceptance or finding of guilt,[286] an examination of pardons does not fall within the scope of Part IV. Reference to pardons throughout Part IV will only be made in so far as such pardons can impinge upon the *ne bis in idem* rule. Just by way of parenthesis, I recall that Part III has already shown that when pardons are granted, it is doubted whether the ICC Prosecutor could trigger the jurisdiction of the ICC under the vertical system of enforcement. This is because the ICC Statute contains a significant *lacuna*[287] since it only addresses flaws in the conduct of proceedings, but leaves unaffected measures that take effect post-conviction in proceedings which were not for the purposes of shielding the individual and were otherwise conducted independently and impartially.[288] It is therefore highly likely[289] that such clemency measures would not fall within the purview of the vertical system of enforcement, strengthening impunity by leaving it untouched. Though increasingly unpopular in human rights discourse, amnesties accorded in the executing member State still constitute one of the only three mandatory grounds

[282] For an in-depth analysis of the potential impact of amnesties on the admissibility of cases before the ICC, see El Zeidy 2008, pp. 157–211; see also van den Wyngaert and Ongena 2002, p. 726; see also Kleffner 2008, pp. 261–272.

[283] The IACmmHR held that truth commissions fail to fulfil a State's obligation to compensate victims and punish perpetrators [IACmmHR, *Alicia Consuelo Herrera et al. v Argentina*, 2 October 1992, Report No. 28/92, Cases 10.147, 10.181, 10.240, 10.262, 10.309 and 10.311, para 50].

[284] Laplante and Theidon 2010, p. 297.

[285] See, for example, Decree 2741/90 issued by the then President of Argentina Carlos Menem on 29 December 1990, pardoning the military *juntas* who were sentenced on 9 December 1985 [Decree (1990) Decree No. 2741/90, Argentina, issued by the then President of Argentina Carlos Menem, 29 December 1990].

[286] Urtubey 2005, p. 128.

[287] Schabas 2004, p. 88.

[288] van den Wyngaert and Ongena 2002, p. 727.

[289] This is not necessarily always the case. Jann Kleffner identifies circumstances wherein such clemency measures could anyhow render the case admissible before the ICC. This would occur when the clemency measure under national law constitutes the expunging of a conviction, such as in the French *Nouveau Code Pénal* {French *Nouveau Code Pénal* (1992)}, whereupon such State could be treated as genuinely unwilling to investigate and prosecute (Kleffner 2008, p. 267). This would have an ulterior latent effect, which is of relevance to this book. In practice, rendering a trial null and void *ab initio* conveys that the *ne bis in idem* defence would be inapplicable, allowing for ICC admissibility (Siebert-Fohr 2003, p. 565).

for the non-execution of the EAW.[290] They are not deemed inconsistent with, nor are they nullified, as a result of the mere existence of an express prohibition of statutory limitations attaching to particular crimes under domestic law.[291] A former Judge of the ICJ and former President of the IACtHR[292] strikingly sums up the effect of amnesties in his recent work. He refers to self-amnesties,[293] rather than amnesties, to stress the unilateral dimension of such laws and to personalize the juridical fact. By means of a pun, he conveys that amnesties negate the law by *ab initio* infringing the *derecho al Derecho*, the right to the law.[294] The progressive IACmmHR took a firm stand outlawing amnesties which do not acknowledge responsibility, which apply to crimes against humanity and which eliminate any possibility of obtaining adequate pecuniary compensation, primarily for victims,[295] whereas the IACtHR referred to the 'manifest incompatibility of self-amnesty laws and the American Convention on Human Rights'.[296] Amnesties 'are prohibited for contravening irrevocable rights recognised by International Law of Human Rights'.[297] The IACtHR did not only invalidate amnesties imposed by an outgoing regime which had perpetrated core crimes, but also those adopted democratically further to the promulgation of a law which was approved after a national referendum, such as Uruguay's Expiry Law.[298] Similarly the HRC maintained that non-prosecution could be tantamount to a breach of the victim's right to a national effective remedy, another violation of yet another fundamental human right *per se*.[299] More categorically it affirmed that amnesty laws in regard to serious human

---

[290] As mentioned earlier on, Article 3 of the Framework Decision on the EAW, above n. 71, stipulates that the other two grounds are *ne bis in idem* in one of the member States and the non-fulfilment of the age of criminal responsibility in terms of the law of the executing State.

[291] *Cour de Cassation, Chambre Criminelle* [Court of Cassation, Criminal Division], *France, Wladyslaw Sobanski v George Boudarel*, 1 April 1993, 98-85902.

[292] Olivier de Schutter speaks of an approach of the I-ACtHR which has been largely influenced by Judge Cançado Trindade between 1995 and 2008, when he was a member of the I-ACtHR, but especially between 1999 and 2004 when he was its President (de Schutter 2014, p. 1031).

[293] This is a term also used by Ellen Rutz and Caitlin Reiger in their introduction to their book (Lutz and Reiger 2009, pp. 5–6).

[294] Cançado Trindade 2011, p. 192.

[295] IACmmHR, *Report on the Situation of Human Rights in El Salvador*, 11 February 1994, Doc. OEA/Ser.L/II.85 Doc. 28 rev. with regard to El Salvador's General Amnesty Law for Consolidation of Peace (1993), cited in ECtHR Grand Chamber, *Fred Marguš v Croatia*, 27 May 2014, Application No. 4455/10, para 58.

[296] IACtHR, *Chumbipuma Aguirre and Others v Perú (Barrios Altos* case*)*, 14 March 2001, Series C No. 75, para 44.

[297] IACtHR, *Gomes Lund et al. (Guerrilha Do Araguaia) v Brazil*, Preliminary Objections, Merits, Reparations and Costs, 24 November 2010, Series C No. 219, para 172.

[298] Weiner 2016, p. 237.

[299] HRC, *Bautista de Arellana v Colombia*, 27 October 1995, Communication No. 563/1993.

rights violations are incompatible with the ICCPR.[300] Though the above positions are firm and assertive, 'so far no international treaty explicitly prohibits the granting of amnesty in respect of grave breaches of fundamental human rights'.[301] An ambiguous state of affairs hence subsists. In fact, amnesties are not looked upon only negatively. Some circumstances, such as the Lomé Peace Accord, may subsist whereby impunity 'offers immense benefits in exchange'.[302] Various national supreme courts 'upheld their countries' amnesty laws because such laws contributed to the achievement of peace, democracy and reconciliation'.[303] Julie Flint and Alex de Waal, co-authors of 'Darfur: A New History of a Long War', have argued that the pursuit of *Omar Al Bashir* could jeopardize attempts for peace and reconciliation.[304] Darryl Robinson also concedes that truth and reconciliation efforts, if used to supplement criminal investigations and prosecutions, offer important benefits that are not provided by prosecution alone.[305] He perceptively notes that 'the problem arises where truth commissions are accompanied by amnesties',[306] certainly not a rare contingency at all. He identified the following exceptional instances, derivative of necessity, which merit a rather favourable consideration of amnesties, all of which must be carefully and narrowly construed:

(a) groups responsible for core crimes (non-State actors) may not be willing to cease hostilities or cede power unless amnesties are granted to them and to their close associates; and
(b) where a new democracy has a fragile hold on power, and the former military is still intact and threatened, launching prosecutions may amount to political suicide.

Evaluating current practice, he cited the Sierra Leone blanket amnesties and the *Slobodan Milošević* case[307] as examples to show, respectively, that such blanket amnesties reinforced a culture of impunity in which brutal acts of mutilation and lawlessness continued, also reminding his readers that the Dayton peace agreement shortly followed the indictment of *Slobodan Milošević*.[308] Hence, prosecutions do

[300] HRC, *Hugo Rodríguez v Uruguay*, 9 August 1994, Communication no. 322/1988, paras 12.3 and 12.4, cited in IACtHR, *Juan Gelman v Uruguay (Merits and Reparations)*, 24 February 2011, Series C No. 221, para 206, n. 249.

[301] *Fred Marguš v Croatia*, above n. 295, para 131.

[302] Schabas 2012, p. 5.

[303] *Fred Marguš v Croatia*, above n. 295, para 112.

[304] Flint J and de Waal A (2009) To Put Justice Before Peace Spells Disaster for Sudan: The Overzealous Pursuit of Omar al-Bashir Could Ruin Years of Diplomatic Progress. The Human Cost Will be Massive, The Guardian. http://www.theguardian.com/commentisfree/2009/mar/06/sudan-war-crimes. Accessed 13 January 2015.

[305] Robinson 2003, p. 484.

[306] Ibid.

[307] For a comprehensive analysis of the factual, historical background and of the prosecution thereof, see Suljagić 2009, pp. 176–204.

[308] Robinson 2003, p. 496.

not necessarily disrupt attempts for peace and reconciliation. It thus seems that the growing distate for amnesties is based upon objective reasons and upon reliable and empirical data which evidences a disconnection between amnesties and democratization.

In so far as suppression conventions[309] are concerned, the granting of amnesties infringes the duties of State parties to these treaties, emanating therefrom. Firstly, such amnesties violate the principle of *bonafide*, the maxim *pacta sunt servanda*, which is the very essence of conventional international law. If a State ratifies a treaty, the specific and sole object of which is the prosecution of individuals for their alleged conduct, it may not, subsequent to such ratification perform a positive act of the will which is diametrically opposed to its initial voluntary decision, that is, the State's decision to sign and ratify the treaty which penalizes that same conduct. Diane Orentlicher categorically states that 'it is widely agreed, however, that international treaties that require State Parties to prosecute a defined offence, such as genocide or torture, would be breached by an amnesty exempting perpetrators of these offences from criminal prosecution'.[310] In her comprehensive review, she later places the Genocide Convention, the CAT and the Geneva Conventions (together with its Additional Protocol) in the same basket to signify that treaties which demand extradition or prosecution are violated by means of an amnesty which effectively prevents prosecution of the same crimes the treaty is intended to prevent and punish.[311] Several treaty bodies have reached the same conclusion even without an explicit stipulation requiring prosecution.[312]Although these conventions do not stipulate that amnesties or pardons are expressly prohibited, the above conclusion is implicit in the nature and objects of the suppression conventions. Additionally, when a State is called upon to prosecute on the basis of customary international law,[313] it also acts on behalf of other States, and therefore owes its obligations towards other States, not only towards State parties to international conventions. This is especially so when a situation arises wherein there exists an *erga omnes* obligation to prosecute either a crime prohibited by a *jus cogens* norm or, at least, a crime subject to universal jurisdiction. At that point, *de lege*, the custodial State loses its right, even if it ever had such right, to grant pardon or amnesty as a means of circumventing the international treaty which penalizes such conduct. In other words, the *aut dedere aut judicare* rule necessarily precludes the validity of amnesties. *Aut dedere aut judicare*, on the one hand, and amnesties on the other hand, seem to be mutually exclusive. A State having a duty to

[309] See, *inter alia*, those enlisted in n. 204.

[310] Orentlicher 2011, p. 217.

[311] Orentlicher 2011, pp. 218–219.

[312] HRC, *Nature of the General Legal Obligation Imposed on State Parties to the Covenant Eighteenth Session*, General Comment, No. 31 [80], 26 May 2004, Doc. CCPR/C/21/Rev.1/Ad.13, para 18, cited in Orentlicher 2011, p. 219.

[313] Kolb states that 'by the practically universal ratification of (or accession to) these conventions, the mandatory jurisdiction over grave breaches has become part of customary international law' (Kolb 2004, p. 260).

prosecute for not extraditing an individual in its custody cannot issue an amnesty in relation to the individual's impugned conduct without violating its international obligations. This duty is easily discernible under conventional international law but may be tougher to identify in customary international law, especially if the custodial State has consistently refused to prosecute individuals in analogous situations, hence possibly being entitled to such inaction by virtue of being a persistent objector. Gerhard Werle has found that 'an across-the-board exemption from criminal responsibility is unacceptable, to the extent that international law imposes a duty to prosecute and punish. This means that general amnesties for crimes under international law are impermissible under customary international law'.[314] In other words, 'if international law imposes on States an uncompromising duty to prosecute and punish every violation, the possibility of adopting amnesties also for low-ranking perpetrators should be ruled out'.[315] But to say that this is settled law might be a bit over the top. Therefore, the sweeping statement to the effect that 'it is now settled law consistent with the letter and spirit of the Nuremberg Principles that amnesties for international crimes are prohibited under international law',[316] might not be so accurate since it does not show the full picture. Such a sweeping statement does not portray that amnesties can be dealt with somewhat differently by conventional international law on the one hand and customary international law on the other hand. Moreover, it does not differentiate between across-the-board (blanket) amnesties on the one hand and specific amnesties with due regard to some rights of victims on the other hand.

Most importantly, it seems that amnesties can be *de facto* rendered externally null and invalid as a result of the application of universal jurisdiction. In *FIDH et al. vs Ould Dah*,[317] the Court was asked to examine the extent to which a Mauritanian amnesty law[318] could bar proceedings for torture against a Mauritanian army captain residing in France. The Court concluded that whatever the legitimacy of an amnesty in the context of a local policy of reconciliation, this law has effect only in the territory of the State concerned and is not opposable to third countries in the context of the application of international law. To this extent, amnesties cannot excuse or restrict a State from prosecuting. A duty to punish offenders has been stressed mainly with regard to extra-judicial and summary executions, disappearances, cases of torture, ill-treatment, and arbitrary arrest and detention.[319] Widespread consensus subsists to the effect that States exercising universal jurisdiction are not bound by any amnesty law enacted or any amnesty deal struck

---

[314] Werle 2009, p. 77.

[315] Sullo 2018, p. 83.

[316] Thompson 2015, p. 105.

[317] *Cour d'Appel de Montpellier, France* (examining magistrate), *FIDH et a l. vs Ould Dah*, Referral of the Case to the *Cour d'Assises*, 25 May 2001, 99/14445.

[318] Article 1 of Mauritanian Amnesty Law (1993) *Journel officiel de la republique islamique de Mauritanie : Loi numero 93-23 du 14 juin 1993 portant Amnistie*, Law No. 93-23, 14 June 1993.

[319] HRC, *Comments on Nigeria*, 24 July 1996, Doc. CCPR/C/79/Add.65 (1996), para 32.

elsewhere.[320] It is now[321] settled that across-the-board exemptions, or rather, general amnesties[322] for core crimes are not allowed under customary international law.[323] Gerhard Werle, referring to *Prosecutor v Kallon and Kamara*,[324] correctly notes that this has a crucial ramification because 'an amnesty in contravention of international law does not prevent prosecution by third States'.[325] Furthermore the IACmmHR has suggested that the national reconciliation context is not enough to validate amnesties[326] whereas the IACtHR went a step further establishing that amnesties for serious violations of fundamental human rights are incompatible with the IACtHR and hence inadmissible.[327] Christine Bakker notes that 'the Inter-American case law indeed constitutes a strong precedent prohibiting the State Parties to the American Convention from passing amnesty laws. Although formally a decision of the IACtHR in a particular case only has legal consequences for the State in question, e.g. Perú in the *Barrios Altos* case, they provide authoritative interpretations of the Convention'.[328] The Icelandic Supreme Court determined that decisions of the Strasbourg authorities are important for the purposes of the interpretation and application of the legal provisions of the ECvHR within the Icelandic domestic system itself.[329] Besides having this desirable quality, decisions of human rights courts can also permeate the field of criminal jurisdiction within the defendant State. The judgment of the IACtHR in the *Barrios Altos* case prompted the Peruvian Courts to prosecute army personnel for the killing of civilians, despite municipal amnesty laws.[330] The Argentinian Supreme Court of Justice relied on the *Barrios Altos* pronouncement in so far as it 'represents an "essential interpretation guideline" which is of "imperative" application to the Argentinian case'.[331] The IACtHR also solicited the Guatemalan Supreme Court to reinstate a verdict (which

---

[320] *Prosecutor v Anto Furundžija*, above n. 35, para 155.

[321] Before the millennium John Dugard opined that the law is 'to put it mildly, unsettled' (Dugard 1999a, p. 1015).

[322] Brown 2002, pp. 203 et seq.; Schwartz 2004, pp. 317 et seq.

[323] Article 10 of the Statute of the SCSL (2002) Statute of the Special Court for Sierra Leone and Principle 7 of the Princeton Principles on Universal Jurisdiction (2001) Princeton Project on Universal Jurisdiction, 23 July 2001. William Schabas, quoting various authors, recently stated that 'there is a growing body of authority indicating that amnesties are not only frowned upon by human rights law, they may even be prohibited' (Schabas 2011, p. 373).

[324] SCSL Appeals Chamber, *Prosecutor v Morris Kallon and Brima Bazzy Kamara, Decision on Challenge to Jurisdiction: Lomé Accord Amnesty*, 13 March 2004, Case No. SCSL-2004-15-AR72 (E) and Case No. SCSL-2004-16-AR72(E), paras 67 et seq.

[325] Werle 2009, p. 77.

[326] Roht-Arriaza 2000, p. 79.

[327] *Barrios Altos* case, above n. 296, paras 41–44.

[328] Bakker 2005, p. 1112.

[329] *Hæstiréttur Íslands* [Supreme Court, Iceland], *Jón Kristinsson v Iceland*, 25 November 1985, Case No. 77/1985, cited by Björgvinsson 2015, pp. 144–148, and especially p. 147, n. 58.

[330] Cassese 2002a, pp. 1–29, cited in Ferdinandusse 2004, p. 1047, n. 20.

[331] Ayala 2016, p. 311.

was overturned on appeal) which found three senior officials responsible for the murder of *Myrna Mack Chang*, an outspoken Mayan-Chinese anthropologist.[332] By doing so, the regional human rights court exerts pressure on States to suppress impunity.[333] The penetration of such *dicta* does not only occur within the domestic State itself, but in internationalized (hybrid) criminal tribunals. The jurisprudence of the IACtHR has been explicitly referred to by the SCSL when it declared without effect the Lomé Peace Accords which granted absolute pardon to all combatants for anything done by them in pursuit of their objectives.[334] Yasmin Naqvi predicates that, in the absence of an explicit international conventional rule prohibiting amnesties over core crimes, domestic courts habitually take the following factors into account when examining whether they have jurisdiction over an individual, these being:

1. the scope of the obligation to prosecute core crimes;
2. whether victims' fundamental human rights vitiate the amnesty law; and
3. whether States are constrained not to amnesty core crimes due to their peremptory character.[335]

The latter element, the *jus cogens* status of the prohibition of core crimes, is, in the words of William Schabas, the reason why amnesties over core crimes are generally prohibited.[336] Yet, this is not necessarily a favourable outcome since it can cause friction between two important areas of law, international human rights law on the one hand and international criminal law on the other hand. The synergy between these areas of law stumbles because victims of horrific crimes which do not constitute core crimes do not benefit from the general prohibition of amnesties.[337] Notwithstanding that the two areas of law are deemed to be complementary for the purposes of most grounds of refusal of extradition being considered within Part IV, this does not apply to amnesties.

Jurisprudence points to the fulfilment of the following five State obligations in confronting gross violations of fundamental human rights committed by a previous regime:

i. investigate the identity, fate and whereabouts of victims;
ii. investigate the identity of major perpetrators;
iii. provide reparation or compensation to victims;

[332] IACtHR, *Myrna Mack Chang v Guatemala*, Merits, Reparations and Costs, 25 November 2003, Ser. C No. 101, cited in Robinson 2016, p. 119, n. 92.

[333] Robinson 2016, p. 119.

[334] *Prosecutor v Morris Kallon and Brima Bazzy Kamara*, above n. 324, para 84, cited in Aksenova 2017, p. 76, n. 31.

[335] Naqvi 2010, pp. 110–143.

[336] Schabas 2013, p. 219.

[337] Ibid.

iv. take affirmative steps to ensure that fundamental human rights abuses do not recur; and
v. punish those guilty of fundamental human rights abuses.[338]

It is thus becoming increasingly evident that amnesties are constantly skating on thin ice. At the very least, though not categorically prohibited in all circumstances, as recommended by Anja Siebert-Fohr, a rebuttable presumption that amnesties are detrimental to the protection of human rights should subsist.[339] Ward Ferdinandusse broadens this by identifying a strong presumption, under current international law, against amnesties for serious crimes.[340] This is more so where core crimes are concerned. The HRC, for example, upheld that crimes against humanity may not be amnestied,[341] whereas the UN Committee Against Torture reached the same conclusion specifically in relation to torture.[342] State practice also seems to undertake such path.[343] Congo and Ecuador have legislated specifically to the effect that core crimes 'cannot be the object of an amnesty or a pardon'.[344] On the same lines, amnesties for core crimes are outlawed under international law, especially since 'it is now more and more acknowledged that the granting of amnesty is either totally prohibited where universal jurisdiction is mandatory, or inappropriate where there is a customary international law duty to prosecute or extradite…There are strong legal reasons to believe that amnesties are invalid in the case of international crimes. Furthermore, there are also important moral arguments suggesting the total inadequacy of such measures when applied to international core crimes'.[345] I remark, whilst citing the above, that since universal jurisdiction is not mandatory, Caroline Fournet must have been referring to compelling reasons to exercise universal jurisdiction in the above extract of her work.

In the *Miguel Ángel Sandoval Rodríguez* case, the Supreme Court of Chile,[346] considering the Villa Grimaldi torture centre in Santiago operated by *DINA* between 1974 and 1976 and the aggravated abduction[347] and subsequent disappearance of

338 Scharf 1999, p. 514.

339 Vandeginste 2012, p. 243.

340 Ferdinandusse 2006, p. 202.

341 HRC, *Concluding Observations on Guatemala*, 27 August 2001, CCPR/CO/72/GTM, para 12.

342 Committee Against Torture (2000) Report: Twenty-third session (8–19 November 1999) and Twenty-fourth session (1–19 May 2000), UN GAOR, 55th Session, Supp. 44, UN Doc. A/55/44, para 59(g).

343 The amnesty called for in Guatemala's peace agreement {Guatemala's Peace Agreement (1996) The Accord for a Firm and Lasting Peace between the Government of Guatemala and the *Unidad Revolucionaria Nacional Guatemalteca* [Guatemalan National Revolutionary Unit], 29 December 1996} explicitly excludes very serious crimes (Seibert-Fohr 2005, p. 576, n. 84).

344 Zahar and Sluiter 2008, p. 519.

345 Fournet 2006, pp. 228 and 231.

346 *Corte Suprema de Justicia de Chile* [Supreme Court, Chile], *Juan Contreras Sepúlveda y Otros (Crimen) Casación Fondo y Forma*, 17 November 2004, 517/2004.

347 *Secuestro calificado* [aggravated abduction].

Sandoval, held that such abduction is tantamount to the crime of enforced disappearances, which crime, in turn, constitutes a crime against humanity entailing a multitude of consequences, one of which is the non-applicability of amnesties and statutes of limitations.[348] The *Julio Hector Simón* case is the icing on the cake, the destination point of this trend. Here, the Argentinian Supreme Court,[349] whilst declaring the *Obediencia Debida* and *Punto Final* amnesty laws[350] unconstitutional and retroactively null and void, categorically held that 'all amnesty provisions, provisions on prescription and …measures designed to eliminate responsibility are inadmissible, because they are intended to prevent the investigation and punishment of those responsible for serious human rights violations …, and violate non-derogable rights recognized by international human rights law'.[351] Most importantly, in this case the Argentinian Supreme Court determined that, besides violating the IACvHR, amnesty laws also infringe the duty to prosecute that derives from other sources of international law, both of a customary and of a conventional nature, the ICCPR and the CAT being examples of the latter. Judge Maqueda went as far as opining that the State obligation to prosecute crimes against humanity emanates from a *jus cogens* norm which already existed at the time when the crimes were consummated.[352] The HRC also found that a state of impunity 'encourages further violations of Covenant rights',[353] inferring that the punishment of those committing core crimes has a deterrent effect. It further held that impunity constitutes 'a retroactive ratification of the offences committed'.[354]

There exist instances, however, where amnesties have a substitutive effect in that they could effectively replace an obstacle to extradition. In this way, amnesties can block an extradition for reasons which are different from those which were initially pleaded. They hence appear to facilitate extradition because they abate serious concerns relating to the initial grounds which were pleaded by the extraditee, only to constitute a separate and new ground for refusal. Tom Obokata upholds that amnesties or pardons 'are appropriate particularly when criminals receive harsh punishments, such as the death penalty'.[355] This, however, does not lead to a situation where two negatives, two pitfalls, coincide to make a positive, to allow extradition, keeping in mind that extradition may also be prompted post-conviction. For the two negatives to make a positive, Article 6(4) of the ICCPR must be

[348] Lafontaine 2005, pp. 469–470 and 479–484.

[349] *Corte Suprema de Justicia de la Nación, Argentina, Julio Héctor Simón y otros v Poder Judicial de la Nación*, 14 June 2005, 17.768 S.1767. XXXVIII.

[350] *Obediencia Debida* [Due Obedience] Law No. 23-521, Argentina, 4 June 1987, and *Punto Final* [Full Stop] Law No. 23-492, Argentina, 23 December 1986.

[351] *Julio Héctor Simón y otros v Poder Judicial de la Nación*, above n. 349.

[352] *Julio Héctor Simón y otros v Poder Judicial de la Nación*, above n. 349, Opinion of Justice Dr. Don Juan Carlos Maqueda, para 57.

[353] HRC, *Hugo Rodríguez v Uruguay*, 9 August 1994, Communication no. 322/1988, para 2.4.

[354] HRC, *Summary Record of the 1519th Meeting, Peru*, 1 November 1996, Document CCPR/C/SR.1519 (1997), para 44.

[355] Obokata 2010, p. 99.

rigorously followed, in that those 'sentenced to death have the right to seek pardon or commutation of the sentence'. Rather than applying to amnesties, however, this legal provision seems to apply to special cases dealing with the infliction of the death penalty. To secure that the rights of victims are duly safeguarded, it will then be up to the domestic criminal courts to ensure that such sentences are commuted rather than pardons are granted. The discussion on amnesties can be summed up by quoting the conclusions of the ECtHR to the effect that 'a growing tendency in international law is to see such amnesties as unacceptable because they are incompatible with the unanimously recognised obligation of States to prosecute and punish grave breaches of fundamental human rights'.[356] This trend has permeated domestic politics, which penetration can be noted in the rejection of the *FARC*-Government proposed peace deal by the Colombian electorate in the October 2016 referendum.[357]

16.6 Plea Bargaining

A plea-bargain is not to be confused with an out-of-court settlement or a compromise agreement undertaken in another State.[358] It is hard to identify a uniform definition of a plea bargain because plea bargains vary from one legal system, be it a common law system or else a continental law system, to another, especially in terms of their validity, application and execution.[359] Although technically it can take the form of a fully-fledged agreement or contract, in some jurisdictions between the defence, prosecution and the court itself, it generally presupposes an admission of guilt and a concession or discount in sentencing, and has, for this reason, been looked upon negatively by many scholars.[360] As a result of the uncontested gravity and the potential trans-national nature of core crimes, it is hard to conceive of any plea-bargaining as a barrier to extradition since this would imply that the requesting State has made an agreement with the offender in relation to his/her plea and sentencing/punishment without even consulting/informing the requested State which, with the growth in cross-frontier and trans-boundary crime, is most likely to be of assistance in evidence-collection and information. Extradition

---

[356] *Fred Marguš v Croatia*, above n. 295, para 139.

[357] Brodzinsky S (2016) Colombia's Brexit Moment as Politicians Misjudge Popular Anger at FARC Amnesty: All Sides Left Shocked by Narrow Rejection Which Would Have Seen Guerrillas Guilty of War Crimes Escape Jail, The Guardian, Bogotá. https://www.theguardian.com/world/2016/oct/03/colombias-peace-further-away-is-further-away-but-it-may-still (accessed 2 May 2017).

[358] In accordance with Article 68 of the Dutch Criminal Code (1881) Criminal Code of the Kingdom of the Netherlands, as supplemented by the Criminal Policy Plan on Society and Crime (1985), this would have a similar effect as *ne bis in idem* since it bars re-prosecution before Dutch Courts provided that the accused complied with the terms and conditions set out in the settlement.

[359] For a comparative analysis between the USA system and the German system, see Schuon 2010, pp. 76–108.

[360] Amoury Combs 2008, p. 561.

should thus proceed anyway, and, in the worst scenario/hypothesis the extradited individual would be able either to plead *ne bis in idem* once he is brought before the judicial authorities of the requesting State or sue the requested State for failure to uphold the plea-bargain/agreement. There have rarely been plea bargains both in relation to core crimes[361] and also in relation to crimes which lie on the brink of being categorised as core crimes.[362] Whereas the vertical system of enforcement admitted plea-bargaining for various reasons,[363] the horizontal system of enforcement has not attached equal importance to such mechanism. Moreover, as stated in relation to speciality, a deal consummating a plea bargain can be struck only with the State enjoying jurisdiction over the extradited person. Thus, a plea bargain, *per se*, would generally follow rather than obstruct an extradition. It would only hinder the extradition process if and when the plea bargain is being negotiated on a tri-partite level, *id est* involving the requesting State, the requested State and the individual. It could also be agreed to by the respective States as a pre-condition to an extradition. In any case, its potential to constitute a pitfall within the extradition process is indeed restricted. In fact State practice to this effect is scant, if not inexistent.

The most damaging dimension of a plea-bargain is elicited when it is made conditional upon the fulfilment of certain factors. A plea-bargain may, for example, subsist in circumstances whereby it is being tendered and predicated contemporaneously with a significant discount/reduction in a sentence, which discount/reduction verges on being categorised as an amnesty. The plea-bargain would lead to a final and definitive judgment which benefits the prosecution, hence avoiding time and expenses to try the accused, whilst it also benefits the accused who, rather than enduring a trial and risking a hefty punishment, receives a much milder sentence. It however triggers *ne bis in idem* protection, both locally/domestically (within the same jurisdiction) and probably also vis-à-vis other States, *id est* within the horizontal system of enforcement. To this extent, it can hamper extradition. The same cannot be said about surrender to the ICC because, as explained within Part III, any accompanying pardon or amnesty would probably not escape the 'genuinely unwilling' criterion.

[361] Court of BiH, *Prosecutor's Office of BiH v Slavko Šakić*, Verdict, 29th October 2008, X-KR-05141-1.

[362] High Court, Transvaal Provincial Division, South Africa, *The State v Johannes Velde van der Merwe and four others*, Plea and Sentencing Agreement in Terms of Section 105A of Act 51 of 1977 (as amended), 17 August 2007.

[363] The main reasons are to avoid a backlog of cases and instead expedite investigations and prosecutions, to acquire the testimony of witnesses, to obtain information and prosecute those most responsible for having committed core crimes, and finally, in so far as ICTY and ICTR are concerned, 'to comply with the Security Council's insistence that the international tribunals close their doors' (Amoury Combs 2008, p. 577).

16.7 Human Rights General Exceptions to Extraditions

Grounds under Sects. 16.7.1–16.7.4 are largely of a constitutional nature, in that they are tantamount to reasons which may be invoked by individuals before municipal courts either to prevent extradition or to challenge the exercise of criminal jurisdiction and eventual prosecution. Such grounds may be invoked both domestically and regionally because the human right to individual petition is exercisable, as a last resort,[364] against the State before a regional court or supervisory body which monitors human rights protection within a particular region,[365] or internationally before the HRC. These mechanisms entail that when a State extradites an individual subject to its jurisdiction to another State, the former State is directly responsible for any foreseeable violation of a fundamental human right the extraditee may suffer in the latter State.[366] The extent to which the violation is foreseeable and the degree of foreseeability remain prerogatives of the sending State.[367] These regional courts may be considered to be standardized balancing devices, because they are frequently called upon to effectively decide which right prevails over the other, given a multi-dimensional scenario containing various stakeholders of rights, such as, *inter alia*, the State, the community, the victims of crime and the individual, whether he is a deportee, an extraditee or an asylum seeker. To this extent, the impact which international human rights law and practice have on extradition is substantial,[368] particularly in relation to the absolute rights since 'human rights do not enjoy equal weight when it comes to extradition'.[369] International human rights law equips individuals with a *locus standi* they would not possess in a rigid inter-State and executive matter such as extradition. Such *locus standi* is more pronounced in some jurisdictions rather than others. For example, in the Netherlands, although good faith[370] is generally presumed, Courts allow the defendant in extradition proceedings to raise the argument that their fundamental human rights have been or may be violated in the requesting State,[371]

---

[364] This conveys that ordinary and domestic remedies at law would have to be exhausted first.

[365] The ECtHR, the IACtHR and the ACmmHPR.

[366] ECtHR, *Hector Cruz Varas et al. v Sweden*, 20 March 1991, Application No. 15576/89, Series A No. 201, para 70; ECtHR, *Félix Tomasi v France*, 27 August 1992, Application No. 12850/87, Series A No. 241-A, para 115.

[367] The Federal Constitutional Court of Germany [*Bundersverfassungsgericht*] has found that 'extradition to States that have a consistent pattern of comprehensive and systematic violations of human rights will, as a general rule, establish the probability of a violation of the fundamental principles of the German constitutional order' {*Bundesverfassungsgericht* [Federal Constitution Court, Germany], *G, a citizen of Vanuatu and his motion for a temporary injunction, Order of the Second Senate*, 24 June 2003, 2 BvR 685/03, para 37}. States must hence ensure their track record remains untainted.

[368] Reydams 2003a, p. 18.

[369] Dugard and van den Wyngaert 1998, p. 210.

[370] *Vertrouwensbeginsel.*

[371] Swart 1997, p. 95.

whereas the Irish courts can scrutinize the requesting State's judicial system to determine whether the prevailing standards in the requesting State meet Irish constitutional standards.[372] In this way the Irish adopt an internalized test by measuring the potential risk of a violation in the requested State against its own laws. If the requested extradition would 'expose him to practices or procedures which if exercised within this State would amount to infringements of this constitutional right to fair and just procedures',[373] Irish Courts will refuse extradition. This approach shows the extent to which human rights exceptions to extradition are rooted in domestic extradition laws and serve to block extradition.

Due process rights have a broad jurisdictional reach. In discharging the defendant *Ejup Ganic*, the City of Westminster Magistrates' Court found that a politically motivated prosecution 'at a time when the Serbian Government was attempting to pass a resolution in the Serbian Parliament apologising for the *Srebrenica* massacre of 1995' amounted to an abuse of process consisting in the fact 'that there would be enormous pressure to convict because if he were acquitted there would be uproar in Belgrade'.[374] On the other hand, in so far as the EAW is concerned, although an important reference to human rights is expressly made within the twelveth and thirteenth paragraphs of the Preamble[375] and although the EAW has 'some bars to surrender, a potential breach of fundamental human rights in the issuing State is not explicitly listed amongst them'.[376] EU Member States seem to have a sufficient degree of trust in their respective judicial systems.

Not all fundamental human rights could actually bar extradition, notwithstanding the fact that the ICJ has acknowledged that the UDHR conveys some persuasive, if not binding, obligations,[377] although leading experts John Dugard and Chistine van den Wyngaert have recognized a nascent but expanding 'human rights' general exception to extradition.[378] It seems that this exception can be curtailed by resorting to a mutual understanding of certain binding treaty provisions which infer the necessity to conduct trials fairly. For example, in the case of *Jean Claude Iyamuremye*,[379] since both the Netherlands and Rwanda are parties to the Genocide Convention (the sixth and seventh articles of which imply the fair trial requisite),

[372] Supreme Court, Ireland, *Finucane v McMahon*, 13 March 1990, [1990] 1 I.R. 165; Supreme Court, Ireland, *Seamus Shannon v Ireland*, January 1984, Irish Reports 548, cited in Dugard and van den Wyngaert 1998, p. 191, n. 24.

[373] Supreme Court, Ireland, *Ellis v O'Dea*, 1989, Irish Reports 530, cited in Forde and Kelly 2011, p. 116, n. 145.

[374] City of Westminster Magistrates' Court, Great Britain, UK, *The Government of the Republic of Serbia v Ejup Ganić*, Decision on Extradition, 27 July 2010, [2010] EW Misc 11 (MC), paras 26 and 30.

[375] Framework Decision on the EAW, above n. 71.

[376] Mackarel 2007, p. 41.

[377] ICJ, *United States Diplomatic and Consular Staff in Tehran (USA v Iran) (Iranian Hostages Case)*, 24 May 1980, [1980] ICJ Rep. 3, para 91.

[378] Dugard and van den Wyngaert 1998, p. 187.

[379] *The State of The Netherlands (Ministry of Security and Justice) v Jean Claude I*, above n. 62.

the Extradition Chamber of the District Court of The Hague applied a marginal test ruling that extradition would not lead to 'a flagrant denial of a fair trial'.[380] Reliance on a treaty or on the incorporation of its provisions into domestic law is also crucially important to establish both a jurisdictional basis in the first place and an eventual extradition. In fact, even if universal jurisdiction is not relied upon, if genocide is a crime both under Danish Law and Rwandan Law, extradition may proceed accordingly even for a crime committed outside Denmark. Although this demonstrates the double (dual) criminality requirement, a term not referred to within the judgment of the Danish Supreme Court, the focus of the Danish Supreme Court's reasons and findings was on the universal scope of the prohibition of genocide. Genocide committed outside Denmark (in this case, in Rwanda) anyway violates the Danish Genocide Act which penalises genocide for the purposes of Danish law.[381]

What applies to a mere declaration of principles such as the UDHR, *multo magis*, applies to the binding provisions of the ICCPR, a multi-lateral instrument which is closely linked to the UNC by means of its Preamble, which generally uses mandatory language and which has been ratified by a large majority of States. To this extent, the jurisdictional reach of the ICCPR is overwhelming particularly because it 'applies wherever a person is subject to the jurisdiction or effective control of a party to the treaty'.[382] As a result of this, the decisions of the HRC will be given due weight within Sects. 16.7.1–16.7.4, all of which relate to human rights which could potentially obstruct extradition. It has been argued that most ICCPR legal provisions have helped create norms of customary international law, binding even States which have yet to ratify it.[383] This conclusion has also been reached jurisprudentially when the prohibition of torture was being scrutinized.[384] As a

[380] The 'flagrant denial of a fair trial' requirement carries a very high burden of proof, a sort of *diabolica probatio*. Harmen van der Wilt notes that the *Al-Moayad* case shows that the requirements for a prospective violation of fair trial rights which would impede extradition are quite demanding. The European Court of Human Rights has until now never accepted such a claim [ECtHR Fifth Section, *Mohammed Ali Hassan Al-Moayad vs Germany, Decision on Admissibility*, 20 February 2007, Application No. 35865/03, para 101, cited in van der Wilt 2012a, p. 159].

[381] *Højesteret* [Supreme Court of Denmark], *Prosecution Service v T* (Attorney Bjørn Elmquist, appointed), Order, 26 April 2012, Case 2/2012.

[382] ICJ, *Legal Consequences of the Construction of a Wall in the Occupied Palestinian Territory (Israeli Wall Advisory Opinion)*, Advisory Opinion, 9 July 2004, ICJ GL No. 131, [2004] ICJ Rep. 136, paras 108–111.

[383] Lillich 1984, pp. 115–170. Here one must state that whereas Meron opines that the amount of evidence necessary for the establishment of a customary norm often depends on whether a violation of it triggered a broad condemnation by the international community, hence rendering *opinio juris* alone as the sole and exclusive determining factor, Cassese supports the formation of customary international criminal law under the influence of *opinio juris* alone if the new customary rule is reflected in the *Martens* clause, that is, the laws of humanity or the dictates of public conscience (Schlutter 2010, pp. 42–44).

[384] USA Court of Appeals, Second Circuit, *Dolly and Joel Filártiga v Americo Norberto Peña-Irala*, 30 June 1980, No. 191, Docket 79-6090, 630 F.2d 876.

matter of fact, the ICCPR, by virtue of its above mentioned judicial body,[385] also aided the ECtHR in reaching its decisions within some landmark cases.[386] Conversely, the ECtHR has played a major role in coining customary international law since the *Soering* jurisprudence[387] predated important *dicta* of the HRC such as *Ng*[388] and *Kindler*.[389] Jurists acknowledge both the significance of the pronouncements of the HRC, particularly as a result of the legally binding obligations emanating from the ICCPR itself,[390] and the fact that the HRC's pronouncements play an important role at national level.[391] At this juncture, mention must be made of the fact that a recent and reliable study has found that 'a general supremacy of all human rights over extradition obligations does not exist'.[392] This is so only unless an express clause within an extradition treaty explicitly stipulates otherwise. I will now separately consider (under Sects. 16.7.1–16.7.4) the grounds for refusal of extradition which have a human rights dimension.

16.7.1 The Right to a Fair Trial

This right 'is a fundamental element of international human rights law as it applies to the criminal trial process at both the domestic and the international level'.[393] The prospect of a real risk of an unfair trial,[394] *per se*, has, before the EAW was

---

[385] HRC, *Glenn Ashby v Trinidad and Tobago*, 21 March 2012, Communication No. 580/1994, wherein the HRC was asked to consider a State party's refusal to comply with its request to stay an execution of the petitioner.

[386] Forowicz refers to cases *Mamatkulov and Abdurasulovic v Turkey* [ECtHR First Section, *Rustam Mamatkulov and Askarov Z. Abdurasulovic v Turkey*, 6 February 2003, 46827/99 and 46951/99], and *Mamatkulov and Askarov v Turkey* [ECtHR First Section, *Rustam Mamatkulov and Zainiddin Abdurasulovic Askarov v Turkey*, 4 February 2005, 46827/99 and 46951/99] to the effect that interim measures have a mandatory character under the ECvHR (Forowicz 2010, p. 181).

[387] ECtHR, *Jens Soering v UK*, 7 July 1989, Application No. 14038/88, Series A, Vol. 161.

[388] HRC, *Charles Chitat Ng v Canada*, 7 January 1994, Communication No. 469/191.

[389] HRC, *Joseph Kindler v. Canada*, 11 November 1993, Communication No. 470/1991.

[390] Seibert-Fohr 2002, p. 310.

[391] McGoldrick 1996, p. 504.

[392] van der Wilt 2012a, p. 153.

[393] Boas 2007, p. 15.

[394] The requirements for a fair trial within the horizontal system of enforcement may be said to emerge from Article 14 of the ICCPR. These include equality before courts and tribunals, the right to a public hearing by a competent, independent and impartial tribunal established by law, the right to be presumed innocent until proven guilty and the right to have one's conviction and sentence reviewed by a higher court or tribunal according to law. The following minimum guarantees also fall within the remit of the fair trial regime. These include the right:

(a) to be informed promptly and in detail in a language which he understands of the nature and cause of the charge against him;

established, barred extradition, but not always necessarily to protect the extraditee. In *ex parte Ramda*, the English High Court held that the extradition of *Ramda*, who was wanted for trial in France to respond to changes of involvement in the 1995 Paris Metro bombings, would violate Article 6 of the ECvHR since allegations that incriminating evidence against him had been obtained through torture would not be considered in the substantive trial against him in France.[395] Besides the 'real risk' requirement, the violation of the rights of the extraditee in the territory of the requesting State must be a direct and foreseeable consequence of the decision to extradite.[396] Situations might arise wherein an extradition treaty permits the extradition of an extraditee, but the customary international law status of the protection of the right to a fair trial[397] might get in the way of such extradition. Such status is not to be confused with *jus cogens* status, although Orakhelashvili elevates due process requirements to the *jus cogens* category of norms[398] and eminent experts have categorised due process rights as 'core human rights'.[399] A State may be obliged to extradite under the *aut dedere aut judicare* rule in the absence of its domestic prosecution of an extraditee but may be simultaneously duty bound to refuse such extradition since it is likely to lead to an unfair trial. It seems that, in such instances, the protection of the right to a fair trial would not eliminate the international obligation to extradite. This is because such right is not *jus cogens*, unlike the prohibition of torture which would override the State's international obligation. Where a State effectively refuses to extradite on the basis of a 'lack of

---

(b) to have adequate time and facilities for the preparation of his defence and to communicate with counsel of his own choosing;
(c) to be tried without undue delay;
(d) to be tried in his presence, and to defend himself in person or through legal assistance of his own choosing; to be informed, if he does not have legal assistance, of this right; and to have legal assistance assigned to him, in any case where the interests of justice so require, and without payment by him in any such case if he does not have sufficient means to pay for it;
(e) to examine, or have examined, the witnesses against him and to obtain the attendance and examination of witnesses on his behalf under the same conditions as witnesses against him;
(f) to have the free assistance of an interpreter if he cannot understand or speak the language used in court; and
(g) not to be compelled to testify against himself or to confess guilt.

Within the vertical system of enforcement, Articles 66 and 67 of the ICC Statute, above n. 20, cater for the applicable fair trial rights.

[395] Fletcher et al. 2008, p. 124.

[396] *Soering v UK*, above n. 387, para 91.

[397] Swart, considering the right to a fair trial, upholds that 'the importance of human rights treaties for criminal justice at the national level is mainly that they state meta-principles of fairness which all systems of justice have to respect. These principles may have different consequences for different national systems, and each State has to integrate them in the framework of its own specific system of justice. They create obligations of result and leave States free to determine how these results can be achieved' (Swart 2009, p. 100).

[398] Orakhelashvili 2006, p. 60.

[399] Dugard and van den Wyngaert 1998, p. 193.

effective or fair prosecution' in the requesting State, it is left 'with the duty to initiate prosecution'.[400] Most cases wherein the right to a fair trial is made use of by defendants to hinder their extradition to the requesting State relate:

i. to the requirement of an independent and impartial court or tribunal,[401] which requirement is negated by prejudice or bias;
ii. to the right to cross-examine prosecution witnesses;[402] and
iii. to the right to produce witnesses in one's defence, the latter being reflective of the doctrine of equality of arms.[403]

The concept of 'equality of arms'[404] is an important component of a fair trial, although its ultimate rationale is what may be described as the 'right not to be

---

[400] Paust et al. 2007, p. 17.

[401] See the report of the appointed expert, William Schabas, in High Court of Justice, Divisional Court, on Appeal from the City of Westminster Magistrates' Court (District Judge Evans) and in the Matter for Judicial Review, Great Britain (UK), *Vincent Brown aka Vincent Bajinja, Charles Munyaneza, Emmanuel Nteziryayo & Celestin Ugirashebuja v The Government of Rwanda and the Secretary of State for the Home Department*, Appeal Against Extradition, 8 April 2009, Case CO/6247/2008, para 108. In this report, Schabas reached the conclusion that, subject to international scrutiny, fair trials in Kigali were not an unlikely prospect predominantly because:

i. a vigorous defence bar subsisted;
ii. detention occurred in places which meet international standards; and
iii. transfer from ICTR to domestic Rwandan criminal courts met international standards.

A few days after this landmark judgment, which determined that extraditing four suspected *genocidiaires* to Rwanda constituted a real risk that the men would suffer a 'flagrant denial of justice' both by reason of their likely inability to adduce the evidence of supporting witnesses and by interference in the judiciary by the government of Rwanda, leading to the release of the four men, the Supreme Court of Sweden {*Högsta Domstolens* [Supreme Court], Sweden, *Decision on Sylvère Ahorugeze Extradition to Rwanda*, 26 May 2009, Ö 1082-09} authorised *Sylvère Ahorugeze's* extradition to Rwanda notwithstanding alleged shortcomings of the Rwandan criminal justice system, the extraditees' poor health and his refugee status. The extraditee resorted to the Strasbourg authorities. The ECtHR decided that Sweden could extradite a Rwandan genocide suspect to Kigali, Rwanda [ECtHR Fifth Section, *Sylvère Ahorugeze v Sweden*, 27 October 2011, Application No. 37075/09].

[402] *Zentai v Honourable Brendan O'Connor*, above n. 82, para 224. Defence counsel submitted that reliance by the prosecution on statements of deceased persons meant that such witnesses may not be cross-examined at trial and that consequently *Zentai's* trial in Hungary, wherein he would be asked to answer for war crimes, would breach Article 14(3)(e) of the ICCPR [*vide* para 38.3]. *Zentai's* lawyer, concluding his remarks, submitted that 'extensive particulars are supplied in support of the contention that there could be no guarantee of a fair trial before the Military Panel' [*vide* para 76].

[403] In *Vincent Brown aka Vincent Bajinja, Charles Munyaneza, Emmanuel Nteziryayo & Celestin Ugirashebuja vs The Government of Rwanda and the Secretary of State for the Home Department*, above n. 401, the appellants contended that a fair trial would be negated by the apprehension that witnesses who could give important evidence for the defence will be too afraid either of possible reprisals to testify or to travel to Rwanda for such purpose [*vide* para 37].

[404] This concept 'requires a fair balance between the parties' (White and Ovey 2010, p. 261). The ECtHR held that what matters is that parties are afforded a reasonable opportunity to present their case – including their evidence under conditions that do not place them under a substantial

convicted of offences of which one is innocent'.[405] The above list (*id est* i–iii) is not exhaustive. Other due process guarantees successfully made use of by defendants to block an extradition include, for example, the right to be tried within a reasonable time.[406]

Nowadays, it is settled that the ECtHR would require a rampant violation of fair trial rights for an extradition to conflict with Article 6 of the ECvHR,[407] this being the legal provision which safeguards fair trial rights.[408] In their joint partly dissenting opinion, Judges Bratza, Bonello and Hedigan motivated their reasoning which led to the establishment of their conviction that a flagrant violation would subsist, should the applicants be extradited to Uzbekistan. In the process they defined the term 'flagrant' and held as follows:

> 'What constitutes a "flagrant" denial of justice has not been fully explained in the Court's jurisprudence, but the use of the adjective is clearly intended to impose a stringent test of unfairness going beyond mere irregularities or lack of safeguards in the trial procedures such as might result in a breach of Article 6 if occurring within the Contracting State itself'.[409] 'As in the case of the risk of treatment proscribed by Article 3 of the Convention, the risk of a flagrant denial of justice in the receiving State for the purposes of Article 6 must be assessed primarily by reference to the facts which were known or should have been known by the respondent State at the time of the extradition'.[410]

The ECtHR delved into the extent to which the above test was stringent and the *onus probandi* required to prove such flagrant denial of justice. It held that:

> It should be noted that, in the twenty-two years since the *Soering* judgment, the Court has never found that an extradition or expulsion would be in violation of Article 6. This indicates that the "flagrant denial of justice" test is a stringent one. A flagrant denial of

disadvantage vis-à-vis the other side [ECtHR, *Dombo Beheer BV v The Netherlands*, Application No. 14448/88, 27 October 1993, Series A No. 274, para 33]. Jurists, noting that due process rights also apply to civil proceedings, have commented to the effect that 'for criminal cases, where the very character of the proceedings involves a fundamental inequality of the parties, this principle of "equality of arms" is even more important' (van Dijk et al. 2006, p. 580).

405 Choo 1995, p. 865.

406 *The Government of the Russian Federation v Akhmed Zakaev*, above n. 136. For an understanding of the criteria used by the ECtHR to determine the reasonableness or otherwise of the time, see ECtHR, Fourth Section, *Nazzareno Zarb v Malta*, 4 July 2006, Application No. 16631/04, para 34.

407 Some eminent jurists have argued that the 'European Convention on Human Rights can be considered to reflect customary international law. It is true that this is only a regional convention and therefore the ensuing State practice is by definition limited, but this Convention dates from 1950 and served as a model for the ICCPR' (Zahar and Sluiter 2008, p. 279).

408 *Rustam Mamatkulov and Zainiddin Abdurasulovic Askarov v Turkey*, above n. 386, Joint Partly Dissenting Opinion of Judges Bratza, Bonello and Hedigan. For an understanding of the concept of a fair trial and of the evolution of this concept in international criminal law, see Soler 1999, pp. 12–38.

409 *Mamatkulov and Askarov v Turkey*, above n. 386, Joint Partly Dissenting Opinion of Judges Bratza, Bonello and Hedigan, para 14.

410 *Mamatkulov and Askarov v Turkey*, above n. 386, Joint Partly Dissenting Opinion of Judges Bratza, Bonello and Hedigan, para 15.

> justice goes beyond mere irregularities or lack of safeguards in the trial procedures such as might result in a breach of Article 6 if occurring within the Contracting State itself. What is required is a breach of the principles of fair trial guaranteed by Article 6 which is so fundamental as to amount to a nullification, or destruction of the very essence, of the right guaranteed by that Article. In executing this test, the Court considers that the same standard and burden of proof should apply as in the examination of extraditions and expulsions under Article 3. Accordingly, it is for the applicant to adduce evidence capable of proving that there are substantial grounds for believing that, if removed from a Contracting State, he would be exposed to a real risk of being subjected to a flagrant denial of justice. Where such evidence is adduced, it is for the Government to dispel any doubts about it (see, *mutatis mutandis*, *Saadi v. Italy* [GC], no. 37201/06, § 129, ECHR 2008-...).[411]

The Strasbourg Court has also recently undertaken a comparative analysis of the 'flagrant denial of justice'[412] test, whilst differentiating clearly between the prevailing facts and circumstances in the *Mamatkulov* case and those in the important *Abu Qatada* case. In the latter case,[413] the ECtHR concluded that the applicant's deportation to Jordan would violate his fair trial rights on account of the real risk of the admission at the applicant's retrial of evidence obtained by torture of third persons, namely *Abu Hawsher* and *Al-Hamasher*. *Abu Qatada* was deported to Jordan in July 2013 following the signature of a treaty signed by Jordan and the UK by means of which Jordan guaranteed that evidence obtained by torture would not be used against *Abu Qatada*[414] who was not found guilty on charges of conspiracy to carry out terrorist attacks.[415] Besides being of a ground-breaking nature, the ECtHR *dictum* fascinatingly blends the right to a fair trial with the general prohibition of torture, this symbiosis having already been adopted by domestic courts.[416] In all fairness, the ECtHR had already done so in considering the application by Yemeni national *Mohammed Ali Hasan Al-Moayad*, where it authoritatively held as follows:

> The Court reiterates that it cannot be ruled out that an issue might exceptionally arise under Article 6 of the Convention by an extradition decision in circumstances where the fugitive has suffered or risks suffering a flagrant denial of a fair trial in the requesting country (see *Soering*, cited above, p. 45, § 113; *Einhorn*, cited above, § 32; and *Mamatkulov and Askarov*, cited above, § 88). It considers that, like the risk of treatment proscribed by Article

[411] *Sylvère Ahorugeze v Sweden*, 27 October 2011, above n. 401, paras 115–116.

[412] As opposed to European jurists, Jan Paulsson notes that Latin American jurists came to take the narrowest possible view of of the scope of denial of justice (see Paulsson 2005, p. 24).

[413] ECtHR Fourth Section, *Omar Othman (Abu Qatada) v UK*, 17 January 2012, Application No. 8139/09, para 282.

[414] Most domestic courts tend to uphold that when an accused person is not able to hear witnesses, this does not *ipso facto* lead to the exclusion of such statements. In fact, these could be used if they are adequately supported by additional evidence [District Court of Rotterdam, The Netherlands, *Prosecutor v V15*, 10 January 2014, 10/960227-12 (ECLI:NL:RBROT:2014:119)].

[415] Corera G (2014) BBC News, *Abu Qatada* Found Not Guilty by Jordan Court of Terror Plot. http://www.bbc.com/news/uk-28033749. Accessed 24 March 2016.

[416] Court of Appeal (Civil Division), England and Wales, *Othman v Secretary of State for the Home Department*, 9 April 2008, T1/2007/9502, EWCA Civ 290, cited in van der Wilt 2012a, p. 160, n. 47.

2 and / or Article 3, the risk of a flagrant denial of justice in the country of destination must primarily be assessed by reference to the facts which the Contracting State knew or should have known when it extradited the person concerned (see *Mamatkulov and Askarov*, cited above, § 90; and *Olaechea Cahuas v. Spain*, no. 24668/03, § 61, European Court of Human Rights 2006).

...

A flagrant denial of a fair trial, and thereby a denial of justice, undoubtedly occurs where a person is detained because of suspicions that he has been planning or has committed a criminal offence without having any access to an independent and impartial tribunal to have the legality of his or her detention reviewed and, if the suspicions do not prove to be well-founded, to obtain release (see, *a fortiori* and among many other authorities, *Papon*, cited above, § 90). Likewise, a deliberate and systematic refusal of access to a lawyer to defend oneself, especially when the person concerned is detained in a foreign country, must be considered to amount to a flagrant denial of a fair trial within the meaning of Article 6 §§ 1 and 3 (c). The Court refers to its well-established case-law in these fields (see, *a fortiori* and among many other authorities, *John Murray v. the United Kingdom*, judgment of 8 February 1996, *Reports* 1996-I, pp. 53–56, §§ 59–70; and *Öcalan*, cited above, §§ 131–137, 148). The extradition of the applicant to the United States would therefore raise an issue under Article 6 of the Convention if there were substantial grounds for believing that following his extradition he would be held incommunicado without having access to a lawyer and without having access to and being tried in the ordinary United States criminal courts.

...

In order to determine whether the German authorities can be considered to have obtained sufficient guarantees to avert the danger of the applicant's suffering a flagrant denial of a fair trial in breach of Article 6, the Court refers to its above finding under Article 3 that the German Government was entitled to infer from the assurance given that the applicant would not be transferred to one of the detention facilities outside the United States of America – that is, the facilities in which terrorist suspects were held without being granted access to a lawyer or to the ordinary criminal courts (see paragraphs 66–69 above)

...

In these circumstances, the German authorities could reasonably infer from the assurance given to them in the course of the extradition proceedings that the applicant would in fact be committed to stand trial for the offences in respect of which his extradition had been granted and that he would therefore not be detained for an indefinite duration without being able to defend himself in court. The Court further attaches importance to the thorough examination of the circumstances of the present case carried out by the German authorities and courts and to their long standing experience of extraditions to the United States of America, and in particular to the fact that the assurances given to them up to that point had been respected in practice. It refers to its reasoning under Article 3 in this respect

...

Having regard to the foregoing, the Court finds that at the time of the applicant's extradition there were no substantial grounds for believing that he would subsequently suffer a flagrant denial of a fair trial by being detained without access to a lawyer and to the ordinary United States criminal courts.

Such important judgments are pre-emptive since they act to prevent a potential, or rather likely, violation. However, when cases are dealt with *ex post facto, id est* after the extradition is executed and when the extraditee is already in the custody of the requesting State, the remedy would consist in either a re-trial or the payment of compensation to the extraditee, but not in his acquittal.[417] Indeed the right to a fair trial seems to be all-pervasive and multi-faceted, all this having been shown by the relevant extracts of the *Al-Moayad* judgment cited here above. Additionally, its link with the prohibition of discrimination, for example, has already been underscored here above. In practice, it impinges upon other rights and determines the applicability or otherwise of other grounds for refusal, creating a situation of comorbidity. Its muscle is epitomized in the fact that 'an unfair trial in a death penalty context can give rise to a form of inhuman treatment'.[418] This citation, in and of itself, concurrently subsumes and gathers (within a few words) three grounds for refusal which are being considered autonomously within Part IV.

Ben Saul acknowledges that 'whereas non-return to torture is a universal international obligation, non-return to the death penalty or an unfair trial are judgments within the discretion of national extradition law and policy'.[419] In fact it has been admitted that 'extradition practices vary from jurisdiction to jurisdiction, including in the *locus* and level of decision-making by executive/administrative and judicial decision-makers, and in the degree of legislative prescription framing those decisions'.[420] Analysing genocide, for example, William Schabas contemplates a right of States not to extradite those who, should they be extradited, would incur risks of being tortured, executed or denied a fair trial.[421]

All this constitutes yet another ultimate reason which justifies the use of the word 'pitfall', as opposed to 'impediment', when and where grounds for refusal are concerned. In other words, should the required minimum guarantees be implemented, notwithstanding the risk of a sentence of death, the right to a fair trial would no longer constitute a ground for refusal. The prosecuting State would have successfully avoided the pitfall. It would have approached the quicksand without falling into it by means of an Alberto Tomba-like *slalom*. Yet another interesting correlation between the right to a fair trial and universal jurisdiction has been identified by Mohammed Cherif Bassiouni, who states that, since universal jurisdiction gives rise to conflicting claims of jurisdiction, different regimes, divergent criminal justice systems, varied standards of prosecution and unequal lengths of sentences inflicted upon convicts, the right to a fair trial is endangered.[422] Such margins of appreciation reflect the non-peremptory nature of the right to a fair trial. In the light of a prospective extradition, the right is also problematically monitored because it presupposes a value judgment of the fair trial standards adopted by the requested State, of its prevailing judicial practice and any other allegations of the possibility of dependence and partiality in relation to an identifiable individual.

---

417 van Dijk and van Hoof 1990, pp. 171–185.

418 Clapham 2003, p. 488.

419 Saul 2009, p. 71.

420 Saul 2009, p. 69.

421 Schabas 2000, p. 402.

422 Bassiouni 2001, p. 82.

Consequently, diplomatic and political rows are feared and avoided, sometimes to the detriment of extraditees.[423]

Fair trial rights might also stand in the way of an extradition at the post-conviction stage within EU member States which are mutually obliged to recognise the judicial decisions of other member States. Though in principle trials *in absentia* are allowed, the document instituting proceedings must have been duly served on the defaulting defendant at a moment that allows the defendant sufficient time and facilities to prepare his defence.[424] Such pre-requisites bear a resemblance with criteria enabling trials *in absentia* before the STL.[425] The above has shown the multi-faceted nature of the right to a fair trial and its rather limited potential to constitute a ground for refusal of extradition.

16.7.2 The Ne Bis in Idem *Rule*

The *ne bis in idem* rule, being also intricately linked to the ICC's complementarity regime,[426] may be synthesised in the legal maxim *nemo debet bis vexari pro una et eadem causa*. The prohibition of double jeopardy[427] or *autrefois acquit*[428]/ *convict*,[429] which is not catered for by the UDHR, is considered to be a minimum guarantee which safeguards due process rights of individuals. Since it belongs to

423 See http://www.fairtrials.org.uk/fair-trials-international.html. Accessed 12 September 2018.

424 ECJ, *Isabelle Lancray SA v Peters und Sickert KG*, Reference for a preliminary ruling from the *Bundesgerichtshof*, 3 July 1990, Case C-305/88, ECR I-2725; ECJ, *Leon Emile Gaston Carlos Debaecker and Berthe Plouvier v Cornelius Gerrit Bouwman (Reference for a preliminary ruling from the Hoge Raad der Nederlanden*, 11 June 1985, Case 49/84; ECJ, *Peter Klomps v Karl Michel (preliminary ruling requested by the Hoge Raad der Nederlanden)*, 16 June 1981, Case 166/80, ECR 1593.

425 Article 22 of the Statute of the STL (2007) Statute of the Special Tribunal for Lebanon, which is attached to UNSC Resolution 1757 {UNSC (2007) Resolution 1757 (2007) UN Doc. S/RES/ 1757}, and is considered to be an innovation by some jurists (Aptel 2007, p. 1116).

426 See Part III; see also Stigen 2010, pp. 133–159.

427 This is not the exact equivalent of the *ne bis in idem* rule of general international law. The SCSL clarified that 'unlike double jeopardy, the principle of *ne bis in idem* prevents repeated prosecutions for the same conduct in different or the same legal systems, whereas the notion of double jeopardy is a double exposure to sentencing which is applicable to all the different stages of the criminal justice process in the same legal system: prosecution, conviction and punishment' [SCSL, *Prosecutor v Sam Hinga Norman, Moinina Fofana and Allieu Kondewa, Decision on the First Accused's Motion for Service and Arraignment on the Consolidated Indictment*, 29 November 2004, Case No. SCSL-04-14-T, p. 14].

428 This promotes the civil liberties of defendants by ending the fear of renewed prosecution after acquittal (de Than and Shorts 2000, p. 627).

429 This prevents double punishment but does not necessarily bar the hardship of a second trial. In other words, if no sentence was handed down in the first trial, a second trial is possible because this plea would be unsuccessful (de Than and Shorts 2000, p. 625).

the realm of the fair trial rights,[430] leading to its designation as 'one of the pillars of due process',[431] it should also be considered in this context. This means that, just like other due process rights, it is not an absolute human right. As seen in the light of the admissibility test within Part III, courts may have to 'set aside fraudulent *res judicata* in criminal matters, because of the symbolic punishment, or because of the way in which evidence was gathered during the investigation and presented in the indictment, or because of the way in which the trial court came to its verdict'.[432] Moreover, a breach of the rule is prohibited, *inter alia*, by Article 14(7) of the ICCPR, the due process clause, although its application is limited to proceedings within the same jurisdictional remit. In other words, it does not prohibit successive prosecutions for the same offence in different countries,[433] but effectively shields a person from being harassed by a State, protecting him from multiple prosecutions therein. This is the exclusively domestic dimension of the prohibition and is commonly termed as 'internal *ne bis in idem*', whereas the external *ne bis in idem* rule conveys the prohibition to expose an individual to trial a second time for the second conduct in two different States.[434] Regional human rights courts also do not apply the rule to foreign *res judicata* but only give it domestic legal effect.[435] This domestic dimension of *ne bis in idem* quells concerns that a previous prosecution within another (third) State can block later efforts of prosecution in the custodial State, largely subduing any detriment which may accrue as a result of the exercise of universal jurisdiction by a bystander State.[436]

In so far as it is a fundamental feature of procedural due process in criminal justice, it constitutes a principle which is 'rooted in the law'.[437] Although a minimum guarantee, together with the prohibition of retroactive criminal laws which falls within the parameters of due process rights,[438] as has been shown here above, the *ne bis in idem* rule is not the only principle which could effectively bar an extradition.[439] Notwithstanding this, although it falls within the parameters of due process guarantees, *ne bis in idem* is so important that it deserves express and

[430] 'The *ne bis in idem* rule offers an important principle of judicial protection for the individual in the context of a fair trial' (Fletcher et al. 2008, p. 132).

[431] Poels 2005, p. 347.

[432] IACtHR, *La Cantuta v Perú* (Merits, Reparations and Costs), 29 November 2006, Series C No. 162, para 153, and IACtHR, *Almonacid-Arellano et al. v Chile*, Preliminary Objections, Merits, Reparations and Costs, 26 September 2006, Series C No. 154, para 154, both cited in Vervaele 2013, p. 214, n. 12.

[433] HRC, *AP v Italy*, 2 November 1987, Communication No. 204/1986, para 7.3.

[434] Petronio et al. 2014.

[435] Vervaele 2013, p. 214.

[436] van der Wilt 2015, pp. 241–242.

[437] Thompson 2015, p. 103.

[438] Martin et al. 1997, p. 632.

[439] Article 9 of the ECE, above n. 16.

autonomous consideration as a separate ground for refusal. This distinct categorisation as a separate ground for refusal also finds justification in the fact that Article 4 para 1 of the Seventh Protocol to the ECvHR indicates that the scope of *ne bis in idem* as a human right is restricted to the domestic legal order.[440] Similarly, the HRC has ruled that Article 14, para 7 does not apply to foreign *res judicata*.[441] It would hence, *in partem*, be misleading to consider *ne bis in idem* as a minimum guarantee falling solely within the rubric of the general right to a fair trial. Indeed, the rule has its goalposts shifted depending upon the underlying *corpus juris* within which it is being considered and applied.[442] In fact, the ECJ has already warned of the risk of such shifting of goalposts:

> 117. To interpret and apply the *ne bis in idem* principle so differently depending on the area of law concerned is detrimental to the unity of the European Union legal order. The crucial importance of the *ne bis in idem* principle as a founding principle of European Union law which enjoys the status of a fundamental right means that its content must not be substantially different depending on which area of law is concerned. For the purposes of determining the scope of the guarantee provided by the *ne bis in idem* principle, as now codified in Article 50 of the Charter of Fundamental Rights, the same criteria should apply in all areas of European Union law. This point has rightly been made by the EFTA Surveillance Authority.
>
> 118. There is no objective reason why the conditions to which the *ne bis in idem* principle is subject in competition matters should be any different from those applicable to it elsewhere. For, in the same way as, within the context of Article 54 of the CISA, that principle serves to guarantee the free movement of European Union citizens in European Union territory as a "single area of freedom, security and justice", so, in the field of competition law, it helps to improve and facilitate the business activities of undertakings in the internal market and, ultimately, to create uniform conditions of competition (a "level playing field") throughout the EEA.
>
> 119. For the purposes of identifying the relevant criteria for defining *idem*, it must be borne in mind that the *ne bis in idem* principle is based largely on a fundamental right enshrined in the ECHR, more specifically, Article 4(1) of Protocol No 7 to the ECHR, although that protocol has not yet been ratified by all the European Union Member States. That close proximity to the ECHR is indicated not only by the Explanations on Article 50 of the Charter of Fundamental Rights, which must be duly taken into account by the courts of the European Union and of the Member States, but also by the previous case-law of the Court of Justice concerning the general European Union-law principle of *ne bis in idem*.

---

[440] Sometimes, as is the case with the Netherlands, 'the interpretation of *the ne bis in idem* principle on an international level does not differ from the one applied in the domestic context' (van der Wilt 2005b, p. 114).

[441] van der Wilt 2005b, p. 100.

[442] For a comprehensive study of the extent to which *ne bis in idem* serves as an impediment to international cooperation in general and to the surrender of suspects in particular, see van der Wilt 2005b, pp. 99–106.

> 120. The requirement of homogeneity is therefore applicable. It follows from that requirement that rights contained in the Charter which correspond to rights guaranteed by the ECHR are to have the same meaning and scope as those laid down by the ECHR. In other words, Article 4(1) of Protocol No 7 to the ECHR, as interpreted by the European Court of Human Rights (ECtHR), describes the minimum standard that must be guaranteed in the interpretation and application of the *ne bis in idem* principle in European Union law.
>
> 121. Whereas the case-law of the ECtHR on the meaning of *idem* had lacked uniformity for a long time, the ECtHR held, in a landmark judgment in 2009, that Article 4 of Protocol No 7 to the ECHR prohibits the prosecution or trial of a second offence in so far as it arises from identical facts or facts which are substantially the same. This means that the ECtHR has regard only to whether or not the facts are identical and expressly not to the legal classification of the offence. Moreover, in so doing, it is itself guided primarily by the case-law of the Court of Justice on the area of freedom, security and justice. In addition, the form of words used by the ECtHR to define the meaning of identical facts is very similar to that employed by the Court of Justice. There is nothing to indicate that the ECtHR might be inclined to the view that the scope of the guarantee provided by the *ne bis in idem* principle is less extensive specifically in the area of competition law. On the contrary, while the judgment of the Court of Justice in *Aalborg Portland*, which establishes the criterion of unity of the legal interest protected, is cited by the ECtHR, it does not rely on it as a basis for its interpretation of the *ne bis in idem* principle.
>
> 122. It follows that, for the purposes of interpreting and applying *idem* in the context of the prohibition against prosecution and punishment for the same cause of action under European Union law also, account should henceforth be taken only of the identity of the facts (which necessarily includes the unity of the offender).[443]

The extracts cited here above show that there is no common and equivalent standard of *ne bis in idem* between the EU member States.[444] *Ne bis in idem* 'functions differently at the horizontal and vertical levels'.[445] The following considerations will show the veracity of this statement, especially when it is dealt with in the light of Sect. 11.1.2 which postulated the dual importance and significance of *ne bis in idem* within the ICC statutory regime. Although this heading may seem rather Eurocentric, the developments of the law on *ne bis in idem* in Europe (both at EU and CoE level) have been, comparatively speaking, more significant and ground-breaking.

[443] ECJ, *Toshiba Corporation and Others v Úřad pro ochranu hospodářské soutěže*, Opinion of AG Kokott, 14 February 2012, C-17/10, cited in *Qorti Kriminali* [Criminal Court], Malta, *Ir-Repubblika ta' Malta vs Christian Grech*, Akkuza 6/2011, 14 May 2012, pp. 6–7.

[444] Vervaele 2013, p. 212.

[445] Mégret 2010, p. 192.

Since *ne bis in idem*[446] entails that a person should not be tried[447] twice for the same offence,[448] the offshoot of this rule is the *res judicata*[449] general principle of law. Because of this close connection, the applicability or otherwise of *ne bis in idem* can revolve around the determination as to whether a judgment is final or not.[450] The prevailing position seems to be that a decision is final 'if, according to the traditional expression, it has acquired the force of *res judicata*. This is the case when it is irrevocable, that is to say when no further ordinary remedies are available or when the parties have exhausted such remedies or have permitted the time-limit to expire without availing themselves of them'.[451] The decision must generally be of a penal nature. If decisions by administrative authorities have a punitive and deterrent character, they can trigger *ne bis in idem* protection.[452] On these lines, administrative proceedings which lead to administrative fines may bar criminal proceedings for the same offence.[453] Matters can become very complex, but do not fall within the scope of my book, when the 'Court encounters the same combination of double jeopardy (*ne bis in idem*) on the one hand and the notions of concurrence

---

446 ICTY Statute (1993) Statute of the International Criminal Tribunal for the Former Yugoslavia and ICTR Statute (1994) Statute of the International Criminal Tribunal for Rwanda use the nomenclature *non bis in idem*.

447 The pre-requisite of a trial conveys that pardons can only trigger the *ne bis in idem* rule 'where a trial has actually taken place' (Naqvi 2010, p. 179). This also means that amnesties do not trigger such rule.

448 André Klip, however, whilst analysing Article 54 of the CISA (1990) Convention Implementing the Schengen Agreement, 19 June 1990, [2000] OJ L239/19, defines the principle by stating that it conveys a prohibition 'of a second prosecution if the accused has already been tried for the same facts by another State' (Klip 2009, p. 231). His conclusion seems to be strengthened by *dicta* of the Luxembourg-based ECJ {ECJ, *Criminal Proceedings Against Leopold Henri van Esbroeck*, 9 March 2006, Case C-436/04, 2006 E.C.R. I-2333, paras 25–42 and ECJ, *Criminal Proceedings Against Norma Kraaijenbrink*, 18 July 2007, Case C-367/5, [2007] ECR I-6619, paras 26–36}. Moreover, Article 4 of Seventh Protocol to the ECvHR (1984) Protocol No. 7 to the Convention for the Protection of Human Rights and Fundamental Freedoms as Amended by Protocol No. 11 'does not refer to the same offence but rather to trial and punishment again for an offence for which the applicant has already been finally acquitted or convicted' [ECtHR Third Section, *Franz Fischer v Austria*, 29 May 2001, Application No. 37950/97, para 25].

449 This entails that a judgment is final, definitive, irrevocable and may not be subject to any further appeal or re-consideration. In other words, it implies that a case has been decided and settled conclusively (Duncan 1993, p. 55).

450 Emmerson et al. 2007, pp. 436–438.

451 CoE 1984, para 22; see also ECtHR Second Section, *Aleksandr Konstantinovich Nikitin v Russia*, 20 July 2004, Application No. 50178/99, para 37, and ECtHR Second Section, *Horciag v Romania*, 15 March 2005, Application No. 70982/01, all cited in Neagu 2012a, p. 963, notes 40 and 41.

452 Put 2002, pp. 937–949, cited in van der Wilt 2005b, p. 107, n. 22.

453 ECtHR, *Affaire Grande Stevens et autre contre Italie*, 4 March 2014, Application Numbers 18640/10, 18647/10, 18663/10.

of offences (ideal and real/material) on the other'.[454] Complications arise also when parallel proceedings are concerned. There is no violation of the *ne bis in idem* rule when the second set of proceedings are discontinued after the first set of proceedings have become final.[455] In the absence of such discontinuance, a violation subsists.[456] It would be interesting to see the outcome of a Court judgment when criminal proceedings in State A against an individual who is present in State A overlap with criminal proceedings against the same individual in State B which exercises universal jurisdiction *in absentia*. This is not such an unlikely predicament when one notes that 'any judgment rendered *in absentia* and any *ordonnances pénales* which have not yet been the subject of appeal or opposition may, as soon as they have been rendered, be transmitted to the requested State for the purposes of notification and with a view to enforcement'.[457] *Eshetu Alemu*, a naturalized Dutch citizen, has been sentenced to death *in absentia* in Ethiopia which requested his extradition from The Netherlands where his trial commenced on 21 November 2016.[458] He was found guilty and imprisoned for life on 15 December 2017.[459] More so, what if the latter proceedings were undertaken with very little prospect of success, both in terms of the evidence to be produced and in terms of the ability to arrest and incarcerate, and deliberately to shield the individual? This predicament is possible in view of the fact that the *ne bis in idem* principle 'is not an absolute right, and therefore, is not applicable where:

i. the intervention of the Court that heard the case and decided to dismiss it or to acquit a person responsible for violating human rights or international law, was intended to shield the accused party from criminal responsibility;
ii. the proceedings were not conducted independently or impartially in accordance with due process guarantees; or
iii. there was no real intent to bring those responsible to justice'.[460]

---

[454] ECtHR, Fourth Section, *Vaidas Dungveckis v Lithuania*, Concurring Opinion of Judge Zupančič, 12 April 2016, Application No. 32106/08, p. 15, para 1.

[455] ECtHR First Section, *Generoso Zigarella v Italy*, Admissibility, 3 October 2002, Application Number 48154/99, cited in ECtHR, Fourth Section, *Alexander Boman v Finland*, 17 February 2015, Application No. 41604/11, para 41.

[456] ECtHR, *Kaj-Erik Torsten Glantz v Finland*, 20 May 2014, Application No. 37394/11, para 62, cited in *Boman v Finland*, above n. 455, para 41.

[457] Article 22 of the European Convention on the International Validity of Criminal Judgments (1970) signed in The Hague on 28 May 1970.

[458] Coeuret E (2016) Ethiopia: After Years on the Run Eshetu Alemu Will Face Trial. *iLawyer*. http://ilawyerblog.com/ethiopia-years-run-eshetu-alemu-will-face-trial/. Accessed 12 December 2016.

[459] The Hague District Court, *Prosecutor v Eshetu Alemu*, 15 December 2017, ECLI:NL:RBDHA:2017:14782; see also ICD (2018) News Archive, 4 January 2018. http://www.internationalcrimesdatabase.org/home/newsarchive#p2. Accessed 27 December 2018.

[460] *Almonacid-Arellano et al. v Chile*, above n. 432, para 154, cited in *Marguš v Croatia*, above n. 295, para 61.

Ne bis in idem does not protect an individual from a second prosecution where a 'sentence from 2008 passed by the Gacaca court must be cancelled in advance'[461] in terms of Rwandan law. Such judgments have been tagged as 'an apparent or fraudulent *res judicata*'[462] which merely constitute 'fictitious or fraudulent grounds for double jeopardy'.[463] These exceptions could also subsist where a State exercises universal jurisdiction, possibly for political motives, without using the necessary diligence (wherein the trial and its effects were subsequently annulled by a higher court enjoying jurisdiction) or else where a State paroled and/or pardoned an individual prematurely. Hence they mirror the ICC's admissibility test which was dealt with in Part III. Reversing matters, what if the proceedings before State A are not conducted diligently and lead to the individual's acquittal? Could any other State which eventually enjoys custodial jurisdiction over the individual, including State B, invoke the nullity of proceedings undertaken within State A in terms of their (the custodial State which now exercises a ground of jurisdiction) own laws? These are questions which show how multi-faceted the prevailing scenario can be.

The ECJ has however extensively interpreted the finality of the judgment, which interpretation has ramifications both on the domestic but especially on the international level. In *Hüseyin Gözütok* and *Klaus Brügge*,[464] it determined, in terms of Article 54 of the CISA,[465] that proceedings are deemed to have been finalized if they are discontinued by the Public Prosecutor without involvement of the Court following a settlement with the accused. A plea-bargain (see Sect. 16.6), the special procedure of *patteggiamento*,[466] could hence trigger the *ne bis in idem* protective cover. Covering such out of court settlements ensures that the *ne bis in idem* principle would benefit perpetrators of petty crimes, rather than simply benefit those who commit serious crimes.[467] The implications are far-reaching because by equating such out of court settlements with final judgments, States may invoke out of court settlements in other Member States as a bar to compliance with a EAW.[468]

---

461 *Director of Public Prosecutions v T (Attorney Bjørn Elmquist, appointed)*, above n. 165, para 7.

462 *Almonacid-Arellano et al. v Chile*, above n. 432, para 154, cited in *Marguš v Croatia*, above n. 295, para 61.

463 *La Cantuta v Perú*, above n. 432, para 153, cited in *Marguš v Croatia*, above n. 295, para 62.

464 ECJ, *Criminal Proceedings Against Hüseyin Gözütok and Klaus Brügge, Reference for a preliminary ruling from the Oberlandesgericht Köln, Germany, and the Rechtbank van eerste aanleg te Veurne, Belgium*, 11 February 2003, Joined Cases C-187/01 and C-385/01. For an exposition of the facts of these cases, see Neagu 2012b, pp. 67–71.

465 The CISA is the first multi-lateral treaty which establishes an international *ne bis in idem* principle as an individual right *erga omnes*, though this is restricted to the regional Schengen area (Vervaele 2013, p. 218).

466 ECJ, *Criminal Proceedings Against Hüseyin Gözütok and Klaus Brügge, Reference for a preliminary ruling from the Oberlandesgericht Köln, Germany, and the Rechtbank van eerste aanleg te Veurne, Belgium*, Opinion of AG Ruiz Jarabo Colomer, 19 September 2002, Joined Cases C-187/01 and C-385/01, para 72.

467 van der Wilt 2005b, p. 110.

468 van der Wilt 2005b, p. 111.

In these cases, the ECJ held that 'there is a necessary implication that the Member States have mutual trust in their criminal justice systems and that each of them recognises the criminal law in force in the other Member States even when the outcome would be different if its own national law were applied'.[469] In Nadine Thwaites' words, this was the only interpretation the ECJ could undertake and adopt in order to ensure 'the object and purpose of Article 54 of the CISA as well as the *effet utile* of the provision'.[470] Nadine Thwaites concludes that the *Gözütok and Brügge* preliminary rulings not only constitute a vivid expression of the concepts of mutual trust and mutual recognition in penal matters, but are also an indirect appeal for some harmonisation of the member States' criminal justice systems.[471]

Although the *Filomeno Mario Miraglia dictum*,[472] involving parallel proceedings instituted in another EU member State, departed from this line of throught, the ECJ reconfirmed its line of thought in the *Giuseppe Francesco Gasparini dictum*[473] where it held that *ne bis in idem* applies in the case of a final acquittal because prosecution of the offence is time-barred. However the *Vladimir Turansky* judgment[474] determined that in order to be considered as a final disposal for the purposes of Article 54 of the CISA, a decision must bring the criminal proceedings to an end and definitively bar further prosecution.[475] To this extent, the EAW is ground-breaking since by recognising *res judicata* as a bar to surrender, 'it considers final judgments of all member States of the European Union on the same par as those emanating from the requested State'.[476] In other words, it established the principle of mutual recognition of judicial decisions within the EU.[477] The Framework Decision on the EAW provides for a mandatory non-execution of the request to surrender in terms of Article 3(2) thereof on the one hand and an optional non-execution of the request to surrender in terms of Article 4 of the same. The former, as opposed to the latter, applies when a *res judicata* subsists. Here one must note that the jurisprudence of the ECJ has inspired the ECtHR which, with reference to such case-law, ruled in favour of factual *idem* in the Grand Chamber's

---

[469] *Criminal Proceedings Against Hüseyin Gözütok and Klaus Brügge*, above n. 464, para 33.

[470] Thwaites 2003, p. 258.

[471] Thwaites 2003, p. 261.

[472] ECJ, *Criminal Proceedings Against Filomeno Mario Miraglia, Reference for a preliminary ruling from the Tribunale di Bologna*, 10 March 2005, C-469/03. For an exposition of the facts of this case, see Neagu 2012b, pp. 71–73.

[473] ECJ, *Criminal Proceedings Against Giuseppe Francesco Gasparini and Others (Reference for a preliminary ruling from the Audiencia Provincial de Málaga*, 28 September 2006, C-467-/04). For an exposition of the facts of this case, see Neagu 2012b, pp. 73–77.

[474] ECJ, *Criminal Proceedings Against Vladimir Turanský. Reference for a preliminary ruling: Landesgericht für Strafsachen Wien – Austria*, 22 December 2008, C-491/07. For an exposition of the facts of this case, see Neagu 2012b, pp. 81–87.

[475] Neagu 2012a, pp. 964–965.

[476] van der Wilt 2005b, p. 102.

[477] van der Wilt 2005b, p. 103.

Sergey Zolotoukhin v Russia judgment.[478] Whereas the above mentioned may reveal that 'the European principle of *ne bis in idem* is open for interpreting "*idem*" (the same) as "*idem crimen*" (in normative terms of the offence) or as "*idem factum*" (in terms of the act as the historical event the indictment is based on)', the wording of the American counterpart, *id est* the double jeopardy clause in the Fifth Amendment, is attached to the 'offence'.[479]

Coming back to the conduct or offence-oriented *ne bis in idem*, one must consider a crucial matter at this stage. Some definitions refer to the same offence rather than the same conduct. In other words the rule refers to the same crime (offence)[480] rather than the same fact (conduct) [being an act of commission or of omission]. This seems to be the prevailing position in State practice,[481] especially in some continental law States. The consequences of this are obviously very far-reaching.[482] If *ne bis in idem* refers to the same offence, rather than the same conduct, it would be possible for an individual to be tried for a different offence (with a different criminal charge) arising from the same conduct. This seems to be the position which prevails in a few common law jurisdictions.[483] From an analysis of such systems, I predicate that the Irish system seems to be the most well-balanced system. Irish law on the matter is based upon the *Connelly* principles.[484] These establish a test which is evidence-oriented and succinctly connote an analysis as to whether the evidence which is necessary to support the second indictment would have been sufficient to produce a legal conviction on the first indictment either as to the offence charged or as to an offence of which, on the indictment, the accused could have been found guilty. However, the test must be subject to the proviso that the offence charged in the second indictment had in fact been committed at the time of the first charge.

---

[478] ECtHR Grand Chamber, *Sergey Zolotoukhin v Russia*, 10 February 2009, Application No. 14939/03, cited in Weyembergh and Armada 2016, p. 196, n. 39.

[479] Eser 2004, p. 968.

[480] According to the South African Constitutional Court, 'the double jeopardy rule prevents anyone being tried twice for the same crime' [*The State vs Wouter Basson*, above n. 272, para 252].

[481] The French Supreme Court upheld that 'the export of drugs to Canada, committed in France, constitutes an offence which is distinguishable from the import of the same drugs in Canada' {*Cour de Cassation*, *Chambre Criminelle* [Court of Cassation, Criminal Chamber], *Edouard*, 22 November 1973, 73-91840}, cited in van der Wilt 2005b, p. 115, n. 59.

[482] Sedman 2010, pp. 259–266.

[483] USA District Court for the Eastern District of New York, *Ancel Vincent Elcock, Petitioner v United States of America, Respondent*, 26 January 2000, Civil Action No. CV-99-1757 (DGT), 80 F. Suppl. 2d 70 (E.D.N.Y. 2000); USA District Court for the Eastern District of New York, *United States of America v Jose Franklin Jurado-Rodriguez and Edgar Alberto Garcia-Montilla, Defendants*, No. CR 94-547, 907 F. Supp. 568 (1995).

[484] In the *Connelly* case [HoL, *Charles Connelly v Director of Public Prosecutions*, 1 October 1964, 3727/63, DPP 2/3771, 2 WLR 1145], the HoL had allowed a subsequent prosecution for robbery after the suspect had been acquitted of murder. Hence, a second prosecution is permissible if two offences with a different scope coincide in a particular event/incident (van der Wilt 2005b, p. 113).

Thus, if there is a prosecution and conviction in respect of this, there is no obstacle to a charge of murder if the assaulted person subsequently dies[485] as a result of the blows endured in such assault. The Irish test seems to strike the right balance between the fact or offence conundrum by ensuring that 'no person should be tried twice for an offence arising out of the same, or substantially the same, set of acts' and 'there should be no consecutive trial for offences on an ascending scale of gravity'.[486] There is no perfect system. Bottlenecks can subsist anyway. In such system as the Irish one, various issues, ranging from the weight which ought to be given to circumstantial evidence, to the relevance and (in)admissibility of such evidence, may lead to juridical complications. Yet I assert that such system is juridically sound and reliable.

I also subscribe to the conclusions reached by the Buenos Aires Appeals Court in the *Jorge Videla* case. Videla was tried, convicted for murder and torture in Argentina, and sentenced to life imprisonment in 1985, but pardoned by President Carlos Saúl Menem in 1990. He was re-arrested in 1998 on the basis of the abduction and kidnapping of children of persons who had disappeared whilst being in the custody of the armed forces. However, the Court established that since the abduction and kidnapping charges were not included within the charges issued in the 1985 indictment, *ne bis in idem* did not apply.[487] Had the Buenos Aires court interpreted *ne bis in idem* to refer to the same conduct, *Videla's* plea would have most likely been successful.

The ECtHR has shifted interpretations in so far as *ne bis in idem* is involved. Its first approach, epitomised by the Gradinger decision, it focuses on the 'same conduct'[488] and may be said to be the most akin to the position prevailing within the ICC Statute. It may be deemed to be the horizontal counterpart of the vertical system, or at least, a similar version thereof. The second approach determined that 'a single act constituted various offences, thus allowing different charges to be brought at a later point'.[489] It hence postulated that the same conduct may constitute several criminal offences (*concours idéal d'infractions*) which may be tried in separate proceedings,[490] adopting the same view in the *Göktan* case.[491] In its third approach, it placed emphasis on the constitutive elements of the two criminal offences in question. Relying on the *concours idéal d'infractions*, although being tried and punished again for offences which were nominally different would violate the *ne bis in idem* rule, one ought to examine whether or not such offences would

[485] van der Wilt 2005b, pp. 112–113.

[486] van der Wilt 2005b, p. 113.

[487] *Cámara Federal de Buenos Aires*, *Jorge Rafael Videla (first junta)*, Appeals Court Judgment, 23 May 2002, Case No. 33714.

[488] Neagu 2012a, p. 969.

[489] ECtHR, *Maria Celeste Vieira Veloso de Oliveira v Switzerland*, 30 July 1998, Application No. 84/1997/868/1080.

[490] Neagu 2012a, p. 969.

[491] ECtHR Second Section, *Ali Riza Göktan v France*, 2 July 2002, Application No. 33402/96, para 50, also cited in Neagu 2012a, p. 969, n. 70.

subsist upon the existence of the same ingredients. The *ne bis in idem* rule does not apply where the constitutive elements of the respective offences overlap slightly.[492] The ECtHR followed suit in other decisions, most of which involved Austria as defendant State, such as, for example, *W.F. v Austria*,[493] *Sailer v Austria*,[494] *Bachmaier v Austria*,[495] *Hauser-Sporn v Austria*[496] and *Schutte v Austria*.[497] By means of a surprising *volte-face*,[498] the ECtHR reverted to the same conduct (second) approach, qualifying it *rationae temporis* and *rationae loci.* The incidents which occurred on 4 February 2002 were, in the view of the ECtHR, not equivalent to being the same acts although they were characterised by the same pattern/course of conduct and although they occurred over a short span of time, namely on the same day. In other words, there was no spatial or temporal unity between the incidents. The incidents were not a single continuous act but different manifestations of the same conduct shown on a number of distinct occasions.

Having comprehensively examined the prevailing jurisprudence, Norel Neagu summaries the prevailing position at law as follows. He found that 'the criteria for establishing a breach of the *ne bis in idem* principle as regards the *idem* concept in respect of certain offences against natural persons should read as a set of facts inextricably linked together in time and space, as well as by their object and subjects. Since no such particularity could be included in a tendency of the ECtHR to harmonize its previous case law and offer a new set of criteria of universal value, the only option remains that of considering the conduct in the *Zolothukin* case as a breach of the temporal and spatial criteria.[499]

Continentally and conventionally, Article 2 of the 1975 Additional Protocol to the ECE expands the protection to final judgments, including acquittals, by a third State which must be a party to the ECE. On a communitarian level, the rule surfaced when the Amsterdam Treaty[500] integrated the *Schengen Acquis* into the framework of the EU, and was tweaked by Article 50 of the EU Charter of Fundamental Rights

492 *Franz Fischer v Austria*, above n. 448, para 22, also cited in Neagu 2012a, p. 970, n. 72.

493 ECtHR, *W.F. v Austria*, 30 May 2002, Application No. 38275/97, also cited in Neagu 2012a, p. 970, n. 73.

494 ECtHR, First Section, *Gerhard Sailer v Austria*, 6 June 2002, Application No. 38237/97, also cited in Neagu 2012a, p. 970, n. 74.

495 ECtHR, *Bachmaier v Austria*, Decision on Admissibility, 2 September 2004, Application No. 77413/01, also cited in Neagu 2012a, p. 970, n. 74.

496 ECtHR, First Section, *Alois Hauser-Sporn v Austria*, 7 December 2006, Application No. 37301/03, also cited in Neagu 2012a, p. 970, n. 74.

497 ECtHR, First Section, *Roland Schutte v Austria*, 26 July 2007, Application No. 18015/03, also cited in Neagu 2012a, p. 970, n. 74.

498 *Zolotukhin v Russia*, above n. 478, paras 70–84, also cited in Neagu 2012a, pp. 970–971.

499 Neagu 2012a, p. 971.

500 Amsterdam Treaty (1997) Treaty of Amsterdam amending the Treaty of the European Union, the Treaties establishing the European Communities and certain related acts. This was signed on 2 October 1997.

proclaimed by the Lisbon Treaty.[501] Notwithstanding this, the *Miraglia* case[502] had been cited to show that 'the European Court of Justice does not recognise the significance of the *ne bis in idem* principle *per se*, i.e. as the expression of a fundamental right, but has regarded this principle merely as the underpinning principle of the freedom of movement of persons, one of the four freedoms of the Common Market'.[503] This is rather one-sided since, considering *ne bis in idem*, the ECJ upheld that 'a person must be regarded as someone whose case has been "finally disposed of" in relation to the acts which he is alleged to have committed, even if no court has been involved in the procedure and the decision taken on the conclusion of the procedure does not take the form of a judicial decision'.[504] In a rigid and divergent tone, the Advocate General Ruiz Jarabo Colomer has opined that 'the classic formulation of the *ne bis in idem* principle requires that three identical circumstances should be present: the same facts, the same offender and the same legal principle – the same value – to be protected'.[505] Yet, the ECJ departed from this approach by finding that only the same acts should be taken into account.[506] The meaning of the term 'same acts' relies upon 'the identity of the material acts, understood as meaning a set of concrete circumstances which are inextricably linked together in time and space and by their subject-matter as assessed by national judges.[507] Whilst analysing the European approach to *ne bis in idem* under the law of Schengen and the ECvHR, Michael Bohlander states that 'the general rule would still appear to be that there is no international ban on a subsequent prosecution by a different State'.[508] In fact Alexander Poels considers this as a 'major human rights concern'.[509]

Ne bis in idem undoubtedly varies widely in the way it is applied,[510] approached and interpreted by national courts of various criminal justice systems. Since States foster different interpretations to the *ne bis in idem* rule,[511] such inconsistencies consequently persist at international level too.[512] In substantiation of this, approximately four decades ago, Italy's *Corte Costituzionale* had stated that the

[501] Lisbon Treaty (2007) Treaty of Lisbon Amending the Treaty on European Union and the Treaty Establishing the European Community. This was signed on 12 December 2007.

[502] *Criminal Proceedings against Filomeno Mario Miraglia, Reference for a preliminary ruling from the Tribunale di Bologna*, above n. 472.

[503] Rafaraci and Belfiore 2007, cited in van Bockel 2010, p. 132.

[504] Tchorbadjiyska 2004.

[505] Opinion of AG Ruiz Jarabo Colomer, above n. 466, para 56.

[506] *Criminal Proceedings Against Hüseyin Gözütok and Klaus Brügge*, above n. 464, para 44.

[507] *Criminal Proceedings Against Leopold Henri van Esbroeck*, above n. 448, paras 36, 38, cited in Rosanò 2017, p. 42, n. 12.

[508] Bohlander 2008, p. 551.

[509] Poels 2005, p. 340.

[510] Emmerson et al. 2007, p. 424.

[511] van der Wilt 2005b, p. 103.

[512] For a comprehensive account of such divergent applications, see Neagu 2012a, pp. 956–958.

principle had not turned into customary international law,[513] allowing a prosecution of the same person for the same offence in more than one State with the exception of instances wherein both States are party to a treaty, be it bi-lateral or milti-lateral, which prohibits such successive trials between States. On the same lines, 'there is no rule of international customary law prohibiting double jeopardy',[514] although defendants may be able to argue that 'double jeopardy is barred by general principles of international law'.[515] This contention is widely supported, with Morosin going as far as stating that *ne bis in idem* is not even a general principle of law,[516] a submission backed by others who suggest that 'it has not achieved the status of a general principle of international law'.[517] However, on a continental/regional (European) level, there is a propensity towards uniformization in interpretation[518] as a result of the fact that both the ECJ and the ECtHR apply the same test in respect of the notion of *idem*.[519] Whereas the international *ne bis in idem* rule is not cast in stone, it is both a general principle of law and a fundamental human right within domestic jurisdictions and/or regionally. The same cannot be said about *ne bis in idem* on the domestic level. What seems to be needed, as evidenced by Harmen van der Wilt, is ongoing harmonisation with an eye to bridging the lingering gap between civil law and common law legal systems, a solid mechanism for dispute settlement and a common European policy (possibly compiled by EUROJUST) which identifies factors and criteria to be used to search for the best place for prosecution.[520] Such a *forum prosequi* would ensure the avoidance of multiple prosecutions, whilst enhancing mutual consultation and reciprocity.[521]

It remains to be seen whether *ne bis in idem* could be deemed to apply equally in the face of serious crimes, or whether an exception thereto can be applied where core crimes are concerned. Nowadays, it seems that at communitarian level, that is, under EU law, whether *ne bis in idem* is triggered or not depends largely on the crime in question to which it is subject. Analysing the right to prosecute, in *Gözütok*[522] and *Brügge*,[523] Advocate General Ruiz-Jaraba Colomer upheld that:

> Indeed, I have pointed out that the settlement procedure is a means of administering criminal justice in minor or medium offences, but that it is not used in the field of more serious crimes. Therefore the approach taken by the German, French and Belgian Governments would provide better treatment for the perpetrators of major offences, who

513 *Corte Costituzionale* [Constitutional Court], Italy, *Zennaro* case, 8 April 1976, Case no. 69.
514 D'Amato 2008, p. 287.
515 D'Amato 2008, p. 288.
516 Morosin 1995, p. 261.
517 Cassese et al. 2011, p. 100.
518 Neagu 2012a, p. 956.
519 Neagu 2012a, p. 977.
520 van der Wilt 2005b, p. 117.
521 Ibid.
522 Opinion of AG Ruiz Jarabo Colomer, above n. 466.
523 *Criminal proceedings Against Hüseyin Gözütok and Klaus Brügge*, above n. 464.

> would benefit from the *ne bis in idem* rule, than to the perpetrators of minor transgressions, which are less socially reprehensible. The perpetrator of a more serious crime, who may be convicted only by a final judgment, could not be judged again in another State signatory to the Convention, quite unlike the perpetrator of a petty offence who has accepted and completed the punishment suggested by the Prosecutor.[524]

More recently, a similar conclusion was reached in the case dealing with *Criminal Proceedings Against Jürgen Kretzinger*.[525] On this pretext, core crimes, owing to their uncontested gravity, would be caught within the *ne bis in idem* tangle. It might sound paradoxical, but the more serious the offence committed, the greater are one's chances to be a direct beneficiary of the *ne bis in idem* rule. Yasmin Naqvi identifies six circumstances which have already arisen in State practice and militate in favour of the non-applicability of *ne bis in idem* to core crimes, these being:

1. legal arguments countering a transnational *ne bis in idem* principle;
2. the exception for fundamental defects, or sham trials, pertaining to the first trial;
3. newly discovered, *id est* fresh, facts or evidence;
4. the State claim to exercise jurisdiction over offences committed on its own territory;
5. exceptions for certain offences; and
6. the exception in case of additional serious offences.[526]

Probably no case fascinatingly mingles amnesties and pardons, in the context of statutory limitations and the *ne bis in idem* rule, in a more pronounced and intellectually stimulating way than the controversial *Finta* one, where the Canadian Supreme Court[527] held that:

> On January 27, 1958, as a result of a statutory limitation that existed under Hungarian law, the punishment of *Finta* in that country became statute-barred. In 1970, the Presidential Council of the Hungarian People's Council issued a general amnesty which, by its terms, applied to *Finta*. In Canada, the trial judge found that the general amnesty did not, either in its own terms or by operation of Hungarian law, constitute a pardon. Further, he found that the Hungarian trial and conviction were nullities under Canadian law. As a result, he concluded that *Finta* was not entitled to plead *autrefois convict* or pardon.[528]

Yasmin Naqvi states that 'this suggests that had the amnesty been considered as a pardon, the Canadian court would have declined to exercise jurisdiction'.[529] State practice, even in Common Law countries, seems to allow the subsequent trial of the same person for having committed the same conduct, be it an act or omission,

---

[524] Paras 115 and 116 respectively.

[525] ECJ, *Criminal proceedings Against Jürgen Kretzinger (Reference for a preliminary ruling from the Bundesgerichtshof)*, 18 July 2007, Case C-288/05, para 43.

[526] Naqvi 2010, pp. 310–325.

[527] Supreme Court, Canada, *Regina v Imre Finta*, 24 March 1994, Case No. 23023, 23097.

[528] *Regina v Imre Finta*, above n. 527, p. 106.

[529] Naqvi 2010, p. 178.

which however constituted a different criminal offence in both States wherein prosecutions were undertaken.[530] The *Omar Mohammed Ali Rezaq* case is a classical example of this scenario. *Rezaq* and two other Palestinian members of the Abu Nidal group[531] hijacked an Egyptair plane and ordered pilots to land the plane in Malta, whereupon *Rezaq* started shooting and killing Israeli and American passengers whom he had separated from others passengers after releasing some females from Egypt and The Philippines. On 25 November 1985, two days after the hijack had begun, Egyptian commandos, in liaison with Maltese authorities, stormed the plane. As a result of the shootout fifty-seven passengers were killed. *Rezaq* was wounded but survived, to be subsequently tried and convicted in Malta, by virtue of Malta's *Kodiċi Kriminali*,[532] for the wilful homicide of those killed, the attempted homicide of those wounded and the illegal possession of arms and explosives. A twenty-five year jail term was inflicted on *Rezaq* by the Maltese Criminal Court, which was confirmed by the Maltese Court of Criminal Appeal on 20 April 1989. However *Rezaq* was released by the Maltese authorities after serving merely seven years, less than a third of his jail term as a result of remissions he gained by virtue of the then prevailing penitentiary system. By means of extraordinary rendition,[533] Federal Bureau of Investigation agents secured his abduction in Lagos, Nigeria in July 1993. A USA Court judge sentenced *Rezaq* to life imprisonment[534] for the criminal offence of air piracy for which Rezaq was not prosecuted in Malta, hence ensuring that the *ne bis in idem rule*[535] be circumvented in a fascinatingly shrewd manner. The judgment was confirmed on appeal on 6 February 1998, hence becoming a *res judicata*. In her concise and flowing opinion, Circuit Judge Patricia Wald, who subsequently served as Judge at ICTY, acknowledged that it is possible that a treaty could contain a double jeopardy clause which is more restrictive, that is, barring more prosecutions, than the Constitution's double jeopardy clause. She referred to *Sindona v Grant*[536] wherein the Court so read a double jeopardy provision in an extradition treaty with Italy but found that *Rezaq* had not shown that the Convention for the Suppression of Unlawful Seizure of Aircraft,[537] on the basis of which *Rezaq* was prosecuted in the District of

[530] For *ne bis in idem* to apply a mere investigation does not suffice. A previous trial is necessary.

[531] For an analysis of Abu Nidal's connection with Malta, see Mifsud and Bugelli 2014, pp. 187–213.

[532] Maltese *Kodiċi Kriminali, Kapitolu 9 tal-Liġijiet ta' Malta* [Criminal Code, Chapter 9 of the Laws of Malta] (1854).

[533] Though this practice is not rare and not novel, it has been referred to as 'one of the most contentious counter-terrorism policies utilized by the USA administration in the post-9/11 era' (Fabbrini 2010, p. 3).

[534] USA Court of Appeals, District of Columbia Circuit, *USA v Omar Mohammed Ali Rezaq*, 6 February 1998, 134 F.3d 1121 (D.C. Cir. 1998), 96-3127.

[535] This is the USA Constitution's double jeopardy clause.

[536] *Michele Sindona v George V. Grant*, above n. 181.

[537] Convention for the Suppression of Unlawful Seizure of Aircraft, above n. 203.

Columbia, fell within this category.[538] This also shows that the prohibition of double jeopardy in the USA is very treaty-dependent. In fact it has been referred to as a 'treaty defense' or a 'treaty right'.[539] She concluded that:

> The *travaux preparatoires* for the Hague Convention reinforce our conclusion that the treaty does not incorporate a special bar on sequential prosecution. They show that the treaty's negotiators considered and rejected the possibility of expressly barring sequential prosecutions through a *ne bis in idem* provision (a term for double-jeopardy provisions in international instruments; another term is *non bis in idem*). The States opposed to this idea, whose views carried the day, argued that "the principle was not applied in exactly the same manner in all States", and that "[i]n taking a decision whether to prosecute, and, similarly, a decision whether to extradite, the State concerned will, in each case, apply its own rule on the subject of *ne bis in idem*". International Civil Aviation Organization, Legal Committee, 17th Session, Document 8877-LC/161, at 8 (1970). This is, of course, exactly what the United States has done in applying its own double jeopardy rules.
>
> Nor is there any indication that Congress, in enacting section 1472(n), read the Hague Convention differently, or intended to subject prosecutions under section 1472(n) to a heightened double jeopardy standard. The text and legislative history of section 1472(n) are both devoid of evidence pointing to such a conclusion. In the absence of any sign that either section 1472(n) or the Hague Convention undertook to impose a more stringent than usual double-jeopardy rule, we conclude that Rezaq's prosecution in Malta was not an obstacle to his subsequent prosecution, in this proceeding, on air piracy charges.[540]

The above has shown how *ne bis in idem* can bring to the fore and how it can encompass other grounds for refusal such as amnesties and double criminality, not to mention fair trial rights. One must note that *aut dedere aut judicare* might be violated if a State fails to either extradite or prosecute. However, it may be misused if a State first decides to prosecute an individual and then opts to extradite him. In this way the alternative or disjunctive *aut dedere aut judicare* obligation could be misused or abused by States to infringe the *ne bis in idem* rule. This is subject to an exception. Circumstances may subsist whereby a prosecution is undertaken in State A. *Pendente lite*, State C assumes possession of reliable and important evidence which ought to be preserved [or may only be produced] in State C. If State A suspends its criminal proceedings and extradites the accused to State C (at this stage, the *forum* which is best positioned/qualified to prosecute), it would not be violating the *ne bis in idem* rule.

---

[538] USA Court of Appeals, District of Columbia Circuit, *USA v Omar Mohammed Ali Rezaq*, Opinion of Judge Patricia Wald, 6 February 1998, 134 F.3d 1121 (D.C. Cir. 1998), 96-3127, para 23.

[539] USA Court of Appeals, Second Circuit, *John Peter Galanis, Petitioner-appellant v Ermen Pallanck, U.S. Marshal for the District of Connecticut, Respondent-appellee,* 22 November 1977, 568 F.2d 234 (2d Cir. 1977), and USA Court of Appeals, Fifth Circuit, *Albert Gusikoff and Paul Rosen, Plaintiffs-Appellants v United States of America, Respondent-Appellee*, 6 June 1980, No. 79-3500, 620 F.2d 459 (5th Cir. 1980).

[540] Opinion of Judge Patricia Wald, above n. 538, paras 28–29.

This shows that the *ne bis in idem* juncture becomes a puzzling predicament when multiple sovereigns are involved as stakeholders of rights.[541] The USA Constitution's Fifth Amendment, for example, has been interpreted to accommodate dual sovereignty between the States and federal systems, each with overlapping jurisdictions over certain crimes.[542] Situations have also arisen whereby prosecutions were deliberately undertaken to shield[543] the accused from any further criminal proceedings.[544] In this context, upon undertaking an analysis of Article 14 (7) of the ICCPR and the case-law of the HRC,[545] it has been stated that *ne bis in idem* 'only prohibits retrials after an acquittal by the same jurisdiction. This limitation on the scope of the principle can serve international justice by permitting other States to step in when the territorial state or the suspect's State fails to conduct a fair trial'.[546] The same author, however, qualifies this by stating that 'the principle applies equally to judgments in other countries under certain conditions'.[547] This sub-heading has shown that *ne bis in idem* can hinder extradition both on a domestic level and on an international level, with the former being more noteworthy than the latter.

16.7.3 The Prohibition of Torture and Other Cruel, Inhuman and Degrading Treatment or Punishment

As shown earlier on, the *jus cogens* nature of the prohibition of torture[548] is not contested, to the extent that the House of Lords emphasized that 'there can be few issues on which international legal opinion is more clear than on the condemnation of torture',[549] whereas jurists upheld that 'if any human rights norm enjoys the

---

[541] This is more so in the international domain, the vertical system of enforcement, which has already been dealt with in Part III.

[542] Cassese et al. 2011, p. 105.

[543] As noted in Part III (particularly Sect. 11.1.1), shielding is constituted by means of a sham undertaking designed specifically to protect the accused from criminal liability.

[544] Cassese et al. cite the successive federal prosecution of four police officers accused of beating *Rodney King* in Los Angeles, California, as a typical example of an attempt to curb shielding (Cassese et al. 2011, p. 105).

[545] *AP v Italy*, above n. 433.

[546] Erikson 2009, p. 65.

[547] Erikson 2009, p. 75.

[548] For a distinction between torture on the one hand, and cruel, inhuman or degrading treatment or punishment on the other, with the former being an aggravated form of the latter, see Rodley 1999, p. 85 and pp. 96–100.

[549] *HoL, A and Others (Appellants) (FC) and Others v Secretary of State for the Home Department (Respondent)* (Conjoined Appeals), Opinion of Lord Bingham of Cornhill, 8 December 2005, {2005}, UKHL 71.

status of *jus cogens*, it is the prohibition on torture'.[550] The net effect of such status is the refusal of extradition where an evident threat of torture subsists. Such threat may be re-defined to the effect that it shall subsist should there exist reasonable grounds to believe that an extraditee could be subjected to torture in the requesting State. Thus, though belonging to the *domaine reserve* of the State, jurists insist that States are prevented from extraditing a person to a country where such person runs the risk of being tortured.[551] Estimating such risk is a difficult task for the requested State which, amidst its power to investigate the human rights record of the requesting State, finds itself in a catch-22 situation.[552] If it refuses extradition out of concern for the prospective fate of the requested person, it elicits the wrath of the requesting State. If it extradites, the requested State itself may turn out to be co-responsible for violating human rights both vis-à-vis the victimized individual and also towards State Parties to a human rights convention.[553]

Rather than invoking reasonable grounds to believe that the extraditee could be subjected to torture,[554] the CAT, in the context of provisional measures, habitually adopts the test of reasonableness in order to protect an extraditee from irreparable harm.[555] However, a mere evident threat of cruel, inhuman and degrading treatment or punishment might not be enough to justify refusal of extradition, although under the ECvHR, the absolute prohibition[556] does not only apply to torture but also applies to inhuman and degrading treatment, nullifying any margin of appreciation.[557] Important jurisprudence has occasionally failed to distinguish between torture on the one hand and cruel, inhuman, degrading treatment or punishment on the other hand. The ECtHR has stated that:

> It is the settled case-law of the Court that the decision by a Contracting State to extradite a fugitive – and, *a fortiori*, the actual extradition itself – may give rise to an issue under Article 3, and hence engage the responsibility of that State under the Convention, where substantial grounds have been shown for believing that the person in question would, if extradited, face a real risk of being subjected to treatment contrary to Article 3 in the receiving country. The establishment of such responsibility inevitably involves an assessment of conditions in the requesting country against the standards of Article 3 of the Convention.[558]

[550] Dugard and van den Wyngaert 1998, p. 198.

[551] de Wet 2004, p. 97.

[552] van der Wilt 2012a, pp. 160 and 149.

[553] van der Wilt 2012a, p. 149.

[554] For such purpose, naturally the Strasbourg authorities reserve the right to review not only the domestic judicial procedures of the custodial [requested] State but also the risk to which the individual might be exposed in the State to which he is to be sent, that is, in the requesting State (Gomien et al. 1996, p. 112).

[555] Committee Against Torture, *Cecilia Rosana Núñez Chipana v Venezuela*, 10 November 1998, Communication No. 110/1998, para 8.

[556] This entails that the prohibition applies even during times of armed conflict or when national security is threatened.

[557] For a comprehensive understanding of the 'margin of appreciation' doctrine, see Legg 2012.

[558] *Mohammed Ali Hassan Al-Moayad vs Germany*, above n. 380, para 62.

Even at municipal level, occasionally, torture on the one hand, and inhuman and/or degrading treatment and/or punishment on the other hand, have not been distinctively categorised. In the *Lewis Muscat* extradition case, as counsel and on behalf of *Lewis Muscat*, I successfully obtained a constitutional reference which the Maltese Court of Criminal Appeal (presided by the then Chief Justice Vincent De Gaetano, currently Judge at the European Court of Human Rights) made owing to concerns that overcrowding in Californian prisons was rampant, and that Californian prisons had been condemned by the UN Committee Against Torture for subjecting inmates to excessive force, psychological harassment and degrading treatment.[559] These concerns were subsequently quelled by means of a written assurance furnished, in September 2006, by the then California governor Arnold Schwarzeneger.[560] *Lewis Muscat* was extradited to the USA and detained at Sacramento County Main Jail on 25 April 2007.[561] Where, in connection with a mass prison escape, evidence is adduced that if extradited to Northern Ireland there existed a likelihood that the extraditee would be subjected to abuse by prison officers particularly since other escapees in comparable circumstances were assaulted by police officers who were never brought to trial, the extraditee is deemed to be a 'probable target for ill-treatment' and should not be extradited.[562] In the request brought within the parameters of the Framework Decision on the EAW, a mere possibility of ill-treatment will not satisfy the burden of proof, but reasonable grounds showing a real risk of ill-treatment are required.[563] Nevertheless a marked distinction between torture on the one hand, and inhuman and/or degrading treatment and/or punishment on the other hand has been detected. To clarify the prevailing distinction, 'torture was inhuman treatment which has a purpose, such as the obtaining of information or confessions, or the infliction of punishment, and it is generally an aggravated form of inhuman treatment. So, for torture to occur, a scale of criteria has to be climbed. First, the behaviour must be degrading treatment; second, it must be inhuman treatment; and third, it must be an aggravated form of inhuman treatment, inflicted for certain purposes'.[564]

---

559 Court of Criminal Appeal, Malta, *The Police (Inspector Raymond Cutajar & Inspector Raymond Aquilina) v. Lewis Muscat*, 31 August 2016, Criminal Appeal No. 278/2006.

560 http://www.timesofmalta.com/articles/view/20060901/local/chief-justice-upholds-request-by-man-wanted-in-the-us.42773 (accessed 2 October 2016) and related newspaper articles at http://www.independent.com.mt/articles/2006-09-01/news/court-mans-case-referred-to-constitutional-court-96143/. Accessed 2 October 2016. http://www.maltamedia.com/artman2/publish/law_order/article_1613.shtml. Accessed 2 October 2016.

561 http://www.independent.com.mt/articles/2007-05-04/news/fbi-announces-that-lewis-muscat-is-in-us-custody-172868/. Accessed 2 October 2016.

562 *Finucane v McMahon*, above n. 372, para 206, cited in Forde and Kelly 2011, p. 120, n. 175.

563 Supreme Court, Ireland, *Minister for Justice, Equality and Law Reform v Robert Rettinger*, Appeal No: 165 & 189 of 2010, [2010] IESC 45 [2010], 1 L.R.M. 157, cited in Forde and Kelly 2011, p. 120, n. 177.

564 Rodley 1999, pp. 77–78.

This distinction can have far-reaching legal consequences which may be compared to water which seeps and percolates through cracks in a wall. In fact, domestic courts have been willing to prioritise the freedom from torture over the requested extradition[565] but have not done the same when the level of severity of the prospective violation did not exceed the threshold of 'inhuman and degrading'. In such case 'courts have adapted (and downplayed) the concept of 'inhuman and degrading treatment' and balanced it against the "'beneficial purpose of extradition'".[566] Extradition, or rather the extradition request, acts as an elastic measuring tape because it has the capacity to lengthen a short measurement. Harmen van der Wilt cites the case of '*Bary* and *Al Fawwaz*, who faced surrender to the United States on the suspicion of having been involved in the synchronized bombings of the United States embassies in Nairobi and Dar Es Salaam'.[567] In this case 'the Court quoted with approval Lord Hoffmann who had expressed in the Wellington case his opinion that:

> The desirability of extradition is a factor to be taken into account in deciding whether the punishment likely to be imposed in the receiving State attains the "minimum level of severity" which would make it inhuman and degrading. Punishment which counts as inhuman and degrading in the domestic context will not necessarily be so regarded when the extradition factor has been taken into account.

Following this track, the Court concluded that:

> Neither SAMs (Special Administrative Measures) or life without parole cross the article 3 threshold in the present case. Although near to the borderline the prison conditions at ADX Florence, although very harsh do not amount to inhuman or degrading treatment either on their own or in combination with SAMs and in the context of a whole life sentence. Whether the high article 3 threshold for inhuman or degrading treatment is crossed depends on the facts of the particular case. There is no common standard for what does or does not amount to inhuman or degrading treatment throughout the many different countries in the world. The importance of maintaining extradition in a case where the fugitive would not otherwise be tried is an important factor in identifying the threshold in the present case.[568]

The phrase 'would not otherwise be tried' may infer that no extradition would be authorised if another State can exercise jurisdiction elsewhere. The CAT,[569] which established a Committee Against Torture, introduced the concept of non-

[565] *Ústavní Soud* [Constitutional Court], Czech Republic, *V. M. against a decision of the Regional Court in Ostrava of 4 December 2000 (Danger of Torture* case), 15 April 2003, I. ÚS 752/02, cited in van der Wilt 2012a, p. 156, n. 34.

[566] van der Wilt 2012a, p. 156.

[567] van der Wilt 2012a, pp. 156–157.

[568] High Court of Justice, Queen's Bench Division, Divisional Court, UK, *Regina (on the application of Adel Abdul Bary and Khalid Al Fawwaz) v Secretary of State for the Home Department*, 7 August 2009, CO/5577/2008 and C0/5511/2008, [2009] WL 2392232, cited in van der Wilt 2012a, p. 157, n. 37.

[569] Article 3(1).

refoulement in the event of a threat of torture,[570] provided for a system of universal jurisdiction and established the *aut dedere aut judicare* rule in relation to the crime of torture. This fits like a glove in the scenario postulated by myself within Part IV, especially because 'strands of the Strasbourg jurisprudence were generally marked by the Court's implicit tendency to follow the case law of the Committee' Against Torture[571] and the reports of the Special Rapporteur on Torture.[572] Such reports have occasionally constituted a persuasive source of law, or rather an interpretative tool.[573]

Although the *Pinochet* case is deeply associated with the core crime of torture within the context of extradition proceedings,[574] I affirm that Lord Bingham's opinion is the most comprehensive and juridically sound expression on the status of torture under international law and the ensuing consequences that such status has on an extradition request, notwithstanding the fact that this opinion primarily dealt with the use of evidence resulting from involuntary confessions.[575] In this opinion, Lord Bingham of Cornhall eloquently postulates three fundamental factors which can influence the impact that the prohibition of torture could have on extradition proceedings. A close look at these fundamental features is a *sine qua non* in the light of the matter under scrutiny. He starts off by referring to the *Filartiga* paradigm and by speaking of a 'current universal revulsion against torture'.[576] He proceeds to enlist and elaborate upon the three peculiar features of torture, portraying a remarkable command of the subject-matter and critically analysing case-law, conveying that:

1. the prohibition covers potential breaches, which entails that it is insufficient for a State to intervene after the infliction of torture, but States must put in place all those measures that may pre-empt the perpetration of torture;
2. the prohibition imposes obligations *erga omnes*, entailing a correlative right of all members of the international community, the violation of which gives rise to a claim for compliance accruing to each and every member which acquires the right to insist on the fulfilment of the obligation or to call for the breach to be discontinued;

[570] The existence of a pattern of gross, flagrant or mass violations of human rights does not automatically give rise to the application of the *non-refoulement* principle. The applicant must show that he or she would be individually at risk of torture if removed [*Chipana v Venezuela*, above n. 555].

[571] Forowicz 2010, p. 213.

[572] Forowicz 2010, p. 217.

[573] ECtHR Grand Chamber, *Karamjit Singh Chahal v UK*, 15 November 1996, App. No. 22414/93, and ECtHR First Section, *Ilhomjon Ismoilov and others v Russia*, 24 April 2008, App. No. 2947/06.

[574] This is particularly so because the Law Lords limited the scope of the extradition inquiry in England to two offences, torture and conspiracy to torture (Wilson 1999, p. 977).

[575] Opinion of Lord Bingham of Cornhill, above n. 549.

[576] Opinion of Lord Bingham of Cornhill, above n. 549, para 147.

3. the prohibition has acquired the status of *jus cogens* which, firstly, gives rise to a *locus standi* of potential victims before a competent international or national judicial body, secondly, entitles States to investigate, prosecute and punish or extradite individuals accused of torture who are present in a territory under its jurisdiction, and thirdly precludes the application of statutory limitations and the political offence exemption to extradition.[577] To this extent the *jus cogens* nature of the prohibition has consequences on other grounds for refusal.

On the same lines, where a prohibition, such as freedom from torture, is dictated by a *jus cogens* norm, a Mauritanian amnesty law becomes superfluous since it did not preclude France from exercising jurisdiction over army captain *Ely Ould Dah*, an intelligence officer at the Jreida prison base who was charged for having ordered and participated in the torture carried out against two black Mauritanian soldiers during the Senegalese-Mauritanian conflict between 1989 and 1991.[578] In a regional context, the absolute character of the general prohibition on torture, which also results from Article 4 of the EU Charter of Fundamental Rights,[579] constitutes a hurdle for the execution of the EAW. A two-step screening test is adopted. First the executing authority must rely on objective, reliable, specific and properly updated information on the prevailing detention conditions in the issuing Member State which display the existence of deficiencies. In the second step the executing authorities must ascertain whether in the specific case the requested person would face such a real risk of inhuman or degrading treatment. However, this does not constitute a direct ground of refusal, but a mandatory ground for postponement of the request[580] which is not expressly provided for within the Framework Decision on the EAW,[581] the object of which is to provide additional information which would enable the executing judicial authority to exclude the existence of such real risk within a reasonable time.[582] Szilard Gaspar-Szilagyi, analysing the last sentence of the operative part of the *Aranyosi* and *Caldararu* judgment, states that if the risk subsists 'the executing authority must decide whether it should terminate the surrender procedure'.[583] The prevailing procedural iter therefore allows defaulting States to cure their default by means of a method which partially resembles the granting of assurances to the requested State further to an extradition

577 Opinion of Lord Bingham of Cornhill, above n. 549, paras 147–159.

578 *Cour de Cassation* [Court of Cassation], France, *Public Prosecutor v Ely Ould Dah*, 23 October 2002, 02-85379.

579 By virtue of Article 6 sub-article 1 of the Treaty on the Functioning of the EU (as amended by the Lisbon Treaty, above n. 501), the EU Charter of Fundamental Rights (2000) Charter of Fundamental Rights of the European Union, Official Journal of the European Communities, (2000/C 364/01), has been given the same legal value as the EU treaties.

580 ECJ, *Pál Aranyosi and Robert Căldăraru v Generalstaatsanwaltschaft Bremen*, 5 April 2016, C-404/15 and C-659/15 PPU, para 98, cited in Gaspar-Szilagyi 2016, p. 208, n. 71.

581 Gaspar-Szilagyi 2016, p. 211.

582 Gaspar-Szilagyi 2016, p. 208.

583 Gaspar-Szilagyi 2016, p. 209.

request. It also converges standards of the ECJ with those of the ECtHR.[584] However, the ground for postponement can ultimately constitute a *de facto* ground of refusal to surrender the requested person.[585]

The prohibition of torture, cruel, inhuman and degrading treatment or punishment has been tested in the light of the prospect of a judicial sentence imposing life imprisonment. This punishment is meted out, albeit in a differential manner,[586] both in Europe[587] and beyond.[588] Although Portugal, a EU and CoE member State, has prohibited life imprisonment,[589] as a general rule, the mere fact that a life sentence could eventually be served in full, does not render it contrary to Article 3 of the ECvHR.[590] The sequential reasoning of the ECtHR is self-explanatory and deserves to be reproduced here under:

> The Court has consistently stressed that the suffering and humiliation involved must in any event go beyond that inevitable element of suffering or humiliation connected with a given form of legitimate treatment or punishment. Measures depriving a person of his liberty may often involve such an element. In accordance with Article 3 of the Convention, the State must ensure that a person is detained under conditions which are compatible with respect for his human dignity and that the manner and method of the execution of the measure do not subject him to distress or hardship exceeding the unavoidable level of suffering inherent in detention (see *Kudła v. Poland* [Grand Chamber], no. 30210/96, §§ 92–94, European Court of Human Rights 2000-XI).
>
> The imposition of a sentence of life imprisonment on an adult offender is not in itself prohibited by or incompatible with Article 3 or any other Article of the Convention (see, *inter alia*, among many authorities, *Kotälla v. the Netherlands*, no. 7994/77, Commission decision of 6 May 1978, Decisions and Reports (DR) 14, p. 238; *Bamber v. the United Kingdom*, no. 13183/87, Commission decision of 14 December 1988, DR 59, p. 235; and *Sawoniuk v. the United Kingdom* (dec.), no. 63716/00, ECHR 2001-VI). At the same time, however, the Court has also held that the imposition of an irreducible life sentence on an adult may raise an issue under Article 3 (see, *inter alia*, *Nivette v. France* (dec.), no. 44190/

---

584 Gaspar-Szilagyi 2016, pp. 217–218.

585 Gaspar-Szilagyi 2016, p. 216.

586 Italy, France, Australia and Canada 'tailor different minimum terms with reference to the crimes committed … in order to render the system more flexible' (Marchesi 2018, pp. 113–114).

587 *Prosecutor v Eshetu Alemu*, above n. 459. As stated here above, Eshetu Alemu has been sentenced for life by a Dutch Court in The Hague in 2017 [DutchNews.nl (2018) https://www.dutchnews.nl/news/2018/01/dutch-ethiopian-jailed-for-war-crimes-appeals-against-his-life-sentence/. Accessed 30 January 2018]. Moreover, the Stockholm District Court, on 27 June 2018, sentenced *Théodore Rukeratabaro*, a Rwandan, to life imprisonment after finding him guilty of genocide and crimes against humanity committed against the Tutsi [Karuhanga (2018) https://www.newtimes.co.rw/news/government-welcomes-life-sentence-against-genocide-suspect-sweden. Accessed 11 September 2018].

588 Judges in Buenos Aires sentenced 29 former officials to life imprisonment in a case documenting the former military dictatorship's widespread practice of killing civilians by throwing them from aircraft [Politi D, Londoño E (2017) https://www.nytimes.com/2017/11/29/world/americas/argentina-death-flights-trial-dictatorship.html. Accessed 9 January 2018].

589 Appleton and Grover 2007, p. 608, n. 39.

590 ECtHR, *László Magyar v Hungary*, 20 May 2014, Application No. 73593/10, cited in ECtHR Press Unit 2017, pp. 4–5.

> 98, European Court of Human Rights 2001-VII; *Einhorn*, cited above; *Stanford v. the United Kingdom* (dec.), no. 73299/01, 12 December 2002; and *Wynne v. the United Kingdom* (dec.), no. 67385/01, 22 May 2003).
>
> In determining whether a life sentence in a given case can be regarded as irreducible, the Court has sought to ascertain whether a life prisoner can be said to have any prospect of release. An analysis of the Court's case-law on the subject discloses that where national law affords the possibility of review of a life sentence with a view to its commutation, remission, termination or the conditional release of the prisoner, will be sufficient to satisfy Article 3. The Court has held, for instance, in a number of cases that, where detention was subject to review for the purposes of parole after the expiry of the minimum term for serving the life sentence, it could not be said that the life prisoners in question had been deprived of any hope of release (see, for example, *Stanford*, cited above; *Hill v. the United Kingdom* (dec.), no. 19365/02, 18 March 2003; and *Wynne*, cited above). The Court has found that this is the case even in the absence of a minimum term of unconditional imprisonment and even when the possibility of parole for prisoners serving a life sentence is limited (see, for example, *Einhorn*, cited above, §§ 27–28). It follows that a life sentence does not become "irreducible" by the mere fact that in practice it may be served in full. It is enough for the purposes of Article 3 that a life sentence is *de jure* and *de facto* reducible.
>
> Consequently, although the Convention does not confer, in general, a right to release on licence or a right to have a sentence reconsidered by a national authority, judicial or administrative, with a view to its remission or termination (see, *inter alia*, *Kotälla*, and *Bamber*, both cited above; and *Treholt v. Norway*, no. 14610/89, Commission decision of 9 July 1991, DR 71, p. 168), it is clear from the relevant case-law that the existence of a system providing for consideration of the possibility of release is a factor to be taken into account when assessing the compatibility of a particular life sentence with Article 3. In this context, however, it should be observed that a State's choice of a specific criminal-justice system, including sentence review and release arrangements, is in principle outside the scope of the supervision the Court carries out at European level, provided that the system chosen does not contravene the principles set forth in the Convention (see, *mutatis mutandis*, *Achour v. France* [Grand Chamber], no. 67335/01, § 51, European Court of Human Rights 2006-IV).

I note that the ECtHR has not conclusively established objective criteria or explicit guidelines to aid it in its assessment of the prospect of release, nor did it identify the threshold, percentage, extent or degree of success of such prospect. In fact it held that:

> In the instant case, the Court must determine whether the sentence of life imprisonment imposed on the applicant in the particular circumstances has removed any prospect of his release.
>
> In reaching its decision the Court has had regard to the standards prevailing amongst the member States of the Council of Europe in the field of penal policy, in particular concerning sentence review and release arrangements (see *Soering v. the United Kingdom*, 7 July 1989, § 102, Series A no. 161; and *V. v. the United Kingdom* [GC], no. 24888/94, § 72, European Court of Human Rights 1999-IX). It has also taken into account the increasing concern regarding the treatment of persons serving long-term prison sentences, particularly life sentences, reflected in a number of Council of Europe texts (see paragraphs 68–73 above).
>
> At the outset the Court notes that in Cyprus the offence of premeditated murder carries a mandatory sentence of life imprisonment (see paragraphs 31–33 above), which under the Criminal Code, as confirmed by the domestic courts, is tantamount to imprisonment for the

rest of the convicted person's life. Furthermore, it observes that Cypriot law does not provide for a minimum term for serving a life sentence or for the possibility of its remission on the basis of good conduct and industry. However, the adjustment of such a sentence is possible at any stage irrespective of the time served in prison. In particular, under Article 53 § 4 of the Constitution as it has been applied since 1963, the President of the Republic, on the recommendation of the Attorney-General, may suspend, remit or commute any sentence passed by a court (see paragraphs 36–37 above). The President can therefore at any point in time commute a life sentence to another one of a shorter duration and then remit it, affording the possibility of immediate release. Moreover, section 14 of the Prison Law of 1996 provides for the conditional release of prisoners, including life prisoners (see paragraph 59 above). In line with this provision, subject to the provisions of the Constitution, the President, with the agreement of the Attorney-General, can order by decree the conditional release of a prisoner at any time.

Admittedly, it follows from the above provisions that the prospect of release for prisoners serving life sentences in Cyprus is limited, any adjustment of a life sentence being only within the President's discretion, subject to the agreement of the Attorney-General. Furthermore, as acknowledged by the Government, there are certain shortcomings in the current procedure (see paragraph 91 above). Notwithstanding, the Court does not find that life sentences in Cyprus are irreducible with no possibility of release; on the contrary, it is clear that in Cyprus such sentences are both *de jure* and *de facto* reducible. In this connection, the Court notes that from the parties' submissions it transpires that life prisoners have been released under Article 53 § 4 of the Constitution. In particular, nine life prisoners were released in 1993 and another two in 1997 and 2005 respectively (see paragraphs 52 and 90 above and paragraph 158 below). All of these prisoners, apart from one, had been serving mandatory life sentences. In addition, a life prisoner can benefit from the relevant provisions at any time without having to serve a minimum period of imprisonment. Consequently, it cannot be inferred that the applicant has no possibility of release and he has not adduced evidence to warrant such an inference.

In his submissions, the applicant has placed great emphasis on the lack of a parole board system in Cyprus. However, the Court reiterates that matters relating to early release policies including the manner of their implementation fall within the power member States have in the sphere of criminal justice and penal policy (see, *mutatis mutandis*, *Achour*, cited above, § 44). In this connection, the Court observes that at the present time there is not yet a clear and commonly accepted standard amongst the member States of the Council of Europe concerning life sentences and, in particular, their review and method of adjustment. Moreover, no clear tendency can be ascertained with regard to the system and procedures implemented in respect of early release.

In view of the above, the Court considers that the applicant cannot claim that he has been deprived of any prospect of release and that his continued detention as such, even though long, constitutes inhuman or degrading treatment. However, the Court is conscious of the shortcomings in the procedure currently in place (see paragraph 91 above) and notes the recent steps taken for the introduction of reforms.

Furthermore, with regard to the applicant's second complaint, although the change in the applicable legislation and consequent frustration of his expectations of release must have caused him a certain amount of anxiety, the Court does not consider that in the circumstances this attained the level of severity required to fall within the scope of Article 3. Bearing in mind the chronology of events and, in particular, the lapse of time between them, it cannot be said that the applicant could justifiably harbour genuine expectations that he would be released in November 2002. In this connection, the Court notes that apart from the clear sentence passed by the Assize Court in 1989 the relevant changes in the domestic law happened within a period of approximately four years, that is, between 1992 and 1996, thus about six years before the release date given by the prison authorities to the applicant

> came around. Therefore, any feelings of hope on the part of the applicant linked to the prospect of early release must have diminished as it became clear with the changes in domestic law that he would be serving the life sentence passed on him by the Assize Court.
>
> It is true that a life sentence such as the one imposed on and served by the applicant without a minimum term necessarily entails anxiety and uncertainty related to prison life but these are inherent in the nature of the sentence imposed and, considering the prospects for release under the current system, do not warrant a conclusion of inhuman and degrading treatment under Article 3.
>
> Accordingly, the Court finds that there has been no violation of that provision.[591]

It is noteworthy that in the *Kafkaris* case partly dissenting Judge Javier Borrego Borrego opined that:

> The applicant's "future [is] death in prison" (paragraph 85). Why?
>
> Because "any adjustment of a life sentence [is] only within the President's discretion" (see paragraph 103), and the President, who is precisely the highest State institution, visited the applicant in an (unsuccessful) attempt to request his cooperation.
>
> If the applicant does not identify the person who hired him to carry out the crime, he will not leave prison alive. He is aware of this, as are his lawyer and the entire country. Surprisingly, it seems that the majority of the Court do not realise this, hence the reasoning concerning Article 3, which to my mind has been produced from an ivory tower. Several paragraphs, such as paragraph 106, display a lack of sensitivity that is unworthy of a court of human rights.[592]

The above extracts discloses the stark differences in the perception that Judges may have when they evaluate, weigh and assess the prospects of release, or otherwise, of applicants. Admittedly, this is a difficult task. Following this important case, *Babar Ahmad and others* contested the extradition from the UK to the USA because, in their view, if convicted in the USA, they would be held at ADX Florence where conditions of detention violated Article 3 of the ECvHR, they would be subjected to special administrative measures and would face life sentences without parole.[593] The ECtHR[594] spelt out criteria which must be considered when determining whether the alleged ill-treatment attained the required minimum level of severity or otherwise. These include all the circumstances of the case, which ought to be considered cumulatively, particularly:

---

[591] ECtHR Grand Chamber, *Panayiotis Agapiou Panayi alias Kafkaris v Cyprus*, 12 February 2008, Application No. 21906/04, paras 96–108.

[592] *Panayiotis Agapiou Panayi alias Kafkaris v Cyprus*, above n. 591, *Partly Dissenting Opinion of Judge Francisco Javier Borrego Borrego*, para 9.

[593] One can speak of a general right of eligibility for parole but not of a right to parole. The latter right to parole was identified by Judge Pinto de Albuquerque in his dissenting opinion in ECtHR Grand Chamber, *Arthur Hutchinson v UK*, Dissenting Opinion of Judge Pinto de Albuquerque, 17 January 2017, Application No. 57592/08, paras 2–6.

[594] ECtHR Fourth Section, *Babar Ahmad and Others v UK*, 10 April 2012, Application Numbers 24027/07, 11949/08, 36742/08, 66911/09 and 67354/09.

i. the duration of the treatment;
ii. the physical and mental effects of the treatment; and
iii. the state of health of the victim.[595]

It further considered relevant issues dealing with detention, including recreation and outdoor exercise in prison, together with solitary confinement in the context of the European Prison Rules. Most importantly, although, in principle, matters relating to the infliction of punishment are dealt with exclusively by domestic courts which enjoy the necessary discretion *de lege*, hence falling outside the scope of the ECvHR, 'a grossly disproportionate sentence could amount to ill-treatment contrary to Article 3 at the moment of its imposition'.[596] The ECtHR distinguished between three types of life sentences, namely:

1. one with eligibility for release after a minimum period has been served;
2. another being a discretionary sentence of life imprisonment without the possibility of parole;[597] and
3. a third being a mandatory sentence of life imprisonment without the possibility of parole.

It held that the first type raises no issue under Article 3 of the ECvHR, that the second may be imposed after due consideration of all relevant mitigating and aggravating factors is made, whereas in relation to the latter type, greater scrutiny was necessary. This was because the third type of life sentence deprives the defendant of any possibility to put any mitigating factors or special circumstances before the sentencing court. The ECtHR concluded that a mandatory sentence of life imprisonment without the possibility of parole is not *per se* incompatible with the ECvHR. However, such sentence is 'more likely to be grossly disproportionate than any of the other types of life sentence, especially if it requires the sentencing court to disregard mitigating factors which are generally understood as indicating a significantly lower level of culpability on the part of the defendant, such as youth or severe mental health problems'.[598] Since, when dealing with core crimes, the likelihood of the infliction of a sentence imposing life imprisonment is high, it seems that *ergastolani*[599] will not be able to avoid such penalty on human rights grounds. The same may be said to apply should the prison conditions in the requesting State be poor as a result of, *inter alia*, overcrowding. This is because

595 *Babar Ahmad and Others v UK*, above n. 594, para 170, paras 200–204.

596 *Babar Ahmad and Others v UK*, above n. 594, para 170, para 237.

597 Parole is commonly equated to conditional release [ECtHR Grand Chamber, *Arthur Hutchinson v UK*, 17 January 2017, Application No. 57592/08, para 20]. For an understanding of the relevant principles which constitute requirements for compliance with an accepted parole mechanism, see ECtHR Grand Chamber, *James Clifton Murray v The Netherlands*, 26 April 2016, Application No. 10511/10, paras 99–100.

598 *Babar Ahmad and Others v UK*, above n. 594, para 242.

599 These are persons sentenced to imprisonment for life, referred to as 'lifers' by Judge Pinto de Albuquerque in his dissenting opinion [Dissenting Opinion of Judge Pinto de Albuquerque, above n. 593, para 35].

such matters, though constitutive of inhuman and degrading punishment and though in breach of the UN Standard Minimum Rules for the Treatment of Prisoners, would fall short of being categorized as 'torture'. Notwithstanding the above, States are given sufficient leeway (margin of appreciation) in determining the measures which are required in order to give a life prisoner a prospect of release,[600] or, in more elegant terms, 'a right to hope'.[601] Yet, State Parties to the ECvHR are obliged to devise and enact a procedure which constitutes a mechanism in order to review life sentences for the purposes of compatibility with Article 3 of the ECvHR.[602] In other words, States must create a juridical framework against which life sentences should be measured to ensure that they do not cross the line which precedes their categorization as inhuman and degrading treatment. This framework should cater for a prospect of release together with a possibility to have the sentence reviewed.[603] One would have to see whether States can circumvent such requirements when, rather than convicting an individual to life imprisonment, it convicts such individual to one hundred and twenty years and/or to two hundred and forty years.[604]

Subsequently, the ECtHR has upheld that:

> For the foregoing reasons, the Court considers that, in the context of a life sentence, Article 3 must be interpreted as requiring reducibility of the sentence, in the sense of a review which allows the domestic authorities to consider whether any changes in the life prisoner are so significant, and such progress towards rehabilitation has been made in the course of the sentence, as to mean that continued detention can no longer be justified on legitimate penological grounds.
>
> However, the Court would emphasise that, having regard to the margin of appreciation which must be accorded to Contracting States in the matters of criminal justice and sentencing (see paragraphs above), it is not its task to prescribe the form (executive or judicial) which that review should take. For the same reason, it is not for the Court to determine when that review should take place. This being said, the Court would also observe that the comparative and international law materials before it show clear support for the institution of a dedicated mechanism guaranteeing a review no later than twenty-five years after the imposition of a life sentence, with further periodic reviews thereafter (see paragraphs above).

---

600 *Murray v The Netherlands*, above n. 597, cited in ECtHR Press Unit 2017, p. 7.

601 ECtHR Former Fifth Section, *Nizar Trabelsi v Belgium*, Separate Opinion of Judge Power-Forde, 4 September 2014, Application No. 140/10, cited in ECtHR Former Fifth Section, *Nizar Trabelsi v Belgium*, Concurring Opinion of Judge Yudkivska, 4 September 2014, Application No. 140/10. The Concurring Opinion has no paragraph numbers.

602 *Nizar Trabelsi v Belgium*, above n. 601, para 137.

603 ECtHR Grand Chamber, *Douglas Gary Vinter and Others v UK*, 9 July 2013, Application Numbers 66069/09, 130/10, 3896/10, para 110, cited in *Qorti Kostituzzjonali* [Constitutional Court] Malta, *Ben Hassine Ben Ali Wahid v Honourable Prime Minister and Advocate-General of the Republic of Malta*, 7 November 2016, Constitutional Application 60/13 AF, para 50, n. 17.

604 Guatemala sentenced *Esteelmer Reyes Giron* and *Heriberto Valdez* for crimes against humanity [High Risk Tribunal, Guatemala City, Guatemala, *Prosecutor v Esteelmer Reyes Girón* and *Heriberto Valdez Asij, Verdict*, 26 February 2016].

> It follows from this conclusion that, where domestic law does not provide for the possibility of such a review, a whole life sentence will not measure up to the standards of Article 3 of the Convention.
>
> Although the requisite review is a prospective event necessarily subsequent to the passing of the sentence, a whole life prisoner should not be obliged to wait and serve an indeterminate number of years of his sentence before he can raise the complaint that the legal conditions attaching to his sentence fail to comply with the requirements of Article 3 in this regard. This would be contrary both to legal certainty and to the general principles on victim status within the meaning of that term in Article 34 of the Convention. Furthermore, in cases where the sentence, on imposition, is irreducible under domestic law, it would be capricious to expect the prisoner to work towards his own rehabilitation without knowing whether, at an unspecified, future date, a mechanism might be introduced which would allow him, on the basis of that rehabilitation, to be considered for release. A whole life prisoner is entitled to know, at the outset of his sentence, what he must do to be considered for release and under what conditions, including when a review of his sentence will take place or may be sought. Consequently, where domestic law does not provide any mechanism or possibility for review of a whole life sentence, the incompatibility with Article 3 on this ground already arises at the moment of the imposition of the whole life sentence and not at a later stage of incarceration.[605]

Sometimes the nature of the crime, *per se*, can detract the prospect of release. Since *Öcalan* was a convicted Kurd sentenced to aggravated life imprisonment for a crime against State security, 'it was clearly prohibited for him to apply for release throughout the duration of his sentence'.[606] The nature of the crime[607] which forms the subject of the conviction is also relevant when the extent to which the discretionary[608] life sentence is proportional or otherwise is considered.[609] Therefore, life sentences can be legitimately inflicted, but 'they must provide a prospect for release and a possibility of periodic review, even if, in a specific case, release is never attained'.[610]

The potential imposition of life imprisonment with special provisions (conditions), solitary confinement (also referred to as 'isolation') being a type thereof, has also stood in the way of the transfer (referral) of cases from ICTR to Rwandan criminal courts on the grounds that, without adequate safeguards, the right not to be subjected to cruel, inhuman or degrading punishment would be breached. This

---

605 *Vinter and Others v UK*, above n. 603, paras 119–122.

606 ECtHR Second Section, *Abdullah Öcalan v Turkey* (No. 2), 18 March 2014, Applications numbers 24069/03, 197/04, 6201/06 and 10464/07, cited in ECtHR Press Unit 2017, p. 4.

607 Trabelsi was prosecuted in the USA for *al-Qaeda* inspired acts of terrorism [*Trabelsi v Belgium*, above n. 601, para 121].

608 This denotes that the Judge could have imposed a less severe (lighter) sentence of imprisonment [*Trabelsi v Belgium*, above n. 601, para 121].

609 *Trabelsi v Belgium*, above n. 601, para 121.

610 Gianelli 2017, pp. 407–408.

happened in *Prosecutor v Yussuf Munyakazi*[611] and in *Prosecutor v Ildephonse Hategekimana*.[612] These cases abated a ruling of the Rwandan Supreme Court[613] which found that the imposition of solitary confinement did not amount to torture, this being a decision that did not reassure ICTR and foreign States which requested the extradition of genocide fugitives from Rwanda.[614] An Irish Court has recently refused extradition to the USA, *inter alia*, on the grounds of long periods of solitary confinement associated with one USA prison.[615]

Article 5(2) of the Framework Decision on the EAW also stipulates that when the offence carries a custodial life sentence or life-time detention order, surrender may be refused where the requesting State has no law or practice for reviewing it at least after twenty years have been served. The compatibility of the infliction of life imprisonment with human rights law has also been tested by domestic courts. Courts in South Africa, Namibia, Germany and the USA (in cases of juveniles convicted of non-homicidal offences) have declared that the sentence of life imprisonment, only without the possibility of parole, is cruel and inhuman, hence unconstitutional.[616] The Supreme Court of the Netherlands, the *Hoge Raad*, dismissed claims that the imposition of a life sentence constituted inhuman treatment since Dutch law caters for a pardon and for the possibility to appeal to the civil judge on the basis of a supposed unlawfulness of further execution of the sentence.[617] Reynaldo Bignone, the *de facto* President of Argentina between 1982 and 1983, was punished by means of various sentences of life imprisonment after being convicted of crimes against humanity in several trials on the basis of his involvement in the *Guerra Sucia*, the so-called Dirty War.[618] In conclusion, one may

---

611 ICTR Trial Chamber III, *Prosecutor v Yussuf Munyakazi, Decision on Prosecutor's Request for Referral of the Indictment to the Republic of Rwanda, Rule 11bis of the Rules of Procedure and Evidence*, 28 May 2008, Case No. ICTR-97-36A-T, paras 22–32, cited in Rugege and Karimunda 2014, p. 106, n. 105.

612 ICTR Trial Chamber III, *Prosecutor v Ildephonse Hategekimana, Decision on Prosecutor's Request for the Referral of the Case of Ildephonse Hategekimana to Rwanda*, 19 June 2008, Case No. ICTR-00-55BR11bis, para 78, also cited in Rugege and Karimunda 2014, p. 107, n. 112.

613 Supreme Court, Rwanda, *Tubarimo Aloys v The Government*, 29 August 2008, Case. No. RS/INCONST/Pén. 0002/08/CS, also cited in Rugege and Karimunda 2014, p. 106, n. 107.

614 Rugege and Karimunda 2014, p. 106.

615 High Court, Ireland, *Attorney General v Damache*, 30 June 2015, IEHC 339, cited in Boister 2016, p. 25, n. 148.

616 Mujuzi 2011, p. 107.

617 *Public Prosecutor v Joseph Mpambara*, 21 October 2008, above n. 36.

618 See the various cases against *Bignone*, including Federal Criminal Oral Tribunal No. 6, Buenos Aires, Argentina, *Public Prosecutor v Reynaldo Benito Antonio Bignone* [*Plan Sistemático'* case], *Verdict*, 17 September 2012, 1351; *Cámara Federal de Casación Penal* [Federal Chamber of Criminal Appeals], Argentina, *Public Prosecutor v Reynaldo Benito Antonio Bignone* [*Hospital Posadas'* case], *Appeals decision*, 28 November 2012, 1696/1742; *Cámara Federal de Casación Penal* [Federal Chamber of Criminal Appeals], Argentina, *Public Prosecutor v Reynaldo Benito Antonio Bignone* [*'Campo de Mayo'* case (1)], *Appeals decision*, 7 December 2012, 2023, 2031, 2034 and 2043; *Cámara Federal de Casación Penal* [Federal Chamber of Criminal Appeals], Argentina, *Public Prosecutor v Reynaldo Benito Antonio Bignone* [*Campo de*

observe that the *jus cogens* nature of the prohibition of torture, with its broad jurisdictional reach (which encompasses not only violations which have been already committed but also likely infringements, duly qualified as explained hereabove), may serve as a vigorous ground for refusal of extradition.

16.7.4 Death Row and the Death Penalty

An analysis as to whether the death penalty is justified or otherwise, from a philosophical, ethical and/or moral perspective, is beyond the scope of the juridical study I undertake in my book. What counts is that, as explained by Caleb Wheeler, 'the move towards abolishing the death penalty as an acceptable punishment is no more evident than in international criminal law'.[619] Torture does not only arise and is not only practiced in States which retain the death penalty. Yet it also ought to be considered in the light thereof. It can partake of various modes, types and forms. When Chechnyan former Deputy Prime Minister *Akhmed Zakaev* was wanted by Russian authorities who promised fair treatment should extradition take place, Senior District Judge Timothy Workman, relying on clear and unequivocal evidence given by the credible witness Doshuev, found that if the Russian 'authorities are prepared to resort to torturing witnesses there is a substantial risk that Mr. *Zakaev* would himself be subject to torture. I am satisfied that such punishment and detention would be by reason of his nationality and political opinions'.[620] Since torture was widespread in Russia, the Chechens were particularly susceptible to torture and because the Russian government did not have effective control over the vast prison system, *Akhmed Zakaev* was not extradited but discharged. The scope of the prohibition under Article 3 of the ECvHR also covers extraordinary rendition, *id est* extra-judicial transfers. This conveys situations where persons are transferred from one jurisdiction or State to another, for the purposes of detention and interrogation outside the normal legal system and where there subsists a real risk of torture or cruel, inhuman or degrading treatment or punishment.[621] The ECtHR has held that where the sending State knew, or ought to have known at the relevant time, that the extraditee would be subjected to extra-judicial transfer, 'the possibility of a breach of Article 3 is particularly strong and must be considered intrinsic

Mayo' case (2)], *Appeals decision*, 7 December 2012, 2023, 2031, 2034 and 2043; Federal Criminal Oral Tribunal No. 1, San Martin, Argentina, *Public Prosecutor v Reynaldo Benito Antonio Bignone* [*'Campo de Mayo'* case (3)], *Verdict*, 12 March 2013, 2047.

619 Wheeler 2018, p. 358.

620 *The Government of the Russian Federation v Akhmed Zakaev*, above n. 136.

621 ECtHR, Former Fourth Section, *Abd Al Rahim Hussayn Muhammad Al Nashiri v Poland*, 24 July 2014, Application No. 28761/11, para 454; ECtHR, Former Fourth Section, *Husayn (Abu Zubaydah) v Poland*, 24 July 2014, Application No. 7511/13, para 451.

in the transfer'.[622] Whereas the capital punishment has been eliminated by the vertical system of enforcement, it is gradually being eroded by the horizontal system of enforcement. Whilst in no way conveying that the outlawing of the death penalty is a rule of customary international law,[623] this infers that it is still commonplace in certain jurisdictions, which jurisdictions have habitually faced non-extradition by the requested State. Hence one may say that 'neither *usus* nor *opinio juris*'[624] supports the prohibition of the death penalty under international law. The *Soering* case[625] has had a massive impact on this ground for refusal.[626] In this case the ECtHR considered the death row phenomenon[627] *per se* as constitutive of cruel, inhuman and degrading treatment or punishment, engaging the responsibility of the requested State to measure the conditions in the requesting State in terms of Article 3 of the ECvHR 'where substantial grounds have been shown for believing that the person concerned, if extradited, faces a real risk of being subjected to torture or to inhuman or degrading treatment or punishment in the requesting country'.[628] It found that the evidence showed that it would probably take at least six years to decide *Soering's* fate after conviction, and that there was a

---

[622] *Al Nashiri v Poland*, above n. 621, para 454; *Husayn (Abu Zubaydah) v Poland*, above n. 621, para 451.

[623] The non-customary status of the prohibition featured domestically in various States, including South Africa [Constitutional Court, South Africa, *S v T Makwanyane and M Mchunu*, 6 June 1995, CCT3/94].

[624] Dugard and van den Wyngaert 1998, p. 196.

[625] *Soering v UK*, above n. 387.

[626] By way of example, and following *Soering* to the letter by rejecting the Chinese request for the extradition of couple *Mandugeqi*, the Polish Supreme Court, on 29 July 1997, held that 'the European Convention on the Protection of Human Rights and Fundamental Freedoms is applicable *ex proprio vigore* to the extradition and the competent authorities in Poland, as the requested State, are bound by its provisions' (Plachta 1998, pp. 100–101). Similarly, 'the possibility of capital punishment and the lack of an extradition treaty remain the main reasons behind the refusal of many States to hand over suspected former Derg officials, including the top Derg leader, *Mengitsu Hailemariam*. For instance, Italy has repeatedly refused to hand over Derg officials who took refuge in its embassy in Addis Ababba after the fall of the Derg in 1991' (Alemu Aneme 2006, p. 80). The domino effect was also felt in Jamaica in 1994 [Judicial Committee of the Privy Council, *Earl Pratt and Ivan Morgan v The Attorney-General for Jamaica and The Superintendent of Prisons, Saint Catherine's, Jamaica*, 2 November 1993, 210/1986 and 225/1987] when 'the Privy Council decision in *Pratt and Morgan* followed the decision of the European Court of Human Rights in *Soering*' (Mukherjee 2004, pp. 511–512). All in all, the 'substantial grounds' test adopted by the ECtHR in *Soering* has served as a point of reference for municipal courts in their assessment of the likelihood of a violation of the rights of the extraditee {High Court of Justice, Queen's Bench Division, Divisional Court, UK, *Miklis v Deputy Prosecutor General of Lithuania*, 11 May 2006, CO/1489/2006 [2006] EWHC 1032 (Admin), and Queens Bench Division, Divisional Court, England and Wales, UK, *Bite v Latvia*, 6 October 2009, [2009] EWHC 3092, both cited in van der Wilt 2012a, p. 171, notes 94 and 95}.

[627] 'This phenomenon may be described as consisting in a combination of circumstances to which the applicant would be exposed if, after having been extradited to Virginia to face a capital murder charge, he were sentenced to death' [*Soering v UK*, above n. 387, para 81].

[628] *Soering v UK*, above n. 387, para 91.

substantial possibility that he would experience the severely damaging psychological and physical conditions of death row for a period ranging between six to eight years.[629] On the pretext of the particular circumstances of the case,[630] the anticipated torture, inhuman or degrading treatment and severe prison conditions in Mecklenburg Correctional Center, Virginia, the ECtHR unanimously determined that in the event of the Secretary of State's decision to extradite the applicant to the USA being implemented, there would be a violation of Article 3 of the ECvHR. Having found a violation of Article 3, the ECtHR felt the need to eloquently explain the nature and content of the prohibition of inhuman and degrading treatment. It authoritatively held that:

> Treatment has been held by the Court to be both "inhuman" because it was premeditated, was applied for hours at a stretch and "caused, if not actual bodily injury, at least intense physical and mental suffering", and also "degrading" because it was "such as to arouse in [its] victims feelings of fear, anguish and inferiority capable of humiliating and debasing them and possibly breaking their physical or moral resistance" (see the above-mentioned Ireland v. the United Kingdom judgment, p. 66, § 167). In order for a punishment or treatment associated with it to be "inhuman" or "degrading", the suffering or humiliation involved must in any event go beyond that inevitable element of suffering or humiliation connected with a given form of legitimate punishment (see the Tyrer judgment, *loc. cit.*). In this connection, account is to be taken not only of the physical pain experienced but also, where there is a considerable delay before execution of the punishment, of the sentenced person's mental anguish of anticipating the violence he is to have inflicted on him.[631]

Although the *Öcalan* case[632] was slightly diverted when the Turkish government commuted the death penalty to life imprisonment, the ECtHR traced an evolution of State practice since *Soering*, referring to an 'almost complete abandonment of the death penalty in times of peace in Europe'.[633] The same reasoning was echoed by municipal courts in some subsequent landmark decisions.[634] In this context, the ECtHR held that all Contracting States had signed Protocol 6 and that all such

[629] *Soering v UK*, above n. 387, para 56.

[630] 'These circumstances to which Soering would be exposed as a consequence of the implementation of the Secretary of State's decision to return him to the USA, namely the "death row phenomenon", cumulatively constituted such serious treatment that his extradition would be contrary to Article 3 of the ECHR. These included the delays in the appeal and review procedures following a death sentence, during which time *Soering* would be subject to increasing tension and psychological trauma, the fact that the judge or jury in determining sentence is not obliged to take into account the defendant's age and mental state at the time of the offence, the extreme conditions of *Soering's* future detention on "death row" in Mecklenburg Correctional Center, where he expects to be the victim of violence and sexual abuse because of his age, colour and nationality, and the constant spectre of the execution itself, including the ritual of execution' [*Soering v UK*, above n. 387, para 105].

[631] *Soering v UK*, above n. 387, para 100.

[632] ECtHR Grand Chamber, *Abdullah Öcalan v Turkey*, 12 March 2003, Application No. 46221/99.

[633] *Öcalan v Turkey*, above n. 632, paras 195–196.

[634] *Hoge Raad* [Supreme Court, The Netherlands], *Short v The Netherlands*, 30 March 1990, 13.949 and 13.950; see also *Venezia v Ministero di Grazia e Giustizia*, above n. 60.

States, except Turkey, Armenia and Russia ratified it. As of today, the death penalty in time of peace has been abolished *de jure* in all member States of the Council of Europe,[635] with the exception of Russia, which, in any case, has declared a moratorium on capital executions in 1996. Within the European continent, only Belarus[636] retains the death penalty.[637] Other non-EU States have retained it, and applied it in the context of proceedings leading to the conviction for core crimes.[638] In fact, 'it is difficult to state that abolition of the death penalty has sperad beyond Europe',[639] to the extent that it is deemed to be one example 'where the so-called regional *jus cogens* takes precedence over an obligation created under the United Nations Charter'.[640] Indeed the *Soering* precedent, though rejected by the HRC, in the USA and in Canada, was followed within the municipal judicial sphere by 'several Indian decisions and has been endorsed by the Supreme Court of Zimbabwe and the Privy Council.'[641] It seems that since the trauma involving the death row phenomenon 'has been largely ascribed to the uncertainty in relation to the date of execution coupled with conditions on death row',[642] each and every case will depend upon its various identifiable and surrounding circumstances. The time factor remains of the essence.[643] To this extent, 'there is no consensus as to the exact parameters of the death row phenomenon'[644] probably because different jurisdictions possess distinct legislative infrastructures and systems which must be assessed independently and on a case-by-case basis.

The EU Charter of Fundamental Rights follows the footsteps of the ECE[645] in the prohibition of extradition to a State where there is a serious risk that he or she would be subjected to the death penalty.[646] The Protocol confirmed the abolitionist

---

635 Such list is available at http://www.coe.int/. Accessed 22 November 2018.

636 It is neither a EU member State nor a CoE member State.

637 Belarus has, on 14 March 2012, executed, by gunshots, two of its nationals, *Dzmitry Kanavalaw and Uladzislaw Kavalyow*, for the bombings of the Minsk Metro on 11 April 2011, drawing widespread international condemnation {*Вярхоўны суд Беларусі* [Belarus Supreme Court], *Public Prosecutor v Dzmitry Kanavalaw and Uladzislaw Kavalyow, Death Sentences*, 30 November 2011}.

638 *Vide, inter alia, Tribunal de Première Instance de Kigali* [Court of First Instance of Kigali], Rwanda, *Public Prosecutor v Froduald Karamira*, 14 February 1997, Case No. 7, leading to the public execution by firing squad in the Nyamirambo Stadium on 24 April 1998 of *Froduald Karamira*, former vice-President of the *Mouvement Démocratique Républicain.*

639 Obokata 2010, p. 75.

640 Vidmar 2012, p. 22.

641 Dugard and van den Wyngaert 1998, p. 198.

642 Bojosi 2004, p. 309.

643 Supreme Court, Zimbabwe, *Catholic Commission for Justice and Peace in Zimbabwe v Attorney-General and Others*, 20 May 1993, 21 May 1993, 24 June 1993, 1993 (4) SA 239 (ZS); see also Bradford 2010–2011, pp. 85–92.

644 Bojosi 2004, p. 309.

645 Article 11 of the ECE, above n. 16.

646 Article 19, above n. 579.

trend[647] established by the practice of contracting States, concluding that the death penalty [not merely the death row phenomenon] can be regarded as inhuman and degrading treatment, especially when such punishment followed an unfair trial.[648] This was the case in *Öcalan*.[649] To this extent, in my opinion, the abolition of the death penalty cannot be completely detached from the general right to a fair trial. It stands to reason that, given that the death penalty leads to an irreversible state of affairs consisting in the loss of a human life, due process safeguards must be enforced with the highest level of rigour. Andrew Clapham notes that 'the argument linking fair trial to the prohibition of the death penalty could have enormous consequences in other jurisdictions both at international and at national level',[650] whereas William Schabas highlighted that the death penalty itself has been linked to other human rights violations. He refers to the 1994 Parliamentary Assembly of the CoE which upheld that the death penalty itself 'may well be compared with torture and be seen as inhuman and degrading punishment within the meaning of Article 3 of the European Convention on Human Rights'.[651] This is the conclusion reached by Silvia Borelli who, post-*Öcalan*, determined that for the State parties to the ECvHR, but not parties to the Protocol, it follows that 'the extradition of individuals facing capital punishment in the requesting country can now be considered *per se* a violation of the Convention, and in particular of Article 3, regardless of the circumstances of each single case'.[652]

The emerging, or rather the developing, abolitionist movement[653] might not be enough, on its own and unaided, to justify a refusal to an extradition request, although John Dugard and Christine van den Wyngaert held that retentionist States 'cannot be confident that their extradition treaties will be honoured where the death penalty is a possible punishment'.[654] For example, in *Kindler v Canada*,[655] Judge La Forest approved the extradition on the basis of the 1976 Extradition Treaty between Canada and the USA, following the escape of the convict after a verdict of guilt was delivered in his trial by jury in Pennsylvania. He held that 'the extradition of an individual who has been accused of the worst form of murder, to face capital

---

647 This trend is also spurred by the International Commission of Jurists (International Commission of Jurists 2000, p. 8). This does not convey that there are no States in Europe which are considering the reintroduction of the death penalty. A legislative proposal for the reintroduction of the death penalty has been tabled before Turkey's Parliament on 1 October 2018 (Çali 2018).

648 The HRC spelt out, in no unclear terms, that 'in capital punishment cases, the duty of States parties to observe rigorously all the guarantees for a fair trial set out in Article 14 of the Covenant is even more imperative' [HRC, *Carlton Reid v Jamaica*, 20 July 1990, Communication No. 250/1987, para 12.2].

649 *Öcalan v Turkey*, above n. 632, para 197.

650 Clapham 2003, pp. 484–485.

651 Schabas 1997, p. 255.

652 Borelli 2004, cited in Kolb 2004, p. 347.

653 Manacorda 2003, pp. 265–271.

654 Dugard and van den Wyngaert 1998, p. 199.

655 *Kindler v Canada*, above n. 389.

prosecution in the United States, could not be said to shock the conscience of the Canadian people nor to be in violation of the standards of the international community'.[656] This is more so since retentionist States amount to fifty-eight,[657] whilst the ICCPR still fails to outlaw the death penalty[658] and cultural relativism[659] still inhibits international consensus on the matter.[660] However, with the likelihood or the manifest prospect of an unfair trial, such refusal acquires a sufficient level of justification. This assumes a degree of relevance because some acknowledge that 'national courts, in spite of the famous doctrine of separation of powers, are often wary to disentangle themselves from the executive'.[661] In practice, throughout various domestic systems the judiciary is appointed by the executive. Judges, in turn, might be hesitant either to take a decision which is unfavourable to the current government especially in politically sensitive cases or after an armed conflict, or to take a decision which is prejudicial to a neighbouring State or any of its nationals throughout a regional democratization process wherein various States are about to strike a Peace Accord.[662] Jann Kleffner refers to the *iter* by means of which a 'trafficking of influence through the politicized processes for the appointment of judges' is consummated as 'political corruption'.[663] This influence is stronger when judges obtain their positions through political connections and favours, as a result of which they feel indebted to the government authorities, but particularly indebted to the individuals who have decided to appoint them, some of whom might either be the subjects of allegations of the commission of core crimes or else nationals of 'friendly States' who enjoy close diplomatic, political and economic ties with the prosecuting State. Consequently, the objectivity of municipal criminal courts is not always guaranteed. This is more so when the prosecution of core crimes is involved, given the fact that such core crimes are typically committed by State actors using the State's machinery, and hence 'often have a highly political connotation'.[664]

Obstacles to extradition emanating from the legality of capital punishment in the requesting State are habitually circumvented by means of guarantees (assurances) that the death penalty will not be executed should there subsist a finding of guilt,

---

[656] Paust et al. 2007, pp. 369–370.

[657] Death Penalty Information Centre 2018.

[658] Article 6(2) allows the capital punishment only for the most serious crimes.

[659] Donders 2010, pp. 15–35.

[660] Rehman states that 'the position in international law is not established and State practices are inconsistent' (Rehman 2003, p. 72).

[661] Nollkaemper 2011, cited in van der Wilt 2012b.

[662] Hans Kochler states that 'when addressing the question of power and enforcement in the field of international criminal law, one must not ignore the *status quo* of international relations (which is also the predicament of the United Nations Organization as "guarantor" of the international rule of law)' (Kochler 2003, p. 46).

[663] Kleffner 2008, p. 54.

[664] Ryngaert 2008, p. 115.

especially outside Europe.[665] In some cases, the death penalty exception to extradition is a discretionary ground for refusal but becomes operative *de lege* if the requesting State fails to provide such assurances.[666] Where this requirement has not been incorporated within the domestic legal system, practice reveals that extradition is generally undertaken upon suspensive or resolutive conditions, one of which is the non-execution of the death penalty.[667] This will however depend on the legal and constitutional infrastructure of States, some of which do not allow the revocation or variation of a court judgment by the executive because the judiciary is an independent possessor of its unfettered discretion, its exclusive prerogative.[668] Other criminal justice systems might need to legislate directly on the matter without necessarily forfeiting their fundamental values, the crux of their entire juridical infrastructure. By way of example, 'Muslim States can, therefore, curtail the death penalty by legislation and remain consistent with the *Shari'a*'.[669] Abdullah Ahmen An-Na'im believes that 'a modern version of Islamic law can and should be developed. Such a modern *Shari'a* could be, in my view, entirely consistent with current standards of human rights', and concludes that 'human rights advocates in the Muslim world must work within the framework of Islam to be effective. They need not be confined, however, to particular historical interpretation of Islam known as *Shari'a*'.[670] The practice of the HRC shows that the infliction of the death penalty *per se* does not constitute a ground for refusal of an extradition,[671] provided that the capital punishment is lawfully imposed as a sanction for the consummation of the most serious crimes, as stated by Article 6(2) of the ICCPR. It follows, from this legal provision, that the expression 'for the most serious crimes' must be read restrictively, because the lawful execution of a convict is quite an exceptional measure, which necessitates the death of the victim.[672]

The value of the prevailing State practice dealing with the weight, reliability and trustworthiness which States attach to such assurances is important because it cements a distinction between torture on the one hand and the infliction of the death penalty on the other hand.[673] The former smells of illegality, wherever and

[665] Supreme Court, Canada, *Minister of Justice, USA v Glen Sebastian Burns and Atif Ahmad Rafay*, 15 February 2001, File No. 26129, 2001 SCC 7 {see Martin 1998–1999, pp. 243–261}; Constitutional Court, South Africa, *Mohamed and Dalvie v The President of the Republic of South African and Others*, 28 May 2001, CCT 17/01.

[666] Section 30(2) of the New Zealand Extradition Act (1999) No. 55, cited in Boister 2016, p. 24, n. 141.

[667] Goodwin and McAdam 2007, p. 261.

[668] Dean et al. 2003, p. 515.

[669] Bassiouni 2000, p. 83. The content and scope of the Shari'a is dealt with by Rehman 2005, pp. 15–17.

[670] An-Na'im 1990, p. 13.

[671] Others have opined that 'the death penalty *per se* is not a violation of human rights' (Obokata 2010, p. 75).

[672] HRC, *Webby Chisanga v Zambia*, 18 October 2005, Communication No. 1132/2002, para 5.4.

[673] van der Wilt 2012a, pp. 166–168.

whenever it is resorted to, but in terms of international law, capital punishment is a legitimate punishment.[674] Rather than following the *Soering* precedent and domestic *dicta*, the HRC has intricately linked the death penalty to a more potent ground for refusal, the prohibition of torture, inhuman and/or degrading treatment or punishment. It found that the possible sentence of gas asphyxiation in California, a method which could take around ten minutes to cause death, was tantamount to prolonged suffering constituting cruel and inhuman treatment in terms of Article 7 of the ICCPR.[675] Thus, in practice, it determined that the extradition of a person 'depends on the particular mode of execution of the death penalty'.[676] This could have a domino effect in extradition law because other methods of execution, such as electrocution, stoning and hanging could be found to constitute prolonged suffering. As a matter of fact the ACmmHPR found that the latter method of execution, i.e. hanging, breaches the African Charter on Human and Peoples' Rights.[677] Hence, such domino effect can be of a truly global nature owing to 'an increasing symbiosis between the applications of the European Convention on Human Rights and other human rights regimes', as a result of which the *Öcalan* judgment 'has important implications not only for the future application and interpretation of the European Convention on Human Rights; it may also have considerable impact on the interpretation of human rights law outside the Council of Europe system'.[678] Some jurisdictions which retain the death penalty, however, do not consider hanging as constitutive of cruel, inhuman and degrading punishment since 'there was no evidence that other methods of execution, such as lethal injection, were less painful than hanging'.[679] In any case, even if this were not so, a global trend towards performing an execution without divesting the would-be-executed of his dignity seems to be developing.[680]

It seems to be still premature to state that the death penalty is on its death bed. Most probably the death penalty is here to stay. Whether this is morally and/or legally ethical and/or correct is beyond the scope of this work. Retentionist States do not seem to be dissuaded by the possible rejection of their extradition requests by abolitionist States on the basis of the likely execution of the death penalty. The prospect of non-extradition (or qualified extradition, dependent on assurances) because of the death penalty is not sufficient enough an incentive for them to change their views and policies thereupon. The net effect of all this is that the death penalty (especially where it is not executed in a humane manner and/or where it

---

674 van Heugten and van Laar 2011, p. 270, citing IHT Appeals Commission, *Public Prosecutor v Saddam Hussein Al Majeed et al.* [*Dujail* case], 26 December 2006, Case No. 29/c/2006.

675 *Chitat Ng v Canada*, above n. 388.

676 De Merieux 1996, p. 31.

677 Windridge 2018.

678 Clapham 2003, pp. 475–476.

679 Supreme Court, Uganda (at Mengo), *Attorney-General v Susan Kigula and 417 Others*, 21 January 2009, Constitutional Appeal No. 3 of 2006, cited in Mujuzi 2009, pp. 577–578.

680 Asia Pacific Advisory Council 2001, p. 175.

causes unnecessary suffering) may still be said to constitute a robust ground for the refusal of extradition.

Sections 16.7.1–16.7.4 have shown that the requirement to protect certain fundamental human rights (namely those enjoying a *jus cogens* status) renders such grounds for refusal more resilient. In this field, more than anywhere else, courts must endeavour to strike 'a restored balance between effective enforcement and adequate protection of fundamental human rights'.[681] Keeping aside issues dealing with the criminal sanction, be it life imprisonment and/or the death penalty, I shall now briefly embark onto proposing the use of some legal principles which may be borrowed from another *corpus juris* with an eye to identifying the extent/degree (level) of the risks an extraditee would potentially undergo in case he would be extradited.

16.7.4.1 International Refugee Law: A New and Reliable Measuring Tape?

There are some levels of interaction between international refugee law, international human rights law and international criminal law.[682] Suffice to note that 'the limits of the refugee law principle of *non-refoulement* have, however, come to be filled by the progressive development of international human rights law' and that 'compared to its refugee law counterpart, the principle of *non-refoulement* in international human rights law has a broader scope of application'.[683] Although I do not deny that, as noted by Zoë Egelman, there is misalignment between the principles of international criminal law and the international refugee regime,[684] I[685] identify some common ground between the legal regime under scrutiny (this containing shades of both international criminal law and international human rights law) and international refugee law, which common ground could serve to guide requesting States in their assessment of the foreseeability of the likelihood of a violation. The latter *corpus juris* necessitates a well-founded fear of persecution (which could include torture) for the attainment of refugee status.[686] General State practice shows that such test ought to be both subjective and objective,[687] the latter requirement emanating from the qualification 'well-founded', the nature and scope of which

[681] Ouwerkerk 2018, p. 104.

[682] Gilbert 2017, p. 56.

[683] Bauloz 2018, p. 535.

[684] Egelman 2018, pp. 467–475.

[685] I hold the public office of Chairperson of one of the three Chambers of Malta's Refugee Appeals Board which is a tribunal set-up in terms of Chapter 420 of the Laws of Malta.

[686] See Article 1A(2) of the Refugee Convention (1951) Convention Relating to the Status of Refugees.

[687] This is considered as the combined subjective-objective approach. It is favoured by domestic courts and by the UN High Commissioner for Refugees (Zimmermann and Mahler 2011, p. 338).

connotes and necessitates a good, reasoned and solid foundation. In other words, for the purposes of refugee law, though fear is intrinsically of a subjective nature, it needs to be proved objectively to satisfy a claim for refugee status. This line of though is supported jurisprudentially.[688] The counterpart of this within the extradition regime is easily detectable by the fact that 'the review should inquire whether the subjective fear is so objectively concretized that the person is in fact threatened, and should include an assessment of the general situation in the requesting State as well'.[689]

Judicial or quasi-judicial authorities which determine whether to grant refugee status or otherwise are hence called to determine whether repatriation is likely to expose the asylum seeker to a risk of being tortured. Other startling similitudes with an extradition scenario subsist. Persecution is generally endured at the hands of the State itself or of non-State actors over whom the State has no tangible control. This state of affairs is highly reminiscent of characteristics pertaining to crimes against humanity. That refugee status is habitually granted by municipal authorities in cases of asylum seekers who derive from countries where crimes against humanity were committed or are being investigated is not coincidental. Similary, I can confirm that it is no rare occurrence at all that some asylum seekers claim a well-founded fear of being persecuted by virtue of a politically motivated (unfair) trial in their country of nationality in the event of their repatriation. They hence avail themselves of their right to a fair trial as an obstacle to deportation and/or repatriation, in the same way as an extraditee avails himself of the same right by way of a ground for refusal in extradition proceedings. Moreover, judicial or quasi-judicial authorities necessarily have to analyse the country-specific situation, shedding a light on the human rights record and the judicial remedies available within the country of origin/nationality of the asylum seeker. The universally accepted definition of a refugee also explicitly encapsulates the criteria of unwillingness and inability which are cemented, as seen in Part III, in the complementarity principle.[690] Last but not least, in refugee law,

---

[688] Such *dicta* result from an analysis of case-law in France, Germany, UK, New Zealand and Australia (Zimmermann and Mahler 2011, pp. 340–341).

[689] *Ustavno sodišče Slovenije* [Constitutional Court, Slovenia], *Annullment of the second subparagraph of para 2 of Article 40 of the Asylum Act (Official Gazette of the Republic of Slovenia, No. 61/99)*, 29 June 2000, Official Gazette RS, No. 66/2000, para 15, cited in van der Wilt 2012a, p. 172, n. 97.

[690] Article 1A(2) of the Refugees Convention (above n. 686) stipulates that a refugee is a person who 'owing to well-founded fear of being persecuted for reasons of race, religion, nationality, membership of a particular social group or political opinion, is outside the country of his nationality and is unable or, owing to such fear, is unwilling to avail himself of the protection of that country; or who, not having a nationality and being outside the country of his former habitual residence as a result of such events, is unable or, owing to such fear, is unwilling to return to it'.

more than in extradition law, the analysis is intrinsically and exclusively prospective (forward-looking). Fear, for the purposes of refugee law, 'expresses a forward-looking expectation of risk'.[691]

Indeed, the judicial or quasi-judicial authority determining whether to grant refugee status or otherwise is placed in an analogous position to the Magistrate or Judge who is determining whether an extradition request should be adhered to or otherwise. Some of the juridical considerations in extradition law replicate those being made under refugee law. I detect an overlap between the concepts of 'substantial grounds' (expounded by the ECtHR in the *Soering* case which has been considered in Sect. 16.7.4) and 'well-founded fear'. A well-founded fear, in fact, protrudes directly from the subsistence of such substantial grounds. In the absence of such substantial grounds, the fear, for all intents and purposes of refugee law, cannot be well-founded. The subsistence of such substantial grounds does not necessarily equate to a well-founded fear since other elements (such as a link of causation and past persecution, the latter also being instrumental in the context of an extradition)[692] might have to be proved. State practice shows that, when assessing an extradition request, 'domestic courts have been guided by the case law of the international human rights organs'.[693] I am not at odds with this. However, I suggest that extradition law, duly applied by domestic courts, can make use of refugee law at least in so far as the identification, application and implementation of the standard of proof to evaluate the likelihood or otherwise (the degree and the extent) of the risk of torture is concerned. Refugee law can constitute a normative point of reference by becoming a meaningful utensil in the toolkit of domestic courts which are called to determine the extraditability or otherwise of an individual. Refugee law can be made use of in a multitude of ways by municipal courts which are being constantly called to determine 'the standard of probability which is required to tip the balance in favour of human rights'.[694] Just to give a concrete example, the 'substantial grounds' test can be re-shaped to comprehend and necessitate a 'well-founded risk of torture', hence using refugee law as a new and reliable measuring tape to measure the risk involved (to assess the foreseeability of the likelihood of a violation). Though this would probably fall short of the 'flagrant violation' test, it would raise the standard of proof to create an equitable balance between the interest of the requesting State and the rights of the extraditee, keeping in mind the preference to restrict grounds for refusal in manners which render such limitations anyway compliant with contemporary international norms and standards.

---

[691] Zimmermann and Mahler 2011, p. 341.

[692] van der Wilt 2012a, p. 172.

[693] Ibid.

[694] Ibid.

16.8 Diplomatic Privileges and Immunities

At the outset, one must note that, for the sake of avoiding unnecessary repetitions in this book, some cases dealt with in Part III will not be given due importance again herein. This notwithstanding the fact that they may have kicked-off as situations being contemplated as falling within the parameters of the horizontal system of enforcement but ended up being triggered directly within the vertical system of enforcement, leading to, for example, the former Liberia President *Charles Taylor*'s[695] conviction for war crimes.[696] The purpose of this heading does not solicit an examination of all kinds of immunities, together with a study on the distinction between, on the one hand, sovereign immunity, and on the other, immunities *rationae personae* and *rationae materiae*, but only an analysis of how and to what extent such immunities can effectively hinder the prosecution of core crimes within the horizontal system of enforcement. It must be stated however that although there exists a trend to limit immunities in order to suppress impunity, there still subsist circumstances, to date, where immunities are absolute.[697] Just because the UN is a conglomeration of States, no equivalent absolute immunity necessarily applies to States. Hence a collectivity of States enjoys privileges which an individual State does not enjoy. However, State immunity *per se*[698] falls outside the scope of this work. Similarly, the immunity of Heads of State in civil actions[699] is not relevant therefor.

The same may be said about the *Yerodia* judgment which was also dealt with in the context of the vertical system of enforcement in as much as it also, albeit partially, limitedly and indirectly, had an impact on the vertical system of enforcement itself. Analysing *Yerodia*, which dealt only incidentally with the issue of functional immunities before foreign courts, one cannot turn a blind eye at the negative vibe that it left within jurists[700] who argue that customary international law 'allows for an exception to the rule of *rationae materiae* immunity in the context of international crimes (including but not limited to genocide)'.[701] Gerhard Kemp states that the ICJ's statements 'are indeed unfortunate' since the ICJ failed to 'draw

---

695 SCSL, *Prosecutor v Charles Ghankay Taylor, Judgment*, 26 April 2012, SCSL-2003-1-I.

696 This judgment followed an important decision delivered by the SCSL which divested *Charles Taylor* from diplomatic protection and immunity from jurisdiction [SCSL Appeals Chamber, *Prosecutor v Charles Ghankay Taylor, Decision on Immunity from Jurisdiction*, 31 May 2004, Case No. SCSL-2003-01-I; see also Tejan-Cole 2009, pp. 205–232].

697 *Hoge Raad* [Supreme Court of the Netherlands] First Division, *Mothers of Srebrenica Association et al. v State of The Netherlands and the United Nations* [*Mothers of Srebrenica* case], 13 April 2012, 10/04437. Here, the Supreme Court, by virtue of Article 105 of the UNC (1945) Charter of the United Nations, decided that the UN's immunity under international law is absolute.

698 For an analysis of the relationship between State immunity, human rights and *jus cogens*, see Caplan 2003, pp. 741–781, and see also Knuchel 2011, pp. 149–183.

699 For an analysis of such matters, see Taylor 2001, pp. 114–118.

700 See a list of these jurists and their respective papers/articles in Schlutter 2010, p. 161, n. 218.

701 Gaeta 2009, p. 325.

a clearer distinction between immunity *rationae personae* (relating to the individual's office, status or position) and immunity *rationae materiae* (referring to acts performed in an official capacity)',[702] the latter being commonly referred to as 'official acts' which must necessarily be committed by a *de jure* or *de facto* State official.[703] The former immunity generally applies to heads of State, heads of government and senior ministers, protecting them against criminal prosecution in a foreign State for the duration of their period in office. They will be dealt with first.

16.8.1 Immunities Rationae Personae

The rationale of personal immunities is premised firstly on the respect that sovereign equals owe each other (*par in parem non habet imperium*) and secondly on the fact (of a functional dimension) that such immunities enable certain officials to perform their duties without interference.[704] There is indeed an interaction between the vertical and the horizontal systems of enforcement when personal immunities are at stake. Firstly, the *Yerodia dictum* established that immunities *rationae personae* are not applicable before the criminal courts of the person benefiting from such immunities.[705] Secondly, incumbent foreign ministers 'may be subject to criminal proceedings before certain international criminal courts, where they have jurisdiction'.[706] Personal immunities for core crimes are still solidly rooted. The same may not be said about functional immunities especially in view of a gradual, but steady and increasing, articulation of a customary international law human rights exception to immunities.[707] Even the 2009 Resolution on 'Immunity from Jurisdiction of the State and of Persons who act on Behalf of the State in Case of International Crimes' acknowledged this.[708]

A Swiss court has found that 'for acts committed before taking office as Minister of Defence of the Republic of Algeria, as well as for acts committed after the end of

---

[702] Kemp 2010, p. 180.

[703] In the words of the ICTY, immunity *rationae materiae* means that 'State officials cannot suffer the consequences of wrongful acts which are not attributable to them personally but to the State on whose behalf they act' [ICTY Appeals Chamber, *Prosecutor v Tihomir Blaškić, Judgment on the Request of the Republic of Croatia for Review of the Decision of the Trial Chamber II of 18 July 1997*, 29 October 1997, Case No. IT-95-14-AR 108*bis*, para 38].

[704] Orentlicher 2011, p. 213.

[705] ICJ, *Arrest Warrant of 11 April 2000 (DRC v Belgium)*, 14 February 2002, ICJ Rep. 2002, p. 3, para 61.

[706] Ibid.

[707] Webb 2012, p. 147.

[708] *IDI* 2009, cited in Webb 2012, p. 146.

his term, no jurisdictional immunity can be granted to *A*'.[709] However, this does not mean that senior State officials, such as serving Heads of State, may not enjoy any immunity whatsoever. It is a settled matter that they are still entitled to personal immunities 'as long as they hold office',[710] that is, as incumbents, 'unless a treaty to which the States in question have consented stipulates otherwise'.[711] Irrespective of such immunities, current practice in any case discloses an apparent incapability both of the ICC and of western jurisdictions of dealing with suspects who still wield political power.[712] They would lose such immunity when they relinquish their post as Prime Minister,[713] Head of State, head of government or Minister of Foreign Affairs. A distinction between these senior positions is articulated conventionally.[714] Max du Plessis analyses the consequences of personal immunities in the light of the requests within South Africa to prosecute *Robert Mugabe*, the former President of Zimbabwe, in terms of the South African ICC Act. He concludes that 'if one accepts that under international law personal immunity attaches to incumbent senior cabinet officials such as heads of State, then not only would any prosecution by South Africa under the ICC Act of a current head of State of a country that is not party to the ICC Statute be possibly inconsistent with its (South Africa's) obligations under customary international law, but the ICC would also be prevented from requesting the surrender of that person'.[715] Senior District Judge at Bow Street Magistrates' Court (UK), Tim Workman, had already upheld that Common Law provides absolute immunity to any Head of State, concluding that:

> I am satisfied that *Robert Mugabe* is President and head of State of Zimbabwe and is entitled whilst he is head of State to that immunity. He is not liable to any form of arrest or detention and I am therefore unable to issue the warrant that has been applied for.[716]

The Spanish *Audiencia Nacional* had also reached a decision on these lines further to the criminal complaint for acts of genocide and terrorism allegedly

[709] Federal Criminal Court, Switzerland, *A, represented by Jacques Michod, Marc Bonnant and Magali Buser, lawyers v Office of the Attorney General of Switzerland, and B and C, both represented by Damien Chervaz, lawyer*, 25 July 2012, File No. BB.2011.140, paras 5.4.3 and 5.55.

[710] Cassese 2004b, cited in Kemp 2010, p. 181, n. 732.

[711] Drumbl 2008, p. 238.

[712] van der Wilt 2011, p. 1064.

[713] *Cour de Cassation* [Court of Cassation], *Belgium, H.S.A. et al. v S. A. et al., Decision related to the Indictment of Defendant Ariel Sharon, Amos Yaron and Others*, 12 February 2003, Case No. P.02.1139.F/1.

[714] See Article 1 of the Convention on the Prevention and Punishment of Crimes against Internationally Protected Persons, including Diplomatic Agents (1973), providing for the definition of 'protected person' for the purposes of this legal instrument.

[715] du Plessis 2007, pp. 476–477.

[716] Bow Street Magistrates' Court, UK, *Application filed by Peter Tatchell (under Britain's Criminal Justice Act, 1988), Decision rejecting the issue of an arrest warrant for Robert Mugabe*, 14 January 2004, cited in Warbrick 2004, p. 770.

committed by the then President of the Republic of Cuba, *Fidel Castro Ruz*.[717] The impact of personal immunities and the way it still shields the unwanted regime of impunity is hence underscrored.

From the very first words on the subject, one notices that in this field, customary international law, exemplified by State practice, which in turn is reflected by domestic jurisprudence, is of the essence. The reason for this being the fact that conventional international law is generally silent on matters dealing with the immunity, or otherwise, of State officials. In fact it is customary international law that 'does not permit a defendant to plead immunities in prosecutions within courts of that defendant's own State'.[718] Rémy Prouvèze, whilst identifying 'a trend toward general restriction of immunities',[719] cites the *Muhammar Gaddafi*[720] case to 'confirm the *rationae personae* immunity of incumbent heads of State' but to implicitly recognise 'that conventional exceptions are possible for certain crimes'.[721] The same *ratio* is employed by Yasmin Naqvi, who however goes a step further. In her detailed study, she enlists and examines six legal arguments, which she appropriately traces from State practice, to reject both functional and personal immunities in cases dealing with core crimes, these main arguments being:

1. treaty obligations to prosecute or extradite persons accused of core crimes are incompatible with immunities;
2. States have impliedly waived immunity of their officials by signing treaties criminalising certain international offences;
3. customary international law lifts functional (and personal) immunity in case of core crimes;
4. the *jus cogens* nature of core crimes overrides immunity;
5. core crimes fall outside the notion of 'acts performed in a sovereign capacity'; and
6. the fundamental right of victims are incompatible with immunities.[722]

These valid arguments are the living proof of the inter-connectedness, inter-dependence and, at times, inter-changeability of the matters considered under Part IV. Legal argumentation within Part IV is hence significantly cross-fertilized. Naqvi seems to suggest that as a result of the commission of core crimes the distinction between immunities *rationae personae* and immunities *rationae materiae* evaporates. The nature of core crimes outweights the solidity upon which personal immunities are grounded. On the other hand, Thomas Weatherall

[717] *Audiencia Nacional* [Central Criminal Court], Spain, *Fidel Castro Ruz, Ruling*, 4 March 1999, cited in Cassese et al. 2011, pp. 89–91.

[718] Drumbl 2008, p. 238.

[719] Prouvèze 2011, p. 360.

[720] *Cour de Cassation*, France, *Public Prosecutor v Muhammar Gaddafi*, 13 March 2001, examined *funditus* in Zappalà 2001, pp. 595–612.

[721] Prouvèze 2011, p. 362.

[722] Naqvi 2010, pp. 253–284.

postulates that 'judicial authority indicates that immunity *rationae personae* prevails as a rule of customary international law in domestic courts for the prosecution of international crimes', adding that such immunities endure 'at the national level to preclude incumbent high officials from appearing before domestic courts notwithstanding the offences with which they are accused'.[723] Although Naqvi might not be fully correct, there might be a time (not in the too distant future) when immunities *rationae personae* will find it difficult to resist the increasing development of an immunity-free international criminal justice system.

16.8.2 Immunities Rationae Materiae

An important consequence which derives from a relevant distinction should be noted at the very start. Diane Orentlicher, after vividly distinguishing between immunities *rationae personae* and immunities *rationae materiae*, perceptively posits that the latter become relevant when a potential defendant's official status comes to an end, *id est* when he is no longer entitled to enjoy any immunity *rationae personae*.[724] Thus, in relation to immunity *rationae materiae*, Orentlicher righly highlights that such immunities remain applicable even after the person leaves office.[725] In fact Elizabeth Helen Franey refers to it as status immunity.[726] This contrasts sharply, as seen already, with the position at law relating to immunities *rationae personae*.[727] The main rationale of immunities *rationae materiae* is that 'when they act in an official capacity, [individuals representing a] State do not engage their own responsibility, but that of the State; consequently their acts enjoy the immunities of the State'.[728]

Immunities *rationae materiae*, particularly as a result of the *Pinochet*[729] landmark judgment, can hardly be applied when an individual, for example, a former Head of State, is charged with core crimes. According to the House of Lords, the nature of the crimes committed by *Pinochet*, such as torture, even though purportedly perpetrated in an official capacity, divested *Pinochet* of any immunity he may have been entitled to. State practice reveals that domestic courts give

723 Weatherall 2015, p. 295.

724 Orentlicher 2011, p. 203.

725 Orentlicher 2011, p. 204.

726 Franey 2015, p. 214.

727 Orentlicher 2011, p. 204.

728 ICJ, *Certain Questions of Mutual Legal Assistance in Criminal Matters* [*Djibouti v France*], *Pleadings*, CR 2008/7, Statement of Alain Pellet, Counsel for France, 25 January 2008, General List No. 136, cited in Orentlicher 2011, p. 203, n. 9.

729 HoL, *Regina v Bartle and Commissioner of Police for the Metropolis and Others (Appellants) ex parte Pinochet (Respondent); Regina v Evans and another and Commissioner of Police for the Metropolis and others (Appellants) ex parte Pinochet (Respondent), On Appeal from a Divisional Court of the Queen's Bench Division*, 24 March 1999, 2000 1 AC 147 HL.

substantial weight to the nature of the crimes when determining whether an accused individual is entitled to functional immunity at law or otherwise.[730] Though recognised by some jurists as ground-breaking and influential,[731] Torsten Stein is sceptical as to whether the Pinochet dictum 'constitutes a precedent on which State and jurisprudential practice can build upon to establish customary international law'.[732] Such scepticism, and the reasons therefor, have already been dealt with in Sect. 11.4.2 and will be referred to at a later stage throughout this sub-heading. Irrespective of such scepticism, 'it is now clear that the criminal proceedings against *Pinochet* in England were the leading edge of a profound transformation…'[733] This leads me to highlight such significant developments which may have been triggered by an important dissenting opinion of Judge *ad hoc* Christine van den Wyngaert,[734] to which I fully subscribe, in so far as it stressed the importance and need to take into account the nature of the crimes *Yerodia* was accused with. A joint separate opinion of three judges in the same case identified a 'discernible trend to limiting immunity and strengthening accountability'.[735] This trend is a result of three phenomena:

a. the development of the principle of individual criminal responsibility;
b. the ascendance of human rights; and
c. the expansion of domestic jurisdiction over human rights violations, most of which followed the ratification of States to the ICC Statute.[736]

The District Court of Amsterdam, divesting *Desiré Delano Bouterse* of his immunity, had also held that the commission of very serious crimes cannot be attributed to the official functions of a Head of State.[737] Crimes against humanity can never constitute official acts for the purposes of functional immunity. This judgment echoes the logical and purposive conclusion that it would be highly incongruous for international law to protect, by means of functional immunity, the very conduct which it criminalizes and for which it imposes the *aut dedere aut*

---

730 *Corte di Cassazione, Sezione Prima Penale* [Supreme Court of Cassation, First Criminal Section], Italy, *Mario Luiz Lozano v The General Prosecutor for the Italian Republic*, 24 July 2008, Case No. 31171/2008, sub-heading No. 8, pp. 19–20. In this case the Italian court decided that since the crimes Lozano, who was born in NY, was accused of having committed were neither '*crimini contro l'umanità*' [crimes against humanity] nor '*crimini di guerra*' [war crimes], the Italian courts lacked jurisdiction by virtue of his functional immunity which results from customary international law.

731 Bernaz and Prouvèze 2010, pp. 368–369; see also Barker et al. 1999.

732 Stein 2006, p. 258.

733 Orentlicher 2004, p. 1057 and pp. 1132–1133.

734 ICJ, *Arrest Warrant of 11 April 2000 (DRC v Belgium), Dissenting Opinion of Judge Christine van den Wyngaert*, 14 February 2002, ICJ Rep. 2002, p. 3, para 5.

735 ICJ, *Arrest Warrant of 11 April 2000 (DRC v Belgium), Joint Separate Opinion of Judges Higgins, Kooijmans and Buergenthal*, 14 February 2002, ICJ Rep. 2002, p. 3, para 75.

736 Webb 2012, pp. 114–116.

737 Court of Appeal, Amsterdam, *R. Wijngaarde and R.A.L. Hoost v Desiré Delano Bouterse*, Order, 20 November 2000, LJN: AA8395, cited in Keijzer and van Sliedregt 2000, p. 548.

judicare obligation upon States. Arguing otherwise would be tantamount to a juridical *reductio ad absurdum*. Salvatore Zappalà also concludes that functional immunity (immunity *rationae materiae*) and core crimes cannot co-exist,[738] recapitulating a ruling which had already been delivered by the Appeals Chamber of the ICTY.[739] Roman Kolodkin, appointed as Special Rapporteur by the ILC, found that 'grave crimes under international law could not be considered as acts performed in an official capacity'.[740] Andrea Bianchi wrote that 'reliance on the hierarchy of norms in the international legal system is a viable argument to assert non-immunity for major violations of international human rights'.[741] Even the USA Appeals Courts have determined that 'we believe there is respectable authority for denying head-of-State immunity to a former head-of-State for private or criminal acts in violation of American law'.[742] Some important State practice rests on such basis. The Swiss Federal Criminal Court upheld that 'it would be contradictory and futile to, on the one hand, affirm the intention to combat against these grave violations of the most fundamental human values and, on the other hand, to accept a wide interpretation of the rules governing functional or organic immunity (*rationae materiae*), which would benefit former State officials with the concrete result to hinder, *ab initio*, any investigation. In such case, it would be difficult to admit that conduct contrary to fundamental values of the international legal order can be protected by rules of that very same legal order. Such situation would be paradoxical and the criminal policy adopted by the legislator would be condemned to remain a dead letter in almost all cases. This is not what the legislator wanted. It follows that, in the present case, the suspect cannot claim any immunity *rationae materiae*'.[743]

In *Luigi Ferrini v Federal Republic of Germany*[744] the Italian Supreme Court reversed the Court of Appeal's judgment and denied State immunity to Germany, hence rejecting the reasoning adopted by the Greek Supreme Court in the

---

[738] Zappalà 2006, pp. 602–622.

[739] *Prosecutor v Tihomir Blaškić*, above n. 703, para 41.

[740] Kolodkin 2011, para 99, cited in ECtHR Fourth Section, *Jones and Others v UK*, 14 January 2014, Application Numbers 34356/06 and 40528/06, para 212.

[741] Bianchi 1994, p. 220.

[742] USA Court of Appeals, Second Circuit, *Re Mr. and Mrs. Doe, Witnesses Before the Grand Jury*, 6 December 1988, 860 F.2d 430; see also USA Court of Appeals, Fifth Circuit, *Marcos Perez Jimenez, Appellant v Manuel Aristeguieta, Intervenor, Appellee, and John E. Maguire, Appellee*, 12 December 1962, No. 19507, 311 F.2d 547, presenting Act of State arguments, cited in Taylor 2001, p. 120, n. 147.

[743] See *A, represented by Jacques Michod, Marc Bonnant and Magali Buser, lawyers v Office of the Attorney General of Switzerland, and B and C, both represented by Damien Chervaz, lawyer*, above n. 709; Federal Criminal Court, Switzerland, *Khaled Nezzar alias A v Ministère Public de la Confédération, B and C (Office of the Attorney-General of Switzerland)*, 25 July 2012, Case No. BB.2011.140, para 5.4.3.

[744] *Corte di Cassazione* [Supreme Court], Italy, *Luigi Ferrini v Federal Republic of Germany*, 11 March 2004, Case No. 5044/04.

Prefecture of Voiotia case.[745] The Court of Cassation transferred the case again to the Tribunal of Arezzo for examination of the merits. The Italian Supreme Court held that while customary law prescribes immunity from jurisdiction of a foreign State for acts which are the expression of its sovereign authority, such immunity should be lifted when such acts amount to core crimes. For the Court, violations of fundamental human rights encroach upon universal values protected by *jus cogens* norms, which lie at the top of the hierarchy of norms in the international legal order, and thus take precedence over conflicting law, including State immunity, considered as an 'underdeveloped theory' by Rosanne van Alebeek.[746] The judgement paved the way for hundreds of damage claims against Germany in Italian courts. Although this case dealt with State immunity, rather than immunity *rationae personae* and/or *rationae materiae*,[747] the Court's conclusion echoes van den Wyngaert's dissenting opinion in *Yerodia*.[748] Notwithstanding the evident trends referred to here above, immunities are still conferred upon diplomats,[749] although this is increasingly becoming a rarity.

It is thus evident that immunities, described by Ilias Bantekas as 'counter-productive' to international relations,[750] cannot all be placed into one basket, especially when one recalls that their validity and applicability or otherwise

---

[745] *ανώτατο δικαστήριο της Ελλάδας* [*Areios Pagos*/Greek Supreme Court], *Prefecture of Voiotia v Federal Republic of Germany*, 4 May 2000, 11/2000 (288933); see also such cases being cited in the light of the 'implied waiver' argument in Knuchel 2011, pp. 166–168; see also a detailed analysis of this judgment in Caplan 2003, pp. 768–770.

[746] van Alebeek 2008, p. 416.

[747] The ICJ has correctly found that immunity *rationae materiae* is treated as derivative of the State's immunity because any proceeding against a State official acting in his official capacity is considered to be a proceeding against the State itself [ICJ, *Certain Questions on Mutual Assistance in Criminal Matters (Djibouti v France), Judgment*, 4 June 2008, General List No. 136, paras 187–188, cited in Trapp 2011, p. 95, n. 173]. The ICJ categorically upheld that a claim to functional immunity 'is, in essence, a claim of immunity for the Djiboutian State, from which the *Procureur de la République* and the Head of National Security would be said to benefit' [ICJ, *Certain Questions on Mutual Assistance in Criminal Matters (Djibouti v France), Judgment*, 4 June 2008, General List No. 136, para 188]. Moreover, Craig Barker contends that immunity *rationae materiae* of a diplomat or Head of State is in fact State immunity (Barker 2002, p. 4). Similarly, Elizabeth Helen Franey contends that 'immunity *rationae materiae* protects a State by protecting conduct performed on behalf of a State from interference from, and the scrutiny of, another State. Any protection thereby afforded to an individual is incidental' (Franey 2015, p. 213).

[748] In her view, the *Yerodia* judgment failed to recognize the customary international law status of the principle of individual criminal responsibility and consequently failed to balance the 'two divergent interests in modern international (criminal) law: the need of international accountability for such crimes as torture, terrorism, war crimes and crimes against humanity, and the principle of sovereign equality of States, which presupposes a system of immunities' [*Dissenting opinion of Judge van den Wyngaert*, above n. 734, p. 141, para 5].

[749] See the charges against *General Jean-Francois N'dengue*, dropped by a French Court of Appeal on 9 April 2008, in the *Brazzaville Beach* case [*Cour de Cassation* [Court of Cassation], *France, Re General Jean-Francois N'dengue (Brazzaville Beach case)*, 9 April 2008], cited in Rikhof 2010, p. 58.

[750] Bantekas 2010, p. 128.

could be largely dependent upon the nature of the crimes involved in the matter being dealt with. They differ in nature, in context and in application. This also results from a comprehensive study of the position at law on immunities which was undertaken by the ECtHR.[751] Additionally, being a discretionary political matter, immunity, as established in the *Yerodia* case, may be waived by the sending State, provided that such waiver, be it explicit or implicit, is certain.[752] This is so since 'the immunity protecting foreign officials for their official acts ultimately belongs to the sovereign rather than the official'.[753] The Government of Bolivia waived the immunity of former President of Bolivia *Gonzalo Daniel Sánchez de Lozada Sánchez Bustamante*.[754] No counterpart, no waiver or renunciation of rights, may be undertaken in relation to the other grounds for refusal of extradition, such as, for example, in relation to the prohibition of torture. For the sake of the argument and for all intents and purposes of international law, should an individual renounce to his right to freedom from torture, such waiver would be null and void *ab initio* and the torturer would still be criminally liable, with the sole qualification that a domestic criminal court may take the waiver into account to mitigate the punishment, the criminal sanction.

At this stage, it must be stated, in the light of the horizontal system of enforcement, that 'no conclusive decision has been reached as yet as to whether the Vienna Convention on Diplomatic Relations extends to extradition requests'.[755] In so far as State practice is concerned, nowadays it may be safe to reach the conclusion, as stated by Gerhard Kemp, that 'State officials (including the Head of State and other senior government officials) may not claim immunity from jurisdiction (or functional immunity)'[756] for core crimes. Another Gerhard, this time Werle, opines that 'modern international law has resolved the tension between immunity and international criminal law almost exclusively in favour of international criminal law'.[757] He reaches this conclusion by citing, *inter alia*, Antonio Cassese's examples of State practice,[758] notwithstanding that he determines that the immunity *rationae materiae* is literally 'anchored in customary international law'.[759]

---

[751] *Jones and Others v UK*, above n. 740, paras 44–56, 81–109, and 150–154.

[752] Article 7 of *IDI* 2009 Resolution on Immunity from Jurisdiction of the State and of Persons who act on Behalf of the State in Case of International Crimes, cited in Naqvi 2010, p. 230. See also Denza 2016, pp. 273–287.

[753] USA Court of Appeals for the Fourth Circuit, *Bashe Abdi Yousuf, John Doe 1, John Doe 2, Aziz Deria, Plaintiffs–Appellees, John Doe 3, John Doe 4, Jane Doe 1, Plaintiffs v Mohamed Ali Samantar, Defendant–Appellant*, 2 November 2012, 11-1479, Part I, p. 5.

[754] USA Court of Appeals for the Eleventh Circuit, USA, *Mamani et al. v Sánchez de Losada, and Mamani et al. v Sánchez Berzain*, 28 August 2011, Case Numbers 09-16246 & 10-13071.

[755] Gilbert 1998, p. 199.

[756] Kemp 2010, p. 181.

[757] Werle 2009, p. 236.

[758] Cassese 2002b.

[759] Werle 2009, p. 238.

The matter, as of today, at least in so far as immunities *rationae materiae* are concerned, seems to be a *fait accompli.* What might have been a bit nebulous pre-*Pinochet*, is now more visible and clear. Robert Cryer, Hakan Friman, Darryl Robinson and Elizabeth Wilmshurst, in fact, declare that 'a considerable body of international cases, national cases, other State practice and academic commentary supports the view that functional immunity does not preclude prosecution for serious international crimes, which is consistent with the broader reading of Pinochet'.[760] Indeed, in this case, Lord Browne-Wilkinson queried: 'How can it be for international purposes an official function to do something, which international law itself prohibits and criminalizes? Further, Lord Millett noted, 'the official or governmental nature of the act, which forms the basis of the immunity, is an essential ingredient of the offence. No rational systems of criminal justice can allow an immunity which is coextensive with the offence'.[761] He correctly found that 'international law cannot be supposed to have established a crime having the character of a *jus cogens* and at the same time to have provided an immunity which is co-extensive with the obligation it seeks to impose'.[762] He added that third States were permitted, and indeed required, to convict and punish individuals responsible for torture if the offending State declines to take action.[763]

Diane Orentlicher however appropriately warns everyone not to either over-estimate or misconstrue the precedential value of the House of Lords *dictum*. She notes that the reasoning of the Law Lords varied considerably, and rather than relying on the *jus cogens* nature of the prohibition of torture, it relied upon the legal provisions of the CAT. As a matter of fact, three Law Lords (Browne-Wilkinson, Hope and Saville) relied on the implied waiver of immunities *rationae materiae* that State Parties to the CAT must have intended, whereas another three (Millett, Hutton and Phillips) opined that the development of core crimes and extra-territorial jurisdiction are inconsistent with the existence of immunities *rationae materiae.*[764] Since reliance was placed upon Chile's obligation to exercise universal criminal jurisdiction over acts of torture by virtue of the CAT, the Pinochet *dictum* cannot be deemed to have established a general principle that functional immunity is unavailable to those suspected of core crimes.[765] To this Rosanne van Alebeek adds that the lack of such precedential value stems from the fact that not all States are parties to the CAT, not all crimes are subject to a conventional *aut dedere aut judicare* rule, and not all core crimes can only be committed by State officials.[766]

---

[760] Cryer 2010, p. 542.

[761] *Regina v Bartle and Commissioner of Police for the Metropolis and Others (Appellants) ex parte Pinochet (Respondent); Regina v Evans and another and Commissioner of Police for the Metropolis and others (Appellants) ex parte Pinochet (Respondent), On Appeal from a Divisional Court of the Queen's Bench Division*, above n. 729, cited in Ferstman 2007, p. 154.

[762] *Opinion of Lord Millett*, above n. 729, cited in Webb 2012, p. 124.

[763] *Opinion of Lord Millett*, above n. 729, cited in Webb 2012, p. 134.

[764] Webb 2012, p. 129.

[765] van Alebeek 2012, p. 7.

[766] Ibid.

Though, in theory, van Alebeek's arguments cannot easily be rebutted, I am, to some extent, at odds with such observations. Firstly, not to mention various UN resolutions dealing with torture, a great majority of world States (precisely 165) have ratified the CAT.[767] Secondly, the CAT, the Genocide Convention and the Geneva Conventions are subject to a conventional *aut dedere aut judicare* rule. These cover acts which constitute nearly all core crimes penalized by the ICC Statute. Certain crimes against humanity are not equally subject to such rule not because such stigma does not attach thereto, neither because legislators decided to deliberately omit such rule from such treaties, but because they are not conventionally proscribed in the first place. The lack of a treaty to penalize crimes against humanity does not and should not be used as an argument to aid the application of immunities. In fact, Article 6 of the proposed convention on crimes against humanity expressly prohibits the invocation of immunities, bringing such provision in line with Article 27 of the ICC Statute, Article 3 of the 1954 ILC Draft Code of Offences Against the Peace and Security of Mankind and Article 7 of the 1996 Draft Code of Offences Against the Peace and Security of Mankind.[768] Thirdly, although core crimes can be committed by non-State entities,[769] even if and when they are so committed, the perpetration of the core crime by members of non-State entities does not exonerate highest State officials from their responsibility to protect, to prosecute and to punish. Fourthly, it has been acknowledged that the *Pinochet dictum* 'not only constitutes State practice and *opinio iuris*, but also provides a useful argument for an approach towards the problem of immunity for core crimes under customary international law'.[770] Finally, at worst, the application of diplomatic privileges and immunities can be deemed to cause a situation of 'norm conflict' which necessitates a hierarchical prioritisation of one over the other since it entails that a State party to two treaties cannot simultaneously comply with its obligations under both treaties.[771] In this persistent tension, Rosanne van Alebeek seems to infer that some diplomatic privileges and immunities are more solidly grounded than the quest (or better, the duty) to punish core crimes which, in other words, translates itself into the quest (or better, the duty) to punish gross violations of human rights. Such distinct prioritisation probably stems from an omission (possibly deliberate) to distinguish between procedural and substantive rules.

---

767 See https://treaties.un.org/pages/ViewDetails.aspx?src=TREATY&mtdsg_no=IV-9&chapter=4&lang=en. Accessed 31 December 2018.

768 See The Crimes Against Humanity Initiative, launched by Leila Nadya Sadat (the Henry H. Oberschelp Professor at Washington University School of Law), which is a Rule of Law project of the Whitney R. Harris World Law Institute. A Conference report was published on 17 July 2014 following an experts' (including members of the ILC) meeting in Geneva entitled 'Fulfilling the Dictates of Public Conscience: Moving Forward with a Convention on Crimes Against Humanity'. A day after, on 18 July 2014, the ILC voted to add the drafting of a treaty on crimes against humanity to its active agenda (Sadat and Pivnichny 2014, pp. 19–20).

769 See Sect. 4.1.

770 Wirth 2002, p. 434.

771 Webb 2012, p. 117.

Whereras immunity from jurisdiction belongs to the former (procedural) regime, the prohibition of human rights violations belongs to the latter substantive regime, as a result of which some 'human rights norms prevail over the immunity of State officials', namely functional immunities.[772] In fact, 'courts have set aside immunity *rationae materiae* when officials are accused of international crimes' by undertaking two approaches.[773] In the first (adopted by the ICJ and by judges in the UK, the Netherlands and the USA)[774] core crimes cannot constitute official acts of a State but must qualify as private acts of an individual. In disagreement with this approach, Judge Christine van den Wyngaert (in her dissenting opinion in Yerodia), upheld that it distorts reality to say that such acts are 'private'.[775] In the second approach, to which I subscribe, a core crime exception to immunities subsists. This approach was adopted by Law Lords Millett and Phillips in *Pinochet* (wherein immunities *rationae materiae* could not apply to core crimes) and by the *Corte di Cassazione* in *Lozano v Italy* wherein immunity *rationae materiae* of a USA serviceman can be lifted in the case of core crimes, and where, uncharacteristically, the *jus cogens* nature of the breach was essential to resolving the norm conflict.[776] The word 'uncharacteristically' is being used here above since the role of *jus cogens* in solving the norm conflict is still rather obscure.[777] Even in the *Pinochet dictum* Lord Browne-Wilkinson and Lord Hope upheld that notwithstanding the *jus cogens* status of the prohibition of torture, immunity rules applied and prevailed.[778] Only the provisions of CAT tilted the balance.[779] Brunnee, to this effect, observes that 'States have been largely unwilling to realize the normative ambition of *jus cogens* in international practice'.[780] This sharply contrasts with the formidable opinion of Lord Millett which is cited here above.

This said, Orentlicher is correct in observing that the erosion of immunities largely stems from legal provisions within treaties. This is so because treaties 'may endow human rights with a normative superior quality'.[781] Besides the CAT, the Genocide Convention explicitly provides that persons who have committed genocide 'shall be punished, whether they are constitutionally responsible rulers, public

[772] Webb 2012, pp. 118–120.

[773] Webb 2012, pp. 121–125.

[774] USA courts have set aside immunities of State officials accused of serious human rights violations, basing such decisions on the Alien Tort Claims Act (1789) Alien Tort Statute, 28 U.S.C. § 1350, ATS, United States of America, and the Torture Victim Protection Act (1991) H.R.2092, United States of America, which provide federal courts with jurisdiction to hear cases brought by aliens seeking damages for human rights infringements (Webb 2012, p. 132).

[775] *Dissenting opinion of Judge van den Wyngaert*, above n. 734, para 36, cited in Webb 2012, p. 122.

[776] Webb 2012, pp. 123–124.

[777] Webb 2012, p. 124.

[778] Opinions cited in Webb 2012, p. 124.

[779] Webb 2012, p. 124.

[780] Brunnee 2010, cited in Webb 2012, p. 125.

[781] Webb 2012, p. 125.

officials or private individuals'.[782] Likewise Rosanne van Alebeek emphasized that the prevailing State practice after the *Pinochet dictum* did not follow the footsteps of the House of Lords.[783] Nobody can have qualms on van Alebeek's observation. Her conclusion to the effect that the question on the relation between the rule of functional immunity and core crimes is still far from settled,[784] unfortunate as it may be, is a correct analysis of the current position at law on immunities. It is thus correct to conclude that the *Pinochet* case is 'not indicative of the emergence of a hierarchy of norms within international law',[785] but that 'in some cases, the scope of the human rights protection might encompass an ancillary obligation not to recognize immunity'.[786]

Yet, other case-law may be utilised to demonstrate that 'courts deny foreign officials functional immunity from criminal jurisdiction'[787] in so far as core crimes are concerned. Robert Cryer, Hakan Friman, Darryl Robinson and Elizabeth Wilmshurst trace a clear 'shift in the law toward the narrowing of immunities',[788] epitomised by the ruling of the House of Lords by means of which 'international crimes are exempt from traditional international immunities'.[789] This shift is tantamount to an increasing trend in international law to abrogate foreign official immunity for individuals who commit acts, otherwise attributable to the State, that violate *jus cogens* norms'.[790] This is because *jus cogens* violations 'are not legitimate official acts and therefore do not merit foreign official immunity'.[791] Irrespective of this current reality, notwithstanding such state of affairs, Yitiha Simbeye had anyway portrayed the circumvention of immunities by promoting the so-called implied waiver theory as a result of which the immunity of state officials is waived by implication, particularly as a result of the *jus cogens* nature of core crimes.[792] In colloquial terms, even Heads of State will not get away with murder.

782 See Article IV of the Genocide Convention, above n. 155, cited in Orentlicher 2011, p. 211.

783 van Alebeek 2012, p. 6.

784 Ibid.

785 Webb 2012, p. 129.

786 Webb 2012, p. 145.

787 Riccardo Pisillo Mazzeschi refers to, *inter alia*, a few landmark cases, some of which do not deal exclusively with core crimes {[העליון המשפט (Supreme Court), Israel, *Attorney-General of Israel v Adolf Eichmann*, 29 May 1962, Criminal Appeal 336/61]; *Cour de Cassation* [Court of Cassation], Belgium, *Sharon and Yaron*, 12 February 2003; *Corte di Cassazione, Sezione Penale V* [Supreme Court, 5th Criminal Chamber], Italy, *Kidnap of Abu Omar*, 19 September 2012} (Pisillo Mazzeschi 2017, pp. 523–524).

788 Cryer et al. 2010, p. 558.

789 Swart and Sluiter 1999, p. 121.

790 *Bashe Abdi Yousuf, John Doe 1, John Doe 2, Aziz Deria, Plaintiffs–Appellees, John Doe 3, John Doe 4, Jane Doe 1, Plaintiffs v Mohamed Ali Samantar, Defendant–Appellant*, above n. 753, Part III A, p. 20.

791 *Bashe Abdi Yousuf, John Doe 1, John Doe 2, Aziz Deria, Plaintiffs–Appellees, John Doe 3, John Doe 4, Jane Doe 1, Plaintiffs v Mohamed Ali Samantar, Defendant–Appellant*, above n. 753, Part III A, p. 21.

792 Simbeye 2004, pp. 136–146.

Since immunity from criminal jurisdiction, at least *rationae materiae*, has become the exception, rather than the rule, 'it may become still more questioned or even disappear completely'.[793] It may nowadays be correct to endorse the view that individual criminal responsibility has been globalized, whereas the rule of law has been internationalized. The prospects of seeing more Heads of State in the dock (after they relinquish their official duties) have thus been boosted significantly.

Rosanne van Alebeek, throughout her detailed study, critically examines *funditus* various arguments militating both in favour and against the applicability of immunities in the light of the research question she poses, this being: are the well-established immunity rules that shield States and their officials from the adjudicative jurisdiction of other States and that are rooted in the classic inter-state system of international law, affected by the relatively recent developments in international human rights law and international criminal law? She concludes that 'the rule of functional immunity does not apply in the face of allegations of crimes against international law, and that the rule of State immunity and the rules on personal immunity may clash with the fundamental rights of individuals under international law'.[794] In pursuance of this, she suggests that 'international law immunity rules are not affected by the developments in international human rights law'[795] and opines that 'ironically, the human rights movement may thus harm rather than promote the effective protection of the fundamental rights of individuals'.[796] As a result of her latter conclusions, amidst the inconsistency of State practice, a *cadit quaestio* attitude seems to be unwarranted, although I contend that international law discourse is likely to be value-driven in the next years and that such a tailor-made approach is most likely to gradually erode, rather than protect immunities, because of the evident explosion of awareness-oriented human rights legal discourse within the parameters of contemporary international law. To sum up, it would be fair to say that the literature on immunity is still diverse and confusing.[797] Philippa Webb's list of factors and circumstances wherein international and domestic courts tend to remove immunities is probably one of the best and most succinct (to the extent that she refers to it as a simple list which belies a messy reality) restatements of the position of immunities under international law. She contends that the removal of immunities is steadily gaining ground when more than one of the following five factors is present:

(1) the immunity being invoked is immunity *rationae materiae*;
(2) the alleged human rights violation is a core crime;
(3) there is an applicable treaty that lifts immunity or removes the defence of official capacity;

[793] Prouvèze 2011, p. 362.
[794] van Alebeek 2008, p. 418.
[795] van Alebeek 2008, p. 416.
[796] van Alebeek 2008, p. 417.
[797] Murungu 2011, p. 33.

(4) there is domestic law that lifts immunity in human rights litigation;
(5) the proceedings are criminal in nature.[798]

Although jurisprudence suggests a developing exception to immunities *rationae materiae* for core crimes and although this exception is supported by many jurists, the existence of such an exception has not yet fully crystallized partly because the *Yerodia dictum* may be read to construe that there is no exception to immunity *rationae materiae* for core crimes.[799] It 'apparently limited the exception to functional immunity in relation to international crimes to acts performed by State agents in the exercise of their duties, but only for private purposes',[800] disrupting the trend which was being established and the momentum which was being garnered by, *inter alia*, the *Bouterse*, *Pinochet*, *Ríos Montt, Lucas Garcia and Meija Victores*, and by the *Bignone*, *Lambruschini*, *Massera* and *Videla* cases.[801] The announcement of the Supreme Court of Appeal of South Africa to the effect that 'it would go too far to say that there is no longer any sovereign immunity for *jus cogens* (immutable norm) violations',[802] seems apposite and timely, especially because it was 'unable to hold that at this stage of the development of customary international law there is an international crimes exception to the immunity and inviolability that heads of State enjoy when visiting foreign countries and before foreign national Courts'.[803] To remove any lingering doubts it would be preferable if international law were to admit of an exception to State immunity for the prosecution of individuals for core crimes and that such exception develops as an independent head.[804] This should be explicitly inserted within a prospective 'International Convention for the Prevention, Prosecution and Punishment of Core Crimes'[805] and would cement the contention that nobody can be immune because 'no one is above the law'.[806]

In the meantime, in a side event held on 7 December 2017 during the 16th ASP, Argentina, Belgium, Mongolia, Senegal, Slovenia and The Netherlands have jointly proposed a new multilateral Treaty for Mutual Legal Assistance and Extradition for Domestic Prosecution of Crimes of Genocide, Crimes Against Humanity and War

798 Webb 2012, p. 144.

799 Trapp 2011, pp. 98–99.

800 *Arrest Warrant of 11 April 2000 (DRC v Belgium)*, above n. 705, para 61, cited in Pisillo Mazzeschi 2017, p. 532, n. 74.

801 Pisillo Mazzeschi 2017, pp. 531–532. With the exception of the *Ríos Montt* case, which has been cited repeatedly in Chap. 13 of my book, *Lucas Garcia* and *Meija Victores*, *Lambruschini*, and *Massera*, all of these cases are referred to and cited throughout this chapter.

802 Supreme Court of Appeal, South Africa, *The Minister of Justice and Constitutional Development v The Southern African Litigation Centre*, 15 March 2016, 867/15 [2016] ZASCA 17, para 84.

803 Ibid.

804 McLachlan 2002, p. 959, cited in Franey 2015, p. 242, n. 104.

805 See references to this proposed treaty in Chap. 23, the last chapter of my book.

806 Tutuianu 2013, p. 131.

Crimes, this being an initiative which is rapidly gaining support.[807] A preliminary background document has been compiled by PGA.[808] Final negotiations and the conclusions intended to devise a draft treaty are expected in 2019.[809] These observations conclude the specific analysis of each and every ground for refusal.

References

ACHPR (1981) African Charter on Human and Peoples' Rights

Additional Protocol I (1977) Protocol Additional to the Geneva Conventions of 12 August 1949, and relating to the Protection of Victims of International Armed Conflicts, 8 June 1977

Additional Protocol (1975) to the European Convention on Extradition, European Treaty Series No. 86, 15 October 1975

Additional Protocol to the ECE (1975) Additional Protocol to the European Convention on Extradition, ETS No. 086

AI (2012) Sierra Leone: End Impunity Through Universal Jurisdiction. No Safe Haven Series No. 9. https://www.amnesty.org/en/documents/AFR51/007/2012/en/. Accessed on 31.12.2018

AI (2018) Perú: Fujimori may be Tried After Decision Not to Apply Grace in Pativilca Case. https://www.amnesty.org/en/latest/news/2018/02/peru-fujimori-podra-ser-juzgado-tras-decision-de-no-aplicar-gracia-en-caso-pativilca/. Accessed 10 May 2018

Aksenova M (2017) Human Rights at the International Criminal Court: Testing the Limits of Judicial Discretion. NJIL 86(1):68–90

Alemu Aneme G (2006) Apology and Trials: The Case of the Red Terror Trials in Ethiopia. AHRLJ 6(1):64–84

Alien Tort Claims Act (1789) Alien Tort Statute, 28 U.S.C. § 1350, ATS, United States of America

Ambos K (2009a) Epilogue: Future Developments of International Criminal Law in Relation to the Responsibility of Superiors for International Crimes. In: Olásolo H (ed) The Criminal Responsibility of Senior Political and Military Leaders as Principals to International Crimes. Hart Publishing, Oxford, pp. 331–336

Ambos K (2009b) The Legal Framework of Transitional Justice: A Systematic Study with a Special Focus on the Role of the International Criminal Court. In: Ambos K, Large J, Wierda M (eds) Building a Future on Peace and Justice: Studies on Transitional Justice, Pace and Development: The Nuremberg Declaration on Peace and Justice. Springer, Berlin/Heidelberg, pp. 19–103

Ambos K, Urquizo G (2018) Pardons for Crimes Against Humanity: Some Critical Considerations Regarding the Pardon of Former Peruvian President Alberto Fujimori. EJIL: Talk! https://www.ejiltalk.org/pardons-for-crimes-against-humanity-some-critical-considerations-regarding-the-pardon-of-former-peruvian-president-alberto-fujimori/. Accessed 22 March 2018

Amoury Combs N (2008) Plea Bargains in International Criminal Prosecutions. In: Bassiouni MC (ed) International Criminal Law: International Enforcement, Vol. III, 3rd edn. MNP, Leiden, pp. 561–579

Amsterdam Treaty (1997) Treaty of Amsterdam amending the Treaty of the European Union, the Treaties establishing the European Communities and certain related acts

[807] Cocan 2017.

[808] See https://www.pgaction.org/pdf/Background-Information-MLA-Initiative.pdf. Accessed 26 February 2018.

[809] Cocan 2017.

Anderson K (2002) An Asian Pinochet? - Not Likely, The Unfulfilled International Law Promise in Japan's Treatment of Former Peruvian President Alberto Fujimori. SJIL 38(2):177–206

Anglo-Indian Extradition Treaty (1992) Extradition Treaty Between the United Kingdom and India

Anglo-USA Supplementary Extradition Treaty (1985) Supplementary Extradition Treaty (Supplementary Treaty) between the United States of America and the United Kingdom

An-Na'im AA (1990) Human Rights in the Muslim World: Socio-Political Conditions and Scriptural Imperatives – A Preliminary Inquiry. HHRJ 3:13–52

Apartheid Convention (1973) Convention on the Suppression and Punishment of the Crime of Apartheid

Appleton C, Grover B (2007) The Pros and Cons of Life Without Parole. British Journal of Criminology 47(4):597–615

Aptel C (2007) Some Innovations in the Statute for the Special Tribunal for Lebanon. JICJ 5 (5):1107–1124

Arab League Agreement (1952) Arab League Collective Security Pact

Asia Pacific Advisory Council of Jurists (2001) Reference on the Death Penalty. A-P JHR 2 (2):155–229

Ayala C (2016) The Judicial Dialogue between International and National Courts in the Inter-American Human Rights System. In: Scheinin M, Krunke H, Aksenova M (eds) Judges as Guardians of Constitutionalism and Human Rights. EE, Cheltenham, UK/Northampton, MA, USA, pp. 306–328

Bakker CAE (2005) A Full Stop to Amnesty in Argentina: The *Simón* Case. JICJ 3(5):1106–1120

Bantekas I (2010) International Criminal Law, 4th edn. HP, Oxford/Portland, Oregon

Barker C (2002) Immunity *Rationae Personae* and *Jus Cogens* Norms – Approach with Caution. Conference Paper of the ILA, British Branch, Spring Conference

Barker C, Warbrick C, McGoldrick D (1999) The Future of Former Head of State Immunity After *Ex Parte Pinochet.* ICLQ 48(4):937–949

Bassiouni MC (1974) International Extradition and World Public Order. Sijthoff, Leiden

Bassiouni MC (1986) The United States Model. In: Bassiouni MC (ed) International Criminal Law: Volume II: Procedure. TP, Dobbs Ferry, NY, pp. 405–425

Bassiouni MC (1994) The Protection of Human Rights in the Administration of Criminal Justice: A Compendium of United Nations Norms and Standards. TP, Irvington-on-Hudson, NY

Bassiouni MC (1996) International Crimes *Jus Cogens* and *Obligatio Erga Omnes.* LCP 59(4):63–74

Bassiouni MC (1999) Law and Practice of the United States. In: Bassiouni MC (ed) International Criminal Law, Procedural and Enforcement Mechanisms, Vol. II, 2nd edn. TP, NY, pp. 191–275

Bassiouni MC (2000) Death as a Penalty in the *Shari'a*, International Commission of Jurists, *The Death Penalty Condemned.* Extended Version of Papers Presented in the Roundtable Organised by the International Commission of Jurists with the Support of the European Union and the Council of Europe on 12 April 1999 in Geneva, Published in Chatelaine, Switzerland

Bassiouni MC (2001) Universal Jurisdiction for International Crimes: Historical Perspectives and Contemporary Practice. VJIL 42(1):81–162

Bassiouni MC (2007) International Extradition: United States Law and Practice, 5th edn. OPI, Dobbs Ferry, NY

Bassiouni MC (2008) The Need for International Accountability. In: Bassiouni MC (ed) International Criminal Law: International Enforcement, Vol. III, 3rd edn. MNP, Leiden, pp. 3–28

Bauloz C (2018) Non-Refoulement. In: Djukić D, Pons M (eds) The Companion to International Humanitarian Law. International Humanitarian Law Series No. 55, Brill Nijhoff, Leiden/Boston, pp. 534–536

Bederman DJ, Semmelman J (2010) International Decisions. AJIL 104(4):641–647

Belgian Act Concerning the Punishment of Grave Breaches of the Geneva Conventions of 12 August 1949 and their Additional Protocols I and II of 18 June 1977 (1993), Official Journal of

5 August 1993, at 17751–17755, as amended by the Act Concerning the Punishment of Grave Breaches of International Humanitarian Law (1999) Official Journal of 23 March 1999, at 9286–9287, (adopted in 1993, expanded in 1999, and repealed on 5 August 2003)

Belgian Code of Criminal Procedure (1808) Book III, Title I, Articles 137–216, amended 30 November 2011

Bellelli R (2010) Obligation to Cooperate and Duty to Implement. In: Bellelli R (ed) International Criminal Justice: Law and Practice from the Rome Statute to Its Review. MPG Books Group, Ashgate, Farnham, Surrey, pp. 211–240

Benelux Treaty on Extradition and Mutual Assistance in Criminal Matters (1962) T2064 41.8, 27 June 1962

Bernaz N, Prouvèze R (2010) International and Domestic Prosecutions. In: Bassiouni MC (ed) The Pursuit of International Criminal Justice: A World Study on Conflicts, Victimization, and Post-Conflict Justice, Vol. 1. Intersentia, Antwerp, Oxford, Portland, pp. 269–398

Bernhardt R (1981) (ed) Encyclopedia of Public International Law: Settlement of Disputes, Vol. 1. North-Holland Publishing, Amsterdam, pp. 148–150

Bianchi A (1994) Denying State Immunity to Violators of Human Rights. AJPIL 46:195–229

Björgvinsson DT (2015) The Intersection of International Law and Domestic Law: A Theoretical and Practical Analysis. EE, Cheltenham, UK and Northampton, Massachusets, USA

Boas G (2007) The Milošević Trial: Lessons for the Conduct of Complex International Criminal Proceedings. CUP, Cambridge

Bohlander M (2008) *Ne Bis in Idem*. In: Bassiouni MC (ed) International Criminal Law: International Enforcement, Vol. III, 3rd edn. MNP, Leiden, pp. 541–560

Boister N (2016) The Simplification of the Law of Extradition at a Global Level: Some Reflections on the Implications of the Move Towards a No Dress Rehearsal Rule. Paper submitted for the purposes of an ACIL lecture, *UvA*, Amsterdam

Bojosi KN (2004) The Death Row Phenomenon and the Prohibition Against Torture and Cruel, Inhuman or Degrading Treatment. AHRLJ 4(2):303–333

Borelli S (2004) The Rendition of Terrorist Suspects to the United States: Human Rights and the Limits of International Cooperation. In: Bianchi A (ed) Enforcing International Law Norms Against Terrorism. HP, Oxford and Portland, Oregon, USA, pp. 331–373

Bradford CD (2010–2011) Waiting to Die, Dying to Live: An Account of the Death Row Phenomenon from a Legal Viewpoint. IDJHRL 5(1):77–96

Brazilian Criminal Code (1940) *Código Penal, Decreto-Lei n.° 2.848 de 7 de Dezembro de 1940* [Decree-Law No. 2.848 of 7 December 1940]

Brown AS (2002) *Adiós* Amnesty: Prosecutorial Discretion and Military Trials in Argentina. TILJ 37(1):203–225

Brunnee J (2010) The Prohibition on Torture: Driving *Jus Cogens* Home? Proceedings of the 104th ASIL Annual Meeting, International Law in a Time of Change. ASIL, Washington, DC, 104:454–457

Çali B (2018) The Spectre of Trexit: Proposal to Reintroduce the Death Penalty in Turkey. EJIL: Talk! https://www.ejiltalk.org/the-spectre-of-trexit-proposal-to-reintroduce-the-death-penalty-in-turkey/. Accessed 25 November 2018

Cançado Trindade AA (2011) The Access of Individuals to International Justice. OUP, Oxford

Cançado Trindade AA (2001a) *El Acceso Directo Del Individuo a los Tribunales Internacionales de Derechos Humanos* [The Right to Individial Petititon Before International Courts of Human Rights]. *Universidad de Deusto*, Bilbao, Spain

Cançado Trindade AA (2001b) *Vers la Consolidation de la Capacité Juridique Internationale des Pétitionnaires dans le Système Interaméricaine des Droits de la Personne* [Towards the Consolidation of a *Locus Standi* of Petitioners in the Inter-American System of Human Rights], *Revue Québécoise de Droit International*, 14(2):207–239

Cançado Trindade AA (2001c) *El nuevo Reglamento de la Corte Interamericana de Derechos Humanos* [The New Laws of the Inter-American Court of Human Rights] (2000): *La emancipación del ser humano como sujeto del derecho internacional de los derechos humanos*

[The Emancipation of the Human Being as a Subject of International Human Rights Law]. *Revista del Instituto Interamericano de Derechos Humanos*. 30/31:45–71
Caplan LM (2003) State Immunity, Human Rights, and *Jus Cogens*: A Critique of the Normative Hierarchy Theory. AJIL 97(4):741–781
Cassese A (2002a) *Y a-t-il un conflit insurmontable entre souveraineté des Etats et justice pénale internationale*? [Is there an insurmountable conflict between state sovereignty and international criminal justice?] In: Cassese A, Delmas-Marty M (eds) *Crimes Internationaux et Juridictions Internationales* [International Crimes and International Jurisdictions]. Paris, Puf, pp. 1–29
Cassese A (2002b) When May Senior State Officials Be Tried for International Crimes? Some Comments on the *Congo v Belgium* Case EJIL 13(4):853–875
Cassese A (2004a) Terrorism as an International Crime. In: Bianchi A (ed) Enforcing International Law Norms Against Terrorism. HP, Oxford and Portland, Oregon, USA, 2004, pp. 213–225
Cassese A (2004b) International Law, 2nd Edn. OUP, Oxford
Cassese A, Acquaviva G, Fan M, Whiting A (2011) International Criminal Law: Cases and Commentary. OUP, Oxford
CAT (1984) Convention Against Torture and Other Cruel, Inhuman or Degrading Treatment or Punishment
Charter of Paris for a New Europe (1990)
Chigara B (2000) Pinochet and the Administration of International Criminal Justice. In: Woodhouse D (ed) The Pinochet Case: A Legal and Constitutional Analysis. HP, Oxford/Portland, Oregon, pp.115–128
Choo A L-T (1995) Halting Criminal Prosecutions: The Abuse of Process Doctrine Revisited. CLR 864–874
Ciampi A (2009) Extradition In: Cassese A (ed) The Oxford Companion to International Criminal Justice. OUP, Oxford, pp. 321–322
CISA (1990) Convention Implementing the Schengen Agreement, 19 June 1990, [2000] OJ L239/19
Clapham A (2003) Symbiosis in International Human Rights Law: The *Öcalan* Case and the Evolving Law on the Death Sentence. JICJ 1(2):475–489
Cocan S (2017) Fighting Impunity: The Mutual Legal Assistance Initiative for Domestic Prosecution of the Most Serious Crimes. Canadian Partnership for International Justice. https://ilg2.org/2017/12/07/fighting-against-impunity-the-mutual-legal-assistance-initiative-for-domestic-prosecution-of-the-most-serious-crimes/. Accessed 26 February 2018
Code Pénal, France (1810)
CoE (1984) Explanatory Report to the Protocol No. 7 to the Convention for the Protection of Human Rights and Fundamental Freedoms. 22 November 1984, European Treaty Series No. 117, Strasbourg. https://rm.coe.int/16800c96fd. Accessed 1 July 2013
Committee Against Torture (2000) Report: Twenty-third session (8–19 November 1999) and Twenty-fourth session (1–19 May 2000), UN GAOR, 55th Session, Supp. 44, UN Doc. A/55/44
Commonwealth Scheme for the Rendition of Fugitive Offenders (1990)
Constitution of the International Labour Organization (1946) Instrument for the Amendment of the Constitution of the International Labour Organization, adopted by the International Labour Conference at its 29th Session, International Labour Office Official Bulletin, Vol. XXIX, No. 4
Convention Against the Taking of Hostages (1979)
Convention for the Suppression of Terrorist Bombings (1997)
Convention for the Suppression of the Financing of Terrorism (1999)
Convention for the Suppression of Unlawful Acts against the Safety of Civil Aviation (1971)
Convention for the Suppression of Unlawful Acts against the Safety of Maritime Navigation (1988)
Convention for the Suppression of Unlawful Seizure of Aircraft (1970)
Convention on the Physical Protection of Nuclear Material (1980)
Convention on the Prevention and Punishment of Crimes against Internationally Protected Persons, including Diplomatic Agents (1973)

CREMS (1996) Convention Relating to Extradition between the Member States of the EU, drawn up on the basis of Article K.3 of the Treaty on European Union, relating to extradition between the Member States of the European Union

Criminal Justice Act, UK (1988)

Cryer R, Friman H, Robinson D, Wilmshurst E (2010) An Introduction to International Criminal Law and Procedure, 2nd Edn. CUP, Cambridge

D'Amato A (2008) National Prosecution for International Crimes. In: Bassiouni MC (ed) International Criminal Law: International Enforcement, Vol. III, 3rd edn. MNP, Leiden, pp. 285–295

Danish Constitution (1953) The Constitutional Act of Denmark, 5 June 1953

Danish Genocide Act (1955) Act No. 132 Concerning the Punishment of Genocide, 29 April 1955

de Bondt W, Vermeulen G (2010) Appreciating Approximation: Using Common Offence Concepts to Facilitate Police and Judicial Cooperation in the EU. In: Cools M, Easton M, Ponsaers P, van der Beken T, Vermeulen G, de Ruyver B, Pauwels L, van der Walle G, van der Laenen F, Vynckier G (eds) EU and International Crime Control. Governance of Security Research Paper Series, Associatie Universiteit Gent, Maklu Publishers, Antwerpen, pp. 15–40

De Merieux M (1996) Extradition as the Violation of Human Rights: The Jurisprudence of the International Covenant on Civil and Political Rights. NQHR 14(1):23–33

De Schutter O (2014) International Human Rights law, 2nd edn. CUP, Cambridge

de Than C, Shorts E (2000) Double Jeopardy – Double Trouble. JCL 64(6):624–641

de Wet E (2004) The Prohibition of Torture as an International Norm of *Jus Cogens* and Its Implications for National and Customary Law. EJIL 15(1):97–121

Dean F, D'Innocenzio M, Pugliese P, Ricci A (2003) *Diritto Penale Internazionale: Lezioni agli Studenti* [International Criminal Law: Lectures for Students], *Terza Edizione. Marghiacci, Galeno Editrice*, Roma

Death Penalty Information Centre (2018) Abolitionist and Retentionist Countries. http://www.deathpenaltyinfo.org/abolitionist-and-retentionist-countries. Accessed 11 December 2018

Decree (1990) Decree No. 2741/90, Argentina, issued by the then President of Argentina Carlos Menem, 29 December 1990

Deen-Racsmany Z, Blekxtoon R (2005) The Decline of the Nationality Exception in European Extradition? EJCCLCJ 13(3):317–364

Deen-Racsmany Z (2006) The European Arrest Warrant and the Surrender of Nationals Revisited: The Lessons of Constitutional Challenges. EJCCLCJ 14(3):271–306

Denza E (2016) Diplomatic Law: Commentary on the Vienna Convention on Diplomatic Relations, 4th edn. Oxford Commentaries on International Law, OUP, Oxford

Donders Y (2010) Do Cultural Diversity and Human Rights make a Good Match? ISSJ 61(199): 15–35

Draft Code of Offences Against the Peace and Security of Mankind (1954) International Law Commission Draft Code of Offences Against the Peace and Security of Mankind, adopted in the ILC's sixth session

Draft Code of Offences Against the Peace and Security of Mankind (1996) International Law Commission Draft Code of Offences Against the Peace and Security of Mankind, adopted in the ILC's forty-eighth session

Drumbl MA (2008) Immunities and Exceptions. In: Bassiouni MC (ed) International Criminal Law, Vol. II, Multilateral and Bilateral Enforcement Mechanisms, 3rd edn. MNP, Leiden, pp. 231–242

du Plessis M (2007) South Africa's Implementation of the International Criminal Court Statute: An African Example. JICJ 5(2):460–479

Duffy H (2007) The War on Terror and the Framework of International Law. CUP, Cambridge

Dugard J (1999a) Dealing with Crimes of a Past Regime. Is Amnesty still an Option? LJIL 12(4): 1001–1015

Dugard J (1999b) South Africa's Truth and Reconciliation Process and International Humanitarian Law. YIHL 2:254–263

Dugard J, van den Wyngaert C (1998) Reconciling Extradition with Human Rights. AJIL 92 (2):187–212
Duncan AGM (1993) Trayner's Latin Maxims. 4th edn. S & M, Edinburgh
Dutch Criminal Code (1881) Criminal Code of the Kingdom of the Netherlands, as supplemented by the Criminal Policy Plan on Society and Crime (1985)
ECE (1957) European Convention on Extradition
ECMAC (1959) European Convention on Mutual Assistance in Criminal Matters
Economic Community of West African States Convention on Extradition (1994) Convention on Extradition of the Governments of the Member States of the Economic Community of West African States, A/P.1/8/94
ECvHR (1950) European Convention for the Protection of Human Rights and Fundamental Freedoms
Egelman Z (2018) Punishment and Protection, Two Sides of the Same Sword: The Problem of International Criminal Law under the Refugee Convention. HILJ 59(2):461–499
El Salvador's General Amnesty Law for Consolidation of Peace (1993)
El Zeidy M (2008) The Principle of Complementarity in International Criminal Law: Origin, Development and Practice. MNP, Leiden/Boston
Emmerson B, Ashworth A, Macdonald A (2007) Human Rights and Criminal Justice. 2nd Edn. S & M, London
Epps V (1996) In re Requested Extradition Smyth 61 F.3d. 711 US Court of Appeals, 9th Cir., July 27 1995. AJIL 90(2):296–300
Erikson CJ (2009) Sweden: End Impunity Through Universal Jurisdiction, Amnesty International, No Safe Haven Series. London. https://www.amnesty.org/download/Documents/48000/eur420012009en.pdf. Accessed 31 July 2013
Eser A (2004) For Universal Jurisdiction: Against Fletcher's Antagonism. UTLR 39(4):955–978
EU Charter of Fundamental Rights (2000) Charter of Fundamental Rights of the European Union, Official Journal of the European Communities, (2000/C 364/01)
European Communities Convention (1952) Treaty Establishing the European Coal and Steel Community
European Communities Convention (1957) Treaty Establishing the European Economic Community
European Convention on the International Validity of Criminal Judgments (1970)
European Convention on the non-Applicability of Statutory Limitations to Crimes Against Humanity and War Crimes (1974)
European Convention on the Suppression of Terrorism (1977)
Evans AE (1980) *Narenji v Civiletti* No. 79-2460: US Court of Appeals, D.C. Cir., Dec. 27, 1979. AJIL 74(2):433–434
Extradition treaty between France and Algeria (1964), *Décret n° 65-679 du 11 août 1965 portant publication de la convention entre la France et l'Algérie relative à l'exequatur et à l'extradition et de l'échange de lettres complétant le protocole judiciaire signés le 27 août 1964* [Decree No. 65-679 of 11 August 1965 relating to the publication of the Convention between France and Algeria on Extradition and on the Exchange of Letters Supplementing the Judicial Protocol signed on 27 August 1964]
Extradition Treaty between the Government of Canada and the Government of the USA (1971)
Extradition Treaty Between the Government of the United States of America and the Government of Jamaica (1983)
Extradition Treaty Between the Government of the United States of America and the Government of the Republic of Costa Rica (1982)
Extradition Treaty Between the United States of America and Canada (1976)
Fabbrini F (2010) Understanding the Abu Omar Case: The State Secret Privilege in a Comparative Perspective. International Association of Constitutional Law Workshop 6 entitled 'The Rule of Law in the Age of Terrorism'. Paper submitted in the World Congress, Mexico City, Mexico
Ferdinandusse W (2004) The Interaction of National and International Approaches in the Repression of International Crimes. EJIL 15(5):1041–1053

Ferdinandusse WN (2006) Direct Application of International Criminal Law in National Courts. Asser Press, The Hague

Ferstman C (2007) The Approach of the United Kingdom to Crimes under International Law. In: Kaleck W, Ratner M, Singelnstein T, Weiss P (eds) International Prosecution of Human Rights Crimes, Springer, Berlin/Heidelberg, pp. 149–158

Filletti S (2017) Towards a European Criminal Law System. Kite Group, Malta

Fletcher M, Loof R, Gilmore B (2008) European Union Criminal Law and Justice. EE, Cheltenham, UK/Northampton, Massachusets, USA

Flint J, de Waal A (2009) To Put Justice Before Peace Spells Disaster for Sudan: The Overzealous Pursuit of Omar al-Bashir Could Ruin Years of Diplomatic Progress. The Human Cost Will be Massive. The Guardian. http://www.theguardian.com/commentisfree/2009/mar/06/sudan-war-crimes

Forde M, Kelly K (2011) Extradition Law and Transnational Criminal Procedure, 4th edn. Round Hall, Dublin

Forowicz M (2010) The Reception of International Law in the European Court of Human Rights. International Courts and Tribunals Series, OUP, Oxford

Fournet C (2006) International Crimes: Theories, Practice and Evolution. CMP, London

Framework Decision on the EAW (2002) Council Framework Decision on the European Arrest Warrant and the Surrender Procedures Between the Member States, Doc. 2002/584/JHA

Franey EH (2015) Immunity from the Criminal Jurisdiction of National Courts. In: Orakhelashvili A (ed) Research Handbook on Jurisdiction and Immunities in International Law. Research Handbook in International Law, EE, Cheltenham, UK/Northampton, MA, USA, pp. 205–252

Frazer E (2010) Reviewing Slomp G (2009) Carl Schmitt and the Politics of Hostility, Violence and Terror. Palgrave Macmillan, NY. In: Ethics and International Affairs 24(3):339

French *Nouveau Code Pénal* (1992)

Gaeta P (2009) Immunities and Genocide, In: Gaeta P (ed) The United Nations Genocide Convention: A Commentary. Oxford Commentaries on International Law, OUP, Oxford, pp. 310–333

Gamarra R (2009) A Leader Takes Flight: The Indictment of Alberto Fujimori. In: Lutz EL, Reiger C (eds) Prosecuting Heads of State. CUP, Cambridge, pp. 95–110

Garner BA (2009) Black's Law Dictionary. Thomson West, Saint Paul, MN, USA

Gaspar-Szilagyi S (2016) Joined Cases *Aranyosi* and *Caldararu*: Converging Human Rights Standards, Mutual Trust and a New Ground for Postponing a European Arrest Warrant, Case Report. EJCCLCJ 24(2–3):197–219

General Treaty of Peace and Amity (1907)

Geneva Convention (1949a) Geneva Convention (I) for the Amelioration of the Condition of the Wounded and Sick in Armed Forces in the Field

Geneva Convention (1949b) Geneva Convention (II) for the Amelioration of the Condition of the Wounded, Sick and Shipwrecked Members of Armed Forces at Sea

Geneva Convention (1949c) Geneva Convention (III) relative to the Treatment of Prisoners of War

Geneva Convention (1949d) Geneva Convention (IV) relative to the Protection of Civilian Persons in Time of War

Genocide Convention (1948) Convention on the Prevention and Punishment of the Crime of Genocide

German-Polish Upper Silesian Convention (1922) German-Polish Convention concerning Upper Silesia

Gianelli A (2017) The Place of Rehabilitation of the Offender Among the Purpose of Penalties According to International Law. In: Acconci P, Donat Cattin D, Marchesi A, Palmisano G, Santoni V (eds) International Law and the Protection of Humanity: Essays in Honour of Flavia Lattanzi. MNP, Leiden/Boston, pp. 397–412

Gilbert G (1991) Aspects of Extradition Law. MNP, Dordrecht

Gilbert G (1998) Transnational Fugitive Offenders in International Law: Extradition and Other Mechanisms. MNP, Leiden/Boston

Gilbert G (2017) Undesirable but Unreturnable: Extradition and Other Forms of Rendition. JICJ 15(1):55–74

Gomien D, Harris D, Zwaak L (1996) Law and Practice of the European Convention on Human Rights and the European Social Charter. Council of Europe Publishing, Strasbourg

Goodwin SG, McAdam J (2007) The Refugee in International Law, 3rd edn. OUP, Oxford

Gorski A (2008) Summary. In: Gorski A, Hofmanski P (eds) The European Arrest Warrant and its Implementation in the Member States of the European Union. Wydawnictwo C.H. Beck, Warszawa. http://www.law.uj.edu.pl/~kpk/eaw/other/220_EAW.pdf. Accessed 11 January 2013

Guatemala's Peace Agreement (1996) The Accord for a Firm and Lasting Peace between the Government of Guatemala and the *Unidad Revolucionaria Nacional Guatemalteca* [Guatemalan National Revolutionary Unit], 29 December 1996

Haas G (2002) State Security Interests in the French Extradition Procedure. In: Roggemann H, Šarcevic P (eds) National Security and International Criminal Justice. KLI, The Hague/London/NY, pp. 193–207

Hague Convention XII (1907) Convention (XII) Relative to the Creation of an International Prize Court

Harris D, O'Boyle M, Bates EP, Buckley CM (2009) Harris, O'Boyle and Warbrick: Law of the European Convention on Human Rights, 2nd edn. OUP, Oxford

Hungarian Criminal Code (1875) Law No. V

Hungarian Code of Criminal Procedure (1998) Criminal Procedure Code of the Republic of Hungary, Act XIX on Criminal Proceedings, as amended in 2011

IACvHR (1969) Inter-American Convention on Human Rights

ICC Statute (1998) Rome Statute of the International Criminal Court

ICCPR (1966) International Covenant on Civil and Political Rights

ICTR Statute (1994) Statute of the International Criminal Tribunal for Rwanda

ICTY Statute (1993) Statute of the International Criminal Tribunal for the Former Yugoslavia

IDI (2009) Resolution on Immunity from Jurisdiction of the State and of Persons who act on Behalf of the State in Case of International Crimes, Napoli Session, Third Commission. Rapporteur: Lady Fox. http://www.idi-iil.org/app/uploads/2017/06/2009_naples_01_en.pdf. Accessed 13 November 2018, also available at *IDI* (2009) *Annuaire de l'Institut de droit international - Session de Naples* - Volume 73, Third Commission, Rapporteur: Lady Fox. http://www.idi-iil.org/app/uploads/2017/06/Lady-Fox.pdf. Accessed 12 April 2018

Instrument Amending the Treaty Between Belgium and the United States of America of 27 April 1987 (2004) 16 December 2004

Inter-American Convention Against Terrorism (2002)

Inter-American Convention to Prevent and Punish Torture (1985)

International Commission of Jurists (2000) The Death Penalty Condemned, Extended Version of Papers Presented in the Roundtable Organised by the International Commission of Jurists with the Support of the European Union and the Council of Europe on 12 April 1999 in Geneva, Published in Chatelaine, Switzerland.

International Convention on the non-Applicability of Statutory Limitations to War Crimes and Crimes Against Humanity (1968)

Irish Extradition (Amendment) Act (1994), No. 6 of 1994

Italian Law on the EAW (2005) *Mandato d'arresto europeo e procedure di consegna tra Stati membri* [EAW and Transfer Procedures Between Member States], Law No. 69, 22 April 2005

Jennings RY, Watts A (1992) Oppenheim's International Law, 9th edn. Longman, London

Joint Action on Trafficking in Human Beings (1997) Joint Action adopted by the Council on the basis of Article K.3 of the Treaty on European Union concerning action to combat trafficking in human beings and sexual exploitation of children, 24 February 1997, 97/154/JHA

Karuhanga J (2018) Government Welcomes Life Sentence Against Genocide Suspect in Sweden. The New Times, Rwanda's Leading Daily. https://www.newtimes.co.rw/news/government-welcomes-life-sentence-against-genocide-suspect-sweden. Accessed 11 September 2018

Kay A (2016) Former Georgian Minister of Defence and Aide to President Misha Saakashvili Discharged in UK Extradition Proceedings. Bedford Row International. http://9bri.com/former-georgian-minister-of-defence-and-aide-to-president-misha-saakashvili-discharged-in-uk-extradition-proceedings/. Accessed 11 January 2018

Keijzer N, van Sliedregt E (2000) A Guide to State Practice Concerning International Humanitarian Law: Correspondents' Reports. YIHL 3:405–616

Kelly MJ (2003) Cheating Justice by Cheating Death: The Doctrinal Collision for Prosecuting Foreign Terrorists – Passage of *Aut Dedere Aut Judicare* into Customary Law and Refusal to Extradite based on the Death Penalty. AJICL 20(3):491–532

Kemp G (2010) Individual Criminal Liability for the International Crime of Aggression. Intersentia, Antwerpen/Oxford/Portland

Kielsgard MD (2013) The Political Offence Exception: Punishing Whistleblowers Abroad. EJIL: Talk! http://www.ejiltalk.org/the-political-offense-exception-punishing-whistleblowers-abroad/. Accessed 22 March 2018

Kleffner JK (2008) Complementarity in the Rome Statute and National Criminal Jurisdiction, International Courts and Tribunals Series. OUP, Oxford

Klimek L (2015) European Arrest Warrant. Springer, Heidelberg/NY/Dordrecht/London

Klip A (2009) European Criminal Law, An Interactive Approach. *Ius Communitatis* Series, Vol. 2, Intersentia, Cambridge/Antwerp/Portland

Klouckova S (2006) Introduction into the Czech Constitutional Court's Decision on the European Arrest Warrant; The Decision of the Czech Constitutional Court No. PI. US 66/04 of 3 May 2006. http://www.asser.nl/upload/eurowarrantwebroot/documents/cms_eaw_id863_1_Introduction%20into%20the%20Czech%20Constitutional%20Court.doc. Accessed 1 August 2018

Knuchel S (2011) State Immunity and the Promise of *Jus Cogens*. NJIHR 9(2):149–183

Kochler H (2003) Global Justice or Global Revenge? International Criminal Justice at the Crossroads. Springer, Vienna/NY

Kok RA (2007) Statutory Limitations in International Criminal Law. Asser Press, The Hague

Kolb R (2004) The Exercise of Criminal Jurisdiction over International Terrorists. In: Bianchi A (ed) Enforcing International Law Norms Against Terrorism. HP, Oxford and Portland, Oregon, USA, pp. 227–281

Kolodkin RA (2011) ILC Report, Immunity of State Officials from Foreign Criminal Jurisdiction. 2nd Report considered by the ILC and by the Sixth Committee of the UNGA, 63rd Session of the ILC, Doc. A/CN.4/631

Lafontaine F (2005) No Amnesty or Statute of Limitation for Enforced Disappearances: The *Sandoval* Case before the Supreme Court of Chile. JICJ 3(2):469–484

Lagondy O (2003) Expert Opinion for the Council of Europe on Questions Concerning Double Criminality. PC-OW/WP, Strasbourg, 24 June 2003

Laplante LJ, Theidon K (2010) Commissioning Truth, Constructing Silences: The Peruvian Truth Commission and the Other Truths of "Terrorists". In: Clarke KM, Goodale M (eds) Mirrors of Justice: Law and Power in the Post-Cold War Era. CUP, Cambridge, pp. 291–315

Legg A (2012) The Margin of Appreciation in International Human Rights Law: Deference and Proportionality. OUP, Oxford

Lillich RB (1984) Civil Rights In: Meron T (ed) Human Rights in International Law: Legal and Policy Issues. Vol. 1, CP, Oxford, pp. 115–170

Lisbon Treaty (2007a) Treaty of Lisbon Amending the Treaty on European Union and the Treaty Establishing the European Community

Lisbon Treaty (2007b) Treaty of Lisbon Amending the Treaty on the European Union and the Treaty Establishing the European Community

London Agreement (1945) Agreement by the Government of the United States of America, the Provisional Government of the French Republic, the Government of the United Kingdom of Great Britain and Northern Ireland and the Government of the Union of Soviet Socialist Republics for the Prosecution and Punishment of the Major War Criminals of the European Axis

London Scheme for Extradition Within the Commonwealth (2002)

Long N (2009) Implementation of the European Arrest Warrant and Joint Investigation Teams at European Union and National Level. European Parliament, Brussels
Lutz EL, Reiger C (2009) Introduction. In: Lutz EL, Reiger C (eds) Prosecuting Heads of State. CUP, Cambridge, pp. 1–24
Mackarel M (2007) The European Arrest Warrant – the Early Years: Implementing and Using the Warrant. EJCCLCJ 15(1):37–65
Maltese *Kodiči Kriminali, Kapitolu 9 tal-Liġijiet ta' Malta* [Criminal Code, Chapter 9 of the Laws of Malta] (1854)
Manacorda S (2003) Restraints on Death Penalty in Europe: A Circular Process. JICJ 1(2): 263–283
Marchesi D (2018) Imprisonment for Life at the International Criminal Court. ULR 14(1):97–115
Martin FF, Schnably SJ, Slye RC, Wilson R, Falk R, Simon JJ, Koren E (1997) International Human Rights Law and Practice: Cases, Treaties and Materials. KLI, Alphen aan den Rijn, The Netherlands
Martin MK (1998–1999) A One-Way Ticket Back to the United States The Collision of International Extradition Law and the Death Penalty. Capital Defense Journal 11(2):243–261
Mauritanian Amnesty Law (1993) *Journel officiel de la republique islamique de Mauritanie: Loi numero 93-23 du 14 juin 1993 portant Amnistie*, Law No. 93-23, 14 June 1993
McDermott H (2015) The Structure of International Cooperation in the Transfer of Suspects. Extradite or Abduct? ICLR 15(2):254–297
McGoldrick D (1996) The Human Rights Committee: Its Role in the Development of the International Covenant on Civil and Political Rights. Oxford Monographs in International Law, OUP, Oxford
McLachlan C (2002) Pinochet Revisited. ICLQ 51(4):959–966
Mégret F (2010) In Search of the 'Vertical': Towards an Institutional Theory of International Criminal Justice's Core. In: Stahn C, van den Herik L (eds) Future Perspectives on International Criminal Justice. Asser Press, The Hague, pp. 178–224
Mifsud J, Bugelli M (2014) Terror's Footprints: Shadows of International Terrorism Over Malta. Kite Group, Malta
Model American Convention (1980) Model American Convention on the Prevention and Punishment of Serious Forms of Violence Jeopardizing Fundamental Rights and Freedoms, Division of Public Service Activities, ABA
Morosin MN (1995) Double Jeopady and International Law: Obstacles to Formulating a General Principle. NJIL 64(2):261–274
Mujuzi JD (2009) International Human Rights Law and Foreign Case Law in Interpreting Constitutional Rights: The Supreme Court of Uganda and the Death Penalty Question. AHRLJ 9(2):576–589
Mujuzi JD (2011) Life Imprisonment Before the International Criminal Tribunal for the Former Yugoslavia. EJCCLCJ 19(2):103–112
Mukherjee A (2004) The ICCPR as a "Living Instrument": The Death Penalty as Cruel, Inhuman and Degrading Treatment. JCL 68(6):507–519
Murungu C (2011) Immunity of State Officials and the Prosecution of International Crimes. In: Murungu C, Biegon J (eds) Prosecuting International Crimes in Africa. PULP, Pretoria, pp. 33–60
Naqvi YQ (2010) Impediments to Exercising Jurisdiction over International Crimes. Asser Press, The Hague
Neagu N (2012a), 'The *Ne Bis In Idem* Principle: Interpretation of European Courts: Towards Uniform Interpretation'. LJIL 25(4):955–977
Neagu N (2012b), 'The *Ne Bis In Idem* Principle in the Case-Law of the European Court of Justice (II). The "Final Judgment" and "Enforcement' Issues"', *Lex Et Scientia*, Juridical Series, 2 (XIX):67–87
New Zealand Extradition Act (1999) No. 55
Nollkaemper A (2011) National Courts and the International Rule of Law. OUP, Oxford

Nordic Extradition Act (1960) Act on Extradition of Offenders to Finland, Iceland, Norway and Sweden, No. 27, 3 February 1960
O'Brien J (1999) Smith's Conflict of Laws, 2nd edn. CPL, London
O'Shea A (2002) Amnesty for Crime in International Law and Practice. Kluwer, The Hague/London/NY
Obediencia Debida [Due Obedience] Law No. 23-521, Argentina, 4 June 1987
Obokata T (2010) Transnational Organised Crime in International Law. Studies in International and Comparative Criminal Law, Vol. 5, HP, Oxford/Portland, Oregon
Olásolo H (2009) The Criminal Responsibility of Senior Political and Military Leaders as Principals to International Crimes. Studies in International & Comparative Criminal Law, HP, Oxford and Portland, Oregon, USA
Ongena T, van Daele I (2002) Universal Jurisdiction for International Core Crimes: Recent Developments in Belgium. LJIL 15(3):687–701
Orakhelashvili A (2006) Peremptory Norms in International Law. Oxford Monographs in International Law, OUP, Oxford
Orentlicher D (2004) Whose Justice? Reconciling Universal Jurisdiction with Democratic Principles. GLJ 92(6)1057–1134
Orentlicher D (2011) Immunities and Amnesties. In: Sadat LN (ed) Forging a Convention for Crimes Against Humanity. CUP, Cambridge, pp. 202–222
Ouwerkerk J (2018) Balancing Mutual Trust and Fundamental Rights Protection in the Context of the European Arrest Warrant: What Role for the Gravity of the Underlying Offence in CJEU Case Law? EJCCLCJ 26(2):103–109
Padfield N (2007) The European Arrest Warrant: Between Trust, Democracy and the Rule of Law – The Implementation of the European Arrest Warrant in England and Wales. EUCLR 3 (2):253–268
Paraguayan Penal Code (1997) *Ley Nº 1.160/97, Código Penal*, Law No. 1.160/97, Criminal Code
Paulsson J (2005) Denial of Justice in International Law. CUP, Cambridge
Paust JJ, Bassiouni MC, Scharf M, Gurulé J, Sadat L, Zagaris B (2007) International Criminal Law: Cases and Materials, 3rd edn. CAP, Durham, NC, USA
Petersen AC (1992) Extradition and the Political Offense Exception in the Suppression of Terrorism. ILJ 67(3):767–796
Petronio F, Hyeraci M, Contesso M (2014) *The Ne Bis in Idem* Principle Among International Treaties and Domestic Rules: The Recent Case-Law of the European Court of Human Rights on Italy. Insights, Paul Hastings, Milano. http://www.paulhastings.com/publications-items/details/?id=1943e169-2334-6428-811c-ff00004cbded. Accessed 29 May 2016
Pinzauti G (2005) An Instance of Reasonable Universality: The *Scilingo* Case. JICJ 3(5): 1092–1105
Pisillo Mazzeschi R (2017) The Functional Immunity of State Officials from Foreign Jurisdiction: A Critique of the Traditional Theories. In: Acconci P, Donat Cattin D, Marchesi A, Palmisano G, Santoni V (eds) International Law and the Protection of Humanity: Essays in Honour of Flavia Lattanzi. MNP, Leiden/Boston, pp. 509–534
Plachta M (1989) The Role of Double Criminality in International Cooperation in Penal Matters. In: Jareborg N (ed) Double Criminality: Studies in International Criminal Law. Iustus Forlag, Uppsala, pp.84–134
Plachta M (1998) Extradition and the Principle *Aut Dedere Aut Judicare* in the New Polish Legislation. EJCCLCJ 6(2):94–105.
Plachta M (2001a) The Lockerbie Case: The Role of the Security Council in Enforcing the Principle *Aut Dedere Aut Judicare*. EJIL 12(1):125–140
Plachta M (2001b) Contemporary Problems of Extradition: Human Rights, Grounds for Refusal and the Principle *Aut Dedere Aut Judicare*, UNAFEI Annual Report for 1999 and Resource Material Series No. 57. http://www.unafei.or.jp/english/pdf/PDF_rms/no57/57-07.pdf. Accessed 9 August 2012
Plachta M (2005) Joint Investigation Teams: A New Form of International Cooperation in Criminal Matters. EJCCLCJ 13(2):284–302

Poels A (2005) A Need for Transnational *Non Bis In Idem* in International Human Rights Law. NQHR 23(3):329–347

Pollicino O (2008) European Arrest Warrant and Constitutional Principles of the Member States: A Case Law-Based Outline in the Attempt to Strike the Rights Balance Between Interacting Legal Systems. German LJ 9(10):1313–1355

Poncet D, Hart PG (1999) The European Model. In: Bassiouni MC (ed) International Criminal Law: Procedural and Enforcement Mechanisms, Vol. II, 2nd edn. TP, Ardsley, NY, pp. 277–328

Princeton Principles on Universal Jurisdiction (2001) Princeton Project on Universal Jurisdiction, 23 July 2001

Prosecutor v Tadić, Judgment, 15 July 1999, IT-94-1-A. In: Klip A, Sluiter G (2001) (eds) Annotated Legal Cases of International Criminal Tribunals: The International Criminal Tribunal for the Former Yugoslavia, 1997–1999, Vol. 3, Intersentia, Cambridge, pp. 761–850

Protocol for the Suppression of Unlawful Acts against the Safety of Fixed Platforms Located on the Continental Shelf (1988) supplementary to the Convention for the Suppression of Unlawful Acts against the Safety of Maritime Navigation

Protocol on the Suppression of Unlawful Acts of Violence at Airports Serving International Civil Aviation (1988) supplementary to the Convention for the Suppression of Unlawful Acts against the Safety of Civil Aviation

Protocol Relating to the Status of Refugees (1967) supplementary to the Convention Relating to the Status of Refugees

Prouvèze R (2011) Immunities. In: Schabas WA, Bernaz N (eds) Routledge Handbook of International Criminal Law. Routledge, T & F, London/NY, pp. 355–367

Punto Final [Full Stop] Law No. 23-492, Argentina, 23 December 1986

Put J (2002) *Bis, sed non in idem, Een denkoefening over de toepassing van het non bis in idembeginsel op de cumulatie van administratieve en strafsancties, [Bis, sed non in idem:* Reflections on the application of the *non bis in idem* principle to the cumulative consideration of administrative and criminal sanctions], in: *Rechtskundig Weekblad* 65(27):937–949

Rafaraci T, Belfiore R (2007) Judicial Protection of Individuals under the Third Pillar of the European Union. Jean Monnet Working Paper 10/07, NY University School of Law, NY. http://jeanmonnetprogram.org/wp-content/uploads/2014/12/071001.pdf. Accessed 31 December 2016

REDRESS, African Rights (2008) Extraditing Genocide Suspects From Europe to Rwanda: Issues and Challenges, Report of a Conference Organised by REDRESS and African Rights at the Belgian Parliament. http://www.redress.org/downloads/publications/Extradition_Report_Final_Version_Sept_08.pdf. Accessed 22 June 2014

Refugee Convention (1951) Convention Relating to the Status of Refugees

Rehman J (2003) International Human Rights Law: A Practical Approach. Pearson Education Limited, London

Rehman J (2005) Islamic State Practices, International Law and the Threat from Terrorism: A Critique of the 'Clash of Civilisations' in the New World Order. HP, Oxford/Portland, Oregon

Reydams L (2003a) Universal Jurisdiction: International and Municipal Legal Perspectives. OUP, Oxford

Reydams L (2003b) Belgium's First Judicial Application of Universal Jurisdiction: The *Butare Four* Case. JICJ 1(2):428–436.

Rikhof J (2010) Fewer Places to Hide? The Impact of Domestic War Crimes Prosecutions on International Impunity. In: Bergsmo M (ed) Complementarity and the Exercise of Jurisdiction for Core International Crimes. Forum for International Criminal and Humanitarian Law Publication Series N. 7. TOAEP, Oslo, pp. 7–81

Robinson A (2016) Challenges to Justice at Home: The Domestic Prosecution of Efrain Rios Montt. ICLR 16(1):103–133

Robinson D (2003) Serving the Interests of Justice: Amnesties, Truth Commissions and the International Criminal Court. EJIL 14(3):481–505

Rodley N (1999) The Treatment of Prisoners under International Law, 2nd edn. OUP, Oxford

Roht-Arriaza N (2000) Amnesty and the International Criminal Court. In: Shelton D (ed) International Crimes, Peace, and Human Rights: The Role of the International Criminal Court. TP, Ardsley, NY, pp. 77–82

Ronco M, Ardizzone S (2007) *Codice Penale Ipertestuale: Commentario con Banca Dati di Giurisprudenza e Legislazione* [Electronic Criminal Code: Commentary on Materials, Jurisprudence and Legislation], 2nd edn. WK, *Italia Giuridica srl, UTET Giuridica*

Rosanò A (2017) *Ne Bis Interpretatio In Idem*? The Two Faces of the *Ne Bis In Idem* Principle in the Case Law of the European Court of Justice. German LJ 18(1):38–59

Roth R (2009) The Extradition of *Genocidaires*. In: Gaeta P (ed) The United Nations Genocide Convention: A Commentary. Oxford Commentaries on International Law, OUP, Oxford, pp. 278–309

Rugege S, Karimunda AM (2014) Domestic Prosecution of International Crimes: The Case of Rwanda. In: Werle G, Fernandez L, Vormbaum M (eds) Africa and the International Criminal Court. International Criminal Justice Series, Vol. 1, Asser Press, The Hague, pp. 79–116

Ryngaert C (2008) Jurisdiction in International Law. Oxford Monographs in International Law, OUP, Oxford

Sadat LN, Pivnichny DJ (2014) Fulfilling the Dictates of Public Conscience: Moving Forward with a Convention on Crimes Against Humanity, Conference Report, Whitney R Harris World law Institute, 17 July 2014. http://law.wustl.edu/harris/documents/Final-CAHGenevaReport-071714.pdf. Accessed 28 May 2018

Saul B (2009) The Implementation of the Genocide Convention at the National Level. In: Gaeta P (ed) The UN Genocide Convention: A Commentary. Oxford Commentaries on International Law, OUP, Oxford, pp. 58–83

Schabas W (1997) The Abolition of the Death Penalty in International Law, 2nd edn. CUP, Cambridge

Schabas W (2012) Unimaginable Atrocities: Justice, Politics, and Rights at the War Crimes Tribunals. OUP, Oxford

Schabas W (2013) International Criminal Law and Tribunals and Human Rights. In: Sheeran S, Rodley N (eds) Routledge Handbook of International Human Rights Law. Routledge Handbooks, Routledge, T & F, London, pp. 215–229

Schabas WA (2000) Genocide in International Law. CUP, Cambridge

Schabas WA (2011) National Amnesties, Truth Commissions and International Criminal Tribunals. In: Brown BS (ed) Research Handbook on International Criminal Law. Research Handbooks in International Law, EE, Cheltenham, UK/Northampton, MA, USA, pp. 373–390

Schabas W (2004) An Introduction to the International Criminal Court. 2nd edn. CUP, Cambridge

Scharf MP (1999) The Amnesty Exception to the Jurisdiction of the International Criminal Court. CILJ 32(3):507–527

Schengen Acquis (1999) The Schengen Convention to Implement the Schengen Agreement of 14 June 1985

Schlutter B (2010) Developments in Customary International Law: Theory and Practice of the International Court of Justice and the International ad hoc Criminal Tribunals for Rwanda and Yugoslavia. MNP, Leiden/Boston

Schuon C (2010) International Criminal Procedure: A Clash of Legal Cultures. Asser Press, The Hague

Schwartz DW (2004) Rectifying Twenty-Five Years of Material Breach: Argentina and the Legacy of the "Dirty War" in International Law. EILR 18(1):317–370

Schwarzenberger G (1950) The Problem of International Criminal Law. CLP 3(1):263–296

Sedman D (2010) Should the Prosecution of Ordinary Crimes in Domestic Jurisdictions Satisfy the Complementarity Principle? In: Stahn C, van den Herik L (eds) Future Perspectives on International Criminal Justice. Asser Press, pp. 259–266.

Seibert-Fohr A (2002) The Fight Against Impunity under the International Covenant on Civil and Political Rights. MPYUNL 6:301–344

Seibert-Fohr A (2005) Reconstruction Through Accountability. MPYUNL 9:555–578

Seventh Protocol to the ECvHR (1984) Protocol No. 7 to the Convention for the Protection of Human Rights and Fundamental Freedoms as Amended by Protocol No. 11

Shearer IA (1971) Extradition in International Law. MUP, Manchester

Siebert-Fohr A (2003) The Relevance of the Rome Statute of the International Criminal Court for Amnesties and Truth Commissions. MPYUNL 7:553–590

Simbeye Y (2004) Immunity and International Criminal Law. Ashgate, Farnham, Surrey

Simpson JA, Weiner ESC (1989) The Oxford English Dictionary, 2nd edn, Vol. XI. CP, Oxford

Sixth Protocol to the ECvHR Concerning the Abolition of the Death Penalty (1983) Protocol No. 6 to the Convention for the Protection of Human Rights and Fundamental Freedoms Concerning the Abolition of the Death Penalty as Amended by Protocol No. 11

Sluiter G (2003) The Surrender of War Criminals to the International Criminal Court. LLAICLR 25:605–651

Slye RC, van Schaack B (2009) Essentials: International Criminal Law. WK, Alphen aan den Rijn, The Netherlands

Soler C (1999) Reconciling Conflicting Human Rights in the New International Criminal Law Regime. Thesis Submitted to the Centre for Legal Studies of the University of Sussex in partial fulfilment of the degree of Master of Laws (LL.M.) in International Criminal Law, pp. 12–38.

Soler C (2004) Why is Freedom From Tortue an Absolute Right? – A Multi-disciplinary Analysis. Mediterranean Journal of Human Rights 8(1):369–380

South Asian Association for Regional Cooperation Regional Convention on Suppression of Terrorism (1987)

Special Genocide Law of Rwanda (1996) *Loi organique no. 8196 du 30/08/1996 sur l'organisation des poursuites des infractions constitutives du crime de génocide ou de crimes contre l'humanité, commises à partir du 1er octobre 1990* [Organic Law no. 8196 of 30/08/1996 on the Prosecution of Offences Constituting the Crimes of Genocide or Crimes against humanity, Committed as of 1 October 1990], Official Gazette of the Republic of Rwanda, 1 September 1996

Spector JS (1998) Extraditing Mexican Nationals in the Fight Against International Narcotics Crimes. UMJLR 31(4):1007–1037

Spencer JR (2013) Extradition, The European Arrest Warrant and Human Rights. CLJ 72(2): 250–253

Statute of the SCSL (2002) Statute of the Special Court for Sierra Leone

Statute of the STL (2007) Statute of the Special Tribunal for Lebanon

Stein T (2006) Limits of International Law Immunities for Senior State Officials in Criminal Procedure. In: Tomuschat C, Thouvenin J-M (eds) The Fundamental Rules of the International Legal Order: *Jus Cogens* and Obligations *Erga Omnes*. MNP, Leiden/Boston, pp. 249–263

Stigen J (2010) The Relationship Between the Principle of Complementarity and the Exercise of Universal Jurisdiction for Core International Crimes. In: Bergsmo M (ed) Complementarity and the Exercise of Jurisdiction for Core International Crimes. Forum for International Criminal and Humanitarian Law Publication Series No. 7, TOAEP, Oslo, pp. 133–159.

Suljagić E (2009) Justice Squandered? The Trial of Slobodan Milošević. In: Lutz EL, Reiger C (eds) Prosecuting Heads of State. CUP, Cambridge, pp. 176–204.

Sullo P (2018) Beyond Genocide: Transitional Justice and *Gacaca* Courts in Rwanda: The Search for Truth, Justice and Reconciliation. International Criminal Justice Series, Vol. 20. Asser Press, The Hague

Supplementary Extradition Treaty Between the United States of America and the United Kingdom of Great Britain and Northern Ireland (1985)

Supplementary Treaty to the Treaty Between the USA and the Federal Republic of Germany Concerning Extradition (1986) Treaty Doc. 100-6, 21 October 1986

Swart AH (1992) Human Rights and the Abolition of Traditional Principles. In: Eser A, Lagondy O (eds) Principles and Procedures for a New Transnational Criminal Law. *Freiburg im Breisgau, Max-Planck-Institut fur auslandisches und internationals Strafrecht*, pp. 505–534

Swart B (1997) Extradition. In: Swart B, Klip A (eds) International Criminal Law in the Netherlands. *Freiburg im Breisgau, Edition iuscrim, Max-Planck-Institut fur Auslandisches und Internationales Strafrecht, Freiburg; Bd. S 66*, pp. 85–122

Swart B (2009) International Criminal Justice and Models of the Judicial Process. In Sluiter G, Vasiliev S (eds) International Criminal Procedure: Towards a Coherent Body of Law. CMP, London, pp. 93–118

Swart B, Sluiter G (1999) The International Criminal Court and International Criminal Co-operation. In: von Hebel HAM, Lammers JG, Schuking J (eds) Reflections on the International Criminal Court. Asser Press, The Hague, pp. 91–127

Taylor RH (2001) Pinochet, Confusion and Justice: The Denial of Immunity in US Courts to Alleged Torturers who are Former Heads of State. TJLR 24:101–120

Tchorbadjiyska A (2004) Joint Cases C-187/01 and C-385/01, *Gözütok and Brügge*, *CJEL*, Vol. 10, European Legal Study Center, Columbia Law School. http://www.cjel.net/print/10_3-tchorbadjiyska/. Accessed 28 March 2011

Teitel R (2002) Transitional Justice. OUP, Oxford

Tejan-Cole A (2009) A Big Man in a Small Cell: Charles Taylor and the Special Court for Sierra Leone. In: Lutz EL, Reiger C (eds) Prosecuting Heads of State. CUP, Cambridge, pp. 205–232

Third Supplementary Extradition Treaty Between the United States of America and the Kingdom of Spain (1996) Treaty Doc. 105-15, 12 March 1996

Thompson B (2015) Universal Jurisdiction: The Sierra Leone Profile. International Criminal Justice Series, Vol. 3, Asser Press, The Hague

Thwaites N (2003) Mutual Trust in Criminal Matters: The European Court of Justice Gives a First Interpretation of a Provision of the Convention Implementing the Schengen Agreement: Judgment of the European Court of Justice of 11 February 2003 in Joined Cases C-187/01 and C-385/01, *Hüseyin Gözütok and Klaus Brügge*. German LJ 4(3):253–262

Torture Victim Protection Act (1991) H.R.2092, United States of America

Trapp KN (2011) State Responsibility for International Terrorism: Problems and Prospects. OUP, Oxford

Treaty Between the United States and the Federal Republic of Germany Concerning Extradition (1978)

Tutuianu S (2013) Towards Global Justice: Sovereignty in an Interdependent World. Asser Press, The Hague

UN Model Treaty on Extradition (1990) Model Treaty on Extradition 45/116, UNGA, 68th Plenary Meeting, 14 December 1990, UN Doc. A/RES/45/116

UN Standard Minimum Rules for the Treatment of Prisoners (1955) adopted by the First United Nations Congress on the Prevention of Crime and the Treatment of Offenders, and approved by the Economic and Social Council by means of Resolutions 663 C (XXIV) of 31 July 1957 and 2076 (LXII) of 13 May 1977

UNC (1945) Charter of the United Nations

UNSC (2007) Resolution 1757 (2007), UN Doc. S/RES/1757

Urtubey LM (2005) Non-Applicability for Statutes of Limitation for Crimes Committed in Argentina: *Barrios Altos*. Southwestern Journal of Law and Trade in the Americas 11(1): 109–132

Uruguay's Expiry Law (1986) *Ley de Caducidad*, Uruguay, Law 15.848

USA and Canada Supplementary Extradition Convention (1952) T.I.A.S. No. 2454 (1952), U.S. Dep't of State Pub. No. 4709 (1952); Can. T. S., 1952, No. 12 (1953)

USA Constitution's Fifth Amendment (1789)

USA-Italy Extradition Treaty (1983) Extradition Treaty Between the United States of America and Italy

van Alebeek R (2008) The Immunity of States and Their Officials in International Criminal Law. Oxford Monographs in International Law, OUP, Oxford

van Alebeek R (2012) National Courts, International Crimes and the Functional Immunity of State Officials. NILR 59(1):5–41 van Bockel B (2010) The *Ne Bis in Idem* Principle in European Union Law. KLI, Alphen aan den Rijn, The Netherlands

van den Wyngaert C (1980) The Political Offence Exception to Extradition: The Delicate Problem of Balancing the Rights of the Individual and the International Public Order. Kluwer, Alphen aan den Rijn, The Netherlands

van den Wyngaert C, Ongena T (2002) *Ne Bis in Idem* Principle, Including the Issue of Amnesty. In: Cassese A, Gaeta P, Jones JRWD (eds) The Rome Statute of the International Criminal Court: A Commentary, Vol. I. OUP, Oxford, pp. 705–729

van der Wilt H (1997) The Political Offence Exception in Extradition Law: An Antidote to Prefixed Ideas About Political Integration in Europe? MJECL 4(1):25–58

van der Wilt H (2005a) The Principle of Reciprocity. In: Blekxtoon R, van Ballegooij W (eds) Handbook on the European Arrest Warrant. Asser Press, The Hague, pp. 71–81

van der Wilt H (2005b) The European Arrest Warrant and the Principle *Ne Bis In Idem*. In: Blekxtoon R, van Ballegooij W (eds) Handbook on the European Arrest Warrant, Asser Press, The Hague, pp. 99–117

van der Wilt H (2011) Universal Jurisdiction under Attack: An Assessment of African Misgivings Towards International Criminal Justice as Administered by Western States. JICJ 9(5): 1043–1066

van der Wilt H (2012a) On the Hierarchy Between Extradition and Human Rights. In: de Wet E, Vidmar J (eds) Hierarchy in International Law: The Place of Human Rights. OUP, Oxford, pp. 148–175

van der Wilt H (2012b) Domestic Courts' Contribution to the Development of International Criminal Law; Some Reflections, Amsterdam Law School Legal Studies Research Paper Number 2012-15, ACIL, *UvA*, Amsterdam. http://ssrn.com/abstract=1995469. Accessed 3 September 2016

van der Wilt H (2015) "Sadder but Wiser"?: NGOs and Universal Jurisdiction for International Crimes. JICJ 13(2):237–243

van Dijk P, van Hoof F, van Rijn A, Zwaak L (2006) Theory and Practice of the European Convention on Human Rights. 4th edn. Intersentia, Antwerpen/Oxford

van Dijk P, van Hoof GH (1990) Theory and Practice of the European Convention on Human Rights, 2nd edn. Kluwer, Alphen aan den Rijn, The Netherlands

van Heugten E, van Laar PA (2011) (eds) The Iraqi Special Tribunal for Crimes Against Humanity: The *Dujail* Case. Wolf Legal Publishers, Nijmegen

van Sliedregt E (2009) The Dual Criminality Requirement. In: Keijzer N, van Sliedregt E (eds) The European Arrest Warrant in Practice. Asser Press, The Hague, pp. 51–70

Vandeginste S (2012) Reviewing Siebert-Fohr A (2009) Prosecuting Serious Human Rights Violations. OUP, Oxford. In: LJIL 25(1):239–243

Versailles Treaty (1919) *Traité de Versailles*

Vervaele JAE (2013) *Ne Bis In Idem*: Towards a Transnational Constitutional Principle in the EU? ULR 9(4):211–229

Vestergaard J (2003) Implementation of the Framework Decision Regarding the European Arrest Order - the Danish Extradition Legislation: Appendix 3, The Danish Extradition Act 2003. In: Alegre S, Leaf M (eds) European Arrest Warrant: A Solution Ahead of its Time? Justice, pp. 91–95.

Vidmar J (2012) Norm Conflicts and Hierarchy in International Law: Towards a Vertical International Legal System? In: de Wet E, Vidmar J (eds) Hierarchy in International Law: The Place of Human Rights. OUP, Oxford, pp. 13–41

Warbrick C (2004) Immunity and International Crimes in English Law. ICLQ 53(3):769–774

Weatherall T (2015) *Jus Cogens*: International Law and Social Contract. CUP, Cambridge

Webb P (2012) Human Rights and the Immunities of State Officials. In: de Wet E, Vidmar J (eds) Hierarchy in International Law: The Place of Human Rights. OUP, Oxford, pp. 114–147

Weiner AS (2016) Ending Wars, Doing Justice: Colombia, Transitional Justice, and the International Criminal Court. SJIL 52(2):211–241

Werle G (2009) Principles of International Criminal Law. 2nd edn. Asser Press, The Hague

Westphalian Peace Treaties (1648) Peace Treaties of Westphalia, 14–24 October 1648
Weyembergh A, Armada I (2016) The Principle of *Ne Bis In Idem* in Europe's Area of Freedom, Security and Justice. In: Mitsilegas V, Bergstrom M, Konstadinides T (eds) Research Handbook on EU Criminal Law. EE, Cheltenham, UK/Northampton, MA,USA, pp. 189–209
Wheeler CH (2018) Rights in Conflict: The Clash Between Abolishing the Death Penalty and Delivering Justice to the Victims. ICLR 18(2):354–375
White RCA, Ovey C (2010) The European Convention on Human Rights, 5th edn. OUP, Oxford
Williams SA (1991) Nationality, Double Jeopardy, Prescription and the Death Sentence as Bases for Refusing Extradition. International Review of Penal Law 62(1–2):259–280
Wilson RJ (1999) Prosecuting *Pinochet*: International Crimes in Spanish Domestic Law. HRQ 21 (4):927–979
Windridge O (2018) Two Times Too Many: Botswana and the Death Penalty. EJIL: Talk! https://www.ejiltalk.org/author/oliverwindridge/. Accessed 2 July 2018
Wirth S (2002) Immunities, Related Problems, and Article 98 of the Rome Statute. CLF 12:429–458
Zahar A, Sluiter G (2008) International Criminal Law. OUP, Oxford
Zappalà S (2001) Do Heads of State in Office Enjoy Immunity from Jurisdiction for International Crimes? The *Ghaddafi* Case Before the French *Cour de Cassation*. EJIL 12(3):595–612
Zappalà S (2006) The German Federal Prosecutor's Decision Not to Prosecute a Former Uzbek Minister: Missed Opportunity or Prosecutorial Wisdom? JICJ 4(3):602–622
Zimmermann A, Mahler C (2011) Article 1A, para. 2: Definition of the term 'Refugee'. In: Zimmermann A (ed) Dorschnerp J, Machts F (assistant eds) The 1951 Convention Relating to the Status of Refugees and its 1967 Protocol: A Commentary. OUP, Oxford, pp. 281–465

Chapter 17
Concurrent State Obligations

Contents

References 553

Abstract If and when a State is faced with an international obligation to extradite an individual, but simultaneously it is constitutionally precluded from extraditing the individual owing to human rights concerns or constitutionally-entrenched provisions, what should the State do? A solution can be provided by a State's ordinary legislation or by the State's Constitution itself. Where domestic law remains silent on this dilemma international law should prevail to the detriment of a constitutionally-entrenched domestic provision, especially if the international law being invoked is of a customary nature, unless this would entail a breach of a *jus cogens* norm. What should a State do if faced with two international obligations emanating from norms of equal hierarchical status, or of seemingly equal hierarchical status? In the case of a conflict between two international norms of equal hierarchical status, the usual rules governing conflict between international norms may lead to the priority of the international norm that corresponds to the fundamental right. Here no question of supremacy arises. When the fundamental right in question is a rule of *jus cogens*, at the international level, the former would trump the latter and the State in question would be free and, indeed, compelled to prioritize the fundamental right. In this situation, again, no issue of supremacy arises. However, when the conflict of norms exists between an internationally protected human right, not rising to the level of *jus cogens*, and an obligation arising under a resolution of the UNSC, the latter would be superior over conflicting obligations.

Keywords Customary international law · Concurrent State obligations · Fundamental human rights · Amnesty laws · *Aut dedere aut judicare* · Conflicts · Equal hierarchical status · Human rights norms · International obligations · *Julio Héctor Simón et al.* · Supremacy · *Jus cogens* norms

C. Soler, *The Global Prosecution of Core Crimes under International Law*,
https://doi.org/10.1007/978-94-6265-335-1_17

Having considered the grounds for refusal, one must pose some final questions. If and when a State is faced with an international obligation to extradite an individual, which obligation emanates either from a treaty it ratifies or from customary international law, but simultaneously it is constitutionally precluded from extraditing the individual owing to fundamental human rights concerns or constitutionally-entrenched provisions, such as the non-extradition of its nationals, what should the State do? Should its international legal obligations prevail? Or should its constitutional provisions override such international duties?[1] A solution to this conundrum can be provided by a State's ordinary legislation or by the State's Constitution itself. For example, in the USA probably a domestic legal constraint would override international law. Article 6 of the USA Constitution 'places treaties and federal statutes as co-equal articulations of the supreme law of the land'.[2] If, however, this entails that a person may not be extradited, he would still have to be prosecuted on USA soil, this being yet another manifestation of *aut dedere aut judicare*. Effectively, States enjoy freedom in means and method of implementation of international law.[3] Contrarily, Article 15, Section 4 of the Russian Federation Constitution confers supremacy unto international law.[4] On the other hand, where domestic law remains silent on this dilemma, I opine that international law should prevail to the detriment of a constitutionally-entrenched domestic provision, especially if the international law being invoked is of a customary nature, unless adherence to the obligation emanating from customary international law entails a violation of a *jus cogens* norm, such as the prohibition of torture. This is substantiated by the fact that 'States cannot invoke the provisions of their internal law as justification for their failure to perform international obligations'.[5] Commentators have generally concluded that 'primacy is in fact accorded to human rights norms over the extradition treaty', paying 'little attention to the reason for this primacy'.[6] In this context, reference must again be made to the *Julio Héctor Simón and others* landmark judgment, where the Argentinian Supreme Court gave precedence to international law over Argentinian national legislation, namely amnesty laws.[7]

A final question must now be posed. What should a State do if faced with two international obligations emanating from norms of equal hierarchical status, or of seemingly equal hierarchical status? André Nollkaemper, whilst considering such

---

[1] Similar questions are posed by Matilde Ventrella within a EU context. Her study addresses whether EU supremacy should also mean setting aside national Constitutions if they can prevent the application of the EAW (Ventrella 2008, pp. 225–251).

[2] Kelly 2003, p. 517.

[3] ICJ, *Germany v USA* (*LaGrand* Case), 27 June 2001, [2001] ICJ Rep. 466, para 125.

[4] Kelly 2003, p. 517.

[5] PCIJ, *Treatment of Polish Nationals and Other Persons of Polish Origin or Speech in the Danzig Territory* (*The Polish Nationals in Danzig* case), Advisory Opinion No. 23, 4 February 1932, [1932] PCIJ, Series A/B, No. 44, para 24.

[6] Dugard and van den Wyngaert 1998, p. 194.

[7] *Corte Suprema de Justicia de la Nación* [Supreme Court], *Argentina. Julio Héctor Simón y otros v Poder Judicial de la Nación*, 14 June 2005, 17.768 S.1767. XXXVIII; see also, Sect. 16.5.

hypothetical scenario, concludes that 'in case of a conflict between two international norms of equal hierarchical status, the usual rules governing conflict between international norms may lead to the priority of the international norm that corresponds to the fundamental right; if so, no question of supremacy need arise. When the fundamental right in question is a rule of *jus cogens*, at the international level, the former would trump the latter and the State in question would be free and, indeed, compelled to prioritize the fundamental right in question. In this situation, again, no issue of supremacy will arise. And when the conflict of norms exists between an internationally protected human right, not rising to the level of *jus cogens*, and an obligation arising under a resolution of the Security Council, the latter by virtue of Article 103 would be superior over conflicting obligations. The outcome will be that on the international level, the obligation arising under the resolution would have to prevail'.[8] Indeed, conflicts can result not only on an international scale, but also regionally/continentally in that 'the greatest obstacles to the development of a functioning European criminal justice system seem to exist on the horizontal level, in the field of constitutional and ideological conflict between the member States'.[9] These considerations enable me to conclude this part dealing with the horizontal system of enforcement by taking stock of some pertinent jurisdictional issues in the next chapter.

References

Dugard J, van den Wyngaert C (1998) Reconciling Extradition with Human Rights. AJIL 92 (2):187–212

Groning L (2010) A Criminal Justice System or a System Deficit? Notes on the System Structure of the European Union Criminal Law. EJCCLCJ 18(2):115–137

Kelly MJ (2003) Cheating Justice by Cheating Death: The Doctrinal Collision for Prosecuting Foreign Terrorists –Passage of *Aut Dedere Aut Judicare* into Customary Law and Refusal to Extradite based on the Death Penalty. AJICL 20(3):491–532

Nollkaemper A (2011) National Courts and the International Rule of Law. OUP, Oxford

Russian Federation Constitution (1993)

UNC (1945) Charter of the United Nations

USA Constitution (1787)

Ventrella M (2008) Making the Fight Against Criminal Organisations in the European Union More Effective by Setting Aside National Constitutions. EJCCLCJ 16(2):225–251

---

[8] Nollkaemper 2011, p. 293.

[9] Groning 2010, p. 135.

Chapter 18
The Self-assumption of Jurisdiction: An Abuse of Process or a Necessary Evil?

Contents

References 559

Abstract The self-conferment of jurisdiction by domestic criminal courts, especially when universal jurisdiction is being relied upon, should not be construed to mean that such courts are acting *ultra vires*. It has become a necessary evil. The recent expansion of universal jurisdiction is a commendable development especially because international courts and tribunals have not always been up to the job for reasons which are not always imputable to them, *Omar Al Bashir* being a typical case in point. It does not necessarily entail an abuse of process. Domestic prosecutions need to be encouraged. The ensuing uncertainty as to where an individual will be prosecuted and as to where an individual should be prosecuted is the by-product of the failure of international law to set up a clear hierarchy which establishes the proper prosecuting *forum*. The default allows practical factors, such as the whereabouts of the suspect and the domestic application of *aut dedere aut judicare* rule by the custodial State, to determine the prosecuting *forum*. The value of positive complementarity is best appreciated when States embark onto prosecuting. Criminal courts and human rights courts could claim to be endowed with inherent powers. The *compétence de la compétence* doctrine has been used by the IACtHR, amongst others. The principle of mandatory prosecutions, the escalation of which owes its existence to the increasing crystallization of the *aut dedere aut judicare* rule and to the complementarity principle of jurisdiction, seems to be gaining impetus rapidly. Grounds for refusal of extradition should be restrictively interpreted.

Keywords Universal jurisdiction · International Courts · *Ultra vires* · Self-assumption of jurisdiction · Necessary evil · Abuse of process · International community · *Aut dedere aut judicare* · Balance · *Compétence de la compétence* · Complementarity · Dialectical relationship · Inherent powers · Human rights

C. Soler, *The Global Prosecution of Core Crimes under International Law*,
https://doi.org/10.1007/978-94-6265-335-1_18

courts · Implied powers · Mandatory prosecutions · Regional human rights mechanisms · Grounds for refusal of extradition

To conclude this Part, there is no doubt that international criminal law is a victim of a constant struggle: the demand to strike an equitable but effective balance between the interests it seeks to protect, particularly the rights of individuals who are accused of having committed core crimes, and, on the other hand, the ever-present need to exact the prosecution and punish those responsible of the most henious crimes both on behalf of and in representation of the victims of such crimes, and also to produce a deterring effect. As a result of the appalling nature of core crimes, the jurisdictional regime governing core crimes 'is arguably subject to different jurisdictional criteria than other areas of international law'.[1] The jurisdictional regime of international criminal law is, inevitably, intrinsically extra-ordinary. Consequently, the self-conferment of jurisdiction by domestic criminal courts, especially when universal jurisdiction is being relied upon, should not be construed to mean that such courts are acting *ultra vires* or that they should not exercise jurisdiction within the particular circumstances of a particular case. On the contrary, 'where international tribunals have not been created, as in the case of Guatemala, other States may invoke the principle of universal jurisdiction in order to prosecute genocide committed outside their borders'.[2] Several European States, such as Sweden, Germany, Belgium and the UK, are undertaking prosecutions of individuals who have allegedly committed core crimes during the Syrian armed conflict.[3] Therefore, such self-assumption of jurisdiction has become a necessary evil. Alicia Robinson considers domestic criminal justice by the custodial State and/or the invocation of universal jurisdiction by another State as 'the only cognizable courses of action'.[4] The recent expansion of universal jurisdiction and the current increase in universal jurisdiction statutes and trials[5] are therefore a commendable development especially because international courts and tribunals have not always been up to the job for reasons which are not always imputable to them, *Omar Al Bashir* being a typical case in point. It does not necessarily entail an abuse of process especially because 'the most recent cases on the international level evidence a heavy presumption in favour of exercising jurisdiction in spite of prejudice to the defendant where they are accused of international crimes'.[6] This notwithstanding the fact that, as

[1] Bianchi 1992, p. 384.

[2] Robinson 2016, p. 113.

[3] ICD (2018) News Archive. http://www.internationalcrimesdatabase.org/Case/3296 ;http://www.internationalcrimesdatabase.org/Case/3283 ;http://www.internationalcrimesdatabase.org/Case/3288 ;http://www.internationalcrimesdatabase.org/Case/3286 .Accessed 28 December 2018.

[4] Robinson 2016, p. 114.

[5] Langer 2015, p. 249.

[6] Naqvi 2010, p. 330.

observed in Part III, the abuse of process doctrine derives from the right to a fair trial.[7] Put simply, if the international community wants to get rid of safe havens, the self-assumption of jurisdiction is really and truly a necessary evil that ought to be exercised equitably, proportionately and in the least arbitrary fashion possible. Domestic prosecutions need to be encouraged especially since, as Mark Osiel warns, some domestic States may have the tendency to refer prosecutions 'to the ICC despite an apparent ability to conduct them at home' in order to conveniently blame them 'for imposing an unpopular result that municipal courts should rightly be prepared to reach on their own'.[8] The ensuing uncertainty as to where an individual will be prosecuted and as to where an individual should be prosecuted is the by-product of the failure of international law to set up a clear hierarchy which establishes the proper prosecuting *forum*. The default allows practical factors, such as the whereabouts of the suspect[9] and the domestic application of *aut dedere aut judicare* rule by the custodial State, to determine the prosecuting *forum*. Where States take the bull by the horns, the value of positive complementarity can be appreciated. A case in point is Uruguay which made inroads for the purposes of the establishment of a prosecutor's office which will specialize in the prosecution of crimes against humanity.[10]

The rules, norms and principles discussed here above, should not only be considered theoretically or academically. Indeed they have the potential of equipping courts and tribunals with special tools which are conducive to the attainment of the objectives of international criminal law. Hence the *aut dedere aut judicare* rule, the ground of universal jurisdiction, *jus cogens* norms and *erga omnes* obligations do not confer rights or impose duties *in abstracto*. This must be counter-balanced with another reality, being the dialectical relationship between, on the one hand, State sovereignty[11] and, on the other, the inalienability and indivisibility of fundamental human rights. Referring to P*i*CT, Chester Brown, in terms of the doctrine of inherent powers,[12] states that 'international courts have also relied on another source of law relating to procedure and remedies; that is, the exercise of powers that are not expressly conferred on them by their constitutive instruments, but which are nonetheless necessary for the performance of their functions'.[13] I posit that the doctrine does not belong merely to international courts and tribunals, but also to the

[7] Knoops 2006, p. 181.

[8] Osiel 2009, p. 182.

[9] Ferdinandusse 2004, p. 1048.

[10] Buenos Aires Herald (2016) Uruguay Moves to Tackle Dictatorship Crimes. http://www.buenosairesherald.com/article/221642/uruguay-moves-to-tackle-dictatorship-crimes. Accessed 5 November 2017.

[11] See an analysis thereof in Part II, particularly in Chap. 5.

[12] These are powers existent in something as a permanent attribute or quality, forming an element, especially a characteristic or essential element of something, belonging to the intrinsic nature of that which is spoken of. Such powers derive from an office, position or status. An inherent power of a court might then be thought to derive from its nature as a court of law (Mason 1983, p. 449). For a better understanding of such powers, see Chap. 21.

[13] Brown 2005, p. 195.

domestic realm of law, particularly because its source can be found either in general principles of law recognized by States,[14] being a source of international law, or in the doctrine of implied powers,[15] being powers which are not express but are considered to be conferred by the terms of a constitutive instrument. In fact Chester Brown adds that the courts of many common law jurisdictions have claimed inherent powers, whereas continental law countries[16] have also invoked such powers.[17] Hence, it would be fair to conclude that, on a global scale, criminal courts, especially those enjoying superior jurisdiction,[18] and human rights courts, or rather Constitutional Courts, could claim to be endowed with such inherent powers. By way of example, the *compétence de la compétence* doctrine has been used by the IACtHR.[19]

Whilst core crimes are fought on many fronts, employing the relative *corpus juris*, be it the prevailing horizontal one or the vertical one, the principle of mandatory prosecutions (referred to also within Sect. 2.1) seems to be gaining impetus rapidly within the systems of enforcement. This escalation owes its existence to the increasing crystallization of the *aut dedere aut judicare* customary international law rule and to the complementarity principle of jurisdiction. Although regional human rights mechanisms might not be the best example of this trend, the practice of domestic criminal courts and international bodies protecting human rights convey this *iter*.[20] In substantiation of the principle of mandatory prosecution,[21] Luc Reydams concludes that the Austrians, who experienced a massive influx of refugees as a result of the Balkan wars,[22] prosecuted *Duško Cvjetković* for genocide on the basis of universal jurisdiction rather than for war crimes on the basis of *Strafgesetzbuch* 64(1) sub-para 6, because the prosecutor is precluded from preferring a lesser charge if he possesses enough evidence to prove a graver crime, namely genocide.[23] Part IV has shown that the engagement of domestic prosecutions unmasks ‘a growing international *opinio juris* holding that

[14] Article 38(1) of the ICJ Statute (1946) Statute of the International Court of Justice.

[15] Gunther and Sullivan 1997, pp. 98–107.

[16] ‘Civil law’ countries that invoked such powers include France, Germany, Sweden and Norway.

[17] Brown 2007, p. 56.

[18] This connotes the ‘particular aspects of the general legal competence of States often referred to as sovereignty’ [Brownlie 2003, p. 297]. It is habitually divided into three types which signify three separate forms of powers or competences, *id est* prescriptive (legislative), adjudicative (judicial) and enforcement (executive).

[19] IACtHR, *Ivcher Bronstein v Peru (Competence)*, 24 September 1999, Series C No. 54, paras 31–33.

[20] Seibert-Fohr 2005, p. 564, n. 40.

[21] *Legalitatsprinzip*.

[22] Such influx also led to the first conviction for grave breaches of the 1949 Geneva Conventions by a third State, being Denmark [Eastern Division of the Danish High Court, 3rd Chamber, *Public Prosecutor v Refik Sarić*, 25 November 1994, S-3396-94; *Højesteret* (Danish Supreme Court), *Public Prosecutor v Refik Sarić*, 15 August 1995, S-3396-94].

[23] Reydams 2003, p. 101.

the perpetrators of the most henious crimes should not escape punishment'.[24] In the wise words of George Fletcher challenging *impunidad* (these being a few words which should serve as an eye opener to the international community), 'the failure to prosecute serious crimes is considered as bad, if not worse, than the crime itself'.[25] This would explain why a 94-year-old German national is being accused, before a juvenile court in Münster, of being an accessory in the killings of hundreds, in a Nazi concentration camp near Gdańsk in Poland, during World War II.[26]

In my final remarks, by means of which I conclude Part IV, I hereby call for a restrictive interpretation of the grounds for refusal of extradition. André Klip, considering grounds for refusal, states that the 'contribution of the European Union has been to reduce the number of grounds or to remove them'.[27] Under contemporary international criminal law, such grounds for refusal of extradition should be interpreted as restrictively as possible, especially if international criminal law is striving to defeat impunity. This is also consonant with a principled approach to the application of the *aut dedere aut judicare* rule in State practice, at least in so far as the *ratio decidendi* of domestic *dicta* is concerned. Indeed, domestic *dicta* 'can also shape international law when looked to by foreign courts as persuasive judicial authority'.[28] Such approach connotes the application of broad (and arguably hierarchically superior) principles upon which a rule is founded and has also been advocated within a regional context.[29] Therefore, there exists room for a rigid and restrictive interpretation of the above grounds for refusal. Within the horizontal system of enforcement States have control and latitude, but such discretion must be exercised in a manner which is not arbitrary and which safeguards the interest of other States and the human rights of the extraditee.

References

Bianchi A (1992) Extraterritoriality and Export Controls: Some Remarks on the Alleged Antinomy Between European and United States Approaches. GYIL 35:366–435

Bjorge E (2013) The Courts and the European Court of Human Rights: A Principled Approach to the Strasbourg Jurisprudence. CLJ 72(2):289–300

Brown C (2005) The Inherent Powers of International Courts and Tribunals. BYIL 76(1):195-244

Brown C (2007) A Common Law of International Adjudication. International Courts and Tribunals Series in Cooperation with the Project on International Courts and Tribunals, OUP, Oxford

[24] van der Wilt 2011, p. 1045.

[25] Fletcher 2003, p. 580.

[26] Georgiou A (2018) 94-Year-Old Nazi War Crimes Suspect Faces Trial in German Juvenile Court. https://www.newsweek.com/94-year-old-nazi-war-crimes-suspect-faces-trial-german-juvenile-court-1134435. Accessed 30 November 2018.

[27] Klip 2009, p. 322.

[28] O'Keefe 2013, abstract, p. 541.

[29] Bjorge 2013, pp. 289–290.

Brownlie I (2003) Principles of Public International Law, 6th edn. OUP, Oxford

Ferdinandusse W (2004) The Interaction of National and International Approaches in the Repression of International Crimes. EJIL 15(5):1041–1053

Fletcher GP (2003) Against Universal Jurisdiction, Editorial Comments. JICJ 1(3):580–584

Gunther G, Sullivan KM (1997) Constitutional Law, 13th edn. FP, Westbury, NY

ICJ Statute (1946) Statute of the International Court of Justice

Klip A (2009) European Criminal Law: An Interactive Approach, *Ius Communitatis* Series, Vol. 2. Intersentia, Cambridge

Knoops G-JA (2006) Redressing Miscarriages of Justice: Practice and Procedure in National and International Criminal Law Cases. TP, Ardsley, NY

Langer M (2015) Universal Jurisdiction is Not Disappearing: The Shift From "Global Enforcer" to "No Safe Haven" Universal Jurisdiction. JICJ 13(2):245–256

Mason K (1983) The Inherent Jurisdiction of the Court. ALJ 57(8):449–459

Naqvi YQ (2010) Impediments to Exercising Jurisdiction over International Crimes. Asser Press, The Hague

O'Keefe R (2013) Domestic Courts as Agents of Development of the International Law of Jurisdiction. LJIL 26(3):541–558

Osiel MJ (2009) Making Sense of Mass Atrocity. CUP, Cambridge

Reydams L (2003) Universal Jurisdiction: International and Municipal Legal Perspectives. OUP, Oxford

Robinson A (2016) Challenges to Justice at Home: The Domestic Prosecution of Efrain Rios Montt. ICLR 16(1):103–133

Seibert-Fohr A (2005) Reconstruction Through Accountability. MPYUNL 9:555–577

Strafgesetzbuch StGB (1974) Penal Code, Austria

van der Wilt H (2011) Universal Jurisdiction under Attack: An Assessment of African Misgivings Towards International Criminal Justice as Administered by Western States. JICJ 9(5):1043–1066

Part V
Conclusion

Chapter 19
The Obligation of States to Prevent, Prosecute and Punish Core Crimes

Contents

References 577

Abstract A collective subsidiary responsibility of the international community exists when the State manifestly fails in its duties of protection. Yet, the obligation to exercise universal jurisdiction is not absolute, but subsidiary and conditional. Both conventional and customary international law recognise that the State *locus delicti*, which is also usually the *forum conveniens*, has a duty to prosecute core crimes. This duty should not be misconstrued as to denote an obligation to prosecute *in absentia*. International human rights law imposes, at the very least, upon the States *locus delicti commissi*, a duty to investigate. The duty to submit to prosecution necessitates, as a bare minimum, that the State fulfils ancillary (accessory) obligations. These ancillary obligations should certainly include the duty to notify the international community that an individual is within the custodial jurisdiction of a State, which notification can trigger either a decision of the international community to establish a court or tribunal to prosecute the individual or any potential extradition request of another State. The custodial State would also be obliged to preserve any evidence it might possess or come across which could be used in the eventual prosecution of such individual. These are, to date, good practices but they can gradually assume a more onerous and mandatory dimension. War crimes prosecutions in Europe based on universal jurisdiction have become possible because of the arrival in Europe of both victims and suspects during the refugee crisis. Such prosecutions safeguard access to justice, an enabling right and an empowering tool.

Keywords ICC cooperation regime · Countermeasures · Compliance Committee · Positive complementarity · Part 9 · State obligations · Proliferation · Cross-fertilization · *Devoir* · *Deber* · Grounds for refusal · Interactive community of courts · *Aut dedere aut judicare* · Extradition · Duty to submit to prosecution · *Jus cogens* norms · *Erga omnes* obligations · Duty to prosecute · Duty of the territorial State · Accessory obligations · Ancillary obligations · Customary

C. Soler, *The Global Prosecution of Core Crimes under International Law*,
https://doi.org/10.1007/978-94-6265-335-1_19

international law · Self-delegitimization process · Universal jurisdiction · Custodial State · Obligation to investigate and prosecute · *Pinochet* · *Locus delicti commissi* · *Forum conveniens* · Territorial State · *Desaparecidos* · Case of the *Street Children* · Right to the truth · Right to know · Positive obligations of the State · Victims · Basic Principles and Guidelines · *Villagrán-Morales et al. v Guatemala* · *Locus standi* · Effective remedy · Custodial universal jurisdiction · UNSC Resolution · *Furundžija* · UNGA Resolution · IIIM · Prevent · Prosecute · Punish · Collective subsidiary responsibility

Part V is cumulatively intended to strengthen the replies to the research questions posed in the introduction to this book, the body of which has revealed a number of obstacles which surface when the surrender and/or extradition of an individual wanted for core crimes and his prosecution thereafter are at stake. The research which has been conducted has shown that States can take advantage of the relatively fragile ICC cooperation regime and fail to surrender an individual wanted by the ICC without incurring drastic consequences. *Kenya* is a case in point.[1] To counter this fragility, some suggestions have been offered in Sect. 10.3. The ICC, may, in so far as this is worth the time, effort and energy, confirm the charges in the absence of the non-surrendered person even prior to such person's initial appearance before the ICC. Furthermore, nothing stops State Parties from adopting countermeasures vis-à-vis the defaulting State. Moreover, it might be legitimate for international institutions to exercise economic pressure on defaulting States in order to entice their cooperation with the ICC. Additionally, Article 112(4) of the ICC Statute could be used to establish a 'Compliance Committee' as a subsidiary body of the ASP. Finally, though various States might be reluctant, one should not exclude the possibility of an amendment to the ninth part of the ICC Statute. This could, as a start and at the very least, send a message to the effect that priority should be given to mandatory compliance and adherence to obligations rather than to mere cooperation and assistance by prior consent. Besides undertaking amendments to some legal provisions, the title of Part 9 could be changed to read, unequivocally, 'State Obligations'. Although fragile, the vertical system of enforcement is still necessary for many reasons. It fills the impunity gap, it diversifies mechanisms intended to deliver international criminal justice, it contributes to the progressive development of international law and, most of all, it buttresses the horizontal system of enforcement by virtue of a process called 'positive complementarity'. In fact, notwithstanding its shortcomings, the trend to limit grounds for refusal, in so far as the vertical system of enforcement is concerned,[2]

---

[1] See references to ICC Trial Chamber V(B), *Prosecutor v Uhuru Muigai Kenyatta, Decision on the Withdrawal of Charges Against Mr. Kenyatta*, 13 March 2015, Case No. ICC-01/09-02/11, in Kenyans for Peace, Truth and Justice 2014, pp. 2–10.

[2] The ICC Statute precludes States from circumventing their surrender obligations by relying on the traditional extradition-based grounds for refusal, such as the non-extradition of nationals, the political offence exemption and double criminality.

is discernible even by virtue of domestic legislation.[3] This direction was undertaken even throughout the ICC's drafting history[4] and is also currently reflected, by way of example, in international agreements.[5] The nationals of States not parties to the ICC Statute clearly have no guarantee they can never be subjected to the ICC's jurisdiction, hence to the parameters of the vertical system of enforcement. Their minds cannot be put indefinitely at rest. Jann Kleffner aptly notes that other language versions of the ICC Statute use mandatory terms which connote a duty of ICC State Parties to investigate and prosecute, such as '*devoir*' in French and '*deber*' in Spanish.[6] After all, this is also why the vertical system of enforcement has been projected as a valuable frame of reference.

The horizontal system of enforcement, though not flawless, is more robust. Irrespective of the complementarity principle, it stands to reason that the horizontal system of enforcement should be the main system of enforcement. It is the one with the highest chances of success especially because States are managing to circumvent its pitfalls by means of some measures. These measures range from assurances given by the State requesting extradition, to the unification of some procedural laws on a regional level,[7] to the proliferation and cross-fertilization[8] of courts and tribunals, not to mention recourse to universal jurisdiction which is a luxury the vertical system of enforcement is constrained to envy. The net result is an interactive community of courts[9] that streamline some comforting State practice which restrictively interprets bars to extradition, at times eliminating them all together, to the extent that States now enjoy less flexibility and discretion to determine whether an individual wanted for prosecution should be extradited to another domestic State or otherwise. Where they enjoy such leeway and exercise it by refusing to extradite, they remain obliged to submit the wanted individual to prosecution in terms of the customary international law rule of *aut dedere aut judicare*.

The preceding Part has constructed a solid edifice to sustain the contention that *aut dedere aut judicare* can be deemed to be a rule of customary international law. For the sake of avoiding repetitions, these arguments will not be reproduced herein but will occasionally be referred to since they constitute a platform upon which I

[3] See Chapter 2 of the Dutch ICC Implementation Act (2002), The International Criminal Court Implementation Act, The Netherlands, namely Articles 11–44, by means of which the traditional extradition law grounds for refusal have been deliberately omitted.

[4] See Committee Report, 1996, Vol. I, paras 316 and 324, cited in Young 2001, p. 344.

[5] By virtue of the EU-ICC Agreement [EU-ICC Agreement, Council Decision 2002/494/JHA of 13 June 2002, Official Journal L 167, 26 June 2002], cited in Antoniadis and Bekou 2007, *passim*, the EU is obliged to waive the privileges and immunities of persons within the scope of the ICC, where appropriate, in order to allow the ICC to exercise jurisdiction over such persons.

[6] Kleffner 2008, p. 241, n. 26.

[7] See references to the EAW in Chap. 16.

[8] Such cross-fertilization 'produces a process of harmonization, which, although slow, ultimately leads to *rapprochement* and eventually to unification' (Bassiouni 2008a, p. 12); see also van der Wilt and Lyngdort 2009, p. 43.

[9] Burke-White 2002, p. 75.

ground my main submissions sustaining a nascent obligation of custodial States to prevent, prosecute and punish core crimes. The duty to submit to prosecution and the duty to prosecute are not one and the same thing. The duty to prosecute is a duty of the territorial State. Such State cannot extradite in the absence of an extradition request, nor can it surrender if international courts and/or tribunals do not tender a request for surrender owing to their lack of jurisdiction. Moreover, the territorial State possesses all the evidence and means available for the purposes of a successful prosecution. It is hence expected to prosecute. Some States, including Ecuador, Ethiopia and Venezuela, have constitutionalised the duty to prosecute core crimes.[10] The duty to submit to prosecution belongs to and burdens the custodial State. The former, *id est* the duty to prosecute, is mandatory and absolute, whereas the latter, *id est* the duty to submit to prosecution, is optional and alternative since it may lead to surrender, extradition or to a prosecution by the custodial State itself. Yet, it cannot lead to nowhere. There is no option to do nothing. Some form of engagement, consisting, at the very least, in the fulfilment of accessory and related obligations,[11] is required. Whereas the duty to prosecute of the territorial State nowadays forms part of the customary international law regime, the duty of the custodial State to submit to prosecution,[12] at least in some identifiable circumstances which shall be shortly considered, is ripening into a rule with customary international law status. A jurist has asserted that 'the prosecution of violations of *jus cogens* is itself endowed with the status of *jus cogens*'.[13] This said, the fact that the *jus cogens* status of core crimes may engender a duty to submit an individual to prosecution, does not mean that the duty to submit to prosecution is itself a *jus cogens* norm. This is so notwithstanding widespread recognition for the argument that the punishment of core crimes, an intrinsic and necessary part of their prevention, necessitates that the duty to prosecute must enjoy the same peremptory character as the duty to prevent.[14] The acquisition of customary law status of the *aut dedere aut judicare* rule should not be dealt with in isolation. The acquisition of this status finds support in other related developments, to which, in part, it owes its very existence. This journey owes its foundation to the following steps:

I. core crimes are crimes under customary international law, as affirmed in *Tadić*, *Čelebići* and *Jelisić*;[15]

---

[10] Ferdinandusse 2006, p. 196.

[11] An analysis of these obligations will be undertaken with some examples to be given at a later stage of this chapter.

[12] This owes its origin to the duty to submit the individual to prosecution which encompasses the option to either surrender to an international criminal tribunal (or a hybrid or special court) or to extradite to a domestic court. Hence it connotes and mirrors the *aut dedere aut judicare* rule.

[13] Ryngaert 2008, p. 112.

[14] *Suprema Corte de Justicia de la Nación* [Supreme Court], Mexico, *Ricardo Miguel Cavallo, Amparo en Revision*, 10 June 2003, Case No. 14/2002, paras 493–494, cited in Ferdinandusse 2006, p. 183.

[15] See Chap. 13, notes 46, 47, 48.

II. customary international law allows for universal jurisdiction[16] over core crimes[17] since core crimes violate *jus cogens* norms[18] in so far as they infringe the most fundamental human rights the prohibition of which, in and of themselves, constitute *jus cogens* norms. A breach of these hierarchically superior norms is a consequence, not a cause, of core crimes. Thus, *aut dedere aut judicare*-based jurisdiction may become a form of universal jurisdiction if the underlying crime constitutes a violation of *jus cogens*,[19] a status which attaches to a few norms and which is accepted and used by courts and tribunals.[20] In fact, 'the duty to prosecute or extradite (*aut dedere aut judicare*) applies to international crimes and more particularly to *jus cogens* crimes'.[21] It is generally agreed that core crimes 'require the application of universal jurisdiction when other means of carrying out the obligations deriving from *aut dedere aut judicare* have proved ineffective'.[22] Put in simpler terms, States must protect people within their jurisdictional reach by investigating and prosecuting crimes committed in their regard and to their detriment. If they fail to do so, a duty blossoms and the defaulting State can incur responsibility on various fronts. Moreover by means of sufficient time and State practice, it may be argued that universal jurisdiction over certain crimes, including hostage-taking and hijacking,[23] has passed onto customary international law as a result of State acquiescence[24] by virtue of the absence of international protest[25] against the exercise of such jurisdiction

[16] Here one must make reference to the self-delegitimization process which triggers universal jurisdiction [see Chap. 5]. The consequence of a violation of *jus cogens* norms (these norms consisting in the prohibition of core crimes) is the *erga omnes* obligation to prosecute and punish such core crimes [see Sect. 5.5].

[17] van der Wilt 2011, p. 1049.

[18] ICTY found that prohibitions that have reached the level of *jus cogens* may be safely categorised as core crimes [ICTY Appeals Chamber, *Prosecutor v Zejnil Delalić et al.*, 20 February 2001, IT-96-21-A, para 172, n. 225].

[19] Randall 1988, p. 821.

[20] ILC 2006, cited in D'Aspremont 2016, p. 87, n. 8.

[21] Bassiouni 2008b, p. 483. The relationship between *aut dedere aut judicare*, universal jurisdiction, *erga omnes* obligations and *jus cogens* norms was also acknowledged by the ILC in 2014 during its sixty-sixth session (ILC 2014).

[22] Bassiouni 2008c, p. 194.

[23] *Vide, inter alia*, USA District Court, District of Columbia, *USA v Fawaz Yunis*, 12 February 1988, 681 F.Supp. 896 (D.D.C. 1988) Crim. A No. 87-0377; USA District Court for the Southern District of New York, *USA v Ramzi Ahmed Yousef et al.*, 29 May 1996, 927 F.Supp. 673 (S.D.N.Y. 1996), S12 93 Cr.180 (KTD); and USA Court of Appeals, District of Columbia Circuit, *USA v Omar Mohammed Ali Rezaq*, 6 February 1998, 134 F.3d 1121 (D.C. Cir. 1998), 96-3127.

[24] Watson notes that it is indeed difficult to determine whether a government has, in fact, acquiesced to another government's actions or practices (Watson 1993, p. 39).

[25] Zimmerman upholds that 'no State has with regard to the exercise of universal jurisdiction concerning genocide, crimes against humanity or war crimes, so far acted as a persistent objector' (Zimmermann 2006, p. 353). One must also remember that the tacit acquiescence of a State is relevant for the purposes of such State practice.

over nationals of States which are not necessarily parties to the treaties penalizing such conduct.[26] It may thus be stated that 'in view of the widespread State practice as to the exercise of universal jurisdiction over core crimes, such jurisdiction is lawful under customary international law'.[27] Lord Slynn of Hadley, in the *Pinochet* case, went as far as noting that 'universality of jurisdiction is subject to customary international law rules';[28]

III. Customary international law does not only allow but demands the exercise of universal jurisdiction over core crimes when an obligation *erga omnes* stems from the consummation thereof,[29] signifying that 'all States are, in a legal sense, injured by the violation'.[30] This, in turn, presupposes that the territorial state has failed to investigate and prosecute, that an international criminal tribunal, a hybrid tribunal and/or a special court have not been set up to prosecute, and that the ICC has no jurisdiction. At this point the *erga omnes* nature of the obligation to investigate and prosecute transforms itself into an *aut dedere aut judicare*, an obligation to either extradite or prosecute. The latter contention pointing to a customary international law obligation of States to exercise universal jurisdiction is far more compelling where the consummation of such core crimes constitutes a threat to international peace and security, which, in turn, exacts the responsibility to protect.[31] In some conventional regimes, such as, for example, the grave breaches under the Geneva Conventions, a mandatory universal jurisdiction is implied within the *aut dedere aut judicare* obligations.[32] In the case of genocide such obligations also emanate from the existence of the customary international law rule entailing a duty to prosecute. The evidence substantiating this, consisting of national and international practice, has already been described as 'convincing' by commentators.[33]

The obligation to exercise universal jurisdiction is not absolute. It is of a subsidiary nature entailing that it ought to be exercised only when other judicial institutions have failed to investigate and prosecute the core crime. It is also conditional upon the third (bystander) State enjoying custodial jurisdiction over the

---

26 Morris 2001a, p. 64.

27 Ryngaert 2008, p. 117.

28 HoL, *Regina v Bartle and the Commissioner of the Police for the Metropolis and Others (Appellants) Ex parte Pinochet (Respondent) on Appeal from a Divisional Court of the Queen's Bench Division; Regina v Evans and Another and the Commissioner of the Police for the Metropolis and Others (Appellants) Ex parte Pinochet (Respondent) on Appeal from a Divisional Court of the Queen's Bench Division*, Lord Slynn of Hadley, 25 November 1998, 37 ILM (1998) 1302, cited in Poels 2005, p. 69.

29 See Sect. 13.1.

30 Posner 2009, p. 14.

31 This responsibility anyway subsists where the territorial State has failed to investigate and prosecute core crimes (see Sects. 5.4 and 5.5).

32 Zahar and Sluiter 2008, p. 498.

33 Zahar and Sluiter 2008, p. 498, n. 72.

individual. In other words, there exists an unqualified and absolute duty of the territorial State to investigate and prosecute only where the alleged perpetrator has committed a core crime within the territorial State. Both conventional[34] and customary[35] international law recognise that the State *locus delicti*, which is also usually the *forum conveniens*,[36] has a duty to prosecute core crimes. International human rights law, as outlined in Part IV, imposes, at the very least, upon the States *locus delicti commissi*, a duty to investigate. An obligation of the territorial State to investigate clearly subsists under international law,[37] both conventional and customary, the corollary of which is the victim's [and/or his next-of-kin's,[38] especially his mother's][39] right to truth[40] and/or the right to know.[41] Hence, beyond its individual and collective dimensions, 'the truth has also a legal dimension, with the

---

[34] Article IV of the Genocide Convention (1948) Convention for the Prevention and Punishment of the Crime of Genocide, Article 129 of the Geneva Convention (1949) Geneva Convention (III) relative to the Treatment of Prisoners of War, Article 146 of the Geneva Convention (1949) Geneva Convention (IV) relative to the Protection of Civilian Persons in Time of War, and Article 7 of the CAT (1984) Convention Against Torture and Other Cruel, Inhuman or Degrading Treatment or Punishment.

[35] Triffterer 2008, Preamble, Marginal No. 17.

[36] Pocar and Maystre 2010, p. 251.

[37] This obligation has been recognised by the HRC, *id est* internationally, in terms of the ICCPR, by the ECtHR and by IACtHR, *id est* regionally in terms of these supervisory mechanisms. The latter Court has gone furthest in its interpretation of victims' rights, widening them considerably by detecting and applying 'an individual right to criminal prosecution and punishment of those found responsible of serious human rights violations' upon the pretext that 'punishment serves as a measure to prevent human rights violations and as a measure to protect the individual victim' (Siebert-Fohr 2009, p. 191).

[38] It is settled practice that certain crimes against humanity do not only violate the victim's rights. In the case of enforced disappearances, for example, the term 'victims' is broadly interpreted to include close family members of the *desaparecidos* [IACtHR, *Nicholas Chapman Blake v Guatemala*, 24 January 1998, Series C No. 36, and ECtHR, *Koçeri Kurt v Turkey*, 25 May 1998, Application No. 15/1997/799/1002]. When no adequate investigations are conducted after the abduction, torture and homicide of persons, the victims' next of kin rights to be heard and to a fair trial are breached [IACtHR, *Anstraum Aman Villagrán-Morales et al. v Guatemala* (Case of the *Street Children*), 19 November 1999, Series C No. 63, paras 229 and 238]. Yet another human rights regional system has pronounced that 'even where it cannot be proved that violations were committed by government agents, the government had a responsibility to secure the safety and the liberty of its citizens, and to conduct investigations into murders. Chad therefore is responsible for the violations of the African Charter' [ACmmHPR, *Commission Nationale des Droits de l'Homme et des Libertés v Chad*, 11 October 1995, Communication No. 74/92, para 22].

[39] IACtHR, *Anstraum Aman Villagrán-Morales et al v Guatemala* (*Case of the Street Children*), Joint Concurring Opinion of Judges Antônio Augusto Cançado Trindade, Alirio Abreu Burelli and Manuel E. Ventura-Robles, 19 November 1999, Series C No. 63, paras 9 and 10.

[40] Yasmin Naqvi contends that this right is approaching a customary right and a general principle of law (Naqvi 2006, pp. 245–273).

[41] Lisa Ott acknowledges that 'while the right to the truth was initially referred to explicitly with respect to missing persons, its existence is today generally confirmed in the context of crimes against humanity, genocide, war crimes and gross human rights violations' (Ott 2011, p. 112).

emerging right to know the truth.'[42] However, Liesbeth Zegveld observes that notwithstanding the applicant's explicit reference to the *Velásquez Rodríguez v Honduras* ground-breaking *dictum*, in *Kurt v Turkey* the ECtHR ignored the IACtHR's decision. In Zegveld's view, the difference between these two decisions might be taken to suggest that the State's obligation to protect individuals against other private individuals is not applicable if the individuals belonged to armed opposition groups.[43] In practice, the right to know the truth[44] may have led to the establishment of truth commissions, particularly in Latin American States, where fully-fledged prosecutions were habitually barred by amnesty laws.[45] The *ad hoc* tribunals have also determined that 'punishment must therefore reflect both the calls for justice from the persons who have – directly or indirectly – been victims of the crimes'.[46] Part IV, particularly Sect. 13.5, has in fact shown that this right is considered as a derivative of the State's duty to investigate events that lead to human rights violations, and that a breach thereof may also give rise to an infringement of the prohibition of torture, other cruel, inhuman and/or degrading treatment. This has been commonly referred to as 'the inalienable right to know the truth vis-a-vis gross human rights violations and serious crimes under international law',[47] this right being autonomous, widely recognised and not subject to any limitations.[48] It entails the imprescriptible right of family members to know what happened to the disappeared, to know their fate and their whereabouts.[49] The positive obligation of the State to investigate was unanimously endorsed by the ECtHR in *Assenov and Others v Bulgaria*.[50] This emanated predominantly from Article 3 of the ECvHR and implicitly from its first Article, prompting the Strasbourg Court to decide that the effective official investigation should be capable of leading to the identification and punishment of those responsible for any ill-treatment. The *Assenov* positive obligation, though followed in *Sevtap Veznedaroğlu v Turkey*,[51] was debilitated *in partem* in *İlhan v Turkey*,[52] only to find unfading refuge in *Satik and Others v Turkey*,[53] and, scantily, more recently in

[42] Boutruche 2013 p. 305.

[43] Zegveld 2002, p. 171.

[44] See Sect. 13.5.

[45] See Sect. 16.5.

[46] ICTY Trial Chamber I, Section A, *Prosecutor v Momir Nikolić*, 2 December 2003, Case No. IT-02-60/1-S, para 86.

[47] UN High Commissioner for Human Rights 2006, para 4.

[48] UN High Commissioner for Human Rights 2006, paras 55 and 60.

[49] UN 2005, Principle 4.

[50] See Sect. 13.5.

[51] Ibid.

[52] Ibid.

[53] Ibid.

Anguelova v Bulgaria.[54] The Basic Principles and Guidelines[55] recall, *inter alia*, 'that international law contains the obligation to prosecute perpetrators of certain international crimes...'.[56] These Basic Principles and Guidelines encompass several overarching rights[57] and make explicit reference to the right of victims to equal and effective access to justice[58] which includes 'equal access to an effective judicial remedy as provided for under international law. Other remedies available to the victim include access to administrative and other bodies, as well as mechanisms, modalities and proceedings conducted in accordance with domestic law. Obligations arising under international law to secure the right to access justice and fair and impartial proceedings shall be reflected in domestic law'.[59] Although the Basic Principles and Guidelines merely confer soft law obligations, these have the potential to evolve into binding State obligations, a concern expressed by Japan in the consultations preceding adoption.[60] It is hence not surprising that these Basic Principles and Guidelines have been considered as a 'monumental milestone in the history of human rights as well as international criminal justice'.[61] Additionally, international human rights law demands an effective remedy and deems it to be a right which is 'amply recognised in all the global human rights instruments'.[62] Bantekas notes that a trend towards an automatic individual right to a remedy seems to have been shared by the ICJ and cites the Advisory Opinion in the *Israeli Wall* case[63] in substantiation thereof. Bassiouni could be correct in upholding that 'a victim's right to access justice includes the State duty to prosecute those responsible for human rights violations',[64] which right emanated from the interpretation (by international human rights tribunals) of provisions within human rights treaties which establish a right to access to justice or to be heard and a right to an effective remedy.[65] We must here recall that access to justice is an enabling right and an empowering tool.[66] Whilst appropriately citing *Villagrán-Morales et al. v Guatemala*,[67] he adds that 'a victim's right to prosecution, however, is not a

54 Ibid.

55 UNGA (2005) Resolution 60/147 (2005) UN Doc. A/RES/60/147, adopted on 16 December 2005 in the Sixtieth Session of the UNGA.

56 Preambular para 8.

57 Principle 11.

58 Principle 3(c) and 11(a).

59 Principle 12.

60 Bassiouni 2008d, p. 671, n. 256.

61 Bassiouni 2008d, p. 693.

62 Bantekas 2010, p. 548.

63 ICJ, *Legal Consequences of the Construction of a Wall in the Occupied Palestinian Territory (Israeli Wall Advisory Opinion)*, Advisory Opinion, 9 July 2004, ICJ GL No. 131, [2004] ICJ Rep. 136, paras 149–160, cited in Bantekas 2010, p. 549.

64 Bassiouni 2008d, p. 680.

65 Ibid.

66 FRA et al. 2016, pp. 3, 16.

67 *Villagrán-Morales et al. v Guatemala*, above n. 38.

substitute for the State's duty to ensure respect for international human rights and humanitarian law, but rather co-exists with it. Victims' claims to prosecution have, therefore, become a justifiable right that victims should be able to claim against a state'.[68] This was accentuated by the fact that the case concerned the homicides of *Henry Giovani Contreras, Federico Clemente Figueroa-Túnchez, Julio Roberto Caal-Sandoval, Jovito Josué Juárez-Cifuentes and Anstraum Aman Villagrán-Morales et al. v Guatemala* at the hands of State agents.[69] In this context one must note that the duty to investigate does not only emanate from the right to a national, effective remedy but also 'from the infringed substantive right itself'.[70] This idea of retrospective protection, as Anja Siebert-Fohr refers to it,[71] has gained ground. This obligation to submit to prosecution may be said to constitute the second layer of obligations, the first being the above mentioned general duty to investigate. A duty to investigate an event whereby a human rights violation has allegedly subsisted necessarily presupposes that such duty must be exercised firstly by the State *locus delicti* and secondly in good faith. This, however, can be equivalent to a dead letter. Reference must be made to the dynamics of system criminality which underlies the consummation of core crimes and is susceptible to situations wherein political control over the judiciary is rampant. There exists however no fully-fledged right to exact prosecution, no correlative individual right of action. No duty to punish flows from Article 13 of the ECvHR, the right to a national, effective remedy.[72] Under international law, no individual right either to national criminal justice or to international criminal justice exists, so far. An absolute duty to prosecute may be said to apply only to the State where the core crime was committed.[73] On the other hand, the obligation to prosecute of the State enjoying custodial jurisdiction, which is not to be confused with the inadmissibility of amnesty laws, is thus qualified to the effect that a State is obliged to either prosecute or extradite to another State or surrender to an international criminal tribunal (including the ICC) which wants and is competent to prosecute. It is, therefore, a duty to submit to prosecution, rather than a *strictu sensu* obligation to prosecute. In other words, the obligation to prosecute of the bystander (third) State in this context is a duty either to prosecute on one's own soil or to ensure and exact prosecution by either extraditing or surrendering the individual elsewhere. The option to surrender to the ICC is accomplished in furtherance of a forthcoming prosecution because by the time the ICC issues an international arrest warrant its Pre-Trial Chamber would have already ruled that there are reasonable grounds to

[68] Bassiouni 2008d, p. 680.

[69] *Villagrán-Morales et al. v Guatemala*, above n. 38, paras 142–143, and 213.

[70] ECtHR First Section, *Torquil Dick Erikson v Italy*, Decision as to Admissibility, 26 October 1999, Application No. 37900/97.

[71] Siebert-Fohr 2009, pp. 126–130.

[72] ECtHR Grand Chamber, *Maşallah Öneryildiz v Turkey*, 30 November 2004, Application No. 48939/99, paras 96 and 148.

[73] Ambos 1999, cited in Ferdinandusse 2006, p. 202, n. 1195.

believe that the person has committed a crime within the ICC's jurisdiction.[74] Put differently, the Pre-Trial Chamber decision precedes the arrest warrant itself and the eventual appearance of the person before the ICC. In actual fact the obligation to submit to prosecution is therefore, tangibly and in practice, the duty to prosecute, or extradite or surrender.

This duty should not be misconstrued as to signify or denote an obligation to prosecute *in absentia*, although Judge Christine van den Wyngaert found that neither conventional nor customary international law expressly prohibit this.[75] Were this to be the case, all the States in the world, except the one where the alleged perpetrator is physically present, would have to fulfil such a duty and a multiplicity of prosecutions would lead to massive juridical uncertainties. Furthermore, universal jurisdiction *in absentia* is also likely to exacerbate tensions between States involved within a conflict.[76] Additionally, the risk and prospect of States abusing the system by prosecuting nationals of enemy States increases drastically.[77] The obligation to prosecute is hence only vested upon States enjoying custodial jurisdiction. To this effect, I advocate what I term as 'custodial universal jurisdiction', as opposed to universal jurisdiction *in absentia*. These constitute what many jurists refer to as the narrow and broad applications of universal jurisdiction respectively.[78] The obligation to submit to prosecution is therefore strictly conditional upon the presence requirement. This is why by means of the pre-requisite of custodial jurisdiction, I expect that universal jurisdiction should not be exercised *in absentia*. This also dispels difficulties related to ranking, some of which were dealt with in *Pinochet*, where various States wanted to exercise their right to prosecute. In truth, the theory I juxtapose will not be accompanied by difficulties related to ranking because only one State may exercise custodial jurisdiction. A person cannot physically be within the territorial jurisdiction of two States simultaneously. The element of custodial jurisdiction establishes a physical and corporeal link to the crime (the presence requirement), not a retrospective one. It hence creates a link *ex post facto*, whereas generally forms of jurisdiction precede the crime or accompany it.

To illustrate all this in a simplistic but tangible way, suffice to give a classical example. Individual C, a Minister of Home Affairs in State S, orders the attack of a civilian population by members of the armed forces of State S who are, by reason of their employment, loyal and subservient to individual C. The attack, consisting of rape, torture, enforced disappearances and murder, is consummated as part of a widespread and systematic attack against a civilian population and is hence tantamount to a crime against humanity, for all intents and purposes of international law.

---

[74] See Article 58(1)(a) of the ICC Statute.

[75] ICJ, *Arrest Warrant of 11 April 2000 (DRC v Belgium)*, Dissenting Opinion of Judge Christine van den Wyngaert, 14 February 2002, ICJ Rep. 2002, p. 3, paras 54–55.

[76] Rabinovitch 2004, p. 522.

[77] Morris 2001b, p. 355.

[78] Philippe 2006, pp. 379–380.

The attack is not investigated by the State S and no prosecutions are undertaken. Individual C is subject to individual criminal responsibility in terms of international law. He is therefore criminally liable. State S has infringed various fundamental human rights of victims and their families, including the right to life and the prohibition of torture,[79] in terms of international human rights law, by failing to investigate, by not guaranteeing access to justice, *id est* a judicial hearing, and by failing to provide redress by way of an effective domestic remedy. State S is responsible under international law both for having failed to legislate and penalise crimes against humanity and for not having prevented such crimes against humanity in the first place. The example given is more easily verifiable if State S were a signatory of an international convention which penalises the proscribed conduct (assuming that the acts committed were to be genocidal, *id est*, accompanied by the *dolus specialis*), such as the Genocide Convention, which has been widely ratified and, in any case, engenders rules of customary international law, such as the duty to prosecute.[80] By way of example, in so far as the CAT is concerned, 'extradition is an option offered to the State by the Convention, whereas prosecution is an international obligation under the Convention, the violation of which is a wrongful act engaging the responsibility of the State'.[81] Even in the absence of an applicable conventional regime, jurists increasingly opine that a general obligation on States to prosecute core crimes subsists when such core crimes were committed within the State's territory.[82] If individual C is to be found on the territory of another State (not being State S), that other State (State J) enjoying custodial jurisdiction over individual C, presuming there is such an obligation, would be obliged to submit individual C to prosecution in the absence of a request for individual C's extradition from State S or surrender to the ICC. The latter will depend upon whether State S ratified the ICC Statute and/or whether an international arrest warrant was issued as a result of a UNSC Resolution. Now, if no extradition and/or surrender request is forthcoming, State J must submit individual C to prosecution in State J, especially if State S does not intend prosecuting individual C. If State J fails to prosecute individual C, besides violating conventional provisions such as the *aut dedere aut judicare* rule, State J could be liable under the State responsibility regime for breaching *aut dedere aut judicare*. Whether State J could be held liable, under the State responsibility regime, for not prosecuting in the absence of a conventional provision, and hence on the premise of customary international law, is certainly still flimsy and tenuous. However, a trend is developing by means of which State J, under customary international law, would be obliged, in the absence of having conducted a prosecution, to ensure that individual C be prosecuted in another State

---

[79] The *jus cogens* status of this prohibition has been reiterated by the ICJ {ICJ, *Questions Relating to the Obligation to Extradite or Prosecute* (*Belgium v Senegal*), 20 July 2012, ICJ Rep. 2012, p. 422, para 99} and by the former UN Special Rapporteur on Torture (Rodley 2007, pp. 185–200).

[80] Siebert-Fohr 2009, p. 265.

[81] *Belgium v Senegal*, above n. 79, para 95.

[82] Ward Ferdinandusse cites Sadat, Cassese, Delmas-Marty, Ratner and Abrams, Dugard and Kleffner to this effect (Ferdinandusse 2006, p. 193).

(not S and not J) which has a juridical interest in the prosecution of individual C or else to surrender to the ICC or to another *ad hoc* or hybrid tribunal or a special Court. State J would, in the meantime, be certainly obliged to safeguard the pre-trial detention of individual C by eliminating any dangers that individual C absconds. It would be obliged to preserve any evidence it might possess or come across which could be used in the eventual prosecution of individual C (irrespective of where and when such prosecution would be conducted), and it would be further obliged to determine where, when and how should individual C be prosecuted, besides applying and enforcing its own legislation which should cater for such scenarios, and in the absence of which State J might also be responsible in line with the *Furundžija dictum*.[83] All this comes at a cost consisting of the erection of a structural framework conducive to 'preserving evidence, maintaining contact with witnesses, monitoring security and mitigating threats [to victims and witnesses]'.[84] State competent authorities are required 'to investigate allegations of ill-treatment when they are "arguable" and "raise a reasonable suspicion"', the corollary of which is the obligation to take all the necessary steps to secure evidence such as detailed statements from victims, eyewitness testimony, forensic evidence and medical reports.[85] Such obligations have already been impliedly established by a recent UNGA Resolution which demands the collection, preservation and analysis of evidence of core crimes 'to prepare files in order to facilitate and expedite fair and independent criminal proceedings, in accordance with international law standards, in national, regional or international courts or tribunals that have or may in the future have jurisdiction over these crimes, in accordance with international law'.[86] These ancillary and accessory obligations of State J fall within the rubric of the 'duty to submit to prosecution'. If State J fails to fulfil such ancillary (accessory) obligations, State J's act or omission would entail State responsibility, both in terms of conventional international law if such treaty provision binds State J to such effect, and on the basis of customary international law, hence even in the absence of such treaty provisions. In the latter case the other State (the plaintiff State) which complains of State J's State responsibility must have some connection, albeit remote, to the crime because it needs to prove, at least *prima facie* and on a preliminary basis, a juridical interest to possess a *locus standi* in the first place.

---

[83] ICTY Trial Chamber, *Prosecutor v Anto Furundžija*, 10 December 1998, IT-95-17/1-T, para 149.

[84] ICC 2013, para 64, cited by van Schaack 2014, p. 3, n. 3.

[85] ECtHR, Third Section, *Carol Ciorcan and Others v Romania*, 27 January 2015, Application Numbers 29414/09 and 44841/09, para 147.

[86] The UNGA Resolution {UNGA (2016) Resolution 71/248 (2016) UN Doc. A/RES/71/248} adopted, in its seventy-first session, the International, Impartial and Independent Mechanism to Assist in the Investigation and Prosecution of those Responsible for the Most Serious Crimes under International Law Committed in the Syrian Arab Republic Since March 2011 [Doc. A/71/L.48, 19 December 2016, para 4]. This led to a Report of the Independent International Commission of Inquiry on the Syrian Arab Republic which was adopted by the Human Rights Council in its thirty-fourth session (UN Human Rights Council 2017).

International law, although it is increasingly mandating States to prosecute individuals who perpetrated core crimes, has not matured enough to allow any other State, which enjoys absolutely no connection to the crime perpetrated, to claim the responsibility of State J and exact it before the ICJ. The most such State could do is trigger a resolution at UN level. Thus, whereas the duty to prosecute requires that the State enjoying territorial jurisdiction undertakes a prosecution of individual C, the duty to submit to prosecution necessitates, as a bare minimum, that the State fulfils the ancillary and related obligations referred to here above. These ancillary and related obligations should certainly include the duty to notify the international community that individual C is within the custodial jurisdiction of State J, which notification can trigger either a decision of the international community to establish a court or tribunal to prosecute individual C or any potential extradition request of another State. Yet, these obligations should not commence when a suspect is on one's territory. The German Attorney-General has issued an international arrest warrant against a *Daesh* commander further to identifications thereof by means of testimonies of *Yezidi* victims.[87] Some States, such as Germany, undertake best practices consisting in the setting up of specialized units which collect and preserve evidence obtained directly from asylum seekers, migrants and/or refugees who have witnessed atrocities in States where core crimes are committed, after which such evidence is passed onto the respective domestic police crimes unit.[88] An Innsbruck court has convicted an asylum seeker to life imprisonment for war crimes committed in Syria further to reports confirming that he had told other asylum seekers at a refugee shelter that he had shot dead government soldiers when he was fighting with an Islamic rebel group called the *Farouq* Brigade.[89]

These are, to date, good practices, but they can gradually assume a more onerous and mandatory dimension. In fact, war crimes prosecutions in Europe based on universal jurisdiction have become possible 'because of the arrival in Europe of

---

[87] *Die Welt* (2017) In: ICD, News Archive. 16 February 2017. http://www.internationalcrimesdatabase.org/home/newsarchive. Accessed 18 July 2017; van Wilgenburg W (2017) Germany Issues Arrest Warrant Against ISIS Leader for War Crimes. Ara News, Pulse of the North. http://aranews.net/2017/02/germany-issues-arrest-warrant-isis-leader-war-crimes/. Accessed 27 January 2018. International human rights lawyer Amal Clooney held that she aims to have *Daesh* group members at the ICC [Mostafa N (2017) Yazidi Genocide Evidence Mounting Against Islamic State: Legal Experts, Iraqi News. http://www.iraqinews.com/iraq-war/yazidi-genocide-evidence-mounting-islamic-state-legal-experts/. Accessed 10 April 2018]. In 2019 a UN team will commence investigative activities relating to massacres of the Yezidi minority and other atrocities perpetrated by jihadists in Iraq [*Agence France – Presse* (2018) In Early 2019, UN Team to Begin Probe of IS Crimes in Iraq. https://www.voanews.com/a/in-early-2019-un-team-to-begin-probe-of-is-crimes-in-iraq/4687322.html. Accessed 22 December 2018].

[88] TRIAL International (2016), News Release, EU Day Against Impunity, Highlights, Progress, Challenges. https://trialinternational.org/latest-post/eu-day-against-impunity/. Accessed 18 October 2017.

[89] BBC News (2017) Austria Convicts Asylum Seeker of Syria War Crimes. http://www.bbc.com/news/world-europe-39879305. Accessed 22 August 2017.

both victims and suspects during the refugee crisis'.[90] Besides Germany, France and The Netherlands have also set up specialized war crimes units which 'can help domestic law enforcement units and prosecutors overcome the investigative difficulties of universal jurisdiction cases'.[91] The recognition of such ancillary and related duties under international law is proliferating steadily because these are inevitable corollaries of the generic duty to submit to prosecution. Thus, nowadays it can be safely contended that there subsists a 'collective subsidiary responsibility of the international community in case the State manifestly fails in its duties of protection'.[92] This is materialising by means of the unprecedented momentum which universal jurisdiction has gathered in the recent months.[93] This movement possesses the potential to gel various *instituti legis* in order to sow the seeds which may culminate in an emerging duty to prosecute, this being the main thrust of Part V of my book.

References

Ambos K (1999) *Völkerrechtliche Bestrafungspflichten bei Schweren Menschenrechtsverletzungen* [International Penalties for Serious Human Rights Violations], *Archiv des Völkerrechts* 37(3–4):318–356

Antoniadis A, Bekou O (2007) The European Union and the International Criminal Court: An Awkward Symbiosis in Interesting Times. ICLR 7(4):621–655

Bantekas I (2010) International Criminal Law. HP, Oxford

Bassiouni MC (2008a) The Discipline of International Criminal Law. In: Bassiouni MC (ed) International Criminal Law, Vol. I, Sources, Subjects and Contents, 3rd edn. MNP, Leiden/Boston, pp. 3–40

Bassiouni MC (2008b) Crimes Against Humanity. In: Bassiouni MC (ed) International Criminal Law: Sources, Subjects and Contents, Vol. I, 3rd edn. MNP, Leiden/Boston, pp. 437–492

Bassiouni MC (2008c) Universal Jurisdiction for International Crimes: Historical Perspectives and Contemporary Practice. In: Bassiouni MC (ed) International Criminal Law: Multilateral and Bilateral Enforcement Mechanisms, Vol. II, 3rd edn. MNP, Leiden/Boston, pp. 153–199

Bassiouni MC (2008d) International Recognition of Victims' Rights. In: Bassiouni MC (ed) International Criminal Law: International Enforcement, Vol. III, 3rd edn. MNP, Leiden, pp. 635–701

[90] HRW (2016) War Crimes Prosecutions in Europe: Video, Q & A Highlight Cases Spurred by Syrian, Iraqi Refugees. https://www.hrw.org/news/2016/10/20/war-crimes-prosecutions-europe. Accessed 10 July 2017.

[91] HRW (2014) The Long Arm of Justice: Lessons from Specialized War Crimes Units in Germany, France and the Netherlands, Summary, p. 3. https://www.hrw.org/report/2014/09/16/long-arm-justice/lessons-specialized-war-crimes-units-france-germany-and. Accessed 9 June 2016.

[92] Lugato 2017, p. 258.

[93] *FIDH* (2017) Syria, Iraq, Rwanda: Universal Jurisdiction has Gathered Unprecedented Momentum in 2017. https://www.fidh.org/en/issues/international-justice/universal-jurisdiction/syria-iraq-rwanda-universal-jurisdiction-has-gathered-unprecedented. Accessed 2 January 2018.

Boutruche T (2013) Seeking the Truth About Serious International Human Rights and Humanitarian Law Violations: The Various Facets of a Cardinal Notion of Transitional Justice. In: Matthee M, Toebes B, Brus M (eds) Armed Conflict and International law: In Search of the Human Face. *Liber Amicorum* in Memory of Avril McDonald. Asser Press, The Hague, pp. 303–325

Burke-White WW (2002) A Community of Courts: Towards a System of International Criminal Law Enforcement. MJIL 24(1):1–101

CAT (1984) Convention Against Torture and Other Cruel, Inhuman or Degrading Treatment or Punishment

d'Aspremont J (2016) *Jus Cogens* as a Social Construct Without Pedigree. Amsterdam Law School Legal Studies Research Paper No. 2016-59, ACIL Research Paper No. 2016-19, UvA, Amsterdam

Dutch ICC Implementation Act (2002) The International Criminal Court Implementation Act, The Netherlands

EU-ICC Agreement, Council Decision 2002/494/JHA of 13 June 2002, Official Journal L 167, 26 June 2002

Ferdinandusse W (2006) Direct Application of International Criminal Law in National Courts. Asser Press, The Hague

FIDH (2017) Syria, Iraq, Rwanda: Universal Jurisdiction has Gathered Unprecedented Momentum in 2017. https://www.fidh.org/en/issues/international-justice/universal-jurisdiction/syria-iraq-rwanda-universal-jurisdiction-has-gathered-unprecedented. Accessed 2 January 2018

FRA, ECtHR, CoE (2016) Handbook on European Law Relating to Access to Justice. Publication Office of the EU, Luxembourg. file:///C:/Users/csol1/Downloads/handbook-on-access-to-justice_en-pdf.pdf. Accessed on 17 December 2017

Geneva Convention (1949a) Geneva Convention (I) for the Amelioration of the Condition of the Wounded and Sick in Armed Forces in the Field

Geneva Convention (1949b) Geneva Convention (II) for the Amelioration of the Condition of the Wounded, Sick and Shipwrecked Members of Armed Forces at Sea

Geneva Convention (1949c) Geneva Convention (III) relative to the Treatment of Prisoners of War

Geneva Convention (1949d) Geneva Convention (IV) relative to the Protection of Civilian Persons in Time of War

Genocide Convention (1948) Convention for the Prevention and Punishment of the Crime of Genocide

HRW (2014) The Long Arm of Justice: Lessons from Specialized War Crimes Units in Germany, France and the Netherlands, Summary. https://www.hrw.org/report/2014/09/16/long-arm-justice/lessons-specialized-war-crimes-units-france-germany-and. Accessed 9 June 2016

HRW (2016) War Crimes Prosecutions in Europe: Video, Q & A Highlight Cases Spurred by Syrian, Iraqi Refugees. https://www.hrw.org/news/2016/10/20/war-crimes-prosecutions-europe. Accessed 10 July 2017

ICC (2013) ICC Report on Cooperation for the 12th ASP, 9 October 2013, I-ASP/12/35

ICC Statute (1998) Rome Statute of the International Criminal Court

ICCPR (1966) International Covenant on Civil and Political Rights

ILC (2006) Fragmentation of International Law; Difficulties Arising from the Diversification and Expansion of International Law. Report of the Study Group of the ILC, 58th Session. UN Doc. A/CN.4/L.682

ILC (2014) Obligation to Extradite or Prosecute (*Aut Dedere Aut Judicare*). Office of Legal Affairs, Codification Division, UN. http://legal.un.org/docs/?path=../ilc/texts/instruments/english/reports/7_6_2014.pdf&lang=EF. Accessed 14 November 2018

Kenyans for Peace, Truth and Justice (2014) All Bark No Bite?: State Cooperation and the International Criminal Court. Africa Centre for Open Governance, Nairobi, Kenya

Kleffner JK (2008) Complementarity in the Rome Statute and National Criminal Jurisdictions. International Courts and Tribunals Series, OUP, Oxford

Lugato M (2017) Conceptualizing the Responsibility to Protect: A Short Contribution. In: Acconci P, Donat Cattin D, Marchesi A, Palmisano G, Santoni V (eds) International Law and the Protection of Humanity: Essays in Honour of Flavia Lattanzi. MNP, Leiden/Boston, pp. 245–261

Morris M (2001a) High Crimes and Misconceptions: The International Criminal Court and Non-Party States. LCP 64(1):13–66

Morris MH (2001b) Symposium: Universal Jurisdiction: Myths, Realities and Prospects: Universal Jurisdiction in a Divided World: Conference Remarks. NELR 35:337–361

Naqvi Y (2006) The Right to the Truth in International Law: Fact or Fiction? IRRC 88(862):245–273

Ott L (2011) Enforced Disappearance in International Law. Intersentia, Cambridge

Philippe X (2006) The Principles of Universal Jurisdiction and Complementarity: How Do the Two Principles Intermesh? IRRC 88(862):375–398

Pocar F, Maystre M (2010) The Principle of Complementarity: A Means Towards a More Pragmatic Enforcement of the Goal Pursued by Universal Jurisdiction? In: Bergsmo M (ed) Complementarity and the Exercise of Universal Jurisdiction for Core International Crimes. Forum for International Criminal and Humanitarian Law, Publication Series No. 7, TOAEP and PRI, Oslo, pp. 247–303

Poels A (2005) Universal Jurisdiction *In Absentia*. NQHR 23(1):65–84

Posner EA (2009) *Erga Omnes* Norms, Institutionalization, and Constitutionalism in International Law. JITE 165(1):5–23

Rabinovitch R (2004) Universal Jurisdiction *In Absentia*. FILJ 28(2):500–530

Randall K (1988) Universal Jurisdiction under International Law. TLR 66:785–841

Rodley NS (2007) The Prohibition of Torture: Absolute Means Absolute. In: Kaleck W, Ratner M, Singelnstein T, Weiss P (eds) International Prosecution of Human Rights Crimes. Springer, Berlin/Heidelberg, pp. 185–200

Ryngaert C (2008) Jurisdiction in International Law. Oxford Monographs in International Law, OUP, Oxford

Siebert-Fohr A (2009) Prosecuting Serious Human Rights Violations. OUP, Oxford

Triffterer O (2008) Preamble Margins 16-17. In: Triffterer O (ed) Commentary on the Rome Statute of the International Criminal Court – Observers' Notes, Article by Article, 2nd edn. Nomos, Baden-Baden, pp. 1–11

UN (2005) (Principles to Combat Impunity) Report of Diane Orentlicher, Independent Expert, to Update the Set of Principles to Combat Impunity - Updated Set of Principles for the Protection and Promotion of Human Rights through Action to Combat Impunity. 8 February 2005, U.N. Doc. E/CN.4/2005/102/Add. 1

UN High Commissioner for Human Rights (2006) Study on the Right to the Truth, 62nd Session, 8 February 2006, U.N. Doc. E/CN.4/2006/91

UN Human Rights Council (2017) Report of the Independent International Commission of Inquiry on the Syrian Arab Republic, 34th Session, UNGA Doc. A/HRC/34/64

UNGA (2005) Resolution 60/147 (2005) UN Doc. A/RES/60/147

UNGA (2016) Resolution 71/248 (2016) UN Doc. A/RES/71/248

van der Wilt H (2011) Universal Jurisdiction under Attack: An Assessment of African Misgivings Towards International Criminal Justice as Administered by Western States. JICJ 9(5):1043–1066

van der Wilt H, Lyngdort S (2009) Procedural Obligations under the European Convention on Human Rights: Useful Guidelines for the Assessment of "Unwillingness" and "Inability" in the Context of the Complementarity Principle. ICLR 9(1):39–75

van Schaack B (2014) International Criminal Court Fugitives: The Need for Bespoke Solutions. Santa Clara Law Digital Commons, Santa Clara University School of Law. http://digitalcommons.law.scu.edu/cgi/viewcontent.cgi?article=1856&context=facpubs. Accessed 19 March 2017

Watson GR (1993) The Passive Personality Principle. TILJ 28(1):1–46

Young SNM (2001) Surrendering the Accused to the International Criminal Court. BYIL 71 (1):317–356

Zahar A, Sluiter G (2008) International Criminal Law: A Critical Introduction. OUP, Oxford

Zegveld L (2002) The Accountability of Armed Opposition Groups in International Law. Case Studies in International and Comparative Law. CUP, Cambridge

Zimmermann A (2006) Violations of Fundamental Norms of International Law and the Exercise of Universal Jurisdiction in Criminal Matters. In: Tomuschat C, Thouvenin J-M (eds) The Fundamental Rules of the International Legal Order: *Jus Cogens* and Obligations *Erga Omnes*. MNP, Leiden/Boston, pp. 335–353

Chapter 20
The Development of Functional International Constitutionalism

Contents

References 584

Abstract The interaction of some *instituti legis* may have led to functional international constitutionalism, the main cause of which is the hierarchically superior nature of *jus cogens* norms, and the effect of which justifies the exercise of universal jurisdiction. Such process is a similar development to the constitutionalization of international law. The obligation to submit to prosecution also stems from international human rights law, rather than from international criminal law *strictu sensu*. Core crimes breach rights in an actual and tangible manner but also prospectively. This is also why the duty to punish a core crime can be equated to the duty to prevent another core crime. Consequently, the responsibility to protect, or rather to prevent, is triggered. Owing to international human rights law, by failing to conduct investigations and undertaking prosecutions, States violate the rights of victims to an effective remedy. Human rights act like a double-edged sword. On the one hand, a duty to investigate and prosecute core crimes flows from a State's human rights obligations. On the other hand, most barriers to extradition (and hence to eventual prosecution) assume legitimacy for the ultimate protection of human rights in so far as the respect of human rights can entitle States to limit cooperation in some circumstances. The two prongs of human rights counter one another. There exists the need to constantly strike an equitable balance between conflicting interests. This is why the juridical framework is counter-productive. Thus, a restrictive interpretation of grounds for refusal becomes more essential.

Keywords International law · Criminal law · Human rights law · Protection of human rights · International judges · National judges · Interaction · Functional international constitutionalism · Hierarchically superior norms · Constitutionalization of international law · VCLT · Universal jurisdiction · Obligation to submit to prosecution · Effective remedies · Double-edged sword · Duty to investigate and prosecute · *Velásquez-Rodríguez v Honduras* · Equitable

C. Soler, *The Global Prosecution of Core Crimes under International Law*,
https://doi.org/10.1007/978-94-6265-335-1_20

balance · Conflicting interests · Human being-oriented approach · Human rightism · *Actio popularis*

The interaction of some doctrines, principles and rules[1] leads to a fascinating patchwork of international law with a penal and constitutional dimension, of criminal law with an international and constitutional dimension, and of human rights law with a penal and international dimension. The ensuing patchwork demonstrates that a holistic and global approach must be undertaken for the purposes of the overall and ultimate protection of human rights by virtue of the fight against impunity. Here too, a global dimension, consonant with the title of this work, is reverberated. Anita Usacka upholds that 'justice and the protection of human rights must be viewed in a global context, requiring multi-layered and inclusive discussion between national judges, international judges and academics working on constitutionalism and international law and practice, as well as international human rights'.[2] The interaction of the above mentioned *instituti legis* may have led to functional international constitutionalism, the main cause of which is the hierarchically superior nature and scope of Article 53 of the VCLT, and the effect of which justifies the exercise of universal jurisdiction.[3] Such functional international constitutionalism is a similar development to the constitutionalization of international law.[4] The former is specifically geared and intended to curb impunity whereas the latter has a broader and more general reproach which exceeds the application of criminal law and human rights law. The obligation to submit to prosecution can hence also stem from international human rights law, rather than from international criminal law *strictu sensu*. One must keep in mind that the first bases of the principle of independence in human rights law is the obligation to provide effective remedies. In terms of Article 13 of the ECvHR 'and other comparable articles in other human rights treaties, remedies are only effective if the courts are independent', hence not subservient to political control.[5] The commission of core crimes, therefore, may be said to presuppose not only that human rights have been violated, from a substantive viewpoint, but that human rights are most likely to be trampled upon even procedurally. In other words, whereas crimes against humanity generally violate the right to life, or else, for example, constitute torture, inhuman and/or degrading treatment, they also, in so far as their nature necessarily connects them to State power, carry a significant risk of ulterior infringements. Put differently, core crimes breach rights in an actual and tangible manner but also prospectively. This is also why the duty to punish a core crime can

[1] These include the *aut dedere aut judicare* rule, the principle of universal jurisdiction, *jus cogens* norms and *erga omnes* obligations.

[2] Usacka 2016, pp. 281–282.

[3] Fischer-Lescano 2007, pp. 15–19 and p. 25.

[4] In relation to the latter, see Klabbers et al. 2009.

[5] Nollkaemper 2011, p. 60.

be equated to the duty to prevent another core crime. Consequently, the responsibility to protect, or rather to prevent, is triggered.

Indeed, this work shows that human rights act like a double-edged sword. On the one hand it shows that a duty to investigate and prosecute core crimes flows from a State's human rights obligations. It is hence correct to deduce that 'there exists a general duty to investigate grave violations of human rights that have been the object of specific judgments.'[6] The *Velásquez-Rodríguez v Honduras* landmark case,[7] referred to in Sect. 13.5, is a clear example thereof. This case shows that investigation, prosecution and punishment are measures required to ensure the respect of the conventional rights,[8] namely the right to life, the right to liberty[9] and the prohibition of inhuman and degrading treatment.[10] Suffice to note, in order to place a spotlight on the relevance of international human rights law, that 'most international judgments to date about the legitimacy of amnesties have been made in the context of State obligations under regional or international human rights law and not in the context of individual criminal prosecutions.'[11] On the other hand, most barriers to extradition (and hence to eventual prosecution)[12] assume validity and legitimacy for the ultimate protection of human rights in so far as the respect of human rights can entitle States to limit cooperation in some circumstances. The two prongs of human rights work in opposite directions and counter one another. Hence there exists the need to constantly strike an equitable balance between conflicting interests, especially within domestic criminal justice systems. This is why the juridical framework is particularly vulnerable and counter-productive. Its shortcomings are innate. Consequently, a restrictive interpretation of grounds for refusal becomes more essential. The major challenge is 'how will justice be delivered?', since this presupposes a level of fairness, in the absence of which international criminal (in) justice would be counter-productive and would increase scepticism of this dynamic and intriguing *corpus juris*. As seen throughout this work, today's international criminal law is becoming flooded with what Alain Pellet calls 'human rightism'.[13] The ICC too must apply and interpret law in a manner consistent with

---

6 Gamarra 2012, p. 83.

7 IACtHR, *Velásquez-Rodríguez v Honduras*, 29 July 1988, Series C, No. 4.

8 Siebert-Fohr 2009, p. 55.

9 Siebert-Fohr 2009, p. 57.

10 Siebert-Fohr 2009, p. 105.

11 Meintjies 2000, p. 89.

12 As per the previous analysis, since the requesting State is habitually the *locus delicti commissi*, the requesting State is probably in the best position to prosecute for many reasons, including the availability of evidence which is necessary to prove the crime.

13 'Human rightism may be defined as the stance that consists in being absolutely determined to confer a form of autonomy (which, to my mind, it does not possess) on a 'discipline' (which, to my mind, does not exist as such): the protection of human rights' (Pellet 2000). For a seemingly contrary view, see Vanneste 2010, p. 195 and pp. 457–458.

internationally recognised human rights.[14] The transformation from a State-sovereignty approach to a human being-oriented approach was also acknowledged in the *Duško Tadić dictum*.[15] This is accompanied by a clear trend towards accountability[16] which necessitates the undertaking of prosecutions as a *sine qua non*.

As shown in the preceding chapter, owing to international human rights law, by failing to conduct investigations and undertaking prosecutions, States violate the rights of victims to an effective remedy. This same omission exposes the State to international responsibility and may trigger international jurisdiction consisting in either universal jurisdiction or else the ICC's jurisdiction. Bassiouni clearly considers universal jurisdiction not only as an *actio popularis*[17] but also as a mechanism by virtue of which victims obtain reparation.[18] Frédéric Vanneste optimistically opines that 'the right to individual petition for certain international (human rights) violations is becoming part of general international law'.[19] Yet sometimes, courts, especially international courts, must take certain initiatives and must be pro-active to enforce the protection of certain basic human rights, especially amidst a rather complex and fragile juridical framework which suffers from the drawbacks of *realpolitik*, namely of State power and diplomacy. However, these initiatives should be undertaken cautiously since 'there must be limits to judicial creativity'.[20] The next chapter will explain why and how these initiatives could and should be undertaken.

References

Aksenova M (2016) Complicity in International Criminal Law. Studies in International Law Series, Vol. 63, Hart, Bloomsbury, London

Bassiouni MC (2008a) Universal Jurisdiction for International Crimes: Historical Perspectives and Contemporary Practice. In: Bassiouni MC (ed) International Criminal Law: Multilateral and Bilateral Enforcement Mechanisms, Vol. II, 3rd edn. MNP, Leiden/Boston, pp. 153–199

Bassiouni MC (2008b) International Recognition of Victims' Rights. In: Bassiouni MC (ed) International Criminal Law: International Enforcement, Vol. III, 3rd edn. MNP, Leiden/Boston, pp. 635–701

[14] ICC Pre-Trial Chamber I, Situation in the DRC, *Prosecutor v Thomas Lubanga Dyilo, Decision on the Prosecutor's Application for a Warrant of Arrest*, 10 February 2006, Case No. ICC-01/04-01/06, para 12.

[15] ICTY Appeals Chamber, Prosecutor v *Duško Tadić, ICTY Decision on the Defence Motion for Interlocutory Appeal on Jurisdiction*, 2 October 1995, Case No. IT-94-1-AR72, para 97.

[16] Cryer et al. 2010, pp. 582–584.

[17] Bassiouni 2008a, pp. 157 and 162.

[18] Bassiouni 2008b, p. 657.

[19] Vanneste 2010, p. 196.

[20] Aksenova 2016, p. 257.

Cryer R, Friman H, Robinson D, Wilmshurst E (2010) An Introduction to International Criminal Law and Procedure, 2nd edn. CUP, Cambridge

Fischer-Lescano A (2007) Global Constitutional Struggles: Human Rights Between *Colère Publique* and *Colère Politique*. In: Kaleck W, Ratner M, Singelnstein T, Weiss P (eds) International Prosecution of Human Rights Crimes. Springer, Berlin/Heidelberg, pp. 13–27

Gamarra Y (2012) National Responses in Latin American to International Events Propelling the Justice Cascade: The *Gelman* Case. In: Beneyto JM, Kennedy (eds) Varela JC, Haskell J (assistant eds) New Approaches to International Law: The European and the American Experiences. Asser Press, The Hague, pp. 75–96

Klabbers J, Peters A, Ulfstein G (2009) The Constitutionalization of International Law. OUP, Oxford

Meintjies G (2000) Domestic Amnesties and International Accountability. In: Shelton D (ed) International Crimes, Peace, and Human Rights. TP, Ardsley, NY, pp. 83–91

Nollkaemper A (2011) National Courts and the International Rule of Law. OUP, Oxford

Pellet A (2000) 'Human Rightism' and International Law, Gilberto Amado Memorial Lecture delivered on 18 July 2000, NY. http://pellet.actu.com/wp-content/uploads/2016/02/PELLET-2000-Human-rightism-and-international-law-G.-Amado.pdf. Accessed 1 October 2018

Siebert-Fohr A (2009) Prosecuting Serious Human Rights Violations. OUP, Oxford

Usacka A (2016) Constitutionalism and Human Rights at the International Criminal Court. In: Scheinin M, Krunke H, Aksenova M (eds) Judges as Guardians of Constitutionalism and Human Rights. EE, Cheltenham, UK/Northampton, MA, USA, pp. 281–305

Vanneste F (2010) General International Law Before Human Rights Courts: Assessing the Specialty Claims of International Human Rights Law. Intersentia, Cambridge

Chapter 21
The Exercise of *Kompetenz-Kompetenz* in the Determination of Presumptive Jurisdiction

Contents

21.1 International Courts 589
21.2 Domestic Courts 592
References 595

Abstract Universal jurisdiction purports to extend judicial power by overstretching jurisdiction. Recourse to implied powers may be justifiable in terms of the need to enforce victims' rights. The ICC, as arbiter of its own jurisdiction, enjoys such power. Within the framework of admissibility proceedings, it may actually press a State to start or to reopen an investigation. International courts enjoy such inherent powers, but the same may not necessarily apply to domestic courts. In so far as such courts are concerned, the inaction of a State could anyway fall within the rubric of international human rights law. Where a *nolle prosequi* subsists, the only way a case can be brought to the court's cognisance is by means of a private prosecution. Many States cater for this. When proceedings are discontinued by the prosecutor, courts should be allowed, *de lege*, to order prosecutors to continue such proceedings. This, however, could be useless if the prosecutor makes no effort to produce the relevant incriminating evidence. When shielding occurs the role of a domestic criminal court assumes significance. This is because the criminal court could allow the alleged victim to take over by acting as a subsidiary prosecutor. Alternatively, the criminal court should at least acknowledge, in its judgment, that there subsists the suspicion that the accused has been (deliberately) shielded. Its judgment will hence possess a marked declaratory dimension which may be referred to by other courts, be they domestic or international, which subsequently assume a ground of jurisdiction to prosecute the suspect.

Keywords *Compétence de la compétence* · *Kompetenz-kompetenz* · Presumptive jurisdiction · Inherent powers · Implied powers · Rights of victims · Prevention · Prosecution · Punishment · Failure to prosecute · Emerging duty to submit to

C. Soler, *The Global Prosecution of Core Crimes under International Law*,
https://doi.org/10.1007/978-94-6265-335-1_21

prosecution · Duty to prosecute · Amnesty · *Lacunae* · Judicial bodies · Teleological approach · *Nolle prosequi* · Discontinue criminal proceedings · Private prosecution · Arbiter of its own jurisdiction · International courts · Domestic courts · *Actio popularis* · Subsidiary prosecutor · Declaratory function · Judicial dialogue · International Convention for the Prevention, Prosecution and Punishment of Core Crimes

The ultimate power possessed by courts is the *compétence de la compétence* doctrine. The *kompetenz-kompetenz* doctrine[1] allows court to assess, to determine and restrict their own jurisdictional competence. It is hence the very same courts which determine their own jurisdictional competence and the limits to be imposed there upon. Such inherent powers could be exercised for various reasons, such as the right and power to adjudicate.[2] Inherent powers are 'powers that are not expressly conferred on them by the terms of their statutes and rules of procedure',[3] these being their constitutive instruments, 'but which are nonetheless necessary for the performance of their functions'.[4] The exercise of inherent powers by some courts could also lead to presumptive jurisdiction. Admittedly, one major problem in this context is that inherent powers may only be exercised by courts enjoying jurisdiction since these are powers necessary for their functioning. Hence they cannot be exercised by courts which want or vaunt the right to enjoy (assume) jurisdiction. *Ergo*, probably, the only ways such powers may become exercisable before the determination of the enjoyment of jurisdiction is by means of presumptive jurisdiction. In any case, in order to be able to assume jurisdiction, implied, rather than inherent, powers could be availed of for such purpose. Whereas inherent powers are necessary for the effective functioning of the entity which resorts to their use, implied powers 'arise by necessary implication as being essential to the performance of the organ's duties and which can be derived from the express powers of an organization or its functions'.[5] Thus, implied powers are more directly commensurate with the assumption of jurisdiction since they may be availed of in such a way as to precede the determination of the enjoyment of jurisdiction of a criminal court. Here a distinction should be drawn between international courts and domestic courts.

[1] See Sects. 10.1 and 10.3.

[2] Kor 2006, p. 64.

[3] Brown 2007, p. 41.

[4] Brown 2007, p. 55.

[5] Skubiszewski 1989, pp. 856–857, and White 1996, both cited in Zahar and Sluiter 2008, p. 21, n. 97.

21.1 International Courts

Recourse to implied powers may be justifiable in terms of the need to respect and enforce victims' rights. Its need arises from the developing trend of functional international constitutionalism. In other words, universal jurisdiction (which has been analysed particularly within Chap. 13) purports to dramatically extend judicial power, hence significantly overstretching jurisdiction itself. The exercise of implied powers is therefore not a unique and completely novel way of assuming jurisdiction in a justifiable manner, because the exercise of universal jurisdiction embodies the very essence of the assumption of such powers. Such powers are more easily prone to be exercised and enjoyed by courts because 'an inherent power of a court might then be thought to derive "from its nature as a court of law",[6] and also because judicial institutions, being endowed with specific jurisdictional competences, 'have those powers which are necessary to enable them to act effectively'.[7] This functional international constitutionalism, in turn, demands that courts exercise their *kompetenz-kompetenz* to fulfil their States' obligations. Exercising *kompetenz-kompetenz* hence safeguards the rights of victims to access to justice, which 'is an intrinsic part of the rule of law',[8] and protects the virtual (hypothetical) rights of would-be victims. The need to permit the assumption of jurisdiction, and hence presumptive jurisdiction, also logically flows, at least under international human rights law, from the requirement to allow access to a court and to enable such court and/or tribunal to exercise remedial powers, in the absence of which international justice would remain a mere *desideratum*. The three P's of international criminal law, being prevention, prosecution and punishment, in the words of Ilias Bantekas, constitute 'the threefold objective of international criminal law'.[9] Ward Ferdinandusse focuses on deterrence when he considers the object and purpose of international criminal law.[10] Enabling prosecutions by assuming jurisdiction 'can serve to discourage future human rights abuses, to deter vigilante justice, and to reinforce respect for law and a new government'.[11] It has a significant domino effect. The reverse is also true because the 'failure to prosecute leaders responsible for human rights abuses breeds contempt for the law and encourages future violations. The UNCHR and its Sub-Commission on Minorities have concluded that impunity is one of the main reasons for continuing grave violations for human rights throughout the world'.[12] Moreover, 'when the international community encourages or endorses an amnesty for human rights abuses, it sends a signal that others have nothing to lose by instituting repressive measures: if things start going

[6] Brown 2007, p. 56.

[7] Brown 2007, p. 57.

[8] FRA 2016.

[9] Bantekas 2010, p. 14.

[10] Ferdinandusse 2006, p. 176.

[11] Scharf 2000, p. 182.

[12] UNCHR 1990, cited in Scharf 2000, p. 182, n. 23.

badly, they can always bargain away their crimes by agreeing to peace'.[13] Thus, the need to enable prosecutions (which must necessarily precede punishments) further legitimises the assumption of implied powers, the exercise of which may be said to inspire presumptive jurisdiction. In sum, this presumptive jurisdiction acts as a safety-valve and as a tool which incentivises the desired curtailment of impunity. It is the prelude to the duty to submit to prosecution, but it is an end in itself. The emerging duty to submit to prosecution largely depends on this presumptive jurisdiction which, in turn, heavily relies on implied powers. On the other hand, it is the nature, scope and content of the duty to submit to prosecution itself which enables presumptive jurisdiction to come into existence in the first place. This is also because the nature, scope and content of such a duty allows, enables (and sometimes arguably obliges) States and their domestic criminal courts to exercise inherent and implied powers in order to discharge and exert international jurisdiction. Paradoxically, the duty to submit to prosecution is thus both the cause and the effect of presumptive jurisdiction. This is the very essence of inter-dependence in its most complete and broad manifestation. *Lacunae* and ambiguities, in so far as these are legally permissible, should be set aside by criminal courts. Alexander Zahar and Göran Sluiter have conceded that 'if there is a clear omission one would accept that a claim for an implied power to "fill the gap" would satisfy the test of legality and would not encounter much opposition from the state parties'.[14] The pre-emptive and teleological role of international criminal courts and tribunals, is thus hereby emphasized. Such courts should not only be the *bouche de la loi*. These implied powers can be availed of to pave the way for a dynamic interpretation of legal instruments[15] intended to mete out international criminal justice. This is permissible, within this context, particularly because dynamic interpretation is a human rights law technique.[16] Rather than soliciting judicial restraint, judicial activism would emboss customary international law rules which are ripening, one of which being the duty to prosecute core crimes which cannot be said to be limited to paper practice anymore.[17]

The ICTY, which was shut down by November 2017,[18] held that it possessed the inherent power to determine its own jurisdiction.[19] It is noteworthy to cite the *Nuclear Tests* case wherein the ICJ upheld that 'such inherent jurisdiction, on the basis of which the Court is fully empowered to make whatever findings may be

---

[13] Scharf 2000, p. 183.

[14] Zahar and Sluiter 2008, p. 24.

[15] For an understanding of the evolutive interpretation of legal instruments, see Forowicz 2010, pp. 11–12; see also Vanneste 2010, pp. 243–264.

[16] Robinson 2010, p. 145.

[17] Ferdinandusse 2006, p. 202.

[18] Ristic (2017) Balkan Transitional Justice, Hague Tribunal Prepares for Shutdown in 2017. http://www.balkaninsight.com/en/article/the-last-year-for-the-icty-01-02-2017-1. Accessed 27 November 2017.

[19] ICTY Appeals Chamber, *Prosecutor v Duško Tadić, Decision on the Defence Motion for Interlocutory Appeal on Jurisdiction*, 2 October 1995, Case No. IT-94-1, para 18.

necessary for the purposes just indicated, derives from the mere existence of the Court as a judicial organ established by the consent of states, and is conferred upon it in order that its basic judicial functions may be safeguarded'.[20] This suggests firstly that, unlike implied powers, inherent powers belong to judicial bodies.[21] Probably, in part for this reason, some have argued that inherent powers are a broader conceptual category than implied powers.[22] Secondly, it suggests that all international courts and tribunal do enjoy such inherent powers, but that the same may not necessarily be said about domestic courts.[23] The ICC, as arbiter of its own jurisdiction, is not devoid of such power. This jurisdictional endowment of the ICC is crucially important because there can be no greater power than being able to determine one's own powers. The ICC's latitude is therefore a priceless and unparalleled virtue.[24] Chester Brown concluded that 'a review of international jurisprudence reveals that many international courts have considered that they have a source of competence to fill in such gaps, and they have engaged in a process of cross-fertilization of the principles which has had a harmonising effect on the way they approach questions of procedure and remedies'.[25] A strong and authoritative ICC which successfully performs its functions is a powerful tool for the enforcement of the responsibility to protect norm as a robust 'part of the international normative architecture'.[26] This can be accomplished by the exercise of inherent powers. Indeed inherent powers do not only fill loopholes. They can determine the boundaries of the operationalization of positive complementarity[27] by incentivising domestic prosecutions. Rather than merely filling gaps, they can, in turn, elicit compliance with certain international obligations of States. Bert Swart, after concluding that a failure to investigate and prosecute 'may itself create international responsibility of the State concerned and give rise to complaints before international supervisory bodies',[28] went as far as stating that 'within the framework of admissibility proceedings, the International Criminal Court may actually press a State to

[20] ICJ, *Nuclear Tests Case (Australia v France)*, 20 December 1974, ICJ Rep 1974, p. 253, paras 259–260.

[21] Paola Gaeta in fact held that only once, this being the *Blaškić subpoena duces tecum* case, have implied powers been invoked by an international court of law (Gaeta 2003, pp. 364–365).

[22] Verdirame 2011, p. 77.

[23] The same conclusion can be reached from an analytical interpretation of the *Lotus* case [PCIJ Twelfth Ordinary Session, *Case of S.S. Lotus (France v Turkey)*, 7 September 1927, PCIJ Series A, no. 10, paras 242–250]. For a succinct explanation of the *S.S. Lotus* case and the ensuing legal consequences, see Vos 2013, pp. 176–177.

[24] This is so not only in terms of jurisdictional issues. In procedure, judges have discretion to decide whether trials will be more adversarial than inquisitorial, or vice-versa. In substantive law, recourse to general principles and comparative criminal law will be pivotal to fill any *lacunae* (Ambos 2010, p. 170).

[25] Brown 2007, p. 41.

[26] Contarino and Negron-Gonzales 2013, p. 411.

[27] Kleffner 2006, p. 89.

[28] Swart 2006, p. 173.

start or to reopen an investigation'.[29] Such a teleological approach is reflected in the evolution of international criminal law by means of judicial decisions.[30]

Given the presumption of international jurisdiction explained here above, a presumption which is closely related to the State's qualified duty to submit to prosecution (this constituting the main suggestion within Part V), domestic criminal courts and/or tribunals should be inclined to assume jurisdiction. To this extent, presumptive jurisdiction is a *juris tantum* presumption, not a *juris et de jure* one. The former presumption is a rebuttable one, meaning that 'the Court may find that the presumed facts exist unless sufficient evidence to the contrary is adduced, e.g. that a child conceived in wedlock is held to be the child of the mother's husband'.[31] The latter is an irrebuttable presumption 'where the Court must find that the presumed fact exists upon proof of some other fact, e.g. that a child under nine years is not criminally responsible for his/her acts'.[32] The assumption of jurisdiction should be the rule, not the exception. A compelling argument in support of this is the functional justification of the role and remit of criminal courts in general, but particularly those which are not exclusively domestic and are hence international. Indeed, by means of the *Blaškić dictum*, the ICTY Appeals Chamber authoritatively upheld that 'the International Tribunal must possess the power to make all those judicial determinations that are necessary for the exercise of its primary jurisdiction'.[33] *Ergo*, it was imperative to examine, *a priori*, the functions of courts endowed on the one hand with international criminal jurisdiction, and on the other with national criminal jurisdiction, unless one can somehow place both types of jurisdiction within the same basket. This examination was undertaken in Parts III and IV respectively.

21.2 Domestic Courts

In the absence of a world legislator which is the counterpart of domestic legislative bodies (such as national parliaments), implied and inherent powers largely belong to international courts and tribunals. It remains to be seen whether, if at all, implied and inherent powers may be availed of by domestic courts which function within mature legal systems. It seems that this could be permissible only if domestic courts are allowed to overrule decisions of prosecutors either not to prosecute or to discontinue criminal proceedings. These decisions are habitually camouflaged in

[29] Swart 2006, p. 174.

[30] Mettraux 2009, p. 8.

[31] Aquilina 2018b, p. 542.

[32] Ibid.

[33] ICTY Trial Chamber II, *Prosecutor v Tihomir Blaškić, Decision on the Objection of the Republic of Croatia to the Issuance of Subpoena Duces Tecum*, 18 July 1997, Case No. IT-95-14, para 704.

excuses such as ‘there is not enough evidence’, which often translates to ‘we cannot be bothered’, ‘it will cost too much’ and it is ‘not in the public interest’.[34] In these circumstances, more than ever, victims of crimes deserve special protection.[35]

Where a *nolle prosequi* subsists the only way a case can be brought to the court’s formal cognisance is by means of a private prosecution. Many States admit of this possibility. In fact ‘the decision not to prosecute is susceptible to some form of judicial review or appeal to a court of law in at least twenty-five Contracting States and in these countries the standard of review varies considerably’.[36] However, where a victim can be a private prosecutor, the additional burden in terms of resources, time, expenses and costs is vested upon him and ‘it is questionable if this burden may be mitigated by the provision of free legal aid and other assistance’.[37] In the light of the collective dimension of core crimes, at the very least, victims as private prosecutors should be allowed a collective *locus standi* which would enable them to pursue a prosecution by means of a joint/class action, a sort of *actio popularis*,[38] without any need for authorization and/or any intervention of the public prosecutor, both before but even after the commencement of criminal proceedings. Besides guaranteeing access to justice, this would also alleviate the financial burden of the victims. This should constitute a right, not a victim support service, and should arise ‘where the public prosecutor is unable or unwilling to prosecute’.[39] In the absence of this prerogative, in ‘refusing to institute or discontinuing the criminal proceedings against the police officers’, the ECtHR considered that ‘the investigation was not prompt and thorough and the proceedings showed a lack of will on the part of the authorities to hold the police officers to account. By failing in its duty to carry out an effective investigation, the State fostered the police officers’ sense of impunity’.[40] The inaction could hence anyway fall within the rubric of international human rights law.

---

[34] Gurney Harden Solicitors 2018.

[35] ECJ, *György Katz v István Roland Sós* (Opinion of AG Kokott), 10 July 2008, Case C-404/07, para 39.

[36] ECtHR Grand Chamber, *Patricia Armani da Silva v UK*, 30 March 2016, Application Number 5878/08, para 279.

[37] European Commission 2013, Article 11, Recitals 43, 44 and 45, para 39, p. 31. For a comparative analysis of the different ways how this directive was transposed in Germany, Italy, France and Croatia, see Novokmet 2016, pp. 95–107.

[38] Some jurisdictions allow individuals to impugn a law by means of an action, known as the *actio popularis*, for a declaration of invalidity of that law. This is the case, for example, with Article 116 of the Maltese Constitution (Aquilina 2018a, p. 73). My conception of an *actio popularis* in the context of this book is obviously different to what it ordinarily conveys in such jurisdictions.

[39] Ddamulira Mujuzi 2016, p. 131.

[40] ECtHR Third Section, *Anton Shestopalov v Russia*, 28 March 2017, Application No. 46248/07, paras 53–54.

When proceedings are discontinued by the prosecutor,[41] as opposed to circumstances when proceedings are not conducted in the first place, courts should be allowed, *de lege*, to order prosecutors to continue such proceedings. If the right to order prosecutors to continue proceedings is not established by an express legal provision, nothing should stop courts from asking the prosecutor to continue a prosecution by issuing an interlocutory decree to such effect. This, however, could be useless if the prosecutor makes no effort to produce the incriminating evidence and to tender submissions pointing to the guilt of the accused. So when shielding occurs the role of a domestic criminal court assumes significance. This is because the criminal court could allow the alleged victim to take over by acting as a subsidiary prosecutor, hence pursuing the prosecution. This does not necessarily solve the problem anyway because a subsidiary prosecutor does not possess the resources of the public prosecutor. He is not best placed and best equipped to conduct a prosecution. Alternatively, the criminal court should at least acknowledge, in its judgment, that there subsists the suspicion that the accused has been (deliberately) shielded. Where the judgment of the court is not a *res judicata*, it may equip victims (the *partie civile*) with grounds to appeal the judgment. Where the judgment does not constitute a *res judicata*, in and of itself, it may be an indicator of unwillingness which could satisfy the ICC admissibility test. If the ICC's jurisdiction will not be triggered and the accused would eventually be found within the custodial jurisdiction of another State willing to exercise universal jurisdiction over him, the declaratory judgment may be cited to rebut the *ne bis in idem* plea especially when evidence which was not produced before the court of the State which acquitted the individual is subsequently produced before the court within the State which grounded the prosecution on universal jurisdiction. In this way, judgments of courts, even when they acquit owing to lack of evidence, have a deep 'declaratory function'. I use the term 'declaratory function' in a broader sense than the meaning conveyed to it by means of declaratory judgments of the ICJ, the import of which is explicated by Ian Brownlie.[42] By means of their declaratory judgments, courts can legitimately communicate with one another without colluding and without interfering in the performance of the duties of other courts. This is more so if courts recognise the declaratory function of other courts in the field of core crimes. The mandatory recognition of such judgments could also constitute an undertaking by means of a legal provision within a prospective 'International Convention for the Prevention, Prosecution and Punishment of Core Crimes' which could sow the seeds for a more harmonised (global) approach intended to consolidate special cooperation devices designed to repress system criminality.

The extent to which core crimes can be subjected to prosecution is a complex task which merits attention, most of which must pivot around the relevant

---

[41] This presupposes that the investigation stage has been completed. Should this not be the case, in inquisitorial criminal justice systems members of the judicial branch anyway have investigative powers which would generally allow them to pursue investigations [see, for example, Articles 546–569 of the *Kodiċi Kriminali* {Criminal Code} (1854) Chapter 9 of the Laws of Malta].

[42] Brownlie 1983, pp. 200–208.

differentiation between international courts on the one hand and domestic courts on the other hand. The outcome does not only depend on the courage of courts to take the bull by the horns, but also on other stakeholders who are directly involved in the administration of criminal justice. These include investigators, witnesses, victims, defence lawyers, prosecutors and other public administrators who work in the delicate, and often thorny, field of criminal justice. The following chapter will explore the judicial dialogue between courts and will make reference to the integrated system which relies upon consultative cooperation between a seemingly coordinated community of courts, the ultimate objective of which is the delivery of criminal justice.

References

Ambos K (2010) International Criminal Law at the Crossroads: From *Ad Hoc* Imposition to a Treaty-Based Universal System. In: Stahn C, van den Herik L (eds) Future Perspectives on International Criminal Justice. Asser Press, The Hague, pp. 161–177

Aquilina K (2018a) Constitutional Law in Malta. KLI, Alphen aan den Rijn, The Netherlands

Aquilina K (2018b) Human Rights Law: Selected Writings of Kevin Aquilina. Department of Media, Communications and Technology Law, Faculty of Laws, University of Malta, Malta

Bantekas I (2010) International Criminal Law. HP, Oxford

Brown C (2007) A Common Law of International Adjudication, developed in cooperation with P*i*CT. OUP, Oxford

Brownlie I (1983) System of the Law of Nations: State Responsibility, Part I. CP, Oxford

Contarino M, Negron-Gonzales M (2013) The International Criminal Court. In: Zyberi G (ed) An Institutional Approach to the Responsibility to Protect. CUP, Cambridge, pp. 411–435

Ddamulira Mujuzi J (2016) Victim Participation in the Criminal Justice System in the European Union Through Private Prosecutions: Issues Emerging from the Jurisprudence of the European Court of Human Rights. EJCCLCJ 24(2–3):107–134

European Commission (2013) DG Justice Guidance Document Related to the Transposition and Implementation of Directive 2012/29/EU of the European Parliament and of the Council of 25 October 2012 Establishing Minimum Standards on the Rights, Support and Protection of Victims of Crime, and Replacing Council Framework Decision 2001/220/JHA, 19 December 2013.

Ferdinandusse WN (2006) Direct Application of International Criminal Law in National Courts. Asser Press, The Hague

Forowicz M (2010) The Reception of International Law in the European Court of Human Rights. OUP, Oxford

FRA (2016) Fundamental Rights Report 2016. http://fra.europa.eu/en/publication/2016/fundamental-rights-report-2016. Accessed 3 March 2018

Gaeta P (2003) Inherent Powers of International Court and Tribunals. In: Vohrah LC, Pocar F, Featherstone Y, Fourmy O, Graham MF, Hocking J, Robson N (eds) Man's Inhumanity to Man: Essays on International Law in Honour of Antonio Cassese. MNP, Leiden/Boston, pp. 353–372

Gurney Harden Solicitors (2018) Edward Hayes Lawyers, Private Prosecutions for Individuals. http://www.edwardhayes.co.uk/legal-services-for-you/private-prosecutions-for-individuals. Accessed 9 April 2018

Kleffner JK (2006) Complementarity as a Catalyst for Compliance. In: Kleffner JK and Kor G (eds) Complementary Views on Complementarity: Proceedings of the International Roundtable on the Complementary Nature of the International Criminal Court, Amsterdam, 25/26 June 2004. Asser Press, The Hague, pp. 79–104

Kodiċi Kriminali (Criminal Code) (1854) Chapter 9 of the Laws of Malta

Kor G (2006) Sovereignty in the Dock. In: Kleffner JK, Kor G (eds) Complementary Views on Complementarity: Proceedings of the International Roundtable on the Complementary Nature of the International Criminal Court, Amsterdam, 25/26 June 2004. Asser Press, The Hague, pp. 53–71

Mettraux G (2009) The Law of Command Responsibility. OUP, Oxford

Novokmet A (2016) The Right of a Victim to a Review of a Decision not to Prosecute as Set Out in Article 11 of Directive 2012/29/EU and an Assessment of its Transposition in Germany, Italy, France and Croatia. ULR 12(1):86–108

Ristic M (2017) Balkan Transitional Justice, Hague Tribunal Prepares for Shutdown in 2017. http://www.balkaninsight.com/en/article/the-last-year-for-the-icty-01-02-2017-1. Accessed 27 November 2017

Robinson D (2010) The Two Liberalisms of International Criminal Law. In: Stahn C, van den Herik L (eds) Future Perspectives on International Criminal Justice. Asser Press, The Hague, pp. 115–160

Scharf MP (2000) Justice *versus* Peace. In: Sewall SB, Kaysen C (eds) The United States and the International Criminal Court: National Security and International Law, American Academy of Arts and Sciences, RLP, Lanham, Maryland, USA, pp. 179–193

Skubiszewski K (1989) Implied Powers of International Organisations. In: Dinstein Y, Tabory M (eds) International Law at a Time of Perplexity: Essays in Honour of Shabtai Rosenne. MNP, Leiden/Boston, pp. 855–868

Swart B (2006) Comment on Chapter 5 of Rod Jensen. In: Kleffner JK, Kor G (eds) Complementary Views on Complementarity: Proceedings of the International Roundtable on the Complementary Nature of the International Criminal Court, Amsterdam, 25/26 June 2004. Asser Press, The Hague, pp. 171–175

UNCHR (1990) Report on the Consequences of Impunity, U.N. Doc. E/CN.4/1990/13

Vanneste F (2010) General International Law Before Human Rights Courts: Assessing the Specialty Claims of International Human Rights Law. Intersentia, Cambridge

Verdirame G (2011) The UN and Human Rights: Who Guards the Guardians? Cambridge Studies in International and Comparative Law. CUP, Cambridge

Vos JA (2013) The Function of Public International Law. Asser Press, The Hague

White N (1996) The Law of International Organisations. MUP, Manchester

Zahar A, Sluiter G (2008) International Criminal Law: A Critical Introduction. OUP, Oxford

Chapter 22
The Proliferation of Judicial Panels and Judicial Partnerships

Contents

References 601

Abstract The prosecution of core crimes is a challenging experience which can justify the adoption of extra-ordinary mechanisms for such purpose. What will most likely save the need to continue relying upon the ICC is the prosecution of senior leaders and high-level suspects. Judicial panels and judicial partnerships are gradually morphing. These noteworthy developments can lead to an integrated system which relies upon consultative cooperation between, what should hopefully become, a coordinated community of courts. The outcome of the proliferation of courts of tribunals is a system of ongoing and constructive judicial dialogue, the genesis of which precedes the ICC itself, wherein courts and tribunals no longer operate in isolation from each other. Courts and tribunals must interact when international judges and/or internationalized courts/tribunals apply domestic law. Interaction is also necessary when international rulings are domestically enforced and when judgments of international courts are implemented domestically. Since complementarity and subsidiarity presuppose that the State *locus delicti commissi* either did not investigate and prosecute or did not do so with the necessary vigour, some form of interaction between various judicial systems is inevitable. Interaction is habitually required in other crucial matters and throughout the entire procedural iter, such as the surrender and/or extradition of a suspect pre-trial, the production of evidence during the trial and the execution of judgments further to the *res judicata,* post-trial. The interaction is multi-dimensional and multi-faceted. It does not only play a role either vertically or horizontally. It can intersect the entire enforcement spectrum at various levels.

Keywords International courts · ICC · Credibility · Senior leaders · High-level suspects · Judicial panels · Judicial partnerships · Integrated system · Consultative cooperation · Coordinated community of courts · Unfair trial · Complementarity · Subsidiarity · *Locus delict commissi* · International judges · Internationalized courts · Interactive judicial dialogue · Preliminary examination phase · Sharing of

C. Soler, *The Global Prosecution of Core Crimes under International Law*,
https://doi.org/10.1007/978-94-6265-335-1_22

information • Documentary evidence • Hybrid court • Liaison body • Constructive judicial dialogue

The proper prosecution of core crimes, given their phenomenological peculiarities, is such a challenging experience that it can justify the adoption of extra-ordinary mechanisms for such purpose. This is why judicial panels and judicial partnerships are gradually morphing to the extent that 'there are more international courts than ever before'.[1] The ETSPSC, which were established by the UN acting as the transitory authority between the end of the Indonesian occupation in 1999 and the Independence of East Timor in 2002,[2] is an example of the former. The CAR Special Criminal Court,[3] which partners the ICC, is a hybrid tribunal which exemplifies the latter. This is an altogether different beast[4] since it complements an ICC intervention whereas we are generally accustomed to see the ICC complement other judicial systems by virtue of the complementarity regime. The ensuing state of affairs is queer. The ICC has an interest in cooperating with the CAR Special Criminal Court both to ensure that all, even low-level individuals, be prosecuted, and particularly to prove that positive complementarity, evidence sharing and capacity building, really work. If so, the ICC makes a solid case for its own continued existence. At the same time, if the ICC complements special courts and hybrid tribunals over and above, and besides, complementing domestic criminal justice systems, the need for its existence may dwindle since the formation of new special courts and hybrid tribunals may overshadow, if not substitute altogether, the ICC which could gradually become redundant. Mathias Holvoet predicates that 'as it currently stands, hybrid or internationalized courts will not play a secondary role but, to the contrary, will be a crucial complement to the ICC's and domestic courts' work'.[5] Such diversified judicial mechanisms can also benefit from some of the same advantages which characterise the international commissions carried out by non-nationals under the auspices of the UN, these being 'distance from domestic political squabbles, a claim to objectivity and disinterestedness, a greater degree of protection from reprisals, and the clout to bring its recommendations to the attention of international public opinion and to use international pressure to have its recommendations implemented.[6] What will most likely save the need to continue relying upon the ICC is the prosecution of senior leaders and high-level suspects. In fact, as long as those who ordered and planned core crimes are prosecuted domestically, it seems unlikely that the ICC would exercise jurisdiction over lower

---

[1] Usacka 2016, p. 284.

[2] IBA 2018.

[3] Mudge 2017.

[4] Kersten 2015.

[5] Holvoet 2016, p. 36.

[6] Roht-Arriaza 1995, p. 283.

level perpetrators, 'particularly those not connected to notorious or mass crimes'.[7] Even if it did, it would be unlikely that the ICC, 'in view of the resource constraints it faces, would exercise jurisdiction over more than a small handful of such persons'.[8] Anyway, the intricacies of prosecuting these high-profile individuals are such that probably no special court and/or hybrid tribunal can successfully perform the ICC's job in a like manner. This is so from various viewpoints, ranging from the conceptual, to the political, to the administrative, and also to the operational. It also explains why 'there can hardly be a one-size-fits-all prosecutorial strategy'[9] of and for core crimes, and/or a prosecutorial strategy which is dependent and reliant upon the *forum prosequi*. The ICC statutory framework, which can soon boast of two decades of experience, protects fundamental human rights of all stakeholders. In this way, *inter alia*, the ICC earns credibility. Credibility is something you do not have, unless you earn it. Consequently the ICC legitimises the delivery of international criminal justice in a way which no new special court or new hybrid tribunal can easily parallel. Admittedly, the achilles heel of the ICC is its slow pace. Yet, any swifter prosecution of a high-level suspect by a special court or a hybrid tribunal will not necessarily be met with praise. It is likely to be criticised as a political facade embedded within a seemingly unfair trial, which could, in turn, cause a more volatile political atmosphere within the respective State or region, especially during the troublesome process of post-conflict transitional justice.

This does not mean that such developments are to be frowned upon. These noteworthy developments can lead to an integrated system which relies upon consultative cooperation between, what should be, a coordinated community of courts wherein *l'unité fait la force*. In many circumstances these courts must acknowledge that they cannot do all the work alone, that they should accept the assistance and cooperation of their counterparts, and that they should, as far as practicable, accept to ultimately share the responsibility to prosecute core crimes if they are unable to do so alone, unaided. The acceptance by States of any foreign know-how, resources, expertise and cooperation is not reflective of any domestic default. On the contrary, just like a car which needs some diesel to arrive safely at the destination point, States which diligently collect and preserve evidence for it to be produced before non-domestic and/or international panels and/or tribunals and/or courts fulfil their duties under international law by portraying a willingness to prosecute and by minimizing their inability to do so alone. The outcome of the proliferation of courts of tribunals is a system of ongoing and constructive judicial dialogue, the genesis of which precedes the ICC itself,[10] wherein courts and tribunals no longer operate in isolation from each other. Courts and tribunals must

[7] Weiner 2016, p. 238.

[8] Weiner 2016, pp. 235–236.

[9] Yau 2018.

[10] O'Shea 1996, pp. 332–333. For this reason, *inter alia*, I do not agree with Zachary Kaufman's finding to the effect that such proliferation suggests that the international community 'does not necessarily view the ICC as a default or desired venue' (Kaufman 2018, p. 109).

interact when international judges and/or internationalized courts/tribunals apply domestic law, this having been the case with the STL. Interaction is also necessary when international rulings are domestically enforced and when judgments of international courts are implemented domestically.[11] Ultimately, 'judges engage in regional and international decision-making by virtue of a dialogue, which can take different shapes or forms'.[12] Such courts and tribunals interact with one another partly out of choice, and partly out of necessity. Whereas Judge Anita Usacka traces this connection to the 'shared duty to adhere to and interpret international human rights norms',[13] I suggest that it owes its existence predominantly to other factors ranging from the customary law status of the prohibition of core crimes, to the incorporation and penalisation of core crimes in many domestic laws, to the cross-fertilization of doctrines, norms and principles, and to the very nature of the systems of enforcement of international criminal law which, in the absence of the exercise of territorial jurisdiction or upon the misuse thereof, are reliant on complementarity and subsidiarity, as shown in Parts III and IV of this work.

Since complementarity and subsidiarity presuppose that the State *locus delicti commissi* either did not investigate and prosecute or did not do so with the necessary vigour, some form of interaction between various judicial systems is inevitable. The need to interact is ingrained, embedded and inherent within the framework of the system of enforcement because of its very structure and scope. This happens *ipso facto* when the territorial State fails to investigate and prosecute or fails to do so diligently. Yet, even when the territorial State investigates and prosecutes, especially post-conflict, it tends to do so by asking for and/or obtaining external assistance which may come in various types, shapes and forms. Moreover, interaction is habitually required in other crucial matters and throughout the entire procedural iter, such as the surrender and/or extradition of a suspect pre-trial, the production of evidence during the trial and the execution of judgments further to the *res judicata*, post-trial. The interaction is multi-dimensional and multi-faceted. It does not only play a role either vertically or horizontally. It can intersect the entire enforcement spectrum at various levels. For example, if one targets just one situation, being core crimes committed by *Daesh* militants in Syria, various efforts by distinctive judicial bodies can, and possibly should, be undertaken. States must exercise universal jurisdiction on individuals within their custodial jurisdiction, a network of specialized judicial panels can be set up (possibly) in neighbouring States to prosecute the large majority of responsible individuals, and the ICC can prosecute nationals of ICC State Parties whose criminal liability falls within the parameters of Article 25 of the ICC Statute, be they direct, indirect perpetrators or accomplices. A hybrid court in Syria itself should be considered only upon the cessation of hostilities. These efforts can, and should, be undertaken simultaneously. They are not mutually exclusive. They just require the sharing of

[11] Aksenova and Ulfstein 2016, p. 356.

[12] Aksenova and Ulfstein 2016, p. 354.

[13] Usacka 2016, p. 304.

responsibilities by virtue of synchronised and ongoing judicial cooperation. They can also benefit from the mutual sharing of information, including documentary evidence. Any court exercising universal jurisdiction, any specialized judicial panels, any special court and/or any hybrid court can, for example, make use of any and of all the evidence collected by the ICC during its preliminary examination phase even when the ICC's jurisdiction is limited. By way of example, further to two case studies conducted by HRW, Emeric Rogier has assessed the impact, on Colombia and Guinea, of the preliminary examinations of the OTP.[14]

In sum, an interactive judicial dialogue looms on the horizon. It is now up to these judicial bodies to make a success story out of the ensuing interactive judicial dialogue. With this aim in sight, it might be worthwhile to ponder over whether a specific organ, being a liaison body consisting of various legal experts with diverse backgrounds, could be established to facilitate, manage and maintain the ongoing, constructive judicial dialogue.

References

Aksenova M, Ulfstein G (2016) The Task of Regional and International Courts in Guarding Constitutionalism and Human Rights. In: Scheinin M, Krunke H, Aksenova M (eds) Judges as Guardians of Constitutionalism and Human Rights. EE, Cheltenham, UK/Northampton, MA, USA, pp. 352–369

Holvoet M (2016) The Continuing Relevance of the Hybrid or Internationalized Justice Model: The Example of the Kosovo Specialist Chambers. CLF 28(1):35–73

IBA (2018) Special Panel for Serious Crimes (East Timor). https://www.ibanet.org/Committees/WCC_EastTimor.aspx. Accessed 31 December 2018

ICC Statute (1998) Rome Statute of the International Criminal Court

Kaufman ZD (2018) The Prospects, Problems and Proliferation of Recent UN Investigations of International Law Violations. JICJ 16(1):93–112

Kersten M (2015) Why Central African Republic's Hybrid Tribunal Could be a Game-Changer. Justice in Conflict. https://justiceinconflict.org/2015/05/14/why-central-african-republics-hybrid-tribunal-could-be-a-game-changer/. Accessed 2 April 2017

Mudge L (2017) A Step Towards Justice in the Central African Republic: New Court Can Help End Impunity, HRW. https://www.hrw.org/news/2017/02/21/step-toward-justice-central-african-republic. Accessed 22 November 2017

O'Shea S (1996) Interaction Between International Criminal Tribunals and National Legal Systems. In: Franck TM, Fox GH (eds) International Law Decisions in National Courts. TP, Irvington-on-Hudson, NY, pp. 285–333

Rogier E (2018) The Ethos of "Positive Complementarity". EJIL:Talk! https://www.ejiltalk.org/the-ethos-of-positive-complementarity/. Accessed 30 December 2018

Roht-Arriaza N (1995) Conclusion: Combating Impunity. In Roht-Arriaza N (ed) Impunity and Human Rights in International Law and Practice. OUP, NY/Oxford, pp. 281–304

Usacka A (2016) Constitutionalism and Human Rights at the International Criminal Court. In: Scheinin M, Krunke H, Aksenova M (eds) Judges as Guardians of Constitutionalism and Human Rights. EE, Cheltenham, UK/Northampton, MA, USA, pp. 281–305

[14] Rogier 2018.

Weiner AS (2016) Ending Wars, Doing Justice: Colombia, Transitional Justice, and the International Criminal Court. SJIL 52(2):211–241

Yau SSM (2018) The Decentralisation of International Crimes: A Shift from the Central Criminal Apparatus at the ICC? EJIL:Talk! https://www.ejiltalk.org/the-decentralisation-of-international-crimes-a-shift-from-the-central-criminal-apparatus-at-the-icc/. Accessed 31 December 2018

Chapter 23
Concluding Observations and Final Remarks

Contents

References 615

Abstract An International Convention for the Prevention, Prosecution and Punishment of Core Crimes could constitute evidence of a duty to prosecute of the territorial State and of an obligation to submit to prosecution of the custodial State. If it will be widely ratified it would impose such duties. If not, it could still pave the way for the formation of a rule of customary international law. The exercise of universal jurisdiction by States, provided it be undertaken fairly and not *in absentia*, could anyway be a preferred course of action to a prosecution under the vertical system of enforcement. Criminal justice will be predominantly meted out by domestic criminal courts, exercising various forms of jurisdiction, particularly territorial, but also resorting to and availing themselves of universal jurisdiction. It will also be delivered by the ICC, and by hybrid tribunals which are most likely to gain importance in the near future since their flexible and customised nature facilitate their creation and establishment. Since the ICC's jurisdiction can never be all-encompassing due to limitations *rationae temporis, rationae loci, rationae personae* and *rationae materiae*, hybrid tribunals are likely to blossom in countries and/or regions post-conflict. There might be some place for *sui generis* trials, such as the *Lockerbie* trials. These could also take the form of specialized country-specific tribunals. There is increasingly more room for special courts, such as, *inter alia*, the EAC. One notes that the UNGA has adopted a Resolution establishing the IIIM which has a unique quasi-prosecutorial role, scope and functions.

Keywords Normative point of reference · Refugee law · Equitable balance · Foreseeability of the likelihood of a violation · Standard of proof · Obligation to prosecute · Territorial State · International Convention for the Prevention · Prosecution and Punishment of Core Crimes · Universal jurisdiction · State practice · ECtHR · Customary international law · Failure to act · Pre-emptive role · *Bona fide* prosecution · Catalyst for compliance · Duty to submit to

C. Soler, *The Global Prosecution of Core Crimes under International Law*,
https://doi.org/10.1007/978-94-6265-335-1_23

prosecution · IIIM · Asian dissent · Quasi-prosecutorial role · Selective prosecutions · Resources · Infrastructure · Variables · Greatest responsibility · Regionalizing international criminal justice · *Sui generis* trials · *Lockerbie* · Statutory limitations · Dualism of core crimes · Hybrid model · Special courts · EAC · Internationalized justice model · Proliferation of judicial panels · UNITAD · Division of labour · Burden sharing · Domestication of international criminal law

This book has revealed that the horizontal system of enforcement has primacy, and that the vertical system of enforcement requires some surgical intervention. This should not lead one to think that the horizontal system is flawless. Had it been perfect there would have not been the need for the vertical system in the first place. There exists room for improvement in the horizontal system of enforcement too. Part IV has shown that the major stumbling blocks emanate from human rights grounds for refusing extradition. This is where, in the absence of an International Court of Human Rights and/or an International Human Rights Court,[1] domestic constitutional courts and the human rights regional mechanisms ought to strike the right balance between, on the one hand, the protection of the extraditee from arbitrary and illegal treatment and, on the other hand, the rights both of the alleged victims of crimes and of the State requesting extradition. In this context, extradition law, duly applied by domestic courts, can make use of refugee law at least in so far as the identification, application and implementation of the standard of proof to evaluate the likelihood or otherwise (the degree and the extent) of the risk of torture is concerned. Refugee law can constitute a normative point of reference by becoming a meaningful utensil in the toolkit of domestic courts which are called to determine the extraditability or otherwise of an individual. Refugee law can be made use of in a multitude of ways by municipal courts which are being constantly called to determine 'the standard of probability which is required to tip the balance in favour of human rights'.[2] Just to give a concrete example, the 'substantial grounds' test can be re-shaped to comprehend and necessitate a 'well-founded risk of torture', hence using refugee law as a new and reliable measuring tape to measure the risk involved (to assess the foreseeability of the likelihood of a violation). Though this would probably fall short of the 'flagrant violation' test, it would raise the standard of proof to create an equitable balance between the interest of the requesting State and the rights of the extraditee, keeping in mind the

---

[1] Although 'the ECtHR has been described as a "sort of world court of human rights" due to the fact that its jurisprudence exercises formal authority over courts within Europe and is of persuasive force in courts outside Europe' (Attanasio 1996, p. 16, cited in Usacka 2016, p. 294, n. 57), it is not the human rights counterpart of the ICC. One must also keep in mind that 'at the international level, there are no individual complaints mechanisms available to the victims of violations of international humanitarian law.' (Hastie and Crepeau 2015, p. 1320).

[2] van der Wilt 2012, p. 172.

preference to restrict grounds for refusal in manners which render such limitations anyway compliant with contemporary international norms and standards.

It is settled that 'under international human rights law, States' obligations are directed first and foremost towards ensuring the rights of people on their territory; therefore it may be assumed that States have the most intricate web of obligations to prevent gross human rights violations within their own territory.'[3] But although prevention can be exercised by prosecuting, the strongest evidence of an obligation to prosecute of the territorial State and of an obligation to submit to prosecution of the custodial State would be an explicit conventional disposition to this effect. A treaty which is widely ratified would hence impose such duties. A treaty, though not widely ratified, could pave the way for the formation of a rule of customary international law. An 'International Convention for the Prevention, Prosecution and Punishment of Core Crimes' could be the next recommended step in this regard, particularly in the absence of an international convention which penalises and punishes crimes against humanity. Besides acknowledging and codifying 'the three P's of international law', referred to in sub-heading 21A, it would constitute a progressive restatement of international law in so far as the repression of core crimes is concerned. Such a treaty, in and of itself, can also constitute, from a procedural perspective, an international law on extradition. Its broad ratification could lead to a crystallisation of a new rule of customary international law, or else, at the very least, it will strengthen the argument for the ripening of the custodial State's duty to submit to prosecution.

In the realization that 'universal jurisdiction is best understood as being based in an individual's right of access to justice for victims of serious international crimes',[4] States must exercise universal jurisdiction more. The ensuing State practice will engender important legal consequences. Rod Rastan upholds that 'universal jurisdiction will therefore continue to form a significant component of an overall global strategy to combat impunity'.[5] In the exercise of universal jurisdiction, States such as Canada, Norway, France, Germany, Spain and Belgium, just to cite a few, are at the forefront.[6] Nowadays permissive universal jurisdiction is customary international law, but mandatory universal jurisdiction is so gradually becoming. In terms of international law, the breach of conventional international law, possibly the *aut dedere aut judicare* rule,[7] besides entailing State responsibility, leads to the obligation to uphold customary international law. Examining the interaction between complementarity and universal jurisdiction, Britta Lisa Krings advocates the following three permutations:

1. complementarity improves the use and implementation of universal jurisdiction;
2. with complementarity there is no room left for nationally prescribed universal jurisdiction;

[3] van der Have 2018, p. 30.

[4] Hovell 2018, p. 455.

[5] Rastan 2010, p. 127.

[6] Carter 2013, p. 461, cited in Usacka 2016, p. 285, n. 17.

[7] This is deemed to be the cornerstone of international penal matters (Bassiouni 2008, p. 45).

3. universal jurisdiction enforces the principle of complementarity effectively by increasing the number of potential national States that are able to deal with the commission of core crimes.[8]

In the absence of the exercise of such universal jurisdiction the impact of the failure to investigate and prosecute is multi-faceted in that it does not only have external consequences, but also internal ones. This is particularly so because the failure to act, *per se*, can (or should) be considered as tantamount to complicity in the perpetration of the core crime itself. Commentators, such as Thomas Buergenthal, state that this theory is applicable when widespread impunity subsists. This leads to a 'retroactive ratification of the offences committed'.[9] Anja Siebert-Fohr upholds that 'the complicity rationale can be applied only if there is a *nexus* between the shortcomings and the violation'.[10] The ICC cooperation regime is more robust when a case has been referred to it following a UNSC Resolution, at which point the system of enforcement looks less like a Tower of Pisa but more like the former *ad hoc* international criminal tribunals of former Yugoslavia and Rwanda, firm and vertical.

The exercise of jurisdiction necessarily implies the undertaking of an investigation, at least as a bare minimum. The extent to which it necessitates a prosecution is another matter. However, the admissibility procedure within the ICC Statute clearly conveys that if an investigation discloses and reveals that a core crime has been committed and identifies its alleged perpetrator, a *bona fide* prosecution ought to be genuinely undertaken, in the absence of which the case could become admissible before the ICC. Crimes committed on the territory of ICC State Parties or else by nationals of such ICC State Parties are therefore more likely to be subjected to prosecution and punishment. This illustrates the pre-emptive role of positive complementarity, referred to as a 'catalyst for compliance' by Jann Kleffner[11] and as a 'global compliance system for the enforcement of international criminal law' by Rod Rastan.[12] Some commentators have gone a step further by not confining such duties to core crimes, stating that the purpose of preambular para 6 is not only to evoke the obligation to investigate and prosecute all core crimes, but also that there is a class of crimes under international law for which States have an obligation to prosecute although these crimes do not fall within the jurisdiction of the Court.[13] This view is not wholly shared by myself in so far as the duty only refers to crimes falling under the ICC radar. It remains to be seen, however, whether the accession of 123 States of the ICC Statute could either start to pave the way or strengthen the case in favour of the establishment of a customary international law

[8] Krings 2012, p. 740.

[9] HRC, Summary Record of the 1519th Meeting: *Perú*, Fifty-seventh session, U.N. Doc., CCPR/C/SR.1519, para 44.

[10] Siebert-Fohr 2009, p. 205.

[11] Kleffner 2008, pp. 309–339.

[12] Rastan 2010, p. 131.

[13] Triffterer 2008, pp. 1–11, cited in Kleffner 2008, p. 244, n. 41.

rule entailing the duty to prosecute core crimes, not merely the duty to submit to prosecution.[14] Jann Kleffner provides a comprehensive list of ICC State Parties which have understood the ICC regime as permitting, or indeed demanding, the establishment of universal jurisdiction in their implementing legislation.[15] Such State practice,[16] coupled with the *obiter dicta* referred to throughout this work, has the potential to solicit the commencement of a customary international law rule necessitating the conditional and qualified duty of States enjoying custodial jurisdiction to submit an individual to prosecution, as explained here above. Although such rule is still ripening and is hence not yet fully mature,[17] it is, gradually but steadily, creating a presumption to the effect that, at least on a *prima facie* basis, non-extradition and non-prosecution are, simultaneously and cumulatively, incompatible with international law. Somehow and somewhere the alleged perpetrator of the core crime must be submitted to prosecution.[18] The whole point is

---

[14] Within the Islamic world, only Jordan, Afghanistan and Uzbekistan have ratified the ICC Statute. In central, southern and eastern Asia [besides the above mentioned States], only Cambodia, Mongolia, Japan and South Korea have ratified it. Most importantly, Russia, China and the USA are not State Parties thereto. A graphic look at the State Parties shows that a very great majority of those States which have neither signed nor ratified the ICC Statute are neighbouring Asian States, to the extent that one may speak about quasi-global consensus with the marked exception of a region (continent) [http://en.wikipedia.org/wiki/States_parties_to_the_Rome_Statute_of_the_International_Criminal_Court. Accessed 19 October 2016]. In other words, the phrase 'Asian dissent to the ICC', coined by myself, could be fitting nowadays. In fact in a courtesy visit paid by myself in my capacity as Chairperson of the *COJUR*-ICC Working Group of the Council of the EU, at the ICC on 23 May 2017 (EU Day Against Impunity), the ICC President Silvia Fernández de Gurmendi expressed concern in view of a low rate of ratifications by Asian States to the ICC Statute. In truth, however, African States have increasingly shown discomfort with the ICC notwithstanding that the Chief Prosecutor is African too. This has evidently emerged from the 11 October 2013 ministerial meeting and the 12 October 2013 summit of AU member States in Ethiopia, where, in the light of the international arrest warrants issued against Kenya's *Uhuru Kenyatta* and Sudan's *Omar Al Bashir*, a resolution was adopted to the effect that no sitting African Head of State should appear before an international court [http://www.reuters.com/article/2013/10/11/us-africa-icc-idUSBRE99A0BS20131011, accessed 29 August 2016, and http://www.france24.com/en/20131012-africa-nations-african-union-attacks-unfair-icc-international-criminal-court-trial-Kenyatta-Ruto, http://www.bbc.co.uk/news/world-africa-24506006, accessed on 29 August 2016] and culminated in the withdrawals of Burundi, South Africa and The Gambia [see Chap. 2, notes 41–43]. Yet only the former withdrawal still stands [see Chap. 2, notes 46 and 47].

[15] See the list in Kleffner 2008, p. 276, n. 201.

[16] A detailed analysis of such practice, particularly in Australia, Austria, Belgium, Canada, Denmark, France, Germany, Israel, the Netherlands, Senagal, Spain, Switzerland, the UK and the USA until 2003 may be found in Reydams 2003, pp. 86–219.

[17] A few, amongst whom Bruce Broomhall, contend that Nuremberg created a duty to prosecute core crimes on behalf of the international community on the grounds of universal jurisdiction, this duty being an obligation *erga omnes* (Broomhall 2003, p. 56, cited in Melandri 2009, p. 534, n. 12).

[18] This is generally undertaken by elimination and hierarchically. The first port of call, the territorial State, is initially examined. If this is either unwilling or unable to investigate and prosecute, the prospects of a UNSC Resolution are realistically analysed. If this is not a realistic prospect, a hybrid tribunal can be examined next (see, for example, Sayapin 2016).

where, when and how, keeping in mind that the conundrum involves hefty financial, operational and administrative considerations too. If States, even when they are bystander States, who have the custody of the individual suspected of having committed core crimes, decide not to exercise universal jurisdiction, the international community must pull its socks up. One must here positively remark that the UNGA adopted a Resolution establishing the IIIM[19] which has been termed a 'game changer'[20] in view of its unique quasi-prosecutorial role, scope and functions. The IIIM has already collected an overwhelming and unprecedented amount of evidence which includes depositions of witnesses, images and videos documenting atrocities committed by all stakeholders in Syria's war.[21] Similarly, the UN Investigative Team for Accountability of *Daesh*, also known as UNITAD, established by the S-G pursuant to UNSC Resolution 2379 (2017), is mandated to support domestic efforts to hold *Daesh* accountable by collecting, preserving and storing evidence of core crimes committed by *Daesh* in Iraq. More recently the Human Rights Council has voted to establish an independent mechanism to collect, consolidate, preserve and analyse evidence of violations of international humanitarian law and of human rights in Myanmar.[22]

The exercise of universal jurisdiction by States, provided it be undertaken fairly and not *in absentia*, could anyway be a preferred course of action to a prosecution under the vertical system of enforcement. It is hence appropriate to identify it as an option which should be considered before recourse to the vertical system of enforcement. States willing to exercise universal jurisdiction already have resources and infrastructure in place which are conducive to a smoother and faster prosecution. Besides having their intact criminal justice systems, such States make use of agreements, be they bilateral or multilateral, to entice other States to make evidence available to the requesting (prosecuting) State. The exercise of universal jurisdiction can also set aside the dangers and challenges of selective prosecutions which are commonly associated with the vertical system of enforcement.[23] Consequently the

---

[19] The UNGA Resolution [UNGA (2016) Resolution 71/248 (2016), UN Doc. A/RES/71/248] adopted, in its seventy-first session, the IIIM [see UN Doc. A/71/L.48, para 4].

[20] This term was used by Deputy Permanent Representative of Liechtenstein to the EU, Stephan Barriga, in a keynote address undertaken at a meeting of *COJUR (*Public International Law) Working Group of the Council of the EU chaired by myself and held at Justus Lipsius building, Brussels, on 1 June 2017.

[21] Nebehay S (2018) War Crimes Evidence in Syria Overwhelming, Not All Can be Pursued: UN. Reuters World News. https://www.reuters.com/article/us-mideast-crisis-syria-warcrimes/war-crimes-evidence-in-syria-overwhelming-not-all-can-be-pursued-u-n-idUSKBN1H22GN. Accessed 25 August 2018.

[22] Mahnad 2018.

[23] The fact that only high-level suspects will be prosecuted before the ICC may be deduced from Articles 1 and 5(1) of the ICC Statute (which allow the ICC to exercise jurisdiction over persons for the most serious crimes of international concern). Although it is not associated with (legal) gravity *per se* under Articles 17(1)(d) and 53(2)(b) of the ICC Statute (see Ambos and Stegmiller 2012, p. 401), the criterion mirrors the gravity threshold (see Article 17(1)(d) of the ICC Statute). The OTP policies convey that the focus on those bearing the greatest responsibility for the most

prosecution of all those responsible for core crimes would be undertaken, from the Head of State to the last obedient soldier. This, in turn, would internationalize the rule of law by promoting the equal subjection of all individuals to the law. It would also send a strong message to the international community to the effect that impunity could be defeated when justice is done and when it is seen to be done. Hence rather than leaving the door for universal jurisdiction ajar,[24] the door for the ICC should be left ajar. Although a permanent institution, the ICC needs to exist only when, until and because States remain unwilling or unable to investigate and prosecute core crimes.

At the very end of this work, I will pose a final question which the 'global prosecution of core crimes under international law' elicits. Who is most likely to undertake prosecutions for core crimes in the near future, and how will this be done? Before replying to such question, one must note that the number of indicted individuals and trials is neither the only way to evaluate the record of criminal courts nor necessarily the most insightful. It is also necessary to hold them against the expectations that the international community had when they were created.[25] The following variables need to be presented:

i. international criminal justice will be predominantly meted out by domestic criminal courts, exercising various forms of jurisdiction, particularly territorial, but also resorting to and availing themselves of universal jurisdiction. Maybe Britta Lisa Krings estimates the value and role of universal jurisdiction disproportionately or too optimistically, but she is right in predicting that the enforcement of international criminal law still leaves sufficient room for universal jurisdiction. Time will tell whether, at least in so far as core crimes are concerned, this door will be eventually opened wide or whether, in due course, it would have to be closed (if not locked). It seems that the former is more likely than the latter;
ii. it will be delivered by the ICC, which has been described as a "stigmatizer" in international society,[26] the success of which 'will depend upon the support and commitment of States, international organizations, and civil society.'[27] This is largely because the ICC is 'characterised by the structural weakness that it does not have the competencies and means to enforce its own decisions,' especially with regard 'to the crucial question of the effective execution of

serious crimes should be taken into account for the purposes of the admissibility test [OTP (2013) Policy Paper on Preliminary Examinations. ICC-OTP, November 2013, p. 11. https://www.icc-cpi.int/iccdocs/otp/otp-policy_paper_preliminary_examinations_2013-eng.pdf. Accessed 10 March 2016]. It must be highlighted that this criterion is a policy matter, not a legal requirement (Ambos and Stegmiller 2012, p. 401).

[24] Garcia Ramirez 2004, pp. 154–156.

[25] Mackenzie et al. 2010, p. 244.

[26] Dancy 2017, p. 627.

[27] Kirsch 2008, p. 291.

arrest warrants and surrender of suspects to The Hague.'[28] Yet, this support should not be the pretext to a diminution of autonomy. On the contrary, the ICC's future 'depends on the extent to which political influence can be annihilated by proper and independent investigation of the cases.'[29] The relationship of the ICC with the UNSC will also constitute an indicator of its success, or otherwise, particularly because cooperation between both institutions 'will become more difficult and without doubt at the mercy of States who will exert the power to consent or block the activity of the Court exclusively in relation to the protection of individual national interests.'[30] If the ICC becomes superfluous and dies a natural death, it would be the greatest winner. It seems however that it is here to stay and might actually become more necessary than ever. The ICC can also function as an alternative and neutral forum of prosecution especially when, as was the case with *Lockerbie*, 'the requesting State might have supported the criminal activity'.[31] But this does not mean that it is a loser, in the jigsaw puzzle of international criminal justice, although its excessively slow pace is worrying.[32] Embarking on the road to Rome, though long and often contentious,[33] was necessary. Former ICC President, Judge Sang-Hyun Song, besides hinting at a low quality of previous ICC-judges, expressed concern about the lack of support by States and State Parties.[34] Ultimately, one must recognise that the ICC has a heavy rule of law identity and dimension which it also and particularly fulfils by providing much needed technical assistance to ill-equipped domestic criminal justice systems. Thus, 'even if it is not possible to host trials on local soil, there remains a need to provide training and support for local judicial institutions if they are to be expected not only to host lower level trials not sought by international courts, but to take over, continue and complete outstanding prosecutions once the international court has closed down';[35]

iii. other semi-internationalized/hybrid tribunals[36] could play an important role to fill the impunity gap too. These are most likely to gain importance in the near future since their flexible and customised nature facilitate their creation and establishment, although they have not always accomplished international

[28] Kaul 2012, p. 683.

[29] Tutuianu 2013, p. 135.

[30] Gargiulo 1999, p. 103.

[31] Margariti 2017, pp. 119–120.

[32] A slow pace can however be advantageous for the purposes of establishing admissibility (Akhavan 2016, pp. 1048–1050).

[33] Tofan and van der Wolf 2011, p. 1.

[34] Heinze 2018, pp. 22–23.

[35] Chan and Wouter 2015, p. 168.

[36] For a definition and thorough understanding of hybrid, internationalised tribunals, see Williams 2012, pp. 201–252.

criminal justice in a fair manner.[37] Moreover, since the ICC's jurisdiction can never be all-encompassing due to limitations *rationae temporis*,[38] *rationae loci*,[39] *rationae personae*,[40] and *rationae materiae*,[41] coupled with the prohibition of statutory limitations[42] in the case of core crimes, hybrid tribunals are likely to blossom in countries and/or regions post-conflict. This is particularly so because the goal of such hybrid courts is 'also to buttress the national judiciary and the rule of law in the affected country'.[43] To this extent, such tribunals are regionalizing international criminal justice.[44] Being locally based, besides other advantages they possess, such internationalized (hybrid) tribunals can also have a positive impact on the legitimacy of the ICC and on the consequent political support for it.[45] Irrespective of this impact, the hybrid model could become the preferred option in view of the dualism of core crimes, these being crimes under domestic law and crimes under international law in so far as they assault the local society, this being the primary victim, and the international community at large, this being the secondary victim.[46] This dualism is reflected in the nature, structure and composition of hybrid tribunals. In fact they are often constituted as domestic courts,[47] although they can benefit, *inter alia*, from external funding and foreign personnel, including judges. Whereas the flexibility and customisability are the greatest assets of

---

[37] See, for example, severe criticisms of the IHT in Sect. 9.3.

[38] The ICC cannot prosecute crimes the alleged consummation of which precedes 1 July 2002.

[39] The ICC's jurisdiction is limited over the territories of State Parties.

[40] The ICC's jurisdiction is limited over natural persons who are nationals of ICC State Parties.

[41] The ICC can only prosecute crimes which fall within its subject-matter jurisdiction, these being the four core crimes.

[42] These establish an expiration period during which the competent authorities must prosecute the accused, failing which the criminal action and any potential criminal liability of the accused would be extinguished. It may be safely concluded that customary international law precludes the use of statutes of limitations over core crimes (Naqvi 2010, pp. 192–214). This seems to have been cast in stone when it was decided that 'prescription does not seem to be a principle of international criminal law and appears to be irreconcilable with the character of the offences… Their imprescriptibility is inherent in their nature. Therefore, we find that, as a matter of customary international law, crimes against humanity cannot prescribe and that this principle is directly applicable in the domestic legal order' [Tribunal of First Instance, Brussels (Investigating Magistrate Damien Vandermeersch), *re Pinochet*, 8 November 1998]. Moreover, signatories to the Convention on the non-Applicability of Statutory Limitations to War Crimes and Crimes Against Humanity (1968), must respect the prohibition. The non-applicability of statutory limitations, however, does not *ipso facto* translate itself into an absolute duty of the State to prosecute. In fact, this duty is not expressly stipulated within the above mentioned Convention. It may only be said to be implied, at best.

[43] Mackenzie et al. 2010, p. 245.

[44] Ibid.

[45] Jackson 2016, p. 1069.

[46] Hobbs 2017, p. 191.

[47] Hobbs 2017, p. 190.

such polymorphous tribunals,[48] some hybrid tribunals, such as the ECCC, are integrated in the domestic court structure as a result of which 'the enforcement of its arrest warrants closely resembles the enforcement of arrest warrants in ordinary domestic criminal proceedings'.[49] This gives hybrid tribunals a significant edge. Hybrid tribunals offer other benefits in so far as the 'penetration and development of the norms of international humanitarian law'[50] are concerned. Moreover, since they encapsulate the particular features of core crimes,[51] hybrid tribunals can be considered as a truly 'principled and justifiable response to core crimes';[52]

iv. there might be some place for *sui generis* trials, such as those conducted by the Camp Zeist Court which was specifically tailored to the needs of the *Lockerbie Pan Am bombing*. These could also take the form of specialized 'country-specific tribunals'. It seems that the Camp Zeist court will most likely remain an isolated experiment of international criminal justice, a fishing expedition which went quite wrong, both procedurally and substantively.[53] Although, in 2004, Diane Orentlicher suggested that 'the arrangement may have significant implications for contemporary issues relating to international jurisdiction',[54] this does not seem to have materialised yet. Its nature and set-up are absolutely extra-ordinary, as is the *aut dedere aut transferere* model it introduced, a model which had a very short life indeed and which is now history;

v. last but not least, there is increasingly more room for special courts. *Hissène Habré*, on 2 July 2013, was charged with crimes against humanity and war crimes before the EAC, a special Court created by agreement between Senegal and the AU on 22 August 2012.[55]

The proliferation of judicial panels and partnerships can be subsumed within the latter three mechanisms, *id est* iii-v. Together with the ICC [see (ii) here above], they comprehend and encompass the internationalized justice model which becomes necessary when domestic justice [see (i) here above] fails. In the meantime, international jurisdiction on the one hand and domestic jurisdiction on the

[48] Mackenzie et al. 2010, p. 245.

[49] Ryngaert 2012, p. 652.

[50] Dickinson 2015, p. 493.

[51] Mégret 2005, p. 725, cited in Hobbs 2017, p. 192, n. 115.

[52] Hobbs 2017, p. 193.

[53] Malta's leading newspaper has confirmed that the lead investigator had personally lobbied USA authorities to pay two Maltese witnesses in order to secure the conviction of *Abdelbaset Al Megrahi* for the purposes of the *Lockerbie* case {Appeal Court, High Court of Justiciary, Scotland, *Abdelbaset Ali Mohmed Al Megrahi v Her Majesty's Advocate*, 14 March 2002, C/104/01} [http://www.timesofmalta.com/articles/view/20131124/local/new-documents-on-lockerbie-tragedy-published-in.495996#.UpWO9cri4Ww. Accessed 21 September 2018].

[54] Orentlicher 2004, p. 226.

[55] See Sect. 13.2.

other hand continue to play their respective roles within the 'jurisdictional joint venture'. Somehow, when core crimes are committed, these constituting the action, a reaction is generally undertaken, this being constituted by the establishment of a court, an *ad hoc* tribunal and/or a hybrid tribunal, or a special court for the prosecution of such crimes. Colombia's Senate approved a constitutional reform to set up special war crimes courts[56] whereas both the UN Human Rights Commissioner and the Sri Lankan Panel of the Consultation Task Force on Reconciliation Mechanisms recommended the establishment of a hybrid court to investigate and prosecute core crimes committed in Sri Lanka with the involvement of international investigators and prosecutors.[57] If we can speak of a 'Lockerbie legacy',[58] this is only in so far as it shows that prosecutions are more likely to be undertaken than not, even in politically sensitive and volatile atmospheres. The reaction can actually be multiple, not only singular. In fact, Antonio Cassese, analysing the future of international criminal justice, postulated that this is most likely to be undertaken in the four following ways:

(a) domestic courts will make more use of universal criminal jurisdiction over core crimes;
(b) other States, such as the USA, will begin to grant judicial redress and compensation for crimes committed abroad;
(c) the ICC will gradually assert its authority and increasingly exercise its jurisdiction; and
(d) when resort to the ICC will prove to be difficult, *ad hoc* international criminal tribunals and hybrid, internationalized courts will be established.[59]

With *aut dedere aut judicare* at the apex thereof, the ensuing division of labour constitutes a commendable system of burden sharing. Jeremy Sarkin, with reference to the ICC, contends that 'while its role will be to prosecute those perpetrators who have committed the most egregious of crimes, its Statute makes it clear that the major role in regard to such prosecutions will be played by domestic States that are obliged to prosecute or extradite'.[60] The first port of call for the delivery of criminal justice shall be the territorial State, the *forum conveniens*. Yet, it has been shown that owing to the extraordinary dynamics of system criminality, this is often a dead letter. Other States which are not unwilling and/or not unable to investigate and prosecute would have to intervene on the pretext of a ground of jurisdiction which

[56] Staff Writers (2017) Colombia to Set up Special War Crimes Court, Terra Daily. http://www.terradaily.com/reports/Colombia_to_set_up_special_war_crimes_courts_999.html. Accessed 9 February 2018.

[57] Jurist Twenty 2017.

[58] See Sect. 13.4.

[59] Cassese 2009, p. 130.

[60] Sarkin 2005, pp. 105–106.

connects them to the core crime. In the absence of such connection, States enjoying custodial jurisdiction over an individual would have to submit the individual who is on its soil to a domestic prosecution by exercising universal jurisdiction. Unless it does so, it will have either to extradite him to a State better qualified to prosecute under the horizontal system of enforcement or undertake arrangements to have him prosecuted before a court or tribunal under the vertical system of enforcement. Whether the court or tribunal is the ICC, a hybrid tribunal or a special court is largely immaterial. Although one must acknowledge that, as the experience of certain judicial bodies has shown, 'the creation of legal institutions is not a panacea'[61] and may need to be supplemented by other non-legal initiatives,[62] what ultimately counts, from my standpoint, is that the individual will face criminal charges and that the victims will see their day in court, no matter how long this may take. Courts and tribunals are essential. They settle disputes, they make commitments credible, they produce legal knowledge and embody hope.[63] For this reason, in order to defeat impunity, one should not put all one's eggs in one basket. The above permutations and variables reveal that the decentralization of prosecutions, entailing the domestication of international criminal law, is certainly on the horizon. Similarly, other publicists have spoken about a domestication of international criminal law and have considered it as an unstoppable trend.[64] The domestication of international criminal law should be consolidated and strengthened, where this is possible. The way the framework of international law has enchantingly evolved since Bassiouni completed his doctoral thesis at George Washington University, the product of which was later published[65] and was used by myself to coin the title and research questions of my book, augurs well. Rather than remaining a duty *in status nascendi*, the duty to submit to prosecution could become, by virtue of uniform State practice, a fully-fledged rule of international law. This is what I desire in order to ensure that impunity, which has been categorically condemned by so many harsh words, be curbed by concrete, concerted and combined measures in the interest of the maintenance of international peace and security, this being one of the ultimate goals of international criminal law and a main deliverable of the sixteenth UN Sustainable Development Goal.[66] In the coming years and decades, it is hoped that we should be able to say that the 'international community's abysmal record in halting crimes against humanity and genocide prior to the death of tens of thousands, if not millions, of people',[67] belongs to the past.

---

[61] Roper and Barria 2006, p. 96.

[62] These include 'efforts in economic development and expanded education opportunities' (see Saxon 2012, p. 603).

[63] Kingsbury 2012, pp. 215–221.

[64] Bhuta and Nerlich 2009, p. 575.

[65] Bassiouni 1974, Preface, p. vii.

[66] The 2030 Agenda for Sustainable Development, adopted by all UN member States in 2015, urged countries to take concrete measures and action on seventeen fronts, the penultimate being 'peace, justice and strong institutions' [UN Department of Public Information 2016].

[67] Totten 2007, p. 17.

References

Akhavan P (2016) Complementarity Conundrums: The ICC Clock in Transitional Times. JICJ 14 (5):1043–1059

Ambos K, Stegmiller I (2012) Prosecuting International Crimes at the International Criminal Court: Is There a Coherent and Comprehensive Prosecution Strategy? CLSC 58(4):391–413

Attanasio J (1996) Rapporteur's Overview and Conclusions: Of Sovereignty, Globalization and Courts. Journal of International Law and Politics 28(1–2):1–34

Bassiouni MC (1974) International Extradition and World Public Order. OPI, AW Sijthoff, Leiden

Bassiouni MC (2008) The Duty to Prosecute and/or Extradite: *Aut Dedere Aut Judicare.* In: Bassiouni MC (ed) International Criminal Law: Multilateral and Bilateral Enforcement Mechanisms, Volume II, 3rd edn. MNP, Leiden/Boston, pp. 35–45

Bhuta NC, Nerlich V (2009) National Prosecution of International Crimes: Cases and Legislation. JICJ 7(3):575–576

Broomhall B (2003) International Criminal Justice and the International Criminal Court: Between Sovereignty and the Rule of Law. OUP, Oxford

Carter LE (2013) The Future of the International Criminal Court: Complementarity as a Strength or a Weakness. Washington University Global Studies Law Review 12(3):451–473

Cassese A (2009) The Rationale for International Criminal Justice. In: Cassese A (ed) The Oxford Companion to International Criminal Justice. OUP, Oxford, pp. 123–130

Chan K, Wouters J (2015) Constructing the International Criminal Court's Rule of Law Identity. In: De Baere G, Wouters J (eds) The Contribution of International and Supranational Courts to the Rule of Law. Leuven Global Governance Series. EE, Cheltenham, UK/Northampton, MA, USA, pp. 127–175

Convention on the Non-Applicability of Statutory Limitations to War Crimes and Crime Against Humanity (1968)

Dancy G (2017) Searching for Deterrence at the International Criminal Court. ICLR 17(4):625–655

Dickinson L (2015) The Promise of Hybrid Tribunals. AJIL (2003) 97:295. In: O'Connell ME, Scott RF, Roht-Arriaza N, Bradlow DD (eds) The International Legal System: Cases and Materials, 7th edn. FP, St. Paul, MN, USA, pp. 493–494

Garcia Ramirez S (2004) *Principio de Complementaridad en el Estatuto de Roma, Anuario Mexicano de Derecho Internacional*, Vol. 4. *Universidad Nacional Autónoma de México,* pp. 149–188

Gargiulo P (1999) The Controversial Relationship Between the International Criminal Court and the Security Council. In: Lattanzi F, Schabas WA (eds) Essays on the Rome Statute of the International Criminal Court, Vol. 1. *Il Sirente, Ripa Fagnano Alto, AQ, Italia,* pp. 67–103

Hastie B, Crepeau F (2015) Special Rules on Refugees. In: Clapham A, Gaeta P, Sassòli M (eds) van der Heijden I, Nuzov I, Grignon J, Hylton A, Haeck T (assistant eds) The 1949 Geneva Conventions: A Commentary. OUP, Oxford, pp. 1313–1323

Heinze A (2018) The 20th Anniversary of the Rome Statute: A Review Essay About the Nuremberg Forum 2018. CLF 1-27. https://doi.org/10.1007/s10609-018-9361-z. Accessed 24 December 2018

Hobbs H (2017) Towards a Principled Justification for the Mixed Composition of Hybrid International Criminal Tribunals. LJIL 30(1):177–197

Hovell D (2018) The Authority of Universal Jurisdiction. EJIL 29(2):427–456

ICC Statute (1998) Rome Statute of the International Criminal Court

Jackson M (2016) Regional Complementarity: The Rome Statute and Public International Law. JICJ 14(5):1061–1072

Jurist Twenty (2017) Documenting Law Since 1996, Supported by University of Pittsburgh School of Law. http://www.internationalcrimesdatabase.org/. Accessed 13 December 2018

Kaul H-P (2012) International Criminal Court. In: Wolfrum R (ed) The Max Planck Encyclopedia of Public International Law. Volume V. Published under the Auspices of the Max Planck Institute for Comparative Public Law and International Law. OUP, Oxford, pp. 667–688

Kingsbury B (2012) International Courts: Uneven Judicialisation in Global Order. In: Crawford J, Koskenniemi M (eds) Ranganathan S (assistant ed) The Cambridge Companion to International Law. CUP, Cambridge, pp. 203–227

Kirsch P (2008) The Role of the International Criminal Court in Enforcing International Criminal Law. In: Ellis MS, Goldstone J (eds) The International Criminal Court: Challenges to Achieving Justice and Accountability in the 21st Century. International Debate Education Association, NY, Amsterdam, Brussels, pp. 285–293

Kleffner JK (2008) Complementarity in the Rome Statute and National Criminal Jurisdictions. International Courts and Tribunals Series, OUP, Oxford

Krings BL (2012) The Principles of Complementarity and Universal Jurisdiction in International Criminal Law: Antagonists or Perfect Match? GJIL 4(3):737–763

Mackenzie R, Romano C, Shany Y, Sands P (2010) The Manual on International Courts and Tribunals, 2nd edn. International Courts and Tribunals, OUP, Oxford

Mahnad PL (2018) An Independent Mechanism for Myanmar: A Turning Point in the Pursuit of Accountability for International Crimes. EJIL: Talk! https://www.ejiltalk.org/a-turning-point-in-the-pursuit-of-accountability-for-international-crimes/. Accessed 13 December 2018

Margariti S (2017) Defining International Terrorism: Between State Sovereignty and Cosmopolitanism. International Criminal Justice Series, Volume 15. Asser Press, The Hague

Mégret F (2005) In Defence of Hybridity: Towards a Representational Theory of International Criminal Justice. CILJ 38(3):725–751

Melandri M (2009) The Relationship Between State Sovereignty and the Enforcement of International Criminal Law under the Rome Statute (1998): A Complex Interplay. ICLR 9 (3):531–545

Naqvi YQ (2010) Impediments to Exercising Jurisdiction Over International Crimes. Asser Press, The Hague

Orentlicher DF (2004) The Future of Universal Jurisdiction in the New Architecture of Transnational Justice. In: Macedo S (ed) Universal Jurisdiction: National Courts and the Prosecution of Serious Crimes under International Law. University of Pennsylvania Press, Philadelphia, pp. 214–239

OTP (2013) Policy Paper on Preliminary Examinations. ICC-OTP, November 2013. https://www.icc-cpi.int/iccdocs/otp/otp-policy_paper_preliminary_examinations_2013-eng.pdf. Accessed 10 March 2016

Rastan R (2010) Complementarity: Contest or Collaboration? In: Bergsmo M (ed.) Complementarity and the Exercise of Universal Jurisdiction for Core International Crimes. Forum for International Criminal and Humanitarian law, Publication Series No. 7, TOAEP and PRI, Oslo, pp. 83–132

Reydams L (2003) Universal Jurisdiction: International and Municipal Legal Perspectives. Oxford Monographs in International Law, OUP, Oxford

Roper SD, Barria LA (2006) Designing Criminal Tribunals: Sovereignty and International Concerns in the Protection of Human Rights. Ashgate Aldershot, Hampshire, UK/Burlington, VT, USA

Ryngaert C (2012) Arrest and Detention. In: Reydams L, Wouters J, Ryngaert C (eds) International Prosecutors. OUP, Oxford, pp. 647–699

Sarkin J (2005) Justice for Serious International Crimes, reviewing Lattmer M, Sands S (eds) (2003) Justice for Crimes Against Humanity. HP, Oxford. CLF 16(1):103–106

Saxon D (2012) The Prosecution of Human Rights Abuses. In: Cushman T (ed) Handbook of Human Rights. Routledge, T & F, London/NY, pp. 598–609

Sayapin S (2016) A "Hybrid" Tribunal for Daesh? EJIL: Talk! http://www.ejiltalk.org/a-hybrid-tribunal-for-daesh/. Accessed 29 May 2018

Siebert-Fohr A (2009) Prosecuting Serious Human Rights Violations. OUP, Oxford

Tofan C, van der Wolf R (2011) (eds) The Long and Winding Road to… Rome: A Brief History of the ICC. Wolf Legal Publishers, Nijmegen

Totten S (2007) The Prevention and Intervention of Genocide: An Annotated Bibliography. Routledge, T & F, NY/London

Triffterer O (2008) Preambles, margins 16-17. In: Triffterer O (ed) Commentary on the Rome Statute of the International Criminal Court – Observers' Notes, Article by Article. Nomos, Baden-Baden, pp. 1–11

Tutuianu S (2013) Towards Global Justice: Sovereignty in an Interdependent World. Asser Press, The Hague

UN Department of Public Information (2016) Sustainable Development Goals, Knowledge Platform. https://sustainabledevelopment.un.org/sdgs. Accessed 13 July 2018

UNGA (2016) Resolution 71/248 (2016), UN Doc. A/RES/71/248

UNSC (2017) Resolution 2379 (2017), UN Doc. S/RES/2379

Usacka A (2016) Constitutionalism and Human Rights at the International Criminal Court. In: Scheinin M, Krunke H, Aksenova M (eds) Judges as Guardians of Constitutionalism and Human Rights. EE, Cheltenham, UK/Northampton, MA, USA, pp. 281–305

van der Have N (2018) The Prevention of Gross Human Rights Violations under International Human Rights Law. Asser Press, The Hague

van der Wilt H (2012) On the Hierarchy Between Extradition and Human Rights. In: de Wet E, Vidmar J (eds) Hierarchy in International Law: The Place of Human Rights. OUP, Oxford, pp. 148–175

Williams S (2012) Hybrid and Internationalised Criminal Tribunal: Selected Jurisdictional Issues. HP, Bloomsbury, London

Table of Cases

Cases in Chapter 1

ICC Trial Chamber V(B), *Prosecutor v Uhuru Muigai Kenyatta, Decision on the Withdrawal of Charges Against Mr. Kenyatta*, 13 March 2015, Case No. ICC-01/09-02/11
ICC Trial Chamber V(B), *Prosecutor v Uhuru Muigai Kenyatta, Notice of Withdrawal of the Charges Against Uhuru Muigai Kenyatta*, 5 December 2014, Case No. ICC-01/09-02/11

Cases in Chapter 2

High Court (Guateng Division, Pretoria), South Africa, *Matter between Democratic Alliance and Minister of International Relations and Cooperation et al.*, 22 February 2017, Case No. 83145/2016
ICC Pre-Trial Chamber I, *Situation in the DRC, Decision on the Prosecutor's Application for Warrants of Arrest under Article 58*, 10 February 2006, Case No. ICC-01/04-01/07
ICTR Appeals Chamber, *Jean-Bosco Barayagwiza v The Prosecutor, Decision on the Prosecutor's Request for Review or Reconsideration*, 31 March 2000, Case No. ICTR-97-19AR72
ICTY Appeals Chamber, *Prosecutor v Tihomir Blaškić, Judgment on the Request of the Republic of Croatia for Review of the Decision of the Trial Chamber II of 18 July 1997*, 29 October 1997, Case No. IT-95-14-AR 108*bis*

Cases in Chapter 3

ECtHR Grand Chamber, *Hilal Abdul Razzaq Al-Jedda v UK*, 7 July 2011, Application No. 27021/08

C. Soler, *The Global Prosecution of Core Crimes under International Law*,
https://doi.org/10.1007/978-94-6265-335-1

ECtHR Grand Chamber, *Mazin Jum'Aa Gatteh Al-Skeini and Others v UK*, 7 July 2011, Application No. 55721/07

ECtHR Grand Chamber, *Sabah Jaloud v The Netherlands*, 20 November 2014, Application No. 47708/08

SCSL Appeals Chamber, *Prosecutor v Charles Ghankay Taylor, Decision on Immunity from Jurisdiction*, 31 May 2004, Case No. SCSL-2003-01-I

Cases in Chapter 4

ICC Pre-Trial Chamber II, Situation in the Republic of Kenya, *Decision Pursuant to Article 15 of the Rome Statute on the Authorization of an Investigation into the Situation in the Republic of Kenya*, Dissenting Opinion of Judge Hans-Peter Kaul, 31 March 2010, Case No. ICC-01/09

ICTY Trial Chamber, *Prosecutor v Duško Tadić*, 7 May 1997, Case No. IT-94-1-ICTY

Cases in Chapter 5

Buenos Aires Federal Court, *Simón, Julio, Del Cerro, Juan Antonio, sustracción de menores de 10 años*, Decision of Judge Gabriel Cavallo, 6 March 2001, Case No. 8686/2002000/B

Constitutional Court, South Africa, *National Commission of the South African Police Service and Another v Southern African Human Rights Litigation Centre and Another* (*Zimbabwe Torture Docket Case*), 30 October 2014, [CCT 02/14] ZACC 30

Hoge Raad [Supreme Court], The Netherlands, *Stichting Mothers of Srebrenica v The Netherlands and United Nations*, 13 April 2012, Case No. 10/04437

ICC Appeals Chamber, *Situation in the DRC, Prosecutor v Germain Katanga and Mathieu Ngudjolo Chui, Judgment on the Appeal of Mr. Germain Katanga against the Oral Decision of Trial Chamber II of 12 June 2009 on the Admissibility of the Case*, 25 September 2009, Case No. ICC-01/04-01/07 OA8

ICC Pre-Trial Chamber I, *Prosecutor v Omar Hassan Ahmad Al Bashir, Decision on the Prosecution's Application for a Warrant of Arrest Against Omar Hassan Ahmad Al Bashir*, 4 March 2009, Case No. ICC-02/05-01/09

ICJ, *Application of the Convention on the Prevention and Punishment of the Crime of Genocide* (*BiH v Serbia and Montenegro*), 26 February 2007, ICJ Reports 2007

ICJ, *Questions Relating to the Obligation to Extradite or Prosecute (Belgium v Senegal)*, 20 July 2012, ICJ Rep. 2012, p. 422

ICTY Appeals Chamber, Prosecutor v *Duško Tadić*, 15 July 1999, Case No. IT-94-1-A

STL Appeals Chamber, *Interlocutory Decision on the Applicable Law*, 16 February 2011, Case No. STL-11-01/1

Supreme Court, Canada, *Regina v Imre Finta*, 24 March 1994, Case No. 23023, 23097

The Hague Court of Appeal, *Hasan Nuhanović v The Netherlands*, 5 July 2011, Case No. 200.020.174/01

Cases in Chapter 6

ICC Appeals Chamber, Situation in the CAR, *Prosecutor v Jean-Pierre Bemba Gombo, Judgment on the Appeal of Mr. Jean-Pierre Bemba Gombo against Trial Chamber III's 'Judgment Pursuant to Article 74 of the Statute'*, 8 June 2018, Case No. ICC-01/05-01/08A

ICC Appeals Chamber, Situation in the CAR, *Prosecutor v Jean-Pierre Bemba Gombo, Judgment on the Appeal of Mr. Jean-Pierre Bemba Gombo against Trial Chamber III's 'Judgment Pursuant to Article 74 of the Statute'*, 8 June 2018, Separate Opinion of Judge Christine van den Wyngaert and Judge Howard Morrison, Case No. ICC-01/05-01/08A

ICC Pre-Trial Chamber I, *Prosecutor v Germain Katanga and Mathieu Ngudjolo Chui, Decision on the Confirmation of Charges*, 30 September 2008, Case No. ICC-01/04-01/07

ICC Pre-Trial Chamber I, Prosecutor v *Omar Hassan Ahmad Al Bashir, Decision on the Prosecution's Application for a Warrant of Arrest Against Omar Hassan Ahmad Al Bashir*, 4 March 2009, Case No. ICC-02/05-01/09

ICC Pre-Trial Chamber II, *Decision on the Prosecutor's Application for Summons to Appear for William Samoei Ruto, Henry Kiprono Kosgey and Joshua Arap Sang in Prosecutor v Ruto, Kosgey and Sang*, Dissenting Opinion of Judge Hans-Peter Kaul, 15 March 2011, Case No. ICC-01/09-01/11-2

ICC Pre-Trial Chamber II, Situation in the Republic of Kenya, *Decision Pursuant to Article 15 of the Rome Statute on the Authorization of an Investigation into the Situation in the Republic of Kenya*, Dissenting Opinion of Judge Hans-Peter Kaul, 31 March 2010, Case No. ICC-01/09

ICC Trial Chamber III, Situation in the CAR, *Prosecutor v Jean-Pierre Bemba Gombo, Judgment Pursuant to Article 74 of the Statute*, 21 March 2016, Case No. ICC-01/05-01/08

ICC, Pre-Trial Chamber II, Situation in the Republic of Kenya, *Decision Pursuant to Article 15 of the Rome Statute on the Authorization of an Investigation into the Situation in the Republic of Kenya*, 31 March 2010, Case No. ICC-01/09

ICC, Pre-Trial Chamber II, *Prosecutor v Jean-Pierre Bemba Gombo, Decision Pursuant to Article 61(7)(a) and (b) of the Rome Statute on the Charges of the Prosecutor Against Jean-Pierre Bemba Gombo*, 15 June 2009, Case No. ICC-01/05-01/08

ICJ, *Case Concerning Armed Activities on the Territory of Congo (DRC v Rwanda)*, 3 February 2006, [2006] ICJ Rep. 2006, General List No. 126

ICTR Trial Chamber, *Prosecutor v Kayishema and Ruzindana*, 21 May 1999, Case No. ICTR-95-1-T

ICTY Appeals Chamber, *Prosecutor v Duško Tadić, Decision on the Defence Motion for Interlocutory Appeal on Jurisdiction*, 2 October 1995, Case No. IT-94-1

ICTY Appeals Chamber, *Prosecutor v Goran Jelisić*, 5 July 2001, Case No. IT-95-10-A

ICTY Trial Chamber I, Section A, *Prosecutor v Vidoje Blagojević and Dragan Jokić*, 17 January 2005, Case No. IT-02-60-T

ICTY Trial Chamber II, *Prosecutor v Fatmir Limaj et al.*, 30 November 2005, Case No. IT-03-66-T

ICTY Trial Chamber, *Prosecutor v Goran Jelisić*, 14 December 1999, Case No. IT-95-10-T

ICTY Trial Chamber, *Prosecutor v Radislav Krstić*, 2 August 2001, Case No. IT-98-33-T

ICTY, *Prosecutor v Radovan Karadžić and Ratko Mladić, Consideration of the Indictment Within the Framework of Rule 61 of the Rules of Procedure and Evidence*, 11 July 1996, Case Nos. IT-95-5-R61 and IT-95-18-R61

International Military Tribunal, *The Trial of the German Major War Criminals, Proceedings of the International Military Tribunal Sitting at Nuremberg, Germany*, Part 22, 22 August 1946 to 1 October 1946

Cases in Chapter 7

Hoge Raad [Supreme Court], The Netherlands, *Nuhanović v the Netherlands*, 6 September 2013, Case No. 12/03324

ICJ, *Application of the Convention on the Prevention and Punishment of the Crime of Genocide (Croatia v Serbia)*, 3 February 2015, [2015] ICJ Rep. 2015, p. 3

ICJ, *Application of the Convention on the Prevention and Punishment of the Crime of Genocide (BiH v Serbia and Montenegro)*, 26 February 2007, ICJ Rep. 2007, p. 43

ICJ, *United States Diplomatic and Consular Staff in Tehran (USA v Iran) (Iranian Hostages Case)*, 24 May 1980, [1980] ICJ Rep. 3

ICTY Appeals Chamber, *Prosecutor v Miroslav Kvočka et al., Decision on Interlocutory Appeal by the Accused Zoran Žigić Against the Decision of the Trial Chamber I dated 5 December 2000*, 25 May 2001, Case No. IT-98-30/1

ICTY Trial Chamber I, *Prosecutor v Miroslav Kvočka et al., Decision on the Defence Motion Regarding Concurrent Procedures Before International Criminal Tribunal for the Former Yugoslavia and International Court of Justice on the Same Questions*, 5 December 2000, Case No. IT-98-30/1

ICTY Trial Chamber III, *Prosecutor v Slobodan Milošević, Decision on Preliminary Motions*, 8 November 2001, Case No. IT-02-54

ICTY Trial Chamber, *Prosecutor v Anto Furundžija*, 10 December 1998, Case No. IT-95-17/1-T

Cases in Chapter 8

ICC Trial Chamber II, *Situation in The DRC, Prosecutor v Germain Katanga, Judgment Pursuant to Article 74 of the Statute*, Minority Opinion of Judge Christine van den Wyngaert, Anx. I, 7 March 2014, Case No. ICC-01/04-01/07

ICTY Appeals Chamber, *Prosecutor v Duško Tadić, Decision on the Defence Motion for Interlocutory Appeal on Jurisdiction*, 2 October 1995, Case No. IT-94-1

ICTY Trial Chamber II, *Prosecutor v Fatmir Limaj et al.*, 30 November 2005, Case No. IT-03-66-T

ICTY Trial Chamber II, *Prosecutor v Ljube Boškoski & Johan Tarčulovski*, 10 July 2008, Case No. IT-04-82-T

ICTY Trial Chamber, *Prosecutor v Dragoljub Kunarac et al.*, 22 February 2001, Case Nos. IT-96-23-T and IT-96-23/1-T

USA Court of Appeals, 11th Circuit, *USA v Esteban Marino-Garcia*, 9 July 1982, 679 F.2d 1373

USA District Court for the Southern District of Florida, *USA v Cesar James-Robinson*, 11 June 1981, 515 F. Supp. 1340 (SD Fla. 1981)

Cases in Chapter 9

ECtHR Fourth Section, *Mladen Naletilić v Croatia, Decision as to the Admissibility of the Application*, 4 May 2000, Application No. 51891/99

German Federal Constitutional Court, *Solange II*, Order, 22 October 1986, 2 BvR 197/83, *BVerfGE* 73, 339 (387)

ICC Pre-Trial Chamber I, *Situation in the Republic of Côte d'Ivoire, Prosecutor v Simone Gbagbo, Decision on Côte d'Ivoire's challenge to the admissibility of the case against Simone Gbagbo*, 11 December 2014, Case No. ICC-02/11-01/12

ICTR Appeals Chamber, *Jean Bosco Barayagwiza v Prosecutor, Decision on the Prosecutor's Request for Review or Reconsideration*, Declaration by Judge Rafael Nieto-Navia, 31 March 2000, Case No. ICTR-97-19AR72

ICTR Appeals Chamber, *Jean Bosco Barayagwiza v Prosecutor, Decision on the Prosecutor's Request for Review or Reconsideration*, Separate Opinion of Judge Shahabuddeen, 31 March 2000, Case No. ICTR-97-19AR72

ICTR Trial Chamber I, *Prosecutor v Bernard Ntuyahaga, Decision on the Prosecutor's Motion to Withdraw the Indictment*, 18 March 1999, Case No. ICTR-98-40-T

ICTY Appeals Chamber, *Prosecutor v Tihomir Blaškić, Judgment on the Request of the Republic of Croatia for Review of the Decision of the Trial Chamber II of 18 July 1997*, 29 October 1997, Case No. IT-95-14-AR 108*bis*

ICTY Trial Chamber II, *Prosecutor v Dragan Nikolić, Decision on Defence Motion Challenging the Exercise of Jurisdiction by the Tribunal*, 9 October 2002, Case No. IT-94-2-PT

SCSL Appeals Chamber Judgment, *Prosecutor v Charles Ghankay Taylor, Decision on Immunity from Jurisdiction*, 31 May 2004, Case No. SCSL-2003-01-I

Cases in Chapter 10

District Court, The Hague, *Dragan Opacić v the Netherlands*, 30 May 1997, KG 97/742
ECFI, Second Chamber (Extended Composition) *Ahmed Ali Yusuf and Al Barkakaat International Foundation v Council of the European Union and Commission of the European Communities* [2005], 21 September 2005, T-306/01
ECFI, Second Chamber (Extended Composition) *Yasin Abdullah Kadi v Council of the European Union and Commission of the European Communities* [2005], 21 September 2005, T-315/01
ECtHR Former Third Division, *Vasiliy Kononov v Latvia*, 24 July 2008, Application No. 36376/04
Federal Supreme Court of Switzerland, Appeal Judgment, *Rukundo v Federal Office of Justice*, 3 September 2001, Case Nos. 1A.129/2001 and 1A.130/2001
ICC Appeals Chamber, *Situation in the DRC, Prosecutor v Germain Katanga and Mathieu Ngudjolo Chu i, Judgment on the Appeal of Mr. Germain Katanga against the Oral Decision of Trial Chamber II of 12 June 2009 on the Admissibility of the Case*, 25 September 2009, Case No. ICC-01/04-01/07 OA8
ICC Appeals Chamber, *Situation in the DRC, Prosecutor v Thomas Lubanga Dyilo, Judgment on the Appeal of the Prosecutor Against the Decision of Trial Chamber I Entitled 'Decision on the Consequences of Non-Disclosure of Exculpatory Materials Covered by Article 54(3)(e) Agreements and the Application to Stay the Prosecution of the Accused, Together with Certain Other Issues Raised at the Status Conference on 10 June 2008'*, 21 October 2008, Case No. ICC-01/04-01/06 OA 13
ICC Appeals Chamber, *Situation in the Republic of Kenya, Prosecutor v Uhuru Muigai Kenyatta, Judgment on the Prosecutor's Appeal Against Trial Chamber's V (B)'s 'Decision on Prosecution's Application for a Finding of Non-Compliance under Article 87(7) of the Statute'*, 19 August 2015, Case No. ICC-01/09-02/11 OA 5
ICC Pre-Trial Chamber I, *Prosecutor v Saif Al-Islam Gaddafi and Abdullah Al-Senuss i, Decision on the Postponement of the Execution of the Request to Surrender of Saif Al-Islam Gaddafi Pursuant to Article 95 of the Rome Statute*, 1 June 2012, Case No. ICC-01/11-01/11
ICC Pre-Trial Chamber I, *Situation in Darfur, Sudan, Decision on the Prosecution's Application for a Warrant of Arrest Against Omar Hassan Al Bashi*r, 4 March 2009, Case No. ICC-02/05-01/09
ICC Pre-Trial Chamber I, *Situation in Darfur, Sudan, Prosecutor v Ahmad Muhammad Harun (Ahmad Harun) and Ali Muhammad Ali Abd-Al Rahman (Ali Kushayb), Decision on the Prosecution Application under Article 58(7) of the Statute*, 27 April 2007, Case No. ICC-02/05-01/07

ICC Pre-Trial Chamber I, *Situation in the DRC, Decision on the Applications for Participation in the Proceedings of VPRS 1, VPRS 2, VPRS 3, VPRS 4, VPRS 5 and VPRS 6*, 17 January 2006, Case No. ICC-01/04

ICC Pre-Trial Chamber I, *Situation in the DRC, Decision to Convene a Status Conference*, 17 February 2005, Case No. ICC-01/04

ICC Pre-Trial Chamber I, *Situation in the DRC, Prosecutor v Thomas Lubanga Dyilo, Decision on the Prosecutor's Application for a Warrant of Arrest under Article 58*, 10 February 2006, Case No. ICC-01/04-01/06

ICC Pre-Trial Chamber II, *Situation in Darfur, Sudan, Prosecutor v Omar Hassan Ahmad Al Bashir, Decision on the Cooperation of the DRC Regarding Omar Al Bashir's Arrest and Surrender to the Court*, 9 April 2014, Case No. ICC-02/05-01/09

ICC Pre-Trial Chamber II, *Situation in Darfur, Sudan, Prosecutor v Omar Hassan Ahmad Al Bashir, Decision under Article 87(7) of the Rome Statute on the Non-compliance by South Africa with the Request by the Court for the Arrest and Surrender of Omar Al Bashir*, 6 July 2017, Case No. ICC-02/05-01/09

ICC Pre-Trial Chamber II, *Situation in Darfur, Sudan, Prosecutor v Omar Hassan Ahmad Al Bashir, Decision under Article 87(7) of the Rome Statute on the non-compliance by Jordan with the Request by the Court for the Arrest and Surrender of Omar Al-Bashir*, 11 December 2017, Case No. ICC-02/05-01/09

ICC Pre-Trial Chamber II, *Situation in Uganda, Decision on Prosecutor's Application for Leave to Appeal in Part Pre-Trial Chamber II's Decision on the Prosecutor's Applications for Warrants under Article 58, Unsealed Pursuant to Decision ICC-02/04-01/05-52 dated 13 October 2005, Situation in Uganda*, 19 August 2005, Case No. ICC-02/04-01/05-20-US-Exp

ICC Pre-Trial Chamber II, *Situation in Uganda, Prosecutor v Joseph Kony, Vincent Otti, Okot Odhiambo, Dominic Ongwen, Decision on the Admissibility of the Case under Article 19(1) of the Statute*, 10 March 2009, Case No. ICC-02/04-01/05

ICJ, Advisory Opinion, *Legal Consequences for States of the Continued Presence of South Africa in Namibia Notwithstanding Security Council Resolution 276 (1970) (Namibia case)*, 21 June 1971, 1971 ICJ 16

ICJ, *Application of the Convention on the Prevention and Punishment of the Crime of Genocide (BiH v Serbia and Montenegro)*, 26 February 2007, ICJ Rep. 2007, p. 43

ICJ, *Nuclear Tests Case (Australia v France)*, 20 December 1974, ICJ Rep 1974, p. 253

ICJ, *Questions of Interpretation and Application of the 1971 Montreal Convention Arising from the Aerial Incident at Lockerbie (Libyan Arab Jamahiriya v UK), Provisional Measures*, Order of 14 April 1992, ICJ Rep. 1992, p. 114

ICTR, Trial Chamber II, *Prosecutor v Joseph Kanyabashi, Decision on the Defence Motion on Jurisdiction*, 18 June 1997, Case No. ICTR-96-15-T

ICTY Appeals Chamber, *Prosecutor v Duško Tadić, Decision on the Defence Motion for Interlocutory Appeal on Jurisdiction*, 2 October 1995, Case No. IT-94-1

Cases in Chapter 11

ACHPR, *Tanganyika Law Society et al. v United Republic of Tanzania*, 14 June 2013, Application No. 009/2011

Court of Assize, Tripoli, Libya, *Prosecutor v Saif Al-Islam Gaddafi and Abdullah Al-Senussi et al., Death Sentence*, 28 July 2015, 630/2012

Divisional Court, UK, *Smakowski and Zestfair Ltd v Westminster City Council*, (1990), 154 J.P. 345 DC, Crim. L.R. 1990 Jun 419-421

ECCC, *Prosecutor v. Kaing Guek Eav alias Duch*, 3 February 2012, 001/18-07-2007-ECCC/SC

ECtHR Former Second Section, *İsak Tepe v Turkey*, 9 May 2003, Application No. 27244/95

ECtHR Fourth Section, *Borislav Yevgenyevich Poltoratskiy v Ukraine*, 29 April 2003, Application No. 38812/97

ECtHR Grand Chamber, *Anelia Kunchova Nachova et al. v Bulgaria*, 6 July 2005, Application Nos. 43577/98 and 43579/98

ECtHR Grand Chamber, *McCann and Others v UK*, 27 September 1995, Application No. 18984/91

ECtHR Third Section, *Franz Fischer v Austria*, 29 May 2001, Application No. 37950/97

ECtHR Third Section, *Ponsetti and Chesnel v France*, 14 September 1999, Application Nos. 36855/97 and 41731/98

ECtHR, *Maria Celeste Vieira Veloso de Oliveira v Switzerland*, 30 July 1998, Application No. 84/1997/868/1080

ECtHR, *Sergey Kuznetsov v Ukraine*, 29 April 2003, Application No. 39042/97

HoL, *Regina (on the application of Al-Jedda) (FC) (Appellant) v Secretary of State for Defence (Respondent)*, 12 December 2007, 2007 UKHL 58

HoL, *Regina v Bow Street Stipendiary Magistrate and Others, Ex Parte Pinochet (Spanish request for extradition* case*)*, 24 March 1999, (No. 3) [1999], 2 WLR 827

HoL, *Regina v Horseferry Road Magistrates' Court ex parte Bennett*, 24 June 1993 [1993], 3 WLR 90

HoL, *Stockdale v Hansard*, 15 June 1839, vol. 48 cc301/6

HRC, *A.R.J. v Australia*, 28 July 1997, Communication No. 692/1996

IACtHR, *La Cantuta v Perú* (Merits, Reparations and Costs), 29 November 2006, Series C, No. 162

IACtHR, *Maritza Urrutia v Guatemala*, 27 November 2003, Series C, No. 103

IACtHR, *Paniagua Morales et al. v Guatemala* (*Panel Blanca* {The case of the *White Van*}), 8 March 1998, Series C, No. 37

IACtHR, *Velásquez-Rodríguez v Honduras*, 29 July 1988, Series C, No. 4

ICC Appeals Chamber, *Situation in the Republic of Kenya, Prosecutor v Francis Kirimi Muthaura, Uhuru Muigai Kenyatta and Mohammed Hussein Ali, Judgment on the Appeal of the Republic of Kenya Against the Decision of Pre-Trial Chamber II of 30 May 2011 entitled 'Decision on the Application by the Government of Kenya Challenging the Admissibility of the Case Pursuant to Article 19(2)(b) of the Statute'*, 30 August 2011, Case No. ICC-01/09-02/11 OA

ICC Appeals Chamber, *Situation in Darfur, Sudan, The Hashemite Kingdom of Jordan's Appeal Against the 'Decision under Article 87(7) of the Rome Statute on the Non-Compliance by Jordan with the Request by the Court for the Arrest and Surrender [of] Omar Al-Bashir'*, 12 March 2018, Case No. ICC-02/05-01/09

ICC Appeals Chamber, *Situation in Libya, Judgment on the Appeal of Abdullah Al-Senussi against the decision of Pre-Trial Chamber I of 11 October 2013 entitled 'Decision on the Admissibility of the Case against Abdullah Al-Senussi, Gaddafi and Al-Senussi'*, 24 July 2014, Case No. ICC-01/11-01 OA6

ICC Appeals Chamber, Situation in Libya, *Prosecutor v Saif Al-Islam Gaddafi and Abdullah Al-Senussi, Judgment on the Appeal of Libya Against the Decision of Pre-Trial Chamber I of 31 May 2013 entitled 'Decision on the Admissibility of the Case Against Saif Al-Islam Gaddafi'*, 21 May 2014, Case No. ICC-01/11-01/11 OA4

ICC Appeals Chamber, *Situation in Libya, Prosecutor v Saif Al-Islam Gaddafi and Abdullah Al-Senussi, Decision on the Request for Suspensive Effect and Related Issues*, 18 July 2013, Case No. ICC-01/11-01/11

ICC Appeals Chamber, *Situation in the CAR, Prosecutor v Jean-Pierre Bemba Gombo, Corrigendum to Judgment on the appeal of Mr. Jean Pierre Bemba Gombo Against the Decision of Trial Chamber III of 24 June 2010 entitled 'Decision on the Admissibility and Abuse of Process Challenges'*, 19 October 2010, Case No. ICC-01/05-01/08 OA 3

ICC Appeals Chamber, *Situation in the DRC, Judgment on the Prosecutor's Appeal Against the Decision of the Pre-Trial Chamber I entitled 'Decision on the Prosecutor's Application for Warrants of Arrest under Article 58'*, 13 July 2006, Case No. ICC-01/04

ICC Appeals Chamber, Situation in the DRC in the case of the *Prosecutor v Germain Katanga and Mathieu Ngudjolo Chui*, Judgment on the Appeal of Mr. Katanga Against the Decision of the Trial Chamber II of 20 November 2009 entitled 'Decision on the Motion of the Defence for Germain Katanga for a Declaration on Unlawful Detention and Stay of Proceedings', Dissenting Opinion of Judge Erkki Kourula and Judge Ekaterina Trendafilova, 12 July 2010, Case No. ICC-01/04-01/07 OA 10

ICC Appeals Chamber, *Situation in the DRC, Prosecutor v Germain Katanga and Mathieu Ngudjolo Chui, Judgment on the Appeal of Mr. Germain Katanga Against the Oral Decision of Trial Chamber II of 12 June 2009 on the Admissibility of the Case*, 25 September 2009, Case No. ICC-01/04-01/07 OA8

ICC Appeals Chamber, *Situation in the DRC, Prosecutor v Thomas Lubanga Dyilo, Judgment on the Appeal of Mr. Thomas Lubanga Dyilo Against the Decision on the Defence Challenge to the Jurisdiction of the Court Pursuant to Article 19(2) of the Statute of 3 October 2006*, 14 December 2006, Case No. ICC-01/04-01/06(OA4)

ICC Appeals Chamber, *Situation in the Republic of Kenya, Prosecutor v Francis Kirimi Muthaura, Uhuru Muigai Kenyatta and Mohammed Hussein Ali, Judgment on the Appeal of the Republic of Kenya Against the Decision of Pre-Trial Chamber II of 30 May 2011 entitled 'Decision on the Application by the*

Government of Kenya Challenging the Admissibility of the case Pursuant to Article 19(2)(b) of the Statute', 30 August 2011, Case No. ICC-01/09-02/11 OA

ICC Pre-Trial Chamber I, *Prosecutor v Ahmad Muhammad Harun et al.*, Decision on the Prosecution Application under Article 58(7) of the Statute, 27 April 2007, Case No. ICC-02/05-01/07

ICC Pre-Trial Chamber I, *Prosecutor v Bosco Ntanganda, Decision on the Prosecutor's Application for Warrants of Arrest under Article 58*, 10 February 2006, Case No. ICC-0I/04-02/06-20-Anx2

ICC Pre-Trial Chamber I, *Prosecutor v Omar Hassan Ahmad Al Bashir, Decision Pursuant to Article 87(7) of the Rome Statute on the Failure by the Republic of Malawi to Comply with the Cooperation Requests Issued by the Court with Respect to the Arrest and Surrender of Omar Hassan Ahmad Al Bashir (Malawi* case*)*, 12 December 2011, Case No. ICC-02/05-01/09

ICC Pre-Trial Chamber I, *Prosecutor v Saif Al-Islam Gaddafi and Abdullah Al-Senussi*, Decision on the OPCD Requests in relation to the Hearing on the Admissibility of the Case, 2 October 2012, Case No. ICC-01/11-01/11

ICC Pre-Trial Chamber I, *Prosecutor v Simone Gbagbo, Decision on Côte d'Ivoire Challenge to the Admissibility of the Case Against Simone Gbagbo*, 11 December 2014, Case No. ICC-02/11-01/12

ICC Pre-Trial Chamber I, *Situation in Libya, Prosecutor v Saif Al-Islam Gaddafi and Abdullah Al-Senussi, Decision on the Admissibility of the Case Against Saif Al-Islam Gaddafi*, 31 May 2013, Case No. ICC-01/11-01/11

ICC Pre-Trial Chamber I, *Situation in Libya, Prosecutor v Saif Al-Islam Gaddafi and Abdullah Al-Senussi, Public Redacted Version of the Corrigendum to the 'Defence Response to the Application on Behalf of the Government of Libya Pursuant to Article 19 of the ICC Statute'*, 31 July 2012, Case No. ICC-01/11-01/11

ICC Pre-Trial Chamber I, *Situation in Libya, Prosecutor v Saif Al-Islam Gaddafi and Abdullah Al-Senussi, Decision Requesting Further Submissions on Issues Related to the Admissibility of the Case Against Saif Al-Islam Gaddafi*, 7 December 2012, Case No. ICC-01/11-01/11

ICC Pre-Trial Chamber I, *Situation in Libya, Prosecutor v Saif Al-Islam Gaddafi and Abdullah Al-Senussi, Decision on the Admissibility of the Case Against Abdullah Al-Senussi*, 11 October 2013, Case No. ICC-01/11-01/11

ICC Pre-Trial Chamber I, *Situation in Libya, Prosecutor v Saif Al-Islam Gaddafi and Abdullah Al-Senussi, Decision on the Postponement of the Execution of the Request for Surrender of Saif Al-Islam Pursuant to Article 95 of the Rome Statute*, 1 June 2012, Case No. ICC-01/11-01/11

ICC Pre-Trial Chamber I, *Situation in Libya, Prosecutor v Saif Al-Islam Gaddafi and Abdullah Al-Senussi, Public Redacted Version of the Response to the Libyan Government's Further Submissions on Issues Related to Admissibility of the Case Against Saif Al-Islam Gaddafi*, 18 February 2013, Case No. ICC-01/11-01/11

ICC Pre-Trial Chamber I, *Situation in the DRC, Decision of the Prosecutor's Application for Warrants of Arrest under Article 58*, 10 February 2006, Case No. ICC-01/04-01/07

ICC Pre-Trial Chamber I, *Situation in the DRC, Decision on the Applications for the Participation in the Proceedings of VPRS 1, VPRS 2, VPRS 3, VPRS 4, VPRS 5 and VPRS 6*, 17 January 2006, Case No. ICC-01/04

ICC Pre-Trial Chamber I, *Situation in the DRC, Prosecutor v Callixte Mbarushimana, Decision on the Defence Challenge to the Validity of the Arrest Warrant*, 9 January 2011, Case No. ICC-01/04-01/10

ICC Pre-Trial Chamber I, *Situation in the DRC, Prosecutor v Germain Katanga and Mathieu Ngudjolo Chui*, Initial Appearance of Mathieu Ngudjolo Chui, 11 February 2008, Case No. ICC-01/04-01/07

ICC Pre-Trial Chamber I, *Situation in the DRC, Prosecutor v Germain Katanga, Decision on the Evidence and Information Provided by the Prosecution for the Issuance of a Warrant of Arrest for Germain Katanga*, 6 July 2007, Case No. ICC-01/04-01/07

ICC Pre-Trial Chamber I, *Situation in the DRC, Prosecutor v Katanga, Decision on the Evidence and Information Provided by the Prosecution for the Issuance of a Warrant of Arrest for Germain Katanga*, 5 November 2007, Case No. ICC-01/04-01/07

ICC Pre-Trial Chamber I, *Situation in the DRC, Prosecutor v Thomas Lubanga Dyilo, Decision on the Prosecutor's Application for a Warrant of Arrest, Article 58*, 10 February 2006, Case No. ICC-01/04-01/06

ICC Pre-Trial Chamber I, *Situation in the DRC, Prosecutor v Thomas Lubanga Dyilo, Decision to Unseal the Warrant of Arrest Against Mr. Thomas Lubanga Dyilo and Related Documents*, 17 March 2006, Case No. ICC-01/04-01/06

ICC Pre-Trial Chamber II, *Situation in Darfur, Sudan, in the Case of the Prosecutor v Omar Hassan Ahmad Al Bashir, Decision under Article 87(7) of the Rome Statute on the Non-Compliance by South Africa with the Request by the Court for the Arrest and Surrender of Omar Al Bashir (Decision on South Africa's non-compliance)*, 6 July 2017, Case No. ICC-02/05-01/09

ICC Pre-Trial Chamber II, *Situation in Darfur, Sudan, Prosecutor v Omar Hassan Ahmad Al Bashir, Decision following the Prosecutor's request for an order further clarifying that the Republic of South Africa is under the obligation to immediately arrest and surrender Omar Al Bashir*, 13 June 2015, Case No. ICC-02/05-01/09

ICC Pre-Trial Chamber II, *Situation in Darfur, Sudan, Prosecutor v Omar Hassan Ahmad Al Bashir, Decision on the Cooperation of the DRC Regarding Omar Al Bashir's Arrest and Surrender to the Court*, 9 April 2014, Case No. ICC-02/05-01/09

ICC Pre-Trial Chamber II, *Situation in the Republic of Côte d'Ivoire, Prosecutor v Simone Gbagbo, Prosecution's Request to Access Material and Provide Observations in the Article 19(1) Admissibility Proceedings*, 25 September 2018, Case No. ICC-02/11-01/12

ICC Pre-Trial Chamber II, Situation in the Republic of Kenya, *Decision Pursuant to Article 15 of the Rome Statute on the Authorization of an Investigation into the Situation in the Republic of Kenya*, Dissenting Opinion of Judge Hans-Peter Kaul, 31 March 2010, Case No. ICC-01/09

ICC Pre-Trial Chamber II, *Situation in Uganda, Decision on Prosecutor's Application for Leave to Appeal in Part Pre-Trial Chamber II's Decision on the Prosecutor's Applications for Warrants of Arrest under Article 58*, 19 August 2005, Case No. ICC-02/04-01/05

ICC Pre-Trial Chamber II, *Situation in Uganda, Decision on the Prosecutor's Application for Warrants of Arrest under Article 58 in Relation to the Situation in Uganda*, 8 July 2005, Case No. ICC-02/04

ICC Pre-Trial Chamber II, *Situation in Uganda, Prosecutor v Joseph Kony, Vincent Otti, Okot Odhiambo, Dominic Ongwen, Decision on the Admissibility of the Case under Article 19(1) of the Statute*, 10 March 2009, Case No. ICC-02/04-01/05

ICC Pre-Trial Chamber III, *Situation in the CAR, Prosecutor v Jean-Pierre Bemba Gombo, Decision on the Admissibility and Abuse of Process Challenges*, 24 June 2010, Case No. ICC-01/05-01/08

ICC Pre-Trial Chamber III, *Situation in the Islamic Republic of Afghanistan, Public Redacted Version of 'Request for Authorisation of an Investigation Pursuant to Article 15'*, 20 November 2017, Case No. ICC-02/17

ICC Trial Chamber I, *Situation in the DRC, Prosecutor v Thomas Lubanga Dyilo, Decision on the Consequences of Non-Disclosure of Exculpatory Materials Covered by Article 54(3)(E) Agreements and the Application to Stay the Prosecution of the Accused, Together with Certain Other Issues Raised at the Status Conference on 10 June 2008*, 13 June 2008, Case No. ICC-01/04-01/06

ICC Trial Chamber II, *Situation in the DRC, Prosecutor v Germain Katanga and Mathieu Ngudjolo Chui, Reasons for the Oral Decision on the Motion Challenging the Admissibility of the Case (Article 19 of the Statute)*, 16 June 2009, Case No. ICC-01/04-01/07

ICC, Pre-Trial Chamber I, *Situation in Darfur, Sudan, Prosecutor v Omar Al Bashir, Decision on the Prosecution's Application for a Warrant of Arrest Against Omar Hassan Ahmad Al Bashir*, 4 March 2009, Case No. ICC-02/05-01/09

ICC, Pre-Trial Chamber II, Situation in Darfur, Sudan, *Prosecutor v Omar Hassan Ahmad Al Bashir, Decision under Article 87(7) of the Rome Statute on the non-compliance by Jordan with the request by the Court for the arrest and surrender of Omar Al-Bashir (Decision on Jordan's non-compliance)*, 11 December 2017, ICC-02/05-01/09

ICJ, *Arrest Warrant of 11 April 2000* (*DRC v Belgium*), 14 February 2002, ICJ Rep. 2002, p. 3

ICJ, *Arrest Warrant of 11 April 2000* (*DRC v Belgium*), 14 February 2002, ICJ Rep. 2002, p. 3

ICJ, *Arrest Warrant of 11 April 2000* (*DRC v Belgium*), Dissenting Opinion of Judge Christine van den Wyngaert, 14 February 2002, ICJ Rep. 2002, p. 3

ICJ, *Case Concerning Certain Criminal Proceedings in France (DRC v France)*, Order of Removal of the Case, 16 November 2010

ICTR Appeals Chamber, *Jean Bosco Barayagwiza v Prosecutor, Decision*, 3 November 1999, Case No. ICTR-97-19-AR72

ICTR Appeals Chamber, *Jean Bosco Barayagwiza v Prosecutor, Prosecutor's Request for Review or Reconsideration*, 31 March 2000, Case No. ICTR-97-19-AR72

ICTR Trial Chamber designated under Rule 11bis, *Prosecutor v Fulgence Kayishema, Decision on the Request by Human Rights Watch for Leave to Appear as Amicus Curiae in the Proceedings for Referral of the Indictment Against Fulgence Kayishema to Rwanda: Rule 11bis and 74 of the Rules of Procedure and Evidence*, 8 November 2007, Case No. ICTR-2001-67-I

ICTR Trial Chamber I, *Prosecutor v Jean Kambanda*, Judgement and Sentence, 4 September 1998, Case No. ICTR-97-23-S

ICTR Trial Chamber I, *Prosecutor v Théoneste Bagosora, Gratien Kabiligi, Aloys Ntabakuze and Anatole Nsengiyumva*, Modalities for Presentation of a Witness, 20 September 2006, Case No. ICTR-98-41-T

ICTR Trial Chamber II, *Prosecutor v Joseph Kanyabashi, Decision on the Defence Motion on Jurisdiction*, 18 June 1997, Case No. ICTR-96-15-T

ICTY Appeals Chamber, *Prosecutor v Dragan Nikolić, Decision on Interlocutory Appeal Concerning Legality of Arrest*, 5 June 2003, Case No. IT-94-2-AR73

ICTY Appeals Chamber, *Prosecutor v Radislav Krstić*, 19 April 2004, IT-98-33-A

ICTY Trial Chamber I, *Prosecutor v Mile Mrkšić, Veselin Šljivančanin and Miroslav Radić, Prosecutor's Requests for Deferral to the ICTY of Proceedings Instituted in Serbia (Vukovar Hospital* case*)*, 7 December 1998, Case No. IT-95-13/1

ICTY Trial Chamber II, *Prosecutor v Dragan Nikolić, Decision on the Defence Motion Challenging the Exercise of Jurisdiction by the Tribunal*, 9 October 2002, Case No. IT-94-2

ICTY Trial Chamber III, *Prosecutor v Slobodan Milošević, Decision on Preliminary Motions*, 8 November 2001, Case No. IT-02-54

ICTY Trial Chamber, *Prosecutor v Duško Tadić, Decision on the Defence Motion on the Principle of Non Bis in Idem*, 14 November 1995, Case No IT-94-1-T

ICTY, *Decision on the Prosecutor's Request for Deferral and Motion for Order to the Former Yugoslav Republic of Macedonia*, 4 October 2002, Case No. IT-02-55-MISC.6

ICTY, *Prosecutor v Mrkšić et al.*, Transcript, 9 December 1998, ICTY Case No. IT-95-13/1

SCSL Appeals Chamber, *Prosecutor v Charles Ghankay Taylor, Decision on Immunity from Jurisdiction*, 31 May 2004, Case No. SCSL-2003-01-I

Special Panel for Serious Crimes, *República Democrática de Timor-Leste,* Dili District Court, *The Deputy General Prosecutor for Serious Crimes v Wiranto et al., Legal Ruling Concerning the Applicability of Ne Bis in Idem at the Arrest Warrant Stage of the Proceedings*, 5 May 2005, Case No. 05/2003

Supreme Court of Appeal, South Africa, *State v Ebrahim Ismail Ebrahim*, 26 February 1991, 279/89

Supreme Court of Appeal, South Africa, *The Minister of Justice and Constitutional Development v The Southern African Litigation Centre*, 15 March 2016, 867/15 [2016] ZASCA 17

בית המשפט העליון [Supreme Court], Israel, *Attorney-General of Israel v Adolf Eichmann*, 29 May 1962, Criminal Appeal 336/61

USA Court of Appeals, 9th Circuit, *Susan Siderman de Blake et al. v Argentina*, 22 May 1992, 85-5773, 1992, 965 F.2d 699

USA Court of Appeals, 2nd Circuit, *Dolly and Joel Filártiga v Americo Norberto Peña-Irala*, 30 June 1980, No. 191, Docket 79-6090, 630 F.2d 876

USA Supreme Court, *USA v Humberto Alvarez-Machain*, 15 June 1992, 504 U.S. 655 (112 S.Ct. 2188, 119 L.Ed.2d 441) 91/712

Cases in Chapter 12

ICTY Appeals Chamber, *Prosecutor v Tihomir Blaškić, (subpoena), ICTY Appeals Chamber Judgment on the Request of the Republic of Croatia for Review of the Decision of the Trial Chamber II of 18 July 1997*, 29 October 1997, Case No. IT-95-14-AR 108*bis*

Cases in Chapter 13

African Commission, *Various Communications vs Mauritania*, 11 May 2000, Communications 54/91, 61/91, 96/93, 98/93, 164/97, 210/98

Appeals Commission for Refugees (2nd Division), France, *Agathe Habyarimana neé Kanziga*, 15 February 2007, 564776

Audiencia Nacional [Criminal Chamber, Plenary Session] Spain, *Unión Progresista de Fiscales de España et al. v. Pinochet*, 5 November 1998

Audiencia Nacional, Spain, *Fundación Casa del Tibet and Others v Jiang Zemin and Others*, Appeal Judgment on Admissibility, 10 January 2006, ILDC 1002 (ES 2006)

Audiencia Nacional, Spain, *Graciela P de L and Others v Adolfo Francisco Scilingo Manzorro*, 19 April 2005, ILDC 136 (ES 2005)

Audiencia Nacional, Spain, *Rigoberta Menchu Tum et al. v Ríos Montt et al. (Guatemala Genocide* case*)*, 13 December 2000, 331/99

Bavarian High Court (*Oberlandesgericht*), Munich, *Novislav Djajic Case*, 23 May 1997, 2 St 20/96, 51 *Neue Jusistische Wochenschrisft* (1998) p. 392

Bundesgerichtshof [German Federal Supreme Court], *Public Prosecutor v Nikola Jorgić*, 30 April 1999, 2 BvR 1290/99

Bundesverfassungsgericht, [Federal Constitutional Court, 4th Chamber of the Second Senate, Germany], *Public Prosecutor v Nikola Jorgić*, 12 December 2000, 2 BvR 1290/99

Chambre de mises en accusation [Pre-Trial Chamber of the Belgian Court of Appeal], Brussels, *Samiha Abbas Hijazi et al. v Ariel Sharon*, 26 June 2002

Colombian State Council, *Hector Jaime Beltran Parra, Clara Patricia, Nidia Amanda, Jose Antonio and Mario Beltran Fuentes*, 19 July 2007

Constitutional Court, Guatemala, *Tribunal Primero A Guatemala, Rigoberta Menchu et al. v Ríos Montt et al. (Genocide in Guatemala)*, 20 May 2013, Case No. Exp 1904-2013

Constitutional Court, South Africa, *National Commission of the South African Police Service and Another v Southern African Human Rights Litigation Centre and Another (Zimbabwe Torture Docket* case*)*, 30 October 2014 [2014] ZACC 30

Corte Constitucional [Constitutional Court], *Sala Plena*, Bogotá, Colombia, *Sentencia (In re Corte Penal Internacional)*, 30 July 2002, C-578/02

Corte Suprema de Argentina [Supreme Court], Argentina, *Arancibia Clavel, Enrique Lautaro Homicidio Calificado y Asociación Ilicita y Otros*, 24 August 2004, Case No. 259

Cour d'Assises de Paris, 2ème Section [*Second Chamber of the Criminal Court of Paris*], *Public Prosecutor v Pascal Senyamuhara Safari (alias Pascal Simbikangwa)*, 14 March 2014, Case No. 13/0033

Cour de Cassation, Chambre Criminelle [Court of Cassation (Criminal Chamber)], France, *Elvir Javor et al. contre X, Arrêt (Rejet du pourvoi)*, 26 March 1996, 95-81527

Cour de Cassation, Chambre Criminelle [Court of Cassation, Criminal Chamber], France, *Muhayimana*, Judgment No. 810, 26 February 2014, 13-87888

Cour de Cassation, Chambre Criminelle [Court of Cassation (Criminal Law Chamber)], France, *France v Paul Touvier*, 27 November 1992, 92-82409

Cour de Cassation, Chambre Criminelle [Court of Cassation (Criminal Law Chamber)], France, *Prosecutor v Klaus Barbie*, 6 October 1983, 83-93194

Cour de Cassation, Chambre Criminelle, France, *Prosecutor v Maurice Papon*, 11 June 2004, 98-82.323

Cour Suprême du Sénégal [Supreme Court, Senegal], *Association des Victimes des Crimes et Répressions Politiques au Tchad (AVCRP) et al. v Hissène Habré*, 20 March 2001, Case No. 14

Court of Appeal, Amsterdam, *Chili Komitee Nederland v Pinochet*, 4 January 1995

Court of Appeal, Amsterdam, *R. Wijngaarde and R.A.L. Hoost v Desiré Delano Bouterse*, Order, 20 November 2000, LJN: AA8395

Court of Appeal, Brussels, *Public Prosecutor v Abdulaye Yerodia Ndombasi et al.*, 16 April 2002

Court of Appeal, The Hague, *Public Prosecutor v Habibullah Jalalzoy*, 29 January 2007, 09-751005-04 (LJN: AZ9366)

Court of Appeal, The Hague, *Public Prosecutor v Hesamuddin Hesam*, 29 January 2007, LJN: AZ9365

Court of Appeals, Santiago, Chile, *Fernando Laureani Maturana and Miguel Krassnoff Marchenko v Miguel Ángel Sandoval Rodríguez*, 5 January 2004, 517-2004

Court of Queen's Bench of Manitoba, Canada, *Harvey Swystun v USA*, 30 October 1987, 50 Man.R.(2d) 129 (QB)

District Court for the Central District of California, Los Angeles, California, USA, *The State v Sergeant Stacey Koon, Officer Theodore J. Briseno, Officer Timothy E. Wind, Officer Laurence Powell, (Rodney King* case*)*, 29 April 1992

ECFI, Second Chamber (Extended Composition) *Yasin Abdullah Kadi v Council of the European Union and Commission of the European Communities* [2005], 21 September 2005, T-315/01

ECJ, *Criminal Proceedings Against Maria Pupino*, Opinion of Advocate General Kokott, 11 November 2004, Case C-105/03

ECJ, Fourth Chamber, *SGL Carbon AG v Commission of the European Communities*, 10 May 2007, Case C-328/05 P

ECJ, Third Chamber, *Varec SA v Belgian State*, 14 February 2008, Case C-450/06

ECtHR Chamber, *Alecos Modinos v Cyprus*, Dissenting Opinion of Judge Pikis, 22 April 1993, Application No. 15070/89

ECtHR Fifth Section, *Nikola Jorgić v Germany*, 12 July 2007, Application No. 74613/01

ECtHR Fifth Section, *Sylvère Ahorugeze v Sweden*, 27 October 2011, Application No. 37075/09

ECtHR First Section, *Iovchev v Bulgaria*, 2 February 2006, Application No. 41211/98

ECtHR First Section, *Kadir Satik and Others v Turkey*, 10 October 2000, Application No. 31866/96.

ECtHR Grand Chamber, *Cyprus v Turkey*, 10 May 2001, Application No. 25781/94

ECtHR Grand Chamber, *Hirsi Jamaa and Others v Italy*, 23 February 2012, Application No. 27765/09

ECtHR Grand Chamber, *Hirsi Jamaa and Others v Italy*, Concurring Opinion of Judge Pinto de Albuquerque, 23 February 2012, Application No. 27765/09

ECtHR Grand Chamber, *Nassim Saadi v Italy*, 28 February 2008, Application No. 37201/06

ECtHR Grand Chamber, *Tejedor García v Spain*, 16 December 1997, Application No. 142/1996/761/962

ECtHR Second Section, *Hasan İlhan v Turkey*, 9 November 2004, Application No. 22494/93

ECtHR Second Section, *Peers v Greece*, 19 April 2001, Application No. 28524/95

ECtHR Second Section, *Sevtap Veznedaroğlu v Turkey*, 11 April 2000, Application No. 32357/96

ECtHR Third Section, *Dougoz v Greece*, 6 March 2001, Application No. 40907/98

ECtHR, *Anton Assenov and Others v Bulgaria*, 28 October 1998, Application No. 90/1997/874/1086

ECtHR, *Assya Anguelova v Bulgaria*, 13 June 2002, Application No. 38361/97

ECtHR, Fourth Section, *Anya Velikova v Bulgaria*, 18 May 2000, Application No. 41488/98

ECtHR, *Remetin v Croatia*, 11 December 2012, Application No. 29525/10

ECtHR, Second Section, *M.E. v Denmark*, Application No. 58363/10, 8 July 2014

ECtHR, *Sulaiman Al-Adsan i v UK*, 21 November 2001, Application No. 35763/97

ECtHR, Third Section, *Carol Ciorcan and Others v Romania*, 27 January 2015, Application Nos. 29414/09 and 44841/09

ECtHR, Third Section, *Kelly and Others v UK*, 4 May 2001, Application No. 30054/96

Ethiopia Federal High Court, *The Special Prosecutor v Col Mengistu Hailemariam and 173 Others*, 9 October 1995, Criminal File No. 1/87, 1988 EC [GC], ILDC 555 (ET 1995)

Federal Court of Australia, Canberra, *Nulyarimma v Thompson*, 1 September 1999, [1999] FCA 1192, 165 ALR 621

Federal Court of Canada, Trial Division, Ottawa, Ontario, Canada, *Madeleine Mangabu Bukumba and Gracia Mukumba v Canada (Minister of Citizenship and Immigration)*, 22 January 2004, [2004] FC 93

Hoge Raad [Supreme Court], The Netherlands, Criminal Division, *Public Prosecutor v Habibullah Jalalzoy*, 8 July 2008, 07/10064 (LJN: BC7418)

Hoge Raad [Supreme Court], The Netherlands, *Prosecutor-General of the Supreme Court v Desiré Delano Bouterse*, 18 September 2001, LJN: AB1471

Hoge Raad [Supreme Court], The Netherlands, *Public Prosecutor v Joseph Mpambara*, 21 October 2008, Case No. 09-750007-07

Hoge Raad [Supreme Court], The Netherlands, *Public Prosecutor v Sebastien Nzapali*, 1 December 2009, S/07-12112

HRC, *Bautista de Arellana v Colombia*, 27 October 1995, Communication No. 563/1993

HRC, *Daniel Monguya Mbenge v Zaire*, 8 September 1977, Communication No. 16/1977

HRC, *Hugo Rodríguez v Uruguay*, 9 August 1994, Communication No. 322/1988 (1994)

Human Rights Chamber for BiH, *Ferida Selimović, Šefika Palić, Šefika Palić, Mejrema Junuzović, Mevlida Sulejmanović, Mevlida Sulejmanović, Munira Sulejmanović, Hazreta Delić, Zilha Fejzić, Hafiza Hrustić and Adila Hrustić, Nura Omić, Enver Hamzić, Hajro Okanović, Rabija Smajić, Jusuf Malkić, Šuhra Alić, Raza Jusufović, Ahmija Mujić, Hasena Ahmetagić, Fatija Ibrahimović, Rifet Muhić, Rešida Omerović, Timka Mujić, Ifeta Selimović, Ifeta Selimović, Ifeta Selimović, Ifeta Selimović, Hata Ahmetović, Hata Ahmetović, Hata Ahmetović, Hata Ahmetović, Hanifa Smailović, Amira Gurdić, Tima Gurdić, Fatima Ramić, Fatima Ramić, Fatima Ramić, Enes Dozić, Enes Dozić, Azem Smajić, Tahira Skeledć, Tahira Skeledć, Tahira Skeledć, Hakija Čakanović, Sabra Kabilović, Sabira Jusufović, Emina Salihović, Hamša Čerimović, and Aiša Ademović against The Republika Srpska (Srebrenica* Cases), *Decision on Admissibility and Merits*, 7 March 2003, Case Nos. CH/01/8365, CH/01/8397, CH/01/8398, CH/01/8399, CH/01/8410, CH/01/8411, CH/01/8412, CH/01/8414, CH/01/8428, CH/01/8484, CH/01/8487, CH/01/8521, CH/02/8842, CH/02/8927, CH/02/9357, CH/02/9375, CH/02/9385, CH/02/9390, CH/02/9403, CH/02/9427, CH/02/9431, CH/02/9433, CH/02/9470, CH/02/9484, CH/02/9485, CH/02/9486, CH/02/9487, CH/02/9505, CH/02/9506, CH/02/9507, CH/02/9508, CH/02/9513, CH/02/9514, CH/02/9515, CH/02/9528, CH/02/9529, CH/02/9530, CH/02/9532, CH/02/9542, CH/02/9546, CH/02/9547, CH/02/9548, CH/02/9549, CH/02/9550, CH/02/9552, CH/02/9553, CH/02/9594, CH/02/9595, and CH/02/9596

IACmmHR, *Djamel Ameziane v USA*, *Report No. 17/12 (Admissibility)*, 20 March 2012, P-900-8

IACmmHR, *Michael Domingues v USA*, 22 October 2002, Report No. 62/02, Case 12.285

IACtHR, *Anstraum Aman Villagrán-Morales et al. v Guatemala (Case of the 'Street Children')*, 19 November 1999, Series C, No. 63

IACtHR, *Goiburú et al. v Paraguay*, 22 September 2006, Series C, No. 153

IACtHR, *La Cantuta v Perú* (Merits, Reparations and Costs), 29 November 2006, Series C, No. 162

IACtHR, *Miguel Castro-Castro Prison v Perú*, 25 November 2006, Series C, No. 160

IACtHR, *Nicholas Chapman Blake v Guatemala*, 24 January 1998, Series C, No. 36

IACtHR, *Velásquez-Rodríguez v Honduras*, 29 July 1988, Series C, No. 4

ICJ, *Application of the Convention on the Prevention and Punishment of the Crime of Genocide (BiH v Serbia and Montenegro)*, 26 February 2007, ICJ Rep. 2007, p. 43

ICJ, *Arrest Warrant of 11 April 2000 (DRC v Belgium)*, Dissenting Opinion of Judge Christine van den Wyngaert, 14 February 2002, ICJ Rep. 2002, p. 3

ICJ, *Arrest Warrant of 11 April 2000 (DRC v Belgium)*, Dissenting Opinion of Judge Christine van den Wyngaert, 14 February 2002, ICJ Rep. 2002, p. 3

ICJ, *Case Concerning Military and Paramilitary Activities in and Against Nicaragua (Nicaragua v USA) Nicaragua* case], 27 June 1986, ICJ Rep. 1986, p. 14

ICJ, *Case Concerning Questions of Interpretation and Application of the 1971 Montreal Convention Arising from the Aerial Incident at Lockerbie, Request for the Indication of Provisional Measures (Libyan Arab Jamahiriya v USA)*, Provisional Measures, Order of 14 April 1992, Dissenting Opinion of Judge Weeramantry, ICJ Rep. 1992, p. 114

ICJ, *Case Concerning the Barcelona Traction, Light and Power Company Limited (Belgium v Spain)*, 5 February 1970, ICJ Rep. 1970, p. 3

ICJ, *Ethiopia v South Africa; Liberia v South Africa* [*South West Africa* cases], Judge Tanaka's Dissenting Opinion, 18 July 1966, ICJ Rep. 6

ICJ, *Federal Republic of Germany v Denmark; Federal Republic of Germany v The Netherlands* [*North Sea Continental Shelf* cases], 20 February 1969, ICJ Rep. 1969, p. 3

ICJ, *Portugal v Australia* [*East Timor* case], 30 June 1995, ICJ Rep. 1995, p. 90

ICJ, *Questions Relating to the Obligation to Extradite or Prosecute* (*Belgium v Senegal*), 20 July 2012, ICJ Rep. 2012, p. 422

ICJ, *Reservations to the Convention on the Prevention and Punishment of the Crime of Genocide*, Advisory Opinion, 28 May 1951, 1951-ICJ Reports, p. 15

ICJ, *United States Diplomatic and Consular Staff in Tehran (USA v Iran)* [*Iranian Hostages* Case], 24 May 1980, ICJ Rep. 1980, p. 3

ICTR Trial Chamber I, *Prosecutor v Bernard Ntuyahaga, Decision on the Prosecutor's Motion to Withdraw the Indictment*, 18 March 1999, Case No. ICTR-98-40-T

ICTY Appeals Chamber, *Prosecutor v Duško Tadić*, Decision on the Defence Motion for Interlocutory Appeal on Jurisdiction, 2 October 1995, Case No. IT-94-1-AR72
ICTY Appeals Chamber, *Prosecutor v Tihomir Blaškić, Judgment on the Request of the Republic of Croatia for Review of the Decision of the Trial Chamber II of 18 July 1997*, 29 October 1997, Case No. IT-95-14-AR 108*bis*
ICTY Trial Chamber II, *Prosecutor v Dragan Nikolić, Decision on the Defence Motion Challenging the Exercise of Jurisdiction by the Tribunal*, 9 October 2002, Case No. IT-94-2
ICTY Trial Chamber, *Prosecutor v Anto Furundžija*, 10 December 1998, Case No. IT-95-17/1-T
ICTY Trial Chamber, *Prosecutor v Enver Hadžihasanović and Amir Kubura*, 15 March 2006, IT-01-47-T
ICTY Trial Chamber, *Prosecutor v Goran Jelisić*, 14 December 1999, Case No. IT-95-10-T
ICTY Trial Chamber, *Prosecutor v Slavko Dokmanović, Decision on the Motion for Release by the Accused*, 27 October 1997, Case No. ICTY-95-13a
ICTY Trial Chamber, *Prosecutor v Zejnil Delalić et al.*, (*Čelebići* case), 16 November 1998, Case No. IT-96-21-T
International (Nuremberg) Military Tribunal, *United States of America v. Karl Brandt et al.* (*the Medical* case), 19 August 1947
International (Nuremberg) Military Tribunal, *United States of America v. Erhard Milch et al.* (*the Milch* case), 16 April 1947
International (Nuremberg) Military Tribunal, *United States of America v. Josef Altstötter et al.* (*the Justice* case), 3 December 1947
International (Nuremberg) Military Tribunal, *United States of America v. Oswald Pohl et al.* (*the Pohl* case), 3 November 1947
International (Nuremberg) Military Tribunal, *United States of America v. Friedrich Flick et al.* (*the Flick* case), 22 December 1947
International (Nuremberg) Military Tribunal, *United States of America v. Carl Krauch et al.* (*the I.G. Fabren* case), 29 July 1948
International (Nuremberg) Military Tribunal, *United States of America v. Wilhelm List et al.* (*the Hostages* case), 19 February 1948
International (Nuremberg) Military Tribunal, *United States of America v. Ulrich Greifelt et al.* (*the Rusha* case), 10 March 1948
International (Nuremberg) Military Tribunal, *United States of America v. Otto Ohlendorf et al.* (*the Einsatzgruppen* case), 8 April 1948
International (Nuremberg) Military Tribunal, *United States of America v. Alfried Krupp et al.* (*the Krupp* case), 31 July 1948
International (Nuremberg) Military Tribunal, *United States of America v. Ernst von Weizsäcker et al.* (*the Ministries Case*), 11–13 April 1949
International (Nuremberg) Military Tribunal, *United States of America v. Wilhelm von Leeb et al.* (*the High Command* case), 27 & 28 October 1948
Juzgado Central de Instrucción No. 006 [Sixth Central Court for Preliminary Criminal Proceedings], Madrid, Spain, *Bush Six* case, 13 April 2011

Landesgericht [Trial Court], Salzburg, Austria *Public Prosecutor v Duško Cvjetković*, Acquittal, 31 May 1995, 150s99/94

Oberste Gerichtshof [Supreme Court], Vienna, Austria, *Public Prosecutor v Duško Cvjetković*, Judgment on Interlocutory Appeal Upholding Jurisdiction, 13 July 1994, 150s99/94

Opinion of the Director of Public Prosecution of Denmark, *Lee Urzúa et al. v Pinochet*, 3 December 1998, 555/98

PCIJ Twelfth Ordinary Session, *Case of S.S. Lotus (France v Turkey)*, 7 September 1927, PCIJ Series A, No. 10

Poder Judicial de la Nación, Buenos Aires, *Prosecutor v Ricardo Miguel Cavallo*, Full Verdict, 28 December 2011, Case No. 1298

Public Prosecutor of Amsterdam, *Chili Komitee Nederland v Pinochet*, 6 June 1994

SCSL Appeals Chamber, *Prosecutor v Morris Kallon, Decision on Challenge to Jurisdiction Lomé Accord Amnesty*, 13 March 2004, SCSL-2004-15-AR72(E)

Stockholm District Court, *Prosecutor v Jackie Arklöf*, 18 December 2006, B 4084-04

Suprema Corte de Justicia de la Nación [Supreme Court], Mexico, *Ricardo Miguel Cavallo, Amparo en Revision*, 10 June 2003, Case No. 14/2002

העליון המשפט בית [Supreme Court], Israel, *Attorney-General of Israel v Adolf Eichmann*, 29 May 1962, Criminal Appeal 336/61

The Court of Justice of the Economic Community of the States of West Africa (ECOWAS), *Hissène Habré v Republic of Senegal*, 18 November 2010, Case No. ECJ/CCJ/JUD/06/10

The High Court of Justice, Queen's Bench Division, UK, *Ndiki Mutua, Paulo Nzili, Wambugu Wa Nyigi, Jane Muthoni Mara and Susan Ngondi v The Foreign and Commonwealth Office*, 5 October 2012, HQ09X02666

Tribunal Constitucional, Estado de Bolivia, José Carlos Trujillo Oroza José contra Luis Dabdoub López y Jacinto Morón Sánchez, Sentencia, 12 November 2001, *Resolucion* 1190/01-R

Tribunal Constitucional, Perú, *Huaura, José Enrique Crousillat López Torres*, 8 August 2008, Decision 01271-2008-PHC/TC

Tribunal of First Instance of Brussels, *Aguilar Diaz et al. v Pinochet*, Order, 6 November 1998

Tribunal Oral Federal N° 5, *Prosecutor v Ricardo Miguel Cavallo*, 26 October 2011, Case No. 1298

Tribunal Primero de Sentencia Penal, Guatemala City, Guatemala, *Ríos Montt* Judgment, 10 May 2013, No C01076-2011-00015

UK Supreme Court, *R (on the application of Smith (FC) (Respondent)) v Secretary of State for Defence (Appellant) and another*, 30 June 2010, [2009] EWCA Civ 441

UN Committed Against Torture, *Marcos Roitman Rosenmann v Spain*, 30 April 2002, CAT Committee No. 176/2000

UN Committee Against Torture, *Suleymane Guengueng and Others v Senegal*, 19 May 2006, CAT/C/36/D/181/2001

UN Committee Against Torture, *Tahir Hussain Khan v Canada*, 4 July 1994, Communication No. 15/1994

USA Court of Appeals, 6th Circuit, *John Demjanjuk v Joseph Petrowsky et al.*, 31 October 1985, 776 F.2d 571, 85-3435
USA Court of Appeals, District of Columbia Circuit, *USA v Omar Mohammed Ali Rezaq*, 6 February 1998, 134 F.3d 1121 (D.C. Cir. 1998), 96-3127
USA District Court for the Southern District of New York, *USA v Ramzi Ahmed Yousef et al.*, 29 May 1996, 927 F. Supp. 673 (S.D.N.Y. 1996), S12 93 Cr.180 (KTD)
USA District Court, District of Columbia, *USA v Fawaz Yunis*, 12 February 1988, 681 F. Supp. 896 (D.D.C. 1988) Crim. A No. 87-0377
USA Supreme Court, *Lakhdar Boumediene et al. v Bush et al.*, 12 June 2008, 06-1195
USA Supreme Court, *USA v Humberto Alvarez-Machain*, 15 June 1992, 504 U.S. 655 (112 S.Ct. 2188, 119 L.Ed.2d 441) 91/712

Cases in Chapter 14

Central Criminal Court (Old Bailey), London, *Regina v Faryadi Sarwar Zardad*, 18 July 2005, 200505339/D3
ICJ, *Continental Shelf* Case *(Libyan Arab Jamahiriya v Malta)*, 3 June 1985, [1985] ICJ Rep. 13
ICJ, *Legality of the Threat or Use of Nuclear Weapons (Nuclear Weapons* Advisory Opinion*)*, 8 July 1996, [1996] ICJ Rep. p. 226

Cases in Chapter 15

ICJ, *Continental Shelf* case *(Libyan Arab Jamahiriya v Malta)*, 3 June 1985, [1985] ICJ Rep. 13

Cases in Chapter 16

Acte d'accusation du Procureur général près la Cour d'appel de Bruxelles du 12 février 2001 [Bill of Indictment of the Prosecutor filed before the Court of Appeal on 12 February 2001, Brussels], *Prosecutor v. Vincent Ntezimana, Alphonse Higaniro, Consolata Mukangango & Julienne Mukabutera*, Case No. 23764
Appeals Court, The Hague, *Public Prosecutor v Joseph Mpambara*, 17 December 2007, 09-750007-07
ανώτατο δικαστήριο της Ελλάδας [*Areios Pagos*/Greek Supreme Court], *Prefecture of Voiotia v Federal Republic of Germany*, 4 May 2000, 11/2000 (288933)

Assize Court of Brussels, *Public Prosecutor v Alphonse Higaniro, Vincent Ntezimana, Consolata Mukangango (Sister Gertrude) and Julienne Mukabutera (Sister Maria Kisito), Verdict*, 8 June 2001

Audiencia Nacional [Central Criminal Court], Spain, *Fidel Castro Ruz, Ruling*, 4 March 1999

Audiencia Nacional, Spain, *Graciela P de L and Others v Adolfo Francisco Scilingo Manzorro*, 19 April 2005, ILDC 136 (ES 2005)

Auto de la Sala de lo Penal de la Audiencia Nacional Confirmando la Jurisdicción de España para Conocer de los Crímenes de Genocidio y Terrorismo Cometido Durante la Dictadura Chilena [*Decision of the Penal Chamber Confirming Spanish Jurisdiction to Investigate Genocide in Chile*], First Section, 5 November 1998, Appeal 173/98, File 1/98 from Judicial Chamber 6

Вярхоўны суд Беларусі [Belarus Supreme Court], *Public Prosecutor v Dzmitry Kanavalaw and Uladzislaw Kavalyow, Death Sentences*, 30 November 2011

Bow Street Magistartes' Court, UK, *Application filed by Peter Tatchell (under Britain's Criminal Justice Act, 1988), Decision rejecting the issue of an arrest warrant for Robert Mugabe*, 14 January 2004

Bow Street Magistrates' Court, UK, *The Government of the Russian Federation v Akhmed Zakaev*, Judgment, 23 November 2003

Bundesverfassungsgericht [Federal Constitution Court, Germany], *G, a citizen of Vanuatu and his motion for a temporary injunction, Order of the Second Senate*, 24 June 2003, 2 BvR 685/03

Bundesverfassungsgericht [German Federal Constitutional Court], *Decision on the German European Arrest Warrant Law*, 18 July 2005, 2 BvR 2236/04

Cámara Federal de Buenos Aires, Jorge Rafael Videla (first junta), Appeals Court Judgment, 23 May 2002, Case No. 33714

Cámara Federal de Casación Penal [Federal Chamber of Criminal Appeals], Argentina, *Public Prosecutor v Reynaldo Benito Antonio Bignone* [*'Hospital Posadas'* case], *Appeals decision*, 28 November 2012, 1696/1742

Cámara Federal de Casación Penal [Federal Chamber of Criminal Appeals], Argentina, *Public Prosecutor v Reynaldo Benito Antonio Bignone* [*'Campo de Mayo'* case (1)], *Appeals decision*, 7 December 2012, 2023, 2031, 2034 and 2043

Cámara Federal de Casación Penal [Federal Chamber of Criminal Appeals], Argentina, *Public Prosecutor v Reynaldo Benito Antonio Bignone* [*'Campo de Mayo'* case (2)], *Appeals decision*, 7 December 2012, 2023, 2031, 2034 and 2043

City of Westminster Magistrates' Court, Great Britain, UK, *The Government of the Republic of Serbia v Ejup Ganić*, Decision on Extradition, 27 July 2010, [2010] EW Misc 11 (MC)

Committee Against Torture, *Cecilia Rosana Núñez Chipana v Venezuela*, 10 November 1998, Communication No. 110/1998

Conseil d'Etat, Assemblée, Affaire Aylor (Joy Aylor-Davis), 15 October 1993, 144950

Conseil d'Etat, France, *Lujambio, Galdeano, Garcia Ramirez and Martinez Beiztegui*, 26 September 1984, 62847

Constitutional Court, South Africa, *Mohamed and Dalvie v The President of the Republic of South African and Others*, 28 May 2001, CCT 17/01

Constitutional Court, South Africa, *Azanian Peoples Organization (AZAPO) and Others v President of the Republic of South Africa and Others*, 25 July 1996, CCT 17/96 [1996] ZACC 16, 1996 (8) BCLR 1015, 1996 (4) SA 672

Constitutional Court, South Africa, *S v T Makwanyane and M Mchunu*, 6 June 1995, CCT3/94

Constitutional Court, South Africa, *The State vs Wouter Basson*, 9 September 2005, Case CCT 30/03

Corte Costituzionale [Constitutional Court], Italy, *Zennaro* case, 8 April 1976, No. 69

Corte Costituzionale Italiana [Italian Constitutional Court], *Pietro Venezia v Ministero di Grazia e Giustizia*, 27 June 1996, 223-1996

Corte di Cassazione, Sezione Penale, [Supreme Court, Criminal Chamber], Italy, *Estradizione di Hussain Osman* Hussain Osman's Extradition Order], 13 September 2005, Case No. 33642

Corte di Cassazione [Supreme Court], Italy, *Luigi Ferrini v Federal Republic of Germany*, 11 March 2004, Case No. 5044/04

Corte di Cassazione, Sezione Penale V [Supreme Court, 5th Criminal Chamber], Italy, *Kidnap of Abu Omar*, 19 September 2012

Corte di Cassazione, Sezione Prima Penale [Supreme Court of Cassation, First Criminal Section], Italy, *Mario Luiz Lozano v The General Prosecutor for the Italian Republic*, 24 July 2008, Case No. 31171/2008

Corte Supreme di Cassazione, Sezione Prima Penale [Supreme Court, Criminal Chamber I], Italy, *Public Prosecutor v Karl Hass & Erich Priebke, Sentenza sul ricorso* [Judgment following the application], 16 November 1998

Corte Suprema de Justicia de Chile [Supreme Court, Chile], *Juan Contreras Sepúlveda y Otros (Crimen) Casación Fondo y Forma*, 17 November 2004, 517/2004

Corte Suprema de Justicia de la Nación [Supreme Court], Argentina. *Julio Héctor Simón y otros v Poder Judicial de la Nación*, 14 June 2005, 17.768 S.1767. XXXVIII

Corte Suprema de Justicia de la Nación [Supreme Court], Argentina. *Julio Héctor Simón y otros v Poder Judicial de la Nación,* Opinion of Justice Dr. Don Juan Carlos Maqueda, 14 June 2005, 17.768 S.1767. XXXVIII

Corte Suprema de Justicia de la República, Sala Penal Especial [Supreme Court, Special Criminal Chamber], Perú, *Ministerio Público v Alberto Fujimori Fujimori*, 7 April 2009, A.V. 19-2001

Cour d'Appel de Montpellier [Court of Appeal of Montpellier], *France* (examining magistrate), *FIDH et al. vs Ould Dah*, Referral of the Case to the *Cour d'Assises*, 25 May 2001, 99/14445

Cour d'Assises de Paris, 2ème Section [*Second Chamber of the Criminal Court of Paris*], *Public Prosecutor v Pascal Senyamuhara Safari (alias Pascal Simbikangwa)*, 14 March 2014, Case No. 13/0033

Cour de Cassation [Court of Cassation], *Belgium, H.S.A. et al. v S. A. et al., Decision related to the Indictment of Defendant Ariel Sharon, Amos Yaron and Others*, 12 February 2003, Case No. P.02.1139.F/1
Cour de Cassation, Chambre Criminelle [Court of Cassation (Criminal Law Chamber)], France, *Prosecutor v Klaus Barbie*, 6 October 1983, 83-93194
Cour de Cassation [Court of Cassation], France, *Public Prosecutor v Ely Ould Dah*, 23 October 2002, 02-85379
Cour de Cassation [Court of Cassation], *France, Re General Jean-Francois N'dengue (Brazzaville Beach* case), 9 April 2008
Cour de Cassation, Chambre Criminelle [Court of Cassation, Criminal Chamber], *France, Wladyslaw Sobanski v George Boudarel*, 1 April 1993, 98-85902
Cour de Cassation, Chambre Criminelle [Court of Cassation, Criminal Chamber], *Edouard*, 22 November 1973, 73-91840
Cour de Cassation, France, *Public Prosecutor v Muhammar Gaddafi*, 13 March 2001
Court Martial, Khartoum, Sudan, *Trial of Rolf Steiner*, August-September 1971, 74 International Law Reports 478 (1971)
Court of Appeal (Civil Division), England and Wales, *Othman v Secretary of State for the Home Department*, 9 April 2008, T1/2007/9502, EWCA Civ 290
Court of Appeal, Amsterdam, *R. Wijngaarde and R.A.L. Hoost v Desiré Delano Bouterse*, Order, 20 November 2000, LJN: AA8395
Court of Appeal, The Hague, The Netherlands, *Government in exile of the Republic of South Moluccas (RMS) v The Netherlands*, 22 November 2011, LJN: BU5105, 200.077.445/01
Court of Appeal, The Hague, *The State of The Netherlands (Ministry of Security and Justice) v Jean Claude I.*, 5 July 2016, Case No. 200.182.281/01
Court of Appeals, Ninth Circuit, USA, *William Joseph Quinn v Glen Robinson*, 18 February 1986, 83/2455, 783 F.2d 776 (9th Cir. 1986), ILDC 1584 (US 1986)
Court of BiH, *Prosecutor's Office of BiH v Slavko Šakić*, Verdict, 29 October 2008, X-KR-05141-1
Court of Criminal Appeal, Malta, *The Police (Inspector Raymond Cutajar & Inspector Raymond Aquilina) v. Lewis Muscat*, 31 August 2016, Criminal Appeal No. 278/2006
Ανώτατο Δικαστήριο Κύπρου [Cyprus Supreme Court], *Cypriot European Arrest Warrant Law Ruling*, 7 November 2005, Civil Action No. 294/2005
District Court for the Central District of California, Los Angeles, California, USA, *The State v Sergeant Stacey Koon, Officer Theodore J. Briseno, Officer Timothy E. Wind, Officer Laurence Powell, (Rodney King* case*)*, 29 April 1992
District Court of Rotterdam, The Netherlands, *Prosecutor v V15*, 10 January 2014, 10/960227-12 (ECLI:NL:RBROT:2014:119)
District Court of The Hague, *Prosecutor v Yvonne Basebya*, 1 March 2013, LJN: BZ4292
District Court, Criminal Law Section, Extradition Division, The Hague, *Public Prosecutor v Ahmatasevic*, Judgment, 5 May 2009, 08-3524
Divisional Court, UK, *In re Castioni*, 11 November 1890, [1891] 1Q.B. 149

ECJ, *Advocaten voor de Wereld VZW v Leden van de Ministeraad, Reference for a preliminary ruling from the Arbitragehof*, 3 May 2007, Case C/303-05

ECJ, *Andrea Francovich and Danila Bonifaci et al. v Italy*, 19 November 1991 Cases C-6 and 9/90, [1991] ECR I-5357

ECJ, *Ciprian Vasile Radu, Request for a preliminary ruling from the Curtea de Apel Constanţa*, 29 January 2013, Case No. C-396/11

ECJ, *Criminal Proceedings Against Filomeno Mario Miraglia, Reference for a preliminary ruling from the Tribunale di Bologna*, 10 March 2005, C-469/03

ECJ, *Criminal Proceedings Against Giuseppe Francesco Gasparini and Others (Reference for a preliminary ruling from the Audiencia Provincial de Málaga)*, 28 September 2006, C-467-/04

ECJ, *Criminal Proceedings against Hüseyin Gözütok and Klaus Brügge, Reference for a preliminary ruling from the Oberlandesgericht Köln, Germany, and the Rechtbank van eerste aanleg te Veurne, Belgium*, 11 February 2003, Joined Cases C-187/01 and C-385/01

ECJ, *Criminal Proceedings against Hüseyin Gözütok and Klaus Brügge, Reference for a preliminary ruling from the Oberlandesgericht Köln, Germany, and the Rechtbank van eerste aanleg te Veurne, Belgium*, Opinion of Advocate-General Ruiz Jarabo Colomer, 19 September 2002, Joined Cases C-187/01 and C-385/01

ECJ, *Criminal Proceedings Against Jürgen Kretzinger (Reference for a preliminary ruling from the Bundesgerichtshof)*, 18 July 2007, Case C-288/05

ECJ, *Criminal Proceedings Against Leopold Henri van Esbroeck*, 9 March 2006, Case C-436/04, 2006 E.C.R. I-2333

ECJ, *Criminal Proceedings Against Norma Kraaijenbrink*, 18 July 2007, Case C-367/5, [2007] ECR I-6619

ECJ, *Criminal Proceedings Against Vladimir Turanský. Reference for a preliminary ruling: Landesgericht für Strafsachen Wien – Austria*, 22 December 2008, C-491/07

ECJ, *Isabelle Lancray SA v Peters und Sickert KG*, Reference for a preliminary ruling from the *Bundesgerichtshof*, 3 July 1990, Case C-305/88, ECR I-2725

ECJ, *Leon Emile Gaston Carlos Debaecker and Berthe Plouvier v Cornelius Gerrit Bouwman (Reference for a preliminary ruling from the Hoge Raad der Nederlanden)*, 11 June 1985, Case 49/84

ECJ, *Pál Aranyosi and Robert Căldăraru v Generalstaatsanwaltschaft Bremen*, 5 April 2016, C-404/15 and C-659/15 PPU

ECJ, *Peter Klomps v Karl Michel (preliminary ruling requested by the Hoge Raad der Nederlanden)*, 16 June 1981, Case 166/80, ECR 1593

ECJ, *Toshiba Corporation and Others v Úřad pro ochranu hospodářské soutěže*, Opinion of AG Kokott, 14 February 2012, C-17/10

ECJ, *van Gend en Loos (NV Algemene Transporten Expeditie Onderneming v Nederlandse Administratie der Belastingen)*, 5 February 1963, Case 26/62

ECtHR Fifth Section, *Mohammed Ali Hassan Al-Moayad vs Germany, Decision on Admissibility*, 20 February 2007, Application No. 35865/03

ECtHR Fifth Section, *Sylvère Ahorugeze v Sweden*, 27 October 2011, Application No. 37075/09

ECtHR First Section, *Generoso Zigarella v Italy*, Admissibility, 3 October 2002, Application No. 48154/99

ECtHR First Section, *Ilhomjon Ismoilov and others v Russia*, 24 April 2008, Application No. 2947/06

ECtHR First Section, *Rustam Mamatkulov and Askarov Z. Abdurasulovic v Turkey*, 6 February 2003, Application Nos. 46827/99 and 46951/99

ECtHR First Section, *Rustam Mamatkulov and Zainiddin Abdurasulovic Askarov v Turkey*, 4 February 2005, Application Nos. 46827/99 and 46951/99

ECtHR Former Fifth Section, *Nizar Trabelsi v Belgium*, 4 September 2014, Application No. 140/10

ECtHR Former Fifth Section, *Nizar Trabelsi v Belgium*, Concurring Opinion of Judge Yudkivska, 4 September 2014, Application No. 140/10

ECtHR Former Fifth Section, *Nizar Trabelsi v Belgium*, Separate Opinion of Judge Power-Forde, 4 September 2014, Application No. 140/10

ECtHR Fourth Section, *Babar Ahmad and Others v UK*, 10 April 2012, Application Nos. 24027/07, 11949/08, 36742/08, 66911/09 and 67354/09

ECtHR Fourth Section, *Jones and Others v UK*, 14 January 2014, Application Nos. 34356/06 and 40528/06

ECtHR Fourth Section, *Omar Othman (Abu Qatada) v UK*, 17 January 2012, Application No. 8139/09

ECtHR Grand Chamber, *Abdullah Öcalan v Turkey*, 12 March 2003, Application No. 46221/99

ECtHR Grand Chamber, *Arthur Hutchinson v UK*, 17 January 2017, Application No. 57592/08

ECtHR Grand Chamber, *Arthur Hutchinson v UK*, Dissenting Opinion of Judge Pinto de Albuquerque, 17 January 2017, Application No. 57592/08

ECtHR Grand Chamber, *Douglas Gary Vinter and Others v UK*, 9 July 2013, Application Nos. 66069/09, 130/10, 3896/10

ECtHR Grand Chamber, *Fred Marguš v Croatia*, 27 May 2014, Application No. 4455/10

ECtHR Grand Chamber, *James Clifton Murray v The Netherlands*, 26 April 2016, Application No. 10511/10

ECtHR Grand Chamber, *Jørgen Pedersen and Sten Kristian Baadsgaard v Denmark*, 17 December 2004, Application No. 49017/99

ECtHR Grand Chamber, *Karamjit Singh Chahal v UK*, 15 November 1996, App. No. 22414/93

ECtHR Grand Chamber, *Mocanu and Others v Romania*, 17 September 2014, Application Nos. 10865/09, 45886/07 and 32431/08

ECtHR Grand Chamber, *Mocanu and Others v Romania*, Concurring Opinion of Judge Pinto de Albuquerque, Joined by Judge Vučinić, 17 September 2014, Application Nos. 10865/09, 45886/07 and 32431/08

ECtHR Grand Chamber, *Panayiotis Agapiou Panayi alias Kafkaris v Cyprus, Partly Dissenting Opinion of Judge Francisco Javier Borrego Borrego*, 12 February 2008, Application No. 21906/04

ECtHR Grand Chamber, *Panayiotis Agapiou Panayi alias Kafkaris v Cyprus*, 12 February 2008, Application No. 21906/04

ECtHR Grand Chamber, *Sergey Zolotoukhin v Russia*, 10 February 2009, Application No. 14939/03

ECtHR Press Unit (2017) Life Imprisonment, CoE, Strasbourg. https://www.echr.coe.int/Documents/FS_Life_sentences_ENG.pdf. Accessed 2 July 2018

ECtHR Second Section, *Abdullah Öcalan v Turkey* (No. 2), 18 March 2014, Applications numbers 24069/03, 197/04, 6201/06 and 10464/07

ECtHR Second Section, *Aleksandr Konstantinovich Nikitin v Russia*, 20 July 2004, Application No. 50178/99

ECtHR Second Section, *Ali Riza Göktan v France*, 2 July 2002, Application No. 33402/96

ECtHR Second Section, *Horciag v Romania*, 15 March 2005, Application No. 70982/01

ECtHR Third Section, *Franz Fischer v Austria*, 29 May 2001, Application No. 37950/97

ECtHR, *Affaire Grande Stevens et autre contre Italie*, 4 March 2014, Application Nos. 18640/10, 18647/10, 18663/10

ECtHR, *Bachmaier v Austria*, Decision on Admissibility, 2 September 2004, Application No. 77413/01

ECtHR, *Dombo Beheer BV v The Netherlands*, Application No. 14448/88, 27 October 1993, Series A, No. 274

ECtHR, *Félix Tomasi v France*, 27 August 1992, Application No. 12850/87, Series A, No. 241-A

ECtHR, First Section, *Alois Hauser-Sporn v Austria*, 7 December 2006, Application No. 37301/03

ECtHR, First Section, *Gerhard Sailer v Austria*, 6 June 2002, Application No. 38237/97

ECtHR, First Section, *Roland Schutte v Austria*, 26 July 2007, Application No. 18015/03

ECtHR, Former Fourth Section, *Abd Al Rahim Hussayn Muhammad Al Nashiri v Poland*, 24 July 2014, Application No. 28761/11

ECtHR, Former Fourth Section, *Husayn (Abu Zubaydah) v Poland*, 24 July 2014, Application No. 7511/13

ECtHR, Fourth Section, *Alexander Boman v Finland*, 17 February 2015, Application No. 41604/11

ECtHR, Fourth Section, *Nazzareno Zarb v Malta*, 4 July 2006, Application No. 16631/04

ECtHR, Fourth Section, *Vaidas Dungveckis v Lithuania*, Concurring Opinion of Judge Zupančič, 12 April 2016, Application No. 32106/08

ECtHR, *Hans Eckle and Marianne Eckle v FRG*, 15 July 1982, Application No. 8130/78, Series A, No. 51

ECtHR, *Hector Cruz Varas et al. v Sweden*, 20 March 1991, Application No. 15576/89, Series A, No. 201

ECtHR, *Jens Soering v UK*, 7 July 1989, Application No. 14038/88, Series A, Vol. 161

ECtHR, *Kaj-Erik Torsten Glantz v Finland*, 20 May 2014, Application No. 37394/11

ECtHR, *Karl-Heinz Wemhoff v FRG*, 25 April 1968, Application No. 2122/64

ECtHR, *László Magyar v Hungary*, 20 May 2014, Application No. 73593/10

ECtHR, *Maria Celeste Vieira Veloso de Oliveira v Switzerland*, 30 July 1998, Application No. 84/1997/868/1080

ECtHR, *W.F. v Austria*, 30 May 2002, Application No. 38275/97

Federal Court of Australia, *Zentai v Honourable Brendan O'Connor* (No. 3), 2 July 2010, [2010] FCA 691

Federal Criminal Court, Switzerland, *A, represented by Jacques Michod, Marc Bonnant and Magali Buser, lawyers v Office of the Attorney General of Switzerland, and B and C, both represented by Damien Chervaz, lawyer*, 25 July 2012, File No. BB.2011.140

Federal Criminal Court, Switzerland, *Khaled Nezzar alias A v Ministère Public de la Confédération, B and C (Office of the Attorney-General of Switzerland)*, 25 July 2012, Case No. BB.2011.140

Federal Criminal Oral Tribunal No. 1, San Martin, Argentina, *Public Prosecutor v Reynaldo Benito Antonio Bignone* [*'Campo de Mayo'* case (3)], *Verdict*, 12 March 2013, 2047

Federal Criminal Oral Tribunal No. 6, Buenos Aires, Argentina, *Public Prosecutor v Reynaldo Benito Antonio Bignone* [*'Plan Sistemático'* case], *Verdict*, 17 September 2012, 1351

First Senate in Criminal Matters of the German Reichsgericht, *Spanish-German Extradition Treaty* case, 1925–1926, Annual Digest of Public International Law Cases 308

German Federal Constitutional Court, *Baader-Meinhof Gang {Rote Armee Fraktion} (Red Army Faction)* case, 1 August 1978, 1977, BVerfGE 54, 208 1 BvR 797/78 Böll-decision

Hæstiréttur Íslands [Supreme Court, Iceland], *Jón Kristinsson v Iceland*, 25 November 1985, Case No. 77/1985

High Court of Justice, Divisional Court, on Appeal from the City of Westminster Magistrates' Court (District Judge Evans) and in the Matter for Judicial Review, Great Britain (UK), *Vincent Brown aka Vincent Bajinja, Charles Munyaneza, Emmanuel Nteziryayo & Celestin Ugirashebuja v The Government of Rwanda and the Secretary of State for the Home Department*, Appeal Against Extradition, 8 April 2009, Case CO/6247/2008

High Court of Justice, Divisional Court, on Appeal from the City of Westminster Magistrates' Court (District Judge Evans) and in the Matter for Judicial Review, Great Britain (UK), *Vincent Brown aka Vincent Bajinja, Charles Munyaneza, Emmanuel Nteziryayo & Celestin Ugirashebuja v The Government of Rwanda and the Secretary of State for the Home Department*, Appeal Against Extradition, Report by Appointed Expert William Schabas, Transcript, 22 April 2008, Case CO/6247/2008

High Court of Justice, Queen's Bench Division, Administrative Court, UK, *Artur Krolik v Regional Court in Czestochowa*, Poland, 17 August 2012, CO/2864/2012, CO/2915/2012, CO/2868/2012, CO/2918/2012, CO/2861/2012, CO/2747/2012, [2012] EWHC 2357, [2013] 1 W.L.R. 2390

High Court of Justice, Queen's Bench Division, Divisional Court, UK, *Miklis v Deputy Prosecutor General of Lithuania*, 11 May 2006, CO/1489/2006 [2006] EWHC 1032 (Admin)

High Court of Justice, Queen's Bench Division, Divisional Court, UK, *Regina (on the application of Adel Abdul Bary and Khalid Al Fawwaz) v Secretary of State for the Home Department*, 7 August 2009, CO/5577/2008 and C0/5511/2008, [2009] WL 2392232

High Court, Australia, *Minister for Home Affairs of the Commonwealth v Charles Zentai*, 15 August 2012, P56/2011, [2012] HCA 28

High Court, Australia, *Riley v The Commonwealth of Australia*, 18 December 1985, [1985] HCA 82, 159 CLR 1, 62 ALR 497

High Court, Austrialia, *Republic of Croatia (Appellant) v Daniel Snedden aka Dragan Vasiljkovic (Respondent)*, 19 May 2010, [2010] HCA 14

High Court, Ireland, *Attorney General v Damache*, 30 June 2015, IEHC 339

High Court, Transvaal Provincial Division, South Africa, *The State v Johannes Velde van der Merwe and four others*, Plea and Sentencing Agreement in Terms of Section 105A of Act 51 of 1977 (as amended), 17 August 2007

High Risk Tribunal, Guatemala City, Guatemala, *Prosecutor v Esteelmer Reyes Girón* and *Heriberto Valdez Asij, Verdict*, 26 February 2016

Hoge Raad [Supreme Court, the Netherlands] First Division, *Mothers of Srebrenica Association et al. v State of The Netherlands and the United Nations* [*Mothers of Srebrenica* case], 13 April 2012, 10/04437

Hoge Raad [Supreme Court, The Netherlands], *Public Prosecutor v Joseph Mpambara*, 26 November 2013, Case No. 12/04592 (ECLI:NL:HR:2013:1420)

Hoge Raad [Supreme Court, The Netherlands], *Short v The Netherlands*, 30 March 1990, 13.949 and 13.950

Hoge Raad [Supreme Court, The Netherlands], *Public Prosecutor v Joseph Mpambara*, 21 October 2008, 09-750007-07

Högsta Domstolens [Supreme Court], Sweden, *Decision on Sylvère Ahorugeze Extradition to Rwanda*, 26 May 2009, Ö 1082-09

Højesteret [Supreme Court, Denmark], *Prosecution Service v T* (Attorney Bjørn Elmquist, appointed), Order, 26 April 2012, Case 2/2012

Højesteret [Supreme Court, Denmark], *Prosecution Service v T* (Attorney Bjørn Elmquist, appointed), Order, 6 November 2013, Case 105/2013

HoL, A and Others (Appellants) (FC) and Others v Secretary of State for the Home Department (Respondent) (Conjoined Appeals), 8 December 2005, {2005}, UKHL 71

HoL, *A and Others (Appellants) (FC) and Others v Secretary of State for the Home Department (Respondent)* (Conjoined Appeals), Opinion of Lord Bingham of Cornhill, 8 December 2005, {2005}, UKHL 71

HoL, *Charles Connelly v Director of Public Prosecutions*, 1 October 1964, 3727/63, DPP 2/3771, 2 WLR 1145
HoL, *Dabas v High Court of Justice in Madrid,* Spain, 28 February 2007, [2007] 2 WLR 254
HoL, *Office of the King's Prosecutor (Brussels) v Cando Armas et al.*, 17 November 2005, [2005] UKHL 67, 2005 3 WLR 1079
HoL, *Regina v Bartle and Commissioner of Police for the Metropolis and Others (Appellants) ex parte Pinochet (Respondent); Regina v Evans and another and Commissioner of Police for the Metropolis and others (Appellants) ex parte Pinochet (Respondent), On Appeal from a Divisional Court of the Queen's Bench Division*, 24 March 1999, 2000 1 AC 147 HL
HRC, *AP v Italy*, 2 November 1987, Communication No. 204/1986
HRC, *Bautista de Arellana v Colombia*, 27 October 1995, Communication No. 563/1993
HRC, *Carlton Reid v Jamaica*, 20 July 1990, Communication No. 250/1987
HRC, *Charles Chitat Ng v Canada*, 7 January 1994, Communication No. 469/191
HRC, *Comments on Nigeria*, 24 July 1996, Doc. CCPR/C/79/Add.65 (1996)
HRC, *Concluding Observations on Guatemala*, 27 August 2001, CCPR/CO/72/GTM
HRC, *Glenn Ashby v Trinidad and Tobago*, 21 March 2012, Communication No. 580/1994
HRC, *Hugo Rodríguez v Uruguay*, 9 August 1994, Communication no. 322/1988
HRC, *Joseph Kindler v. Canada*, 11 November 1993, Communication No. 470/1991
HRC, *Nature of the General Legal Obligation Imposed on State Parties to the Covenant Eighteenth Session*, General Comment, No. 31 [80], 26 May 2004, Doc. CCPR/C/21/Rev.1/Ad.13
HRC, *Summary Record of the 1519th Meeting*, Perú, 1 November 1996, Document CCPR/C/SR.1519 (1997)
HRC, *Webby Chisanga v Zambia*, 18 October 2005, Communication No. 1132/2002
IACmmHR, *Alicia Consuelo Herrera et al. v Argentina*, 2 October 1992, Report No. 28/92, Cases 10.147, 10.181, 10.240, 10.262, 10.309 and 10.311
IACmmHR, *Report on the Situation of Human Rights in El Salvador*, 11 February 1994, Doc. OEA/Ser.L/II.85 Doc. 28 rev.
IACtHR, *Almonacid-Arellano et al. v Chile*, Preliminary Objections, Merits, Reparations and Costs, 26 September 2006, Series C, No. 154
IACtHR, *Chumbipuma Aguirre and Others v Perú (Barrios Altos* case*)*, 14 March 2001, Series C, No. 75
IACtHR, *Gomes Lund et al. (Guerrilha Do Araguaia) v Brazil,* Preliminary Objections, Merits, Reparations and Costs, 24 November 2010, Series C, No. 219
IACtHR, *Juan Gelman v Uruguay (Merits and Reparations)*, 24 February 2011, Series C, No. 221
IACtHR, *La Cantuta v Perú* (Merits, Reparations and Costs), 29 November 2006, Series C, No. 162

IACtHR, *Myrna Mack Chang v Guatemala*, Merits, Reparations and Costs, 25 November 2003, Ser. C No. 101

ICJ, *Arrest Warrant of 11 April 2000 (DRC v Belgium)*, 14 February 2002, ICJ Rep. 2002, p. 3

ICJ, *Arrest Warrant of 11 April 2000 (DRC v Belgium), Dissenting Opinion of Judge Christine van den Wyngaert*, 14 February 2002, ICJ Rep. 2002, p. 3

ICJ, *Arrest Warrant of 11 April 2000 (DRC v Belgium), Joint Separate Opinion of Judges Higgins, Kooijmans and Buergenthal*, 14 February 2002, ICJ Rep. 2002, p. 3

ICJ, *Certain Questions of Mutual Legal Assistance in Criminal Matters* [*Djibouti v France*], *Pleadings*, CR 2008/7, Statement of Alain Pellet, Counsel for France, 25 January 2008, General List No. 136

ICJ, *Certain Questions on Mutual Assistance in Criminal Matters (Djibouti v France), Judgment*, 4 June 2008, General List No. 136

ICJ, *Legal Consequences of the Construction of a Wall in the Occupied Palestinian Territory (Israeli Wall Advisory Opinion)*, Advisory Opinion, 9 July 2004, ICJ GL No. 131, [2004] ICJ Rep. 136

ICJ, *Liechtenstein v Guatemala (Nottebohm* case*)*, 6 April 1855, I.C.J. Rep. 1955, p. 4, General List No. 18

ICJ, *United States Diplomatic and Consular Staff in Tehran (USA v Iran) (Iranian Hostages Case)*, 24 May 1980, [1980] ICJ Rep. 3

ICT of Bangladesh, Second Chamber, *Chief Prosecutor v. Moulana Abul Kalam Azad*, 21 January 2013, 05 (2012)

ICTR Trial Chamber II, *Prosecutor v. Joseph Kanyabashi*, Decision on the Defence Motion on Jurisdiction, 18 June 1997, Case No. ICTR-96-15

ICTR Trial Chamber III, *Prosecutor v Ildephonse Hategekimana, Decision on Prosecutor's Request for the Referral of the Case of Ildephonse Hategekimana to Rwanda*, 19 June 2008, Case No. ICTR-00-55BR11bis

ICTR Trial Chamber III, *Prosecutor v Yussuf Munyakazi, Decision on Prosecutor's Request for Referral of the Indictment to the Republic of Rwanda, Rule 11bis of the Rules of Procedure and Evidence*, 28 May 2008, Case No. ICTR-97-36A-T

ICTY Appeals Chamber, *Prosecutor v Tihomir Blaškić, Judgment on the Request of the Republic of Croatia for Review of the Decision of the Trial Chamber II of 18 July 1997*, 29 October 1997, Case No. IT-95-14-AR 108*bis*

ICTY Trial Chamber II, *Prosecutor v Tihomir Blaškić, Decision on the Objection of the Republic of Croatia to the Issuance of Subpoena Duces Tecum*, 18 July 1997, Case No. IT-95-14

ICTY Trial Chamber, *Prosecutor v Anto Furundžija*, 10 December 1998, Case No. IT-95-17/1-T

ICTY, *Prosecutor v Milan Martić*, ICTY Trial Chamber, Decision on the Prosecutor's Motion to Request Leave to File a Corrected Amended Indictment, 18 December 2002, Case No. IT-95-11

IHT Appeals Commission, *Public Prosecutor v Saddam Hussein Al Majeed et al.* [*Dujail* case], 26 December 2006, Case No. 29/c/2006

Judicial Committee of the Privy Council, *Earl Pratt and Ivan Morgan v The Attorney-General for Jamaica and The Superintendent of Prisons, Saint Catherine's, Jamaica*, 2 November 1993, 210/1986 and 225/1987
Juez Sexto de Distrito de Procesos Penales Federales en el Distrito Federal [Sixth District Judge in Criminal Matters of the First Circuit, Mexican Federal Court], *Miguel Angel Cavallo* case, 11 January 2001, Resolution 5/2000
Polski Sąd Najwyższy [Polish Supreme Court], *In the Matter of Extradition of Mandugueqi*, 29 July 1997, II KKN 313/97
Qorti Kostituzzjonali [Constitutional Court] Malta, *Ben Hassine Ben Ali Wahid v Honourable Prime Minister and Advocate-General of the Republic of Malta*, 7 November 2016, Constitutional Application 60/13 AF
Qorti Kriminali [Criminal Court], Malta, *Ir-Repubblika ta' Malta vs Christian Grech*, Akkuza 6/2011, 14 May 2012
Queens Bench Division, Divisional Court, England and Wales, UK, *Bite v Latvia*, 6 October 2009, [2009] EWHC 3092
SCSL Appeals Chamber, *Prosecutor v Charles Ghankay Taylor, Decision on Immunity from Jurisdiction*, 31 May 2004, Case No. SCSL-2003-01-I
SCSL Appeals Chamber, *Prosecutor v Morris Kallon and Brima Bazzy Kamara, Decision on Challenge to Jurisdiction: Lomé Accord Amnesty*, 13 March 2004, Case No. SCSL-2004-15-AR72(E) and Case No. SCSL-2004-16-AR72(E)
SCSL, *Prosecutor v Charles Ghankay Taylor, Judgment*, 26 April 2012, SCSL-2003-1-I
SCSL, *Prosecutor v Sam Hinga Norman, Moinina Fofana and Allieu Kondewa, Decision on the First Accused's Motion for Service and Arraignment on the Consolidated Indictment*, 29 November 2004, Case No. SCSL-04-14-T
SCSL, Trial Chamber II, *Prosecutor v Charles Ghankay Taylor*, Judgment Summary, 26 April 2011, SCSL-03-1-T
Senior District Judge Howard Riddle, Chief Magistrate, UK, *Davit Kezerashvili Extradition Proceedings, Discharge*, 21 March 2016
Stockholm District Court, Sweden, *Prosecutor v Théodore Rukeratabaro*, 27 June 2018
Supreme Court of Appeal, South Africa, *The Minister of Justice and Constitutional Development v The Southern African Litigation Centre*, 15 March 2016, 867/15 [2016] ZASCA 17
Supreme Court, Canada, *Minister of Justice, USA v Glen Sebastian Burns and Atif Ahmad Rafay*, 15 February 2001, File No. 26129, 2001 SCC 7
Supreme Court, Canada, *Regina v Imre Finta*, 24 March 1994, Case No. 23023, 23097
Supreme Court, Ireland, *Ellis v O'Dea*, 1989, Irish Reports 530
Supreme Court, Ireland, *Finucane v McMahon*, 13 March 1990, [1990] 1 I.R. 165
Supreme Court, Ireland, *McGlinchey v Wren*, 7 December 1982, Irish Reports 154
Supreme Court, Ireland, *Minister for Justice, Equality and Law Reform v. Robert Rettinger*, Appeal No: 165 & 189 of 2010, [2010] IESC 45 [2010], 1 I.R.M. 157
Supreme Court, Ireland, *Seamus Shannon v Ireland*, January 1984, Irish Reports 548

Supreme Court, Ireland, *The State {Duggan} vs Tapley*, 1952, Irish Reports 62
בית המשפט העליון [Supreme Court], Israel, *Attorney-General of Israel v Adolf Eichmann*, 29 May 1962, Criminal Appeal 336/61
Supreme Court, Rwanda, *Tubarimo Aloys v The Government*, 29 August 2008, Case. No. RS/INCONST/Pén. 0002/08/CS
Supreme Court, Uganda (at Mengo), *Attorney-General v Susan Kigula and 417 Others*, 21 January 2009, Constitutional Appeal No. 3 of 2006
Supreme Court, Zimbabwe, *Catholic Commission for Justice and Peace in Zimbabwe v Attorney-General and Others*, 20 May 1993, 21 May 1993, 24 June 1993, 1993 (4) SA 239 (ZS)
The Hague District Court, *Prosecutor v Eshetu Alemu*, 15 December 2017, ECLI: NL:RBDHA:2017:14782
The Hague District Court, *Public Prosecutor v Joseph Mpambara*, Interlocutory Decision, 24 July 2007, 09/750009-06 and 09/750007-07
The High Court of Justice, Queen's Bench Division, UK, *Ndiki Mutua, Paulo Nzili, Wambugu Wa Nyigi, Jane Muthoni Mara and Susan Ngondi v The Foreign and Commonwealth Office*, 5 October 2012, HQ09X02666
Tribunal de Première Instance de Kigali [Court of First Instance of Kigali], Rwanda, *Public Prosecutor v Froduald Karamira*, 14 February 1997, Case No. 7
Trybunał Konstytucyjny [Polish Constitutional Court], *Constitutionality of Laws Implementing the Secondary Law of the European Union*, 27 April 2005, Case Number P1/05, OTK-A 2005, No. 4, Item 42
USA Court of Appeals for the Eleventh Circuit, USA, *Mamani et al v Sánchez de Losada, and Mamani et al v Sánchez Berzain*, 28 August 2011, Case Nos. 09-16246 and 10-13071
USA Court of Appeals for the Fourth Circuit, *Bashe Abdi Yousuf, John Doe 1, John Doe 2, Aziz Deria, Plaintiffs–Appellees, John Doe 3, John Doe 4, Jane Doe 1, Plaintiffs v Mohamed Ali Samantar, Defendant–Appellant*, 2 November 2012, 11-1479
USA Court of Appeals, Second Circuit, *Dolly and Joel Filártiga v Americo Norberto Peña-Irala*, 30 June 1980, No. 191, Docket 79-6090, 630 F.2d 876
USA Court of Appeals, Second Circuit, *John Peter Galanis, Petitioner-appellant v Ermen Pallanck, U.S. Marshal for the District of Connecticut, Respondent-appellee*, 22 November 1977, 568 F.2d 234 (2d Cir. 1977)
USA Court of Appeals, District of Columbia Circuit, *USA v Omar Mohammed Ali Rezaq*, Opinion of Judge Patricia Wald, 6 February 1998, 134 F.3d 1121 (D.C. Cir. 1998), 96-3127
USA Court of Appeals, Fifth Circuit, *Albert Gusikoff and Paul Rosen, Plaintiffs-Appellants v United States of America, Respondent-Appellee*, 6 June 1980, No. 79-3500, 620 F.2d 459 (5th Cir. 1980)
USA Court of Appeals, Fifth Circuit, *Marcos Perez Jimenez, Appellant v Manuel Aristeguieta, Intervenor, Appellee, and John E. Maguire, Appellee*, 12 December 1962, No. 19507, 311 F.2d 547

USA Court of Appeals, First Circuit, *George Koskotas, Petitioner, v James B. Roche, United States Marshal for the District of Massachusetts, Respondent*, 30 April 1991, 931 F.2d 169

USA Court of Appeals, Ninth Circuit, *Matter of the Extradition of Smyth*, 27 July 1995, 61 F.3d 711

USA Court of Appeals, Second Circuit, *Dolly and Joel Filártiga v Americo Norberto Peña-Irala*, 30 June 1980, No. 191, Docket 79-6090, 630 F.2d 876

USA Court of Appeals, Second Circuit, *Joseph Patrick Thomas Doherty v Department of Justice, Immigration and Naturalization Service*, 29 June 1990, Nos. 662, 880, Dockets 88-4084, 89-4092

USA Court of Appeals, Second Circuit, *Michele Sindona v George V. Grant*, 21 March 1980, Nos. 618, 764, Dockets 78-2155, 79-2175, 619 F.2d 167 (178)

USA Court of Appeals, Second Circuit, *Re Mr. and Mrs. Doe, Witnesses Before the Grand Jury*, 6 December 1988, 860 F.2d 430

USA Courts of Appeals, Second Circuit, *Muhamed Sacirbey, Petitioner-Appellant, v. Joseph R. Guccione, United States Marshal for the SDNY; Officer Dennis Spitzer, Chief Pretrial Services for the Southern District of New York, Respondents-Appellees*, 9 December 2009, Docket Nos. 06-5137-pr (L), 07-0018-pr (con), 589 F.3d 52

USA District Court for the Eastern District of New York, *Ancel Vincent Elcock, Petitioner v United States of America, Respondent*, 26 January 2000, Civil Action No. CV-99-1757 (DGT), 80 F. Supp. 2d 70 (E.D.N.Y. 2000)

USA District Court for the Eastern District of New York, *United States of America v Jose Franklin Jurado-Rodriguez and Edgar Alberto Garcia-Montilla, Defendants*, No. CR 94-547, 907 F. Supp. 568 (1995)

USA District Court for the Southern District of Florida, *United States of America v Manuel Antonio Noriega*, 8 June 1990, 88-79-CR, 746 F. Supp. 1506 (1990)

USA District Court for the Southern District of New York, *In the Matter of the Extradition of Sergio Locatelli, a/k/a "Sergio Luigi Locatelli", a/k/a "Guido Zaccaria"*, 6 March 1979, No. 78 Cr. Misc. No. 1 (KTD), 468 F. Supp. 568 (1979)

USA District Court, *In the Matter of the Extradition of McMullen*, 11 May 1979, 3-78-1099 MG

Ústavní Soud [Constitutional Court], Czech Republic, *V. M. against a decision of the Regional Court in Ostrava of 4 December 2000 (Danger of Torture* case*)*, 15 April 2003, I. ÚS 752/02

Ustavno sodišče Slovenije [Constitutional Court, Slovenia], *Annullment of the second subparagraph of paragraph 2 of article 40 of the Asylum Act (Official Gazette of the Republic of Slovenia, No. 61/99)*, 29 June 2000, Official Gazette RS, No. 66/2000

Cases in Chapter 17

Corte Suprema de Justicia de la Nación [Supreme Court], *Argentina, Julio Héctor Simón y otros v Poder Judicial de la Nación*, 14 June 2005, 17.768 S.1767. XXXVIII
ICJ, *Germany v USA (LaGrand* case*)*, 27 June 2001, [2001] ICJ Rep. 466
PCIJ, *Treatment of Polish Nationals and Other Persons of Polish Origin or Speech in the Danzig Territory* (*The Polish Nationals in Danzig* case), Advisory Opinion No. 23, 4 February 1932, [1932] PCIJ, Series A/B, No. 44

Cases in Chapter 18

Eastern Division of the Danish High Court, 3rd Chamber, *Public Prosecutor v Refik Sarić*, 25 November 1994, S-3396-94
Højesteret (Danish Supreme Court), *Public Prosecutor v Refik Sarić*, 15 August 1995, S-3396-94
IACtHR, *Ivcher Bronstein v Peru (Competence)*, 24 September 1999, Series C, No. 54

Cases in Chapter 19

ACmmHPR, *Commission Nationale des Droits de l'Homme et des Libertés v Chad*, 11 October 1995, Communication No. 74/92
ECtHR First Section, *Kadir Satik and Others v Turkey*, 10 October 2000, Application No. 31866/96
ECtHR First Section, *Torquil Dick Erikson v Italy*, Decision as to Admissibility, 26 October 1999, Application No. 37900/97
ECtHR Grand Chamber, *Maşallah Öneryildiz v Turkey*, 30 November 2004, Application No. 48939/99
ECtHR Second Section, *Hasan İlhan v Turkey*, 9 November 2004, Application No. 22494/93
ECtHR Second Section, *Sevtap Veznedaroğlu v Turkey*, 11 April 2000, Application No. 32357/96
ECtHR, *Anton Assenov and Others v Bulgaria*, 28 October 1998, Application No. 90/1997/874/1086
ECtHR, *Assya Anguelova v Bulgaria*, 13 June 2002, Application No. 38361/97
ECtHR, *Koçeri Kurt v Turkey*, 25 May 1998, Application No. 15/1997/799/1002
ECtHR, Third Section, *Carol Ciorcan and Others v Romania*, 27 January 2015, Application Nos. 29414/09 and 44841/09
HoL, *Regina v Bartle and the Commissioner of the Police for the Metropolis and Others (Appellants) Ex parte Pinochet (Respondent) on Appeal from a Divisional*

Court of the Queen's Bench Division; Regina v Evans and Another and the Commissioner of the Police for the Metropolis and Others (Appellants) Ex parte Pinochet (Respondent) on Appeal from a Divisional Court of the Queen's Bench Division, Opinion of Lord Slynn of Hadley, 25 November 1998, 37 ILM (1998) 1302

IACtHR, *Anstraum Aman Villagrán-Morales et al v Guatemala (Case of the 'Street Children')*, 19 November 1999, Series C, No. 63

IACtHR, *Anstraum Aman Villagrán-Morales et al v Guatemala (Case of the 'Street Children')*, Joint Concurring Opinion of Judges Antônio Augusto Cançado Trindade, Alirio Abreu Burelli and Manuel E. Ventura-Robles, 19 November 1999, Series C, No. 63

IACtHR, *Nicholas Chapman Blake v Guatemala*, 24 January 1998, Series C, No. 36

IACtHR, *Velásquez-Rodríguez v Honduras*, 29 July 1988, Series C, No. 4

ICC Trial Chamber V(B), *Prosecutor v Uhuru Muigai Kenyatta, Decision on the Withdrawal of Charges Against Mr. Kenyatta*, 13 March 2015, Case No. ICC-01/09-02/11

ICJ, *Arrest Warrant of 11 April 2000 (DRC v Belgium)*, Dissenting Opinion of Judge Christine van den Wyngaert, 14 February 2002, ICJ Rep. 2002, p. 3

ICJ, *Legal Consequences of the Construction of a Wall in the Occupied Palestinian Territory (Israeli Wall Advisory Opinion)*, Advisory Opinion, 9 July 2004, ICJ GL No. 131, [2004] ICJ Rep. 136

ICJ, *Questions Relating to the Obligation to Extradite or Prosecute* (*Belgium v Senegal*), 20 July 2012, ICJ Rep. 2012, p. 422

ICTY Appeals Chamber, *Prosecutor v Zejnil Delalić et al.*, 20 February 2001, Case No. IT-96-21-A

ICTY Trial Chamber I, Section A, *Prosecutor v Momir Nikolić*, 2 December 2003, Case No. IT-02-60/1-S

ICTY Trial Chamber, *Prosecutor v Anto Furundžija*, 10 December 1998, Case No. IT-95-17/1-T

Suprema Corte de Justicia de la Nación [Supreme Court], Mexico, *Ricardo Miguel Cavallo, Amparo en Revision*, 10 June 2003, Case No. 14/2002

USA Court of Appeals, District of Columbia Circuit, *USA v Omar Mohammed Ali Rezaq*, 6 February 1998, 134 F.3d 1121 (D.C. Cir. 1998), 96-3127

USA District Court for the Southern District of New York, *USA v Ramzi Ahmed Yousef et al*, 29 May 1996, 927 F. Supp. 673 (S.D.N.Y. 1996), S12 93 Cr.180 (KTD)

USA District Court, District of Columbia, *USA v Fawaz Yunis*, 12 February 1988, 681 F. Supp. 896 (D.D.C. 1988) Crim. A No. 87-0377

Cases in Chapter 20

IACtHR, *Velásquez-Rodríguez v Honduras*, 29 July 1988, Series C, No. 4
ICC Pre-Trial Chamber I, Situation in the DRC, *Prosecutor v Thomas Lubanga Dyilo, Decision on the Prosecutor's Application for a Warrant of Arrest*, 10 February 2006, Case No. ICC-01/04-01/06
ICTY Appeals Chamber, Prosecutor v *Duško Tadić, ICTY Decision on the Defence Motion for Interlocutory Appeal on Jurisdiction*, 2 October 1995, Case No. IT-94-1-AR72

Cases in Chapter 21

ECJ, *György Katz v István Roland Sós* (Opinion of AG Kokott), 10 July 2008, Case C-404/07
ECtHR Grand Chamber, *Patricia Armani da Silva v UK*, 30 March 2016, Application No. 5878/08
ECtHR Third Section, *Anton Shestopalov v Russia*, 28 March 2017, Application No. 46248/07
ICJ, *Nuclear Tests Case (Australia v France)*, 20 December 1974, ICJ Rep 1974, p. 253
ICTY Appeals Chamber, *Prosecutor v Duško Tadić, Decision on the Defence Motion for Interlocutory Appeal on Jurisdiction*, 2 October 1995, Case No. IT-94-1
ICTY Trial Chamber II, *Prosecutor v Tihomir Blaškić, Decision on the Objection of the Republic of Croatia to the Issuance of Subpoena Duces Tecum*, 18 July 1997, Case No. IT-95-14
PCIJ Twelfth Ordinary Session, *Case of S.S. Lotus (France v Turkey)*, 7 September 1927, PCIJ Series A, No. 10

Cases in Chapter 23

Appeal Court, High Court of Justiciary, Scotland, *Abdelbaset Ali Mohmed Al Megrahi v Her Majesty's Advocate*, 14 March 2002, C/104/01
HRC, Summary Record of the 1519th Meeting: *Perú,* Fifty-seventh session, U.N. Doc., CCPR/C/SR.1519
Tribunal of First Instance, Brussels (Investigating Magistrate Damien Vandermeersch), *re Pinochet*, 8 November 1998

Index

A
A and Others (Appellants), 493, 647
ABA, 343
Abass, 274, 284, 285
Abduction and kidnapping of children, 486
Abdulaye Yerodia Ndombasi et al, 348, 633
Abi-Saab, 24
Abolitionist movement, 511
Abolitionist States, 427, 514
Abolition of the death penalty, 427, 510, 511
Absence of international protest, 340
Absolute immunity, 518, 520
Absolute political offence, 439
Absolute universal jurisdiction, 340, 359
Abu-Bakr al-Siddiq Battalion, 158
Abu Hawsher, 474
Abuja, 362
Abu Omar, 530, 641
Abu Qatada, 474, 644
Abuse of process, 212, 248, 256–260, 262–265, 277, 278, 296, 343, 419, 468, 627, 630
Abuse of process doctrine, 557
Academics, 582
Accessory obligations, 575
Access to justice, 328, 385, 386, 571, 574, 589, 593, 605
Accomplices, 600
Accountability, 584
Achille Lauro, 103
Achour, 500, 501
ACHPR, 384, 426, 436, 444
ACJHR, 34
ACmmHPR, 467, 514
Acquaviva, 370, 371
Acquired rights, 338, 426
Acquittal, 233, 235, 247, 248, 256, 261, 455, 476, 477, 483, 484, 493
Across-the-board exemption, 460
Actio criminalis popularis, 347
Actio popularis, 584, 593
Active nationality principle, 330
Act of war, 102
Acts of aggression, 105
Acts of mutilation, 458
Actus reus, 65, 90, 91, 101, 119
Addis Ababa, Ethiopia, 21
Additional Protocol, 103, 440, 487
Additional Protocol 1975, 440
Additional Protocol II, 129
Additional State Parties, 105
Ad hoc international criminal tribunals, 33
Ad hoc tribunals, 16–19, 125, 127, 148–150, 152–154, 167, 168, 172, 173, 176, 189, 195, 570, 613
Adjustment of a life sentence, 501, 502
Administrative considerations, 608
Administrative proceedings, 481
Admissibility procedure, 606
Admissibility proceedings, 591
Admissibility test, 174, 178, 184, 336, 478, 483, 594, 608
Admissibility threshold, 46
Adolf Eichmann, 334, 359, 638
Adversarial criminal justice system, 373
Adversarial proceedings, 384
Adverse inference, 185
Advisory opinion, 571, 654
Advocaten voor de Wereld, 450–452, 643
ADX Florence, 496, 502

C. Soler, *The Global Prosecution of Core Crimes under International Law*,
https://doi.org/10.1007/978-94-6265-335-1

Affaire Aylor, 427, 640
Affaire Grande Stevens, 481, 645
Afghanistan, 293, 607, 630
Africa, 34, 127
African Charter on Human and Peoples' Rights, 426, 514
African Criminal Court, 34, 120
African Head of State, 607
African National Congress, 21
African Pinochet, 359
African States, 21, 607
Afro-centrist objections, 20
Agathe Habyarimana née Kanziga, 367, 632
Agenda for Sustainable Development, 614
Agents of the State, 385
Age of criminal of responsibility, 457
AG General Ruiz Jarabo Colomer, 488
Aggravated abduction, 463
Aggravated form of inhuman treatment, 495
Aggravated responsibility, 106, 111, 112, 131, 134
Aggression, 44, 104, 105
Aggrieved State, 355, 360
Aguilar Diaz et al. v Pinochet, 340, 341, 638
Ahmatasevic, 449, 642
Ahmen An-Na'im, 513
Ahorugeze, 374, 472, 474, 634, 643, 647
AIDP, 9
Aircraft, 499
Air piracy, 354
Akande, 245, 249, 250, 260, 267, 270–272, 277, 280–283, 286–289, 291
Akehurst, 194
Akhavan, 229, 240
Aksenova, 225, 227
Al-Adsani, 331, 634
Al-Ajami Al-Atiri, 158
Al Bashir, 65, 90, 92, 169, 186, 187, 199, 458, 607, 620, 621, 624, 625
Alecos Modinos v Cyprus, 383, 634
Alemu, 482, 499, 508
Al Fawwaz, 496, 647
Algeria, 436, 454, 519
Al-Hamasher, 474
Alibi, 454
Alien Tort Claims Act, 529
Ali Rezaq, 354
Ali Wahid, 504, 650
Al-Jedda v UK, 34, 619
Allegations of ill-treatment, 381
Al Megrahi, 612, 655
Al Moayad, 469, 474, 476, 494, 643
Almonacid-Arellano, 478, 482, 483, 648
Al Nashiri, 507, 508, 645
Aloys, 506, 651
Al Qaeda, 505
Al-Senussi, 217, 224–229, 231, 237, 239, 240, 250–252, 626–628
Al-Skeini and Others v UK, 34, 620
Alternative duty to prosecute, 355
Alternative enforcement measures, 313
Alternative obligation, 324, 354, 355, 405
Altman, 64
Ambach, 189
Ambiguities, 590
Ambos, 126, 134, 171, 190
American double jeopardy standards, 343
American forces, 293
American prosecutions, 352
American Servicemembers' Protection Act, 295
Amnesia, 454
Amnesties, 135, 193, 222, 243, 246, 418, 419, 428, 434, 454–466, 481, 490, 492, 583, 589, 650
Amnesty laws, 552, 570, 572
Amneus, 70, 74, 76
Amsterdam Court of Appeals, 341
Amsterdam Treaty, 241
Analogical interpretation, 325
Analytical interpretation, 591
Ancillary obligations, 575, 576
Angel of death, 380
Anglo-American Incidence Test, 438
Anglo-Indian Extradition Treaty, 446
Anglo-USA Supplementary Extradition Treaty, 443
Angola, 44, 454
Anguelova, 387
Anonima Sarda, 349
Anstraum Aman Villagrán-Morales et al v Guatemala, 385, 569, 636, 654
Antelope case, 138
Anti-Balaka, 128
Anticipatory measures, 72, 73
Anti-terrorist convention, 357
Anto Furundžija, 321, 637
Anton Assenov and Others v Bulgaria, 387, 634, 653
Antônio Augusto Cançado Trindade, Judge, 426
Anya Velikova v Bulgaria, 387, 634
Apartheid, 424, 441
Apartheid Convention, 177, 441
Applicable procedures, 313
Application of the Convention on the Prevention and Punishment of the Crime of Genocide, 326, 636

Application of the Convention on the Prevention and Punishment of the Crime of Genocide (BiH v Serbia and Montenegro), 113, 177, 622, 625
Application of the Convention on the Prevention and Punishment of the Crime of Genocide (Croatia v Serbia), 622
Appropriate basis, 181, 195
Arab Charter on Human Rights, 345
Arab League Agreement, 432
Arab State, 187
Arancibia Clavel, Enrique Lautaro Homicidio Calificado y Asociación Ilicita y Otros, 383, 633
Aranyosi and Caldararu, 498
Arbiter, 167, 197, 591
Arbitrary arrest, 460
Arbitrary decisions, 349
Arbitrary detentions, 259, 379
Arbour, Judge, 175
Area of freedom, security and justice, 377
Arendt, 74–76
Argentina, 71, 191, 356, 359, 364, 376, 380, 382, 383, 454, 456, 464, 486, 506, 532, 633, 640, 641, 646, 648
Argentina *junta* trials, 366
Argentine Constitution, 71
Argentine intelligence officer, 379
Argentinian national legislation, 552
Argentinian Supreme Court, 552
Argentinian Supreme Court of Justice, 461
Arklöf, 360, 638
Armani da Silva v UK, 593, 655
Armas, 435, 648
Armed actors, 48
Armed conflict, 101–103, 124, 127–129, 138, 440, 494, 512
Armed opposition groups, 44, 570
Armenia, 67, 382, 510
Army Captain Ely Ould Dah, 498
Arnold, 103, 104
Arrangements, 181, 189, 200
Arrest, 16–19, 21, 212–214, 216, 217, 219, 223, 229, 232, 247, 249, 250, 255, 256, 258–261, 263, 264, 266, 269–272, 274, 276–278, 283, 285, 287–290, 292, 313, 434, 450, 455, 482, 520, 619, 627–631
Arrest warrant, 313, 428, 429, 432, 433, 444, 449, 452, 519, 520, 523, 532, 640, 642, 649
Arrest Warrant of 11 April 2000, 349, 636
Arrest Warrant of 11 April 2000 (DRC v Belgium), 573, 654
Arson, 439
Article 98 agreements, 293
Asian dissent, 607
Asian States, 607
ASP, 45, 100, 104, 185–190, 199, 532, 564
ASP prerogatives, 187
Assenov, 387
Assertion of universal jurisdiction, 344, 351
Assessment *in abstracto*, 454
Assessment *in concreto*, 453
Assize Court, 421, 501, 502, 640
Association des Victimes des Crimes et Répressions Politiques au Tchad (AVCRP) et al. v Hissène Habré, 330, 633
Assurances, 417, 427, 475, 498, 512–514, 565
Assya Anguelova v Bulgaria, 387, 634, 653
Asylum seeker, 368, 448, 467, 516, 576
Attempted *coup d'état*, 439
Attorney-General, 421, 501, 508, 510, 514, 524, 530, 646, 650, 651
Attorney General of the USA, 346
AU, 361, 362, 371, 612
AU Commission, 363
Audi alteram partem, 384
Audiencia Nacional, 335, 363, 364, 367, 423, 455, 520, 521, 632, 640
AU member States, 607
AU Resolution, 279
AU statement, 20
Australia, 102, 191, 326, 360, 371, 431, 450, 453, 499, 516, 607, 647
Australia legislation, 326, 360
Australian citizenship, 430, 431
AU strategy, 20
Austria, 607
Austrians, 558
Austrian Supreme Court, 334
Aut dedere aut judicare, 12, 23, 42, 51, 77, 80, 120–123, 153, 174, 216, 251, 290, 320–325, 327, 328, 331, 332, 334, 337–339, 341, 348, 350, 351, 355–358, 361, 367–373, 377, 379, 380, 386, 388, 405, 407, 412, 413, 552, 557–559, 565–568, 574, 582, 605, 613
Aut dedere aut judicare model, 251
Aut dedere aut judicare rule, 424, 425, 447, 459, 471, 497, 527, 528
Aut dedere aut prosequi, 321
Aut dedere aut transferre, 370, 371, 380, 612
Authoritative evidence, 9
Authoritative source, 215
Authorization, 593
Auto-deligitimization, 327

Auto-delegitimization process, 327
Automatic firearm, 446
Autopsy, 12
Autrefois acquit, 477
Autrefois convict, 490
Aventi diritto, 337
Avocats Sans Frontières, 375
Avoidance techniques, 427
Azerbaijan, 382

B
Baader-Meinhof, 443, 646
Babar Ahmad, 502, 503, 644
Bachmaier, 487, 645
Bakker, 461
Balance, 443, 444, 486, 515, 517, 525, 529, 583
Balance of probabilities, 114
Balkan States, 67
Balkan wars, 558
Bamber, 499, 500
Bangladesh Liberation War, 423
Bantekas, 525, 571, 589
Barayagwiza, 154, 157, 261, 262, 623, 630, 631
Barbie, 352, 423, 633, 642
Barcelona Traction case, 330, 331, 337, 338, 343, 347
Bargain, 590
Barriers, 583
Barrios Altos, 428, 457, 461, 648
Barrios Altos massacre, 428
Bar to extradition, 355
Bary, 496, 647
Basebya, 431, 642
Basic Principles and Guidelines, 571
Basque separatists, 445
Bassiouni, 5, 9, 46, 98, 119, 120, 131, 133, 321, 322, 324, 329, 338, 339, 341, 344, 349, 365, 378, 419, 422, 424, 437, 449, 451, 453, 476, 513, 565, 567, 571, 572, 584, 605, 614
Basson, 454, 485, 641
Bautista de Arellana, 457, 648
Bautista de Arellana v Colombia, 381, 635
Bavarian *Oberlandesgericht*, 346
Beast of Bolzano, 348
Becker, 357
Bekou, 171, 196, 252, 264
Belarus, 510, 640
Belfast, 445
Belgian Government, 154, 421, 489
Belgian laws, 358
Belgium, 421, 441, 452, 483, 504, 505, 520, 530, 532, 605, 607, 642–644
Belgium's universal jurisdiction law, 360
Belgium v Senegal, 324, 361, 369, 620, 636
Belgium v Spain, 324, 636
Belgrade, 468
Bellelli, 173
Bemba, 247, 248, 277, 627, 630
Bemba Gombo, 94–96
Benelux State, 421
Benelux Treaty on Extradition and Mutual Assistance in Criminal Matters, 428
Benin, 20
Bensouda three, 217
Benzig, 295
Bergsmo, 221, 242
Berlin Wall, 42
Bernard, 234, 242, 252
Bernard Ntuyahaga, 326, 636
Bianchi, 113, 524
Biased trials, 438
Bignone, 506, 532, 640, 646
BiH tribunals, 36
BiH v Serbia and Montenegro, 77, 82, 326, 356, 620, 636
Bilateral agreements, 608
Bilateral extradition treaties, 322
Bilateral immunity agreements, 292–295
Bilateral treaties, 404, 408
Binding obligation, 323, 331
Binding precedent, 215
Binding rule, 345
Bingham, Lord, 493, 497, 498, 647
Blagojević, 93, 622
Blake, 385, 636
Blanket amnesties, 245
Blaškić, 18, 148, 519, 524, 592, 619, 623, 649, 655
Blaškić Appeals Chamber ruling, 312
Blaškić subpoena *duces tecum* case, 591
Blatant human rights violation, 222
Bo, 230, 240
Bobigny, 327
Bodily harm, 339
Boister, 33, 119–121, 123, 130, 131, 136, 428, 449, 452–454, 506, 513
Bolivia, 376, 383, 638
Boman, 482, 645
Bomb, 446
Bombers, 447
Bombings, 103
Bona fide prosecution, 606
Bonello, Judge, 473
Borelli, 419, 437, 448, 449, 453, 454, 511

Borrego Borrego, Judge, 502, 644
Borsellino, Prosecuting Magistrate and Judge, 350
Boškoski & Tarčulovski, 128
Bottini, 344
Bouche de la loi, 590
Boulevard Voltaire, 103
Bouterse, 341, 348, 523, 532, 642
Bovensmilde incident, 444
Boycott, 293
Braber, 102, 126–129
Bratza, Judge, 473
Brazil, 376
Brazzaville Beach case, 525, 642
British Colonial Rule, 423
British journalists, 377
British Officer, 445
British political incidence theory, 438
British political scientists, 377
Brown, 557, 558, 588, 589, 591
Brown aka Bajinja, 472, 646
Browne-Wilkinson, Lord, 289, 291, 527, 529
Brownlie, 9, 594
Budapest, 437
Buenos Aires, 486, 499, 506, 640, 646
Buenos Aires Appeals Court, 486
Buenos Aires Criminal Tribunal, 380
Buenos Aires Federal Criminal Court, 620
Buergenthal, 606
Buergenthal, Judge, 523, 649
Buk installation, 371
Bulgaria, 329, 387
Bundersverfassungsgericht, 467
Burden sharing, 613
Burden shifting exercise, 312
Bureau of the ASP, 188
Burens, 330, 335–337
Burns, 98, 513, 650
Burundi, 20, 607
Bush Six case, 346, 637
Bustamante, 526
BWCC, 7
Bystander States, 330, 568, 572, 608

C

Caal-Sandoval, 572
Café Bonne Bière, 103
California prisons, 495
Cambodia, 607
Canada, 102, 348, 349, 357, 358, 360, 367, 369, 382, 441, 446, 470, 485, 490, 499, 510, 511, 513, 514, 605, 607, 633, 635, 648, 650
Canada's universal jurisdiction, 349
Canadian Crimes Against Humanity and War Crimes Act, 349
Cançado Trindade, 426, 457
Capacity building, 598
Capacity-oriented approach, 98
Capital murder charge, 508
Capital offence, 427
Capital punishment, 427, 508, 511–514
CAR, 248, 265, 277, 627, 630
Caracas, 376
CAR authorities, 248, 265
Camorra, 349
Campo de Mayo, 506, 640, 646
Camp Zeist, 371, 612
Carol Ciorcan and Others v Romania, 382, 575, 634, 653
CAR Special Criminal Court, 598
Case-by-case basis, 441, 510
Case Concerning Military and Paramilitary Activities in and Against Nicaragua, 345, 636
Case Concerning Questions of Interpretation and Application of the 1971 Montreal Convention Arising from the Aerial Incident at Lockerbie, Request for the Indication of Provisional Measures, 321, 636
Case of the *Street Children*, 385, 569, 636
Cassese, 4, 19, 21, 126, 130, 134, 137, 168, 172, 191, 199, 267, 269, 270, 322, 323, 349, 351, 353, 430, 461, 469, 489, 493, 520, 521, 526, 613
Cassese, Judge, 191
Castioni, 438, 642
Castro Ruz, 521, 640
CAT, 137, 180, 181, 324, 330, 335, 337, 346, 348, 358, 360–362, 369, 387, 459, 464, 494, 496, 527–529, 569, 574, 638
Catalyst, 264
Catalyst for compliance, 22, 606
Catch-22 situation, 494
Category one *génocidaires*, 373
Category one rape cases, 375
Catholic Commission for Justice and Peace in Zimbabwe, 510, 651
Cause of criminalization, 129
Cavallo, 379, 380, 383, 424, 566, 650, 654
Cavallo, Judge, 620
Čelebići case, 325, 566, 637
Central African Republic, 94, 128, 248, 265, 277, 598
Central American *desaparecidos*, 376
Central Court for Preliminary Criminal Proceedings, 346, 637

Cessation of hostilities, 600
Chad, 186, 274, 283, 286, 362, 363
Chadian Truth Commission, 359
Chahal, 497, 644
Challenge of admissibility, 212
Chambre de mises en accusation, 348, 349, 632
Chapeau offence, 370
Chapter VII enforcement mechanisms, 172
Chapter VII powers, 184
Characterized infringement, 190
Charter of Fundamental Rights, 479, 498
Charter of Paris for a New Europe, 426
Chechnyan former Deputy Prime Minister, 507
Chemical weapons, 54, 55
Chief prosecuting officer of the State, 383
Chile, 335, 376, 383, 421, 428, 454, 455, 463, 478, 482, 483, 527, 633, 640, 641, 648
Chilean Supreme Court, 428
Chili Komitee Nederland v Pinochet, 348, 633, 638
China, 199, 293, 607
Chinese officials, 367
Chinese Request, 508
Chipana, 494, 497, 640
Chisanga, 513, 648
Chlorine gas, 55
Chui, 94, 96, 621
CIA officers, 293
Ciorcan, 382, 634
Circumstantial evidence, 91
CISA, 479, 481, 483, 484
Civil Actions, 518
Civil law countries, 432, 448, 558
Civil Proceedings, 455, 472
Civil society, 366
Civitas maxima, 62, 66, 131
Clark, 376
Clemency, 425, 456
Coalition pour la Défense de la République, 431
Cockayne, 155
Code Napoléon, 353
Code of Penal Procedure, 348
Code Pénal, 382
Codification of criminal law, 388
Codification of the law of treaties, 338
CoE, 33, 34, 353, 433, 480, 481, 645
CoE Member State, 499, 510
CoE treaties, 354
COJUR-ICC Working Group, 428, 607
COJUR (Public International Law) Working Group, 608
Collection of evidence, 599, 601
Collective countermeasures, 188
Collective security, 62, 70
Collective subsidiary responsibility, 577
Colombia, 44, 47, 48, 376, 383, 601, 633
Colombian armed conflict, 48
Colombian drug cartels, 349
Colombian electorate, 465
Colombian Senate, 613
Colombian State Council, 383, 632
Comité Juridique (*COJUR*) ICC Working Group of the Council of the EU, 178
Commission Nationale des Droits de l'Homme et des Libertés v Chad, 569, 653
Commission on Human Rights Working Group, 358
Committee against Torture, 463, 494, 496, 640
Common denominator, 9, 42, 118, 125, 129, 153, 236, 388
Common European Policy, 489
Common law, 243, 247, 257, 353, 363
Common law countries, 432, 490
Common law jurisdictions, 485
Commonwealth member State, 353
Commonwealth Scheme for the Rendition of Fugitive Offenders, 436
Communal justice, 372
Communitarian principle, 322
Communitarian regime, 332, 381
Community of courts, 153, 595
Comparative criminal law, 591
Compensation, 613
Compétence de la compétence, 588
Compétence de la compétence doctrine, 558
Competent authorities, 321, 353, 361, 381, 382, 387
Competing values, 368
Complaints, 591
Complementarity, 61, 78, 79, 153, 154, 156, 159, 160, 168, 170, 171, 173–175, 178, 179, 181, 188, 189, 193, 333, 336, 365, 558, 565, 598, 600, 605, 606
Complementarity facet, 233, 237
Complementarity principle, 22, 216, 218, 236, 242, 249, 516
Complementarity regime, 314
Complementarity test, 224
Complementary universal jurisdiction, 325
Compliance Committee, 190, 564
Complicity, 606
Complicity in genocide, 115
Compromise, 195
Compromise agreement, 465
Concept of international community, 48
Concerned States, 194

Concerted action, 259, 260
Concession in sentencing, 465
Concours idéal d'infractions, 486
Concrete and real threat, 92
Concurrence facet, 233
Concurrent jurisdiction, 113
Concurrent State obligations, 551
Concurrent universal jurisdiction, 359
Conditional duty, 607
Conditional extradition, 427
Confession, 255, 260, 262, 263, 373, 374
Confirmation of charges hearing, 265
Conflicting interest, 583
Conflict of interest, 60
Conflicts, 127, 129, 192, 251, 272, 283, 287, 293, 339, 368, 553
Conflicts of jurisdiction, 367
Conforti, 24, 98
Congo, 463
Connected crime, 439
Connelly principles, 485
Connivance of State power, 327
Conseil d'Etat, 427, 445, 640
Consensus, 412
Consequential characteristic, 112
Consequentialist approach, 150
Consequential rights, 426
Constitution, 222, 274, 291, 426, 467, 491, 493, 501, 640
Constitutional Court, 335, 364, 365, 381, 383, 558, 604, 632, 633
Constitutional Court of South Africa, 454
Constitutional Court of the Czech Republic, 652
Constitutional formula, 355
Constitutionalism, 582
Constitutionalization of international law, 582
Constitutional law, 404, 435
Constitutionally-entrenched human rights, 436
Constitutional norms, 332
Constitutional prohibitions against extraditing nationals, 433
Constitutional provisions, 382
Constitutional reference, 495
Constitutional reform, 613
Constitutive elements, 237, 240, 241, 251, 430, 450, 452, 453, 486, 487
Constitutive instruments, 557, 588
Consuelo, 456, 648
Consuetudo, 427
Consultation, 255, 256, 263
Consultative cooperation, 599
Container-type concept, 119
Contemporary international criminal law, 325, 343, 370
Contempt, 589
Contested values, 271
Contextual elements, 43–46, 90, 92, 94, 95, 97
Continental law, 353
Continental Shelf case, 412, 639
Continuing obligation, 113
Contreras, 572
Conventional international law, 322, 345, 350, 404, 408, 412, 605
Conventional rights, 583
Convention for the Suppression of Terrorist Bombings, 441, 447
Convention for the Suppression of the Financing of Terrorism, 441, 447
Convention for the Suppression of Unlawful Acts against the Safety of Civil Aviation, 446, 447
Convention for the Suppression of Unlawful Acts against the Safety of Maritime Navigation, 447
Convention for the Suppression of Unlawful Seizure of Aircraft, 353, 446, 447, 491
Convention on the non-Applicability of Statutory Limitations to War Crimes and Crimes Against Humanity, 611
Convention on the Physical Protection of Nuclear Material, 447
Convention on the Prevention and Punishment of Crimes against Internationally Protected Persons, including Diplomatic Agents, 447, 520
Convention Relating to Extradition Between Member States, 421
Convention Relating to the Status of Refugees, 448, 515
Convict, 425, 444, 468, 477, 511, 513, 527
Conviction, 222, 223, 226, 227, 235, 240, 245, 248, 256, 296, 297, 421, 425, 428, 431, 455, 456, 464, 470, 473, 477, 485, 486, 490, 505, 508, 510, 518, 558
Cooperate fully, 182, 279, 287
Cooperation, 211–216, 246, 250, 255, 256, 258, 266, 267, 270, 272, 274, 279, 284, 286, 292–296, 312, 313, 583, 628, 629
Cooperation in criminal matters, 441
Coordinated community of courts, 599
Core principle, 273
Corpus juris, 479, 515, 583
Corpus Juris Civilis, 353
Corpus juris criminalis, 377
Corpus juris of extradition, 150
Corpus juris relating to extradition, 408

Correlative collective duty, 76
Correlative individual right of action, 572
Correlative right, 327
Corresponding obligation, 381, 385
Corresponding obligation to investigate, 381, 385
Corrosive effect, 120
Corruption, 421
Corte Constitucional, Sala Plena, 383, 633
Corte Costituzionale Italiana, 488, 641
Corte di Cassazione, 523, 524, 529, 530, 641
Cosmopolitan values, 121, 131
Costa Rica, 360, 376
Côte d'Ivoire, 160, 217, 220, 228, 239, 623, 628, 629
Council of the EU, 607, 608
Counterfeiting, 421
Cour d'Assises, 327, 633
Cour de Cassation, 328, 348, 352, 457, 485, 498, 520, 521, 525, 530, 633, 642
Crawford, 129
CREMS, 421, 432, 443, 444
Crime control, 418
Crime of State, 44
Crimes against humanity, 11, 44, 52, 55, 63, 69–71, 93–97, 99, 100, 102, 158, 324, 325, 340–342, 349, 358, 360, 362, 364, 365, 380, 381, 385, 404, 422, 423, 427, 428, 430, 440, 441, 446, 457, 463, 499, 504, 506, 516, 523, 525, 528, 532, 557, 605, 611, 612, 614
Crimes Against Humanity and War Crimes Act, 324, 342, 362, 365
Crimes against public order, 439
Crimes committed abroad, 613
Crimes *jure gentium*, 445
Criminal action, 611
Criminal acts, 524
Criminal code, 594
Criminalization of modes of conduct, 118
Criminal justice, 594, 595
Criminal law provisions, 388
Criminal liability, 422, 450, 452, 493, 600
Criminal networks based in Italy, 349
Criminal policy, 465, 524
Criminal Proceedings Against Maria Pupino, 379, 634
Croatia, 18, 321, 360, 439, 454, 457, 458, 465, 482, 483, 519, 619, 637, 644, 647, 649
Cross-border dimension, 378
Cross-fertilization, 23, 600
Cross fertilization of courts and tribunals, 565
Cross-frontier crime, 465
Cryer, 347, 348, 351, 381, 527, 530
Crystallization of customary international law, 313
Culpable wrongdoing, 384
Cultural denominator, 388
Cultural relativism, 512
Culture of impunity, 376
Custodial jurisdiction, 4, 330, 333, 413, 600, 607, 614
Custodial State, 212, 259, 260, 264, 279–281, 324, 333, 347, 348, 350, 353, 355, 356, 459, 460, 478, 483, 556, 557, 566, 605
Custodial universal jurisdiction, 573
Customary international law, 8, 9, 64, 76, 91, 98, 104, 120, 127, 130, 131, 136, 151, 153, 166, 167, 177, 179, 245, 246, 270–272, 274, 275, 277, 283, 285, 286, 288, 290, 296, 297, 321, 323–326, 330, 331, 333–335, 337–341, 345, 347, 349, 350, 359, 361, 366, 368, 378, 404, 412, 413, 420, 422–424, 428, 443, 450, 459–461, 463, 469–471, 473, 489, 508, 518, 520–523, 525, 526, 528, 532, 552, 565–568, 573–575, 590, 605–607, 611
Customary International Law human rights exception to immunities, 519
Customary law argument, 268, 285
Customary norms, 412
Customary obligation, 321, 323, 330
Customary right, 321
Customary rule of extradition law, 419
Cvjetković, 558
Cybercrime, 370, 421
Cypriot Constitutional provision, 432
Cypriot law, 501
Cypriot Supreme Court, 432
Cyprus, 432, 433, 500–502, 642, 644, 645
Cyprus v Turkey, 385, 634
Czech citizens, 435
Czech Constitutional Court, 435
Czech Republic, 435, 496, 652
Czestochowa Regional Court, 433, 647

D

Dabas, 435, 648
Daesh, 72, 78, 102
Daesh commander, 576
Daesh militants, 600
Dakar Regional Court, 362
Damache, 506, 647
D'Amato, 341
Daniel Monguya Mbenge v Zaire, 349, 635
Danish citizens, 429
Danish Constitution, 429
Danish Genocide Act, 469

Danish law, 469
Danish nationals, 438
Danish Supreme Court, 469
Daqun, 233
Dar Es Salaam, 496
Darfur, 157, 169, 186, 187, 191, 196, 624, 625
Dayton, Ohio, 17
Dayton Peace Agreement, 17
Dead letter, 322
Dean, 404, 405
Death, 437, 465, 476, 482, 502, 508, 510, 513, 514, 610, 614, 640
Death by firing squad, 158
Death flights, 499
Death penalty, 131, 226, 229, 234, 328, 349, 368, 418, 427, 464, 465, 476, 507–515
Death row, 418, 507–511
Death sentence, 417, 509
Deber, 565
Decentralization, 614
De Brouwer, 372, 373, 376, 377
Decentralization of prosecutions, 614
Decision on Challenge to Jurisdiction Lomé Accord Amnesty, 321, 638
Decision on Jordan's non-compliance, 286, 287, 630
Decision on South Africa's non-compliance, 271, 286, 629
Declaratory function, 594
Declaratory judgments, 594
Dedere limb, 405–407
Dédoublement fonctionnel, 323
Deen-Racsmany, 428, 430, 432, 435, 436, 448
De facto regime, 100, 105
Defaulting State, 188–190, 199, 200, 332, 564, 567
Default mechanism, 330
Defence lawyers, 159, 374
Deferral, 192
Definition, 124–127, 132, 134, 137
Definition of a refugee, 516
De Guzman, 48, 49
De Hoogh, 327, 331
Delalić et al., 325, 567, 637, 654
Delegated universal jurisdiction, 340
Delictual act, 114
Delictum iuris gentium, 323
Delitos contra los deberes de humanidad, 365
de Marco, 332
Demjanjuk, 359
Democratization, 156, 246, 267, 459
Democratization process, 454, 512
Denationalization of the administration of criminal justice, 290
Denmark, 429, 430, 441, 444, 455, 469, 558, 607, 644, 647
Depoliticizing *formula*, 437, 441
Deportation, 368, 369
Depositions, 608
Derecho al derecho, 457
Derg crimes, 36
Derg officials, 508
Desaparecidos, 569
De Serpa Soares, 46
Desideratum, 589
Detention, 229, 230, 243, 258–262, 264, 627
Determination of a criminal charge, 455
Deterrence, 78, 329, 589
Detrimental effects, 329
Devoir, 565
De Waal, 458
Diabolica probatio, 469
Dialectical relationship, 557
Dicta, 215, 221, 258
Dictates of public conscience, 469, 528
Dictum, 338, 342, 343, 345, 362, 386
Different charges, 486
Differential treatment, 187, 438
Different modes of liability, 114
Difficult to convict, 226, 229
DiFilippo, 98
Dignity, 337, 376
Dilemma, 327
DINA, 463
Diplomacy, 584
Diplomatic channels, 216, 263
Diplomatic immunities, 418
Diplomatic privileges, 418, 528
Diplomatic privileges and immunities, 212, 265, 267, 269, 270, 274, 280, 418, 518, 528
Diplomatic rows, 477
Diplomatic ties, 512
Direct criminalization theory, 50
Direct enforcement model, 5
Direct enforcement system, 22
Direct injury, 130
Director of public prosecutions, 383
Director of Public Prosecutions v T, 483
Dirty War, 506
Disappearances, 460
Disappeared, 486
Discharge, 590
Discontinue criminal proceedings, 592
Discount in sentencing, 465
Discretionary ground for refusal, 513
Discretionary nature, 405

Discretionary sentence of life imprisonment, 503
Discrimination clause, 438
Disinteressement in cooperation, 435
Disjunctive conception, 354
Disobedience of a direct order, 436
Disproportionate sentence, 503
Dispute settlement method, 188
District Court for the District of Columbia, 339, 567, 639, 654
District Court of The Hague, 431, 642
Division of labour, 312, 613
Djajic, 346, 632
Djamel Ameziane v USA, 347, 635
Djibouti v France, 522, 525, 649
Doctoral thesis, 614
Doctrine de gravité, 438
Doctrine of implied powers, 558
Doctrine of separation of powers, 512
Doe, 524, 526, 530, 651, 652
Doherty, 445, 652
Dolus eventualis, 119
Dolus specialis, 65, 91–93
Dombo Beheer BV v The Netherlands, 472, 645
Domesticated international courts, 36
Domestication of international criminal law, 22, 614
Domestic barriers to surrender, 312
Domestic *corpus juris*, 227
Domestic courts, 412, 588, 591, 592, 595, 604, 611, 613
Domestic crimes, 112, 118, 119, 129–133, 138
Domestic criminal court, 7–9, 24
Domestic criminalization, 121
Domestic criminal justice systems, 583, 598
Domestic default, 599
Domestic human rights law, 134, 224
Domestic jurisdiction, 612
Domestic justice, 612
Domestic law, 224, 227, 228, 259, 274, 290
Domestic legal order, 611
Domestic legislation, 565
Domestic legislative bodies, 592
Domestic police crimes unit, 576
Domestic political squabbles, 598
Domestic politics, 465
Domestic proceedings, 220, 222, 224, 225, 227, 237, 242, 249
Domestic prosecutions, 32, 557, 558
Domestic remedies, 227, 230
Domino effect, 508, 514, 589
Donald Trump, 292
Dos Erres massacre, 364
Double criminality, 417, 427, 435, 448–454, 492, 564
Double criminality requirement, 435, 448, 450–452
Double criminality rule, 418, 448–453
Double criminality rule *in concreto*, 453
Double criminality verification, 434, 450
Double-edged sword, 583
Double jeopardy, 232, 235, 236, 342, 367, 419, 477, 481, 483, 485, 489, 491, 492
Double punishability, 449
Double punishment, 477
Dougoz v Greece, 369, 634
Draft code of crimes against the peace and security of mankind, 353
Draft Code of Offences Against the Peace and Security of Mankind, 426, 528
Dragan Nikolić, 359, 637
DRC, 16, 24, 127, 128, 169, 170, 181, 186, 197, 213, 216, 217, 219, 220, 234, 243, 247, 248, 259, 260, 266, 269, 279, 286, 290, 619, 623–625, 627–630
DRC v Belgium, 349, 350, 361, 519, 523, 532, 636, 649
DRC v Rwanda, 91, 621
Droit d'ingérence, 61
Drugs formula, 355
Drug trafficking, 44, 121, 122
Drumbl, 267, 277, 284
Dual citizen, 430
Dual criminality, 296, 436, 448, 452
Dualism, 611
Due diligence, 383, 417
Due process, 221, 224–227, 230, 231, 233–235, 242, 254, 258, 265, 343, 372
Due process guarantees, 384, 473, 478, 482
Due process rights, 223, 227, 231, 256, 424, 468, 471, 472, 477, 478
Due process safeguards, 444, 511
Due process theory, 225
Due process violations, 226
Dugard, 270, 341, 424, 426, 427, 432, 449, 454, 461, 467, 468, 471, 494, 508, 510, 511
Dujail trial, 158
Dungveckis, 482, 645
Du Plessis, 270, 272, 283, 287, 520
Duration of the treatment, 503
Duško Cvjetković, 334, 638
Duško Tadić, 325, 637
Dutch Constitution, 341
Dutch Court, 499
Dutch jurist, 322
Dutch Law, 506

Dutch Supreme Court, 341
Duty *in status nascendi*, 614
Duty of the territorial State, 566, 569
Duty to cooperate, 149, 152, 177, 180, 197, 198, 286
Duty to intervene, 72, 73
Duty to investigate, 381, 382, 388, 583
Duty to prevent, 566
Duty to prosecute, 339, 344, 355, 381–383, 388, 406, 566–569, 571–574, 576, 577, 590, 607
Duty to submit to prosecution, 590, 592
Dyer, 428
Dynamic interaction, 388
Dynamic interpretation, 590

E

EAC, 362, 363, 612
Ease to convict, 227
Eastern Ukraine, 371
East Timor, 36
East Timor case, 331, 636
East Timor Special Panels for Serious Crimes, 7, 152, 598
East Timorese citizen, 347
EAW, 123, 151, 377, 429, 430, 432–436, 448, 450–453, 457, 468, 470, 483, 484, 498, 552
ECCC, 7, 35, 36, 152, 612
ECE, 419–422, 428, 430, 436, 438, 440, 441, 448, 452, 478, 487, 510
ECJ, 362, 379, 433, 435, 450, 477, 479–481, 483, 484, 488–490, 498, 499, 634, 638, 643
Economic Community of West African States Convention on Extradition, 440
Economic pressure, 190, 564
Economic ties, 512
ECtHR, 34, 170, 172, 422, 424, 427, 455, 457, 465, 467, 469, 470, 472–474, 480–482, 484–487, 489, 494, 497, 499, 500, 502–505, 507–509, 517, 524, 526, 569, 570, 572, 575, 593, 619, 620, 624, 643–646, 653, 655
Ecuador, 376, 463, 566
ECvHR, 222, 227, 262, 349, 384–388, 426, 433, 436, 443, 444, 461, 470, 471, 473, 488, 494, 499, 502–504, 507–509, 511, 570, 572, 582
Effective investigation, 286
Effective official investigation, 385, 387
Effective prosecution, 325, 336, 381
Effective remedy, 571, 572, 582
Effective rights, 443
Effects of the crime, 356
Egregious crime, 613
Egregious violation, 262
Egypt, 199
Eichmann, 334, 359
Einarsen, 42, 43, 134–136
Einhorn, 474, 500
Einsatzgruppen case, 352, 637
Ejusdem generis, 48
Electrocution, 514
El Salvador, 376, 454, 457, 648
Elvir Javor et al. contre X, Arrêt (Rejet du pourvoi), 348, 633
El Zeidy, 216, 219–222, 225, 230, 236, 242, 245, 246, 273
Embassy of the Republic of Malta in The Hague, 158
Embodiment of willingness, 222
Encroachment on the ASP, 187
Enforced disappearance of persons, 326, 385
Enforced disappearances, 464, 569, 573
Enforcement, 320, 322, 325–327, 336, 351, 362, 363, 365, 370, 380
Enforcement mechanism, 5
Enforcement spectrum, 600
England and Wales, 382
English High Court, 471
Enslavement, 123–125
Enumerative method, 451
EPPO, 33, 377, 378
Equal hierarchical status, 552, 553
Equality, 424, 447, 470, 495, 525, 650
Equality of arms, 128, 129, 373, 472
Equatorial Guinea, 34
Equitable balance between conflicting interests, 583
Erga omnes in abstracto, 80
Erga omnes in concreto, 80
Erga omnes obligations, 18, 80, 81, 91, 321, 331, 350, 557, 567, 582
Erga omnes partes, 18
Erga omnes status, 246
Ergastolani, 503
Escuela de Suboficiales de Mecanica de la Armada, 380
Eser, 342, 343
Eshetu Alemu, 482, 499, 508, 651
ESPO, 36
Essential principles of contemporary international law, 332
Estonia, 382
Ethiopia, 482, 566, 607
Ethnic minorities, 371
ETSPSC, 7

EU Charter of Fundamental Rights, 433, 487, 498, 510
EU citizenship, 435
EU Day Against Impunity, 607
EU financial interests, 33
EU-ICC Agreement, 565
EU law, 148
EU Member States, 430, 435, 444, 468, 477, 480
EUROJUST, 378, 489
Europe, 352, 358, 378, 381, 604
European code of criminal procedure, 377
European Commission, 33, 377
European Communities Convention, 426
European Convention for the Suppression of Terrorism, 446
European Convention on Mutual Assistance in Criminal Matters, 420
European Convention on Terrorism, 438
European Convention on the Non-Applicability of Statutory Limitations, 422
European Convention on the Protection of the Environment, 354
European Convention on the Suppression of Terrorism, 354, 355, 446
European Council, 33
European criminal code, 377
European criminal justice system, 553
European Criminal Law, 377, 432
European integration, 388
European Public Prosecutor, 33
European Union (EU), 33, 322, 349, 353, 371, 377–379, 381, 382, 386, 388, 559
EU supremacy, 552
EU transnational network, 349
Evidence, 324, 334, 351, 355, 356, 366, 368, 373, 382, 385, 422, 423, 425, 433, 465, 469, 471, 472, 474, 478, 482, 485, 486, 490, 492, 495, 497, 501, 506–508, 514, 566, 568, 575, 576, 605, 608, 649
Evidence sharing, 598
Evolution of international criminal law, 592
Exception to the exception, 437
Execution of a request, 212, 249, 250
Executive *ad hoc* entities, 456
Executive international institution, 323
Exemption, 421, 436–445, 448
Expertise, 599
Export of drugs, 485
Extension of powers, 168
Extensive criminal networks, 349
External assistance, 600
External intervention, 62–64, 72, 73
External prosecutions, 282
Extinctive prescription, 422, 423
Extraditable offence, 123
Extradite or prosecute, 323–325, 332, 341, 342, 353–355, 636
Extradite-or-prosecute requirement, 354
Extradition, 174, 195
Extradition Act, 429, 433
Extradition bi-lateral agreement, 435
Extradition Chamber of the District Court of The Hague, 469
Extradition Court, 418, 442
Extradition laws, 425, 468, 604
Extradition regime, 352
Extradition request, 323, 324, 328, 334, 336, 342, 416, 417, 420, 437, 438, 445, 448, 450, 496, 497, 499, 511, 517
Extradition Treaty, 425, 426, 429, 432, 436, 442, 443, 446–448, 453, 470, 471, 491, 508, 511, 552
Extradition Treaty between the Government of Canada and the Government of the USA, 446
Extradition Treaty Between the USA and Germany, 441
Extra-judicial executions, 428
Extraordinary African Assize Appeal Chamber, 362
Extraordinary African Assize Chamber , 362
Extraordinary African Indictments Chamber, 362
Extraordinary African Investigation Chamber, 362
Extraordinary rendition, 491, 507
Extra-territorial jurisdiction, 34, 291, 334, 355, 449, 527
Eye witness testimony, 382

F

Fact-finding inquiry, 244
Failed State, 47, 53–55
Failure of international law, 557
Failure to investigate, 47, 568, 606
Failure to prevent, 329
Failure to prosecute, 75, 559, 589, 606
Failure to protect, 74
Failure to punish, 329
Fair balance, 472
Fair defence, 373
Fairness, 583
Fairness of proceedings, 227
Fair trial, 557
Fair trial assessment, 221
Fair trial rights, 469, 470, 473, 474, 477, 478, 492

Faltering State, 47, 54, 55
FARC-Government proposed peace deal, 465
Farouq brigade, 576
Faulty interpretation, 270
Features, 612
FEDEFAM, 376
Federal Court of Australia, 326, 431, 436, 635, 646
Federal prosecutors, 427
Federal Republic of Germany v Denmark, 323, 636
Federal Republic of Germany v The Netherlands, 323, 636
Ferdinandusse, 330, 331, 383, 461, 463, 589, 590
Fernández de Gurmendi, Judge, 607
Fernando Laureani Maturana and Miguel Krassnoff Marchenko v. Miguel Ángel Sandoval Rodríguez, 383, 633
Ferrini, 524, 641
Ferstman, 69, 70
FIDH et al. vs Ould Dah, 460, 641
Feudal lord, 435
Fifth Amendment, 485, 493
Figueroa-Túnchez, 572
Fijnaut, 119
Filártiga, 469, 651, 652
Filártiga v Peña-Irala, 284
Financial considerations, 608
Financial interests of the EU, 377
Financing of terrorism, 378
Finding of non-compliance, 175, 185, 187, 188, 196, 624
Finland, 360, 430, 482, 645, 646
Finta, 71, 621
Finucane v MacMahon, 468, 495, 650
Firing squad, 510
Fiscal offences, 421
Fischer, 481, 487, 645
Flagrant denial of a fair trial requirement, 469, 474, 475
Flagrant denial of justice, 262, 472–475
Flagrant human rights violation, 224
Flagrant violation test, 517, 604
Fleck, 293, 294
Fletcher, 50, 64, 342, 343, 559
Flexibility, 611
Flexible interpretation, 312
Flick case, 352, 637
Flint, 458
Focarelli, 74
Forced disappearance, 368, 381
Forced labour, 368
Foreign aggression, 368
Foreign courts, 518
Foreign know-how, 599
Foreign personnel, 611
Foreign States, 506
Foreign suspect, 349
Forensic evidence, 382
Forensic experts, 37
Foreseeability, 450, 467, 515, 517, 604
Forgiveness, 376
Formal transfer, 420
Former Yugoslavia, 443, 481, 606
Former Yugoslav Republic of Macedonia, 370
Form of universality, 322
Formulae, 331, 351, 354, 356, 370, 377, 404, 405, 412
Forum, 125, 132
Forum conveniens, 24, 25, 80, 253, 254, 333, 353, 356, 357, 375, 405, 407, 613
Forum deprehensionis, 333, 353, 367
Forum prosequi, 599
Forum shopping, 349
Forum State, 325, 326, 337, 342, 366, 412
Forward-looking expectation of risk, 517
Four freedoms of the Common Market, 488
Four Geneva Conventions, 326, 337, 355
Fournet, 463
FRA, 571
Frame of reference, 7, 12, 16, 23, 150, 565
Framework Decision on Combating Terrorism, 378
Framework Decision on the EAW, 419, 429, 434, 444, 450–453, 457, 468, 484, 495, 498, 506
France, 67, 102, 328, 348, 352, 360, 367, 382, 423, 427, 436, 445, 457, 460, 467, 471, 485, 486, 498–500, 516, 521, 522, 525, 558, 576, 577, 605, 607, 632, 633, 640–642, 645, 649
France v Turkey, 339, 638
Francisco Franco, 356
Francovich and Bonifaci, 435
Franey, 522, 525, 532
Fraud, 421, 428, 439
Fraudulent *res judicata*, 478, 483
Fredman, 61
Free movement of judicial decisions in criminal matters, 429
Freetown, 36
French Code of Crimnal Procedure (Torture), 358, 360
French Court of Appeal, 525
French laws, 177, 358, 360
French lawyers, 423
French objective test, 439

French Supreme Court, 485
Friman, 527, 530
Frowein, 180
Frulli, 268, 273, 274, 290
Fugitives, 404, 442, 506
Fujimori, 428, 641
Fully-fledged agreement, 465
Functional immunities, 267, 518, 529
Functional international constitutionalism, 582, 589
Functional justification, 592
Function of international criminal law, 32
Functions, 588, 591, 592
Fundación Casa del Tibet and Others v Jiang Zemin and Others, 367, 632
Fundamental human rights, 6, 12, 183, 313, 326, 328, 337, 381, 386, 388, 423, 424, 428, 454, 455, 458, 461–463, 465, 467, 468, 515, 525, 552, 557, 567, 574
Fundamental legal interests, 335
Fundamental rights, 435, 446, 531
Furundžija, 114, 422, 437, 441, 461, 575, 622, 649, 654
Fundamental safeguards, 373
Future violations, 589

G

Gacaca courts, 372–377, 483
Gacaca law, 375
Gacaca trials, 152
G, a citizen of Vanuatu, 467, 640
Gaddafi, 223, 225, 227, 234, 285, 288, 627
Gaddafi and Al-Senussi, 624
Gaeta, 134, 270, 274
Galanis v Pallanck, 492, 651
Gallant, 166, 167, 179
Gambia, 20, 21, 607
Game-changer, 608
Ganic, 468
Garcia, 367, 445, 485, 532, 640, 652
Garzón, Judge, 380
Gas asphyxiation, 514
Gasparini, 484, 643
Gaspar-Szilagyi, 498
Gbagbo, Laurent, 160
Gbagbo, Simone, 160, 623
Gdańsk, 559
General consensus theory, 328
General Framework Agreement for Peace in BiH and the Annexes thereto, 17
General human rights clause, 438
General principle, 324, 341
General principle of international law, 426, 442, 489
General principle of law, 9, 236, 321, 324, 412, 413, 569
General prohibition, 330, 384
General right to a fair trial, 479, 511
General rule of international law, 345
General Treaty of Peace and Amity, 426
Geneva Conventions, 72, 101, 103, 129, 137, 181, 335, 346, 355, 358, 388, 407, 459, 528, 558, 568
Geneva formula, 355, 356
Génocidaires, 91, 178, 372, 421
Genocide, 44, 51, 91–93, 323, 325–328, 330, 332, 335, 340, 342, 347, 349, 351, 353, 358, 360, 363–365, 372–375, 380, 384, 385, 404, 422, 423, 427, 431, 440, 441, 446, 451, 455, 459, 469, 472, 476, 499, 506, 518, 520, 529, 532, 556, 558, 567–569, 576, 614, 633, 640
Genocide case, 77, 81
Genocide Convention, 6, 66, 91, 92, 113, 115, 137, 177, 178, 180, 181, 282, 283, 326, 334, 335, 349, 359, 363, 440, 441, 459, 468, 528–530, 569, 574
Genuinely unwilling to investigate and prosecute, 456
Genuineness assessment, 220, 221
Genocide in Guatemala case, 365
Genuine willingness or ability, 212, 218, 222, 223, 236
Geographic levels of prosecution, 32
George Washington University, 614
Georgia, 67
Georgia investigation, 217
Georgian Minister of Defence, 438
Germain Katanga and Mathieu Ngudjolo Chui, 78, 620
German Constitutional Court, 443, 467
German Constitutional Order, 467
German Democratic Republic, 42
German Federal Constitutional Court, 148, 432, 433, 443, 623, 640, 646
German Federal Supreme Court, 334, 632
German legislation, 335
German national, 559
German-Polish Upper Silesian Convention, 426
Germans, 74
Germany, 67, 333, 335, 346, 359, 360, 365, 382, 432, 441, 451, 452, 467, 469, 483, 494, 506, 516, 524, 525, 556, 558, 576, 577, 605, 607, 632, 639–641, 643
Germany v USA (*LaGrand* case), 552, 653
Ghana, 382
Gilbert, 430, 439, 442–445, 515, 526

Gillet, 178
Girón and Valdez Asij, 504, 647
Glantz, 482, 646
Glen Ashby v Trinidad and Tobago, 470, 648
Global community, 349
Global dimension, 582
Global enforcement, 167
Global human rights instruments, 571
Global justice, 351
Global prosecution, 32, 42, 609
Global system of international criminal justice, 33
Goiburú et al. v Paraguay, 381, 636
Göktan, 486, 645
Gomes Lund, 457, 648
Good faith, 572
Good practices, 576
Goran Jelisić, 325, 637
Gorski, 435, 441, 449
Government of Bolivia, 526
Government of Kenya, 11
Government soldiers, 576
Graciela P de L and Others v Scilingo, 364
Grave breaches, 421, 458, 459, 465, 558
Gravity, 112, 327, 331, 375, 381, 608
Gravity threshold, 216, 220
Greatest juridical interest, 356
Greatest responsibility, 33, 608
Grech, 480, 650
Greek-Cypriot missing persons, 385
Greek Supreme Court, 524, 525, 639
Grenade, 446
Grievous bodily harm, 430, 436, 451
Gross human rights violation, 222
Grotius, 322
Ground for refusal of extradition, 357, 367, 477, 507
Ground of jurisdiction, 322, 334, 335, 348, 613
Grounds for denial of extradition, 419, 420
Grounds for non-execution of the EAW, 434
Grounds for refusal, 50, 183, 198, 210–216, 237, 249–251, 255, 256, 286, 296–298, 312, 564, 565, 583
Grounds for refusal of extradition, 10, 334, 367
Grounds for refusal of surrender, 150
Group-based crimes, 67
Group-based nature, 134
Group-oriented crimes, 65
Grupo Colina death squad, 428
Guantanamo Bay, 346, 379
Guantanamo detainees, 346
Guarantees, 419, 427, 475, 511, 512
Guatemala criminal code, 365
Guatemala, 363, 365, 376, 385, 462, 463, 504, 556, 633, 636, 638, 647–649
Guatemala City, 365, 638
Guatemala Genocide case, 335, 632
Guatemalan criminal courts, 364
Guatemalan law, 363
Guatemalan Supreme Court, 461
Guatemala's Peace Agreement, 463
Guateng Division, 21, 619
Guengueng, 360, 638
Guerra Sucia, 506
Guerrilla groups, 55
Guinea, 601
György Katz v István Roland Sós, 593, 655

H

Habeas corpus, 347
Habibullah Jalalzoy, 348, 351, 633, 635
Habitual residence, 516
Hadžihasanović, 329
Hague Convention XII, 426
Hague District Court, The, 422, 482, 651
Hague formula, The, 353, 355
Hague, The, 35, 610
Hailemariam, 508
Haiti, 454
Hanging, 514
Harmonised approach, 387, 594
Harmonization, 565
Harmonized European approach, 452
Harsh punishments, 445, 464
Harun and Ali Kushayb, 196, 624
Harvey Swystun v USA, 357, 633
Hasan İlhan v Turkey, 387, 634, 653
Hass, 423, 641
Hategekimana, 506, 649
Hauser-Sporn, 487, 645
HCSS, 371
Head-of-State Immunity, 21, 178, 524
Heads of government, 519
Heads of State, 267–269, 271, 275, 277, 283, 285, 288, 422, 440, 518–520, 522, 525, 526, 530–532, 609
Heathrow Airport, 370
Hector Jaime Beltran Parra, Clara Patricia, Nidia Amanda, Jose Antonio and Mario Beltran Fuentes, 383, 632
Hedigan, Judge, 473
Heller, 222, 227, 229, 234, 269
Henzelin, 406
Hesamuddin Hesam, 351, 633
Hieramente, 328, 329
Hierarchically superior, 582
Higaniro, 421, 639, 640

Higgins, Judge, 523, 649
High Command case, 352, 637
High Court of Australia, 450
High-level State officials, 267
High-level suspects, 598, 608
High-profile individuals, 599
Hijackers, 447
Hijacking, 103, 339, 354, 355, 567
Hill, 500
Hirsi Jamaa and Others v Italy, 368, 369, 634
Hissène Habré, 330, 359–363, 369, 612
Hissène Habré v Republic of Senegal, 362, 638
HIV, 122
Hobbes, 62
Hobbs, 64
Hoge Raad, 326, 341, 348, 379, 635
HoL, 435, 485, 493, 522, 647, 648
Holmes, 221, 231, 245, 246
Holocaust, 48, 51
Holvoet, 598
Honduras, 376
Hope, Lord, 290, 529
Horciag, 481, 645
Horizontal axis, 329
Horizontal complementarity, 336, 337
Horizontal effects, 271
Horizontal system of enforcement, 22–25, 32, 121, 149, 150, 152, 153, 155, 156, 159, 170, 174, 177, 211, 215, 232, 235, 246, 254, 264, 266, 267, 269, 270, 274, 278, 297, 312–314, 333, 336, 351, 352, 362, 365, 404, 407, 408, 412, 413, 417, 420, 424, 425, 434, 466, 470, 508, 518, 526, 564, 565, 604, 614
Hoskins, 134
Hospital Posadas, 506, 640
Hostages case, 352, 468, 637, 649
Hostages Convention, 354, 355
Hostage-takers, 447
Hostage-taking, 103, 127, 339, 354, 567
Hostis humani generis, 71, 131, 350, 442
House arrest, 425
HRC, 349, 381, 384, 457–460, 463, 464, 467, 469, 470, 478, 479, 493, 510, 511, 513, 514, 635, 648
HRW, 601
H.S.A., 520, 642
Huaura, José Enrique Crousillat López Torres, 347, 638
Hugo Rodríguez v Uruguay, 384, 635
Human being-oriented approach, 584
Humanitarian argument, 437
Humanitarian law, 572
Human rightism, 583
Human rights, 328–332, 336, 342, 347, 349, 351, 353, 358, 362, 367–369, 373, 380, 381, 383–386, 388, 604, 605, 608, 613, 633, 635
Human rights abuses, 589
Human Rights Act, 433
Human rights advocates, 513
Human rights chamber of BiH, 385
Human Rights Committee, 222, 237, 349, 381, 384, 457–460, 463, 464, 467, 469, 470, 478, 479, 493, 510, 511, 513, 514, 569, 606
Human Rights Council, 608
Human rights court, 34, 221, 230, 461, 462, 558
Human rights general exceptions to extradition, 467
Human rights instrument, 384
Human rights law, 590
Human rights lens, 230
Human rights mechanisms, 346
Human rights monitoring mechanisms, 222
Human rights movement, 531
Human rights norms, 552
Human rights offences, 388
Human rights protection, 435, 467, 530
Human rights record, 179
Human rights regional systems, 569
Human rights standards, 221, 223, 257
Human right violations, 328, 329, 362, 373, 384, 385, 388, 569–571
Human security, 138
Human security principle, 61
Human trafficking, 378
Humberto Alvarez-Machain, 359, 639
Humiliation, 499, 509
Hungarian Criminal Code, 437
Hungary, 430, 431, 436, 437, 472, 499, 646
Hüseyin Gözütok and Klaus Brügge, 483, 484, 488, 489, 643
Hutchinson, 502, 503, 644
Hutton, Lord, 289
Hutu extremist party, 431
Hybrid courts, 8, 152, 153
Hybridity, 36
Hybrid tribunal, 8, 35–37, 371, 568, 575, 598, 607, 613, 614

I

IACmmHR, 456, 457, 461, 648
IACtHR, 380, 381, 383, 385, 457, 458, 461, 462, 467, 478, 558, 569, 570, 636, 648, 649, 653, 654
IACvHR, 426, 436, 444, 464

ICC, 7, 9–12, 16–24, 42, 44, 46, 48–50, 60–62, 65, 68, 71, 77–79, 81, 124–128, 130, 131, 133, 135, 136, 138, 149–160, 166–200, 322, 325, 328, 330, 333, 334, 336, 337, 341, 343, 347, 353, 360, 363, 365, 370, 372, 425, 444, 451, 456, 466, 477, 480, 483, 520, 557, 564, 565, 568, 572–576, 591, 594, 598–601, 604, 606–614, 619, 620, 623–625, 654
ICC Consequential Amendments Act, The, 360
ICC cooperation legislation, 313
ICC cooperation regime, 564
ICC crimes, 44, 45
ICC drafting history, 565
ICC Elements of Crimes, 90, 91, 93, 96, 101
ICC encroachment, 187
ICC jurisdiction, 312
ICC Legal Tools, 155
ICC orders, 172
ICCPR, 384, 424, 426, 444, 458, 464, 469, 470, 472, 473, 478, 493, 512–514, 569
ICC proceedings, 245, 248, 249, 260, 273
ICC regime, 607
ICC RPE, 6, 69
ICC's Elements of Crimes, 420
ICC's jurisdiction, 431, 453
ICC State Parties, 333, 337, 381, 606, 607, 611
ICC Statute, 7–9, 11, 16, 19, 20, 22, 44, 45, 48–52, 64, 65, 75, 77, 78, 91, 93, 95, 96, 98, 99, 104, 166–173, 175–185, 187–190, 192–200, 210–226, 230–247, 249–259, 261, 263, 264, 266, 267, 270–288, 290–298, 312, 313, 325, 328, 333, 336, 342, 343, 352, 370, 372, 381, 382, 384, 385, 417, 420, 424, 445, 456, 470, 486, 520, 523, 528, 564, 565, 573, 574, 606–608, 628
ICC Statute State Parties, 149
ICD of the HC of Uganda, 35
Iceland, 430, 461, 646
Icelandic domestic system, 461
Icelandic Supreme Court, 461
ICJ, 8, 77, 80, 82, 168, 177, 180, 182–184, 188, 189, 196, 199, 321, 323, 324, 326, 330–332, 337, 345, 347, 349, 353, 356, 360–362, 369, 412, 413, 431, 457, 468, 469, 518, 519, 522, 523, 525, 529, 571, 573, 574, 576, 620, 625, 636, 639, 649, 654
ICRC, 128
ICT of Bangladesh, 35, 423, 649
ICTR, 16, 18, 150–152, 154, 157, 326–328, 351, 373, 374, 431, 466, 472, 481, 505, 506, 619, 623, 636, 649
ICTR Statute, 150, 284
ICTY, 16–19, 21, 148, 150–152, 420, 422, 466, 481, 491, 519, 524, 567, 570, 575, 590, 592, 619, 623, 649, 654, 655
ICTY cooperation regime, 168
ICTY orders, 172
ICTY State cooperation regime, 148
ICTY Statute, 247, 284
IDI, 9, 342
I.G. Farben case, 637
IHT, 7, 36, 159, 363, 514, 611
IIIM, 608
ILA, 9
ILC, 7, 9, 82, 93, 94, 126, 321, 332, 345, 353, 404, 426, 524, 528, 567
ILC Draft Code of Offences Against the Peace and Security of Mankind, 528
ILC report, 94
ILC's Draft Articles on State Responsibility, 115
Illegal restraint and hostage-taking, 430
Illegal treatment, 604
Illicit trade in human organs and tissue, 430
Ill-treatment, 460, 495, 502, 503
Images documenting atrocities, 608
Immediate release, 501
Immunities, 313
Immunities *rationae materiae*, 267, 273, 282, 285, 289–291, 521, 522, 527, 529, 532
Immunities *rationae personae*, 267, 270, 273, 278, 282, 284, 285, 288, 518, 519, 521, 522
Immutable norm, 532
Impartiality, 224–226, 231, 242, 253, 270, 273
Impartial judicial institution, 336
Implementation, 552
Implementing legislation, 607
Implied powers, 197, 558, 588–591
Import of same drugs, 485
Imprescriptibility, 611
Impunidad, 559
Impunity, 62, 78, 186, 191–194, 312, 313, 339, 341, 343, 344, 365, 367, 376, 380, 381, 388, 582, 589, 590, 593
Impunity gap, 36, 564, 610
Inability, 47, 48, 51, 53, 55, 129, 219, 220, 224, 225, 229–231, 236, 277
Inability to prosecute, 599
Inaction, 211, 220, 251
Inactivity, 159, 170, 174, 175
Inadequate heating, 369
Inadequate sleeping, 369
Inadequate toilet facilities, 369
Inadequate ventilation, 369

Inadmissibility, 218, 231, 241, 247
Incarceration, 505
Incommunicado detentions, 379
Incriminating evidence, 594
Incumbent Heads of State, 521
Independence, 224, 225, 231, 242, 253, 582
Independence of East Timor, 598
Independent judicial institution, 336
Independent mechanism, 608
India, 199, 382
Indian decisions, 510
Indicia, 160
Indictment, 420, 421, 458, 477, 478, 485, 506, 520, 639, 642, 649, 650
Indirect enforcement system, 23
Indirect jurisdiction, 326
Indirect perpetrators, 600
Indirect review, 24
Indirect waiver argument, 268, 285
Individual criminal responsibility, 6, 7, 113–115, 238, 289, 290
Individual petition, 584
Indonesia, 199, 425
Indonesian occupation, 598
Inescapable dyads, 314
Inference, 439, 501
Inherent powers, 168, 557, 558, 588, 591, 592
Inhuman and degrading treatment or punishment, 418, 493, 494, 499, 508
Inhuman or degrading treatment, 368
Inquisitorial criminal justice system, 373, 594
Insider trading, 421
Institutional independence of investigators, 387
Institutional levels of prosecutions, 32
Insufficient food, 369
Insufficient medical treatment, 369
Insufficient recreation, 369
Insurrectional movements, 44
Integrated system, 599
Interaction, 582
Interaction between complementarity and universal jurisdiction, 605
Interactive community of courts, 565
Inter-American Convention Against Terrorism, 447
Inter-American Convention to Prevent and Punish Torture, 426
Interests of justice, 244, 246
Intergovernmental organisations, 44
Inter-jurisdictional, 218, 242
Interlocutory decree, 594
Internal political affairs, 437
International agreements, 565
International arrest warrant, 172, 177, 190, 213, 214, 217, 256, 257, 260, 273, 278, 282, 348, 572, 574, 576
International chamber of horizontal complementarity, 336
International Civil Aviation Organization, 492
International Commission of Jurists (Kenya), 158, 427
International community, 323, 325–327, 329, 330, 332, 335, 338, 339, 343, 346, 347, 349, 359, 370, 371, 381, 557, 559, 607–609, 611, 614
International concern, 608
International consensus, 328
International constabulary, 313
International Convention for the Prevention, Prosecution and Punishment of Core Crimes, 532, 594
International Convention on the non-Applicability of Statutory Limitations, 611
International conventions, 404, 605
International cooperation and judicial assistance, 6
International Court Against Terrorism, 138
International Court of Human Rights, 604
International courts, 267, 269, 270, 276, 284, 288, 556, 557, 588, 589, 591, 592, 595, 598, 600
International crimes, 112, 118, 120, 121, 129, 132–136, 138, 139
International Crimes Act, 348, 358, 360
International crimes exception, 532
International crimes proper, 134
International criminal jurisdiction, 592
International criminal justice, 314, 320, 322, 564, 571, 572, 590, 599, 609–613
International criminal law, 4–12, 422, 425, 441, 451, 462, 469, 473, 507, 512, 515, 526, 531
International criminal tribunals, 211, 213, 215, 232, 265, 268, 269, 276, 284, 285, 566, 568, 572
International extradition law, 336, 453
International fair trial rights, 374
International harm, 138
International harm principle, 46, 64, 68, 73
International humanitarian law, 6, 8, 53, 101–104, 128, 129, 138, 335, 349, 358, 360, 404
International Human Rights Court, 604
International human rights instrument, 384

International human rights law, 6, 8, 10, 12, 134, 328, 383, 388, 462, 464, 467, 470, 515, 531, 582–584, 589, 593, 605
International human rights tribunals, 571
International institution, 377, 564
Internationalization of a global rule of law, 291
Internationalization of the rule of law, 349
Internationalized courts, 598, 600, 613
Internationalized domestic courts, 36, 133
Internationalized model of criminal justice, 152
International joint investigative team, 371
International judges, 582
International jurisdiction, 243, 269, 584, 612
International law, 605–607, 609, 611, 614
International legal instruments, 320
International legal order, 412
International legal personality, 426
Internationally recognized human rights, 9
International Marshals Service, 313
International obligation, 471, 476, 552, 591
International organizations, 37
International peace and security, 46, 130, 135, 183, 191–193, 199, 329, 568, 614
International prosecutions, 32
International protection, 368
International protest, 344, 567
International refugee law, 369, 515
International relations, 404, 434, 512, 525
International responsibility, 62, 74, 82, 584, 591
International rule of law, 4, 512
International solidarity, 330
International supervisory bodies, 591
Inter partes, 322, 339, 351
Interpol, 216
Inter-State case, 385
Inter-State cooperation, 167
Inter-state model, 18
Interstate model of cooperation, 149
Interstate rendition, 154
Inter-state system of international law, 531
Inter-State tensions, 433
In the Matter for Judicial Review, 472, 646
Intra-jurisdictional, 242
Intrusion, 60, 63, 72, 77, 79
Investigate or prosecute, 212, 217, 219, 221, 245
Investigation, 213–215, 221, 224, 228, 230, 238–240, 244, 249–251, 260, 290, 292, 293, 295, 296, 629, 630
Investigative steps, 228, 238–240, 251
Investigators, 595
Inviolability, 268, 278, 280
Inyangamugayo, 373
Iovchev v Bulgaria, 369, 634
Iran, 199
Iranian Hostages Case, 324, 636
Iraq, 67, 72, 576, 577
Iraqi criminal procedural law, 363
Ireland, 388
Ireland v UK, 509
Irish citizen, 445
Irish Courts, 468, 506
Irish Extradition (Amendment) Act, 446
Irish Law, 485
Irish Republican Army, 442
Irish Supreme Court, 437, 445
Irish System, 485
Irish Test, 486
Irrebuttable presumption, 592
Irregular capture, 359
Irregularities, 259, 260, 264
Islam, 513
Islamic terrorist groups, 72
Islamic world, 607
Isolation, 505
Israel, 334, 359, 382, 607, 638
Israeli Wall Advisory Opinion, 571, 654
Instituti legis, 8, 235, 388, 577, 582
Institutum legis, 423
Italian Courts, 423, 523, 525
Italian language, 353
Italian Law on the EAW, 453
Italian Supreme Court, 524, 525
Italy, 348, 360, 369, 382, 423, 427, 430, 432, 433, 435, 452, 474, 478, 482, 488, 489, 491, 493, 499, 508, 523, 524, 529, 530, 634, 641, 643, 644, 648
Iudex (loci) deprehensions, 347
Iuris tantum presumption, 245
Ius prosequi, 23, 25, 406
Ius puniendi, 12
Ivcher Bronstein v Peru, 558, 653
Ivorian amnesty process, 228
Ivory tower, 502

J

Jacobs, 80
Jalalzoy, 348, 351
Jalloh, 276
Jaloud v The Netherlands, 34, 620
Jamaica, 446, 508, 511, 648, 650
James-Robinson, 130, 623
Japan, 382, 428, 429, 571, 607
Japanese Yakuza, 349
Javor, 348, 633
Jean Claude Iyamuremye, 427, 468
Jean-Pierre Bemba Gombo, 94, 621

Jelisić, 91–93, 325, 566, 622
JEP, 48
JFK Airport, 370
Jia, 273, 295, 327
Jihadists, 576
Jimenez, 524, 651
John Demjanjuk v Joseph Petrowsky et al, 359, 639
Johnsson, 216, 226, 244–246
Joint Action 97/154 on Trafficking in Human Beings, 452
Jokić, 93, 622
Jones and Others, 524, 526, 644
Jordan, 102, 187, 200, 286, 287, 289, 607, 625, 627, 630
Jordan's appeal, 289, 627
Jørgensen, 126
Jorgić, 334, 335
José Carlos Trujillo Oroza José contra Luis Dabdoub López y Jacinto Morón Sánchez, 383, 638
Jreida Prison, 498
Juárez-Cifuentes, 572
Judge-made law, 168
Judges, 610, 611
Judicare limb, 355, 372, 405–407
Judicial activism, 168–170, 590
Judicial authority, 498, 517, 522
Judicial body, 189, 196, 588, 591, 600, 601, 614
Judicial branch, 594
Judicial cooperation, 601
Judicial cooperation agreement, 363
Judicial creativity, 584
Judicial determinations, 592
Judicial dialogue, 23, 595, 599, 601
Judicial forum, 22, 24
Judicial functions, 591
Judicial international institution, 323
Judicial mechanisms, 32
Judicial organ, 591
Judicial panels, 598, 612
Judicial partnerships, 598, 612
Judicial power, 589
Judicial redress, 613
Judicial restraint, 590
Judicial review, 593
Judiciarisation, 441
Juge d'instruction, 349
Jurid, 226
Juridical infrastructures, 12, 373
Juridical process, 454
Jurisdiction, 148, 151, 152, 157, 166–170, 172–174, 176–184, 188, 194–199, 210, 211, 213, 214, 216–221, 226, 233, 235, 236, 238, 241–245, 247, 249–251, 253, 256, 259, 260, 262–264, 266–269, 271–276, 278–281, 283, 285, 287, 289–291, 293, 295, 297, 298, 417, 422, 429, 431, 432, 441, 451, 455, 456, 461, 462, 466, 467, 469, 476, 483, 490, 493, 496, 498, 507, 518, 519, 523, 525, 526, 529–531, 565–568, 572–576, 623–625, 627, 631, 640, 649, 650
Jurisdictional authority, 363
Jurisdictional claims, 336, 367
Jurisdictional competence, 588
Jurisdictional joint venture, 312, 613
Jurisdictional pointsman, 242
Jurisdictional pretext, 342
Jurisdictional priority, 336
Jurisdictional reach, 121, 127, 131
Jurisdiction-bestowing device, 322
Jurisdiction *in absentia*, 340, 348, 349
Jurisdiction to enforce, 5
Juris et de jure presumption, 592
Juris tantum presumption, 33, 592
Jus cogens, 45, 46, 255, 256, 260, 262–264, 266, 273, 282, 288–291, 295, 324, 325, 327, 331–333, 337–342, 344, 345, 347, 368, 369, 381
Jus cogens norms, 61, 71, 81, 322, 327, 330, 331, 333, 339, 341, 342, 369, 525, 530, 552, 557, 567, 582
Jus cogens violations, 344, 359
Jus de non evocando principle, 431
Jus in bello, 103
Justice case, 352, 637
Justus Lipsius, 428
Juvenile court, 559

K

Kabul government, 293
Kadir Satik and Others v Turkey, 387, 634, 653
Kadi v Council of the European Union and Commission of the European Communities, 167, 624
Kafkaris, 502, 644, 645
Kallon and Kamara, 461
Kambanda, 276, 288, 631
Kampala Conference, 292
Kampala Review Conference, 44
Kanavalaw, 510, 640
Kant, 62, 70
Kantian philosophy, 50
Kanyabashi, 183, 431, 625, 649
Karadžić, 21, 92, 622
Karamira, 510, 651

Katanga, 94–96, 127, 621, 623
Katanga and Chui, 174, 176, 624
Kaul, Judge, 99, 100, 125
Kavalyow, 510, 640
Kayishema, 92, 622
Kelly and Others v UK, 386, 387, 634
Kemp, 518–520, 526
Kennedy, 341
Kenya, 35, 68, 97–100, 125, 136, 186, 187, 215, 217, 220, 238, 283, 423, 564, 621, 624, 626–629
Kenyatta, 11, 186, 187, 564, 607, 619, 624, 654
Keywords, 5, 32, 42
Kezerashvili, 438, 650
Khan, 369, 638
Kidnap, 530
Kidnappers, 447
Kidnapping, 119, 359, 430, 446, 486, 530, 641
Kigali, 472, 510, 651
Kindler, 470, 511, 648
Kinetic social institution, 376
King, 275, 276, 292, 294, 343, 417, 435, 493, 642, 648
Kisimba-Ngoy, Minister, 25
Kiyani, 277, 283, 285
Kjeldgaard-Pedersen, 132
Kleffner, 67, 68, 235, 236, 243, 244, 322, 325, 336, 359, 360, 421, 425, 449, 451, 456, 512, 565, 574, 606, 607
Klein, 341
Klip, 559
Knoops, 313, 314
Koçeri Kurt v Turkey, 569, 653
Kodiči Kriminali, 360
Kok, 422, 424
Kolb, 321, 322, 339, 357, 405, 406, 419, 437, 446, 449, 454, 459, 511
Kompetenz-kompetenz principle, 10, 168, 292, 588, 589
Kononov v Latvia, 172, 624
Kony et al, 168
Kooijmans, Judge, 523, 649
Kosgey, 100, 621
Koskotas v Roche, 443
Kosovo, 36, 44, 371
Kosovo Relocated Specialist Judicial Institution, 371
Kreß, 90–92, 99, 150, 151, 267, 268, 283–286, 288
Krings, 157, 333, 605, 606, 609
Krisch, 180
Kristinsson, 461, 646
Krolik, 433, 647
Krstić, 91, 622
Krupp case, 352, 637
KSC, 35
Kunarac et al., 123, 124, 623
Kurd, 505
Kurdish religious community, 67
Kurds, 102
Kvočka, 113, 622

L

La Belle Équipe, 103
Laboratory, 377
La Cantuta, 428, 478, 483, 648
La Cantuta University, 428
La Cantuta v Perú, 381, 636
La Casa Nostra, 103
Lack of impartiality, 374
La Cosa Nostra, 349
Lacuna, 245, 254
Lacunae, 8, 12, 352, 590, 591
La Forest, Judge, 511
Lagos, 491
Lake Chad, 128
Lakhdar Boumediene et al. v Bush et al., 347, 639
Lambruschini, 532
Language barriers, 452
Larceny, 439
Latin America, 366, 376
Latin American States, 570
Law enforcement, 118, 130
Law Enforcement Network, 313
Law Lords, 290, 497, 527, 529
Law of international responsibility, 115
Law on the Application of the Statute of the ICC, 360
Laws of humanity, 469
Laws of Malta, 491, 515
Leadership requirement, 105
Lebanese law, 132
Lebanon, 378, 382, 454, 477
Le Carillon, 103
Le Comptoir Voltaire, 103
Lee, 60
Lee Urzúa et al. v Pinochet, 348, 349, 638
Legal authority, 342, 406
Legal certainty, 42, 340
Legal characterization, 251
Legal claims, 332
Legal consequences, 135, 605
Legal Consequences for States of the Continued Presence of South Africa in Namibia Notwithstanding Security

Council Resolution 276 (1970) (Namibia case), 183, 625
Legal control, 342
Legal culture, 353
Legal denominator, 388
Legal duty to testify, 375
Legal experts, 601
Legal folk culture, 342
Legal infrastructure, 357
Legal instruments, 360, 378, 421, 422, 426, 441, 590
Legality, 42, 433, 449, 450, 452, 475, 512
Legal literature, 219, 267, 271, 285, 331, 332
Legal representation, 374
Legal rubric, 244
Legal xenophobia, 431
Legibus solutus, 5
Legislative *ad hoc* entities, 456
Legislative international institution, 323
Legislative requirements, 256
Legitimacy of local legislation, 433
Legitimizing link, 349
Lemkin, 66
Lenient prison sentence, 425
Lenient punishment, 242
Lepard, 323, 324, 331, 345, 347, 386, 412
Le Petit Cambodge, 103
Lethal injection, 514
Letter bomb, 446
Lever, 5, 6
Lex ferenda, 265
Lex specialis, 9
Ley Organica del Poder Judicial, 365
Liaison body, 601
Liberia, 35
Liberty, 379
Libya, 81, 157, 158, 191, 217, 223–230, 234, 239, 240, 250–252, 626–628
Libya Dawn, 158
Libyan Arab Jamahiriya v Malta (Continental Shelf case), 412, 639
Libyan Arab Jamahiriya v USA, 321, 636
Libyan court, 158
Libyan Court of Assize, 226, 626
Liechtenstein v Guatemala, 431, 649
Life imprisonment, 131, 362, 372, 380
Life sentence, 496, 499–506
Lifting of immunities, 276, 279
Likelihood of a successful prosecution, 239
Likelihood of a violation, 508, 515, 517, 604
Limaj et al., 97, 128, 622, 623
Limitations of jurisdiction *rationae loci*, 611
Limitations of jurisdiction *rationae materiae*, 611
Limitations of jurisdiction *rationae personae*, 611
Limitations of jurisdiction *rationae temporis*, 611
Limits of jurisdiction, 588
Link of causation, 517
Lithuania, 430, 482, 508, 645, 647
Local crime, 132
Locatelli, 443, 652
Lockerbie, 152, 321, 370, 371, 610, 612, 613, 636
Lockerbie trial, 35
Locus delicti commissi, 11, 35, 75, 113, 118, 124, 355, 365, 381, 405, 569, 583, 600
Locus standi, 426, 467, 498, 575, 593
Locus standi in judicio, 80
Logical formula, 338
Loi organique, 427
Loi relative aux violations graves du droit international humanitaire, 335
Lomé Peace Accords, 462
London Agreement, 426
London Scheme for Extradition Within the Commonwealth, 440
Lord Bingham's opinion, 497
Lords, 114
Lord Slynn of Hadley, 340, 568, 654
Los Angeles, 493, 642
Los Zetas cartel, 96
Lotus, 339, 348, 638
Lotus case, S.S., 591
Lotus, S. S. (France v Turkey), 591, 655
Lower level perpetrators, 599
Low-level individuals, 598
Low-profile criminals, 373
Lozano, 523, 529, 641
Luban, 44, 47, 48, 52
Lubanga, 170, 181, 197, 216, 218, 219, 240, 246, 247, 259, 260, 263, 264, 584, 624, 625, 627, 629, 630, 655
Lujambio, 445, 640
Luo Taliban, 68
Luring, 359
Luxembourg, 33, 191

M

Macro-criminality, 44
Madeleine Mangabu Bukumba and Gracia Mukumba v Canada (Minister of Citizenship and Immigration), 367, 635
Mafias, 349
Mai Mai, 128
Malabo Protocol, 34
Mala fides, 256, 259, 372

Mala in se, 119
Mala prohibita, 119
Malawi, 270, 274, 275, 277, 278, 286, 296, 628
Male captus bene detentus, 258, 359
Malice aforethought, 119
Malta, 353, 354, 360, 382, 612
Malta's Refugee Appeals Board, 515
Maltese Court of Appeal, 491, 495
Maltese Criminal Court, 491
Maltese laws, 353
Malum in se, 119
Malaysia Airlines flight MH17, 371
Mamatkulov and Abdurasulovic, 470
Mamatkulov and Askarov, 470, 473–475, 644
Mandatory compliance, 564
Mandatory duty to investigate and prosecute, 381
Mandatory ground for postponement of the request, 498
Mandatory jurisdiction, 459
Mandatory prosecutions, 344, 558
Mandatory recognition of judgments, 594
Mandatory requirement, 347
Mandatory sentence of life imprisonment, 500, 503
Mandatory universal jurisdiction, 605
Manner of execution, 171
Marchuk, 113, 114
Marcos Roitman Rosenmann v Spain, 324, 638
Marek, 289
Margin of appreciation, 18
Margin of appreciation doctrine, 494
Marguš, 457, 458, 465, 482, 483, 644
Marino-Garcia, 130, 623
Martens Clause, 469
Maşallah Öneryildiz v Turkey, 572, 653
Massera, 532
Matryoshka dolls, 422
Matter between Democratic Alliance and Minister of International Relations and Cooperation et al., 21
Mature legal systems, 592
Mature rule, 607
Mau Mau, 423
Mauritanian amnesty law, 460, 498
Mauritanian soldiers, 498
Maxwell-Fyfe, 9
May, 42, 46, 54, 61–65, 68–70, 77, 79, 92, 134, 620, 622
Mayan-Chinese anthropologist, 462
Mayan Ixil population, 364
Mayotte, 327
Mazzini, 66
McArthur, 324, 325, 330
Meaningful utensil, 517
Mechanism, 466, 489, 503–505
Mecklenburg Correctional Center, 509
MEDAC, 47
Médecins Sans Frontières, 61
Medical case, 352, 637
Medical reports, 382
Mégret, 173
Meloni, 112, 113
Membership of a particular social group, 516
Menem, 456, 486
Mens rea, 90, 92, 119
Mental health problems, 503
Mental suffering, 509
Mercedes Benz plant, 359
Meron, 19, 346, 412
Methods of execution, 514
Mettraux, 270
M.E. v Denmark, 388, 634
Mexican Court, 424
Mexican drug cartels, 349
Mexico, 96, 383, 432
Meyrowitz, 128
Michael Domingues v USA, 331, 636
Michael Seifert, 348
Migrants, 576
Migrant smuggling, 122, 124
Miguel Castro-Castro Prison v Perú, 381, 636
Miklis, 508, 647
Milch case, 352, 637
Military court, 264
Military dictatorship, 499
Military Division of the Budapest Metropolitan Court, 437
Military force, 104, 105
Military *juntas*, 380
Military law, 436
Military offence exception, 437
Military offence exemption, 418, 436
Military offences, 436
Military panel, 472
Military personnel, 294
Millett, Lord, 290, 291, 527, 529
Milošević, 268, 276, 277, 285, 288, 458, 631
Milošević exception, 156
Minimum guarantees, 470, 476
Minimum level of severity, 496, 502
Ministerial meeting, 607
Minister of Defence of the Republic of Algeria, 519
Minister of Foreign Affairs, 520
Minister of Justice and Constitutional Development, 532, 650

Ministries case, 352, 637
Minor, 434, 489, 490
Minsk Metro, 510
Miraglia, 484, 488, 643
Misalignment, 515
Mise en scène, 48, 242
Mitigating factors, 503
Mixed courts, 152
Mixed tribunals, 152
Mladen Naletilić v Croatia, 151, 623
Mladić, 21, 92, 622
Mob rule, 4
Mocanu, 422, 644
Model American Convention, 446
Model of cooperation, 149, 150
Mode of conduct, 339
Mode of repression, 118, 125, 129
Modern crimes, 377
Modinos, 383, 634
Modus operandi, 6, 32, 171, 198
Mohammed and Dalvie, 513, 641
Monageng, Judge, 21
Money laundering, 122, 421
Mongolia, 382, 532, 607
Monitoring mechanisms, 353, 427
Montevideo Convention, 52, 280
Montreal Convention, 321, 354, 355, 636
Montt, 364–366
Monumental milestone, 571
Moral argument, 437
Morris, 92
Morrison, Judge, 95, 621
Mossad agents, 359
Mothers of Srebrenica case, 518, 647
Moulana Abul Kalam Azad, 423, 649
Mouvement Démocratique Républicain, 510
Muammar Gheddafi, 280
Mueller, 119, 120
Mugabe, 520, 640
Muhayimana, 328, 633
Multi-functional, 255
Multilateral agreements, 608
Multilateral conventions, 134
Multilateral extradition treaties, 322
Multi-lateral instrument, 469
Multi-lateral international agreement, 441
Multilateral treaties, 121, 404, 408
Multilateral Treaty for Mutual Legal Assistance and Extradition, 532
Multinational forces, 313
Multinational organizations, 313
Multiple competing requests, 252
Multiple States, 332
Multi-tasking, 234
Mungiki, 68
Municipal courts, 604
Municipal crime, 132
Municipal criminal court, 25
Municipal criminal law, 339
Münster, 559
Munyakazi, 506, 649
Murder, 339, 354, 360, 380, 384, 386, 429, 436, 439, 451, 462, 485, 486, 500, 511, 530, 573
Murphy, Judge, 437
Muscat, 495, 642
Muslim States, 513
Muslim world, 513
Mutual recognition in criminal matters, 378
Mutual recognition principle, 378
Mutyaba, 213, 265, 275, 295
Myanmar, 608
Myers, 344
Myrna Mack Chang, 462, 649

N

Nairobi, 496
Namibia, 198, 454, 506
Naqvi, 417, 419, 422, 423, 462, 481, 490, 521, 522, 526
Narcoterrorism, 121
Narrowing of immunities, 530
National Commission of the South African Police Service, 381, 633
National Constitutions, 552
National courts, 241, 267–270, 274
National crime, 119, 124, 132
National Criminal Court of Perú, 428
National criminalization theory, 50
National criminal jurisdiction, 592
National criminal justice systems, 22
National decision, 221
Nationality, 312, 335, 337, 342, 356, 364, 430–432, 436, 507, 509, 516
Nationalized citizen, 428
National judges, 582
National procedural law, 214, 255
National reconciliation, 244, 246
National security, 213, 214
National Union for the Total Independence of Angola, The, 44
National unity, 454
Nation State, 438
NATO member, 329
Naturalist school of thought, 346
Naturalized Dutch citizen, 482
Nature of the crime, 328, 505
Nazi concentration camp, 559

Ndiki Mutua, 423, 651
Ndiki Mutua, Paulo Nzili, Wambugu Wa Nyigi, Jane Muthoni Mara and Susan Ngondi v The Foreign and Commonwealth Office, 382, 638
Ndombasi, 348, 349
'Ndrangheta, 349
Ne bis in idem, 212, 222, 231–237, 241–243, 246–248, 250, 257, 258, 261, 296, 418, 419, 425, 434, 456, 457, 465, 466, 477–493, 594, 631
Ne bis in idem protection, 466, 481
Necessary evil, 556, 557
Negotiating history, 294, 297
Neighbouring State, 329, 600
Nemo debet bis vexari pro una et eadem causa, 477
Nerve agents, 55
Netherlands, The, 81, 326, 341, 348, 358, 360, 371, 379, 422, 427, 428, 430, 444, 465, 467, 468, 474, 479, 482, 499, 503, 504, 509, 518, 529, 532, 565, 577, 607, 620, 621, 635, 642, 644, 647
Network of specialized judicial panels, 600
New political administration, 245
New Zealand, 348, 360
New Zealand Extradition Act, 513
Next-of-kin, 569
Nexus between the shortcomings and the violation, 606
Nezzar, 524, 646
Ng, 470, 514, 648
NGO reports, 374
Nicaragua v USA, 636
Nicholas Chapman Blake v Guatemala, 385, 569, 636, 654
Nieto-Navia, Judge, 18
Nigeria, 186, 362, 460, 491, 648
Nikitin, 481, 645
Nikola Jorgić, 334, 335, 632
Nikola Jorgić v Germany, 348, 634
Nikolić, 148, 570, 623, 654
Nivette, 499
Nolle prosequi, 386, 454, 593
Nollkaemper, 23, 24, 74, 80–82, 112, 114, 115, 134, 352, 353, 386, 412, 413, 552, 553
Nomenclature, 339, 381
Non bis in idem, 235, 246, 631
Non c'è Pace Senza Giustizia, 44
Non-citizen, 364
Non-cooperation, 211, 260, 263
Non-custodial State, 368
Non-definition, 441
Non-derogable obligation, 326
Non-discrimination, 424, 447
Non-discrimination clause, 419, 439
Non-enforcement, 191
Non-EU States, 510
Non-execution of the death penalty, 150
Non-extradition, 368
Non-extradition of nationals, 312, 418, 428, 430–432, 435, 438, 552, 564
Non-governmental organisations, 44
Non-homicidal offences, 506
Non-judicial accountability, 244
Non-prosecution, 329, 372
Non-refoulement, 367–369, 448, 497, 515
Non-State actors, 44, 47
Non-State entities, 44, 45, 47, 48, 52–55
Non-State Parties, 155, 157, 166, 175–179, 181, 182, 184, 185, 195, 198–200, 217, 218, 250, 253, 254, 270–278, 280, 281, 287, 292, 295, 297
Non-State Parties to the ICC Statute, 367
Non-UN member States, 18
Nordic countries, 429
Nordic Extradition Act, 429, 438
Noriega, 426, 652
Normative point of reference, 517, 604
Northern Ireland, 426, 495
North Korea, 53
North Sea Continental Shelf cases, 323, 636
Norway, 360, 430, 500, 558, 605
Nottebohm Principle, 431
Nouveau Code Pénal, 456
Nouwen, 216, 224, 237, 240, 248, 268, 269, 273
Nowak, 324, 325, 330
Nsereko, 174, 218, 233, 240, 258
Ntezimana, 421, 639, 640
Ntuyahaga, 154, 623
Nuclear Tests case (*Australia v France*), 168, 591, 625, 655
Nuclear Weapons Advisory Opinion, 404, 639
Nuhanović v the Netherlands, 112, 622
Null and void, 245, 259
Nulla poena sine lege, 42, 449
Nullum crimen sine lege, 42, 224, 339, 449
Nulyarimma v Thompson, 326, 635
Nuremberg, 104, 607, 622
Nuremberg Principles, 6, 7, 460
Nyamirambo Stadium, 510
Nzapali, 379

O

OAS, 33
Obediencia debida, 464
Obiter dicta, 607

Objective interpretation, 453
Objectives of international criminal law, 557, 589
Obligation *erga omnes*, 459, 497, 607
Obligation to investigate, 606
Obligation to penalise, 121
Obligation to prosecute, 422, 425, 441, 459, 462, 567, 571–573, 605, 606
Obligation to protect, 72, 81, 82
Obligation to submit to prosecution, 572, 573, 605
Obligation to surrender, 151, 370
Obokata, 321, 338, 349, 357, 378, 449, 464, 510, 513
Obstacles, 4, 8, 10, 418, 427, 428
Obstacles to extradition, 427, 512
Obstacle to deportation, 516
Obstacle to repatriation, 516
Öcalan, 475, 505, 509, 511, 514, 644, 645
Ocampo, 199
Ocampo Six, 217
October 2016 referendum, 465
Office of Public Counsel for Victims, 160
Official acts, 114, 290
Official capacity, 268, 273, 275, 287, 519, 522, 524, 525, 531
Official functions of a Head of State, 523
O'Keefe, 5, 42, 45, 118, 132, 133, 136
OLAF, 377
Olásolo, 213, 243
Omar Al Bashir, 178, 186, 187, 287, 289, 556, 625, 627, 630
Omission, 406, 441, 453, 455, 485, 490, 528, 584, 590
Ongena, 222, 232, 237, 244, 245
Ongoing, 213, 220, 229, 233, 234, 240, 249, 251
Onus probandi, 241
Opacić v the Netherlands, 172, 624
Operational, 214
Operationalization, 591
Opinio juris, 323, 324, 366, 412, 423, 469, 508, 558
Opinion of Advocate General Kokott, 379, 634
Opinion of AG Ruiz Jarabo Colomer, 483, 488, 489
Opposition, 590
Optional grounds for refusal, 419, 434
Orakhelashvili, 471
Order of reparation, 115
Ordinary law, 404
Ordinary legislation, 552
Ordinary responsibility, 114
Ordonnances pénales, 482
Ordre public, 347
Orentlicher, 459, 519, 522, 523, 527, 529, 530, 612
Organic Law of the Judiciary, 360
Organization, 92–98, 100, 588
Organizational policy, 95, 96, 99, 100
Organized armed group, 133
Organized criminal group, 122, 123, 125
Organized guilt, 74
Osiel, 557
Osman, 430, 641
OTP, 313, 601, 608
OTP policy papers, 155, 174
OTP Report, 223
Ott, 357, 368, 385
Ouattara, President, 228
Ould Dah, 460, 498, 641, 642
Out-of-court settlement, 465
Overarching rights, 571
Overcrowding, 369, 495, 503
Overrule decisions, 592

P

Pacta sunt servanda, 166, 459
Pakistan, 199, 369
Palermo, 124
Pan Am bombing, 612
Pan American trans-Atlantic flight 103, 370
Papon, 352, 633
Paraguay, 376
Paraguayan Penal Code, 451
Parallel proceedings, 482, 484
Paramaribo, 348
Parcel bomb, 446
Pardon, 245, 246, 419, 425, 428, 456, 459, 462–466, 481, 490, 506
Paris, 17, 419, 641
Paris attacks, 103
Paris metro bombings, 471
Parliamentary Assembly of the CoE, 511
Parliaments, 456
Parochial crime, 64
Parole, 245, 425, 496, 500, 502, 503
Parole board system, 501
Part 9, 191, 195, 212, 249, 250, 255, 261, 263, 271, 564
Part 9, ICC Statute, 19
Participation in a criminal organisation, 429
Partie civile, 71, 594
Pascal, 19
Pascal Senyamuhara Safari (alias Pascal Simbikangwa), 327, 633
Passive nationality principle, 342
Past persecution, 517

Pativilca, 428
Patrol service, 437
Patteggiamento, 483
Pattern of crimes, 94
Pattison, 72, 73, 79
Paust, 320, 341, 344, 359
Peace, 454, 457–459, 463, 509, 510
Peace Accord, 458, 512
Peace-keeping forces, 313
Peacekeeping operation, 112, 294
Pecuniary compensation, 457
Pedersen and Baadsgaard, 455, 644
Peers v Greece, 369, 634
Pellet, 361, 583
Penological perspective, 383
Peremptory norms, 344, 345
Peremptory plea, 241
Periodic review, 505
Perish, 387
Permanent institution, 16
Permanent International Criminal Court, 443
Permissive universal jurisdiction, 605
Permutations, 404, 407
Perpetrators, 613
Persecution, 368
Persistent objector, 277, 291, 323, 340, 344, 453, 460
Persistent violation, 191
Personal immunity, 266, 270, 283–285, 519–521
Personal liberty and security, 369
Persuasive obligation, 323, 324
Persuasive source, 215
Pert, 129
Perú, 347, 382, 428, 429, 454, 457, 461, 478, 483, 638, 641, 648
Perú's Supreme Court, 428, 429, 641
Peruvian Constitution, 428
Peruvian Constitutional Court, 347
PGA, 533
Phillips, Lord, 290, 529
Philosophy of law, 346
Physical and mental effects of the treatment, The, 503
Physical integrity, 368
Physical suffering, 509
P*i*CT, 557
Pinnacle of criminal justice, 375
Pinochet, 114, 212, 273, 274, 289, 291, 324, 335, 340, 348, 359, 421, 497, 522, 523, 527–530, 532, 568, 573, 611, 626, 648, 653–655
Pinto de Albuquerque, Judge, 422, 502, 503, 644
Piracy, 133, 134, 136–138
Pirates, 136, 137
Place of origin, 368
Plachta, 321, 322, 355, 370, 371, 377, 416, 418, 419, 421, 448, 508
Plan Sistemático, 506, 646
Playing fields, 124
Plea bargain, 415, 465, 466, 483
Plea bargaining, 418, 419, 465, 466
Plural-States hypothetical scenario, 278
Plural-States hypothetical setting, 260
Poels, 478, 488
Pohl case, 352, 637
Point de depart, 379
Poland, 432, 433, 452, 499, 507, 508, 559, 645, 647
Police force, 24, 186, 188, 313
Police officers, 493, 495, 593
Police reform and social responsibility act, 383
Polish Constitutional Court, 429, 432, 651
Polish legislation, 418
Polish Nationals in Danzig case, The, 552, 653
Polish persons, 433
Polish prison conditions, 433
Polish Supreme Court, 508, 650
Political argument, 437
Political bias, 259
Political censure, 185
Political character, 438, 442, 445
Political control, 582
Political corruption, 512
Political crimes, 437, 439, 440, 445
Political disturbance, 438
Political facade, 599
Political implications, 421
Political international criminal law, 371
Politically motivated cases, 375
Politically motivated (unfair) trial, 516
Political offence, 438–441, 443, 448
Political offence exception, 442, 445
Political offence exemption, 418, 419, 437–448, 498, 564
Political offender, 437, 444
Political opinion, 424, 438, 439, 447, 448, 516
Political opponents, 371
Political persecution, 448
Political philosophy, 42, 93
Political rows, 477
Political situation, 215
Political support, 611
Political ties, 512
Political victimization, 122
Polymorphous tribunals, 612
Port of call, 224

Portugal, 360, 432, 448, 499
Portugal v Australia, 331, 636
Positive complementarity, 154, 155, 557, 564, 591, 598, 606
Positive obligations, 384, 387, 388
Positive obligations of the State, 570
Possession of arms and explosives, 491
Possibility of parole, 500, 503, 506
Post-conflict societies, 244
Post-conflict transitional justice, 156, 454, 599
Postponement, 212, 217, 249, 250, 628
Post-surrender, 261, 284
Potential defences, 314
Potential trans-national nature of core crimes, 465
Poursuites, 325
Powerful politicians, 5
Powerful States, 349
Power to adjudicate, 588
Powles, 224, 225
Pratt and Morgan, 508
Preamble, 49, 51, 52, 246, 325, 354, 381
Precede, 213, 232
Pre-emptive, 243
Prefecture of Voiotia case, 525
Preliminary examination phase, 601
Premeditation, 43, 119
Pre-requisite, 172, 177, 213, 481
Prerogative, 265, 270, 593
Prescription, 422, 464, 476
Preservation of evidence, 599
President Carlos Menem, 456
President of Argentina, 456, 506
President of Bolivia, 526
President of the Republic of Cuba, 521
President of Zimbabwe, 520
President's discretion, 501, 502
Press censoring, 428
Presumptio iuris tantum, 160, 407, 433
Presumptio juris tantum, 407, 433
Presumption, 412, 556
Presumption of innocence, 374
Presumption of juridical interest, 59
Presumptive jurisdiction, 588–590, 592
Presumptive order of priorities, 343
Pretoria, 20, 21, 619
Pre-trial detention, 575
Prevention, 77–79, 82, 620
Previous extradition request, 355
Priebke, 423, 641
Primacy, 215, 224, 254
Prima facie case, 355
Primary jurisdiction, 294
Primary obligations of States, 75
Primary responsibility to prosecute, 355
Primary responsibility to punish, 355
Primary victim, 611
Prime Minister, 421, 504, 520, 650
Primo dedere secundo prosequi, 354
Primo prosequi approach, 355
Princeton Principles on Universal Jurisdiction, 461
Princeton Project, 357
Principled and justifiable response to core crimes, 612
Principle of *bona fide*, 459
Principle of complementarity, 322
Principle of legality, 328, 368
Principle of mandatory prosecution, 558
Principle of non-intervention, 349
Principle of prosecutorial fairness, 20
Prioritization, 333, 343, 355, 406
Prior request for extradition, 354, 358
Prior responsibility, 335
Prison authorities, 501
Prison law, 501
Private acts, 529
Private enterprise, 125
Private entity, 96, 97
Private individuals, 294
Private prosecution, 382–384, 593
Privilege against self-incrimination, 345, 375
Privileged position, 167, 170
Privileged State, 333
Privileges and immunities, 565
Privy Council, 508, 510, 650
Procedural bar, 236, 279
Procedural defects, 372
Procedural iter, 386, 600
Procedural laws, 5, 6, 565
Procedural obligations, 385
Procedural perspective, 605
Procedural unfairness, 375
Production of evidence, 214, 600
Progressive, 228, 239, 240, 251
Progressive restatement of international law, 605
Prohibition of discrimination, 424, 448, 476
Prohibition of genocide, 91
Prohibition of inhuman and degrading treatment, 583
Prohibition of torture, 324, 369, 384, 416–418, 424, 427, 431, 469, 471, 474, 493, 497, 499, 507, 514, 526, 527, 529
Proliferation, 612
Proliferation of courts and tribunals, 565
Prolonged suffering, 514
Prominent opponent, 342

Promising prospect for an effective investigation and prosecution, 253
Proprio motu powers, 217, 281
Pro-Russian rebels, 371
Prosecuting forum, 557
Prosecuting state, 476, 512
Prosecution *in absentia*, 573
Prosecution of perpetrators, 71, 115
Prosecution Service v T, 441, 469, 647
Prosecutor-General of the Supreme Court v Desiré Delano Bouterse, 341, 348, 635
Prosecutorial discretion, 246, 379
Prosecutorial strategy, 599
Prosecutor of the ICC, 196
Prosecutors, 321, 363, 373, 383
Prosecutor's policy papers, 218
Prosecutor v Enver Hadžihasanović and Amir Kubura, 329, 637
Prosecutor v Morris Kallon, 321, 638
Prosequi vel dedere, 356
Prospective international law, 352
Prospective violation, 427, 469, 496
Prospect of release, 500, 501, 504, 505
Prost, 150, 151, 167, 195, 266, 271, 275, 292
Prostitution, 124
Protected human rights, 368
Protest, 426
Protocol for the Suppression of Unlawful Acts against the Safety of Fixed Platforms located on the Continental Shelf, 447
Protocol No. 7 to the ECHR, 481
Protocol on the Suppression of Unlawful Acts of Violence at Airports Serving International Civil Aviation, 447
Protocol Relating to the Status of Refugees, 448
Protracted violence, 128
Provisional measures, 321, 362, 636
Public administrators, 595
Public execution, 510
Public interest, 385
Public international law, 8
Publicists, 5, 9, 10, 614
Public Prosecutor, 327, 334, 335, 348, 349, 351, 382, 383, 421–423, 449, 483, 498, 506, 510, 514, 521, 593, 594, 632, 633, 635, 638–642, 646, 647, 649, 651
Public Prosecutor v Joseph Mpambara, 326, 635
Public Prosecutor v Sebastien Nzapali, 379, 635
Punishment, 71, 77, 78, 82, 421, 426, 439–441, 446, 447, 449, 454, 464–466, 477, 478, 480, 481, 490, 493–496, 499, 503–505, 507–509, 511, 514, 520, 526, 532, 559, 566, 569, 570, 589, 594, 605, 606, 620
Punishment of perpetrators, 381
Punto Final, 464
Pure political crime, 439
Pure political offence, 419
Purported amnesty, 222
Purpose of international criminal law, 32, 589
Purposes of the treaty, 244
Purposive interpretation, 224

Q
Qualification, 224, 230, 237
Qualified duty, 607
Qualified erga omnes obligation, 325, 337
Qualitative gravity, 327
Quantitative gravity, 327
Quash, 227
Quasi-judicial *ad hoc* entities, 456
Quasi-judicial authorities, 516
Quasi-prosecutorial role, 608
Querellantes, 71, 366
Questions of Interpretation and Application of the 1971 Montreal Convention Arising from the Aerial Incident at Lockerbie (Libyan Arab Jamahiriya v UK), 180, 183, 625
Questions Relating to the Obligation to Extradite or Prosecute (Belgium v Senegal), 574, 654

R
Race, 424, 516
Radical complementarity, 227
Radu, 433, 643
Ragazzi, 331, 338
Raison d'être, 6
Ramda, 471
Ramsden, 270
Randall, 338, 339, 344
Rape, 362, 375, 430, 573
Rape victims, 375
Rastan, 33, 343, 344, 605, 606
Ratification, 17, 173, 177, 180, 195, 243, 266, 273, 404
Ratio legis, 419
Rationae loci, 362
Rationae materiae, 357
Rationae personae, 357
Rationae temporis, 328, 362, 365
Ratner, 98
Realpolitik, 20, 200, 584
Real risk of ill-treatment, 495
Real risk requirement, 471

Reasonable expedition, 387
Reasonable grounds, 572
Reasonable grounds to believe, 494
Reasonable suspicion, 382, 575
Rebel militia, 55
Receiving State, 293
Reciprocity, 296, 404
Reconciliation, 376, 377, 454, 458–461
Reconstruction, 376
Redress, 327, 360
Reducibility of the sentence, 504
Referendum, 47
Referral, 157, 159, 179, 181–189, 191, 198, 199
Referral to the ICC, 72
Refoulement, 368
Refugee Convention, 78
Refugee laws, 515–517, 604
Refugees, 558
Refugee shelter, 576
Regime, 167–169, 172, 173, 175–177, 181, 188–190, 193, 195, 199, 200
Regime of cooperation, 6
Region, 599
Regional complementarity, 227
Regional court, 381, 433, 467, 496, 647, 652
Regional criminal court, 34
Regional extradition agreements, 420
Regional human rights courts, 478
Regional human rights instruments, 444
Regional human rights law, 134, 583
Regional human rights mechanisms, 558
Regional level, 565
Regional mechanisms, 604
Regional prosecutions, 35
Regional stability, 329
Regional treaties, 404, 406
Registrar of the ICC, 196
Rehabilitation, 504, 505
Related obligations, 566, 576
Related political crime, 439
Relative political offence, 419
Release, 222, 257
Religion, 345, 424, 516
Remedial measures, 73
Remedial powers, 589
Remedy, 190, 200, 222, 256, 261–264
Remetin v Croatia, 384, 634
Remit of criminal courts, 592
Reopen an investigation, 592
Reparation, 114, 584
Repatriation, 368
Reports, 330, 331, 359, 374, 376, 636
Repressive measures, 589
Repressive system, 337
Republic of Chad, 330, 363
Requested State, 214, 233, 252–255, 260, 261, 263, 265, 272, 278, 284, 289, 293, 296, 297, 418, 420, 425, 435, 438, 440–450, 453, 465, 466, 468, 476, 482, 484, 494, 498, 508
Requesting country, 420, 474, 494, 508, 511
Requesting State, 413, 417–420, 425, 427, 428, 435, 438, 441–445, 448, 450, 453, 465–468, 471, 472, 475, 494, 503, 506, 508, 512, 513, 516, 517
Research questions, 10
Reservation, 246, 424
Reservations to the Convention on the Prevention and Punishment of the Crime of Genocide, 330, 636
Residence, 356, 360, 379
Res inter alios acta, 166, 272
Res judicata, 434, 478, 479, 481, 484, 491, 594, 600
Res judicata facet, 232, 237
Resolution on Immunity from Jurisdiction of the State and of Persons who act on Behalf of the State in case of International Crimes, 526
Resolutive conditions, 427, 513
Responsibility to enforce, 314
Responsibility to prevent, 73, 79
Responsibility to prevent atrocities, 194
Responsibility to prosecute, 73
Responsibility to protect, 192, 193, 314, 583
Responsibility to protect norm, 193
Responsibility to protect principle, 73, 74, 76, 77, 386
Responsibility to rebuild, 73, 194
Restorative justice, 376
Restraining device, 336
Restrictive approach, 286
Restrictive interpretation, 244, 246, 286, 583
Retentionist States, 511, 512, 514
Rethinking Criminal Law, 343
Retribution, 78
Retributive justice, 373
Retroactive penal law, 368
Retroactive ratification, 464, 606
Rettinger, 495, 650
Reversal of *aut dedere*, 356
Reverse cooperation, 154
Review, 172, 179, 180, 192, 196–198
Reydams, 558
Ricardo Miguel Cavallo, 380, 638
Right of complementarity, 333
Right of third States, 329, 330, 387

Rights of peoples to self-determination, 331
Rights of the accused, 379
Rights of the defence, 379
Rights of victims, 382, 460, 465, 589
Right to a fair trial, 349, 379, 384, 418, 424, 444, 470–472, 474, 476, 477, 516
Right to a national effective remedy, 384, 457
Right to *habeas corpus*, 347
Right to hope, 504
Right to individual petition, 467
Right to intervene, 73
Right to know, 388, 569, 570
Right to liberty, 583
Right to life, 368, 381, 384, 582, 583
Right to self-determination, 332
Right to truth, 385, 388, 569
Right to vote, 188
Rigid definition, 439
Rigoberta Menchu Tum et al. v Ríos Montt et al., 335, 632
Rikhof, 351, 352, 358, 360
Riley, 450, 453, 647
Ríos Montt, 363–365, 532, 638
Rios regime, 366
Risk of being tortured, 494, 516
Risk of torture, 417, 497, 507, 517
Ritual of execution, 509
Road to Rome, 610
Robertson, 62, 70
Robinson, 71, 94, 98, 100, 313, 314, 440, 458, 462, 527, 530, 556, 642
Rocket, 446
Rodenhauser, 97, 98
Rodney King case, 343, 633
Rodríguez, 383, 636
Rogier, 601
Rogue State, 11, 47, 53–55, 385
Rojo, 258, 265
Role splitting, 323
Rome, 33
Rome Negotiating Text, 312
R (on the application of Smith (FC) (Respondent)) v Secretary of State for Defence (Appellant) and another, 387, 638
Roth, 354–356, 441
Rudimentary rights, 347
RUF, 44
Rukundo v Federal Office of Justice, 172, 183, 624
Rule 58, ICTY RPE, 18
Rule of law, 54, 384, 589, 609–611
Rule of Law Project, 528
Rule of non-inquiry, 420, 443
Rule of speciality, 419
Rules of law, 353
Rules of procedure and evidence, 375
Rumania, 329
Rusha case, 352, 637
Russia, 67, 102, 199, 293, 371, 481, 485, 487, 497, 507, 510, 607, 644, 645
Russian Federation Constitution, 552
Russian mafias, 349
Ruto, 100, 621
Ruvebana, 372, 373, 376, 377
Ruzindana, 92, 622
Rwanda, 52, 53, 327, 328, 351, 358, 372, 374–376, 421, 427, 443, 468, 469, 472, 481, 506, 510, 606, 646, 647, 649, 651
Rwandan Criminal Courts, 472, 505
Rwandan criminal justice, 376
Rwandan genocide, 48
Rwandan government officials, 374
Rwandan law, 469, 483
Rwandan Supreme Court, 506
R. Wijngaarde and R.A.L. Hoost v Desiré Delano Bouterse, 341, 633
Ryngaert, 258, 264, 335, 336, 340, 344, 349, 351, 357, 360, 365

S
Saadi, 369, 474, 634
Saakashvili, 438
Sacramento County Main Jail, 495
Safe havens, 341, 557
Saif Al-Islam Gaddafi, 158, 179, 191, 217, 218, 223–231, 234, 237, 239, 240, 250–252, 624, 626–628
Sailer, 487, 645
Saint-Denis, 103
Same case, 228, 251
Same conduct, 216, 224, 228, 235–240, 248, 249, 251, 253, 254, 297
Same person, 233, 237, 238, 249, 251
Samiha Abbas Hijazi et al. v Ariel Sharon, 348, 349, 632
Sanctions, 184, 188, 190, 191, 199, 200, 325, 332, 406
Sandoval Rodríguez, 463
Sang, 100, 621
San José, 376
Santiago, 463
Sarić, 558, 653
Sarin gas, 54
Sarkin, 613
Satik, 387
Saudi Arabia, 102
Saul, 476

Saville, Lord, 527
Sawoniuk, 499
Schabas, 133, 170, 174, 178, 184, 185, 189, 196, 197, 334, 351, 359, 384, 441, 456, 458, 461, 462, 472, 476, 511, 646
Scharf, 92
Schengen *acquis*, 241
Schlunck, 292
School of thought, 405
Schrijver, 99
Schuerch, 137
Schwarzeneger, 495
Scilingo, 364, 423, 632, 640
Scobbie, 244
Scotland, 360
Scottish criminal law, 371
Scottish judges, 371
SCSL, 7, 33, 35, 36, 127, 132, 152, 267–269, 284, 461, 462, 477, 518, 620, 624, 631, 650
Secondary role, 598
Secondary victim, 611
Second trial, 477
Secretary of State, 421, 472, 474, 493, 496, 509, 642, 646, 647
Secret detention centre, 380
Sectoral conventions, 122
Security, 358, 377, 379
Security Council Sanctions Committee, 185
Security principle, 62–64, 68, 73
Selective approach, 352
Selective prosecutions, 33, 608
Self-amnesties, 457
Self-amnesty law, 457
Self-assumption of jurisdiction, 556, 557
Self-delegitimization, 60, 282, 289, 327, 567
Self-delegitimization process, 60, 282, 327, 567
Self-incrimination, 373
Self-referral, 78, 185, 273
Semi-internationalized tribunal, 16, 153
Sending State, 292–295, 467, 507, 526
Senegal, 532, 612
Senegalese judicial system, 362
Senegalese law, 330, 362
Senegalese-Mauritanian conflict, 498
Senegalese territory, 330
Senior District Judge at Bow Street Magistrates' Court, 520
Senior leaders, 598
Senior ministers, 519
Sentencia (In re Corte Penal Internacional), 383, 633
Serbia, 326
Serbian Government, 468
Serious human rights violations, 458, 464, 529
Seriousness, 48, 51
Seventh Protocol to the ECvHR, 479, 481
Severity of the sentence, 357
Sevtap Veznedaroğlu v Turkey, 387, 570, 634, 653
Sexual abuse, 509
Sexual exploitation, 124
SGL Carbon AG v Commission of the European Communities, 379, 634
Shades of grey, 265
Shah, 260, 289, 291
Sham prosecution, 372
Sham trials, 222, 244
Shared duty, 600
Shared ideology, 118
Shared responsibility, 81
Shari'a, 513
Sharon, 348, 421, 520, 530, 642
Shelton, 345
Shestopalov v Russia, 593, 655
Shielding, 221, 231, 242, 594
Shining Path, 44
Shootings, 103
Short, 487, 496, 504, 509, 517, 647
Sicilian mafia, 349
Siebert-Fohr, 456, 463, 569, 572, 574, 583, 606
Sierra Leone, 44, 450, 454, 461
Sierra Leone blanket amnesties, 458
Simbeye, 168, 267, 275, 290, 291, 325, 530
Simbikangwa, 327, 328, 382, 423, 641
Simón, 71, 464, 620, 641
Simone Gbagbo, 220, 228, 239, 240, 251, 628, 629
Simón et al, 552, 653
Sindona v Grant, 491
Single area of criminal justice, 452
Sixth central court for preliminary proceedings, 346, 637
Sixth Protocol to the ECvHR Concerning the Abolition of the Death Penalty, 427
Slavery, 123–125
Slavko Dokmanović, 359, 637
Slovenia, 360, 432, 452, 516, 532, 652
Sluiter, 148–156, 159, 160, 167, 168, 173, 175, 177, 179–182, 185, 187–189, 195–198, 200, 210, 213, 214, 232, 246, 253, 262, 265, 273, 275, 276, 286, 292, 295–297, 312, 313, 362, 423, 441, 463, 473, 530, 588, 590
Slye, 5
Smith, 387, 638
Smyth, 442, 652

Snedden, 439, 647
Sobanski, 457, 642
Social fabric, 376
Socio-economic growth, 137
Socio-legal experiments, 373
Soering, 470, 471, 473, 474, 500, 508, 509, 517, 646
Soering precedent, 510, 514
Sofaer, 443
Soft law obligations, 571
Solange II, 148, 623
Solid infrastructure, 313
Solid platform, 312
Solitary confinement, 503, 505, 506
Somalia, 53, 136
Song, Judge, 610
Sources, 8, 9, 412, 413
South Africa, 20, 21, 186, 187, 258, 271, 277–279, 286, 332, 360, 381, 424, 454, 455, 466, 506, 508, 513, 520, 532, 607, 619, 625, 629, 631, 633, 636, 641, 647, 650
South African Constitutional Court, 382, 485
South African Defence Force, 454
South African Government, 187
South African High Court, 21
South African ICC Act, 520
South American *desaparecidos*, 376
South Asian Association for Regional Cooperation, 446
South Korea, 358, 382
South Sudanese law, 371
South West Africa cases, 332, 636
Sovereign equality of States, 349
Sovereign equals, 519
Sovereign States, 269, 297
Sovereignty, 5, 60–63, 73, 74, 76, 79, 82
Sovu residents, 375
Spain, 67, 335, 346, 356, 359, 360, 363–365, 367, 380, 383, 421, 423, 435, 441, 475, 521, 605, 607, 632, 637, 640, 648
Spanish *Audiencia Nacional*, 520
Spanish authorities, 347
Spanish-German Extradition Treaty, 442, 646
Spanish jurisdiction, 335, 364
Spanish jurisprudence, 366
Spanish law, 358
Spanish Supreme Court, 364, 380
Special cooperation devices, 42, 55, 594
Special Court Against Terrorism, 138
Special courts, 35, 37, 566, 568, 575, 598, 612–614
Special criminal court for events in Darfur, 363
Special Genocide Law, 427
Speciality, 212, 296, 297
Speciality doctrine, 420
Specialized divisions, 35
Specialized judicial panels, 601
Specialized units, 35
Specialized war crimes units, 577
Special prosecutions, 35
Special Prosecutor v Col Mengistu Hailemariam and 173 Others, The, 358, 635
Special Rapporteur, 524
Special Rapporteur on Torture, 497
Special Referral Bench, 190
Special war crimes court, 613
Specific amnesties, 460
Specific emergency measures, 454
Specific function, 267
Specific requirements, 255, 259
Spectre of the execution, 509
Speculative, 240
Sphere of competence, 214
Spillover effect, 68
Splinter groups, 128
Srebrenica, 81, 112, 468, 518, 620, 647
Srebrenica cases, 385, 635
Srebrenica massacre, 326
Sri Lankan Panel of the Consultation Task Force on Reconciliation Mechanisms, 613
Stade de France, 103
Stages of the criminal justice process, 477
Stahn, 149, 150, 152, 153
Standard of probability, 604
Standard of proof, 114, 517, 604
Standard of protection, 435
Stand-by judicial mechanism, 24
Stanford, 500
State acquiescence, 340
State action assessment, 220, 221
State agents, 572
State aggravated responsibility, 43, 105, 106, 112, 131, 134
State cooperation, 33, 35, 123
State crime, 44
State criminality, 47, 52
State discretion, 353, 417, 444
State immunity, 518, 524, 525, 531, 532
State inability, 90
State investigation, 170, 177
State involvement, 46, 47, 90
State-like entities, 294
State-likeness, 100
State-like organization, 91
Statements from victims, 382

State obligations, 17, 18, 182, 191, 255, 330, 334, 337, 385, 386, 426, 462, 564, 571, 583
State obligation to cooperate, 12
State obligation to prosecute crimes against humanity, 464
State of emergency, 428
State of health of the victim, 503
State of nationality, 329, 330, 332
State ordinary responsibility, 134
State or organizational policy, 93, 95, 100
State Parties, 166, 171–173, 175, 176, 178–180, 182–185, 187–190, 198–200
State party referral, 199
State policy, 99, 434
State power, 582, 584
State practice, 323, 334–336, 339, 340, 344, 345, 349, 357, 366, 367, 412, 413, 423, 424, 427, 440–442, 446, 463, 466, 473, 485, 490, 509, 513, 515, 517, 521, 522, 524, 526–528, 530, 531, 565, 567, 568, 605, 607, 614
State referral, 185, 192
State responsibility, 176, 188–190, 605
States, 321–327, 329–333, 335, 336, 338, 340–345, 347–350, 353, 354, 356–358, 360, 362, 363, 366, 368, 378, 379, 381–384, 386–388, 636, 638
State Sovereignty, 425, 449, 557
State-sovereignty approach, 584
State-sponsored terrorism, 130
State's prerogative, 444
State v Sergeant Stacey Koon, Officer Theodore J. Briseno, Officer Timothy E. Wind, Officer Laurence Powell, The, 343, 633
Stationing of troops, 294
Status of Forces Agreements, 293
Status of international organizations, 37, 79, 112, 195, 280
Statute of the IHT, 7, 36, 159, 363, 514, 611
Statute of the SCSL, 461
Statute of the STL, 378
Statutes of limitations, 419, 422–424, 464
Statutory framework, 277, 599
Statutory limitations, 382, 422–424, 457, 490, 498, 611
Stein, 523
Stigen, 71
Stigma, 425, 528
STL, 7, 35, 36, 64, 65, 152, 329, 600, 620
Stockholm District Court, 499, 650
Stockholm Programme, 378
Stoning, 514
Straffeloven, 349
Strafgesetzbuch, 558
Strasbourg Court, 379, 387, 422, 474, 570
Strasbourg jurisprudence, 497
Street Children case, 385, 569
Strict liability, 197, 198
Structural failure, 54
Structural impunity, 78
Structure of judicial institutions, 379
Stumbling blocks, 604
Sub-Commission on Minorities, 589
Sub iudice, 223, 248, 287, 327
Subjective approach, 453, 454
Subjective fear, 516
Subjectivity, 242
Subject of international law, 377
Submit to prosecution, 566, 572, 575–577
Subpoena, 312, 632
Subsequent proceedings, 236
Subsidiaridad, 335
Subsidiarity, 61, 153, 327, 330, 335, 336, 365, 600
Subsidiary body, 564
Subsidiary obligation, 405
Subsidiary prosecutor, 594
Subsidiary universal jurisdiction, 335, 336
Substantial grounds, 438, 446, 474, 475, 494, 508, 517
Substantial grounds test, 508, 517, 604
Substantial interaction, 388
Substantially collapsed, 219, 226
Substantive international criminal law, 413
Substantive justice, 375
Successful prosecution, 239
Successive federal prosecution, 493
Sudan, 169, 178, 186, 187, 196, 199, 607, 624, 625
Suffering, 474, 475, 499, 509, 515
Sufficient evidence, 224
Sui generis characteristics, 386
Sui generis core crime, 385
Sui generis ICC regime, 173
Sui generis organizations, 294
Sui generis prosecutions, 32
Sui generis (special) courts, 371
Sui generis trials, 612
Sulaiman Al-Adsani v UK, 331, 634
Suleymane Guengueng and Others v Senegal, 360, 638
Summary executions, 460
Super-customary law, 341
Super-customary norm, 341
Superfluous, 610
Supervisory body, 467

Supplementary Treaty, 442, 443
Suppression convention, 65, 120, 130, 131, 406, 407
Suppression of core crimes, 321, 328
Supranational crimes, 44
Supra-national human rights court, 372
Supranational model, 195
Supranational model of cooperation, 149
Supreme Court of Chile, 463
Supreme Court of Israel, 638
Supreme Court of Senegal, 330
Supreme Court of the Netherlands, 348, 379, 422, 506, 518
Supreme Court of Uganda, 514, 651
Supreme Court of Zimbabwe, 510
Supreme law, 552
Supreme National Baathification Commission, 159
Surinam, 341, 348
Surrender, 600
Suspect, 313, 610
Suspensive conditions, 454
Sustainable Development Goals, 614
Swart, 167, 174, 175, 177, 183, 195, 197, 211, 213, 249, 252–254, 273, 276, 297, 591, 592
SWCC, 7
Sweden, 430, 467, 472, 474, 556, 558, 643, 645, 647, 650
Swiss Court, 519
Swiss Federal Criminal Court, 524
Swiss proportionality theory, 438
Switzerland, 360, 607
Sylvère Ahorugeze v Sweden, 374, 634
Synergy, 255
Syria, 54, 55, 67, 72, 74, 600, 608
Syrian armed conflict, 556
Syrian government, 102
Syria's war, 608
Systematic exclusion, 270
Systematic harm, 68, 69, 82
Systematic terror, 103
Systematic terrorism, 103
Systematic torture, 360
Systematic violations of human rights, 467
System criminality, 44, 51, 55, 594

T

Tacit acquiescence, 340
Tacit precondition for extradition, 449
Tadić, 52, 103, 128, 168, 566, 584, 590, 620, 622, 623, 625, 655
Tahir Hussain Khan v Canada, 369, 638
Taliban, 293
Tapley, 442, 651
Tatchell, 520, 640
Taylor, 35, 36, 152, 518, 524, 620, 624, 650
Taylor, Melinda, 230, 267–269, 283–285, 288, 631
Tejedor García v Spain, 383, 634
Teleological approach, 169, 200, 592
Teleological role, 590
Temple of international justice, 367
Tension, 271, 272, 278, 283
Terminological distinctions, 32
Terms of imprisonment, 242
Terra incognita, 378
Territorial jurisdiction, 217, 218, 253, 277, 329, 330, 335, 341, 350, 363, 364, 367, 375, 387, 600
Territorial State, 325, 329, 330, 332, 333, 335, 336, 349, 365, 566, 568, 569
Territory, 605, 606
Terrorism, 120–122, 126, 127, 129, 130, 138, 139, 354, 355, 378, 380, 405–407, 429, 444, 446, 454, 491, 505, 520, 525
Terrorist attack, 102
Terrorist bombing, 370
Terrorist organization, 369
Terrorists, 447
Third State, 36, 135, 181, 568, 572
Third State prosecutions, 328
Thirlway, 412
Threat of Torture, 494, 497
Threat to the peace, 191, 192, 199, 200, 329
Threshold, 114
Threshold of criminality, 220
Tibet, 347, 367
Tihomir Blaškić, 321, 637
Tillier, 179
Time-barring, 382
Tladi, 271, 272, 286, 290
Tobruk, 158
Toolkit, 517
Torquil Dick Erikson v Italy, 572, 653
Torture, 230, 236, 259, 260, 262–266, 269, 289–291, 324–326, 330, 341, 346, 358, 360, 364, 368, 369, 380, 382, 385, 386, 436, 437, 445, 446, 451, 459, 460, 463, 471, 474, 476, 486, 493–498, 504, 506–509, 511, 513, 515, 522, 525–528, 552, 569, 570, 573, 574, 604, 638, 652
Torture Victim Protection Act, 529
Toshiba, 480, 643
Touvier, 352, 633
Tower of Pisa, 167, 606
Trabelsi, 504, 505, 644
Traditional exceptions in extradition, 436

Trafficking in human beings, 120, 123–125, 129, 130, 139, 368, 429, 452
Trafficking of blood diamonds, 44
Trafficking of firearms, 122
Trafficking Protocol, 120, 122, 123
Trahan, 226
Trans-border effects, 329
Trans-boundary crime, 465
Transfer, 17, 18
Transfer of proceedings, 264, 265
Transitional justice institutions, 377
Transitional Period in South Sudan, 371
Transitory authority, 598
Translation difficulties, 452
Transnational corporations, 44
Transnational crimes, 119, 120, 123, 134
Transnational organized crimes, 65, 66, 112, 115, 118–124, 126, 129–132, 135, 138, 349, 377, 404, 421
Travaux preparatoires, 257, 337, 492
Treatment of offenders, 419
Treatment of the accused, 420
Treaty-based crimes, 134
Treaty-crime, 121
Treaty interpretation, 270, 272
Treaty law, 244, 272, 326, 412
Treaty of Amsterdam, 322
Treaty of Rome, 343
Treaty on the Functioning of the European Union, 33
Treaty practice, 323
Treholt, 500
Trials, 609, 610
Trials *in absentia*, 4, 7, 19, 445, 477
Tribunal of Arezzo, 525
Tribunal of First Instance of Brussels, 340, 638
Trickery, 359
Triggering mechanism, 174
Trigger mechanism, 178, 200, 272
Trinidad and Tobago, 360
Tripoli, 158
Trump, President, 292
Trustees, 327, 330
Truth, 345, 357, 373, 376, 385, 388
Truth commissions, 456, 458
Trybunał Konstytucyjny, 429, 651
Tunis, 345
Tunisia, 369
Turansky, 484
Turk, 60, 63
Turkey, 102, 329, 387, 439, 470, 473, 505, 509–511, 644, 645
Turkey's Parliament, 511
Tutsi, 499
Types of immunities, 267
Tyrer, 509
Tzanakopoulos, 171, 179, 180, 194, 198

U

Ubi lex voluit lex dixit, 407
UCK, 371
UDHR, 6, 332, 468, 469, 477
Uganda, 168, 196, 625
UK, 421, 423, 430, 433, 438, 441, 442, 452, 468, 470–472, 474, 496, 497, 502–505, 508, 509, 516, 520, 524, 526, 529, 607, 640, 642, 644, 646, 647, 650, 651
UK High Court of Justice, 423
UK Human Rights Act, 387
Ukraine, 67
UK soldiers, 387
Ulterior infringements, 582
Ultimate arbiter, 218, 241, 264
Ultra vires, 556
Ultra vires acts, 290
UN, 36, 112, 119, 120, 126, 135, 136, 419, 445, 446, 455, 463, 477, 515, 518, 598
Unable, 170, 173, 607, 609, 613
Unable to investigate and prosecute, 78
Unable to prosecute, 364
UN and Sierra Leone Bilateral Agreement, 36
UN-assisted tribunals, 193
UN-authorized operations, 295
UNC, 17, 104, 178, 179, 181–183, 188, 191, 192, 195, 198, 199, 321, 426, 469, 518
UNCATOC, 120, 122–125
UNCHR, 589
UNCLOS, 136
UN Committee against Torture, 463, 495
Uncompromising formula, 381
Unconditional obligation, 355
Uncontested admissibility, 159
UN Convention Against Illicit Traffic in Narcotic Drugs and Psychotropic Substances, 355
Underlying assumption, 384
UN Development Goals, 614
UN Diplomatic Conference of Plenipotentiaries, 44
Unemployment, 137
Unfair trial, 158, 159, 328, 357, 362, 437, 444, 470, 471, 476, 511, 512, 599
UNGA, 7, 9, 21, 180, 185, 191, 193, 325, 332
UNGA official records, 353
UNGA Resolution, 7, 120, 356, 575, 608
UN High Commission for Refugees, 515
UN-ICC Negotiated Relationship Agreement, 189

UN-ICC Relationship Agreement, 283
Uniform international practice, 455
Unilateral exclusion, 323
Unilateral reservation, 323
Unilateral universal jurisdiction, 340
UN International Residual Mechanism for Criminal Tribunals, 21
Unión Progresista de Fiscales de España et al. v. Pinochet, 335, 632
UNITAD, 608
United Nations Committee Against Torture, 463
United States Diplomatic and Consular Staff in Tehran (USA v Iran) (Iranian Hostages case), 622
United States-led coalition, 102
Universal crime, 64
Universal criminal jurisdiction, 527
Universality principle, 344, 348
Universal jurisdiction, 42, 51, 53, 130, 134, 135, 137, 282, 291, 322, 326–330, 333–335, 337, 339–344, 347–352, 356–367, 370, 372, 380, 384, 405–407, 421, 459–461, 463, 469, 476, 478, 483, 497, 556–558, 565, 567, 568, 573, 576, 577, 582, 584, 589, 594, 600, 601, 605–609, 614
Universal jurisdiction *in absentia*, 340, 348, 349, 482, 573
Universal legal injury, 79, 80
Universal responsibility, 74
Universal values, 64, 525
UN Mechanism for International Criminal Tribunals, 328
UN Member States, 18, 148, 157, 329, 366
UN Model Treaty on Extradition, 419, 453
UNODC, 136
UNODC Counter-Piracy Programme, 136
UN peace-keeping force, 421
UN peacekeeping troops, 178
UN Prevention and Criminal Justice Branch, 119
UN protective mechanisms, 77
UN Refugee Convention, 368
UN resolutions, 528
UNSC, 9, 10, 74, 78, 152, 157, 159, 167, 172, 177–180, 182–188, 190–195, 198–200, 325, 329, 341
UNSC referral, 176, 183, 184, 191, 199, 218, 275, 276, 279, 281, 286–289, 329
UNSC Resolution, 16, 19, 72, 81, 105, 157, 173, 176, 178–180, 182, 183, 185, 189, 191, 194, 198, 199, 217, 218, 252, 274–276, 279–281, 287, 288, 322, 341, 574, 606–608
UNSC Resolution 1593, 157, 178, 198, 278, 280, 286, 287
UNSC Resolution 1970, 157
UNSC Resolution 827, 177
UNSC Resolution 955, 177
UNSC Sanctions Committee, 185
UN Standard Minimum Rules for the Treatment of Prisoners, 504
UN Sub-Committee on the Prevention of Torture, 431
UNTAET Regulation, 347
UN Transitory Authority for Eastern Timor, 347
Unwilling, 336, 363, 365, 382, 607, 609, 613
Unwillingness, 47, 48, 51, 129, 155, 160, 372, 594
Unwilling to investigate and prosecute, 77, 170
Unwilling to prosecute, 336
Uruguay, 360, 376, 454, 458, 464, 557, 648
Uruguay's Expiry Law, 457
USA, 67, 78, 154, 157, 199, 200, 426, 427, 429, 432, 439, 440, 442, 443, 446, 465, 468, 485, 491–493, 495, 502, 505, 506, 509–511, 513, 524, 526, 529, 607, 612, 613, 642, 649–652
Usacka, 582, 598, 600
USA Constitution, 552
USA Court of Appeals, 442, 443, 445, 469, 491, 492, 524, 526, 651, 652
USA Courts, 421, 443, 529, 652
USA detention facility at Guantanamo Bay, 346
USA federal system, 427
USA government, 359
USA-ICC relationship, 292
USA-Italy Extradition Treaty, 427
USA law, 44
USA prison, 506
USA sanctions, 293
USA serviceman, 529
USA Supplementary Extradition Treaties, 441
USA Supreme Court, 138
USA territory, 359
USA v Fawaz Yunis, 339, 639
USA v Omar Mohammed Ali Rezaq, 339, 354, 639
USA v Ramzi Ahmed Yousef et al., 339, 639
Use of force, 387
Utility, 22, 23
Uzbekistan, 473, 607

V

Valid detention, 359
Value-driven connotation, 376
van Alebeek, 114, 525, 527, 528, 530, 531
Vandeginste, 328
van den Herik, 91, 99, 152
van den Wyngaert, 222, 232, 236, 237, 244, 245, 290, 630
van den Wyngaert, Judge, 95, 525, 529, 573, 621, 654
van der Merwe and four others, 466, 647
van der Wilt, 44, 54, 55, 63, 64, 68–70, 79, 90, 101, 102, 120, 123, 125–129, 133, 136, 273, 289, 294, 327, 330, 331, 333, 335, 342, 364–367, 383, 427, 433, 434, 438, 441–444, 469, 470, 474, 478, 479, 481, 483–486, 488, 489, 494, 496, 508, 512, 513, 516, 517, 520
van Esbroeck, 481, 488, 643
van Gend en Loos, 435, 643
Vanneste, 583, 584
van Schaack, 5
van Sliedregt, 432–434, 449, 450, 452, 453, 523
van Steenberghe, 322–324, 354, 356
Varec SA v Belgian State, 379, 634
Various Communications vs Mauritania, 321, 632
Various offences, 486
Vasiliev, 169, 197
Vasiljkovic, 439, 647
VCLT, 166, 181, 338, 344, 345, 407, 582
Veil, 214
Velásquez-Rodríguez v Honduras, 383, 570, 583, 636, 655
Velikova, 387, 634
Venezia, 427, 509, 641
Venezuela, 376, 566
Verdict, 362, 373, 380, 638
Versailles Treaty, 426
Vertical axis, 329
Vertical complementarity, 336
Vertical effect, 235
Verticality, 16, 148, 150
Vertical system, 330, 336, 362, 363, 365, 370
Vertical system of enforcement, 16, 19, 22, 23, 25, 32, 139, 148–150, 152, 153, 155–157, 159, 160, 166, 168, 170, 172, 190, 210, 211, 215, 235, 243, 246, 258, 259, 264, 265, 270, 277, 278, 284, 288, 297, 298, 312–314, 417, 420, 425, 434, 456, 466, 470, 493, 508, 518, 564, 565, 604, 608, 614
Vested right, 337
Victims, 122, 124, 125, 129, 138, 155, 190, 200, 236, 245, 248, 262, 264, 328, 342, 343, 355, 364, 366, 376, 378, 379, 382, 383, 455–457, 462, 467, 498, 569–572, 574, 575, 577, 604, 605, 614
Victim support service, 593
Victores, 532
Videla, 486, 532, 640
Videos documenting atrocities, 608
Vienna Convention on Diplomatic Relations, 526
Vigilante jurisdiction, 71
Vigilante justice, 589
Villagrán-Morales, 385, 636
Villa Grimaldi Torture Centre, 463
Vinter, 504, 505, 644
Violations of international humanitarian law, 604, 608
Violence, 334, 376
Virginia, 508
Vučinić, Judge, 422, 644

W

Waiver, 382
Waiver of immunity, 273, 289
Wald, Judge, 491, 651
War crimes, 44, 45, 48, 53, 94, 97, 99, 101–104, 322, 324, 326, 340, 342, 349, 358, 360, 362, 365, 371, 384, 385, 404, 422, 430, 436, 440, 446, 451, 465, 472, 518, 523, 525, 533
War Crimes Act, 349, 421
Watchdog, 216
Weatherall, 288
Weeramantry, 344, 345
Well-developed structure, 96
Well-founded fear, 448, 515–517
Well-founded risk of torture, 604
Wellington, 496
Wellman, 64
Wemhoff, 455, 646
Werle, 43, 267, 424, 460, 461, 526
Westernized juridical world, 373
Westminster Magistrates' Court, 468, 472, 646
Westphalian Peace Treaties, 454
Wetboek van Strafvordering, 348
W.F, 487, 646
Whereabouts, 214, 223, 570
White-collar crimes, 421
Widespread and systematic attack, 573
Widespread consensus, 329
Widespread harm, 68
Widespread or systematic attack, 93, 94, 96–98, 100

Williams, 35, 36
Willingness criterion, 372
Willingness to prosecute, 599
Wilmshurst, 527, 530
Wise, 321, 322, 324, 344
Withdrawal, 20, 607
Without delay, 214, 252, 263
Witnesses, 229, 238, 253, 575, 595, 608, 612
Workable definition of core crimes, 43
Workman, Judge, 507, 520
World court, 604
World legislator, 592
World War II, 352, 559
Would-be-executed, 514
Would-be victims, 589
Wrongful conviction, 229
Wrongful omissions, 425
Wynne, 500

Y

Yaron, 520, 530, 642
Yasin Abdullah Kadi v Council of the European Union and Commission of the European Communities, 332, 634
Yayi, 20
Yekatom, 265
Yemen, 454
Yemeni national, 474
Yerodia, 267, 269, 290, 361, 362, 421, 518, 519, 523, 525, 526, 529, 532
Yeung, 270
Yezidi minority, 576
Yezidis, 67
Yezidi victims, 576
Yudkivska, Judge, 504, 644
Yugoslav wars, 332
Yusuf and Al Barkakaat International Foundation v Council of the European Union and Commission of the European Communities, 167, 624

Z

Zahar, 423, 463, 473, 588, 590
Zairian army officer, 379
Zakaev, 438, 473, 507, 640
Zappalà, 169, 521, 524
Zarb, 473, 645
Zardad, 405, 639
Zegveld, 570
Zejnil Delalić et al., 325, 567
Zemin, 367
Zennaro, 489, 641
Zentai, 430, 431, 436, 437, 450, 451, 472, 646, 647
Zigarella, 482, 644
Žigić, 113, 622
Zimbabwe Torture Docket case, 61, 381, 382, 620, 633
Zintan, 158
Zintani militia, 223
Zintanis, 158, 223, 234
Zintan Revolutionaries' Military Council, 158
Zolothukin, 487
Zuma, 21

The manufacturer's authorised representative in the EU is Springer Nature Customer Service Centre GmbH, Europaplatz 3, 69115 Heidelberg, Germany. If you have any concerns regarding our products, please contact ProductSafety@springernature.com

Printed and bound by CPI Group (UK) Ltd, Croydon, CR0 4YY
30/09/2026
02225447-0019